Find the real Europe.
Go with a friend.

Hertz Affordable Europe.
A friend to travelers for 75 years.

To get to the real Europe, away from the crowds, you need a car. And an experienced companion. Which is why you need Hertz. **H**ertz Affordable Europe offers low rates guaranteed in U.S. dollars throughout Europe on a wide variety of cars. All with Free Unlimited Mileage and Computerized Driving Directions available at many locations. And with 24-Hour Emergency Roadside Assistance, you'll enjoy peace of mind everywhere from Barcelona to Bologna. You'll also find English spoken at each of our 2,500 locations throughout Europe.

For reservations, call your AAA travel office or the Hertz/AAA Desk at **1-800-654-3080**. And let a friend take you around the real Europe.

exactly.

EUROPE
TravelBook™

A CATALOG OF
SELECTED TRAVEL INFORMATION
PREPARED TO ENHANCE THE
TRAVEL EXPERIENCE
IN OTHER LANDS

AAA PUBLISHING
1000 AAA DRIVE, HEATHROW, FL 32746

1998 EDITION

Published by the American Automobile
Association, 1000 AAA Drive, Heathrow,
Florida FL 32746-5063

CONTENTS

This book has been prepared by AA
Publishing, Basingstoke, England
exclusively for the American Automobile
Association

Second edition **1998**
Reprinted with amendments **1997**
First published **1996**
Maps © The Automobile Association 1996,
1997, 1998
Text © American Automobile Association
1996, 1997, 1998

Printed in the United States of America at
Quebecor Printing Kingsport, Kingsport,
Tennessee (on recyclable paper)

The following photographers and libraries
assisted in the preparation of this book:
James Davies Travel Photography 195,
529b; Nature Photographers Ltd 233 (E. A.
James), 537b (C. K. Mylne); Pictures Colour
Library 49, 71, 206, 207, 303b, 461a, 554;
Spectrum Colour Library 40, 48, 162, 163,
232, 529a; Zefa Pictures Ltd 41, 70, 194, 302,
460, 514, 515, 528, 536, 627

The remaining photographs are held in the
Automobile Association's own photo library
(AA PHOTO LIBRARY) and were taken by:
A. Baker 24, 303a; J. Blandford 378; M.
Birkitt 483a; J. Carnie 77b; J. Edmanson
482, 483b, 569b; P. Enticknap 452, 453a,
453b; D. Forss 498, 499; T. Harris 352;
S. Hill 379b; J. Holmes 403a; P. Kenward
241a, 630, 631a; A. Kouprianoff 56, 57,
62; K. Naylor 537a, 555; D. Noble 25; K.
Paterson 184, 185a, 185b, 216, 217b,
461b; D. Robertson 569a; C. Sawyer 174,
175, 240, 402, 403b; M. Short 379a; B. Smith
102; A. Souter 631b; R. Strange 77a, 241b;
W. Voysey 217a; P. Wilson 353, 568

Front cover photographs:
*Village in northern Holland; Annecy, France;
Triumphpforte, Innsbruck, Austria; Royal
Coachman, London, England
– Corel Photos*

EUROPE
TravelBook™

USING THE TRAVELBOOK

The purpose of the AAA Europe TravelBook
is to make your trip as smooth and enjoyable as possible.
Whether you are an explorer, sports enthusiast, history buff or just plain
curious, you'll find many appealing things to see and do. The wealth of
facts, statistics and descriptions in this publication provide detailed
knowledge about places of interest throughout 46 destinations in Europe.
The information in this guide is based on data supplied by the Automobile
Association of Britain. All copy is accurate at press time; however, since
material is necessarily prepared in advance of the publication date, there is
always the possibility that changes will occur after the guide is printed. If
you become aware of material that is inaccurate, please write to us at AAA
Member Comments, Box 61, 1000 AAA Dr., Heathrow, FL 32746-5063.
Each country is separated into two sections: an introductory section
followed by an A-Z listing of the major sights in the country.

INTRODUCTION

Each country chapter begins with a two-page pictorial introduction that provides a broad image of the nation.

This is followed by the *Things to Know* box, which gives helpful information and addresses at a glance. Next is a more detailed introduction that includes such specific topics as history, food, sports, travel, lodging and tipping.

For the larger destinations there is also a *Principal Touring Areas* section that describes the country's various geographical regions.

MAPS

There is a map for each main country that pinpoints listed towns, and there are also city plans for the major centers and capital cities.

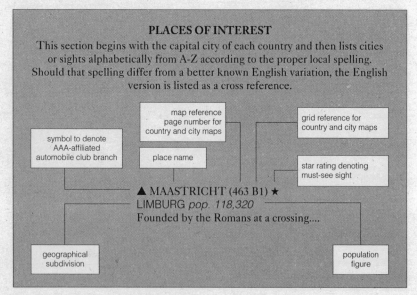

PLACES OF INTEREST

This section begins with the capital city of each country and then lists cities
or sights alphabetically from A-Z according to the proper local spelling.
Should that spelling differ from a better known English variation, the English
version is listed as a cross reference.

map reference
page number for
country and city maps

grid reference for
country and city maps

symbol to denote
AAA-affiliated
automobile club branch

place name

star rating denoting
must-see sight

▲ MAASTRICHT (463 B1) ★
LIMBURG *pop. 118,320*
Founded by the Romans at a crossing....

geographical
subdivision

population
figure

INTRODUCTION TO EUROPE

Draw any line through a map of Europe and you will see the extremes that it covers: from the eternal night of an Icelandic winter to the endless summers of sultry Greece; from Portugal, starting point for explorers to the New World, to the emerging countries of Eastern Europe; from the former Communist countries to the carefree lifestyle of the Republic of Ireland.

Less than half the size of North America, Europe encompasses an infinite variety of cultures that are constantly changing. On January 1, 1993, Czechoslovakia became two new countries, the Czech Republic and the Slovak Republic. The former Yugoslavia has broken into its component parts. The ex-Soviet Republics of Estonia, Latvia and Lithuania regained their independence and turned toward the prosperity of western Europe. Russia is changing, too, but at a slower pace.

CULTURAL DIFFERENCES

Cultural identity in Europe is strong, to the extent that within some nations different groups seek separation. The Basques of northern Spain and the Corsicans of France are just two examples of peoples with strong separatist movements. Corsican culture – reflected in both its language and cuisine – is part French, part Italian. The island of Corsica belongs to France, yet lies closer to Italy. Its southern tip almost touches the Italian island of Sardinia, which itself is geographically closer to North Africa than to Italy.

Sicily, too, is Italian, the largest island in the Mediterranean, marking Europe's southern boundary. Further east, on the island of Crete, cradle of European civilization, visitors will sense the aura of quiet pride that distinguishes a Cretan.

In the cooler climate of Alpine Switzerland, divisions work well. Three official languages – French, German and Italian – happily coexist, and by 1999 the Swiss will be celebrating 500 years as an independent nation.

It seems appropriate that the headquarters of the European Union should be based in Belgium, another country of cultural differences. A third are French-speaking Walloons, while just over half are Flemings, who speak Flemish (a dialect of Dutch).

THE EUROPEAN UNION

The seeds of today's European Union (E.U.), which links the economic and, to some extent, legal systems of its member states, were sown in France in 1950 with the suggestion that the steel and coal resources of the western European nations should be pooled. In 1957, the Treaty of Rome brought together France, (West) Germany, Italy, Belgium, the Netherlands and Luxembourg as the European Economic Community (E.E.C.), also known as the Common Market. The intent of the E.E.C. was to remove trade and duty barriers, thereby improving the economic strength of the member nations in order to compete with the United States and Britain.

However, in 1972 the E.E.C. voted to accept Britain, Ireland, Denmark and Norway, though the citizens of Norway subsequently voted in a referendum to remain outside the E.E.C. Membership was increased to 10 nations in 1981 when Greece was admitted, to 12 members in 1986 with the admittance of Spain and Portugal, and to 15 in 1995 with Finland, Austria and Sweden. The Slovak and Czech republics have shown a desire to join in the future.

Among the sweeping changes introduced by the E.U. was the lifting of restrictions at the end of 1992 on the movement of goods, services, capital, and workers and tourists between member states. This meant that tourists – even non-E.U. citizens – were able to cross between E.U. countries without showing their passport, while at airports, separate channels existed for E.U. and non-E.U. citizens.

Proposed changes go much deeper than this. The Maastricht Treaty of 1991 suggested that there should be a single common European currency for at least some of its members by 1999.

THE WORKINGS OF
THE EUROPEAN UNION

To most people, the concept of Europe is now embodied in the European Union which centers on four main institutions.

The **Council of Ministers** is comprised of government representatives from all member states. This is the most powerful organization, where legislative and political decisions are made.

The **European Commission** is responsible for initiating proposals which are put to the Council of Ministers, and for implementing those proposals that are put into force. It has 20 commissioners, one from each country and, in addition, one extra member from France, Italy, Germany, Britain and Spain.

The **European Parliament** is based in Strasbourg and consists of elected representatives. There are 626 Members of the European Parliament (M.E.P.s), divided roughly on a proportional basis. The European Parliament's main role is to provide some kind of democratic control over the other bodies, though this has not yet been fully realized. It has certain powers over the European Commission, and must be consulted over some legislative matters by the Council of Ministers.

Finally, the **Court of Justice**, based in Luxembourg, is responsible for seeing that the law is applied throughout the E.U., not just as regards the E.U.'s own treaties, but also as a final Court of Appeal on matters referred to it by national courts within member states. It also gives opinions on international agreements entered into by the E.U.

KALEIDOSCOPE OF CULTURES

It is, of course, cultural differences that make Europe what it is. Many citizens fear that this diversity will be lost if, for example, monetary union is imposed and, instead of the *franc, Mark, lira, krone, drachma, guilder, escudo, pound* or *peseta*, the European Currency Unit (E.C.U.) becomes the common currency. A great deal would be lost, certainly, but nothing could ever homogenize the strikingly divergent cultures that exist within Europe's 9.8 million square kilometers (3.8 million square miles), home to millions of very different people.

The people of the Mediterranean countries are generally passionate, extroverted and dramatic. Political arguments rage in squares and cafés, where the men gather – these are still predominantly patriarchal societies.

Similar in many ways – a Portuguese fisherman would have much in common with a Greek fisherman – the inhabitants of this vast land mass are still very different in their national characteristics. All are easygoing and friendly, yet the Portuguese may appear more aloof.

As a people, the Spanish are as hospitable as any on the Mediterranean shores, yet they are much more relaxed than the excitable Italians, or the Greeks, who gave the world drama as well as democracy.

Italians see themselves as sophisticated, with a sharper dress sense than many other Europeans, and living near to the heart of European fashion and culture. They would tend to look north to Paris rather than to Athens or Madrid, though temperamentally they are more at home in the south. The difference between the Italians and the French will be discovered should you try to speak a little of their respective languages. Italians will invariably want to converse; the French are more likely to reply in flawless English, though a smile and a polite word will invariably encourage a positive response.

The British, on the other hand, may be harder to befriend than the Italians or Spanish. Their apparent coolness is a result of both climate and geography, as it was not until 1994 that the 31-mile

Channel Tunnel united Britain with continental Europe.

Just a few miles across the Irish Sea in the Republic of Ireland, no one could be more open-hearted than the Irish. If temperature affects temperament, then the Irish confound the theory. The heavy rainfall that produces the Emerald Isle seems also to produce a sunny disposition in its people.

A more stereotypical example of the theory are the people in the sometimes sun-starved Scandinavian countries – Sweden, Denmark, Finland, Norway and Iceland – who have an undeserved reputation for a certain aloofness.

Some of the most interesting countries in Europe, those that emerged in the late 1980s and early 1990s from behind the Iron Curtain, are now starting to reveal their secrets to the rest of the world. Prague now rivals Paris for popularity, with more people wanting to visit than there are hotel beds available.

The visitor to this part of Europe must expect the unexpected; not merely in the culture and the countryside, but in the people. Most welcome visitors with a warmth suppressed for years, but among the older people are those who cannot shake off the decades when there was no free speech, and for them a mask remains. In this part of Europe travel becomes a much deeper experience, as in Russia, Moldova, Ukraine and Belarus, where the countries have yet to fully regain their culture.

Europe's kaleidoscope also contains tiny countries dwarfed by their big brothers. Surrounded by Rome is the independent state of Vatican City, home to less than a thousand people. San Marino is the world's smallest republic, founded in the 4th century in the Italian Apennine Mountains. Between Switzerland and Austria is Liechtenstein, founded in 1719, and on the French Riviera is the principality of Monaco, ruled by the same Grimaldi family since the 13th century. Andorra is tucked into the Pyrénées between France and Spain, an autonomous republic since 1278. Small, it seems, is not only beautiful, but stable in the changing face of Europe.

FROM MOUNTAINS TO MEDITERRANEAN

Europe offers contrasts of climates and geography. Rivers run through its lands, inspiring music, poetry and legend: the Thames, the Danube, the Rhine, the Loire. It is home to famous peaks like Mount Olympus, the legendary home of the Greek gods, the biblical Mount Ararat, and the peaks of the Alps: Mont Blanc, the Matterhorn and the Jungfrau.

Scandinavia is a dramatic region with fjords and lakes. In Norway the Sognafjord runs for over 161 kilometers (100 miles), and to a depth of 1,219 meters (4,000 feet). Head south to eastern and central Europe and you'll see forests, wolves, wooden huts and the last European bison in the Bialowieza Forest between Poland and Russia. To the west is Germany, land of the Rhine, and of the Black Forest, its pines and mountain peaks. Beyond Germany lie the low countries, the flat Dutch and Belgian landscapes, with much of the land reclaimed from the sea.

Across the water stand the Republic of Ireland and Britain's historical landscapes: Welsh castles and hills, Scottish lochs and remote mountain ranges, green Irish pastures and plunging cliffs, rolling English countryside and quiet villages. The Channel Tunnel connects Britain with the rest of Europe, speeding visitors to northern France and its fertile farmland, and beyond to its Mediterranean beaches and the mountainous borders of the Pyrénées and the Alps. Over the Pyrénées is the hot, high Iberian peninsula, the land of the Spanish *mañana*, and golden beaches that sweep around the Mediterranean's shores through the French and Italian rivieras. Roman remains and the canals of Venice lead to the Balkans, home of the Greek gods, and on to Turkey, where Europe ends at Istanbul, on the Golden Horn, and Asia beckons.

TRAVEL FACTS

With a variety of ways in which to explore Europe, the greatest difficulty will lie in the choice of where to go and where to stay, whether to go independently or on a program organized by a tour operator. Some escorted tours have very tightly packed schedules. Traveling independently will allow you more time to soak up local atmosphere, but will necessitate meticulous planning and perhaps an intrepid spirit. Whichever method you favor, visit a AAA travel agent well in advance to inquire about the options.

BEFORE YOU GO

CLIMATE AND WHEN TO GO

The warm summer months are perennial favorites with vacationers; they go hand-in-hand with enjoyable European festivities. However, off-season rates, hotel availability and fewer tourists make winter a worthwhile alternative.

Weather

Generally, the weather of eastern and central Europe resembles that of the New England states: freezing temperatures in winter, rising to the mid-70s in summer. Naturally, there are exceptions: northern Poland, Russia and the Baltic States have colder winters and cooler, but still pleasant, summers. Areas bordering the Mediterranean and the Black Sea are warmer throughout the year.

Most southern European countries have warmer weather than the latitude suggests. Summers are hot and dry; winters mild and rainy. Snow-covered mountains are never far away.

Despite its reputation, the weather in Britain is more pleasant than in other countries of similar latitude. Trends are hard to predict (there can be snow in June!). As a rule fog and rain are evident in early winter; summer is the driest sea-

---

TRAVEL ADVISORIES

The U.S. Department of State issues Consular Information Sheets and Travel Warnings concerning serious health or security conditions that might affect U.S. citizens. They can be obtained at U.S. embassies and consulates abroad, regional passport agencies in the United States and from the Citizens' Emergency Center, 2201 C Street N.W., Room 4811, Department of State, Washington, DC 20520; tel: (202) 647-5225.

Consular Information Sheets provide information about entry requirements, currency regulations, health conditions, security, political disturbances, areas of instability and drug penalties.

A "Travel Warning" is issued when the situation in a country is dangerous enough for the Department of State to recommend that Americans not travel there.

U.S. CUSTOMS INFORMATION

The helpful booklet *Know Before You Go* lists and explains all U.S. customs regulations for travelers going abroad and returning. It is available from the U.S. Customs Service, 1301 Constitution Avenue N.W., Washington, DC 20229; tel: 202/927-1770.

---

son, and England's sunny "Indian summer" can extend into early November. Temperatures do not often rise above 26°C (80°F) or fall below –6°C (20°F).

Public Holidays

From the religious pageants of Easter and Christmas to folklore festivals, public holidays help reveal a country's character. The *Things To Know* box at the beginning of each country lists public holidays, and the major festivals are described in the appropriate city listings. Banks and stores are often closed on public holidays.

CUSTOMS IN EUROPE

Customs regulations are relatively few when it comes to what you may take into a country. See the *Things To Know* box in each country introduction for more detailed information.

ELECTRICITY

The electricity supply in most countries in Europe is incompatible with U.S.

TEMPERATURE

To convert Fahrenheit to Celsius, subtract 32 from the Fahrenheit temperature, multipy by 5 and divide by 9; to convert Celsius to Fahrenheit, multiply by 9, divide by 5 and add 32.

CELSIUS	FAHRENHEIT
100	BOILING 212
37	100
35	95
32	90
29	85
27	80
24	75
21	70
18	65
16	60
13	55
10	50
7	45
4	40
2	35
0 FREEZING	32
-18	0
-21	-5
-24	-10
-27	-15

electrical appliances, which will be damaged. Some U.S. stores sell electrical items for use overseas, but check the voltage requirements before you buy or ask for a transformer.

HEALTH MATTERS

Health facilities in Europe generally range from good to excellent; physicians, surgeons and specialists are available in all major cities and large towns. Make sure that you have quick access to cash and that your insurance policy is valid outside the United States.

The Centers for Disease Control and Prevention in Atlanta maintain a hot line offering international health requirements – including any requirements and recommendations for inoculation – and general advice for travelers. A touch-tone phone is needed to use the daily 24-hour service; tel: 404/332-4559. In addition, a booklet called *Health Information for International Travelers* can be obtained by sending $5 to the Superintendent of Documents, U.S. Government Printing Office, Washington, DC 20402.

INSURANCE

Automobile

An International Motor Insurance Certificate (Green Card) is advised for any motorist taking their own vehicle overseas; a AAA travel agent can arrange this. In certain eastern European countries (Bulgaria, Estonia, Poland), as well as in Andorra, it is compulsory to have one. The Green Card is not accepted in Belarus, the Baltic States, the Republic of Moldova, Russia or the Ukraine.

In most of Europe, public liability and property damage insurance is required for all vehicles. The charge for this insurance is included in the cost for vehicles that are rented or leased in Europe. U.S. residents who wish to purchase a vehicle while abroad can obtain through AAA clubs a short-term European automobile tourist insurance policy that is valid throughout Europe.

Coverage available to those using their own vehicles includes liability, medical payments and comprehensive and collision loss. Each policy includes a Green Card, proving that the policy conforms with all local insurance laws. For additional information contact your AAA club or phone AAA Foreign Motoring Insurance at 800/222-4599.

Personal Accident and Sickness

Personal accident insurance is sold by many AAA travel agencies. While policy provisions may vary, typically they will provide accidental death and dismemberment benefits when you travel by scheduled airline or another common carrier, including cruises, trains and motorcoaches when tickets are purchased through an AAA travel agency. Coverage of up to $500,000 is available.

TripAssist policies, available from AAA, are designed to provide help for travel-related problems almost anywhere in the world. They offer a broad range of services, including a 24-hour toll-free hot line staffed by multilingual coordinators, medical insurance, document and ticket replacement, legal help, emergency cash transfer, trip cancellation and interruption insurance, baggage insurance and travel accident insurance.

Baggage and Belongings

Baggage and personal effects insurance is available no matter how you travel. Many AAA travel agencies issue a policy that provides coverage for up to 180 days. Included in most plans is coverage for clothing, jewelry and sports gear.

PASSPORTS AND VISAS

Passports

The primary document for U.S. citizens who travel abroad is the U.S. passport. Some countries require as much as six months' validity. Your spouse and young children cannot be included on your passport; each individual must have one. The U.S. Department of State has an inquiries line that provides information

regarding passports; tel: 202/647-0518.

Lost passports should be reported to Passport Services, Bureau of Consular Affairs, 2201 C Street N.W., Washington DC, 20520; tel: 202/647-2423, or to the nearest passport agency, or to the consular officer in any American embassy or consulate (see *Things To Know* box for each country for appropriate addresses and telephone numbers).

Visas

A visa is a stamp affixed to your passport by an official of the country you plan to visit, indicating that travel to that country has been approved.

Visa requirements are specified in each *Things To Know* box. A AAA travel agency can give you detailed information for each country you plan to visit.

WHAT TO TAKE

Clothing

The golden rule is to travel light. The widely differing temperatures (and rainfall) you are likely to encounter on a European vacation point to the need for layers and a light raincoat.

Luggage

International airlines limit baggage by weight or by size. There is usually a charge for baggage that exceeds the maximum weight or size.

GETTING THERE

BY AIR

Air travel falls into three classes – first, business and economy – and rates can vary. Consult a AAA travel agent for reservations and information.

BY SEA

The *Queen Elizabeth II* cruise ship crosses the Atlantic regularly. Costs vary according to the class, type of accommodations, season and itinerary. Numerous air-sea combinations can be arranged. For additional information, contact a AAA travel agency.

CLOTHING CONVERSION CHART

Men's suits

Britain	36	38	40	42	44	46	48
Europe	46	48	50	52	54	56	58
U.S.	36	38	40	42	44	46	48

Dress sizes

Britain	8	10	12	14	16	18
France	36	38	40	42	44	46
Italy	38	40	42	44	46	48
Europe	34	36	38	40	42	44
U.S.	6	8	10	12	14	16

Men's shirts

Britain	14	14½	15	15½ 16 16½	17
Europe	36	37	38	39/40 41	42	43
U.S.		same as Britain				

Men's shoes

Britain	7	7½	8½	9½	10½	11
Europe	41	42	43	44	45	46
U.S.	8	8½	9½	10½	11½	12

Women's shoes

Britain	4½	5	5½	6	6½	7
Europe	38	38	39	39	40	41
U.S.	6	6½	7	7½	8	8½

DUTY-FREE SHOPS

High-quality merchandise from all over the world is featured in most duty-free shops.

Prices are generally about the same as you would expect to pay in the country of origin.

Don't be misled, however, by the word "duty-free." It simply means that the local merchant has been exempted from import taxes. All duty-free goods that return with you to the U.S. are still subject to U.S. import duties if you exceed your $400 limit.

GETTING AROUND

CAMPING

Camping in Europe has become increasingly popular with North Americans. There are thousands of campgrounds ranging from basic to modern; some have bungalows or ready-erected tents for rent. Fully equipped RVs are also available for delivery and collection.

International Camping Carnets, or permits, are available by writing to Family Campers and RVers, 4804 Transit Road, Building 2, Depew, NY 14043; tel: 716/668-6242.

CAR RENTAL

Most car rental companies in Europe will not rent to anyone under 21, even though such persons may have a valid U.S. license and an International Driving Permit (I.D.P.).

European cars are generally small, with manual transmission. Air-conditioning is only rarely available. Costs vary but a AAA travel agent will be able to give you an estimate.

Be sure to inquire about local taxes; in France, for example, taxes increase rental rates by one-third. Make certain that you know exactly what insurance is included, and check whether you need a collision damage waiver (C.D.W.) – you might already be covered through your personal insurance policy or credit card company. Sometimes C.D.W. may not cover certain types of damage – for example, in Greece damage to the underside of a car on a rough road may not be covered.

In some cases, a AAA travel agent can reserve a car for you before you leave, or can arrange for cars to be waiting for you on specified dates in major cities. Be sure to make your arrangements well in advance. If you plan to travel through several countries, ensure that the rental company has been informed and that you have the necessary documents. British rental agencies may require several days' notice to supply a car equipped for travel to continental Europe.

DRIVING

Driving in most western European countries presents no particular issues other than the peculiarities of language, signs, customs and local temperament; driving in some eastern European countries may present hazards of a different order. Seek the latest travel advice for these areas (see Travel Advisories on p.12).

Driving Documents

Although a valid U.S. driver's license is honored in most European countries, several (including Austria and Spain) require you to carry a translation of it in the local language. You should obtain an International Driving Permit (I.D.P.), which serves as an official, internationally recognized translation of your license. The I.D.P. is written in nine languages: English, French, German, Swedish, Italian, Spanish, Russian, Arabic and Chinese. AAA offices can issue I.D.P.s, valid for a year. You must be at least 18, fill out an application form, present a valid U.S. driver's license, submit two passport-size photographs and pay a fee.

Currently I.D.P.s are needed in about 60 countries around the world, including eastern Europe. You must carry both your U.S. driver's license and your I.D.P.

If traveling to Spain, it is highly advisable to obtain a Bail Bond, which is available from your car insurer or as a component of a motoring travel insurance policy. An accident in Spain may result in the impounding of your car and property and the detention of the driver pending trial. A Bail Bond will often facilitate release.

Vehicle Equipment

The display of a warning triangle at the scene of a breakdown or accident is recommended throughout Europe.

The carrying of a first-aid kit is compulsory in Austria, Baltic States, Belarus, Bulgaria, Czech Republic, Slovak Republic, Russia, Greece, Moldavia and the Ukraine. The same countries (except Austria, Czech Republic and Slovak Republic) also require you to carry a fire extinguisher.

A spare set of light bulbs is recommended throughout Europe, but they are compulsory in the Czech Republic, the Slovak Republic and Spain.

In general, it is advisable to check with the motoring organization in the country you plan to visit regarding any requirements for additional equipment.

Accidents and Breakdowns

The procedure to be followed after an accident varies in each country, and you should consult the documentation that accompanies any insurance policy. In most countries, the police will need to be informed if an accident results in injury or substantial damage, and a report will have to be filed. The vehicle should not be moved before this is completed. In some countries in eastern Europe, even minor damage to a vehicle will necessitate a police report; and it may also be necessary to report to the state insurance authority (this is the case in Finland). Drivers should always exchange particulars with the other party; if one of the parties is uninsured, the police should be notified, however slight the damage.

In eastern Europe, any visible existing damage to a vehicle entering the country must be certified by the authorities at the time of entry. Damaged vehicles may only be taken out of these countries on production of such evidence.

Listed below are the European motoring organizations affiliated with AAA through the A.I.T. and F.I.A., the international associations of motoring clubs. If no breakdown service is offered by the motoring organization, the phone numbers given can be used for assistance.

If you are in a rented car, the rental company will have made arrangements with a breakdown service; details of emergency telephone numbers will be given when you receive the car.

Emergency telephone numbers for Fire, Police and Ambulance services are listed in the *Things to Know* boxes.

Austria

Österreichischer Automobil-, Motorrad- und Touring Club (Ö.A.M.T.C.), Schubertring 1–3, 1010 Vienna; tel: (01) 711 990. For 24-hour roadside assistance service (Pannenhilfe) and tow service (Abschleppdienst); tel: 120.

Baltic States
Estonia: Eesti Autoklubi (E.A.K.), Rävaala 91, EE0001 Tallinn; tel: (02) 6317 280. In case of a breakdown contact the E.A.K. roadside assistance tel: 188.
Latvia: Auto-Moto Society of Latvia (L.A.M.B.), Raunas 16b, Lv-1039 Riga; tel: (02) 56 62 22.
Lithuania: The Lithuanian Automobile Association (Lietuvos Automobilininku Sajunka – L.A.S.) Gyneju 8, 2005 Vilnius; tel: (02) 250557. In the event of a breakdown call (02) 722186.

Belgium
Touring Club Royal de Belgique (T.C.B.), 44 rue de la Loi, 1040 Brussels; tel: (02) 233 22 11. T.C.B. has a 24-hour breakdown service: Touring Secours/ Touring Wegenhulp; tel: (070) 34 47 77.

Britain
The Automobile Association (AA) Norfolk House, Priestley Road, Basing-stoke, Hampshire RG24 9NY; tel: (01256) 320123.
A 24-hour rescue service is available to members and courtesy service is available to AAA members by calling (toll free) 0800 887766.
Royal Automobile Club (R.A.C.), RAC House, M1 Cross, Brent Terrace, London NW2 1LT; tel: (0181) 452 8000.

Bulgaria
Union des Automobilistes Bulgares (U.A.B.), 3 Place Positano, Sofia 1090; tel: (02) 8 61 51. U.A.B. patrols main roads daily in summer, until 7pm. In emergencies, tel: 1286, or (02) 883978.

Czech and Slovak republics
Czech Republic: Ústřední Automotoklub CR(Ù.A.M.K;CR), Na Strzi 9, 140 00 Prague 4; tel: (02) 611 04 333. Ù.A.M.K. has 24-hour patrol service throughout the country; tel: 0123
Slovak Republic: Ùstredni Automotoklub (Ù.A.M.K.), Wolkrova 4, 851 01

Bratislava; tel: (07) 81 09 09. Ù.A.M.K. Slovakia s.r.o. has 24-hour patrol service throughout the country; tel: 154 or 0123 in case of breakdown.

Denmark
Forenede Danske Motorejere (F.D.M.), Firskovvej 32, P.O. Box 500, 2800 Lyngby; tel: (045) 270707. In case of breakdown, contact the Falcks Redningskorps A.S. organization; tel:

LIQUID MEASURE

CUSTOMARY
1 fluid ounce = 29.57 milliliters
1 pint = 0.47 liters
1 quart = 0.95 liters
1 gallon = 3.79 liters

METRIC
10 milliliters = 0.34 fluid ounces
1 liter = 2.11 pints
1 liter = 1.06 quarts
1 liter = 0.26 gallons

U.S. LIQUID MEASURE
1 U.S. gallon = 3.79 liters
1 U.S. quart = .95 liter
6 U.S. gallons = 5 imperial gallons
The imperial measure is 20 per cent larger than the U.S. measure

CONVERSION TABLE

GALLONS/LITERS		LITERS/GALLONS	
1	3.79	1	0.26
2	7.57	2	0.53
3	11.36	3	0.79
4	15.14	4	1.06
5	18.93	5	1.32
6	22.71	6	1.59
7	26.50	7	1.85
8	30.28	8	2.11
9	34.07	9	2.38
10	37.85	10	2.64
15	56.78	15	3.96
20	75.71	20	5.28
25	94.64	25	6.60
30	113.56	30	7.93

70 10 20 30 or Dansk Autohjaelp; tel: 70 10 70 80; for 24-hour service.

Finland
Autoliitto (A.L.), Automobile and Touring-Club of Finland, Hameentie 105 A, 00550 Helsinki; tel: (09) 774761. A.L. has a 24-hour patrol service; tel: (09) 77476400 (does not operate Friday–Sunday 6pm–10pm. During these times call (02) 02 00 80 80 for assistance. AAA members receive priority service from A.L.

France
Automobile Club National (A.C.N.), 5 rue Auber, 75009 Paris; tel: (01) 44 51 53 99. French motoring clubs do not provide a roadside breakdown service so it is worth taking out a breakdown insurance policy (available through the AA in the U.K.). Policyholders can get 24-hour assistance by calling (0800) 089222.

Germany
Allgemeiner Deutscher Automobil-Club (A.D.A.C.), Am Westpark 8, 81373 Munich; tel: (089) 76 760. For breakdown assistance, tel: 01802/22 22 22 Deutscher Touring Automobil-Club (D.T.C.), Amalienburgstrasse 23, D-81247 Munich; tel: (089) 89 11 33-0. For breakdown assistance, tel: (089) 811 12 12.

Greece
The Automobile and Touring Club of Greece (E.L.P.A.), Messogion 2-4, Athens; tel: (01) 74 88 800. E.L.P.A. provides a 24-hour breakdown service in all of continental Greece, as well as on some of the islands. For information or assistance, tel: 104.

Hungary
Magyar Autoklub (M.A.K.), Rómer Flóris utca 4/a, 1024 Budapest; tel: (01) 212 29 38. M.A.K. has a patrol service on main roads, and can be called from gas stations, restaurants etc., displaying the yellow sign *Segelyszolgalat;* tel: (01) 212 28 21.

Ireland
Republic of Ireland: The Automobile Association Limited (AA Ireland), 23 Rock Hill, Blackrock, Co. Dublin; tel: (01) 283 35 55. For rescue service, tel: (01800) 667788 (toll free).
Northern Ireland: The Automobile Association (AA), 108 Great Victoria Street, Belfast; tel: (01) 232 328924. The AA's breakdown service is available to members on the same terms as in Britain. Call (01800) 667788 (toll free) for advice in case of breakdown.

Italy
Touring Club Italiano (T.C.I.), 10 Corso Italia, 20122, Milan; tel: (39-2) 85 26 1. Automobile Club d'Italia (A.C.I.), Via Marsala 8, 00185 Rome; tel: (06) 49 98 1. The A.C.I. provides towage from a breakdown to the nearest affiliated garage. Call 116 nationwide on ordinary roads, and push S.O.S. column buttons on highways for assistance.

Luxembourg
Automobile Club du Grand-Duché de Luxembourg (A.C.L.), 54 route de Longwy, l-8007 Bertrange; tel: (02) 45 00 45 1. For breakdown assistance, tel: (02) 45 00 45.

Monaco
Automobile Club de Monaco (A.C.), 23 boulevard Albert 1er, MC 98000, Boite Postale 464, Monaco; tel: (093) 15 26 00.

The Netherlands
Koninklijke Nederlandse Toeristenbond (A.N.W.B.), Wassenaarseweg 220, 2596 EC's-Gravenhage; tel: (070) 314 71 47. A.N.W.B. has a 24-hour patrol service (*Wegenwacht*) throughout the country. Tel: 06 0888 or use yellow call boxes in case of breakdown.

Norway
Norges Automobil-Forbund (N.A.F.), Storgaten 2, 0155 Oslo 1; tel: (022) 34 14 00. N.A.F. operates a limited road patrol service in the summer. For breakdown assistance, tel: (022) 34 16 00.

Poland
Polski Zwiazek Motorowy (P.Z.M.), ul. Kazimierzowska 66, 02-518 Warsaw; tel: (022) 49 93 61.

Portugal
Automóvel Club de Portugal (A.C.P.), rua Rosa Araújo 24-1250, Lisbon tel: (01) 356 3931. A.C.P. operates a 24-hour breakdown service; tel: (01) 942 5059 (Lisbon) and (02) 830 1127 (Porto).

Russia, Belarus, the Ukraine
Russia: Russian Automobile Fédération (R.A.F.), 21/5 Kuznetsky Most. Str., 103895 Moscow; Zelenograd; tel: (095) 921 68 21.
Belarus: The Byelorusian Club of General Assistance and Automobile Service, (A.D.A.S.) Romanovskaya Sloboda Str. 24, Minsk 220004; tel: (0172) 231 055. In Minsk the breakdown telephone numbers are 2231055, 2230893, 2236320. Outside Minsk omit the first digit "2." A CB-radio can also be used to call for assistance on Channel 19; call "Sockol odin."
Ukraine: Féderation Automobile d'Ukraine (F.A.U.), 290000 Lviv, P/b 10697; tel: (0322) 27 21 12.

Spain
Real Automóvil Club de España (R.A.C.E.), Calle Jose Abascal 10, 28003 Madrid; tel: (01) 447 32 00. R.A.C.E. runs a 24-hour breakdown service; tel: (01) 593 33 33.

Sweden
Motormännens Riksförbund (M), Sveavägen 159, 104 35 Stockholm; tel: (08) 690 38 00. M does not operate any roadside service. In cases of breakdown, you may contact the *Assistancekâren* on the green number 020 912 912 and you will be connected with the nearest breakdown center. Breakdown service must be paid for.

Switzerland
Touring Club Suisse (T.C.S.), rue Pierre Fatio 9, 1211 Geneva 3; tel: (022) 737 1212. T.C.S. has a patrol service and 24-hour breakdown service. Call 140 for help, or ask an operator for *Autohilfe*.

Highways
European highways (motorways) vary considerably. In general, highways in northwest Europe are excellent.

There are no standard highways in Belarus, the Republic of Moldova, Russia or the Ukraine. You should seek advice before planning a motoring trip in this area. The Baltic States have one major hard-surfaced highway, the M12, linking Tallinn with Riga and Vilnius. Other countries in eastern Europe (including Czech Republic, the Slovak Republic, Hungary and Poland) have limited systems of varying standards.

Toll Roads
In France, Spain, Greece and Italy, most highways are toll roads. In Italy, an automatic toll card (*Viacard*) can be bought in advance from toll booths and gas (petrol) stations. In Austria you must buy a sticker before driving on highways and some dual carriageways. The sticker is available from O.A.M.T.C. offices, crossing points on the Swiss border and some gas stations. In Switzerland, a disk (*vignette*) is bought in advance at the border. Bulgaria's are paid for at the border.

Route Name Systems
Many main European routes form part of the European International Network, most of which are identified by green and white signs and have the prefix "E." In Austria, Belgium, France, Germany, Italy and the Netherlands, most highways are in the "E" route system. These routes may also be labeled with their national number, usually prefixed with "A" (e.g. in France, the E9, labeled green and white, is also the A71, labeled red and white). Britain and Hungary use the prefix "M" for their highways.

Facilities on the Road
In some countries, there are no gas or service stations along highways, though

they may be signposted off them. There are emergency telephones at intervals (usually 2 kilometers/1½ miles) along most European highways, although in Scandinavia they are infrequent as a result of the increasing use of cell-phones. If you break down on a high-way, you may have to pay a fee for tow-ing, unless you have a motor-breakdown insurance policy offered by one of the national motoring associations.

Gas

Gas (petrol) costs considerably more in Europe than in the U.S., and most gas stations are self-service. Octane levels in gas vary from country to country. Gas is usually graded as "regular" and "super," with "super" having the higher octane level.

The availability of unleaded gas is now widespread throughout Europe, but in some countries leaded "regular" gas is no longer sold. In Britain, for example, only "4-Star" leaded gas is still available with a 98 octane level, but sales of all leaded fuel will stop in the year 2000. Unleaded gas in Britain is available with two octane levels – premium unleaded gas at 95 octane and super unleaded at 98 octane.

LINEAR MEASURE

CUSTOMARY
1 inch = 2.54 centimeters
1 foot = 30.48 centimeters
1 yard = 0.91 meters
1 mile = 1.61 kilometers
1 acre = 0.4 hectare

METRIC
1 centimeter = 0.39 inches
1 meter = 3.28 feet
1 meter = 1.09 yards
1 kilometer = 0.62 miles
1 hectare = 2.5 acres

To convert kilometers into miles multiply by 0.6.

Drinking and Driving

Driving under the influence of alcohol is an offense in all European countries. In most, you exceed the permitted level if you have a jigger of whisky or two cans of beer. Several countries require a zero level of blood alcohol.

On-the-Spot Fines

Fines for traffic violations generally must be paid on the spot, usually in local currency. See *Getting Around* under the appropriate country.

Parking

Designated "blue zones" in major cities are for short-term (usually 1 to 1½ hours) parking. Use of the blue zone requires you to post your arrival time at a conspic-uous place on the automobile. Failure to indicate arrival time may result in a fine. "Red zones" in cities indicate longer-term parking; "green zones" usually des-ignate areas where parking is prohibited.

In cities, watch for the "no parking" sign, usually a circle bisected by a diago-nal line. A circle divided by an "X" indi-cates no stopping.

Pedestrian Crossings

In many cities, bold white parallel lines known as "zebra stripes" cross the road-way. These areas always give the pedes-trian the right of way and cars are required to stop for them. There also are a number of crossings controlled by lights for pedestrian use.

Right of Way

Drive on the right and pass on the left. In Britain and Ireland, however, drive on the left and pass on the right. In either case, passing laws are strictly enforced. Be sure to watch for road markings and do not cross a solid white or yellow line marking the center of the road.

Road Signs

Most countries use the International Road Signs, designed to be easily under-stood. Triangular signs, except the yield sign, warn of danger, and circular signs prohibit certain actions or tell of restrictions. Rectangular signs are informative.

In continental Europe, it is customary to yield to traffic approaching from the right. However, when you see a yellow diamond-shaped sign with a white border, you have the right of way and may keep driving without yielding to traffic from the right. When the sign reappears with a diagonal line through it, then it is again necessary to give right of way to traffic coming along from the right.

Speed Limits
It is important to observe speed limits. Offenders may be fined and have their driver's license confiscated on the spot. It is often illegal to travel so slowly that the traffic flow is obstructed. See *Getting Around* under individual countries

TRAIN TRAVEL
Train travel in Europe is an excellent way to get around, and can be very good value. It is worth doing some homework in advance, investigating the many special offers and passes available. These fall broadly into three categories: unlimited travel within a fixed period (usually 15 or 21 days, or 1, 2 or 3 months); travel on a certain number of days within a longer period (typically 5 days within 15, or 15 within 30), often referred to as a "Flexipass"; and a variety of regional or local discounts or deals.

Many of the fixed-period and "Flexi" passes cover several countries. For example, the EurailPass covers 17 countries; the EuroPass covers five. Others cover eastern Europe, the Benelux countries, Britain, France and Scandinavia. There are several youth passes, applicable to people aged 26 or under. Almost all are available only to nonresidents of participating countries, and can be purchased only outside the country – that is, before you leave the U.S. However, local "Rover" tickets and some other passes are available locally.

In most countries, children under four can travel free of charge, and children aged four to eleven travel for

---

WEIGHT AND PRESSURE

If you know:	Multiply by:	To find:
ounces	28	grams
pounds	0.45	kilograms
grams	0.035	ounces
kilograms	2.2	pounds

Air pressure in automobile tires is expressed in kilopascals. Multiply pound-force per square inch (psi) by 6.89 to find kilopascals (kPa).

24 psi = 165 kPa
26 psi = 179 kPa
28 psi = 193 kPa
30 psi = 207 kPa

---

half price. There are variations, however – for example, in Austria, children under seven travel free. Family passes may prove to be very good value.

For further information, refer to a AAA travel agent.

OTHER PUBLIC TRANSPORTATION
For details of public transportation other than train, see the individual country sections.

EMERGENCIES

EMBASSIES AND CONSULATES
Embassies and consulates give advice and render assistance to their citizens in case of accident, serious illness or death. Consular agents may also be able to help in such matters as lost passports.

In the capitals and larger cities of Europe, U.S. tourists can register at American embassies and, in certain other cities, at American consulates.

It is particularly wise to register with the nearest American embassy or consulate if you are traveling to eastern Europe or if you are staying in any country for longer than one month. The addresses and phone numbers of American embassies and consulates are listed in the *Things To Know* box for individual countries.

VALUABLES

Money

If you are visiting several countries, consider buying traveler's checks in U.S. dollars since few currencies are as easily exchanged and you will save yourself the cost of repeated currency exchanges.

If you will be visiting one country or if the U.S. dollar is declining in value and you want to lock in at the current rate, it might be a good idea to buy traveler's checks in foreign currency.

When exchanging money, it is always advisable to shop around. Banks (other than at international borders) usually offer the best rates, but often charge a commission. Traveler's checks usually get a better rate of exchange than cash.

You can exchange foreign bills when you leave a country, but not coins. Save your exchange transaction receipts; some countries will not let you exchange local currency back to your own unless you can prove that your foreign holdings were originally in your own currency.

The currency of an eastern European country is worthless outside that country, and it is frequently illegal to export (see the *Things to Know* box for each country for further details).

Credit Cards

It is wise to have a backup source of funds in case your money is stolen or an emergency occurs. Take internationally recognized credit cards that will let you draw cash up to your credit limit. You can also use them to pay for purchases at thousands of locations across Europe.

Theft

Travel lightly and do not leave luggage unattended in public places. Be sure not to travel with all of your money, credit cards and traveler's checks in one place. Consider leaving valuables in your hotel safe or a safe deposit box. If possible, take advantage of indoor parking; do not leave your car on the street overnight.

AAA members should consider purchasing AAA baggage insurance.

RETURNING TO THE U.S.

U.S. CUSTOMS REGULATIONS

Declaration of Imports

Hints for returning U.S. residents are in the *Know Before You Go* booklet (see Travel Advisories on p.12). Since customs regulations may change, you are advised to consult the booklet before traveling. Customs Declarations Forms (CF 6059B) are distributed on ships and planes for you to present to customs inspectors upon your arrival in the U.S. You can also obtain one in advance from customs offices. All articles acquired abroad that accompany you on your return must be declared to customs, including any repairs to articles taken abroad, and any gifts received abroad.

To avoid paying duty on foreign-made items that you owned before you went abroad, such as cameras, jewelry or watches, register them at a customs office before leaving the United States.

Duties

Returning residents of the U.S. are allowed a $400 duty-free exemption on articles for personal use or gifts if they have been out of the country a minimum of 48 hours and have not used this exemption within the preceding 30-day period. A flat-rate duty of 10 percent will be applied to the next $1,000 worth of merchandise; above this, various rates apply, depending on the article. Assessment is based on the retail value; remember to keep sales slips, and don't be tempted by a sales clerk's offer to understate the cost of purchase. Genuine antiques (anything more than 100 years old) are duty-free; you'll need written proof of the article's age.

Items bought abroad and sent home by a U.S. resident or by the store will be subject to duty and taxes.

Gifts

Packages containing gifts with a total fair retail value not exceeding $50 in the country where you purchased them may be sent duty-free to persons in the U.S., provided that only one such package is received by the same person in one day. Gifts for more than one person may be mailed in the same package, provided each gift is individually wrapped and labeled with the name of the recipient. Duty on gifts exceeding $50 cannot be prepaid; it is collected by the U.S. Postal Service in the form of postage-due stamps. The gift allowance does not include alcohol-containing perfume valued at more than $5, alcoholic beverages or tobacco products. While traveling in Europe you may not send a gift to yourself, nor can persons traveling together send gifts to one other.

Restricted or Prohibited Articles

To prevent the introduction of plant and animal pests and diseases into the U.S., an agricultural quarantine bans the importation of certain fruits, vegetables, plants, livestock, poultry and meats. For details, request the leaflet *Travelers' Tips* from APHIS (Animal and Plant Health Inspection Service), 14th St. and Independence Avenue S.W., Washington, D.C. 20250; tel: 301/734-7799.

Certain articles considered injurious or detrimental to the U.S. are prohibited, such as *absinthe*, liquor-filled confections, fireworks, lottery tickets and narcotics. Endangered animal or plant species and products made from them are prohibited, and import restrictions are placed on firearms and ammunition.

If you require medicines with habit-forming drugs or narcotics, ensure they are in their original containers, and carry a prescription authorizing their use to avoid customs problems on your return.

Alcoholic Beverages and Tobacco

A returning resident 21 years or older who is entitled to the $400 duty-free exemption may include one quart (U.S.) of alcoholic beverages for personal use or as a gift. Persons of legal age may bring in 100 cigars and 200 cigarettes. Laws concerning the importation of cigarettes and alcohol vary from state to state.

AUTOMOBILE CLUBS IN EUROPE

For the benefit of members traveling abroad, the American Automobile Association maintains reciprocal agreements with many foreign motor clubs, a number of which are in Europe. Presentation of your valid AAA membership card at these participating clubs makes you eligible to receive all the services they give to their own members. This does not mean you'll receive the same services as those provided by AAA at home – operating philosophies differ around the world.

This reciprocal service for AAA members is for short-term visitors only. If you are going abroad for an extended period, you will have to become a member of the local club. Addresses of main offices are provided near the beginning of each country with an automobile club or association.

AAA's *Offices to Serve You Abroad* pamphlet, available from your local AAA club, lists auto club offices to serve you overseas and explains in detail the services you can expect from those clubs with which AAA has a full reciprocal agreement. As a member of both the A.I.T. (Alliance Internationale de Tourisme) and the F.I.A. (Fédération Internationale de l'Automobile), AAA also has additional but more limited sources of worldwide service available through A.I.T./F.I.A. member clubs. They too are listed. A copy of this booklet should be taken along with your AAA membership card.The symbol ▲ before the city or town name in the alphabetical listings denotes the presence ofa main or branch office of an automobile club.

AUSTRIA

AUSTRIA IS A RICH COUNTRY: PROSPEROUS ECONOMI-CALLY, BUT RICH ALSO IN SCENERY AND CULTURE, AND WITH A PEOPLE WHOSE LOVE OF LIFE AND EASYGOING NATURE MAKES THEM RICH IN SPIRIT, TOO. WHOSE SPIRITS WOULD NOT RISE, THOUGH, WITH SUCH A SPLENDID CAPITAL CITY AS VIENNA? ONE OF THE GREAT CENTERS OF THE WORLD, VIENNA IS THE CITY OF SCHUBERT

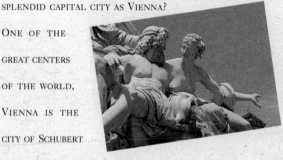

AND STRAUSS, OF HAYDN, MOZART, BEETHOVEN, THE VIENNA WOODS, THE BLUE DANUBE, OF FREUD, THE SPANISH RIDING SCHOOL, OF CAFÉS AND CHOCOLATE CAKE, AND THE MYSTERIES OF *THE THIRD MAN*. BEYOND VIENNA LIES BEAUTIFUL COUNTRYSIDE, FROM LUSH VINE-FILLED VALLEYS WHERE EXCELLENT WINES HAVE BEEN KEPT SOMETHING OF A SECRET, TO THE MOUNTAIN LAKES AND HIGH PEAKS OF THE ALPS.

Left THE PICTURESQUE MARKET TOWN OF HALLSTATT, OVERLOOKING LAKE HALLSTATT, DATES BACK TO PREHISTORIC TIMES
Above THE PALLAS ATHENE FOUNTAIN OUTSIDE THE PARLIAMENT, VIENNA

THINGS TO KNOW

- **AREA:** 83,849 square kilometers (32,374 square miles)
- **POPULATION:** 7,586,400
- **CAPITAL:** Wien (Vienna)
- **LANGUAGE:** German
- **RELIGION:** Mainly Catholic but some Protestants also.
- **ECONOMY:** Industry, agriculture, tourism. Chief exports are machinery, iron and steel, and textiles.
- **PASSPORT REQUIREMENTS:** Required for U.S. and British citizens.
- **VISA REQUIREMENTS:** Not required for stays up to three months.
- **DUTY-FREE ITEMS:** 200 cigarettes or 50 cigars or 250 grams of tobacco; two liters of wine and one liter of distilled liquor; 0.25 liters of toilet water and 60 grams of perfume; two still cameras with one roll of 24-exposure film for each; one small movie camera with 10 rolls of film; one video camera.
  Note: If, on the way to Austria, a stopover of more than 24 hours is made in any European country, the duty-free allowance of cigarettes, tobacco, and distilled liquor is increased.
- **CURRENCY:** The currency unit is the Austrian *schilling*, divided into 100 *groschen*. Due to currency fluctuations, the exchange rate is subject to frequent change. No limit on Austrian and foreign currency brought into the country. Note: No limit on the exportation of foreign currency, but only 100,000 *schillings* may be taken out of the country.
- **BANK OPENING HOURS:** 8am–12:30pm and 1:30–3pm Monday–Wednesday and Friday, 8am–12:30pm and 1:30–5:30pm Thursday.
- **STORE OPENING HOURS:** Generally 8:30am–6pm Monday–Friday, 8:30am–1pm Saturday. In downtown Vienna stores do not close for lunch. Vienna's Dorotheum, a large pawn and loan house, publishes regular auction announcements.
- **BEST BUYS:** Leather goods, wooden crafts, porcelain, knitwear, ski

HISTORY

Because many principal trade routes, including the strategic Donau (Danube River), traverse this small nation, Austria has played an important part in European history. Following centuries of invasions by Romans, Goths, Huns and various barbaric tribes, Charlemagne brought some stability to the country when he made it his eastern frontier (Ost Mark) in AD 799.

In AD 962 Austria became a part of the Holy Roman Empire of the German nation. Leopold of Babenberg was declared Margrave of Austria in AD 976 and established his capital at Melk. His successors ruled the margravate, a duchy after 1156, until the death of the last

male heir in 1246. A 27-year struggle for the throne ended when Rudolph of Habsburg, the elected Holy Roman Emperor, was crowned Duke of Austria, beginning 645 years of that family's rule.

The Emperor Maximilian I, who ruled 1493–1519, increased the extent of the Habsburg lands. Charles V, his grandson, inherited one of the greatest empires in the world; Austria, the Netherlands, Belgium, Spain, Latin America (except Brazil), Naples, Sardinia, Sicily, and a few provinces in eastern France. Charles divided his empire, and his brother Ferdinand got the Austrian lands in 1521, becoming King of Bohemia and Hungary in 1526. With the acquisition of the latter came the responsibility of defending Christian Europe from the Moslem Ottoman Turks, who were at the walls of Vienna by 1529.

During the turmoil of the Napoleonic era, the Holy Roman Empire was replaced by the Empire of Austria in 1806. The Congress of Vienna convened in 1815 to redraw the maps of Europe. As a result, the Habsburgs ruled an empire that included Germans, Romanians, Czechs, Slovaks, Hungarians, Poles, Italians, Croats, Slovenes and Serbs. A revolution, riots and war brought about the exclusion of the Habsburgs from the established kingdom of Italy and the German Empire and resulted in the creation of the Dual Monarchy of Austria-Hungary in 1867.

clothing and equipment, local costumes, copper and iron work.

- **PUBLIC HOLIDAYS:** January 1; January 6 (Epiphany); Easter Monday; May 1 (Labor Day); Ascension Day; Whitmonday; Corpus Christi; August 15 (Assumption Day); October 26 (Austrian National Flag Day); November 1 (All Saints' Day); December 8 (Immaculate Conception); December 25–26.
- **USEFUL TELEPHONE NUMBERS:**
  Police 133
  Fire 122
  Ambulance 144
- **NATIONAL TOURIST OFFICES:**
  Austrian National Tourist Office
  500 Fifth Avenue
  Suite 2009-2022
  New York, NY 10110
  Tel: 212/944-6880
  Fax: 212/73-04 568
  Austrian National Tourist Office
  30 St. George Street
  London W1R 0AL, England
  Tel: 0171-629 0461
  Fax: 0171-499 6038
  Wiener Fremdenverkehrsverband
  Obere Augartenstrasse 40
  A-1025 Wien, Austria
  Tel: 1 211 140
  Fax: 1 216 84 92
  Salzburger Land –
  Tourismus Ges.m.b.H.
  Alpenstrasse 96
  A-5033 Salzburg, Austria
  Postfach 8
  Tel: 662 20 506-0
  Telex: 633076
  Fax: 662 23070
  Tirol Werbung
  Bozner Platz 6
  A-6010 Innsbruck, Austria
  Tel: 512 53 20 170 or 512 53 20 171
  TTX: 3522229
  Fax: 512 53 20 150
- **AMERICAN EMBASSY:**
  Boltzmanngasse-16
  1090 Vienna, Austria
  Tel: 0222 315511 (1-31338 from outside Austria)

On June 28, 1914, the assassination of the heir to the Austrian throne by a Serbian nationalist released the global tensions that escalated into World War I. After the war, the non-German peoples of the empire established their own nations. The German members of the Reichstag, the Imperial Parliament, proclaimed the Republic of German-Austria in November 1918.

Confusion reigned between the world wars while considerable agitation for union with the German Republic was thwarted by the allied powers. In 1938, Hitler annexed Austria to his Third Reich. Seven years later the armies of France, Great Britain, the Soviet Union and the United States occupied the land. After a decade of military occupation, the Austrian Republic was restored.

FOOD AND DRINK

To request a menu in Austria, ask for a *Speisekarte;* if you ask for a menu, you might be brought the daily special. The fatted calf appears on nearly every Austrian table. You can enjoy it as *Wienerschnitzel* (Viennese fillet of veal), or the memorable *Schnitzel cordon bleu* (veal, ham and cheese dipped in egg and breadcrumbs and fried). Pork makes its entrance as *Spanferkel* (roast suckling pig) and *Wildschweinbraten* (roast boar). *Heisse Würstel mit Senf* is simply a frankfurter, served with mustard and a roll.

Noodle dishes are plentiful, but better remembered are the delightfully rich desserts. Among them are *Sachertorte*, Viennese chocolate cake with or without cream, and *Strudel*, made with apples, cherries or pot cheese. Viennese coffee or several varieties of beer and wine make fine dinner endings.

As delightful as the Austrian wines are the *Heurigen* (country wine taverns). The *Nobel-Heuriger* is the city version, sometimes more simply called *Weinstube*. Local coffee houses and *Konditoreien*, or pastry shops, serve light snacks.

SPORTS AND RECREATION

Skiing and mountain climbing top the list of sports in mountainous Austria, where the skiing season lasts from December to late spring.

For fishermen, fly fishing is best in the mountain streams. Apply in advance to the local authorities for permission to fish. Golf and horseback riding can be enjoyed at many resorts. Swimming, water skiing, rowing and sailing are also popular. While no special license is required for sailing boats under 10 meters (33 feet) long, official regulations require you either to prove your ability to operate a sailing craft or to be accompanied by a qualified sailor.

GETTING AROUND

Austria's six major train lines, mostly electrified, range from slower trains serving smaller towns to expresses between Vienna and other large cities. Reduced rates offered by the Austrian Federal Railway system include discounts for travel in any one Austrian province and half fare for children under 15. The "Austria Ticket" gives special rates for travel on trains and buses for those under 26, as well as certain discounts on Danube steamboat cruises, aerial trams and chair lifts. Postal and local buses serve areas off the railroad routes. River and lake cruises provide another enjoyable way to see the country.

AUTOMOBILE CLUB
The **Österreichischer Automobil-Motorrad- und Touring Club** (Ö.A.M.T.C., Austrian Automobile Motoring and Touring Club), Schubertring 1–3, A-1010, Vienna, has branch offices in various cities throughout Austria. The symbol ▲ beside a city name indicates the presence of a AAA-affiliated automobile club branch. Not all auto clubs offer full travel services to AAA members.

Austria has an excellent system of roads and *Autobahnen* (or highways). The local weather conditions can sometimes necessitate the use of tire chains; these can be rented from Austria's automobile club.

Road identification signs use white letters and numbers on a green background for a European highway and white numbers on a blue background for an Austrian federal highway type I; the latter gives the right of way over all intersecting traffic. A yellow circular sign with black numbers is an Austrian federal highway type II, allowing no special right of way.

Visitors must buy stickers before driving on Austrian highways and some dual carriageways. Available from O.A.M.T.C. offices, Swiss border crossing points, post offices and some petrol stations, the stickers do not cover some toll roads and tunnels, whch carry an extra fee.

Seat belts are mandatory for driver and passengers, if the vehicle is so equipped; a child under 12 cannot travel unless using a suitable restraint system. The speed limits are 50 k.p.h. (31 m.p.h.) in town, 100 k.p.h. (62 m.p.h.) on all out-of-town roads and 130 k.p.h. (80 m.p.h.) on highways, unless otherwise posted. Visiting motorists are required to pay fines for motoring violations on the spot with Austrian *schillings*.

ACCOMMODATIONS

Gasthöfe, or small inns, are common in the small towns throughout Austria. Many lodgings include a Continental breakfast in their room rates and some serve *durchgehend warme Küche*, hot meals, between noon and 2pm and between 6pm and 9pm. *Jause*, afternoon coffee, is normally served between 4 and 5pm.

If you prefer luxury, Austria has some 90 spas and resorts. About 100 youth hostels accommodate travelers as well, giving preference to those under 30. Austria also maintains about 400 campgrounds. Some might give a reduced rate if you have an International Camping Carnet, or permit, which, although not usually mandatory, may be required on some sites.

TIPPING

Restaurants in Austria usually include a service charge in the bill, but a tip of about 10 percent on top is expected, rounding off to the nearest 10 *schillings*. Tip taxi drivers 10 to 15 percent of the fare; tip bartenders about 10 percent of your beverage bill. Porters and bellhops normally receive about 20 *schillings* per bag and doormen about 15 *schillings*.

PRINCIPAL TOURING AREAS

Note: For descriptions of attractions in bold type, see individual listings.

CARINTHIA

Kärnten (Carinthia) is an Alpine province descending to the Klagenfurt Plain, with several scenic extremes. Mountains protect the area, resulting in a long, warm season ideal for swimming, water skiing or sunbathing. Mountain climbers have a choice of peaks, the most formidable being Grossglockner, which at 3,797 meters (12,457 feet) is the highest of the Austrian Alps.

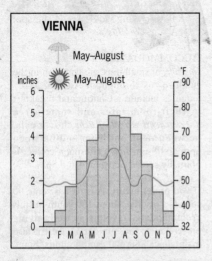

VIENNA

May–August

inches · May–August · °F

LOWER AUSTRIA AND BURGENLAND

Niederösterreich (Lower Austria) encompasses beautiful parts of the Danube, as well as vineyards, castles, museums, palaces, villages and mountains. The Wienerwald (Vienna Woods) is a hiker's paradise. **Wien** (Vienna) is a cosmopolitan city with a rich heritage.

Lower Austria's tiny eastern neighbor, Burgenland, adjoins the Slovak Republic, Hungary and Slovenia. Numerous castles and fortified churches recall a less peaceful past. **Eisenstadt**, the capital, was the home of Franz Joseph Haydn.

SALZBURG AND UPPER AUSTRIA

Oberösterreich (Upper Austia) and the federal province of **Salzburg** are situated futher west. Salt in the springs makes this a good spa center. The surrounding area and the lakes of Salzkammergut are popular all year.

STYRIA

In the mountainous and forested part of central and southeastern Austria there is good walking, climbing and riding. In Steiermark (Styria), there are several mountain and lowland resorts. **Graz**, an old university town, is known for its October Festival of Music and Drama.

TIROL

In the heart of Europe, the Tirol offers rugged, snow-capped peaks and green valleys. Rich with woods and meadows, it is known for its beautiful old villages and for the university town of **Innsbruck**. Many resorts are tucked away in its hills.

VORARLBERG

The subtly changing landscape in western Austria extends from the shores of Bodensee (Lake Constance) up to the glaciers of the Silvretta range. Mountain villages and lakes, meadows and deep valleys are surrounded by snow-capped gray mountains. **Bregenz**, the capital of this small province, holds an open-air music festival during July and August.

PLACES OF INTEREST

▲ WIEN (27 E3)★

WIEN *pop. 1,533,000*

Located at the crossroads of Europe, Wien (Vienna) was for a thousand years the capital of the far-flung Holy Roman and Habsburg empires. Today it is the capital of the Austrian Republic and serves as an international congress city. Though its people and ways have changed, Vienna has retained its imperial monuments of past glories, now symbols of its present freedom.

UNDERGROUND VIENNA

The catacombs of St. Stephen's Cathedral offer a fascinating glimpse into the city's past. For less spiritual refreshment, the 12 Apostelkeller wine cellar at nearby Schönlaterngasse is a good introduction to city life.

Vienna's charm consists of several elements. This metropolis on the Danube River has lush parks and fine stores, hotels and restaurants. It also has some of the most beautiful Renaissance, baroque and rococo buildings in the world, as well as many buildings that embody *Jugendstil*, the Austrian version of art nouveau architecture.

The Ringstrasse, or Ring, is the well-known boulevard which, with the Donaukanal (Danube Canal), encloses the Inner City, or First District, of Vienna. The buildings on the broad, 4-kilometer (2½ mile) street include the *Parlament* (Parliament), State museums, the *Staatsoper* (Opera House), and the *Hofburg* (Imperial Palace) all interspersed with historic gardens. Kärntnerstrasse, Graben, Kohlmarkt and Mariahilfer Strasse are the city's best-known streets for shopping.

If you visit Vienna in winter, you have a special advantage: it is the high season for cultural events. As the home of Franz Joseph Haydn, Wolfgang Amadeus Mozart, Ludwig van Beethoven, Anton Bruckner, Franz Schubert, Johannes Brahms, Gustav Mahler and Johann and Richard Strauss, the city almost breathes music. From September through June the Vienna State Opera performs, and there are operettas, ballets and chamber music. (Opera tickets, however, can be expensive and hard to get, so make sure you plan ahead.)

Vienna's musical offerings extend into summer as well, with such events as the Vienna Festival from mid-May to mid-June, and a program of operettas and open-air and palace concerts taking place in July and August.

The Vienna Boys' Choir performs at the 9:15am Mass in the Hofburg Palace Chapel on any Sunday or Holy Day from the first Sunday after September 15 to the last Sunday in June (except January 6, Corpus Christi and December 26). Written requests for tickets must be made at least eight weeks in advance to Verwaltung der Hofmusikkapelle, Hofburg, 1010 Vienna, Austria.

No matter what time of year you visit, you can buy a three-day inclusive ticket that is valid for the subway, the *Stadtbahn* (city train), *Schnellbahn* (fast city train), trams and buses. You can get the ticket for a small fee from the tourist information offices at Wien West, Wien Süd, the airport, Westbahnhof, and Südbahnhof, as well as at all transport authority ticket offices.

AUSTRIA

BELVEDERE (33 D1), on Prince-Eugen-Strasse 27, with two entrances, on Karolinengasse and Ramweg, consists of two palaces built for Prince Eugene of Savoy. Lower (*Unteres*) Belvedere, is a former summer residence and houses the Museum of Medieval Austrian Art and the Museum of Austrian Baroque. Upper (*Oberes*) Belvedere was built a few years later and used for festivities; it now contains the Austrian Gallery, which displays collections of paintings from the 19th and 20th century. The palaces are linked by elegant terraced gardens.

HOFBURG (Imperial Palace) (33 C2), at 2 Michaelerplatz, dates from the 16th to 20th century and was the residence of Emperor Franz Josef and Empress Elisabeth. The chapel, the only part of the original castle that still stands, dates from the 13th century. The Habsburgs' gold table service is on display. The imperial apartments and staterooms also are open for viewing.

A fire swept through one wing of the palace in 1992, destroying the historical 18th-century Redoutensaal ballroom, among others. The adjacent National Library, with its baroque Great Hall and the Schatzkammer, the treasure room, including a 9th-century holy lance and 10th-century crown, were spared.

Albertina Collection of Graphic Arts contains the Dürer Collection, including the well-known *Praying Hands*, as well as works by Michelangelo, Titian, Raphael and Rembrandt, among others.

Kapuzinerkirche (Capuchin Church) houses the crypt where the imperial family is buried. The church is entered from 2 Tegetthoffstrasse.

Spanische Reitschule (Spanish Riding School), Josefsplatz, is one of Vienna's most popular attractions. Reservations to see the Sunday performances of the Lippizaner horses must be made by written application to the school.

HOHER MARKT (33 D3), the oldest part of Vienna, was the center of the medieval town. Beneath the bustling square lie

the ruins of a Roman settlement. The ruins can be entered at 3 Hoher Markt.

KUNSTHISTORISCHES MUSEUM (Museum of Fine Arts) (33 C2), Maria-Theresien Platz, contains one of Europe's finest collections of paintings, including works by Pieter Bruegel, Diego Velázquez,

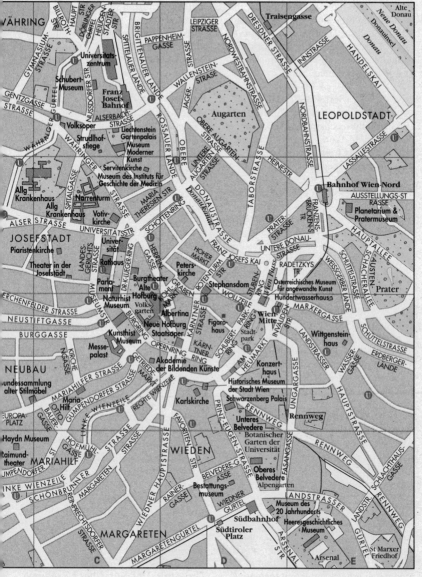

Titian, Rembrandt and Correggio. In addition, Egyptian and Oriental art is represented in the museum's collection.

PARLAMENT (Parliament) (33 C3), 3 Dr. Karl-Renner-Ring, is housed in a neoclassical building that was opened to the public in 1883.

PRATER (33 E3), Hauptallee, was a hunting reserve for the aristocracy, opened by Emperor Josef II; today it has a sports arena and amusement park with the *Riesenrad* (giant wheel), a landmark.

SCHLOSS SCHÖNBRUNN (32 A1), 13 Schönbrunner Schloss Strasse in the suburbs, is

AUSTRIA

a lavish 1,440-room summer palace that has changed little since the time of Maria Theresa. The furnishings of the 45 rooms on view, the fountains, parks and formal terraces, all create a picture of unsurpassed elegance.

STAATSOPER (State Opera House) (33 D2), 2 Opernring, was built in the 1860s and carefully reconstructed following its destruction in World War II. The opera season extends from September to June, with daily performances.

STEPHANSDOM (St. Stephen's Cathedral) (33 D3), Stephansplatz, is an impressive Gothic structure that was consecrated in the mid-12th century. It has a 136-meter (450-foot) spire and many art treasures. The bell tower affords an excellent view of the city and houses the huge brass bell called Pummerin – "the boomer."

ACHENSEE (26 B2)
TIROL *elev. 853m. (2,815ft.)*
The Achensee lies between the Karwendel and Rofan mountains and is Tirol's largest and most attractive lake. The villages of Pertisau and Maurach provide leisure facilities for both summer and winter vacations.

ADMONT (26 D2)
STEIERMARK *pop. 3,100*
A market town in the Enns Valley, Admont has become a popular winter and summer resort.

ALTAUSSEE (27 C2)
STEIERMARK *pop. 1,900*
The little town of Altaussee is a summer and winter spa resort area on pretty Altausseer, in the Styrian section of the mountainous Salzkammergut region.

ATTERSEE (27 C2)
OBERÖSTERREICH *pop. 1,300*
Attersee, bordering the Alpine lake of the same name, dates from Roman times. The Attersee is the largest mountain lake in Austria; it extends from limestone cliffs of the Höllengebirge on the far

southeastern bank to the low hills in the northern bank.

Its west bank is an area of rolling hills and flourishing orchards. A road encircles the lake, passing Schörfling and other picturesque towns.

BADGASTEIN (27 C2) ★
SALZBURG *pop. 5,600, elev. 1,007m. (3,324ft.)*
Built on evergreen-covered slopes overlooking a rushing mountain torrent, Badgastein is revered for its spectacular setting and radioactive thermal springs.

BAD HOFGASTEIN (27 C2)
SALZBURG *pop. 5,960, elev. 795m. (2,623ft.)*
About 1 million liters (265,000 gallons) of thermal water comes daily from nearby Badgastein and fills three indoor pools linked via channels to outdoor pools, enabling visitors to swim inside or out. The water temperature stays between 32 and 34°C (90 and 93°F), providing cures and relaxation in summer and winter.

BAD ISCHL (27 C2)
OBERÖSTERREICH *pop. 13,100*
Once the site of Emperor Franz Josef's summer court, Bad Ischl is among the best equipped spas in Austria.

BAD KLEINKIRCHHEIM (27 C1)
KÄRNTEN *pop. 1,900, elev. 1,094m. (3,609ft.)*
Bad Kleinkirchheim, a popular resort and spa in the Nock Mountains of Kärnten, offers recreational facilities in summer and winter alike.

BREGENZ (26 A2)
VORARLBERG *pop. 24,700*
The capital of Vorarlberg Province, Bregenz is in the Alpine foothills on the shores of Lake Constance (Bodensee), the largest lake in Europe. It is an ideal starting point for trips by boat, bus, car or train to nearby Switzerland, Germany and Liechtenstein. A cable car trip to the top of Pfänder Mountain affords a fine view of the Austrian, Swiss and Bavarian Alps.

DÜRNSTEIN (27 D3) ★
NIEDERÖSTERREICH *pop. 1,030*
Dürnstein is on the Donau (Danube River) between Melk and Krems in the beautiful Wachau region.

It has a ruined castle, where Richard the Lionheart was imprisoned in the 12th century. Surrounding vineyards produce fine wines.

EISENSTADT (27 E2)
BURGENLAND *pop. 10,100*
The capital of Austria's eastern province, Eisenstadt was once the home of Franz Joseph Haydn.

The Haydn home is now a museum, and his tomb is in a local church. The city makes a good starting point for motor trips in eastern Austria.

SCHLOSS ESTERHÁZY is the lavish palace where Franz Joseph Haydn composed and was conductor of a private orchestra at the court of the Esterházy princes.

FELDKIRCH (26 A2)
VORARLBERG *pop. 24,000*
Surrounded by mountains, Feldkirch's well-preserved attractions include the remains of battlements and a small Gothic church.

In June one of the world's best-known music festivals is held in Feldkirch. Called the *Schubertiade*, it focuses on the works of Franz Schubert.

GMUNDEN (27 C2)
OBERÖSTERREICH *pop. 13,000*
Built on the north banks of the Traunsee, east of Salzburg, Gmunden is the principal town of the Salzkammergut region. A popular spa, Gmunden's past is reflected in its 17th-century parish church and the part-Gothic Ort Castle.

GOSAUSEE
OBERÖSTERREICH *elev. 867m. (2,846ft.)*
A stunning Alpine landscape unfolds at the Vorderer Gosausee, easily reached by car or bus. A 90-minute walk leads to Hinterer Gosausee, from where there are spectacular views.

▲ GRAZ (26 D2)
STEIERMARK *pop. 232,400*
Capital of the province of Styria and the second largest city in Austria, Graz is in the southeastern part of the country on the banks of the River Mur. It stages a popular festival of music and drama in October. West at Piber is the stud farm where the Lippizaner stallions are bred for use at the Spanish Riding School in Vienna (see p.32).

DOM (Cathedral) was built in the 15th century by Emperor Frederick III. The exterior fresco depicts the *Divine Torments* – plague, locusts and war.

SCHLOSS EGGENBERG, 3.5 kilometers (2 miles) west, is a splendid baroque castle built in the early 17th century, now housing a hunting museum. The grounds are maintained as a game reserve.

GURK (26 D1)
KÄRNTEN *pop. 2,100*
Gurk, a small market town in a valley to the north of Kärnten, is known for its splendid Romanesque cathedral, built between 1140 and 1200, with baroque domes mounted on twin towers.

HALLEIN (26 C2)
SALZBURG *pop. 15,400*
DÜRRNBERG MINE, a 4-kilometer (2½-mile) long salt mine first used in 700 BC by the Celts, was opened to the public before World War I. Hardwood slides allow visitors to reach a museum and salt lake near the bottom. A cathedral-like cavern that contains marble statues and tablets can be viewed on a boat trip on an illuminated lake.

HALLSTATT (26 C2) ★
OBERÖSTERREICH *pop. 1,130*
Largely untouched by the modern world, the ancient salt-mining town of Hallstatt is built on terraces that climb the steep mountain slopes above Lake Hallstatt. The town is noted for its relics of the pre-Christian Celtic period and also for its exquisite woodcarvings.

AUSTRIA

DACHSTEIN HÖHLEN (Dachstein Ice Caves) form one of Europe's largest underground complexes. They can be reached via cable car from Obertraun, a few miles to the east.

HEILIGENBLUT (27 C1) ★
KÄRNTEN *pop. 1,300, elev. 1,300m. (4,265ft.)*
Picturesque Heiligenblut, the highest town in Kärnten, is a winter resort and southern terminus of the Grossglockner Highway. The Gothic church is famous as a place of pilgrimage. There is also a well-known mountain-climbing school in the town. Heiligenblut is a touring center for Hohe Tauern, the second largest national park in Europe, which includes nearly 275 kilometers (170 miles) of marked trails and Alpine wildlife.

A 13-kilometer (8-mile) excursion over the High Alpine Highway leads to 3,797-meter (12,457-foot) Grossglockner, Austria's highest peak. Traffic is heavy in summer, so an early start is advisable.

IGLS (26 B2)
TIROL *pop. 1,600, elev. 900m. (2,953ft.)*
South of Innsbruck, the hillside resort of Igls provides fine hotels and a variety of recreational facilities — swimming, golf, tennis and riding, as well as a cable car to Patscherkofel.

▲ INNSBRUCK (26 B2) ★
TIROL *pop. 115,000*
In a valley of the mountainous border area, Innsbruck is the capital of the Tirol and within easy reach of the Tirolean Alps. Outside the city, there are beautiful glacier views from the Stubai Valley, which can be reached by way of Fulpmes. A drive along the Brenner road to the 1,374-meter (4,508-foot) Brenner Plateau and the Italian frontier at Brenner Lake abounds in scenic contrasts. The Alpine Expressway to the south crosses the Europabrücke, a 1 kilometer (½ mile) bridge high above the Sill River Valley.

DOM ZU ST. JAKOB (St. Jacob's Cathedral) is a baroque cathedral of the early 18th century. A magnificent painting by Lucas Cranach the Elder, who lived for a short while in Vienna, adorns the space above the high altar.

GOLDENES DACHL (Golden Roof), Herzog-Friedrich-Strasse, is a three-story late-Gothic balcony of a former palace in Stadtplatz, known for its gilded copper roof. The former royal residence was built by Maximilian I in 1500 as a royal box for watching spectacles in the square below.

HOFBURG (Imperial Palace), Rennweg 1, was built 1754-73 during the reign of Empress Maria Theresa. It contains splendid ornamentation, ceiling frescoes, pictures and tapestries.

HOFKIRCHE (Court Church) contains the magnificent marble tomb of Maximilian I, which is covered by 24 carved scenes depicting the emperor's deeds.

KITZBÜHEL (27 B2) ★
TIROL *pop. 7,800*
With its picturesque old houses and ancient archway, Kitzbühel is one of Austria's most fashionable winter sports and health resorts. The summits of the 1,655-meter (5,430-foot) Hahnenkamm and the 1,998-meter (6,555-foot) Kitzbüheler Horn are reached by cable car.

Such summer sports as golf, swimming, tennis and riding also are popular. An annual tennis tournament in early August draws top international talent.

SUMMERTIME REVELRY

Many visitors to Kitzbühel come for the *Kirtag*, a local festival that takes place on the first Saturday in August. Stalls are set up along the main streets, refreshments are served, and there's plenty of good-humored fun.

KREMS (26 D3)
NIEDERÖSTERREICH *pop. 23,100*
The Wachau is an expanse of splendid scenery that stretches east along the

Danube River from Melk to Krems, its principal city. The region is renowned for its wine, and Krems is the center of the wine trade. Founded during the late 10th century, the city has Renaissance, baroque and rococo buildings.

KREMSMÜNSTER (27 D2)
OBERÖSTERREICH *pop. 6,000*
Ancient Kremsmünster is the site of a historic Benedictine abbey. Founded in AD 777, it has ceiling frescoes, plaster moldings and a collection of paintings.

LECH (26 A2)
VORARLBERG *pop. 1,200, elev. 1,450m. (4,757ft.)*
A fashionable winter sports center, Lech lies in the superb skiing country of the Arlberg region. Summer visitors also enjoy this scenic spot, reached by the Flexen Pass road from the Arlberg.

LIENZ (27 C1)
TIROL *pop. 11,700*
The capital of East Tirol, Lienz is an pretty riverside town that attracts winter sports enthusiasts, mountain climbers and sun lovers. Lienz is an excellent starting point for trips over the magnificent Grossglockner road and equally stunning valleys of East Tirol.

▲ LINZ (27 D3)
OBERÖSTERREICH *pop. 202,000*
The Danube River bisects Linz, capital of Upper Austria, and creates a major thoroughfare for rail, highway and river routes. The town has a number of old buildings and makes an ideal stopover for travelers from Salzburg to Wien.

Among the city's places of interest is the Old Cathedral, where the great Austrian composer of church music, Anton Bruckner, was an organist.

STIFT ST. FLORIAN ABBEY, 18 kilometers (11 miles) east, is an excellent example of baroque architecture.

Said to be the largest abbey in Austria, it contains valuable paintings and the tomb of Anton Bruckner.

MARIA WÖRTH (27 D1)
KÄRNTEN *pop. 1,000*
One of the oldest Christian settlements in the area, Maria Wörth lies on the south shores of the warm Wörthersee, and is a flourishing resort away from the bustling tourist routes.

MARIAZELL (27 D2)
STEIERMARK *pop. 1,900, elev. 870m. (2,854ft.)*
In addition to being Austria's leading pilgrimage center, Mariazell is a resort much favored by the Austrians. The town has a ski school and chair lift.

MELK (27 D3) ★
NIEDERÖSTERREICH *pop. 5,000*
Ancient Melk, on the Danube River, marks the beginning of the Wachau, a beautiful stretch of winding river and vine-covered hillsides in Lower Austria.

Between AD 976 and 1110, Melk was the seat of the Babenberg dukes, who ruled Austria. The town was later immortalized in the great German medieval epic poem *Nibelungenlied*.

STIFT MELK (Abbey of Melk), founded in 1089 on a cliff high above the river, was rebuilt between 1702 and 1726 in high baroque style.

It is reputed to be the largest monastic building in Lower Austria – the south façade alone is 262 meters (860 feet) long. The library, containing around 100,000 volumes and treasures, can be viewed.

ROBBER BARONS
In a romantic spot about 13 kilometers (8 miles) north of Melk, the ruined medieval castle of Aggstein has a grisly past. The knights who owned the castle were little more than highwaymen, robbing everyone who passed and incarcerating their victims in a narrow cell, called the *Rosengärtlein* (rose garden), until the ransom was paid.

AUSTRIA

MONDSEE (27 C2)
OBERÖSTERREICH *pop. 2,100*
Mondsee is a scenic summer resort town northwest of the lake of the same name. The 11-kilometer (7-mile) long lake is one of the warmest north of the Alps, making it suitable for water sports.

OBERGURGL (26 B1)
TIROL *pop. 300, elev. 1,930m. (6,332ft.)*
Obergurgl, the highest ski village in Austria, teems with skiers until late spring, when summer visitors begin to arrive. The village can be reached by a mountain road that branches off the main Landeck–Innsbruck road and is a starting point for glacier tours.

RADSTADT (27 C2)
SALZBURG *pop. 4,100, elev. 862m. (2,828ft.)*
A well-known winter sports resort, quaint Radstadt is an ideal starting point for mountain walks and climbs.

SAALBACH (27 C2)
SALZBURG *pop. 2,700, elev. 1,003m. (3,291ft.)*
Saalbach, in the Glemm Valley, is one of the most prestigious ski resorts in the Alps. There are nearly 204 kilometers (125 miles) of ski runs of all grades, and numerous skiing facilities. Other sporting activities, including climbing, hiking and golf, are also available.

ST. ANTON (26 A2)
TIROL *pop. 2,170, elev. 1,287m. (4,222ft.)*
St. Anton is the site of what is said to be the oldest ski school in Europe. The nearby valley station of a cable railroad provides easy access to the 2,650-meter (8,692-foot) Valluga, which offers good views and some unsurpassed ski terrain.

ST. GILGEN
SALZBURG *pop. 3,000*
St. Gilgen is a popular summer resort on the shores of Wolfgangsee, a well-known lake southeast of Salzburg in the lake district. Surrounded by mountains, Wolfgangsee is 10 kilometers (6 miles)

long and 114 meters (375ft) deep, and is a scenic summer resort.

ST. WOLFGANG (27 C2)
OBERÖSTERREICH *pop. 2,500*
Motorboat tours of Wolfgangsee depart from St. Wolfgang, a well-known resort. The town also is the starting point for the cogwheel railroad that ascends the 1,783-meter (5,850-foot) Schafberg from May to October.

▲ SALZBURG (27 C2) ★
SALZBURG *pop. 143,000*
Enchanting Salzburg, capital of the province of the same name, is almost in the center of Austria.

Flanking the Salzach River on the northern edge of the eastern Alps, it is considered one of the most beautiful European cities due to its mountainous countryside and splendid architecture. Hikers head for the 1,853-meter (6,079-foot) Untersberg peak, accessible by cable car, and smaller Gaisberg. Also nearby are several lakes.

The birthplace of Wolfgang Amadeus Mozart, it is host to the Salzburg Festival from late July through August. Palace Concerts are held almost daily between Easter and October and less frequently during the rest of the year. Salzburg also celebrates an Easter Festival and Mozart Memorial Week, which takes place the last week in January.

DOM (Cathedral) is a fine baroque building north of the Alps.

ERZABTEI ST. PETER (Benedictine Abbey of St. Peter), 1 St. Peter Bezirk, was established during the late 7th century and is noted for its catacombs.

SCHLOSS HELLBRUNN (Hellbrunn Pleasure Castle) was built in the early 17th century for Archbishop Marcus Sitticus. Watch out for the trick fountains – some operate mechanical figures, others balance balls on water jets. Wear casual clothes when visiting: hidden spouts can drench sightseers.

MARIONETTENTHEATER, Schwarzstrasse 24 to be found near Mirabell Palace, has a repertory puppet company that performs from mid-April through September and tours the world in other months. The operas of Mozart are a specialty.

SEEFELD (26 B2) ★

TIROL *pop. 2,300, elev. 1,200m. (3,937ft.)*
Seefeld, one of Tirol's most popular and elegant winter resorts, boasts some fine cross-country skiing. The Gothic parish church has elaborate vaulting as well as mural paintings.

Beyond Seefeld, neighboring Bavaria is a pleasant summertime excursion area.

TAKING AIM

In August a special shooting competition is staged on the Prebersee, 8 kilometers (5 miles) northeast of Tamsweg.
Participants have to aim at the mirror image of the target on the lake. The bullets are deflected off the surface and directed onto the target.

TAMSWEG (27 C2)

SALZBURG *pop. 5,260, elev. 949m. (3,114ft.)*
Nestling between mountains is the main town of the area called Lungau. Formerly an important medieval trading center, it is now a particularly favorite place in which to go hiking.

VELDEN AM WÖRTHERSEE (27 C1)

KÄRNTEN *pop. 7,700*
The largest summer resort in the Carinthian lake district, fashionable Velden stretches along the western bay of the Wörthersee.

Watersports are the great attraction by day, while a casino draws crowds at night. Dellach, to the west of the town, has an excellent golf course.

VIENNA – see *Wien* on p.31.

WAGRAIN

SALZBURG *pop. 2,900*
Wagrain is a small resort in a spectacular mountain setting. Among its recreational opportunities are swimming, tennis, skeet shooting, fishing, hiking on mountain paths, and skiing.

ZELL AM SEE (27 C2)

SALZBURG *pop. 8,000*
One of Austria's best known vacation resorts, this charming town derives its popularity from its idyllic position on the shores of an Alpine lake, surrounded by high mountains.

There are extensive facilities for skiers, and the lake is also perfect for many kinds of water sports in summer.

WONDERFUL WATERFALLS

A narrow-gauge railway line connects Zell am See with Krimml, where you can see some of the most impressive waterfalls in Europe. A steam engine makes the journey on certain days (contact the local tourist information office for details).

ZELL AM ZILLER (26 B2)

TIROL *pop. 1,870, elev. 535m. (1,754ft.)*
Surrounded by forests, Zell am Ziller is a busy summer and winter resort.

FESTIVE FROLICS

In May the village of Zell am Ziller celebrates the *Gauderfest*, a folklore festival that features the potent *Gauderbier*, brewed specially for the occasion.

ZÜRS (26 A2)

VORARLBERG *elev. 1,596m. (5,237ft.)*
Zürs is one of Austria's smallest but most exclusive winter sports resorts. It is also one of the oldest, as skiing instruction began here in 1906. Zürs has only a few luxury hotels, but the surrounding terrain and the facilities are superb.

THE BALKANS

The Balkans have long been a crossroads in Europe. In the once ostensibly Communist country of Yugoslavia, Catholic Croats, Orthodox Serbs, Bosnian Muslims and other ethnic groups are now disputing territories. Some areas that are currently unsafe for travel have not been covered in detail here.

However, the ongoing disputes hide the fact that there are beautiful Balkan countries, such as Slovenia and Croatia, which are now considered safe to visit.

Slovenia shares a border and some breathtaking Alpine scenery with Austria, while to the south Croatia faces Italy across a stunning Adriatic coastline. Albania, currently subject to a travel warning, has mountain scenery and archaeological remains.

Left Stunning Lake Bled in Slovenia, once a popular tourist spot
Above Colorful designs adorn houses in the attractive city of Ljubljana, Slovenia

THINGS TO KNOW

- **AREA: Albania:** 28,748 square kilometers (11,100 square miles); **Slovenia:** 20,256 square kilometers (7,821 square miles); **Croatia:** 56,539 square kilometers (21,820 square miles); **Bosnia-Herzegovina:** 51,129 square kilometers (19,740 square miles); **Federal Republic of Yugoslavia:** 102,170 square kilometers (39,450 square miles)
- **POPULATION: Albania:** 3,335,000; **Slovenia:** 2,000,000; **Croatia:** 4,780,000; **Bosnia-Herzegovina:** 4,124,000; **Federal Republic of Yugoslavia:** 11,372,000.
- **CAPITAL: Albania:** Tiranë; **Slovenia:** Ljubljana; **Croatia:** Zagreb; **Bosnia-Herzegovina:** Sarajevo; **Federal Republic of Yugoslavia:** Belgrade
- **LANGUAGES:** Albanian; Slovene; Croatian; Serbo-Croatian; Serbian
- **ECONOMY: Albania:** mining products, copper ore; tobacco, wool, fruit. **Slovenia:** industry, agriculture, forestry, tourism. **Croatia:** tourism, ship building, agriculture, wine, textiles.
- **PASSPORT REQUIREMENTS: Slovenia/ Albania/Croatia:** required for U.S. citizens.
- **VISA REQUIREMENTS: Albania:** no visa required; entrance fee of $20–$25 on arrival. **Croatia:** required for U.S. citizens; obtained at the border or in advance from the Croatian consulates (New York; tel: 212/599-3066; Washington, D.C.; tel: 202/588-5899). There is no charge. **Slovenia:** no visa required for visits up to 90 days.
- **CURRENCY: Albania:** the *lek*, divided into 100 *quindarka*. **Slovenia:** the *tolar*, divided into 100 *stotin*. **Croatia:** the *kuna* , divided into 100 *lipa*. The exchange rate is subject to change.
- **BANK OPENING HOURS: Albania:** 8:30am–1pm Monday–Friday. **Slovenia:** 8am–6pm Monday–Friday; 8am–noon Saturday. **Croatia:** 7:30am–7pm Monday–Friday; 8am–noon Saturday.
- **STORE OPENING HOURS: Albania:** 9am–6pm Monday–Saturday. **Slovenia:** 7:30am–7pm Monday–Friday; 7:30am– 1pm Saturday. **Croatia:** 8am–8pm Monday–Friday; 8am–2pm Saturday.

WARNING

Due to political problems within the Balkans, in particular affecting Bosnia-Herzegovina and the Federal Republic of Yugoslavia, it is not advisable to travel to these places. This section covers Albania, where recent unrest has resulted in the U.S. Department of State issuing a Travel Warning which advises U.S. citizens to avoid traveling there at present. Croatia and Slovenia were considered stable at press time, but contact the U.S. Department of State for updated information before making travel arrangements.

ALBANIA
HISTORY

Albanians are descendants of the Illyrians. The ancient Greek and Roman settlements at Apollonia and Butrinti are among the greatest archaeological sites in the Balkans. Ottoman Turks dominated the country for five centuries until independence in 1912. Following the death of the dictator Enver Hoxha, Albanians rejected 50 years of Communist rule and isolation and held democratic elections in 1991, but widespread unrest led to anarchy and violence in 1997.

FOOD AND DRINK

Greek and Turkish influences are apparent in Albanian cuisine. Typical dishes include *byrek* (pastry filled with meat, cheese or vegetables) and *fërgëse* (cottage cheese, liver, eggs and vegetables). *Koran* is fish from Lake Ohrid. Red wines are much better than the white.

CROATIA
HISTORY

Croatia's towns display a range of historic monuments, from Roman ruins and Byzantine art to Renaissance and baroque architecture. The lovely Adriatic coastline sparkles with 1,185 islands and reefs, while the scenic interior offers mountains, lakes, forests, castles and hundreds of small churches. Croatia was part of the former

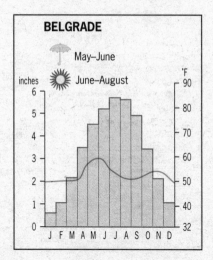

BELGRADE

May–June

June–August

inches

°F

Yugoslavia until it declared independence in 1991. Following the Serbian withdrawal, a major renovation program has helped rebuild Croatia's tourist industry.

FOOD AND DRINK
Croatian cuisine reflects the influences of its Italian, Austrian and Hungarian neighbors. Fish is the staple of the Dalmatian coast, boiled or grilled on an open fire and seasoned with olive oil and herbs. Pork, veal, and lamb predominate inland, along with dumplings and dairy products. The full-bodied dark red Dingac is Croatia's best-known wine.

GETTING AROUND
There are several international airports, rail connections with Europe and ferry links to the Italian coast. Long-distance buses are frequent and inexpensive, and there are two domestic train routes. Roads are currently being improved, and there are a few toll highways. The Adriatic Highway is a narrow but very scenic drive along the stunning coastline. Road information is available from the Croatian automobile club, Hrvatski Autoklub, tel: (01) 4554 433. Unless otherwise posted, speed limits are 130 k.p.h. (80 m.p.h.) on major highways, 90 k.p.h. (55 m.p.h.) on secondary highways and 60 k.p.h. (37 m.p.h.) in town.

ACCOMMODATIONS
Hotels are rated from one to five stars. There are apartment complexes, guesthouses, pensions, and private homes as well as holiday homes, luxury hotels and Adriatic resorts. There are also campgrounds and youth hostels.

SLOVENIA
HISTORY
Slovenia was colonized by the Romans, and in the ensuing centuries its lands were overrun by Huns, Mongols, Slavs, Franks and Magyars. Most of the towns, castles and monasteries were built between the 10th and 13th centuries. The Adriatic ports retain an Italian character from the era of Venetian rule. From the early 14th century until World War I, Slovenian lands were under the control of the Austrian Habsburg Empire. In 1990, Slovenia held free elections and declared its independence.

Northwest Slovenia is a region of Alpine valleys, mountains, wooded hills and glacial lakes; eastern Slovenia has spring waters and thermal spas, and fertile plains and forests in the northeast. The Karst region, west of Ljubljana, has spectacular underground caves.

FOOD AND DRINK
The sausages, dumplings, *schnitzel* and *strudel* of Slovenia's Alpine region display an Austrian influence. Seafood, risotto and pasta dishes along the Adriatic coast reflect a taste of Italy, while Hungarian dishes like *goulash* and pancakes are also popular. Slovenia produces excellent wines and beers. Strong liquors are distilled from various fruits.

GETTING AROUND
Roads are generally good, though roads in the mountains are narrow and are often closed in winter and early spring. A toll will be charged on some highway sections. Seat belts are mandatory. Speed limits are 60 k.p.h. (37 m.p.h.) in towns, 80–100 k.p.h. (50–62 m.p.h.) out of town and 120 k.p.h. (74 m.p.h.) on highways.

- **BEST BUYS: Albania:** crafts, briar pipes, filigree jewelry, rugs, copperware. **Slovenia:** ceramics, glass, woodcarvings, leather goods. **Croatia:** leather goods, crystal, porcelain, ceramics, crafts.
- **PUBLIC HOLIDAYS: Albania:** no information available. **Slovenia:** January 1, 2; February 8; Easter Sunday; Easter Monday; April 27; May 1, 2; June 25; August 15; October 31; November 1; December 25, 26. **Croatia:** January 1, 6, 7; Ramadan-Bairam; Easter Monday; May 1, 30; June 22; August 15; November 1; December 25, 26.
- **NATIONAL TOURIST OFFICES:**
  Albanian Mission
  320 East 79th Street
  New York, NY 10021
  Tel: 212/249-2059
  Fax: 212/535-2917
  Albanian Embassy
  4th floor, 38 Grosvenor Gardens
  London, SW1W 0EB, England
  Tel: 0171 730 5709
  Fax: 0171 730 5747
  All tourist inquiries should be directed to Albania's embassies abroad.
  Slovenian Tourist Office
  122 East 42nd Street, Suite 3006
  New York, NY 10168-0072
  Tel: 212/682-5896; fax: 212/661-2469
  Slovenian Tourist Office
  2 Canfield Place, London
  NW6 3BT, England
  Tel: 0171-372 3767; fax: 0171-372 3763
  Croatian National Tourist Office
  300 Lanidex Plaza, Parsippany,
  NY 07054
  Tel: 201/428-0707; fax: 201/428-3386
  Croatian National Tourism Office
  2 The Lanchesters
  162–164 Fulham Palace Road
  London W6 9ER, England
  Tel: 0181-563 7979; fax: 0181-563 2616
- **AMERICAN EMBASSIES:**
  Rruga E. Libinoti 103, Tiranë, Albania
  Tel: 355 42 32875
  4 Pražakova, 1000 Ljubljana, Slovenia
  Tel: (61) 301 427
  Hebrangova 2, 10,000 Zagreb, Croatia
  Tel: (01) 455-5500

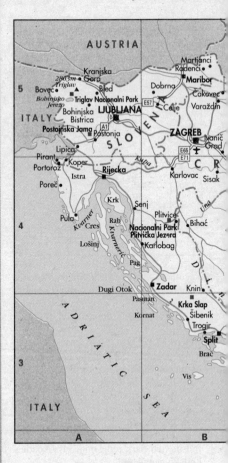

Emergency roadside help is available from Avto-moto zveza Slovenije, the Slovene Automobile Association (A.M.Z.S.); tel: 987. The information center can be contacted by phoning A.M.Z.S. at (061) 34 13 41. Slovenia has three international airports and rail connections to Europe. There are scenic railway journeys through the Julian Alps and Soca River Valley and along the Sava River gorge.

ACCOMMODATIONS
Hotels range from luxury and castle hotels to *gostisce* (inns) and C-class hotels. Rooms can be rented in tourist regions through tourist offices or agencies. There are plenty of campgrounds.

HUNGARY

ROMANIA

Bjelovar Virovitica

Subotica • Kanjiza

Kikinda

Sombor

• ATIA

Našice Osijek Vojvodina

Slavonski Novi Sad Zrenjanin

Brod Vinkovci

•rijedor Sremski Kovačica Vršac

Karlovci

Banja Luka Stremska Dunav (Danube)

Doboj Mitrovica BEOGRAD Pančevo Djerdap,

BOSNIA Brčko Smederovo Tabula Traiana

Tuzla Šabac Golubac Sip Kladovo

Jajce Mladénovac Lepenski Vir

Travnik Zenica Vlasenica Arandjelovac Donji Milanovac

HERZEGOVINA Valjevo Miloševa Negotin

Bugojno Kula

SARAJEVO Trebević Titóva Uziče Kragujevac

Jablanica Jahorina YUGOSLAVIA Zaječar

Bjelašnica Igman Čačak Kraljevo Ljubostaja Soka Barja

Makarska Nacionalni Višegrad Studenica Trstenik Kruševac

Park Sutjeska Mileševo Brzeće Niš Niška

Mostar Pljevlja Tara Kanjon Sopoćani Kopaonik Banja Pirot

Medjugorje Žabljak Novi Leskovac

Metković Durmitor Nacionalni Pazar Titova

2522m Park Durmitor Mitrovica

•rćula Nacionalni Park Ivangrad Peć Priština

Nacionalni Nikšić Biogradska Gora Metohija

Park Mljet Trebinje Visoki Dečani Djakovica Uroševac Vranje

Dubrovnik Kotor Titograd Prizren Brezovica Prohor Pčinjski

Cetinje (Podgorica) Kukës SKOPJE Kumanovo

Nacionalni Shkodër Višegrad Kočani

Park Lovcen Bar Lezhë Tetovo Titov

Ulcinj Skadarsko Gostivar Veles Stip

Jezero Peshkopi Nacionalni Park Mavrovo

Sveti Jovan Bigorski Kičevo Babuna Kanjon Strumica

Vorë MACEDONIA Prilep

Durrës TIRANË Struga Dojransko

ALBANIA Ohrid Ezero

Rogozhinë Elbasan Bitala

Obridsko Ezero Sveti Peter Nacionalni Park Pelister

Apollonia Lushnjë Sveti

Naum Prespansko

• Berat Korcë Ezero

Vlorë

Këlcyrë

Borsh Gjirokastër GREECE

Kakavi

Butrinti

Kérkira

BULGARIA

HERZEGOVINA

Nišava

Vardar

Crni Drim

Crna

Morava

Tamiš

Tisa

Drava

Drina

Bosna

Vrbas

Neretva

Pelješac

Šar planina

Timok

0   50   100   150 km

0   50   100 miles

C   D   E

PLACES OF INTEREST

THE U.S. DEPARTMENT OF STATE HAS ISSUED A TRAVEL WARNING AS A RESULT OF SEVERE UNREST IN ALBANIA IN 1997.

APOLLONIA (45 D2)
ALBANIA

Founded in 588 BC and named for the god Apollo, Apollonia was an important Greek colony and a prosperous stronghold during Roman times. It had a large port until an earthquake altered the coastline in the 3rd century AD. The Fountain of Cephisus is among the well-preserved ruins.

BERAT (45 D1)
ALBANIA

This outstanding Ottoman city, with well-preserved mosques and beautiful buildings, is a U.N.E.S.C.O. World Heritage Site. The hilltop citadel is one of the finest historic monuments in the Balkans. Inside are some 14 churches, with fine 16th-century frescoes and icons and an icon museum.

BUTRINTI (45 D1)
ALBANIA

According to legend, Butrinti (or Buthrot) was founded by refugees from Troy and was settled in turn by Illyrians, Greeks and Romans.

DURRËS (45 C2)
ALBANIA

Founded by Greek colonists in 627 BC, Durrës has long been an important Adriatic port. A Byzantine chapel with 10th-century mural mosaics and a large Roman amphitheater are among the ancient remains.

GJIROKASTËR (45 D1)
ALBANIA

This atmospheric town of Ottoman houses, mosques, a bazaar quarter, and narrow streets winding up to the hilltop citadel is a U.N.E.S.C.O. World Heritage Site. The 13th-century citadel commands the surrounding countryside.

TIRANË (45 D2)
ALBANIA

A small provincial town that became the capital after World War I, Tiranë is now a large, chaotic city. Remnants of its Turkish period were largely destroyed during World War II and the Communist era. At the heart of the city is Skanderberg Square, named for Albania's national hero, whose bronze equestrian statue stands on the south side. The Palace of Culture here houses a concert hall and the National Library.

DUBROVNIK (45 C3) ★
CROATIA

This beautiful stone city on the Dalmatian coast was founded in the 7th century. It is surrounded by medieval walls, and has been almost completely restored since it was attacked in 1991. Among its highlights are the cathedral with its treasury; the Dubrovnik Museum: the Franciscan monastery and cloister, with one of the oldest pharmacies in Europe; and the Dominican monastery with its Gothic cloisters. A festival of classical music and theater is held annually in July and August.

PULA (44 A4)
CROATIA

The port of Pula, a gateway for tourists visiting the northern Istria region, is an old-style Mediterranean city with narrow streets and Italianate architecture. It was a major city of the Roman empire, and it has one of Europe's largest and best-preserved Roman amphitheaters. An international film festival takes place here in July/August.

ZAGREB (44 B5) ★
CROATIA

Zagreb, founded on neighboring hills, became Croatia's capital in 1557. It is a lively university city, with academic and cultural institutions. A funicular, built in 1890, leads to the Upper Town, Zagreb's old quarter. Sights include the twin-spired Gothic cathedral and treasury; the Croatian National Theater, fronted by a beautiful square; Mimara Museum, with artifacts from around the world; and the Mirogoj cemetery, with a wealth of monuments dating from 1876.

BLED (44 A5) ★
SLOVENIA

With its beautiful setting on the shores of emerald-green Lake Bled and surrounded by mountains and forests, Bled has been a fashionable resort since the mid-19th century. It is Slovenia's most popular vacation spot, with thermal baths and numerous outdoor activities. Gondolas ferry visitors to the lake's tiny island, where a church has stood since the 9th century. Bled Castle is perched on a 100-meter (328-foot) cliff overlooking the lake.

BOHINJSKO JEREZO (44 A5) ★
SLOVENIA

The 5-kilometer (3-mile) Bohinjsko Jerezo (Lake Bohinj) lies 32 kilometers (20 miles) west of Bled in Triglav Alpine National Park. Alpine and cross-country skiing in winter are among its outdoor pursuits. Mount Triglav, Slovenia's highest mountain, soars to 2,863 meters (9,395 feet). The tourist office in Bled is able to provide mountain guides and information for experienced hikers.

BOVEC (44 A5)
SLOVENIA

Bovec is a popular alpine resort in the upper Soča Valley. The town is overlooked by Mount Kanin, which rises to 2,585 meters (8,479 feet). Slovenia's only high-mountain ski resort, it has snow from November to May.

KOPER (44 A4)
SLOVENIA

Known as Capodistria in Italian, this town on the Adriatic coast has an old quarter that reflects its period of Venetian rule between 1279–1797.

KRANJSKA GORA (44 A5)
SLOVENIA

This small Alpine village near the borders of Austria and Italy has become Slovenia's largest winter sports center. In summer it is a base for hiking and mountaineering.

LJUBLJANA (44 A5) ★
SLOVENIA *pop. 340,000*

Slovenia's attractive capital is dominated by its castle, on a hill in the center of the old town. Highlights in the old quarter include the Cathedral of St. Nicholas, the open-air market, the 15th-century town hall and the Robba Fountain (1751). The city's famous bridges are also found here: Dragon Bridge and Shoemaker Bridge were lined with craftsmen's shops in the Middle Ages. Triple Bridge, a unique structure by the celebrated architect Jože Plečnik, links the old town to the Center, or new town. Plečnik's outstanding national and university library, as well as several museums and the beautiful Ursuline Church of the Holy Trinity, are all located here.

PORTOROŽ (44 A4)
SLOVENIA

"Port of Roses" is a big, brash coastal resort that grew up in the 19th century around the local spa and mud baths. It has sandy beaches and a casino. Venice is only two hours away by hydrofoil.

POSTOJNSKA JAMA (44 A5)
SLOVENIA

The Postojna Cave system is one of the largest underground caverns in the world, carved out by a subterranean river beneath the limestone plateau of the Karst region. Spectacular rock formations can be viewed on a combined walking and mini-train tour.

BALTIC STATES

The people of Estonia, Latvia and Lithuania have lived through dramatic events and will share their experiences with the visitors their countries are now starting to attract. Guides will tell you where they were when revolution came, delighted that they are no longer under Soviet domination. Now they talk freely of their own cultures, thriving again in different ways.

Estonia and its capital, Tallinn, are the most Westernized, used to receiving visitors from Finland. Above the center of medieval Tallinn stands the 14th-century tower of Pikk Hermann (Tall Hermann), from where, in 1989, a two-million-strong human chain began, trailing to the Lithuanian capital, Vilnius, demanding independence from Moscow.

Left Latvia's medieval capital, Riga, on the banks of the Daugava River
Above The splendid domes of the Alexander Nevsky Cathedral in Tallinn, Estonia

THINGS TO KNOW

- **AREA: Estonia:** 45,216 square kilometers (17,458 square miles);. **Latvia:** 64,589 square kilometers (24,938 square miles);. **Lithuania:** 65,300 square kilometers (25,174 square miles)
- **POPULATION: Estonia:** 1,492,000; **Latvia:** 2,490,600 **Lithuania:** 3,724,000
- **CAPITAL: Estonia:** Tallinn; **Latvia:** Riga; **Lithuania:** Vilnius
- **LANGUAGES: Estonia:** Estonian; **Latvia:** Latvian; **Lithuania:** Lithuanian and Polish.
  Russian is understood by the majority of people in these countries, but not willingly spoken.
- **ELECTRICITY:** 220v/50Hz AC; two round-pin plugs.
- **PASSPORT REQUIREMENTS:** Required for all visitors.
- **VISA REQUIREMENTS:** Required for U.S. citizens to Latvia only.
  For information about obtaining a visa in advance, telephone the Embassy of Estonia on 202/789-0320, the Embassy of Latvia on 202/726-8213 or the Embassy of Lithuania on 202/234-5860.
- **DUTY FREE ITEMS: Lithuania:** 200 cigarettes or 50 cigars or 250 grams of tobacco; 2 liters of table wine; 1 liter of fortified wine; 1 liter of spirits; 10 liters of beer. No limit on personal items. In **Latvia**, as for Lithuania
  Estonia has a lower alcohol allowance of 1 liter of ordinary wine and 1 liter of strong; 200 cigarettes or 50 cigars.
- **CURRENCIES:** The currency unit in **Estonia** is the *Kroon* , divided into 100 *senti*; in **Latvia** it is the *Lat*, divided into 100 *Santími*, and in **Lithuania** it is the *Lita*, divided into 100 *cento*. Remember that the exchange rate is subject to frequent change. Travelers' checks cannot be exchanged at many places; Amex is most widely accepted c redit card. U.S. dollars and German *Deutsch Marks* are the most useful currencies, but the amount exported must not exceed the amount imported. Money can be

HISTORY

The histories of Estonia and Latvia are essentially the same; Lithuania's also would be if not for their entry into an alliance with Poland that was to last for nearly four centuries. Linguistic and cultural differences remain, however.

The Latvians (or Letts) and Lithuanians descend from Indo-European stock while the Estonians belong to the Finno-Ugric group. Estonia and Latvia became considerably Germanized from the 13th to mid-16th centuries, so Lutheranism is the predominant religion. Most Lithuanians are Roman Catholic, as a result of long associations with Poland.

All three republics were forcibly Sovietized following World War II.

The Baltic region was known in ancient times as a source of fine amber. Trade with the Roman Empire and Germanic tribes continued throughout the whole of the 6th century.

With the decline of the Roman Empire came less businesslike encounters. Vikings made their way into the Baltics in about AD 850, followed by the Danes and the Swedes in the 11th and 12th centuries. At the same time the Balts were experiencing their first hostile encounters with the Russians. But it was the Germans who were to gain the first real foothold into the region.

German bishop, Albert of Buxhoevden began to establish his presence along the Daugava River in about 1200. Within 30 years his Knights of the Sword controlled a region comprising all of present-day Latvia and southern Estonia – a land known then as Livonia.

In 1237, the Teutonic Order absorbed the Knights of the Sword and over the next century extended their holdings to include the land of northern Estonia and all of Prussia to the south. During the next 200 years great cultural development, agricultural improvements as well as commercial prosperity were facilitated by the Hanseatic League.

However, the German influence was not all-pervasive. The native Estonians,

Latvians and Livs, though relegated to mere serfdom, managed to maintain their age-old traditions through folklore and craft work.

Meanwhile, various Lithuanian tribes were desperately atempting to resist the

changed at banks, hotels, airports, railroad stations and currency exchange points. Many major hotels, restaurants, stores, and banks accept the major credit cards (Visa, Eurocards, American Express). A few ATMs in the main cities also accept these cards.

- **BANK OPENING HOURS:** 9am–12:30pm Monday–Friday. Some open afternoons and also open on Saturday mornings.
- **STORE OPENING HOURS:** Large stores stay open for nine hours, but may open at 8, 9 or 10am and close at 6, 7 or 8pm. They shut for an hour at lunchtime – sometimes 2–3pm. On Saturday they close at 5pm if open in the afternoon.
- **PUBLIC HOLIDAYS:** January 1; February 16 (Lithuanian Independence Day); February 24 (Estonian Independence Day); Good Friday; Easter Monday (Estonia); May Day (Estonia and Latvia), May 1; June 23 (Victory Day-Estonia and Ligo Holiday - Latvia); St. John's Day (Estonia and Latvia), June 24; July 6 (King Mindaugas' Crowning Day-Lithuania); November 1 (All Saints' Day-Lithuania); November 16 (Rebirth Day-Estonia); November 18 (Latvian Independence Day); December 25/26, New Year's Eve.
- **NATIONAL TOURIST OFFICES:** Pikk 71, EE-0001 Tallinn; Estonia Tel: (372) 6411 420 Pils Square 4, LV-1050 Riga, Latvia Tel: (371) 721 3011 Ukmerges 20, 2600,Vilnius, Lithuania Tel: (370) 262 2610
- **AMERICAN EMBASSIES:** Kentmanni 20 Tallinn, Estonia Tel: 6312 021 Raina Boulevard 7 Riga, Latvia Tel: 7210 005 6 Akmenu Street Vilnius, Lithuania Tel: 222 7371

German threat in a land which was then called Samogitia.

The Lithuanians were united under Grand Duke Mindaugas in 1236 and a succession of powerful leaders extended their territory by 1430 as far east as Moscow and as far south as the Black Sea.

In 1385, to counter the encroaching Teutonic Order, Grand Duke Jogaila made a union with Poland and, in turn, became its king. In 1410, joint Polish-Lithuanian forces broke the German stranglehold on the Baltics. This action followed a decisive victory at Tannenberg that hastened the decline of the Teutonic Order.

However, union with the more culturally advanced Poland only served to diminish a Lithuanian identity. Its citizens fell into serfdom and, like their neighbors to the north, resorted to cultural self-preservation.

With the dissolution of the Teutonic Order in 1561, Estonia and Latvia became a battleground once again when Sweden advanced from the north, Russia from the east led by Ivan the Terrible, and Poland–Lithuania came from the south.

The era of devastation culminated in the Great Northern War of 1700 to 1721, by which Peter the Great finally claimed the Baltics for Russia. The conquest became complete in 1795 with the annexation of Lithuania from Poland.

The 19th century saw the creation of a precarious balance of social reforms on the one hand and acceding to Russian influence on the other.

Advances in education and human rights were countered with strict controls on judicial and political participation and on language and religion. Consequently, although national identities were reawakened, they had to await the opportunity for realization.

That time came with the Bolshevik Revolution of 1917. Each of the Baltic States declared its independence and they managed to maintain it through World War I and a world-wide economic depression, until 1940.

The rise of Nazi Germany ended the independence in the Baltic States. The alliance between the Soviet Union and Germany left them in the hands of Stalin, who dismantled the individual governments and deported or executed nearly 150,000 people.

When the German-Soviet alliance ended in 1941, German forces moved in and the atrocities continued. Nearly 250,000 people, mostly Jews, were executed. At the war's end, another 200,000 fled advancing Soviet troops, and by 1949 about 500,000 had been deported to northern Russia and Siberia as the region was forcibly repopulated.

Over the next several decades farms were collectivized and an industrial economy began.

With the advent in 1987 of Soviet leader, Mikhail Gorbachev, and his campaign of *perestroika* (restructuring) came increases in nationalism. Non-Communist political parties in each of the republics succeeded in legitimizing their native language and establishing freedoms of speech and the press, as well as in religion.

In March 1990, Lithuania became the first republic to declare its independence. Estonia and Latvia followed in August 1991 after the failed Soviet coup.

Formal recognitions of independence were given to the Baltic States by both the United States and the Soviet Union in September 1991.

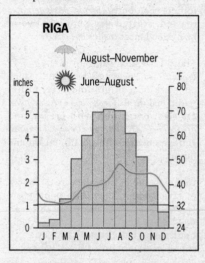

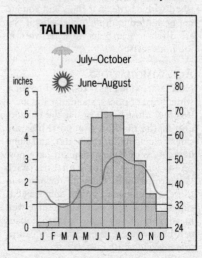

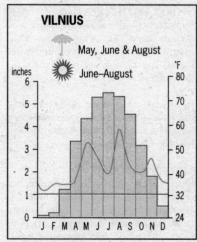

FOOD AND DRINK

The Baltic States offer widely varying cuisines – meat and dairy products feature widely.

Other dishes common to all three are pancakes (filled with fruit, jam or cheese) and sour cream. Surprisingly, there is little fresh fish; most is smoked and salted.

In Estonia some traditional favorites are *seaspraad*, pork with sauerkraut, and *hapukapsa*, sauerkraut soup. *Sult*, or jellied veal, and *taidetud basikarind*, a roasted, stuffed veal, are just two of many good meat dishes.

Many Latvians wake up to a *zamieku brokastis*, or "peasant's breakfast" which consists of a huge omelette. Other traditional meals are *maizes zupa ar putukrejumu*, corn soup with cream, and *biezpiens ar kartupeliem*, *krejumi*, cottage cheese with potato, cream and butter.

Common fare in Lithuania are *virtinukai*, or ravioli-like dishes. Also popular are *bulviniai blynai*, potato pancakes; *cepelinai*, dumplings; and *šaltibarščiai*, cold beet soup. Unique to Lithuania is a strong local spirit called Black Balsam.

SPORTS AND RECREATION

Summer activities along the Baltic coast include sailing and windsurfing, while inland, canoeing (in Latvia and Lithuania) and fishing are popular on the many rivers.

In national parks, horse riding and walking have great appeal. Spectator sports include basketball, for which Lithuania has won Olympic golds.

GETTING AROUND

Since independence, each country has set up its own airline, mostly routed to Germany, Scandinavia and the Netherlands. Many north European carriers fly to the Baltic States, making it easily accessible from the United States via Amsterdam, Frankfurt or Scandinavia. Summer charter flights operate from Chicago to Kaunas. Check flight details with your travel agent.

Ferries take passengers from Helsinki and Stockholm to Tallinn. Riga is served by ferries from Kiel and Travemunde in Germany, from Copenhagen in Denmark and Stockholm in Sweden.

Public transportation in the Baltic States is cheap and slow. Cities are linked by trains (soft class, the highest, is only available on intercity routes) and buses; towns are served by trolley buses, trams, local trains as well as taxis.

Car rental is available from international rental companies – take your driver's license and credit card with you as well as enough cash for a deposit. It is advisable to arrange comprehensive insurance, and cars should always be locked when they are parked.

The speed limits in built-up areas are 50 k.p.h. (31 m.p.h.) and 90 k.p.h. (55 m.p.h.) elsewhere. Estonian drivers keep their lights on in daytime. Many roads are in very poor condition, particularly in Latvia. Driving infringements are punished with on-the-spot fines and you are not permitted to drink any alcohol if you are driving. Seat belts must be worn in the front seats.

ACCOMMODATIONS

Hotels are not classified, and cover a wide range of prices, standards and architecture. Most hotels are at the cheaper end of the market, though things are slowly changing for the better, and some new hotels of luxury standard have now been built as joint ventures with Western partners. Demand for rooms in these and upgraded hotels now exceeds supply, and it is advisable to reserve well in advance. Lodging in private houses can be arranged; there are also campgrounds and youth hostels.

PLACES OF INTEREST

TALLINN (51 B4)
ESTONIA *pop. 434,800*

The capital of Estonia, Tallinn is a well-preserved medieval town with city walls, church spires and buildings with steep tiled roofs.

The old port sits on a hill, Toompea, dominated by Toompea Castle, built in the early 13th century. Now only two walls and three towers remain from the original structure. The 13th-century Toomkirk was destroyed by fire in 1684 and has been restored; it has a baroque-style altar and several carved tombs of Swedish commanders.

The 15th-century bastion Kiek-in-die-Kök, whose name translates as "look in the kitchen," derived its name from the local saying that from the castle heights a person could see through all the chimneys and into the kitchens. It is now a museum with weapons, maps and models of early Tallinn.

The onion-domed Alexander Nevsky Cathedral is nearby.

KUNSTIMUUSEUM (Fine Arts Museum), in Kadriorg Park at 37 Weizenbergi Street, housed in the baroque Kadriorg Palace contains over 17,000 modern Estonian, Russian and European works of art.

RIGA (51 B3)
LATVIA *pop. 840,000*

The capital of Latvia, Riga, sits on the banks of the Daugava River and was a Hanseatic port. It can trace its history back to about AD 1200.

Relics abound in the section between the right bank of the river and the city's canal, and include old fortifications as well as the 14th-century Gunpowder Tower, occupied by the Latvian War Museum.

Riga Castle, from the same era, houses three different museums, including the Museum of Latvian History.

Several well-preserved examples of medieval architecture survive; among these are the 17th-century Dannenstern Mansion, the Mansion of Peter I and 13th-century St. Jacob's Church. Once a walled city, the only surviving remnant is the Swedish Gate, with nine cannon balls embedded in its wall.

A great port and industrial center, Riga also is a city of parks, gardens and theaters. Most notable among these are Mežparks, the opera and ballet and the Latvia Philharmonia Orchestra.

VILNIUS (51 C1)
LITHUANIA *pop. 579,000*

The cultural and industrial center of Lithuania, as well as its capital, Vilnius, at the confluence of the Neris and Vilnia rivers, was important as early as 1323, when it was chosen as the seat of the powerful grand dukes of Lithuania.

Magnificent buildings surviving from the early expansion of the city include the Aušros Vartai (Gates of Dawn) and the Church of Saints Peter and Paul.

Most places of interest are in the area of Gediminas Square in the center of the city; the reconsecrated St. Stanislaus Cathedral, the 16th-century Gothic St. Anne's Church and 14th-century Gediminas Castle are outstanding.

Excursions are available to the nearby lake country and site of Trakai, the 14th-century fortress-capital of Lithuania, 30 kilometers (18½ miles) west, complete with a ruined castle.

KAUNAS (51 B1)
LITHUANIA *pop. 419,900*

Lithuania's second largest city, Kaunas is at the confluence of the Nemunas and Neris rivers.

This important industrial center was the capital of Lithuania between the world wars. Though the architecture is predominantly modern, several historical sites remain.

The 15th-century Gothic Church of Saints Peter and Paul at Aleksotas Street is the city's oldest, while nearby the ruins of 14th-century Kaunas Castle can also be visited.

BELGIUM

Belgium is rather a neglected country on the travel map. Anyone who has been there, though, knows that it offers superb beaches and delightful spa towns, the beautiful town of Bruges, and the lovely mountains of the Ardennes. Visitors will find the best beer, the most delicious waffles and the finest chocolate in Europe. The artists Bruegel and Rubens came from Belgium.

The country illustrates the rainbow nature of Europe. The Walloons from the south speak French, while in the north the Flemings speak Flemish (Dutch). The capital, Brussels, is a historic and attractive city – it is no surprise then that the members of the European Union chose it for their main base.

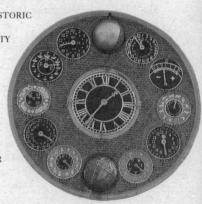

Left One of the colorful parades which Belgium has to offer
Above The astronomical clock on the Zimmer Tower in Lier tells universal time

Things to Know

- **Area:** 30,519 square kilometers (11,799 square miles)
- **Population:** 9,998,000
- **Capital:** Brussel/Bruxelles (Brussels)
- **Languages:** Dutch, French and German
- **Passport Requirements:** Required for U.S. citizens.
- **Visa Requirements:** Not required for stays up to three months.
- **Duty-Free Items:** Visitors from outside the E.U. 200 cigarettes or 50 cigars or 250grams of tobacco; 2 liters of wine, 1 liter of alcoholic beverages, 50 grams of perfume, one large bottle of toilet water, one still camera with 12 rolls of film, one movie camera with six rolls of film; one video camera. See also *The European Union*, p.9.
- **Currency:** The currency unit is the Belgian *franc*, divided into 100 *centimes*. Due to currency fluctuations, the exchange rate is subject to change.
- **Bank Opening Hours:** 9am–4pm Monday–Friday; many close for lunch.
- **Store Opening Hours:** Major stores 9am–8pm Monday–Saturday, 9am–9pm Friday, others 9am–6pm Monday–Saturday.
- **Public Holidays:** January 1; Easter Monday; May 1 (Labor Day); Ascension Day; Whitmonday; July 21 (National Day); August 15 (Assumption Day); November 1 (All Saints' Day); November 11 (Armistice Day); December 25.
- **National Tourist Offices:**
  Belgian National Tourist Office
  780 Third Avenue, Suite 1501
  New York, NY 10017
  Tel: 212/ 758-8130
  Fax: 212/ 355-7675
  Commissariat-General De Tourisme:
  Grasmarkt 61/63 rue Marché-aux-Herbes
  B-1000 Brussel/Bruxelles
  Tel: (02) 504-03-90
- **American Embassy:**
  27 Boulevard du Régent
  B-1000 Brussel/Bruxelles
  Belgium
  Tel: (02) 513-38-30

History

Excellent ports and few natural defences have long made Frankish Belgium a natural battleground. Following Roman and Frankish occupations, the nation began to take shape under 14th-century Philip the Good, who annexed the Low Countries. Extending from the North Sea to the Rhône Valley, the duchy assumed commercial leadership in Europe, while the arts flourished. But with the death of Charles the Bold in 1477, control passed to the Habsburg rulers of Austria.

The Low Countries were allied with the Spanish Empire when the Austrian Charles I became King of Spain in the 16th century. With his abdication, internal tensions divided the area into the United Provinces (Holland) and the Spanish Netherlands (Belgium). France annexed Belgium and the principality of Liège in 1795, but Belgians were dissatisfied with French rule and the subsequent Napoléonic regime. With

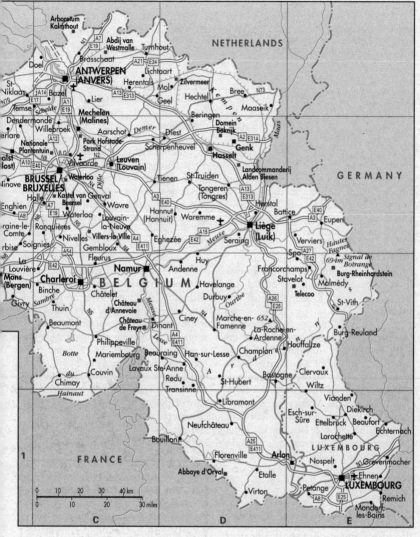

Napoléon's defeat at Waterloo in 1815, the Congress of Vienna united Belgium with the United Provinces to form the Kingdom of the Netherlands. William of Orange, the first king, had to contend with a north that was Protestant and a south that was Catholic. On October 4, 1830, the southern provinces declared their independence, and the major European powers soon recognized the Kingdom of Belgium as a neutral nation.

Although Belgium was the scene of fierce battles in both world wars, its recovery was swift and prosperous. Now governed by a constitutional monarchy; its local affairs are handled by nine provincial authorities.

Belgium's ruler, King Baudouin, was succeeded in 1993 by his brother, who became King Albert II. His wife is Queen Paola.

Internal cultural differences between the northern Flemish provinces and the southern French-speaking Walloon provinces have resulted in an unusual language situation. In the 19th century, French was the dominant language in business, government and education, though more than half of Belgium's population was Flemish-speaking. To diffuse tensions between the two groups, Flemish was made an equally official language in 1898. Today, Dutch (of which Flemish is a dialect) is the official language in the north, French in the south and German in the east. In Brussels, the capital, both Dutch and French are officially recognized. English is widely understood.

FOOD AND DRINK

Surrounded by other countries known for their *haute cuisine*, Belgium has still managed to create a cuisine that is unmistakably its own.

Tomates aux crevettes, tomatoes stuffed with shrimp, are a delight. *Witloof*, or chicory, garnishes a number of main dishes. The sandy Mechelen region produces wonderful asparagus; ham comes from the Ardennes. Mussels are especially good in Brussels and on the coast; in Namur fried eel is a local treat. Many varieties of *boudin*, or sausage, are always available. Seafood specialties such as lobster and *waterzooi* – fish or chicken stew – are invariably delicious. *Frites*, or fried potatoes, are a national favorite. Those with a sweet tooth can enjoy a variety of cakes, chocolates and waffles. Belgium also offers about 400 varieties of beer and nearly 200 types of *genièvre*, or gin.

SPORTS AND RECREATION

Belgian coastal resorts, particularly at Oostende, offer excellent swimming and water sports facilities. Deep sea, surf and trout fishing are available, but permits are required. Horse racing takes place in Brussels, Oostende, Waregem and Spa. Boaters can enjoy their sport at Oostende, Zeebrugge, Blankenberge and Nieuwpoort. Golf, tennis and horseback riding facilities are also available. Other activities include canoeing on several rivers and along the coastline, and skiing in the highlands.

GETTING AROUND

Belgium's excellent transportation system includes electric rail lines throughout the country. Tourist season tickets, available for either five or eight days, are available from most major railroad stations. Bicycles can be rented at many railroad stations as well. Cabs in the large cities are expensive, but trams and buses offer one-day tickets that allow unlimited travel on both services.

Drivers in Belgium usually travel on a comprehensive system of toll-free highways. There are two highway numbering systems. A national network uses black and white signs with the prefix A; an international network uses green and white signs with the prefix E. Some E roads have a new numbering system that was introduced in 1986, so some signs may show two different numbers, an old and a new, for the same road. Road signs are in two languages: in the northern part of the country, signs are in Dutch (Flemish); in the south, they are in French. Brussels is the only area where signs are in both languages.

AUTOMOBILE CLUB

The Touring Club Royal de Belgique (T.C.B., Touring Club Royal de Belgique) 44 rue de la Loi, Brussels, and the **Royal Automobile Club de Belgique**, (R.A.C.B., Automobile Club of Belgium), rue d'Arlon 53, Brussels, have branch offices in various cities throughout Belgium. The symbol ▲ beside a city name indicates the presence of a AAA-affiliated automobile club branch. Not all auto clubs offer full travel services to AAA members.

The wearing of seat belts (if the car is so equipped) is mandatory for the driver and passengers. A child under the age of 12 cannot occupy a front seat unless using a suitable restraint device or unless rear seats are not available or are already occupied by children. Speed limits are 60 k.p.h. (37 m.p.h.) in town, 90 k.p.h. (55 m.p.h.) on out-of-town roads and 120 k.p.h. (75 m.p.h.) on highways. There are stiff penalties for driving while under the influence of alcohol. Nonresidents of Belgium are charged fines for motoring violations on the spot in Belgian currency or U.S. dollars.

ACCOMMODATIONS

Belgium rates its hotels with from one to five stars – five stars is the best rating. The Belgian Tourist Authority publishes a list of lodgings; those approved by the authority post a special sign. The list can be obtained from Belgian tourist offices abroad as well as local tourist offices throughout Belgium. Local tourist offices can also book rooms for you. Breakfast is usually included in the price of a room. More than 800 campgrounds throughout Belgium provide inexpensive accommodations; some campgrounds offer a price reduction if you have an International Camping Carnet.

LANGUAGE

Dutch (Flemish), French and German are the three official languages in Belgium. Brussels is essentially bilingual (Dutch and French), due partly to its cultural and political importance and partly to its central location. Flemish is spoken north of Brussels; French is spoken in the south and German in the east. (For useful expressions in French see p.249, for German see p.311, and for Dutch see p.467).

TIPPING

Generally, tipping is not practiced in Belgium because a service charge is usually included in the bill. If you do leave a tip of 10 percent, however, it will be readily accepted.

PRINCIPAL TOURING AREAS

Note: For attractions in **bold type**, see individual listings.

Although French is widely spoken in Belgium, Flemish is the official language for the northern region of the country and is usually the *only* language spoken in that area. Because of strong Flemish sentiments, all French place names have now been eliminated. Towns that were once known by their French spellings are now only referred to by their original Flemish names. Among the towns whose names have been changed are the following: Bruges is known as Brugge; Courtrai is Kortrijk; Louvain is Leuven; Malines is Mechelen; Ostend is Oostende; and Ypres is Ieper.

All road signs and European maps carry the Flemish designations. Brussels is still bilingual and is known as either Brussel (Flemish) or Bruxelles (French).

BRABANT

Belgium's only province not to be bordered by another country, Brabant is the heart of the nation and a centuries-old crossroads of the Continent.

It was the logical site for metropolitan growth: **Brussel/Bruxelles**, or Brussels, has a population of nearly 1 million. It also seemed to be in an unfortunate position as the site for over six major European wars. **Waterloo**, the site of Napoléon's defeat, is the region's best-known battlefield.

EASTERN WALLOON PROVINCES

Belgium's land begins to rise in the southeast, reaching the provinces of Liège, Luxembourg and Namur. The first region to be settled, this part of the country is an area of traditional Walloon sentiments. The picturesque Meuse River stretches between limestone cliffs, passing such economically important towns as **Dinant**, **Namur** and **Liège**. But

Sunlight reflecting the gabled houses on the River Leie at Korenlei (Corn Quay), in Ghent.

summer visitors flock to the Ardennes region, which includes the best of the scenic Semois and Meuse valleys.

HAINAUT

Hainaut, a part of Walloon Belgium, has long shared economic and historical ties with neighboring France. The French architectural influence is most evident in **Tournai**, which boasts extensive art collections and the largest Gothic cathedral in Belgium. Not to be overlooked are the castle of Beloeil and ancient **Mons**, the provincial capital.

THE KEMPEN

The sandy, pine-strewn plain that supports much of industrialized Belgium is known unofficially as the Kempen; officially, it takes in the province of Antwerpen and Limburg. The port of **Antwerpen**, or Antwerp, on the River Schelde is the center of a large industrial and commercial area. Museum enthusiasts will enjoy the national art treasures to be found in the city. Outside the metropolitan area, **Mechelen**, once the capital of the Netherlands has its lovely 13th-century St. Rombaut's Cathedral.

WEST FLEMISH PROVINCES

East and West Flanders occupy the northern Flemish plain, which is crisscrossed by rivers and canals. In the northwest, the resorts of Zeebrugge and Het Zoute line the North Sea. Farther east, memorials pay tribute to past heroism, particularly in **Ieper (Ypres)**, rebuilt since its devastation in World War I. **Brugge (Bruges)** and **Gent**, once rival city-states, vie for tourist attention with their splendid architecture and museums.

BRUSSELS

July–August

May–September

inches

6

5

4

3

2

1

0

J F M A M J J A S O N D

°F

90

80

70

60

50

40

32

PLACES OF INTEREST

▲ **BRUSSEL/BRUXELLES (59 C3)** ★
BRABANT *pop. 950,000*
Known as Brussel in Flemish, Bruxelles in French and Brussels in English, the capital of Belgium is an important banking, trade and transportation center, as well as the headquarters for the North Atlantic Treaty Organization (N.A.T.O.) and the European Union. The most influential leaders of Europe regularly convene in Brussels.

HOME OF THE EUROCRATS

Officially, there is no capital of Europe, but Brussels is the home of the European Commission, who often appear to be the driving force of the European ideal. As one of the centers of political power, Brussels has a cosmopolitan ambience, with cafés, pubs and restaurants creating a Euro-neighborhood in which the city's civil servants can be at their ease.

Skyscrapers and hotels have modernized the skyline of this French- and Flemish-speaking city. Old Brussels, with its narrow streets, brick stores and houses decorated with ornamental ironwork, recalls the city's medieval past. The *petit ceinture*, boulevards where the city walls once stood, encircles the lower city, and contains the site of the Gothic Cathedral of St. Michel, 13th-century Church of la Chappelle and the Gothic Church of Sablon. The upper city, with tree-lined avenues, has large public squares and magnificent 18th- and 19th-century palaces.

Formerly home of the Renaissance scholar Erasmus, Brussels remains a cultural and educational center. The opera season runs from September to April, and the city has several excellent museums and art galleries.

One of Brussels' most prominent annual events is the Ommegang, a colorful pageant dating from 1549 and held at Grand Place in July. Titled Belgians don the costumes of their ancestors and join a procession led by a figure of Charles V.

Trips into the surrounding countryside can take in the castles and châteaux at Beersel, Gaasbeek, Groot-Bijgaarden, Horst and Rixensart. Nearby are the grape-growing areas of Overijse, Hoeilaart and the Forest of Soignes, and the Abbaye de Villers ruins near Villers-la-Ville. Waterloo and its battlefield are about 16 kilometers (10 miles) south.

More information on the city and its attractions is available from the tourist office, 61 rue Marché-aux-Herbes (Grasmarkt), or Tourist Information Brussels (T.I.B.), City Hall, Grand-Place (Grote Markt).

BRUPARCK is a family leisure park containing a mini-Europe exhibit, which has scale models of famous European buildings. Just outside the park is the Atomium, a spectacular monument composed of nine giant metal spheres that represent the atoms of an iron molecule. Designed for the 1958 World Expo, it is one of the city's best-known symbols. An observation deck inside the topmost sphere affords superb panoramic views.

GRAND-PLACE (64 B2), dominated by the Gothic spire of the Hôtel de Ville (Town Hall) and the gabled Guild Houses, with their ornate Flemish baroque façades, is one of Europe's most beautiful public squares. The buildings are illuminated nightly from June to September.

MANNEKEN-PIS (64 B2), rue de l'Etive, is an early 17th-century bronze statue of a boy using nature's own sprinkling system. A wardrobe of over 500 costumes presented to the statue is in the Musée Communal (Museum of the City of Brussels).

MUSÉE D'ART ANCIEN (Museum of Ancient Art) (64 B2), 3 rue de la Régence, offers a superb selection of paintings from the Flemish School from the 14th

to the early 19th centuries. The museum connects to the Musée d'Art Moderne (see below).

MUSÉE D'ART MODERNE (Museum of Modern Art) (64 B2), place Royale 1, traces Belgian painting since the late 19th century.

PALAIS ROYAL (64 C2), Place des Palais, the 18th-century palace of the dukes of

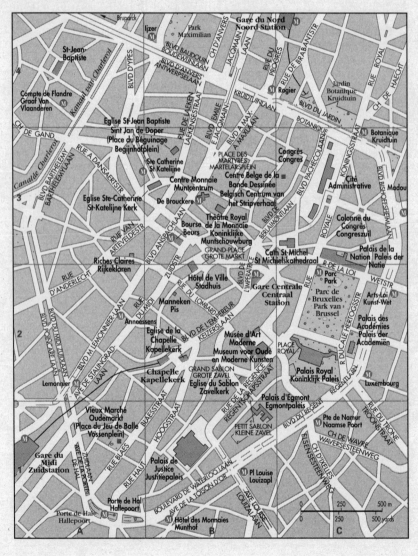

Brabant, was rebuilt at the beginning of the century for King Leopold II.

PLACE ROYALE (64 C2) is an elegant 18th-century square that is dominated by the equestrian statue of Godefroy de Bouillon, leader of the First Crusade.

▲ ANTWERPEN (59 C4) ★
ANTWERPEN *pop. 475,000*
Antwerpen (Antwerp), on the Scheldt River, is one of the world's largest commercial ports and an international business center with a lively nightlife.

During the Renaissance the city flourished as a center of Flemish culture. Rubens, Van Dyck and other well-known painters lived in Antwerp, and several of the city's museums display their works. The city is still culturally important. Theaters and nightclubs provide year-round entertainment, and opera runs from September to May. Exhibitions of diamond-cutting can be seen at the Provincial Diamantsmuseum (Diamond Center) at Lange Herentalsestraat 31.

KONINKLIJK MUSEUM VOOR SCHONE KUN-STEN (Royal Museum of Fine Arts), Leopold de Waelplaats 1–9, is in a 19th-century neoclassical building. Its 2,500 paintings span five centuries.

MAYER VAN DEN BERGH MUSEUM, Lange Gasthuisstraat 19, is a reconstruction of a 16th-century townhouse. The highlight is probably Bruegel's *Dulle Griet* (*Mad Meg*), which shows a woman in an apron and armor charging the gates of hell.

ONZE LIEVE-VROUWE KATHEDRAAL (Cathedral of Our Lady), Groenplaats 21, was completed in the 16th century after over 200 years. The largest cathedral in the Lowlands, it is known for its Gothic architecture and contains several masterpieces by Rubens, including three outstanding altarpieces. The 123-meter (404-foot) spire dominates the skyline.

PLANTIN-MORETUS MUSEUM, Vrijdagmarkt 23, is housed in the mansion of French-born printer Christophe Plantin. Among the exhibits are priceless manuscripts and a Librarium Prohibitorum, a list of "dangerous" books once banned by the Church.

RUBENSHUIS (Rubens' House), Wapper 9, the former home and studio of the great Flemish artist Peter Paul Rubens, who lived here from 1608 until his death in 1640, contains mementoes, a self-portrait and paintings from his school.

SINT-PAULUSKERK (St. Paul's Church), in the Veemarkt, is a 16th-century Gothic-style church with a baroque tower. In addition to fine woodcarvings and over 200 sculptures, the church has paintings by Rubens, Van Dyck and Jordaens.

VLEESHUIS (Butchers' Guild House), Vleeshouwersstraat 38–40, is a Gothic palace whose hall was once used as a meat market. It now houses an archaeological and craft industries museum, and has a noteworthy collection of 17th- and 18th-century musical instruments.

BOKRIJK (59 D3) ★
LIMBURG
Some 10 kilometers (6 miles) northeast of Hasselt is an estate with a park, arboretum, rose garden and several lakes. The open-air museum in the grounds re-creates a medieval Flemish town and a typical Kempen village.

▲ BRUGGE/BRUGES (58 A4) ★
WEST-VLAANDEREN *pop. 120,000*
The medieval aura surrounding Brugge, or Bruges, dates from the city's beginnings during the 9th century and its 13th- to 15th-century rise to importance as an inland trading port. The old buildings, gabled houses, splendid churches, picturesque streets, bridged canals and art treasures attest to this period of prosperity, which reached its peak during the 15th century.

Walking down the cobbled streets, riding in a horse-drawn carriage, boating down a canal or renting a bicycle are all

BELGIUM

satisfying ways to see Brugge. Markt, the city's main square, offers interesting old buildings. The Burg square nearby offers such varied structures as the Basilica of the Holy Blood, the 14th-century Gothic town hall and the Renaissance-era Old Recorder's House.

Several other well-preserved buildings, numerous museums and art galleries, including the Brangwyn, Groeninge, Gruuthuse and Memling museums, are within walking distance.

Special events include Ascension Day, when the Procession of the Holy Blood makes its way through the city streets, bringing to life biblical characters and scenes.

BELFORT EN HALLE (Belfry and Halls), Markt, dates from the 13th to 15th centuries. Reached by a winding staircase of 366 steps, the 83-meter (272-foot) belfry commands an excellent view of the city and has a 47-bell carillon.

GROENINGE MUSEUM, on the Dijver Canal, contains works by such Flemish Primitive painters as Van Eyck, Van der Goes and Memling, as well as art from more recent periods.

GRUUTHUSE MUSEUM, on the Dijver Canal, was the palace of the Lords of Gruuthuse, who owned the monopoly on the sale of *gruut*, a mixture of herbs and spices used in brewing beer. The 15th-century palace now exhibits Flemish pottery, furniture, weapons and goldsmiths' works.

HEILIG BLOEDBASILIEK (Basilica of the Holy Blood) was built between 1139 and 1149 in Romanesque style, evident in the crypt chapel. The upper chapel was remodeled in Gothic style in the 15th century, with later alterations. This chapel contains the Relic of the Holy Blood. The relic is carried around in a colorful procession on Ascension Day.

ONZE LIEVE VROUWEKERK (Church of Our Lady), Mariastraat, is primarily Gothic,

although it combines several different styles. Among its art treasures is a marble *Madonna and Child* by Michelangelo. The church includes the mausoleums of Mary of Burgundy and Charles the Bold.

SINT-JANSHOSPITAAL (St. John's Hospital), Mariastraat 38, founded in the

GUILDS AND SOCIETIES

Guild houses were once a powerful force in Belgian society, and inscriptions such as *brasseurs* (brewers) and *bakkers* (bakers) can still be seen on buildings. Most existing guilds have strict membership and dress codes, and each honors a particular cause, however bizarre – the Confrérie de la Tarte, for example, is dedicated to a special kind of cheesecake!

12th century, now houses the Memling Museum, a small collection of work by the 15th-century painter, Memling.

CHARLEROI (59 C2)
HAINAUT *pop. 220,000*
Named for Charles II of Spain, Charleroi was once an important fortified town. Highlights include the Museum of Fine Arts, with works by Pierre Paulus and Magritte, and, 18 kilometers (11 miles) southwest, is the medieval village of Thuin.

DINANT (59 C2) ★
NAMUR *pop. 12,300*
Dinant is a popular tourist center on the Meuse River, and is crowned with an impressive citadel. Famous for its copperware and *couques* (ginger cookies), Dinant has an amusement park and bathing facilities, and is the starting point for river trips to Namur.

▲ EUPEN (59 E3)
LIÈGE *pop. 17,300*
Eupen is a thriving textile center at the confluence of the Vesdre and Hill rivers.

In addition to its scenery, Eupen is renowned for its annual pre-Lenten carnival, an 18th-century baroque church and the unique Euro Space Center, housed in a futuristic building.

▲ GENT/GHENT(58 B3) ★
OOST-VLAANDEREN *pop. 230,000*

Gent or Ghent, the city of flowers and the capital of East Flanders, is on a series of islands at the confluence of the Leie and Schelde rivers. In medieval times the city was a major commercial center and the seat of the Counts of Flanders. By the end of the 13th century, its flourishing textile industry had transformed it into one of Europe's largest cities. During the Renaissance, Gent became home to several Flemish artists, including the Van Eyck brothers.

The narrow streets and medieval houses lend a picturesque quality to this city, which also is noted for its Gothic town hall, 7th-century Abbey of St. Bavo, attractive Citadel Park, Floralia Palace and nearby Castle of Laarne.

BELFORT EN LAKENHALLE (Belfry and Cloth Hall), on St. Baafsplein, are Gothic structures built between 1321 and 1426. Remodeled in 1913, the building is a symbol of freedom and has a 52-bell carillon.

GILDEHUIZEN (Guild Houses), on the Graslei, date from the 12th to 17th centuries and were built in the Romanesque, Gothic and Renaissance styles.

GRAVENSTEEN (Castle of the Counts of Flanders), St. Veerleplein, was built in 1180 by Philip of Alsace. It resembles the Crusader fortresses built in Syria. The dungeons and a gruesome torture room are still intact.

MUSEUM VOOR SCHONE KUNSTEN (Museum of Fine Arts), Nicolaas de Liemaeckereplein 3, contains paintings by old masters and is particularly noted for Flemish works, including Hieronymus Bosch's *The Carrying of the Cross*.

MUSEUM VOOR VOLKSKUNDE (Folklore Museum), Kraanlei 65, is housed in an attractive courtyard complex of restored almshouses dating from the mid-14th century.

SINT-BAAFSKATHEDRAAL (St. Bavon's Cathedral), St. Baafsplein, houses many treasures, including the *Adoration of the Mystic Lamb* altarpiece by Jan and Hubert van Eyck, one of the most celebrated and enigmatic works in Western art.

DEVILISH CHOCOLATES

Don't leave Belgium without visiting a *chocolatier* (chocolate store), where delectable handmade pralines can be bought either in a presentation box or selected according to your tastes. Remember, real cream doesn't keep, though this is unlikely to be a problem as Belgian chocolates seldom last long.

STADHUIS (Town Hall), Botermarkt, is an intriguing architectural blend of Gothic and Renaissance styles. The Pacification of Gent, a peace treaty between Catholics and Protestants, was signed in 1576 in the Pacificatiezaal, one of a series of halls open to the public. Access by tour.

▲ HASSELT (59 D3)
LIMBURG *pop. 66,900*

Hasselt is a market town on the Demer River and famous for its Cathedral of St. Quintin, constructed on Romanesque foundations and built mainly in the 13th and 14th centuries.

IEPER/YPRES (58 A3)
WEST-VLAANDEREN *pop. 35,000*

After Ieper, or Ypres, was reduced to rubble in World War I, its residents took care in reconstructing the town, especially the 13th-century Gothic Cloth Hall, with its lofty belfry, and the Cathedral of St. Martin. Several museums have art and history displays, and war memorials and cemeteries are nearby.

About 500,000 fallen soldiers lie in 170 military cemeteries in the vicinity. The Lille Gate stands as a reminder of past glory, and the Menin Gate, the place where many thousands advanced toward the front, is an imposing British memorial to World War I dead.

LAKENHALLE (Cloth Hall), Grote Markt, is a magnificent Gothic hall, painstakingly rebuilt in 1933 after destruction in 1914. The 70-meter (230-foot) belfry is reached by 264 steps, and has a carillon of 40 bells. It now houses the Salient Museum, exhibiting artifacts from World War I.

KNOKKE-HEIST (58 A4)
WEST-VLAANDEREN *pop. 32,000*

The resort area of Knokke-Heist consists of five North Sea resort towns: Heist, Duinbergen, Knokke, Albertstrand, and Het Zoute. All are on an expanse of beach near the Dutch border, with Het Zoute regarded as the most sophisticated. The casino, golf course, tennis courts, stores, restaurants and nightspots make it a favorite resort.

▲ LEUVEN (59 C3)
BRABANT *pop. 85,000*

Leuven was a flourishing city in the Middle Ages. The seat of the dukes of Brabant for centuries, it is now known for the University of Leuven. Churches include the 15th-century Gothic St. Pieterskerk and baroque St. Michielskerk. The cobbled Oude Markt (Old Market) is the city's liveliest square and a popular student haunt, while the Stadhuis (Town Hall), in mid-15th-century Flamboyant Gothic style, is one of the most attractive buildings in Belgium.

GROOT BEGIJNHOF, founded in 1234, is the nation's largest community of lay nuns, and has over 70 magnificently restored 17th-century houses.

▲ LIÈGE (59 D3)
LIÈGE *pop. 196,300*

Once ruled by prince-bishops, Liège (Luik in Flemish) is at the confluence of the Meuse and Ourthe rivers and gateway to the Ardennes. In an attractive region of rivers and forests, Liège is the largest French-speaking city in Belgium and a popular tourist destination.

CATHÉDRALE ST-PAUL, rue Bonne-Fortune 6, is a 13th-century Gothic construction with noteworthy statuary, stained glass and a fine interior.

CHÂTEAU DE JEHAY is a 16th-century castle on an islet 25 kilometers (16 miles) southwest of Liège containing a museum of Gothic to 18th-century furniture.

MONTAGNE DE BUEREN (Bueren Hill) off rue Hors-Château, is a steep passageway of some 400 steps leading to the ancient citadel. An impressive view rewards those able to make the climb.

PALAIS DES PRINCES EVÊQUES (Palace of the Prince-Bishops), palace Saint-Lambert, is a vast Gothic palace begun in the 9th century and rebuilt in the 16th and 18th centuries. Now the Palais de Justice, it has magnificent interior decor.

▲ MECHELEN (59 C3)
ANTWERPEN *pop. 75,000*

Mechelen, on the Dijle River, was once the capital of the Netherlands and for centuries the religious center of Belgium. Many of its buildings and much of its medieval atmosphere have survived. Mechelen was the center of Flemish cloth weaving, and is now known for its lace. A bellringing school in St. Rombaut's Cathedral attracts *carillonneurs* from all over the world.

Mechelen is home to two great paintings by Rubens: the *Adoration of the Magi* in the St. Janskerk and the *Miraculous Draft of Fishes* in Onze Lieve Vrouw over de Dijle.

SINT-ROMBOUTS KATHEDRAAL (St. Rombaut's Cathedral) dates from the 13th century and is considered one of the most beautiful in Belgium. Its 97-meter (318-foot) tower has a 49-bell carillon.

Inside the cathedral are some priceless paintings, including works by Van Dyck.

▲ MONS (59 B2)
HAINAUT *pop. 92,400*
A settlement that dates from the 7th century, Mons has quaint buildings, winding streets and old mansions. Its 15th-century Gothic town hall has some fine tapestries. A 17th-century baroque belfry stands on the site of the Castle of the Counts of Hainaut. The 87-meter (285-foot) tower contains a 47-bell carillon and affords splendid views.

▲ NAMUR (59 C2)
NAMUR *pop. 104,000*
Namur is the capital of the province of the same name. The old citadel on a promontory overlooking the city can be reached by road or cable car, and many of its fortifications can be visited.

MAISON DES SOEURS DE NOTRE DAME (House of the Sisters of Notre Dame), 17 rue Julie Billiart, houses the treasure of Oignies Priory, including silverwork from the 13th century.

▲ OOSTENDE (58 A4)
WEST-VLAANDEREN *pop. 69,000*
The most important and one of the oldest Belgian communities, Oostende is a port of embarkation for cross-channel trips to Dover in England. From May to October it is a popular seaside resort, with a racetrack, casino, golf course and beach.

▲ SPA (59 E2)
LIÈGE *pop. 10,300*
Spa has given its name to health resorts throughout the world. It was popular in the 18th and 19th centuries, when Europe's elite used its waters. Today it has a casino, racetrack and 18-hole golf course. Spa is the site of the Battle of Flowers parade on the second Sunday in August.

TONGEREN (59 D3)
LIMBURG *pop. 30,000*
As the oldest town in Belgium (founded in the 1st century) and the first in the country to adopt Christianity, Tongeren has a rich heritage. Its many Roman ruins include remnants of the city wall, while its Gallo-Roman museum has over 18,000 artifacts.

▲ TOURNAI (58 B3)
HAINAUT *pop. 67,800*
Divided by the Scheldt River, Tournai (Doornik in Flemish) was founded by Romans in the 3rd century; only Tongeren is older. It is famous not only for the architects, sculptors, goldsmiths, and painters who were born or lived in the town, but also for tapestries, china and earthenware. The Museum of Fine Arts displays works by such old and modern masters as Rubens, Bruegel, Manet, Ensor and Van der Weyden.

The 13th-century belfry is the oldest in Belgium. A tourist office is opposite the belfry at 14 rue du Vieux Marché-aux-Potèries.

CATHÉDRALE DE NOTRE DAME (Cathedral of Our Lady), place de l'Évêché, is a Romanesque structure, completed in the 12th century. The sculptures on the west face of the cathedral date from the 14th to the 17th centuries and represent Adam and Eve, the apostles and the saints; 12th-century murals as well as paintings by Metsys, Rubens and Jordaens adorn the interior walls.

WATERLOO (59 C3) ★
BRABANT *pop. 26,900*
Napoleon met defeat at Waterloo in 1815; today the famous battlefield has monuments and memorials to those who died during the waning hours of the Napoleonic Empire. A sweeping view of the battlefield is available at the Butte du Lion (Lion Mound), a 40-meter (130-foot) mound which marks the spot where Prince William of Orange was wounded.

The nearby Panorama de la Bataille contains a lifelike panoramic painting of a French cavalry charge, which gives the visitor the frightening illusion of being involved in the action.

LUXEMBOURG

LUXEMBOURG OCCUPIES ONLY 2,590 SQUARE KILOMETERS (1,000 SQUARE MILES) AND LIES BETWEEN FRANCE, GERMANY AND BELGIUM. ITS HISTORY HAS BEEN INFLUENCED BY ITS LARGER NEIGHBORS, WHICH VARIOUSLY ANNEXED THE TERRITORY. INDEPENDENCE WAS ACHIEVED IN 1867 WHEN THEY FINALLY WITHDREW. THE GRAND DUCHY OF LUXEMBOURG IS THE SMALLEST MEMBER OF THE EUROPEAN UNION AND IS HOME TO THE EUROPEAN COURT OF JUSTICE. LUXEMBOURG CITY IS WHERE MANY INTERNATIONAL BANKS KEEP THEIR RESERVES. THERE ARE MANY REMINDERS OF LUXEMBOURG'S 1,000 YEARS OF HISTORY, NOTABLY THE 16TH-CENTURY GRAND DUCAL PALACE AND THE 17TH-CENTURY NÔTRE DAME CATHEDRAL.

Left A TYPICAL LUXEMBOURG VILLAGE IS PRETTY BLICK AUF CLERVAUX
Above THE RIOT OF COLOR IN THE STAINED GLASS AT THE BASILICA IN ECHTERNACH IS OUTSTANDING

THINGS TO KNOW

- **AREA:** 2,585 square kilometers (998 square miles)
- **POPULATION:** 400,000
- **CAPITAL:** Luxembourg
- **LANGUAGES:** French, German and Luxembourgeois. English in main towns.
- **PASSPORT REQUIREMENTS:** Required for U.S. citizens.
- **VISA REQUIREMENTS:** Not required for stays up to three months.
- **DUTY-FREE ITEMS:** 200 cigarettes or 50 cigars or 100 cigarillos or 250 grams of tobacco; two liters of wine, one liter of spirits (or two liters of alcohol not exceeding 22 proof), 25 grams of toilet water, 50 grams of perfume, two movie cameras with a reasonable amount of film, two still cameras with a reasonable amount of film, one video camera and personal goods to the value of 2,000 *francs*.
- **CURRENCY:** The currency unit is the Luxembourg *franc*, divided into 100 *centimes*. Belgian currency also is legal tender. There is no limit on the import or export of any currency.
- **BANK OPENING HOURS:** 8:30 or 9am–noon and 1:30pm or 2–4:30 or 5pm Monday–Friday.
- **STORE OPENING HOURS:** 9am–noon and 2–5:30 or 6pm Monday– Saturday; most large department stores are closed Monday morning.
- **PUBLIC HOLIDAYS:** January 1; Easter Monday; May 1 (Labor Day); Ascension Day; Whitmonday; June 23 (National Day); August 15 (Assumption Day); November 1 (All Saints' Day); December 25 and 26.
- **NATIONAL TOURIST OFFICE:** Luxembourg National Tourist Office 17 Beckman Place New York, NY 10022 Tel: 212/935–8888 Fax: 212/935–5896
- **AMERICAN EMBASSY:** 22 Boulevard Emmanuel Servais L-2535 Luxembourg Tel: 460123 Fax: 461401

HISTORY

In AD 963, young Count Siegfried of the Ardennes acquired the ruins of a Roman fort built high on a cliff over the Alzette River. He rebuilt it into a mighty fortress, becoming the overlord of an independent fief of the Holy Roman Empire named Lucilinburhuc, after his "little fortress." Successive rulers extended their domains, and by the 13th century Luxembourg was a significant power. The next century brought John the Blind, the most prominent warrior of his day and the best remembered figure in the House of Luxembourg. His son, Charles IV, was king of Bohemia and Holy Roman Emperor, and through these positions continued his father's policy of expansion.

In the mid-15th century, the nation lost its independence to Philip the Good of Burgundy. For the next 400 years, Luxembourg's fortunes were closely linked with those of Belgium and Holland, as the Low Countries were alternately united and partitioned under the control of Spain, Austria and France.

In 1815 the Congress of Vienna pulled together the Netherlandic region as the Kingdom of the Netherlands and the supposedly independent Grand Duchy of Luxembourg; an eastern section of Luxembourg was given to the duchy of Prussia. However, in 1830 the southern provinces split from the Netherlands to form the Kingdom of Belgium, taking with them a large section from Luxembourg that is today a Belgian province, and is also called Luxembourg. Nine years later, the Netherlands officially recognized the independence of Belgium and the remaining Grand Duchy. It was not until 1867 that the Prussian occupation of Luxembourg ended and independence, autonomy and neutrality began.

In 1940 the German armies poured over the frontiers, just as they had in 1914. The country was occupied for four years, but if you drive through the peaceful countryside today, it is difficult to imagine this small domain as a battlefield. It has recovered remarkably from the ravages of war, and has become a prosperous modern nation.

As a Grand Duchy, Luxembourg is a constitutional monarchy governed under its Constitution of 1868.

FOOD AND DRINK

Smoked pork, sauerkraut and broad beans are specialties. Jellied suckling pig and the ham of the Ardennes are popular dishes, as is black pudding (*treipen*). Trout, crawfish and pike are choices on summer menus; wild game is an autumn and winter favorite. Moselle wines are light and dry. Brewing is a very old industry, and local beer is excellent. Small plum tarts (*quetsch*) are a specialty during September.

SPORTS AND RECREATION

Visitors will find diversion in a jaunt through the countryside. There is an extensive network of marked pathways, and walking tours are organized most weekends and holidays. There also are marked cycling trails. Fishing rights are often held by hotel owners. The Luxembourg Golf Course, near the capital, has one of Europe's most spectacular settings.

GETTING AROUND

Luxembourg is easily reached by air, rail and bus and via good highways from Belgium, Germany, Switzerland and France. Once inside the country, every corner is accessible by road, rail or bus.

AUTOMOBILE CLUB
The Automobile Club du Grande-Duché de Luxembourg
(A.C.L., Automobile Club of the Grand Duchy of Luxembourg) is at Route de Longwy 54, Bertrange. Not all auto clubs offer full travel services to AAA members.

Excursion buses, leaving from the railroad station in Luxembourg City, make trips of varying lengths into the countryside. Motorists can enjoy a leisurely drive through the Moselle Valley, with its verdant vineyards and rock-hewn wine cellars, reached by Route 1 from Luxembourg City.

Other scenic destinations are the flower gardens at the thermal springs spa and resort of Mondorf-les-Bains, the rugged hills and rock formations of Müllerthal and the artificial lake region of Esch-sur-Sûre and Vianden, both of which offer impressive castles.

The wearing of seat belts, if the car is so equipped, is mandatory for the driver and passengers. A child under 12 cannot occupy a front seat if rear seating is available and must use a special seat if sitting in the front.

Speed limits are 50 k.p.h. (31 m.p.h.) in town, 90 k.p.h. (55 m.p.h.) on out-of-town roads and 120 k.p.h. (75 m.p.h.) on highways. Visiting motorists are required to pay fines for motoring violations on the spot in Luxembourg *francs*.

ACCOMMODATIONS

Hotels are classified using from one to five stars, with five stars the highest rating. There are official campgrounds throughout the country, but camping is permitted everywhere with the landowner's approval.

A list of hotels, inns and campgrounds and accompanying maps can be obtained from the Luxembourg National Tourist Office. If camping, an International Camping Carnet is recommended.

TIPPING

A 15 percent service fee is usually included in hotel and restaurant bills. If you see none listed, ask if it has been included. Tip taxi drivers 15 percent of the fare, and tip bellhops and porters about 20 *francs*.

PLACES OF INTEREST

LUXEMBOURG

LUXEMBOURG (59 E1)
pop. 75,400

More than 1,000 years old, the capital city of Luxembourg was once one of Europe's most important fortresses, with strategic advantages that were the envy of neighboring countries. Through the years the city's rulers encircled it with three protective walls and commissioned an underground labyrinth of connecting passages and shelters. Visitors can explore a section of this maze.

In the Middle Ages, Luxembourg was ringed by three walls and 18 forts, which were linked by 21 kilometers (13 miles) of tunnels and casemates carved from solid rock. A model of the old citadel can be seen on Place d'Armes.

The city of Luxembourg also has a modern side; along with Brussels, it serves as co-capital of the European Union (E.U.), which was created in Luxembourg.

A busy city, Luxembourg usually offers some kind of special event each month. The biggest is Schobermesse, a fair that started as the "Shepherd's Market" in 1340. It is held in late August and early September.

CASEMATES, Pont du Château and Place de la Corniche, are the network of underground fortifications – 21 kilometers (13 miles) in length – built to defend Luxembourg in the Middle Ages.

CATHÉDRALE NOTRE-DAME DE LUXEMBOURG, boulevard Franklin D. Roosevelt, is an imposing Gothic-style structure built in the early 17th century.

MUSÉE NATIONAL (National Museum), Marché aux Poissons, includes some priceless works of art as well as some impressive exhibits illustrating the region's Roman past.

PALAIS GRAND-DUCAL was renovated in the late 19th century, although some portions date back to 1572. There is a Changing of the Guard ceremony every Saturday morning.

ROCHER DU BOCK, the remains of the mighty fortress founded by Count Siegfried in AD 963, stand on the projecting outcrop of the Bock rocks.

BEAUFORT (59 E1)
pop. 1,040

At the heart of the area known as La Petite Suisse (Little Switzerland), the ruined castle of Beaufort occupies a striking position on a plateau surrounded by wooden slopes. Built on the site of a Roman camp, the castle dates from the 12th to 15th centuries.

CLERVAUX (59 E2)
pop. 1,600

Clervaux lies in a deep, narrow valley in the middle of the Ardennes, next to the Clerve River. On a small hill stands the feudal castle of Clervaux. Partially destroyed during World War II, it was once the seat of the Counts of Clervaux, from whom Franklin D. Roosevelt was descended. Clervaux's many historic structures, including the castle, chapel, abbey, parish church and monument of the Peasants' War, are illuminated from Easter through October. In nearby Munshausen and Weicherdange there are ancient churches with fine frescoes.

DIEKIRCH (59 E1)
pop. 5,600

Diekirch, surrounded by forests and orchards, is a resort in the Sûre Valley. Concerts, tennis, fishing and canoeing are favorite diversions. Also of interest is the parish church, which dates from the 5th and 6th centuries.

ECHTERNACH (59 E1)
pop. 4,360

Echternach is a vacation center on the Sûre River, which forms the border between Germany and Luxembourg. Echternach was popular as a vacation spot with the Romans, who built their villas on the town's seven hills. The Benedictine Abbey was founded by the Northumbrian monk St. Willibrord in the late 7th century. The town still has a strong medieval atmosphere, with old patrician houses and pointed gables, narrow streets and ancient ramparts. The Dancing Procession, held annually on Whit Tuesday, lures thousands of pilgrims and spectators.

The surrounding area is known as La Petite Suisse, Luxembourg's "Little Switzerland." The woods here are crisscrossed by hundreds of footpaths, where visitors can find good views and quiet spots among the rocks and waterfalls.

BASILIQUE DE ST. WILLIBRORD, within the Benedictine Abbey, dates from the 11th century and is one of the country's most important religious buildings. The vaults contain frescoes dating back to 1100. In the crypt is the marble sarcophagus of St. Willibrord, who is honored in the Dancing Procession.

EHNEN (59 E1)
pop. 2,100
East of the capital city and close to the German border, Ehnen is a small village of medieval character with narrow streets and a wine museum. The only circular church in Luxembourg is in Ehnen.

ESCH-SUR-SÛRE (59 E1)
pop. 240
The Ardennes market town of Esch-sur-Sûre is bordered on three sides by the Sûre River. Nearby Upper Sûre Lake is a good center for recreation.

GREVENMACHER (59 E1)
pop. 3,000
Attractive Grevenmacher is a wine center in the Moselle Valley. The popular local sparkling wine can be tasted at the Caves Bernard-Massard and the Caves Cooperatives, which are open to visitors from April through October. Grevenmacher also boasts an exotic butterfly garden.

LAROCHETTE (59 E1)
pop. 1,300
The remains of medieval castles overlook Larochette, a picturesque old town in the valley of the Ernz Blanche. This popular tourist destination is a starting point for walks through the beautiful surrounding woodlands.

MONDORF-LES-BAINS (59 E1)
pop. 2,900
Mondorf-les-Bains is in the serene valley of the Gander, which forms the Franco-Luxembourg border. Its modern thermal establishments have excellent facilities. Mondorf also is known for its casino, park and sports facilities. Summer, when the flower parks are in bloom, is the loveliest time to visit.

REMICH (59 E1)
pop. 2,600
This picturesque village on the banks of the Moselle River is an important wine center, the headquarters of the State Viticulture Institute. Visitors can view the local *méthode champenoise* (champagne production method) and sample the sparkling wine at the Caves St. Martin.

VIANDEN (59 E1)
pop. 1,500
Ancient ramparts, watchtowers and gates still stand guard over medieval Vianden, which rises formidably out of the wild and hilly region of the Our River. Its reconstructed castle is an enormous fortress dating from the late 4th century.

WILTZ (59 E1)
pop. 4,000
A scenic Ardennes town, Wiltz straddles a series of cliffs overlooking the Wiltz River. The town features a 17th-century château built on the foundations of a 12th-century castle that now houses the tourist office as well as two museums: the Museum of the Battle of the Bulge and the Musée Arts et Métiers, a museum of arts and crafts. An open-air festival of music and theater is held annually in the château gardens during July and August.

BRITAIN

Britain includes the three separate mainland nations of England, Scotland and Wales, as well as islands such as the Channel Islands. (If you add Northern Ireland it is the United Kingdom of Great Britain and Northern Ireland, or U.K.). Don't worry if you can't remember, most of the citizens can't either, but never refer to the Welsh, Scots or Irish as English – they are not, and many resent being ruled from London when they see themselves as separate. You will certainly see separate cultures, all steeped in history, as well as distinct landscapes: England's rolling green fields and country villages; Wales' hills and castles; Scotland's mountains and lakes; and Northern Ireland's cliffs and glens.

Left Shakespeare's wife, Anne Hathaway, lived here in Stratford upon Avon, England, before she married
Above left One of the famous landmarks of London – Big Ben
Above right Bagpipes produce the traditional music of Scotland

THINGS TO KNOW

- **AREA:** 130,378 square kilometers (50,339 square miles)
- **POPULATION:** 47,536,000
- **CAPITAL:** London
- **LANGUAGE:** English
- **ECONOMY:** Agriculture, industry, mining, finance, tourism, oil and gas extraction and refining. Major crops barley, wheat, potatoes; extensive livestock and dairy production. Chief exports machinery, cars, chemicals, textiles.
- **PASSPORT:** Required for U.S. citizens.
- **VISA:** Not required for stays up to six months.
- **DUTY-FREE ITEMS:** 200 cigarettes or 100 cigarillos or 50 cigars or 250 grams of tobacco; 2 liters of still wine plus 1 liter of spirits or 2 liters of sparkling wine; 60 milliliters of perfume; 250 milliliters ($1/4$ liter) of toilet water; and up to £136 value in other goods. Tobacco and alcohol products cannot be imported by persons under 17. (Allowances are for those arriving from outside the E.U.). Also see *The European Union* on p.9.
- **VALUE ADDED TAX:** Britain levies a Value Added Tax (V.A.T.) on goods purchased in the U.K. You can be reimbursed for the taxes you pay, however, after you leave.
- **CURRENCY:** The currency unit is the *pound sterling* (£), divided into 100 *pence*. Due to currency fluctuations, the exchange rate is subject to frequent change. There is no limit on the import or export of British currency or U.S. traveler's checks. Banks will convert larger amounts into traveler's checks before departure.
- **BANK OPENING HOURS:** 9:30am–4:30pm Monday–Friday. Some banks open on Saturday mornings.
- **STORE OPENING HOURS:** In London 9:30am–5:30pm Monday–Saturday (to 7 or 8pm also on Wednesday or Thursday). In suburbs and provinces 9am–5:30pm (to 1pm on Wednesday in some rural towns). Some stores are open 10am–4pm Sunday. Supermarkets are generally

HISTORY

The Romans occupied England, Wales and southern Scotland until AD 410, when control slowly reverted to tribal kingdoms. The Norman Conquest in 1066 saw England united under William the Conqueror, followed by the gradual expansion of Norman rule into Wales and Ireland. In 1215 King John guaranteed citizens' rights against excessive use of royal power in the Magna Carta, laying the foundation for the future system of parliamentary government.

The Middle Ages saw further constitutional developments and the legal system evolved towards the basis of the current English and U.S. systems. The emergence of universities contributed to this cultural evolution.

The Elizabethan Age brought England into competition with France and Spain for territories in the New World. By the early 19th century a worldwide British Empire was established, spurred by wealth from the Industrial Revolution.

The national system of primary education, begun in 1870, was expanded in the early 20th century to include secondary education. Even before World War I, Britain had instituted pensions as well as health and unemployment insurance. After World War II the welfare system was expanded to include the National Health Service. Under successive governments, led by the Conservative Party, the nation's public utilities were brought under private control. In the national election in May 1997 the Labour Party was voted into office, ending almost 18 years of Conservative rule.

The extent of the British Empire diminished after 1945 as many of Britain's colonies achieved independence in the 1950s and 1960s. Hong Kong, one of the last colonies, was returned to the Chinese in July 1997. Ties to many former colonies, such as Australia, are maintained through the Commonwealth.

ENGLAND

FOOD AND DRINK

Many traditional English dishes center on roast meat: roast beef, accompanied by roast potatoes and Yorkshire pudding; mint sauce served with lamb; currant jelly with poultry; or pork, normally complemented by apple sauce. A treat is salmon, also available smoked, as are haddock and mackerel. Stews and pies are also favorites; Lancashire hot pot is just one celebrated stew. Other traditional fares are Melton Mowbray pork pies. Cornish meat pies, called pasties, are found in Cornwall. Cheeses include Cheddar, Cheshire, Stilton, Double Gloucester, Red Leicester, Lancashire and Wensleydale.

Tea is the national drink, although coffee enjoys almost equal popularity. Pubs serve a wide range of nonalcoholic and alcoholic beverages, including gin, vodka, sherry and whisky. Beer can be one of several distinct brews: mild, bitter (draft and keg), stout or lager; lager resembles the cold, highly carbonated beers of the United States. Permitted drinking hours are generally from 11am to 11pm Monday to Saturday; noon to 3pm and 7pm to 10:30pm on Sunday, Good Friday and Christmas Day, December 25.

SPORTS AND RECREATION

The main spectator sports are cricket, rugby and soccer (called football). The best place for cricket in London is at Lord's or the Oval. Rugby is akin to North American football; Twickenham is the English venue for the Five Nations Series competition between England, Wales, Scotland, Ireland and France. The soccer season runs from August to May, culminating in the Football Association Cup Final at London's Wembley Stadium.

Horse racing is also popular, either flat or steeplechase; the latter includes the Grand National in Liverpool in April. The Lawn Tennis Championship at Wimbledon is held in the last week of June and first week of July. Henley-on-Thames is the setting for the Royal Regatta in July.

GETTING AROUND

A *BritRail Pass* allows unlimited travel on Britain's railroads for periods of 4, 8, 15 or 22 days, or one month. Also available are the *BritRail FlexiPass* for unlimited travel on any 4, 8 or 15 days in

---

AUTOMOBILE CLUB
The Automobile Association (AA), Norfolk House, Priestley Road, Basingstoke, Hampshire RG24 9NY, has branch offices in various cities throughout Britain. The symbol ▲ beside the city name indicates the presence of a AAA-affiliated automobile club branch. Not all auto clubs offer full travel services to AAA members.

---

a one-month period; and *Rail Rover* passes, for unlimited travel within a certain region. Get details from National Rail Enquiries, tel: 0345 484950.

Over 500 properties managed by the National Trust, English Heritage, Cadw (Wales), and Historic Scotland can be visited at no additional charge by purchasing a Great British Heritage Pass, available for 7 or 15 days or one month. Contact the British Travel Centre, 12 Regent Street, London W1Y 4PQ.

ACCOMMODATIONS

Bed and breakfast is a specialty. These establishments are generally inexpensive and well run. Hotels in England are not government rated, but the AA publishes a book of them rated from one to five stars. Many of the country's campgrounds are listed in the AA's *Guide to Camping and Caravanning in Britain and Ireland*.

TIPPING

Hotels include a 10 to 15 percent service fee. Tip chambermaids up to £1 a day and bellmen 50p to 75p per bag; taxi drivers and waiters 10 to 15 percent.

BRITAIN • ENGLAND

open daily.
- **Best Buys:** Porcelain from Worcester and Stoke-on-Trent; pewterware and sterling silver; Sheffield cutlery; antiques; tweeds and woolens, rainwear and leatherware.
  Note: if the purchase is an antique valued at more than £35,000, an export license is required to take it out of the country.
- **Public Holidays:** January 1, or closest weekday; Good Friday; Easter Monday; first Monday in May (May Day); last Monday in May (Spring Bank Holiday); last Monday in August (Late Summer Holiday); December 25 (or closest weekday); December 26 (or closest weekday).
- **Useful Telephone Numbers:** Police, Fire, Ambulance 999
- **National Tourist Office:** British Tourist Authority (B.T.A.) Suite 701 551 Fifth Avenue New York NY 10176-0799 Tel: 212/986 2200 or 1-800-462 2748
- **American Embassy:** 24 Grosvenor Square London W1A 1AE England Tel: 0171 499 9000 (telephone enquiries only)

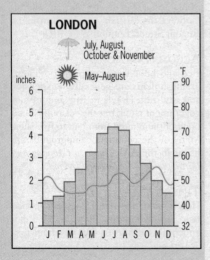

LONDON

July, August, October & November

May–August

PRINCIPAL TOURING AREAS

Note: For descriptions of attractions in **bold type**, see individual listings.

East Anglia

Suffolk has cornfields and marshlands, moated manor houses, and reed-roofed cottages. Norfolk's bow-shaped coast stretches from south of Great Yarmouth to the northwestern tidal inlet called The Wash. Popular among sailing and boating enthusiasts are the Norfolk Broads, 30 open lagoons linked by rivers, lakes and man-made channels to form more than 200 miles of navigable waterways. Cambridgeshire has no coast, but long, straight dikes. **Cambridge** has a famous university – spires, cloisters, chapels and bridges in a setting with gardens and a river.

Home Counties

Northeast of London lies the county of Essex, with the old Roman town of **Colchester**, the ancient royal hunting ground of Epping Forest, and the popular seaside resort of Southend-on-Sea. Hertfordshire is traversed by roads that have been major thoroughfares since prehistory; the Ridgeway is one of Britain's oldest routeways. Within commuting distance north of London, this county has lost much of its rural character. The broad River Great Ouse enters Bedfordshire from Buckinghamshire and meanders across this grassy county. Bedfordshire's south is hillier, dominated by the chalk ridge of the Chiltern Hills and a lower sandstone ridge farther south. Dense forests of beech blanket much of the Chiltern ridge, and there is a network of footpaths. The River Thames forms the northern boundary of Berkshire, while the Lambourn Downs lie to the west. To the north the Vale of the White Horse takes its name from a prehistoric site: a white horse carved into a chalk hillside. Across the Thames from Berkshire is Oxfordshire. Historic **Oxford**, the most famous of the towns along the Thames, is characterized by the dignified lawns and soaring spires of its university.

MIDLANDS

Gloucestershire has a landscape of rivers, woods, old towns and mellow hills. The Forest of Dean dominates the southwest, split from the rest of the county by the River Severn. To the east Gloucestershire offers the Cotswolds plateau with its wool market towns: **Chipping Campden**, North Leach, **Stow-on-the-Wold** and **Cirencester**.

North of Gloucestershire are two closely linked counties, Herefordshire and Worcestershire. Herefordshire is characterized by peaceful meadows with sheep and cattle, and several attractive old market towns. **Hereford**, a cathedral city with a long history, is the political and geographical center of the area.

Worcestershire lies east of Herefordshire, bordered by the Cotswolds in the southeast. The fruit-growing Vale of Evesham, and the Malvern Hills with a vacation spa in their lee, lie in the south of the county. **Worcester**, with its lovely cathedral overlooking a bend of the River Severn, is the largest city. Neighbouring Warwickshire is best-known for William Shakespeare, and contains many sites associated with the poet – notably at **Stratford-upon-Avon**. Other features of this densely populated region include the old county town of **Warwick**, with its famous castle. Northwest is the county of West Midlands, with **Coventry** and Britain's second largest city, **Birmingham**.

Northamptonshire is a county with rural and urban areas. Open fields and pasturelands constitute the northern landscape, while **Northampton**, the county town, dominates the south. Adjacent Leicestershire is associated with manufacturing. This county also is known for its good agricultural lands. On the border with Wales to the west is Shropshire, divided into two contrasting regions by the River Severn. The county town, **Shrewsbury**, lies in a loop of the river. The northern portion of the county is a well-watered plain broken here and there by isolated hills. The southern half is a hilly region that includes a 10-mile heathland ridge called the Long Mynd. Staffordshire, between Shropshire and Derbyshire, is familiar as Arnold Bennett country. In the north are the "Five Towns" of his novels; **Stoke-on-Trent** is the best-known. Collectively called the Potteries, these towns still produce fine porcelain and china. The steep-sided valley of the Dove is a pleasant introduction to Derbyshire. Competing for popularity are several other valleys – Wolfscote, Beresford and Monsal dales – and the rocky crags and peatlands of the Peak District. Today the name Nottinghamshire is inseparable from legends of the outlaw hero Robin Hood. (However, scholars are now of the opinion that the real Robin Hood was not from Nottingham at all.) Truly historic inhabitants of this county were Lord Byron and D.H. Lawrence. Lincolnshire is the easternmost county of the Midlands. Rolling green hills of the chalk Wolds, busy North Sea fishing ports, and seaside resorts are found towards the north. **Lincoln**, with remains dating from the Roman occupation and an immense medieval cathedral, is part of the western region. The landscape in the south of the county is remarkably similar to the Netherlands, with flat, drained fens and Dutch-gabled houses.

NORTHEAST

Northumberland, England's most northern county, is a scenic region rich in history. The Pennine Hills run the length of the county to merge in the north with the Northumberland National Park and the Cheviot Hills, a remote region on the Scottish border. A remarkable feature of this part of the county is the remains of Hadrian's Wall, which once marked the northern boundary of Britain under Roman rule. County Dur-

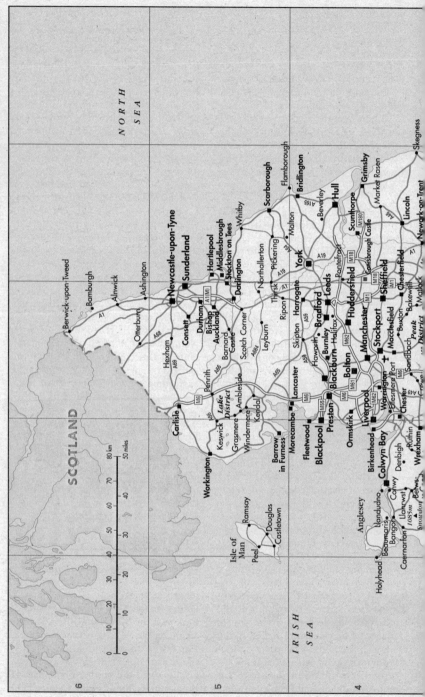

NORTH
SEA

SCOTLAND

IRISH
SEA

80 km
50 miles

70
40

60
30

50

40
20

30

20
10

10

0
0

Isle of
Man

Ramsay
Peel
Douglas
Castletown

Berwick-upon-Tweed
Bamburgh
Alnwick
Ashington
Otterburn

Newcastle-upon-Tyne
Sunderland
Hartlepool
Middlesbrough
Stockton on Tees
Whitby
Scarborough
Flamborough
Bridlington

Hexham
Consett
Durham
Bishop
Auckland
Barnard
Castle
Darlington
Scotch Corner
Northallerton
Pickering
Malton
York
A19
Penrith
A66
Leyburn
Ripon
Thirsk
A1
Harrogate
Leeds
Pontefract
M18
Scunthorpe
Market Rasen
Grimsby
Hull
Beverley
A165
Lincoln
Newark-on-Trent
Skegness
A46
A1
A1

Carlisle
A69
A686
A684
A65
A59
Skipton
Bradford
Huddersfield
Sheffield
Chesterfield
Conisbrough Castle
M18
M1
Bakewell
Matlock
A6

Workington
Keswick
Grasmere
Windermere
Ambleside
Kendal
Lake
District
M6
Barrow
in Furness
Morecambe
Lancaster
M6
Howarth
Burnley
Halifax
M62
Manchester
Stockport
Macclesfield
Buxton
Peak
District
A49
A1

Fleetwood
Blackpool
Preston
M55
M61
M6
Ormskirk
Liverpool
Bolton
Blackburn
Warrington
Ellesmere Port
M62
M6
Sandbach
Crewe

Birkenhead
Colwyn Bay
Chester
Ruthin
Wrexham
Denbigh

Anglesey
Llandudno
Conwy
Bangor
Beaumaris
Llanrwst
Betws-
Snowdon
1085m
Caernarfon
Holyhead

6

5

4

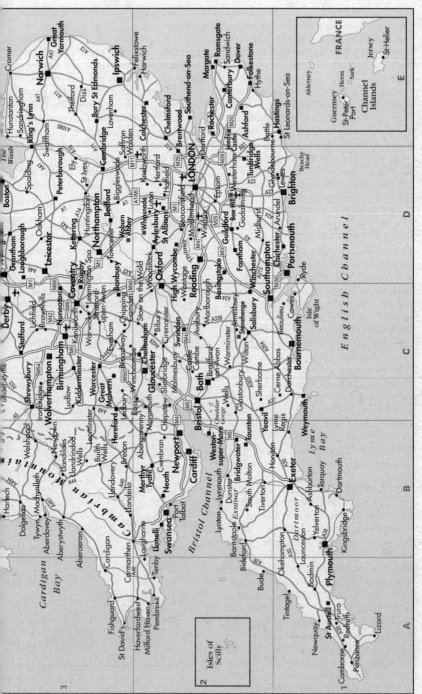

ham is easily divided into east and west. The densely-populated east has been a region of coal mining and shipbuilding since the beginning of the Industrial Revolution. Prominent in this spread of factories, ports and new towns is **Durham**, a medieval city above the winding River Wear. The west of the county is a higher upland; frequent rainfall and flat terrain have formed poorly drained moors. A few small mining towns and villages still dot this landscape. North Yorkshire's seacoast is decorated with holiday towns such as the fishing port of Whitby, once associated with Captain Cook. North Yorkshire also is known for its moorlands, now a national park. The Yorkshire Dales are equally scenic with woods, meadows, streams and waterfalls forming one of the grandest landscapes in England. **York** is the oldest of North Yorkshire's cities. Historic streets and walls, twisting lanes, medieval market squares and timbered houses reflect the city's past; towering over the city is the cathedral of York Minster. South Yorkshire's center is **Sheffield**, the county's steel metropolis. Southeast of North Yorkshire, the East Riding of Yorkshire contains the chalk Yorkshire Wolds, which form an undulous crescent from **Hull** to the Flamborough Peninsula, where they meet the sea as white cliffs. West Yorkshire contains great wool cities, including **Leeds**.

NORTHWEST

On England's northwest border is Cumbria. The northernmost region of the county is not on the usual tourist itinerary, but therein lies its attraction. In the southwest are the austere and boulder-strewn Cumbrian Mountains, among them Scafell Pike, the highest point in England. Here, too, are the largest waters of the Lake District – Windermere and Ullswater – and the peak of Helvellyn. Perhaps the most pleasing scenery is Cumbria's southern region, with green vales, lofty fells and mountain streams. Greater Manchester covers a region devoted to manufacturing. **Manchester**,

for centuries a center of British textile production, is a cultural focus and university city. Just north of the Greater Manchester region are Lancashire's wooded dales, moorlands and beaches. Merseyside contains the estuary of the River Mersey, which meets the sea at **Liverpool**. Cheshire is partly industrial in its Macclesfield textile factories, grain and oil processing centers at Ellesmere Port, and railroad center at Crewe. Even so, the dominant impression of this county is one of woods, meres, and "magpie" houses of darkened timbers and white-painted plaster.

SOUTH AND SOUTHEAST

Wiltshire, in southern England, has grasslands and grainfields, chalk downs, and clear streams. Among the fields and hills are the region's stone-built towns and villages. Historic houses include delightful Littlecote and Elizabethan Longleat. However, one of Wiltshire's best-known sights is **Salisbury**, a spired medieval city rising out of a meadow. Equally well-known is the 4,000-year-old group of megaliths near Amesbury, called Stonehenge – a testimony to the complex ideas and skills of the people who built it. Between Wiltshire and West Sussex is Hampshire. Representing the county's historic aspect are villages of

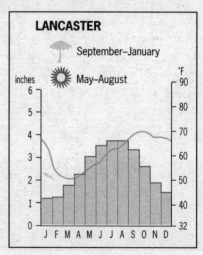

LANCASTER

September–January

inches   May–August   °F

thatched and timber cottages; several old seaside towns, and **Winchester**, the capital of Saxon England. Contradicting its name, among the country's older features is the New Forest, a hunting preserve of Norman kings.

East and West Sussex, with their fine coast, served as an entrance for invasions by the Saxons and Normans. Paralleling West Sussex's coast are the chalk South Downs. Just inland of these hills is the Sussex Weald, a region of quiet hamlets, old market towns and great estates. The northern part of the two Sussex counties is a landscape of heaths and woodlands.

In the hills of west Kent is **Tunbridge Wells**, among the most elegant of English spas. The Pilgrim's Way is an ancient routeway that runs along the high ridge of Kent's North Downs. Though historians today doubt that this was indeed the path of medieval pilgrims, it is nonetheless an enjoyable method of approaching the fine cathedral city of **Canterbury**, once the destination of these travelers. Surrey, south of London, contains lakes and rivers, open heaths and dense woods, and many admirable old towns. The dominant feature of this region is a stretch of the North Downs, a line of hills that crosses the whole county from east to west.

SOUTHWEST

Westernmost is the ancient Celtic land of **Cornwall**, steeped in stories of the sea and Arthurian legend. At the tip of Cornwall, a mass of granite cliffs called Land's End descend into the sea. East of Cornwall is Devon, a county set between the English and Bristol channels. The less populated and perhaps loveliest feature of Devon is its interior, encompassing the timeless and sometimes desolate **Dartmoor National Park**, as well as attractive villages and lush, green farmlands. Dorset, facing the English Channel east of Devon, is a county of stone and thatch villages, rich pastures, and heathy stretches of bracken and briars. Along its coast there are beautiful sandy beaches and chalk or sandstone cliffs. Northwest of Dorset is Somerset, known both for its Bristol Channel coast backed by the rugged upland of Exmoor National Park and for the peaceful green Quantock Hills. To the east, where the coast is gentler, are Somerset's resorts. Inland are the gaunt slopes of the Mendips, pocked with numerous caverns and gorges. Excursions from here lead south to **Glastonbury**, east to the Roman city of **Bath**, and north to **Bristol**.

THE ATLANTIC DIVIDE

Some of the following may help you with the linguistic gulf that separates the United States from Britain:

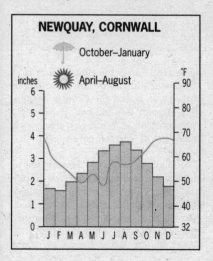

NEWQUAY, CORNWALL

October–January

inches — April–August — °F

American	*British*
elevator	**lift**
collect call	**reverse-charge call**
one-way ticket	**single ticket**
round-trip ticket	**return ticket**
pants	**trousers**
underwear	**pants**
nylons	**tights**
restroom	**toilet**
trunk/hood	**boot/bonnet**
gas	**petrol**
traffic circle	**roundabout**
underground pedestrian passage	**subway**
subway	**tube/underground**
liquor store	**off-licence**
check (in restaurant)	**bill**

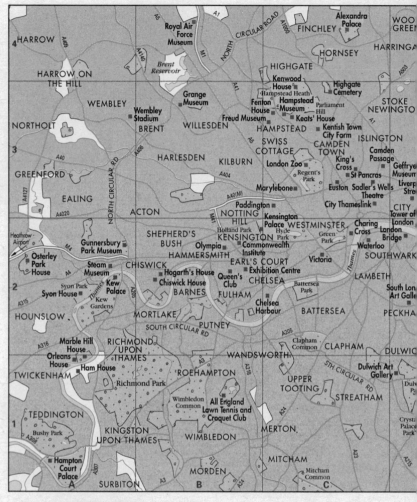

LONDON
pop. 6,800,000

HISTORY

Encompassing 610 square miles and nearly 7 million people, London is a city of tremendous variety. From humble beginnings as a small port on the River Thames, it has grown to incorporate suburban areas.

Despite the creation of a greenbelt in 1938, and the authorities' earnest attempts to encourage industries to locate in other cities, London continues to expand to such a degree that it is sometimes difficult to determine where the city ends and the country begins. The Greater London conurbation is a collection of 32 boroughs, each with some form of local self-government.

The founding of the city is attributed to the Romans in the 1st century AD. They likely chose the site on the north bank near the Thames estuary as being an easy place to cross and providing ready access to the sea. Archaeological evidence indicates that *Londinium* was a

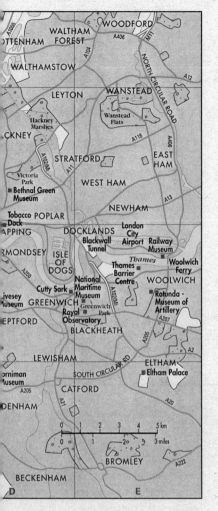

and received – a charter assuring them of special privileges.

Medieval London developed at a phenomenal rate. Preoccupied with commerce, the city had more than 100 craft guilds by the 13th century. Its wharves were piled high with merchandise, and its waterways teemed with vessels from throughout Europe.

By the mid-16th century London controlled more than three-quarters of the country's trade. Its size contributed to the ascendancy of Britain, for in this city were collected the capital and imagination necessary to initiate the nation's great maritime adventures.

With an estimated 500,000 inhabitants, London was one of the most populous European cities by the mid-17th century. It also was among the first cities to experience urban problems: widespread poverty, filth, crime and overcrowding. Not the least of its troubles was the threat of epidemics. In 1665 the city experienced its last and worst bout with the Great Plague; by the end of the year, over 75,000 had perished and thousands had fled.

Soon after this epidemic there was yet another, more devastating, calamity – the Great Fire. Originating in Pudding Lane on September 2, 1666, the blaze consumed much of the city in four days, destroying the cathedral, 80 churches, thousands of dwellings, and virtually all civic buildings. By September 6, hardly a fifth of London remained.

The London that emerged from the ashes was a more durable city. The streets were wider and straighter, houses were built of brick, markets were enlarged, quays were raised, and the River Fleet, long a filthy sewer, was covered over. Though Sir Christopher Wren's sweeping architectural plan was never realized, he did give the city St. Paul's Cathedral and many other new churches.

center of trade by land and water routes. Early in the 2nd century AD, London became the principal city of Roman Britain, defended by enclosing walls and a fortress. By the 3rd century AD the city had its own mint.

Though its national importance had waned during the Saxon period, London was still a city of some consequence by the time of the Norman Conquest. It soon became a political capital with the arrival of William the Conqueror, and from the outset Londoners demanded –

London quickly resumed its dominant position, controlling the economic and political power of Britain, while boasting some of the finest literary and philosophical minds in the kingdom. The metropolis continued to grow: at the time of the first census in 1801, the city and immediate surroundings had more than a million residents.

Technological advances in the 19th century further altered the community. Established as the political and intellectual capital of the British Empire, London assumed the additional role of industrial giant and became the dreary city described by Charles Dickens.

During World War I London became a casualty of modern warfare. Yet, though many were killed and much destroyed, the damage sustained was only a fraction of the destruction the city endured in World War II.

The city's death toll from German air raids in World War II was more than 30,000, and the value of property lost immeasurable. Nevertheless, by the 1950s London had revived and began to prosper again.

London today wears its 2,000 years of history with dignity. Though constantly undergoing renewal of some sort, reminders of the past are carefully guarded. Below the modern skyscrapers, the crumbling remnants of the city's Roman wall are still visible.

The only drawback to exploring London is that there is too much to see and do!

GETTING THERE
BY PLANE AND TRAIN
Most visitors to London arrive via Heathrow Airport. The Airbus express bus service runs to downtown London every 20–30 minutes; taxis are readily available. The Piccadilly Line of the Underground connects Heathrow with central London.

Many scheduled and charter flights operate from Gatwick Airport. There is a direct rail link to Victoria Station and the Gatwick Express fast train service runs frequently. Stansted Airport is approximately 30 miles northeast of London; the airport is linked to central London via Liverpool Street Station, a 45-minute train ride.

GETTING AROUND
Visitors unaccustomed to driving on the left, and unfamiliar with London's street plan, should avoid driving, particularly during morning (7:30–9:30am) and evening (4:30–6:30pm) rush-hour traffic.

PARKING
Parking is a problem. Parking meters operate in the greater part of central London, usually during work hours. Meters, when they must be used, are operable for periods up to two hours; it is illegal to restart a meter for the same vehicle. In addition to the coin-operated meters, there are ticket parking meters.

There also are numerous parking lots above and below ground. Read posted parking restrictions carefully: clamping of illegally parked vehicles is common and fines are costly. Never park on routes that are marked with red lines or two yellow lines alongside the road; the vehicle will be towed away and fined.

CAR RENTAL
Renting a car in London is relatively easy but should be arranged prior to

---

GREEN SPACES

Despite the number of man-made structures, ancient and modern, in central London, there also are large areas of well-tended parks. You can walk for over 2 miles from Kensington Palace to Waterloo Bridge, never far from lawns and trees as you pass through Hyde Park and St. James's Park.

LONDON

arrival, particularly during tourist or holiday seasons. In London, hotels, travel services, major airports and railroads can arrange rental. Most cars have manual gear change but automatics are available. Chauffeured rentals are an option.

PUBLIC TRANSPORTATION

London's traditional black cabs can be hired in the street if their "For Hire" sign is lit, or ordered by telephone. Taxi drivers are regularly tested on their knowledge of the city. Fares are determined on an initial charge plus mileage, with extra fees for large parcels, luggage or pets. A table of fares, extra charges and conditions must be posted in each cab. For longer trips, you and the driver should agree a fare in advance. A tip of 10 to 15 percent is usual.

The Tube, or Underground, is generally the fastest method of traveling, with an extensive network of trains. Where the Underground system ends, there are often connections with suburban trains or buses. Many stations have elevators; all major stations have escalators. Fares are determined by distance traveled. Purchase tickets either from staff at a window or a coin-operated machine. **Note:** Attraction listings in this guide usually include the nearest Tube stop, denoted by a (U) for Underground. The symbol for the Underground is a red circle with a horizontal line (and marked in the London Map, p.92-3).

Slower but more enjoyable are the red double-decker buses. From the upper level of these buses you will be treated to some exceptional views of London.

A *Travel Card* entitles you to one-day unlimited travel on trains, the Underground or city buses in and around London. A photocard is required if you wish to purchase a week, month or longer season ticket. Photocards are free, but you must supply a passport-type photograph. Both the *Travel Card* and the season ticket can be purchased at

train station offices, the British Travel Centre, and Underground stations. London Transport runs a 24-hour information line for Underground and bus services, tel: 0171 222 1234.

WHAT TO DO
SIGHTSEEING AND TOURS

There are tourist information centers at Victoria Station, Heathrow Airport, Waterloo and Liverpool Street train stations, and Selfridges department store on Oxford Street. For additional information, contact the London Tourist Board, 26 Grosvenor Gardens, London SW1W 0DU, or the British Travel Centre, 12 Regent Street, London SW1Y 4PQ. For a list of Visitorcall information telephone numbers, tel: 0171 971 0026.

Sightseeing tours of the capital include London Pride Sightseeing's "Round London" tours (tel: 01708 631122), the Original London Sightseeing Tour (tel: 0181 877-1722), and Blue Triangle Sightseeing Tours (tel: 01708 631001).

A leisurely way to see much of riverside London is by boat. A popular tour begins at Westminster Pier just below Westminster Bridge and goes to Tower Bridge; some boats go onto Greenwich or, in summer, west to Hampton Court. Trips on Regents Canal begin from Camden Lock and Little Venice.

PAGEANTS AND CEREMONIES

No other city in the world is characterized by such pomp and pageantry. There are literally hundreds of ceremonies in London. Listed below are some of the most popular ones, but there are many more to choose from.

CHANGING OF THE GUARD occurs daily (every other day mid-August to March 31) inside Buckingham Palace railings. At 11:30am a band leads the new guard, in full dress, from Chelsea or Wellington barracks to the palace and, after the replacement of the old with the new, leads the old guard back to the barracks.

BRITAIN · ENGLAND

Changing of the Queen's Life Guard takes place every day at 11am (10am Sunday) at the Horse Guards Parade in Whitehall. The new guard rides daily from Hyde Park Barracks. Arrive early.

LORD MAYOR'S SHOW is held on the second Saturday of November, and has been for the last 50 years. The newly elected mayor rides in a great gilded coach from the Guildhall to the Royal Courts of Justice to take the oath of office before the Lord Chief Justice. Pikemen in armor accompany the mayor to the Courts and back to the Guildhall.

MOUNTING THE GUARD is performed on Horse Guards Parade on certain days in May as preparation for the Queen's birthday parade, otherwise known as Trooping the Colour.

STATE OPENING OF PARLIAMENT, in late October or early November, is one of the most colorful events of the ceremonial year. Though closed to the public, it is televised. You can see the grand royal procession of the Queen arriving at the Houses of Parliament in the Irish State Coach. She is met here by the robed and wigged Law Lords and other Officers of State. Inside the House of Lords, she presents a prepared speech outlining the government's program for the coming session.

TROOPING THE COLOUR is such a spectacle that crowds attend the rehearsals. The actual ceremony, marking the official birthday of the Queen, takes place on Horse Guards Parade on a selected Saturday in June. The color, or flag, of one of the five regiments of Foot Guards is displayed to the music of bands. The Foot Guards line up to await the arrival of the Queen and the Household Cavalry. The sovereign inspects the parade while riding in a carriage, and the color is trooped before her. The last part of the ceremony is the great marching display.

It is a matter of pure luck whether you will be able to get a ticket for the ceremony itself (around 50,000 people apply for 4,000 seats). To try, write requesting tickets (maximum of two) to the Brigade Major, Trooping the Colour, Household Division, Horse Guards, Whitehall, between January 1 and March 1. Include a stamped self-addressed envelope. If you do not succeed, however, you can apply for tickets to the dress rehearsals (Mounting the Guard) on the two preceding Saturdays.

SPORTS AND RECREATION
Although not generally regarded as a recreational center, London does offer a wide variety of sporting activities. Outdoor and indoor pools provide opportunities for swimming throughout the year. Ice-skating rinks and tennis courts are scattered throughout the metropolis. Horseback riding is available on the trails of Hyde Park. More than 200 courses provide golf; the courses usually welcome visitors but are often crowded, especially on weekends.

By far the most popular spectator sport is soccer, while hockey, boxing, wrestling, ice hockey, and greyhound, cycle and auto racing excite countless fans. Cricket can be watched at Lords and the Oval, rugby at Twickenham and, of course, lawn tennis at Wimbledon in June and July. Epsom, site of the Derby and Oaks, and Ascot, home of Royal Ascot, are the best horse racing tracks.

For more information on local facilities and events call Sportsline, tel: 0171 222 8000 (weekdays 10am–6pm).

WHERE TO SHOP
Bond Street has jewelers and art galleries; Savile Row is well-known for fine tailoring; Charing Cross Road has old books; and King's Road showcases contemporary fashions. St. James's is for the "discerning gentleman," and Oxford Street and Kensington High Street boast some of the best-known stores. Shops specializing in elegant menswear can be found in the Burlington Arcade.

Harrod's is Britain's best-known department store; its five floors incorporate everything from baked pheasant to fine crystal. Be sure to dress appropriately as visitors without shirts are turned away. Shoppers with less to spend might prefer Selfridges on Oxford Street, with excellent take-home gifts, or nearby Marks and Spencer, noted for value.

A vast selection of delicacies can be found in the food halls of Fortnum and Mason on Piccadilly. Liberty's, on Regent Street, is well-known for its fabrics.

For something old as well as new, London is one of the world's largest centers for antiques and artworks. Christie's and Sotheby's are the most reputable names in the trade, and King's Row one of the best sources. Bermondsey Market (Fridays 5am–12pm), Camden Lock (Saturday and Sunday 9am–6pm), and time-honored Chelsea Antiques Market are best visited early to avoid crowds.

Covent Garden, the old fruit and vegetable market, has been renovated to contain a variety of specialty shops, art galleries and restaurants. Shoppers can easily spend an entire day browsing and watching the street entertainment.

WHERE TO STAY AND WHERE TO EAT

Although there are thousands of hotels in London, from April to August the city is overrun with visitors, and adequate accommodation for impromptu travelers is hard to find. Reservations are essential for the centrally located establishments.

London's finest and most expensive hotels are in the loosely defined West End, which includes Westminster, St. James's and Mayfair. Since the 19th century, the West End has been the stylish place to dine and shop. There are excellent hotels with lower rates outside the West End.

Visitors with special interests can choose hotels convenient to what they wish to do or see. Museum devotees might prefer Bloomsbury or Kensington; those wanting good food might seek lodgings in Soho. Those interested in history might want a place in the City (the area within the original walled city of London).

Many London hotels have restaurants and bars offering complete meal services. Some that serve only breakfast are not usually licensed to serve alcohol. In some inexpensive hotels, services and facilities are at a minimum, but you may prefer these more homey places. Bed and breakfast establishments can offer good value; note that prices are usually per person, not per room. For a small fee the London Tourist Board offices, in Heathrow Airport, and in Victoria Station next to the British Rail ticket office, give advice on budget hotels and hostels for visitors without reservations. To make reservations by credit card, tel: 0171 824 8844.

Along with the city's great hotels, some of the best restaurants are in the West End. Mayfair and adjacent St. James's contain several of the finest eating establishments in London. By far the greatest concentration of foreign restaurants is in the brash, neon quarter of Soho.

The oldest chophouses, simple taverns serving hearty fare, are in the City. Historically interesting as the favorites of Dickens and William Makepeace Thackeray, these places are still popular among the City's business people.

Reservations are usually necessary for the chic or particularly popular restaurants. It is usual to tip around 10 to 15 percent. Before leaving a tip, check to see if a service fee has been added to the bill; if it has, tips should be an extra 5 percent.

ENTERTAINMENT
NIGHTLIFE

Once the pubs close around 11pm, many clubs, late-night restaurants, theaters and cinemas take over. Nightlife thrives

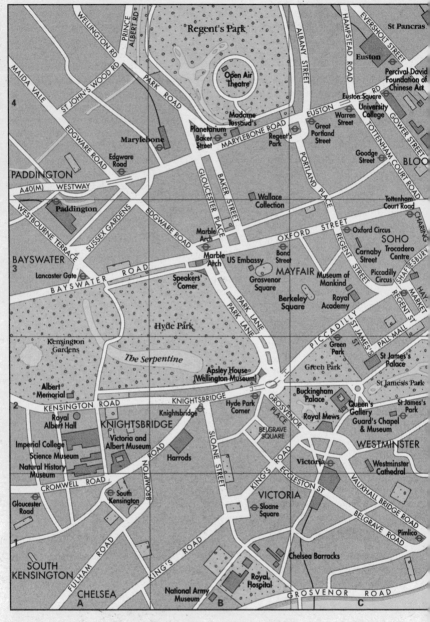

in Mayfair, scene of hotels and restaurants that offer dinner and dancing until late, and nightclubs, invented to circumvent the liquor laws. In the first category are the great hotels-cum-clubs, including The Dorchester, Grosvenor House, Mayfair Intercontinental, and the Hilton. Among those places offering dinner, dancing and floor shows are The Savoy and Quaglino's.

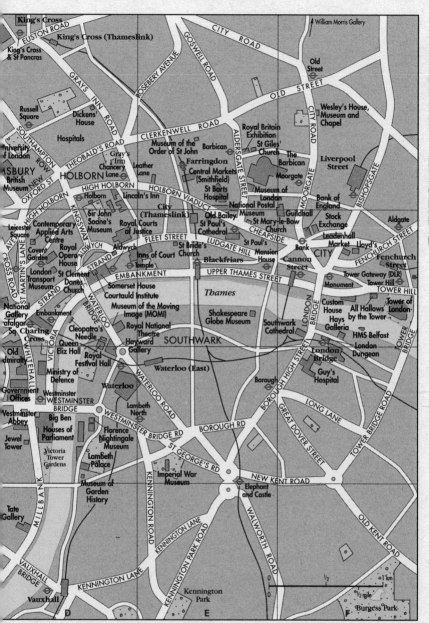

Wine bars are a fashionable alternative to pubs and discos. At Brahms & Liszt in Covent Garden, visitors can buy wine by the glass or bottle, and listen to live jazz and blues music. Another popular night spot and restaurant known for its rock 'n' roll memorabilia is the Hard Rock Café on Piccadilly. Nightclubs, in the British sense, demand either an entrance or membership fee that varies depending on the establishment. Legally there is a 48-hour wait between application and membership, but this technicality may be disregarded. Application must be made in person on the club premises. A passport is an introduction into many clubs where membership is normally restricted. Clubs are subject to the whims of those who patronize them and often appear and disappear almost overnight. The Hippodrome, on Charing Cross Road near Leicester Square, and Stringfellows, 16 Upper St. Martin's Lane, are two of the most famous at press time.

Ordering beverages often poses a dilemma for visiting Americans. When asking for a beer, try to give the brand name or specify the type desired – lager, bitter, ale, etc. If you are fond of ice in mixed drinks or sodas, ask for extra if you want more than a couple of cubes.

London's Underground trains stop running each night at around midnight or 1am. Be sure to make alternative plans for transportation or save sufficient money for a taxi fare. For complete listings of events and venues, consult *Time Out*, London's weekly guide (published Wednesdays) to what's happening around the capital.

Note: The mention of any area or establishment in the preceding sections is for information only and does **not** imply endorsement by AAA.

THEATER AND CONCERTS
Most of London's major theaters are located in or near Shaftesbury Avenue, the Haymarket, or St. Martin's Lane in the West End. Notable exceptions are the Aldwych Theatre in the Strand, the National Theatre on the South Bank, and the Barbican in the City, a center for the Royal Shakespeare Company.

London newspapers advertise plays, and the weekly entertainment guide *What's on in London* describes each very briefly. The selection is excellent: everything from classic works being revived to exciting new plays. Tickets are available from the box office or through agencies that charge nominal fees.

Though plays are in English, a language lesson is still in order! The orchestra to Americans is known as the stalls; the balcony is the dress circle; and the second balcony is the balcony. During intervals (intermissions), drinks and ice creams are available. Curtain time varies but is often at 7:30pm. Some theaters have twice-nightly shows, with the first show at 6 or 6:15pm and the second at 10:30 or 11pm.

London's principal concert halls are the Royal Festival Hall on the South Bank and the Royal Albert Hall in Kensington. Covent Garden is the home of both the Royal Opera and the Royal Ballet. The Coliseum has the English National Opera. Major newspapers and magazines such as *Time Out* and *What's on in London* give details for concerts, recitals, operas and ballets at these and other places.

ESPECIALLY FOR CHILDREN
For children, London is a feast of color and sound: from the clattering red double-decker buses to the multihued crown jewels in the famed Tower of London; from Buckingham Palace's heel clicking, scarlet- and gold-clad Queen's Guard to the blue-helmeted "Bobbies."

London Zoo, within Regent's Park, is where children under 12 can pet or ride certain animals. Youngsters enjoy the comic antics of the pelicans that inhabit St. James's Park, and for the strong at heart there are the Chamber of Horrors at Madame Tussaud's, or the London Dungeon south of the river. A variety of theaters cater exclusively to children. Many have Saturday matinées as well as morning and afternoon performances throughout the week. These include the Little Angel Marionette Theatre and the Young Vic. Several theaters and movie theaters have special shows for children on Saturday mornings.

PLACES OF INTEREST

★ Highlights ★	
British Museum	(see p.95)
Buckingham Palace	(see p.95)
Hampton Court Palace	(see p.96)
Houses of Parliament	(see p.96)
National Gallery	(see p.99)
St. Paul's Cathedral	(see p.100)
Tate Gallery	(see p.100)
Tower of London	(see p.101)
Westminster Abbey	(see p.101)
Whitehall	(see p.102)

BANK OF ENGLAND (93 F3), EC2 (U: Bank), stands on the north side of an open space called simply Bank. It also borders on Threadneedle Street, which gives the bank its nickname: The Old Lady of Threadneedle Street. Founded in 1694, it was rebuilt by Sir John Soane in the late 18th century, but is overwhelmed by the fortresslike enlargements of the 20th century. A museum illustrates the history of the bank.

BRITISH MUSEUM (93 D4) ★, Great Russell Street WC1 (U: Russell Square, Tottenham Court Road), dates from 1753, when the British Government purchased the private collection of Sir Hans Sloane and the Harleian Manuscripts. The museum first opened at Montagu House in Bloomsbury in 1759; the present building was begun behind the site in 1823. Later additions extend well beyond the original location, and the museum has become one of the world's largest.

Its treasures include prints, drawings and manuscripts; coins and medals; ethnographic articles; and an unrivaled collection of antiquities. In addition to relics of ancient Britain there are valuable treasures from Assyria, Babylonia, Egypt, Greece and Rome.

The museum is far too large to be seen in one visit, but entry is free so more than one trip can be made. Those who have limited time but who wish to see samples of all the collections can do so by visiting the Edward VII Gallery.

BUCKINGHAM PALACE (92 C2) ★, SW1 (U: Green Park, St. James's Park), was originally built in 1705 by the Duke of Buckingham. It became the official residence of British sovereigns in 1837 during the reign of Queen Victoria. Today Queen Elizabeth II lives in the palace; when she is in residence the Royal Standard (flag) flies above it. The palace is open to the public for a limited period during the summer. Visitors may tour the State Rooms, which include the Throne Room, State Dining Room and Picture Gallery.

Buckingham Palace is familiar to most visitors as the scene of the Changing of the Guard. The palace is at the western end of The Mall, a broad thoroughfare that serves as the impressive setting for state processions. Along The Mall are other sites, including Clarence House, where the Queen Mother lives; St. James's Palace; Marlborough House; and Carlton House. Opposite these palaces is St. James's Park. The Mall entrance is guarded by the enormous, stately Admiralty Arch.

CENOTAPH, in Whitehall SW1 (U: Westminster), was designed by Sir Edwin Lutyens and commemorates those who died in both world wars.

CENTRAL CRIMINAL COURT (93 E3), EC4 (U: St. Paul's), or more familiarly, Old Bailey, stands on Newgate Street at the site of the notorious Newgate Prison, which was demolished in 1902. The street was widened long ago to accommodate the crowds who came to view executions. The public today enjoys the more peaceful option of watching the courts in session.

CHELSEA ROYAL HOSPITAL (92 B1), Royal Hospital Road SW3 (U: Sloane Square), was founded in 1682 by Charles II for veteran and invalid soldiers, and the building was begun by Sir Christopher Wren that same year. In the central quadrangle of the great Wren building is a bronze statue of the king by Grinling Gibbons. The hospital is the home of the Chelsea Pensioners, known for their tricorne hats and scarlet coats (dark blue in winter).

CLEOPATRA'S NEEDLE (93 D3), Embankment Gardens (U: Embankment), dates from about 1475 BC, which makes it the oldest structure in the city. Its name is a misnomer: the obelisk, though Egyptian, never belonged to Cleopatra. Victorian relics are sealed within its base.

COURTAULD INSTITUTE GALLERIES (93 D3), at Somerset House, Strand WC2 (U: Embankment, Temple), houses the extensive art galleries of the University of London. In addition to the well-known Courtauld Collection of French Impressionist and Postimpressionist paintings, it includes the Lee Collection of old masters; the Roger Fry Collection; the unusual Gambier-Parry Collection of old masters; sculptures, majolica, ivory and metalwork.

CUTTY SARK AND GIPSY MOTH IV (8 D2), Greenwich Pier SE10, are two very different ships. The Cutty Sark is the last survivor of the tea clippers, made obsolete by steam. Reconditioned and permanently berthed at Greenwich, the ship now serves as a museum of ship figureheads. The Gipsy Moth IV is the well-known yacht in which Sir Francis Chichester made his epic solo voyage around the world in 1966.

DULWICH ART GALLERY (86 D1), on College Road SE21, is the oldest public picture gallery in England, and has an outstanding collection of old masters.

GREEN PARK (92 C2), (U: Green Park), was a favorite spot for duels during the 18th century. Today this delightful 53-acre green triangle, bounded by Piccadilly, Constitution Hill and Queen's Walk, seems far removed from the busy streets that surround it.

HAMPSTEAD HEATH (86 C3), (U: Hampstead), encompasses some 800 acres of grassy hills and wooded dells in north London.

HAMPTON COURT PALACE (86 A1) ★, 10½ miles southwest at Hampton Court, was begun by Cardinal Wolsey in 1514 but functioned as a royal residence from 1525 to 1760. In the late 17th century Sir Christopher Wren was commissioned to enlarge the house, and some of the principal façades date from that time. The palace was the favorite country residence of King Henry VIII, who played tennis and jousted in its gardens. Five of his six wives lived in the palace with him; the ghosts of two of them, Jane Seymour and Catherine Howard, are said to haunt the palace.

BLUE PLAQUES

The idea of mounting plaques on houses or sites where distinguished people once lived was devised in 1866 by William Ewart. The first was set on the birthplace of Lord Byron in Holles Street. There are now over 400 blue plaques. To qualify the honoree has to have been dead for more than 20 years, born more than 100 years ago, and to have made "some important contribution to human welfare or happiness."

HMS BELFAST (93 F3), Morgan's Lane, (near London Bridge) SE1 (U: London Bridge). This World War II battle cruiser (Europe's largest preserved warship) served in England's navy up until the 1960s and now houses exhibits of military history.

HOUSES OF PARLIAMENT (93 D2) ★, Parliament Square SW1 (U: Westminster), are known officially as the Palace of Westminster, but little remains of the original structure, and no sovereign has resided here since Henry VIII. Most of the early buildings were lost in a fire in

1834. The present buildings were designed by Sir Charles Barry and constructed 1837–47. The House of Commons was damaged by bombs in World War II and has since been rebuilt. The most familiar symbol of this Victorian Gothic building is the 320-foot Clock Tower with its 13½-ton bell, Big Ben, whose resonant chimes can be heard throughout London.

Parliament traditionally opens with the Queen's Speech from the throne in the House of Lords. No sovereign has entered the House of Commons since Charles I in 1642 (see below). A flag on top of Victoria Tower by day and a light in the Clock Tower by night indicate that Parliament is in session. Parliament normally sits from around the end of October/start of November to the end of

---

THE GUNPOWDER PLOT

On November 5, 1605, Guy Fawkes and a number of other Roman Catholic conspirators attempted to blow up the Houses of Parliament, along with James I and his ministers. To this day, effigies of Guy Fawkes are burned on bonfires, and fireworks are set off throughout England on November 5. Furthermore, before the ceremonial State Opening of Parliament each year, the cellars of the Houses of Parliament are still checked by the Yeomen of the Guard. The Queen presides over the State Opening from the House of Lords, as no monarch has been admitted to the Commons since 1642, when Charles I forced entry and tried to arrest five MPs.

July, except for short breaks after Christmas and Easter.

HYDE PARK (92 B3), (U: Hyde Park Corner, Marble Arch), and adjacent Kensington Gardens make up the largest public park in central London. The 620

acres belonged to Westminster Abbey in the Middle Ages, but with the dissolution of the monasteries in 1536 the land became the private hunting ground of Henry VIII. The park was opened to the public in the 18th century, and its large artificial lake immediately became popular among boating and sailing enthusiasts.

The lake separates the parklands into two unequal sections, with Hyde Park on the east and Kensington Gardens on the west. Kensington Gardens includes the great Kensington Palace, as well as the Round Pond, favored by model yachting enthusiasts, and the delightful statue of Peter Pan. Scenic Hyde Park has a well-known corner dedicated to free speech, Speakers' Corner, where anyone can stand and hold forth on a soapbox on Sunday mornings.

Albert Memorial (92 A2), in the park opposite Royal Albert Hall, depicts Queen Victoria's prince consort examining the catalogue of the Great Exhibition of 1851. In the process of being restored, the memorial will be under scaffolding until the year 2000.

IMPERIAL WAR MUSEUM (93 E2), Lambeth Road SE1 (U: Lambeth North), is dedicated to all aspects of the two world wars and campaigns in which British and Commonwealth forces have been involved during the 20th century.

INNS OF COURT (92 E3) (U: Holborn) are corporate legal societies that have the sole right to prepare barristers and grant permission to establish a barrister's practice in England. The four Inns of Court are the Inner and Middle temples, Gray's Inn and Lincoln's Inn; each is interesting historically and architecturally.

The Temple between Fleet Street and the Embankment houses the first two; its name comes from the Knights Templar who once occupied the site.

Gray's Inn, reached by way of a 17th-century gateway from High Holborn, has long been associated with the teaching of law; a law school existed as early as the 14th century. Shakespeare's *The Comedy of Errors* was first performed in 1594 at Gray's Inn. The beautiful gardens usually are open to the public. Lincoln's Inn is set around the tree-shaded Lincoln's Inn Fields off Chancery Lane. Reached through the magnificent Henry VIII Gateway, its rose-colored brick buildings include a hall, chapel, offices and chambers that are mostly Tudor and Georgian in style.

KENSINGTON GARDENS – *see Hyde Park on p.97.*

KENSINGTON PALACE (86 B2), west end of Kensington Gardens W8 (U: High Street Kensington). The palace was rebuilt by Sir Christopher Wren for William III in the late 17th century. William Kent further remodeled and enlarged the palace for George I. The site served as the royal residence until 1760.

The State Apartments (open to the public), with many sections by Sir Christopher Wren and William Kent, contain paintings, art objects, costumes and furniture that once belonged to royal residents. The Royal Ceremonial Dress Collection displays costumes worn at court from 1750 to the 1930s.

KENWOOD HOUSE – THE IVEAGH BEQUEST (86 C3), 4 miles north at Hampstead Lane NW3 (U: Hampstead), is a remarkable mansion with grounds adjoining London's Hampstead Heath. The architect Robert Adam rebuilt the mansion in its current Georgian style for the first Earl of Mansfield. In 1927 its owner, the first Earl of Iveagh, bequeathed the house and its excellent art collection to the nation. Among the works are Jan Vermeer's *The Guitar Player* and a self-portrait by Rembrandt.

KEW GARDENS (86 A2), 9 miles west on Kew Road (U: Kew Gardens), were landscaped in the 18th century as private botanic gardens in the grounds of Kew Palace, which also can be visited. Today the 300 acres form the Royal Botanic

Gardens, with thousands of species of trees, shrubs and herbaceous plants. Though dedicated to the study of horticulture and botany, the gardens also are interesting to non-botanists; notable are the Succulent and Orchid glasshouses.

MADAME TUSSAUD'S (92 B4), Marylebone Road NW1 (U: Baker Street), contains life-size wax models of such international figures as Margaret Thatcher, Luciano Pavarotti and Michael Jackson. This world-famous collection, which includes the gruesome Chamber of Horrors, was founded in Paris in 1770. It moved to England in 1802 and found a permanent home in London's Marylebone Road.

MARBLE ARCH (92 B3), W1 (U: Marble Arch), at the west end of Oxford Street on the corner of Hyde Park, was designed by John Nash in 1828 as an entrance to Buckingham Palace. However, it was too small for state coaches and was moved to this site in 1851. Marooned in the middle of a huge traffic circle, only members of the royal family are allowed to pass through it.

MONUMENT (93 F3), Monument Street EC3 (U: Monument), was designed by Sir Christopher Wren and erected in 1671–77 to commemorate the Great Fire of 1666. The winding 311-step staircase leads to a gallery 160 feet high, where climbers are rewarded with an elevated view of the City of London.

MUSEUM OF LONDON (93 E4), The Barbican, London Wall EC2 (U: St. Paul's, Barbican), traces the city's history from prehistoric to modern times. The museum combines the collections of Kensington Palace and the Guildhall.

MUSEUM OF THE MOVING IMAGE (MOMI) (93 D3), South Bank, Waterloo SE1 (U: Waterloo), traces the history of the cinema from early experimentation to modern animation. The museum features a replica of a 1950s British movie theater and includes hands-on exhibits and films that visitors can watch. You can also take part and watch yourself interviewing the famous, or reading the news.

NATIONAL GALLERY (93 D3) ★, Trafalgar Square WC2 (U: Charing Cross), houses a collection of paintings by prominant European artists including Leonardo da Vinci, Raphael, John Constable, Jan Vermeer and Rembrandt.

National Portrait Gallery, behind the National Gallery in St. Martin's Place, has paintings and sculptures of well-known British men and women from all walks of life from the Middle Ages to the present day. The collection includes controversial portraits of the late Diana, Princess of Wales and the Queen Mother.

NATIONAL MARITIME MUSEUM (87 E2), 5 miles southeast at Romney Road, Greenwich SE10, has more than 1 mile of galleries showing models, paintings, instruments and relics that collectively depict the maritime history of Britain.

NATURAL HISTORY MUSEUM (92 A2), Cromwell Road SW7 (U: South Kensington), contains large collections of animals, insects and plants – extant and extinct – as well as rocks and minerals. The impressive Victorian building, designed by Alfred Waterhouse, opened in 1881. Noteworthy are the permanent dinosaurs exhibit, and the Whale Hall with a life-size model of a blue whale.

NELSON'S COLUMN, WC2 (U: Charing Cross), rises 170 feet above Trafalgar Square. Built to commemorate Admiral Horatio Nelson's 1805 victory, the column is topped by a 17-foot statue of the admiral and is flanked by four bronze lions.

OLD BAILEY – see *Central Criminal Court* on p.95.

OLD ROYAL OBSERVATORY (87 E2), Greenwich SE10, was founded in 1675 by King Charles II. It is the site of the prime meridian, or longitude zero, and

the place where Greenwich Mean Time is determined. Here you can stand with one foot in the western hemisphere and one foot in the eastern. The observatory has fascinating exhibits on the history of mankind's efforts to map space and measure time. There also is a camera obscura and Britain's largest refracting telescope.

PLANETARIUM (92 B4), Marylebone Road NW1 (U: Baker Street), is generally visited on a combined ticket with Madame Tussaud's (next door). It has interactive exhibit areas and a star show that takes you on a simulated journey through space.

REGENT'S PARK (92 B4), (U: Regent's Park) was laid out by John Nash in the early 19th century. Intended originally as an elegant residential suburb, it became a public park in 1838. Its 487 acres contain playing fields, tennis courts, tree-shaded walks, a rose garden, a pretty lake for boating and sailing, and a fine open-air theater.

London Zoo is one of the most comprehensive and best-housed collections of animals in the world. Particularly outstanding are the children's zoo, the Moonlight Hall of nocturnal animals, the Monkey House, and the giant walk-

> **LONDON ZOO**
> London's Zoological Gardens were an instant hit when they opened in 1828, but in 1993 they nearly closed for lack of funds. The zoo was saved by a public appeal, and today it spearheads conservation and breeding programs for endangered species such as gorillas and tigers. It is also praised for its pioneering architecture and innovative animal habitats.

through aviary designed by Lord Snowdon and inhabited by exotic birds.

ST. JAMES'S PALACE (92 C2), SW1 (U: Green Park), at the corner of St. James's

Street and Pall Mall, is a great brick mansion built in 1532 for Henry VIII. From 1698–1861 it was the sovereign's official London residence. Sentries of the Brigade of Guards parade in front of its picturesque Tudor gatehouse daily – a great opportunity for photographs. However, the palace is not open to the public. Just to the west of the palace is Clarence House (not open), residence of the Queen Mother.

ST. JAMES'S PARK (92 C2), (U: St. James's Park) was a virtual swamp until drained by Henry VIII as a nursery for the royal deer. In the 17th century, Charles II introduced ducks and other birds to its long lake and opened the park to the public. Much later, in 1828, John Nash remodeled the 93-acre site alongside The Mall. The lake and its island are preserved as a refuge for waterfowl and the park's comical pelicans.

ST. MARTIN-IN-THE-FIELDS CHURCH, Trafalgar Square WC2 (U: Charing Cross), was designed by James Gibbs, a pupil of Sir Christopher Wren. The classical church, which was rebuilt 1722–26, stands on one of the busiest squares in the world. Its richly decorated interior is particularly notable.

ST. MARY-LE-BOW CHURCH (93 E3), Cheapside EC2 (U: St. Paul's), was designed by Sir Christopher Wren. Much damaged in World War II, it has since been fully restored. The Renaissance campanile, one of the finest examples of Wren's work, survives intact.

The church's bells have been cast from the metal of the original ones. Each bears a passage from the Psalms, with the first letter of each inscription spelling out D Whittington. According to tradition, it was the Great Bell of Bow that called Dick Whittington, the well-known mayor, back to London.

ST. PAUL'S CATHEDRAL (93 E3) ★, Ludgate Hill EC4 (U: St. Paul's), was built 1675–1710 to replace a Gothic church

destroyed in the Great Fire of 1666. The magnificent baroque structure is the crowning achievement of English architect Sir Christopher Wren. Notable features are the classic proportions of the church and the great dome, a major engineering feat in its time. High above is the circular Whispering Gallery, so called because its acoustics make whispers audible from anywhere around its circumference. From the Stone Gallery there are views of the City, but the finest panoramas are from the Golden Gallery on top of the dome.

The enormous crypt is almost a cathedral in itself. It contains the massive tombs of Lord Nelson, the Duke of Wellington and other notable figures. This also is the burial place of Sir Christopher Wren, whose tomb bears the famous inscription: *Si monumentum requiris, circumspice* – "If you seek a monument, look around you."

SCIENCE MUSEUM (92 A2), Exhibition Road SW7 (U: South Kensington), offers over 40 galleries exploring the world of science, technology, industry and medicine through exciting displays and interactive exhibits. Highlights include the Apollo 10 space capsule.

SHAKESPEARE'S GLOBE THEATRE (93 E3), New Globe Walk SE1, is a reproduction playhouse built using the same materials and techniques as the original. The theater is now open and stages performances.

SYON HOUSE (86 A2), near Isleworth, dates from the early 15th century. In the 18th century Robert Adam redesigned parts of the great Tudor house, and landscape architect "Capability" Brown laid out its grounds, which now include a display of British horticulture. Catherine Howard, the unfortunate fifth wife of Henry VIII, was imprisoned in the house before her execution in 1542.

TATE GALLERY (93 D1) ★, Millbank SW1 (U: Pimlico), has an unrivaled collection of British paintings, including works by John Constable, Thomas Gainsborough and Sir Joshua Reynolds. The Clore Gallery is dedicated to works by J. M. W. Turner. There also are modern paintings and sculptures, notably works by the French Impressionists.

THAMES FLOOD BARRIER (86 E2), downstream from Greenwich Pier SE10. Each of the Thames Flood Barrier's gates weighs 3,000 tons and is 45 feet high. Together they constitute the world's biggest moveable flood barrier. A visitor center on the Unity Way explains the barrier's workings and you can tour around the structure by boat.

TOWER OF LONDON (93 F3) ★, Tower Hill EC3 (U: Tower Hill), is among the oldest of London's buildings. Built as a fortress by William the Conqueror, it served first as a royal residence and later as a prison. The principal keep of the medieval complex is the White Tower, dating from 1078; this and later keeps were prisons of such notables as Sir Walter Raleigh and Princess Elizabeth (later Elizabeth I). A paved square marks the site where many of England's greatest, such as Thomas More, were beheaded.

Of architectural note in the tower is St. John's Chapel in the central keep, the oldest church in London and a fine example of Norman style. The tower's history gallery, near the "Bloody Tower," where the two young princes (heirs to Edward IV) were murdered, offers models, pictures and text relating to the history of the tower. The most prominent among the collections, however, are the crown jewels, displayed under maximum security in the Jewel House. Among these royal riches are enormous serving dishes and gold flagons, jewel-studded coronation robes and the font used in royal christenings since 1841. The tower's famous redcoated Beefeaters, or Yeoman Warders, give entertaining free tours to the public every 30 minutes.

TROCADERO CENTRE (92 C3), 13 Coventry Street W1 (U: Piccadilly Circus), is an entertainment complex whose attractions include the Rock Circus, Segaworld, and the Emaginator, a space-flight simulation.

VICTORIA AND ALBERT MUSEUM (92 A2), Cromwell Road SW7 (U: South Kensington), displays fine and applied arts from all countries and periods. The Raphael cartoons, postclassical sculpture, period dress collection, British miniatures, watercolors and Oriental art are of particular interest. One gallery is devoted to the work of American architect Frank Lloyd Wright. It is not advisable to attempt to see it all in one visit.

WESTMINSTER ABBEY (93 D2) ★, Parliament Square SW1 (U: Westminster), is London's greatest Gothic church. Founded by Edward the Confessor in the 11th century, the abbey was enlarged and embellished by later monarchs. What appears today is mostly the product of the 13th-century reign of Henry III; important additions since that time have been the Tudor chapel of Henry VII as well as the Wren towers at the western entrance.

Since the 11th century, the church has been the coronation site of English kings and queens. The Coronation Chair in Edward the Confessor's Chapel is a 13th-century oak throne. Most sovereigns from Henry III to George II have been interred in the abbey, along with the country's greatest statesmen, scientists and poets.

One of the most visited spots in the abbey is Poets' Corner, which contains the graves of (among others) Edmund Spenser, Geoffrey Chaucer, John Dryden, Samuel Johnson, Robert Browning, Charles Dickens, Thomas Hardy, Rudyard Kipling and Alfred, Lord Tennyson. The Tomb of the Unknown Warrior is a representative of servicemen killed in World War I.

The museum in the abbey's crypt contains surviving pieces of the original abbey and wax effigies of many who lie buried in the church. These images were customarily displayed at the funerals of their subjects.

WESTMINSTER CATHEDRAL (92 C2), Ashley Place SW1 (U: Victoria).

As the seat of England's only cardinal, this is the most important Roman Catholic church in the country. The neo-Byzantine structure was completed in 1903; the inlaid stone piazza is a recent redevelopment. Of note in the interior are the Eric Gill bas-reliefs depicting the Stations of the Cross. The gallery of the 284-foot tower affords views over the whole of London.

WESTMINSTER HALL, Houses of Parliament, New Palace Yard SW1 (U: Westminster),

was built 1097–99, although the great oak roof was added 300 years later.

The hall served as the chief law court until 1883; Charles I was tried and condemned to death at this site in 1649. All visits must be arranged with a member of Parliament.

WHITEHALL (92 D2) ★ SW1,

is the short thoroughfare extending south from Trafalgar Square towards the Palace of Westminster (Houses of Parliament). Along the wide street are Britain's chief government offices, including the Treasury, the Foreign Office and the Admiralty and Horse Guards, which houses some of the departments of the War Office. No. 10 Downing Street, an unimposing side street, is the official residence of the Prime Minister, and No. 11 that of the Chancellor of the Exchequer; the street is normally closed to the public. Nearby are the offices of the original New Scotland Yard – the police headquarters in London.

Banqueting House is all that survived the 18th-century fire that destroyed Whitehall Palace, after which the street is named. Designed in 1619 by Inigo Jones, it is among the most beautiful of London's buildings. Charles I was beheaded in front of the hall, and today a glorious equestrian statue of the king – with his head on – graces a spot nearby.

The Houses of Parliament (or Palace of Westminster) sit splendidly beside the River Thames

PLACES OF INTEREST

```
┌─────────────────────────────────────┐
│         ★ HIGHLIGHTS ★               │
│                                      │
│  Bath              (see p.104)       │
│  Cambridge         (see p.107)       │
│  Canterbury        (see p.108)       │
│  Dartmoor          (see p.111)       │
│     National Park                    │
│  Lake District     (see p.117)       │
│     National Park                    │
│  Oxford            (see p.121)       │
│  Peak District     (see p.122)       │
│     National Park                    │
│  Stratford-upon-Avon (see p.125)     │
│  Windsor           (see p.127)       │
│  York              (see p.129)       │
└─────────────────────────────────────┘
```

ALDERNEY (82 E1) – *see Channel Islands on p.109.*

ALNWICK (82 C6)
NORTHUMBERLAND *pop. 7,200*
Alnwick lies in Northumberland's eerie border country, where medieval barons built grim castles during the centuries of Scottish–English wars. Many of these strongholds still stand; among them are the castles of Alnwick, Dunstanburgh and Warkworth. Alnwick Castle was the Norman stronghold of the Percy family.

AMBLESIDE (82 C5)
CUMBRIA *pop. 3,400*
Ambleside, with its old stone houses and rushing stream, is a popular walking and rock-climbing center as well as a good point from which to journey into the English Lakeland. Lake Windermere is popular with boaters and water skiers.

AMESBURY (83 C2)
WILTSHIRE *pop. 6,500*
On the edge of Salisbury Plain is Amesbury, which took its name from 19th-century Amesbury Abbey. The abbey grounds are a park including a Palladian bridge and Gay's Cave, the site where John Gay composed *The Beggar's Opera.* (See also *Stonehenge* on p.125.)

ARUNDEL (83 D1)
WEST SUSSEX *pop. 3,200*
ARUNDEL CASTLE, which dominates this south-coast town, has been the seat of the Dukes of Norfolk, Earl Marshals of England, and their ancestors for more than 700 years. The building contains rare 16th-century furnishings.

ASCOT – *see Windsor on p.127.*

BAKEWELL (82 C4)
DERBYSHIRE *pop. 4,000*
CHATSWORTH, 3 miles east in a park beside the Derwent River, is a stately house known for its gardens and fountains. The house is filled with pictures, antique furniture and rare books.

BAMBURGH (82 C6)
NORTHUMBERLAND *pop. 400*
The ramparts of Bamburgh Castle dominate the peaceful resort of Bamburgh. Off the coast are the tiny Farne Isles, the site of a noted bird sanctuary. To the northwest and linked to the shore by a causeway is Lindisfarne, or Holy Island.

BAMBURGH CASTLE was once the seat of Northumbrian kings. The armory of the restored Norman fortress contains a large collection of weapons.

BANBURY (83 C3)
OXFORDSHIRE *pop. 39,700*
A sizeable marketing and manufacturing center, Banbury is best-known for its cross of nursery rhyme renown (now a 19th-century replica). Nearby are several noteworthy old houses. Farnborough Hall, a National Trust property 6 miles north of Banbury, is a mostly 18th-century house with extensive grounds. Upton House, 7 miles northwest, also is a National Trust property and is known for its fine furnishings, porcelain, tapestries and paintings.

SULGRAVE MANOR, 7 miles northeast, off B4525 in Sulgrave, is a compact 16th-century manor house that was the home of Lawrence Washington, an ancestor of George Washington.

BATH (83 C2) ★
SOMERSET *pop. 80,000*
Roman colonists suffering from the damp northern climate built large pools to take advantage of the curative hot springs they found around Bath. Today visitors flock to see the baths, which are remarkably complete in layout and are among the finest Roman remains in Britain. The Roman baths were first discovered in the late 19th century, lying 20 feet below street level.

Bath enjoyed its greatest fame in the 18th century, when wealthy Britons vacationed in the town. Spacious houses, public buildings, arches, terraces and colonnades of cream-colored stone recall that era. Recent additions to the well-planned town do not detract from the prevailing Georgian style of architecture, which is preserved in such streets as Royal Crescent, The Circus, Queen's Square and Great Pulteney Street.

Plaques mark the elegant dwellings of Bath's celebrated past residents. Also retaining the history of the city are the 18th-century Pump Room, Assembly Rooms with their Museum of Costume, abbey church, the guildhall and Victoria Art Gallery. For additional information, contact the Tourist Information Center, Guildhall High Street, Bath, Avon BA1 5AW, tel: 01225 462831.

AMERICAN MUSEUM, 2½ miles from town, is housed in Claverton Manor and contains American decorative arts.

NO. 1 ROYAL CRESCENT is a completely restored 18th-century stone town house, now partially converted to a museum.

ROMAN BATHS and PUMP ROOM, next to Bath's hot spring, were built in the 1st century AD and served pilgrims visiting the Temple of Sulis Minerva. The Roman Temple Precinct beneath the Pump Room also can be examined.

BATTLE (83 E2)
EAST SUSSEX *pop. 6,300*
The small market town of Battle lies several miles inland from Hastings. Its name derives from the Battle of Hastings, fought here in 1066.

BATTLE ABBEY, High Street, occupies the site of the historic battle. The monastery was founded soon afterwards by William the Conqueror. The impressive 14th-century gatehouse contains a museum.

BODIAM CASTLE, 6½ miles northeast, is a 14th-century fortress-castle surrounded by a picturesque lily-covered moat.

BEACONSFIELD (83 D2)
BUCKINGHAMSHIRE *pop. 11,100*
Beaconsfield is an elegant old town of inns and 17th-century houses that has not always been so placid: highwaymen once haunted the woods nearby.

A historic monument to more peaceful times is the 17th-century Quaker meeting house in the nearby village of Jordans. The structure has been little altered since it was built. The grave of William Penn, founder of Pennsylvania and Philadelphia, is in the churchyard.

BEAULIEU (83 C1)
HAMPSHIRE *pop. 800*
THE NATIONAL MOTOR MUSEUM, on the grounds of Beaulieu (pronounced Bewly) Abbey, was founded in 1952 by Lord Montagu, commemorating his father, who was a pioneer in motoring. More than 200 vehicles on display detail the history of motoring since 1895.

▲ BEDFORD (83 D3)
BEDFORDSHIRE *pop. 77,000*
WOBURN ABBEY AND DEER PARK, 12½ miles southwest at Woburn, is the ancestral home of the Dukes of Bedford. This palatial 18th-century mansion contains a fine collection of paintings and furnishings.

The well-stocked Wild Animal Kingdom and Leisure Park on the grounds has many rare animals.

BEVERLEY (82 D4)

EAST RIDING OF YORKSHIRE
pop. 23,200
A market town, Beverley was once walled. The ramparts are gone, but one of the five admission gates, the 15th-century North Bar, remains. Reminiscent of the town's early cloth-trading days are the 18th-century guildhall and market cross, as well as Lairgate Hall, an attractive mansion now used as council offices.

BEVERLEY MINSTER, destroyed and re-built several times in its long history, is one of the most notable Gothic churches in the country. Significant features of the interior are the 14th-century Percy Tomb, a monument to that family; the glass in the great east window; and Early English choir stalls and misericords.

BIBURY (83 C2)

GLOUCESTERSHIRE *pop. 500*
ARLINGTON ROW is a collection of early 17th-century stone cottages along the Coln River. The Row is a favorite with photographers. Nearby is Arlington Mill, housing the Cotswold Museum.

BIDEFORD (83 B2)

DEVON *pop. 12,200*
Once a successful port, the town has a big covered market dating to 1883.

CLOVELLY is a small village 8½ miles west of Bideford. The houses and cottages lean together on incredibly steep streets that descend to the harbor. The village is considered one of the most picturesque in England.

BIRMINGHAM (83 C3)

WEST MIDLANDS *pop. 1,024,100*
In William the Conqueror's 11th-century survey of lands, the *Domesday Book*, Birmingham is described as "worth 20 shillings and having nine tenants living under the lord of the manor." Some 10 centuries later, Birmingham is the metropolis of the Midlands, the second largest city in Britain, and a sizeable manufacturing center.

Not an ancient city, Birmingham developed much of its current appearance at the end of the 19th century, a time of extensive urban renewal. Victoria Square, the principal plaza, is surrounded by governmental and commercial buildings, including the city's neoclassical town hall. The Symphony Hall, inside the nearby International Convention Centre, is one of the finest concert halls in Europe.

West of Victoria Square is the Central Library and beyond it is the Hall of Memory, commemorating citizens killed in both world wars. The old market area of the Bull Ring has been redeveloped as a modern shopping center.

Birmingham is most productive in the arts. The City of Birmingham Symphony Orchestra, the Birmingham Royal Ballet and the D'Oyly Carte Opera Company are all resident in the city.

Inland water cruises of the region are available. For additional tourist information, contact either the visitor information center at 2 City Arcade, Birmingham, West Midlands B2 4TX; tel: 0121-643 2514 or the information center at 130 Colmore Row, Birmingham B2 5TJ; tel: 0121-693 6300.

ST PHILIP'S CATHEDRAL, initially designed by Thomas Archer, was consecrated in 1715. This large baroque structure includes several later additions, notably the beautiful Burne-Jones stained-glass windows depicting scenes from the life of Christ.

CITY OF BIRMINGHAM MUSEUM AND ART GALLERY, Chamberlain Square, is noted for its pre-Raphaelite works.

BLACKPOOL (82 B4)

LANCASHIRE *pop. 143,800*
Originally a fishing village, Blackpool has mushroomed into Britain's largest holiday resort, known to Britons as the "playground of the north." The chief attractions are the beach, Blackpool Sea Life Centre and Blackpool Tower, a 520-foot imitation of the Eiffel Tower

that dominates the seafront. The city has three piers, the Winter Gardens and Opera House, and the famous Blackpool Pleasure Beach.

BODMIN (83 A1)
CORNWALL *pop. 14,500*

Bodmin is a sombre-looking granite town on the southwestern edge of Bodmin Moor. On the main Land's End road, Bodmin is a good point from which to explore the tip of Cornwall and the north and south coasts.

LANHYDROCK, 2½ miles southeast, is a restored 17th-century mansion with a gatehouse, Victorian servants' quarters and a picture gallery containing 17th- to 20th-century family portraits.

BOSTON (83 D3)
LINCOLNSHIRE *pop. 36,600*

Ancient Boston on the Witham River enjoyed its heyday as a 13th-century Hanseatic wine- and wool-trading town. However, it is better-known to U.S. visitors for its associations with the Massachusetts city founded by Puritans from the English Boston. Links with the American city are maintained in several different ways.

On Scotia Creek, southeast of Boston, there is a granite memorial to the first pilgrims, who in 1607 attempted to flee to religious freedom in the New World.

▲ BOURNEMOUTH (83 C1)
DORSET *pop. 154,000*

The south coast's largest resort, Bournemouth came of age in the Victorian era and retains the atmosphere of that time. The town is midway along the southern English coast, making it convenient for visits to historic sites in nearby Hampshire and Wiltshire.

COMPTON ACRES GARDEN, 3 miles west on Canford Cliffs Road, is one of the finest gardens of its kind in Europe. It contains exotic plants and priceless statuary; also of note are the Japanese, Italian, Roman and English gardens.

▲ BRADFORD (82 C4)
WEST YORKSHIRE *pop. 295,000*

A primary wool-manufacturing center, Bradford dates from Norman times. The National Museum of Photography, Film and Television has studios, galleries and displays presenting various forms of photography and film-making.

BRONTË PARSONAGE MUSEUM, 8 miles northwest at Haworth, was the home of the Brontë sisters, 19th-century novelists. The house contains mementos of their lives.

▲ BRIGHTON & HOVE (83 D1)
EAST SUSSEX *pop. 233,400*

Brighton became a fashionable health and bathing resort with the patronage of King George IV in the late 18th century. Three miles of seafront, shopping in The Lanes (charming little back streets) and Europe's largest marina add to its charms. It is one of England's most fashionable resorts.

Hove, the adjoining town, is distinguished by imposing Regency-style buildings with spacious lawns.

PIERS OF THE REALM

The pier, that familiar feature of the seaside, is descended from the much earlier quay, built to land cargo and passengers on an open shore. In 1823 Brighton constructed its famous Chain Pier, like a suspension bridge tiptoeing gracefully into the English Channel (which destroyed it in a storm in 1896). Sadly, piers are now an endangered species, being costly to repair and maintain.

ROYAL PAVILION, Old Steine, was built in 1787 for the Prince Regent, later King George IV. The architect John Nash redesigned the pavilion into a whimsical structure of Indo-Chinese and Moorish style. Extensive structural restoration has taken place.

▲ BRISTOL (83 C2)

BRISTOL *pop. 372,600*

At the outlet of the Avon River is Bristol, hailed as the port where many historic voyages began. In 1497 John Cabot sailed from Bristol on a journey that led to the discovery of the northern half of the New World.

Though severely damaged by air attacks in World War II, Bristol retains a number of architectural treasures.

The city's grandest ecclesiastical structure is the 13th-century Church of St. Mary Redcliffe, resembling a cathedral in its floor plan. Bristol's Theatre Royal is the oldest theater in England still in use.

CLIFTON SUSPENSION BRIDGE, over the Avon Gorge, was considered a daring feat of engineering when it was built in the 19th century. It still offers excellent views. A toll is charged for automobiles.

MATTHEW VISITORS' CENTRE, Redcliffe Quay, is the site of a reconstruction of the ship John Cabot sailed to the New World. The *Matthew* actually sailed across the Atlantic in 1997.

BROADWAY (83 C3)

WORCESTERSHIRE
pop. 2,100

A pretty village of honey-colored houses and tidy gardens, Broadway was known as the Painted Lady of the Cotswolds during the 19th century.

BROADWAY TOWER COUNTRY PARK, 1 mile southeast, is a park surrounding a tower built in 1799 by the 6th Earl of Coventry. Three floors of the tower contain exhibits; an observation room and telescope provide splendid views of the 12 nearby counties.

BUXTON (82 C4)

DERBYSHIRE *pop. 20,800*

One of the highest towns in England, Buxton is a mountain spa. Visitors enjoy the invigorating climate, thermal springs, golf courses and sports events; the Easter steeplechase is a yearly contest.

▲ CAMBRIDGE (83 D3) ★

CAMBRIDGESHIRE *pop. 101,200*

The early prosperity of old Cambridge was due in great part to its namesake – a bridge across the Cam River that was the only crossing on a major trade route between eastern and central England. Cambridge began to emerge as a seat of learning early in the 13th century with the town-and-gown troubles at Oxford, although the first college, Peterhouse, was not established until 1284.

In the course of a few centuries, Cambridge gained 22 more colleges and became significant in the shaping of English life. Just a few of the many eminent names associated with the university include William Pitt the Younger; diarist Samuel Pepys; scientists Sir Isaac Newton and Charles Darwin; and several poets, writers and politicians.

The university and college buildings – courts, halls, gates and chapels – form a rich variety of styles from Norman to modern. Most prominent among them is imposing King's College Chapel. Not far away is Queens' College, founded in the 15th century by queens Margaret of Anjou and Elizabeth Woodville.

Other structures worth noting are the old court of Corpus Christi, the 17th-century hall of Clare and the entrance gateway to St. John's.

The city's man-made enchantment is enhanced by gardens and commons with such curious names as Jesus Green, Midsummer Common, Sheep's Green and Christ's Pieces. Most favored are the Backs, landscaped lawns extending for half a mile behind the main row of colleges. The Cam River, winding its way through the Backs, is spanned here and there by a bridge – the graceful stone bridge at Clare, the Bridge of Sighs at St. John's and the Mathematical Bridge at Queens' College. The University Botanic Garden at Cory Lodge comprises 40 acres of excellent botanical collections.

Punting (a type of boating) along the Backs is a favorite Cambridge pastime, and there are facilities for many other kinds of sport as well. For additional tourist information contact the Tourist Information Centre, Wheeler Street, Cambridge, Cambridgeshire CB2 3QB; tel: 01223 322640.

AMERICAN CEMETERY is 3 miles west at Madingley; here is the final resting place for more than 3,800 American soldiers who lost their lives during World War II.

FITZWILLIAM MUSEUM, Trumpington Street, was founded in 1816. The art collection is one of the best in Britain.

KING'S COLLEGE CHAPEL, built from 1446 to 1515, is one of the finest examples of the English Perpendicular style. Visitors come not only to view this impressive building, but also to hear the choral and organ music. The chapel's memorable Festival of Nine Lessons and Carols is broadcast throughout the world every Christmas Eve.

CANTERBURY (83 E2) ★

KENT *pop. 35,000*

A settlement even before the Roman era, Canterbury is one of England's oldest and most historic cities. It was here that St. Augustine, on a mission from Rome in the 6th century, initiated the English people's conversion to Christianity. With the establishment of an abbey and later a cathedral, Canterbury became the prime see of England and functioned as a principal religious and cultural center throughout the Saxon period.

Rich in medieval historical associations, Canterbury is often remembered as the scene of Archbishop Thomas à Becket's murder in 1170 by four knights of King Henry II. Becket was canonized in 1173.

By the 14th century, Canterbury had become a tourist town, its industry based on the pilgrimages to the shrine of St. Thomas. This aspect of the city's history is captured in Geoffrey Chaucer's *Canterbury Tales*, which recounts the journey from London to Canterbury of a group of fictional pilgrims in about 1390.

The city's greatest monument is the cathedral, which bears the stamp of many people and events.

Many old almshouses still stand, among them 11th-century St. John's and 12th-century St. Thomas' of Eastbridge, where pilgrims stopped to rest and eat. For further information contact the Canterbury Tourist Information Center, 34 St Margaret's Street, Canterbury, Kent CT1 2TG; tel: 01227 766567.

CANTERBURY CATHEDRAL, founded by St. Augustine, has been reconstructed and enlarged several times during its long history. The structure today is largely Perpendicular in style, with Norman and Early English sections. A vast and imposing building, it is visible from all parts of Canterbury and beyond. Its most remarkable feature is the 235-foot bell tower, known both as Bell Harry and Angel Steeple, after the gilded angel that once graced its top. Two bulkier towers with tiered buttresses rise from the western front; one is the original structure from 1465, the other a 19th-century copy.

With a long nave and an unusually long choir, the building is more than 300 feet long. At the eastern end is a circular tower known as the Corona, or Becket's Crown. On the northern side of the cathedral are the remains of the once great monastic buildings, which include the 15th-century Great Cloister, the Norman dormitory, the library and the Chapter House.

Chapels extend from the double aisles of the choir, and the choir walls and arcades curve inward. The Trinity Chapel, occupying the eastern end of the church, contained the tomb of St. Thomas until 1538, when Henry VIII ordered the shrine destroyed and the remains of the saint scattered. The 13th-century stained-glass windows, which illustrate the miracles wrought by St. Thomas, were mostly spared.

Near the site of the shrine is the tomb and effigy of Edward, the Black Prince, who died in 1376. Henry IV and Joan of Navarre also are interred in this section.

CHILHAM CASTLE GARDENS, 5 miles southwest on A252 at Chilham, is a 17th-century mansion (not open to the public) reputedly created by architect Inigo Jones and landscaped by the redoubtable "Capability" Brown.

CARLISLE (82 C5)
CUMBRIA *pop. 73,200*
Lying near Scotland, Carlisle figured often in the period of border warfare. The castle was founded in the late 11th century and rebuilt many times; it has carvings on its walls from Scottish prisoners captured in the 1745 rebellion.

HADRIAN'S WALL stretches almost 74 miles from Wallsend to Bowness. Built AD 122–26, it was designed to defend the frontier of the Roman province from ancient northern tribes. At Vindolanda Fort near Hexham, 30 miles east of Carlisle, a section of the wall is reconstructed to its original form.

CERNE ABBAS (83 C1)
DORSET
Secluded Cerne Abbas is known for its row of overhung Tudor cottages and for the remains of a 10th-century abbey. On nearby Giant Hill is the so-called Cerne Giant, a 180-foot fertility figure carved in chalk, thought to have been created during the Roman occupation.

▲ CHANNEL ISLANDS (83 E1)
pop. 142,200
The Channel Islands – Jersey, Guernsey, Alderney, Sark and Herm – are favorite vacation spots in Britain. Visitors are attracted by the mild English Channel climate and tax-free shopping.

Jersey, the largest of the islands, is only 14 miles from the French coast and, even after centuries of British domination, bears a medieval French air. St. Helier, Jersey's capital, is a small but lively town; stores, restaurants and nightspots line its narrow streets.

Although flat sandy beaches flank St. Helier, much of Jersey's coastline consists of tumbling cliffs and heathery slopes dotted with picturesque harbor towns. On the rugged east coast is Gorey, whose tidy cottages are dwarfed by the battlements of Mont Orgueil Castle. The 12th- and 13th-century structure is one of the best-preserved medieval concentric castles in Britain.

Guernsey is well-liked for its placid holiday beaches. Sandy coves and bays are protected by the granite headlands of the indented coast. St. Peter Port, the island's capital, is a pleasant town of stone houses. Granite stairs and cobbled lanes climb the hill and provide views of the harbor and medieval castle below. Colorful markets are stocked with the region's produce.

Alderney, reached by sea from Guernsey, is an unspoiled island of silvery dunes, pools and hidden bays.

On the tiny, rocky island of Sark, motor vehicles are strictly prohibited and travel is limited to bicycles or horse-drawn carriages.

The tiny island of Herm lies between Guernsey and Sark. It has a single hotel, a few cottages, dunes, woods and an old manor house. Shell Beach is a favorite place for swimming.

Jersey and Guernsey are served by daily flights from many locations in Britain, and by ferry from several ports in Britain and from St. Malo in France.

CHELTENHAM (83 C2)
GLOUCESTERSHIRE *pop. 90,500*
The Cotswold town of Cheltenham has been a favorite holiday resort since the 18th century, when its three saline springs were discovered. Much of that era lives on in the Regency buildings, wide tree-lined streets and pleasant parks. Drinking water can still be obtained at the town hall and at the Pittville Pump Room, a masterpiece of Greek Revival style.

Popular as a sports center, the spa is the site of the biggest steeplechase in Britain. The National Hunt Festival (Gold Cup) takes place in March. The town hall, opera house and civic playhouse offer other entertainment. Every

July fans of avant-garde music flock to Cheltenham for the International Festival of Music.

CHEDWORTH ROMAN VILLA, 8½ miles southeast, dates from AD 180 to 350. Rediscovered in 1864, it is probably the best-preserved Roman villa in Britain.

▲ CHESTER (82 C4)
CHESHIRE *pop. 122,000*
Like most English towns with "caster," "cester" or "chester" in their names, Chester dates from the Roman times. These names are derived from the Latin word *castra*, meaning "camp."

Much of medieval Chester was built on top of the Roman city and survives today. The walls surrounding the town follow the line of the Roman walls; even the four main streets were laid along their ancient predecessors.

Chester also is noted for 16th- and 17th-century timber-framed houses. The Rows, a line of "gingerbread" buildings with stores on the first and second stories, are of particular interest. The upper-floor stores have their own arcaded walkways.

The visitor center presents Roman and later local history through a film show, a life-size exhibit of Victorian Chester, and maps and prints. For additional tourist information, write to the Visitor Center, Vicars Lane, Chester, Cheshire CH1 1QX; tel: 01244 351609.

CHICHESTER (83 D1)
WEST SUSSEX *pop. 25,300*
Though now a quiet country town, Chichester was important during the Roman era when it functioned as a *regnum*, or reigning area. Reminders of that time are the city walls, first built about AD 200, and the nearby Roman palace at Fishbourne.

GOODWOOD HOUSE, 3 miles northeast, is the unusual, but stately, home of the dukes of Richmond. The three-sided house, designed by James Wyatt in 1780, is representative of Sussex stonework. It contains collections of paintings and valuable Sèvres porcelain. On the property is Goodwood Racecourse, the site of a prestigious annual meet (horse racing) in late July and early August.

ROMAN PALACE, 1 mile west at Fishbourne, was discovered in 1960 under a few feet of soil. A large structure with four colonnaded wings enclosing a formal garden, it is the largest Roman palace in Britain and famous for its mosaics. The opulent structure was probably built about AD 75 for Cogidubnus, a British king.

THE WEALD AND DOWNLAND OPEN-AIR MUSEUM, 6 miles north on A286 at Singleton, is an assemblage of historic buildings depicting regional life from the Middle Ages to the 19th century.

CHIPPING CAMPDEN (83 C3)
GLOUCESTERSHIRE *pop. 2,000*
The market town of Chipping Campden lies near the northern edge of the Cotswolds; the lovely old houses lining its main street are made of stone from these well-known hills.

HIDCOTE MANOR GARDEN, 3 miles northeast, is a series of formal gardens separated by unusual varieties of hedges.

CIRENCESTER (83 C2)
GLOUCESTERSHIRE *pop. 17,000*
The unofficial capital of the Cotswold region, Cirencester (pronounced Sighren-sester) is an excellent center for touring this land of gentle hills and stone-built villages. In the town itself are many gray stone inns and houses built by medieval merchants.

▲ COLCHESTER (83 E2)
ESSEX *pop. 151,900*
Established as a Roman colony, Colchester is England's oldest Roman town. Ruins include a long stretch of ancient wall, recovered buildings and dikes, many sculptures and inscribed stone tablets. A fine collection of Romano-

British antiquities is housed in the dungeon of Colchester's remarkable 11th-century castle.

▲ COVENTRY (83 C3)

WEST MIDLANDS *pop. 304,400*

Coventry rose to fame in the Middle Ages as a producer of woolen cloth. During the Industrial Revolution the town became a manufacturing city. Its heavy industry made it a prime target for German bombers in World War II, and much of the central city, including the cathedral church, was destroyed.

A new traffic-free shopping center is one feature of the rebuilt city. Standing in this modern sector is a statue of medieval resident Lady Godiva, who according to legend rode naked through town on market day to protest her husband's unfair taxation of the citizens.

Nearby Warwick Castle (see *Warwick* on p.126) lies to the southwest.

CATHEDRAL, designed by Sir Basil Spence, was begun in 1954 and incorporates the ruins of its 14th-century predecessor. Notable features include the Sutherland tapestry and *God's Revelations*, a bronze group by Sir Jacob Epstein depicting St. Michael and the Devil.

DARTMOOR NATIONAL PARK

(83 B1) ★

DEVON

Long before it became a National Park, the desolate Dartmoor plateau was a favorite setting for English detective stories. The bleak unfenced uplands and uninhabited remains of ancient mountains, are pocked with peat bogs and dotted with heather. Weirdly shaped isolated granite headlands, the tors, soar to more than 2,000 feet above sea level.

Not many people live on Dartmoor today, but this land was inhabited as early as 2000 BC. Evidence exists in the form of stone circles, enclosures and monoliths, silent memorials to Britain's Bronze Age denizens.

The best way to explore the park is on foot or by horseback. Hikers should take sturdy boots, a compass, and a competent guide who can circumnavigate the dangerous peat bogs. Small towns on the moor's edge, including Yelverton, Ashburton and Bovey Tracey, are popular as touring centers.

DARTMOUTH (83 B1)

DEVON *pop. 5,600*

Dartmouth, a seaport on the Dart estuary, has figured often in naval history. Richard I's crusaders set off from Dartmouth in 1190 for the Holy Land. A memorial commemorates a more recent event. In 1944, U.S. troops left from Dartmouth to participate in the World War II invasion of Normandy.

Though damaged by World War II bombs, many old buildings have been preserved. Especially worth noting are a row of 17th-century houses on the waterfront at Bayard's Cove.

▲ DERBY (83 C3)

DERBYSHIRE *pop. 220,700*

A market town since the Middle Ages, Derby gained an industrial aspect in the 19th century. Manufacturing a great assortment of goods from engines to underwear, it is best-known for making fine porcelain, an industry created by William Duesbury in 1756.

ALL SAINTS' CATHEDRAL CHURCH dominates the town with its graceful 178-foot tower. Inside, the stained glass is superb.

DERBY MUSEUM AND ART GALLERY, on The Strand, contains items of archaeological and historical interest. Exhibits include a reconstructed public house.

KEDLESTON HALL, 4 miles northwest, was built in neoclassical style by Scottish architect Robert Adam. Some 50 acres of carefully tended grounds surround the country house.

ROYAL CROWN DERBY WORKS rose to fame after their founding by William Duesbury and Andrew Planche in 1750. The identifying crown trademark and the "crown" in the name were permitted by George III, who was favorably impressed when he visited the porcelain company in 1783. In the next century, Queen Victoria appointed the company manufacturers to the Crown and added the "royal" to the name.

The company maintains its standards of excellence and is world-renowned. Reservations for tours must be made well in advance. Contact tours operator, Royal Crown Derby Porcelain Co, Osmaston Road, Derby DE23 8JZ; tel: 01332 712800.

DORCHESTER (83 C1)
DORSET *pop. 14,200*
Founded by the Romans, Dorchester has evidence of an even earlier settlement. It was the home of Judge George Jeffreys who, with four other judges, tried and executed hundreds of rebels in the Bloody Assize of 1685.

HARDY'S COTTAGE is 3 miles northeast at Higher Bockhampton. The writer, Thomas Hardy, was born in this little thatched house in 1840; it contains a small collection of items associated with him. The cottage can be visited by appointment; contact the local National Trust office, tel: 01305 262366.

MAIDEN CASTLE, 1½ miles southwest, is England's greatest prehistoric fort. The multiple ramparts and complicated entrances were finally breached by the Romans.

▲ DOVER (83 E2)
KENT *pop. 34,300*
Dover has long been a cross-Channel port. The Romans, who called it *Dubris*, built a lighthouse here to guide their troops across the Channel. In the Middle Ages, it was chief among the Cinque Ports, and during World War II it withstood heavy German shellfire from Calais. Reminders of earlier times include a 12th-century castle. The road northwest to Canterbury follows the route of Roman Watling Street.

ROMAN PAINTED HOUSE, New Street, is part of an exceptionally well-preserved Roman town house containing 1,800-year-old wall paintings.

DUNSTER (83 B2)
SOMERSET *pop. 800*
Dunster is one of the prettiest villages on Exmoor. In the main street is the octagonal Yarn Market which dates from 1609 when Dunster was an important cloth center. Overlooking the village is Dunster Castle, a National Trust property; opposite lies a small folly on a wooded hillside.

DUNSTER CASTLE AND CORN MILL. The home of the Luttrell family for 600 years, Dunster Castle is well worth visiting. The present corn mill which dates from the 18th century has been restored.

DURHAM (82 C5)
COUNTY DURHAM *pop. 41,200*
The city of Durham, on the Wear River, is dominated by a staid Norman castle and cathedral. The castle is now part of the University of Durham. The cathedral is considered the finest example of Norman architecture in Europe – it is best visited with a guide.

ELY (83 D3)
CAMBRIDGESHIRE *pop. 12,000*
The name Ely means Eel Island, a reference to the dietary staple of its early Saxon dwellers. Ely was an island when Hereward the Wake and his followers held out against William the Conqueror. Not until the 17th and 18th centuries were the flat, low-lying fens drained for farming. A few isolated patches remain, protected by the National Trust.

ELY CATHEDRAL has overlooked the town and surrounding countryside since the Middle Ages. The "Monarch of the Fens," as it is known, was begun in about 1080 on the site of a 7th-century monastery.

A harmonious mix of several architectural styles, it is mainly Norman, but major sections represent Early English, Perpendicular and Decorated Gothic. Alan de Walsingham, who designed the exterior, also contributed the designs for the Lady Chapel and choir stalls.

Beneath the lantern tower is an octagon that separates the great choir from the 208-foot nave. The massive western tower, rising 270 feet, was added in the 15th century as a complement to the lantern.

EPSOM (83 D2)
SURREY *pop. 68,400*

Epsom is primarily known for Epsom Downs Racecourse, where the horse race, the Derby, occurs during the first week of June. Epsom Salts take their name from the mineral springs responsible for the town's origin as a spa.

ETON – *see Windsor on p.127.*

▲ EXETER (83 B1)
DEVON *pop. 103,000*

The county town of Exeter sits on a hill sloping to the Exe River. Its great variety of architectural styles range from medieval to modern. Medieval walls partly surround the city, and passages built in the Middle Ages run under the main streets (guided tours available). There are pubs claiming to have been the regular haunt of people like Sir Francis Drake.

EXETER CATHEDRAL, situated in the town center, was completed in 1369. Of note are the 60-foot bishop's throne and medieval tombs. Two Norman towers date from 1133.

FOLKESTONE (83 E2)
KENT *pop. 45,300*

Folkestone was once an important channel port and terminus of boat services to the Continent. It is now the boarding point for the Hoverspeed Seacat, a service that crosses the channel to Boulogne, France, four times a day. It is also a summer resort and fishing center. The new 32-mile Channel Tunnel,

THE CHANNEL TUNNEL

The project to build a link from England to France had a long germination; diggings were made as far back as Napoleonic times. The Anglo-French venture that has finally come to fruition, a railroad tunnel from Folkestone in Kent to Sangatte near Calais, in France, has created a mountain of complications. British Rail made errors over a high-speed rail link to London, houses were bought up for demolition, but then the route was changed and the houses remained empty. Recession hit and time and financial estimates were way off. Despite all these setbacks, the first trains to cross beneath the Channel finally made their journey in September 1994.

opened in 1994, connects Folkestone with Calais in France.

GLASTONBURY (83 C2)
SOMERSET *pop. 7,500*

Historic Glastonbury has many literary associations. Joseph of Arimathea is said to have brought the chalice of the Last Supper to the town, which is believed to be the Avalon of King Arthur and his knights. The town has numerous monuments and relics.

GLASTONBURY ABBEY, now in ruins, is where King Arthur and his wife, Queen Guinevere are said to be buried. The Glastonbury Thorn, which blossoms each Christmas, allegedly sprang from St. Joseph's staff, and is in the grounds.

GLOUCESTER (83 C2)
GLOUCESTERSHIRE *pop. 97,000*

Gloucester is an old strategic city that once guarded the lowest crossing on the Severn River and the routes into Wales. Fortified first by the Romans, the city was later walled by the Normans. Its most important medieval monument is the cathedral; other historic sites are the City East Gate, with its Roman and medieval gate towers, and moat in an underground chamber; the St. Mary de Crypt Church; the ruins of St. Oswald's Priory; and the New Inn, a medieval hostelry. Bishop Hooper's Lodging is now a folk museum.

GLOUCESTER CATHEDRAL was founded in the 12th century as a monastic church and refounded by Henry VIII as a cathedral. The east window, dating from the 14th century, is the largest stained-glass window in England.

THE PROTECTION OF BIRDLIFE
The Wildfowl and Wetlands Trust at Slimbridge in Gloucestershire is dedicated to the protection of wetland sites and has wildfowl collections at eight centers in Britain. The Royal Society for the Protection of Birds (R.S.P.B.) is the principal body concerned with wild birds and their environment, and has over 100 reserves in Britain.

GLYNDEBOURNE (83 D1)
EAST SUSSEX *pop. 300*
Tiny Glyndebourne, near Lewes, is noted chiefly for its opera house, which is in the middle of an English garden. The Glyndebourne Festival Opera performs from April to August. Dinner is served during intermission or visitors can bring their own meals; reservations must be made well in advance.

BENTLEY WILDFOWL AND MOTOR MUSEUM is 5 miles northeast at Halland. Wildfowl from around the world can be seen on the grounds, including black swans, mandarin ducks and flamingos.

GRASMERE (82 C5)
CUMBRIA *pop. 1,600*
Grasmere is a good point from which to hike to the surrounding mountains and lakes of the Lake District. Poet William

Wordsworth lived in this town for nine years; his grave and those of his family are in the village churchyard.

DOVE COTTAGE AND THE WORDSWORTH MUSEUM are south of the village at Town End. Dove Cottage was the residence of William Wordsworth. The Wordsworth Museum, opposite the cottage, houses manuscripts, paintings and various items associated with the poet.

RYDAL MOUNT, 2 miles southeast at Rydal, was the Wordsworth family home from 1813 until the poet's death in 1850.

GREAT MALVERN (83 C3)
WORCESTERSHIRE
pop. 30,800
Most vacationers have yet to fully discover this charming sheltered town. Modern attractions include a spa, an outdoor swimming pool, a golf course, winter gardens, and a theater long associated with performances of George Bernard Shaw and J.M. Barrie.

GUERNSEY (82 E1) – *see Channel Islands on p.109.*

▲ GUILDFORD (83 D2)
SURREY *pop. 61,600*
Guildford, the county town of Surrey, is set on the Wey River where it has cut through the North Downs. Its steep High Street is lined with old buildings; the half-timbered guildhall dates from the 17th century, as does Abbot's Hospital, a group of almshouses. Modern buildings include the Yvonne Arnaud Theatre and the law courts. Near the cathedral is the University of Surrey. Well-tended parks and gardens recall the town's ancient name, derived from the Saxon phrase meaning "ford of the golden flowers."

CATHEDRAL, on Stag Hill, is the town's most conspicuous landmark. The simplified Gothic structure was designed by Sir Edward Maufe. Begun in 1936, it was completed in 1962.

CLANDON PARK, 3 miles east, at West Clandon, is a Palladian house built about 1735, probably by Giacomo Leoni.

WISLEY GARDEN, 5 miles northeast off the A3 at Wisley, is a 250-acre display of experimental flowers, fruit and vegetables. Walks wind through rock gardens containing heather and alpine plants.

THE BATTLE OF HASTINGS

Every British schoolchild knows the date 1066, when the Battle of Hastings between William of Normandy and King Harold took place at Battle (as it is now called). Strangely, the great turning point in English history was a haphazard affair. The English (Saxons) should have trounced the French, who were vastly outnumbered and fighting uphill. However, they made a strategic blunder in storming downhill when they thought some of the Normans were retreating; this left a hole in the Saxon defenses on the top of the slope, which the Normans promptly filled.

HARROGATE (82 C4)
NORTH YORKSHIRE pop. 69,300
Harrogate is a well-known, fashionable spa and convention center; wide streets and spa gardens are typical. At the edge of the town gardens is the Royal Pump Room, an 1804 octagonal structure built over a sulphur spring. The Pump Room is now a museum of local history, and the sulphur spring can be tasted.

HAREWOOD HOUSE AND BIRD GARDEN, 6 miles south, is the home of the Earl and Countess of Harewood, designed in 1759 by John Carr and Robert Adam. The bird garden has exotic species.

KNARESBOROUGH CASTLE is 3 miles northeast at Knaresborough. This ruin of a 14th-century stronghold above the Nidd River includes two baileys, a keep and gatehouses.

HASTINGS AND ST. LEONARDS-ON-SEA (83 E1)
EAST SUSSEX pop. 81,900
Despite its popularity, the coastal resort of Hastings retains much of the character of its fishing port past. In the eastern part of town, narrow streets lined with tiled cottages lead down to the old harbor area. The remains of a Norman castle are on a cliff overlooking the beach.

West is St. Leonards-on-Sea, principally a residential area with family hotels and boarding houses. Along the 3 miles of seafront stretches a continuous promenade, with many vacation amenities.

There are fine views over the Channel and the countryside from East Hill, Ecclesbourne Glen and the Fire Hills.

HATFIELD (83 D2)
HERTFORDSHIRE pop. 29,000
HATFIELD HOUSE was built by the first Earl of Salisbury from 1607 to 1611 and has been the home of the Cecil family since then. In the garden are the remains of the Old Palace, where Queen Elizabeth I was imprisoned by her half sister Mary I from 1555 to 1558. The house contains some of Elizabeth's personal items, as well as notable works of art.

HEREFORD (83 C3)
HEREFORDSHIRE
pop. 48,400
Hereford is a flourishing agricultural town. Its 12th-century sandstone cathedral contains a collection of rare books and the *Mappa Mundi*, a 13th-century world map. Of additional interest are the 15th-century Booth Hall. Not far from the Welsh border, Hereford is a good base for excursions into Wales.

HERM – see Channel Islands on p.109.

HERTFORD (83 D2)
HERTFORDSHIRE pop. 22,400
Hertford is an ancient county town at the convergence of the Lea, Beane and

Rib rivers. Elizabeth I spent much of her childhood in the town's castle, of which only a gatehouse remains. Wings were added in the 18th and 20th centuries. The castle grounds, often the site of band concerts, are open to the public.

▲ HULL (82 D4)
EAST RIDING OF YORKSHIRE
pop. 245,100

Hull, or more properly Kingston-upon-Hull, is an important seaport 20 miles from the east coast at the confluence of the Hull and Humber rivers. Places to visit include Ferens Art Gallery, the Transport and Archaeological Museum, the Town Docks Museum, and the Holy Trinity Church, with its notable brickwork. Significant among Hull's old houses is the Wilberforce House, 17th-century home of William Wilberforce, who instigated the abolition of slavery.

▲ IPSWICH (83 E3)
SUFFOLK *pop. 119,600*

The port of Ipswich lies at the head of the Orwell estuary. An industrial town, Ipswich is not without historic interest. The painter Thomas Gainsborough was a resident for a long time; many of his works, along with those of John Constable, are on display at the museum and art gallery of Christchurch Mansion. Also in Ipswich is the beautiful Sparrowe's House, a 16th-century dwelling that now serves as a bookshop.

IRONBRIDGE (83 C3)
SHROPSHIRE *pop. 1,500*

Ironmaster Abraham Darby first smelted iron using coke as a fuel in Ironbridge in the early 18th century. The process contributed significantly to Britain's leadership in the Industrial Revolution. Locally, it was responsible for the creation of the world's first iron bridge. His 196-foot bridge still spans the town.

IRONBRIDGE GORGE MUSEUM is a series of seven museums preserving major sites of the iron industry along a 4-mile section of the Severn River.

JERSEY (83 E1) – *see Channel Islands on p.109.*

KENDAL (82 C5)
CUMBRIA *pop. 23,600*

The old market town of Kendal, in the lush Kent Valley, is a good starting point for exploring the English Lake District. Kendal also is interesting in itself, with cobbled streets and quaint archways.

ABBOT HALL, in Kirkland, houses both an art gallery and the museum of Lakeland Life and Industry.

LEVENS HALL, 5 miles southwest, is a well-preserved Elizabethan mansion with a topiary garden.

SIZERGH CASTLE, 3½ miles southwest, has been the home of the Stricklands for more than 700 years. The oldest section of the current structure is the pele tower, built about 1340. Notable interior features are the fine paneling and ceilings, antique furniture, works of art and Stuart and Jacobite relics.

LAKELAND TERMS
Small lakes are called tarns, mountains are fells, streams are known as becks, spotted black-faced sheep are Herdwicks, white-faced ones are Swaledales. Force means waterfall.

KESWICK (82 B5)
CUMBRIA *pop. 5,600*

Keswick on Derwent Water is an excellent base for touring the northern part of the Lake District. Most of the attractions in this part of the country are purely scenic. Castle Head, half a mile south, offers splendid views of Derwent Water and Bassenthwaite Lake; Latrigg, to the northeast, affords a higher vantage point and more extensive vistas. John Ruskin praised Friar's Crag, which overlooks the northeastern end of Derwent Water, for its panoramas. The area is also well-known for its associations with the

English Romantic poets. William Wordsworth was born in Cockermouth, and Sir Walter Scott and Samuel Taylor Coleridge visited him in Grasmere.

MIREHOUSE, 3 miles northwest, is a fine 17th-century manor house with well-preserved rooms and original furniture.

LAKE DISTRICT NATIONAL PARK (82 C5) ★
CUMBRIA

In northwest England, the Lake District National Park, just 40 miles across, is an area of rugged windswept mountains, interspersed by tranquil lakes. Spring and fall are the best times to visit, when the area is less crowded. The western district is more remote, with England's highest peak, Scafell Pike (3,210 feet). Walking, climbing and sailing are popular, while there are strong literary connections with the 18th-century poets Wordsworth and Coleridge.

VISITOR CENTER, on A591 at Brockhole in 32 acres of woodland on the eastern shore of Lake Windermere, has exhibits relating to Lakeland. Tel: 01539 44660.

▲ LEEDS (82 C4)
WEST YORKSHIRE *pop. 454,700*

Leeds has a diversified industrial base. One of the prices of obvious success has been a coat of grime on its fine Victorian buildings, including the Corn Hall, the Infirmary and the town hall. More utilitarian complexes of glass and reinforced concrete have risen nearby.

Leeds has three fine theaters, a leading British university and an excellent art gallery, as well as Britain's only remaining music hall, the City Varieties.

TEMPLE NEWSAM HOUSE AND PARK, 3 miles east, is a Jacobean house with 18th-century additions. The prominent landscape architect "Capability" Brown redesigned the large (more than 900-acre) grounds as a park in the 18th century. The Knights Templar once had a farm on these extensive grounds.

LEEDS CASTLE (83 E2)
MAIDSTONE, KENT

Some 4 miles southeast of Maidstone on the B2163, Leeds Castle has its origins in Anglo-Saxon England and was a gift from William the Conqueror to a cousin who fought with him in the Battle of Hastings. The grounds incorporate parkland, aviaries, wildlife and a golf course. The most spectacular views of the castle are from the air.

LEWES (83 D1)
EAST SUSSEX *pop. 15,000*

The old market town of Lewes bears the stamp of hundreds of years of history. Oldest among its extant monuments is a Norman castle, largely in ruins. Barbican House, on the castle grounds, contains archaeological finds. Along the town's narrow medieval streets are many old buildings, including tile-hung houses of the 17th century, Georgian buildings of local stone and several old inns. The town is renowned for its fires and torchlight processions on November 5, Guy Fawkes' night (see p.97).

BLUEBELL RAILWAY, 7 miles north off the A275, is a renovated steam train on which passengers can take a 9-mile trip from Sheffield Park Station through the Bluebell Woodland.

▲ LINCOLN (82 D4)
LINCOLNSHIRE *pop. 80,400*

On a high plateau above the Witham River, Lincoln dominates much of Lincolnshire and is itself commanded by its magnificent cathedral, founded in the 11th century. Close by the cathedral are the ruins of an 11th-century castle built by William the Conqueror. Steep cobbled streets go down to the lower, newer town.

CATHEDRAL CHURCH OF ST. MARY was begun late in the 12th century and completed in the 14th century. It remains one of the best examples of the Early English and Decorated styles of English Gothic architecture.

The cathedral's 365-foot spire is visible for miles. Like much of medieval Lincoln, it is built of local limestone.

LINCOLN CASTLE, Castle Hill, was begun in the 11th century by William the Conqueror. A Norman bailey and two motte mounds survived the period; a Victorian prison chapel also is intact.

MUSEUM OF LINCOLNSHIRE LIFE, Burton Road, paints a picture of local life since the late 18th century.

▲ LIVERPOOL (82 C4)
MERSEYSIDE *pop. 457,500*
King John granted a charter to the fishing village of Liverpool on the north bank of the Mersey River in 1207. By the 18th century, the village had become a sizeable port, participating actively in England's West Indies trade. All of this contributed to the busy city of today.

Though a great seaport with miles of docks, Liverpool also is known for its generous patronage of the fine arts and education. The city also contributed several bands to the "British Invasion" of music in the 1960s, foremost among them, the Beatles.

Two tunnels connect Liverpool to Birkenhead across the Mersey, but the finest views of the city's docks and landing platforms are from the ferries. The Royal Liver Building dominates the waterfront. On top of its 295-foot towers are statues of the mythical Liver Bird, which according to local tradition gave Liverpool its name. Once a functioning dock, Albert Dock has been restored to include stores, restaurants and museums.

For further tourist information, contact the Merseyside Welcome Centre, Clayton Square Shopping Centre, Liverpool, Merseyside L1 1QR; tel: 0151-709 3631; or the Tourist Information Center, Atlantic Pavilion, Albert Dock, Liverpool, Merseyside L3 4AE, tel: 0151 708 8854.

ANGLICAN CATHEDRAL, occupies a commanding position at the summit of St. James Mount. Designed by Sir Giles Gilbert Scott, the red sandstone building is a modern version of the Gothic style. With an interior height of 119 feet and a length of 619 feet, it is the largest ecclesiastical structure in England and the largest Anglican cathedral in the world.

BEATLES STORY, Britannia Pavilion at Albert Dock, has exhibits featuring recreations of Liverpool's Cavern Club, Hamburg's Star Club, Brian Epstein's record shop and London's Abbey Road Studios.

PORT SUNLIGHT HERITAGE CENTRE is situated 4½ miles south at 95 Greendale Road, within the 130-acre garden village of Port Sunlight, built by the soap baron Lord Leverhulme in the late 1800s.

ROMAN CATHOLIC CATHEDRAL OF CHRIST THE KING is a vast modern structure on Mount Pleasant designed by award-winning architect Frederick Gibberd.

TATE GALLERY, Albert Dock, houses works from the national collection of 20th-century art.

WALKER ART GALLERY, William Brown Street, houses a collection of paintings, sculptures and drawings dating from the 1300s to the present day.

LUTON (83 D2)
BEDFORDSHIRE *pop. 169,000*
Luton is an industrial and manufacturing town, easily reached via the M1 freeway from London.

KNEBWORTH HOUSE, GARDENS AND COUNTRY PARK, 8½ miles east at Stevenage, includes a 250-acre park and the home of the Lytton family. The house contains a Jacobean banquet hall and a Gothic state drawing room. The parkland includes a deer park.

LUTON HOO, 2 miles southeast on B653, was designed and built by Robert Adam in the 18th century. The gardens were designed by "Capability" Brown. The house contains a fine collection of paintings, porcelain and jewels.

WHIPSNADE WILD ANIMAL PARK, 6 miles southwest, encloses 600 acres on the edge of the Chiltern Hills. Over 3,000 animals can be seen in mostly natural surroundings.

LYME REGIS (83 B1)
DORSET *pop. 3,500*
The Georgian fishing village of Lyme Regis is a seaside resort with charming houses and fossil-studded cliffs.

THE FOWLES' CONNECTION
The Cobb at Lyme Regis is a windswept wall, curving out to sea, that gained international fame through the film *The French Lieutenant's Woman*, based on the novel by John Fowles.
The Cobb is medieval in origin, and the undercliff, riddled with landslips, is designated a National Nature Reserve.

MALMESBURY (83 C2)
WILTSHIRE *pop. 4,200*
WESTONBIRT ARBORETUM, 5½ miles northwest, was laid out in 1829 by the squire of Westonbirt. The 600-acre tree reserve is especially colorful in the fall

▲ MANCHESTER (82 C4)
GREATER MANCHESTER *pop. 450,100*
Manchester is the capital of England's cotton manufacturing industry and one of the country's busiest cities. It dates from Roman times, but gained prominence in the 18th and 19th centuries after construction of the Manchester Ship Canal provided access to the flourishing port of Liverpool. Growth accelerated as trade was established with the New World.

Although most of the Victorian architecture of old Manchester has been destroyed, a few areas still survive. For further information, contact Manchester Visitor Centre, Town Hall Extension, Lloyd Street, Greater Manchester M60 2LA; tel: 0161-234 3157.

CITY ART GALLERIES, Mosley Street, has paintings by the old masters, George Stubbs, Thomas Gainsborough, J.M.W. Turner and the Pre-Raphaelites.

WHITWORTH ART GALLERY, University of Manchester, Whitworth Park. The gallery was founded in 1889 by royal charter. Principal collections include watercolors by Blake, Turner, and the Pre-Raphaelites as well as Cézanne, Van Gogh and Picasso, and the *Whitworth Tapestry*, designed by Paolozzi in 1968.

MAN, ISLE OF (82 B5)
pop. 50,500
Between Northern Ireland and the northwest coast of England, surrounded by the Irish Sea, is the colorful Isle of Man, 31 miles long and 13 miles wide. One of the smallest independent countries under the British Crown, the island retains its own parliament, the Tynwald, and makes its own laws, and controls taxation. The official language is a form of Celtic Manx similar to Gaelic.

Douglas, the capital and main port, also is the largest city and leading resort. On Prospect Hill is the House of Keys, home of the Manx parliament. Annual events include the Manx Grand Prix in September and the International Tourist Trophy races in June.

Castletown, south of Douglas, is the island's former capital. Its leading attraction is Castle Rushen, a beautifully preserved medieval stronghold that guards the harbor's entrance.

Ramsey is the principal northern resort and boasts a fine golf course.

Port Erin is a quiet resort town from which side trips to the uninhabited island, the Calf of Man, can be arranged.

Peel is an old fishing port on the west coast noted for its kippers. Also in Peel are the ruins of 15th-century Peel Castle and the Cathedral of St. German. On its outskirts rises tiered Tynwald Hill, from where new laws are proclaimed.

MARLBOROUGH (83 C2)
WILTSHIRE pop. 7,000

The small downland town of Marlborough is known for its wide High Street, lined with excellent Georgian buildings, coaching inns and stores.

Ancient remains on the chalk downlands near Marlborough include the Iron Age hill fort of Barbury Castle, 4 miles northwest. The White Horse, carved into the chalk in 1804, is 1 mile southwest beside the A4.

AVEBURY, 6 miles west, is a village that stands in the middle of a huge prehistoric stone circle, dating to around 2500 BC. It is larger and, for some, more impressive than Stonehenge.

MIDHURST (83 D2)
WEST SUSSEX pop. 4,660

PETWORTH HOUSE, about 5½ miles east, was rebuilt in the late 17th century and is famous for its fabulous art collection, on loan to the National Trust from the Treasury. There are works by Turner, Gainsborough, Holbein, Frans Hals and Rembrandt. A deer park, designed by "Capability" Brown, surrounds the house.

▲ NEWCASTLE-UPON-TYNE (82 C5)
TYNE AND WEAR pop. 203,600

Though very old, Newcastle-upon-Tyne has the face of a modern industrial town. As early as the 1830s urban renewal began; congested areas were cleared, and streets became broad thoroughfares. Rebuilding continues with the civic center, the modern library, the Laing Art Gallery and a modern shopping district. With so much building and rebuilding, the city still boasts 1,400 acres of open spaces, including the vast Town Moor.

BEDE'S WORLD, Jarrow, 9 miles east, is a museum and working farm commemorating the Venerable Bede, the Anglo-Saxon monk who wrote one of the first ever history books in AD 731.

▲ NORTHAMPTON (83 D3)
NORTHAMPTONSHIRE pop. 186,000

On the banks of the Nene River, this is an industrial center famous for boots and shoes. Charles II destroyed part of the town during the Civil War because shoes for Cromwell's army were made here.

ALTHORP HALL, 5 miles northeast on A428, has been the Spencer family home since 1508. It was the childhood home of Diana, Princess of Wales. The collection of pictures, furniture and china is very impressive.

▲ NORWICH (82 E3)
NORFOLK pop. 173,300

Ancient Norwich spreads comfortably over the low Norfolk hills, the spire of its prominent landmark – the Cathedral of the Holy Trinity – is easily noticeable. A thriving settlement at the time of the Norman Conquest, Norwich has prospered since the 10th century as the see of East Anglian bishops.

Probably the most picturesque area is Elm Hill, with old houses and cobbled streets.

Near to the Norfolk Broads and the coast, Norwich is a good center for touring these areas.

CATHEDRAL OF THE HOLY TRINITY was begun in the 12th century, but has many later additions. The nave and tower are typically Norman, but the magnificent spire above the tower is from the 15th century. The tower soars to 315 feet; the varied tracery of the cloister arches required 130 years to complete.

NORWICH CASTLE, occupying the city's highest hill, retains its Norman keep; gardens fill the ancient moat.

▲ NOTTINGHAM (83 D3)
NOTTINGHAMSHIRE pop. 279,700

Nottingham gained fame as the home of Robin Hood, the medieval outlaw whose lair was in Sherwood Forest. The city has long been noted as the center of the English lace trade.

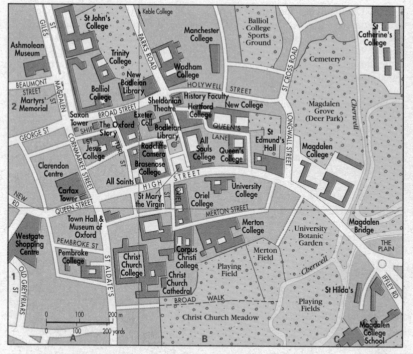

The Goose Fair, a three-day event, is held on the first Thursday of October in the Forest Recreation Ground, a surviving fragment of Sherwood Forest.

D.H. LAWRENCE BIRTHPLACE MUSEUM, 8a Victoria Street, Eastwood, is the birthplace of the English novelist. The house has been restored and furnished in typical Victorian blue-collar style.

NEWSTEAD ABBEY, 11 miles north, is the former home of Lord Byron. The house contains relics of his life and works.

NOTTINGHAM CASTLE MUSEUM, once the home of Robin Hood's arch-enemy, the Sheriff of Nottingham, is now a museum and art gallery.

▲ OXFORD (83 C2) ★
OXFORDSHIRE *pop. 115,800*

The venerable university and cathedral city of Oxford originated as a religious settlement in the Saxon period. Though tradition has it that Alfred the Great founded the university, it was probably not until the 12th century that students flocked to Oxford to study in the monastic establishments. In the 13th century several colleges – University, Balliol and Merton – emerged; each considers itself the oldest.

Since the 13th century, the history of Oxford has been the history of the university, with its far-reaching academic and religious activities and its influential lecturers and scholars. From the few colleges in the 13th century, the university has grown to include some 35 colleges, as well as important scientific research facilities, museums and several excellent libraries, including the Bodleian.

Though factories and houses now stretch across the suburbs, this "City of Dreaming Spires" remains largely unchanged. Old Oxford's showpiece is the High Street, simply called the "High," an ancient street lined with the imposing stone buildings of the university's schools. Dating mainly from the 15th to 17th centuries, the colleges are built around traditional quadrangles; each has its own chapel, hall, library and gardens.

In addition to the popular and traditional pastimes of college life, rowing, punting, swimming and fishing or simply strolling along the riverbank, are favorite leisure activities. For additional information contact the Tourist Information Center, The Old School, Gloucester Green, Oxford, Oxfordshire OX1 2DA; tel: 01865 726871.

ASHMOLEAN MUSEUM (121 A2), Beaumont Street, is England's oldest museum. It contains European, Egyptian and Near Eastern antiquities and world art.

BODLEIAN LIBRARY (121 B2), in four buildings on Parks Road and Broad Street, was founded in 1602 by Sir Thomas Bodley. It has over 3 million volumes, none of which may leave the library.

COLLEGES OF THE UNIVERSITY are clustered in the central part of the city; most are on or within a short walk of the High. The following is by no means a complete list of Oxford's colleges. Access to some colleges is restricted; get details from the tourist information center.

All Souls (121 A2), High Street, was established in 1438 by Archbishop Chichele of Canterbury. The gateway and front quadrangle date from that time.

Brasenose (121 B2), Radcliffe Square, dates from 1509. The present buildings were constructed on top of the site of several older halls; the gate tower and hall date from the founding.

Christ Church (121 A1), St. Aldates, known as The House, was founded in 1546 as Cardinal College by Thomas Wolsey. When Wolsey fell into disfavor, it was renamed King Henry VIII College. After its chapel became the cathedral of the diocese in 1546, the college gained its present name. A local landmark is Wren's Tom Tower, wherein hangs the 7½-ton bell Great Tom, dedicated to St. Thomas of Canterbury.

Magdalen (121 C2), High Street, has changed little in appearance since the 15th century. The college is at the end of the High, on the Cherwell River; the Magdalen Walks follow the river and there is a deer park on the grounds.

Merton (121 B1), Merton Street, was founded in Malden in 1264, and transferred here in 1274.

Trinity (121 A2), Broad Street, founded in 1555, is the traditional rival of adjacent Balliol. It incorporates parts of the 14th-century Durham College.

University (121 B2), High Street, although one of the oldest colleges, the present buildings are only 300 years old.

SAINT MARY THE VIRGIN (121 B2), next to All Souls College, is the university church and is mentioned in William the Conqueror's 11th-century *Domesday Book*.

SHELDONIAN THEATRE (121 B2), Broad Street, designed by Sir Christopher Wren and built in 1669. The theater is the scene of the Encaenia every June in which honorary degrees are conferred.

PEAK DISTRICT NATIONAL PARK
(82 C4) ★
If the image of pastoral Britain is manifest anywhere, it is in the Peak District National Park, 452 square miles of heather and peat-laden moorland hills, wooded dales, tunnels and caverns.

The park extends to Oldham in the north, Ashbourne in the south, and Sheffield and Chesterfield in the east; in the west it neatly surrounds Buxton.

For more information, contact the Peak District National Park, Aldern House, Baslow Road, Bakewell, Derbyshire DE45 1AE; tel: 01629 816200 or visit the tourist information center at The Crescent in Buxton, or Old Market Hall in Bakewell; tel: 01629 813227.

PENZANCE (83 A1)
CORNWALL *pop. 19,600*
As a port for the Cornish tin trade and a haven for smugglers, Penzance prospered long before its development as a

seaside resort. The most westerly town in England, it has a particularly mild climate and 4 miles of fine sandy beach.

LAND'S END, 9 miles southwest, is the 200-acre western tip of English mainland, perhaps best known as one of two points that mark the farthest distance one can travel in Britain. The other point is John O'Groats in Scotland.

MINACK THEATRE, 8 miles southwest, at Porthcurno, is a Greek-style open-air theater built on rugged cliffs.

ST. MICHAEL'S MOUNT, across the bay, is linked to the mainland at low tide by a causeway; a ferry runs in summer.

▲ PLYMOUTH (83 B1)
DEVON *pop. 242,600*
Plymouth has been the starting point for several pivotal historical events. From here Sir Francis Drake sailed to engage the Spanish Armada, and it was from this port that the Pilgrim Fathers sailed in the *Mayflower* to found a colony in the New World – an event marked by a memorial stone. The town suffered considerable damage during World War II, but a few historic areas remain; inside the Barbican area is the Old Quarter, with narrow streets, old houses and a busy harbor.

▲ PORTSMOUTH & SOUTHSEA (83 D1)
HAMPSHIRE *pop. 181,100*
Portsmouth, an important naval dockyard, is linked with the busy seaside resort of Southsea, on the small peninsula of Portsea Island, across from the Isle of Wight. These two settlements form the city of Portsmouth. The city lies between two natural harbors: Portsmouth and Langstone.

PORTSMOUTH HISTORIC SHIPS, The Hard. Three famous ships are on display here.
  HMS *Victory* was Nelson's flagship during the Battle of Trafalgar in 1805. The nearby Royal Naval Museum depicts the military hero and his exploits. HMS *Warrior* was launched in 1860 as the world's first iron-hulled armored warship. Now restored, it portrays life aboard a 19th-century warship.

  Mary Rose Shiphall and Exhibition features Henry VIII's flagship which sank off Portsmouth during a battle in July 1545. The ship was raised in 1982 after lying for four centuries in the mud and is remarkably well-preserved.

RIPON (82 C5)
NORTH YORKSHIRE *pop. 14,600*
RIPON CATHEDRAL is a small structure embodying a variety of architectural styles from the 12th to the 15th century. Saint Wilfred's Needle is a narrow opening through which supposedly only the virtuous can squeeze.

FOUNTAINS ABBEY AND STUDLEY ROYAL, a World Heritage Site, 4 miles southwest off B6265, is the largest monastic ruin in Britain. The abbey was founded by Cistercian monks in 1132 and the vast park and landscape garden were laid out from 1720 to 1740.

NORTON CONYERS, 3 miles north, is a Jacobean house believed to have figured in Charlotte Brontë's *Jane Eyre*. A display of Brontë family relics includes a collection of furniture.

ST. ALBANS (83 D2)
HERTFORDSHIRE *pop. 77,200*
Founded before the time of Christ, St. Albans is a market town built on the site of the Roman city of *Verulamium*. Among the ancient ruins are a large theater dating from the 2nd century AD and a hypocaust (Roman heating system).

ST. ALBANS CATHEDRAL, an 11th-century church named after the first British saint, stands on the site of his martyrdom. The 550-foot abbey has one of the longest naves in Britain.

SHAW'S CORNER, 6½ miles north at Ayot St. Lawrence, was George Bernard Shaw's home for 44 years and the place of his death in 1950. Several rooms remain preserved as they were during his residence.

▲ SALISBURY (83 C2)
WILTSHIRE *pop. 37,000*
Salisbury, known for its cathedral, is a charming town surrounded by hills and four rivers. It was laid out on a grid plan by Bishop Poore in the 13th century. For further information contact the Tourist Information Centre, The Council House, Bourne Hill, Salisbury, Wilts SP1 3UZ; tel: 01722 334956.

SALISBURY CATHEDRAL, built from 1220 to 1280, with some later additions, is a masterpiece of early Gothic architecture. The spire, added in the 14th century, is the tallest in England.

OLD SARUM, 2 miles north, on A345, was probably an Iron Age camp; later it was the site of a Norman castle and cathedral town. Its foundations can still be seen; there is a small museum.

SANDRINGHAM (83 E3)
NORFOLK
SANDRINGHAM ESTATE is the royal family's country home and the place George V loved "better than anywhere in the world." Closed to the public when the royal family are in residence, the house contains ancestral paintings of the royal family that date from 1845.

SANDWICH (83 E2)
KENT *pop. 4,600*
For hundreds of years Sandwich was an important port on England's east coast. During the past centuries the sea has withdrawn, leaving the town center more than 2 miles from the shore. Many ancient buildings survive, lending their medieval charm. The exclusive Royal St. George's golf course is nearby.

SARK – *see Channel Islands on p.109.*

SCILLY ISLES (83 A2)
The Isles of Scilly, a group of about 130 islands roughly 28 miles off the south-west tip of England, are part of an almost submerged granite mass that has been broken up by the sea. They can be reached from Penzance by boat (summer only), by helicopter and from Land's End by fixed-wing aircraft.

Five of the islands are inhabited: St. Mary's, Tresco, St. Martin's, St. Agnes and Bryher. St. Mary's, the largest, is really three islands joined by a sandbar; Hugh Town is the largest settlement. Tresco is the home of the islands' governor and offers gardens, the ruins of an abbey and two crumbling fortifications.

▲ SHEFFIELD (82 C4)
SOUTH YORKSHIRE *pop. 528,300*
Sheffield, an industrial city on the Don River, is known for the manufacture of steel and cutlery.

Of note are the City Museum and the 15th-century cruciform Church of St. Peter and St. Paul. The church bishop's house is a 15th-century, half-timbered structure, preserved as a museum of domestic life. In Sheffield Castle, Mary, Queen of Scots was held captive by the Earl of Shrewsbury for 14 years.

SHREWSBURY (83 C3)
SHROPSHIRE *pop. 63,900*
Shrewsbury is an old town on a neck of land formed by the Severn River. The town is thought to have been founded by Britons who abandoned the Roman city of *Viroconium*, 5 miles southeast. Shrewsbury Castle is an old landmark, built soon after the Norman Conquest; the present structure dates mostly from the 14th century.

▲ SOUTHAMPTON (83 C2)
HAMPSHIRE *pop. 196,500*
Southampton has distinguished itself as a major commercial port for more than 1,000 years. The city offers shopping centers, a university and sports facilities.

Tudor House is a half-timbered building now used as a museum containing antiques and historical exhibits. The Bargate, a medieval gateway, is now the focal point of the city center.

▲ STOKE-ON-TRENT (82 C4)

STAFFORDSHIRE *pop. 247,000*

Fine pottery and porcelain have been made in Stoke-on-Trent since before the Romans. Josiah Wedgwood set up a pottery business in 1759 and developed his famous blue and cream china, stamped with John Flaxman's classical design. The Wedgwood Visitor Centre is 5 miles south at Baralston. Josiah Spode and his son, specialists in bone china and pottery, were contemporaries. There are tours of their factory on Church Street.

At the beginning of the 19th century, Thomas Minton developed his fine transfer-printed earthenware; his work can be seen at the Minton Museum.

A few of the old bottle-shaped brick ovens remain; Gladstone Pottery Museum at Longton is a restored Victorian pottery that contains a few examples.

ALTON TOWERS, 12 miles east, is Britain's biggest theme park, with over 100 rides, shows and attractions.

STONEHENGE (83 C2)

AMESBURY

A World Heritage Site, 2½ miles west off the A303, this is an imposing collection of prehistoric stone monuments and one of history's most baffling mysteries. Experts believe the monoliths, which can only be viewed from behind a perimeter fence, were set in place about 5,000 years ago as a religious and cultural center for early herding clans.

STOW-ON-THE-WOLD (83 C2)

GLOUCESTERSHIRE *pop. 2,100*

At the junction of eight roads, Stow-on-the-Wold, a busy market town and site of an annual fair, is a favorite as one of the prettiest Cotswold villages.

STRATFORD-UPON-AVON (83 C3) ★

WARWICKSHIRE *pop. 20,900*

Had it lacked one 16th-century poet, this medieval market town would never have become known to so many. But William Shakespeare is believed to have been born, married and buried here, and visitors come to trace his life. Many sites associated with him remain; most belong to the Shakespeare Birthplace Trust, which has restored the buildings to their original appearance. An admission ticket to all trust properties is available at any of the five houses.

Although actor David Garrick established something in the way of a Shakespearean festival as early as 1769, a permanent theater was not built until 1879. Today's Royal Shakespeare Theatre was built in 1932 to replace an older building destroyed by fire. Shakespearean dramas take place from April to January.

Many shops and hotels have been renovated in half-timbered, 16th-century style, so the town seems similar to how it must have looked in Shakespeare's day. The town is best investigated on foot.

A typical exploration might begin with the house on Henley Street where Shakespeare was born. From this point, it is just a short walk to Chapel Street, site of the town hall and the Shakespeare Hotel, supposedly the original great house of Hugh Clopton, a 15th-century mayor of London. Where Chapel Street meets Chapel Lane is Thomas Nash's House, now a museum, next to the foundations of the house in which Shakespeare died. Also on Chapel Lane is the 15th-century Guild Chapel of the Holy Cross.

On nearby Church Street is the grammar school that Shakespeare probably attended and the Guildhall where he might have seen plays by traveling companies. Church Street continues to Old Town, site of two noteworthy old houses, Hall's Croft and Avoncroft. At the end of Old Town on Trinity Street is the 15th-century church where Shakespeare and some of his family are buried.

For additional information contact the Tourist Information Center, Bridgefoot, Stratford-upon-Avon, Warwickshire CV37 6YY; tel: 01789 293127.

ANNE HATHAWAY'S COTTAGE, at Shottery, a mile's walk from Stratford, has been well-preserved and is probably the most photographed farmhouse in England.

HALL'S CROFT, Old Town, is a fine Tudor house that was the home of William Shakespeare's daughter Susanna and her husband, Dr. John Hall.

NEW PLACE, Chapel Street, adjoining the foundations of the house where William Shakespeare spent his last five years, has an Elizabethan knot garden. Entry is through the adjoining Nash's House.

SHAKESPEARE'S BIRTHPLACE, Henley Street, is where Shakespeare's father worked as a glover and wool dealer and where the poet was born in 1564.

TINTAGEL (83 A1)
CORNWALL *pop. 1,800*
Legend names picturesque Tintagel as the birthplace of King Arthur. The town faces the Atlantic on the rugged coast of Cornwall, which has been designated an Area of Outstanding Natural Beauty.

TINTAGEL CASTLE, on a rocky headland above the sea, is a ruined, mainly 13th-century fortress. Excavations have revealed remains from the 5th century.

TORQUAY (83 B1)
DEVON *pop. 58,700*
Torquay is on a promontory above Tor Bay. The exceptionally mild climate has promoted the cultivation of subtropical vegetation. With its palm trees, unusual plants and Italianate style architecture, Torquay has a Mediterranean appearance and is the focus of the "English Riviera."

TUNBRIDGE WELLS (ROYAL) (83 D2)
KENT *pop. 45,300*
This delightful town became a fashionable spa resort in the 17th century. The famous Pantiles, a row of stores beside a tree-lined promenade, lie at the heart of the town.

CHIDDINGSTONE CASTLE, 6½ miles northwest in the well-preserved village of Chiddingstone, is a 19th-century building restored from a 17th-century house.

HEVER CASTLE AND GARDENS, about 7 miles northwest toward Edenbridge, is remarkable for its age – it dates from the 13th century – but is best-known as the childhood home of Anne Boleyn, second wife of Henry VIII.

KNOLE, 9½ miles north in Sevenoaks, is one of the largest and finest private houses in England. Begun in the 15th century, it was greatly expanded in the 17th century.

PENSHURST PLACE AND GARDENS, about 5 miles northwest off B2176 amid beautiful parklands, was the birthplace of Elizabethan poet Sir Philip Sidney; it has been the home of his descendants since the 16th century.

WARMINSTER (83 C2)
WILTSHIRE *pop. 16,500*
LONGLEAT HOUSE, 4 miles southwest, is the home of the Marquess of Bath. A Renaissance structure in a park-like setting, Longleat is considered one of the finest Elizabethan houses in the country. The 200-acre Safari Park contains freely roaming African animals.

WARWICK (83 C3)
WARKWICKSHIRE *pop. 22,800*
WARWICK CASTLE, parts of which date from Norman times, is an imposing, well-preserved medieval fortress that is still inhabited. The state apartments display furniture and armor collections; the parkland, designed by "Capability" Brown, offers many lovely walks.

WELLS (83 C2)
SOMERSET *pop. 9,400*
Wells is an ancient settlement in a valley between the Mendip Hills to the north, and the plains to the south. The narrow, twisting streets and the aged buildings create a medieval atmosphere.
Make an excursion to the great caves of Wookey Hole, 2 miles northeast.

CATHEDRAL OF ST. ANDREW is the third church to be erected on the site, and dates from the 12th to 14th century. The church is noted for its carvings of angels, prophets and saints, considered some of the best of their kind in England.

WESTERHAM (82 D2)
KENT *pop. 3,400*

CHARTWELL, 2 miles southeast off the B2026, is the home in which Winston Churchill spent the happiest years of his private life. Many of his mementos and paintings can be seen.

WESTON-SUPER-MARE (83 B2)
SOMERSET *pop. 66,600*

CHEDDAR GORGE, 10 miles southeast, is a ravine enclosed by 450-foot limestone outcrops. A series of caverns includes stalagmites, stalactites and deep lakes.

WIGHT, ISLE OF (83 C1)
pop. 125,000

The Isle of Wight, 23 miles long and 13 miles wide, lies a mile off the southern coast of England. Its 147 square miles encompass towns, lush vegetation, rolling farmlands and craggy cliffs.

Newport is the capital and chief town. Cowes is a principal port and center for sailing and yachting. Osborne House at East Cowes was Queen Victoria's residence at the time of her death in 1901.

Carisbrooke, the old island capital, has a 12th-century castle built on the site of a Saxon fort. Freshwater Peninsula, on the western end of the island, is marked by the Needles, three huge chalk pinnacles rising from the water.

Other resorts are Ryde, Sandown, Ventnor and Yarmouth.

WINCHCOMBE (83 C3)
GLOUCESTERSHIRE *pop. 4,100*

SUDELEY CASTLE AND GARDENS, ½ mile southeast off A46, date from the 12th and 15th centuries. The castle is the former home of Catherine Parr and Charles I.

WINCHESTER (83 C2)
HAMPSHIRE *pop. 35,600*

Winchester was the capital and regional seat of government under the Romans,

Saxons, Danes and Normans until William the Conqueror moved his court to London. Kings and princes, including Alfred the Great and Edward the Confessor, were crowned or buried in Winchester.

WINCHESTER CASTLE preserves the 13th-century Great Hall, with a table once said to be King Arthur's Round Table.

WINCHESTER CATHEDRAL is surpassed only by Westminster Abbey as the shrine of royalty. The present cathedral was built sometime after the Norman Conquest, but investigation has revealed evidence of earlier cathedrals. The writer Jane Austen is buried here.

WINCHESTER COLLEGE, College Street, is one of the oldest public schools in England and has been largely unaltered since its founding in 1382.

WILLIAM WORDSWORTH
The famous poet was born in Cockermouth in 1770. His childhood here influenced his poetry in later life. He lived from 1799 to 1808 at Dove Cottage in Grasmere, following a life of plain living and high thinking, with his wife Mary and sister Dorothy. He is appropriately buried in Grasmere churchyard.

WINDERMERE (82 C5)
CUMBRIA *pop. 8,000*

Windermere lies at the foot of Orrest Head beside the largest lake in England, Lake Windermere.

A region of extremes and contrasts, the surrounding area has some of the best scenery in the English Lakeland, immortalized by William Wordsworth.

WINDSOR (83 D2) ★
BERKSHIRE *pop. 31,500*

The Victorian riverside town of Windsor owes its fame to the great royal castle. The history of the immediate region, however, is traceable for centuries prior to King William I's establishment of the royal dwelling. Saxon kings maintained a palace in Windsor, and the Romans built a fortress.

ASCOT, located south of Windsor Great Park, is the site of the famous racecourse. The Royal Ascot meeting, initiated by Queen Anne in 1711, is held in late June.

ETON COLLEGE, at the end of High Street, is a prestigious public school, founded in 1440 by Henry VI. Many politicians and statesmen attended this school. Much of the original atmosphere is maintained; the Early English chapel retains rare Flemish-style murals, and the cloisters date from the 16th century.

THORPE PARK, 7 miles southwest, combines fun with history in a lake and parkland setting. The theme park has over 70 attractions, and there are exhibits on the achievements of Britons from the Stone Age to the Norman invasion. Lessons in waterskiing and sailboarding are also available.

WINDSOR CASTLE, the royal residence, is set on the 4,800-acre Great Park and represents every major stage in the history of English architecture. Aside from its historic and architectural importance, it is a veritable museum of fine furnishings and artwork. In November 1992 a fire caused extensive damage that resulted in major renovation.

WOODSTOCK (83 C2)
OXFORDSHIRE pop. 2,800
BLENHEIM PALACE, off A44, is the estate given by the nation to John Churchill, 1st Duke of Marlborough, in gratitude for his victory at Blenheim in 1704. Sir John Vanbrugh designed the stately palace, which is surrounded by a beautiful 2,000-acre park. Displays include the iron bed in which Churchill was born. His burial place is in the village churchyard of Bladon, south of the park.

WORCESTER (82 C3)
WORCESTERSHIRE
pop. 80,000
An old city on the Severn River, Worcester is an industrial center noted for glove-making and porcelain. The town might be best-known for the sauce that takes its name.

WORCESTER CATHEDRAL, dating from the 11th to 14th centuries, was begun by Bishop Wulfstan on a much older site and built in the shape of a double cross. The sandstone structure contains a number of chapels and the tomb of King John.

SIR EDWARD ELGAR
(1857–1934)

Elgar's musical education was derived mainly from his experience as a violin player, as a singer at the church where his father was an organist, and from browsing the scores in his father's music shop in Worcester. Elgar's early works were recognized only locally, but his international reputation was assured when Richard Strauss acclaimed the popular *Enigma Variations* (1899). Then the *Pomp and Circumstances Marches* (1901–30) won widespread popularity. His music epitomizes Edwardian England in its nostalgic qualities.

ELGAR'S BIRTHPLACE MUSEUM, 3 miles west off A44 at Crown East Lane, Lower Broadheath, is the cottage where British composer Sir Edward Elgar was born in 1857. Inside are scores, photographs, letters and other memorabilia.

YEOVIL (83 C2)
SOMERSET pop. 38,000
MONTACUTE HOUSE, 4 miles west, is an Elizabethan mansion completed in 1601. It includes collections of china, old glass, Jacobean and Tudor portraits, tapestries and paneling. There is also a Jacobean garden and a landscaped park.

▲ YORK (82 D4) ★

NORTH YORKSHIRE *pop. 100,00*

York, on the Ouse River, remains remarkably complete as a fort town of the Middle Ages; The Shambles and Stonegate are among the best-preserved medieval streets in Europe. Four medieval bars, or gates, lead through walls that stretch for 3 miles around the city. A walk on the rampart walls evokes the time when Constantine the Great was proclaimed emperor in York; the town was then a Roman fortress known as *Eboracum.*

In the 8th century, York became the northern ecclesiastical capital and gained world acclaim as a learning center under Alcuin, an English scholar. With its outstanding cathedral and other churches, the city ranks second only to Canterbury in ecclesiastical importance. The curfew bell of St. Michael's has tolled nightly, with few exceptions, since 1066.

In addition to its medieval and half-timbered houses and fine churches, York possesses the Georgian mansions Micklegate House and Bootham School. Young's Hotel, a charming old inn near the cathedral, is the birthplace of Guy Fawkes, who created a stir in 1605 by trying to blow up Parliament.

For additional information about the city contact the Tourist Information Center, De Grey Rooms, Exhibition Square, York, North Yorkshire YO1 2HB; tel: 01904 621756.

BENINGBROUGH HALL, 6½ miles northwest off A19, is an early 18th-century house that features a fine hall, staircase, friezes and paneling.

CASTLE HOWARD, lying 14 miles northeast was built between 1699 and 1726. The great domed mansion contains exhibits of china, furniture and paintings, as well as an extensive collection of 18th- to 20th-century clothing. The Temple of the Four Winds, by architect John Vanbrugh, and a mausoleum are also on the grounds.

CASTLE MUSEUM, housed in an old prison on Tower Street, next to Clifford's Tower, has reconstructions of period streets, parks, interiors and costumes. Of special note is the extensive display devoted to past Yorkshire regiments; exhibited are uniforms, swords, rifles, medals and ceremonial artifacts. There is also a collection of toys, domestic items and a corn mill to be viewed.

JORVIK VIKING CENTRE, Coppergate, is a former Viking settlement site uncovered by archaeologists. Visitors board "time cars" at a platform and watch the 20th century recede as they descend to a Viking city re-created beneath modern York. The authentic 10th-century buildings have been reconstructed on the sites where they were found.

YORK MINSTER, whose three towers dominate the entire city, is the largest medieval cathedral in England. Built over a period of 250 years and completed in the 15th century, it is an intriguing jumble of architectural styles. The present church is the third on the site since the early 7th century. Exhibits show models of the Roman, Anglo-Saxon and Norman structures once present.

Also displayed in the minster are the gold, silver and jewelry of the Minster treasury. The Great East Window and 128 other stained-glass windows are outstanding, with the *Five Sisters* considered the loveliest.

YORKSHIRE MUSEUM AND GARDENS, Museum Street, displays some of the finest Roman, Anglo-Saxon, Viking and medieval treasures found in Britain. It is set in 10 acres of botanical gardens containing a section of the Roman city wall, observatory and the ruins of a medieval abbey and its guesthouse.

THE YORK STORY, at the Heritage Centre at Castlegate, is devoted to the social and architectural aspects of York. There are exhibits, artwork, films and craft demonstrations.

- AREA: 5,463 square miles
- POPULATION: 1,578,000
- CAPITAL: Belfast
- LANGUAGE: English
- ECONOMY: Agriculture, industry, tourism.
- PASSPORT REQUIREMENTS: *See England*
- VISA REQUIREMENTS: *See England*
- DUTY-FREE ITEMS: *See England*
- CURRENCY: *See England*
- BANK OPENING HOURS: 9:30am–4:30pm Monday–Friday.
- STORE OPENING HOURS: 9am–5:30pm Monday–Saturday (to 9pm Thursday in Belfast). In some areas stores close on Wednesday afternoon.
- BEST BUYS: Linen, damask, lace, Belleek porcelain, Irish whiskey. Note: An export license is required to export any antique valued at more than £35,000.
- PUBLIC HOLIDAYS: January 1 (or closest weekday); March 17 (St. Patrick's Day); Good Friday; Easter Monday and Tuesday; first Monday in May (May Day); last Monday in May (Spring Bank Holiday); July 12 (Orangeman's Day); last monday in August (Late Summer Holiday); December 25, or closest weekday; December 26, or closest weekday.
- NATIONAL TOURIST OFFICES:
  Northern Ireland Tourist Board
  Suite 701, 551 Fifth Avenue
  New York
  NY 10176-0799
  Tel: 212/922-0101
  Fax: 212/922-0099
  Northern Ireland Tourist Board
  St Anne's Court
  59 North Street
  Belfast, BT1 1NB
  Tel: 01232 231221
  Fax: 01232 240960
- AMERICAN CONSULATE:
  Queen's House
  14 Queen Street
  Belfast, BT1 6ER
  Tel: 01232 328239 or 242520
  Fax: 01232 248482

NORTHERN IRELAND

HISTORY

After more than 25 years of troubles, Northern Ireland is, at time of writing, experiencing an uneasy peace. The Provisional Irish Republican Army (I.R.A.) and its political wing Sinn Fein both agreed to a ceasefire in the summer of 1997 in order to participate in all-party talks as to the future of the province.

Political and social turmoil has historically been a feature of life in the six counties known as Ulster. The political division of Ireland by an act of the British government in 1920 was not an unexpected move. As far back as the 12th century, colonies of English and Scottish settlers were "planted" in the fertile areas around the ancient province of Ulster. But it was the confiscation and redistribution by Oliver Cromwell in 1650 of some 750,000 acres of Catholic land that laid the foundation for strife in future centuries.

With a population more than two-thirds Protestant, and resisting any form of Irish Catholic control, the six counties of Northern Ireland chose self-government within the United Kingdom when Ireland became an independent republic in 1922. Protestant control of the government meant the Catholics had virtually no political or economic power. Belfast became the home of vast shipyards and engineering works – resulting in a larger, more diverse economic base than that enjoyed by citizens of the agrarian-based republic.

The Catholic minority of Ulster, however, gained little from this union with Britain. Over time, economic disparity led to a shift in attitude within the Catholic community, with a growing emphasis on full and equal rights as British citizens rather than the previous insistence on a united Ireland.

Violent clashes between civil rights marchers and Unionist extremists in 1968 set the stage for more militant postures from both the I.R.A., who were defending the Catholic minority, and the Ulster Volunteer Force and Ulster Defence Association, who were in support of the Protestant majority.

The situation grew even more volatile with the decision by the Unionist government to institute internment of I.R.A. members without trial. Terrorism increased, fierce rioting took place in Belfast and Londonderry, and the Catholic population (both in Northern Ireland and the Irish Republic) joined in their rejection of the government and the demand for a united Ireland. In 1969, the British army was dispatched to Northern Ireland to act as a peacekeeping force.

A significant blow to any peaceful solution came in 1972. Increased tension and violence from all the various factions culminated in the killing of 13 civil rights protesters in what became known as "Bloody Sunday." Within a few weeks, Britain suspended Northern Ireland's parliament and imposed direct rule.

On August 31, 1994, the I.R.A. announced a ceasefire. The British military presence in the province was substantially reduced. After two years of talks, however, instances of violence resumed, especially in sensitive areas, and particularly during the traditional Protestant "marching" season of July and August. At the time of going to press there is a new ceasefire; but due to the fragile political situation it may be advisable to check with local authorities before traveling. Be aware that travel intineraries may be affected by demonstrations and security alerts.

Sports and Recreation
Golfers will find some 80 courses to

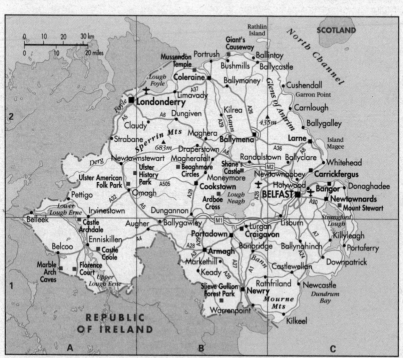

tempt them, including championship links at Newcastle and Portrush. Belfast and Londonderry boast museums, theaters, stores and historic monuments. The countryside, dotted with castles and legend-haunted sites, is equally enticing. Fishing and boating enthusiasts flock to the lakes and rivers. Horseback riding through the countryside is popular, while forests, lakes and unspoiled stretches of coast delight nature lovers.

TIPPING

A gratuity charge is usually included in the restaurant check, otherwise a tip of 10 percent is customary.

PRINCIPAL TOURING AREAS

Note: For descriptions of attractions in **bold type**, see individual listings.

Conveniently, a coast road provides an easy means of visiting most of County Antrim's attractions. The scenic drive starts in **Belfast** and skirts Belfast Lough to the coast proper. The Coast Road itself originates at **Larne**, a seaside resort and terminus of ferry crossings from Scotland.

Continuing north, the road passes headlands, bays and coastal towns. Some of

---

AUTOMOBILE CLUBS
The Automobile Association (AA) has an office at Fanum House, 108 Great Victoria Street, Belfast. **The Royal Automobile Club** (RAC) has an office at RAC House, 79 Chichester Street, Belfast. Not all auto clubs offer full travel services to AAA members.

these small resorts are good bases for traveling inland to the Glens of Antrim – sheltered valleys of woods and waterfalls. Farther north is Ballycastle, and not far away is the **Giant's Causeway**. One of the country's best-known tourist sites is not even near the coast; Lough Neagh is a 153-square-mile lake that County Antrim shares with four other counties.

West is County Londonderry, with an expansive coast. Its principal town, **Londonderry,** is the second largest in the province and a tourist destination.

South of County Londonderry is County Tyrone, the largest but least populous of the six counties. Dominating the region are the wild moorland summits of the Sperrins. The road leading from Newtonstewart to Draperstown is a good way to see these lonely heights.

In the far southwest lies pretty County Fermanagh, best known for its lakeland. The historic county town of **Enniskillen** is the starting point of a 57-mile circuit around Lough Erne, the largest of County Fermanagh's lakes.

Smallest of the six counties is County Armagh, noted for its fruit orchards, roses and fine, old towns. The chief attraction in the county is the town of **Armagh,** with an ecclesiastical history stretching far back into the Irish past.

County Down is known for its scenery, particularly for the Mountains of Mourne, which in the words of a well-known song "sweep down to the sea."

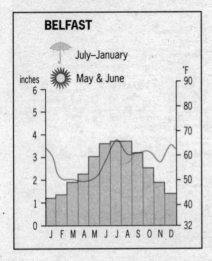

BELFAST

July–January

May & June

inches

6
5
4
3
2
1
0

°F
90
80
70
60
50
40
32

J F M A M J J A S O N D

PLACES OF INTEREST

▲ BELFAST ★
BELFAST *pop. 416,700*

The capital of Northern Ireland, Belfast is a modern city situated in a district of mountains, loughs and rivers. Built on the linen and shipbuilding industries, it has a unique character and an impressive industrial past; it was here that the *Titanic* was built.

For additional tourist information contact the Tourist Information Centre, St. Anne's Court, 59 North Street, Belfast, Co. Antrim BT1 1NB; tel: 01232 246609.

ALBERT MEMORIAL CLOCK TOWER, one of Belfast's most familiar sites, it was erected in 1865 by William Barre, in memory of Albert Prince Consort of Queen Victoria.

BELFAST CASTLE, Antrim Road, is a handsome edifice built in 1870 by the 3rd Marquis of Donegal in the Scottish fortified-house style. Presented to the city in 1934, it was restored and is now open to the public. It stands on the wooded Cave Hill slopes, and is part of the 200-acre Belfast Castle Estate.

BELFAST ZOOLOGICAL GARDENS, Antrim Road, is a 50-acre award-winning zoo, set on the side of Cave Hill. Attractions include the primate house, penguin enclosure, African enclosure and free-flight aviary.

BOTANIC GARDENS, Stranmillis Road, is a 38-acre park on the south side of the city, containing the Ulster Museum. It also has a Tropical Ravine and the Palm House, a glass house that predates the one in Kew Gardens in London; this is one of the earliest curved-glass and iron structures in the world.

CITY HALL, in Donegall Square, is marked by a copper dome, Portland stone façade and sculptured pediment. Inside is a fresco depicting the city's history. The grounds contain statues and monuments including a memorial to the *Titanic*, which was built in Belfast.

CROWN LIQUOR SALOON, Great Victoria Street, is a splendidly ornate, gaslit Victorian pub now in the care of the National Trust. Its interior is all tiles, mirrors, marbles and paneled booths.

LINEN HALL LIBRARY, Donegall Square, was founded in 1788 and is housed in the Old White Linen Hall. It has a fine collection of volumes in its old-fashioned interior.

ULSTER MUSEUM, Botanic Gardens, is a nationally important museum and art gallery. Permanent displays include The Dinosaur Show, Made in Belfast and Early Ireland. There is also a program of temporary exhibitions.

QUEEN'S UNIVERSITY, University Road, was built in the 1840s in a similar style to Oxford University in England, with spires and turrets.

ST. ANNE'S CATHEDRAL, Donegall Street, is the city's Anglican cathedral; an austere neo-Romanesque structure, enlivened inside by mosaics.

ST. MALACHY'S CHURCH, Alfred Street, was built in 1844. This Roman Catholic church has a plain red-brick exterior disguising an interior of glorious plasterwork.

BELFAST'S SHIPYARDS

In 1859 Belfast had the largest shipyards in the United Kingdom. It was here that the most famous of all the world's ocean-going liners, the ill-fated *Titanic*, was built. Now sadly in decline, the city's industrial past is recalled by the two enormous yellow cranes that dominate the dockland skyline.

BRITAIN · NORTHERN IRELAND

★ **HIGHLIGHTS** ★

Belfast (see p.133)
Giant's Causeway (see p.135)
Larne (see p.135)
Ulster-American (see p.135)
Folk Park

ARMAGH (131 B1)
CO. ARMAGH *pop. 12,700*
Capital of the county, Armagh has been the ecclesiastical center of Ireland since the 5th century. Today it is the seat of both Protestant and Roman Catholic archbishoprics and has two cathedrals. Navan Fort, 2 miles west, is an important prehistoric site, with a center nearby that portrays its history.

ST. PATRICK'S CATHEDRALS, crown hills, on opposite sides of the city. Sections of the Protestant cathedral date from the 8th century. The Roman Catholic cathedral was completed in 1873.

BALLINTOY (131 B2)
CO. ANTRIM *pop. 200*
The striking white tower of Ballintoy parish church dominates this village, which lies between Knocksaughey and the sea. A winding road leaving the harbor takes drivers past a house of cubes built by a Belfast artist.

CARRICK-A-REDE ROPE BRIDGE, spanning a 60-foot wide chasm, is a swinging bridge originally built by salmon fishermen. Traditionally the bridge only had one handrail, but even with the second rail, crossing the bridge, 80 feet above sea level, requires courage and care.

To satisfy a 300-year-old tradition, the bridge is erected every year at Easter and dismantled in the fall. It is a National Trust property.

BALLYGALLEY (131 C2)
CO. ANTRIM *pop. 400*
Ballygalley, a little seaside town, is in a good location for exploring the Glens of Antrim. It offers opportunities for golf, tennis, yachting, swimming and fishing.

BANGOR (131 C2)
CO. DOWN *pop. 46,600*
Once the site of one of Europe's great monastic schools (the history of which is traced in the North Down Heritage Centre), Bangor is popular for its fine beaches. Ward Park offers a nature trail, a children's zoo and sports facilities; Castle Park features an arboretum, and there is a museum of childhood.

BUSHMILLS (131 B2)
CO. ANTRIM *pop. 1,400*
The two mills that give the town its name can be seen on the River Bush.

OLD BUSHMILLS DISTILLERY, said to be the world's first licensed distillery, was founded in 1608. Tours of the distillery and its visitor center are available.

DOWNPATRICK (131 C1)
CO. DOWN *pop. 8,200*
St. Patrick is reputed to have been buried at Downpatrick, in the grounds of the cathedral. The site where St. Patrick built his first church in Ireland, in AD 432, is in nearby Saul.

ENNISKILLEN (131 A1)
CO. FERMANAGH *pop. 10,400*
Enniskillen is an island town between two channels of the Erne River. Enniskillen Castle embraces the Water Gate, a 17th-century, turreted, fairy-tale building on the Erne River; the barracks, a square of massive 18th- and 19th-century buildings; and Maguire's Castle, a three-storey keep. The keep houses the Fermanagh County Museum and Regimental Museum.

FLORENCE COURT, 8 miles southwest, is a fine Georgian house built by John Coles, father of the first Earl of Enniskillen. The house is noted for its rococo plasterwork.

MARBLE ARCH CAVES, 12 miles southwest off the A4 Enniskillen–Sligo Road, is one of Europe's most prominent historic limestone cave systems.

LARNE (131 C2) ★
CO. ANTRIM *pop. 18,200*
Larne is an ideal base for touring the magnificent Antrim Coast Road and the Glens of Antrim. The Mountains of Mourne and the Ulster Lakeland District are both less than a 2-hour drive from Larne.

LONDONDERRY (131 A2)
CO. LONDONDERRY *pop. 62,700*
Derry, the widely accepted, older name of Londonderry, comes from the Irish *doire*, a place of oaks. The area has been the site of repeated conflicts since an abbey was built by St. Columba in AD 546. Derry was renamed by the City of London, at whose expense the town was rebuilt and its protective walls erected in the early 15th century.

CITY WALLS were built in 1617. Averaging 20 feet in height and thickness, they have survived three attacks and nearly four centuries. Their protection has given Derry the title of "Maiden City." Platforms, monuments and cannon surmount the walls.

NEWCASTLE (131 C1)
CO. DOWN *pop. 6,200*
Newcastle is a small seaside resort on the west end of Dundrum Bay, where the Mountains of Mourne sweep down to the sea. The Royal County Down Golf Course, one of the best in Britain, stretches along the seafront at the northern end of town.

DUNDRUM CASTLE, 4 miles north, is a 12th-century fortification built by John de Courcy. Noted for its round keep, the castle is very well-preserved.

NEWTOWNARDS (131 C2)
CO. DOWN *pop. 20,500*
MOUNT STEWART HOUSE AND GARDEN, 5 miles southeast, was the home of the Marquesses of Londonderry, of whom Lord Castlereagh is best-known.
The house is filled with a stunning collection of family treasures, including *Hambletonian*, one of George Stubbs' most celebrated paintings.

OMAGH (131 A2)
CO. TYRONE *pop. 14,600*
OMAGH MELLON HOUSE AND ULSTER-AMERICAN FOLK PARK ★, 5 miles northwest, is an outdoor museum that tells the story of Ulster's link with the United States. The park is centered on the ancestral home of the Mellon family, who were founders of the Mellon Bank of Pittsburgh. Costumed guides demonstrate traditional crafts, including horseshoeing in a reconstructed forge.

PORTRUSH (131 B2)
CO. ANTRIM *pop. 5,100*
Portrush is a popular seaside town above basalt cliffs. Its golf course and coastal rock formations are world-renowned.

GIANT'S CAUSEWAY ★, 7 miles east, consists of more than 40,000 basalt columns formed millions of years ago from cooling lava. The pillars are to be found in peculiar groupings often resembling such objects as an organ and a cannon.

PRESIDENTIAL LINKS
A dozen Americans of Ulster stock have made it to the White House, 11 as presidents. Some of the more memorable are Andrew Jackson; Ulysses S. Grant; Woodrow Wilson, whose ancestral home is at Dergalt near Strabane; and Theodore Roosevelt, whose family came from Antrim.

STRABANE (131 A2)
CO. TYRONE *pop. 9,300*
The second largest town in Co. Tyrone, below the Mourne River, Strabane is of considerable historic interest. Gray's Print Shop, where John Dunlap, printer of the American Declaration of Independence, was apprenticed, is on the main street. President Woodrow Wilson's ancestral home is a few miles away.

THINGS TO KNOW

- **AREA**: 30,405 square miles
- **POPULATION**: 5,094,000
- **CAPITAL**: Edinburgh
- **LANGUAGES**: English and Gaelic
- **ECONOMY**: Agriculture, mining, whisky distilling.
- **PASSPORT REQUIREMENTS**: *See England*
- **VISA REQUIREMENTS**: *See England*
- **DUTY-FREE ITEMS**: *See England*
- **CURRENCY**: The currency unit is the Scottish pound (£), equal in value to the English pound. Currencies of the two countries are generally interchangeable, although many stores in England do not accept Scottish pounds (banks will). *See England.*
- **BANK OPENING HOURS**: 9am–4pm Monday–Friday. Hours may vary; some banks may be open Saturday morning.
- **STORE OPENING HOURS**: 9am–6pm Monday–Saturday (to 7:30 or 8:30pm Thursday in some larger towns); some sstores close one afternoon at 1pm.
- **BEST BUYS**: Tweeds, woolens, silks from Paisley and Glasgow, Scotch whisky. **Note:** If the purchase is an antique valued at over £35,000, an export license is required to take it out of the country.
- **PUBLIC HOLIDAYS**: January 1 or closest weekday day; Good Friday; first Monday in May (May Day); last Monday in May (Spring Bank Holiday); first Monday in August (Summer Holiday); December 25 or closest weekday; December 26 or closest weekday.
- **NATIONAL TOURIST OFFICES**: British Tourist Authority (B.T.A.) Suite 701, 51 Fifth Avenue New York, NY 10176-0799 Tel: 212 /986-2200; fax: 212/9860-1188 Scottish Tourist Board 23 Ravelston Terrace Edinburgh EH4 3EU, Scotland Tel: 0131 332 2433; fax: 0131 343 1513
- **AMERICAN CONSULATE**: 3 Regent Terrace Edinburgh EH7 5BW, Scotland Tel: 0131 556 8315

SCOTLAND

HISTORY

By the 7th century AD, the Picts, Scots, Britons and Angles had formed distinct tribal kingdoms in the parts of the island that are today represented by northern England, Scotland and Wales. The emergence of a kingdom of Scotland in the 11th century led to a period of fractious relations with the English monarchy. The death of the last legitimate Scottish heir 250 years later left the country struggling to maintain a separate identity. Robert Bruce, crowned king in 1306, was ultimately successful and independence was recognized by the Treaty of Northampton in 1328. Scottish autonomy was doomed however, for in 1567 Mary, Queen of Scots, was forced to abdicate her throne. Upon the death of Elizabeth I, Mary's son James ascended to the English throne, bringing the two countries together under one crown.

THE LOVER OF MARY, QUEEN OF SCOTS

James Hepburn, Earl of Bothwell, was the lover of Mary, Queen of Scots, the possible father of James VI of Scotland (James I of England), and the murderer of Darnley, the queen's second husband. He then divorced his wife and secretly married the queen at Dunbar Castle in 1567. The lovers were forced to part after continued pressure from enemies, and Bothwell was imprisoned in the Danish Castle of Dragsholm, where he died insane.

The 1707 Act of Union formally united England and Scotland as Great Britain. The Scots gained representation in Parliament and control of their church and legal system, but sacrificed their autonomy in many other respects. The peace did not last long. In 1714 Queen Anne of Great Britain died, ending the Stuart line with its Scottish ancestry.

Scotland's desire to restore the Stuarts to power resulted in failed rebellions in 1715 and 1745. England retaliated with the Act of Proscription, outlawing many aspects of the native Highland culture. Although the act was subsequently repealed in 1782, the face of Scotland was changed permanently.

The Industrial Revolution in Scotland began in the early 19th century. It saw the majority of the population shift to the Central Lowlands and the new culture of an industrial economy. This led to the emergence of the labor movement as a political force in the 1880s. Scotland played an important industrial role in World War I, but swift and uncontrolled growth resulted in a severe depression at the war's end. The crisis encouraged the rise of liberalism and the organization of the Scottish National Party in 1934. It was under a Conservative government, however, that the country's administration was returned to Edinburgh in 1939.

A strong nationalistic pride continues to develop in Scotland, but has been slow to gain momentum in the political arena. The Scottish National Party nevertheless continues to campaign for an independent state of Scotland.

FOOD AND DRINK
Scottish fare is one tradition that has survived, although English dishes are found throughout Scotland. *Finnan haddie* and *Arbroath smokie*, smothered in butter or cream, head the fish menu; they are most properly enjoyed at breakfast, along with the traditional porridge. Haggis is not an elusive three-legged animal, as canny Scots would have you believe, but a spicy mixture of chopped meat and oatmeal cooked in a sheep's stomach. A specialty of the Isle of Skye is the *partan*, or crab, which is made into pies. Equally intriguing is late-afternoon high tea, in which the beverage is accompanied by assortments of baps, bannocks, scones, shortbreads and other pastry surprises. Best remembered by many visitors, however, is a product born of the thrifty tradition of mashing surplus barley – Scotch whisky. A visit to one of the many distilleries is perhaps the best way to appreciate this native liquor. As cafés can be few and far between on the road, it is common practice to ask your hotel to pack a lunch for traveling.

SPORTS AND RECREATION
Geographically, Scotland can boast that it has something for everyone. The mountains, lochs and rivers attract mountain climbers, fishermen, hikers and walkers. Classic salmon streams include the Tweed, Tay, Dee and Spey. The sport of golf, as we know it today, originated in Scotland. As a result, some of the oldest and most prestigious courses in the world are in this country – among them St. Andrews, Turnberry, Troon, Gleneagles and Carnoustie.

Other sports have a home in Scotland, also – horseback riding is popular around Callander and Aberfoyle, and mountain climbing in the Highlands can provide a challenge even to experienced climbers. A network of hiking trails and hostels allows the hardy to penetrate Scotland's more remote countryside. Skiing is popular at Glencoe, Braemar and Aviemore. Aviemore also offers swimming, skating, racket ball, movie theaters and discos.

GETTING AROUND
The *Scotrail Rover* pass gives unlimited travel on Scottish railways on any 4 days during a period of 8 consecutive days, or for any 12 out of a period of 15 consecutive days. In addition, there are *Area Rover* passes covering specified regions of Scotland for rail travel on 3 out of 7, or 4 out of 8 days. For further information, contact National Rail Enquiries, tel: 0345 4849.

Historic Scotland and the National Trust for Scotland offer passes which allow entry to their properties for a discounted price.

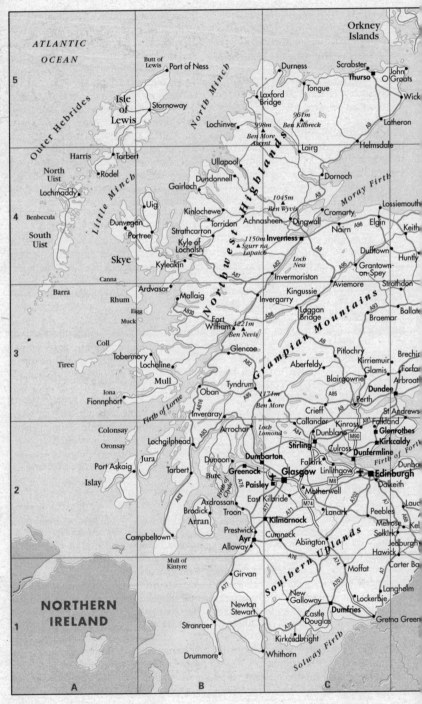

ATLANTIC
OCEAN

Orkney
Islands

Butt of
Lewis
Port of Ness
Durness
Scrabster
Thurso
John
O'Groats
Wick

Isle
of
Lewis
Stornoway
North Minch
Lochinver
998m
Ben More
Assynt
961m
Ben Kilbreck
Lairg
Tongue
Laxford
Bridge
Helmsdale
Latheron

Harris
Tarbert
North
Uist
Rodel
Little Minch
Gairloch
Ullapool
Dundonnell
1045m
Ben Wyvis
Dingwall
Cromarty
Moray Firth
Lossiemouth
Elgin
Keith

Lochmaddy
Benbecula
South
Uist
Uig
Dunvegan
Portree
Skye
Kyle of
Lochalsh
Kyleakin
Kinlochewe
Torridon
Strathcarron
Achnasheen
1150m
Sgurr na
Lapaich
Inverness
Loch
Ness
Nairn
A96
Dufftown
Grantown-
on-Spey
Huntly
Strathdon

Canna
Ardvasar
Mallaig
A87
Invermoriston
Kingussie
Invergarry
Aviemore
Ballate

Barra
Rhum
Eigg
Muck
A830
Fort
William
1221m
Ben Nevis
Laggan
Bridge
Grampian Mountains
Braemar

Coll
Tiree
Tobermory
Lochaline
Mull
Glencoe
Aberfeldy
Pitlochry
Kirriemuir
Glamis
Brechir
Forfar
Arbroath

Iona
Fionnphort
Oban
Tyndrum
1174m
Ben More
Firth of Lorne
Inveraray
Crieff
Blairgowrie
Dundee
Perth
St Andrews

Colonsay
Oronsay
Lochgilphead
Arrochar
Loch
Lomond
Callander
Dunblane
Kinross
Falkland
Glenrothes
Kirkcaldy

Jura
Tarbert
Dunoon
Dumbarton
Stirling
Culross
Dunfermline

Port Askaig
Islay
Bute
Greenock
Paisley
Glasgow
Falkirk
Linlithgow
Firth of Forth
Edinburgh
Dunba

Ardrossan
Saltcoats
Troon
East Kilbride
M74
Motherwell
Lanark
Dalkeith
A7
Laud

Bradick
Arran
Prestwick
Kilmarnock
Cumnock
Abington
Peebles
Melrose
Selkirk
Jedburgh
Kel

Campbeltown
Mull of
Kintyre
Ayr
Alloway
Girvan
Southern Uplands
Moffat
Hawick
Carter Ba
Langholm

NORTHERN
IRELAND
Newton
Stewart
New
Galloway
Castle
Douglas
Dumfries
Lockerbie
Gretna Green

Stranraer
Drummore
Kirkcudbright
Whithorn
Solway Firth

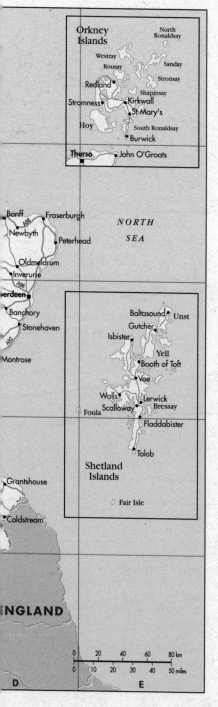

AUTOMOBILE CLUBS
The Automobile Association (AA) has an office at Fanum House, Erskine Harbour, Erskine, Glasgow.
The **Royal Scottish Automobile Club** (RSAC) has an office at 11 Blythswood Square, Glasgow. The symbol ▲ indicates the presence of a AAA-affiliated automobile club branch. Not all autoclubs offer full travel services to AAA members.

PRINCIPAL TOURING AREAS

Note: For descriptions of attractions in **bold type**, see individual listings.

HIGHLANDS AND ISLANDS

Scotland's Highlands are minuscule alongside the world's great mountains, but the peaks are nevertheless impressive, for they share the landscape with a wild sea, tumbling streams and peaceful inland lochs. It is a lonely land, where members of the animal kingdom thrive: golden eagles and sea birds soar, wildcats and red deer roam the moors and forests, and salmon and trout abound in the streams.

The region of peaks, lochs and moors to the north of Glasgow and the Lowlands is best-known for its history. To the northwest across the Firth of Lorne lies **Mull**, a large island among the Inner Hebrides; to the north lies Stirling, with its imposing castle, and the Trossachs, a collection of lakes, streams and high hills that resound with tales of Rob Roy, a Scottish Robin Hood; the connection with Sir Walter Scott's lovely Lady of the Lake adds to the enchantment of this region. Golfers find **Perth**, in Perthshire and Kinross, attractive for the nearby Gleneagles courses.

Northeast, from **Dundee** to **Aberdeen**, lies a fertile land of farms, forests, rugged shores and small fishing ports. Inland, the Grampian Mountains form a majestic wall across the centre of Scotland with the lofty Cairngorms and the Monadhliaths to the north. The Highland Wildlife Park at Kincraig, 7 miles southwest of **Aviemore**, features many species of Highland wildlife.

The northeast coast along Moray Firth is often referred to as the Scottish Riviera, an indication of this region's vacation atmosphere. A principal magnet of the central Highlands is neither coast nor mountain, but a lake – long Loch Ness, part of the Great Glen across Scotland. According to folklore, a sea monster makes its home in the loch.

North and west of historic **Inverness** rise the loneliest and wildest lands in Britain, forming the tip of the Highland region. Scotland's north also includes its far-flung islands. Off the west coast are the Hebrides, where Gaelic is still the first language of most of the islanders. Once part of a vast Viking kingdom, the more distant **Orkneys** and **Shetlands** off the northeast coast bear a Nordic stamp.

LOWLANDS
Tradition dictates that the southern half of Scotland be called the Lowlands, although this region is low only in a relative sense. Composed of grassy hills and dales, the Lowlands are devoted largely to grain farming and sheep raising. Yet this portion of Scotland holds two-thirds of the population and virtually all of Scottish industry.

The southernmost region on the Solway Firth is known as Dumfries and Galloway. This area of few towns is the hilly home of red deer, curly-horned sheep and hardy Galloway cattle. Farther north, in South Ayrshire, the Firth of Clyde's shoreline is dotted with such seaside and golf resorts as **Ayr**, Ardrossan, Troon and Girvan. **Arran**, an island of glens, streams and lochs, rises in the firth.

West of the islands of Arran and **Bute** is the long Kintyre Peninsula. Close by are the islands of Islay and Jura.

Though the Firth of Clyde is edged by quiet towns and uncrowded beaches, it reaches inland to one of the largest and busiest cities in Britain – **Glasgow. The route alongside** Loch Lomond leads north from the city. The Southern Uplands to the south, where both the Tweed and Clyde rivers originate, are the green, hilly home of sheep. The Uplands have many great old houses and castles. On the Tweed River, **Peebles** is a small textile town specializing in, not surprisingly, the manufacture of tweeds and knitwear.

Northeast of Peebles is East Lothian. Manufacturing and market towns are typical of this region, but so are castle ruins and resorts. Here, too, is Scotland's capital, **Edinburgh**. Across the Firth of Forth lies the former Kingdom of Fife, with its fine old city of **St. Andrews**, where golf was invented; the Royal and Ancient Golf Club remains.

Southeast of Peebles are the Borders, where ruined abbeys, impressive houses and grim castles recall a long history of border warfare.

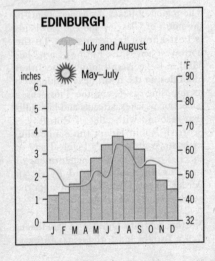

EDINBURGH

☂ July and August

☀ May–July

inches

	°F
6	90
5	80
4	70
3	60
2	50
1	40
0	32

J F M A M J J A S O N D

PLACES OF INTEREST

▲ **EDINBURGH** (138 C2) ★
CITY OF EDINBURGH DISTRICT
pop. 438,700
Edinburgh, the administrative and cultural capital of Scotland, rises from among the Lowland hills along the Firth of Forth. Though evidence suggests habitation as early as the Iron Age, the present city dates from the 11th-century reign of Malcolm II and Queen Margaret. The Middle Ages were times of continual fluctuation as the citizens fought invasion and poverty. As a result, Edinburgh's early development was greatly impeded.

Two walls were erected around the city, inhibiting expansion. The last, Flodden Wall, was built in a fearful reaction to the English victory at Flodden in 1513 and contained the city for almost 250 years. Crowded and confined as they were, 17th- and 18th-century residents built upward. Some structures reached 14 stories.

Not until the Act of Union in 1707 joined Scotland to its traditional enemy did the city begin to spread beyond its old boundaries. Edinburgh began to emerge as an intellectual capital of Europe. The golden age of the late 18th and early 19th centuries included such literary figures as James Boswell, Robert Burns and Sir Walter Scott, as well as philosopher David Hume and political economist Adam Smith.

Although today's Edinburgh has landscaped gardens and squares and busy thoroughfares, it still bears the stamp of its long and often grim history. This is particularly true of Old Town. Here, dominating the city from atop Castle Rock, is Edinburgh's oldest and most prominent survivor – the castle-fortress.

Between the castle and the gates of Holyroodhouse, the 16th-century palace associated with the ill-fated Stuarts, stretches the aptly named Royal Mile, the center of oldest Edinburgh. A walk down these ancient streets – Lawnmarket, High Street and Canongate – is like a promenade through the past.

Near St. Giles' Cathedral two relics mark historic sites: the Old Tolbooth and the Mercat Cross. A heart-shaped pattern in the street is all that remains of the Old Tolbooth, an ancient prison. At the Mercat Cross, townspeople gathered in 1513 to hear about the death of James IV and 10,000 Scots at Flodden.

Closer to the palace, in what was the separate burgh of Canongate, there are many restored 17th-century buildings. Beyond the Palace of Holyroodhouse, Edinburgh evolves into a vast park, out of which rises the 823-foot summit of Arthur's Seat, an extinct volcano that can be easily climbed for a panorama of the city and surrounding countryside. In the southern quarter of Old Town is Edinburgh University.

Though Old Town is of more historic interest, it is in New Town (characterized by Georgian architecture) that the heart of the city lies. Princes Street marks the division between the old and new and is the main thoroughfare. Stores, hotels, clubs and restaurants line its northern side, while its opposite side is formed by Princes Street Gardens.

A particularly enjoyable time to visit the city is during the Edinburgh International Festival, which takes place the last three weeks in August. The official program includes opera, ballet, symphony concerts, plays, movies and art exhibitions. On the unofficial Fringe program are numerous theatrical, musical and comedy events. The Military Tattoo, staged by Scottish regiments each evening (except Sundays) on the floodlit castle esplanade, ranks among Edinburgh's most spectacular events.

For further information on contact the Tourist Information Centre, Waverley Market, 3 Princes Street, Edinburgh EH2 2QP; tel: 0131-557 1700.

THE CASTLE (142 B1), Royal Mile, has been occupied by both Scottish and English rulers. Although it stands on a high strategic rock used as a fortress since the 7th century, reliable records date the castle from the 11th century. St. Margaret's Chapel (1076) is the oldest building.

Inside is the Crown Room, with the Honours of Scotland (the Scottish crown jewels) and the Stone of Scone – the Stone of Destiny on which Scottish kings were traditionally crowned (returned to Scotland in 1997). The Royal Apartments were where in 1566 Mary, Queen of Scots, gave birth to James VI. Though haunted from birth by the question of his legitimacy, the young prince first became the King of Scotland, then King James I of England.

On one side of the Castle Yard, the 16th-century Great Hall, with its former banquet rooms, now is an armory; below the hall are the Casemates, large vaulted rooms with ancient doors bearing the carved pictures and signatures of prisoners held during the Napoleonic Wars.

On the opposite side of the yard is the Scottish National War Memorial, commemorating the 100,000 Scots who died in World War II.

CITY ART CENTRE (143 C2), 2 Market Street, is the home of Edinburgh's permanent fine arts collection of 3,000 paintings, drawings, prints and sculptures, most of them by Scottish artists.

EDINBURGH ZOO, at the Scottish National Zoological Park, Corstorphine Road, is considered one of the finest zoos in Europe. Birds, reptiles and mammals are displayed on 80 acres of grounds which offer panoramic views.

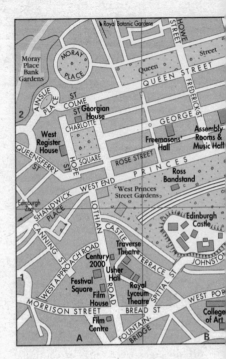

JOHN KNOX HOUSE (143 D2), 43–5 High Street, is a 15th- to 16th-century house built by a goldsmith to Mary, Queen of Scots.

The house is traditionally associated with John Knox, the preacher and reformer. Displays document the building and development of the house from the 15th century to the present.

MUSEUM OF ANTIQUITIES (143 C2), Queen Street, illustrates the history of Scotland from the Stone Age to the present.

NATIONAL GALLERY OF SCOTLAND (143 B2), The Mound, contains paintings by Scottish and European masters from the 14th to 19th centuries.

PALACE OF HOLYROODHOUSE (143 E2), surrounded by the Queen's Park, is the official Scottish residence of the Queen.

Begun during the 16th century by James IV, the palace was expanded and redecorated by succeeding royalty. Among its occupants were Bonnie

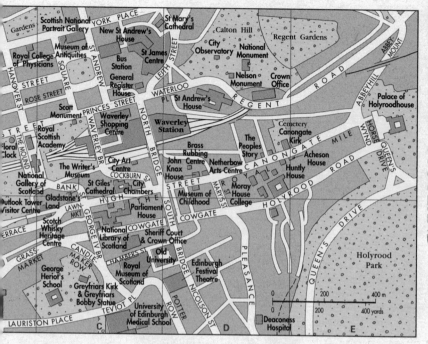

Prince Charlie, a resident in 1745 during his unsuccessful attempt to win the Crown, and Mary, Queen of Scots, who lived in the palace from 1561 to 1567.

The palace also was the scene of two historic events. It was here that in 1566 Queen Mary saw her secretary and alleged lover, David Rizzio, murdered by a group of nobles that included her consort Lord Darnley. In 1603 James VI learned of his succession to the English throne in the palace.

The Royal Apartments, the Throne Room and the present State Apartments, with their rich tapestries and period furnishings, are of particular interest.

Holyrood Abbey, next to the palace, was founded in 1128 by David I, who, according to legend, built it as a penance for hunting on a holy day.

On that day, on the site of the abbey, a miracle is said to have occurred as the king was about to be attacked by a stag. As he grabbed the animal by the antlers, it disappeared and was replaced by a Holy Cross – or Rood.

ROYAL BOTANIC GARDENS, Inverleith Row, originated in 1670 as a medicinal garden at Holyrood and was moved to its present site in 1820. The 70 acres of gardens include an arboretum.

ROYAL MUSEUM OF SCOTLAND (143 C1), Chambers Street, is ranked among the finest of Britain's museums. Its exhibits encompass decorative arts of the world, archaeology, ethnography, natural history and other sciences.

ST. GILES' CATHEDRAL (143 C2), Royal Mile, is the site where John Knox, leader of the Protestant Reformation, preached his fiery sermons, from 1559 to his death in 1572. Built in the 14th and 15th centuries, the church was greatly altered during the 16th-century Reformation and restored in the 19th century. A feature is the 15th-century spire.

SCOTT MONUMENT (143 C2), in East Princes Street Gardens, has a marble statue of the author at its base. Towering above is a 200-foot Gothic spire adorned by statuettes of characters from Sir Walter Scott's novels and poems.

SCOTTISH NATIONAL PORTRAIT GALLERY (143 C2), Queen Street, displays portraits of individuals who have contributed to Scottish history. These figures, which include royals, rebels, soldiers and writers, are portrayed in various media.

THE WRITER'S MUSEUM (143 C2), off Lawnmarket, is a 17th-century dwelling containing manuscripts and relics of literary greats Robert Burns, Sir Walter Scott and Robert Louis Stevenson.

ABERDEEN (139 D3) ★
ABERDEEN CITY *pop. 211,100*
The noble northern city of Aberdeen fairly bristles with history; its motto "Bon Accord" was the rallying cry of the ruling Bruce family.

A number of buildings in Aberdeen are of historical interest. The Church of St. Nicholas is largely a product of the Middle Ages, as is the castle-like St. Machar's Cathedral. The Mercat Cross in Castle Street and Provost Skene's House date from the 17th century; Provost Ross' House in Shiprow is a century older and houses the Aberdeen Maritime Museum.

A grim relic now incorporated into municipal buildings is the Old Tolbooth, the scene of public executions until 1857. A part of the tolbooth that remains is the "Maid of Aberdeen," said to have been the prototype of the guillotine. A statue of Lord Byron in front of Aberdeen Grammar School recalls that the poet attended the school 1794–98.

The Granite City, as Aberdeen is known, is on the coast and has three major industries – fishing, tourism and oil.

Aberdeen lies near the most "castled" part of Scotland. Between the Grampians and the coast, in the valleys of the Don, Dee and Ythan, are castles remarkable for their their variety. *Bouchmorale* is the Gaelic word meaning "majestic

dwelling," and Balmoral is just that in its role of summer residence for the British Royal Family. They have traditionally come to Balmoral each summer since 1853.

ABERDEEN MARITIME MUSEUM, Provost Ross's House, Shiprow, depicts the highlights of Aberdeen's maritime history through drama and pictures. The museum is housed in the third oldest building in Aberdeen.

CRAIGIEVAR CASTLE, 24 miles west, remains virtually unchanged since its construction in the 17th century. Its solid lower walls rise to a riot of turrets, gables and conical roofs. Inside are magnificent plaster ceilings.

CRATHES CASTLE AND GARDEN, 14 miles west, was finished in 1596 on land given to the Burnett family by Robert the Bruce. Inside are painted ceilings; outside are gardens with yew hedges planted in 1702.

PITMEDDEN GARDEN, 14 miles north, near the village of Udny, is a fine example of a 17th-century Great Garden. Its elaborate floral designs, fountains, pavilions and sundials are carefully arranged on four spacious parterres, three of which are based on designs once used at Holyrood Palace.

ARBROATH (138 D3)
ANGUS *pop. 24,500*
The pleasant odor of woodchip fires pervades Arbroath; this fishing port is the home of Scotland's "smokies," North Sea haddock smoked over oak fires. Arbroath is also a holiday destination, with a beach, seaside walks and a golf course; there is a world-renowned course 8 miles south at Carnoustie.

ARBROATH ABBEY, now in ruins, dates from the 12th century. It was the temporary hideaway of the Stone of Scone after the Coronation Stone's removal from Westminster in 1950.

ARRAN (138 B2)

NORTH AYRSHIRE *pop. 3,600*

Called "Scotland in Miniature," the island of Arran has sandy bays, glens and lochs, rolling hills and lofty ridges. Its caves have sheltered fugitive kings. Vacation resorts are Brodick, Machrie and Blackwaterfoot.

BRODICK CASTLE, GARDEN AND COUNTRY PARK, at Brodick, was built in 1456 as a residence for the Dukes of Hamilton. The 60-acre grounds enclose two gardens, one formal, dating from 1710, and the other a woodland with a notable display of rhododendrons.

AVIEMORE (138 C3) ★

HIGHLAND *pop. 2,400*

The Speyside village of Aviemore, lying at the foot of the Cairngorm Mountains, is a popular year-round vacation spot. A sports center in winter, it is a favorite base for hikers and mountain climbers during the summer months. Fishermen fish for salmon and trout in the Spey River, while boating enthusiasts take to nearby Loch Morlich.

The Aviemore Centre includes stores, restaurants, hotels, a theater, a concert hall, a swimming pool, an artificial ski slope and rinks for skating and curling. Scotland's Whisky Festival takes place in Aviemore in late November.

AYR (138 B2)

SOUTH AYRSHIRE *pop. 56,000*

Ayr is principal among the vacation towns and steamer ports that dot the coast along the Firth of Clyde. It also has connections with the poet Robert Burns. The Brig o' Doon of *Tam o' Shanter* fame still spans the river, as does the Auld Brig o' Ayr. Here also is Kirk Alloway, where the poet's father is buried.

Of non-literary interest in this Burnsian landscape are the granite cliffs, sand and shingle beaches and barren moorlands. Within a 20-mile radius of Ayr there are several standing castles and houses, as well as the ruins of many others – among them Blair House, Dunure, Dundonald and Seagate.

ALLOWAY is perhaps best-known as the birthplace of Scotland's national poet, Robert Burns.

Burns' Cottage is the thatched house where Robert Burns was born in 1759; it is now a museum. In the grounds is Burns' Monument, built in 1823.

CULZEAN CASTLE, 12 miles south on A719, is an enormous mock-Gothic mansion set on a 563-acre park overlooking the Firth of Clyde. It was designed by Robert Adam in 1777.

BRAEMAR (138 C3)

ABERDEENSHIRE *pop. 400*

Braemar, a village in the typical Highland country of Lower Grampian, is especially popular with summer visitors. The Royal Highland Gathering is an exhibition of Scottish sports held in September and usually attended by the Royal Family. Balmoral Castle is 6 miles east from Braemar.

BUTE (138 B2)

ARGYLL AND BUTE *pop. 14,400*

The hilly Cowal Peninsula partly encircles Bute, an island separated from the mainland peninsula by a curve of water called the Kyles of Bute. Boats of every kind cruise this sheltered stretch of water. Settled in prehistoric times, the island abounds in barrows, cairns, cists and other stone monuments. The scenery, mild climate and proximity to the most populous part of Scotland have made Bute a

---

CURLING

For at least 350 years this team game, similar to bowls, but played on ice, has been played all over Scotland. The curling stones are made from granite and have handles let into the top. The object is to slide the stones along the ice into a target circle. The team with the most stones at the center is the winner.

favorite vacation site. The coastal town of Rothesay is its chief resort and steamer port.

CALLANDER (138 C2) ★
STIRLING pop. 2,500

Callander is on an ancient route to the Highlands and perhaps represents Scotland at its romantic best. During the early 18th century the outlaw Rob Roy roamed the surrounding countryside. A century later Sir Walter Scott immortalized the benevolent bandit in his well-known novel. Scott also wrote of *The Lady of the Lake*, the lady being Ellen Douglas and her lake Loch Katrine.

West of Callander are three lochs – Venachar, Katrine and Ard – and south of these lakes are the birch-covered hills and sweeping moorland known collectively as the Trossachs.

CAMPBELTOWN (138 B2)
ARGYLL AND BUTE pop. 6,100

Campbeltown is the main settlement of the long Kintyre Peninsula, the first Kingdom of Scotland. The town, originally called Dalruadhain, was the seat of the Dalriadan kings. Today visitors fish from the rocky seashore and play golf at Machrihanish, 5 miles west.

CULLODEN – *see Inverness on p.149.*

CULROSS (138 C2)
FIFE pop. 4,800

Picturesque Culross, with its cobbled streets and 16th-century houses, is a well-preserved period town. Culross Abbey is a Cistercian monastery that contributes substantially to the town's medieval aura. Founded by Malcolm, the Earl of Fife, in 1217, the abbey is still used. The choir functions as a parish church; parts of the nave remain, and the central tower is still intact.

DUFFTOWN (138 D4)
MORAY pop. 1,600

The "capital of Scottish Malt Distilling," ancient Dufftown is also noted for its medieval buildings. The Mortlach parish church, just south of Dufftown, reputedly dates from the 11th century. Balvenie, on a hill above the Fiddich River, is one of Scotland's earliest and largest stone castles, dating from the 15th and 16th centuries.

GLENFIDDICH DISTILLERY, near Balvenie Castle, was founded in 1887. The visitor center has a whisky museum and a bar.

DUMFRIES (138 C1)
DUMFRIES AND GALLOWAY pop. 31,600

Dumfries straddles the Nith River, its halves joined by five bridges. Located close to the English border, the town suffered from frequent raids.

Dumfries is best-known as the home of Robert Burns from 1791 to his death in 1796. Here, while working as an excise officer, he wrote some of his finest songs, including *Auld Lang Syne*. His statue graces High Street. Additional reminders of the poet are in the municipal museum, the Globe Inn and the Hole in the Wa' Tavern.

BURNS HOUSE, on Burns Street, is where Robert Burns died in 1796. Memorials and personal relics are on display.

BURNS MAUSOLEUM, St. Michael's Churchyard, is a Grecian temple that is the burial site of the poet, his wife Jean Armour and their five sons. For access contact the attendant at Burns House.

▲ DUNDEE (138 D3)
CITY OF DUNDEE pop. 174,300

Despite attempts by the English to destroy the town, medieval trappings survive in historic Dundee. The cross near the City Churches dates from 1586.

Places of interest include the Barrack Street Natural History Museum, featuring natural history and wildlife exhibits, and the McManus Galleries Museum, which focuses on shipping and industry. Dundee's 1,300 acres of parks include Camperdown, the site of Camperdown House, a 19th-century mansion that contains a tearoom; east on the Firth is Broughty Ferry, a resort and residential suburb developed from a fishing village.

▲ DUNFERMLINE (138 C2)
FIFE *pop. 52,100*

Now devoted to the production of textiles, Dunfermline was once capital of Scotland. Examples of its past history are the 11th-century abbey and the crumbling royal palace, birthplace of the unfortunate Charles I, the British king whose authoritarian rule in the first half of the 17th century provoked a civil war that resulted in his execution.

Another major figure born in Dunfermline was Andrew Carnegie, who made his fortune in the United States and gained renown as an industrialist and philanthropist. Remembering his roots, Carnegie gave the town the park that surrounds the 17th-century Pittencrieff House.

ELGIN (138 C4)
MORAY *pop. 20,300*

Elgin, on the Lossie River, is a principal market for a large garden area and a convenient center for visiting this region of salmon rivers and medieval castles.

Lossiemouth, 5 miles north on the Firth, is a seaside resort. The town of Forres, 12 miles west, is mentioned in William Shakespeare's *Macbeth*.

FORT WILLIAM (138 B3)
HIGHLAND *pop. 11,100*

In "Scotland's Great Glen," Fort William began as an earth and wattle fort; today it is a point of departure for touring the Western Highlands. The history of the region is kept alive in the West Highland Museum, and local folk traditions are revived in the Highland Games each August.

BEN NEVIS, 4,406 feet, is the tallest mountain in Britain. It also may be one of the oldest; its age is estimated to be 500 million years. Only experienced climbers should attempt to scale the dangerous northern flanks, but the less seasoned

---

HIGHLAND GAMES

Athletes compete at these traditional Highland gatherings, held all over Scotland during the summer. Events include putting the stone and tossing the caber. It is believed that the games began as martial contests held by King Malcolm Canmore in the 11th century to find the strongest men to fight the Normans.

---

can conquer the mountain via the stony 5-mile trail that originates near Fort William, on the bank of the Nevis River. Wear sturdy footwear and warm, waterproof clothing.

GLAMIS (138 C3)
ANGUS *pop. 240*

GLAMIS CASTLE is the celebrated home of the Earls of Strathmore. The present Queen Mother is the daughter of the 14th earl. According to William Shakespeare's *Macbeth*, Duncan was murdered at this site. Architecturally as well as historically interesting, the castle's 13th-century nucleus is enhanced by corbels, wings and turrets in the 17th-century French-château style.

▲ GLASGOW (138 C2) ★
CITY OF GLASGOW *pop. 697,000*

Founded by the missionary St. Mungo in about AD 550, Glasgow on the Clyde spent its first few centuries as an obscure religious center.

The 19th century ushered in the Industrial Revolution and with its nearby source of coal and substantial labor pool, Glasgow competed with other industrial giants. Foundries and factories of many varieties appeared, and when the Clyde River was widened and dredged, shipbuilding grew.

Obviously a city of industry and commerce, Glasgow has other faces as well. Acres of green space can be found in Linn Park, on the banks of a small lake in Botanic Gardens, and in Glasgow

Green in the city center. Such scenic spots as the Trossachs, Loch Lomond and the Kilpatrick Hills are all within a few hours of the city.

Glasgow is architecturally a product of the early and mid-19th century, and a few Victorian confections survive. Just as interesting are examples of Charles Rennie Mackintosh's early modern style. A handful of pre-19th-century structures remain, such as the cathedral, Trades House, Provand's Lordship and Provan Hall, a delightful restored 15th-century house.

For additional tourist information, contact the Tourist Information Centre, 35 St. Vincent Place, Glasgow G1 2ER; tel: 0141-204 4400.

BOTANIC GARDENS, Queen Margaret Drive, off Great Western Road, was established in 1817. In addition to the 42 acres of flowers, herbs and shrubs, there are greenhouses sheltering such exotic flora as orchids and tree ferns.

BURRELL COLLECTION, Pollok Country Park, was opened in 1983 by Queen Elizabeth II. Over 8,000 items on display include Chinese bronzes; Turkish pottery; Near Eastern rugs and carpets; and artifacts from Iraq, Egypt, and Greece.

GLASGOW ART GALLERY AND MUSEUM, in Kelvingrove Park, was financed by profits from Glasgow's 1888 International Exhibition. The neo-Gothic buildings house important collections of works by both old and new artists.

GLASGOW CATHEDRAL stands on a hill in the oldest part of the city and dates mostly from the 13th century. There has been a church on the site since St. Mungo founded one in the 6th century.

PROVAND'S LORDSHIP, 3 Castle Street, was built in 1471 and is the oldest domestic building in Glasgow. It now contains a museum of Flemish tapestries and *petit point*, period furniture and historical paintings.

TENEMENT HOUSE, 145 Buccleuch Street, Garnethill, is a carefully restored 1892 first-floor apartment, the parlor, bedroom, kitchen and bath of which contain their original fixtures. The apartment and its contents, preserved by The National Trust for Scotland, paint a picture of life in Glasgow in the early 1900s.

UNIVERSITY OF GLASGOW was established by papal order in the mid-15th century. The institution has occupied its impressive neo-Gothic quarters on Gilmorehill since 1870.

Hunterian Art Gallery maintains a major collection of works by James McNeill Whistler and Charles Rennie Mackintosh as well as reconstructed interiors from Mackintosh's Glasgow home, collections of Dutch, Flemish, Italian and British 17th- and 18th-century paintings, and a collection of 19th- and early 20th-century Scottish paintings.

GLENCOE (138 B3) ★
HIGHLAND pop. 200
Stretching from Rannoch Moor to Loch Leven, mountainous Glencoe has been described as the most scenic glen in Scotland. Tradition claims Ossian's Cave as the birthplace of the 3rd-century poet. Signal Rock, north of the Coe River, has a more infamous history. It was here in 1692 that the signal was given for the treacherous massacre of the MacDonald Clan by Robert Campbell and his troops, who had been guests of the MacDonalds for 12 days. A monument honoring those slain stands near the road to Invercoe.

GLENCOE VISITOR CENTRE, Ballachulish, is surrounded by more than 14,000 acres of Highland country which are very popular for walking and hiking.

GRANTOWN-ON-SPEY (138 C4)
MORAY pop. 1,500
In summer Grantown-on-Spey, on the winding Spey River, is a favorite resort of salmon fishermen; in winter, skiers flock to its ski school and the Cairngorm slopes. The town itself is an attractive

collection of 18th-century Georgian buildings; walks thread through nearby Beachan Wood and Glen Beg.

INVERARAY (138 B3)
ARGYLL AND BUTE *pop. 500*
Inveraray is relatively new by Scottish standards, having been rebuilt in the 18th century after its destruction by Royalists a century earlier. The cottages and parish church of the white-walled town have changed little since then. The church has an unusual dividing wall, which makes possible simultaneous services in English and Gaelic.

AUCHINDRAIN TOWNSHIP OPEN-AIR MUSEUM, 6 miles southwest, re-creates 18th- and 19th-century folklife in restored period buildings on farmland. Traditional crops and livestock are on display.

▲ INVERNESS (138 C4) ★
HIGHLAND *pop. 42,600*
A county town steeped in British history, Inverness has reminders of such historical figures as St. Columba, Mary, Queen of Scots, and Oliver Cromwell. Its monuments include the remains of a Pictish fort, a 17th-century clock tower, part of a fort erected by Cromwell's army, and a 19th-century cathedral.

CULLODEN, a few miles southeast at Drummossie Muir, was the scene of a battle in 1746 that was the last Scottish bid for independence and began the breakdown of the traditional clan system.
   Here Bonnie Prince Charlie, the last hope of the Scottish Stuarts, was defeated by the English Duke of Cumberland.
   Old Leanach Cottage, around which the battle raged, contains the Battlefield Museum with its collection of historical maps, relics and a battle plan.

URQUHART CASTLE, 17 miles southwest, was once Scotland's largest castle. On the banks of Loch Ness, the ruins date from the 14th century when the castle was built on the site of an earlier fort.

THE LOCH NESS MONSTER
The legend of the Loch Ness monster, or "Nessie," still continues to intrigue passing travelers. She is supposedly a dinosaur-like beast whose alleged appearances on the surface of the water, supported by disputed photographic evidence, make even the most cynical of visitors stop a little longer – just in case. The Official Loch Ness Monster Exhibition at Drumnadrochit, 14 miles southwest of Inverness, tells the legend of the monster from the Middle Ages to the present and demonstrates the latest technology employed to solve the mystery.

ISLAY ISLAND – *see Mull on p.150.*

JEDBURGH (138 D2)
SCOTTISH BORDERS *pop. 4,500*
One might never guess that peaceful Jedburgh and its hilly, green surroundings have had a stormy past. Jedburgh's castle changed hands often during the Border Wars and was destroyed in 1409. Historically interesting are Queen Mary's House, where she lived in 1566, and the remains of medieval Jedburgh Abbey.

JURA ISLAND – *see Mull on p.150.*

KELSO (138 D2)
SCOTTISH BORDERS *pop. 5,500*
On the Tweed River and just north of the Cheviot Hills, Kelso is a salmon-fishing center and a point from which to explore the gentle countryside. The medieval abbey, mostly in ruins, was once among the wealthiest in Britain.

▲ KILMARNOCK (138 C2)
EAST AYRSHIRE *pop. 47,200*
Kilmarnock's fame as the site of the world's largest whisky-bottling concern began in 1820, when grocer Johnny Walker began blending his well-known product in the town. Robert Burns pub-

lished his first book of poems in Kilmarnock, a success that reversed his decision to emigrate to Jamaica. The town's museum, housed in a monument to Burns, contains a copy of that book.

KINLOCHEWE (138 B4)
HIGHLAND *pop. 100*
At the head of Loch Maree, Kinlochewe is a good point of embarkation for exploring the remote Highlands.

BEINN EIGHE NATIONAL NATURE RESERVE, west of Kinlochewe, was founded in 1951 as the first nature reserve in Britain. Its 10,000 acres include remnants of the Caledonian pine forests, part of Loch Maree, and the Coire Mhic Fhearchair, an impressive hollow nestling in the shadow of Beinn Eighe.

KINROSS (138 C2)
PERTHSHIRE AND KINROSS *pop. 4,000*
The county town of Kinross lies in the scenic countryside between the Ochil Hills and the Firth of Forth.

LOCH LEVEN CASTLE, on an island in the lake, is an impressive reminder of a once-forbidding fortress. Though mostly 15th-century in design, it incorporates masonry from a besieged predecessor. Mary, Queen of Scots, was a guest in the castle – much against her will – in 1567. Inaccessible during winter, the castle is reached by ferry when it is open.

▲ KIRKCALDY (138 C2)
FIFE *pop. 49,600*
FALKLAND PALACE AND GARDEN, 11 miles north, was built in 1542 for James V and was a favorite hunting lodge of Scottish kings for a century thereafter. Of note are its state apartments and tennis court, one of the oldest in existence.

LAIRG (138 C4)
HIGHLAND *pop. 700*
At the foot of Loch Shin, where five roads converge, Lairg is a good starting point for touring the country's northern areas. There are lochs and mountains to

the west, moorlands to the north, and beaches and golf courses to the east.

LINLITHGOW (138 C2)
WEST LOTHIAN *pop. 11,100*
Old, if not old looking, Linlithgow preserves its 17th-century town hall, a medieval parish church and the ruins of a royal palace. The church was first consecrated in 1242 and largely rebuilt after a fire in 1424. Its spire of gilded aluminum was added in 1964.

HOPETOUN HOUSE, 6 miles east, was begun in the late 1600s by Sir William Bruce of Kinross. Most of the mansion is the creation of 18th-century architect William Adam and his sons. Among its valuable contents are original Chippendale furniture.

LINLITHGOW PALACE occupies a knoll overlooking the town's lake. Built between the 15th and 17th centuries, the palace was a favorite residence of Scotland's royalty.

LOCH NESS – *see Inverness on p.149.*

MELROSE (138 D2)
SCOTTISH BORDERS *pop. 2,100*
Called Kennaquhair in two of Sir Walter Scott's novels, Melrose is in the center of the region associated with this great Romantic. Scott is interred 5 miles southeast at Dryburgh, another ruined abbey.

ABBOTSFORD HOUSE, 2 miles west, was Sir Walter Scott's home from 1817 until his death in 1832. It contains mementos of the writer as well as collections of rare books, armor and weapons.

MULL (138 B3)
ARGYLL AND BUTE *pop. 2,700*
Cliffs and beaches, lakes, forests and moors characterize Mull, the second largest island of the Inner Hebrides archipelago off Scotland's west coast.

Overlooking the Sound of Mull and the Firth of Lorne, the small port of Craignure is the ancestral home of the

Clan MacLean. Nearby is 13th-century Duart Castle; another castle, in ruins, is on the edge of Loch Buie. Mull's chief town and fishing port is Tobermory.

From Fionnphort on the island's southwestern coast it is possible to take a trip to tiny Iona, where St. Columba initiated his missionary work in the 6th century, or to tinier Staffa, an uninhabited island remarkable for its basaltic caves and columns. Fingal's Cave, whose Gaelic name *An Uamh Ehinn* means "musical cave," inspired the *Hebrides* Overture of Felix Mendelssohn. The nearby Treshnish Isles are the domain of sea birds.

Farther south over the Firth of Lorne lie Colonsay and rugged Jura, a large island with many beautiful beaches. A narrow strait separates Colonsay from Oronsay, site of a ruined medieval priory. Southernmost of the principal islands in the Hebrides is Islay (*EYE-la*), with its beaches and bays and reminders of much earlier denizens.

OBAN (138 B3)
ARGYLL AND BUTE *pop. 8,100*
Oban's harbor is always busy with fishing boats, yachts and the steamers that carry travelers to Scotland's western islands. Yachts are most plentiful during the West Highland Yachting Week, held from late July to early August.

In addition to Oban's tiny granite cathedral, there are several interesting castles nearby. The 13th-century castle of Dunollie was once the seat of the Lords of Lorn; Gylen, on the nearby

FINGAL'S CAVE
The cathedral-like cave that inspired Mendelssohn's *Hebrides* overture is one of several on the tiny uninhabited island of Staffa north of Iona. Boat trips leave from Oban in summer to see the black columns of smooth basalt rising up out of the sea, the results of volcanic action.

island of Kerrera, is still the home of the MacDougalls. Dunstaffnage, 3 miles north, is an impressive and formidable castle with 10-foot-thick walls.

ORKNEY ISLANDS (139 E5)
ORKNEY *pop. 17,000*
Settled by Vikings in the 9th century, the Orkney Islands were ruled from Norway and Denmark until 1468, when a Norwegian king gave them to Scotland in lieu of a dowry for his daughter, who married James III.

Though politically part of Britain, the islands seem different – Norse crafts and traditions are obvious everywhere. In the summer the days are long, but even in this northern archipelago, at the same latitude as southern Greenland, the Gulf Stream tempers the climate.

About half the 60-odd islands are inhabited; the rest belong to seals and sea birds. Most of the islanders, who draw their livelihoods from the fertile hills rather than the sea, live on Mainland, largest of the islands.

Here is the capital, the harbor town of Kirkwall, its steep-roofed, stone houses set on streets that wind around a medieval cathedral. St. Mary's on Holm Sound is very popular among yacht enthusiasts, and Stromness in the west is known for its lobster and crab exports.

Ferries cross to Stromness from Aberdeen twice daily and from Scrabster twice a week. In summer a ferry runs from John O'Groats to Burwick.

EARL PATRICK'S PALACE, Kirkwall, was built about 1607 by Patrick Stewart, Earl of Orkney. Although now roofless, the Renaissance palace is one of the finest buildings of its kind in Scotland.

MAES HOWE CHAMBERED CAIRN, 9 miles west of Kirkwall at Finstown, is Britain's best-preserved megalithic tomb; it dates from 1800 BC. Viking carvings and runes are visible.

SKARA BRAE, 17 miles northwest of Kirkwall, is a Stone Age village that, because it was covered with sand for most of its existence, is very well preserved. Stone furniture and fireplaces can be seen as their owners left them.

PEEBLES (138 C2)
SCOTTISH BORDERS *pop. 6,700*
An unhurried town on the Tweed River, Peebles was once frequented by Scottish royalty, who hunted in Ettrick Forest.

Now devoted to the manufacture of tweeds and knits, the town keeps some of its past intact: the Mercat Cross, the ruins of 13th-century Cross Kirk, portions of the town walls, a 15th-century bridge and several old houses.

Anglers fish for trout and salmon in season.

TRAQUAIR HOUSE, 6 miles southeast, was built largely in the 17th century but dates from the 10th century. This gray stone house of small-paned windows and miniature turrets has been an occasional home to 27 British monarchs.

There are many reminders of Mary, Queen of Scots, as well as valuable silver and glass, books and manuscripts, tapestries and 13th-century embroideries.

▲ PERTH (138 C3)
PERTHSHIRE AND KINROSS *pop. 42,100*
One would never know by looking at Perth that this city on the Tay River is centuries old and was once the capital of Scotland. Several invasions and later demolitions in the name of progress or religion have taken their toll.

Significant among what remains of the old is St. John's Kirk, a mostly 15th-century structure on the site of an early medieval church. In 1559, reformer John Knox preached a sermon denouncing the "idolatry" of the Roman Catholic Church; his congregation set about destroying monasteries and all art arbitrarily deemed "idolatrous."

Just north of the city is Scone, where Scottish kings were once crowned. The Stone of Scone, traditionally regarded as Jacob's Pillow, is said to have been brought from the Holy Land in the 9th

century. In 1296, the English King Edward I took the Stone of Destiny to London, where it remained for the most part until it was returned in 1997; it is now in Edinburgh Castle.

SCONE PALACE, 1 mile north, is a castle-like house built on the site of a 12th-century abbey destroyed by zealous followers of John Knox. A religious center until the Reformation, it was for several centuries the scene of Scottish coronations. The present 19th-century palace contains extensive collections of china, ivory, French furniture, Vernix Martin vases, and art objects.

PITLOCHRY (138 C3)
PERTHSHIRE AND KINROSS *pop. 2,300*
Set on Tayside's splendid rivers and hills, Pitlochry is a fine inland vacation spot. Chief among its attractions are local streams where the salmon run. The town has an excellent golf course and the modern Festival Theatre, scene of almost continuous concerts and plays during the warmer months.

BLAIR CASTLE, 7 miles northwest at the village of Blair Atholl, was first built in 1269 for the Duke of Atholl and is now owned by the present duke. Altered over the years, it was restored to its present castle-like appearance by David Bryce, a 19th-century architect. Visitors can see tapestries, portraits, furniture and porcelain, as well as Jacobite relics.

PORTREE – *see Skye on p.153.*

PORTREE – *see Skye on p.153.*

ST. ANDREWS (138 D3) ★
FIFE *pop. 14,000*
Originating in the 6th century as a Celtic religious settlement, St. Andrews quickly became a cultural center in Scotland.

Augustinians erected the yellow-stone cathedral in the 12th century, and additional holy orders established communities. Bishops and archbishops inhabited the castle, set on a rocky promontory above St. Andrews Bay. A society of scholars formed Scotland's very first university in St. Andrews in 1412. Although still important as a university town, St. Andrews is best-known as a vacation center and the home of golf. The Royal and Ancient Golf Club has been the world's principal rule-maker for the sport since its founding in 1754. For a fee, visitors to St Andrew's may play this or any of the city's other six courses.

ST. ANDREW'S CATHEDRAL is a 12th- and 13th-century ruin of the largest cathedral in Scotland. Many of the precinct walls have survived; a museum contains an important collection of Celtic and medieval sculpture.

SCONE – *see Perth on p.152.*

SHETLAND ISLANDS (139 E3) ★
SHETLAND *pop. 22,000*
It is difficult to imagine a part of Scotland in which Gaelic has never been the native tongue and where the kilt is a rarity, but Shetland is that part. Away from the mainstream of Scottish history, these far-flung islands have a unique past.

Monuments from eons past prove the islands were settled by an anonymous neolithic people, but the settlers who left the distinct cultural stamp were the Norsemen, who arrived here in the 9th century and stayed. Their language, Norn, disappeared, but sea birds, places and parts of boats, among other things, still bear Viking names.

Officially known as Zetland, from the Nordic Hjaltland, this county is a collection of more than 100 rocky islands and skerries. Of the 24 that are inhabited, Mainland is the largest.

Slightly fewer than a third of the islanders live in the capital and fishing port of Lerwick. The small island of Bressay shelters the harbor, a haven to fleets fishing the northern seas. Every January the town revives its Viking past in the uproarious festival of Up-Helly-Aa, a pagan plea for the sun to return.

The nearby town of Scalloway preceded Lerwick as capital and is the seat of the judicial branch of the government.

North of Mainland is Yell, second-largest of the islands, and beyond it, Unst. Unst's lighthouse at Muckle Flugga is the northernmost inhabited spot in Britain. Lying to the south midway between the Shetlands and the Orkneys is Fair Isle. Owned and protected by the National Trust for Scotland, this tiny island is a favorite for sea birds and of the ornithologists who observe them. Fair Isle is also known for its knitwear of colorful Norse-inspired patterns.

JARLSHOF PREHISTORIC SITE, 25 miles south of Lerwick at Sumburgh, encompasses Bronze Age, Iron Age, Viking and medieval settlements.

SKYE (138 B4) ★
HIGHLAND *pop. 8,800*
The island of Skye remains much as Bonnie Prince Charlie must have seen it more than 200 years ago – its coastal hamlets still unhurried and attractive and its interior rocky and brooding. Portree is the capital. A new road bridge links Kyle of Lochalsh on the mainland to Kyleakin, while ferries run from Mallaig to Armadale on Skye or from Glenelg to Kylerhea. Broadford, in the south of the island, is a good touring base for the beautiful Cuillin hills.

▲ STIRLING (139 C2)
STIRLING *pop. 29,200*
The royal burgh of Stirling lies between two of Scotland's most famous battle-fields. Northeast is where Sir William Wallace rallied his countrymen to defeat an English army in 1297. A few miles southeast is Bannockburn, where in 1314 Robert the Bruce led the Scots to victory against an English army three times their size. Bannockburn Centre has audiovisual progams on the battle.

STIRLING CASTLE, Upper Castle Hill, rises on a steep crag above the town. Fortresses have occupied this site since early medieval times, and the present structure dates from the 16th century.

- **AREA:** 8,019 square miles
- **POPULATION:** 2,857,000
- **CAPITAL:** Cardiff
- **LANGUAGES:** English and Welsh
- **ECONOMY:** Agriculture, manufacturing, engineering; beef and dairy cattle, sheep, wool; coal, zinc, slate; crude steel is a major export.
- **DUTY-FREE ITEMS:** *See England*
- **CURRENCY:** *See England*
- **BANK OPENING HOURS:** 9:30am–4 or 5pm Monday–Friday.
- **STORE OPENING HOURS:** 9am–5:30pm Monday–Saturday. Outside Swansea and Cardiff stores can sometimes close at 1pm on Wednesday.
- **BEST BUYS:** Handicrafts, including ironwork, leatherwork, basketry, pottery, wooden love spoons, dolls; woolens. Note: If purchase is an antique valued at over £35,000, an export licence is required to take it out of the country.
- **PUBLIC HOLIDAYS:** *See England*
- **USEFUL TELEPHONE NUMBERS:** Police 999; Fire 999; Ambulance 999
- **NATIONAL TOURIST OFFICES:** British Tourist Authority (BTA) Suite 701, 551 Fifth Avenue New York, NY 10176-0799 Tel: 212/986-2200 or 1-800-462-2748 (toll-free) Fax: 212/986-1188 British Tourist Authority (BTA) Thames Tower Black's Road Hammersmith London W6 9EL, England (written enquiries only) Wales Tourist Board Brunel House 2 Fitzalan Road Cardiff CF2 1UY, Wales Tel: 01222 499909 Fax: 01222 485031
- **AMERICAN EMBASSY:** 24 Grosvenor Square London, W1A 1AE England Tel: 0171 499-9000 (telephone enquiries only)

WALES

HISTORY

As a social entity, Wales had its origins between the 5th and 7th centuries, when Saxon invasions forced some of Britain's inhabitants into the mountainous west. In the 8th century the Celtic Wealhs, as these people were called by the Anglo-Saxons, were confined to their hilly land by a great earthwork, Offa's Dyke, which stretched from the River Dee in the north to the Mouth of the Severn in the south. Wales, the region west of the earthwork, remained largely independent until the late 13th century. Edward I, the English king, then overcame the last native princes, built castles to subdue the population, and made his son the Prince of Wales.

The ascendance of the Welsh Tudor dynasty to the English throne assured the unity of England and Wales. The Act of Union in the reign of Henry VIII barred Welsh as the language of law and administration. Meanwhile, the principality was carved into English-style shires, and Welsh representatives were sent to the parliament in London. Nonetheless, although England and Wales are legally one state, strong regional sentiments and an interest in the conservation of Welsh culture remain, defining the character of this proud principality.

SPORTS AND RECREATION

With its rugged mountains, Wales is naturally a favorite among climbers. More gentle than the heights of Snowdonia are the Brecon Beacons in the south. Horseback riding is popular – and a good way to travel the rolling green hills.

The Welsh coast, with its sandy bays and quiet seaside towns, attracts those seeking less strenuous activities. Golfers can enjoy excellent courses – more than 100 – including two of championship caliber at Harlech. Freshwater fishing, however, is undoubtedly the most popular outdoor pastime. Angling associations and some riverside hotels own coveted stretches of water; ask local river authorities about where to obtain permission to fish.

Souvenir seekers will find a colorful assortment of handicrafts, from hand-painted pottery to copper lusterware. Many items are decorated with a leek design, a national symbol of Wales. An old and romantic art is the carving of wooden love spoons: traditionally given by young men to their sweethearts, they are today more sought after by tourists. Wales also is popular for its woolens, which combine ancient patterns with bright, new colors.

PRINCIPAL TOURING AREAS

Note: For descriptions of attractions in **bold type**, see individual listings.

NORTH

North Wales is a rugged land of wild mountains, ruined castles, rocky headlands and long, sandy bays. Crossing into Wales from the old English border stronghold of Chester, the road passes the friendly seaside towns of Rhyl, Prestatyn and Colwyn Bay, before reaching the bold headland of Great Orme and the elegant Victorian resort of Llandudno.

The medieval fortress and city walls of Conwy guard the route west to the university town of Bangor. Beyond is the great medieval castle of Caernarfon which once controlled the narrow Menai Strait. To the south of Chester and just across the border lies Llangollen, home of the International Eisteddfod.

The Menai Strait, which has been spanned by two bridges since the 19th century, separates the mainland from the island of Anglesey. This large, flat island with its beautiful coastline is famous for containing the little town with the longest and most unpronounceable

name in Britain – Llanfairpwllgwyngyll-gogerychwyrndrobwllllantysiliogogogoch (usually abbreviated to Llanfair PG). Anglesey's attractions include many prehistoric tombs; the magnificent, moated castle at **Beaumaris** (the last of the Welsh castles built by Edward I; and the scenic sea cliffs of Holy Island, near **Holyhead**.

> ### SNOWDON SAFETY
> If you intend climbing Mount Snowdon, beware that, although it may not look like the Alps or the Rockies, it is full of dangers and has claimed many lives. Make sure you are properly clothed and equipped: check the weather forecast, take a good map, compass, and provisions, and tackle only those walks well within your capabilities. Tell someone where you are going and when you expect to return – perhaps by leaving a note with your hotel.

On the mainland side of the Menai Strait lies **Snowdonia National Park**, an incomparable region covering a large part of the Cambrian Mountains. The park is named after Snowdon, its majestic central peak which is, at 3,560 feet, the highest mountain in England and Wales. Wild Llanberis Pass and the valleys around the villages of Beddgelert and **Betws-y-coed** provide fine hiking country.

The isolated Lleyn Peninsula strikes out southwest from Porthmadog, a Welsh-speaking region of farms, villages and sandy vacation beaches. Tremadog Bay lies to the south and is overlooked by the brooding castle of **Harlech**, a historic fortress whose name is remembered in the well-known traditional song, *Men of Harlech*.

Nearby, **Portmeirion** provides a contrast with the Mediterranean-style village, built by the early 19th-century architect and designer, Sir Clough Williams-Ellis.

BRITAIN · WALES

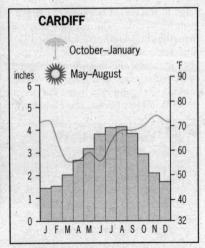

CARDIFF

October–January

inches | May–August | °F

SOUTH AND CENTRAL

The green valleys and grassy hills of central Wales are renowned for being good walking country. The region is crisscrossed by a number of long distance paths, but many walkers head for the hills of the Brecon Beacons and Black Mountains.

North of **Brecon** lie the sheep-farming country of Radnor Forest, and the old spa towns of Llandridnod Wells, Builth Wells and Llanwrtyd Wells.

One of the most colorful areas in the country is around the pleasant resort and university town of **Aberystwyth**. This is a center for traditional craftworkers and Welsh is the first language of the largely rural population. A prime vacation area, it is known for its splendid coastline and peaceful seaside towns.

Pembrokeshire, in the southwestern corner of the country, has a beautiful rugged coast of limestone cliffs, and is dotted with fishing villages and seaside resorts like **Tenby**.

The little village of St. David's, named for the partron saint of Wales, is the site of the country's finest cathedral. The cliffs peter out eastward into the sand-fringed expanse of Carmarthen Bay and the charming village of **Laugharne**, once home to the poet Dylan Thomas.

Carmarthen itself is said to be the birthplace of Merlin, the legendary magician.

The region of South Wales between Swansea and Newport has been heavily industrialized and the valleys stretching north into the hills are scarred from a century and a half of coal mining.

At the heart of the southern region is **Cardiff**, the Welsh capital, where an ambitious scheme is under way to build a barrier across Cardiff Bay to create a freshwater lake and marina.

West is the rural Vale of Glamorgan, with its attractive coast. The flourishing port of **Swansea** is gateway to the scenic Gower Peninsula, with its gray limestone crags, pretty villages and sandy bays, including the beautiful Caswell Bay.

To the east are the border county of Monmouthshire and the beautiful Wye Valley. **Chepstow**, at the mouth of the Wye where it flows into the Severn Estuary, is known for its racecourse and the evocative ruins of nearby Tintern Abbey. **Monmouth**, further inland, has fine medieval fortifications.

Abergavenny lies at the southern edge of the Black Mountains, guarding the route north into central Wales.

AUTOMOBILE CLUBS
The Automobile Association
(AA) has an office at Fanum House, 140 Queen Street, Cardiff. The **Royal Automobile Club** (R.A.C.) has an office on Newport Road, Cardiff. The symbol ▲ indicates the presence of a AAA-affiliated automobile club branch. Not all auto clubs offer full travel services to AAA members.

PLACES OF INTEREST

★ HIGHLIGHTS ★	
Beaumaris	(see p.158)
Betws-y-Coed	(see p.158)
Brecon	(see p.158)
Caernarfon	(see p.158)
Conwy	(see p.159)
Harlech	(see p.159)
Llandudno	(see p.160)
Llangollen	(see p.160)
St David's	(see p.161)
Tenby	(see p.161)

▲ CARDIFF (83 B2)
CARDIFF *pop. 279,500*

The busy city of Cardiff, in the most populous part of Wales, has only been the country's capital since 1955, although it has been a major coal-shipping port and manufacturing center for more than a century.

Visitors enjoy the broad tree-lined streets, National Museum of Wales, Civic Centre and City Hall as well as arcaded shopping streets, the Cardiff Market and the New Theatre. Parks, gardens, restaurants, movie houses, and facilities for a wide range of sports enhance the city.

Within easy reach from Cardiff are Caerphilly, known for its castle and the crumbly cheese that bears its name, and Bridgend, with its 12th-century castle and fortified monastery. Penarth, with its esplanade and marina, is 4 miles from the capital.

For additional information contact the Tourist Information Centre, Central Railway Station, PO Box 48, Cardiff CF1 2AX; tel: (01222) 227281.

CARDIFF CASTLE, dating from 1093, occupies the site of an earlier Roman fort. Though remodeled in the 19th century, it has its original well-preserved keep.

LLANDAFF CATHEDRAL lies 2½ miles northwest in Llandaff, a small town now incorporated into Cardiff. The first structure on this site was a 6th-century wooden church; its 12th-century stone successor was rebuilt after suffering serious damage in World War II. An obviously recent addition is Sir Jacob Epstein's aluminum sculpture of Christ in Majesty.

NATIONAL MUSEUM OF WALES, Cathays Park, has exhibits on archaeology, botany, zoology, geology, industry and art.

ABERDOVEY (83 B3)
GWYNEDD *pop. 1,000*

The name Aberdovey (Aberdyfi) describes this port's position at the Dyfi's River mouth. The coastline was once more distant, evidenced by the sunken tree trunks visible at low tide. Local legend claims that a drowned city also lies in the bay; its bells ringing from the deep are said to portend trouble.

Known for its harbor and miles of sandy beach, the town also is popular as a center for exploring inland.

ABERGAVENNY (83 B2)
MONMOUTHSHIRE *pop. 14,900*

Set among wooded hills, Abergavenny is an excellent center from which to explore the Brecon Mountains region and the castles that lie along the Welsh border. Of interest in the town are St. Mary's Church and its monuments.

ABERGAVENNY MUSEUM AND CASTLE dates from between the 12th and the 14th century; its walls, towers and gateway remain. A museum contains exhibits that document local history.

BIG PIT MINING MUSEUM, 5 miles southwest at Blaenavon, allows a close look at a mine that operated until 1980. Visitors are given mining helmets and lamps to descend the 300-foot shaft. Sturdy shoes and warm clothing are recommended.

ABERYSTWYTH (83 B3)
CARDIGANSHIRE *pop. 11,200*

In addition to its beaches, harbor and promenades, Aberystwyth boasts an arts

BRITAIN • WALES

center in its university and the National Library of Wales. There are gardens on the seafront near the ruined 13th-century castle built by Edward I.

DEVIL'S BRIDGE, 12 miles east, is reached by a 1-hour steam railroad ride up the wooded Rheidol Valley. Of the three bridges spanning the Mynach River as it plunges 300 feet to join the Rheidol, the Devil's Bridge is the oldest.

NATIONAL LIBRARY OF WALES, Penglais Hill, is one of Britain's six copyright libraries. It specializes in Welsh and Celtic literature and contains *The Mabinogion*, a medieval collection of Welsh legends.

BANGOR (82 B4)
GWYNEDD *pop. 16,000*
Built on the site of an early monastery, the northern town of Bangor took its name from the wattled fence, or *bangor*, that once surrounded the holy house. Though no longer a monastic settlement, Bangor is a cathedral city, its present church a 19th-century creation of Sir Gilbert Scott.

PENRHYN CASTLE lies 3 miles east at Landegai off A5122. It was built in neo-Norman style between 1820 and 1845. The Norman-style furniture, paneling and ceilings were designed by Thomas Hopper. An industrial railroad, a doll museum and a Victorian walled garden are of interest.

BEAUMARIS (82 B4) ★
ANGLESEY *pop. 1,500*
With its early Victorian terraces, its half-timbered houses and old inns, Beaumaris on Anglesey Island is among the prettiest towns in Wales.

BEAUMARIS CASTLE was begun in 1295 by Edward I to guard the strait separating Anglesey from the mainland. The low, turreted, outer curtain, and the higher inner walls that formed the main part of the fortress still stand.

BETWS-Y-COED (82 B4) ★
ABERCONWY AND COLWYN *pop. 800*
Tiny Betws-y-Coed, whose name means Chapel in the Wood, is tucked away in the wooded hills of the Gwydir Forest. Recreational activities available include fishing, horseback riding, skiing and golf. Long regarded as a good base for touring the Snowdonia region, the community is near several enchanting spots: 15th-century Pont-y-Pair, or Bridge of the Cauldron, near a wild reach of the Llugwy River; Swallow Falls on the same stream; and Fairy Glen and Conwy Falls on the Conwy River.

LOVE SPOONS
Throughout rural Wales between the 17th and 19th centuries, young men would spend many an evening carving wooden "love spoons." These would be presented to the ladies they courted. If accepted, it was a sign that courtship would lead to marriage.

BRECON (83 B3) ★
POWYS *pop. 7,500*
A center popular with tourists, Brecon has two museums, medieval castle ruins and a cathedral dating from the 13th century. Visitors can enjoy golf, canal cruising, and trout fishing in the Usk.

The principal attraction of the region, however, is Brecon Beacons National Park, encompassing high hills and empty moorlands, peaceful lakes and tumbling streams, and occasional reminders of early human habitation. At Storey Arms Youth Hostel, 8 miles southwest, is the beginning of a trail up the 2,906-foot Pen y Fan, the highest of the mountains called "beacons" and a vantage point for much of Wales.

CAERNARFON (82 B4) ★
GWYNEDD *pop. 9,400*
Dominating this otherwise peaceful-looking resort is the enormous bulk of 13th-century Caernarfon Castle. The first English Prince of Wales, Edward II,

was born in Caernarfon in 1284. His investiture at the castle in 1301 began the tradition that extends through to the investiture of Prince Charles in 1969.

SNOWDON MOUNTAIN RAILWAY, 7 miles south at Llanberis, operates coal-fired steam locomotives which climb the 4½ miles to the summit of Snowdon.

CARMARTHEN (83 B3)
CARMARTHENSHIRE *pop. 14,500*
The appearance of much of Carmarthen belies its ancient origins, but "Merlin's town" is very old, as proven by the ruin of a Roman fort, remaining medieval streets, and the remnants of a Norman castle. A monument in Nott Square marks the martyrdom site of a bishop burned in Carmarthen in 1555.

Carmarthen lies at the center of a region notable for both its scenery and historic sites. Scattered over the green hills are the impressive remains of medieval castles and such reminders of Iron Age inhabitants as the great hill fort Carn Goch in the Vale of Tywi.

CHEPSTOW (83 C2)
MONMOUTHSHIRE *pop. 10,400*
Chepstow is a good center for excursions through the Wye River valley; 4 miles north is 13th-century Tintern Abbey, the Cistercian church that inspired William Wordsworth's poem.

COLWYN BAY (82 B4)
ABERCONWY AND COLWYN
pop. 27,700
A north-coast resort long favored by families, Colwyn Bay has a 3-mile promenade and a safe, sandy beach.

WELSH MOUNTAIN ZOO overlooks Colwyn Bay. Elephants, deer, reptiles, tropical birds, bears and penguins are among the animals displayed in natural settings.

CONWY (82 B4) ★
ABERCONWY AND COLWYN *pop. 3,900*
Guarding the mouth of the Conwy River is massive Conwy Castle, its walls extended to encompass what was once the entire town. Though no longer needed, the town's defenses are in good condition; you can walk along the 15-foot-thick ramparts of the turreted castle. Boating enthusiasts enjoy the river.

BODNANT GARDENS, 4 miles south on the opposite bank of the river, were laid out in 1875 by Henry Pochin and extended by several of his descendants. The 87 acres of gardens include collections of camellias, rhododendrons, magnolias, roses and azaleas. The hillside site offers views of nearby Snowdonia.

CONWY CASTLE, reigning over the town, was built in the 13th century for Edward I and figured in centuries of medieval warfare. An unusual feature is the castle's shape – the ½ mile of walls form the outline of a Welsh harp.

DOLGELLAU (83 B3)
GWYNEDD *pop. 2,300*
Sombre, slate-built Dolgellau is a good center for walking or horseback riding. More challenging are several possible climbs up Cader Idris, the 3,000-foot mountain that dominates the skyline south of Dolgellau. Visitors are warned of the myth attached to the mountain: whoever spends the night on Cader Idris risks waking the next day mad or a poet.

HARLECH (83 B3) ★
GWYNEDD *pop. 1,100*
HARLECH CASTLE, built by Edward I, is a vast stronghold dominating Tremadog Bay. Protected by the sea on one side and a moat on the other, it was the last Welsh castle to fall to the English. The three-story gatehouse and four towers are prominent features, offering views of the Snowdon Range and Lleyn Peninsula.

PORTMEIRION, 8 miles north at Porthmadog, is a re-creation of an Italian village on a wooded peninsula that juts into Cardigan Bay. The sandy beach here is about 1 mile long.

BRITAIN · WALES

HOLYHEAD (82 A4)
ANGLESEY *pop. 13,300*

Holyhead is an ancient settlement on rocky Holy Island in northernmost Wales. The island, which bears the stamp of ages of human habitation, is reached by a causeway from Anglesey Island. As long ago as 2000 BC, Holyhead was a port for Welsh–Irish trade.

In addition to its many prehistoric sites, Holy Island has many natural attractions. Most obvious is Holyhead Mountain, the summit of which provides views of the Cumberland Mountains, Snowdonia, the Isle of Man and, on clear days, Ireland.

LAUGHARNE (83 A2)
CARMARTHENSHIRE *pop. 1,000*

Picturesque Laugharne, by the sea, has a harbor and castle but is best-known as the home of writer Dylan Thomas, who lived by the Taf River. Many contend – though Thomas denied it – that the town and its residents served as models for *Under Milk Wood*.

DYLAN THOMAS' BOAT HOUSE was the riverside home of the poet for 16 years. Family furniture and photographs remain; an audiovisual presentation and information panels tell about the poet.

▲ LLANDUDNO (82 B4) ★
ABERCONWY AND COLWYN *pop. 17,600*

The large resort of Llandudno is on a spit of land between two sandy beaches. From the quieter West Shore there are panoramas of Conwy Bay and more distant Snowdonia. A statue of Lewis Carroll recalls that the author often came to Llandudno to visit the Liddells and their daughter Alice, for whom he wrote his best-known story.

Enclosing the principal beach, North Shore, are two rocky headlands; 676-foot Great Orme Head, the larger of the promontories, is a playground in itself. Of the several approaches, the most pleasant is on foot through the Happy Valley, a garden remarkable for its rare flowers and trees.

LLANGOLLEN (83 B3) ★
DENBIGSHIRE *pop. 3,100*

Tiny Llangollen lies at the head of the Vale of Llangollen. In addition to its unspoiled surroundings the town has several historic attractions: the 14th-century stone bridge across the Dee River; the remains of an 18th-century castle; the well-known old house Plas Newydd; and the ruined abbey of Valle Crucis.

Llangollen is well-known among music lovers as it is the site of the International Musical Eisteddfod, held since 1947. Early every July, folk singers and dancers from around the world descend upon the town to compete with one another. In order to be certain of good seats, make reservations many months in advance; tel: 01978 860236 or write Llangollen International Musical Eisteddfod Office, Llangollen LL20 8NG.

CHIRK CASTLE stands about 6 miles southeast near the village of Chirk. Built in 1310 by Roger Mortimer, it has been continuously occupied. The massive retangular castle includes some remarkable features – elaborately worked iron gates dating from the 18th century, interesting 16th-century decorative interior features and some excellent portraits of the Stuart kings. On the grounds are traces of Offa's Dyke, the extensive earthwork built by the 8th-century King of Mercia.

HORSE DRAWN BOATS AND CANAL EXHIBITION CENTRE, The Wharf, combines exhibits and 45-minute boat rides to enlighten visitors about Britain's canal era. The museum contains models, photographs, murals and slides pertaining to the canal commerce of the 18th century. Horse-drawn boats (schedule varies) travel the Vale of Llangollen.

PLAS NEWYDD is east of town on A5. From 1780 to 1831, this black-and-white half-timbered house was the home of two Irish aristocrats, Miss Sarah Ponsonby and Lady Eleanor Butler. Though locally regarded as eccentric, the "Ladies of Llangollen" were widely known for their wit and hospitality. Their many friends included such personages as William Wordsworth and the Duke of Wellington. Aside from its historical associations, the house is interesting for its furnishings and interior details, especially the stained glass.

MACHYNLLETH (83 B3)
POWYS *pop. 2,000*
The great champion of Welsh independence, Owain Glyndwr, made Machynlleth his capital in 1404. The town grew in succeeding centuries as a result of its position at the junction of a number of coach roads.

CENTRE FOR ALTERNATIVE TECHNOLOGY, Llwyngwern Quarry, promotes the development of natural energy sources. Solar collectors, windmills, waterwheels and a conservation house demonstrate energy-saving techniques; organic gardening and fish cultures show self-sufficient ways of food production.

MONMOUTH (83 C2)
MONMOUTHSHIRE *pop. 9,000*
On the border at the junction of the Wye, Monnow, and Trothy rivers, historic Monmouth provides a convenient center for touring the Wye Valley. The castle, now in ruins, was built by William FitzOsbern and was the birthplace of Henry V in 1387.

ST. DAVID'S (83 A3) ★
PEMBROKSHIRE *pop. 1,500*
St. David's takes its name from the 16th-century patron saint of Wales. Though seemingly in the middle of nowhere, the town is at the junction of what were once well-traveled routes across the coastal region. The 12th-century cathedral was the object of pilgrimages during the Middle Ages.

Close to St. David's are many scenic bays, beaches, cliffs and islands. A half-mile from the coast lies Ramsey Island, a privately owned nature reserve accessible by way of a boat service offered by local fishermen.

▲ SWANSEA (83 B2)
SWANSEA *pop. 282,600*
The seaport of Swansea has long been the metallurgical capital of Wales. Still mainly industrial, this is the second largest city in Wales as well as is the site of the University College of Swansea, the Glynn Vivian Art Gallery and the Royal Institution of South Wales. The last includes a museum devoted to the natural and cultural history of the district.

TENBY (83 A2) ★
PEMBROKESHIRE *pop. 5,000*
A popular resort on a rocky promontory overlooking two sandy bays, Tenby preserves several medieval monuments: St. Mary's Church, the Tudor Merchant's House and 13th-century walls. Caldy Island, 2½ miles south, is the site of an old priory and a modern monastery.

Pembroke Castle, 10 miles west, is an impressive 12th- to 13th-century fortress with a 80-foot round keep.

WELSHPOOL (83 B3)
POWYS *pop. 4,900*
POWIS CASTLE, on the southern edge of Welshpool, was built by Owain ap Gruffyd in 1250. Though it is obviously a medieval castle, the structure has undergone some interior renovation. The plasterwork and paneling are late 16th-century, and the ornate staircase is 17th-century. The 18th-century gardens are the creation of "Capability" Brown.

▲ WREXHAM (82 B4)
WREXHAM *pop. 41,700*
Wrexham is the industrial center of northern Wales. The pinnacled steeple of St. Giles' Church rises above the city; the church is known for its wrought-iron gates. In the churchyard lies the tomb of Elihu Yale, the 17th-century merchant who founded the American university that bears his name.

BULGARIA

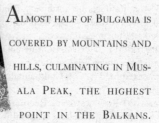

Almost half of Bulgaria is covered by mountains and hills, culminating in Musala Peak, the highest point in the Balkans. Part of the Rila Mountains, it shelters the remote Rila Monastery. In the thick forests on these slopes are bears, wolves, wildcats and elk. To the north is the capital, Sofia. After many years behind the Iron Curtain, Bulgaria is trying to find its place on the economic map of Europe. It stands between Greece and Turkey to the south, and the Carpathian Mountains to the north. On its western edge a former Communist ally, Yugoslavia, has fragmented. To the east it shares the Black Sea shores with Russia. Vacation resorts on the Golden Coast are becoming rapidly Westernized. The northeast corner boasts Bulgaria's greatest river, the Danube.

Left In the small village of Shipka, near Kazanluk, the gold domes and brightly colored façade of the Memorial Church attract the eye
Above During May and June, the scent of Damask roses fills the air

THINGS TO KNOW

- **AREA:** 111,000 square kilometers (42,857 square miles)
- **POPULATION:** 8,900,000
- **CAPITAL:** Sofiya (Sofia)
- **LANGUAGE:** Bulgarian
- **RELIGION:** Bulgarian Orthodox, Moslem
- **ECONOMY:** Industry, agriculture, tourism. Products are machinery, chemicals, steel, textiles; wheat, corn, barley, seed oils, potatoes, tobacco.
- **ELECTRICITY:** 220 volts, Continental two round-pin plugs. Adaptor and/or transformer required for non-Continental appliances.
- **PASSPORT REQUIREMENTS:** Required for U.S. citizens (with at least six months left before expiry).
- **VISA REQUIREMENTS:** Not required for stays of up to 30 days by U.S. citizens. Visas take about seven working days to process and are valid for three months.
- **DUTY-FREE ITEMS:** 200 cigarettes or 50 cigars or 250g tobacco; 1 liter of liquor; 2 liters of wine; 100g perfume; objects and foodstuffs for personal use during stay.
- **CURRENCY:** The currency unit is the *lev* divided into 100 *stotinki*. Due to currency fluctuations, the exchange rate is subject to frequent change. No limit on import or export of foreign currency, but amounts over 1,000 U.S. dollars must be declared. Visitors are not permitted to either import or export any Bulgarian currency at any time. *Leva* not spent in Bulgaria may be exchanged on presentation of a receipt of origin.
- **BANK OPENING HOURS:** 8–11:30am and 2–6pm Monday–Friday, 8:30–11:30am Saturday. Money can be exchanged at hotels and private exchange bureaus. Credit cards are not widely accepted.
- **STORE OPENING HOURS:** 10am–8pm Monday–Friday, 8am–2pm Saturday.
- **BEST BUYS:** Ceramics, embroidered clothing, linens, carpets, Valley of the Roses perfume, leather, coffee sets.
- **PUBLIC HOLIDAYS:** January 1; March 1 (Liberation Day); Easter Sunday and Monday; May 1 (Labor Day); May 24 (Education Day); December 25.

HISTORY

Bulgaria, northern Greece and European Turkey were home to the Thracians, an Asiatic people, who were conquered by Philip II of Macedonia and his son Alexander the Great in the 4th century BC. After the defeat of Macedonia in 168 BC, the Romans became the dominant power in the Balkans.

By the 1st century AD they had established the provinces of Moesia and Thrace. But Roman rule collapsed with the invasions of the Bulgars, who merged with the great migration of Slavic tribes in the 6th and 7th centuries. Not until the first Bulgarian kingdom was established in AD 681 was the flowering of a national identity possible. St. Cyril and St. Methodius created the Slavonic alphabet in AD 863; Christianity was declared the state religion two years later and the country became the center of Slav culture. Under King Simeon, who ruled from AD 893 to 927, Bulgarian literature attained its golden age and the empire's land holdings expanded to their greatest limits. Internal friction weakened the country and led to the Byzantine occupation from 1018 to 1185.

Independence was regained during the second Bulgarian kingdom, which brought about a renaissance in architecture, painting and literature. In the late 14th century central authority was weakened by opposition from powerful nobles. This led to the Turkish occupation, which ended religious, cultural and political freedom, and brutally suppressed resistance. Monasteries such as Rila and Troyan kept the Bulgarian spirit alive, until in the late 18th century national feelings and political expectations could grow once more.

A failed uprising in 1876 and subsequent Turkish massacres roused international consciousness and enlisted Russian help in the successful Liberation War of 1877–8, which inaugurated the third Bulgarian kingdom of 1879–1944.

Tempted by the offer of Macedonia, which many thought to be part of their country, Bulgaria sided with the Germans in both world wars.

When the former Soviet Union declared war on Bulgaria in 1944, the country subsequently signed an armistice with the Allies. The monarchy was overthrown and the People's Republic of Bulgaria was founded on September 8, 1946, after a referendum.

Communist rule lasted for nearly 50 years, until on November 10, 1989, the country's leader Todor Shivkov resigned. Parliament subsequently voted to revoke the constitutionally guaranteed dominance of the Communist Party.

Today Bulgaria is transforming its political and economic role in Europe. In August 1990, the leader of the opposition party, Dr. Zhelyu Zhelev, was chosen as Bulgaria's first non-Communist president. The first non-Communist government came to power in November 1991, after the Union of the Democratic Forces won the elections. In January 1992, President Zhelev was re-elected in the country's first direct presidential elections.

FOOD AND DRINK
Bulgarian cuisine is mainly influenced by its neighbors, the Turks. Meals begin with salads, usually accompanied by a shot of *rakiya* (grape or plum brandy). Grilled meats are very popular, and there are excellent stews with meat and vegetables cooked slowly together. Bulgarian yoghurt is delicious and is served at breakfast and used in cooking.

Typical dishes include *tarator*, whipped yoghurt soup; *gyuvech*, a mixture of green beans and tomatoes, eggplant, peppers, potatoes and meat; *drob surma*, lamb's liver baked with fried rice; *kebapeheta*, peppery meatballs; and *shopska salat*, salad with grated white cheese, cucumber and tomatoes.

Melnik, Misket, Muscatel and Tamyanka are good local wines. Bulgarians like their food hearty, traditional and varied, and they take time to savor meals; service in restaurants is characteristically unhurried and the *smetkata* (check) will not be brought to you until you ask for it. The main meal is usually eaten in the middle of the day.

SPORTS AND RECREATION
Bulgaria offers many sporting activities for both spectators and participants alike, including tennis, mini-golf, horseback riding and cycling. Downhill skiing takes place at the resorts of Borovets, Vitosha and Pamporovo.

Soccer, volleyball and basketball are popular nationally, and the Black Sea beaches are excellent for water sports. Trout are fished in the Rila Mountain lakes, and pike and carp in the Black Sea and the Dunav (Danube) River. Hunters can contact a variety of new travel agents to arrange vacations in a number of game preserves. Quarry include deer, game birds and wild boar.

GETTING AROUND
Passing through Sofiya (Sofia) and Plovchiv, the main Bulgarian railroad connects to Belgrade in Serbia, and Istanbul in Turkey. Other important routes are the Trans–Balkan, which includes the Sofia–Burgas and Sofia –Varna lines, and the Ruse–Varna route. There are three international airports, and a network of internal flights; regular

---

AUTOMOBILE CLUB
The Union des Automobilistes Bulgares
(U.A.B., Union of Bulgarian Automobilists) has offices at 3 Place Positano, Sofiya 1090. The symbol ▲ beside a city name indicates the presence of a AAA-affiliated automobile club branch. Not all auto clubs offer full travel services to AAA members.

- **USEFUL TELEPHONE NUMBERS:**
  Police 166; Fire 160; Ambulance 150
- **NATIONAL TOURIST OFFICES:**
  Balkan Holidays (U.S.A.) Ltd
  41E 42nd Street
  Suite 508
  New York
  NY 10017
  Tel: 212/573-5530
  Fax: 212/573-5538
  Balkan Holidays
  Sofia House
  19 Conduit Street
  London W1R 9TD,England
  Tel: 0171 491 4499; fax: 0171 491 7068
  Balkantourist
  Boulevard Vitosha 1
  1040 Sofiya
  Bulgaria
  Tel: (2) 88 37 39 or (2) 83 25 45
  Shipka Tourist Agency
  Sveta Sofiya Street 6
  1000 Sofiya, Bulgaria
  Tel: (2) 88 38 56 or (2) 88 42 93
  Fax: (2) 81 96 49 or (2) 81 53 89
- **AMERICAN EMBASSY:**
  Suborna Street 1, Unit 1335
  Sofiya
  Bulgaria
  Tel: (2) 980-5341-8
  U.S. citizens are encouraged to register with the consular section to obtain up-to-date travel information.

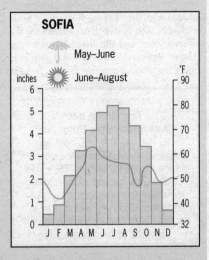

SOFIA

May–June

June–August

inches °F.

passenger boats and hydrofoils serve Varna and Burgas on the Black Sea coast and ports along the Danube River. Several international bus routes pass through Sofia.

Although some are potholed, highways and secondary roads are mostly well-maintained. Bulgaria's main east–west approach runs from Serbia to Turkey and passes through Sofia. Other major highways connect Sofia to Burgas on the Black Sea coast, and link the Black Sea resorts. Driving is on the right and international road signs are used.

The wearing of seat belts (if the car is so equipped) is mandatory for the driver and front-seat passenger outside populated areas; a child under 12 cannot travel in the front seat. Speed limits are 60 k.p.h. (37 m.p.h.) in town, 80 k.p.h. (49 m.p.h.) out of town and 120 k.p.h. (74 m.p.h.) on highways. A U.S. driver's license is not considered valid; only an International Driving Permit is accepted. It is illegal to drive after consuming alcohol. Drivers are required to pay fines for motoring offences on the spot.

In rural areas gas stations are often far apart and sometimes run out of gas; few are open 24 hours. Fill up often when traveling off the beaten track.

ACCOMMODATIONS
Hotels and private rooms for rent in Bulgaria are classified as deluxe, first class, second class and third class. The number of private hotels is growing.

Campers will find a large number of campgrounds in the country, rated as special, first or second class. The top two categories have hot and cold water, showers, electricity, grocery stores and restaurants, telephones and sports facilities. Most sites have chalets for rent. An International Camping Carnet is recommended. The Bulgarian authorities allow camping only at officially designated campgrounds.

TIPPING
Waiters will expect a *stotinki*, or small tip, usually about 10 percent.

SPECIAL EVENTS
The god of wine, Dionysus, is said to have taught viticulture to the ancient Thracians, and the February feast of Tryphon Zarezan honors him with singing, dancing and drinking. Other events include June fire-dancing rituals in the Stranja Mountains and Easter week celebrations featuring Bulgarian costumes. Sofia's National Folk Ensemble is internationally known for its song and dance programs.

PRINCIPAL TOURING AREAS

Note: For descriptions of attractions in **bold type**, see individual listings.

THE BALKANS AND NORTHERN BULGARIA
The Danubian Plain and the Balkan range make up northern Bulgaria. This richly forested region is crisscrossed by a network of rivers and roads. High above a bend in the Jantra River, the city of **Veliko Tŭrnovo** is built on a slope of the Balkan Mountains.

In the western foothills is Belogradchik, a resort area known for its unusual geological formations. Nearby Magoura Cave (Magura Peshtera) contains guano paintings by Bronze Age inhabitants. Situated on the Danube River is Vidin, which has a fortress and 15th-century monuments. Pleven, farther into the Danube Valley, has monuments and museums commemorating the Russo–Turkish War of 1876–78. Kailuka Park, nearby, has accommodations and campgrounds. On the banks of the Danube River is **Ruse**, a sophisticated city with an opera house, theaters, museums and art galleries.

BLACK SEA COAST
The Black Sea washes Bulgaria's eastern coast. Furrowed by coves and headlands, the long stretches of fine sand attract visitors in spring, summer and fall.

North of **Varna**, itself a popular beach resort, there are three modern beach resorts, the tranquil Sts. Konstantin and Elena, **Albena** and **Zlatni Pyasŭtsi** (Golden Sands), Bulgaria's second-largest resort.

Burgas is a lively cultural, industrial and fishing center with its own beach. Just north of Burgas are the therapeutic mud baths of Pomorie. Pomorie also produces a choice wine, Pomorie Dimiat. **Nesebŭr** has architecture recalling a long period of Byzantine rule. **Slŭnchev Bryag**, or Sunny Beach, is a leader among the Black Sea resorts.

South of Burgas, the slopes of the Strandja Mountains stretch to the sea. At the ancient port of **Sozopol**, rustic buildings and fishermen tending their nets contribute to a charming seascape. Beyond Sozopol there is little development, the beaches are often deserted. Towards the Turkish border, the coastline is rocky and there are attractive coves. One of the charms of Bulgaria's Black Sea coast is that, despite its popularity, it is always possible to get away from the crowds. Much of the coast is undeveloped; empty beaches are backed by forests, villages, vineyards and farmland.

PLOVDIV AND THE VALLEY OF THE ROSES
Plovdiv, on the plain between Sofia and Istanbul, Turkey, is a convenient starting point for touring central Bulgaria. Nearby are the Bachkovo Monastery, 13th-century Assen Fortress, Hissarya Spa and Rosova Dolina (the Valley of the Roses).

North of Plovdiv, the Valley of the Roses has acres of damask roses which provide the oil base for the world's perfumes. The best time to tour is in May and

June, when the fragrance of roses fills the valley as workers harvest the blooms, and donkey carts carry the sacks to nearby distilleries. There are several attractive small towns in the valley: Sopot, Karlovo and Kalofer, and at the eastern end, the city of **Kazanlŭk**; a short drive southeast leads to Stara Zagora. Both of these cities have sites of ancient civilizations.

SOFIA AND THE WEST

Sofiya (Sofia), Bulgaria's capital, is set against a background of mountains. Trips by bus or automobile from Sofia to the spa Yavovir Iskúr (Isker Lake), **Rila Manastir** (Rila Monastery), Bankya, Mount Vitosha, or the popular mountain resort of **Borovets** can be made in a day.

SOUTHERN MOUNTAIN REGION

Southern Bulgaria has the country's highest and most extensive mountain region. The Rila Planina and Pirin Planina (the Rila and Pirin ranges) have rocky peaks interspersed with lakes and brooks. The Rodopi Planina (Rhodope Mountains) to the east encompass rolling hills, pastureland and dense forests.

In the Rila range is the south's major tourist draw, the Rila Monastery. The chief ski resort is Borovets, lying about 70 kilometers (43½ miles) south of Sofia; nearby 2,925-meter (9,596-foot) Mount Musala is the highest peak on the Balkan Peninsula. Melnik, in the southwestern region of the Pirin Mountains, is

noted for its architecture, its rich red wine, and the strange-shaped sandstone cliffs which surround it. The mountain resort of **Pamporovo**, 84 kilometers (52 miles) south of Plovdiv in the Rodopi Planina (Rhodope Mountains) has ski areas and coniferous forests.

USEFUL EXPRESSIONS IN BULGARIAN

Bulgarian, the official language, is a South Slavonic tongue and is closely related to Russian. The Cyrillic alphabet is used, and it is important to remember that a sideways shake of the head means "yes," while a nod means "no." English is generally only understood in Sofia, Plovdiv and the main tourist resorts.

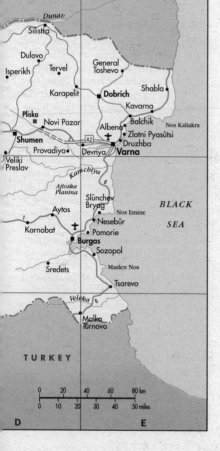

hello	zdraveí (singular/familiar) sdravéite (plural/polite)
good-bye	dovizhdane
good morning	dobró útro
please	mólya
thank you	blagodaryá, mercí
yes/no	da/ne
excuse me	izvinéte
you're welcome	nyáma zashtó
Do you speak English?	Govórite li anglíski?
I do not understand.	Ne vi razbíram.
What is the time?	Kólko e chasút?
How much does it cost?	Kolko struva tova?
I have broken down.	Kolata me se povrédi.
Where is the nearest service station?	Kudé e naiblízkiya ávtoservíz?
Which is the road to Sofiya?	Koi e pútyat za Sófiya?
Where is ...?	Kudé se namira ...?
Where are the restrooms, please?	Kudé e toalétnata, mólya?
museum	muzéi
art gallery	hudózhestvena galériya
restaurant	restoránt
open/closed	otvóreno/zatvóreno

NUMBERS

1	edin/edna/edno
2	dve/dva
3	tri
4	chetiri
5	pet
6	shest
7	sedem
8	osem
9	devet
10	deset
20	dvadeset
30	tridesset
40	chetiridesset
50	petdeset
60	shestdeset
70	sedemdeset
80	osemdeset
90	devetdeset
100	sto

PLACES OF INTEREST

▲ SOFIYA (168 A2) ★

SOFIYA *pop. 1,300,000*

The nation's capital since 1879, Sofiya (Sofia) is fringed by the western mountains of Bulgaria. The city's history began in the 8th century BC, when it was known to the Thracians as *Serdica*.

It was occupied by the Romans in the 1st century BC. During the Middle Ages, under the intermittent rule of Constantinople, it acquired its Byzantine architecture. Later, the Ottoman Empire left Sofia a heritage of Moslem architecture, and succeeding styles include those of the Bulgarian Renaissance.

Sofia's cultural calendar revolves around the Opera House, Concert Hall, the National Art Gallery and theater.

The History Museum has outstanding exhibits. Borisov Park has an open-air theater and sports facilities. There are several monasteries near the city.

Nearby are Bankya, a mineral spa; Pancharevo and Isker lakes; Borovets, a mountain resort and ski center; the rocks of Belogradchik and Magoura Cave.

BUJUK DJAMIJA (Great Mosque), Alexander Stamboliiski Boulevard 2, dates from the 15th century. With its nine lead-covered domes, it is the finest surviving example of Moslem architecture in Bulgaria.

Archeologiceski Musei (Archaeological Museum) has ceramic, silver and bronze historical artifacts.

CERKVA ALEKSANDER NEVSKI ★ (Alexander Nevsky Memorial Church) dominates the impressive square of the same name. The church was begun in 1882 and consecrated in 1924. The great gold-domed structure is built in the style of a Byzantine basilica, with Renaissance, Russian and Oriental elements. Under the largest dome, which is 51 meters (167 feet) high, are the great bells, whose peals can be heard 32 kilometers (20 miles) away. Features are the carved marble iconostasis and thrones, alabaster and onyx columns and paintings by well-known Bulgarian and Russian artists.

CERKVA SVETA SOFIYA (Church of St. Sofiya), Alexander Nevsky Square, was built in the 6th century as a Christian church under Byzantine rule. St. Sofiya's architecture reflects strong Byzantine and Romanesque styles. Later it served as a mosque while under Ottoman rule.

CERKVA SVETI GEORGI (Rotunda of St. George), off St. Nedelya Square, dates from the Roman occupation, when it was possibly a temple or public bath. Under the rule of Constantine the Great, the first Roman emperor to be converted to Christianity, it became a church. It was vandalized by nomads and rebuilt, but much of the church's beauty remains, particularly in the medieval frescoes.

ETHNOGRAFSKI MUSEI (Ethnographic Museum), Alexander Battenberg Square, shares the former royal palace with the National Art Gallery. Regional costumes, tapestries and jewelry are on display.

NATIONAL HISTORY MUSEUM ★, in the old Palace of Justice on Vitosha Boulevard, contains exhibits illustrating Bulgaria's role in world history and culture. The Rogozen silver and Panagyurishte gold treasures are spectacular.

BULGARIA

VITOSHA is a 2,290-meter (7,513-foot) mountain in a recreational park, 8 kilometers (5 miles) south. There are rivers, gorges and waterfalls, hiking trails and excellent skiing facilities.

Bojanska Cerkva (Church of Boyana) is an 11th-century church with 13th-century frescoes that have been compared to the greatest works of the Italian Renaissance. The anonymous paintings are remarkable for their realistic style and as predecessors to the early Italian masters.

ALBENA (169 E3)
VARNA

A resort on the Black Sea coast north of Varna, Albena has a modern skyline and spacious beach with water sports, tennis, cycling, volleyball and basketball. Entertainment includes concerts and folklore displays. The restaurants are moderately priced and often have live music.

BOROVETS (168 B2)
SOFIYA *pop. 500*

A popular winter and summer resort on the northern slopes of the Rila Mountains, Borovets is at the foot of Mount Mussala. The scenery, comfortable climate and winter sports facilities makes it a popular venue for international events.

▲ BURGAS (169 D2)
BURGAS *pop. 200,000*

Burgas is a cultural and busy commercial center, and popular resort on the southern Black Sea coast. The oil refinery makes the port one of the busiest on the Black Sea. There are cafés, stores, historic buildings, theaters and museums.

▲ GABROVO (169 C2) ★
GABROVO *pop. 80,000*

Gabrovo is situated on the banks of the River Yantra and has some attractive buildings in its older riverside quarter. A statue of its 14th-century founder, Racho the Blacksmith, stands on a rock in the river. Gabrovo has the Domna Humorai Satirata (House of Humor and Satire) and hosts a comedy festival in May every odd-numbered year.

KAZANLŬK (168 C2)
STARA ZAGORA *pop. 58,000*

Kazanlŭk is the chief town in the Valley of the Roses. To the north, excavations

---

ROSES

Bulgaria's Rosova Dolina (Valley of the Roses) lies between Kazanlŭk and Klisura. Here over 70 percent of the world's *attar* (oil) of roses is produced. It is, literally, worth its weight in gold. The rose was brought to Europe by Crusaders returning from the Holy Land, hence its name, the Rose of Damascus, or Damask Rose. The roses are harvested in late May/early June, and picked between 3 and 8am, before the sun is hot enough to evaporate the oil. Each acre yields about 3 million rosebuds, but it takes over 1 hectares (2.5 acres) of roses to produce just 1 liter (1½ pints) of the precious *attar*. Rose oil is the basis of most modern perfumes. The residual products are used to make medicines, cosmetics, rose jam and liqueurs, as well as the seductive Turkish delight.

---

have uncovered a 4th-century Thracian tomb decorated with murals of abstract design and battle scenes. There is no public access to the site, but an impressive replica of the tomb is nearby.

MUSEUM OF THE ROSE INDUSTRY gives an introduction to the area's main industry; the production of rose *attar* (oil) for the international perfume industry.

KOPRIVSHTITSA (168 B2) ★
SOFIYA

Koprivshtitsa is situated in the Gora Mountains. Houses lining its narrow, cobbled streets have intricately carved ceilings, bay windows and verandas. The whole town has been declared an architectural monument.

NESEBŬR (169 E2) ★
BURGAS *pop. 7,000*
Nesebŭr is an ancient fishing village on the Black Sea coast. It has pretty houses, cobbled streets and some notable Byzantine churches.

PAMPOROVO (168 B1)
SMOLIJAN
Pamporovo, set at an altitude of 1,600 meters (5,249 feet) in the Rhodope Mountains near Plovdiv, is the most southerly ski resort in Europe. It has good facilities, with runs for all levels of experience.

▲ PLOVDIV (168 B1) ★
PLOVDIV *pop. 360,000*
Settled long before Philip II of Macedonia conquered it and named it Philippopolis in the 4th century BC, Plovdiv is one of the oldest cities in Europe. The well-preserved Hissar Kapiya (Gate of the Fortress) leads to the Old City, Plovdiv's major attraction, with its cobblestone alleys and quaintly decorated houses from the National Renaissance period.

Just south of Plovdiv, the forests and rocky peaks of the Rhodope Mountains are a favorite excursion and camping area.

ARCHEOLOGICESKI MUSEI (Archaeological Museum), in the Old City, is known for its cache of gold and silver objects, which date from the Thracian period.

BACHKOVSKI MANASTIR (Bachkovo Monastery), founded in 1089, contains priceless icons, frescoes and works by the most famous of Bulgaria's National artists, Zahari Zograf.

DJUMAYA DJAMIYA, on Stambolijski Square, is a 15th-century mosque, built on the site of a Christian church.

GEORGIADI HOUSE, Starinna Street, was built 1846–48 by the master builder Georgi of Constantinople. A fine example of a graceful house, it contains the Museum of the Renaissance and an exhibition on the political history of Bulgaria.

HOUSE OF ARGYR KOUYUMDJIOGLOU, on Dr. Comakov Street, was designed by the builder Georgi in the mid-19th century. The symmetrical house has richly ornamented exteriors and interiors. An ethnological museum inside contains reproductions of craftsmen's workshops, old farming tools, spinning and weaving implements and national costumes.

RILA MANASTIR (168 A2) ★
SOFIYA
RILA MANASTIR (Rila Monastery), had considerable religious influence in the Middle Ages and was a center of resistance against Ottoman domination. The monastery as it stands today is what remains of the 10th-century buildings of John of Rila, who fled the excesses of court life to found a hermitage. Over the centuries succeeding restorations were carried out, with the final form established in the mid-19th century during the Bulgarian National Renaissance.

Hrelyo Tower, 23 meters (75½ feet) tall, and its valuable murals date from the 14th century. The commanding outer walls contrast with the striped arcades, columns, flights of stairs and flowing fountains of the inner courtyard. The church has vaults and walls covered with frescoes, heavily ornamented chandeliers and a carved wooden iconostasis.

Rila Museum, on the ground floor, contains parchment manuscripts, icons, weapons, vestments, coins and various other exhibits.

▲ RUSE (168 C3)
RUSE *pop. 151,500*
Ruse was a Roman fort built in the 1st century BC. Captured by the Ottomans in the 14th century, it became an important commercial town. Today it is a major port and industrial center. Interesting sights include fine baroque buildings, the Museum of Transportation and spacious Lipnik Park.

Ruse is linked with Romania by the Danube Bridge. About 25 kilometers (16 miles) south of Ruse is the medieval town of Cerven; 10 kilometers (6 miles) farther is the monastery of Ivanovo, cut from solid rock.

STREET NAMES

In Bulgaria many streets are named after political figures. This has resulted in recent changes as the names of Communist heroes are replaced by those of former kings and figures from Bulgarian history. However, three old street names are certain to survive.

Vassil Levski was a leading revolutionary against the Ottoman occupation, who was captured and executed by the Turks.

Hristo Botev was an inspiring revolutionary and poet, who was killed in action during the April Uprising in 1876.

Ivan Vazov was a contemporary of Levski and Botev. His poems and novels, especially the famous *Under the Yoke*, give a vivid picture of the brutality and corruption of life in the Ottoman Empire.

SLŬNCHEV BRYAG (169 E2)
BURGAS

White sand beaches have made Slŭnchev Bryag (Sunny Beach) a modern resort popular with families.

Traditional Bulgarian food and music can be found at folk-style restaurants, and the streets are busy with artists and musicians.

SOZOPOL (169 E2) ★
BURGAS *pop. 4,000*

The ancient fishing village of Sozopol, on the Black Sea coast, is a popular resort distinguished by winding, cobbled streets, old buildings and architecturally interesting churches.

▲ VARNA (169 E3)
VARNA *pop. 300,000*

Inhabited since the Stone Age, Varna was known to 6th-century Greek settlers as Odessos and is today the capital of the Black Sea coastal resorts. The city is also an important cultural and industrial center, with a wide range of historical sights and attractions. The Museum of History and Art has an impressive collection of Greek, Thracian and Roman artifacts as well as Bulgarian gold and silver from the 14th century.

Trips from Varna include the scenic nature reserve of Kamchiya to the south, the rock monastery of Aladzha to the north, and the bizarre geological formations of the Stone Forest to the west.

▲ VELIKO TŬRNOVO (168 C2) ★
TŬRNOVO *pop. 90,000*

This town achieved its greatest prominence as the medieval capital of the second Bulgarian kingdom, 1187–1396. The Old Town lies on the western bank of the Yantra. Most of its churches and civic buildings were erected during the 19th-century National Renaissance. The town can be reached by rail or road, including the route to the southwest through the Valley of the Roses.

ARBANASSI, about 4 kilometers (2½ miles) northeast of Tŭrnovo, reached the height of its prosperity in the 17th and 18th centuries. From outside the houses look like small fortresses, but inside the carved wooden ceilings and comfortable furnishings are evidence of the wealth of the inhabitants. The town's prosperous merchants also endowed local churches, which have beautiful frescoes.

ZLATNI PYASŬTSI (169 E3)
VARNA

The resort of Zlatni Pyasŭtsi (Golden Sands) is just north of Varna. Its fine beach is over 4 kilometers (2½ miles) long, and slopes gently to the sea, which has no dangerous currents. Historic and interesting Aladza Monastery is 3 kilometers (2 miles) southwest of the town.

CZECH REPUBLIC

PRAGUE WAS ALWAYS THE GOLDEN CITY, ITS WEALTH OF BAROQUE BUILDINGS AND GOTHIC CHURCHES SCARCELY TOUCHED BY WARS. IT WATCHED OVER THE 1968 PRAGUE SPRING AND THE VELVET REVOLUTION OF 1989, WHEN A PLAYWRIGHT, VÁCLAV HAVEL, BECAME PRESIDENT. MUCH OF THIS OCCURRED IN WENCESLAS SQUARE, A FIRST STOP ON ANY ITINERARY, CLOSELY FOLLOWED BY THE OLD TOWN SQUARE AND CHARLES BRIDGE, WHICH LEADS TO HRADČANY – PRAGUE CASTLE. PRAGUE IS ONE OF THREE U.N.E.S.C.O. WORLD HERITAGE SITES IN THE CZECH REPUBLIC; THE OTHERS ARE TELČ AND ČESKÝ KRUMLOV. THE INCOMPARABLY BEAUTIFUL TOWN OF ČESKÝ KRUMLOV STANDS, LIKE PRAGUE, ON THE VLTAVA RIVER. TELČ IS AN ALMOST PERFECTLY PRESERVED 16TH-CENTURY TOWN. THE CZECH REPUBLIC MAY CENTER ON PRAGUE, BUT WITH ITS MANY CHÂTEAUS AND SPA TOWNS IT OFFERS MUCH MORE.

Left THE SMALL WINE-PRODUCING TOWN OF KARLŠTEJN NESTLES IN THE VALLEY BELOW THE IMPRESSIVE BOHEMIAN KARLŠTEJN CASTLE
Above THE ASTRONOMICAL CLOCK IN STAROMĚSTSKÉ NÁMĚSTÍ

Things to Know

- **Area:** 78,864 square kilometers (30,442 square miles)
- **Population:** 10,300,000
- **Capital:** Praha (Prague)
- **Language:** Czech
- **Religion:** Roman Catholic, Protestant
- **Economy:** Engineering, vehicles, chemicals, textiles, brown coal, iron ore, mixed agriculture.
- **Electricity:** 220 volts, Continental two round-pin plugs (in older parts 120 volts). An adaptor and/or transformer is required for non-Continental appliances.
- **Passport Requirements:** Required for U.S. citizens.
- **Visa Requirements:** Not required for stays of less than 30 days.
- **Duty-Free Items:** 250 cigarettes or tobacco equivalent; 1 liter of liquor, 2 liters of wine; ¼ liter of cologne; gifts up to 3,000 *koruna česká* in value.
- **Currency:** The currency unit is the *koruna česká* (Czech crown), divided into 100 *haléř* (hellers). The exchange rate is subject to frequent change. There are no restrictions on the import and export of foreign currency and travelers' checks up to the amounts declared on entry. Czech currency may not be imported or exported.
- **Bank Opening Hours:** 8am–5pm Monday–Friday, may close during lunch.
- **Store Opening Hours:** 9am–6pm Monday–Friday, 9am–1pm Saturday. Food stores open from 6am. Late-night shopping Thursday. Increasing numbers of stores open Sunday.
- **Best Buys:** Bohemian glass and crystal, gems, jewelry, porcelain, toys, dolls, puppets, handicrafts, CDs.
- **Public Holidays:** January 1; Easter Monday; May 1 (May Day); May 8 (Liberation Day); July 5 (Saints Cyril and Methodius); July 6 (Master John Huss); October 28 (Independence Day); December 25, 26.
- **Useful Telephone Numbers:** Police 158; Fire 150; Ambulance 155

History

The area of the Czech Republic (comprising the historic lands of Bohemia, Moravia and part of Silesia) was first occupied by the Celts, then the Teutons, followed in the 6th century AD by Slav tribes, who formed the Great Moravian Empire. Under Charles IV, Praha (Prague) became the political and cultural center of the empire. In later years, the country was riven with political and religious strife; preacher Jan Hus was burned at the stake in 1415, while the Thirty Years' War was heralded in 1618 by the defenestration of Catholic councillors from Prague's Hrad (castle). After the Battle of the White Mountain in 1620 the Czechs were ruled from Vienna by the Habsburgs.

The collapse of the Habsburg Empire led to the creation of the new state of Czechoslovakia in 1918. In 1938, the Munich Conference left the prosperous and politically stable Czechoslovakia powerless in the face of Nazi Germany, and in 1939 the country was dismembered and Bohemia and Moravia become a Nazi protectorate. In 1945, U.S. troops liberated western Bohemia, and the Red Army freed the rest of the country. Communists seized power in 1948, and an attempt in 1968 by reformists to establish "Socialism with a human face," led by Alexander Dubček, was crushed by Soviet-led troops.

With the collapse of Communism throughout Eastern Europe in 1989, the Czechs brought about the Velvet Revolution. Playwright Václav Havel was elected president. Differences between Czechs and Slovaks on how to form a new democratic state led to an agreement in 1992 to separate. The Czech Republic was proclaimed on January 1, 1993.

Food and Drink

Meals might begin with cold meats and pickles and end with a cream cake. Smoked foods and soups are Czech specialities. Meat, very often pork, is served well done and accompanied by gravy, dumplings and sauerkraut or red cabbage. Fresh vegetables and fruit are rare. The national drink is beer; Czech beers are among the best in the world.

SPORTS AND RECREATION
The country has a good reputation in tennis, ice hockey and gymnastics. Soccer is popular both for fans and players. Outdoor activities like climbing, fishing and rambling are popular. Water sports take place on the many large reservoirs.

GETTING AROUND
International flights center on Praha Ruzyně Airport and there is a network of internal services. Railroads are good, with low fares. Buses serve every settlement in the country, and there are also international services. Public transportation in cities, by tram and bus, is generally excellent. Prague has its own metro (subway).

AUTOMOBILE CLUB
Ústřední Automotoklub
CR (U.A.M.K., Central Automobile Club) has its headquarters at Na Strzi 9, 140 00 Praha 4. The symbol ▲ indicates the presence of a AAA-affiliated automobile club branch. Not all auto clubs offer full travel services to AAA members.

The highway system is good, though some minor roads are in poor condition.

Seat belts must be worn by everyone. Children under 12 may not travel in the front seat. Speed limits are 60 k.p.h. (37 m.p.h.) in urban areas, 90 k.p.h. (55 m.p.h.) in the country and 110 k.p.h. (68 m.p.h.) on highways. Motoring fines must be paid on the spot.

ACCOMMODATIONS
Hotels are classified by star ratings which range from one (basic) to five (deluxe).

The number of hotels is growing and older hotels are being modernized. An increasing number of private residents are providing bed and breakfast, particularly in Prague, and there are numerous campgrounds, many of which have chalets.

TIPPING
It is customary at a restaurant to give a gratuity of 10 percent, likewise with taxis. Hotel porters should receive a few *koruna česká*, as should lavatory attendants.

PRINCIPAL TOURING AREAS

Note: For descriptions of attractions in **bold type**, see individual listings.

PRAGUE AND SURROUNDING AREA
Praha (Prague) is a beautifully preserved city at the heart of Europe, unscathed by the devastation of war. Its architectural heritage is incomparable, and since the fall of Communism it has become one of Europe's liveliest and culturally most vibrant cities. It is at the heart of the province of Bohemia and many of the major tourist attractions are within easy reach. These include romantic castles, as well as the richly wooded gorges of Vltava, Sázava and Berounka.

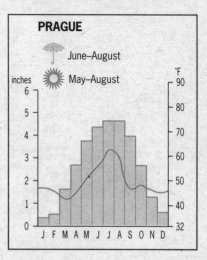

PRAGUE

June–August
May–August

WESTERN BOHEMIA

The border with Bavaria is marked by the cool green uplands of the Šumava (Bohemian Forest) – wonderful walking country. In woodlands are the spa towns **Mariánské Lázně** and, **Karlovy Vary** and the medieval city of Cheb. Plzeň is home to Pilsner beer and heavy industries.

NORTHERN BOHEMIA

An industrialized region, with many power plants; acid rain has damaged some of the forest, but much remains. The Krkonoše (Giant Mountains) are popular with hikers and skiers.

SOUTHERN BOHEMIA

Delightful villages with high-gabled houses and baroque churches typify this area. Most of the towns date from the

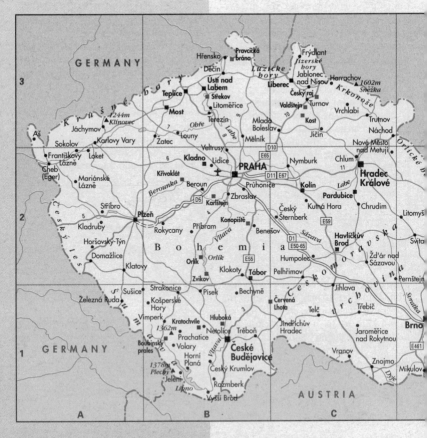

CZECH CASTLES

Richly endowed with castles and fine country houses, the country-side of the Czech Republic reflects an aristocratic past. Under communism there was no place for these splendid residences and they either became museums, were turned into schools and hostels, or simply crumbled away. After 1989, the process of restitution began, with many buildings returned to their owners and slowly restored to something resembling their former glory.

Middle Ages and many, like tiny **Český Krumlov**, or **České Budějovice** with its Renaissance square, are well-preserved.

MORAVIA

In the north, forested highlands provide a green background to the industrialized area around Ostrava. There are exquisite small towns, like Kroměříž and **Telč**, some of the finest castles and châteaus, and villages among the vineyards.

USEFUL EXPRESSIONS IN CZECH

hello	ahoj
good-bye	na shledanou
please	prosím
thank you	děkuji
yes/no	ano/ne
good morning	dobrý den
good evening	dobrý večer
good night	dobrou noc
why?/when?	proč?/když?
where?/what?	kde?/co?
how much?	kolik?
Do you speak English?	mluvíte anglicky?
I don't speak Czech.	nemluvím česky.
I don't understand.	nerozumím.
sorry	promiňte
you're welcome	děkuji
quickly/slowly	rychle/pomalu
cold/hot	studený/horký
left/right	nalevo/napravo
open/closed	otevřeno/zavřeno
expensive/cheap	drahý/levný
near/far	blízko/daleko
day/week	den/týden
month/year	měsíc/rok
café/restaurant	kavárna/restaurace
church	kostel
cathedral	chrám
castle	hrad
town	město
bridge	most
tower	věž
palace	palác
garden	zahrada
monastery/convent	klášter
square	náměstí
market	trh
pharmacy	lekárna
city hall	radnice
station	nádraži
avenue	třída

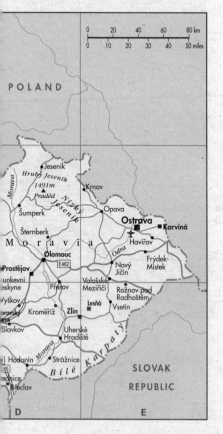

PLACES OF INTEREST

PRAHA ★
CENTRAL BOHEMIA *pop. 1,210,000*

Praha, or Prague, is an ancient metropolis that has preserved its rich heritage through centuries of war and discord.

Divided by the Vltava River, the city has four historic quarters: Hradčany, the castle district high above the river; Malá Strana (Lesser Quarter), on the west bank; Staré Město (Old Town), centered on Old Town Square; and the Nové Město (New Town), centered on Václavské náměstí, Wenceslas Square.

In the 14th century, under Emperor Charles IV, the city became the capital of the Holy Roman Empire; the great Gothic Katredrála Sv. Vita (St. Vitus' Cathedral) and Karlův Most (Charles Bridge) were built and the Nové Město laid out. The 19th century left a legacy of great public buildings such as the national theater and national museum. Prague was at the forefront of art nouveau and early modern building.

The city offers numerous theater performances, several orchestras, organ concerts in churches, and puppet shows. The Prague Spring music festival in May attracts many visitors. Prague's *hospody* (pubs) are just as famous. There are wine bars and an increasing number of restaurants. The city center is compact

and best explored on foot with help from the superb public transportation system.

There are many interesting castles around Prague; Karlštejn Castle, 28 kilometers (17½ miles) southwest, was built by Charles IV as a holy shrine and reposi-

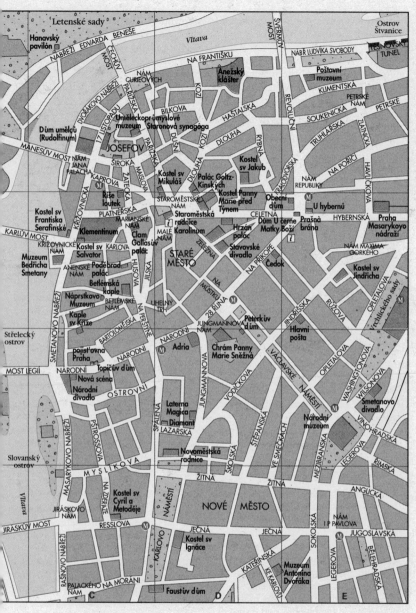

tory for the crown jewels. Other castles include Křivoklát and Konopiště.

ANEŽSKÝ KLÁŠTER (St. Agnes' Convent) (181 D4), Staré Město, is a convent dating from 1233 and painstakingly restored to

house the National Gallery's collection of 19th-century Czech art.

BERTRÁMKA (Mozart Museum), Mozartova 169, is where Mozart completed his opera *Don Giovanni*, only hours before its

CZECH REPUBLIC

first performance at the Estates Theater in the Staré Mesto (Old Town).

HRAD (180 A4) ★, Hradčany, Prague's enormous castle, now the residence of the president, has been a Slav fortress, a princely palace and a seat of empire. As well as presidential offices, it contains churches, concert halls, museums, gardens and restaurants. The views from here are the best in the city.

Bazilika Sv. Jiří (St. George's Basilica) has a baroque west front, but the twin towers and sober interior are Romanesque. Concerts are held here, while the adjoining monastery has been converted into a gallery of Czech art.

Katedrála Sv. Víta' (St. Vitus' Cathedral), has a distinctive outline of twin spires and a central tower capped by a Renaissance helmet. The interior has treasures from all periods of Bohemian art and includes the spectacularly decorated Gothic St. Wenceslas Chapel.

Královská zahrada (Royal Garden). Among the fine old trees and formal gardens is the Renaissance belvedere, a graceful summer palace.

Starý Královský palác (Royal Palace). Above the 12th-century cellars is the Vladislavský sál (Vladislav Hall). It was from a window in the St. Louis Wing that the Catholic councillors were thrown in 1618, the incident that set off the Thirty Years' War.

Zlatá ulička (Golden Lane) is lined with pretty but tiny houses, the dwellings of the alchemists employed to turn base metal into gold for Emperor Rudolph II.

JOSEFOV (Joseph's Town) (181 C4), is the former Jewish quarter. Its principal monuments include the Old Jewish Cemetery, the Jewish Town Hall with its baroque clock tower, and the Gothic Old-New Synagogue.

KARLŮV MOST (Charles Bridge) ★ (180 B3–C3), built in 1357, is carried on 16 massive Gothic arches across the Vltava. It is lined with impressive statuary.

KOSTEL SV. CYRIL A METODEJE (Church of Saints Cyril and Methodius) (181 C1), is where the Czech assassins of the Nazi leader, Reinhard Heydrich, were trapped and killed. There is a small exhibition in the crypt.

KOSTEL SV. MIKULÁŠE (Church of St. Nicholas) Old Town Square, is Prague's most breathtaking baroque church, with an impressive dome and lavish sculpture.

MALOSTRANSKÉ NÁMĚSTÍ (Little Town Square) ★ (180 A4–B4) lined with palaces and fine town houses is dominated by the huge St. Nicholas' Church.

OBECNÍ DŮM (Municipal House) (181 E3), a complex of concert halls, restaurants and bars, the greatest example of art nouveau architecture in Prague.

PETŘÍN HILL (180 A3) offers fine walks and views of the city. There is a funicular railroad here, and it is the site of Strahov Monastery.

STAROMĚSTSKÉ NÁMĚSTÍ (Old Town Square) ★ (181 D3) has a memorial to Jan Hus. The square is especially crowded when the figures above the ancient astronomical clock appear. The towers of Tyn Church rise above the square.

SVEJK TO THE RESCUE

One of the foremost characters of Czech literature is Jaroslav Hasek's Good Soldier Svejk, a seeming simpleton whose cheerful innocence reduces the oppressive Austrian army of World War I to chaos and confusion. Like most male Czechs, Svejk likes his beer, arranging to meet his mate Vodicka in his favorite pub, the Chalice, "at half-past six" when the war is over. The Chalice is still there in Prague's New Town, a mecca for lovers of beer and Hasek's subversive soldier.

ŠTERNBERSKÝ PALÁC (Sternberg Palace) (180 A4–B4), Hradčany, houses the national gallery's collection of European art.

VÁCLAVSKÉ NÁMĚSTÍ (Wenceslas Square) (181 D2–E2) is Prague's shopping and nightclub center. In front of the national museum is the statue of St. Wenceslas.

VYSEHRAD (High Castle), above the Vltava, is the legendary home of Prague's first Slavic settlers. A public park since the 1920s, it had earlier been used as a fortified barracks by the Habsburgs. The nearby cemetery is the burial place of many great Czech scientists and artists, including Dvorák and Smetana.

BRNO (178 D1)
MORAVIA pop. 400,000
Brno has many historic buildings and interesting museums. To the east is the Napoleonic battlefield of Austerlitz (Slavkov) with its Memorial to Peace and the baroque palace where the cease-fire was signed. The Moravian Karst district to the north has a deep chasm and over 400 caves.

ČESKÉ BUDĚJOVICE (178 B1)
SOUTHERN BOHEMIA pop. 97,000
Founded in the 13th century, the city is focused on a central square. Arcaded buildings line its long sides, with baroque façades concealing the medieval structure behind. The Radnice (city hall) has towers and gargoyles. The square is overlooked by the Černá věž (Black Tower), which houses the bells of the cathedral. České Budějovice's name in German is Budweis, and it is famous for its beer, a rival to Plzeň's Pilsner.

ČESKÝ KRUMLOV (178 B1) ★
SOUTHERN BOHEMIA pop. 14,000
The medieval town is laid out around a little square with a Renaissance town hall, while the 300-room moated castle is high above. A ballroom is painted with trompe l'oeil figures and there is a baroque theater, still with its original stage machinery and equipment.

KARLOVY VARY (178 A3) ★
WESTERN BOHEMIA pop. 58,000
Guests have been coming here since the 16th century to sample the healing sulfurous springs. It reached the peak of its prestige at the turn of the century. Karlovy Vary regularly hosts international film festivals and music festivals. The town is famous for its porcelain and herbal liqueur, Becherovka.

KUTNÁ HORA (178 C2) ★
CENTRAL BOHEMIA
Kutná Hora is 65 kilometers (40 miles) southeast of Prague. The royal mint was established here when silver deposits were discovered in the 13th century (Kuntá Hora minted the first silver dollars). The mint – known as the Italian Court – can be visited. The medieval mine workings are now a museum. The spectacular St. Barbara Cathedral is a massive, tentlike construction and has frescoes dedicated to the town's miners. In the suburb of Sedlec is a macabre ossuary that has over 40,000 skeletons arranged in bizarre designs by 19th-century artist František Rint.

MARIÁNSKÉ LÁZNĚ (178 A2) ★
WESTERN BOHEMIA pop. 15,000
There are fine late 19th-century hotels built to serve the cosmopolitan guests who once flocked to this ultra-fashionable spa town.

OLOMOUC (179 D2)
MORAVIA pop. 106,000
Every July Olomouc hosts the national garden festival, Flora Olomouc. Its spacious Horní náměstí (Upper Square) has a huge baroque column and an astronomical clock.

TELČ (178 C1) ★
MORAVIA pop. 5,000
Surrounded by fishponds, and entered through defensive gateways, this tiny medieval town in southern Moravia has a cobbled square, arcaded houses and stores. The Renaissance palace of Telč castle is on the west side of the square.

HUNGARY

Hungary, a country with a rich cultural history, has produced many influential figures in the arts and sciences, including brilliant pianist and composer Franz Liszt and Nobel Prize-winning physicist Edward Teller.

The Iron Curtain came down on Hungary in 1949 and was not lifted for 40 years, despite brave attempts in 1956. A strong-willed people, two million Hungarians — one-fifth of the entire population — live in the capital Budapest, which is divided by the Danube River into Buda and Pest. It is one of the three great cities of central and eastern Europe, along with Prague and Vienna. Beyond its cities, Hungary's countryside has many rivers and lakes. The largest is Lake Balaton in the west, its shores dotted with popular resorts.

Left Budapest's magnificent Parliament Building on the Danube
Above left Detail on the main door of St. Stephen Basilica in Budapest
Above right Hungarian doll in traditionally embroidered costume

185

Things to Know

- **Area:** 93,030 square kilometers (35,919 square miles)
- **Population:** 10,400,000
- **Capital:** Budapest
- **Language:** Hungarian
- **Religion:** Roman Catholic
- **Economy:** Industry, construction, agriculture. Exports are machinery, fruit, bauxite, vegetables, textiles, footwear.
- **Electricity:** 220 volts.
- **Passport:** Required for U.S. citizens.
- **Visa Requirements:** Not required for stays up to three months.
- **Duty-Free Items:** 250 cigarettes or 50 cigars or 250 grams tobacco; 1 liter of liquor, 2 liters of wine; food for three days; gifts up to 8,000 *forints*; personal belongings. Valuable personal effects must be declared on entry.
- **Currency:** The currency unit is the *forint*, divided into 100 *fillérs*. The exchange rate is subject to frequent change. No limits on import of foreign currency, but a declaration is required.
- **Bank Opening Hours:** 9am–5pm Monday–Friday.
- **Store Opening Hours:** 10am–6pm Monday–Friday, 9am–1pm Saturday; most department stores open 10am–7/8pm weekdays.
- **Best Buys:** Herend porcelain, silverware, hand-made pottery, embroidery, lace, costumed dolls, shoes.
- **Public Holidays:** January 1; March 15 (National Holiday); Easter Monday; May 1 (Labor Day); Whit Monday; August 20 (St. Stephen's Day); October 23 (Proclamation of the Republic); December 25, 26.
- **National Tourist Offices:**
  Hungarian Tourist Board
  150 East 58th Street, New York,
  NY 10155, Tel: 212/355-0240
  Tourinform
  Süto Utca 2, Budapest, Hungary
  Tel: 117 9800; Fax: 117 9578
- **American Embassy:**
  Szabadság Tér 12,
  Budapest H-1054, Hungary,
  Tel: 267 4400; fax: 269 9326

History

The founders of the Hungarian nation, the Magyars, crossed the Carpathian Mountains in the late 9th century AD. By AD 907 they had defeated the Slavs and Germans and were secure in their new homeland. In 1241–42 the Mongols stormed in from the east, leaving a trail of destruction, but the country recovered, pushing its boundaries outwards in the 14th century and enjoying a Golden Age from 1458 to 1490.

In 1485 Hungary's king stormed Vienna and occupied Austria, Styria and Carinthia. All these lands were soon lost, and in 1526, Turks routed the Hungarian army in the disastrous battle at

Mohács. In 1541 Turkish forces occupied Buda, and virtually the whole of Hungary remained a part of the Ottoman Empire until the Habsburgs recaptured Buda in 1686. In 1848 Lajos Kossuth led a revolt that the Habsburgs only managed to put down with the help of the Russian tzar. In 1867, what became known as "The Compromise" allowed the Hungarian state a high degree of autonomy within the Habsburg Empire.

On the losing side in World War I, the rule of the Habsburg monarchy ended and Treaty of Trianon (1920) stripped Hungary of two-thirds of its territory. Siding with the Germans in World War II, Hungary attempted to regain its lost territory, but after its defeat the country was occupied by Soviet forces. Resistance to Soviet control broke out in 1956 under the leadership of Imre Nagy. Soviet suppression was swift, Nagy was executed and many Hungarians fled to the West.

Gorbachev's reforms in Russia loosened the Eastern bloc's control over Hungary. In 1989 the country's Communists relinquished their absolute power and in 1990 the Democratic Forum formed the first non-Communist government in more than 40 years. The country has embraced democracy and a market economy – with the aim of full integration within the European Union.

HUNGARY

FOOD AND DRINK

The red pepper gives Hungary its best known spice – paprika. It is combined with flour, onions and pork to create several Hungarian specialties. Potatoes and tomatoes added to the mixture produces *gulyás* (goulash). A similar dish is *pörkölt*, often made with vegetables, game or poultry; with the addition of sour cream, *pörkölt* becomes *paprikas*. *Rétes* is a thin, flaky pastry with apple, sour cherry or nuts. *Palacsinta* are thin pancakes that come with sweet or savory fillings. Around Eger are red wines, including the dry, dark Bull's Blood, *Egri Bikavér*. Part of the harvest of the orchards is distilled into fiery spirits like *barackpálinka* – apricot brandy.

SPORTS AND RECREATION

Soccer and basketball are the main sports. Horseback riding and horse racing are popular pursuits. Swimming and water polo are also popular and the lakes offer sailing and windsurfing. There are over 100 thermal baths and spas across the country. There is some skiing in the mountains in the north, as well as skating in Budapest's City Park.

GETTING AROUND

Budapest's international Ferihegy Airport is linked to most European capitals by direct flights and there is also a direct service to New York operated by Malev, Hungary's national airline. Most internal trips are made by rail using the network operated by the Hungarian State Railway. There are rail connections with neighboring countries, as well as with a number of European capitals including Paris and London. The network of internal bus services is well-developed.

Public transportation in cities is efficient and cheap, though often overcrowded. Some cities have trams and trolley buses as well as ordinary buses, and Budapest has a three-line subway. Boat trips on the Danube and on Balaton are a must, and there is a hydrofoil linking Budapest with Vienna.

The road system is well-developed and, by east European standards, well-maintained. Driving after drinking alcohol is strictly forbidden and the use of dimmed headlights is compulsory in daylight

---

AUTOMOBILE CLUB
Magyar Autóklub
(M.A.K. Hungarian Auto Club) is at Rómer Flóris Utca 4/A, 1024 Budapest. The symbol ▲ beside a city name indicates the presence of a AAA-affiliated automobile club branch. Not all auto clubs offer full travel services to AAA members.

---

hours outside built-up areas. Speed limits are 50 k.p.h. (31 m.p.h.) in urban areas, 80 k.p.h. (49 m.p.h.) on ordinary highways, 100 k.p.h. (62 m.p.h.) on limited access highways, and 120 k.p.h. (74 m.p.h.) on freeways. Seat belts must be worn and children under 12 may not ride in the front seat. Motoring fines must be paid on the spot.

ACCOMMODATIONS

Scálbda (hotels) are graded from one (basic) to five (deluxe). Travel agencies

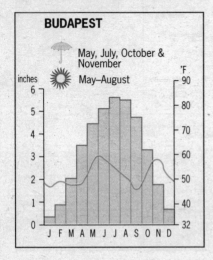

BUDAPEST

May, July, October & November

May–August

offer a regulated system of private rooms *(fizetövendég szolgálat)* with bed and breakfast. Roadside signs also advertise vacant rooms. Look out for *kastélyszálló*, hotels located in historic castles or mansions. For more modest surroundings, farmhouses and cottages can be rented, and there are plenty of campgrounds.

ARTS AND ENTERTAINMENT

Hungary is a music-loving country, the birthplace of Liszt, Kodály and Bartók. The major cities offer symphony orchestras – the Budapest Philharmonic is particularly fine – chamber music and organ recitals as well as theater and ballet. The cultural highlight, Budapest's Spring Festival in mid-March, includes symphonic concerts, opera, jazz and folklore nights, operetta and ballet.

TIPPING

Tipping is an accepted practice. Tip waiters and taxi drivers 10 to 15 percent. Gypsy violinists expect a small gratuity.

PRINCIPAL TOURING AREAS

Note: For descriptions of attractions in **bold type**, see individual listings.

BUDAPEST AND THE DANUBE

The Danube River divides **Budapest** into two, Buda and Pest. A fascinating holiday destination, the city is also a good place to start tours of this strech of the river, called the Danube Bend. The river runs through a gorge at the fortress of **Visegrád**, and extends west to **Esztergom**, headquarters of Hungarian Catholicism. Farther west are the regional centers of **Győr** and **Sopron**.

GREAT PLAIN (ALFÖLD)

Alföld (Great Plain) begins on the outskirts of Pest and covers most of eastern Hungary. It is mostly farmland and home to cattle, sheep and the almost-extinct bustard. The region is especially popular for riding. Kecskemét is known for its apricot brandy and stunning art-nouveau architecture. Debrecen, the second largest city, is a Protestant stronghold.

LAKE BALATON

Lake Balaton is a vacation favorite. The flat, southern shore has several resorts known as the Hungarian Riviera. Siófok is the largest, but Balantonföldvár, Balatonlelle and Fonyód are also popular, with sandy beaches, good accommodations and fine views. The north shore has vines, woods and volcanoes.

NORTHERN MOUNTAINS

The northeastern border with the Slovak Republic, is lined by the Northern Mountains, containing the finest vineyards in Hungary. The mountains are good for skiing and delightful for walks by lakes and castles. At the foot of the Mátra is Gyöngyös, capital of the country's wine industry. To the east are the Bükk, or Beech Mountains, with wineries at **Eger**.

WESTERN HILLS

The foothills of the Alps form the border with Austria; towns in the region include **Sopron, Kőzeg, and Szombathely,** the oldest town in Hungary. The "Little Plain" stretches south to rolling hills above Lake Balaton and east past the old town of Győr to charming **Tata**.

USEFUL EXPRESSIONS IN HUNGARIAN

hello	szia!/szervusz!
(can also mean good-bye)	
good-bye	viszontlátásra
good morning	jó reggelt kivánok
please/thank-you	kérem/köszönöm
yes/no	igen/nem
excuse me	bocsánat
you're welcome	szivesen
Do you speak English?	beszél angolul?
I don't understand.	nem értem
What is the time?	hány óra?
Where are the restrooms?	hol van a WC/ mosdó?

PLACES OF INTEREST

HUNGARY

★ HIGHLIGHTS ★	
Budapest	(see p.190)
Fertőd	(see p.191)
Lake Balaton	(see p.192)

▲ BUDAPEST (187 C2) ★

BUDAPEST *pop. 2,009,000*

Originally three separate settlements, Buda and Óbuda on the west bank and Pest on the east merged in the late 19th century to form Budapest. Each historic core has kept a distinctive identity.

The walled city of Pest was outgrown in the 19th century when grand boulevards were laid out, but the medieval Inner City is still the commercial, financial and governmental district.

Across the river on the hilly west bank is Buda. Medieval Buda grew on the narrow plateau of Castle Hill.

Even older is Óbuda, built on the site of the Roman town of Aquincum at the foot of the hill. The hot springs here were well-known to the Romans and the Turks.

Budapest has opera houses, numerous concert halls and theaters and a large sports stadium. The city hosts a variety of music festivals.

Excursions along the Duna (Danube) are an enjoyable way to view the city. A ride on Europe's oldest subway, which runs between Vörösmarty Tér (Vörösmarty Square) in the Inner City and City Park, and a scenic trip on the ski lift that climbs to the highest point of Buda's wooded hills should not be missed.

AQUINCUM, the Roman city, has left many traces on the modern face of Óbuda, including the Amfiteátrum, the Herkules-Villa and Military Baths.

BUDAI-HEGYSÉG (Buda Hills) rise to a height of 530 meters (1,735 feet). A chair lift takes visitors to the top, or there is a cog-wheel railroad that connects with a narrow-gauge line running 2.4 kilometers (1½ miles) through the hills.

GELLÉRT-HEGY (Gellert Hill) (192 B1). This limestone cliff rears up on the west bank of the Danube. It is named after a saint who fell to his death from the summit, now largely occupied by the

TIME FOR A DIP

Springs and spas supply Hungary with a profusion of mineral waters. Both Roman and Turkish rulers exploited the thermal springs of Aquincum in Budapest. No visitor should miss a dip, perhaps among the half-submerged chess players in the open-air Széchenyi Gyógyfürdö (Szechenyi baths), or in the mysterious vaulted pools deep beneath the wonderful art-nouveau Gellert Hotel.

high Citadella, housing a hotel, a restaurant and a café.

HŐSÖK TERE (Heroes' Square) (192 D4) contains the Millenary Monument, erected in 1896 in celebration of the country's thousand-year existence. The square is enclosed by the neoclassical Szépmuvészeti (Museum of Fine Arts) and the Mucsarnok (Art Gallery). Beyond is the City Park, with boating lake, a mock Transylvanian castle, zoo, amusement park, and the triple-domed Széchanyi Baths with hot spring waters.

MAGYAR NEMZETI GALÉRIA (Hungarian National Gallery) (192 B2), in the Budavári Palace, displays Hungarian paintings and sculptures.

MAGYAR NEMZETI MÚZEUM (Hungarian National Museum) (192 D2), Múzeum körút 14–16, has exhibits on the history of the Hungarian people from prehistoric times.

MARGIT-SZIGET (Margaret Island) (192 B4) lies between two arms of the Danube. It is an island of tranquility.

ORSÁGHÁZ (Hungarian Parliament Building), a neo-Gothic structure with pinnacles, gables, turrets and a great dome, was the largest building in the world on completion in 1902. Admittance is allowed when parliament is not in session, but only to groups organized by tour companies.

SZENT ISTVÁN BAZILIKA (St. Stephen Basilica) (192 C3) is the largest church in Budapest and has a neo-Renaissance dome that is a landmark of the Inner City.

SZÉPMŰVÉSZETI MÚZEUM (Museum of Fine Arts) (193 D4), Hősök Tere, houses a world-renowned collection of non-Hungarian art.

THE HUNGARIAN CROWN

The Hungarian crown is a powerful symbol of statehood. Over the years it has been hidden, stolen, spirited away, bought and sold. At the end of World War II it was taken to Vienna, to Fort Knox and only returned to Hungary in 1978.

VÁRHEGY (Castle Hill) (192 A2–3), the castle district of Buda and a World Heritage Site, has fortifications containing cobbled streets, royal palaces and museums.

Budavári Palota is the Royal Palace which contains the Magyar Nemzeti Galeria (Hungarian National Gallery), the Országos Széchenyi Kőnyvtár (Széchenyi National Library) and the Budapesti Történeti Múzeum (Budapest's history museum).

Halászbástya (Fishermen's Bastion) is one of the best viewpoints in the city. It was completed in 1903 and is named in honor of the fishermen who defended this section of the ramparts.

Mátyás-templom (Matthias Church) was founded in the 13th century and dedicated to the Virgin Mary. A much-rebuilt Gothic church, it is named after King Matthias. Orchestra, choral and organ performances are held here.

▲ EGER (187 D3)
HEVES *pop. 66,000*

Eger takes pride in the products of its orchards and vineyards, and visits can be made to the town's wine cellars. Eger's heavily restored fortress provides a fine view, and the city's neoclassical cathedral, Cisztercita templom, is the second-largest in Hungary.

▲ ESZTERGOM (187 B3)
KOMÁRP *pop. 62,000*

The medieval capital of Hungary, King Stephen I was born and later crowned here.

Esztergomi Székesegyház, the neoclassical Basilica of Esztergom, is the center of the Catholic faith in Hungary and is its largest church. From the 72-meter (236-foot) dome, there are great views of the Danube.

▲ FERTŐD (186 A2) ★
GYŐR-SOPRON *pop. 2,900*

Fertőd is dominated by its magnificent palace, built in the 18th century for Hungary's imperial governor Miklós Eszterházy.The main building is a fine example of Hungarian rococo architecture. Of its 126 rooms, over 20 are on view – opulent, mirrored salons with lavishly gilded ornamentation and furniture. The 250-hectare (610-acre) gardens contain statues, fountains and a waterfall. Weekend music recitals and the mid-September Fertőd Music Festival are held in the palace.

▲ GYŐR (186 B2)
GYŐR-SOPRON *pop. 130,000*

Situated on the Danube River, Győr was once a border fortress. It has an 18th-century old core surrounded by a modern industrial city.

Széchenyi tér, the central square and medieval marketplace, is overlooked by the Church of St. Ignatius, dating from 1641.

KÁPTALAN DOMB (Chapter Hill), overlooking the Raba River just before it joins the Danube, is the pedestrianized,

HUNGARY

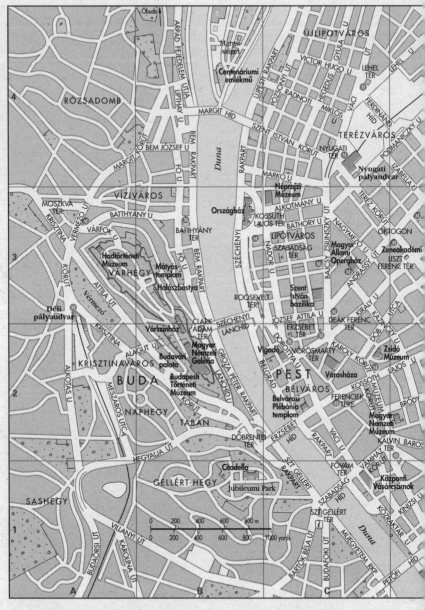

historic old town. The Székeségyház (cathedral) was built in a mixture of styles dating from the 11th century; the Héderváry chapel contains the famed golden reliquary of St. László (Ladislas), from around 1400.

LAKE BALATON (186 B2) ★
SOMOGY AND VESZPRÉM
Stretching 77 kilometers (48 miles), this warm, shallow lake is the largest in continental Europe, and a favorite vacation area for Hungarians.

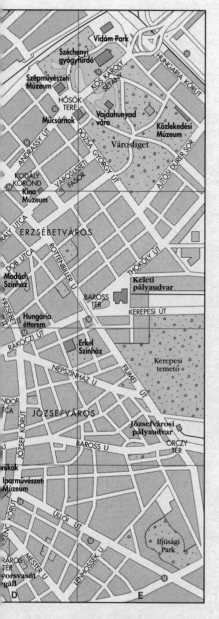

HÉVÍZ, northeast of Keszthely, is an internationally recognized spa, with Europe's largest hot-water lake.

SIÓFOK has 16 kilometers (10 miles) of beach, and is generally regarded as the vacation capital of Balaton.

▲ PÉCS (187 B1)
PÉCS *pop. 179,000*
Pécs is at the confluence of the Danube and Drava rivers. There is a 4th-century Christian chapel and cemetery, and an 11th-century cathedral. The Pasha Kasim mosque dates back to the Turkish occupation of 1543–1686.

Among the many museums are the Early Christian mausoleum, dating from 350, and the Janus Pannonius Museum with its Zsolnay art-noveau porcelain.

▲ SOPRON (186 A2)
GYŐR-SOPRON *pop. 56,700*
Many of the original defensive ramparts remain in this medieval border town. The Tűztorony (fire tower), with its medieval base, provides a gate into the old town and the best views of the town are from its top.

SZENTENDRE (187 C3)
PEST *pop. 17,000*
An 18th-century baroque town, today Szentendre is popular with artists, and works by local painters hang in the Ferenczy and Czóbel museums.

TATA (187 B2)
KOMÁROM *pop. 23,000*
Tata's lakeside setting makes it a natural resort. The Cifra Mill dates from 1587, and the Kisebb Kastely was an estate of the Esterházy princes.

VISEGRÁD (187 C3)
PEST
In the 14th century, King Charles Robert of Anjou built a palace at Visegrád which was rebuilt in Renaissance style by King Matthias. Rediscovered in the 1930s, part of the 18-hectare (44½-acre) site has been excavated and reconstructed.

BADACSONY is a beautiful nature preserve featuring conical volcanic hills planted with vines.

BALATONFÜRED, the oldest spa on the lake, has a relaxed 19th-century charm.

POLAND

Poland was reborn in December 1989 when the new political party, Solidarity, replaced the old Communist government. It is used to being reborn. In the 15th and 16th centuries it became a leading light before being swallowed up by neighbors. Born again after World War I, the invasion of Poland by Germany led to World War II.

Polish people have a love of life and seem to bounce back from anything. Warsaw was all but destroyed during World War II, and reconstruction of the Old Town involved close examination of prints and paintings before rebuilding took place. The countryside is mostly farmland, devoted to plowing, hoeing and haymaking. In the south are the High Tatra Mountains; although shared with the Slovak Republic, they provide more than enough splendor for both countries.

Left THE OLD TOWN MARKET SQUARE IN WARSAW IS SURROUNDED BY FINE
RENAISSANCE AND BAROQUE ARCHITECTURE
Above TRADITIONAL DRESS IS STILL WORN IN THE TATRA MOUNTAINS

THINGS TO KNOW

- **AREA:** 312,683 square kilometers (120,727 square miles)
- **POPULATION:** 38,600,000
- **CAPITAL:** Warszawa (Warsaw)
- **LANGUAGE:** Polish. German also widely spoken.
- **RELIGION:** Mostly Catholic
- **ECONOMY:** Coal, copper, steel production, engineering, chemicals, shipbuilding; fishing and forestry; much agricultural production in the hands of small farmers.
- **PASSPORT REQUIREMENTS:** Required by all visitors.
- **VISA REQUIREMENTS:** Not required for stays up to three months (six months for U.K. citizens).
- **DUTY-FREE ITEMS:** 250 cigarettes or tobacco equivalent; ¼ liter of liquor or ¾ liter of wine; gifts up to a value of U.S. $100; certain items for personal use e.g. cameras (still and movie), video recorder, sporting equipment.
- **CURRENCY:** The unit of currency is the *zloty* divided into 100 *groszy*. From January 1, 1995, the *zloty* was divided by a factor of 10,000. However, it is likely that the exchange rate will continue to fluctuate.
- **BANK OPENING HOURS:** 8am–5pm Monday–Friday, 8am–2pm Saturday.
- **STORE OPENING HOURS:** Variable. Food stores 6 or 7am–6pm (earlier in country areas) Monday–Friday, supermarkets 7am–7pm, other stores 10am–6pm Monday–Friday. Many stores are closed Saturday, others open 7am–1pm.
- **MUSEUM OPENING HOURS:** Variable, but most closed Monday and on days following a public holiday.
- **BEST BUYS:** Dolls in folk costumes, handwoven rugs, handicrafts, woodcarvings, ceramics, leather goods, silverware, jewelry, amber, cut glass. Specialist stores include Cepelia (folk products), Desa (handicrafts and works of art), Jubiler and Orno (jewelry).

HISTORY

The Polish nation originated with the Polanian, Vistulan, Silesian, East Pomeranian and Mazovian tribes that shared a common culture and formed city-states with regional leaders, thus establishing the dynasties that were to rule Poland.

In 1320, after several centuries of invasions and internal chaos, King Wlayslaw Lokietek I unified Poland, and in 1333 the last of the Piast dynasty, Casimir the Great, came to power. During his reign he codified common law, established a university, protected minorities, fortified castles and built roads. The Polish victory over the Teutonic Order (Germanic crusaders) at the Battle of Tannenberg in 1410, marked the beginning of Poland's Golden Age. The economy flourished, and the intellectual and artistic growth were exemplified by the scientific contributions of Nicolaus Copernicus, the poetry of Jan Kochanowski and the political philosophy of Andrzej Frycz-Modrzewski.

Russia, Prussia and Austria took more than a quarter of Poland's territory in the First Partition of Poland in 1772. This sparked Polish patriotism and led to economic and political reforms. A new constitution in 1791 granted peasants and the middle class political rights, while the elective monarchy was abolished.

During this time education flourished, democracy dominated politically, and art and literature became important again. This was the beginning of the independent Polish state, but it all came to an abrupt end when Catherine II of Russia ordered an invasion in 1793, resulting in the Second Partition of Poland.

Polish nationalists battled but could not repel the powerful Russian, Prussian and Austrian troops. In 1795, the three powers divided the rest of Poland among themselves in the Third Partition of Poland, marking the disappearance of the country from the European map.

The 19th century was marked by a number of patriotic uprisings that were quickly suppressed. Despite the unrest, this period was noted for great advances in literature, the arts and science.

In 1918, with the fall of Germany and Austria in World War I, Poland gained its freedom. In 1920 soldier-politician Jósef Pilsudski led the Polish legionnaires against the Russian Bolsheviks in the Polish-Soviet War, and the Treaty of Riga following the war granted Poland former Russian territories.

In 1939 the country was attacked by Nazi Germany and, despite heroic resistance, was swiftly defeated. A new partition followed. Much of the country was absorbed into Germany, while an area centering on Cracow and Warsaw was contemptuously named the *General-gouvernement*. The whole of the east part of Poland was then annexed by the Soviet Union.

The Polish *intelligentsia* (teachers, lawyers and priests) was systematically killed by the Nazis, as were nearly all of the Jews. The Soviets also exacted their toll: hundreds of thousands of Poles were deported to Siberia, and more than 10,000 Polish officers were massacred at Katyn, victims of Joseph Stalin's brutality. Poles in exile fought on several fronts against Germany: with the western Allies in the Middle East, Italy and France, and, after the Nazi attack on the Soviets in 1941, with the Red Army.

Pemex and Baltona shops sell a variety
of imported goods.

- **PUBLIC HOLIDAYS:** January 1; Easter
  Monday; May 1 (Labor Day); May 3
  (Constitution Day); May/June (Corpus
  Christi); August 15 (Feast of the
  Assumption); November 1 (All Saints'
  Day); November 11 (Independence
  Day); December 25–26.
- **USEFUL TELEPHONE NUMBERS:**
  Police 997
  Fire 998
  Ambulance 999
- **NATIONAL TOURIST OFFICES:**
  Orbis
  342 Madison Avenue
  New York
  NY 10173
  Tel: 212/867-5011
  Polorbis Travel
  82, Mortimer Street
  London
  W1N 7DE
  Tel: 0171 637 4971
- **AMERICAN EMBASSY:**
  al. Ujazdowskie 29
  Warsaw
  Poland
  Tel: 02 6283 041/9

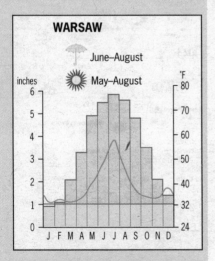

Postwar Poland lay in a state of economic
despair; over 6 million people had died
in the war and the land was in ruin. At
the Potsdam Conference in 1945,
Poland's eastern territories went to the
Soviet Union, but the country was compensated with former German lands to
the west. Stalin's goal after the war was
the Sovietization of Poland. The
Communist Party of Poland was revived
in Warsaw under the name of the Polish
United Workers' Party, and created the
kind of totalitarian regime acceptable to
its Soviet masters.

When Wladyslaw Gomulka came to
power in 1956, Poland's hopes for greater
freedoms rose, but Gomulka soon
abandoned the principles of shared leadership. His attacks on the Roman
Catholic church and outdated economic
policies led to more unrest. By 1970, the
deteriorating economy led Polish shipyard workers to strike. Gomulka was
removed from the Politburo and replaced
by Edward Gierek, who introduced
economic reforms.

Despite Gierek's new program, the
economy worsened and by 1980 Poland
faced severe shortages of food and electricity. The people were frustrated with
the government, and Gierek's overthrow
was hastened by union-inspired strikes
in the shipyards and coal mines.

The Politburo then began negotiations
with Lech Walęsa, the leader and co-
founder of the independent trade union
called Solidarity. An agreement was
signed and concessions were made to
the strikers. However, unrest continued
and in 1981 Solidarity's increased
demands for democratic reforms led
Wojciech Jaruzelski, who had taken over
as leader, to impose martial law and to
outlaw Solidarity, a bitter decision which
nonetheless saved the country from the
dreadful possibility of a Soviet invasion.

Martial law was lifted in 1983, following
a visit by Pope John Paul II. In 1985,

when Mikhail Gorbachev was appointed as the Soviet leader, hopes for the future soared. Gorbachev's liberal theories, the determination of Wałęsa and Solidarity, the backing of Pope John Paul II and the persistence of Polish citizens forced the Communists to take part in talks in 1989. In April 1989 legal status was restored to Solidarity, and the Communist Party agreed to the formation of a new law that allowed non-Communist representation through freely elected candidates.

In the general elections held in June 1989, Solidarity won the overwhelming support of the people, and although many parliamentary seats had been reserved for the Communists, the movement was able to form a government. Tadeusz Mazowiecki became prime minister – the first non-Communist to head the government of a Warsaw Pact nation. Jaruzelski was re-elected to the office of president.

In 1990 the first free presidential elections since World War II were held. Solidarity leader Lech Wałęsa became the new president. In 1993 the government, then headed by the country's first woman prime minister Hanna Suchocka, suffered defeat on the issue of privatization. In subsequent elections the Communist Party, now re-formed and renamed the Social Democracy of the Republic of Poland, received a substantial number of votes and, together with the Peasant Party, formed a government.

The transition to a free-market economy has been rapid and painful, bringing unemployment, rising prices, falling production, and rising crime. Wałęsa's popularity declined and in 1995 he was replaced by Kwasniewski, head of the Democratic Left Alliance. Despite continued problems, the economy is slowly improving and the new government aims to maintain a program of reform and to forge stronger relations with the West.

FOOD AND DRINK

Soups, fish and rich desserts are characteristic. Specialties include *karp po polsku*, carp cooked in raisin sauce; *barszcz*, beetroot soup; *chlodnik*, iced soup with beetroot and sour cream; *golabki*, meat, rice and cabbage leaves; *kolduny*, small mutton turnovers; *pierogi*, large dumplings with meat, plums or white cheese; *bigos*, a stew made with sour cabbage and a variety of meats; and *kuropatwa w smietanie*, young partridge in cream sauce.

Tea and Turkish coffee are popular. Polish beer is good and imported wine is plentiful. The national drink is vodka, which is consumed in a variety of forms and flavors. Popular brands include *wisniowka*, sweet or dry cherry; *jarzebiak*, dry vodka flavored with rowan berries; and *zubrowka*, flavored with bison grass found only in one region of the country. Polish cognac is called *viniak*. *Miod* (mead) is a delicious liqueur made from honey.

SPORTS AND RECREATION

Poland has numerous resorts with sports facilities on mountain slopes, at the seaside and lakeshore. The Masurian and Augustow lake district is a fishing and boating paradise. The nation's love of horses is reflected in the country's reputation for outstanding breeds. You can take horse riding vacations at resorts or stud farms. The slopes of the Tatra are dotted with hikers and mountain climbers in summer and skiers from December to March. Hunting trips can be arranged in advance, and various activity vacations are arranged by the major tour operators.

AUTOMOBILE CLUB
Polski Zwiazek Motorowy
(P.Z.M., Polish Motor Union),
which has its offices at ul.
Kazimierzowska 66, Warsaw, is
the Polish club affiliated with AAA.
Not all auto clubs offer full travel
services to AAA members.

GETTING AROUND

There are direct scheduled flights linking Warsaw with New York and Chicago, and with a number of European cities. L.O.T. (Polish Airlines) connects Warsaw with major cities throughout Poland. Ferry services operate from the Baltic harbor towns of Świnoujście and Gdańsk to ports in Denmark, Sweden and Finland, and there is a weekly service linking Gydnia with Hull or Felixstowe in England; the crossing takes three to four days. Local ferries and hydrofoils connect towns and resorts along the Baltic coast. The Polish State Railroad operates a dense network of internal passenger services, though trains on some lines may be slow and crowded. Fast and comfortable, Eurocity trains link Warsaw with Berlin and Vienna. From Warsaw there is an express service to Brussels, with a connections to London. Public transportation in cities is comprehensive and cheap, though often crowded.

The main roads in Poland usually have good surfaces, but other roads can be narrow and their quality varies greatly. Some larger gas stations are open 24 hours, but away from tourist areas they can be far apart and unleaded gas may not be available. The driver and all passengers must wear seat belts. Children under 10 are not permitted to travel in the front seat.

Speed limits are 60 k.p.h. (37 m.p.h.) in urban areas, 90 k.p.h. (55 m.p.h.) on country roads and 110 k.p.h. (68 m.p.h.) on highways. Drinking and driving is forbidden. Motorists must pay fines for motoring violations on the spot.

ACCOMMODATIONS

In major centers an increasing number of hotels reach international standards. Elsewhere, facilities are likely to be basic, but prices are correspondingly low. Good facilities are often found in private pensions and most cities have offices arranging accommodation in private houses and apartments. There are campgrounds throughout the country.

ARTS AND ENTERTAINMENT

The Polish arts are a source of national pride. Most cities have a theater and in the recent past experimental companies have won an international reputation for their boldness and innovation. There are many annual music festivals.

PRINCIPAL TOURING AREAS

Note: For descriptions of attractions in **bold type**, see individual listings.

BALTIC COAST

Some 520 kilometers (325 miles) of beaches along the Baltic Coast offer national parks, resorts, spas and quiet fishing villages. The summer season lasts from June to September. During these months temperatures average between 18 and 27°C (65 and 80°F) and water temperatures are around 21°C (70°F).

In northwest Poland, Świnoujście is a good base for touring Wolin Island, a national park with lakes, spectacular sand dunes and the resort of Międzyzdroje. Kamień Pomorski and Kolobrzeg combine medieval monuments with modern resort attractions. Darlowo has preserved parts of its medieval past. East is the fishing village of Leba, near two lakes which are part of a national park.

The Hel Peninsula is a pleasant combination of pine woods and beaches. The Amber Coast, the name given to the beaches around the Wisla (Vistula) Delta on the northeast Baltic Coast, was so named because of the yellowish tint of the sand and the amber found there. Forests alternate with resorts and fishing villages, while along the shore of Gdańsk Bay stretches the great conurbation known as the "Tri-City," consisting of the modern port of Gdynia, the resort of Sopot, and historic **Gdańsk**.

CENTRAL POLAND

Central Poland is the main food-producing region and a major touring area, with forests, parks and the Odra, Wisla (Vistula), Warta and Bug rivers. **Poznań**, on the banks of the Warta, is a busy marketplace and cultural center. **Toruń** was the birthplace of Copernicus. Highway E30 leads to a cluster of cities around **Warszawa** (Warsaw). Zelazowa Wola, Chopin's birthplace is 53 kilometers (33 miles) west, and Puszcza Kampinoska (Kampinos Forest), a national park, is 20 kilometers (12 miles) northwest.

Southeast of Warsaw is the academic and architectural center of **Lublin**. On the border with Belarus to the east is the great Bialowieza, the largest virgin forest in Central Europe, covering 582 square kilometers (225 square miles). Part of it is a reserve for European bison, extinct elsewhere, and "backward" breeding techniques have reproduced the tarpan.

LAKE DISTRICTS

Inland from the Baltic Coast are literally thousands of lakes in secluded, wooded hills. West of the Vistula River is the Pomeranian lake district and to the east, the Mazurian lake district. About 20 kilometers (12 miles) west of Gdańsk, medieval Kartuzy is a center for touring the Kashubian region renowned for the beauty of its lakes, forests and hills.

This whole region is ideal for fishing (particularly pike), sailing, canoeing and swimming. Ostróda is the focal point for water sports on Lake Drweckie; Olsztyn, on the Lyna River, is the chief vacation center of the Masurian district. About 100 kilometers (60 miles) east of Olsztyn are Giżycko, popular for sports, and Ruciane-Nida, a lovely resort deep in the Piska Forest. The best time to visit the area is from May to September.

MOUNTAIN REGIONS

The mountainous region of southern Poland abounds with magnificent scenery and opportunities for winter and summer recreation. The Sudety (Sudeten) Mountains, in the southwest, have yet to be discovered by tourists. Spruce forests

and clean lakes typify this sparsely inhabited land. The Jelenia Góra has many villages and spas and is a good center for excursions into the Sudeten.

The Tatra Mountains (Tatry), in the southeast, are the most beautiful of the Western Carpathian Mountains. Winter resorts and spas dot the area. At **Zakopane**, an international ski center, the season lasts from December to April. Spring and summer are equally enjoyable here. From Zakopane excursions can be made east to the Pieniny range, crossed by the Dunajec River gorge.

SOUTHWEST POLAND

Silesia is a major industrial zone. The area around Katowice is one of Poland's most densely populated areas. Factories are one aspect of Silesia, but there are also cool green forests and quiet streams. The Kingdom of the Frogs is a fisherman's paradise on the banks of the Vistula River. It begins 60 kilometers (37 miles) south of Katowice at the twin city of Bielsko-Biala. **Wrocław** has been completely rebuilt after wartime devastation. To the east of Katowice is ancient **Kraków** or Cracow, for centuries the country's capital, which survived the war with most of its treasures intact.

USEFUL EXPRESSIONS IN POLISH

good morning	**dzień dobry**
good evening	**dobry wieczór**
good night	**dobranoc**
please/thank you	**proszę/dziękuję**
yes/no	**tak/nie**
excuse me	**przepraszam**
you're welcome	**witam**
Do you speak English?	**Czy ktoś mówi po angielsku?**
I don't understand.	**Nie rozumiem**
What is the time?	**Która godzina?**
How much is that?	**Ile płacę?**
Where are the restrooms?	**Gdzie są toalety?**
I'd like ...	**Chciał (a) bym ...**
Can you help me, please?	**Proszę mi pomóc?**

PLACES OF INTEREST

POLAND

▲ **WARSZAWA** (197 B2) ★

WARSZAWA *pop. 1,640,000*

Warszawa (Warsaw) the capital, lies on the banks of the Wisla (Vistula) River. The city, believed to have been founded in the early 14th century, became the capital of the Polish-Lithuanian state in 1596 under King Sigismund III.

A long history of foreign rule includes 18th-century oppression by Prussia and Russia, under whose rule it became capital of the Kingdom of Poland in the 19th century. Following World War I, Warsaw became the capital of the restored Polish State.

In 1939 the Germans humiliated Warsaw by making Kraków (Cracow) the capital of their *General-gouvernement*. In 1944, as the Red Army approached, the city rose against the Nazis, but in spite of incredible heroism the Warsaw Uprising was defeated. In an act of vengeance the city was razed to the ground and the population deported.

After the war, Warsaw, abandoned and ruined, made its reconstruction a national priority. The historic core has been rebuilt as it was and today it is a thriving metropolis.

Several monuments recall a heroic past; among them the *Heroes of the Warsaw Ghetto* – Jews who took up arms and fought against the Nazis.

In Ogrod Saski, the Tomb of the Unknown Soldier commemorates Polish soldiers who have lost their lives in centuries of battle.

Warsaw has numerous theaters and museums. The Filharmonia presents concert and opera performances, and folk dance groups often appear. The magnificent Grand Theater of Opera and Ballet houses the State Opera.

Annual events include the Festival of Contemporary Music (September/October) and the Jazz Jamboree (late October).

About 50 kilometers (31 miles) west of Warsaw is Zelazowa Wola, whose most famous son was Chopin. Leading Polish pianists give weekly concerts of his music. Chopin memorabilia is exhibited in the beautifully restored and charming house where he was born.

At Lowicz, about 85 kilometers (53 miles) west of Warsaw, Polish customs are observed, particularly in late May or early June at Corpus Christi. Costumes are worn at church festivals all year.

ŁAZIENKI ★, a park, was laid out in the 18th century. The Palace on the Water once housed King Stanislaw August, the last Polish monarch. The theater on the island offers summer musical productions. Pianists give recitals in summer at the foot of the Chopin memorial.

MUZEUM NARODOWE (National Museum) Al Jerozolimskie 3, has a large collection of Polish art dating from the 14th century to the 20th century. The frescoes, especially those of St. Anne, are particularly noteworthy.

PALAC KULTURY I NAUKI ★ (Palace of Culture), Plac Defilad, was a gift from Stalin to the Polish people. The 37-story skyscraper is in the bizarre Stalinist Wedding-cake style. It houses theaters, movie theaters, restaurants, museums, galleries, a swimming pool, and casino. The top floor has views of the city.

PUSZCZA KAMPINOSKA, a national park 20 kilometers (12 miles) northwest, is a rare example of wild countryside coming right to the edge of a major city. Wildlife includes wild boar, elk and beavers. The memorial cemetery for the heroes of Warsaw is here.

STARE MIASTO ★, The Old Town on the left bank of the Vistula, is a vision of the past, a re-creation based on architectural plans and detailed paintings of Bernardo Bellotto. The Old Town market square is surrounded by 17th- and 18th-century Renaissance and baroque houses. Medieval fortifications still stand.

Katedra Sw. Jana (Cathedral of St. John), Swietojanska, a serene Gothic structure, is one of Poland's oldest churches. Henryk Sienkiewicz, author of the 19th-century novel *Quo Vadis* is buried here.

Muzeum Historyczne M. St. Warszawy (Warsaw Historical Museum), 48 Rynek Starego Miasta, inhabits reconstructed houses in the Old Town market square. Its collection traces the history of Warsaw. The documentary films telling the story of resistance are very moving.

WILANÓW PALACE, a baroque palace built by King Jan III Sobieski, is 10 kilometers (6 miles) away at the end of the Royal Way.

ZAMEK KRÓLEWSKI ★ is the royal castle, blown up by the Nazis in 1944 and restored using furnishings and fittings hidden away during the war. As well as the royal apartments, it contains the chambers where the Sejm – Poland's parliament – used to meet. In Castle Square is the King Sigismund Column, the symbol of Warsaw.

CRACOW – *see Kraków p.204.*

CZETOCHOWA (197 B1)
KATOWICE *pop. 274,000*
This industrial city is best-known for the 14th-century shrine at Jasna Góra (Bright Mountain) whose greatest treasure is the icon the *Black Madonna*, which became a key symbol of Poland in the 18th century.

▲ GDAŃSK (197 B3) ★
GDAŃSK *pop. 462,000*
This ancient city symbolises the old conflict between Poland and Germany.

CHOPIN
Chopin (1810–49) was born Fryderyk Szopen, and although his family lived in the house in Zelazowa Wola for only a year after his birth, he often returned to the area, where his talent found inspiration in the local, vibrant music traditions. Echoes of Mazovian folk music can be heard in many of his compositions.

Between the two world wars Gdańsk (Danzig in German) was nominally a free city, but the status of its predominantly German population was used by Hitler as one of his pretexts for invading Poland in September 1939.

In the 1970s and 80s. Gdańsk was the cradle for popular discontent against the government, with workers at the city's shipyards striking in protest under the leadership of Lech Wałęsa. It was here that the political party Solidarity was born.

Almost totally destroyed in World War II, the old town has been restored. Places of interest include the 14th-century town hall, the city's medieval fortifications, and several canals along with the 14th-century Wielki Mlyn, or Great Mill.

The city's Gothic Church of St. Mary accommodates 25,000 people. The quayside Gdańsk Crane dates from the 15th century and is the biggest of its kind in Europe. It houses part of the city's excellent maritime museum.

MALBORK CASTLE, 55 kilometers (34 miles) southeast, is one of the best-preserved medieval structures in the whole of Europe.

Works of art include a huge painting of the Battle of Grunwald.

POLAND

▲ KRAKÓW (197 B1) ★
KRAKÓW *pop. 746,000*

Kraków (Cracow) on the Vistula River to the north of the Tatra Mountains, was capital of Poland between the 11th and the 16th centuries. It was one of the few cities not devastated in World War II and is on the list of sites of significant cultural value compiled by U.N.E.S.C.O.

Here are superb examples of Gothic, baroque and Renaissance architecture in the main market square as well as in the Wawel complex. Churches from different periods are scattered around, among them the Church of St. Andrew and the Roman baroque Church of St. Peter and St. Paul.

The city's cultural life is well-developed, with theater, cabaret, rock and jazz clubs, and classical concerts. In June there are several major arts festivals.

MUZEUM CZARTORYSKICH, a branch of the National Museum at sw. Jana 19, houses fine artworks including Leonardo da Vinci's *Lady with the Ermine.*

OJCÓWSKI PARK NARODOWY (Ojców National Park), 20 kilometers (12 miles) northwest, is a deep gorge on the Pradnik River with hundreds of caverns, rock formations, rare bird species, and castle ruins that date from the 13th century.

OSWIÉCIM, 70 kilometers (43 miles) southwest, is the location of the Auschwitz concentration camp. Some 1½ to 2 million people died here in Nazi gas chambers. The great majority were Jews, but many gypsies died here too, as well as people from virtually every European nation.

RYNEK GLOWNY (Main Market Square) and the site of many fine, old residences.

Kočsciól Mariacki (St. Mary's Church) is one of the finest Gothic churches in Poland. Stained-glass windows enhance the gilding of the interior. Every hour a trumpeter sounds his horn briefly from the taller of two towers, commemorating the Tartar siege of 1241 and the brave trumpeter who died trying to warn the town of the danger.

Sukiennice was established by the Guild of the Textile Merchants as a cloth hall to display and sell their wares. The first floor houses the National Gallery of Polish Painting, with works dating from the 18th to 20th century.

UNIWERSYTET JAGIELLONSKI (Jagiellonian University), southwest Anny Street, built in 1364, was where Copernicus studied.

Collegium Maius, the university museum contains the Golden Globe of Copernicus, one of the first globes to show the American continent.

THE FALL OF GDAŃSK

Some of the first shots of World War II were fired in Gdańsk, then nominally a free city under League of Nations protection, but whose German population were cónverted to Nazism. Stormtroopers attacked the defended Poczta Polska, an event described with great gusto in the novel *The Tin Drum,* by Gunter Grass.

WZGORZE WAWELSKIE (Wawel Hill), with its castle and cathedral towering over the city centre, is a reminder of the centuries when Cracow was the capital of Poland.

Katedra na Wawelu was built in the 14th century. It is the mausoleum of no fewer than 41 of the country's 45 monarchs. The great Zygmunt bell in the tower was cast in 1520 in honor of King Sigismund I. There is a fine view over the city from the top of the tower.

Zamek Wawelskie is a Renaissance fortress with an arcaded courtyard. Until the 16th century, it was the home of Polish kings. Collections include priceless Flemish tapestries, the crown treasury, the armory and oriental art.

▲ LUBLIN (197 C2)
LUBLIN *pop. 350,000*

Lublin is of great historical and cultural interest. An ancient settlement, it was one of the first cities to be liberated during World War II and became the capital of Poland in 1944.

The old town has houses in Renaissance and baroque style. The Market Square is a charming area leading to the 14th-century Church of the Dominicans.

The fortified Kraków Gate is all that survives of the medieval city walls, and it now houses a museum on the city's history.

POZNAŃ (197 A2)
POZNAŃ *pop. 583,000*
Poznań has been a famed marketplace for a thousand years. Visitors will find a number of museums, theaters, churches and palaces. The town hall, Dzialynski Palace and Przemyslaw Castle are both worth visiting.

Biskupin, 85 kilometers (53 miles) northeast, offers an Iron Age village with an archaeological museum and a reconstruction of 2,500-year-old buildings.

MUZEUM INSTRUMENTOW MUZYCZNYCH (Museum of Musical Instruments), Old Town Square, has a collection of stringed instruments from the 16th to the 20th centuries. A room devoted to Chopin contains his piano.

▲ SZCZECIN (197 A3)
pop. 418,000
Szczecin (Stettin in German) is a cultural and industrial center as well as home to famous shipyards. Rebuilt after World War II, it has many restored historic buildings and monuments.

Among the attractions are a cathedral and neo-Gothic town hall. A baroque palace, part of the National Museum, has medieval sculptures and Renaissance jewelry. The harbor is best-viewed by boat.

ZAMEK KSLAZAT POMORSKICH (Castle of the Pomeranian Dukes), on Kusnierska Street near the Odra, houses a museum, art gallery and wine cellar.

The castle's impressive south wing has two Gothic towers, a prison and clock tower.

TORUŃ (197 B3) ★
BYDGOSZCZ *pop. 202,000*
Toruń, one of Poland's best-preserved - medieval towns, was the birthplace in 1475 of the astronomer Copernicus, whose theory of the earth's position in the solar system revolutionized man's concept of the universe. Among sites remaining are the house where he was born and a church where he studied. Facing the Market Square is the Gothic town hall where Copernicus' father was councillor. The Copernican tradition continues to be followed at Toruń's Copernicus University.

Toruń's reputation for confectionery originated in the Middle Ages. The town's traditional specialties include honey-and-spice gingerbread.

WROCŁAW (197 A2)
WROCŁAW *pop. 643,000*
Wrocław is the capital of Lower Silesia and one of Poland's oldest cities. Towards the end of World War II, the Nazis declared the city a fortress. The siege that followed left the city in ruins. After the expulsion of its German inhabitants the city was repopulated by Poles, many of them from the old city of L'vov which had become part of the Soviet Union.

The old city is laid out around the Odra River. There is a wealth of restored historic buildings, among them the magnificent Gothic town hall. Houses near the Market Square were rebuilt in their original Renaissance and baroque styles. Other attractions include the university buildings, the cathedral and the national museum.

ZAKOPANE (197 B1)
KRAKÓW *pop. 30,000*
The timber chalets of Zakopane lie at the foot of the spectacular peaks and crags of the Tatra Mountains, which reach their highest point at the summit of Rysy (2,500 meters/8,199 feet). The largest mountaineering and winter sports center in Poland, the town also is a health resort.

ROMANIA AND REPUBLIC OF MOLDOVA

KNOWN THROUGHOUT THE WORLD AS THE LAND OF COUNT DRACULA (THE TRANSYLVANIAN MOUNTAINS RUN ACROSS ITS CENTER), IT IS OTHERS WHO HAVE SUCKED THE BLOOD FROM ONCE-PROSPEROUS ROMANIA.

NOW, FOLLOWING THE NICOLAE CEAUŞESCU ERA, THE COUNTRY IS STARTING OVER, AND VISITORS SHOULD ALLOW FOR THE LACK OF SERVICES AND EXPECT SOME POVERTY. HOWEVER, THE PEOPLE ARE WELCOMING, AND YOU WILL FIND SOME OF THE MOST MAGNIFICENT SCENERY IN EUROPE.

THE CAPITAL, BUCHAREST, ONCE CALLED THE "PARIS OF THE BALKANS" BECAUSE OF ITS GRACIOUS ARCHITECTURE AND GRAND BOULEVARDS, HAPPILY HAS LIFE ONCE MORE COURSING THROUGH ITS VEINS.

THE INDEPENDENT REPUBLIC OF MOLDOVA BORDERS NORTHEAST ROMANIA AND HAS STRONG HISTORICAL LINKS TO THE COUNTRY. THE CAPITAL, CHIŞINĂU, IS THE REPUBLIC'S CULTURAL CENTER AND HAS A UNIVERSITY AND OTHER CENTERS OF LEARNING.

Left BRAN CASTLE IN TRANSYLVANIA, HOME OF THE FAMOUS VAMPIRE, DRACULA, IS FULL OF ATMOSPHERE

Above THE SIBIU TRADITIONAL COSTUME IS SOMBER BUT IMPRESSIVE

- **AREA**: Romania: 237,500 square kilometers (91,699 square miles); Republic of Moldova: 33,700 square kilometers (13,012 square miles)
- **POPULATION**: Romania: 23,397,000; Republic of Moldova: 4,362,000
- **CAPITAL**: Romania: Bucureşti; Republic of Moldova: Chişinău
- **LANGUAGE**: Romanian; Moldovan
- **RELIGION**: Romanian Orthodox
- **ECONOMY**: Romania: agriculture, mining, wine making industry, wheat, corn, gasoline, natural gas, minerals, machinery, metals, food processing, electronics, chemicals, oil. Republic of Moldova: wine making, tobacco, food processing, gypsum mining.
- **ELECTRICITY**: 220 volts, Continental two round-pin plugs. Adaptor and/or transformer required.
- **PASSPORT REQUIREMENTS**: Required for U.S. citizens.
- **VISA REQUIREMENTS**: Romania: visas for American citizens are obtained free of charge at the Romanian border. Moldova: visas are obtained at the Romanian/Moldovan border and at Chişinău airport. Visas are valid for 30 days.
- **DUTY-FREE ITEMS**: Within reasonable limits, tourists may import duty-free goods for personal use, and food and medicines necessary for their stay. All valuable goods must be declared on entering and leaving the country. It is forbidden to introduce radioactive substances, drugs, guns of any caliber ammunition. Pets require antirabies vaccination certificates.
- **CURRENCY**: Romania: the currency unit is the *lei*. Republic of Moldova: the currency unit is the *leu*. The exchange rate is subject to frequent change. The import and export of Romanian *lei* is prohibited. Foreign currency can be exchanged into *lei* at any branch of the Romanian national bank, at the national tourist office exchange offices, or at other authorized organizations. Before leaving Romania, unspent *lei* must be exchanged and the exchange slip presented.

ROMANIA

HISTORY

The inhabitants of what is now Romania, known as Dacians, were conquered by Rome in AD 106. This Latin ancestry survives in the Romanian language. The Romans withdrew in AD 275 pressured by invading tribes. Incursions continued until the 9th century, when the dominant Bulgars were displaced by the Magyars.

As these tribes swept through the land, the Romanized Dacians retreated to the security of Transylvanian mountains.

Between the 10th and 14th centuries new organizational structures began to emerge. In the 14th century a number of small Romanian duchies joined to form

the two independent principalities of Walachia and Moldavia.

For successive centuries the Magyars, Turks, Austrians and Poles vied for supremacy. The Turks dominated during the 16th and 18th centuries; Russia held control during the first half of the 19th century. The Treaty of Paris ended the Russian protectorate, and in 1859 Walachia and Moldavia united under the name Romania, electing Alexandru Ioan Cuza as prince. Cuza abdicated in 1866 and Carol I was elected prince. Romania joined Russia during the Russo-Turkish War, and its independence was secured through the Treaty of Berlin, which settled the war in 1878.

Romania sided with the Allies in World War I and sent troops into Hungary. At the end of the war it greatly expanded its territories, now including most of Transylvania. Although Romania was an ally of Germany at the beginning of World War II, Hitler awarded northern Transylvania back to Hungary, and Romania also lost the Moldavian region of Bessarabia to the Russians. This fueled widespread discontent, and in 1944, following a military coup led by King Michael, Romania was liberated and allied with Russia to drive out the Nazis. After the Allies' victory, Romania was effictively sold to Russia at Yalta.

As the Communists gained control, the monarchy was abolished and a people's republic was declared in 1947. In 1965, Nicolae Ceaușescu came to power and

- **BANK OPENING HOURS:** 9am–noon and 1–2pm Monday–Friday; 9am–12:30pm Saturday.
- **STORE OPENING HOURS:** 8am–8pm Monday–Friday; 8am–2pm Saturday; 8am–noon Sunday.
- **BEST BUYS:** Handwoven fabrics (including carpets and wall hangings); woodcarvings, embroideries and other handicrafts; food specialties; wines; records.
- **PUBLIC HOLIDAYS:** January 1 and 2; May 1 and 2 (May Day); December 1 (Romanian National Holiday).
- **USEFUL TELEPHONE NUMBERS** (Romania): Police 955; fire 981; ambulance 961; emergency hospital (Bucharest): 679 4310
- **MEDICAL ASSISTANCE:** Romania: no vaccines are needed. Medical assistance can be obtained at any hospital, clinics or dispensary.
  Moldova: certain vaccines may be needed; medical facilities are limited – immediate cash payment is expected.
- **EMERGENCY RADIO MESSAGES:** On the Black Sea Coast *Radio Vacances* transmits urgent messages in Romanian, French, English, German and Russian daily from mid-May to September 30.
- **NATIONAL TOURIST OFFICES:**
  Romanian National Tourist Office
  342 Madison Avenue, Suite 210
  New York, NY 10173
  Tel: 212/697-6971
  Fax: 212/697-6972
  Romanian National Tourist Office
  183a Marylebone High Street
  London W1M 3RD, England
  Tel/fax: 0171 224 3692
  Romanian State Travel Agency
  Carpaţi, 7 Magheru Boulevard
  Sector 1, Bucureşti
  Romania
  Tel: (401) 614 5160
  Fax: (401) 312 2594
- **AMERICAN EMBASSIES:**
  Strada Tudor Arghezi 7–9
  Tel: (401) 210 4042
  Strada Alexei Mateezicie 103
  Chişinău, Republic of Moldova
  Tel: (3732) 233772

unleashed 25 years of tyranny and human rights abuses. Finally, with the country on the verge of economic collapse, a revolution broke out in 1989, and he and his wife were executed on December 25, 1989. The National Salvation Front rapidly took control and in the ensuing years President Ion Illiescu slowly moved the country toward economic, social and political reform. Romania joined the Council of Europe in 1993, and in the same year was granted Most Favored Nation status by the United States.

REPUBLIC OF MOLDOVA

HISTORY

During the 15th century, Bessarabia – the historic region of Moldova – became part of the independent principality of Moldavia. Control over Bessarabia was disputed first by the Ottoman empire and Russia and later by Russia and Romania.

NADIA COMANECI

Nadia Comaneci, now a U.S. citizen, was the first Olympic gymnast to receive a perfect all-around score of 10.

Following the collapse of the Russian empire, Bessarabia declared itself an independent Moldavian republic and united with Romania. But the newly formed Soviet Union refused to recognize its status and annexed the region in 1940. Romania retook Bessarabia the following year, holding it until 1944, when it was once more taken by the Soviet Union, becoming the Moldavian Soviet Socialist Republic.

In 1991, after the breakup of the Soviet Union, the Republic of Moldova declared its independence, becoming a member of the Council of Europe in 1995. However, two separatist movements instigated armed conflict in 1992 and continue to threaten stability in some areas.

SPORTS AND RECREATION

Romanians enjoy soccer, hardball, tennis, volleyball, gymnastics, boxing, mountaineering, winter sports and water sports.

STEAUA

Steaua, Bucharest's leading soccer club, was managed by Valentin Ceauşescu, the late president's elder son. A frustrated player, not allowed to play by his parents, he helped lead Romania's international squad to victory in the European Cup in 1986, and to second place in 1989. He joined the World Cup squad in 1994 and watched Romania's near success in the United States.

They have been world champions in handball, European cup winners at soccer and Olympic gold medallists in gymnastics. The national sport is *oina*, which resembles American baseball. There are thermal spas are at Felix, Sovata, Herculane, Mangalia and Neptun.

FOOD AND DRINK

Romanian food has a Turkish influence. Pork, a national favorite, is served grilled, as are beef, veal, chicken and fish. Carp on the spit is a specialty in the Danube Delta. Typical dishes are *mititei*, chopped, spiced sausage; *sarmale*, spiced meat and rice in vine leaves; *mamaliga*, corn-flour pancakes; and Moldavian *pirjoale*, meat croquettes. Middle Eastern pastries like *baklava* and *cataif* are popular as well.

Romania produces excellent red and white wines. *Tuica* (fiery plum brandy) is highly potent as is the brandy *palinka*. Vodka is liberally consumed. Romanians drink a Turkish-type coffee.

GETTING AROUND

Motorists should strictly adhere to speed limits: 60 k.p.h. (37 m.p.h.) in town and 70 to 90 k.p.h. (40 to 55 m.p.h.) out of town. Seat belt use is not mandatory. A child under 12 may not ride in the front seat. All vehicles must be equipped with a first-aid kit and warning triangle. Fines for motoring violations must be paid on the spot with Romanian *lei*. Accidents must be reported to the police before repairs are undertaken. Establish the cost of a taxi ride before getting in. Some hotels can arrange cars with a driver. Note: special care should be taken in Moldova where roads are generally unlit.

ACCOMMODATIONS

Hotels follow the international star system and prices are good by Western standards. There are many campgrounds throughout Romania.

TIPPING

Tip in U.S. dollars. Salaries are low and everyone expects to be tipped.

PRINCIPAL TOURING AREAS

Note: For descriptions of attractions in **bold type**, see individual listings.

BLACK SEA COAST

Romania's Black Sea coast stretches for 245 kilometers (152 miles) from the wetland nature reserves of the Dunarea (Danube) Delta – whose focal point is the ancient city of **Tulcea** – to the sandy beaches and lively resorts of the southern shores. **Constanţa**, a thriving seaport, is the gateway to the southern coast. A few miles north is popular Mamaia, and on an inland waterway lies ancient Istria. To the south, Eforie Nord, with its curative Tekirghiol mud treatments, is one of the largest spas in Europe.

BUCHAREST AND THE SOUTHERN PLAINS

Romania's capital **Bucureşti** (Bucharest) lies between the Danube River and the Carpathian foothills and is surrounded by the fertile Walachia plain. Padurea Băneasa (Baneasa Forest), 10 kilometers (6 miles) north of Bucharest, is a good place to see the region's wildlife. Farther north is Breaza, where traditional houses and folk costumes can be seen. Museums at Craiova, Curtea de Argeş, Tirgovişte and Cimpulung Muscel display the area's archaeological riches.

CARPATHIANS

The Carpatii Mountains (Carpathians) dominate the countryside from the north to the southwest. The Făgăraşuli Range, with its waterfalls and glacial lakes, extends over 72 kilometers (45 miles). At the foot of the Bucegi Range, the road through Romania traverses the Prahova Valley, which features deep ravines and grottoes. The Rodnei Range has a lovely alpine lake, Lala, and the winter sports resort of Borsa. The 1,904-meter (5,803-foot) Ceahlău Massif, legendary home of the Dacien gods, is characterized by strangely shaped peaks; in the calcified Giurgeului Massif the winding Bicaz River has created a number of dramatic gorges. Where the Oltul River meets the southern Carpathians is medieval **Sibiu.**

NORTHERN MOLDAVIA

Northern Moldavia has Romania's richest legacy of folk art; monasteries, churches, and citadels all display frescoes. Notable examples are the Last Judgement scenes of Voronet Church; a poem in pictures at Humor Monastery; delightful, delicate wall portraits at Arbore Church; the *Siege of Constantinople* at Moldavia Monastery; and other works at Sucevita Church.

TRANSYLVANIA

Romania's best-known region was made famous by the fictional vampire Dracula.

The character was based on a 15th-century nobleman, Prince Vlad Tepes, known as "Vlad the Impaler" for his battles against the Turks. A popular excursion can be made from **Braşov** to Bran Castle, said to have been his home. The medieval towns of Sighisoara and lovely **Sibiu** are delightful to visit. The historic sights of **Cluj-Napoca,** the region's capital, and the royal resort of Sinaia, with the castle of Peles, are also worth seeing.

USEFUL EXPRESSIONS IN ROMANIAN

Pronunciation Tip: read each letter individually. Do not pronounce single "i" at the end of a word. Read: ce as che as in chair; ci as chi as in chip; ţ as tz; ş as sh as in shop; â as a in map.

good morning	**bună dimineaţa**
good evening	**bună seara**
good-bye	**la revedere**
yes/no	**da/nu**
please	**vă rog**
thank you	**mulţumesc**
excuse me	**scuzaţi-mă**
Do you speak English?	**Vorbeşte cineva aici engleza?**
I don't understand	**Nu inţeleg**
Where is?	**Unde est?**
How much is that?	**Cât costă?**
today/tomorrow	**azi/mâine**

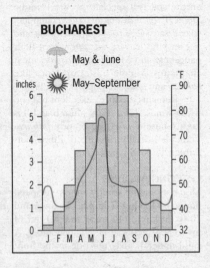

BUCHAREST

☂ May & June

☀ May–September

PLACES OF INTEREST

▲ BUCUREŞTI (209 C1) ★
BUCUREŞTI, ROMANIA *pop. 2,300,000*
Bucureşti (Bucharest) has earned several nicknames in its 500-year history as Romania's capital: The Garden City and Little Paris of Eastern Europe are two, both justified.

Like Paris, there's an Arc de Triomph, with five boulevards radiating outward. One leads from tree-lined Şoseaua Kiseleff into Calea Victoriei, the busy heart of Bucharest. There are a number of leafy parks, including central Cismigiu, Parcul Libertăţii in the south and fine botanical gardens. The parks have boating lakes and cafés.

Nestling between the huge apartment blocks are ancient palaces, churches and monuments. One sight not to be missed is the People's Palace. Piaţa Revoluţiei (Revolution Square) is the site of the former royal palace.

International fairs and exhibitions are held annually in Bucharest, as well as both classical and rock music festivals. Bucharest has many theaters and a beautiful opera house. The George Enescu Philharmonic Orchestra performs at the neoclassical Atheneul Roman.

CASĂ POPORULUI (People's Palace) ★, a reminder of Ceauşescu's rule, is Europe's largest building, and has marble floors and enormous chandeliers.

LACUL SI PADUREA SNAGOV (Snagov Lake and Forest) ★ is 40 kilometers (25 miles) north. Its beach offers facilities for water sports, including fishing. On a tiny island in the lake stands the 15th-century Snagov Monastery.

MUZEUL COLECTILOR DE ARTA (Art Collections Museum), 111 Calea Grivitei and Calea Victoriei, exhibits works by Romanian classical painters, old masters and Oriental artists.

MUSEUL DE ARTA AL ROMÂNIEI (Art Museum of Romania), 1 Calea Victoriei, has galleries of medieval, modern and contemporary art with works by Romanian and European masters.

MUSEUL NATIONAL DE ISTORIE (National History Museum), 12 Calea Victoriei, covers the history of Romania from the neolithic age.

PADUREA BĂNEASA (Băneasa Forest), 10 kilometers (6 miles) north, has botanical gardens, a zoo and a deer reserve.

PARCUL HERĂSTRĂU (Herăstrău Park) ★ offers water sports, recreational facilities, an amusement park, an open-air theater and a library.

Museul Satului (Village Museum) boasts more than 300 authentic buildings from all parts of Romania.

▲ BRAŞOV (209 C2) ★
BRAŞOV, ROMANIA *pop. 353,000*
Braşov dates back to the 12th century. Its medieval walls and landmarks chronicle a rich and varied history.

Poiana Braşov, an all-year-round sports resort, lies nearby, and Predeal, with superb skiing, is 30 kilometers (19½ miles) away. Bran Castle, the 14th-century fortress and fictional home of Dracula, is also close by. From Poina Braşov's Cristianul Chalet, some 1,198 meters (3,930 feet) above sea level, there is a great view of the Bucegi Range. Etched into the range is a magnificent sphinx. Also nearby is Sinaia and Peles Castle.

BISERICA NEAGRA (Black Church), a large Gothic cathedral begun in 1385 and completed almost 100 years later, derives its name from its blackened walls, the result of a fire in 1689. Inside, the walls are white and decorated with Turkish carpets.

CASA SFATULUI (Council Hall) is a 15th-century construction with thick walls, vaulted halls and a Trumpeter's Tower. It houses the Regional Museum of History with exhibits on the Saxon guilds who once ruled the city.

CHIŞINĂU (209 D3)
REPUBLIC OF MOLDOVA
pop. 665,000
Chişinău is the capital of the Republic of Moldova. The monument to Stephen the Great, erected in the city center in 1925, pays tribute to the region's great medieval king and hero. The underground cellars of the Cricovo Winery stretch for 60 kilometers (37 miles). It is open for excursions and tastings of its sparkling wines.

ORGEIEV (209 D3), 50 kilometers (31 miles) north of Chişinău, was built by the Golden Horde khans in the 14th century. Archaeological remains are displayed at the Old Orgeiev Museum Reserve.

▲ CLUJ-NAPOCA (209 B3)
CLUJ-NAPOCA, ROMANIA *pop. 318,000*
Cluj-Napoca was the Hungarian capital of Transylvania. It has a university and several museums and theaters. Much of its charm stems from medieval architecture, displayed in the Tailor's Bastion, the Franciscan monastery and churches.

BOTANICAL GARDENS AND MUSEUM is Romania's largest, with a 10-hectare (25-acre) collection of various plant species.

CASĂ NATALA A LUI MATEI CORVIN (Matthias Corvinus' Birthplace) is at Piaţa Muzeului. The 15th-century Hungarian king Corvinus successfully held the Turks at bay during his reign.

MUZEUL ETNOGRAFIC AL TRANSILVANIEI (Transylvania Ethnography Museum), Str. 30 Decembrie 21, has one of the best collections of folk costumes in the country and a fine open-air museum.

▲ CONSTANŢA (209 D1) ★
CONSTANŢA, ROMANIA *pop. 320,000*
According to legend, the ancient Greeks founded the city of *Tomis* here following a battle with the Argonauts. The Roman poet, Ovid, lived in exile here in the 1st century AD.

Today this cosmopolitan city is Romania's main port and the hub of the Black Sea coastal resorts. Its Turkish mosques and Greek and Roman remains are of historical interest, while the Genovese lighthouse and large aquarium reflect its marine traditions. For entertainment, the city has an opera house, theater and casino.

Trips can be taken to the Black Sea resorts including nearby Mamaia and Murfatlar, the main wine-producing area of the country.

MAMAIA, the Miami of Romania, is a narrow tongue of golden sand washed on the east by the Black Sea and on the west by the freshwater Lake Siutghiol. Its hotels, shops, cafés and casinos are set amid rose gardens and lawns. The resort has an open-air theater and a 7-kilometer (4½-mile) beach fully equipped for water sports. The National Folklore Festival is held in late July or early August.

IAŞI (209 D3)
IAŞI, ROMANIA *pop. 330,000*
This fine 14th-century city has a diverse culture. The Yiddish Theater originated here and today Iaşi is the seat of Minority Group Studies, attached to a fine university. The area has produced many of Romania's great literary figures.

▲ SIBIU (209 C2)
SIBIU, ROMANIA *pop. 175,000*
The capital of Sibiu county and a major university city, Sibiu has preserved its walled old town. The baroque Bruken-

thal Palace, converted in 1817 into the Brukenthal Museum, features noted natural history sections. The art section has folk and fine art, and works by world masters.

Modern Sibiu is a commercial city that provides wide cultural opportunities. Nearby at the commune of Simbata de Jos is a Lippizana stud farm where visitors can ride the famous Lippizaner horses.

▲ SUCEAVA (209 C3) ★
SUCEAVA, ROMANIA *pop. 90,000*

Suceava, the medieval capital of the princes of Moldavia, has had a long and colorful history. A former market town, it is now a modern city, with industrial and residential districts beside medieval monuments and churches.

The surrounding hill country of northern Moldavia is known for beautiful painted churches and monasteries with unusual exterior frescoes. As well as the five main churches and monasteries around Suceava (in the area historically known as Bukovina) there are some impressive 12th- to 15th-century ruins.

BISERICA SFINTU DUMITRU (St. Demetrius Church) was founded by Prince Petru Rareş in the 16th century. The exterior is decorated with glazed discs and bricks; the interior has fine frescoes.

CITADELA, on a hill overlooking the town, dates from the 14th century.

MANASTIREA DRAGOMIRNA (Dragomirna Monastery) was founded by Metropolitan Anastsie Crimca in 1609. The tall church introduced elements that became characteristic of Moldavian architecture.

MANASTIREA PUTNA (Putna Monastery), founded in the 15th century by Stephen the Great, houses his tomb and a medieval museum.

MANASTIREA VORONET (Voronet Monastery), 12 kilometers (7 miles) southwest, is perhaps the finest of the painted churches. The exterior frescoes include *The Last Judgement*, which covers the entire western façade.

TIMIŞOARA (208 A2)
TIMIŞ, ROMANIA *pop. 333,000*

Capital of Timiş county, this is a pleasant university town, that will be remembered as the starting point of the 1989 revolution. The main square, Piaţa Libertăţii, dates back to the Austro-Hungarian Empire, and mirrors those of Sibiu and Braşov.

PELE'S CASTLE, SINAIA

Having led a coup in 1944 to overthrow Hitler's ally, Ion Antonescu, King Michael of Romania was led away from the castle at gunpoint and exiled by the Communists in 1947. Antonescu was executed by them in 1946. King Michael, cousin to Queen Elizabeth of England, now resides in Geneva. He has been allowed to return to his homeland only once, in 1992, but proved so popular that he has been escorted away from the airport twice, the last time in October, 1994. Statues are being erected martyring Antonescu.

Decebal's bridge depicts the Dacian King's crossing in Roman times, his elephants supporting the bridge on either side.

▲ TULCEA (209 D2) ★
TULCEA, ROMANIA *pop. 70,000*

Founded by the ancient Greeks and now a thriving fishing center, Tulcea is a picturesque town with a number of attractions. The imposing Azizir Mosque, the Delta Museum, and an aquarium with species of fish found along the Danube River's path should be included in a walking tour of the town.

Along the riverfront, pelicans, waterlilies and rustling reeds create a pleasant setting. The Danube Delta can be toured by organized boat trip.

RUSSIA, UKRAINE AND BELARUS

Russia, the world's largest country, stretches from eastern Europe across northern Asia to within sight of Alaska. The European corner centers on Moscow and St. Petersburg. Its western neighbors, Ukraine and Belarus, have related languages and closely linked histories, but now are independent nations, forging their own identities.

Travel in the region is not as restricted as it was, but there is a lack of good facilities. However, this is more than compensated for by seeing these mysterious countries, hidden for so long behind the Iron Curtain. Travelers can visit Red Square and stroll inside Moscow's Kremlin; marvel at the beauty of St. Petersburg; or wander along the elegant boulevards of Kiev.

Left The fairy-tale onion domes of St. Basil's Cathedral in Moscow
Above left Matryoshka dolls make delightful gifts to take home
Above right Rooftop spires on the Terem Palace in Moscow's Kremlin

217

THINGS TO KNOW

- **AREA: Russia:** 17,075,000 square kilometers (6,590,950 square miles); **Ukraine:** 603,700 square kilometers (233,028 square miles); **Belarus:** 207,600 kilometers (80,133 square miles).
- **POPULATION:** Russia: 149,500,00; Ukraine: 52,027,000; Belarus: 10,374,000
- **LANGUAGES: Russia:** mainly Russian, with more than 100 others also spoken; **Ukraine:** Ukrainian, spoken mostly in the west, as well as Russian; **Belarus:** Belarusian, and also Russian.
- **ECONOMY:** Industry, agriculture. Chief exports include machinery, iron and steel, timber and petroleum products.
- **PASSPORT:** Required for U.S. citizens.
- **VISA:** Required for all visitors. **Russian Embassy,** 1825 Phelps Street, N.W., Washington, DC 20008; **Ukrainian Embassy,** 3350 M. Street N.W., Suite 711, Washinton, DC 20007 (tel: 202/333-0606/fax: 202/333-7510); **Belarusian Embassy,** 1619 New Hampshire Avenue N.W., Washington, DC 20009 (tel: 202/986-1604; fax: 202/986-1805).
- **CUSTOMS RESTRICTIONS:** Items such as prescription drugs, computers and cassettes may be imported for your own personal use. Recorded video cassettes (i.e. commercial movies) are prohibited. Do not export icons or objects of historical value without consulting the relevant country's authorities.
- **CURRENCY:** In **Russia** the currency unit is the *ruble*; in **Ukraine** it is the *Hyryvnya*, divided into 100 *kopiyky* (replacing the old "Cupon" or *Karvovanets*); in **Belarus** it is the *Belarusian ruble*. Remember that the exchange rate is subject to frequent and dramatic change. All currency and travelers' checks must be declared at customs. Local currency can be brought into and taken out of each country, but you cannot take out more currency than you imported. The limit (in Russia) is R500,000. There is no limit on the amount of U.S. currency that may be imported; however, the amount exported must not exceed the amount imported. The State Bank Certificate

HISTORY

The history of the Russian, Ukrainian and Belarusian peoples is, like their Slavic languages, closely linked. Earliest remains show traces of successive nomadic tribes in the region sweeping west across the steppes. By the 10th century AD the Varangians dominated the area, contributing to the foundation of Kievan Rus, a forerunner of both Russia and Ukraine that held control of Belarus.

The Kievan ruler Prince Vladimir introduced Christianity in AD 988, and trade brought prosperity. Developing principalities in the north, particularly Novgorod, Suzdal' and Vladimir, gradually asserted their independence. This culminated in the sack of Kyïv (Kiev) by Andrey Bogolyubsky, Prince of Suzdal', in 1169.

In 1237, Mongol armies crossed the Urals, destroyed Kiev and crushed the Kievan Rus principalities. From its base on the Volga, the Golden Horde, as this part of the Mongol Empire became known, subjugated the region for over 200 years. Indeed, though Mongol control had dissipated by the 16th century, it lingered on in the Crimea and southern Russia until the 18th century.

The Muscovite prince Dmitry Donskoy began the rebellion against the Mongols with a victory at Kulikovo Field, near Moskva (Moscow), in 1380. This marked Moscow's rise in importance. The growth of the Muscovite state and centralization of power allowed Ivan IV (The Terrible) to strike the crucial blow against the Tartars at Kazan in 1552.

To the east, Lithuania and then Poland had extended their control over Belarus and Ukraine. To counter this threat, the Cossacks (independent Tartar bands in Ukraine) allied with Muscovy in 1654. This uneven union proved a major step in the growth of the Russian Empire, further accelerated by Peter the Great. His vision of Russia as a European power led him to found the new capital city of Sankt-

Peterburg (St. Petersburg) on the Gulf of Finland, providing a window to the West.

Catharine the Great pushed territorial expansion south. The partition of Poland added Belarus and parts of Ukraine to the Russian Empire and the rebellious Cossacks were subjugated in 1775. In 1812, Napoléon Bonaparte invaded Russia, entering Moscow after the bloody but inconclusive battle of Borodino. A disastrous campaign, it ended in retreat and the decimation of Napoléon's army by winter.

The harsh social conditions in Russia, the virtual slavery of the peasantry and the autocratic nature of tsarist rule fueled unrest. Rebellions, first by the aristocratic Decembrists in 1825, then in 1905 by striking workers, were crushed. However, military collapse in World War I finally destabilized the weak Tsar Nicholas II, and his resignation in February 1917 led the way to the Bolsheviks' coup in October, masterminded by Lenin and Trotsky. A civil war saw the consolidation of Bolshevik control and the creation of the Soviet Union (U.S.S.R.) of 15 nominally independent republics, including Ukraine and Belarus.

The early years of Communist rule saw the transformation of society and economic advances. However, this was founded on one-party dictatorship, savagely exploited by Lenin's successor, Stalin. He enforced collectivization of agriculture, bringing devastating famine in the 1930s, particularly to Ukraine; and he implemented the "Terror" – mass executions of political opponents. Despite these crippling factors, the Soviet Union managed to survive and repulse Hitler's assault in World War II. Estimates of 10 million Soviet dead in the conflict are probably conservative.

The postwar settlement split Europe in two, with an ideological confrontation between the Soviet bloc and the West. However, despite the military strength of the Soviet Union, its communist policies meant economic stagnation. The desperate need for economic reform prompted Mikhail Gorbachev's revolution in the late 1980s: a restructuring (*perestroika*) of the economy, increased openness (*glasnost*), leading to free elections in 1989.

Boris Yeltsin accelerated change in 1991 by banning the Communist Party and breaking up the Soviet Union. Ukraine voted in favor of independence, and along with the newly formed Belarus (old Belorussia) it became a member of the new Commonwealth of Independent States. The breakup of the Soviet Union into 15 independent states was surprisingly bloodless; however, within the new states conflicts have emerged, specifically in Chechnya, in the south.

The transition to a market-based economy is proving traumatic, bringing new ills of poverty, inflation and organized crime. Politically, an uneasy balance exists between democracy and the need for decisive action to introduce social reforms. The old certainties in foreign policy within the Warsaw Pact have also disappeared: Russia must cope with its loss of superpower status, Belarus is evaluating closer union with Russia, while Ukraine faces the uncertain future armed with its precious independence.

FOOD AND DRINK

Russia's rich culinary tradition provides surprisingly varied fare, starting with assorted *zakusky* (appetizers). These will invariably include red or black caviar (*ikra*). *Borshch* (beet) and *shchee* (cabbage) are popular soups.

Ukrainian dishes include *varenky* (small filled dumplings), *holubtsi* (cabbage leaves with rice and meat) and the well-known *kotleta pokyyivski* (chicken kiev). Asian influences include *shashlik* (skewered lamb) and *plov* (lamb pilau).

Russian cuisine includes delicious fish dishes. *Bliny* (pancakes) come in sweet and savory styles. *Morozhenoye* (ice cream) often ends the meal.

(F-377), which shows the amount of currency converted, is needed to exchange unused *rubles* on leaving Russia. Transactions in hard (Western) currencies are forbidden, although many people will ask to be paid in U.S.$ which is the most widely accepted currency. It is important that notes presented for exchange are in good condition. Beware of counterfeit notes. Credit cards are now accepted by major hotels and restaurants.

- BANK HOURS: 9am–5pm Monday–Friday.
- STORE HOURS: Large stores 9am–7pm Monday–Saturday, small stores 11am–7pm Monday– Saturday. All stores, except G.U.M. and other department stores, close one hour for lunch.
- MUSEUM HOURS: Most museums are open 11am–7pm Tuesday–Saturday, 11am–5pm Sunday. Some close on the last day of the month.
- BEST BUYS: Chess sets, books, records, fur hats, wooden dolls, jewelry, embroidered blouses and hats, crystal, decorative objects and caviar.
- USEFUL TELEPHONE NUMBERS (Russia): Police: 02; Ambulance: 03; Fire: 01
- NATIONAL TOURIST OFFICES:
  Intourist
  630 Fifth Avenue, Suite 868
  New York, NY 10111
  Tel: 212/757-3884
  Intourist
  219 Marsh Wall
  Isle of Dogs
  London E14 9PD, England
  Tel: 0171 538-8600
- AMERICAN EMBASSIES:
  Novinskiy bulvar 19/23
  Moskva, Russia
  Tel: 252 2451/252 2459
  Furshtadtskaya ul 15
  Sankt-Peterburg, Russia
  Tel: 275 1701/274 8692
  Vulitsya Kotsybynskoho 10
  Kyïv 254053, Ukraine
  Tel: (44) 244 7344; fax: (44) 244 7350
  Vulitsa Staravilenskaya 46
  Minsk, Belarus
  Tel: (17) 347761; fax: (17) 347853

Ukraine produces some good red wines. Russian vodka is taken ice cold. *Kvas* is a weak alcoholic beer; *soki* (fruit juice) and *chai* (tea) are also popular.

ARTS AND ENTERTAINMENT

There is a rich artistic tradition from the 19th century, sustained during the Communist period. An opportunity to see the Bolshoi or Mariinskiy (Kirov) ballet companies should not be missed; the Bolshoi Theater in Moscow in particular is a glorious venue. There are also excellent ballet and opera houses in L'viv, Odesa and Kiev.

Music ranges from the great Russian composers (Tchaikovsky, Mussorgsky, Rachmaninov) to colorful Ukrainian folk dance. The best-known festivals are St. Petersburg's White Nights at the end of June, and the Kiev International Music Festival in early October.

For children there are circuses (Moscow and Kiev) and puppet theaters.

SPORTS AND RECREATION

The most popular sport in Russia, Ukraine and Belarus is soccer. During the winter, cross-country skiing and skating are popular pursuits. The summer brings swimming, particularly in the Black Sea resorts. A visit to a *banya* (bathhouse) is a traditional way to relax.

GETTING AROUND

Russia's major international airports are Sheremetevo II (Moscow) and Pulkovo II (St. Petersburg); Boryspil is the main entry point to Ukraine, and Minsk-2 International Airport to Belarus.

Travel within town is quick and fairly safe in the excellent metro (subway) systems in Moscow, St. Petersburg and Kiev. Above ground, buses, trolleybuses and streetcars provide cheap and extensive travel; tickets need to be validated during the journey. Car rental firms operate in major cities, for those determined to brave local driving habits. Some agencies provide a chauffeur service; it can be cheaper to bargain with a taxi driver for his services for the day.

Full documentation must be carried. It is illegal to drive after drinking alcohol.

ACCOMMODATIONS

Although the situation is gradually improving, there is still a limited choice and restrictive regulation on accommodations. In major cities, joint ventures with Western corporations provide luxury accommodation in either new hotels or refurbished old ones – but at prices that make Moscow and St. Petersburg the most expensive cities in Europe.

Unlike the rest of Eastern Europe, the travel restrictions of the Communist era have not yet fully disappeared. Accommodations have to be reserved and specified on your visa before traveling. Travel companies will make these reservations for you. Alternatively, a personal invitation allows staying with a friend, or "sponsor," at a specified address.

Russia contains a number of campgrounds, open from May to September; reservations must be made in advance.

SHOPPING

The shortages of the Communist era no longer apply in the major cities. Using U.S. dollars in Russia is illegal, except at authorized establishments. To compensate for inflation, some stores have prices marked in dollars, which are then converted by the sales clerk into *ruble* prices at the current exchange rates.

Credit cards are not widely accepted. Indeed, the traditional payment system is still prevalent in most stores: first select your item at the relevant counter, then pay for it in cash at a *kassa* (cash desk), taking the receipt back to the original counter to collect your purchase.

Changing currency on the black market is illegal. It is also unwise; you will probably be cheated.

TIPPING

A small gratuity is advised for hotel porters, restroom attendants and tourist guides. Waiters should be tipped 5–10 percent in smarter restaurants.

PRINCIPAL TOURING AREAS

Note: For descriptions of attractions in **bold type**, see individual listings.

BELARUS

The terrain of Belarus, the former Soviet Republic of Belorussia, is predominantly flat steppe, birch forests and the Pripet Marsh, Europe's largest wetland area. The country stands on the route between Poland and Moscow, a position that explains the appearance of the capital **Minsk** – totally rebuilt after its destruction during World War II. For more historic surroundings, you will need to look to the elegance of Vitsebsk; the picturesque city of Hrodna, an out-

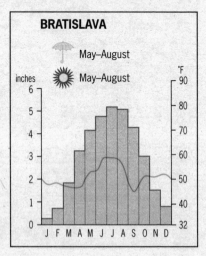

BRATISLAVA

☂ May–August

☀ May–August

RUSSIA, UKRAINE AND BELARUS

post of Kievan Rus; or the bustling border town of Brest.

Southwestern Belarus suffered the worst contamination from the Chernobyl nuclear disaster in 1986.

BLACK SEA COAST

Odesa stands between the estuaries of the Dnister and Dnipro, a major seaport and vacation resort. Also in Ukraine, though with a predominantly Russian population, is the subtropical Crimean peninsula. The naval port of Sevastopol is a closed city; Bakhchysaray provides a glimpse of the region's Mongol past; and **Yalta** is the finest and the most cosmopolitan resort on the coast.

Further east, the foothills of the Caucasus provide the backdrop for the leading resorts of Sochi and Dagomys.

NORTHWEST RUSSIA

Sankt-Peterburg (St. Petersburg) stands facing the West; the more historic cities of **Novgorod** and **Pskov** lie to the south. A string of rivers, lakes and canals link St. Petersburg to the great Volga River, and by waterways to **Moskva** (Moscow), capital of the largest country in the world.

Moscow is surrounded by the "Golden Ring," a string of historic towns with fortresses, monasteries and churches. These include Yaroslavl, Rostov-Veliky, Kostroma, Zvenigorod and the twin cities of **Vladimir** and **Suzdal'**.

UKRAINE

Ukraine is almost entirely steppe (prairie), crossed by great rivers running into the Black Sea. **Kyïv** (Kiev), the birthplace of east Slavic culture and capital of modern Ukraine, stands on the Dnister River. To its west lie the border towns of **L'viv** (Lvov), with its Western church architecture, and **Uzhhorod**, the gateway to the Carpathian Mountains. Attractive historic towns in the region include Chernivtsi and Kamyanets-Podilsk.

VOLGA

The lower reaches of the Volga flow south through green steppe, past the old city of Nizhniy Novgorod, the Tartar city of Kazan', Lenin's birthplace at Simbirsk, and Volgograd, scene of the horrific Battle of Stalingrad (1942–3), commemorated by the Mamaev Kurgan memorial. Here the Volga turns southeast to Astrakhan' and into the Caspian Sea, while a canal at Volgograd connects to the Don, which flows southwest through attractive Rostov-na-Donu and into the Black Sea.

USEFUL EXPRESSIONS IN RUSSIAN

hello	zdrávstvuytye
good morning	dobroye utro
good afternoon	dobriy dyen'
good evening	dobriy vyechyer
good night	spokoynoy nochi
good-bye	dosvidaniya
please	pozhalusta
thank you	spasibo
yes	da
no	nyet
good	khoroshiy
bad	plokhoy
how long	skol'ko
how far	kak dalyeko
left	lyeviy
right	praviy
you're welcome	pozhalusta
Do you speak English?	Zdyes' kto-nibud' govorit po-angliyski?
I don't understand.	Ya nye ponimayu.
What is the time?	Kotoriy chas?
Waiter!	Ofitsiant!
Waitress!	Ofitsiantka!
How much is that?	Skol'ko eto stoit?
Do you take credit cards?	Vi byeryotye Kryeditniye Kartochki?
Where are the restrooms?	Gdye tualyety?
I'd like ...	Ya khotyel(a) bi ...
Can you help me, please?	Pomogitye mnye, pozhalusta?
Please write it down.	Pozhalusta, napishitye.
where?	gdye?
when?	kogda?
how?	kak?
free (vacant)	svobodniy
occupied	zanyatiy

PLACES OF INTEREST

NOTE

Due to the changing political situation, it has not always been possible to provide up-to-date information on attractions.

▲ MOSKVA (221 B3) ★

RUSSIA *pop. 8,957,000*

A major manufacturing center, Moskva (Moscow) is also a city of arts and learning, with ballet and opera, drama and musical comedy, theaters, concert halls, museums and art galleries.

Take a boat trip along the river for fine views of spires, gold domes and wedding-cake-style buildings, or ride round the city on its excellent subway.

ANDRONIKOV MONASTYR (Andronikov Monastery) (226 E3), Andronevskaya ploshchad 10, was founded in 1359 and now contains the Rublev, a museum of ancient Russian culture and art. The monastery holds within its turreted walls the 15th-century Savior's Cathedral, admired for its narrowing tiers of spade-shaped gables, as well as the baroque Archangel Michael's Church, now a workshop for icon restoration.

ARBAT (226 B3) was the cultural center of Moscow, home to Pushkin, Lermontov and Tolstoy. It is now the city's main shopping area, complete with street musicians and artists.

DOM-MUZEY CHEKHOVA (Chekhov House Museum) (226 B4), Sadovaya-Kudrinskaya Ulitsa 6, was the home of Anton Chekhov from 1896 to 1900. The museum has manuscripts, photographs from theatrical productions of his plays, and personal effects on display.

G.U.M. (226 C3), the Universal State Store, runs along the eastern side of Red Square. A three-story building of glass-covered passages and linking bridges, it replaced the old merchant arcades (1888–93). Western boutiques now predominate.

KRASNAYA PLOSHCHAD (Red Square) (226 E3) is Moscow's famous parade ground.

Khram Vasiliya Blazhennovo (St. Basil's Cathedral), at the south end, has its seven brightly colored cupolas and is one of the world's most recognizable buildings. Built by Ivan the Terrible to commemorate victory over the Tartars at Kazan in 1552, it survived Stalin's directive to be knocked down.

Mavzoley Lenina (Lenin Mausoleum), alongside the Kremlin wall, is the black-and-red marble resting place of Vladimir Lenin, founder of the Soviet Union. The gardens behind contain the graves of Josef Stalin and Leonid Brezhnev.

KREML (226 C3) ★, (Kremlin – fortress), in the heart of Moscow, is an essential stop for any visitor to the city. The pentagon-shaped red-brick walls, dating from 1485, are punctuated by 20 towers; Troitskaya (Trinity) Tower provides the only public access. Inside is a spacious ensemble of ancient cathedrals and palaces, 19th-century neoclassical buildings and the modern Palace of Soviets (1961).

Uspenskiy Sobor, Dormition Cathedral (1479) is a beautifully proportioned five-domed building, combining Russian and Italian styles. Its interior is heavily decorated with frescoes, but its greatest treasures are the icons, some of which

MOSCOW METRO

Recognizable by the large, red letter M on the pavement, the entrances to Metro stations lead you to another world. The first line, from Sikolniki to Park Kultury, opened in the 1930s. Stations on this line are resplendent with marble, mosaics and murals, and lit with chandeliers.

MONSTER CANNON

In the Kremlin grounds stands the beautifully decorated cast-iron King of Cannons. Weighing 40 tons, with a bore of 91 centimeters (36 inches), it was cast in 1586 for the feeble-minded son of Ivan the Terrible, but never fired.

date back to the 12th century. There are two side chapels, one containing Ivan the Terrible's Throne.

Blagoveshchenskiy Sobor (Cathedral of the Annunciation), a nine-domed building, contains original 15th-century icons by the great iconographers Theophanes, Prokhor and Rublev.

Arkhangeliskiy Sobor (Cathedral of Archangel Michael) is a five-domed cathedral with Venetian external ornamentation commissioned by Ivan III in 1505 as a burial place for tsars, who lie here in bronze-encased sarcophagi. Also of note are the frescoes and iconostasis.

Kolokolnya Ivan Veliky (bell tower of Ivan the Great) stands 82 meters (269 feet) high. Built in 1505–8, the tower narrows as it rises toward its dome, holding 21 bells.

KUSKOVO, the estate of the Sheremetiev family, lies in the western suburbs. The grand park, described as "The Moscow Versailles," dates from the 1760s. Although the grandiose palace has not survived, a Russian classical house remains, overlooking an artificial lake. The rooms are decorated with paintings, sculptures and tapestries. The gardens contain a Dutch house, an Italian house, an orangery that now houses a ceramics museum, and a watery grotto.

MUSEY IZOBRAZITELNYKH ISKUSSTV IM A.S. PUSHKINA (Pushkin Museum of Fine Arts) (226 B3), Ulitsa Volkhonka 12, has an excellent collection of French Impressionist and Post-Impressionist art (Van Gogh, Cézanne), French sculpture (Rodin), as well as classical Greek treasures. Opened in 1912 and expanded by private collections, it was nationalized following the 1917 revolution.

NOVODEVICHY MONASTYR (226 A2), in a tranquil setting in a bend of the Moscow River, is a beautiful convent of golden domes surrounded by white walls and red-topped turrets, founded in 1524. Peter the Great had both his half-sister and first wife banished here and forced to take the veil. The ensemble includes the grand Smolensk Cathedral (1525), covered with magnificent 16th-century frescoes and a stunning iconostasis, an octagonal-tiered bell tower (1690) and two fine gate churches.

The cemetary behind contains the tombs of many of Russia's greatest figures: Chekhov, Gogol, Mayakovsky, Prokofiev, Eisenstein and Stanislavsky, as well as Khrushchev and Gromyko.

SERGIEV POSAD ★, 70 kilometers (43 miles) northeast of Moscow, is the home of the magnificent monastery Trinity-St. Sergius Lavra. Within its walls stand the Church of the Descent of the Holy Cathedral (1476) and Troitsky Sobor (Trinity Cathedral), built on the site of St. Sergius' grave. The blue and gold-domed Assumption Cathedral, which was commissioned by Ivan the Terrible, holds the tomb of Tsar Boris Godunov.

TRETYAKOVSKAYA GALERYA (226 C2), Lavrushinskiy Pereulok 10, was founded by the industrialist Pavel Tretkyakov in 1892. The newly restored building contains one of the greatest collections of

RUSSIA, UKRAINE AND BELARUS

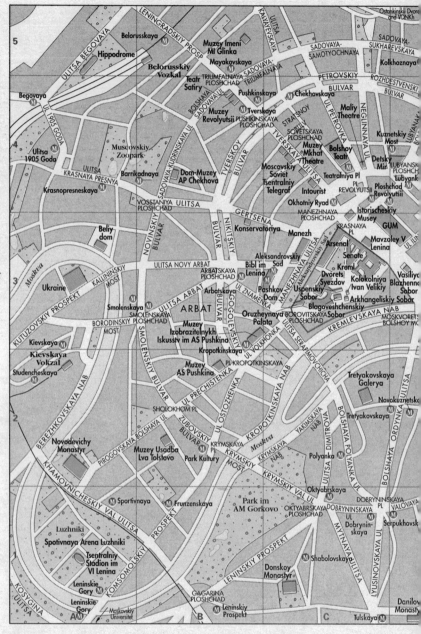

Russian art, ranging from 11th-century Kievan icons and the revered *Old Testament Trinity* by Andrei Rublev, to Ilya Repin's 19th-century portraits and historical landscapes. The Tretyakovka (New Tretyakov Gallery), situated on Krymskiy Val Ulitsa, is devoted to Soviet art.

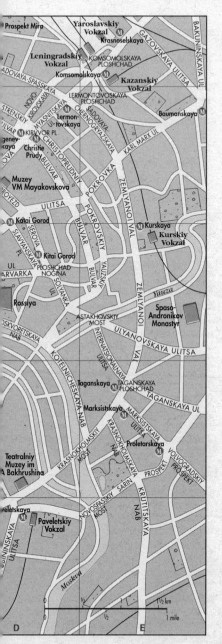

ICONS

A feature of Orthodox Christianity is the veneration of the icon, which has left a superb artistic legacy. The aim of the icon is to evoke spiritual communion between observer and the subject; the work of the greatest iconographers – Theophanes the Greek, Prokhor the Elder, Daniil Cherniy and Andrei Rubnev – were valued for this mystic quality. Often the icons of saints are framed with scenes from their lives.

was founded on the Dnipro River in AD 482. Kiev is now an attractive capital, combining quaint historic quarters, like Podil, with grand wide boulevards, such as Khreshchatyk. Among its many fine museums are the Russian Fine Art Museum, Kiev History Museum and Ukrainian Folk Decorative Art Museum. The grand Shchevchenko Opera and Ballet Theater is the best in the country.

PECHERSK LAVRA (Caves Monastery) was the first monastery of the Kievan Rus state. It contains ruins of the Dormition Cathedral, museums, monastic buildings and underground labyrinths with the mummified remains of monks.

SOFISKIY SOBOR (St. Sophia Cathedral) was built in 1017–31 to honor Prince Yaroslav's victory over the Pechenegs. The internal mosaics and frescoes are original, some dating from the 11th century, but the exterior has been greatly altered.

▲ MINSK (221 A3)

BELARUS *pop. 1,603,000*

Minsk was flattened during World War II, and the rebuilding exemplifies Soviet planning with its uniform façades, wide streets and parks. The city has an invigorated cosmopolitan air as capital of the new Belarusian state.

▲ KYÏV ★ (221 A3)

UKRAINE *pop. 2,643,000*

Capital of Ukraine and historic mother-city of the Eastern Slavs, Kyïv (Kiev)

TOURIST CAVEAT

The internal situation in Russia and the former republics is unstable, and changes may affect tourists. The process of de-Leninization, for example, means that towns, streets and buildings named after Lenin and his comrades are being renamed, so be prepared for some changes.

NOVGOROD (221 A4) ★

RUSSIA *pop. 190,000*

A fortress town established in the 9th century, Great Novgorod was a powerful principality in the Middle Ages. It was then eclipsed by Moscow, and brutally subjugated in 1570 by Ivan the Terrible.

KREML (Fortress), dating from the 11th century, overlooks the Volkhov River. Within the impressive walls, punctuated by nine robust 15th-century towers, is St. Sophia Cathedral (1050). The grandiose monument of Russia's Millenium fea-

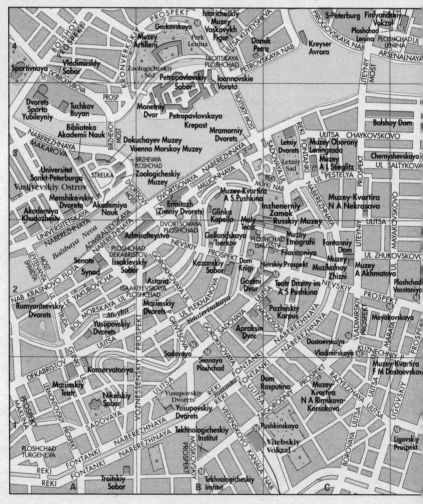

RUSSIA, UKRAINE AND BELARUS

tures statues of the great historical figures that shaped the country's history up to 1862.

YAROSLAVOVO DVORISHCHE I TORG (Yaroslavl's Court) was the commercial center. It now contains an arcade, gate tower and unique goup of churches dating from the 12th to the 19th centuries.

ODESA (221 A2)
UKRAINE *pop. 1,096,000*
A busy city on the Black Sea, Odesa (Odessa) is also a fascinating resort.

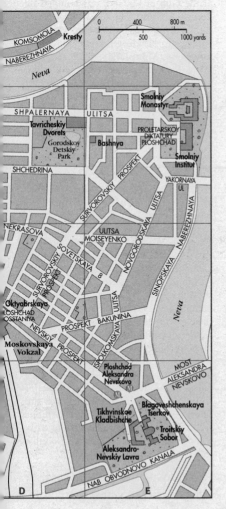

TEATR OPERI TA BALETA (Opera and Ballet Theater), was designed by Viennese architects Flener and Gelmer in the 1880s.

POTEMKINSKY STUPENY (Potemkin Steps) run down 192 steps towards the quayfront. The location was made famous by Eisenstein's film *The Battleship Potemkin*.

PSKOV (221 A3)
RUSSIA *pop. 255,000*
Founded between the 6th and 8th centuries, this fortress city was originally known as "Novgorod's little brother."

KREML (Fortress) dates from the 10th century, when the turreted walls, surrounded on two sides by river, proved almost impregnable. Within, the imposing five-domed Trinity Church dates from the 17th century.

▲ SANKT-PETERBURG (221 A4) ★
RUSSIA *pop. 5,004,000*
Sankt-Peterburg (St. Petersburg) has in its short history also been known as Petrograd and Leningrad. Only the force of will of Peter the Great could have raised this city from such inhospitable watery surroundings in 1703. The result is a strikingly beautiful European city of pastel-colored baroque streets, lined with rivers, canals and over 300 bridges.

PETER THE GREAT
Born in 1672, Peter became tsar when he was 10 years old, and that year traveled to Holland and England incognito to learn about shipbuilding. He returned with the plan of Westernizing Russia, built up a large navy to dispatch the Turks, and extended northern Russia by defeating the Swedes in the 21-year Northern War. He created St. Petersburg, his "Window to the West," at great cost to human life, drafting thousands of laborers to work on the cold, marshy land.

RUSSIA, UKRAINE AND BELARUS

ERMITAZH (Hermitage) ★ (228 B3), built between 1754 and 1762 by Italian architect Rastrelli, is one of the world's great museums. It contains 2.8 million exhibits, ranging from ancient Scythian gold to the Impressionists and Picasso, in over 400 exhibition rooms. Part of the museum is the former Winter Palace, the tsar's residence in St. Petersburg.

Given the scale and range of exhibits, the visitor is advised to be selective. However, the State Rooms in the Winter Palace are definitely not to be missed for their chandeliers, and opulent marble and gold-leaf decoration.

ISAAKIEVSKIY SOBOR (St. Isaac's Cathedral) (228 A2), with one of the largest domes in the world, was begun in 1818, but took over 40 years to build and a further 15 years to decorate. Used as a museum in the 1930s, it is now a working cathedral. Note the magnificent dome, with its viewing gallery and painting of the Virgin. The vast interior contains marble, malachite and stucco decoration, frescoes and mosaics.

LETNIY DVORETS (Summer Palace) (228 B3) stands overlooking the Neva in the corner of the Summer Gardens. Built for Peter the Great, this modest building was one of the first in the city; on display are the tsar's bedroom, turnery and dining room.

MUZEY-KVARTIRA A.S. PUSHKIN (Pushkin House-Museum) (228 B3), on the Moyka River, is where Russia's national poet spent the last years of his life (1836–37) before an ill-fated duel with his wife's lover. The museum includes his study, where the clock was stopped at the time of his death.

NEVSKIY PROSPEKT (228 B2), the city's grand thoroughfare, runs for 4.5 kilometers (3 miles) from Admiralteystvo (Admiralty) to the Alexander Nevskiy Monastery. It displays a variety of architectural syles from baroque to *style moderne* (Russian art nouveau). Chief landmarks include the Dom Knigi (bookstore) with its huge globe, Kazan Cathedral and the City Duma.

PAVLOVSK, 30 kilometers (18½ miles) south of the city, is one of the largest landscaped gardens in the world, with alleys and elaborate paths running between temples, pavilions and ponds. The central palace was built between 1782 and 1786 for the future Tsar Paul I by Scottish architect Charles Cameron.

PETERHOF, west of the city on the shores of the Gulf of Finland, was founded by Peter the Great. The Great Palace contains a stunning ceremonial staircase leading to dazzling state rooms. Two pavilions, Monplaisir and Catherine Wing, flank the palace; others are in the gardens. The Grand Cascade, when working, is the highlight of the estate: a magnificent fountain of 37 sculptures, 29 bas-reliefs and 142 water jets centered around a statue of Samson slaying the lion.

PETROPAVLOVSKAYA KREPOST (Peter and Paul Fortress) (228 B3), begun in 1703 and now largely converted into museums, was both fortress and prison. Among the prisoners held here were Peter the Great's son (whom the tsar had tortured to death), the Decembrists, Lenin's brother, Gorky and Trotsky.

The cathedral is the burial place of the Romanovs. The gilded spire, at 122 meters (400 feet) high, was the tallest in the city until the 1960s.

RUSSKIY MUZEY (Russian Museum) (228 C2), Ploshchad Iskusstv, is housed primarily in the former Mikhailovsky palace. Founded in 1895, the museum rivals Moscow's Tretyakovskaya as the finest collection of Russian art. Exhibits are chronologically arranged, from early iconography to avant-garde and socialist realist art.

TSARSKOE SELO ★, a small town 25 kilometers (15½ miles) south of St.

Petersburg, is the location of Yekaterinskiy Dvorets (Catherine Palace), which is a baroque masterpiece that has come to encapsulate the splendor of St. Petersburg. The sparkling blue-and-white façade is adorned with atlases, pilasters and columns. The interior, particularly the fabulously ornate Grand Hall and Amber Room, is equally stunning. The outbuildings in the parks include the Agate Room and Cameron Gallery, all restored at a huge cost following their destruction in World War II.

VASILYEVSKIY OSTROV (228 A3) (Vasilyevskiy Island) provides an impressive waterfront, featuring the former Stock Exchange (now a naval museum), the Kunstkammer (housing a museum of anthropology and ethnography, including grotesques collected by Peter the Great), and the Menshikov Palace (one of the finest in the city, with guided tours).

SUZDAL' (221 B3) ★
RUSSIA *pop. 12,000*
Suzdal' is a charming town of decorated wooden houses and market gardens, interspersed with a remarkable number of churches and monasteries that demonstrate the town's past importance. Snow-clad in winter with sun sparkling on cupolas, there is no prettier sight in Russia.

The oldest building in the town's *kremlin* (fortress) is the Cathedral of the Nativity (1222–5), notable for its external carving, late 17th-century iconostasis and 13th-century golden gates.

Outside the town is a museum of wooden architecture and peasant life.

VLADIMIR (221 B3)
RUSSIA *pop. 350,000*
Vladimir is an industrial town that contains superb monuments to its earlier religious significance and position as capital of Russia.

DIMITRIEVSKY SOBOR, St. Demetrius Cathedral), built in 1194–7, exudes grace with its single golden dome and slender pilasters. One of the great Russian cathedrals, its exterior white-stone carvings are remarkable.

USPENSKY SOBOR, or Cathedral of the Assumption (Dormition), was built by Prince Andrei Bogolyubsky between 1158 and 1160. Inside, it contains *The Last Judgement* fresco by Andrei Rublev and an 18th-century iconostasis.

BOGOLUBOVO, 14 kilometers (8½ miles) east, is a small village blessed with the enchanting Tserkov Porkova na Nerli (Church of the Intercession on the River Nerl) and an architectural ensemble, including the Cathedral of the Mother of God, dating from the 12th to the 18th centuries.

YALTA (221 B2)
UKRAINE *pop. 90,000*
Yalta occupies a spectacular setting on the Black Sea at the foot of the Crimean mountains.

It became the most popular resort of the Russian Empire in the 19th century, spawning many sanatoria and hotels. Its subtropical climate has fostered the splendid Botanical Gardens.

CHEKHOV MEMORIALNY MUSEI, vulitsa Kirova 112, is the *dacha* (cottage) Chekhov had built in 1904, once he contracted tuberculosis. Tolstoy visited Chekhov here, as did Rachmaninov and Chopin, who would play the piano. Memorabilia and editions of the writer's works are on display in the museum.

LIVADIA, a Renaissance-style palace 3 kilometers (2 miles) west of Yalta, was a summer residence built for Tsar Nicholas II.

In February 1945, toward the end of World War II, it was the scene of the Yalta Conference involving Roosevelt, Stalin and Churchill. Exhibits cover this meeting, as well as Nicholas II and his family. There are also delightful gardens and a clifftop lookout over the Black Sea.

SLOVAK REPUBLIC

THE SLOVAKS SAW THEM-SELVES AS THE NEGLECTED HALF OF CZECHOSLOVAKIA, AND THIS EVENTUALLY CAUSED THE COUNTRIES TO SPLIT ON JANUARY 1, 1993.

ALTHOUGH IT MAY BE ECONOMICALLY POOR, THE SLOVAK REPUBLIC IS RICH IN NATURAL BEAUTY, PARTICULARLY THE IMPRESSIVE AND IMPOSING HIGH TATRA MOUNTAINS. THIS IS AN AREA FOR WALKING IN SUMMER, SKIING IN WINTER, AND PERHAPS GLIMPSING WILD BOAR AND BEARS THAT STILL LIVE IN THE FORESTS. THE APTLY NAMED SLOVENSKY RAJ (THE SLOVAK PARADISE) IS A GEN-TLER REGION OF RIVERS AND GORGES, FORESTS AND FALLS, INCLUDING THE DOBSINA ICE CAVE, A HUGE UNDERGROUND FROZEN LAKE.

IF EMPHASIS IS PLACED ON THE COUNTRYSIDE, IT IS BECAUSE THE SLOVAK CAPITAL, BRATISLAVA, CAN-NOT YET HOPE TO COMPETE WITH NEIGHBORS PRAGUE, VIENNA AND BUDAPEST.

Left BEAUTIFUL STRBSKE PLESO IN THE HIGH TATRA MOUNTAINS
Above THERE ARE STILL BROWN BEARS TO BE SPOTTED IN THE MOUNTAINS IN THE SLOVAK REPUBLIC

THINGS TO KNOW

- **AREA:** 49,000 square kilometers (18,919 square miles)
- **POPULATION:** 5,310,000
- **CAPITAL:** Bratislava
- **LANGUAGE:** Slovak
- **RELIGION:** Roman Catholic
- **ECONOMY:** Engineering and chemicals, textiles and electronics, livestock production, arable crops, fruit, wine, forestry.
- **ELECTRICITY:** 220 volts, Continental two round-pin plugs. An adaptor and/or transformer is required for non-Continental appliances.
- **PASSPORT REQUIREMENTS:** Required for U.S. citizens.
- **VISA REQUIREMENTS:** Not required for stays of under 30 days.
- **DUTY-FREE ITEMS:** 250 cigarettes or corresponding amounts of other tobacco products; 2 liters of wine; 1 liter of liquor; ½ liter of cologne; gifts of up to 1,000 *crowns* in value and personal items suitable to the length and purpose of visit (clothing, personal jewelry, tools, sports equipment, video cameras, still cameras, portable typewriters, radios, cassette players, etc). The import of pure alcohol or pornographic items is prohibited.
- **CURRENCY:** The currency unit is the Slovak *crown* or *koruna*, divided into 100 *hellers* (*halé*). Remember that the exchange rate is subject to frequent change. Visitors may not import or export any local currency; though if you keep exchange receipts you can convert excess *crowns* back into U.S. dollars on departure. There is no limit to the import of foreign currency, but it must be declared on a written attachment to the visa. German *Marks* and U.S. dollars are easily exchanged and sometimes accepted in payment.
- **STORE OPENING HOURS:** 8am–6pm Monday–Friday, 8am–7 or 8pm Thursday, 8am–2pm Saturday.
- **BANK OPENING HOURS:** 8am–12 noon Monday–Friday and often 1:30–3:30pm.
- **BEST BUYS:** Carved wooden items (kitchen articles, toys), ceramics from Modra and Stupava, leather, fur coats

HISTORY

Slav tribes occupied the historic region of Slovakia (the present-day Slovak Republic) during the 5th century AD. The arrival of the Magyars in the 10th century spelled the end of the Great Moravian Empire of which Slovakia had been a part.

For the next thousand years the country was part of Hungary, ruled by Hungarian lord-bishops and when Budapest fell to the Turks in 1541 Bratislava became the capital of Hungary.

The Magyars' political dominance meant that any Slovak with ambitions to rise from the peasantry had no choice but to become "Magyarized," an intolerable situation in the 19th century, with the age of nationalism.

Slovak writers and clerics promoted their native language and culture, but independence from Hungary only came after World War I, when Slovaks joined with the Czechs to form the new Republic of Czechoslovakia.

The occupation of Bohemia and Moravia by Nazi Germany in 1939 established a nominally independent Slovak state. The Slovak National Uprising of 1944 was put down by the German army after months of fierce fighting. At the end of World War II, the Slovaks joined a reconstituted Czechoslovak state, and between 1948 and 1989 experienced (along with the Czechs) Communist rule as part of Czechoslovakia.

Nationalist grievances remained, and found expression after the fall of communism. Slovak and Czech politicians agreed to separate their countries, and in January 1, 1993, the Slovak Republic became truly independent for the first time in its history.

FOOD AND DRINK

A typically rather heavy Central European cuisine is made more exciting by

Hungarian influences like the extensive use of paprika.

Mutton, goose, pork and chicken are all eaten, and fish such as trout and carp are bred in ponds.

Sheep's cheese is widely available, and a favorite dish with just about everyone is *halušky*, noodles with cheese sauce and diced bacon.

Pastries usually accompany Turkish-style coffee (strong), while alcoholic drinks include excellent wines from the vineyards in the plains and, from along the southern fringe of the mountains, the gin-like *borovička* and the plum-based spirit, *slivovice*.

SPORTS AND RECREATION
Soccer and tennis in particular enjoy an enthusiastic following in the Slovak Republic, and the country's rugged terrain makes it a leader in the provision and enjoyment of outdoor recreation of all kinds.

Skiing and ice hockey are very popular sports. There are endless opportunities for walking and climbing in the Slovak mountains.

Sailing and other water sports take place on a number of large artificial lakes and there are plenty of swimming pools.

Mountains and forests harbor an abundance of game for the hunter.

GETTING AROUND
Numerous border crossings link the Slovak Republic to the Czech Republic, Austria, Hungary, Ukraine and Poland. Bratislava (Ivánka) Airport is served by an increasing number of international flights. Internal flights however are limited, but you can fly from Bratislava to Poprad to get to the Vysoké Tatry (High Tatra Mountains).

Public transportation by train and bus is cheap and every settlement is served, but local trains can be very slow.

The road system has been extensively modernized, though there are few freeways and drivers should observe special caution on the sometimes dangerous mountain roads. Drivers and passengers must wear seat belts. Children under 12 may not travel in the front seat. Never consume alcohol before driving; it is an offense to do so.

Speed limits are 65 k.p.h. (40 m.p.h.) in town (indicated by the place-name sign), 90 k.p.h. (55 m.p.h.) out of town and 110 k.p.h. (68 m.p.h.) on highways. Fines must be paid on the spot.

ARCHITECTURAL BEAUTY
Traditional rural architecture has been preserved in many Slovak villages. Timber farmhouses, set at right angles to the street, have steeply pitched roofs and are usually only one room wide. Perfectly conserved examples can be seen in a number of open-air museums or *skanzens*, like the one outside the town of Martin in the central Slovak Republic, but perhaps the most evocative buildings are those in the village of Vlkolinec, saved from change by the village's remoteness – until recently it could only be reached on foot! Near the town of Ruzomberok, Vlkolinec has now been declared a World Heritage Site by U.N.E.S.C.O.

AUTOMOBILE CLUB
Ustrecdny Automotoklub SR
(U.A.M.K. SR) has its headquarters at Wolkrova 4, 851 01, Bratislava. The symbol ▲ beside a city name indicates the presence of a AAA-affiliated automobile club branch. Not all auto clubs offer full travel services to AAA members.

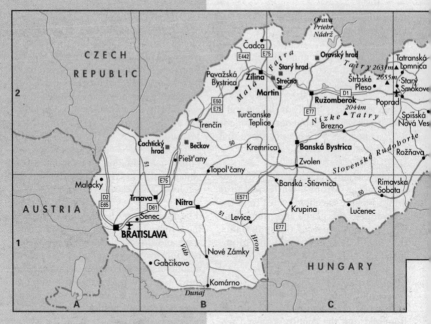

and hats, sheepskins, traditional blouses and shirts, liquor (*slivovice* plum brandy, *borvicka* gin), glass.

- **PUBLIC HOLIDAYS:** January 1 (New Year's Day and establishment of Slovak Republic); Easter Monday; May 1 (May Day); May 8 (Day of Liberation); July 5 (Saints Cyril and Methodius); August 29 (Anniversary of Slovak National Uprising); September 1 and 15; November 1; December 24, 25, 26.
- **NATIONAL TOURIST OFFICES:** SATUR is the Slovak body of the former state-owned ČEDOK agency and has branches in most towns.
  2201 Wisconsin Avenue
  Washington, DC 20007
  Tel: 202/965-5161
  East-West Travel
  109 39th Street
  New York
  Tel: 212/545-0737
- **AMERICAN EMBASSY:** Hviezdoslavovo námestie 4, Bratislava Slovak Republic Tel: (07) 33 08 61

ACCOMMODATIONS

The large number of hotels in the country are classified by star ratings from one (basic) to five (deluxe). Many older hotels are undergoing modernization. Bed-and-breakfast accommodations are often available in private homes and there are numerous campgrounds.

TIPPING

It is customary to round up the bill at a restaurant or give a gratuity of 10 percent, likewise with taxis. Hotel porters and restroom attendants should be given a tip of a few *crowns*.

USEFUL EXPRESSIONS IN SLOVAK

good morning	**dobré ráno**
good afternoon	**dobré odpoledne**
good-bye	**na shledanou**
please	**prosím**
thank you	**dekuju**
castle	**hrad**
château	**zámok**
church	**skostol**
square	**námestie**
city hall	**radnica**

like Kremnica, **Banská Bystrica** and Banská Štiavnica. The Great and Little Fatra ranges are little-known to outsiders, but immensely popular with local ramblers and skiers.

River gorges are guarded by romantic castles, like ruined Strečno on the Váh River or Oravský Zámok, perched on a high crag above the Orava River.

HIGH TATRAS AND EASTERN SLOVAK REPUBLIC

The Low Tatra ranges attract locals for winter sports and summer fresh air, but the Slovak Republic's most spectacular mountains are the **Vysoké Tatry** (High Tatras), a series of jagged peaks rising abruptly from the plain. Here are old upland resorts like Štrbské Pleso, Starý Smokovec and Tatranská Lomnica, with ski runs and hiking trails, and some of Europe's last bears lurking in the forest.

The Spiš region is dominated by the huge ruined fortress of **Spišský Hrad**, and has several fine old towns like Kežmarok and **Levoča**, founded by German settlers who migrated here in the Middle Ages.

Košice, the metropolis of the Eastern Slovak Republic, has a minority ethnic Ukrainian population and villages with wonderful timber churches.

Ždiar is noted for its folk costumes, worn on Sundays and holidays.

PRINCIPAL TOURING AREAS

Note: For descriptions of attractions in **bold type**, see individual listings.

BRATISLAVA AND THE SURROUNDING AREA

In the southwest corner of the country, almost within sight of Vienna, 64 kilometers (40 miles) upstream on the Danube, is the Slovak Republic's cosmopolitan capital, **Bratislava**, with many excellent museums and architectural treasures.

Beginning in the suburbs, the forested heights and vine-clad lower slopes of the Little Carpathian Mountains stretch away to the northeast.

With its many churches, the old town of Trnava (the Slovak Rome) is 48 kilometers (30 miles) away, while 32 kilometers (20 miles) further on is the most prestigious of the country's many spa towns, Piešt'any, which became one of Europe's most fashionable resorts in the years before World War I.

CENTRAL SLOVAK REPUBLIC

This is the country's mountainous heartland, centered on industrial towns like Žilina and Martin, and old mining cities

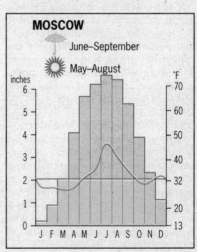

MOSCOW

☂ June–September

☀ May–August

PLACES OF INTEREST

★ HIGHLIGHTS ★	
Bardejov	(see p.239)
Bratislava	
Dóm (Cathedral)	(see p 238)
Hrad (Castle)	(see p.238)
Námestie (Square)	(see p 238)
Levoča	(see p.239)
Vysoké Tatry	(see p.239)

▲ **BRATISLAVA (236 A1)** ★
BRATISLAVA-VIDIEK *pop. 450,000*
One of the most fascinating cities along the Danube, Bratislava straddles the mighty river at the point where the Slovak, Hungarian and Austrian frontiers meet. Its formidable-looking castle perches on the last crag of the Carpathian Mountains. At its foot are the intricate lanes and alleyways of the medieval city which grew up in the 12th and 13th centuries, but whose character has been ruined by insensitive building during the Communist years.

BRATISLAVSKÝ HRAD (Castle) ★ With its four corner towers, the massive and much rebuilt castle has a very distinctive outline earning it the nickname "the upturned table."
Since independence it has become one of the symbols of Slovak statehood and is used for government and ceremonial purposes as well as housing the collections of the National Museum. The hard climb up to the castle terrace is well worth it for the marvelous view over the Danube and the city.

DÓM SV. MARTINA ★ (St. Martin's Cathedral) was the setting for the coronation of no fewer than 11 Hungarian monarchs, crowned here during the Turkish occupation of Budapest. An outstanding example of Gothic architecture, it has been joined as a prominent city landmark by the modern S.N.P. (Slovak National Uprising) Bridge which carries an expressway over the Danube River.

HLAVNÉ NÁMESTIE ★ (Main Square) is at the heart of the old town. A Renaissance fountain with a statue of Roland looks towards the Radnica (old town hall) housing collections of the City Museum.

MICHALSKÁ BRÁNA (Michael's Gate) is the last remaining gateway of the city's fortifications. Its lower parts are Gothic, its cap, 51 meters (167 feet) high, is baroque. The streets running south from its archway are lined with splendid burghers' houses and aristocratic palaces. This is the university quarter, scene of the ferment that helped to bring down communism in late 1989, when students and citzens formed the movement called Public Against Violence, the Slovak equivalent of the Czech Civic Forum.

NÁRODNÁ GALÉRIA (National Gallery), housed in a converted naval barracks facing the Danube, is the best place in which to get acquainted with Slovak art, whose 20th-century practitioners have depicted scenes of traditional life.

PRIMATE'S PALACE in Primaciálne námestie is where Napoléon and the emperor of Austria signed the Treaty of Pressburg in 1805, after the Battle of Austerlitz. Much of the city's art collection is on display and the aptly named mirror hall is a spectacular example of baroque design.

▲ **BANSKÁ BYSTRICA (236 C2)**
CENTRAL SLOVAK REPUBLIC
pop. 51,000
This medieval city above the lush valley of the Hron River was built with the profits from mining the silver and copper ores in the surrounding mountains. The long and sloping marketplace is lined with fine 15th- and 16th-century houses. Banská Bystrica was at the center of the Slovak National Uprising (S.N.P.) of 1944, when the army joined partisans to redeem the country from the strain of collaboration with Nazi Germany. The

revolt was crushed after bitter fighting. These stirring events are commemorated in the futuristic S.N.P. Memorial building. Other old mining towns in the area include Kremnica, with its ancient royal mint, and Banská Štiavnica, with a developing open-air museum of mining.

SOCIAL CONSCIENCE

Juraj Janosik (1688–1713) was Slovakia's Robin Hood, a genial brigand who is supposed to have robbed the rich to pay the poor. Janosik was born in the village of Terchova in the mountains of the Central Slovak Republic, and turned to brigandage when his father was punished by his feudal master for nursing his sick wife rather than working in the fields. Janosik's short life came to an end when he was betrayed and put to death in the marketplace of the little town of Liptovsky Mikulas. Terchova is now a mountain resort, dominated by a stunning metal sculpture of its local hero.

BARDEJOV (237 D2) ★
EASTERN SLOVAK REPUBLIC
pop. 30,000
This ancient town was at its most prosperous in the 15th and 16th centuries. Its well-preserved walls date from the 14th century. The marketplace is surrounded by colorful merchants' houses, while the town hall has a fine collection of icons. Bardejov has a substantial minority population of Ukrainians. Close to the town's spa, 6 kilometers (4 miles) north is an open-air museum with timber buildings.

LEVOČA (237 D2) ★
EASTERN SLOVAK REPUBLIC
pop. 13,000
The most exquisite of the old towns of the Spiš district, Levoča has a broad main square lined with burghers' mansions. In the middle of the square stands the town hall, a fine example of Renaissance architecture, while St. James's Church has one of the country's greatest art treasures – the wonderful altarpiece by the famous 14th-century woodcarver Master Paul. A nearby hilltop is crowned by a church, which is the scene in July of a popular pilgrimage.

SPIŠSKÝ HRAD (237 D2)
EASTERN SLOVAK REPUBLIC
Now a spectacular ruin, Spišský Hrad (Spis Castle) was once the largest castle in Central Europe, dominating the main east–west route through the Slovak Republic. The castle withstood attack by Tartars in 1241, but was abandoned in the 18th century. Destroyed by fire in 1781, most of the remains date from the 13th to 15th centuries.

VYSOKÉ TATRY (237 D2) ★
EASTERN SLOVAK REPUBLIC
The main range of the Vtsoké Tatry (High Tatras) is only a few miles long, but with its series of jagged peaks it is one of the most spectacular mountain chains in Europe. Tourism is exceptionally well developed, with a railway which links a string of mountain resorts among the glorious conifer forests which cover the lower slopes of the mountains.

Štrbské Pleso, the most modern resort, is centered around a lake and is characterized by ultramodern hotels and excellent ski facilities, while the older resorts of Tatranská Lomnica and Starý Smokovec have a charming turn-of-the-century atmosphere.

The High Tatras are as popular in summer as in winter, with many miles of hiking trails leading up from the forest towards the peaks. The highest summit is 2,655-meter (8,711-foot) Gerlachovský štít, while 2,631-meter (8,635-foot) Lomnický štít can be reached by cable car. The whole area is a national park, aimed at preserving the beauty and wildlife that includes wolves and bears, which are still rare in other parts of Europe. There is a good museum of the national park at Tatranská Lomnica.

FRANCE

FRANCE IS ART AND HISTORY, ARCHITECTURE AND LAND-SCAPE, PARIS AND PROVENCE. BUT ABOVE AND BEYOND ALL OF THESE, IT IS FOOD AND DRINK. INDEED, THE MAP OF FRANCE READS LIKE A WINE LIST AND A MENU: ARMAGNAC, CHAMPAGNE, BEAUJOLAIS, BORDEAUX, COGNAC, CAMEMBERT, ROQUEFORT, BRIE. TOWNS AND VILLAGES ARE UNITED BY THEIR BUTCHERS, BAKERS, CAFÉS AND MARKETS. YOU WILL FIND BETTER FOOD IN FRANCE THAN ANYWHERE ELSE IN THE WORLD.

THIS IS A CULTURED COUNTRY, WHERE POLITICS AND ART ARE NOT JUST RESERVED FOR AN EDUCATED ELITE; THE WRITER IS RESPECTED AND THE ARTIST REVERED. ZOLA, SARTRE, FLAUBERT, MONET, CÉZANNE, TOULOUSE-LAUTREC, DEGAS AND MANET ARE JUST SOME OF THE NAMES ASSOCIATED WITH FRENCH CULTURE, AND AS FAMILIAR AS THOSE OF FRENCH CUISINE.

Left THIS *BOULANGERIE* BOASTS "BREAD FOR EVERY OCCASION"
Above left SUNFLOWERS WERE AN INSPIRATION FOR VINCENT VAN GOGH
Above right BEAUJOLAIS GRAPES PRODUCE THE WORLD-FAMOUS WINES

Things to Know

- **Area:** 551,670 square kilometers (220,668 square miles)
- **Population:** 56,184,000
- **Capital:** Paris
- **Language:** French
- **Religion:** Largely Roman Catholic.
- **Economy:** Industry. mining, agriculture. aircraft, autos, textiles, chemicals. Large coal, iron ore, bauxite deposits. Main crops: wheat, barley, dairy products; many small, diversified farms. Leading wine producer; tourist-related industries are important.
- **Passport Requirements:** Required for U.S. citizens.
- **Visa Requirements:** Not required for stays up to three months.
- **Duty-Free Items:** Purchased duty-free or outside of the European Union (E.U.) – 200 cigarettes or 100 cigarillos or 50 cigars or 250 grams tobacco; 1 liter of spirits or 2 liters of fortified wine; 60ml of perfume; 250ml of toilet water; 500 grams of coffee; 100 grams of tea; 300 *francs*' of other goods, sports equipment; two still cameras of different sizes with 10 rolls of film for each; one movie camera with 10 rolls of film; video equipment; other personal belongings. Also see *The European Union*, p.9.
- **Value Added Tax:** France levies a Value Added Tax on goods purchased within its borders. You can avoid paying the V.A.T., however, by asking to have the tax deducted from the price of almost any object you buy to take home as part of your luggage. You also can be reimbursed by applying for a refund when you leave the country.
  You can claim a tax refund on purchases in store of over 1,200 *francs* if you reside outside the E.U. Present the pink copy of your sales invoice and a stamped envelope supplied by the vendor to the French customs official before you register your luggage. The customs official will mail the sales ticket back to the vendor from whom you made your purchases and he or she will mail you a refund in 30 days.

History

Inhabited by the Celts and known as Gaul, southern France became a Roman province with Julius Caesar's conquest in 58–52 BC. Barbarian invasions ended Roman domination in the 5th century and resulted in the formation of a kingdom under the Franks. Clovis I was the first Christian king of France, but Charlemagne, who ruled from AD 768 to 814, was historically more important, for he was the first of a succession of rulers of the Holy Roman Empire. Charlemagne's death resulted in partition of the empire into domains – Normandy, Aquitaine, Burgundy, Flanders and others.

From this period until the 17th century, successive French kings struggled to control the great vassalries and unite the country politically and territorially. These were the times of the Hundred Years' War, the Thirty Years' War and numerous struggles with English and Spanish kings, popes and barons. The land became a checkerboard, with pieces alternately lost and gained. Civil war further divided the populace over religious policies. Eventually a centralized monarchy emerged, only to perish with the capture of the Bastille in 1789. With the rise of Napoléon Bonaparte, France embarked upon a glorious era that lasted until the "Little Corporal's" defeat at Waterloo in 1815.

The Bourbons returned to power, and France was again a monarchy until the revolution of 1848 made the country a republic. Napoléon III established the Second Empire in 1852, but the country reverted to being a republic after the Franco-Prussian War in 1870. In the 20th century, France endured both world wars and following the second, the Fourth Republic was established. Numerous governments, political parties and a fight to retain Algeria as a French possession were some of the country's concerns during the 1950s. As France sought to solve these problems, General Charles de Gaulle was recalled to power in 1958 as premier, and the people of France voted to establish the Fifth Republic, which continues today.

FOOD AND DRINK

Whether selecting from the menus of tiny bistros on the Riviera or those of elegant Parisian restaurants, dining is always a pleasure. The French custom of eating the main meal between noon and 2pm may seem sensible after a strenuous morning of sightseeing. To accompany a meal, inexpensive local wines in carafes rather than bottles are a wise selection. The *plat du jour* (dish of the day) is invariably delicious. Meals generally consist of *hors d'oeuvres* (appetizer), an *entrée* of meat or fish with vegetables, then cheese and fruit or dessert.

Each region of France has its own culinary specialties. Burgundy, noted in particular for fine food and wine, is known for *boeuf bourguignon*, a stew made from beef marinated in red wine, as well as for *quenelles* (pike dumplings) and artichoke hearts stuffed with *foie gras* (goose liver), *chaucrâite* (sauerkraut), and Strasbourg apple tarts with cream. In Brittany the emphasis is on seafood, including oysters, crawfish and sardines. *Homard à l'américaine* (lobster with cream) is a specialty. The Provençal dishes of the Riviera are heady with garlic. Other acclaimed dishes are the *bouillabaisse* of Marseilles, a fish soup, and the *salade niçoise* of Nice, a combination of anchovies, celery, olives, peppers, tomatoes and tuna. The Île-de-France boasts *Châteaubriand aux pommes* (steak with apples) and *crêpes suzette*; Rouen, in Normandy, is noted for duck; and Languedoc for its *cassoulet*, a stew of goose, mutton, pork and beans. From the Champagne region come preparations of succulent ham, shrimp, trout and the celebrated Champagne wine. Salmon from the Loire, chicken dishes of Gascony and the fluffy omelettes of Mont-Saint-Michel are other fine examples of French gastronomy. France produces around 350 different cheeses, including Camembert, Brie, Roquefort, and many other blue cheeses.

SPORTS AND RECREATION

The French relish spectator sports like bicycle racing, soccer, boxing and horse racing. The national Tour de France bicycle race draws international attention for three weeks at the beginning of July. Boxing takes place in Paris at the Palais des Sports and at the Stade Pierre de Coubertin. The Palais Omnisports de Paris-Bercy is the main stadium for basketball. Tennis, notably the French Open in early June, takes place at the Stade Roland-Garros in Paris. Popular horse racetracks near Paris are Auteuil, Chantilly, Longchamp, Vincennes, and St. Cloud. The latter two also have golfing greens. Golf and tennis are generally found in French resorts. Yachting, swimming, fishing, golf, tennis and horseback riding can be enjoyed at the Riviera resorts and at the Atlantic coastal resorts of Biarritz and Deauville. International yachting regattas at coastal resorts are held in summer. Ski resorts in the Alps and Pyrénées offer all winter sports.

GETTING AROUND

Driving through the French countryside is an experience no one should miss, but navigating a car through the large cities, especially Paris, should be avoided. Many country roads are tree-lined, clean, fast and well marked. Generally, road surfaces are in good repair. Rules of the road are similar to those in the United States. Driving is on the right and passing on the left. Priority is given to traffic emerging from the right, unless otherwise signposted. In areas where there is no street lighting, parking lights should be left on wherever possible during evening hours.

The wearing of seat belts, if fitted, is mandatory for the driver and passengers. A child under 10 cannot occupy a front seat apart from a baby under 9 months in an approved rear-facing restraint. The speed limit is 50 k.p.h. (31 m.p.h.) in town. In good weather, out-of-town limits

- **CURRENCY:** The currency unit is the French *franc*, divided into 100 *centimes*. Due to currency fluctuations, the exchange rate is subject to frequent change. There is no import duty on the import or export of currency.
- **BANK OPENING HOURS:** 9am–noon and 2–4pm Monday–Friday; some banks are open Saturday and closed Monday.
- **STORE OPENING HOURS:** 9am or 10am to 6:30pm or 7:30pm Monday–Saturday; some food stores open Sunday morning; small stores are closed Monday; some department stores are closed Monday morning; stores in small towns often close noon to 2pm.
- **BEST BUYS:** Fashionable clothing, perfume, jewelry, gloves, antiques.
- **PUBLIC HOLIDAYS:** January 1; Easter Sunday and Monday; May 1 (Labor Day); May 8 (Anniversary 1945 Victory in Europe Day); Ascension Day; Whitsunday and Whitmonday; July 14 (Bastille Day); August 15 (Assumption Day); November 1 (All Saints' Day); November 11 (Armistice Day); December 25.
- **USEFUL TELEPHONE NUMBERS:**
  Police 17
  Fire 18
  Ambulance 18
- **NATIONAL TOURIST OFFICES:**
  444 Madison Avenue
  16th Floor
  New York
  NY 10022/6903
  Fax: 212/838-7855
  Tel: 900/990-0040
  France-On-Call Hotline
  Tel: 1-900-990-0040
  Also offices in:
  Chicago and Beverly Hills
  French Government Tourist Office
  178 Piccadilly, London, W1V 0AL
  Tel: 0891 244123
  Fax: 0171 493 6594
- **AMERICAN EMBASSY**
  2 Avenue Gabriel
  75382 Paris 8, France
  Tel: 01 42 96 12 02
  Fax: 01 42 66 97 83

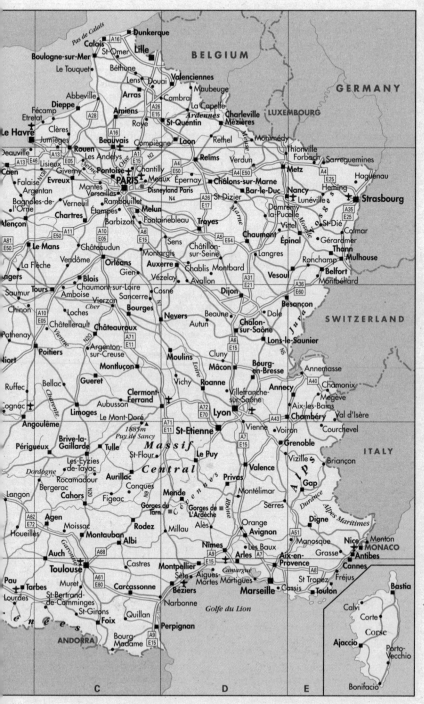

are between 90 k.p.h. (55 m.p.h.) and 110 k.p.h. (68 m.p.h.), depending on the type of road, reduced to between 80 k.p.h. (49 m.p.h.) and 100 k.p.h. (62 m.p.h.) in wet weather. Limits on toll motorways are 130 k.p.h. (80 m.p.h.) during good weather and 110 k.p.h. (68 m.p.h.) during wet, and 50 k.p.h. (31 m.p.h.) in fog when visibility is less than 50 meters (55 yards). There is a minimum

---

AUTOMOBILE CLUB
Automoblile Club National (A.C.N.), 5 rue Auber, 75009 Paris; tel: (01) 44 51 53 99. French motoring clubs do not provide a roadside breakdown service. It is worth taking out a breakdown insurance policy (available through the AA in the U.K.); policyholders can get 24-hour assistance by calling 0800 089222

---

speed limit of 80 k.p.h. (49 m.p.h.) for the outside lane on motorways during daylight hours with good visibility, on level ground. Visiting motorists are required to pay fines for violations on the spot with French *francs* or travelers' checks.

ACCOMMODATIONS

Hotels in France are rated from one to four stars. In special circumstances, an "L" is used to designate a deluxe rating. Hotels in Paris usually include breakfast in the price of the room though hotels in the provinces may not.

ACCOMMODATION BOOKING OFFICES

Many French departments have accommodation booking offices under the name of Loisers d'Accueil. Usually charging no fee, they reserve hotels, gîtes and campgrounds. For a list of these offices send a stamped, addressed envelope to the French Government Tourist Office.

Logis de France, a state-run concern, operates more than 4,000 small, family-run, mostly one- and two-star hotels around France, except Paris. They are often near major highways, reasonably priced, and offer a good way to experience rural French customs.

Relais Routier signs inform travelers of nearby restaurants that offer substantial meals and often lodging at reasonable prices. Local tourist offices (*Syndicates d'Initiative* or *Offices de Tourisme*) can help you with hotel selections and other forms of lodging.

Youth hostels in France give priority to traveling young people. There are about 10,000 campgrounds, including 35 on castle grounds. Local tourist offices have specific information. While not required, an International Camping Carnet may be requested at "*castels et camping-caravanning*" campgrounds or the "*forêts domaniales*" sites in state forests.

TIPPING

Tipping is a way of life in France. Nearly everyone who serves you expects a tip. Hotels and restaurants include a service fee up to 15 percent in their bills, but waiters look for an additional 5 to 7 percent. The cloakroom attendant should receive a tip per item; a washroom attendant 2 francs and a doorman 5 francs. Some cabs have an official scale of charges, but it is usual to give about 10 percent of the fare.

PRINCIPAL TOURING AREAS

Note: For descriptions of attractions in **bold type**, see individual listings.

ALPS

This mighty barrier of mountains in the southeast of France has some of the most spectacular scenery in Europe. Vacationers flock to its winter and summer resorts: **Courchevel**, Gap, Tignes, **Val d'Isère** and many other winter resorts beckon skiers; **Annecy**, **Digne** and Talloires attract summer sunbathers; and **Aix-les-Bains**, **Briançon**, **Chamonix** and Megève provide all-year enjoyment.

AUVERGNE
In the heart of the Massif Central, this spa center has watering places at Le Mont-Dore, Royat and **Vichy**. The terrain near **Clermont-Ferrand** and Le Puy is known for its volcanic rock formations.

BASQUE COUNTRY AND THE PYRÉNÉES
The Pyrénées is one of the most attractive parts of France, with Atlantic beach resorts such as **Biarritz** and Hendaye, and scenic mountains. The Basque people express themselves through dancing, carnivals, poetry, pelota and campaigning for status as an independent nation.

BRITTANY
The sea plays a dominant role in the lives of the Bretons, whose 1,200-kilometer (746-mile) western coast is a jagged line of rocky cliffs and sandy beaches. This is a colorful region of fishing hamlets, native customs, prehistoric megaliths and unusual churches and cottages. Among the coastal resorts are La Baule, Bénodet, Concarneau, **Dinan** and Quiberon; cities are **Nantes**, **Rennes**, **Brest** and **St-Malo**.

BURGUNDY
The ancient province of Bourgogne is renowned for incomparable wines and wonderful food. September and October are grape harvesting months. From May to September Burgundy is alive with concerts, wine fairs, festivals, plays and art exhibitions. **Dijon**, ancient capital of the Burgundian dukes, holds an annual gastronomic fair in November. Autun is rich in museums and art. **Mâcon** produces many high-quality wines; Vézelay was one of the most important pilgrimage sites during the Middle Ages.

CHAMPAGNE AND ALSACE-LORRAINE
Lying between Alsace-Lorraine and Paris in northeast France, Champagne hardly needs an introduction for its well-known bubbling wine. A good time to visit is during the autumn grape harvest. Visit the cathedral at **Reims**, where the kings of France were crowned, and the ancient city of **Troyes**. Alsace-Lorraine is French with a German accent. The region is best known for its beer, white wines and rich, distinctive cuisine. **Strasbourg** is here with its great rose-colored cathedral; **Mulhouse** is a major printing and textile center; and there are the resort towns of Gérardmer and Vittel. The Wine Road of the Vosges,

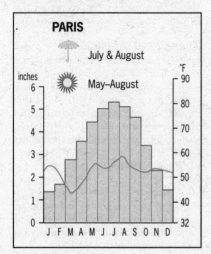

PARIS
July & August
May–August
inches 6 5 4 3 2 1 0
°F 90 80 70 60 50 40 32
J F M A M J J A S O N D

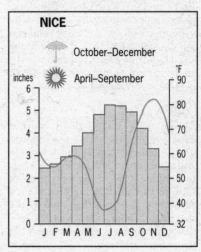

NICE
October–December
April–September
inches 6 5 4 3 2 1 0
°F 90 80 70 60 50 40 32
J F M A M J J A S O N D

FRANCE

vineyards and medieval villages and cities also are in this area.

DORDOGNE AND LES LANDES

One of the longest rivers in the country, the Dordogne is associated with wooded valleys, cliffs and the prehistoric caves around Les Eyzies-de-Tayac. Fortified towns, such as Rocamadour Domme and Monpazier, recall the medieval struggles between France and England. Here, between the Gironde River and almost to the Basque coast, lie Les Landes, a vast area of pine forests, lakes, sand dunes and beaches, noted for oysters, marinas and vineyards.

ÎLE-DE-FRANCE

Feudal castles, ancient forests, peaceful villages and scenes taken from the pages of French classics are everywhere. Discover the palaces of Chantilly, Vaux-le-Vicomte, **Versailles**, **Fontainebleau** and Malmaison, the cathedrals of **Chartres** and **St. Denis**, and the famous artists' haunt, the village of **Barbizon**.

JURA MOUNTAINS

The Jura Mountains form a barrier some 240 kilometers (150 miles) long between France and Switzerland and make up a region of great natural beauty. The mountains are a challenge to those wanting to rough it and a haven to those seeking solitude and tranquility. The city of Bourg-en-Bresse, a striking combination of old and new, is at the foot of the Jura Mountains. Other important towns are the industrial centers of Champagnole and **Dole**, the home of Louis Pasteur.

LOIRE VALLEY

This magnificent château country attracts many visitors and the countryside is as beautiful as the fairy-tale castles that were built by French kings and nobles. One of the best ways to explore this enchanting area is on a leisurely cruise ship that stops at the châteaux along the way. **Blois**, Cheverny, **Amboise**, **Chinon**, **Tours** and **Saumur**, are particularly worth visiting.

NORMANDY

Fertile farmlands, sandy beaches and resorts attract vacationers to the north west province of Normandy in summer. Alençon is a former fortress noted for its lace making; **Honfleur** is the birthplace of Impressionist art; Louviers has its church of Notre-Dame; and Avranches boasts a view of **Le Mont-St-Michel** on its rocky island. **Deauville**, Trouville and Le Touquet are popular seaside resorts. The scene of Allied landings in World War II, many towns and buildings in this region were destroyed, but have since been rebuilt.

RHÔNE VALLEY, LANGUEDOC AND PROVENCE

From **Lyon** to **Marseille**, the Rhône Valley is a treasure trove of Roman ruins. The vast arena and baths of **Nîmes**, the paved streets, mosaics and theater at Vaison-la-Romaine, and the great amphitheater and pagan burial grounds of **Arles** are found in this area. **Orange**, **Avignon** and Valence are a few of the cities steeped in centuries of history. Languedoc is another area for unusual historical excursions. **Toulouse**, foremost city in southern Gaul for many centuries, and the medieval city of **Carcassonne** merit a visit, as well as the hilltop villages of Manosque, Méjanes and Meyragues. Les Stes. Maries-de-la-Mer is in a marshy fen known as the Camargue that serves as a natural reserve.

RIVIERA AND CORSICA

From Marseille to Menton extends one of the world's most publicized playgrounds – the French Riviera, otherwise known as the Côte d'Azur. Along this strip of Mediterranean coast are colorful fishing ports and villages, luxury hotels, casinos, blue waters and the spectacular Corniche drive from Nice to Monaco. Visit La Napoule, Cassis, Èze, Le Lavandou, Miramar, Théoule-sur-Mer, Ste.-Maxime and St.-Tropez. For a change of pace, enjoy the mountainous beauty of Corsica. Ajaccio, the capital of Corsica (**Corse**), and Bastia, a medieval port, are accessible by air and sea.

USEFUL EXPRESSIONS IN FRENCH

hello	bonjour	railroad station	la gare
good morning	bonjour	railroad platform	le quai
good evening	bon soir	subway station	la station de métro
good night	bonne nuit	gas station	un poste à essence
good-bye	au revoir	parking lot	un parking
please/thank you	s'il vous plaît/merci	straight on	tout droit
yes/no	oui/non	right	à droite
excuse me	excusez-moi	left	à gauche
you're welcome	de rien/je vous en prie	opposite	en face de
Do you speak English?	Parlez vous anglais?	behind	derrière
I don't understand.	Je ne comprends pas.	in front of	devant
sorry	pardon	before	avant
What is the time?	Quelle heure est-il?	near	près
How much is that?	Combien est-ce?	here/there	ici/là
Where are the restrooms?	Où sont les toilettes?		

DAYS OF THE WEEK

I'd like...	Je voudrais...

Sunday	dimanche
Monday	lundi
Tuesday	mardi
Wednesday	mercredi
Thursday	jeudi
Friday	vendredi
Saturday	samedi

Can you help me, please?	Pouvez-vous m'aider, s'il vous plaît?
Can you speak more slowly?	S'il vous plaît, parlez moins vite.
Do you take credit cards?	Acceptez-vous les cartes de crédit?
where/when/how	ou/quand/comment
hot/cold	chaud/froid
old/new	vieux/vieille (f) nouveau/nouvelle (f)

NUMBERS

open/closed	ouvert/fermé	1 .... un/une
no smoking	défense de fumer	2 .... deux
The check, please.	L'addition, s'il vous plaît.	3 .... trois
yesterday	hier	4 .... quatre
today	aujourd'hui	5 .... cinq
tomorrow	demain	6 .... six
breakfast	le petit déjeuner	7 .... sept
lunch	le déjeuner	8 .... huit
dinner	le dîner	9 .... neuf
entrance	entrée	10 .... dix
exit	sortie	11 .... onze
stores	les magasins	20 .... vingt
market	le marché	21 .... vingt-et-un
bakery	la boulangerie	22 .... vingt-deux
butcher	la boucherie	30 .... trente
food store	l'alimentation	40 .... quarante
pharmacy	la pharmacie	50 .... cinquante
delicatessen	la charcuterie	60 .... soixante
fishmonger	la poissonnerie	70 .... soixante-dix
		80 .... quatre-vingt
		90 .... quatre-vingt-dix
		100 .... cent
		1,000 .... mille

FRANCE

PARIS

pop. 2,152,333
(Metropolitan area pop.10, 651,000)

If it seems that everything has been said about Paris, then it is up to the visitor to discover the city for themselves, for it offers infinite variety. It is a city for late-nighters, early risers, strollers, culture-vultures, for high fashion, gourmands, ascetics, flower-givers, artists, wine-drinkers, the *avant-garde*, the old hat, lovers of buildings, lovers of art, or just plain lovers.

Spend time walking in parks, along leafy boulevards, looking in store windows, sitting in cafés, or overdosing on art in the overwhelming Louvre or the Musée d'Orsay. Visit Versailles, Montmartre and Montparnasse. Paris is the sum of the great names that have lived, loved, painted, described and shaped her: Eiffel, Trotsky, Picasso, Piaf, Rodin, Hemingway and Scott Fitzgerald. It combines the great with the everyday: markets, *boulangeries*, unshaven men carrying *baguettes* through back streets, chic dressers leading poodles in parks.

Images of the Eiffel Tower, of book-stalls along the Seine and the gardens surrounding the Louvre are all enhanced by the city's grand perspective.

Culturally, Paris easily lives up to expectations. The Louvre, Notre-Dame, the architecturally tradition-shattering Centre Pompidou, theaters and opera all delight the eye as well as the ear.

Paris is a contemporary collage of very different communities, with a backdrop of narrow streets, village-style shops, bars, bistros and markets, faded old apartment buildings and striking new ones, parks and gardens, courtyards and shadowed alleys.

As a mecca for lovers, Paris casts a romantic net across café tables and along the banks of the Seine. High-fashion Paris centers in the *salons* of the great *couturiers* and at ultra-chic boutiques.

Gastronomically, Paris manages to continue to specialize in elaborate and calorific delicacies in an age of health consciousness and fast food.

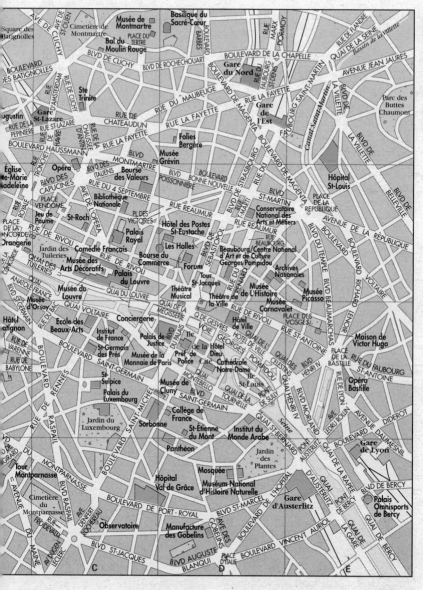

HISTORY

The history of Paris stretches back over 2,000 years. A Gallic tribe, the Parisii, erected fortifications around their settlement on an island in the Seine now known as Ile de la Cité. The Romans razed it and built their own city, *Lutetia*. A series of Hun invasions were later repelled under the strong leadership of Geneviève, who was to become the city's patron saint. The besieging Franks and their Christian king, Clovis I, made Paris their capital in 508.

It remained the capital until 584 when later Franks removed the crown and the

FRANCE

settlement's political importance. The Carolingians, under Charlemagne, moved the capital to Aix-la-Chapelle during the 8th century. The election of Hugh Capet to the throne in AD 987 gave power back to Paris.

The Capetian monarchy reigned for 350 years. The Cathédrale de Notre-Dame and the Sorbonne College, founded by Robert de Sorbon for poverty-stricken students, are of this period. The school was later to become the core of the University of Paris. Development in the 14th century was slowed not only by the Black Death, which plagued the city from 1348 to 1349, but by the Hundred Years' War against England, which was waged between 1337 and 1453.

Prosperity began to return to the city in the latter half of the 15th century. The influence of the Italian Renaissance gave new splendor to city architecture as Paris became the center of the French royal family in the 1500s.

Paris entered a golden age in the 17th century. Blaise Pascal brought distinction to philosophy, and Jean-Baptiste Racine and Molière the same to the theater. The arts continued to flourish in the 18th century with the painters Antoine Watteau and Jean-Honoré Fragonard, the musician Christoph Willibald von Gluck (born in Germany but a Paris resident), and the writers Voltaire and Jean-Jacques Rousseau.

Streets were expanded and homes and public buildings constructed, including the École Militaire, the Panthéon and the Église-Ste.-Marie Madeleine. The French Revolution, beginning with the storming of the Bastille on July 14, 1789, established Paris as the new capital of a centralized France.

Rapid industrialization followed; gas lighting was introduced and the city received its first railroad in 1837. The social consequences of these changes combined with overpopulation, brought squalor to older parts of the city and in part accounted for the revolutions of 1830 and 1848. City Prefect Baron Georges Eugène Haussmann was commissioned by Emperor Napoleon III to remedy the situation.

Haussmann designed a network of wide avenues and boulevards that are still in use today. He also inaugurated the city's modern sewer and water system and rebuilt the ancient market of Les Halles. The Eiffel Tower was constructed in 1889 and a World Exposition held alongside it. The first Métro line opened 10 years later.

In the 20th century, Paris weathered the battering of two world wars and emerged undaunted. Drastic redevelopment in the 1960s and 1970s not only housed a growing population but produced a string of startling new buildings. Recent rebuilding has been on a more intimate scale, and attention has been given to cleaning and renovating decaying quarters and providing housing.

Paris is a multi-faceted city, each face revealing its own distinctive features. One is the Place de l'Opéra, in the city's center, from which radiate streets filled with shops, elegant restaurants and cozy bistros and cafés. Another is the Champs Élysées, one of the world's best known avenues. At one end of this tree-lined boulevard stands the focal point of the Place Charles de Gaulle, the massive Arc de Triomphe; at the other is the huge Place de la Concorde. In between are a children's fair and the Grand et Petit Palais, as well as parks, restaurants, cafés and movie theaters.

The Seine River and its two islands, a geographically and historically significant section of Paris, provide an easy escape from city noise and congestion. The Île de la Cité, Paris' oldest section, is the ancient setting for "La Grande Dame" of European Gothic architecture:

the Cathédrale de Notre-Dame. Île Ste.-Louis, once the home of such famous French citizens as Baudelaire and Theophile Gautier, retains its 17th-century charm along quiet, house-lined streets.

Prominent in both legend and geography is Montmartre, which to many constitutes the heart of Paris. The name is a distillation of "Mont des Martyres," the Mount of Martyrs, and recalls the martyrdom of Paris' first bishop, St.-Denis, who was beheaded on the slopes of this hill, which at 130 meters (427 feet), is the highest point in the city. The area attracted such artists as Toulouse-Lautrec, Pierre Auguste Renoir, Georges Seurat, Pablo Picasso and Georges Braque.

Today parts of Montmartre have become either shoddy or blatant tourist traps. Despite this, there are still numerous pretty back streets, churches and cemeteries, and in addition there is the only vineyard in Paris. The area is also a setting, for nightclubs, cabarets and restaurants. You may quite likely have your portrait painted or caricature drawn in the main square at the top of Montmartre.

No overview of the city would be complete without a mention of the Rive Gauche, or Left Bank. Traditionally associated with romance and unconventionality, the area is a center for students from the nearby Sorbonne and the University of Paris. Artists congregate on the Left Bank; their work is frequently to be seen on display.

Artists and writers also inhabit Montparnasse, another well-known area. Le Dôme, at the intersection of boulevards Raspail and Montparnasse, was a favorite spot for Hemingway, Miller and other famous authors. From the Tour Montparnasse you can enjoy some of the best views of the city.

Farther west, in the Invalides district, rises the proud spire of the Eiffel Tower, perhaps the most widely recognized symbol of the city.

GETTING THERE
BY CAR, PLANE AND TRAIN
Paris is as accessible by car as any large European city, with highways leading in and out in every direction. Trans-Europe arteries are the following autoroutes: A1 north, A4 east, A6 south, A10 southwest and A13 west.

Two international airports service Paris: Orly, 14 kilometers (9 miles) south, and Roissy-Charles de Gaulle, 23 kilometers (14 miles) northeast. Air France shuttle buses run every 12 minutes from Orly and between 15 and 20 minutes from Roissy-Charles de Gaulle into the center of Paris where you can connect with the metro or a taxi. There is also an RATP (Régrie Autonome des Transports Parisiens) shuttle that links with Roissy-Rail on RER (Réseau Express Regional) line B. The Orlyval train line runs every four to eight minutes from Orly to suburban Anjony station, where connections can be made into the city.

French trains, highly regarded throughout Europe, approach Paris from 12 routes into one of six main line stations.

GETTING AROUND
Driving in Paris is, at best, difficult and, at worst, hazardous. Traffic is very heavy, and many areas are constantly beset with traffic jams. Most streets are one way, and it is possible to drive miles out of your intended way if you are unfamiliar with the city's intricate layout. The best advice may be to garage your car upon arrival and use public transportation. The use of front and back seat belts is mandatory and children under 10 years are not permitted to travel in the front seat.

PARKING
On-street parking is limited and illegally parked cars will be fined or towed away. Pay facilities can be found throughout the city. There are large underground

FRANCE

parking lots at all main *portes* on the ring road, from where you can take the metro into the center.

CAR RENTAL
Paris has numerous car rental agencies. A comprehensive list of these, along with contract requirements, is available at the Paris Convention and Visitors' Bureau. To rent a car, you must have been in possession of a valid driver's license for at least one year and be at least 18 years old, though with most international companies it is 20 to 25, with an upper age limit (Avis excepted) of between 60 and 65. Third party insurance is compulsory.

TAXIS
Should you need to use a taxi, opt for a metered cab. There is a standard pickup charge and an extra charge for pickups at airports and railroad stations, for luggage weighing more than 5 kilos (11 pounds) and for more than three passengers. You can usually hail a cab from the street or pick one up from a stand, except during rush hours (8–9am and 5–6:30pm). If you cannot flag a cab, check with the doorman at your hotel, or refer to the phone directory for assistance, but be warned: the time it takes a taxi to reach you is added to the pickup charge.

PUBLIC TRANSPORTATION
The quickest and most efficient transportation is the Paris Métro, one of the best subway systems in the world. Its passageways are well marked and its color-coded maps easy to follow. Only one fare is charged, regardless of distance. This, coupled with the comfortable trains running on 13 lines every two to ten minutes, makes the Métro the ideal way to get around.

The Métro operates from 5:30am to 12:30am. (The letter "M" throughout this guide denotes the nearest Métro station or stations to the relevant sight). Tickets – single, or books of ten (*carnet*) can be purchased at newsagent shops (*tabacs*) or subway stations. *Formule*, a card valid for one day for unlimited travel on the Métro and buses can be bought at the Paris Convention and Visitors' Bureau and subway stations. If you plan to use the Métro extensively, you can buy a *coupon jaune*, which allows unlimited travel on the subway or Parisian bus system for one week, or a *carte orange*, which is good for one month. You must supply a photograph of yourself to purchase these tickets.

Also available are special *Paris Visite* multi-mode tickets, designed for tourist travel in and around Paris. The tickets can be purchased from the R.A.T.P. for travel aboard the Métro or buses; discounts on several entrance fees also are included. *Paris Visite* tickets are available for three or five day consecutive periods. The *formule*, *coupon jaune*, *carte orange* and the *Paris Visite* also allow you to travel on the R.E.R. suburban train service, plus some suburban services of the national S.N.C.F. rail network.

Buses operate daily from 6:30am to 8:30pm; some lines run until 12:30am and night buses also run. Tickets can be bought singly or in books of ten (*carnet*). Each route is divided into three sections, a ticket is valid for one or two sections.

WHAT TO DO

SIGHTSEEING
BOAT TOURS
The sightseeing boats that ply the Seine offer an exhilarating way to see some of the finest sights of central Paris. *Bateaux-mouches*, perhaps the best known of the large tour boats, depart from Pont de l'Alma on the Rive Droite from 10am to noon, and 2 to 6pm. The cruises last approximately 75 minutes.

HELICOPTER TOURS
For a bird's eye-view of Paris, helicopter sightseeing trips are offered by Hélifrance, Héli-port de Paris, tel: 01 45 54 95 11.

SPORTS AND RECREATION

Although typically characterized as a city of art and cuisine, Paris also offers varied recreational opportunities. Professional soccer takes place on Sundays at the Parc des Princes and Colombes stadium; rugby also has a following. The French Open Tennis Tournament takes place at Stade Roland-Garros in early June. Horse races take place daily at any one of eight city race tracks; the most important meeting is the Prix de l'Arc de Triomphe at Longchamp. Boxing, held at the Palais des Sports, is also a favorite. The new Palais Omnisports, 2 kilometers (1 mile) southeast of Notre Dame in the Bercy section, is the setting for a variety of top sporting events as well as musical events that draw large crowds.

If you'd rather play sports than watch them, there are all-year facilities for tennis, bowling and swimming. A leisure complex including a swimming pool, sports hall, billiard room, photographic collections and a tropical greenhouse is in the vicinity of the Centre Pompidou. Facilities for golf, riding, hunting and fishing are all within reach of the city. Cycling enthusiasts can take advantage of rentals in or out of Paris.

Details in English regarding sporting events taking place in Paris are recorded on tape and available daily 24 hours; tel: 01 47 20 88 98.

WHERE TO SHOP

Whether you're seeking a pair of shoes or a first edition novel, you'll delight in what occupies the shelves and store windows of Paris. If your budget allows, you can purchase high-fashion originals by the demigods of design. Fortunately, most of the leading fashion houses, including Christian Dior, Chanel, Givenchy, Yves St. Laurent and Cardin, have boutiques that sell lower-priced accessories and ready-to-wear clothing.

The dozens of shops on the principal shopping streets – rue Faubourg St.-Honoré, rue de Rivoli, avenue Montaigne and their offshoots – stock the perfumes, silk scarves, rainwear, leather goods, jewelry, antiques, crystal and ceramics for which the city is internationally known. The bastion of the "good life," the hotel Ritz, shares place Vendôme with several perfumeries, excellent menswear stores and Wilmart, which sells lovely fabrics. Major department stores to search out are Printemps, Galeries Lafayette and Au Bon Marché.

There also are shopping malls. The Palais des Congrès de Paris Boutiques, at 2 place de la Porte-Maillot, features a Japanese department store, craft stores, restaurants and boutiques. Montparnasse shopping center, at the intersection of rue de l'Arrivée and rue du Départ, has a Chinese department store and swimming pool among its attractions. The Forum les Halles, 1–7 rue Pierre-Lescot, is a four-level shopping center with movie theaters, restaurants and a pool.

Generally, department stores are open 9am–7pm Monday–Saturday; some are open until 9 or 10pm one night a week. Fashion boutiques, perfumeries and other smaller stores are open 9 or 10am–7pm Monday–Saturday (some close for lunch, noon–2pm). Hair salons are usually closed on Monday.

Several unusual stores deserve special mention. Trousselier, boulevard Haussmann, resembles a florist's shop, but all its bouquets are hand-crafted from silk. Au Nain Bleu, rue Faubourg St.-Honoré, has a selection of delightful toys. For elegant edibles go to Fauchon, 26 place de la Madeleine.

A complex comprised of nearly 300 fashion and jewelry stores and eating establishments is close to the Centre Pompidou. On the small streets of Montparnasse and St.-Germain-des-Prés are tiny galleries showing and selling about-to-be-discovered artworks. On the quays of the Seine, the *bouquinistes*, or book-

FRANCE

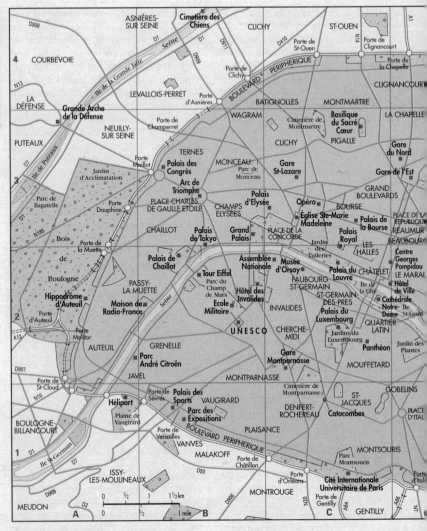

sellers, dispense secondhand books, new and old postcards, old prints and maps.

Nearby, on the Île de la Cité, is the multicolored *marché aux fleurs* (flower market), its wares subject to wilting, but well worth photographing. The market is open 9am to 5pm Monday to Saturday; on Sunday it becomes a bird market.

Somewhat out of the way, but worth the visit, is the Porte de Clignancourt's *marché aux puces*, the flea market, in St.-

Ouen, just past the northern boundary of Paris. It features fine antiques and designer furniture along with traditional flea market bric-à-brac.

Other sections of the market include Marché Vernaison, at 99 rue de Rosiers and 136 avenue Michelet; Marché Paul-Bert, at 16 rue Paul-Bert; Marché Jules-Valles at 5 rue Jules-Valles; and Marché Mailik at 60 rue Jules-Valles. The market is open from 7am to 7:30pm china and silver; it is open from 7:30am to 12:30pm Monday to Saturday.

WHERE TO STAY AND WHERE TO EAT

Like many other Parisian endeavors, running a hotel has evolved into something of an art form; hoteliers have established a tradition of excellent service for their patrons. The large number of accommodations is rated by the government according to quality and price range and given a rating from one-star to four-star luxury. Moderately priced hotels, which usually have a bath in each room, are abundant on both the Left and Right banks.

Although the height of the tourist season in Paris, Easter to October, results in less of a squeeze than in some other cities, it is always advisable to make a reservation. The months of September and October are particularly jammed with trade shows and conventions that flood the city with additional visitors, making reservations even more necessary.

Many hotels offer special deals for weekend breaks in winter. If you do not have reservations, check with the local tourist office, who can reserve a room for you for a small fee. If you decide to look for a room on your own, your chances of finding something suitable are much better early in the day.

Parisian restaurants range from small, economical bistros to celebrated gastronomic shrines. The largest concentration of eating spots is to be found near the Champs-Élysées. Foreign and French cuisine abounds throughout the city.

All restaurants must, by law, display their prices in the window, and in addition to the *à la carte* choice there is also a *formule* or *menu fixe* (fixed-price menu) that is often an excellent value. Most restaurants close one day per week, and many shut down entirely for the Parisian vacation period, in late July and August. It is advisable to make reservations to

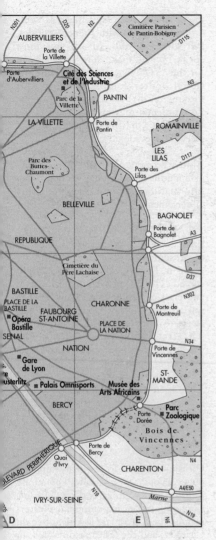

Saturday to Monday, though hours vary among stores.

The Vanves flea market on avenue Georges-Lafenstre has a variety of items for sale, including books, secondhand clothes, old photographs, toys and tableware, and general bric-à-brac. It is open from 7am to 7:30pm Saturday to Sunday.

The Aligre flea market, at place d'Aligre, specializes in secondhand clothing, old

FRANCE

dine at the most popular establishments well in advance.

ENTERTAINMENT
NIGHTLIFE

The best way to find out what is going on in Paris is to buy one of the weekly listings magazines that have details of movies, theatres, concerts, nightclubs, sports events, and much more. *Pariscope*, *7 Jours à Paris*, and *L'Officiel des Spectacles* are available from *tabacs* (news dealers) and street stalls. Whatever your tastes in evening entertainment, Paris can satisfy them all. From the sophisticated, bejeweled Paris Opéra to the endless throngs of people on busy streets, the night breathes life into this age-old city.

There is no limit to the variety in entertainment and àtmosphere offered by Parisian bars and music halls, so a tour of them, which can be arranged through your hotel, is a good way to begin. Many of the clubs emphasise jazz, burlesque or an international theme. Jazz clubs include Caveau de la Huchette, 5 rue de la Huchette, and Le Petit Opportun, 15 rue des Lavandières-Ste.-Opportun. Possibly the most popular show in town is the Folies Bergères at 32 rue Richer, but reserve your seat well in advance – the show is always sold out.

Other extravaganzas are offered at the Lido, 116 Champs-Élysées; the Moulin Rouge, 82 boulevard de Clichy; and the Paradis Latin, 28 rue Cardinal Lemoine.

Discotheques include Les Bains, 7 rue du Bourg L'Abbé; Olivia Valère, 40 rue du Colisée; and Le Palace, 8 rue du Faubourg-Montmartre. The City Rock Café, rue de Berri, is an American restaurant that contains the first rock 'n' roll museum in France. Mementoes of Bill Haley, Buddy Holly and the Beatles are displayed. Bands perform in the basement several times weekly. Cafés and hotel cocktail bars can be amusing and entertaining, particularly if you speak French. Most movies are shown in the original version (advertized as "VO" – *version original*) with French subtitles, but some are dubbed – if you don't speak French, make sure you look out for the "VO" sign. Paris is an international center for experimental art movies, and they feature regularly. Experimental movies are shown at the Palais de Chaillot Cinémathèque, place du Trocadéro.

Note: The mention of any area or establishment in the preceding sections is for information only and does not imply endorsement by the AAA.

THEATER AND CONCERTS

Parisian theaters offer a broad selection of presentations, but the majority are acted in French. Mysteries and light comedies have long been popular; operas and classics also have a following. You can see the works of Molière and others at the Comédie Française and at the Théâtre National de l'Odéon. The Théâtre National de Chaillot also has an interesting repertoire.

The Opéra Garnier (Opéra de Paris) is now devoted almost entirely to traditional ballet, and the huge new Opéra Bastille hosts opera, with fine repertoires and artists.

On the lighter side of theater are the musicals and variety shows commonly held at the Théâtre du Châtelet. Contemporary or experimental theaters include the Théâtre de la Ville, place du Châtelet, and the Théâtre du Soleil, in an old warehouse at Vincennes, avenue de la Pyramide. In addition to private theater, several state-operated stages offer a schedule of medium-priced, enjoyable performances.

Tickets can be purchased from box offices or through several ticket agencies throughout Paris, including Agence Chèque Théâtre, telephone: 01 42 46 72 40, but service fees can run as high as 25 percent of the total ticket price. Music runs the gamut from classical to rock. The Paris Orchestra performs on a regular basis at the Salle Pleyel. Concerts and recitals of many kinds are given at the Palais de Chaillot, Salle Gaveau. Check with local churches and cathedrals, which also sponsor recitals.

The Olympia, 28 boulevard des Capucines, and the Palais des Sports, Porte de Versailles, are concert centers for showcasing new and contemporary music. The Palais Omnisports de Paris-Bercy and Le Zenith at La Villette feature pop concerts and occasional opera.

ESPECIALLY FOR CHILDREN

To make the most of a Parisian vacation, if traveling with children, avoid August, when many of the shops they may find exciting and interesting are closed. Bastille Day (July 14), though crowded, offers a feast of sound and color. The chimeras and gargoyles of Notre Dame will delight the young sightseer, as will the view from Montmartre, a visit to the the Arc de Triomphe or the top of the Eiffel Tower.

Perhaps the best bet is the Disneyland Paris theme park at Marne-La-Vallée, 32 kilometers (20 miles) outside Paris (see p.278 for more details).

Museums with a special appeal for children are the Musée de la Marine, Palais de la Découverte and the Musée Grévin (waxworks museum). Another alternative is Aquarium/Musée des Arts Africains et Océaniens at 293 avenue Daumesnil. Discovery is the key word at the Inventorium of the Cité des Sciences et de l'Industrie.

Zoos are another remedy for restlessness. The Parc Zoologique de Paris, 53 avenue de St.-Maurice, is the city's largest. The Jardin des Plantes, on the Left Bank at 57 rue Cuvier, contains a zoo as well as plant and insect exhibits. Parisian parks provide an excellent outlet for excess energy.

PLACES OF INTEREST

★ PARIS HIGHLIGHTS ★	
Arc de Triomphe	(see p.259)
Beaubourg	(see p.259)
(Centre Pompidou)	
Cité des Sciences	(see p.260)
et de l'Industrie	
Hôtel des Invalides	(see p.261)
Louvre	(see p.262)
Musée d'Orsay	(see p.262)
Notre-Dame	(see p.263)
Opéra	(see p.263)
Sacré-Coeur	(see p.264)
Tour Eiffel	(see p.264)

ARC DE TRIOMPHE (250 A4) ★, place Charles-de-Gaulle (M: Charles-de-Gaulle Étoile), was built 1806–36 to commemorate the victories of Napoléon Bonaparte. Beneath the vault of the arch is the Eternal Flame and the tomb of the Unknown Soldier of World War I. The roof provides a splendid view of the 12 broad, tree-lined streets that radiate from place Charles-de-Gaulle. Access is via the underpasses beneath the chaos of surrounding traffic.

BEAUBOURG (CENTRE GEORGES POMPIDOU) (251 D3) ★, rue Rambuteau at rue St.-Merri (M: Hôtel-de-Ville, Rambuteau, Châtelet). Opened in 1977 amid some controversy, the large structure is a steel and glass box suspended from beams supported by visible scaffolding. Escalators run through brightly painted tubes on the exterior of the building.

Inside is the National Gallery of Modern Art; the Public Information Library, the city's first public library; the exhibition hall of the Industrial Design Center, with a variety of extensive displays illustrating the impact of design on all facets of modern life. Other highlights are the Institute of Research and Coordination of Acoustic Music; a movie theater; rooms for temporary exhibitions; and a restaurant.

BIBLIOTHÈQUE NATIONALE (251 C3), rue de Richelieu (M: Bourse, Palais-Royal, Quatre-Septembre, Pyramides), is one of Europe's largest libraries. It was founded on the collections of the French kings and now contains over 12 million volumes (which were moved in 1997 to the new Bibliothèque de France). The main reading room, roofed over by nine glass-topped domes, dates from 1873.

BOIS DE BOULOGNE (256 A2), in the western part of the city (M: Porte d'Auteuil, Porte Dauphine, Porte Maillot), open for public access, is a 845-hectare (2,088-acre) forest park. Once the hunting ground of kings, it was transformed by Haussmann during the 19th century into a delightful park with a variety of attractions from gardens, lakes and restaurants to the popular Auteuil and Longchamp racetracks.

BOIS DE VINCENNES (257 E1), in the east of the city (M: Château-de-Vincennes), is a 995-hectare (2,459-acre) forest park that contains the city's largest zoo. and the Château de Vincennes with its 14th-century tower, the keep, and Holy Chapel. The château has been a royal residence, a prison, a World War II headquarters and German occupation arms depot.

BOURSE DU COMMERCE (251 C3), in the business district southeast of place de l'Opéra (M: Bourse), is the French Stock Exchange. Built on the site of a convent in 1826 and remodeled in 1888, it once served as a corn exchange. The domed hall is now a busy commodities market.

CATACOMBES (256 C1), place Denfert-Rochereau (M: Denfert-Rochereau), were built as limestone quarries in Gallo-Roman times. For many years they were used as a cemetery – bones and skulls are piled up along the walls of the twisting passages. During World War II, they were used as a headquarters by the French Resistance. Guided tours only – bring a sweater and a flashlight.

CIMETIÈRE DES CHIENS (256 B4), Île d'Asnières, is a cemetery dedicated to dogs. Two of the most well-known occupants are Alsatian Rin-Tin-Tin and Barry, a lifesaving St. Bernard of the Swiss Alps.

CIMETIÈRE DU PÈRE LACHAISE (257 E2), east of the Marais district on avenue de la République (M: Père-Lachaise), is the largest and best-known Parisian cemetery. The burial ground dates from the Middle Ages and is noted not only for its monuments and sculptures by well-known artists, but for the graves of such famous figures as Isadora Duncan, Edith Piaf, Sarah Bernhardt, Chopin, Victor Hugo and Oscar Wilde. Singer Jim Morrison of the pop group the Doors is also buried here.

CIMETIÈRE SURESNES, 8 kilometers (5 miles) west, contains the graves of over 1,500 Americans who died in the two world wars. A memorial chapel lists those lost and gives the location of all overseas cemeteries where Americans killed in action are buried.

CITÉ DES SCIENCES ET DE L'INDUSTRIE (257 D4) ★, 30 avenue Corentin-Cariou (M: Porte de la Villette), on the northeast perimeter, showcases modern science and technology through exhibits, shows, games and other experiences. Featured is a planetarium; La Médiathèque, a multimedia library; a discovery area for children and a flight simulator. In Parc La Villette is La Géode, a shiny steel globe housing a stainless steel spherical movie theater, Le Cinaxe travel simulator and a World War II submarine. Other highlights include the Parc de la Villette.

CITÉ INTERNATIONALE UNIVERSITAIRE DE PARIS (256 C1), boulevard Jourdan (south part of the Left Bank) (M: Cité-Universitaire), was built for students during the 1918 housing shortage.

COLLÈGE DE FRANCE (251 D2), rue des Écoles (M: Maubert-Mutualité), was founded in 1530 by François I. The professors are appointed by government.

DÉFENSE, GRANDE ARCHE DE LA (256 A3), northwest at Parvis de la Défense (M: Grande Arche de la Défense), is a cubic unit weighing 300,000 tons and measuring 109 meters (358 feet) on each side. It is encased in marble and has a vault that could hold Notre-Dame complete with spire. Elevators take visitors to the summit, which provides extensive views of the city.

DISNEYLAND PARIS – *see p.278.*
see p.278.

ÉCOLE MILITAIRE (250 A2) (M: École Militaire), is a magnificent 18th-century structure facing the Eiffel Tower across the broad Champs-de-Mars. Officers of the French military train here; Bonaparte is among its renowned graduates. Not accessible to the public.

ÉGLISE STE.-MARIE MADELEINE (251 B3), place de la Madeleine (M: Madeleine), is an exquisite marble structure built in the 18th and 19th centuries in the style of a Greek temple. The bronze doors are impressive; the murals on the inside façade depict the life of Mary Magdalene, for whom the church was named.

ÉGOUTS (250 A3), place de la Résistance (M: Alma-Marceau), is a massive network of sewers laid out by the engineer Belgrand in 1810–78. They have been popularized in several films, including *Phantom of the Opera*. Guided tours are available.

ESPACE SALVADOR DALI, rue Poulbot, Montmartre, (M: Anvers, Blanche, Pigalle), is an exhibition displaying over 300 original works of Salvador Dali, the 20th-century Spanish surrealist painter.

GRAND ET PETIT PALAIS (250 B3), avenue Winston Churchill (M: Champs-Élysées-Clemenceau), were built for the Universal Exhibition of 1900 and now display artistic and technical exhibits.

The Grand Palais houses the Palais de la Découverte, a center for scientific study with a planetarium. The Musée du Petit Palais has art exhibits that date from antiquity up to the 20th century.

HÔTEL DES INVALIDES (250 B2) ★, Esplanade des Invalides (M: Invalides, Latour-Maubourg, École-Militaire, Varenne). The Hôtel des Invalides was designed by Libéral Bruant and completed by Jules Hardouin-Mansart who added the magnificent Dôme des Invalides. Napoléon Bonaparte's tomb rests under the apex of the gold dome. The 196-meter (643-foot) edifice of the Hôtel also houses the Musée de l'Armée, among others.

INSTITUT DE FRANCE (251 C2), 23 quai de Conti (M: Pont-Neuf, St.-Germain-des-Prés), houses five French academies, including the Académie Française. Its members, the "Forty Immortals," edit the French dictionary. Guided tours are available.

INSTITUT DU MONDE ARABE (Arab Cultural Exhibit Center) (251 D2), rue des Fossés St.-Bernard (M: Cardinal-Lemoine, Jussieu), houses a museum of Arabic culture, a library, an auditorium and a display area for exhibitions of Islamic and contemporary Arabic art.

JARDIN DES PLANTES (251 D1), 57 rue Cuvier (M: Jussieu, Monge, Gare d'Orléans-Austerlitz), contains 10,000 species of classified plants and some of the oldest trees in Paris, including a cedar of Lebanon, the Musée National d'Histoire Naturelle and a small zoo.

JARDIN DES TUILERIES (251 C3), extending from the Louvre to the place de la Concorde (M: Concorde, Tuileries), are 17th-century gardens laid out by André Le Nôtre.

JARDINS DU TROCADÉRO (250 A3) (M: Trocadéro), facing the Eiffel Tower, are known for their fountains and lake.

JEU DE PAUME (251 C3), place de la Concorde (M: Concorde), has been completely reconstructed. The gallery features 20th-century art exhibitions, including plastic arts, a movie and video.

LOUVRE (251 C3) ★, place Carrousel (M: Palais-Royal-Musée du Louvre). The Palais du Louvre houses one of the world's great museums, the Musée du Louvre; an encyclopedic museum divided into seven departments, from ancient times to the mid-19th century. Works of art include the *Venus de Milo* and Leonardo Da Vinci's enigmatic *Mona Lisa*.

Access to the museum is through Chinese-American Ieoh Ming Pei's glass pyramid, which stands in striking contrast to the historic palace.

MAISON VICTOR HUGO (251 E2), 6 place des Vosges (M: St.-Paul, Chemin-Vert, Bastille), contains drawings, furniture, paintings and documents relating to the life of the 19th-century French writer.

MALMAISON ET BOIS-PRÉAU, avenue du Château de Malmaison, 10 kilometers (6 miles) northwest of Paris, was one of Napoléon's homes. Malmaison was the favorite residence of Joséphine, and where she lived after her divorce in 1809. Together with the neighboring Château Bois-Préau, Malmaison forms two museums dedicated to Napoléon.

MANUFACTURE DES GOBELINS (251 D1), 42 avenue des Gobelins (M: Gobelins), is the site of a tapestry workshop founded in 1440. Visitors can view artisans at work. Guided tours are available.

MARCHÉ AUX FLEURS (251 D2), place Louis-Lépine, and adjoining quays on the Île de la Cité (M: Cité), is one of the largest and prettiest flower markets in the city. On Sunday it is transformed into a colorful – and noisy – bird market.

MUSÉE DES ARTS DÉCORATIFS (251 C3), 107 rue de Rivoli (M: Palais-Royal, Tuileries), houses interesting historical collections of interior furnishings from the Middle Ages to the present in addition to a fashion museum.

MUSÉE CARNAVALET (251 E3), 23 rue de Sévigné (M: St.-Paul, Chemin-Vert), depicts through a group of furnished rooms the history of Paris since the reign of Henri IV. The mansion was originally the home of Madame de Sévigné, noted chronicler of the 17th century.

MUSÉE DE CLUNY (251 D2), 6 place Paul-Painlevé (M: St.-Michel, Cluny, Odéon), an attractive 15th-century building containing one of the richest medieval collections in the world, with tapestries, enamels, and ceramics and the remains of 2nd-century Roman thermal baths.

MUSÉE GRÉVIN (251 C4), 10 boulevard Montmartre (M: Richelieu-Drouot, Rue Montmartre), is a wax museum similar to Madame Tussaud's in London.

MUSÉE DE LA MONNAIE DE PARIS (Museum of Coins and Medals) (251 C2), 11 quai de Conti, tells the story of the French people through coins and medals dating from 300 BC to the present.

MUSÉE D'ORSAY (251 C3) ★, 1 rue de Bellechasse (M: Solférino), is in a restored hotel and railroad station originally built for the Universal Exhibition of 1900. It specializes in 19th-century paintings and sculptures, with a particularly fine exhibit on architecture. Some rooms have a section devoted to decorative arts of the Third Republic.

A collection of Impressionist and Post-Impressionist art has works by Cézanne, Manet, Monet, Pissarro and Van Gogh.

MUSÉE PICASSO (251 E2), 5 rue de Thorigny in the Hôtel Salé Juigné (M: Chemin-Vert, St.-Paul), contains over 200 paintings, 158 sculptures, 16 collages, 29 relief paintings and 1,500 drawings by Picasso, the pioneer artist of Cubism.

MUSÉE RODIN (250 B2), 77 rue de Varenne (M: Varenne), in an elegant 18th-century mansion, contains a priceless collection of the great sculptor's works, including *The Thinker*, *The Gateway of Hell* and *Meditation*.

NOTRE-DAME, CATHÉDRALE (251 D2) ★, Île de la Cité (M: Cité), is considered one of the most beautiful cathedrals in the world and a masterpiece of medieval art. Begun in 1163 and completed in 1345, its flying buttresses make it an excellent example of Gothic architecture. Its size and three rose windows are awe-inspiring. Road distances in France are calculated from the "0 km" point on the square on which the cathedral stands.

OPÉRA (251 C3) ★, place de l'Opéra (M: Opéra), was designed by Garnier. Opened in 1875, the Opéra is one of the world's largest theaters, with a gold and red auditorium and an enormous stage, ornate sculptures, works of art and other lavish decorations.

The Grand Staircase is 10 meters (33 feet) wide at its base; the steps are white marble with balustrades of Algerian onyx. The Grand Foyer (open for viewing along with the auditorium when there are no rehearsals) has a vaulted mosaic ceiling, mirrors and columns.

PALAIS BOURBON-ASSEMBLÉE NATIONALE (251 B3), facing place de la Concorde (M: Assemblée Nationale Invalides), was the former official residence of the Dowager Duchess of Bourbon and now home to the Assemblée Nationale, the French parliament. The library painting by Delacroix is impressive.

PALAIS DE CHAILLOT (250 A3), place du Trocadéro (M: Trocadéro), built for the Paris Exhibition of 1937, houses museums, a theater and a movie theater.

Musée de la Marine displays marine vessels and an interesting collection of marine paintings, designs and models covering the naval history of France since the 17th century.

Musée de l'Homme is an ethnological/anthropological museum with exhibits from every corner of the world.

Musée du Cinéma Henri Langlois follows the history of motion pictures with costumes, models, and technical apparatus.

Musée National des Monuments Français presents casts of major works of French architecture and sculpture from the 10th to 19th centuries.

PALAIS DE JUSTICE (251 D2), Île de la Cité (M: Cité), was the headquarters of the Counts of Paris during the Norman invasions. Today it houses the Law Courts, Conciergerie and Sainte-Chapelle.

Conciergerie was the prison where thousands awaited their fate during the Revolution. The silent rooms and cells vividly evoke events of the reign of terror. Among the guests were Marie Antoinette, Robespierre and Danton.

Sainte-Chapelle is considered the finest specimen of Gothic architecture in Paris. Louis IX built the shrine to hold his most valued relics, notably the Crown of Thorns.

PALAIS DU LUXEMBOURG (251 C2), 15 rue de Vaugirard (M: Luxembourg), was built in the 17th century as a residence for Marie de Médicis. Today the palace is the seat of the French Senate and only accessible to the public by appointment. Sculptures and fountains adorn the extensive gardens, popular with picnickers.

PALAIS ROYAL (251 C3), situated behind the Théatre Comédie Française (M: Palais-Royal), was a home of Cardinal de Richelieu. Today old houses and shops border the palace gardens on three sides. Visitors can see the well-known black and white striped Buren's Columns.

PANTHÉON (251 D1), place du Panthéon, (M: Cardinal-Lemoine, Jussieu), was originally designed to be a church but in 1791 became a burial place for prominent French citizens, including Victor Hugo, Jean-Jaurès, Rousseau, Voltaire and Zola.

FRANCE

PARC ANDRÉ-CITROËN (256 A2), between rue St.-Charles and the Seine (M: Balard, Javel), is a futuristic garden opened in 1992 on the site of a former Citroën automobile factory. A huge lawn is graced by several gardens and over 2,000 trees. Guided tours of the park are available.

PARISTORIC, 78 boulevard des Batignolles (M: Villiers), depicts the 2,000-year history of Paris on a giant movie screen.

PLACE DE LA BASTILLE (251 E2) (M: Bastille) was once the site of the fortress prison. The liberation of prisoners by rioting crowds on July 14, 1789, marked the beginning of the French Revolution. Today it is a large square with a memorial column rising from its center and topped by the statue *Spirit of Liberty*.

It is also the home of the Opéra de la Bastille, designed by Canadian architect Carlos Ott and completed in 1989. It can seat up to 2,700 spectators. Guided tours are available – write to Opéra de la Bastille, Service des Visites, 120 rue de Lyon, 75102 Paris, France.

PLACE DE LA CONCORDE (251 B3), at the eastern end of the avenue des Champs-Élysées (M: Concorde), was the scene of bloody executions during the French Revolution. Today it is one of Paris' loveliest squares, but it is surrounded by one of the busiest traffic circles in the world. The obelisk, symbolizing harmony and peace, was given to Charles X by Mohammed Ali in 1829.

PLACE VENDÔME (251 C3), rue de la Paix (M: Tuileries), has harmonious buildings, now taken over by stores and hotels, surrounding a column erected in 1810 by Bonaparte in honor of his German and Austrian campaigns. The column is covered with the bronze from over 200 cannons captured at Austerlitz in 1805.

SACRÉ-COEUR (BASILIQUE DU) (251 D4) ★, Montmartre (M: Abbesses, Château-Rouge, Lamarck-Caulaincourt), was built to fulfill a vow after the Franco-Prussian War. The outside gallery of the 90-meter (259-foot) dome provides a magnificent view of Paris. The interior of the basilica is lavishly decorated with exquisite mosaic and enamel work.

ST.-GERMAIN-DES-PRÉS (251 C2), place St.-Germain-des-Prés (M: St.-Germain-des-Prés) is the oldest church in Paris, dating from the 10th century.

ST.-JULIEN-LE-PAUVRE, 17 rue du Petit-Pont (M: St.-Michel, Maubert-Mutualité), is a tiny 13th-century Gothic church, tucked away in a quiet square in the Latin quarter.

ST.-SÉVERIN, 1 rue des Prêtres-St.-Séverin (M: St.-Michel), is one of the oldest Gothic churches in Paris; started in the 13th century. It is noted for its fine stained-glass windows.

SORBONNE (251 D2), off boulevard-St.-Michel (M: Cluny-La Sorbonne, Maubert-Mutualité, Luxembourg), is one of the oldest universities in Europe. It was founded as a theological school for poor students in 1253 by Robert de Sorbon, a chaplain of St.-Louis. The school is now affiliated with the University of Paris. Particularly impressive is the Grand Amphitheater.

TOUR EIFFEL (250 A3) ★, Champs-de-Mars (M: Champs-de-Mars, Bir Hakeim), is perhaps the most recognizable Paris landmark. The 300-meter (984-foot) iron masterpiece was built 1887–90 for the Paris Exhibition of 1889 by Alexandre Eiffel. It recently underwent structural renovation and shed about 1,000 of its 7,300 tons.

The first level houses a restaurant and museum depicting its history. A mezzanine offers views of the interior and the Palais de Chaillot Gardens. The second level has another restaurant, and the third floor, at 276 meters (905 feet), offers spectacular views as far as 67 kilometers (42 miles) on a clear day.

PLACES OF INTEREST

AIGUES-MORTES (245 D1)
GARD *pop. 5,000*
Rising out of the low-lying marshes of the Camargue, the Rhône delta area of southern France, Aigues-Mortes was founded in the 13th century by St. Louis as a port from which to launch the 7th and 8th Crusades. His son, Philip the Bold, completed fortifications whose ramparts and towers have remained virtually intact.

AIX-EN-PROVENCE (245 D1) ★
BOUCHES-DU-RHÔNE *pop. 123,800*
Aix-en-Provence was founded as a thermal springs resort in 122 BC on the site of the first Roman settlement in Gaul. It has long been a cultural center, with museums, stately buildings, old churches and a university that was established in 1409. The city is still an important therapeutic spa with a variety of thermal treatment centers and many types of resort entertainment – casinos, theater and facilities for most sports. The International Music Festival is held in July and August.

ATELIER DE CÉZANNE, Paul Cézanne's studio, is a short distance north on the road to Entremont. Personal belongings and tools are on display.

CATHÉDRALE ST.-SAUVEUR, rue Gaston-de-Saporta, dates from the 4th to 18th century. The church is best known for its triptych *Les Buissons Ardents* "The Burning Bushes," painted during the 15th century. The cloisters, carved door panels and tapestries also are distinctive.

MUSÉE GRANET, place St.-Jean-de-Malte, houses a collection of paintings including eight of Paul Cézanne's works, others by the Provençal artist Granet, and pre-Roman sculpture.

AIX-LES-BAINS (245 E3)
SAVOIE *pop. 24,700*
Aix-les-Bains, a fashionable spa dating from the Roman occupation of Gaul, is best known for its treatment of rheumatoid conditions. In addition to the casino, racetrack, pools and baths, the resort offers sailing and water skiing, as well as winter sports facilities at Mount Revard. Extensive Roman ruins include the Arch of Campanus, the Temple of Diana and the baths. The town also maintains a modern art collection with works by such artists as Corot, Degas and Rodin.

Side trips can be taken to the summit of Mount Revard, to the nearby Abbey of Hautecombe and around Lake Bourget, France's largest natural lake, on a boat that leaves from the Grand Port. The abbey was founded by St.-Bernard and was used as a burial place by the princes of the House of Savoy.

MUSÉE FESCH, 50 rue Fesch, exhibits over 1,000 paintings in a fine collection donated by Cardinal Fesch, Napoléon's uncle. Its Italian Primitive works are second to only those of the Louvre in Paris.

ALBI (245 C2)
TARN *pop. 46,600*
The Cathédrale de Ste.-Cécile here is a monumental fortress built to protect the

FRANCE

clergy during the Inquisition. Paintings, carvings and ornamentation richly enhance its interior.

MUSÉE TOULOUSE-LAUTREC in the Palais de la Berbie, has the world's largest collection of the painter's works.

AMBOISE (245 C3)
INDRE-ET-LOIRE *pop. 11,000*

The medieval church of St.-Denis, with its 16th-century works of art, the Hôtel de Ville, which houses a historical museum and the Musée de la Poste are all in the center of town.

CHÂTEAU D'AMBOISE is a late Gothic castle that served as a royal residence during the 15th and 16th centuries. Its huge round towers with wide spiral ramps accommodated kings and chariots and were the scene of merciless killings. Leonardo da Vinci is said to be buried in the Chapel of St. Hubert, once a part of the Queen's Apartments. Former residents include Catherine de' Medici. Floodlit in summer, the château is the setting for sound-and-light shows.

CHÂTEAU DE CHENONCEAU, 12 kilometers (7 miles) southeast, is a Renaissance château built on a bridge across the Cher River. Erected in the early 16th century, it belonged to six women in succession, including Diane de Poitiers and Catherine de' Medici. Sound-and-light shows take place in summer.

CHÂTEAU DU CLOS-LUCÉ is the 15th-century manor house where the artist Leonardo da Vinci died. It contains machine models based on the drawings of da Vinci's inventions, including the first self-propelled vehicle, airplane, helicopter, parachute, and swing bridge. A 55-minute audio-visual presentation documents the life of da Vinci.

AMIENS (245 C5)
SOMME *pop. 131,900*

Amiens, on the Somme River, is the capital of the Picardy region. It is where

Jules Verne, renowned author of fantasy, lived until his death; his former home is now the Jules Verne Information Center. The Musée de Picardie has archaeological finds and paintings. Old Amiens, near the cathedral, has been restored and is lively with cafés and restaurants.

Nearby is the underground village of Naours. Constructed as a fort during the 3rd and 4th centuries, it was used during World War II as a secret hideaway from German invaders.

CATHÉDRALE DE NOTRE DAME, which dates from the 13th century, is remarkably beautiful and harmonious in its design. One of the largest Gothic cathedrals in France, it measures more than 145 meters (475 feet) long and 112 meters (367 feet) to the top of the spire.

LES ANDELYS
EURE *pop. 8,500*

The product of the merged twin settlements of Grand and Petit Andely, Les Andelys is a small town beside the Seine River. To the south of Petit Andely are the imposing remains of Château Gaillard, built by Richard the Lionheart in the late 12th century. There are fine views of the Seine Valley from this clifftop site.

ANGERS (245 B4)
MAINE-ET-LOIRE *pop. 141,400*

Angers is known for its horticultural exhibitions and superb public gardens. The regional wines (white, red and rosé d'Anjou) are world-renowned. There is a museum devoted to the vine and the Anjou Wine Fair is held in winter. The liqueur Cointreau is also produced in Angers; the distillery may be visited.

CATHÉDRALE ST.-MAURICE, which dates from the 12th century, dominates the town with its Gothic spires; the stained-glass windows, The Romanesque doorway and the nave are impressive.

CHÂTEAU, a 13th-century fortress, houses the 14th-century Apocalypse Tapestry, which is the largest surviving medieval tapestry in the world.

HÔPITAL SAINT-JEAN is a 12th-century hospital that features cloisters, cellars and a series of tapestries by Jean Lurçat.

HÔTEL PINCÉ, a fine example from the Renaissance period, houses the Pincé Museum with its collection of oriental art.

ANGOULÊME (245 B3)
CHARENTE *pop. 42,900*
The old fortified town of Angoulême overlooks the Charente River. The town walls have been converted into boulevards that afford views of the surrounding countryside. The ornate 12th-century Cathédrale St.-Pierre, restored during the 19th century, is a good example of Romanesque architecture; 75 figures depicting Judgement Day cover one side of the building. Also of interest are the Chapelle des Cordeliers, the Musée Archéologique and the Centre National de l'Image (National Cartoon Museum).

ANNECY (245 E3)
HAUTE-SAVOIE *pop. 49,600*
Annecy is a well-known health resort and attractive vacation spot on the shore of the beautiful Lake Annecy. The picturesque old quarter, with its medieval houses and winding canals, contains the château, an old castle with 13th- and 15th-century towers, and the Palais de l'Île, a fortress and former prison built on an island in the Thiou canal. Boat excursions can be made on the lake to the pretty resort of Talloires.

ANTIBES (245 E2)
ALPES-MARITIMES *pop. 70,000*
Antibes has been a resort since the mid-19th century, but vestiges of Greek and Roman occupation indicate that the spot was popular much earlier. Offering the best in resort entertainment, Antibes is host to several international festivals. Picasso presented a number of his works to the city, and they are now in the Musée Picasso. A museum in nearby

Biot contains paintings and mosaics by Ferdinand Léger, who with Picasso founded Cubism.

Cap d'Antibes, a 4-kilometer (2½-mile) long peninsula, is an exclusive playground covered with luxurious villas and gardens. To the west is the sandy beach of Golfe-Juan and the exclusive resort of Juan-les-Pins.

MUSÉE PICASSO, in the Château Grimaldi, the former residence of the Prince of Antibes and later the home and studio of Picasso, now houses one of the largest collections of his works.

ARCACHON (244 B2)
GIRONDE *pop. 11,800*
Arcachon is a well-known resort overlooking the Bay of Biscay. A resort much frequented by European aristocracy in the 19th century, the slightly eccentric architecture of the villas of the Ville d'Hiver (Winter Town) dates from that period. Today visitors flock to the yacht marina, sports facilities and the local museum, with its aquarium and archaeological and historical collections.

ARLES (245 D1) ★
BOUCHES-DU-RHÔNE *pop. 52,100*
Arles, situated on the Rhône River, has a prestigious past. Founded by Julius Caesar in 49 BC, it became the most important settlement in Roman Gaul.

In and near the city are many Roman ruins, including statuary, a superb amphitheater, aqueducts and baths. The paleo-Christian burial ground, Les Alyscamps, lies on the outskirts of town.

Vincent Van Gogh lived in Arles and made the city the subject of several paintings shortly before his death; the Office de Tourisme provides a map guiding you to the many sites he painted in the region.

LES ARÈNES ROMAINES is a spectacularly well-preserved amphitheater from the 1st century, once seating 20,000, now seating 12,000 for bullfights and concerts in summer.

CATHÉDRALE ST.-TROPHIME, which dates from the 12th century, is well-known for its sculptured portal and cloister behind the church.

THÉÂTRE ANTIQUE, begun by Caesar Augustus in the 1st century BC and finished 150 years later, provides the setting for various summer events.

ARROMANCHES-LES-BAINS (244 B4)
CALVADOS *pop. 400*
Arromanches-les-Bains is a seaside resort that attracted international attention during World War II when it was the site of "Mulberry B," one of two artificial harbors used for landing Allied troops and supplies after the D-Day invasion. The best view is from the viewpoint indicator at the top of the cliff.

MUSÉE DU DÉBARQUEMENT (Landings Museum) is on the beach. Films and exhibits depict the Allied invasion of June 6, 1944, and the construction of the artificial harbors.

AUXERRE (245 D4)
YONNE *pop. 38,800*
Ancient Auxerre, near the wine-producing district of Chablis, dates back to the Gallo-Roman era. A beautiful city, Auxerre borders the Yonne River and is surrounded on three sides by orchards. The Musée Leblanc-Duvernoy is one of several local museums; its 18th-century Beauvais tapestries and artifacts are of particular interest.

CATHÉDRALE ST.-ETIENNE was founded in AD 400 by St.-Amâtre. Most of the structure that stands today, however, was built much later. Of note are the 11th-century crypt with 12th- and 13th-century frescoes, the 16th-century stained-glass window, the choir and three portals with sculptures depicting the Last Judgement.

AVIGNON (245 D2) ★
VAUCLUSE *pop. 87,000*
One of the great art centers of France, Avignon was the residence of the Popes from 1309 to 1377. The city abounds in reminders of the lavish 14th-century papal courts. Villeneuve-les-Avignon, across the Rhône River, contains a fort, a Carthusian monastery and a museum with *The Coronation of the Virgin*. Avignon has been designated as European City of Culture for the year 2000.

There are the remains of a Roman bridge and aqueduct, the Pont du Gard, 20 kilometers (12 miles) west.

CATHÉDRALE-DE-VAUCLUSE, about 24 kilometers (16 miles) east of Avignon, was immortalized by the 14th-century love poet Petrarch, who spent 30 years at the site.

MUSÉE DU PETIT PALAIS, place du Palais, is a 14th-century structure converted into an art museum. Rooms display Italian and French paintings of the 14th to 16th centuries; two rooms contain sculptures from the 12th, 13th and 14th centuries. It was the residence of the Cardinal of Avignon and has been renovated to reflect its original appearance.

PALAIS DES PAPES, place du Palais, a grand example of medieval architecture, was built in the 14th century as a fortress and papal residence.

PONT ST.-BENÉZET, dating from the 12th century, is a bridge made popular by the folk song *Sur le Pont d'Avignon*.

AZAY-LE-RIDEAU – *see Tours p.298*.

BAGNOLES-DE-L'ORNE (245 B4)
ORNE *pop. 900*
Together with neighboring Tessé-la-Madeleine, Bagnoles-de-l'Orne is the largest spa in western France. The area adjoins a wooded lake that is fed by the Vée River. Waters from the river, a therapeutic 25°C (77°F), are particularly beneficial to persons with circulatory disorders. Bagnoles-de-l'Orne has a variety of entertainments, sporting facilities and a casino.

BARBIZON (245 C4)
SEINE-ET-MARNE *pop. 1,400*
Barbizon derives its name from the 19th-century landscape painters who worked in the city and founded the Barbizon school of painting. The studios of Jean-François Millet and Théodore Rousseau are open to the public; the Inn of Père Ganne, where artists once gathered, is now a museum.

LES BAUX-DE-PROVENCE (245 D2)
BOUCHES-DU-RHÔNE *pop. 500*
A medieval village on top of a high hill overlooking rugged countryside. Les Baux-de-Provence was once a stronghold of lords who claimed descent from Balthazar, one of the biblical three kings. Today Les Baux is a collection of white limestone buildings and huge rocks. The Cité Morte (Dead City) contains the ruined shells of the ancient town, which includes an imposing medieval fortress in a clifftop setting. In accordance with the ancient rites of Provence, a midnight procession bearing candles makes its way to the old church in place Saint Vincent on Christmas Eve. The town gave its name to the aluminum ore, bauxite. In a disused quarry just outside Les Baux, the Cathédrale d'Images presents a *son-et-lumière* (sound-and-light) show of the town's history.

BAYEUX (244 B4)
CALVADOS *pop. 14,700*
Bayeaux rose to importance in the 10th century as the principal town of the Duchy of Normandy. It also was the first French town to be liberated during World War II.

Famed for the Bayeux Tapestry, a medieval embroidery depicting the events that led to the Battle of Hastings in 1066, Bayeux still has cobbled streets and timbered houses, escaping damage during World War II.

CATHÉDRALE DE NÔTRE-DAME is a Gothic church. Although originally completed in 1077, only two Romanesque towers and the crypt remain from that era. The interior contains frescoes, ironwork and woodcarvings.

CIMETIÈRE COLLEVILLE-ST.-LAURENT, 15 kilometers (9 miles) northwest, contains the graves of 9,000 American troops killed during World War II.

On a cliff overlooking Omaha Beach and the English Channel, the site has a garden and a memorial with maps and narratives describing the huge military operation that took place. A bronze statue honors the Americans killed.

MUSÉE MÉMORIAL DE LA BATAILLE DE NORMANDIE, boulevard Fabian Ware, chronicles the events of the Battle of Normandy, which occurred between June 6 and August 22, 1944, through models and dioramas.

TAPISSERIE DE BAYEUX is in the Centre Guillaume le Conquérant. This 900-year-old band of linen, 70 meters (229 feet) long and 0.5 meters (20 inches) wide is a masterpiece of medieval crafts-manship. The 58 scenes, embroidered in worsteds of eight colors, depicted for an illiterate audience the historic event of the defeat of Harold II of England by William, Duke of Normandy at the Battle of Hastings, which established the Normans as rulers of England, as well as showing many facets of Norman life. Wrongly credited to William's Queen Mathilde, the tapestry (it is actually an embroidery) is now believed to have been commissioned by the city's Bishop Odo, William's half brother, as well as being produced by an English workshop.

Protected by glass and special lighting, the tapestry is accompanied by a recorded multilingual commentary. Viewing of the tapestry is preceded by a slide-show and an exhibition explaining the background to the events it depicts.

BAYONNE (244 B1)
PYRÉNÉES-ATLANTIQUES *pop. 40,100*
Capital of the French Basque country, Bayonne is tucked into the southwest corner of France.

The Musée Basque is dedicated to the region's folklore, and the Musée Bonnat features priceless paintings. The 13th-century Cathédrale de Ste.-Marie adds Gothic beauty to the town.

MUSÉE ÎLE-DE-FRANCE, at Cap-Ferrat, contains Baroness Ephrussi de Rothschild's rich art collection including Gothic and Italian Renaissance pieces, tapestries, porcelain and paintings and canvases by Fragonard, Boucher, Renoir and Sisley. Gardens surround the villa.

BEAUNE (245 D3)
CÔTE-D'OR *pop. 21,300*

Beaune is a wine center in the Burgundy region celebrating with several wine and grape festivals. The Museum of Burgundy Wine, housed in the Hôtel des Ducs de Bourgogne, displays documents and tools pertaining to the history of the vineyards and wines from ancient times.

Beaune is also noted for its historical treasures. The 15th-century Hôtel-Dieu, built as a hospital for the poor, has a painting collection.

BESANÇON (245 D3)
DOUBS *pop. 113,800*

Besançon is the capital of the Franche-Comté region. It has been important since the Roman era and was once under the control of the Spanish. Medieval buildings are the 16th-century Palais Granvelle and the Cathedral of St.-Jean, with its astronomical clock.

Besançon is the center of France's watchmaking industry; it is also the birthplace of Victor Hugo. The International Music Festival is held in September.

CITADELLE, rue des Fusillés-de-la-Résistance, is on a hill overlooking Besançon. Built by the Spanish and the military engineer Vauban, the fort houses the Museum of the Resistance and Deportation, the Museum of Natural History, including a zoological park and a folklore museum.

MUSÉE DES BEAUX ARTS ET D'ARCHÉOLOGIE, place de la Révolution, is one of the oldest and richest museums in France. It contains European paintings, drawings and sculpture from the Middle Ages to present day; also a collection of Egyptian, Greek and Roman antiquities. The museum has an unsurpassed collection of timepieces of all shapes and sizes.

BÉZIERS (245 D1)
HERAULT *pop. 72,500*

Béziers, on the Orb River near the Mediterranean, is the wine-producing center of the Languedoc-Roussillon region.

An old city, Béziers has a macabre history: as many as 20,000 residents were slain when the town was taken in the Albigensian Crusade of the 13th century.

A source of pride is the Cathédrale St.-Nazaire, built mainly in the 13th and 14th centuries. The Allées Paul-Riquet, named after the Béziers native who built the Canal du Midi, is a maze of attractive

FRANCE'S NATIONAL MUSEUMS

This country's 34 state-owned national museums hold some of its richest treasures. They are closed on Tuesday, with the exception of Versailles (see p.299), the Trianon Palace (see p.299) and the Musée d'Orsay (see p.262) which all are closed on Monday. Under 18 admitted free; 18–25 and over 60 are half-price; half-price admission is offered to all on Sunday.

narrow streets dotted with art galleries and museums devoted to the history of wine and winemaking, leading to a garden – Plateau des Poètes – with busts of famous writers and a panoramic view.

BIARRITZ (244 B1)
PYRÉNÉES-ATLANTIQUES *pop. 28,700*

Biarritz is a fashionable summer and

winter resort on the Atlantic coast at the foot of the Pyrénées. In addition to several beaches and splendid mountain views it has casinos and sports facilities. Also of interest is the Musée de la Mer with an aquarium and seal pool, and the Musée de l'Automobile Miniature, housing 6,000 scale models of cars.

BLOIS (245 C4)
LOIR-ET-CHER *pop. 49,300*

Blois, with its own stunning castle, marks the center of the Loire Valley's great château region. Several of the Loire's mansions, including those at Chambord, Chaumont, Cheverny and Ménars, are near this old industrial town.

CHÂTEAU DE BEAUREGARD, 6 kilometers (4 miles) southeast, has exceptional decoration, which has remained unchanged since the 16th and 17th centuries. Its portrait gallery is the largest in Europe, and there is a rare 16th-century kitchen.

CHÂTEAU DE BLOIS is an excellent example of French architecture; it contains elements from the Middle Ages to the classical period. Known for its handsome 16th-century stairway, it also contains the Musée des Beaux-Arts consisting of frescoes, paintings and religious art.

CHÂTEAU DE CHAMBORD, 18 kilometers (11 miles) southeast, is an enormous 16th-century structure of 440 rooms, the largest château in the Loire Valley. The palace has a double spiral staircase and rich ornamentation throughout.

CHÂTEAU DE CHEVERNY, 14 kilometers (9 miles) southeast, is a 17th-century mansion with original classical furnishings. A hunter's museum features a collection of antlers and maintains a kennel.

BORDEAUX (244 B2)
GIRONDE *pop. 210,300*

A major port on France's Atlantic coast and one of the world's wine capitals, Bordeaux and the surrounding vineyards are dotted with châteaux that have given their names to many prestigious red and white wines.

CATHÉDRALE ST.-ANDRÉ, place Pey-Berland, dates from several periods and has interesting sculptures.

GRAND THÉÂTRE, place de la Comédie, is considered one of the most beautiful theaters in Europe.

MUSÉE DES BEAUX-ARTS, 20 cours d'Albret, houses a collection of impressive paintings from the Renaissance to the 20th century.

BOULOGNE-SUR-MER (245 C5)
PAS-DE-CALAIS *pop. 43,700*

Boulogne-sur-Mer is a leading commercial and passenger port with a hovercraft and catamaran service to Dover, England as well as a catamaran service to Folkestone, England. The upper portion of the town, built on the site of a Roman fortress, contains historic buildings including a 13th-century castle, the 19th-century Cathedral of Notre-Dame and remains of the medieval town walls.

NAUSICAÀ, built on the beach at the entrance to Boulogne harbor, has 15,000 square meters (161,450 square feet) of aquarium space. The center provides an insight into the sciences related to the sea and its natural resources.

BOURGES (245 C3)
CHER *pop. 75,600*

The town of Bourges is an important cultural focal point in central France. Despite modernization, medieval and Renaissance history still lives in its buildings and streets.

Important structures include the 13th-century Cathedrale St.-Étienne, with its stained-glass windows; the Musée du Berry in the Hôtel Cujas, with a fine archaeological collection and art objects; the Musée des Arts Decoratifs in the Hôtel Lallemant; and the Palais Jacques-Coeur, former home and trade center of the medieval financier.

FRANCE

FRANCE

BREST (245 A4)
FINISTÈRE *pop. 148,000*

One of the best natural harbors in France, Brest has a long history as a naval and commercial port. The city dates from before the 14th century, but bombings in both world wars destroyed almost all the historic buildings. As a result, Brest is a very modern city.

Places of interest are the Arsenal and the naval dockyard, the Naval Museum and the Museum of Old Brest. The Pont de Recouvrance across the Penfeld River is said to be the biggest drawbridge in Europe, but opening its 87-meter (285-foot) span takes only a few seconds.

OCÉANOPOLIS, Port de Plaisance du Moulin Blanc, is a culture and marine science center that contains over 500,000 liters (132,100 gallons) of aquarium space.

CAEN (245 B4)
CALVADOS *pop. 112,800*

Caen, a prosperous industrial and commercial city in northern France, was almost entirely destroyed in the 1944 Normandy invasion. Excellent city planning, however, has brought about complete reconstruction and Caen's monuments have been restored and industries have been rebuilt.

Important at the time of the Norman Conquest, Caen has notable 11th- and 12th-century buildings. The massive Abbaye aux Hommes and the Abbaye aux Dames, constructed respectively by William the Conqueror and his queen, Mathilde, are well worth a visit.

CHÂTEAU FÉODAL, dating from the 11th century, is one of the oldest castles in France. It now contains two museums, the Musée des Beaux-Arts, particularly good for French and Italian works from the 17th and 18th centuries and the Musée de la Normandie.

MÉMORIAL, avenue de Maréchal Montgomery, covers the history of the 20th century through exhibits, a film of D-Day and a modern film – *Espérance* (*Hope*) – on the consequences of World War II and the dangers threatening the planet. It also houses a Nobel Peace Prize gallery.

CAGNES-SUR-MER
ALPES-MARITIMES *pop. 34,900*

Cagnes-sur-Mer, between Antibes and Nice, encompasses the old Provençal city of Haut-de-Cagnes, with its imposing castle, and the fishing village of Cros-de-Cagnes, with its fine beach. Haut-de-Cagnes, still an artists' colony, was one of Renoir's favorite spots.

CHÂTEAU-MUSÉE, originally built as a fortress, has a collection of paintings, 17th-century furnishings and superb coastal views. The Château-Musée served as the town's prison until the 17th century, when Baron Jean-Henri Grimaldi made it into a palatial home. An ethnographic museum traces the making of olive oil through the ages.

MUSÉE RENOIR, in Les Collettes, was the last home and studio of Renoir and houses some of the artist's best work.

CAHORS (245 C2)
LOT *pop. 19,700*

Ancient towers and belfries lend the town a medieval atmosphere. The 14th-century Pont Valentré is a particularly fine example of French military architecture; its three battlemented towers have guarded the western approaches since the 14th century.

St.-Cirq-Lapopie, on an escarpment overlooking the Lot River, 33 kilometers (21 miles) east of Cahors, is a medieval settlement so well preserved that the entire village is classified a historic site.

CALAIS (245 C5)
PAS-DE-CALAIS *pop. 75,300*

Calais, an industrial center, is the cross-Channel port for ferry services from Dover, England. At Fréthum, 5 kilometers (3 miles) to the south, is the 50-kilometer (30-mile) cross-Channel rail link, from which two regular services operate.

FRANCE

Eurostar is the high-speed rail passenger service from London (Waterloo, England) via Lille, to Paris (Gare du Nord) (3 hours), while Le Shuttle accommodates vehicles and their passengers for the 35-minute trip between Folkestone, England and Calais.

MONUMENT AUX BOURGEOIS DE CALAIS, in front of the Flemish-style town hall, is a moving memorial sculpture by Rodin, dated 1895, honoring local citizens starved into submission during the seige of Calais by Edward III at the beginning of the Hundred Years' War. Copies of the sculpture can be seen in Los Angeles and Washington.

CANNES (245 E1)
ALPES-MARITIMES pop. 68,700
Cannes, though not as large as Nice, is also an elegant year-round resort on the French Riviera. Between the beach and some of the city's most fashionable hotels is the palm-lined boulevard de la Croisette, with the Casino Municipal at the west end and the Palm Beach Casino. The Palais des Festivals is host to the famous International Cannes Film Festival in May.

West of the yacht harbor is the old town, with narrow streets that lead to the public market and up Mount Chevalier to a section called Le Suquet. Here are the 17th-century Gothic church of Notre-Dame d'Espérance; and the 12th-century Tour du Suquet, a watchtower built by the Monks of Lérins containing the Musée de la Castre, which displays artifacts from ancient Mediterranean civilizations.

The Lérins Islands of Ste.-Marguerite and St.-Honorat are worth visiting (20 minutes by boat). Ste.-Marguerite is the site of the prison that held the *Man in the Iron Mask*, also the subject of a book by Alexandre Dumas.

CARCASSONNE (245 C1)
AUDE pop. 43,500
Carcassonne has a long history as a frontier fortress. The Aude River divides it into two sections: the Ville Basse (Lower Town), which was founded in the 13th century and now forms the modern town; and the center of Carcassonne, the Cité, which dates from the Roman occupation in the 1st century. It developed into a thriving medieval town with formidable fortifications. These fell into disrepair after the Wars of Religion, but were comprehensively restored in the 19th century. The Cité's double-walled and turreted fortress, rising from a preciptous plateau, is illustrated at night to stunning effect.

CARNAC (244 A4)
MORBIHAN pop. 4,200
This town is known for its prehistoric megaliths. Over 2,000 standing stones, erected between 5500 and 1000 BC, are set in rows that stretch across the surrounding countryside for several miles.

The site is best viewed from the roof of the intepretation center, Archéoscope. Menec, and the megaliths of Keriavel, or Kermario are of particular interest.

CASSIS (245 D1)
BOUCHES-DU-RHÔNE pop. 8,000
Cassis is a picturesque fishing port and resort sunk between towering limestone cliffs. The old port, frequented by artists earlier this century, is lined with waterfront cafés, fish restaurants and small hotels. Southwest are three *calanques*, dramatic deep-water inlets slashed into the cliffs, reached by boat or footpath; they are popular with scuba divers and rock climbers.

CASTRES (245 C1)
TARN pop. 44,900
Castres is a sizable town on the banks of the Agoût River within easy reach of the regional Parc du haut Languedoc. It makes an excellent base for exploring the surrounding countryside, including the Montagne Noire (Black Mountain) to the south and the Sidobre area to the northeast. The region is noted for its bizarre rock formations and its stunning natural beauty, much of which can be

FRANCE

appreciated from the numerous tourist trails that traverse the park.

MUSÉE GOYA is situated in the 17th-century Hôtel de Ville, formerly the Bishops' Palace. Paintings by the great master are displayed alongside notable works by other acclaimed Spanish painters, including Velázquez.

CHABLIS (245 D4)
YONNE *pop. 2,600*
On the Serein River, Chablis lends its name to the popular crisp, white wine produced in the town for centuries; a festival in late November celebrates the end of the winemaking season.

CHÂLONS-SUR-MARNE (245 D4)
MARNE *pop. 48,400*
Ancient Châlons-sur-Marne is the center of the surrounding area's wine trade and has 17th- and 18th-century buildings.

BASILIQUE NOTRE-DAME-EN-VAUX, 8 kilometers (5 miles) east, at L'Épine, is a striking example of Romanesque-Gothic architecture. The Basilique de Lumière, a laser light show, dramatically accents its beauty.

CATHÉDRALE St.-ÉTIENNE dates from the 12th century. Its renowned stained glass can be seen in the transept and the choir.

MUSÉE DU CLOÎTRE DE NOTRE-DAME-EN-VAUX is a 12th-century church housing a fine collection of religious sculpture.

MUSÉE GARINET is a reconstruction of a bourgeois house of the 19th century.

MUSÉE MUNICIPAL displays medieval sculpture and exhibits pertaining to archaeology and folklore. A collection of paintings dates from the 16th century to the present.

CHALON-SUR-SAÔNE (245 D3)
SAÔNE-ET-LOIRE *pop. 54,600*
A bustling town in eastern Burgundy, Chalon-sur-Saône is the scene of one of the most joyous Mardi Gras carnivals in France. Of historical interest are the towers, the wooden houses, the Denon Museum containing collections of local archaeology, art and furniture, and the Cathedral of St.-Vincent, dating from the 11th century. Other highlights include the Photography Museum. Chalon-sur-Saône is the birthplace of Joseph-Nicéphore Niepce, the inventor of photography.

CHAMONIX (245 E3)
HAUTE-SAVOIE *pop. 9,700*
The popular Alpine resort of Chamonix is near the French-Swiss border. Perpetually snowy, Europe's highest peak, 4,807-meter (15,771-foot) Mont Blanc towers above the scenic valley. In 1786, Michel-Gabriel Paccard became the first person to scale Mont Blanc. The Musée Alpine gives a history of Mont Blanc and its conquerors.

The Mont Blanc Tunnel enables motorists to drive from Chamonix to Courmayeur in Italy.

The site of the first Winter Olympic Games in 1924, Chamonix has facilities for all winter sports, as well as tennis, golf, swimming and mountain climbing.

CHANTILLY (245 C4)
OISE *pop. 11,300*
Elegant Chantilly has long been a great center of horse racing, horseback riding and dressage, and is still a training center for thoroughbreds.

FRANCE PAST AND PRESENT

"France is the most brilliant and dangerous nation in Europe, best suited to become in turn an object of admiration, hatred, pity, terror, but never of indifference."
These are the words of Alexis de Toqueville in the 19th century, but the notion is just as relevant today.

A popular attraction is the 16th-century castle of the Dukes of Condé, set among ornamental lakes and gardens.

CHÂTEAU, rebuilt in the 19th century, is flanked by stone stables built in the 18th century to house 240 horses and 500 hunting dogs. The Musée Condé displays paintings, jewels, manuscripts and miniatures and is within the palace.

Musée Vivant Du Chevalet Du Poney, in the large 18th-century stables, has horses and ponies of different breeds as well as wooden models representing various equestrian disciplines. Also depicted are trades and activities associated with horses and equestrian shows.

PARC ASTÉRIX, at Plailly, 14 kilometers (9 miles) southeast, is a theme park based on the adventures of French comic-strip hero Astérix. The park has more than 100 attractions, including reconstructions of the Astérix village and a Paris street. In the Roman Arena and Camp, actors portray Roman soldiers and gladiators. Roller coasters, water rides and a dolphinarium also are featured.

CHARTRES (245 C4)
EURE-ET-LOIR pop. 39,600
Chartres is best known for its Cathedral of Notre-Dame, an architectural wonder that dominates the town's gabled houses and cobbled streets.

CATHÉDRALE NOTRE-DAME, which dates from the 13th-century, is a masterpiece of early Gothic architecture. Although some parts of the cathedral have been restored, the stained-glass windows remain as they were seven centuries ago.

CHÂTEAU DE MAINTENON, 18 kilometers (11 miles) northeast, is largely 16th and 17th century, but the square tower dates from the 12th century.

CHÂTILLON-SUR-SEINE (245 D4)
CÔTE-D'OR pop. 6,900
A city in a park, Châtillon-sur-Seine is dominated by its 11th-century Church of St. Vorles. The old church and many houses rise on a hillock above the Seine River, but the little town offers much more than a pleasant setting. At Vix, 7 kilometers (4 miles) north, in the Renaissance house of Philandrier, is the Treasure of Vix, one of the most sensational archaeological discoveries of the 20th century. The collection includes relics dating from about the 6th century BC, as well as Celtic antiquities.

CHAUMONT-SUR-LOIRE (245 C4)
LOIR-ET-CHER pop. 900
Château de Chaumont, above the Loire River, is a grand 15th-century Gothic structure. Inside are fine tapestries and furniture; a cedar tree park, gardens and stables with carriages can be enjoyed in the grounds.

CHERBOURG (244 B5)
MANCHE pop. 27,100
A principal ferry port with connections to England and Ireland, commercial port, shipbuilding and naval center, Cherbourg is on the northern coast of the Contentin Peninsula.

It was the western end of the coast that suffered in the Normandy invasion of 1944. The Musée de la Guerre et de la Libération above nearby Fort du Roule traces the invasion and the subsequent course of war.

Rewarding side trips include the coastal drives around the Cap de la Hague, the wild, rocky coast northwest of Cherbourg, and the Val de Saire region to the east.

CHINON (245 B3)
INDRE-ET-LOIRE pop. 8,600
The riverside town of Chinon has retained much of its medieval appearance manifested in its three ancient, ruined fortresses. Fort St.-Georges was built by King Henry II and is reputedly where he died in 1189; the Château du Milieu is where Joan of Arc was received by the Dauphin in 1429; and the Fort du Coudray is where she slept during her stay.

The Château du Milieu has displays on medieval royal architecture, Joan of Arc and historical scenes with waxworks.

Maison des États-Généraux, where Richard the Lionheart died in 1199, is now the Musée du Vieux Chinon.

CLERMONT-FERRAND (245 D3)
PUY-DE-DÔME *pop. 136,200*

Clermont-Ferrand is considered to be the capital of the Auvergne, with spectacular scenery and extinct volcanoes. The city overlooks a valley to the east and the Monts Dômes to the west. It has a number of old buildings built of black volcanic rock. The Musée du Bargoin contains Roman and prehistoric relics.

CLUNY (245 D3)
SAÔNE-ET-LOIRE *pop. 4,400*

Cluny's history revolves around the Benedictine abbey built in the 10th century. The abbey became a learning center in the Middle Ages, and its monks traveled across Europe founding brother orders. The original abbey church was 187 meters (613 feet) long; it was the biggest church in the Christian world until St. Peter's in Rome was built.

Although much of the structure was destroyed in the early 19th century, some sections remain, giving a good impression of what the whole edifice looked like. The best view of the abbey and of the many old houses in town is from the top of the Tour des Fromages.

COGNAC (245 B3)
CHARENTE *pop. 19,500*

The old city of Cognac is in the heart of brandy country; it is surrounded by vineyards that are the source of the well-known cognac brandies. In addition to its distilleries, which may be visited, the region is known for the 12th-century Church of St. Léger, Renaissance houses and towers, and the Château de Valois, birthplace of François I, surrounded by an attractive park.

MUSÉE DU COGNAC can be found within the Musée Municipal, 48 boulevard Denfert-Rochereau, has displays on the history, distillation and sale of cognac.

CONQUES (245 C2)
AVEYRON *pop. 400*

The old village of Conques is known for its church of Ste.-Foy, considered one of the best examples of Romanesque architecture in southern France. A carving of the *Last Judgement* is inside. There are also examples of 9th- to 16th-century religious art, including a gilded wooden statue of Ste.-Foy, one of the oldest Christian statues.

CORSE (CORSICA) (245 E1)
pop. 249,700

The Mediterranean island of Corsica, 183 kilometers (113 miles) long and 83 kilometers (50 miles) wide, lies off the French and Italian coasts in the Gulf of Genoa. It has been called a continent in miniature because of mountains soaring to over 2,000 meters (6,560 feet), an abundance of rivers and streams, and a rich diversity of flora and fauna. The island has a history stretching back over 8,000 years and contains many monuments of great architectural value.

Corsica can be reached by regular scheduled flights from Paris, Lille, Lyon, Marseille, Nice and Toulon, and also by frequent ferry services from Marseille, Toulon and Nice to the two main ports of Ajaccio and Bastia.

AJACCIO *pop. 55,500*

The seaport and capital of Corsica was Napoléon Bonaparte's birthplace. Today Ajaccio is the principal town on the island with numerous monuments and museums commemorating Napoléon; including the house where he was born, and the church where he was baptized.

BASTIA *pop. 45,000*

Bastia, the ancient port of Corsica, was once a Genoese stronghold. The fishing settlement lies at the foot of vine-clad hills. Visit the old Governor's Palace housing the Ethnographic Museum, the citadel and the local churches.

COURCHEVEL (245 E2)
SAVOIE

Regarded as one of the greatest skiing centers in Europe, Courchevel is the core of a complex of resorts. Along with nearby Albertville, Courchevel was the center for the 1992 Winter Olympics. This lively community in the Savoie region of the Alps consists of four towns ranging in elevation from 1,300 meters (4,265 feet) to 1,850 meters (6,070 feet). Courchevel also supports an active and lively cultural life.

DEAUVILLE (245 B4)
CALVADOS *pop. 4,300*

Deauville, in northwest France, is an extremely fashionable seaside resort where the well-to-do Parisians spend their holidays; in summer, its population swells to 40,000.

The height of the tourist season is in August, when the racetrack holds one of the most popular meets in France and the world polo championship takes place. Les Planches is a wooden promenade lined with gardens and nightclubs that runs the length of the beach.

Sports facilities are excellent, and there is a casino. Deauville is also the setting of the Festival of American Cinema each September.

DIEPPE (245 C5)
SEINE-MARITIME *pop. 35,900*

Dieppe is probably France's oldest seaside resort. Although the city is now a major commercial and passenger port with a ferry service to Newhaven in England, it has retained many of its old alleys and its castle, which contains a museum of the history of Dieppe and its coastline.

A plaque commemorates the August 1942 raid during which over 3,500 Canadian commandos lost their lives.

DIGNE (245 E2)
ALPES-DE-HAUTE-PROVENCE
pop. 16,400

A popular tourist center beside the Bléone River, Digne enjoys a warm, dry climate. The town is known for the production of lavender and fruit.

The southern Alps and the Bès Valley are within easy traveling distance.

MUSÉE MUNICIPAL has exhibits pertaining to prehistory, archaeology, mineralogy and natural history. The paintings on display include works from the French, Flemish, Dutch and Italian schools.

NOTRE-DAME-DU-BORG is a Romanesque cathedral that dates from the 13th and 14th centuries.

DIJON (245 D3)
SEINE-MARITIME *pop. 146,700*

In its heyday, Dijon served as capital of the Burgundian dukes. These wealthy, independent nobles contributed many of the city's fine artistic and architectural treasures. Their most conspicuous monument is the Palais des Ducs et des États de Bourgogne, now the Hôtel de Ville; another palace, the Palais de Justice, was the meeting place of the duchy's 16th-century parliament. Dijon's nobles built spectacular mansions, many of which stand in the city center.

Remarkable among the several churches are St.-Philibert, with its Romanesque nave, and Notre-Dame and St.-Michel, with elaborately carved exteriors. The Cathédrale St.-Bénigne, originally an abbey church, dates from the 14th century. Nearby in a monastery is an archaeological museum with many interesting relics of Dijon's earliest residents, the Romans, who maintained a prominent military installation.

An art center since the Renaissance, Dijon also is an epicurean capital. The surrounding countryside produces some of the finest wines in the world. Dijon itself is recognized for *cassis* (blackcurrant liqueur), *escargots* (snails), *pain d'epice* (spice bread) and mustard. From the end of October to the beginning of November, gastronomes gather in the city for the Foire Internationale et Gastronomique, a magnificent display of good food and drink.

HÔTEL DE VILLE, in the city center, incorporates the substantial remains of the 14th-century Palais des Ducs et des États de Bourgogne.

MUSÉE DES BEAUX-ARTS, one of the outstanding art museums in Europe, was founded in the 18th century and contains European paintings and sculptures.

MUSÉE DE LA VIE BOURGUIGNONNE, 13 avenue Albert I, displays historical waxwork scenes which portray Burgundy's varied past.

DINAN (244 B4)
COTES-D'AMOR pop. 11,600
Dinan is a wonderfully preserved medieval town enclosed within 600-year-old walls and guarded by an impressive fortress. Visitors can stroll the narrow cobbled streets and admire the timberfront houses, little port and craft shops. The Jardin Anglais offers fine panoramic views over the valley of the Rance River. In October, the town is animated by the colorful Fête des Ramparts, a vibrant medieval pageant.

DINARD
ÎLE-ET-VILAINE pop. 19,900
A seaside resort, Dinard became popular with Britons and Americans in the 19th century. Today tourists visit the town for its sports facilities, beaches and casino, or just to stroll the beachfront Promenade Clair-de-Lune.

AQUARIUM ET MUSÉE DE LA MER shows visitors the marine life of the Brittany coast and details the deep-sea expeditions of Commander Charcot, a local explorer.

DISNEYLAND PARIS (245 C4)
SEINE-ET-MARNE
Disneyland Paris is situated 32 kilometers (20 miles) east of Paris at Marne-la-Vallée. It can be reached via Autoroute A4 exit 14, or by RER railroad, line A, Chessy-Marne-La-Vallée Station, or by the shuttle bus. It is based on the Disney theme parks in the United States

and comprises 2,000 hectares (4,940 acres). Visitors can walk along Main Street USA; relive Disney classics and European culture in Fantasyland and Adventureland; ride a roller coaster in Frontierland; travel through space in a flight simulator at Discoveryland's Star Tours, or take a trip in a flying machine based on a design by Leonardo da Vinci. Disneyland Paris also has seven hotels, a log cabin and an 18-hole golf course.

DOLE (245 D3)
JURA pop. 26,600
Dole borders both the Doub River and the Rhine-Rhône Canal. This attractive industrial city is the birthplace of Louis Pasteur and contains an interesting museum illustrating his work.

DOMRÉMY-LA-PUCELLE (245 D4)
VOSGES pop. 200
Joan of Arc was born in tiny Domrémy beside the Meuse River in 1412. Her birthplace, Maison Natale de Jeanne d'Arc, has been preserved. A museum next to the house contains mementos of her life. Just over 1.5 kilometers (1 mile) south is the Basilique du Bois-Chenu, marking the spot where Joan first heard voices summoning her to fight for France.

DOUARNENEZ (244 A4)
FINISTÈRE pop. 16,500
Ancient Douarnenez gradually merged with the neighboring towns of Ploaré, Pouldavid and Tréboul to form one of France's major fishing ports. Lobster and sardines are the town's chief commodities. Visitors are drawn to the beaches, water sports, old churches, Port-Musée laid out along the quays of the Port-Rhu, and the Musée du Bateau, with its extraordinary and interesting collection of traditional European boats.

DUNKERQUE (245 C5)
NORD pop. 70,300
Dunkerque, or Dunkirk, is noted as the embarkation point for the retreat of British troops in June 1940. During the war, more than 75 percent of the city

was destroyed, but it has been almost entirely rebuilt. There are museums of fine art, contemporary art and of the port. A cross-Channel ferry service connects the city with Ramsgate, England.

ÉPERNAY (245 D4)
MARNE *pop. 26,700*
Surrounded by vine-covered hills, Épernay is known for its champagne. The town shares with nearby Reims its status as the core of this region's champagne trade. The avenue de Champagne is lined with neo-Renaissance or classical-style buildings connected with champagne. Beneath the avenue you can visit over 100 kilometers (62 miles) of tunnels storing millions of bottles of champagne. The town museum contains a section devoted to all processes of champagne production.

ÉTRETAT (245 C5)
SEINE-MARITIME *pop. 1,600*
The popular seaside resort of Étretat is distinguished by two imposing chalk cliffs that stand at either end of its beach. Falaise d'Amont (Downstream Cliff) is surmounted by a small museum and a memorial dedicated to aviators Charles Nungesser and François Coli, who attempted unsuccessfully to fly across the Atlantic in 1927; Falaise d'Aval (Upstream Cliff) is cut in its center by a huge natural archway. The distinctive L'Aiguille (The Needle) stands slightly offshore.

A restored covered market in the place Maréchal Foch is of interest.

ÉVREUX (245 C4)
EURE *pop. 49,100*
Évreux is the administrative and religious capital of the Eure *département*. An important agricultural market town, it has achieved considerable industrial and economic growth in recent years.

CATHÉDRALE NOTRE-DAME dates from the 10th century. Although severely damaged in the French Revolution and World War II, the cathedral retains 13th- to 16th-century stained-glass windows, fine woodwork and small chapels.

LES EYZIES-DE-TAYAC (245 C2)
DORDOGNE *pop. 900*
Les Eyzies-de-Tayac is an archaeologist's delight, for it was in this area that some of the first Cro-Magnon skeletons were discovered. Extensive caves near the town such as Grotte de Font-de-Gaume and Grotte des Combarelles contain prehistoric drawings and paintings. A 10th-century castle/fortress houses the Musée National de la Préhistoire.

FALAISE (245 B4)
CALVADOS *pop. 8,100*
William the Conqueror was born in the huge castle here in 1027; the ruins of the fortress can still be seen.

The place Guillaume-le-Conquérant contains a statue of the illegitimate son of Robert, Duke of Normandy, and Arlette, a Falaise tanner's daughter; other statues commemorate the first six dukes of Normandy.

MUSÉE AOÛT commemorates the Battle of the Falaise Gap with documents, models and photographs, and the ultimate end to the Battle of Normandy, with armored vehicles, uniformed soldiers and models demonstrating the arrival of Canadian soldiers in Falaise.

NOËL, NOËL
Christmas is a magical time in France. Falaise is one of many towns that has a special Christmas street market, with colorful stalls brimming with festive fare, decorations and gifts, and seasonal local produce, all accompanied by lively entertainment. Strasbourg has concerts and fun-filled activities for children, including Santa Claus in a tram and a chocolate cruise on the river. For more information, contact the French Government Tourist Office (see p. 244).

FRANCE

FÉCAMP (245 C5)
SEINE-MARITIME *pop. 20,800*
Fécamp was once France's most important cod port, with trawlers embarking as far away as Newfoundland in search of the fish. A museum devoted to the fishing industry remembers those days. The town also is the home of 19th-century novelist Guy de Maupassant, born at nearby Miromesnil Castle, and the place of origin of Bénédictine liqueur.

Fécamp's church of La Trinité contains the Precious Blood relic; pilgrimages are made on the Tuesday and Thursday following Trinity Sunday.

FIGEAC (245 C2)
LOT *pop. 9,500*
Figeac is best known for the Needles of Figeac, two 15-meter (49-foot), 12th-century obelisks on the outskirts of town that are believed to mark the original limits of the local abbey's jurisdiction. Several well-preserved buildings in the vicinity of rue Delzhens and rue Gambetta are of interest.

ÉGLISE ST.-SAUVEUR, the former abbey church, dates from the 12th century. Some of its additions are more recent.

HÔTEL DE LA MONNAIE is a restored Gothic building, once the town mint and now a tourist information center.

MUSÉE CHAMPOLLION, rue des Frères Champollion, birthplace of Egyptologist Jean-François Champollion, one of the first scholars to decipher hieroglyphics, has three showrooms. One focuses on Champollion's life, another contains Egyptian items on loan from the Louvre, and the third, the script room, holds a reproduction of the Rosetta stone.

FONTAINEBLEAU (245 C4) ★
SEINE-ET-MARNE *pop. 15,700*
Fontainebleau's palace, gardens and forest are thought by some to symbolize the spirit of France even more than Versailles. It was at Fontainebleau that Napoléon Bonaparte signed his abdication papers. Because of its outstanding natural beauty, the area was a favorite subject of the 19th-century Barbizon School painters, who included Millet and Rousseau.

Le Fôret de Fontainebleau is one of Europe's most magnificent forests, covering 20,000 hectares (49,420 acres). These woods were a favorite hunting preserve of the French nobility.

PALAIS DE FONTAINEBLEAU is the grandiose castle on which French kings once lavished their tastes and fortunes. Built in the 12th century, it reflects François I's taste for the Italian Renaissance style. Henri IV, Napoléon Bonaparte and Louis Philippe later made additions to the palace and gardens. Some of their apartments, as well as those of Marie Antoinette, are open to visitors.

Of special interest are the Red Room, scene of Napoléon's abdication, the Council Room and Throne Room. The Royal Apartments contain the Gobelin tapestries and a mantelpiece designed by Italian Francesco Primaticcio. Today one wing of the palace houses a summer school with courses in music and arts.

FRÉJUS (245 E1)
VAR *pop. 41,500*
The port of Fréjus was founded by the Romans as a shipbuilding town. Here Octavius built the ships that defeated Mark Antony and Cleopatra at the Battle of Actium.

Now Fréjus is a resort known for its beach; extensive Roman ruins, including a theater, amphitheater and aqueduct; and vineyards and orchards. Also of interest is the 4th-century baptistry next to the town's cathedral.

GIEN (245 C4)
LOIRET *pop. 16,500*
Gien's strategic location on the north bank of the Loire River made it a frequent target for bombings in World War II, but much of the town has been restored to its original charm. Gien is

known for the manufacture of *faïence*, a high-glaze, decorative pottery.

MUSÉE INTERNATIONAL DE LA CHASSE, in a 15th-century château, contains displays of *faïence*, armor, trophies and paintings.

GIVERNY (245 C4) ★
EURE *pop. 500*

The small village of Giverny, 5 kilometers (3 miles) southeast of Vernon, was where the leading French Impressionist painter Claude Monet lived from 1883 until his death in 1926.

Giverny is normally crowded with tourists, particularly in spring and summer – the only time you can visit Monet-associated sights.

MAISON ET JARDIN DE CLAUDE MONET, the country home in which the famous artist lived and painted for more than 40 years, has been restored as a museum. It is surrounded by the gardens he designed and developed as his private painting environment.

The house displays furnishings Monet used, reproductions of some of the artist's masterpieces and his famed collection of Japanese prints.

In the grounds, the main gardens are a kaleidoscope of fruit tree blossoms and seasonal flowers. The water garden, with its Japanese bridge, weeping willows and lily pond, is itself an expression of Monet's art.

MUSÉE D'ART AMERICAIN, 99 rue Claude Monet, features works of 19th- and 20th-century American Impressionist painters who were influenced by their stay at Giverny, and whose works are now famous in their own right.

GORGES DE L'ARDÈCHE (245 D2)
ARDÈCHE

Here the Ardèche River has carved out 27 kilometers (17 miles) of extraordinary gorges. The best views are from the D290 from Vallon-Pont-d'Arc to Pont-St.-Esprit, a succession of roadside belvederes hundreds of feet above the river.

The main feature is the Pont d'Arc, a spectacular natural archway over the Ardèche River, 66 meters (217 feet) wide, which is a popular spot for canoeists. Canoes can be rented from Vallon.

At Suze-la-Rousse, 16 kilometers (10 miles) east of Pont-St.-Esprit, is the only wine university in Europe. Located in a 15th-century château, the university is open to all lovers of wine.

GORGES DU TARN (245 D2) ★
LOZÈRE

One of the natural wonders of western Europe, at Gorges du Tarn where the Tarn River has carved out a dramatic deep gorge, rising to a height of 600 meters (1,968 feet), in the limestone hills of the Cévennes. The canyon is at its most impressive between the villages of Le Rozier and Ste.-Énimie. The roads through the canyon and along the cliff offer scenic views at every turn.

The village of Ste.-Énimie is acknowledged as one of the most beautiful in the whole of France. Boat and canoe trips down the Tarn (spring to fall only) start from La Malène.

At the northern end of the canyon the Tarn River leads to Florac, where a wide mountain road (the Corniche des Cévennes), with breathtaking views, runs to St.-Jean-du-Gard.

GRAND CANYON DU VERDON ★
ALPES-DE-HAUTE-PROVENCE ET VAR

Between Castellane and Moustiers-Ste.-Marie, where the Verdon River cuts through the mountainous Plateau de Valensole, is the most spectacular gorge in Europe. The Grand Canyon du Verdon, more than 21 kilometers (13 miles) long, comprises a series of deeply incised gorges with limestone cliffs plunging 700 meters (2,296 feet). The best way to see it is from the Corniche Sublime on its southern side or the route des Crêtes on its northern side; both offering fine lookout points.

The main tourist center of the area is Moustiers-Ste.-Marie, at the lower end

FRANCE

of the canyon; an interesting village famous for its distinctive pottery displayed in the local Musée de la Faïence.

GRASSE (245 E2)
ALPES-MARITIMES *pop. 42,400*
Grasse is a city of flowers and aromas. It is the world capital of the perfume industry and three perfume distilleries, each with a retail outlet, can be toured: the Fragonard on boulevard Fragonard, the Galimard on the Cannes road and the Molinard on boulevard Victor Hugo. Alternatively you can visit the Musée de la Parfumerie.

The old town center has an attractive tumbledown appeal. Places of interest are the Hôtel de Ville, which once served as a bishop's palace; the fine 12th-century cathedral; and the 18th-century Villa-Musée Fragonard with works by Jean Honoré Fragonard, who was born in Grasse.

GRENOBLE (245 D2)
ISÈRE *pop. 150,800*
Surrounded entirely by the French Alps, Grenoble was a popular winter sports center long before it was selected as the center for the 1968 Winter Olympics. Bolstered by the excellence of its industries and prestige of its university, Grenoble has a worldwide reputation.

Despite the modern bustle, the city carefully conserves the treasures of its past, which include the 11th-century Cathedral of Nôtre Dame, the Renaissance Palais de Justice and the 15th-century Hôtel de Ville. Grenoble has many museums; Musée de Peinture et de Sculpture houses one of the finest collections outside of Paris.

You can get a bird's-eye view of the city from the distinctive *téléférique* (cable car) that spans the Isère River from the quai Stéphanie Jay to the 16th-century fort on a high clifftop on the opposite bank.

LE HAVRE (245 B5)
SEINE-MARITIME *pop. 195,900*
King François I founded Le Havre, originally called Le Havre de Grace, in the 16th century. Now France's second port with ferries to England and Ireland; it was completely rebuilt after the ravages inflicted during World War II. The city's museums include the Musée de l'Ancien Havre, which chronicles local history, and the Museé des Beaux-Arts, which houses a rich collection of Impressionist and modern paintings. Next to the city is the resort suburb of Ste.-Adresse, which has a fine beach.

HONFLEUR
CALVADOS *pop. 8,300*
Honfleur served as an important fishing and commercial port for several centuries and received such explorers as Samuel de Champlain, who founded Québec in 1608. The town grew until the 19th century, when Le Havre, across the Seine River, supplanted it in economic importance.

The Impressionist school was founded in the 19th century by Boudin, Corot and other painters and the Musée Eugène Boudin exhibits some of their works. Ste.-Catherine, is a 15th-century-wooden church built by shipwrights.

Honfleur is a living postcard of a town, with timber-framed houses overlooking winding streets, creating old-world charm but with a thriving atmosphere.

The greatest pleasure is simply wandering the streets, quays and squares of the town. Art galleries and artists' shops line the Vieux Bassin, or Old Harbor, maintaining artistic traditions.

HUELGOAT (244 A4)
FINISTÈRE *pop. 1,750*
Considered one of the most beautiful inland towns in Brittany, Huelgoat benefits from its picturesque setting. Fishermen frequent Huelgoat's lake and the Argent River; hikers and nature lovers walk the Allée Violette, a trail through the Arrée Mountains that passes streams, lush vegetation and mounds of granite rocks. Of particular interest is Roche Tremblante, or Trembling Rock, an imposing massive slab of granite that trembles when gently pushed.

JUMIÈGES (245 C5)
SEINE-MARITIME *pop. 1,600*

Abbaye de Jumièges was founded in the 7th century and grew into a well-known center of learning during the Middle Ages. Now partly ruined, the abbey retains its nave, chancel and portions of the transept. The chapter house and the storeroom date from the 12th century.

KAYSERSBERG
HAUT-RHIN *pop. 2,800*

This tiny wine-producing town is the birthplace of Nobel Peace Prize winner Albert Schweitzer. The town still retains a number of 16th- and 17th-century half-timbered buildings and stores, as well as a centuries-old fortified bridge that spans the Weiss River.

CENTRE CULTUREL ALBERT SCHWEITZER, 126 rue du Général-de-Gaulle, is a monument to the theologian, philosopher, musician and doctor, who was awarded the Nobel Peace Prize in 1952. From 1913 until his death in 1965 he directed the hospital he founded in the jungles of Gabon. The center contains a museum dedicated to his life and work.

LILLE (245 C5)
NORD *pop. 172,100*

Lille, capital of Flanders, is the leading industrial and commercial city in northern France. It is known for textiles, metal products and various foodstuffs. Representative of Lille's historic past and character are several 16th- to 18th-century churches, a number of imposing old houses and a 17th-century citadel.

MAISON NATALE DU GÉNÉRAL DE GAULLE, 9 rue Princesse, is General de Gaulle's birthplace and now a museum including personal mementos of the President and the black Citröen in which he narrowly avoided assassination in 1962.

MUSÉE D'ART MODERNE, 4 kilometers (2½ miles) east of Lille in Villeneuve d'Ascq, features a collection of works by Braque, Picasso, Léger, Miró and Modigliani.

MUSÉE DE BEAUX-ARTS, place de la République, is the second-largest museum in France, after the Louvre. Among its many valuable works are paintings by Goya, Van Gogh, Rubens and Van Dyck.

LIMOGES (245 C3)
HAUTE-VIENNE *pop. 133,500*

Artisans use the pure white clay of St.-Yrieix, a short distance south, to produce the exquisite Limoges porcelain, famed for its delicacy and translucence. David Haviland, an American, built a factory in the town to produce china utilizing the same fine materials but with designs more suited to American tastes. The porcelain factories and enamel workshops can be visited.

Other points of interest include the 1786 Bishop's Palace, which contains a museum of Limousin history; and the Musée National Adrien-Drubouché, which displays a history of porcelain.

LISIEUX (245 C4)
CALVADOS *pop. 23,700*

Pilgrims from all over the world visit Lisieux to pay homage to Ste.-Thérèse. As a child, Thérèse Martin lived in Les Buissonnets, now considered a shrine. The vast Basilique Ste.-Thérèse, consecrated in 1954, contains the tombs of the saint's parents; her own shrine is in the Carmelite chapel. Also in the town is Cathédrale de St.-Pierre, one of the oldest Gothic churches in Normandy.

LOURDES (245 B1)
HAUTES-PYRÉNÉES *pop. 16,300*

It was in Lourdes on February 11, 1858 that Bernadette Soubirous, a young peasant girl, witnessed an apparition of the Virgin Mary; near the site of the vision a curative spring miraculously appeared. Today Lourdes is visited by millions of people each year.

BASILIQUE, begun in 1871 at the site of Ste.-Bernadette's visions, is filled with banners and tablets of gratitude for miraculous cures. In front of the basilica is the richly decorated Church of the

Rosary; next to the basilica is the fountain from which pilgrims drink. Esplanade des Processions extends before the church, with a crucifix 12 meters (39 feet) high at one end and a colossal statue of the Virgin Mary at the other. Nearby is the Grotte de Massabielle, the site of the apparitions.

LYON (245 D3) ★
RHÔNE *pop. 415,500*
At the confluence of the Rhône and Saône rivers, Lyon has been the center of communications since Roman times, gaining international importance with the introduction of the silk industry in the Middle Ages. Its textile industry expanded with the use of power looms, and today Lyon remains France's chief manufacturer of silk. The International Fair of Lyon is held every spring.

As well as museums and Roman monuments, Lyon has a university, theaters, concert halls, stadiums and a botanical garden. The restored old quarter on the right bank of the Saône is now the focus of Lyonnais *chic*, with Renaissance palaces, designer shops and eating places. Lyon is renowned for its fine food, from exclusive restaurants to the typical Lyonnais, bistro-style *bouchon*, and for its Beaujolais and Côtes-du-Rhône wines.

Via highway N84 is Pérouges the medieval village which has been scrupulously restored and old crafts revived.

MUSÉE DE L'AUTOMOBILE is 12 kilometers (7 miles) north at Rochetaillée, off highway D433 on the Saône River. Restored automobiles, motorcycles, bicycles and public transport vehicles are housed in two buildings. Many historic cars are displayed, including Hitler's bullet-proof Mercedes, along with photographs, posters and automotive accessories.

MUSÉE DES ARTS DÉCORATIFS, 30 rue de la Charité, houses 17th- and 18th-century furniture, ceramics, silver and tapestries.

MUSÉE DES BEAUX-ARTS, 20 place des Terreaux housed in a former 17th-century abbey, contains a selection of paintings and sculpture including works by Veronese, Tintoretto and Rubens.

MUSÉE DE LA CIVILISATION GALLO-ROMAINE 17 rue Cléberg, has architecture as exceptional as the collections it contains. On display are examples of Roman relics, including mosaics, sculptures, jewelry, ceramics, weapons, tools and coins.

MUSÉE HISTORIQUE DES TISSUS, 34 rue de la Charité, displays priceless examples of Lyon's rare and exquisite silks from the 17th to the 20th centuries, as well as European tapestries and textiles.

MÂCON (245 D3)
SAÔNE-ET-LOIRE *pop. 37,300*
Mâcon is a peaceful, dignified city on the Saône River, surrounded by the Mâconnais wine-producing area. A Romanesque cathedral and a Louis XV pharmacy are among its attractions. The poet Alphonse Marie Louis de Lamartine was born in Mâcon, and the town is a pilgrimage center for admirers of his works. The Musée Lamartine is housed in the Hôtel Sennecé.

LE MANS (245 B4)
SARTHE *pop. 145,500*
Le Mans is known for its 24-hour motor race, held each June. Of architectural interest is the mainly Gothic Cathedral of St.-Julien, with a Romanesque nave dating from the 12th, 13th and 14th centuries, while its medieval center was the setting for the film *Cyrano de Bergerac*. The city's several museums encompass archaeology, automobiles, painting and sculpture.

MARSEILLE (245 D1)
BOUCHES DU RHÔNE *pop. 880,500*
Ancient Marseille, on the Mediterranean, began as the Greek settlement of Massalia in 600 BC and was a thriving commercial port well into the 19th century, when the growth of France's colonial interests and the opening of the Suez Canal made it a vital southern gateway.

Today, the loss of the French colonies along with a worldwide shipping slump has brought about a relative decline. The city, however, has grown and modernised significantly since World War II.

Marseille, France's largest port and second-largest city, is crowded and cosmopolitan. The main street, La Canbière, was in the days of sea travel a mighty boulevard where sultans and princes met for business. Today it is lined with more modest stores and cafés.

Used primarily by fishing boats and small pleasure craft, the Vieux Port is still the heart of the city. There are boat trips from here to the rocky island of Château d'If, a forbidding 16th-century castle and former prison. Marseille's modern port lies to the north.

Among old treasures to be found are the Ancienne Cathédrale de la Major, an unusual combination of 12th- and 19th-century architectural styles, and the 12th-century Abbey of St.-Victor, with its 5th-century catacombs. There are also museums of history, fine art and the decorative arts.

The stirring French national anthem, composed in 1792 by Claude Joseph

---

LAND OF CHEESE

"The French will only be united under the threat of danger. Nobody can simply bring together a country that has 265 kinds of cheese."
(Charles de Gaulle)

Rouget de Lisle as *The War Song of the Army of the Rhine*, was renamed *The Marseillaise* by Marseille volunteers as they marched together in support of the Revolution.

MUSÉE DE LA VIEILLE CHARITÉ contains Egyptian and Mediterranean archaeology and African art.

PALAIS LONGCHAMP, dating from 1860, houses the Museé des Beaux-Arts and the natural history collections.

MENTON (245 E2)
ALPES-MARITIMES *pop. 29,100*
Menton, near the Italian border, consists of two districts: the old town, with typical Mediterranean buildings, narrow streets and Italian baroque churches, and the modern town, with broad avenues and contemporary buildings. The Musée des Beaux-Arts, in the 18th-century Palais Carnolès, houses a collection of paintings by 18th- to 20th-century artists. The town offers a lively festival program, with its annual Fête du Citron, a chamber music festival, and a biennial art exhibition.

METZ (245 D4)
MOSELLE *pop. 119,600*
Metz is an ancient city at the confluence of the Moselle and Seille rivers. First colonized by the Romans, Metz persevered through the Middle Ages, withstanding many sieges.

An early center of Christianity, it was the seat of great bishops. The Cathédrale St.-Étienne (13th- to 16th-century), rising impressively above the town, has magnificent stained glass. A smaller but older Christian landmark is the 4th-century Church of St.-Pierre-aux-Nonnains, one of the oldest churches in France. Many buildings from the Middle Ages and the 18th century survive.

MUSÉE D'ART ET D'HISTOIRE, rue du Haut Poirier, is housed in the structural remains of the walls of Roman baths, the façade of a Renaissance convent and a 15th-century granary.

MOISSAC (245 C2)
TARN-ET-GARONNE *pop. 12,100*
Situated on the Tarn River, Moissac was a religious center in the Middle Ages. Today it is known for dessert grapes.

ÉGLISE ST.-PIERRE, the former abbey church, was built in Gothic and Romanesque styles in the 11th century.

Additions include cloisters and the south doorway, carved with scenes pertaining to the Apocalypse.

MONTPELLIER (245 D1)
HÉRAULT *pop. 208,000*

Montpellier, capital of the Languedoc-Roussillon region, is a dynamic modern city of high-tech industry and bold new architecture with a thriving university. Its many 17th- and 18th-century buildings and gardens around rue de l'Ancien Courrier in the Quartier Ste.-Anne preserve the elegance of another era.

NEW ROME?
The most extraordinary city project is that of Montpellier in southern France, where Catalan architect Ricardo Bofill has designed medium-rent social housing in neoclassical style that is, in the words of the local mayor, "the Rome of tomorrow."

Modern Montpellier is centered on Antigone, an ambitious neoclassical architectural project.

MUSÉE FABRE, rue Montpellier, contains old masters and 19th-century paintings including works by d'Angers, Delacroix and Courbet.

PROMENADE DU PEYROU, with views of the Mediterranean, Alps and Pyrénées, is noted for its 18th-century bathing pavilion, fountains and aqueduct. The 1593 botanical gardens, Jardin des Plantes, are said to be the oldest in France.

LE MONT-ST.-MICHEL (244 B4) ★
MANCHE *pop. 72*

Photographers have long been captivated by France's premier tourist attraction, Le Mont-St.-Michel, a granite islet about 2 kilometers (1 mile) off the Normandy coast.

Rising majestically from the slopes of the mount the town is topped by a formidable monastery. Though not entirely surrounded by water during low tide, the stretch of sand connecting it to the mainland is not safe for walking; use the permanent connecting causeway.

Le Mont-St.-Michel was established in the 10th century when St. Aubert, Bishop of Avranches, was instructed by the Archangel Michael to build an oratory on the rock. The small chapel was replaced by a Benedictine monastery, which was a celebrated seat of learning. For centuries, Le Mont-St.-Michel resisted not only the ravages of sea water and weather but also the onslaught of the English in the Hundred Years' War by and the attempted invasions of the Huguenots.

By 1800, the monastery had lost its monks, and the island became a state prison. Not until 1874 was the restoration of the monastery begun, and today Le Mont-St.-Michel is a national shrine.

Along the Grande Rue, the steep main thoroughfare leading up to the monastery, there are stores, restaurants and even hotels. There is also a waxwork museum with figures associated with Le Mont-St.-Michel's history, and a maritime museum.

The monastery is illuminated at night and during the summer evenings it is the setting for *son-et-lumière* shows.

MORLAIX (244 A4)
FINISTÈRE *pop. 16,700*

Morlaix, on a narrow estuary of the English Channel, was once a prominent port; today's marine commerce consists of pleasure craft and a small fishing fleet. The town's most visible and impressive landmark is the two-story, 280-meter (919-foot) viaduct. The best place to view the structure, built in 1864, is from the place des Otages near the station.

Other places of interest are rue Grand, a street filled with venerable houses and old-fashioned stores; and the 16th-century Duchess Anne's House, with its ornately carved staircase.

MULHOUSE (245 E4)
HAUT-RHIN *pop. 108,400*

Despite industrialisation, Mulhouse retains traces of the former medieval fortified town that once existed. These include Bollwerk Tower, dwarfed now by the modern European Tower. The town hall, with its painted façade, is a fine example of Renaissance architecture. However, it is for its array of outstanding museums that Mulhouse mainly attracts visitors.

A zoo southeast of town offers views of the city, the Black Forest, the Jura Mountains and the Bernese Alps.

MUSÉE FRANÇAIS DU CHEMIN DE FER is the most important railway museum in continental Europe, with around 100 locomotives and carriages; railway memorabilia is displayed in a disused station.

MUSÉE DE L'IMPRESSION SUR ÉTOFFES, 3 rue des Bonnes Gens, displays printed fabrics from around the world produced since the mid-18th century. An information center contains 3 million samples of fabrics, designs and textile prints, with demonstrations of printing processes taking place in summer.

MUSÉE NATIONAL DE L'AUTOMOBILE, 192 avenue de Colmar, has an extensive collection of automobiles dating from the late 19th century. More than 500 vehicles are displayed, including the highly acclaimed Royale limousine.

NANCY (245 D4)
MEURTHE-ET-MOSELLE *pop. 99,400*
The historic capital of Lorraine, Nancy is well known for place Stanislas, an 18th-century architectural complex that has been listed by U.N.E.S.C.O. as a World Heritage Site. The square is dominated by the ornate Hôtel de Ville, with exits from the square guarded by richly gilded ironwork grilles. The 16th-century place de la Carrière has been completely renovated and is the site of the Musée Historique Lorrain, housed in the Ducal Palace.

NANTES (244 B3)
LOIRE-ATLANTIQUE *pop. 247,000*
Nantes is an Atlantic port on the Loire River, once France's most important port. The city boasts a fine Gothic cathedral, museums, concert halls, theatres, a planetarium, sports facilities and a university and is also known for its restaurants and pre-Lenten carnival. Jules Verne was born in Nantes in 1828.

CHÂTEAU DES DUCS DE BRETAGNE, place Marc Elder, is the former residence of the dukes of Brittany and where Gilles de Rais, Baron de Retz, the original Bluebeard, was imprisoned and subsequently condemned to death. It now houses three museums: of popular art, decorative art, and maritime history.

MUSÉE DES BEAUX-ARTS, 10 rue Georges Clémenceau, displays paintings from the 13th century to the present day and is considered one of the best fine-art museums in France.

MUSÉE JULES-VERNE, 3 rue de l'Hermitage, depicts the life of the author of *Journey to the Centre of the Earth*, *Twenty Thousand Leagues Under the Sea* and *Around the World in Eighty Days*.

NEVERS (245 C3)
NIÈVRE *pop. 42,000*
Nevers, at the junction of the rivers Loire and Nièvre, has been called the "Pointed Town" because of its many gables, belfries and towers. Ste.-Bernadette of Lourdes is buried in the convent of St.-Gildard.

The first French china factory was established in Nevers in the 16th century; its Musée Municipal Frédéric Blandin has fine exhibits of china and glass. Of architectural interest are the Romanesque church of St.-Etienne, as well as the Renaissance ducal palace.

NICE (245 E2) ★
ALPES-MARITIMES *pop. 342,400*
Colonized by the Greeks in the 4th century BC, Nice is a dynamic Riveria resort with hotels, golf courses and promenades. Its incomparable setting on the hill-framed curve of the Baie des Anges, and the region's benevolent climate, made this role almost inevitable.

Dominating the front is the château. A hill rather than a castle, it held the city's fortress until the 18th century. Shaded walks and lookout points accommodate today's invaders, with fine views from the top. On the eastern side of this hill is the harbor, which is always busy with yachts, merchant ships, fishing boats and the steamers that carry tourists and supplies to Corsica.

West of the château is the cramped and quaint Vieille Ville, where tall, shuttered houses crowd the crooked streets. The quarter also contains the Marché aux Fleurs and the 17th-century cathedral. The Paillon River forms the unofficial boundary that separates the Vieille Ville from the modern city. Along the 6-kilometer (4-mile) seafront is the flower-decked Promenade des Anglais, named after the English who underwrote its construction in the 19th century.

Lining the town side are the white-washed façades of hotels, private mansions and such public buildings as the Palais Masséna, now a museum of art and history. A shingle beach is on the sea side of the promenade and beyond this is the blue water that gave the Côte d'Azur its name.

Catering for sun-worshipers and fun-lovers the whole year, Nice is especially lively from January to April. Horse racing, regattas, theaters, casinos, nightclubs, and festivals vie for a share of the tourist's time and energy. The highlight of the season is the boisterous, but exhausting Carnival, which occurs during the two weeks preceding Lent, with processions, masked balls and fireworks.

Contrasting with Nice's coastal setting and winter warmth are the Alpine ski resorts which are less than 2 hours away by road. Only 12 kilometers (7 miles) away is Èze, with its feudal castle and gardens.

CIMIEZ is a fashionable suburb to the north of the harbor and the site of notable Roman ruins. Gladiatorial contests were once held in the arena, which

seated 4,000. Statues, sarcophagi and other objects from these sites are in the archaeological museum. The Gallo-Roman amphitheater in the gardens is the site of a jazz festival in July.

MUSÉE D'ART ET D'HISTOIRE, 65 rue de France, is housed in the elegant Palais Masséna. Provençal pottery, arms, local archives, 15th- and 16th-century local primitive art, Italian Renaissance paintings and works by the French Impressionists.

MUSÉE DES BEAUX-ARTS, 33 avenue des Baumettes, houses more than 600 sculptures and paintings by the creator of the modern poster, Jules Chéret, and smaller collections by Rude, Rodin, Fragonard and Raoul Dufy.

MUSÉE NATIONAL MESSAGE BIBLIQUE MARC CHAGALL, avenue du Docteur Ménard, contains a superb collection of Chagall's paintings, including the *Biblical Message* cycle, which encompasses 17 canvases. There are also sculptures, stained-glass windows, and tapestries on display.

NÎMES (245 D2) ★
GARD *pop. 128,500*
Nîmes was a Gaulish settlement before it fell to the Romans around 121 BC. Emperor Augustus looked favorably on the city and granted it many privileges, which in turn paved the way for a new prosperity and a thriving metropolis.

Nîmes is also the birthplace of the sturdy blue serge that became known as denim (*de Nîmes*), subsequently exported to the southern United States.

LES ARÈNES, dating from the 1st century, is one of the best-preserved Roman amphitheaters in the Roman world. It seats more than 20,000 spectators. Today bullfights and assorted programs are presented.

JARDINS DE LA FONTAINE, laid out in the 18th century, contain a magnificent display of both Roman and 18th-century architecture, including the Fountain of Nîmes, the Temple of Diana and the Magne Tower, built in 16 BC.

MAISON CARRÉE, a 1st-century Roman temple, encloses the Museum of Archaeology and its famed *Venus of Nîmes*.

NIORT (245 B3)
DEUX-SÈVRES *pop. 57,000*
Niort, the principal town of the province of Deux-Sèvres in western France, was once a Huguenot stronghold. Of interest are the Romanesque keep housing the Musée Ethnographique et Archéologique, and the nearby Roman town of Sanxay, between Niort and Poitiers via highways N11 and D5/A62.

West of Niort and extending to the ocean is the Marais Poitevin, a maze of arable and pasture fields sometimes called Green Venice.

Between the *conches* (large ditches) and channels lined by poplars, ashes,

---

FRENCH CUISINE

French cuisine epitomizes the complexities of the national character. Science, sensuality and creativity combine to produce, at its best, food fit for the gods. Every region has its specialties, refined from generation to generation.

---

alders and willows are many forms of wildlife, including eel, pike, heron, snipe, duck and kingfishers. This very appealing half-aquatic, half-countryside landscape can be discovered by a small flat-bottomed boat or pleasure boat.

ORANGE (245 D2)
VAUCLUSE *pop. 27,000*
Orange, in the Rhône Valley, traces its history back to the Roman Empire. Its Roman buildings include the Arc de Triomphe, dedicated to Julius Caesar in the 1st century AD, a theater and a Roman gymnasium. Dutch residents in the 17th century carried the name of

their town to America, where they founded a city in New Jersey.

THÉÂTRE ANTIQUE, place des Mounets, which dates from the 1st century BC, is one of the best surviving examples of a theater from early Mediterranean civilization with superb acoustics. It now offers dramatic performances in summer.

ORLÉANS (245 C4) ★
LOIRET *pop. 105,000*
Former royal city and capital of France during the 10th and 11th centuries, Orléans is above all remembered as the city liberated by the peasant heroine Joan of Arc. She drove the English from the city on May 8, 1429, ending an eight-month siege, and is honoured in annual events. World War II bombings destroyed many of the original structures associated with Joan of Arc. You can, however, retrace her steps in the 17th- to 19th-century Cathédrale de Ste.-Croix and the Maison de Jeanne d'Arc, a replica of the house (it was rebuilt in 1964) in which she stayed in 1429.

ST.-BENOÎT-SUR-LOIRE, 35 kilometers (22 miles) east, was one of the most celebrated intellectual centres of the Middle Ages. The Abbaye de Fleury is an 11th- to 13th-century Romanesque masterpiece, with a noteworthy chancel and a crypt containing the relics of St. Benoît.

SULLY-SUR-LOIRE, 42 kilometers (26 miles) east, includes an outstanding 14th-century château.

PAU (245 B1)
PYRÉNÉES-ATLANTIQUES *pop. 82,500*
On a steep hill overlooking the valley of the Gave de Pau, Pau is the birthplace of French King Henri IV. The town is a popular year-round resort and a good base for excursions into the Pyrénées. The boulevard des Pyrénées offers a spectacular mountain panorama. In the town's 13th-century château are the Musée Béarnais and a fine collection of Flemish and Gobelin tapestries.

PÉRIGUEUX (245 C2)
DORDOGNE *pop. 30,300*

On the left bank of the Isle River, Périgueux, the centre of Périgord, is known for its prehistoric relics and art. Rich prehistoric collections can be found in the Musée de Périgord. Of particular architectural interest is the mostly Byzantine Cathédrale St.-Front.

About 40 kilometers (25 miles) southeast is the village of Les Eyzies-de-Tayac, where the 30,000-year old Cro-Magnon skeleton and the first drawing of a mammoth were discovered.

PERPIGNAN (245 C1)
PYRÉNÉES–ORIENTALES *pop. 106.000*

Perpignan, near the Spanish border, is permeated with Catalan influence. Among noteworthy buildings are the Castillet, a 14th-century brick fortress, now a museum, the Cathédrale St.-Jean, a majestic example of medieval architecture; and the Palais des Rois de Majorque, a well-restored 13th- to 14th-century castle surrounded by ramparts.

South of Perpignan, from Argèles to the Spanish border, the Pyrénées drop sheer into the sea, creating a magnificent rocky coastline known as the Côte Vermeille. Prettiest of the resorts along this stretch is Collioure, a haunt of artists from the beginning of the century.

MUSÉE CASA PAIRAL (Musée Catalàn des Arts et Traditions Populaires), in Castillet, has exhibits relating to local history, agriculture and traditions.

PETIT TRAIN JAUNE, 49 kilometers (30 miles) east at Villefrance-de-Conflent, is the starting point of the open-air "Little Yellow Train" that trundles its way delightfully for over two hours through the Pyrénées to the border town La-Tour-de-Carol.

POITIERS (245 C3)
VIENNE *pop. 78,900*

Poitiers, regional capital and university center, is a charming city that contains many rich examples of Romanesque architecture. Of note are the churches of Notre-Dame-La-Grande, St.-Hilaire-le-Grand and the Bapistère St.-Jean; built in the 4th century and one of the oldest Christian buildings in France. There are splendid stained-glass windows in the Gothic Cathedral of St.-Pierre.

FUTURSCOPE, at Jaunay-Clan, 7 kilometers (4 miles) north, is a high-tech entertainment center featuring the Kinémax cinema, with a giant 600-square-meter (2,153-square-foot) screen; the Dynamic cinema, with seats that move; the 3-D cinema; the 180° cinema; the 360° cinema; the Omnimax 180° cinema; the Show-Scan 60-frame-a-second cinema; and the Gyrotour.

There are scores of attractions for children including an enchanted lake, magic carpet gardens of Europe and Aquascope.

LE PUY (245 D2)
HAUTE-LOIRE *pop. 21,800*

Le Puy occupies an extraordinary site on enormous volcanic peaks and plateau that jut from the green plain of Velay. The city is celebrated for its delicate lace; displays of which can be seen in the Musée Crozatier.

CATHÉDRALE NOTRE-DAME-DU-PUY was built on the site of a Roman temple.

Noted for its façade of multicolored lava and the Carolingian Bible of Theodulph, the 12th-century church is overshadowed by Notre-Dame-de-France, a statue that was cast in 1860 from the melted-down Russian cannon captured in the Battle of Sebastopol.

CHAPELLE ST.-MICHEL D'AIGUILLE a 10th-century chapel, is perched on a 82-meter (268-foot) volcanic needle; and it is a 268-step climb.

QUIMPER (244 A4)
FINISTÈRE *pop. 53,500*

The thriving commercial community of Quimper, on the Odet River, is known for its decorative pottery, a twin-towered cathedral, festivals and museums. Musée de la Faïence has 2,500 examples of the pottery (*faïence*) for which the town is famous. Musée Breton, in the former Bishop's Palace, has exhibits relating to Breton history and traditions.

RAMBOUILLET (245 C4)
YVELINES *pop. 24,300*
Rambouillet is a charming town noted for its 14th- to 18th-century château, one of the official residences of the president which can be visited when the president is not in residence. Also of interest are a sheep farm founded by Louis XVI, and nearby Rambouillet Forest.

REIMS (245 D4)
MARNE *pop. 180,600*
Reims, one of the ancient capitals of the province of Champagne, was badly damaged during both world wars, and much of its architecture is contemporary.

The region is famed for its prestigious and exclusive sparkling wines. The viticulture zone, with its special chalky sub-soil, is officially protected by French law covering 33,994 hectares (84,000 acres); more than 24,281 hectares (60,00 acres) are planted with vines.

BASILIQUE DE ST.-RÉMI IS an 11th-century abbey and now the city's museum of history and archaeology, with collections from prehistoric to medieval times, including a large military history section.

CATHÉDRALE NOTRE-DAME is illuminated inside and out in the evenings in summer. The cathedral's most well-known sculpture is the *Smiling Angel*.

CENTRE DE L'AUTOMOBILE FRANÇAISE, 84 avenue Georges Clemenceau, contains a collection of 150 old French motors, including some rarities, as well as over 2,000 toy automobiles.

MUSÉE DES BEAUX-ARTS, 8 rue Chanzy, is housed in an 18th-century former abbey and is one of the most highly acclaimed fine arts museums in France.

SALLE DE LA REDDITION, 12 rue Franklin Roosevelt, in Reims technical college, contains the room where the German surrender was signed on May 7, 1945. The walls are covered with the operational maps used by Eisenhower.

RENNES (2445 B4)
ÎLLE-ET-VILAINE *pop. 197,500*
Rennes was once the capital of Brittany and was almost destroyed by fire in 1720. All that remained was a corner of the city known as Les Lices, containing the Palais de Justice, the city's sole surviving monument from that time. The city has been rebuilt in a handsome classical style. The Jardin du Thabor botanical gardens and the collections of Renaissance and Breton works in the Musée des Beaux-Arts are of interest.

The Brittany Cemetery at St. James, 50 kilometers (31 miles) northeast, is the resting place for Americans who lost their lives during the 1944 Normandy and Brittany campaigns.

ÉCOMUSÉE DE LA BINTINAIS, an ancient farm south of Rennes, is now an open-air museum displaying local farming implements and machinery.

ROCAMADOUR (245C2)
LOT *pop. 600*
Tiny Rocamadour lies near a narrow gorge of the Alzou River. Its single street is lined with houses built in the Middle Ages to shelter pilgrims coming to pay homage to St. Amadour, to whom a chapel in the cliff is dedicated.

GOUFFRE DE PADIRAC, northwest of Rocamadour, is a series of galleries that have been carved by a subterranean river 103 meters (338 feet) below ground.

LA ROCHELLE (244 B3)
CHARENTE-MARITIME *pop. 71,100*
An ancient fortified town with a rich history connected with the sea, it was from here that pioneer ships set sail for the New World.

La Rochelle has many works of art and features several museums, including the Musée du Noveau-Monde (New World Museum) linking the town and the Americas. La Rochelle is also known for its yachting. To the south are the seaside resorts of Angoulins and Châtelaillon.

Just off the coast of La Rochelle, but connected to the mainland by a toll-bridge, is Île de Ré. This is an island of sandy beaches and flower-filled villages.

LA ROCHE-SUR-YON (244 B3)
VENDÉE *pop. 45,200*

The capital of the state (*département*) of Vendée, La Roche-sur-Yon was laid out by Napoléon Bonaparte during the early 19th century.

In place Napoléon, several neoclassical buildings surround an equestrian statue of the conqueror.

CHÂTEAU DE GILLE RAIS, 55 kilometers (34 miles) northeast at Tiffauges is a medieval castle with secret corridors, dungeons and a whispering gallery.

ECOMUSÉE, 45 kilometers (28 miles) northeast at Les Eppesses, features attractive Vendéen period villages as well as several craft activities.

The complex has been created around the 15th- and 16th-century Château de Puy du Fou.

MEMORIAL DE VENDÉE, 24 kilometers (15 miles) north at St.-Sulpice-le-Verdon; a 16th- and 17th-century fortified manor house, La Chabotterie, contains relics of the Vendée Wars which took place from 1793 and ended here in 1796.

RONCHAMP (245 E4)
HAUTE-SAÔNE *pop. 3,100*

CHAPELLE NOTRE-DAME-DU-HAUT, built on a hilltop site in the Jura between 1951 and 1955 by Swiss architect and city planner Le Corbusier, is one of the most affecting examples of 20th-century religious architecture producing a truly modern sacred space.

Its massive sculptured walls, sweeping roof and unusual dimensions create a dramatically modern contrast to the country's many medieval churches.

ROUEN (245 C4) ★
SEINE-MARITIME *pop. 102,700*

Settled by Celts, Ratumakos, as Rouen was first called, became Rotomagus to the Romans before evolving into Rouen in the Middle Ages. Its easily bridgeable location in a loop of the Seine River rendered the town important as a commercial and cultural center, but also made it the target of sieges and sackings.

The most memorable invasion was that of the English in the Hundred Years' War. After subjecting the city to a six-month siege in 1418–19, Les Goddones, as these unwelcome guests were called, settled down and stayed until 1449. It was during their occupation that national heroine Joan of Arc was brought to Rouen, interrogated and finally, in 1431, burned at the stake as a heretic.

The Wars of Religion in the following century brought additional woe, depressing economic activity and depopulating the city. Rouen's worst devastation, however, came during the 20th century when bombings in World War II reduced much of the commercial and industrial center to rubble.

Despite serious battering over the centuries, Rouen still earns its title of Ville Musée, or Museum City. This applies not only to the number and excellence of the city's museums, but also to the well-preserved quarters of medieval and Renaissance Rouen. The grandest monument is the cathedral. Several other churches are notable, including the Gothic St.-Maclou and 14th-century St.-Ouen. Ste.-Jeanne d'Arc contains a rare collection of 16th-century stained glass.

In the place du Vieux-Marché, now a busy, modern square, a stone marker indicates where the Maid of Orléans was burned at the stake. The Musée Jeanne d'Arc on the square and the Tour Jeanne d'Arc, where the French national heroine was briefly held, recall various episodes from her career as a leader. Nearby on rue de la Pie is another museum, the birthplace of 17th-century dramatist Pierre Corneille. Novelist Gustave Flaubert was born in Rouen; his house on rue de Lecat contains mementos of his family, and medical curiosities.

The Palais de Justice, a wedding cake of chiseled stone, is an unbridled expression of the grandeur of the French Renaissance. From the simpler 14th-century Beffroi the curfew is still rung nightly at 9pm. This belfry once housed the giant clock, Le Gros Horloge, which now occupies an adjacent arch. The belfry adjoining Gros Horloge can be entered by a staircase dating from 1447 housing a small museum of old clocks. From the top there is a view of the city.

In addition to its wealth of architectural treasures, Rouen has facilities for most conventional sports. Small passenger boats cruise the Seine, allowing a closer look at the city's large commercial port. If arriving by car, take time to drive around the Corniche de Rouen, a curved road that climbs the hills above the city to the southeast and provides bird's-eye views of the vista below.

CATHÉDRALE NOTRE-DAME, place de la Cathédrale, received its library, staircase and other finishing touches in the 15th century from the hand of master stonemason Guillaume Pontifs. Exterior features of the church are the two dissimilar towers of the west front, the richly decorated doorways and the great cast-iron spire which rises 151 meters (495 feet) above the city.

Worth viewing outside are the 14th-century sculptures in the transept gables; inside, the beautiful staircase leading to the library, and the 13th-century choir with its stained glass. A tomb containing the heart of Richard the Lionheart is in the ambulatory.

ARCHEVÊCHÉ PALAIS is separated from the cathedral by the picturesque Cour-des-Libraires. A part of the chapel where Joan of Arc was tried still remains.

ÉGLISE ST.-MACLOU, in the shadow of the cathedral, the church was was completed in 1517. Aside from its flamboyant Gothic architectural design, the building is noteworthy for its Renaissance door panels and organ.

MUSÉE DES ANTIQUITÉS, rue Thiers, is the largest fine arts museum in Normandy, boasting notable collections of Impressionist paintings and other art objects from the 16th to the 20th century.

MUSÉE DES BEAUX-ARTS, 198 rue Beauvoisine, is a particularly noteworthy museum in the cloister galleries of a former convent. In addition to the Greek, Egyptian and Oriental collections, there are good exhibits that trace the history of Rouen from its occupation by the Romans to its architectural and commercial zenith during the Renaissance.

MUSÉE LE SECQ DES TOURNELLES, adjoining the Musée des Beaux-Arts, is housed in the former Church of St.-Laurent. The displays, 12,000 pieces in total, including grilles, balconies, doorknockers and keys, form the largest collection of wrought iron in Europe.

St.-Bertrand-de-Comminges
(245 C1)
HAUTE-GARONNE *pop. 200*
Tiny St.-Bertrand-de-Comminges dates from a tribal settlement between 350 and 250 BC. In the 1st century, the Romans discovered the town's thermal springs; today many Roman relics can be viewed, including the forum baths, amphitheater and basilica.

The present settlement was founded on a hill in the 12th century when St.-Bernard constructed a cathedral and monastery here. Originally built in Romanesque style, the structure underwent alterations between the 14th and 16th centuries. Several old houses also remain; of particular interest are the two beside the town gate, which itself is a remnant from the 1st century.

GROTTOES DE GARGAS, 7 kilometers (4 miles) northwest, are caves that contain paintings of animals and stencils of human hands thought to be around 30,000 years old.

ST.-ÉTIENNE (245 D2)
LOIRE *pop. 199,400*
St.-Étienne was once an important industrial city in the center of a rich metallurgical basin. One of its several schools is devoted to the study of mining. Today, the city manufactures such diverse products as silk and chocolates. St.-Étienne also has several fine museums; a chamber of commerce housing works of art and the fine gardens of Rez. A church bearing the city's name dates from the 15th century.

MUSÉE D'ART ET D'INDUSTRIE is devoted to the past industry of St.-Étienne and includes a working mine and a collection of contemporary art.

MUSÉE D'ART MODERNE exhibits a wide variety of modern art, including works by Pablo Picasso and Henri Matisse.

ST.-GERMAIN-EN-LAYE
YVELINES *pop. 39,900*
St.-Germain-en-Laye is a popular vacation spot for Parisians. One of its main attractions is a Renaissance château built by François I, now housing the Musée des Antiquités Nationales, one of the world's premier archaeological collections including the first known image of a human face dating from over 22,000 years ago. The long terrace and beautiful gardens were designed by André Le Nôtre. The terrace is known for its superb view of Paris, the valley of the Seine and the surrounding countryside. Mary Stuart, Queen of Scots, lived in this château until her marriage to the French Dauphin, and James II spent his last years of exile there.

MUSÉE DU PRIEURÉ, 2 rue Maurice-Denis, is devoted to the work of the late 19th-century French artists. The house containing the museum has a varied history. In 1678, the Marchioness of Montespan had it built for deprived people; in 1681, the house was turned into the Royal General Hospital by Louis XIV and retained this status until 1803, when it became a warehouse and painter's studio.

From 1875 to 1905 the house was a retirement home for Jesuit fathers; in 1910, the painter Maurice Denis came to live and work at the property, acquired it in 1914 and began the development of the art collection.

ST.-JEAN-DE-LUZ
PYRÉNÉES-ATLANTIQUES *pop. 13,000*
As well as being a picturesque Basque summer resort, St.-Jean-de-Luz is the chief tuna port of France. In 1660, in the Cathédrale St.-Jean Baptiste, Louis XIV married María Theresa of Spain; the Musée du Souvenir contains their marriage contract. Across the harbor, Ciboure is the birthplace of early 20th-century composer, Maurice Ravel.

ST.-MALO (244 B4)
ÎLLE-ET-VILAINE *pop. 48,100*
Bordered by the sprawling modern city, the ancient citadel, or Ville Close, lies on a rocky island which is connected to the mainland by a causeway called the Sillon. It was from this site that mariner Jacques Cartier sailed to discover the St. Lawrence River. The island's location and fortifications made it an ideal pirate stronghold. The medieval Tour Quic-en-Groigne is a museum displaying wax figures illustrating events in history and also contains souvenirs of the buccaneers who frequented the island.

Île du Grand Bé, where the desolate tomb of French romantic author François René de Châteaubriand is located, can be reached at low tide. The tides of St.-Malo Bay have a range that ranks among the world's greatest, sometimes extending to a difference of 13 meters (43 feet).

ST.-OMER (245 C5)
PAS-DE-CALAIS *pop. 14,400*
St.-Omer, an elegant town on the banks of the Aa River, is surrounded by marshland and is the market garden of the region. Highlights of the town include the Grand Palace flanked by 17th- and 18th-century merchants' houses with a market held at the palace every Saturday. The Notre Dame Cathedral, built from the 13th to 16th centuries, contains many notable works of art. The 18th-century Hôtel Sandelin houses a museum, that displays Flemish, Dutch and French paintings from the 15th century as well as tapestries and archaeological finds. At Argues is the renowned glass and crystal works.

ST.-RÉMY-DE-PROVENCE
BOUCHES-DU-RHÔNE *pop. 9,300*
In St.-Rémy-de-Provence are the ruins of the ancient Greco-Roman town Glanum. Among the 1st-century structures still standing are the municipal arch and the mausoleum erected in honor of the grandsons of Emperor Augustus. Van Gogh came to St.-Rémy to convalesce after cutting off his ear. The 16th-century astrologer and prophet Nostradamus was born in the town; his predictions are still studied world-wide.

ST.-TROPEZ (245 E1)
VAR *pop. 5,800*
An old Provençal town on the Riviera, St.-Tropez was first popular as an artists' colony and now attracts yachtsmen and tourists. "St. Trop," as it is known, became one of the world's top spots for displays of fashion and fashionable behavior in the 1950s and 1960s. Though losing some of its exclusivity, the heart of the resort, the Vieux Port, retains exorbitant restaurants, glitzy yachts and attracts famous people. The 16th-century citadel has a fine view over the town. A festival of music, dancing and flowers is in mid-May.

MUSÉE DE L'ANNONCIADE, place Georges Grammont, exhibits a collection of early 20th-century works by such artists as Paul Signac, Georges Rouault, Henri Matisse and Raoul Dufy.

STE.-MÈRE-ÉGLISE
MANCHE *pop. 1,600*
The market town of Ste.-Mère-Église was the target of the U.S. 82nd Airborne Division's parachute drop on June 5, 1944; it was the first French town to be liberated during the Battle of Normandy. The first milestone on Liberty Road, the road taken by the Americans as they moved inland, is outside the town hall.

MUSÉE DU DÉBARQUEMENT À UTAH BEACH, in Ste.-Marie-du-Mont to the southeast, illustrates the plight of American troops in the fierce battle of Utah Beach. A glassed viewing gallery overlooks the battle site.

MUSÉE DES TROUPES AEROPORTÉES, in the center of the town, is in the form of a parachute and documents the story of the town's liberation by American troops on June 5, 1944.

LES STES.-MARIES-DE-LA-MER
BOUCHES-DU-RHÈNE *pop. 2,200*
Unofficial capital of the Camargue region, Stes.-Maries-de-la-Mer is known for its *course libre* and *abrivado*, variations on the bloodless bullfight popular in Pamplona, Spain.

On the feast days of May 24–25, gypsies from throughout Europe converge to worship their patron saint Sarah. Legend claims her as servant to the Biblical Mary Salome and Mary Jacobaeus, for whom the town was named.

The gypsies carry the statue of Sarah to the sea where it is bathed. The 12th-century fortified church, center of the pilgrimage, contains relics of the French Revolution.

SALINS-LES-BAINS
JURA *pop. 3,600*
Salins takes its name from the saltworks responsible for the town's prosperity.

FRANCE

FRANCE

Today thermal waters are its main attraction with fountains set against a backdrop of historic monuments.

SALINE ROYALE, in the village of Arc-et-Senans, 20 kilometers (12 miles) northwest of Salins-les-Bains, is an exceptional piece of industrial architecture. Built in 1775, but not used for salt production since 1895, it is listed on U.N.E.S.C.O.'s Register of World Monuments.

SARLAT-LA-CANÉDA
DORDOGNE *pop. 9,900*
Yellow ocher stone houses and quaint narrow streets have been carefully restored to preserve the old-world charm of Sarlat-La-Canéda, a typical French country town. *Pâté de foie gras* and walnuts, the town's specialties, can be found in local restaurants.

Sarlat-La-Canéda offers a lively market every Saturday, a drama festival in July and August and regular concerts in the 16th-century cathedral. Places of interest are the cathedral and the Lanterne des Morts ("Lantern of the Dead"), a 12th-century cylindrical tower that was probably built to commemorate the miracles performed in the town by St. Bernard. Of architectural note are the hôtels Maleville and Plamon, the latter a private home of local cloth merchants.

Near Montignac, 25 kilometers (16 miles) northwest, the Grotte de Lascaux contains some of the best-preserved prehistoric cave paintings ever discovered. A replica cave, Lascaux II, nearby, show the authentically copied drawings.

SAUMUR (245 B3)
MAINE-ET-LOIRE *pop. 30,300*
Saumur, in the château region of the Loire Valley, has a distinguished history as a fortified medieval city. Today it is renowned for its riding school and 14th-century château. Heavily damaged during World War II, Saumur has been rebuilt. It is a prestigious wine center, with the sparkling wine caves, in suburban St.-Hilaire-St.-Florent of particular

interest. About 16 kilometers (10 miles) southwest at Doué-La-Fontaine lies the highest concentration of troglodyte dwellings in France. The caves now house a zoo, where many endangered species are kept.

CHÂTEAU, which dates from the 14th century, dominates the valley with its elaborate towers and walls. There are two museums are in the grounds.

Musée Des Arts Décoratifs contains collections of porcelain and ceramics, Limoges enamel, tapestries and a variety of other furnishings.

Musée Du Cheval chronicles the history of horsemanship displaying antique saddles, stirrups, bits and engravings.

VILLAGE TROGLODYTIQUE, about 17 kilometers (11 miles) west at Rochemenier, is an underground troglodyte village. Many of the caves were occupied in the Middle Ages. Several underground houses were inhabited druing the 19th century, and a few are still used.

STRASBOURG (245 E4) ★
BAS-RHIN *pop. 252,300*
Originally Celtic, briefly Roman and for much of its existence Germanic, old Strasbourg, on the Ill River, wears its centuries gracefully.

La Petite France is the name given to the well-preserved and pedestrianized medieval quarter in the southwest section of the city. Its fine high-gabled gingerbread houses on narrow streets and canals date from the 16th and 17th centuries, when millers, tanners and fishermen thronged the area.

The area is best viewed from the *ponts couverts* (covered bridges), which are no longer covered, and better still from the walkway on top of the Barrage Vauban.

Strasbourg's rose-colored cathedral recalls the city's early ecclesiastical importance and the several centuries of struggles between bishops and citizens. The river port, east of the city on the Rhine, points to Strasbourg's long-time role as inland port and trading center.

Known for its printing industry, Strasbourg was the site of Johann Gutenberg's early experiments with movable type. A statue of the 15th-century inventor stands in the square named after him. Seven centuries earlier, two nobles took the Strasbourg Oath; the text of this *Serment de Strasbourg* is considered the oldest written French document.

Also associated with the town is the French national anthem, composed in 1792 and later given its southern French name *La Marseillaise*. Important today as an industrial and administrative enclave, Strasbourg is the headquarters of both the multinational Council of Europe and European Parliament. Gourmets know the city for Alsatian cuisine in general and *pâté de foie gras* in particular.

The Parc de l'Orangerie contains a beautiful formal garden laid out in honor of Empress Joséphine in 1804, together with a zoo and facilities for bowling and canoeing.

Boat trips are available along the Rhine and the Ill rivers. A mini-train makes daily tours of Strasbourg's old section in summer.

CATHÉDRALE NOTRE-DAME, with its 142-meter (464-foot) spire, dominates the city. Built between the 11th and 15th centuries in Romanesque to High Gothic styles, it has fine stained glass, statuary and windows with lacelike tracery. It is most visited for the 19th-century astronomical clock whose figures spring to life at 12:30pm. A figure representing Death strikes the hour; Christ appears and blesses his Apostles; and a cock crows in memory of Peter's denial. Arrive by 12:15pm for a good view.

CHÂTEAU DES ROHAN, the former palace of the bishops dating from the 18th century, now contains several museums. One has local archaeological finds while another is devoted to decorative arts.

Best known is the Musée des Beaux-Arts, with works from the 14th to 19th centuries by Giotto, El Greco, Peter Paul Rubens and Rembrandt. Also displayed is the mechanism of the city cathedral's original astronomical clock, which was replaced in 1842.

MUSÉE ALSACIEN, 23–25 quai Saint-Nicolas, contains displays relating to religious art, viticulture and clog, rope and artificial flower making.

MUSÉE DE L'ŒUVRE NOTRE-DAME, 3 place du Château, houses much of the art assembled in the cathedral over the centuries, as well as exhibits tracing the evolution of distinctive Alsatian art from the 11th to 17th centuries.

TOULOUSE (245 C1)
HAUTE-GARONNE *pop. 358,700*
Known for its rose-red brick buildings, Toulouse's beginnings can be traced to the Roman period. It was capital of the Visigoths through much of the 5th century and was the chief town of the Carolingian kingdom of Aquitaine.

Toulouse contains many medieval churches, notably the Cathédrale St.-Étienne and the Romanesque basilica of St.-Sernin. The church of Notre-Dame-du-Taur has an interesting gabled façade with ornamentation achieved entirely through the use of brick. There are also opulent Renaissance and 16th-century buildings. Many are houses built by merchants who prospered from the discovery of obtaining dye from the woad plant; today they operate as hotels.

Toulouse is rich in museums. The Musée des Augustins, housed in a former convent, contains sculptures and religious paintings by Peter Paul Rubens and Eugène Delacroix. The Musée Paul Dupuy displays a variety of works by artisans from the medieval period to the present; included are coins, clocks and a re-creation of an early 17th-century pharmacy. Toulouse also has more than 100 gardens, including the Royal Gardens, created in 1754.

Modern Toulouse has prospered from extraordinary development in aeronautics and the aerospace industry leading to the development of the Hermes space

FRANCE

shuttle. The city also serves as a trading center well situated between the Mediterranean and the Aquitaine basin, marketing its farm products.

TOURS (245 C3)
INDRE-ET-LOIRE *pop. 129,500*

An important center of learning and commerce since the Middle Ages, Tours, capital of Touraine, is a popular stopping place for travelers exploring the Loire Valley.

The well-restored 15th-and 16th-century half-timbered houses around the place Plumereau are of special interest, as is the beautiful Gothic Renaissance Cathédrale St.-Gatien, with a collection of fine stained glass.

Tours has a number of excellent museums. The Hôtel Gouin, formerly a stately Renaissance dwelling, houses archaeological finds from the time when Tours was a prosperous Roman city. The Musée des Beaux-Arts is located in the 18th-century Bishop's Palace, and two other museums are devoted to craft guilds and wine-making.

AZAY-LE-RIDEAU, 28 kilometers (17 miles) southwest, is well known for its 16th-century Renaissance château, which is surrounded by parkland and rests partly on the bank of the Indre River. Fine furnishings, tapestries and an impressive main staircase highlight the interior.

CHÂTEAU ET JARDIN DE VILLANDRY, about 15 kilometers (9 miles) southwest, is a 16th-century castle overlooking magnificent Renaissance gardens laid out on three levels.

TROYES (245 D4)
AUBE *pop. 59,300*

A prosperous city on a tributary of the Seine, Troyes was once capital of the Champagne province.

Merchants traveled to Troyes in the Middle Ages to attend trade fairs and in the 16th century to buy hosiery, which is still manufactured.

The houses built during Troyes' golden age can still be seen in La Ruelle aux Chats. Here are half-timbered Renaissance dwellings with turrets and porch roofs. Troyes also has many noteworthy churches. Of particular interest are the Cathédral of St.-Peter et St.-Paul, with its stained-glass windows and rich treasury, and the churches of Ste.-Madeleine and St.-Jean.

Floodlights illuminate the cathedral during the Cathédrale de Lumière spectacle from June to September.

MAISON DE L'OUTIL ET DE LA PENSÉE OUVRIÈRE, 7 rue de la Trinité, exhibits a vast collection of tools and books used by French craftsmen through the ages.

MUSÉE D'ART MODERNE, Old Episcopal Palace, place St.-Pierre, features more than 2,000 works of French art dating from 1850 to 1950.

Exhibits include paintings, drawings, sculptures, ceramic pieces, glassware and tapestries, as well as African and Oceanic art. The garden area displays pieces of sculpture amid pleasant surroundings.

MUSÉE DES BEAUX-ARTS, D'ARCHÉOLOGIE ET MUSÉE D'HISTOIRE NATURELLE is in the former Abbaye de St.-Loup. Displays include weapons and gold jewelry from the tomb of a barbarian chief and a large archaeological collection.

MUSÉE DE LA BONNETERIE chronicles the history of Troyes' hosiery industry with old looms, knitting machines and displays of stockings, gloves, bathing costumes and underwear.

VAL D'ISÈRE (245 E3)
SAVOIE *pop. 1,700*
elev. 1,840m (6037ft)

One of the best equipped European ski resorts in eastern France, Val d'Isère is the home of the Low Countries' ski championships.

The season usually continues through May on slopes that can sometimes rise as high as 3,749 meters (12,300 feet).

VERDUN (245 D4)
MEUSE *pop. 20,700*

Verdun is often considered a "warrior town" both because of its location in northeastern France and its long history in military affairs. The most noted occasion was in 1916, when the town's gallant resistance to a long and cruel siege saved Paris in one of the bloodiest battles of World War I. Tributes to this resistance are *Défence*, a group of statuary by Auguste Rodin, and the *Monument to Victory and the Dead* by Jean Boucher. Excursions can be made to the battlefields.

The Meuse-Argonne Cemetery lies 35 kilometers (22 miles) northwest at Romagne-sous-Montfaucon. This is the last resting place of the largest number of American military men killed in Europe, most of whom died in the Meuse–Argonne offensive of World War I.

About 44 kilometers (27 miles) southeast is the St.-Mihiel Cemetery at Thiaucourt, where over 4,000 American soldiers who died between 1914 and 1918 are buried.

MUSÉE ALPHONSE-GEORGE POULAIN, 12 rue du Pont, is housed in a 15th-century mansion and contains collections of French and American Impressionist art and specialises in animal art.

VERSAILLES (245 C4) ★
YVELINES *pop. 87,800*

CHÂTEAU DE VERSAILLES, which dates from the 17th century, is the magnificent centrepiece of the former royal city of Versailles. Built by Le Van and Jules Hardouin-Mansart for Louis XIV, this sumptuous prototype of French classical architecture has been the setting for many dramatic and ironic events – the meeting of the Estates General in 1789, the proclamation of the German Empire in 1871, the direction of France's government 1871–9 and, finally, the signing of the 1919 Treaty of Versailles.

The most interesting parts of the building are its historic first-floor apartments, which include the King's Grand Apartment, with six opulent drawing rooms; the Hall of Mirrors, a beautiful extravagance from the days when mirror glass was extremely expensive; the apartments of Louis XIV and Louis XV; and the Queen's Great and Small Apartments. All of these rooms are decorated with numerous works of art by the reigning masters of the period.

The Musée Historique in the palace has exhibits depicting French history from the 15th century; the 17th- and 18th-century rooms house portraits of the royal family and the court of Versailles. Parts of the château are now being restored, a project that will take place over 50 years.

The symmetry of the largest palace gardens in Europe is impressive. They contain statues, fountains and the Trianon, two more modest residences; Grand Trianon was built for Louis XIV, and Petit Trianon for Louis XV.

The palace can be reached from Paris by car (take Autoroute de l'Ouest), by an organised bus excursion, or by train.

VICHY (245 D3)
ALLIER *pop. 27,700*

Vichy is a world-renowned spa that dates from Roman times; it is vibrant with flowers and parks. Festivals, horse racing, sailing, golf, swimming, rowing, tennis and riding are available in season. Vichy's success as a spa town really took off in the 19th century and the famed Vichy water is bottled in a state factory near the railroad station. The Musée de Vichy and the Maison du Missionaire are also worth a visit.

VIENNE (245 D2)
ISÈRE *pop. 29,500*

Vienne was the "Vienna Pulchra" of the Roman poet Martial, and there are numerous vestiges of the beautiful Vienna of Roman times. Among the many ruins are the Temple of Augustus and Livia, the Temple of Sybil, the Circus Pyramid, aqueducts and a theater. Interesting medieval monuments include the 6th-century church of St-Pierre and the 7th-century tomb of St.-Léonien.

THINGS TO KNOW

- **AREA:** 1.8 square kilometers (7 square miles).
- **POPULATION:** 28,000
- **CAPITAL:** Monaco
- **LANGUAGE:** French
- **RELIGION:** Largely Roman Catholic
- **ECONOMY:** Tourism, light industry; stamp sales; cosmetics; chemicals.
- **PASSPORT:** Required for U.S. citizens.
- **VISA:** Not required for up to 3 months.
- **DUTY-FREE ITEMS:** 400 cigarettes, 50 cigars or 500 grams of tobacco; 1 liter of spirits (over 22 percent proof) or 2 liters (up to 22 percent proof) and 2 liters of wine; two still cameras with 10 rolls of film; one movie camera with 10 rolls of film; video equipment, which should be declared verbally to customs on entry.
- **CURRENCY:** The unit of currency is the French *franc*, 1 franc=100 *centimes*. No limit on import or export of foreign currency, but for amounts exceeding 50,000 *francs*, visitors should complete a currency declaration form upon arrival.
- **BANK OPENING HOURS:** 9am–noon and 2–4pm Monday–Friday.
- **STORE OPENING HOURS:** 9am–noon and 2:30–7pm Monday–Saturday; many stores are closed Monday morning.
- **BEST BUYS:** Cosmetics, costume jewelry, dolls, paintings, antiques.
- **PUBLIC HOLIDAYS:** January 1; January 27 (Festival of St. Dévote); Good Friday; Easter Monday; May 1 (Labor Day); Ascension Day; Whitmonday; Corpus Christi; July 14 (National Day, Bastille); August 15 (Assumption Day); November 1 (All Saints Day); November 19 (National Day); December 8 (Immaculate Conception); December 25–26.
- **NATIONAL TOURIST OFFICE:** Tourist and Convention Bureau 845 Third Ave, 19th Floor, New York, NY 10022 Tel: 800/753-9696
- **AMERICAN EMBASSY:** 2 Avenue Gabriel 75382 Paris 8, France Tel: 01 42 96 12 02

MONACO
(245 E2)

HISTORY

The Phoenicians and Greeks were among the first settlers of Monaco, and the area passed from one ruler to another until 1297, when the Grimaldi family took control. The current ruler is Prince Rainier III, who was married to the movie star Grace Kelly – tragically killed in a car accident in 1982. Their children are Prince Albert and the princesses Caroline and Stephanie. True Monegasques speak an ancient Italian dialect (Monegasco) as well as French, and account for less than 16 percent of the population.

SPORTS AND RECREATION

Once a popular destination for aristocrats, Monte Carlo now has over 2 million visitors a year. Attractions include the Grand Prix, a world-famous car race held through the streets of Monte Carlo in May, and the Fête du Prince, on November 19, with fireworks, pageants, golf tournaments, and yacht races as well as dining, dancing and gambling.

GETTING AROUND

Monaco is noted for a mild climate and magnificent scenery. At the foot of the Maritime Alps, it can be reached by air, land, sea or road, along the Route de la Moyenne Corniche, extending west to Nice, in France, and east to the Italian border. Insurance requirements and traffic regulations are the same as in France.

ACCOMMODATIONS

Monaco classifies hotels with one to four stars. Many of the most luxurious hotels are in Monte Carlo. Breakfast is not usually included in the price of a room. There are no campgrounds in Monaco.

TIPPING

Nearly every bill you are handed will include a gratuity charge, so unless the service is particularly outstanding do not leave a tip.

PLACES OF INTEREST

★ HIGHLIGHTS ★

Jardin Exotique	(see p.301)
Musée Océanographique	(see p.301)
Palais du Prince	(see p.301)
Casino	(see p.301)

MONACO
pop. 2,000

The historic center of the principality is its diminutive capital Monaco, perched on a rocky peninsula 60 meters (196 feet) above the sea. Guarded by ramparts, narrow streets climb the slope to the Prince's Palace high above the sea. The Romanesque Cathedral of St.-Nicolas contains works of art by Bréa.

JARDIN EXOTIQUE ★ contains thousands of species of cacti, flowering plants and palm trees. The Grotte de l'Observatoire, an underground prehistoric cave, and the Musée d'Anthropologie Préhistorique can be visited.

MUSÉE OCÉANOGRAPHIQUE ET AQUARIUM ★, avenue St.-Martin, is an architectural masterpiece dedicated to the marine sciences. The 90-tank aquarium is considered one of the best in Europe.

PALAIS DU PRINCE ★ can be visited when the Prince is not at home. Rooms on view are the gallery with 16th-century frescoes, the Louis XV and the Mazarin salons, the Throne Room, the main Courtyard of Honor, and the Ste.-Marie Tower. The changing of the guard takes place in the square daily at 11:55am.

LA CONDAMINE
pop. 11,000

La Condamine is Monaco's residential district and business center. Numerous exotic yachts are moored in the harbor. The local church is dedicated to Ste.-Dévote, a 3rd-century martyr.

MONTE-CARLO
pop. 9,500

Monte-Carlo is synonymous with the jet set; every year the *crème de la crème* of the business and entertainment world gather to bask in the sun, gamble at the Casino and watch each other. There are many excellent hotels, restaurants and several theaters. The Monte-Carlo Sporting-Club, with its dance clubs and gambling salons, contributes to an unsurpassed nightlife. The city's gardens, parks and beaches enhance its natural beauty.

CASINO ★, famed as the world's largest, this is Monte-Carlo's main attraction. Established in the 19th century, the grandiose building is replete with marble, gilt mirrors and crystal chandeliers. There is an admission charge to both public and private rooms. Minimum age for admission is 21 and passports must be presented. The Casino also offers several bars, a cabaret and restaurant. The atrium leads into the Salle Garnier Opera House.

EXPOSITION DE LA COLLECTION DE VOITURES ANCIENNES DE S.A.S. LE PRINCE DE MONACO, Terrasses de Fontvieille, displays the prince's private collection of vintage and classic automobiles and will appeal to all ages.

MUSÉE DE POUPÉES ET AUTOMATES, 17 avenue Princesse Grace, is housed in the Sauber Villa, designed by the noted architect Charles Garnier. The fine doll collection dates from the 18th and 19th centuries. The miniature furnishings and rose garden also are well worth seeing.

AUTOMOBILE CLUB

L'Automobile club de Monaco is at 23 boulevard Albert 1er, Monte-Carlo. Not all auto clubs offer full travel services to AAA members.

GERMANY

ALTHOUGH UNITED, GERMANY IS STILL DIVIDED INTO THE PROSPEROUS WEST AND THE STRUGGLING EAST. THE SYMBOL OF THAT DIVISION, BERLIN, NEVERTHELESS REMAINS ONE OF THE MOST EXCITING CITIES IN EUROPE.

THERE ARE MANY OTHER ATTRACTIVE, HISTORIC CITIES, TOO, FROM HAMBURG IN THE NORTH TO MUNICH IN THE SOUTH. MUNICH'S LIVELY *OKTOBERFEST* BEER FESTIVAL BELIES THE FACT THAT IT IS ONE OF EUROPE'S MOST CULTURED CITIES, WITH ENVIABLE MUSEUMS AND GALLERIES. CLOSE BY, THE BAVARIAN LAKES AND THE SNOW-CAPPED ALPS ARE REGIONS OF GREAT BEAUTY. FARTHER WEST IS THE MOUNTAINOUS BLACK FOREST, SOURCE OF THE DANUBE, WHILE TO THE NORTH, THE RHINE RIVER CUTS THROUGH ITS GORGE, OVER-LOOKED BY MAGNIFICENT HISTORIC CASTLES.

Left SPECTACULAR NEUSCHWANSTEIN, SET AGAINST A MOUNTAIN BACKDROP
Above left BRASS BANDS PLAY AT THE *OKTOBERFEST* IN MUNICH
Above right STEINS ARE POPULAR IN PASSAU

THINGS TO KNOW

- **AREA:** 357,000 square kilometers (137,838 square miles)
- **POPULATION:** 80,300,000
- **CAPITAL:** Berlin
- **LANGUAGE:** German
- **RELIGION:** Some three-quarters of the population of Germany is Christian, of these, half are Protestant and half Roman Catholic. Every town has a church, and religious festivals are an important part of the calendar (see *Public Holidays* p.306). Other religions are represented in the cities; for addresses of local places of worship, ask at the tourist office.
- **ECONOMY:** Industry and agriculture. Steel, machinery (Ruhr Valley, Berlin, etc.), vehicles, chemicals, textiles. Shipbuilding at North Sea ports; smaller skilled industries in the southwest. Cattle, potatoes, grains, sugar beets, fruit, wine. Transportation, communications, tourism, energy production (coal, hydroelectric, oil-fired, nuclear).
- **ELECTRICITY:** The current in Germany is 220 volts, 50 cycles. Plugs are the round two-pin type.
- **PASSPORT:** Required for U.S. citizens.
- **VISA:** Not required for stays up to three months.
- **DUTY-FREE ITEMS:** 200 cigarettes or 100 cigarillos or 50 cigars or 250 grams of tobacco; 1 liter of spirits or 2 liters of spirits with less than 22 percent alcohol; 2 liters of wine; 500 grams of coffee or 200 grams of instant coffee; cameras and film in reasonable amounts for personal use; 50 grams of perfume; 0.25 liter of cologne.
- **CURRENCY:** The currency unit, the German *Mark*, is divided into 100 *Pfennigs*. Coins come in 1, 2, 5, 10 and 50 *Pfennigs* and 1,2 and 5 *Marks*; notes in 5, 10, 20, 50, 100, 200, 500 and 1,000 *Mark* denominations. Because of currency fluctuations, the exchange rate is subject to frequent change. There is no limit on the import or the export of German or foreign currency.

HISTORY

Germany was originally settled by numerous tribes; the Franks controlled the area when Charlemagne was crowned emperor of the Holy Roman Empire in AD 800. Feudalism hastened the empire's disintegration into regional duchies and kingdoms. In the early Middle Ages, merchants of several German towns, most notably Hamburg, Bremen and Lübeck, formed the Hanseatic League to promote mercantile interests. Their influence on commerce was widespread and is still reflected in the old quarters of these cities.

By the time Frederick II ascended the throne in 1740, the stage was set for the rise of the Kingdom of Prussia. The ruler had inherited a small but flourishing empire. Under his direction, the building of theaters, palaces and monuments transformed Berlin from a provincial city on the Spree River into a cultural center that attracted the world's aristocrats.

In the early 19th century Prussia and the other German states, as well as most of Europe, became part of Napoléon Bonaparte's French empire until 1813. Germany existed as a loose federation of states until 1848, when the popular desire for more unified rule led to widespread civil unrest. It was not until 1871, however, that Otto von Bismarck, the "Iron Chancellor," molded these small states into a great empire that assumed an increasing role in international affairs. The empire crashed with Germany's defeat in World War I.

The Nazi Party came to power for several reasons: lack of confidence in the Weimar Republic, Germany's first foray into democratic government; resentment over the severe terms of the Treaty of Versailles, which took German land and natural resources and demanded the payment of enormous reparations; and concern over the Depression. Named chancellor by President Paul von Hindenburg in 1933, Adolf Hitler took complete control of the government in 1934 and pursued an imperialistic policy that by 1939 had resulted in war.

At its defeat in 1945, Germany was divided into four zones of occupation: American, English, French and Russian. The American, English and French zones consolidated in 1949 to form the Bundesrepublik Deutschland (Federal Republic of Germany), with Bonn as its capital. The Soviet zone became the Deutsche Demokratische Republik (German Democratic Republic).

Under Konrad Adenauer, chancellor from 1949 to 1963, West Germany embarked on a full-scale economic recovery through a combination of U.S. aid and a modified version of free-enterprise capitalism. Meanwhile, East Germany's highly centralized and oppressive Communist regime also experienced revivification but lagged behind the more successful West Germany. In 1961 the Berlin Wall was erected literally overnight and marked the end of free movement between East and West Germany.

The call for change was not heard until 1989, when the dramatic increase in economic defectors from East Germany, reforms in neighboring Poland and the former Soviet Union's *glasnost* policy

---

AUTOMOBILE CLUBS
Allgemeiner Deutscher Automobil-Club (A.D.A.C., National German Automobile Club), Am Westpark 8, 81373 München, and Automobilclub von Deutschland (A.v.D., Automobile Club of Germany), Lyoner Strasse 16, Frankfurt, have branches in various cities throughout Germany. The symbol ▲ beside a city name indicates the presence of an AAA-affiliated automobile club branch. Not all auto clubs offer full travel services to AAA members.

---

resulted in relaxed travel restrictions and emigration policies with Eastern Europe. The Berlin Wall began to tumble in late 1989; the unification of the two Germanys became official on October 3, 1990. The Federal Republic of Germany, with Berlin as its capital, continues to consolidate its status as one of Europe's most prosperous nations.

FOOD AND DRINK

The cities of Hamburg, Braunschweig (Brunswick) and Frankfurt have given their names to familiar meat specialties, and much German food reflects regional modes of preparation. In eastern Germany the food is hearty and simple; pork, fish, potatoes, sausages and chicken are among the staples. Restaurants can be crowded at peak times.

Western Germany is known for its dark breads, and Bavarian beer is world-renowned. Many areas also produce good local beer that is drunk with *Schnapps*, another German favorite. Of the many white wines produced in Germany, perhaps the best known are those from the Rhine and Mosel regions.

SPORTS AND RECREATION

Germans are great sports enthusiasts. Nearly every town of substantial size has a stadium and athletic field for soccer games and track meets. Soccer, called *Fussball*, is the national sport. Other popular athletic pursuits are swimming, tennis, sailing, boxing, hunting, mountain climbing and skiing. Automobile, motorcycle and bicycle races are also common. Germany has some excellent water sports and winter recreation facilities, and its many lakes and streams provide good fishing. Golf courses are open to tourists in almost a dozen cities.

GETTING AROUND

To fly direct, there are international airports at Berlin (northeast), München or Munich (south), Düsseldorf (west), and Hamburg (south). Ferry services operate from other European countries.

- **BANK OPENING HOURS:**
  8:30am–12:30pm and 1:30–3:30pm
  Monday–Friday, to 5:30pm Thursday.
- **STORE OPENING HOURS:** 9am–8pm
  Monday–Friday (some close earlier),
  9am–6pm Saturday
- **BEST BUYS:** Hand-carved clocks, beer
  tankards, toys; peasant dresses and
  costumed dolls; fashions, including
  leather and woolens; porcelain figurines
  and dishes, including antiques; silver
  and steel tableware; luggage, cameras,
  binoculars.
- **PUBLIC HOLIDAYS:** January 1; Good
  Friday; Easter Sunday and Monday;
  May 1 (Labor Day); Ascension Day;
  Whitmonday; Corpus Christi; October 3
  (Unification Day); Repentance Day;
  November 1 (All Saints' Day);
  December 25–26.
- **USEFUL TELEPHONE NUMBERS:**
  Police 110
  Fire 112
  Ambulance 112
- **NATIONAL TOURIST OFFICE:**
  German National Tourist Office
  122 E. 42nd Street
  Chanin Building, 52nd Floor
  New York
  NY 10168-0072
  Tel: 212/661-7200
  German National Tourist Office
  444 South Flower Street
  Suite 2230
  Los Angeles
  CA 90071
  Tel: 213/688-7332
  German National Tourist Office
  65 Curzon Street
  London
  W1Y 7PE
  England
  Tel: 0171 495 3990
- **AMERICAN EMBASSY:**
  Delchmanns Avenue 29
  53170 Bonn
  Germany
  Tel: (30) 0228 3391

There is an ultramodern, efficient, toll-free *autobahn* (highway) system, allied to a dense network of generally well-maintained major and minor roads. Roads in eastern Germany are generally poor and in need of repair. If your vehicle has seat belts, wearing them is mandatory. A child under 12 may not travel unless using a suitable restraint system. Speed limits in built-up areas do not exceed 50 k.p.h. (31 m.p.h.). On all open roads the speed limit is 100 k.p.h. (62 m.p.h.); 130 k.p.h. (81 m.p.h.) is the maximum on the *autobahn* unless otherwise posted. Visiting motorists have to pay fines or deposits for motoring violations on the spot with German *Marks* or travelers' checks.

Rail travel is efficient and convenient. Urban rail services – S-Bahn and U-Bahn – are usually good. Stations are marked on the Berlin, Frankfurt and Munich city maps as S or U in red circles. Special rail rates are available through Eurailpass, Europass or with the German Rail Pass, available through German Rail, D.E.R. Tours, 11933 Wilshire Boulevard, Los Angeles, CA 90025. Major cities sell visitors a 24-hour public transportation ticket, available at local tourist offices, in train stations and airports. Trains throughout eastern Germany can be crowded; reservations should be made at least several hours in advance.

ACCOMMODATIONS

The German National Tourist Office (D.Z.T.) distributes a list of hotels and has a tourists' computer reservation system. Local tourist offices can usually help you find a room. More than 600 hostels are available to members of any association that is affiliated with the International Youth Hostel Federation. Information is available from Deutsches Jungendherbergswek, Postfach 1455, D-32756. Campers will find thousands of campgrounds, and some give discounts to holders of International Camping Carnets; some campgrounds require them.

TIPPING

Hotels and restaurants normally add a 10 to 12 percent gratuity charge to the bill, but satisfied customers often leave a small additional tip. Taxi drivers and hairdressers expect a tip of 10 to 15 percent of the bill. Tip porters and doormen 1 *Mark* per bag; coatroom attendants expect ½ to 1 *Mark*. Bartenders should also be given a small tip.

PRINCIPAL TOURING AREAS

Note: For descriptions of attractions in **bold type**, see individual listings.

BAVARIA

Bayern (Bavaria) is Germany's most popular tourist destination, as much for its spectacular mountain scenery as for its well-preserved old cities and numerous fairy-tale castles. Geographically, Bavaria comprises four regions. Franconia, in the north, has been part of Bavaria for nearly 200 years. Its capital is **Würzburg**, and it includes former imperial cities such as **Bamberg**, the medieval city of **Nürnberg** (Nuremberg) and **Bayreuth**, with its Wagner Festival. In the south, Upper Bavaria includes **München** (Munich), the state capital, and the snow-capped Bavarian Alps in

the south. In the southwest is the region of Allgäu/Bavarian-Swabia, with the Allgäuer Alpen mountains in the south and rolling countryside further north. **Augsburg** is its imposing capital, with origins dating back to Roman times. East Bavaria is less visited than the other areas, but has equally fine scenery. **Regensburg** is the capital of Lower Bavaria; **Passau** is famous for its Italianate baroque architecture.

BLACK FOREST

Cuckoo clocks, spectacular scenery, mountain lakes and health spas all are characteristic of the well-known Schwarzwald (Black Forest) region in southwestern Germany. A good way to see the Black Forest is by car. The Hochstrasse (High Route) extends from **Baden-Baden** to Freudenstadt; the Tälerstrasse (Valley Route) traverses the Murg and Kinzig valleys between Rastatt and Wolfach; and the Badische Weinstrasse (Wine Road) connects Baden-Baden with Basel, Switzerland, via the Rhine Valley.

BRANDENBURG

Contained within the historic Brandenburg region are many of the roots of what is now Germany. Centers include **Potsdam**, the royal city of Frederick the

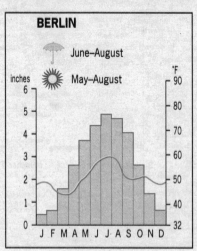

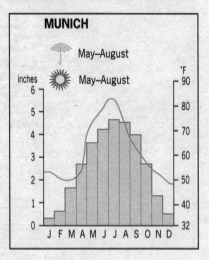

GERMANY

Great, and **Berlin**, the capital. Many of its magnificent baroque buildings have been restored or were rebuilt after their destruction in World War II. Southeast of Berlin is the Spreewald (Spree Forest), a peaceful conservation area crisscrossed by canals and rivers.

BREMEN AND EAST FRIESLAND
The old Hanseatic port of **Bremen** is a good starting point for exploring this region of northwestern Germany.

FRANKFURT AND HESSE
The capital of Hesse is the town of Wiesbaden, but its main city is cosmopolitan **Frankfurt am Main**, center of finance and culture. Nearby are the pretty Taunus hills.

HANNOVER, WESERBERGLAND AND HARZ MOUNTAINS
Industrial **Hannover** has many interesting museums and medieval buildings, while Weserbergland, a scenic area along the Weser River, has Renaissance houses and several spas. Meanwhile, the Harz Mountains provide excellent hiking. Medieval towns such as **Quedlinburg** have beautiful half-timbered buildings, as well as a strong tradition of keeping old customs.

LAKE KONSTANZ AND THE SWABIAN JURA
The Bodensee (Lake Constance) is in the Alpine foothills where Germany, Switzerland and Austria meet. This popular resort center offers swimming, boating and fishing. Upper Swabia, bounded by the Donau (Danube) in the north, is noted for baroque architecture.

LÜNEBURGER HEIDE
Lüneburger Heide (Lüneburg Heath) is a vast region in northern Germany that is now a national park and wildlife reserve.

MECKLENBURG-WEST POMERANIA
A former duchy and province of the German Reich, Mecklenburg-West

Pomerania occupies northeastern Germany. It is a land of geographic variety: grassy marshland and sandy soil characterize hilly central Mecklenburg. Along the coast, steep cliffs give way to sandy beaches and shifting dunes; in the north, hard clay soils support a variety of vegetation. **Schwerin**, the capital, has a large castle on a lake; Wismar is a scenic harbor town on an inlet of the Baltic; **Rostock** is an important fishing center. Güstrow has a famous cathedral and palace. Inland there are over 1,000 lakes, popular for pursuits including bathing, boating and fishing.

Mosel Valley

The Mosel (Moselle) River loops its way along a glorious valley full of vineyards into the Rhine at **Koblenz** (Coblence); the gentler of the two rivers, it passes through old wine towns, such as Beilstein and Cochem with their hilltop castles. **Trier**, a Roman town, is the center of the Moselle wine trade.

The Ahr River, with terraced vineyards (producing red wine) and ruined castles on its crags, flows through the Eifel area north of the Moselle to join the Rhine near Remagen. In the north is **Aachen**, Charlemagne's first capital.

Neckar Valley

This beautiful region of vineyards and woodlands includes some of Germany's most acclaimed tourist destinations: **Mannheim**, with its Fasching celebration; the university town of **Heidelberg**; the wine city of **Heilbronn**; and the cultural center of **Stuttgart**.

Castles are plentiful in the Neckar Valley: the town of Neckarsteinach boasts four, and Zwingenberg and Neckarzimmern each have one. Of particular interest is **Bad Wimpfen**.

Rheinland

The Rhein (Rhine) is Germany's longest river, and while its northern part is wide and sluggish, and flows through heavily populated cities such as **Düsseldorf** and **Köln** (Cologne), and stretches further south are very attractive. The most appealing section is the Rhine gorge, between Coblence and Bingen. Just before **Rüdesheim**, the river swings east, and this section, with the wooded Taunus hills to the north, as far as **Mainz**, is called the Rheingau. A special route, the Deutsche Weinstrasse (wine route), has been created from Bockenheim, west of Worms, running south to Schweigen, just on the French border.

The small area to the west of the Rhine in the south of Germany is the Pfälzer Wald (the Palatinate Forest). The country's smallest state, Saarland, known for its coal fields, is on the French border. Most of Saarland is a national park, heavily wooded and dotted with castles and villages. North of the Palatinate runs the Nahe River, which flows into the Rhine just after Bingen. This area does not hold a great deal of interest for the tourist apart from Idar-Oberstein, where precious stones are cut and displayed, and two spa towns, Bad Münster and Bad Kreuznach.

The Lahn River cuts through the Westerwald and Taunus, flowing into the Rhine on its eastern side at Lahnstein, which is dominated by the restored castle of Burg Lahneck. Much of the scenery is undramatic, apart from Kaiser Wilhelm's favorite resort of Bad Ems, medieval **Limburg**, and the picturesque town of **Marburg** clustered around its hilltop castle.

Sachsen

Sachsen (Saxony) was the name of several overlapping territories in German history. Today known as the area that stretches north from Thüringen (Thuringia) to Brandenburg and east to Lusatia, Saxony is a fertile, mountainous farming region that is almost wholly within the Elbe River basin. The region's major centers include Zwickau, a manufacturing city; industrial Chemnitz; Freiberg; **Dresden**; **Bautzen**; **Meissen**, home of the famed porcelain; and **Leipzig**, in the heart of Saxony.

SCHLESWIG-HOLSTEIN

Schleswig-Holstein, a hilly region of forests and meadows, shares a peninsula with Denmark. On the western side it faces the North Sea, while offshore are several islands. Strung along the north coast are the Dutch-looking Ostfriesische Inseln (East Frisian Islands); off the west coast are the Nordfriesische Inseln (North Friesian Islands).

The region's two biggest towns are the Hanseatic ports of **Bremen** and **Hamburg**, both with plenty of sights. **Kiel**, the province's capital, was badly bombed in the war. However the Kiel Canal, linking the North Sea with the Baltic, makes the city a busy shipping and industrial center.

THÜRINGEN

Thüringen (Thuringia), home of the ancient Thuringian Forest, is an area of rounded hills and gentle forests. It also includes the small but thriving Nordhausen, at the southern foot of the Harz Mountains, Mühlhausen; **Eisenach** with its Wartburg Castle; and **Weimar**, the stately town from which rose the short-lived republic of the same name.

USEFUL EXPRESSIONS IN GERMAN

hello	**Guten Tag**	to the right	**nach rechts**
good morning	**Guten Morgen**	straight ahead	**gerade aus**
good evening	**Guten Abend**	vacant/occupied	**frei/besetzt**
good night	**Gute Nacht**		
good-bye	**Auf Wiedersehen**	**DAYS OF THE WEEK**	
please/thank you	**bitte/danke**	Sunday	**Sonntag**
yes/no	**ja/nein**	Monday	**Montag**
excuse me	**Verzeihung**	Tuesday	**Dienstag**
you're welcome	**bitte**	Wednesday	**Mittwoch**
Do you speak	**Sprechen Sie**	Thursday	**Donnerstag**
English?	**Englisch?**	Friday	**Freitag**
I don't understand.	**Ich verstehe nicht.**	Saturday	**Samstag/**
What is the time?	**Wie spät ist es?**		**Sonnabend**
How much is that?	**Wieviel kostet das?**		
Where are the	**Wo sind die**	**NUMBERS**	
restrooms?	**Toiletten?**	1 **ein**	30 **dreizig**
I'd like ...	**Ich würde ...**	2 **zwei**	40 **vierzig**
Can you help	**Können Sie mir**	3 **drei**	50 **fünfzig**
me, please?	**helfen, bitte?**	4 **vier**	60 **sechzig**
where/when/how	**wo/wann/wie**	5 **fünf**	70 **siebzig**
hot/cold	**heiss/kalt**	6 **sechs**	80 **achtzig**
old/new	**alt/neu**	7 **sieben**	90 **neunzig**
open/closed	**offen/geschlossen**	8 **acht**	100 **hundert**
big/small	**gross/klein**	9 **neun**	1,000 **tausend**
Do you take	**Akzeptieren Sie**	10 **zehn**	
credit cards?	**Kreditkarten?**	20 **zwanzig**	
yesterday/today/	**gerstern/heute/**	21 **ein-und-zwanzig**	
tomorrow	**morgen**	22 **zwei-und-zwanzig**	
to the left	**nach links**		

PLACES OF INTEREST

▲ BERLIN (309 D4) ★

BERLIN *pop. 3,500,000*

Berlin, a city once divided by the Berlin Wall, is now free of the imposing barrier of concrete and barbed wire erected in August 1961 by the German Democratic Republic (East Germany).

The 1989 destruction of this symbol of the postwar division of Germany signaled the move toward the unification of the two Germanys.

Berlin first knew glory in the 15th century under the Hohenzollerns, who governed from the city on the Spree River initially as electors of Brandenburg, then as kings of Prussia and later as emperors of Imperial Germany.

Berlin gained further prominence as the cradle of the Second Reich, which was established by Otto von Bismarck in 1871 and served as the capital until 1914, with the outbreak of World War I. The Weimar Republic that rose five years later was short-lived, due to an ailing economy that produced a depression. The republic fell in 1933 when Hitler became chancellor, but Berlin remained the capital, this time of the Third Reich.

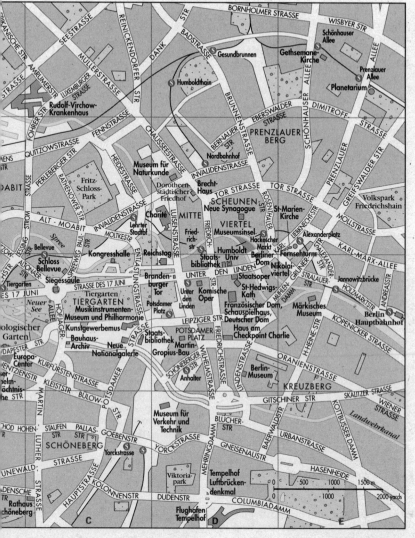

The bombings of World War II destroyed half of Berlin, leveling almost all of its baroque structures. During the Soviet battle for the city, Hitler took his own life in a bunker near the Brandenburger Tor (Brandenburg Gate). The postwar governments, anxious to forget Hitler and recall Berlin's former luster, set about rebuilding and restoring.

Berlin is both a modern showpiece and a monument of Germany's rich, and sometimes chaotic, past. Restored baroque palaces and medieval churches adjoin high-rise apartment complexes and glass-walled buildings. The main avenue of the former eastern sector, Unter den Linden (Under the Lime Trees), dates from the Imperial Berlin of the Hohenzollerns, and sweeps gracefully through the core of the city before ending in front of the historic Brandenburger Tor.

GERMANY

In the former western sector, the Kurfürstendamm and the surrounding streets are the center of tourist activity; the majority of the city's theaters, opera houses, museums, nightclubs and restaurants are in this area.

As a result of being a divided city, Berlin has over 80 museums, several duplicated. It is possible that some will strive to stay separate, but others will want to unite. The same applies to arts venues. There are three opera houses of international standing: the Deutsche Oper Berlin (west); Staatsoper Unter den Linden (east), next door to the Staatskapelle; and the Komische Oper Berlin (east), where comic operas are performed. Operettas and musicals are performed at the Theater des Westens.

The standard of music is world-class. The Berlin Philharmonic performs in its own modern building (Philharmonie) near Kemperplatz, while the Berlin Symphony Orchestra, the city's other main orchestra, plays frequently at east Berlin's main concert venue, the Konzerthaus. Waldbühne is a huge open-air arena where concerts – classical and pop – are performed in summer. Jazz, rock and folk music are easily found in the city.

Theaters offer a full range of entertainment. Nightlife is still livelier in the west, with bars, discos, nightclubs and café-restaurants. Cinemas are numerous, and the annual Film Festival (February) is always popular.

(Urban railroad stations – S-Bahn stations – are marked on the city map in red circles as S.)

ÄGYPTISCHES MUSEUM – *see Schloss Charlottenburg on p.316.*

ALEXANDERPLATZ (313 E3) marks the end of the processional route from the Brandenburger Tor, via Unter den Linden. It was named after Tsar Alexander I in 1805 and was first a marketplace. In the centre of the square is The World Clock and Friendship Fountain.

ALTE NATIONALGALERIE, Bodestrasse, Museuminsel, contains drawings and paintings from the late 18th century, French 19th-century art, German Impressionist paintings, and modern paintings and sculpture.

ANTIKENSAMMLUNG – *see Schloss Charlottenburg on p.316.*

BODEMUSEUM ★, am Kupfergraben, Museuminsel, exhibits objects of art and culture from ancient Egypt, early medieval Italy and the early Christian era of the western Roman Empire. It also contains European paintings dating from the Gothic period to the 18th century. The Skulpturesamm-lung (Sculpture Collection) has mainly German works.

BRANDENBURGER TOR (Brandenburg Gate) (313 D2) ★, at the end of Unter den Linden, was built 1788–91 as the imperial entrance to Berlin. Napoléon confiscated the Quadriga, the four-horse chariot of the Goddess of Victory which sits on top of the gate, when he captured Berlin in 1806; it was returned to the city after the emperor's defeat in 1814.

The gate was a stronghold for government troops in the 1919 Communist uprising and was badly damaged in World War II. A replica of the Goddess of Victory, a gift from the former West Berlin, now decorates it.

FERNSEHTURM (313 E3), a tall television tower topped by a revolving globe with a protruding spike, is Berlin's tallest structure at 365 meters (1,198 feet). The globe, at the 207-meter (679-foot) level, has a viewing gallery and café.

HAUS AM CHECKPOINT CHARLIE (313 D2), Friedrichstrasse 44, near the former border crossing point, describes in films and photos the escape attempts by East Berliners, many of which failed.

JAGDSCHLOSS GRÜNEWALD (Hunting Palace), Grünewaldsee, is a Renaissance mansion dating from 1542. It is now a museum housing art and hunting-trophy collections. Among its treasures are portraits of Roman emperors and works by Rubens and Cranach the Elder.

KAISER-WILHELM-GEDÄCHTNIS-KIRCHE (313 B2), Breitschieldtplatz, commemorates the first ruler of the Second Reich. The west tower remains from the original church, built between 1891–95.

KUNSTGEWERBEMUSEUM (Museum of Applied Arts) (313 C2) is in the Köpenick Palace in the Köpenick district and at Tiergarten – Matthäiskirchplatz 10, Berlin 30. Both museums contain beautiful European items of gold, silver, glass, ceramics and furniture.

MÄRKISCHES MUSEUM (313 E2), am Köllnischen Park 5, focuses on Berliners' contributions to literature, art and science.

MARTIN-GROPIUS-BAU (313 D2) is at Stresemannstrasse 110, Kreuzberg. This Renaissance-style, 19th-century building contains sculptures and paintings spanning the styles of Expressionism to New Objectivity. It also displays an exhibition on the role of the Jewish community in Berlin.

MUSEEN DAHLEM is a huge building containing several worthy collections, originally funded by the Henry Ford Foundation to vie with East Berlin's Pergamon collection.

MUSEUM FÜR NATURKUNDE (Natural History Museum) (313 D3), Invalidenstrasse 43, is one of the largest natural history museums in the world.

MUSEUM FÜR VÖLKERKUNDE (Ethnography Museum) is very extensive, with displays of bronzes from Africa, boats from the South Seas, and pottery and sculpture from South America. (Use the Lansstrasse entrance.)

MUSIKINSTRUMENTEN MUSEUM (313 C2), Tiergartenstrasse 1, has a collection of musical instruments that spans five centuries.

NEUE NATIONALGALERIE (313 C2) ★, Potsdamer Strasse 50, Tiergarten, is a modern structure designed by Ludwig Mies van der Rohe. The building combines the National Gallery, which displays 19th-century works, and the Gallery of the 20th Century. In the Art Library are costumes and photographs.

PERGAMONMUSEUM ★, Bodestrasse 1–3, Museuminsel, is considered one of the finest museums of ancient art in the world. It includes Hellenic and Roman architecture from Asia Minor, the Pergamon Altar and the Market Gate of Miletus, Babylonian sculptures, the Ishtar Gate and the Processional Way.

RATHAUS SCHÖNEBERG (313 C1), John-F.-Kennedy-Platz, was the seat of the West Berlin Government beginning in 1948. It was here that John F. Kennedy made his 1963 speech *Ich bin ein Berliner.* The Freiheitsglocke in the tower, a replica of the Liberty Bell, was donated by the United States. In the room at the base of the tower is the Freedom Scroll, signed by 17 million Americans to express solidarity with West Berliners.

REICHSTAG (313 D2) ★, Platz der Republik, once housed the German Parliament, but was burned down by the Nazis in 1933. Rebuilt in the 1950s, it is again undergoing refurbishment, and will become seat of the Bundestag in 1998.

ST.-MARIEN-KIRCHE (313 E3) is at Karl-Liebknecht-Strasse 8. Built in Gothic style in the 13th century, the nave survives. The fresco entitled *Totentanz,* or *Dance of Death,* is believed to have been painted in 1484.

SCHLOSS BELLEVUE (313 C2), Tiergarten, was built in 1785. The palace, rebuilt since its destruction in World War II, has been the official Berlin residence of the president since 1959.

SCHLOSS CHARLOTTENBURG (312 A3) ★, Luisenplatz, was completed in 1695 as the summer palace for the future queen, Sophie Charlotte, and later enlarged to become the country home of Prussian kings. It was restored after World War II and is Berlin's most impressive example of baroque architecture. On the ground floor of the Knobelsdorff wing are 19th-century paintings from the Nationalgalerie, and above is the reconstructed gilt Golden Gallery built for Frederick the Great. The Royal Apartments are a series of ornate baroque rooms, the most sumptuous being the Ovale Saal and the Porzellankabinett (Porcelain Collection); the Chapel is remarkable. In the informal Palace Gardens are the Schinkel Pavilion, the domed Belvedere and the Royal Mausoleum.

ÄGYPTISCHES MUSEUM (Egyptian Museum), Schloss Strasse 70. This is one of Berlin's split museums – other Egyptian exhibits are in the Bode Museum. Highlights are a bust of Queen Nefertiti and the 2,000-year-old Kalabasha Gate.

ANTIKENSAMMLUNG (Antiquities Collection), Schloss Strasse 1, has Minoan, Greek and Etruscan treasures from the former imperial collection, and Roman silver from Caesar Augustus' time.

MUSEUM FÜR VOR-UND FRÜHGESCHICHTE (Museum of Pre- and Early History) in the west wing of Charlottenburg, contains material from early cultures, particularly the Bronze and Iron Ages.

SCHLOSS PFAUENINSEL (Peacock Island Palace) is on the west edge of Berlin on an island in the Havel River. The palace is built along the lines of a late 18th-century ruined castle.

SIEGESSÄULE (313 C2), Strasse des 17 Juni, a column nearly 60 meters (200 feet) tall, commemorates the successful German campaigns of the Franco-Prussian War.

SPANDAU, a 12th-century moated castle 10 kilometers (6 miles) northwest, served as the fortress, state prison and treasury of the German kaisers over several centuries.

TIERGARTEN (313 C2) ★, a former royal hunting ground, is now a large park replanted with trees, and offers canal and lakeside walks. In the southwest corner is the Zoologischer Garten (Zoo), and in the northeast corner is the Sowjetisches Ehrenmal (Soviet War Memorial, Strasse des 17 Juni).

ZEUGHAUS (Arsenal), Unter den Linden 2, was rebuilt after bombing to become the Deutsches Historisches Museum (German Historical Museum). It displays arms and weapons as well as masks of dying warriors.

AACHEN (308 A3)
NORDRHEIN-WESTFALEN *pop. 253,000*
Aachen is a noted spa with the hottest springs 76°C (168°F) in northwestern Europe. Once Charlemagne's capital, it is also known as Aix-la-Chapelle. The 9th-century octagonal chapel within the cathedral contains Charlemagne's tomb and a valuable treasury; a restored 14th-century *Rathaus* (town hall) stands on the site of Charlemagne's palace.

COUVEN MUSEUM, Hühnermarkt 17, chronicles the history of Aachen. Exhibits here include furniture, fireplaces, Italian stucco work and household utensils.

INTERNATIONALES ZEITUNGSMUSEUM (International Press Museum), Ponstrasse 13, displays newspapers, magazines and journals from around the world, some dating from the 17th century.

ANSBACH (308 C2)
BAYERN *pop. 40,000*
The quiet Frankish town of Ansbach became the seat of the margraves of Brandenburg-Ansbach, who endowed it with many fine buildings. Every two years a Bach Festival is held in early

August. St.-Gumpert-Kirche is a Gothic church, with three towers.

MARKGRAFENSCHLOSS is an ornately furnished 18th-century rococo palace, with state rooms, a two-story frescoed Great Hall and the Margrave's Audience Room. It is surrounded by a fine park, the baroque Hofgarten.

ASCHAFFENBURG (308 B2)
BAYERN *pop. 65,000*
Aschaffenburg, overlooking the Main River, is famous for parks and imposing buildings, many decorated by the 16th-century painter Matthias Grünewald.

SCHLOSS JOHANNISBURG is a large Renaissance palace built 1605–14 as a residence for the bishops of Mainz. The state rooms are hung with pictures by German and Flemish masters.

SCHÖNBUSCH, 3 kilometers (2 miles) west, is a small summer residence built in 1780. It is surrounded by delightful formal gardens with a lake and classical buildings.

STIFTSKIRCHE is a Gothic church with a Romanesque cloister and a later tower. Inside are paintings by Matthias Grünewald and Lucas Cranach.

AUGSBURG (308 C1)
BAYERN *pop. 265,000*
Augsburg is Bavaria's oldest city. Its position at the confluence of two rivers made it an ideal trade route from southern Europe to northern Italy, a fact recognized by the Emperor Augustus, who founded the city in 15 BC. It reached its economic peak as a financial center in the 16th century when it was ruled by two wealthy merchant families, the Fuggers and the Welsers.

The town played an important role in the Reformation: the Peace of Augsburg finally recognized the right of Protestants to follow their own faith. Augsburg was also the birthplace of Leopold Mozart, father of Wolfgang Amadeus (the Mozarthaus has memorabilia), and the home and workplace of the painters Holbein the Elder and Younger and, more recently, of Rudolf Diesel and Wilhelm Messerschmidt.

DOM, on Hoher Weg, was built in AD 995 and rebuilt in the 14th century in Gothic style. Within are five stained-glass windows that are reputedly the oldest in Germany, and Romanesque bronze doors with panels depicting the story of Adam and Eve. Altar paintings are by Hans Holbein the Elder.

RATHAUS (Town Hall), with its two onion-domed towers, is regarded by some as the finest secular Renaissance building in Germany. It was designed by Elias Holl (1615–20). Its Golden Hall has a coffered ceiling and frescoes.

STS.-ULRICH-UND-AFRA, at the southern end of Maximilianstrasse, is a 15th-century Gothic basilica containing the plain Romanesque tomb of St. Afra and the rococo tomb of St. Ulrich.

SCHAETZLERPALAIS, Maximilianstrasse, was built 1512–15 and includes the German baroque gallery and an ornate Festsaal (Banqueting Hall). The adjacent State Gallery displays works by Hans Holbein and Albrecht Dürer.

BADEN-BADEN (306 B2)
BADEN-WÜRTTEMBERG *pop. 50,000*
Baden-Baden has long been a popular German spa: the Roman Emperor Caracalla knew the virtues of its waters almost 2,000 years ago. The town has a neo-classical spa building (*Kurhaus*) overlooking a well-kept park (*Kurgarten*).

NEUES SCHLOSS (New Palace), Römerplatz, dates from the 15th century. Held within is the Zähringer Museum's notable art collection.

RÖMISCHE BADRUINEN, beneath the Römerplatz, were the baths of the Emperor Caracalla. The ancient heating

GERMANY

system and a small church (Spitalkirche) are of interest.

BAD HOMBURG (308 B2)
HESSE *pop. 52,000*
This town is known for its springs, found in the *Kurpark* laid out in English style during the mid-19th century, when the spa was very fashionable.

SCHLOSS, 4 kilometers (2½ miles) northwest on the south slope of the Taunus hills, was built for Prince Friedrich II von Homburg, the title figure in Heinrich Wilhelm von Kleist's drama *Prinz Friedrich von Hamburg*.

BAD MERGENTHEIM (308 C2)
BADEN-WÜRTTEMBERG *pop. 21,000*
A center for the Teutonic Knights, this spa town is on the Romantische Strasse.

DEUTSCHORDENS SCHLOSS was the Renaissance residence of the Teutonic

---

KNIGHT'S TALE

The Grand Order of Teutonic Knights was founded in the Holy Land in 1128. After the Order adopted Lutheranism in 1525, those loyal to Roman Catholicism established themselves and continued their charitable works until Napoléon dispossessed the order in 1809.

Order from 1525 to 1809 and is situated on the eastern edge of the old town. The exterior of the building is highly ornate. Inside is a fine staircase, the Knights' Museum and a baroque church.

BAD WIMPFEN (308 B2)
BADEN-WÜRTTEMBERG *pop. 6,000*
The splendid old fortified town of Bad Wimpfen overlooks the Neckar River. Many of the winding, cobbled streets are lined with half-timbered, gabled houses. The 13th-century church has a fine Gothic cloister, and the upper town is

dominated by the remains of the Hohenstaufens' former imperial palace.

BURG GUTTENBERG, 20 kilometers (12 miles) north, is one of the oldest and best-preserved castles in the Neckar Valley; the property has belonged to the same family for 18 generations.

BAMBERG (308 C2)
BAYERN *pop. 70,000*
Bamberg, set on seven hills above the Regnitz River, has been a religious center since the Emperor Heinrich II established a bishopric here in 1007. As a result, the city has a wealth of churches, abbeys and cloisters, as well as an ancient university. Other attractions are "Little Venice," a row of fishermen's houses along the riverfront; the baroque Church of St. Martin, built by the Dientzenhofer brothers around 1690; and the Gothic Obere Pfarrkirche.

ALTE HOFHALTUNG, the partly ruined former residence of Bamberg's prince-bishops, now houses a museum.

ALTES RATHAUS, the Old Town Hall, is a half-timbered building standing on an island in the river. Originally Gothic, it was later decorated in rococo style.

DOM, on the Domplatz, is Bamberg's impressive Gothic cathedral. Inside, the 13th-century statue of the Knight of Bamberg, the tomb of Heinrich and the renowned Marienaltar (Nativity Altar), carved by Viet Stoss (1523), are outstanding among the statuary.

KLOSTERKIRCHE ST. MICHAEL, founded in 1015 as part of a Benedictine Abbey, is approached by a baroque flight of steps. Inside are bishops' tombs, Romanesque columns and a vault-ceiling painting of 600 herbs. The terrace offers fine views.

NEUE RESIDENZ (New Residence), 8 Domplatz, was built around 1700 as the official residence of the prince-bishops. Magnificently decorated rooms in baroque style include the State Library, the Chinese Room and the Emperor's Room. Outside is the Rose Garden.

POMMERSFELDEN, 21 kilometers (13 miles) southwest, is famous for its imposing castle, Schloss Weissenstein, built 1711–18 for the local bishop by Johann Dientzenhofer. The double staircase was designed by the bishop and has a *trompe-l'oeil* ceiling. The Hall of Mirrors, the Banqueting Hall and the five-story Marble Hall (scene of summer concerts) are all sumptuous.

SCHLOSS ALTENBURG, once a bishop's castle, is 3 kilometers (2 miles) outside Bamberg on the highest hill. Inside is a neo-Gothic chapel. There are fine views.

BAUTZEN (309 E3)
SACHSEN *pop. 47,000*
Built on a granite promontory above the Spree River, Bautzen was known to be a Slavic settlement as early as the 11th century. Germans took the town in 1033 and made it a part of Bohemia; then it became a part of Saxony in the Middle Ages. Named the capital of the Federation of Lusatian Cities in 1346, Bautzen was and is a cultural and political center for the Lusatian Sorbs (Wends), a people of West Slavic descent who migrated here over 1,000 years ago.

The late-Gothic cathedral (Petridom) serves both Catholics and Protestants. Much of the old town wall and bastions survive, and there are good views from the leaning Reichenturm, once a defensive tower. The Alte Wasserkunst (Water Tower) of 1588, now houses a Technological Museum. The Schloss Ortenburg, a 15th-century castle with later additions, dominates the town and houses a Sorb Museum.

BAYREUTH (308 D2)
BAYERN *pop. 72,300*
Bayreuth's cultural tradition began with the Margrave Christian of Hohenzollern, who established his capital here in the 17th century and built many baroque and rococo buildings. A century later, Margravine Wilhelmina, sister of Frederick the Great, continued his policies. Her husband commissioned an Italian architect to build a baroque opera house (Markgräfliches Opernhaus); each May the Fränkische-Festwoche (18th-century opera and music festival) takes place here. It was this building that attracted Richard Wagner when he was looking for a suitable venue for the production of his opera cycle, *The Ring*. Today his works are performed at the annual Bayreuth Festival (July and August) in the Festspielhaus.

ALTES SCHLOSS, Maximilianstrasse, dates from the early 14th century and was rebuilt in the 1750s. Damaged by fire in 1945, it has not been rebuilt.

EREMITAGE SCHLOSS, 5 kilometers (3 miles) east, was the second residence of the Margrave of Brandenburg-Bayreuth and his wife, Wilhelmina. The 18th-century old castle contains some bare cells, while the new castle features an ornate Sun Temple. Fountains play in the landscaped English gardens.

MARKGRÄFLICHES OPERNHAUS (Margrave Opera House) is on the Opernstrasse and was erected between 1745 and 1748 by order of Margravine Wilhelmina for use as a private theater. This rococo structure hosts the Franconian Festival Weeks of 18th-century concerts and ballets during July and August.

NEUES SCHLOSS, Ludwigstrasse, is a lavish rococo palace (1753–4) hastily constructed at the request of Wilhelmina. It has a series of lovely rooms, each decorated in a different style. Outstanding are the Japanese Room, the Mirror Room and the Ballroom. Next to the palace is the Hofgarten, a 17th-century park.

RICHARD WAGNER FESTSPIELHAUS, on the Nibelungenstrasse, is the Festival Theater that Richard Wagner designed.

GERMANY

Its inward and outward appearance of simplicity reflects his desire to create an ideal setting for his musical dramas.

RICHARD WAGNER MUSEUM, Haus Wahnfried, Richard-Wagner-Strasse, has a collection of Wagnerian mementos.

BERCHTESGADEN (309 D1)
BAYERN *pop. 8,200*
Well-known for skiing, Berchtesgaden has also long been recognized for its talented woodcarvers. Nearby is the village of Au, where local costumes are displayed. Natural attractions include the Gorge of the Wimbach (passable from May to mid-October) and the Eis Höhle, an ice cave at Schellenberg.

In a deep, quiet gorge 5 kilometers (3 miles) south lies one of the most popular Alpine lakes: Königssee. On either side rise tremendous jagged cliffs formed in part by the Watzmann, one of the highest Bavarian peaks. Boat trips can be made on the lake: at one of the stops, the Chapel of St. Bartholomä is framed in an Alpine setting.

HEIMAT MUSEUM (Folklore Museum), Schroffenbergallee 6, displays woodcarvings, Berchtesgaden wood-chip boxes, toys and folk crafts.

SALZBERGWERK (Salt Mines), Bergwerk-Strasse, has brought the city prosperity since it began in 1515. A guided trip through the mines is available.

SCHLOSS, first a monk's priory and then a palace for the royal family of Bavaria, this is now a museum of artistic treasures collected by Crown Prince Rupert.

STIFTSKIRCHE, Schlossplatz, is a twin-spired abbey church built in the 12th century in Romanesque style, with part rebuilt in Gothic style after a fire.

▲ BIELEFELD (308 B4)
NORDRHEIN-WESTFALEN *pop. 316,000*
As the Linenweaver's Fountain with its pipe-smoking figure suggests, Bielefeld is historically an industrial town, and today is a center for engineering, electronics and food-processing.

BURG SPARRENBURG affords an extraordinary view over the Ravensburg region and the Teutoburger Forest. Built in the 13th century, the palace was restored in the 19th century. There are catacombs and a playing-card museum.

BONN (308 B3)
NORDRHEIN-WESTFALEN *pop. 312,000*
Bonn is the former capital of the Federal Republic of Germany. In December 1990 Berlin was reinstated as the German capital, but Bonn remains the center of government and administration. Although Bonn dates from Roman times, clusters of

---

FESTIVE BONN

From May to October Bonn offers a free cultural events program on the market square. Known as "Bonner Sommer," it features theater presentations, musical productions and puppet shows. The historic town hall serves as the stage setting. A Beethoven Festival is held here every three years.

---

modern buildings have sprouted amid its ancient churches, quiet parks and elegant 18th-century homes. The German parliament, which meets in Bonn, is to move to Berlin in 1998.

Bonn is surrounded by one of Europe's most striking landscapes. Seven kilometers (4 miles) south of Bonn is Bad Godesberg. This spa and summer resort is the site of the ruins of a castle that was erected by the archbishops of Cologne in the 13th and 14th centuries. The terrace of this castle offers one of the best panoramas of the area.

BEETHOVENHAUS, Bongasse 20, is where the composer was born in 1770. It now houses a museum, containing musical works, portraits and instruments.

MÜNSTER, Münsterplatz, dates from the 12th century. This mainly Romanesque church contains some baroque furnishings and some fine cloisters.

POPPELSDORFER SCHLOSS (Prince Elector's Palace), 171 Meckenheimer Allee, is a striking 18th-century palace showing French and Italian influences. The building today is part of Bonn University, while the grounds serve as the Botanical Gardens.

RHEINISCHES LANDESMUSEUM, at 14 Colmantstrasse, houses a collection of Roman and Frankish relics, medieval paintings and a Neanderthal skull found near Düsseldorf.

BRAUBACH
RHEINLAND-PFALZ *pop. 3,800*
MARKSBURG, above the town, is the only completely preserved 11th-century castle on the Rhine. It is unusual in that it has been inhabited continuously since the 12th century.

BRAUNSCHWEIG (308 C4)
NIEDERSACHSEN *pop. 260,000*
Braunschweig (Brunswick) reached its peak in the 12th century under Henry the Lion, who commissioned many works of art for his city. Brunswick became an important trading center and later (1753–1918) the residence of the dukes of Brunswick. Although heavily damaged in World War II, several pockets of old buildings remain. The most appealing is the Altstadtmarkt with half-timbered houses, the cathedral and some Gothic churches.

BURGPLATZ is the medieval center of the old town; it faces the Burg Dankwarderode, an early fortress Henry chose as his residence. The present edifice was built in the 19th century and houses a museum of medieval art and artifacts.

DOM, Burgplatz, is a Romanesque cathedral dedicated to St. Blasius. Interior features include the tomb of Henry the Lion, a seven-branch candelabrum and 13th-century wall paintings.

HERZOG (DUKE) ANTON ULRICH MUSEUM on Museumstrasse was built in the 1880s and named after this duke, as his own art collection forms the core. The paintings in this collection, including those by Cranach, Holbein and Van Dyck, went on display in 1754, making this Germany's first museum.

▲ BREMEN (306 B4)
BREMEN *pop. 552,000*
Although 65 kilometers (40 miles) from the North Sea, this Hanseatic city on the Weser River is the oldest seaport in Germany. Along the river is the old area of Schnoorviertel, with narrow streets and small cottages, many of which have been restored.

BÖTTCHERSTRASSE, off Marktplatz, once a narrow lane of coopers' workshops, was transformed in the 1920s to a fashionable street. At No. 6 is Kunstsammlung Roseliushaus, a 15th-century merchant's mansion with collections of medieval furniture and paintings.

DOM, Marktplatz Sondstrasse 10–12, is the 11th-century Cathedral of St. Peter. The interior features Romanesque and Gothic styles. The bronze font dates from the 13th century, and an 11th-century crypt lies beneath the organ loft. The Bleikeller (lead cellar) contains several mummies.

FOCKE-MUSEUM, Schwachhauser-Heerstrasse 240, the Bremen State Museum of Art and History, charts the town's eventful history.

KUNSTHALLE (Bremen Art Gallery), am Wall 207, is more than 150 years old and features works by many European artists.

MARKTPLATZ, surrounded by the city's finest old buildings, is considered the most architecturally significant main square in the country.

GERMANY

NEUES MUSEUM WESERBURG BREMEN (New Museum Weserburg), Teerhof 20, displays works by German and American artists on loan from private collections.

RATHAUS, opposite the cathedral, is a 15th-century town hall with a Renaissance façade. A bronze statue of the Bremen Town Musicians adorns its western side.

BRUNSWICK – *see Braunschweig, p.321.*

BURGHAUSEN (309 D1)
BAYERN *pop. 18,000*
The 1,000-year-old town of Burghausen maintains a medieval atmosphere in the ancient houses of its *Altstadt* (old town).

BURG, a 13th-century fortress that overlooks the town, is the longest castle in Europe. It includes a Gothic chapel and houses an art gallery, photograph collection and local history museum.

CELLE (308 C4)
NIEDERSACHSEN *pop. 74,000*
Celle is an old ducal city that retains a medieval atmosphere through its wealth of 16th- and 17th-century timbered houses in the attractive *Altstadt* (old town). In the fall, horses bred in the former ducal stables take part in the spectacular Parade of Stallions.

HERZOGSSCHLOSS (Palace of the Duke) was originally a fortress built in the late 13th century. Here the dukes of Braunschweig-Lüneburg resided for 300 years. The castle was rebuilt in

Renaissance style and has a lovely 15th-century chapel and a moat. The theater, the oldest of its kind in Germany (1674), still offers performances of classical plays.

CHIEMSEE (309 D1)
BAYERN
In Bavaria's largest lake are two islands with 8th-century Benedictine abbeys, accessible by steamer from Prien. The smaller island, Frauensel (Women's Island), retains its nunnery. The larger island is Herreninsel (Men's Island), which had a monastery; all that remains today is a Gothic church and old palace. The island is also the site of King Ludwig's Schloss Herrenchiemsee, modeled on Versailles but unfinished.

COBLENCE – *see Koblenz on p.333.*

COBURG (308 C2)
BAYERN *pop. 44,000*
This 900-year-old town reflects both Renaissance and Gothic influences in its attractive buildings, but is best known for its massive castle-fortress, the "Crown of Franconia."

SCHLOSS EHRENBURG, in the city center, was the residence of the dukes of Coburg from 1547 to 1918 and the boyhood home of Prince Albert, consort to Queen Victoria of England. The Riesensaal (Giants' Room) has 28 huge figures supporting the ceiling.

VESTE COBURG, 2 kilometers (1 mile) east, is one of Germany's largest and strongest citadels. This 12th-century castle-fortress brought Coburg prominence during the Middle Ages. The structure was remodeled and strengthened in the 16th century by Duke Johann Casimir and completely restored around 1900.
  Of special note is the paneled Luther Room, where Martin Luther took refuge during the Augsburg Diet in 1530. The castle houses significant collections of paintings, engravings, carriages, porcelain and weapons.

COLDITZ (309 D3)
SACHSEN
The village's main attraction is striking Colditz Castle, a top-security prisoner-of-war camp during World War II.

COLOGNE – *see Köln on p.333.*

CONSTANCE – *see Konstanz on p.334.*

DETMOLD (308 B4)
NORDRHEIN-WESTFALEN *pop. 70,000*
Detmold is the former capital of the Lippe principality. The Lippisches Landesmuseum has a collection of relics from the Stone, Bronze and Iron ages. The Residenzschloss still belongs to the family and has period rooms and fine Brussels tapestries.

Near Detmold are the medieval towns of Lemgo, Blomberg and Schwalenberg. Also nearby is Horn, known for its early Romanesque bas-relief of the *Descent from the Cross.*

DINKELSBÜHL (308 C2) ★
BAYERN *pop. 11,000*
Dinkelsbühl borders the Wörnitz River in Bavaria. The medieval town has been preserved, and its architecture is typical of southern Germany. The 15th-century church of St. George and the Deutsches Haus are of special interest.

Dinkelsbühl has particular appeal to children, not only for its gingerbread, but also for its Kinderzeche, a week-long children's festival (July).

DONAUESCHINGEN (308 B1)
BADEN-WÜRTTEMBERG *pop. 20,000*
Donaueschingen is a popular tourist center at the head of the Danube; a tremendous 19th-century fountain marks the river's source. The Karlsbau displays the works of Swabian artists, and the Furstenburg castle has a fine collection of porcelain.

▲ DRESDEN (309 D3) ★
SACHSEN *pop. 480,000*
Ancient Dresden began as a Slav settlement on the north bank of the Elbe River sometime before the 13th century. Later, a second settlement was founded on the opposite riverbank, and in 1270 Margrave Henry the Illustrious chose the twin towns as the capital of Saxony. After Henry's death Dresden was transferred from ruler to ruler until Duke Albrecht of the Wettin dynasty moved his residency here from Meissen in 1485.

In the late 17th and 18th centuries, electors Augustus I and Augustus II remodeled Dresden in fabulous rococo and baroque style, making it one of the showplaces of Europe. Many splendid buildings survived the Seven Years' War (1756–63), and the city prospered during the 19th century. Sadly, Dresden was bombed heavily in 1945.

Several of the baroque and rococo buildings that once clustered around the castle have since been rebuilt, among

SAXON SWITZERLAND
In the 19th century, this area (southeast of Dresden and now a national park) was a source of inspiration for many artists of the Romantic School. A "Painters Path" was created, leading through valleys and across mountains from Dresden, via Pillnitz, to the Czech border.

them the Semperoper (opera house), the Japanisches Palais, the Zwinger complex and the Hofkirche. The ruins of the Frauenkirche, until recently preserved as a memorial in its ruined state, are currently being restored.

ALBERTINUM is one of Dresden's two museum complexes. Built in 1559, the glass-domed structure contains various works of art.

The Gemäldegalerie Neuer Meister (Picture Gallery of New Masters) has paintings by 19th- and 20th-century masters, as well as works by German Impressionists, 20th-century socialist artists and 19th-century genre painters.

Grünes Gewölbe (Green Vault)

contains one of Germany's largest royal collections of 15th- to 18th-century silver, gold and jewelry.

KREUZKIRCHE, by the Altmarkt, is one of Dresden's finest baroque structures, and includes the impressive and famous boys' choir (*Kreuzchor*) which dates from the original church.

MUSEUM FÜR GESCHICHTE DER STADT DRESDEN (Museum of the Town of Dresden) is in the Landhaus, an 18th-century palace. Exhibits include photographs that show Dresden before and after the bombings of World War II.

THE ZWINGER is the pride of Dresden. Designed by Pöppelmann and built 1711–32, the Zwinger was planned as part of a large palace. The square court with its U-shaped extensions is considered one of the most successful baroque designs ever conceived. The galleries and pavilions, some now used as museums, are linked to form a court that functions as an outdoor theater.

Gemäldegalerie Alter Meister (Picture Gallery of Old Masters), in the Semper Gallery, contains Raphael's *Sistine Madonna* and Giorgione's *Sleeping Venus* in addition to a dozen Rembrandts, five Tintorettos and works by Titian, Rubens and Van Dyck.

Historisches Museum (Historical Museum), in the Semper Gallery's east wing, displays costumes from the Saxon court, weapons and oriental objects.

Porzellansammlung (Porcelain Collection) consists of early porcelain from the Han, Tang and Ming dynasties and from the Meissen factory. The Museum füre Tierkunde (Zoological Museum) displays 17th- and 18th-century hunting weapons and artifacts.

▲ **DÜSSELDORF** (308 B3)
NORDRHEIN-WESTFALEN *pop. 570,000*
Düsseldorf is an important Rhine city that was founded in the 13th century. It is one of the most significant economic and cultural centers in Germany and offers many restored buildings, fine museums and art collections, private residences, theaters and concert halls.

Cafés, fashionable boutiques, dress shops, art shops and jewelers are found along Königsallee, Düsseldorf's main street, together with two new shopping malls. The town is proud of its open

---

DÜSSELDORF DIARY

Düsseldorf is host to theatrical productions and festivals throughout the year. Drama is performed at the Schauspielhaus, comedies and satires at Komödchen, and opera at Deutche Operam Rhein. In July the Grand Marksmen's Contests and Local Fair are held on the Oberkassel bank of the Rhine. More than 3,000 booths and numerous rides are set up during the nine-day event, culminating in a grand parade and fireworks display. The winter carnival season lasts from mid-November until mid-February.

---

spaces: the L-shaped Hofgarten in the center; the Südpark to the south and Nordpark to the north.

ALTES RATHAUS (Old Town Hall), Marktplatz, is a 16th-century restored brick building with Renaissance gables, and imposing equstrian statue outside.

KUNSTMUSEUM, Ehrenhof 5, contains European art from the Middle Ages to the present, with emphasis on German art of the 19th and 20th centuries.

KUNSTSTAMMLUNG NORDRHEIN-WESTFALEN (State Art Collection of North Rhine-Westphalia), Grabbepl 5, features 20th-century works by Klee, Ernst, Mondrian, Miró and Chagall.

LAMBERTUSKIRCHE, Schlossufer, is a 14th-century church with a crooked spire. Inside is the Renaissance tomb of Duke William the Rich.

SCHLOSS BENRATH, 10 kilometers (6 miles) southeast at Benrather Schossalle 104, is an 18th-century rococo castle with a museum and baroque gardens.

SCHLOSS JÄGERHOF, at the east end of Jägerhofstrasse, is an 18th-century baroque-style hunting palace. It houses the Goethe Museum and the Ernst Schneider Foundation, which contains Meissen porcelain and silverware.

▲ EISENACH (308 C3)
THÜRINGEN *pop. 44,000*

Eisenach was founded around 1150 by the landgraves of Thuringia. It is renowned as the site of the 11th-century Wartburg Castle, where Martin Luther began translating the New Testament into German in 1521. The town was also the birthplace of J. S. Bach in 1685.

BACHHAUS, am Frauenplan 21, was the Bach family home. Inside is a collection of musical instruments, 17th-century

---

MINSTRELS

In the Middle Ages, music and poetry competitions were held for wandering minstrels. The culture-loving descendants of Count Ludwig I promoted art and music at their court in Wartburg Castle in Eisenach and hosted the competition (*Sängerkrieg*) for the German troubadors (*Minnesänger*). One minstrel was Wolfram von Eschenbach, who wrote part of the epic *Parzifal* here; many years later Wagner used the theme in his opera.

---

furniture and a chronicle of the lives and works of the family.

LUTHERHAUS, where Martin Luther stayed as a student, has a collection of Bibles and 16th-century religious books.

THÜRINGER MUSEUM, in the 18th-century former ducal palace, contains glassware,

a picture gallery, wood sculpture, Thuringian porcelain and items from the Middle Ages.

WARTBURG CASTLE was known to exist as early as 1067. Built by landgraves on a hill above the village, it was where Luther sought refuge during the Reformation. Inside the castle are Gothic and baroque furniture, a Romanesque Knights' Hall, and a huge Festsaal (banquet hall) decorated with frescoes by Moritz von Schwind.

▲ ERFURT (308 C3)
THÜRINGEN *pop. 215,000*

Many of Erfurt's buildings date from the 16th century, when Martin Luther was a novice at the monastery, most notable of which are the half-timbered houses lining the 600-year-old Krämer Bridge. The cathedral has fine stained-glass windows and a baroque high altar; next to it is the Church of St. Severus, an early Gothic hall church. The Angermuseum contains many medieval works of art.

ESSEN (308 B3)
NORDRHEIN-WESTFALEN *pop. 670,000*

Sightseeing highlights in this industrial city are Gruga Park and the Münsterkirche, a 9th-century Romanesque basilica that contains some medieval works of art in its Schatzkammer (treasury). Of artistic importance is the Folkwang Museum, which houses a collection of prominent modern works.

FLENSBURG (308 C5)
SCHLESWIG-HOLSTEIN *pop. 87,000*

Flensburg's location on the fiord of the same name near Denmark has earned it the nickname "Gate to the North." Sights of interest include the Nordertor (a city gate), the Nordermarkt, the fishing quarter of Jügenby, and the Städtisches Museum.

SCHLOSS GLÜCKSBURG, about 9 kilometers (6 miles) northeast, is a Renaissance-style lake palace that was built around 1585.

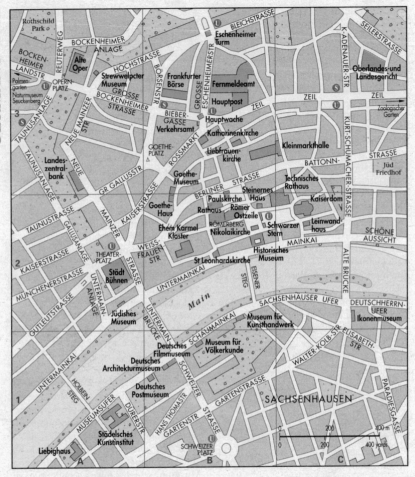

▲ FRANKFURT AM MAIN (308 B2)

HESSE *pop. 660,000*

A trade center since Roman times, Frankfurt has long played a key role in German history. It was the city where early German kings were elected, and Holy Roman emperors were crowned in the cathedral.

Opposed to Prussianism but never radical, Frankfurt later became a stronghold of liberalism and a major trading center. Much of the city, including Germany's largest *Altstadt* (old town), was devastated in 1944; some of the older buildings have since been sensitively restored.

In front of the cathedral, excavated remains from Roman and Carolingian times now constitute the Historischer Garten (Historical Gardens).

The Alte Oper (Old Opera House) has been restored but is now used for conferences – Frankfurt is an important commercial center – and concerts, while operas and plays are performed in the Städtische Bühnen complex. Many venues around the city host concerts of all types, along with plays and and films. A string of museums lines the south bank of the river (Museumsufer) in Sachsenhausen, which has an old quarter full of inns offering local foods.

(Urban railroad stations – S-Bahn and U-Bahn – are marked on the city map in red circles as S and U.)

ESCHENHEIMER TURM (Eschenheimer Tower) (326 B3), a five-turreted tower built in 1428 that is nearly 50 meters (164 feet) tall, is part of the old town walls.

GOETHEHAUS UND GOETHEMUSEUM, Grosser Hirschgraben 23 (326 B2/B3), is a reconstruction of the home of Johann Wolfgang von Goethe (1749–1832). The adjoining museum displays documents and paintings by artists of his day.

HISTORISCHES MUSEUM (326 B2) incorporates the medieval *Rententurm* (tower), the 12th-century castle founded by Emperor Frederick I (Barbarossa), and its Saalhof Kapelle (Romanesque chapel), the city's oldest building. Inside are scale models of old Frankfurt, a children's museum and coins.

JÜDISCHES MUSEUM (326 A2) deals with the history of the city's former influential Jewish community. The displays include mementos from the Nazi period.

KAISERDOM (326 C2), St. Bartholomew's red-sandstone cathedral where emperors were crowned beginning in 1562, rests on Carolingian foundations that date from AD 852. Between the 13th and 15th centuries it was enlarged in the Gothic style. The 90-meter (310-foot) tower, choir stalls and treasury can be toured.

LIEBIGHAUS MUSEUM (326 A1), on Museumsufer, exhibits early sculpture collected from Sumeria, Egypt and Greece, and also later pieces from Germany and Western Europe.

MUSEUM FÜR KUNSTHANDWERK (Museum of Applied Arts) (326 B2) has an outstanding collection of European glass, ceramics and furniture; Islamic carpets; Oriental jade and lacquerwork; and a section which is devoted to books and manuscripts.

NATURMUSEUM SENCKENBERG, Senckenberganlage 25, displays large fossils, animals, plants and geological items in a hands-on learning environment.

RÖMERBERG (326 B2), a cobbled square where royal ceremonies were once held, was rebuilt in the 1980s. Along the west side are some Römer (half-timbered houses) with stepped gables, which once formed the *Rathaus* (town hall), originally built 500 years ago. In the upper stories is the Kaisersaal (Imperial Hall), where coronation banquets of Holy Roman Emperors took place. On the east side, six more houses have been rebuilt in traditional style. On the south side is the Romanesque Nikolaikirche (St. Nicholas' Church); opposite stands Paulskirche, built in the 18th century as a Lutheran preaching hall.

ST. LEONHARDSKIRCHE (326 C2), on Mainkai, west of Eiserner Steg, retains octagonal towers and doorways from a 13th-century Romanesque basilica. Gothic modifications were made in the 15th century.

STÄDELSCHES KUNSTINSTITUT (326 A1), Schaumainkai 63, is an art gallery boasting works by Dürer, Cranach, Grien, Botticelli, Rubens, Rembrandt, Renoir, Goya and others.

ZOOLOGISCHER GARTEN, on Alfred-Brehm-Platz, is a leader in the breeding of rare animals that are difficult to care for in captivity.

▲ **FREIBURG IM BREISGAU (308 B1)**
BADEN-WÜRTTEMBERG *pop. 197,000*
The old university city of Freiburg im Breisgau is the entrance to the southern Black Forest. The cathedral, medieval gates, the university (founded in 1457), and Kaufhaus are sightseeing highlights. Schlossberg (Castle Hill), 460 meters (1,509 feet) high, offers a fine view. The Augustinermuseum houses Upper Rhenish art from the Middle Ages, as well as baroque sculpture.

GERMANY

MÜNSTER, Münsterplatz, is a Gothic cathedral reflecting the architectural styles of the 13th, 14th and 15th centuries. The 116-meter (381-foot) spire is a lattice-work of stone; artwork adorns the tympanum, west porch and south side. The tower offers views over the 18th-century Münsterplatz (Market Square).

FULDA (308 C3)
HESSE *pop. 60,000*

Ancient Fulda, on the Fulda River, originated with a once-celebrated abbey founded by Sturmius, a disciple of St. Boniface, in AD 744. The present St. Boniface Cathedral exemplifies Italian baroque style. Also of interest is the 9th-century Michaelskirche, the oldest undamaged church in Germany.

SCHLOSS FASANERIE, 4 kilometers (2½ miles) northwest, was the summer palace of the archbishops of Fulda. The baroque structure was later developed into an entertainment center.

STADTSCHLOSS has evolved from a 14th-century medieval castle into a baroque residence. Of interest are the princes' and emperor's halls, mirror cabinet, orangery and local history museum.

FÜSSEN (308 C1) ★
BAYERN *pop. 16,500*

This attractive old town, in a gorge on the Austrian border, has a 15th-century castle, once the summer palace of the prince bishops of Augsburg. The beauty of Füssen's mountain backdrop and lake-dotted countryside make it a popular resort and winter sports center. Nearby, outside the village of Schwangau, 3 kilometers (2 miles) from Füssen are two *Königsschlösser* (royal castles) connected with Ludwig II.

HOHENSCHWANGAU was a medieval fortress of the Knights of the Swan, demolished by Napoléon and restored by King Maximilian II, who tried to re-create a medieval castle. Ludwig II lived here as a child.

HOHES SCHLOSS dates from the 15th century and was once the summer palace of the prince-bishops of Ausgsburg.

NEUSCHWANSTEIN is a turreted granite structure that served as the model for the castles at Disneyland and Walt Disney World. The extravagantly decorated castle, built in the 1870s but unfinished, was the inspiration of Ludwig II.

ST.-MANG-KIRCHE, Lechhalde, is a former Benedictine monastery founded in the 8th century. The present church was reconstructed in baroque style in the 18th century and is now a local museum. It incorporates the earlier Chapel of St. Anne, on the walls of which is painted the *Totentanz* (*Dance of Death*).

GARMISCH-PARTENKIRCHEN
(308 C1) ★
BAYERN *pop. 26,500*

The relatively flat ground of Germany's foremost winter sports center (two towns joined together) is surrounded by mountains, including 2,966-meter (9,731-foot) Zugspitze, the country's highest point. Snow can be expected from mid-December through March; the peak tourist season is Christmas.

GOSLAR (308 C4)
NIEDERSACHSEN *pop. 47,000*

Goslar is an old imperial town on the northern edge of the Harz mountains that traces its origins back to the 11th century. The town prospered from silver mining until about 1350 and was a founder member of the Hanseatic League. Local buildings reflect the town's former wealth. Also here are impressive 19th-century murals, found in the German emperors' Romanesque palace. The *Rathaus* (town hall) has a splendid *Huldigungssaal* (council chamber), with frescoes dating from 1500.

HALLE (308 D3)
SACHSEN-ANHOLT *pop. 296,000*

Salt deposits near Halle were discovered around 4000 BC and, as a result, supported a flourishing salt trade on the Saale River. In AD 968, Halle was chartered as a town of the Holy Roman Empire. During the Middle Ages, feuds between the salt-workers and the owners of the salt flats prompted the archbishop to build the Moritzburg fortress. Destroyed by fire in 1637 and rebuilt after 1897, the fortress now contains Staathiche Galerie, an art gallery with 19th- and 20th-century works.

In addition to its industrial history, Halle was the birthplace of Handel in 1685. Today Halle honors its most prominent resident with the annual Handel Festival, and his statue stands in the Marktplatz close to the Roter Turm (Red Tower), a late-Gothic belfry.

DOM (HALLE CATHEDRAL) was built in the 13th century as a Dominican monastery and contains statues of several saints.

HALLOREN UND SALINENMUSEUM (Salt-works Museum) demonstrates how salt was extracted and portrays the lifestyle of the salt workers.

HANDELHAUS is the baroque house where Handel was born. A collection of instruments and exhibits detailing his life and works are displayed.

MARKTKIRCHE UNSER LIEBEN FRAUEN (Market Church) is a late Gothic hall church with four towers, each pair originating from two earlier Romanesque churches. Martin Luther preached here, Handel learned the organ, and Johann Sebastian Bach's son, Friedmann, served as the church organist.

▲ HAMBURG (308 C5) ★
HAMBURG *pop. 1,650,000*
Almost completely destroyed in World War II, Hamburg, on the Elbe River, is one of Europe's major ports, Germany's second largest city, and is today an out-standing example of urban modernity. The city owes much of its character to Lake Alster, which is separated by the Lombard Bridge into Aussen (Outer)

and Binnenalster (Inner Alster). The banks of the Outer Alster are dotted with the city merchants' white villas; along the Inner Alster are hotels and commercial buildings. One row of attrac-tive gabled warehouses from the 17th century still stands in Diechstrasse, near the Nikolai Fleet Canal.

In the lively St. Pauli entertainment quarter, the Reeperbahn and side streets are lined with restaurants, nightclubs, dance halls, shooting galleries and other amusement spots. Hamburg has three municipal theaters, over 30 private ones, and Germany's oldest opera house.

HAUPTKIRCHE ST. MICHAELIS, Krayen-kamp and Ost-West-Strasse, is a baroque church built between 1751 and 1762. Michel, the rotunda-topped tower, provides a panorama of the city.

KUNSTHALLE (City Art Museum), off Glockengiesserwall 1, specializes in German medieval, Romantic and primitive paintings, but also has 17th- and 18th-century European art. Special exhibitions are presented.

MUSEUM FÜR HAMBURGISCHE GE-SCHICHTE, off Holstenwall, traces the development of the city from medieval times. Displays include models of Old Hamburg, railways and ships.

MUSEUM FÜR KUNST UND GEWERBE (Museum for Arts and Crafts) one block west of Steintorwall, contains exhibits from Europe and Asia arranged chrono-logically beginning with the Middle Ages.

RATHAUS, Rathausmarkt, is a neo-Renaissance building with a fine vaulted ceiling where the city's parliament meets. The spire rises nearly 113 meters (371 feet).

HAMELN (308 C4)
NIEDERSACHSEN *pop. 60,000*
According to legend, all the rats of Hameln (Hamelin) were driven out of

GERMANY

town in 1284 by the ratcatcher. When the townspeople refused to pay him, he charmed the children away with his magic pipe and became known as the Pied Piper.

Hamelin, is also known for its stone Renaissance Weser houses with timbered façades and gables, decorated with coats of arms and carvings. Fine examples are in Osterstrasse including the Dempterhaus, Hochzeitshaus (House of Weddings) and Leisthaus.

LEISTHAUS, 9 Osterstrasse, is an old patrician building that now houses the Städkisches Museum (municipal museum), with a religious art collection and several rooms in period style.

HANNOVER (306 C4)
NIEDERSACHSEN *pop. 510,000*

Lively, industrial Hannover is the capital of Niedersachsen (Lower Saxony). The royal House of Brunswick was based in Hannover from the late 17th century, and subsequently inherited the British throne in 1714 through a marriage to the House of Stuart. It then became known as the House of Hannover. This situation prevailed until 1837, when the dynasty split. The city was bombed in World War II but has been reconstructed.

The oldest part of town is the charming *Altstadt* (old town), with many half-timbered and gabled buildings, including the 17th-century Ballhof, a former sports hall and now a theater, and the *Altes Rathaus* (old town hall), built in 1455. The Roter Faden (Red Thread) is a walking tour painted in red on the ground leading to 36 places of interest. From late May to early September, the annual Herrenhausen Festival of concerts, plays, ballets is held.

HERRENHÄUSER GARTEN, off Nienburgerstrasse, is an extensive, immaculately kept garden complex developed in the late 17th and early 18th centuries by the Brunswick family. These are Germany's only unspoiled baroque gardens and include an orangery and garden theater.

HISTORISCHES MUSEUM, am Hohen Ufer, incorporates the Beginen Tower, a remaining piece of the old city walls. Apart from telling the history of the city, the museum displays four state coaches still owned by the House of Hannover.

KESTNER MUSEUM, Trammplatz 3, was founded in 1889; in addition to its Egyptian collection, the museum has examples of ancient Mediterranean and medieval arts and crafts, china and porcelain, and miniature works of art.

LEIBNIZHAUS, in old town, was the home of philosopher and mathematician Gottfried Wilhelm von Leibniz. Once regarded as one of the finest houses in Germany, this Renaissance building was

---

BIG DRINKER

In the *Fassbau* (wine vat building) of the Heidelberg Schloss is the celebrated Great Vat, a symbol of the Bacchanalian spirit of the Palatine. Nearby is the figure of dwarf court jester Perkeo, who, according to legend, drank unaided the contents of the 2,500-liter (5,550-gallon) receptacle.

---

opened in 1983 as a meeting place for scientists from all over the world.

LEINESCHLOSS (Leine Palace) is at Heinrich-Wilhelm-Kopf-Platz 1. Built 1636–40 and reconstructed 1817–42, the palace is now a meeting place of the *Landtag* (parliament).

MARKTKIRCHE, just off Kamarshstrasse, is a 14th-century Gothic church with a fine altarpiece and stained glass.

NEUES RATHAUS (New Town Hall), Trammplatz 2, was built 1901–13 by Hermann Eggert and Gustav Halmhuber. Models of the city from 1689 to the present are displayed in the dome hall. An elevator ride up the dome tower affords a pleasant view of the area.

NIEDERSÄCHSISCHES LANDESMUSEUM (Museum of Lower Saxony), am Maschpark 5, is devoted to archaeology, natural history and ethnology. The art gallery exhibits European art.

OPERNHAUS, on Georgstrasse, is one of the finest opera houses in Germany; it was designed in the 19th century by architect Georg Laves.

HECHINGEN (306 B1)
BADEN-WÜRTTEMBERG pop. 16,600
Hechingen is an old town in the Swabian Jura often visited by travelers to the nearby castles.

BURG HOHENZOLLERN is 5 kilometers (3 miles) south on Zollern Mountain. Here the Hohenzollerns ruled their small Swabian fiefdom prior to becoming margraves of Brandenburg, kings of Prussia and emperors of Germany. The present castle, built 1850–67 on the site of earlier structures, employs the ground plan of the medieval fortress that preceded it. Inside are the tombs of several Prussian kings, a museum with art objects and documents depicting Prussian history, and two chapels.

HEIDELBERG (308 B2)
BADEN-WÜRTTEMBERG pop. 132,000
The tranquil riverside setting of Heidelberg was an inspiration to several 19th-century German writers, including Goethe. The 16th-century castle is the most prominent landmark, but the colorful Church of the Holy Spirit and Renaissance buildings associated with the university are also of interest. As a result of French attacks and a fire, much of the early town was destroyed at the end of the 17th century, although many baroque buildings remain.

KURPFÄLZISCHES MUSEUM (Palatinate Museum), Hauptstrasse 97, exhibits prehistoric items, coins and porcelain. Displays include the Twelve Apostles Altar, carved in 1509 by Tilman Riemenschneider and discovered over

two centuries later under many thick coatings of paint.

SCHLOSS, overlooking the slate-roofed old city and Neckar Valley, is majestic even in its half-ruined state. For five centuries, electors of the Palatinate Dynasty lived here until its virtual destruction in 1693.

Its fortifications include towers and gates, and now house noteworthy collections. The Friedrichsbau boasts an extensive gallery of German notables: Charlemagne; Ruprecht III, founder of the university; and Friedrich II, creator of the Ottheinrichbau, in whose vaults is the Deutches Apothekenmuseum.

HEILBRONN (308 B2)
BADEN-WÜRTTEMBERG pop. 111,000
Heilbronn is a thriving and important industrial community. It was devastated in World War II, but is now rebuilt.

Two buildings date back to the 13th century the House of the Order of the Teutonic Knights; and the Church of St. Peter and St. Paul. The city holds many festivals – a nine-day one for wine (Weinfest), and a boat pageant (Neckarfest) which alternates with the town festival (Stadtfest). A horse fair (Pferdmarkt) is held in February.

BURG GUTTENBERG, 20 kilometers (12½ miles) north, is one of the oldest and best-preserved castles in the Neckar Valley. It has a wooden library, and the defense structures are of interest. It also contains Europe's largest collection of birds of prey.

HILDESHEIM (308 C4)
NIEDERSACHSEN pop. 106,500
Hildesheim's places of interest include the cathedral, known for its bronze doors with biblical scenes; a purportedly 1,000-year-old rosebush; the Basilica of St. Godehard; St. Michael's Church; and the 15th-century Templarhaus.

ROEMER-PELIZAEUS MUSEUM, Am Steine to the west of the cathrdral, is housed in

GERMANY

the old Franciscan monastery. It contains the most important Egyptological collection in Germany after the Egyptian Museum in Berlin, as well as outstanding collections of natural history and ethnography. There are periodic special exhibitions.

▲ KARLSRUHE (308 B2)
BADEN-WÜRTTEMBERG *pop. 268,500*

Shaped like a fan with majestic avenues radiating from its 18th-century Margrave's Palace, Karlsruhe so impressed Thomas Jefferson that he suggested it as a model for Washington, D.C. The city is an important inland harbor and one of Germany's major industrial centers.

SCHLOSS is a reconstruction of the mid-18th-century, late-baroque residence of the margraves of Baden. Surrounded by gardens, the palace is now the home of the Badisches Landesmuseum (Baden

---

THE GRIMM BROTHERS

Jacob and Wilhelm Grimm were born in Hanau in 1785 and 1786, and came to live in Kassel to take up their posts as court librarians. They wrote down stories and fairy tales which had been transmitted by word of mouth for centuries. Many tales, such as *Hansel and Gretel* and *Red Riding Hood*, originated from the area around Trendelburg (Hesse). A third brother illustrated the tales, and the first collection was published in 1812. Kassel devotes a museum to them.

Museum of Local History), which has exhibits of antiques and arts and crafts of the region.

KASSEL (308 C3)
HESSE *pop. 205,000*

In 1277, Landgrave Heinrich of Hesse chose Kassel, on the Fulda River, as his residence, and the family remained here for over 600 years. In the early part of the 18th century they created the grand park of Wilhelmshöhe and encouraged industry. Much of the town was destroyed during World War II (arms were manufactured here), but it has now been rebuilt.

Kassel proudly preserves its parks and gardens, and every five years holds a multimedia avant-garde art festival, Documenta.

DEUTSCHES TAPETENMUSEUM, Brüder-Grimm-Platz 5, features wall coverings from the late Middle Ages to the present, including tapestries from the 16th to 19th centuries.

LANDESMUSEUM (Hessian Provincial Museum – same building as Tapeten Museum) contains applied art, physics and astronomy exhibits, prehistoric finds and displays of amber.

SCHLOSS WILHELMSHÖHE is on a slope of the Häbichtswald forest area, about 14 kilometers (9 miles) west. The layout, in the form of an inverted V, is unique in Europe. The ornately decorated *Schloss* houses the State Art Collection, first assembled by the landgraves of Hesse. The Gallery of Old Masters contains over 600 paintings, with a large number of Rembrandts, as well as works by Van Dyck, Titian and Tintoretto. The museum also has an excellent sculpture gallery.

Löwenburg, in the southern section of the park, was built in 1793–98 in the form of a Gothic-style English castle ruin. An armor collection is inside.

SCHLOSS WILHELMSTAL is a small rococo palace about 15 kilometers (9½ miles) northwest of Kassel, set deep in the forest. Built about 1760, it houses period furniture, porcelain and portraits by Johann Heinrich Tischbein.

▲ KIEL (308 C5)
SCHLESWIG-HOLSTEIN *pop. 250,000*

Kiel is the capital of Schleswig-Holstein, and stands at the western end of the canal that connects the Baltic with the North Sea. On land, visitors can enjoy parks and beaches; at sea, an annual regatta is held in June.

SCHLESWIG-HOLSTEIN FREILICHTMUSEUM is 6 kilometers (3½ miles) southwest at Molfsee. Farms and buildings dating from the 16th through 19th centuries have been reassembled here.

▲ KOBLENZ (308 B3)
RHEINLAND-PFALZ pop. 108,000
Patricians' houses and noblemen's mansions give evidence of the cultural past of Koblenz (Coblence), now a thriving wine center. The Romans established a fort as early as 9 BC, making Coblence one of the oldest towns in Germany. It was a royal seat of the Franks and later, after World War I, served as the headquarters of the Joint Allied Commission for the Rhineland. Because the majority of Coblence was destroyed in World War II, the rebuilt city has a modern appearance.

Ninth-century St. Kastor's is said to be the oldest church; the more recent St. Florin's was built in the 12th century. The 18th-century *Rathaus* reflects the elaborate baroque style.

FESTUNG EHRENBREITSTEIN, rising more than 117 meters (384 feet) above the Rhine, is a massive neo-classical fortress that commands a panoramic view of the river valley. An earlier defense built in the 11th century by Erembert was destroyed by the French in 1801. The present structure, built by Prussians (1817–28), is one of the strongest fortresses in Europe. Today, the fortress houses a memorial to the German army, a youth hostel and the Landesmuseum (Regional Museum).

▲ KÖLN (308 B3)
NORDRHEIN-WESTFALEN pop. 1,005,000
Köln (Cologne), founded by the Romans in 38 BC, is now traversed by entire streets of new buildings to replace the medieval ones destroyed during the war; luckily the twin-towered cathedral and a group of Romanesque churches survived. Museums, a concert hall, small theaters and the Rhine Garden Recreation Area are all near the cathedral. The liveliest time of year is January and February, which is carnival season.

DOM (Cologne Cathedral) is one of the largest Gothic structures in the world. Its foundation dates from 1248, but the edifice was not complete until 1880. The first monumental crucifix in northern Europe, created before 1000, and the Golden Shrine of the Three Magi are of special interest.

Schatzkammer (Cathedral Treasury) includes collections of medieval codices, sacred relics, and gold and ivory items.

RÖMISCH-GERMANISCHES MUSEUM, on the south side of the cathedral, portrays early Roman life along the Rhine. The extensive glassware and earthenware collections from the 1st to 5th centuries are augmented by the Dionysus Mosaic. and the Tomb of Poblicius.

ST.-GEREON KIRCHE, Gereondriesch 2–4, is a ten-sided tower constructed in the late 4th century as a memorial chapel for martyrs. A later Romanesque church was built adjoining it.

SCHLOSS AUGUSTUSBURG is in Brühl, 14 kilometers (8½ miles) southwest, and was the 18th-century residence of the Archbishop of Cologne. The palace contains valuable furnishings; the grand staircase by Balthasar Neumann is especially noteworthy. Formal gardens surround the palace. Brühl also has Germany's largest theme park, Phantasieland, which is similar to Disneyland.

SCHNÜTGEN-MUSEUM, in Cäcilienkirche, just off Cäcilienstrasse 29, contains ecclesiastical art from the early Middle Ages to the baroque era. Collections include ivory carvings, goldsmiths' work, sculptures, textiles and paintings.

WALLRAF-RICHARTZ LUDWIG MUSEUMS are at Bischofsgartenstrasse. The Ludwig Museum houses modern art from Impressionist works to the most recent trends. In the other museum are medieval paintings, 17th- and 18th-century Dutch masterpieces, and 20th-century German and French works.

KONSTANZ (308 B1)
BADEN-WÜRTTEMBERG *pop. 75,000*

Surrounded by Switzerland except for its Bodensee (Lake Constance) waterfront, Konstanz (Constance) blends medieval and cosmopolitan atmospheres.

Remnants of its distinguished past include the Council of Constance, which was invoked by Emperor Sigismund in 1414 to end the schism in the Christian world, during which three men claimed to be the rightful pope. Population grew over the Council's four-year duration, as Constance became the residence of bishops and kings. By 1418, Martin V had been elected pope, and Jan Hus, one of the most noted precursors of Protestantism, had been condemned for heresy and burned at the stake.

Constance is a cultural and economic center, due primarily to its ideal location on shipping routes. The town has a Renaissance *Rathaus* and local museum (Rosgartenmuseum) with a collection of historic and cultural treasures. The city offers facilities for a variety of water sports, gambling and cruises.

MÜNSTER, Münsterplatz was begun in the 11th century. This fine Romanesque cathedral reflects the architectural styles of 600 years during which construction continued. Of note are carved panels in the main façade's doorway, the rich treasury, the 9th-century crypt and the tombs.

LANDSHUT (308 D1)
BAYERN *pop. 59,000*

The seat of Bavarian dukes from 1204–1503, Landshut retains much of the atmosphere of a medieval capital despite the growth of modern suburbs.

The banks of the Isar River are lined with Gothic buildings, including 15th-century St. Martinskirche, with a 133-meter (436-foot) brick steeple said to be the highest in the world. The city's main event is the Landshuter Hochzeit, a triennial commemoration of a medieval duke's wedding.

Landshut's other points of interest include its Gothic churches – Dominikanerkirche, St.-Jodokskirche and Heilig-Geist-Kirche – and the Kloster Seligenthal, a Cistercian convent (1259).

The Burg Trausnitz, a medieval fortress high above the city, and the Stadtresidenz, reputed to be the oldest Renaissance palace in Germany, once housed the dukes of Landshut. The Stadtresidenz is now an art gallery.

LANGENBURG
BADEN-WÜRTTEMBERG *pop. 1,900*

SCHLOSSMUSEUM, in Schloss Langenburg, has a good collection of historic weapons, porcelain, portraits and hunting trophies, as well as displays pertaining to 12th-century fortifications. The *Schloss* is also home to the Deutsches Automuseum.

▲ LEIPZIG (309 D3)
SACHSEN *pop. 530,000*

Leipzig's position above the confluence

RICHARD WAGNER

Richard Wagner was born in Leipzig in 1813 and studied musical composition at Leipzig University. His *Symphony in C Major* was performed at the Leipzig Gewandhaus in 1833, a dozen years before he earned public acclaim for *Rienzi*, a five-act grand opera first performed in Dresden.

---

of the Piesse, Parthe and West Elster rivers earned the town a mention in written history as early 1015, when it was called Urbs Libzi. A burgeoning foreign trade in the Middle Ages helped to establish two annual fairs at Leipzig, and by 1700 it was Germany's most powerful commercial center.

Cultural stirrings began in Leipzig when Johann Sebastian Bach was appointed the city's musical director in 1728. The city entered military history during the Napoleonic Wars with the Battle of Leipzig in 1813.

Leipzig is important as an intellectual, cultural and industrial city. The ancient Leipzig Trade Fairs still take place in early March and in September.

In spite of being severely damaged in World War II and neglected in the ensuing 40 years, Leipzig is now picking up the pieces and re-establishing itself. Historic buildings include the Altes Rathaus, the Old Stock Exchange, Auerbach's Cellar and the 13th-century Thomaskirche.

LIMBURG (308 B3)
HESSE *pop. 31,100*
The 13th-century Cathedral of St. George stands on a rocky height, dominating Limburg an der Lahn. Murals in the early Gothic church date from the building's construction. The city itself contains many old half-timbered houses.

SCHLOSS WEILBURG, 20 kilometers (12½ miles) northeast on the B49 road at Weilburg, is a 16th-century Renaissance palace renovated in baroque style around 1700. Richly furnished rooms reflect the styles of the period from the 16th to 19th centuries.

LINDAU (308 C1) ★
BAYERN *pop. 25,000*
Lindau am Bodensee is an island resort on Lake Constance with Renaissance and baroque houses built by rich merchants in the Middle Ages. The baroque Hans Carazzen has a museum of local history.

LÜBECK (308 C5) ★
SCHLESWIG-HOLSTEIN *pop. 215,000*
Lübeck's docks, old streets and brick buildings testify to the prosperity the city enjoyed in the late Middle Ages,

when it was the seat of the powerful Hanseatic League. Architectural monuments include the towered Holsten Gate, the cathedral with its carved triumphal cross, and the brick *Rathaus*.

Between the town's main streets is a maze of secluded interconnecting courts and passageways, which have been restored and are open to the public. The fashionable Baltic resort town of Travemünde is 15 kilometers (9½ miles) northeast, with ferry connections to Denmark, Finland and Sweden.

LÜNEBURG (308 C4)
NIEDERSACHSEN *pop. 65,000*
Lüneburg is an ancient spa town with many restored Gothic and Renaissance buildings, including the churches of St. John and St. Nicholas. The medieval *Rathaus* is the oldest in Germany and contains notable artworks.

▲ MAGDEBURG (308 D4)
SACHSEN-ANHALT *pop. 289,000*
Magdeburg was a tiny settlement on the Elbe River near Slavic territories when Otto I founded the Benedictine Abbey of Sts. Peter, Maurice and Innocent here around AD 937. Until it was burned down in the 12th century, Magdeburg played an important role in the German colonization of the lands east of the Elbe.

Magdeburg rose from its ashes to become a thriving and important commercial center by the 13th century and went on to function as a leading member of the Hanseatic League. The town survived the attacks of imperial forces during the Thirty Years' War, but fell in 1631 to the Count of Tilly, who burned the city again and murdered 20,000 of its 30,000 inhabitants. Magdeburg became a secular duchy under the Peace of Westphalia in 1648, and was passed on to the electorate of Brandenburg in 1680. It became part of the Kingdom of Westphalia in 1806 after being defeated by Napoléon Bonaparte. The city gained new prominence in 1815, when it was chosen as the capital of the Prussian province of Saxony.

The town was badly damaged in World War II. Magdeburg has, however, restored several of its historic buildings.

DOM ST. MAURITIUS UND KATHERINA (Cathedral of Saints Maurice and Catherine) exemplifies Gothic and Romanesque styles. Its basilica has a polygonal choir aisle and Ernst Barlach's memorial to the fallen of World War I.

KLOSTER UNSER LIEBEN FRAUEN (Convent of Our Lady) exemplifies the Romanesque style of the 11th and 12th centuries. The church, cloisters and refectory (now restored) are considered some of the best examples of monastic architecture of this period.

MAINZ (308 B2)
RHEINLAND-PFALZ *pop. 186,000*
Mainz is the capital of Rhineland-Palatinate. In medieval times the intelligentsia and the church dignitaries of the Holy Roman Empire assembled here. Reflecting the city's past are the Romanesque cathedral, the Gutenberg Museum and the Central Romano-Germanic Museum in the south wing of the electoral palace. The windows in St. Stephanskirche were created by Chagall. The city holds a wine festival in August and September. *Fastnacht*, a German version of Mardi Gras, is of particular interest.

ST.-MARTINS DOM (St. Martin's Cathedral) was begun in AD 975, but most of it was constructed from the 11th through the 13th centuries. It is one of the best examples of Romanesque religious architecture on the upper Rhine. Dom und Diözesan Museum (Cathedral and Diocesan Museum), in the cloister, displays medieval sculpture.

MANNHEIM (308 B2)
BADEN-WÜRTTEMBERG *pop. 324,000*
Mannheim is an important industrial crossroads at the junction of the Rhine and Neckar rivers. The castle, the Jesuit church and the *Rathaus* are the city's most admired buildings.

THE MARBURG COLLOQUY

Held in Marburg Schloss in 1529, the Marburg Colloquy had as its main participants Martin Luther and Ulrich Zwingli, who debated the question of the Eucharist. Although the question was not resolved, other points raised at the meeting had far-reaching effects on the development of the Reformation movement.

MARBURG (308 B3)
HESSE *pop. 75,000*
Marburg has remained intact since medieval times, and is attractively situated on the steep banks of the Lahn Valley. In the lower town, several buildings which once belonged to the Order of Teutonic Knights cluster around Elisabethkirche, the first Gothic building in Germany, elaborately decorated with statues, frescoes and winged altars. In the upper town is the Marktplatz (with half-timbered houses) and the attractive late-Gothic *Rathaus*.

SCHLOSS, 1.5 kilometers (1 mile) west of the town, is a massive 13th-century Gothic palace inhabited by the descendants of St. Elizabeth. It has a fine chapel and Rittersaal (Knights Hall).

MAULBRONN (308 B2)
BADEN-WÜRTTEMBERG *pop. 6,200*
The highlight of this small town is Kloster Maulbronn, one of the oldest Cistercian abbeys in the country. The Romanesque abbey church dates from the mid-12th century. There is also a 14th-century chapter house and a 13th-century refectory and cloisters.

MEERSBURG (308 B1)
BADEN-WÜRTTEMBERG *pop. 5,000*
Meersburg means "sea castle." Its location on Lake Constance makes it a popular place for rowing and sailing.

ALTES SCHLOSS was originally begun in the 7th century and was the residence of the prince-bishops of Constance, who made several structural changes and additions. It later became the home of the Westphalian 19th-century poet Annette von Droste-Hülshoff. The four gables, dungeons and castle keep are noteworthy.

MEISSEN (309 D3)
SACHSEN *pop. 36,000*
Slaves founded Meissen, formerly Misni, on the Elbe River just northwest of Dresden before the 10th century. King Henry I proclaimed the settlement a German town in AD 929, and 39 years later the community became the seat of the Margrave of Meissen.

In 1205, having become one of the largest German settlements in the east, the town was chartered as Meissen. The golden age of the town was in the 13th and 14th centuries, when the Albrechtsburg Castle and several Gothic cathedrals were built. The surviving 13th-century cathedral is in the courtyard of the castle. Meissen is, however, best known for its fine hard-paste porcelain industry, which was moved from Dresden in the early 18th century.

MICHELSTADT (308 B2) ★
HESSE *pop. 16,000*
The Odenwald mountain town of Michelstadt boasts architecture that dates almost exclusively from the 15th century. Among the buildings are the half-timbered 1484 *Rathaus*, the Stadtkirche, and the library. In the market square is St. Michael's Fountain. The Oldenwaldmuseum displays local art and handicrafts.

MINDEN (308 B4)
NORDRHEIN-WESTFALEN *pop. 84,000*
Minden, an old Hanseatic city, has a cathedral and Renaissance houses.

SCHLOSS BÜCKEBURG, about 10 kilometers (6 miles) southeast, is a lake castle with Renaissance and baroque additions. Inside are a baroque chapel and golden hall, and an art gallery.

MITTENWALD (308 C1)
BAYERN *pop. 8,300*
Mittenwald, in the valley of the 2,160-meter (7,087-foot) Karwendel Mountains, is noted for its ski facilities. It is also a health resort and offers good walking and climbing. The town itself is very attractive: many of the old houses lining the streets are decorated with murals.

▲ MÜNCHEN (308 D1) ★
BAYERN *pop. 1,300,000*
München (Munich), once regarded as the "German Rome," is Germany's third largest city and the capital of Bavaria. Its early rulers wanted Munich to become one of the leading cultural centers of Europe, and today its museums house some of the best collections in Germany.

Although the city dates from the 9th century, it did not begin to prosper until it was granted market rights in 1158. About a century later Munich became the home of the Wittelsbachs, a ducal family linked to the town for more than 700 years. These Bavarian rulers fortified their capital and decorated it with magnificent residences, elegant parks and gardens, regal streets and squares, churches, art galleries, theaters and concert halls. The Wittelsbachs were largely responsible for Munich's ascendancy as a center of German music, literature and visual arts.

The last Bavarian king, Ludwig III, abdicated the throne in 1918, and Munich pursued its image as a city of industry and innovation. Politically significant as the headquarters of the Nazi Party, it was the scene of the 1923 *putsch* against Bavarian authorities and the setting for the conference of 1938.

Munich was heavily bombed during World War II, but reconstruction was rapid and dramatic. Today the architecture illustrates different eras the city has survived.

The traditional center of the old city is the Marienplatz, which marks the intersection of medieval trade routes. South of this square lies the medieval section of the city, a triangular area

GERMANY

roughly delineated by Sendlinger Strasse and Zweibrücken.

The center of Munich is easily explored on foot, as much of the old part is traffic-free. A good starting point is the Hauptbahnhof (Central Railroad Station); east of this is Karlsplatz, also called Stachus, and down Neuhauser Strasse, and Kaufingerstrasse is the heart of the city, Marienplatz. Southeast of Marienplatz is the Heiliggeistkirche (Holy Trinity Church), founded in the 13th century. Close by is the Viktualienmarkt, a large open-air food market.

Further north is Max-Joseph Platz, dominated by the huge Nationaltheater and rococo Ehemaliger Postamt (former main post office). The Hofbräuhaus, Munich's best-known beer hall (founded in 1589), is nearby.

The most dignified of Munich's squares is the Odeonsplatz. From here you can see the baroque Theatinerkirche and, opposite it, the Feldernhalle (Generals' Hall), built in 1837. The nearby Hofgarten is a relaxing place to escape the city bustle.

The Isar River runs on the east side of the city and along its banks, northward, extends the Englischer Garten. On the far side is the Maximilaneum, now the seat of the Bavarian Parliament. Also to the north is Schwabing, an area popular with Munich's youth.

There is no shortage of cultural entertainment: the Nationaltheater hosts the Bayerishche Staatsoper (Bavarian State Opera), as well as ballet and varied concerts. Maximilianstrasse is the area for theater, and the Residenztheater and Kammerspiele are venues for both classical and modern drama.

Munich has two resident professional orchestras, with the Gasteig Arts Center on the Kellerstrasse one of the city's main concert venues. Jazz is popular, mostly heard in Schwabing, while discotheques and nightclubs thrive throughout the city.

Munich is famous for its 16-day *Oktoberfest*, which begins on the last Saturday in September. The celebration

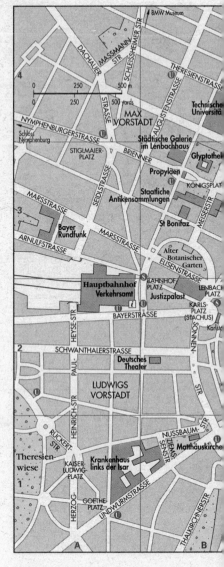

originates from the large fair held in 1810 to celebrate the marriage of Prince (later King) Ludwig I to Therese of Saxe-Hildburghausen. *Fasching* is the pre-Lenten carnival, with colorful decorations and masquerades.

Modern Franz Josef Strauss Airport lies 29 kilometers (18 miles) northeast of the city center. Trains and express buses depart for the Hauptbahnhof every 20

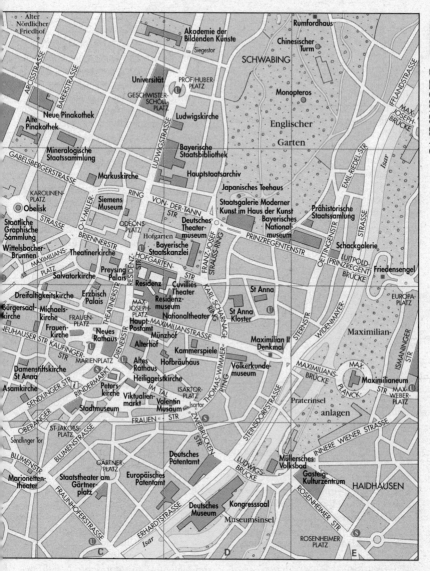

minutes during the day. The city's public transport system is excellent: as well as the rapid transit rail system there is an underground railway, streetcars and buses. Tickets can be bought from machines, for a single journey or for several journeys. A day travel ticket may be more economical – always remember to cancel the ticket in a special machine once you have boarded the vehicle.

(Urban railroad stations – S-Bahn and U-Bahn – are marked on the city map in red circles as S and U.)

ALTE PINAKOTHEK (339 B4), Barerstrasse 27, contains one of the most impressive art collections in the world. The gallery houses European masterpieces from the 14th through the 18th centuries. Notable are works by Dürer, Rubens, Van Dyck,

Rembrandt, El Greco and Pieter Brueghel.

ASAMKIRCHE (339 B2), Sendlinger Strasse 61, is a masterpiece of rococo architecture built by the two Asam brothers (1733–46) as a private family church. Dedicated to St. Johann Nepomuk, (one bone and his wax effigy lie in a glass reliquary), the white and gold interior displays a profusion of statuary and decoration; a ceiling fresco depicts the saint's life.

BAYERISCHES NATIONALMUSEUM (Bavarian National Museum) (339 D3), main building at Prinzregentenstrasse 3, houses Bavarian arts and crafts from the Middle Ages to the 18th century.

BMW-MUSEUM, Petuelring 130, houses a collection of cars, motorcycles and airplane engines and traces modern technological developments.

DACHAU – *see box opposite*.

DEUTSCHESMUSEUM, on the Isarinsel (Isar Island), is one of the best science and technology museums in the world. Exhibits include the latest scientific and technological innovations.

ENGLISCHER GARTEN (339 D4) was the idea of an American soldier, Benjamin Thompson, who in 1789 persuaded officials to drain some marshland and create a garden. The area is really a large city park and is a popular picnic spot. From the Monopteros (rotunda), built in 1837, is a good view of the city skyline.

FRAUENKIRCHE (339 C2), just west of Neues Rathaus, is a mammoth Gothic church with twin onion-shaped towers. The structure, badly damaged in World War II, has been restored and holds many works of Gothic art.

GLYPTOTHEK (338 B3), Königsplatz 3, is a classical building that contains Greek and Roman statues collected by Ludwig I. Do not miss the carved pediment from

---

CONCENTRATION CAMPS

Part of Germany's history which many wish had never happened are the concentration camps. The sites are now preserved as memorials, containing permanent exhibitions and showing films recording conditions. At Dachau, near Munich, the first such camp, the gas chambers and crematorium still stand. Sachsenhausen, in a Berlin suburb, has only recently been opened and the large site remains much as it was, with the addition of photographs and exhibits depicting the horrors. At Buchenwald, 10 kilometers (6 miles) northwest of Weimar, over 50,000 people died.

---

the Aphaia Temple in Aegina. The adjacent Antikensammlungen (Antique Collection) holds Etruscan jewelry, Greek vases and small statues.

MICHAELSKIRCHE (St. Michael's Church) (339 C2), Neuhauser Strasse 52, was built at the end of the 16th century in Renaissance style; the baroque features were added later. The vaulted aisle is said to be the second largest in Europe, after St. Peter's in Rome. In the crypt is the tomb of "mad" Ludwig II.

NEUE PINAKOTHEK (New Picture Gallery) (339 C4), Barerstrasse, is a repository of 18th- and 19th-century paintings and sculpture, many by Bavarian artists such as Gustav Klimt and Carl Spitzweg. French Impressionists (Cézanne and Gauguin) are represented, and one of van Gogh's *Sunflowers* paintings is exhibited here. There is also a collection of art nouveau works.

NEUES RATHAUS (339 C2), Munich's "new" town hall, was completed in the 19th century and dominates Marienplatz. Crowds gather in the square to watch the hall's *glockenspiel*, a mechanical timepiece with many dancing figures.

PETERSKIRCHE (St. Peter's Church) (339 C2), Rindermarkt, is the oldest of the city's parish churches, a mixture of ornate styles from Gothic to 17th and 18th centuries. Notable statues include a 15th-century representation of St. Peter. The bones of St. Munditia, patron saint of single women, lie in a jeweled shroud inside a glass box.

RESIDENZ (339 C3), entered from Residenzstrasse 1, is a complex of buildings built by the Wittelsbach family between the 16th and 19th centuries as a royal residence. Though destroyed in World War II, the opulent palace has been painstakingly rebuilt. The Residenzmuseum, entered from Max Joseph Platz 3, must be visited twice to see all the rooms, as they open at various times.

Highlights include the Ahnengalerie (Ancestors' Gallery) with over 100 family portraits; the Grotto Court; and the Antiquarium, a huge, vaulted chamber originally built to display the family's antiquities and later decorated with frescoes. The eight Reiche Zimmer (Rich Rooms) are sumptuous, as are two 17th-century chapels.

The Schatzkammer (Treasury – entrance from Residenzstrasse) contains crowns, clocks, caskets and religious treasures. The charming rococo Cuvilliés-Theater (named after its designer, a former court dwarf) is decorated with gold and stucco; Mozart's opera *Idomeneo* was first performed here and the theater is still in use. From Hofgartenstrasse, there is access to the Ägyptischer Kunst (Egyptian Collection).

SCHLOSS NYMPHENBURG (Nymphenburg Palace), 11 kilometers (7 miles) northwest, was built 1664–1758 as a summer residence for Bavarian rulers. The Schönheitsgallerie (Gallery of Beauties) contains portraits of the 36 ladies most admired by Ludwig I. In the two-story Grand Marble Hall are frescoes by Clemens von Zimmerman. The Marstall museum displays royal coaches. The lovely park, part formal, part wild and romantic, includes the Amelienburg hunting lodge, which is sumptuously decorated.

SPIELZEUGMUSEUM (Toy Museum), in the tower of Altes Rathaus (339 C2), Marienplatz, has a collection of toys covering a 200-year period. The Festsaal (Dance Hall), in the other part of the building, can also be visited.

STÄDTISCHE GALERIE IM LENBACHHAUS (339 B3), Luisenstrsse 33, is an Italianate villa once owned by Franz von Lenbach, a 19th-century Bavarian painter. His furnishings and portraits, together with paintings by 20th-century Expressionists such as Kandinsky, Klee, Maske and Marc, are on display.

STADTMUSEUM (City Museum) (339 C2), St. Jakobsplatz 1, is a museum devoted to Munich's past. Dancing puppets carved by Erasmus Grasser in 1480 are unusual examples of secular German Gothic art. There are also separate collections of weapons, musical instruments and a history of the brewing industry.

MUNICH – *see München on p.337.*

MÜNSTER (308 B4)

NORDRHEIN-WESTFALEN *pop. 278,000*
Münster is the capital of Westphalia and an attractive university town. The Prinzipalmarkt, regional museums and the Aasee (lake) area attract sightseers.

DOM, Hortsberg, is a large Romanesque Cathedral built in the 13th century. Highlights are the transept's altarpiece of St. John and the silver tabernacle. The Domkammer (Cathedral Chamber) displays treasures that include an 11th-century gold reliquary of St. Paul.

RATHAUS (Town Hall), Prinzipalmarkt, is a high-gabled Gothic mansion dating from the 14th century. It was destroyed in World War II, then rebuilt to its original style. The Friedessaal (Peace Hall) contains precious Gothic wood furnishings.

GERMANY

Naumburg (308 D3)
SAXON-ANHALT *pop. 31,000*
Situated high above the Saale Valley, Naumburg was founded in the early 11th century as a fortress by the Margrave of Meissen. Many old buildings survive, including a 15th-century gate (Marientor) and a late-Gothic *Rathaus*.

DOM is early Gothic/late Romanesque, with four towers, two choirs and a cloister. Situated in the west choir are the famous life-size sculptures of the world-famed 12 founder figures, carved in limestone around 1250.

▲ Neustadt An Der Weinstrasse (308 B2)
RHEINLAND-PFALZ *pop. 50,000*
Neustadt celebrates every October with the selection of the German Wine Queen and baptism of the new wine. The Festival Hall and busy Market Square testify to the town's involvement in the wine trade, and along its streets there are numerous wine inns where you can taste the products. On the slopes of the Hardt Mountains are the 700-year-old ruins of Wittelsbach Castle.

Nördlingen (308 C2)
BAYERN
In the 14th century, Bavarian traders flocked here for the Whitsun Fair held near the *Rathaus* (the outside stairway was added later). The town's subsequent economic stagnation kept it intact, so today it is a complete medieval town with ramparts. From the tower of the late Gothic St. George's Church, which is situated in the town center (365 steps up), is a view over the town and the Ries (crater) formed by a meteorite that fell here 15 million years ago.

Nürnberg (306 C2) ★
BAYERN *pop. 498,000*
Nürnberg (Nuremberg), a former imperial center dating from the 11th century, is today the principal city of Franconia and one of the largest cities in Bavaria. The city was founded in 1040 as a stronghold by Henry III, Duke of Bavaria and Emperor of Germany. It became a trading center devoted to building and patronage of the arts in the 12th and 13th centuries, reaching its economic and cultural peaks during the 15th and 16th centuries when it was the unofficial capital of Germany.

The Thirty Years' War brought devastation, but industrialization in the 19th century re-established the city's eminence. It was badly bombed in World War II, and subsequently, in 1945, the Allied trials of German war criminals were held here.

The *Altstadt* is the most charming part of the city: medieval walls guarded by 80 towers and pierced by four gateways still enclose it. Much of the charm stems from the high-roofed, half-timbered dwellings and gabled façades. Nuremberg was the home of Albrecht Dürer and Hans Sachs, immortalized in Wagner's opera *Die Meistersinger von Nürnberg*. A toy trade fair (February) and the Christkindlmarkt (the weeks leading up to Christmas) are Nuremberg's most celebrated events.

DÜRER-HAUS, in the *Altstadt*, is where painter and engraver Albrecht Dürer (1471–1528) lived from 1509. Several of his drawings are displayed.

FRAUENKIRCHE (Church of Our Lady), Hauptmarkt, is a 14th-century church with a mechanical clock that presents its "Seven Electors" daily at noon, paying homage to the Holy Roman Emperor.

GERMANISCHES NATIONALMUSEUM (German National Museum), Kornmarkt, sits on the site of a former Carthusian monastery. It surveys German art and cultural history. Also here are works by Dürer and Cranach, woodcarvings by Tilman Riemenschneider, old apothecary shops and an antique toy collection.

KAISERBURG, overlooking the city from the north, was the home of emperors from the 11th to the 15th centuries. The castle was destroyed during World War II, but has since been restored. The Romanesque Imperial Chapel is impressive, as is the view of the town from the Sinwellturm (tower).

ST. LORENZKIRCHE, on Lorenzerstrasse, the largest church in Nuremberg and one of the few to have survived the bombing of World War II, is noted for its exquisite rose window. Other items of interest are an early 15th-century crucifix and the *Annunciation*, a wood-carving by Veit Stoss.

ST. MARTHAKIRCHE, between Königstormauer and Königstrasse, is where the Meistersingers held their classes from 1578 to 1620. Glass paintings from the 14th and 15th centuries can be seen.

ST. SEBALDUSKIRCHE, facing the *Altes Rathaus*, is a 13th-century church with a bronze shrine of St. Sebald by Peter Vischer and his sons. Other noted works are the St. Peter altarpiece, the bronze font and fine stained-glass windows.

SCHÖNER BRUNNEN, Hauptmarkt, a 14th-century Gothic fountain, is ornamented at its base by figures of the Seven Electors, and heroes of the Old Testament and the Middle Ages. A statue of Moses surrounded by the prophets tops the 18-meter (59-foot) spire-like structure.

OBERAMMERGAU (308 C1)
BAYERN *pop. 5,400*
When Germany's Black Plague of 1634 stopped short of tiny Oberammergau, the townspeople vowed to present a play honoring the Passion of Christ every ten years. The continuing tradition has won world fame, as confirmed by half a million visitors during the 100-day presentation period.

This scenic Bavarian town, at 834 meters (2,736 feet), sustains interest in non-play years with its 18th-century rococo church covered with frescoes, including the dome. Many houses in the village are also decorated.

SCHLOSS LINDERHOF is 14 kilometers (9 miles) southwest of town. Built by Ludwig II in Italian Renaissance and French rococo styles, this lavish palace includes a hall of mirrors, and gilded furniture and ornamentation. It is surrounded by gardens dotted with several small buildings and the strange Venus Grotte, modeled on the set of *Tannhäuser*.

OBERSTDORF (308 C1)
BAYERN *pop. 11,000*
Oberstdorf, at 815 meters (2,674 feet), is among the best-known Bavarian winter sports centers. Its tennis, swimming and fishing facilities also make it a favorite summer resort. Oberstdorf leads to the peaceful Kleinwalsertal Valley, a curious Austrian enclave accessible only from Germany.

ÖHRINGEN (306 C2) ★
BADEN-WÜRTTEMBERG *pop. 16,700*
Öhringen has a 17th-century castle and a Gothic church. Its museum exhibits collections of pewter and pottery objects.

NEUENSTEIN SCHLOSS is 6 kilometers (3½ miles) east. This 16th-century castle belonged to the ruling Hohenlohe family, and its Renaissance furnishings recall court life in centuries past.

OSNABRÜCK (306 B4)
NIEDERSACHSEN *pop. 161,000*
Charlemagne laid the foundation for modern Osnabrück, and the fortified city subsequently became an important commercial center and judicial seat. Its place in history was assured when negotiations for the Treaty of Westphalia were held in 1648, forging the way for the end of the Thirty Years' War. Modern Osnabrück is a commercial and industrial town, and as the seat of a bishopric is the largest diocese in northern Germany.

Much of the city was rebuilt after World War II, but the medieval town hall remains as Osnabrück's best-known tourist attraction. Also worth a visit are St. Mary's Church, St. Peter's Cathedral and the Church of St. John, all Gothic buildings featuring unusual ornamentation and artwork.

RATHAUS (Town Hall), on Markt, features a statue of Charlemagne surrounded by eight emperors. The Treaty of Westphalia was proclaimed from its steps, and in the Friedensall (Peace Hall), where the talks took place, are portraits of the negotiators and the original chandelier (1554).

OTTOBEUREN (308 C1)
BAYERN pop. 8,000
OTTOBEUREN KLOSTER was founded by the Benedictines in AD 764 and flourished under Charlemagne's patronage. The church was rebuilt beginning in 1737 by Johann-Michael Fischer and is now Germany's largest baroque church, with an airy nave 90 meters (295 feet) long. It has a rich and ornately decorated interior, full of statues and paintings, with stuccowork by J. M. Feuchtmayr and frescoes by J. J. Zeiller. Its two fine organs were built by K. J. Kniepp. The abbey buildings include a museum with exquisite furniture, and a lavishly decorated baroque library with marble columns and painted ceilings.

PASSAU (309 D1)
BAYERN pop. 50,000
Passau is the medieval town where, in 1552, the Holy Roman Emperor Charles V yielded to Protestant prince-bishops at the Treaty of Passau. The city reflects the influence of Italian architects and occupies the point where the Danube, Inn and Ilz rivers all converge. The streets are built on various levels, rising to the hill in the town's center, and quaint archways join the houses. The Residentsplatz, by the cathedral, is an attractive square lined with handsome merchants' houses and bishops' palaces.

DOM ST. STEFAN is a 15th-century Gothic cathedral with an unusual octagonal dome. After the Great Fire of 1662, the building was transformed into a masterpiece of Italian baroque architecture. It houses one of the world's largest church organs.

NEUE RESIDENZ was the 18th-century former palace of Passau's prince-bishops. The elaborate baroque interior contains lavish furnishings and houses a museum and treasury.

RATHAUS (Town Hall), built in the 14th century near the Danube, is decorated with murals representing scenes from the Niebelungen sagas.

VESTE OBERHAUS, on a hill across the Danube River, is a fortress begun in the 13th century by the prince-bishops and added to over the centuries. It is now a local and regional history museum.

▲ POTSDAM (309 D4) ★
BRANDENBURG pop. 130,000
Potsdam, at the confluence of the Nuthe and Havel rivers, is the former capital of Brandenburg province. Founded by Slavs before the 11th century, Potsdam was an electoral residence of Frederick William, the Great Elector, in the mid-17th century. A century later Frederick the Great selected the town for a royal residence, and Potsdam became the intellectual and military center of Prussia. Frederick and the succeeding kings of Prussia built many of the baroque structures for which Potsdam is known.

In the 18th century, Dutch settlers added their own architectural accents to Potsdam, enhancing the city's collection of ornate buildings. Although it sustained heavy damage during the bombings of World War II, several of Potsdam's most beautiful buildings have survived.

SCHLOSS CECILIENHOF, built in the early 20th century, was the site of the Potsdam Conference during July and August 1945.

NEUES PALAIS was built 1763–9 as a summer residence for Prussia's royal family. The walls of the 19th-century receiving room are embedded with semiprecious stones and seashells.

SCHLOSS SANSSOUCI, built by Knobelsdorff (1745–53), is considered one of the finest examples of German rococo architecture in the world. The picture gallery displays works by artists such as Rubens and Tintoretto, and in the landscaped park is a Chinese teahouse and a grand fountain.

THE POTSDAM AGREEMENT

Signed in August 1945 by leaders of the Allied Powers, this agreement divided Germany and Austria into zones controlled by the Soviet and Western Allies. It also decided the future of Germany.

QUEDLINBURG (308 C3)
SACHSEN-ANHALT *pop. 27,000*
Henry I established Quedlinburg in AD 922 as a fortress on the Bode River in the Lower Harz Mountains. Otto I added a new dimension to town life when he built an imperial abbey in AD 968 and designated his daughter as the abbess. As a member of the Hanseatic League in the 1400s, Quedlinburg flourished. It came under the rule of Saxony before becoming part of the Kingdom of Prussia in the 18th century.

Today Quedlinburg is an industrial and manufacturing city that has preserved a number of its half-timbered houses, medieval churches and battlements. The 16th-century castle stands on the site of the original fortress. The 11th- and 12th-century Church of St. Servatius includes the remains of the original abbey church.

RASTATT (308 B2)
BADEN-WÜRTEMBERG *pop. 40,000*
LUSTLOSS FAVORITE, 8 kilometers (5 miles) southwest, was the pleasure palace of Margravine Sibylla Augusta, wife of Ludwig the Turk. The interior decorations are opulent and unusual.

REGENSBURG (308 D2) ★
BAYERN *pop. 128,000*
"Regensburg's situation is enchanting," Johann Wolfgang von Goethe once said. As early as AD 179, the Romans had established a military encampment here and called it Castra Regina.

Regensburg claims to be Germany's largest medieval town, which fortunately escaped damage in World War II. In the Middle Ages, it was one of Europe's most prosperous cities; about 20 Italian-style tower houses survive. Its attractive features include the 12th-century Schottenkirche St. Jakob, the 12th-century Steinerne Brücke (Stone Bridge) that extends nearly across the Danube, and the *Rathaus*, the Gothic town hall. The Porta Praetoria, a ruined Roman gate, was once the northern watchtower on the Danube River.

DOM, Domplatz, is one of the finest examples of German Gothic architecture. Built between the 13th and 15th centuries, with spires added in the 19th century, it contains some 14th-century stained-glass windows and medieval sculptures. Gothic cloisters include two chapels, one is Romanesque and contains original frescoes. Regensburger Domspatzen (Sparrows of Regensburg Cathedral) boys' choir is one of the best-known in Germany.

SCHLOSS THURN UND TAXIS incorporates the former Benedictine Monastery of St. Emmeram, founded in the 8th century. Its baroque interior was designed by the Asam brothers. Ornate royal tombs stand here, and three crypts lie below.

STADTMUSEUM, in a former monastery on Berthodstrasse, recounts the town's social and cultural history.

▲ ROSTOCK (308 D5)
MECKLENBURG-VORPOMMERN
pop. 240,000
At the head of the Warnow River estuary 13 kilometers (8 miles) below its entry into the Baltic Sea, Rostock is a fishing

and shipbuilding center that has preserved many of its medieval monuments. Formed by the union of three separate towns in 1265, Rostock was an influential member of the Hanseatic League in the 14th century. The city became part of Mecklenburg province in 1314 and later passed to the Dukes of Mecklenburg-Schwerin, then to the Schwerin and Güstrow rulers before gaining independence. In 1419, one of Europe's first universities was founded here.

Significant medieval structures, many now restored, include the 1230 Gothic Church of St. Mary, the early 15th-century St. Peter's Church and the 15th-century *Rathaus*, which has a 18th-century baroque façade. Portions of the ruined town walls and gates can still be seen. Apartments and officesare now occupying the tower and roof space of Nikolaikirche, the town's oldest church.

MARIENKIRCHE (St. Mary's Church), built in 1230, is a well-preserved example of Gothic architecture. Notable features include the late-Gothic altarpiece, an astronomical clock, a baroque high altar and a bronze font.

ROTHENBURG OB DER TAUBER
(308 C2) ★
BAYERN *pop. 12,000*
Set high above the Tauber Valley, Rothenburg is one of the most picturesque towns in Bavaria, with its well-preserved walls along which visitors can walk. Within, the crooked, cobbled streets are lined with half-timbered houses and dotted with fountains.

The Reichsstadt-museum (Imperial City Museum; Rothenburg became an imperial city in 1274) contains a most interesting medieval workroom. The Mitteälterliches Kriminnalmuseum (Middle Ages Crime Museum) contains cells and instruments of torture.

Other points of interest are the 14th-century double bridge, and the Burggarten, on the site of a former castle, from where there are good views

of the townscape. The finest work of the master sculptor Tilman Riemenschneider, the Holy Blood Altar, is in the Gothic Church of St. Jakob.

On Whit Sunday, the Meistertrunk (Masterdraught) is celebrated to recall a turning point in the Thirty Years' War, when the mayor saved the town by quaffing 3 liters (5 pints) of wine.

Rothenburg's location on the Romantische Strasse and the Burgstrasse means that it is usually crowded.

RATHAUS (Town Hall) stands in the Marktplatz. Half of the building is 13th-century Gothic and half is Renaissance (1572–8), with arches added later.

RÜDESHEIM (308 B2)
HESSEN *pop. 10,000*
The importance of Rüdesheim as a wine center is reflected in its unusual wine museum and in the wine festival held every September. This Rhine town is known for its old houses with turrets and gables, as well as its busy tourist street, Drosselgasse. Ehrenfels Castle and St. Hildegard's Church are of interest. Nearby, the huge Neiderwald monument overlooks the Rhine.

BRÖMSERBURG, on the banks of the Rhine, was built during the 12th century and reconstructed seven centuries later. Here are the Rheingau Museum and a wine museum.

▲ SAARBRÜCKEN (308 A2)
SAARLAND *pop. 200,000*
Saarbrücken, on the Franco-German border, is a university and cultural city as well as a major European trade center. The Prince's Palace and the Ludwigskirche are excellent examples of 18th-century baroque architecture. There is also an industrial and natural history museum.

SCHLESWIG (308 C5)
SCHLESWIG-HOLSTEIN *pop. 27,000*
The old capital of the Dukes of Gottorf is situated at the head of the Schlei

River, an inlet of the Baltic. A Viking museum at Haithabu recalls the town's earliest history.

DOM is a Gothic cathedral dedicated to St. Peter. The chancel contains the fine 16th-century carved Bordesholm Altar.

NYDAMBOOT is a 14th-century ship discovered in the marshes of Nydam during the 18th century.

SCHLOSS GOTTORF is a 16th-century castle. Inside are the Landesmuseum and a museum of archaeology.

SCHWÄBISCH HALL (308 C2) ★
BADEN-WÜRTTEMBERG *pop. 33,200*
Schwäbisch Hall, on the banks of the Kocher River, is one of the most picturesque towns in the Swabian Forest. The 15th-century parish church, reached by an imposing 18th-century staircase, contains tombs and unusual furnishings. The *Rathaus* (town hall) is an important baroque building. The town contains medicinal springs, and the Hällisch Fränkisches Museum, in a former mansion (the Keckenburg), chronicles the town's history.

An outdoor summer theater festival is held on the Marktplatz.

▲ SCHWERIN (308 C5)
MECKLENBURG-VORPOMMERN
pop. 130,000
Schwerin was settled by Sorbs before the 11th century. The town first gained official recognition when Henry the Lion granted it a charter in 1160. A bishopric was established 10 years later, and the town became the seat of a countship around the same time. During the Middle Ages, Schwerin was made the capital of the Mecklenburg-Schwerin region. In 1934 it was named capital of the Mecklenburg state.

The Gothic cathedral, begun in 1270 and completed in 1890, includes a library, museums and a conservatory. The huge ducal palace, which served as the residence of the Mecklenburg

dukes, was rebuilt in 1843 in the style of a French château and now houses the state parliament. In one wing is the palace church, dating from the 16th century. To the south is a large baroque garden with an orangery, exotic trees and a canal. In another area of the garden is the state theater and the Staatisches Museum, which houses a famous collection of 17th-century Dutch paintings.

SCHWETZINGEN
BADEN-WÜRTTEMBERG *pop. 20,000*
Schwetzingen is known for its baroque palace park, the Schlossgarten, inspired by Versailles. A stage festival takes place in May and June in the town's 18th-century rococo theater.

SIGMARINGEN (308 B1)
BADEN-WÜRTTEMBERG *pop. 16,000*
Sigmaringen's strategic position on the upper Danube made it the minor capital of the Hohenzollern princes.

SIGMARINGEN SCHLOSS, a palace on a rock high above the upper Danube Valley, was for centuries the headquarters of the Swabian Catholic branch of the Hohenzollerns. The Renaissance palace was constructed on the site of an older castle in the 16th century. Restored in 1893, the castle contains exhibits of arms and a rococo chapel.

SOLINGEN (308 B3)
NORDRHEIN-WESTFALEN *pop. 163,000*
Solingen is one of Europe's oldest producers of cutlery. Berg, which is now incorporated into Solingen, was the capital of Bergische Land in the Middle Ages. It also was the seat of the counts of Berg, residents of Schloss Burg.

DEUTSCHES KLINGENMUSEUM (German Museum of Blades), Wuppertaler Strasse 160, has exhibits tracing the development of cutting weapons from the Stone Age to the present. The museum also commemorates the town's 600-year-old sword-making tradition.

GERMANY

SCHLOSS BURG, an early medieval castle overlooking the Wupper River, houses the Bergisches Museum, which provides a history of the castle and the region.

▲ STUTTGART (308 B2)

BADEN-WÜRTTEMBERG *pop. 559,000*
Stuttgart is set amid wooded hills, orchards and vineyards, and its modern buildings stand in gardens and parks.

The largest city in southwestern Germany and capital of Baden-Württemberg, Stuttgart is an important railroad junction and prosperous industrial center. Its ballet and opera are world-famous, and every three years it hosts an international Musikfest with leading world orchestras.

Nearby are the popular health resort of Bad Cannstatt, the rococo Schloss Solitude and Schwäbisch-Gmünd, a jewelry and silversmith center. Some of the best scenery of the Neckar Valley is just north of Stuttgart.

ALTES SCHLOSS (Old Palace) is in the center of town facing the Schillerplatz. The original moated castle, now the Karlsplatz wing, was erected in the 14th century, and the other Renaissance sections were added in the 16th century. It was reconstructed in 1948 after being gutted by fire in 1944. The palace surrounds a Renaissance courtyard and houses a Protestant chapel.

Württembergisches Landesmuseum (Württemberg State Museum) displays prehistoric and religious relics and medieval art. An interesting highlight is the Württemberg crown jewels.

FERNSEHTURM is a 483-meter (1,585-foot) television tower on the Hoher Bopser; there is a spectacular view from its restaurant and observation platform at 150 meters (492 feet).

LUDWIGSBURG SCHLOSS, 14 kilometers (8½ miles) north, is a huge baroque palace. Of its 450 rooms, 75 with ornate rococo and classical furnishings are open to the public. A formal park surrounds

---

SOLINGEN STEEL

The swords that brought medieval fame to Solingen have been succeeded by Solingen steel knives, razor blades and scissors. Many of the city's foundries are relatively small, and some are quite picturesque.

---

the palace and a highlight is the Märchengarten (fairy-tale garden), where the tales of the brothers Grimm are performed by mechanical figures.

DAIMLER-BENZ MUSEUM contains a collection of commercial and luxury cars, plus ship and airplane engines.

PLANETARIUM, Neckarstrasse 47, is one of the most modern in the world. Changing presentations, lectures, seminars and exhibits reflect the latest developments in space technology.

PORSCHE MUSEUM is at Porschestrasse 42 in Zuffenhausen. Fifty vehicles illustrate the development of the Porsche car.

SCHILLER NATIONALMUSEUM, in Marbach am Neckar, exhibits fine artifacts pertaining to the poet Friedrich von Schiller and other Swabian writers.

SCHLOSS SOLITUDE (Solitude Palace), 10 kilometers (6 miles) southwest, is a rococo castle perched on the edge of a plateau. It was built 1763–67 by the French architect La Guépière as a summer residence for the Württemberg court.

STAATSGALERIE, Konrad-Adenauer-Strasse 30–32, contains a collection of 14th- to 16th-century works by old German masters and members of the Dutch and Italian schools. There is also a display of modern art by French and German Expressionists.

STIFTSKIRCHE (Collegiate Church) was founded in the 12th century and rebuilt in the 15th century; although damaged in World War II, it has since been restored. In the choir is an important piece of Renaissance sculpture showing a series of 11 counts of Württemberg.

WILHELMA is a zoo originally built as a summer residence for Wilhelm I; it is now home to a harmonious combination of plant and animal species.

TRAVEMÜNDE – *see Lübeck on p.335.*

TRIBERG (308 B1)
BADEN-WÜRTTEMBERG *pop. 6,000*
This Black Forest clockmaking town is best known for Gutach Falls, the highest in Germany at 162 meters (531 feet).

TRIER (308 A2)
RHEINLAND-PFALZ *pop. 99,000*
Remnants of Trier's past give an almost continuous account of European history. Among the traces of Roman civilization are a bridge across the Moselle River, three baths, the basilica, a 20,000-seat amphitheater and the Porta Nigra, a massive city gate. Medieval buildings include the Romanesque cathedral, the Basilica of St. Matthias and the baroque St. Paulinuskirche.

TÜBINGEN (308 B1)
BADEN-WÜRTTEMBERG *pop. 82,000*
Tübingen is an old university city on the banks of the Neckar River noted for its peaceful, medieval appearance. It has been a home to such poets and philosophers as Eduard Mörike, Hegel, Schelling and Friedrich Hölderlin, whose house has been converted to a museum. The Platanenallee is a popular promenade on an island in the Neckar. Sights include the castle and the 15th-century Church of St. George.

ÜBERLINGEN (308 B1)
BADEN-WÜRTTEMBERG *pop. 20,000*
Überlingen, on the shore of Bodensee (Lake Constance), has lakeside walks that cross former fortifications. The *Rathaus*, with its Gothic council chamber, the Münster, and the Städtisches Museum,

with 18th-century woodcarvings, are well worth visiting. Gothic Salem Abbey and the castle of Heiligenburg lie 21 kilometers (13 miles) east.

ULM (308 C1)
BADEN-WÜRTTEMBERG *pop. 110,000*
Ulm, on the Danube River, is a major entrance to the Swabian and Algäu mountain districts and the birthplace of Albert Einstein. The 14th-century stately Gothic cathedral is said to have the highest church steeple in Germany – 161 meters (528 feet). Its highlights include detailed reliefs, numerous sculptures, colorful stained-glass windows and masterful stone filigree work.

Also of interest in Ulm is the Deutsches Brotmuseum (Bread Museum) and the Ulm Museum, which is concerned with art and culture from the Middle Ages. The Fischerviertel (Fishermen's Quarter), containing picturesque half-timbered houses, is also worth a visit.

WEIMAR (308 C3) ★
THÜRINGEN *pop. 58,000*
Weimar is noted in historical records as early as AD 975, but the city earned a permanent place in history during the 18th and 19th centuries as the intellectual center of Germany. The home of such literary giants as Goethe and Schiller, Weimar attracted other intellectuals of the period, including Liszt and Nietzsche, who came to Weimar to live and work.

By 1919, Weimar's impressive history made it the ideal venue for leaders of the German National Assembly to draw up the constitution of the new German Republic. The Weimar Republic, as the government was known, lasted from 1919 until 1933, when Adolf Hitler secured the chancellorship of Germany. Although damaged in World War II, many of the city's most impressive structures have now been restored, including the 1767 Wittumspalais; Schloss Weimar, built 1790–1803; Schloss Belvedere, built 1724–50; and Schloss Tiefurt.

Other places of interest are Sts. Peter and Paul Church; the Goethehaus, which includes a musem and Goethe's Gartenhaus, his retreat in Ilm Park; the homes of Schiller and Liszt; and the Goethe-Schiller Mausoleum. The Wittumspalais was built in the 1770s for Duchess Anna Amalia, who was a bastion of the town's cultural life.

WERTHEIM (308 C2)
BADEN-WÜRTTEMBERG *pop. 21,700*
Distinctly medieval in appearance, Wertheim is at the confluence of the Main and Tauber rivers. Gabled, half-timbered houses line the streets; the view of the town from the left bank of the Tauber is particularly scenic. Sights include the 16th-century Renaissance Engelsbrunnen (Angel's Well) monument, the church and the ruins of a castle.

WIESBADEN (308 B2)
HESSE *pop. 260,000*
This pleasant city on the Rhine, now the capital of Hesse, was created by the Romans around thermal springs. The *Kurhaus*, a neo-classical building completed in 1906 and set in a large park, houses the spa. Wiesbaden, with its lively theaters, orchestras and ballet company, is host to the International Festival of Music and Drama in May.

WITTENBERGE (308 D4)
SACHSEN-ANHALT *pop. 55,000*
An old town on the Elbe River, Wittenberg is famed as the place where Martin Luther posted his 95 theses on the doors of the Roman Catholic Church of All Saints in 1517, starting the Reformation. The doors were burned in 1760 and much of the church was damaged, but the building has since been restored; it contains Luther's grave. His theses are engraved in Latin on the bronze doors that were installed in 1858.

A settlement as early as 1180, Wittenberg was an official residence for the electors of Saxony and the House of Wettin. Although the French, who occupied the town in 1806, improved its fortifications, the Prussians successfully stormed Wittenberg in 1814 and officially took over the city by 1815.

LUTHERHAUS is where Martin Luther lived and worked during his stay in Wittenberge. The Lutherhalle Museum inside contains an extensive collection of Luther's manuscripts, along with several portraits of the reformer, a number of Bibles from before and after the Reformation, and many fine paintings by Lucas Cranach, Daniel Hopfer and other notable artists.

MELANCHTHONHAUS (1536) was the home of reformer Phillipp Melanchthon until his death in 1560. Displays chronicle the life and works of the theologian, who worked closely with Martin Luther.

STADTKIRCHE ST. MARIEN (CHURCH OF ST. MARY) is where Martin Luther preached. The altar, designed by Lucas Cranach, commemorates the Reformation with scenes of Martin Luther and Phillipp Melanchthon. The church's Gothic features are also of interest.

WOLFENBÜTTEL (308 C4)
NIEDERSACHSEN *pop. 50,000*
This small town of half-timbered houses has changed little since it was built as Germany's first planned town in the 15th century. The dukes of Brunswick and Lüneburg lived in the grand, white *Schloss*, the largest in Lower Saxony. Only the original moat survives; the rest is a mixture of Renaissance and baroque styles.

HERZOG-AUGUST-BIBLIOTHEK houses the books of Augustus the Younger, whose library was the largest in Europe in the 17th century. Early printed books and manuscripts are shown here and in the Zeughaus (Arsenal); the most famous is Henry the Lion's 12th-century Gospel.

LESSINGHAUS, a late-baroque building, which from 1770 to 1781 was occupied by the great playwright and critic,

Gotthold Lessing, who wrote *Nathan der Weise* here.

WORMS (308 B2)
RHEINLAND-PFALZ *pop. 76,000*
The old Rhine town of Worms is very important in religious history. It was in this town in 1521 that the edict against Martin Luther was issued by the Diet of Worms. A monument is dedicated to his memory.

Worms also has the oldest Jewish cemetery in Europe, dating from the 11th century. The Backfischfest in late August and early September is one of Rhineland's liveliest wine festivals.

DOM (Cathedral) was built in the 11th and 12th centuries and is said to be the purest example of Romanesque architecture in Germany. Five late Gothic sandstone reliefs from the demolished Gothic cloisters adorn the north aisle.

WÜRZBURG (308 C2)
BAYERN *pop. 128,000*
St. Boniface established a bishopric in the 8th century, changing this Roman outpost on the Main River into an important ecclesiastical center. Over the centuries, Würzburg was host to several imperial diets, and in the 16th century it joined the ranks of Germany's university cities. Würzburg was badly destroyed in World War II, but today is a thriving commercial city. It still has strong links with the wine industry and is famous for its wine festivals; the September fair is the biggest. Würzburg also hosts music festivals – baroque in May, Mozart in June and Bach in September.

ALTE MAINBRUECKE, a bridge erected across the Main in the 15th century, is adorned with baroque statues of 12 saints.

DOM, Parade-Platz, dates from the 11th century. Destroyed during World War II, this predominantly Romanesque cathedral has been rebuilt. Opposite is Neumünster, a Romanesque basilica; its

TILMAN RIEMENSCHNEIDER
An abundance of trees and the importance of religion may go a long way toward explaining the extraordinary skill of Bavarian woodcarvers. The most famous is Tilman Riemenschneider (1460–1531) who came to Würzburg in his early 20s and sculpted in sandstone, wood and marble with equal ease, capturing the folds of clothing and facial expressions.

His greatest work is the Holy Blood Altar in the Church of St. Jakob in Rothenburg ob der Tauber. Other sculptures can be found in Bamberg, Würzburg and smaller churches in Bavaria.

crypt contains the grave of Irish missionary St. Kilian.

FESTUNG MARIENBURG, high above the city, was first a Celtic hill fort and later a fortified castle that served as a residence of Würzburg's prince-bishops from the 12th until the 17th century.

It has Renaissance and baroque additions and now houses the Mainfränkisches Museum, with displays depicting local history and including works by Bavaria's greatest sculptor, Tilman Riemenschneider. In the courtyard stands an 8th-century circular church.

RESIDENZ, Residenzplatz, is one of the largest baroque palaces in Germany; Balthasar Neumann had this structure built in 1744 to house the prince-bishops. Its huge rooms are sumptuously decorated. Tiepolo painted the ceiling above the grand staircase – said to be the biggest in the world – and also the frescoes in the Kaisersaal (Emperor's Hall).

SCHLOSS VEITSHOECHHEIM, 7 kilometers (4½ miles) northeast, was the summer palace of the prince-bishops. Built in 1682, it was reconstructed in the 18th century, as was the exquisite rococo garden.

GREECE

THE BLUE AND WHITE ON THE FLAG OF GREECE REFLECT THE COLORS OF THE COUNTRY: VIVID BLUE SUMMER SKIES, AND PROUDLY WHITEWASHED HOUSES AND CHURCHES THAT DAZZLE THE EYES. AGAINST THIS BACKGROUND THE BLACK-GARBED ORTHODOX PRIESTS PASS BY, WHILE BLACK-CLAD WIDOWS SHOW THE LOYALTY OF MARRIAGE AND FAMILY TIES. GREECE IS ITS PEOPLE: AMONG THE MOST WELCOMING IN THE WORLD, THEIR LANGUAGE HAS THE SAME WORD FOR BOTH STRANGER AND GUEST.

GREECE IS A LANDSCAPE OF MOUNTAINS AND ISLANDS, MANY ONLY TINY SPECKS WHERE A HANDFUL OF PEOPLE LIVE. IT WAS IN THE CAPITAL, ATHENS, THAT THEATER, DEMOCRACY AND PHILOSOPHY WERE BORN. THE PARTHENON STILL DOMINATES THE MODERN CITY CENTER, A REMINDER OF A NOBLE PAST.

Left EXPERIENCE THE TRANQUILITY OF SOÚNIO'S TEMPLE OF POSEIDON AT SUNSET
Above A GUARD OUTSIDE THE VOULÍ, PARLIAMENT BUILDING, IN ATHENS

THINGS TO KNOW

- **AREA:** 238,536 square kilometers (92,075 square miles), including all islands
- **POPULATION:** 10,500,000
- **CAPITAL:** Athína
- **LANGUAGE:** Greek
- **RELIGION:** Greek Orthodox
- **ECONOMY:** Tourism, shipping, mining, agriculture; textiles (mostly cotton); chemicals, lead, zinc, iron ore, lignite; wheat, grain, olives, raisins, wine grapes, citrus fruit, tobacco, food processing.
- **PASSPORT REQUIREMENTS:** Required for U.S. citizens.
- **VISA REQUIREMENTS:** Not required for stays up to three months.
- **DUTY-FREE ITEMS:** Items for personal use, including camping equipment; 200 cigarettes, 50 cigars, or 250 grams of tobacco; 1 liter of spirits and 2 liters of wine; 500 grams of coffee or 200 grams of coffee extract; 100 grams of tea or 40 grams of tea extract; 50 grams of perfume and ¼ liter of toilet water; 1 still and 1 movie or video camera (with reasonable amount of film or tape); portable radio; record player; tape recorder; typewriter; musical instrument; bicycle; sports equipment; camping equipment. Also gifts and personal articles under $200 (from outside the European Union) and not intended for resale. See also *The European Union* on p.9.
- **CURRENCY:** The currency unit is the Greek *drachma*. Due to currency fluctuations, the exchange rate is subject to frequent change. There is no limit on foreign currency brought into the country. Visitors may import up to 100,000 *drachmas*; no more than 20,000 *drachmas* may be exported in bank notes of 500 *drachmas*. Up to U.S. $1,000 in foreign currency may be exported freely by short-term visitors. Declaration of imported currency must be made at time of entry into Greece.
  Some stores, particularly those selling gifts, will accept U.S. dollars as payment for purchases.
- **BANK OPENING HOURS:** 8am–2pm

HISTORY

Greek culture originated in the late 3rd millennium BC with the Minoan civilization on the island of Kríti (Crete). A series of invasions from the north, initially by the Myceneans about 1600 BC and later the Dorians, gradually shifted the center of culture to the mainland, and by the 8th century BC city-states had become well-established. The greatest of these city-states were Athína (Athens), a maritime power and cultural leader, and Spárti (Sparta), Athens' chief rival. An alliance between the two deflected the threat of Persian invasion, heralding the Golden Age of Greece in the 5th century BC. A period of over 40 years of peace saw extraordinary achievements, many of which have later served as models for Western civilizations. Democracy flowered, the Parthenon and other temples were built, great strides were made in the arts and sciences, and the study of philosophy reached its zenith.

The emergence of Spartan hostility ended this golden era with the Peloponnesian War of 431–404 BC. Following this period of instability, the city-states became an irresistible target for Philip II of Macedon, the barbarian who overpowered and united them early in the 4th century BC. Philip was succeded by his son – Alexander the Great. Alexander soon conquered the Persian Empire and set off to extend his successes into Asia. Though he died before he could achieve his goal, Alexander did succeed in spreading Greek culture throughout the civilised world. However, his untimely death resulted in the gradual dissolution of the Macedonian Empire, paving the way for Roman occupation of Greece in the 2nd century BC.

The Romans may have conquered the land, but Greek culture remained influential. Christianity spread throughout the Roman Empire, mainly due to the prevalence of the Greek language. The empire was split in the 4th century AD,

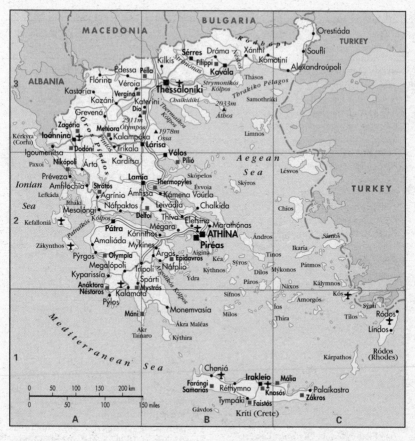

creating the Byzantine Empire in eastern Greece and Turkey. Constantinople, the former Greek city of Byzantium, became its capital, and despite succesive invasions by Goths, Huns, Slavs and Arabs, the Byzantine Empire grew in wealth and power. It then entered a period of renaissance, shaken only by the iconoclastic movement in the 8th and 9th centuries which eventually led to the Great Schism between the Roman Catholic and Greek Orthodox churches in the 11th century.

The sack of Constantinople in the Fourth Crusade of 1202-04 proved fateful for the Byzantine Empire. Greece was divided among the victors and again subjected to a series of conquests.

Finally, Constantinople fell to the Turks in 1453 and came within the orbit of the Ottoman Empire. Centuries of oppression followed, spurring a Greek revolt in 1770. Although the rebellion failed, dissension and international pressure significantly weakened the Ottoman Empire and a second revolution began in 1821. Independence was at last won in 1829 and the Bavarian prince Otto was installed on the throne in 1833. He was replaced 30 years later by George I who, during his 50-year reign, regained much of Greece's former territory. In 1913 Crete became part of Greece.

Greece was declared a republic in 1924, but the monarchy was restored under George II in 1935. The invasion by Italy

Monday–Thursday, 8am-1pm Friday; certain foreign exchange counters are open Saturday, Sunday, and afternoons and evenings.

- **STORE OPENING HOURS:** 8am–2 or 3pm Monday, Wednesday and Saturday, 8.30am–1.30pm and 5–8 or 9pm Tuesday, Thursday and Friday. Stores catering for tourists sometimes have longer opening hours.
- **BEST BUYS:** Pottery from the islands, silver and copper items, embroideries, handwoven textiles, rugs, costumed dolls, gold jewelry, shoes. Only antiquities that have been imported into the country may be exported.
- **PUBLIC HOLIDAYS:** January 1; January 6 (Epiphany); Shrove Monday*; March 25 (Independence Day); Good Friday*; Easter*; Pentecost Monday*; May 1 (Labor Day); Whitmonday; August 15 (Assumption Day); October 28 (Greek National Day); December 25–26. *Movable holidays based on the Eastern Orthodox calendar
- **USEFUL TELEPHONE NUMBERS:** Police 100 Fire 199 Ambulance 199
- **NATIONAL TOURIST OFFICES:** Greek National Tourist Organization 645 Fifth Avenue, Olympic Tower New York NY 10022 Tel: 212/421-5777 Greek National Tourist Organization 4 Conduit Street London W1R 0DJ England Tel: 0171-734 5997 Greek National Tourist Organization Amerikis 2 10564 Athens Greece Tel: (01) 322 3111
- **AMERICAN EMBASSY:** Vasilissis Sofias 91 10160 Athens Greece Tel: (01) 721 2951 or (01) 721 8401

in October 1940 brought Greece into World War II and German occupation lasted from 1941–1944. A civil war between Communist rebels and royalists was waged from 1946 to 1949. Under a democratic coalition government Greece joined N.A.T.O. in 1951.

A *coup d'état* in 1967 placed Greece under military rule and the monarch went into exile in Italy. In 1974 General Ioannides planned an assassination of the president of Cyprus in an attempt to unite the island with Greece. His plan failed: Turkish troops seized the chance to further their own claim by occupying the northern half of the island, and Cyprus remains divided to this day. The junta crumbled, and in 1974 the monarchy was abolished in favor of a republic.

Greece joined the European Economic Community in 1981. In the same year the country elected its first socialist government under Andreas Papandreou. The Panhellenic Socialist party promised populist reforms, but a series of scandals led to its replacement in 1990 by the New Democracy party, led by Constantine Mitsotakis. Its economic reforms proved unpopular, and in 1993 Papandreou returned as premier until his death in 1996. Konstantinos Simitis is the current premier.

FOOD AND DRINK

Greek cuisine features fresh, healthy foods, simply prepared, seasoned with olive oil, lemon, garlic and herbs. It is customary to visit the kitchen and select the dish of your choice. For starters, try *tzatzíki* (a yogurt-cucumber-garlic dip) or *dolmádes* (cabbage or vine leaves stuffed with meat or rice). Favourite dishes include *souvláki* (spit-roasted meat) and *moussaká* (layers of eggplant and minced meat baked in a white sauce). A Greek salad with *féta* (goat's milk cheese) can be a meal in itself. And though it is expensive, fresh seafood is usually excellent: *kalamari* (squid), swordfish, red mullet, sole and shrimp.

Traditional Greek coffee can be ordered strong, medium or sweet. Instant coffee is also widely available. Greek wine can be excellent, although *retsina*, flavoured with pine resin, is an acquired taste; you can specify *aretsinoto* (no resin) if you prefer. *Ouzo* is a strong, aniseed-flavored liquor.

SPORTS AND RECREATION

Although Greece was the birthplace of the Olympic Games in 776 BC, today's favorite spectator sports are soccer and basketball. With its many islands and extensive coastline, Greece has excellent beaches and abundant harbors; these provide opportunities for water-skiing, paragliding, diving, fishing and sailing. Walking, mountaineering, horseback riding and skiing are among the land-based activities. There are golf courses near Athens, and on Kérkyra (Corfu) and Ródos (Rhodes).

GETTING AROUND

A variety of tours around mainland and insular Greece can be made by a combination of land, sea and air transport. Single- or multi-day guided bus tours depart from Athens for mainland sites. Cruises and regular ferry services leave Athens' port of Piréas (Piraeus) for the eastern island groups, while Pátra (Patras) is the mainland port for the Ionian Islands. You should make local reservations for ferry services: ferry travel requires a reasonable amount of time and careful scheduling. Ellinikó Airport is 12 kilometres (7½ miles) south of Athens; Olympic Airways provide domestic flights to the larger islands.

A ferry route leaves Piréas for the island of Sýros, Tínos and Mýkonos to the east, and travelers can continue to Náxos and Thíra (Santorini). These are all part of the Kikládes (Cyclades). More extensive ferry tours to the eastern islands proceed from Piréas around Cape Soúnio and cross the Aigaia Pélagos (Aegean Sea) to the island of Chíos. From Chíos connections are available north to

the islands of Lésvos (Lesbos), Límnos, Samothráki and Thásos, or south to Sámos, Kálymnos, Kós (Cos) and Rhodes.

Buses are available on many of the islands, as are rental cars. Visitors are advised to deal only with established car rental agencies. Mopeds and scooters can also be rented, but many roads are poor and helmets should be worn.

There is a well-developed road system across mainland Greece. Road signs are generally in both Greek and English. Speed limits for cars are 50 k.p.h. (31 m.p.h.) in town, 80 k.p.h. (49 m.p.h.) out of town, and 100 k.p.h. (62 m.p.h.) on highways. Seat belts must be worn, and children under 12 must ride in the back seat. Motorists must pay the fine for a motoring violation in Greek *drachmas* at a public treasury office within 10 days.

An ambitious tour from Athens begins with a drive northwest to Elefsína (Eleusis), Thíva, Leivádia, Delphi, Ámfissa and Náfpaktos. The route partly follows the northern shore of the Korinthiakós Kólpos (Gulf of Corinth), opposite the mountainous Peloponissos peninsula. A trip west from Athens to Pátra can be made on the highway that runs along the north coast of the Peloponissos.

Another tour, of about 90 kilometers (56 miles), goes north from Athens and crosses the Evvoïkós Kólpos by bridge to

---

AUTOMOBILE CLUB
The Automobile and Touring Club of Greece (E.L.P.A.), Messogion 2-4, Athens, tel: (301) 74 88 800, has branch offices in various cities throughout Greece. The symbol ▲ beside a city name indicates the presence of a AAA-affiliated automobile club branch. Not all auto clubs offer full travel services to AAA members.

Chalkída on the island of Évvoia. From here you can proceed east then north for about 90 kilometers (56 miles) to the port of Kými, where there are views of the distant island of Skýros. This tour might continue by ferry to Skýros, or one of its sister islands of the northern Sporádes.

ACCOMMODATIONS

Hotels are classified as either luxury or from A down to E. Rates for each category are set by the government and must be posted in each room. All rooms rated C or above have private bathrooms. Prices are considerably lower out of season. There is also a good network of campgrounds, many run by the Greek National Tourist Organization.

SHOPPING

Beautiful rugs and carpets, as well as needlepoint, lace and embroidery, are on sale throughout the country. Look for handmade traditional items; wood carving and pottery are other good craft souvenirs. There are many jewelry stores selling gold and silver by weight.

True antiquities require an export permit. Replicas of Byzantine icons are expensive; the best ones can often be found in monastery gift stores.

TIPPING

Hotels and restaurants include a service charge in their bills; it is customary to tip an extra 5 to 10 percent. Chambermaids and and porters expect a tip. The minimum tip is usually 100 *drachma*. Tipping taxi drivers and tour guides is optional.

USEFUL EXPRESSIONS IN GREEK

hello/good-bye	*yássas*
please/thank you	*parakaló/efcharistó*
yes/no	*ne/ókhi*
good morning	*kaliméra*
good evening	*kalispéra*
good night	*kaliníkta*
How much is ...?	*póso káni?*
Do you speak English?	*milate angliká?*
I do not speak Greek.	*then miló elliniká*
you're welcome	*parakaló*
where is ...?	*poo íne ...?*
bank	*trápeza*
church	*eklisía*
doctor	*iatrós*
entrance/exit	*isothos/éxothos*
hotel	*xenodokhío*
hospital	*nosokomío*
post office	*takhithromío*
police	*astinomía*
pharmacy	*farmakío*

DAYS OF THE WEEK

Sunday	*Kiriakí*
Monday	*Deftéra*
Tuesday	*Tríti*
Wednesday	*Tetárti*
Thursday	*Pémpti*
Friday	*Paraskeví*
Saturday	*Sávato*

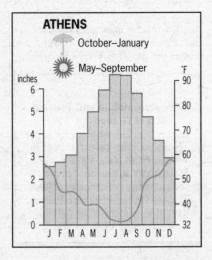

ATHENS

October–January

May–September

inches / °F

NUMBERS

1	*éna*	9	*enniá*
2	*dío*	10	*déka*
3	*tria*	20	*íkosi*
4	*téssera*	30	*triánda*
5	*pénde*	40	*saránda*
6	*éxi*	50	*penínda*
7	*eptá*	100	*ekató*
8	*októ*	1,000	*khília*

PLACES OF INTEREST

Note: Places in **bold type** have individual listings.

▲ ATHÍNA (355 B2) ★

CENTRAL GREECE *pop. 4,000,000*
Cosmopolitan Athína (Athens) is a show-place of antiquity. Every year countless vacationers come to the capital of Greece to see classical art and architecture, and also to enjoy the exciting nightlife and varied cultural offerings.

Athens dates from about 1200 BC. It gained prominence in the 6th century BC when Solon encouraged the growth of agriculture and commerce, and set up a constitution that advanced equality under the law. From 508 BC Kleisthenes directed the city-state in perhaps the most outstanding accomplishment of the classical era – the creation of democracy.

Following several remarkable victories over the Persians in the early 5th century BC, Athens assumed a supremacy among the Greek city-states and established a far-flung empire that included most of the Aegean Islands. Under Perikles monumental buildings sprang up, the arts flourished, several fine schools opened, and the city gained renown as the cultural capital of the ancient world.

Athens maintained its position as a cultural center during Roman times, but it lapsed into relative obscurity under Byzantine and Turkish rule. When King Otto arrived in the capital of the newly independent nation of Greece in 1834, he found an impoverished town with only a few thousand inhabitants. Today Athens is a thriving metropolis, an important commercial headquarters, and again a center of learning.

Many of the remains of ancient Athens lie on or near the Akropolis. To the west, the Athenian Assembly met on the hill of the Pnyx, while in AD 51 St. Paul preached to the Athenians from the Ários Págos, home of the ancient court of justice. Southwest, on the summit of the Mouseíon Hill, stands the Monument of Filopapou dating from the 2nd century AD. Also of interest are the Library of Hadrian, and the Plaka, or old quarter, to the north of the Acropolis.

In addition to the historic sites, Athens is a city of parks, boulevards, outdoor cafés, and various sports and entertainment facilities. Most places of interest are within walking distance of downtown hotels.

The carnival season is celebrated from late February to mid-March. The outstanding event of the year is the Athens Festival, from mid-June to September. Performances are given by national and international bodies, including folk dance groups, guest orchestras, and ballet and opera companies. One of the highlights of the festival is the production of ancient drama held in the Odion Iródou Attiko; the authentic setting provides a spell-binding atmosphere.

Athens is also a convenient center for exploring the attractions of rural Attiki. The Apollo Coast southeast of Athens is dotted with resorts that boast fine seafood restaurants.

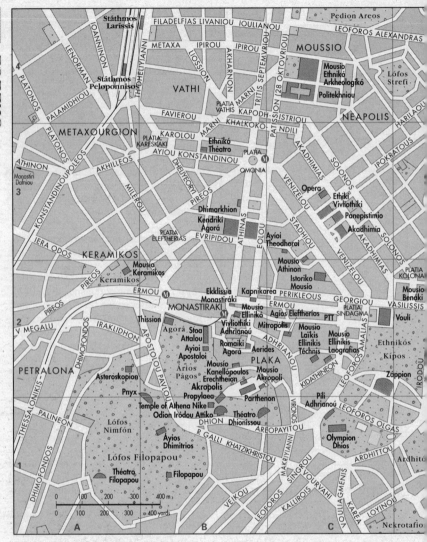

AERIDES (360 B2) (Tower of the Winds), is an octagonal Roman structure, and was designed as a hydraulic clock, sundial and weather vane. It is inscribed with allegorical reliefs of the winds.

AGORÁ (360 B2) (Marketplace), was the focal point of city life in ancient times, and it was here Socrates held his famous dialogues. The ruins of this complex lie north of the Akropolis.

Stoa Attalou, a long open-air arcade, was reconstructed in 1953–56, and has Doric columns on the first floor and Ionic columns on the upper story. Originally a fashionable shopping area, it now houses archaeological finds from the *Agorá*.

Thission, the temple of Athena and Hephaistos, dates from the 5th century BC. This is one of the best-preserved Doric temples in Greece.

AVEROF

LEOFOROS ALEXANDRAS

TRIKOUPI
IPOKRATOUS

Panathinaikos Stadion

L i k a v i t ó s

Ayios Yeoryios

KLEOMENOUS

VASILISSIS SOFIAS

PAPADHIAMANDOPOULOU

KOLONAKI

ILISSIA

Mousío Goulandrí Kikládhiki Texni

Ethniki Pinakothiki

Polemiko Mousío

ILISSION

OFIAS

Vizandinó Mousío

Alsos Singrou

KONSTANDINOU

RIZARI

MERKOURI

VASILEOS ALEXANDHROU

VASILEOS
Anáktora

YEORYIOU II

FORMIONOS

IMITOU

VASILEOS

SPIRIDHION

ERATOSTHENOUS EFRANOROS

Stadion

EFTIKHIDHOU

KHREMONIDOU

FILOLAOU

KHIMIDHOUS

EMPEDOKLEOUS

IMITOU

Profitis Ilias

KONSTANDINOU

PANGRATI

ANALIPSEOS

D

E

first wooden temples. Perikles had them rebuilt in everlasting marble, with the Parthenon as the crowning glory of the complex.

The Akropolis remained a center of sacred activity until the Christian Roman Emperor Theodosius I banned pagan worship in AD 391. During the Byzantine period the site was converted to Christian use, and the Turks later established a garrison here.

The Akropolis is the primary tourist attraction in Greece. Automobiles must be parked at the base of the hill; it is about a 10-minute walk to the gate.

Erechtheion, completed about 395 BC, was the last building raised on the Akropolis. It had temples dedicated to the Greek gods Athena, Poseidon and Erechtheus. On its south side is the famous Caryatid Porch, whose columns are carved in the shape of graceful female figures.

Mousío Akropoli contains many of the archaeological finds uncovered on the Akropolis since the mid-19th century. Highlights include sections of the Parthenon, Erechtheion and Temple of Athena Nike, and a collection of classical female statues.

Parthenon, or the temple of Athena, was erected 447–438 BC. Built of Pentelic marble, it is perfectly proportioned and the largest Doric temple in Greece. It measures 70 meters (230 feet) long and 30 meters (98 feet) wide, and has 46 exterior columns rising 10 meters (33 feet) high. Over the years, most of its magnificent decoration was destroyed or removed, including the Elgin Marbles that comprised the Parthenon's frieze (now in the British Museum, London).

Propylaea was the monumental entrance to the Akropolis. It was begun in 437 BC but never completed. The *Pinakotheke*, the north wing, once held a picture gallery.

Temple of Athena Nike, an attractively proportioned structure with Ionic columns, was built by Callicrates about 427–424 BC. The temple has been restored several times.

AKROPOLIS (360 B2) ★, a limestone hill rising above the city, is the location of the city's greatest monuments. Settlements were first attracted here in prehistory by the defensive position and abundance of natural springs. In the 7th century BC the focus of urban life shifted to the site of the *Agorá*. A temple to Athena was built on the rock, and the Akropolis became a sacred place of worship. The Persians sacked the city in 480 BC, destroying the

GREECE

KERAMIKOS CEMETERY (360 A2), Ermou, was a fashionable burial place in ancient times and contains beautiful sculptured memorials in the burial plots. The Mousío Keramikos displays artifacts from the cemetery.

LIKAVITÓS HILL (361 D3) offers panoramic views from its 277-meter (909-foot) summit. A cable car service runs to the top from Odos Ploutárchou in Kolonaki.

MITROPÓLIS (360 C2), the city's cathedral, stands within a large square. Built in the 19th century, its stunning interior is adorned with marble, mosaics and religious paintings. Beside the cathedral stands Agíos Eleftherios, a 12th-century church known also as "little Mitrópolis."

MONASTIRAKI (360 B2) is a small square that gets its name from a monastery that once stood here. This is one of the focal points of the city, with a host of lively cafés and market stalls.

MONASTIRI DAFNIOU, 10 kilometers (6 miles) west of Athens, is an 11th-century Byzantine monastery. The *Christos Pantokrator* on the dome is the finest of its many superb mosaics. A wine festival is held here in the fall.

MOUSÍO BENÁKI (360 D2), Vasilissis Sofias, houses a private collection of Greek relics and artworks from the prehistoric, classical, Byzantine and post-Byzantine periods. Also of special note are the Chinese ceramics.

MOUSÍO ELLINIKON MOUSIKON ORGANON (360 B2) (Museum of Greek Musical Instruments), Dhioyénous 1, has three floors, each devoted to a different type of instrument. Headphones allow visitors to hear recorded samples while reading the explanations.

MOUSÍO ETHNIKÓ ARKHEOLOGIKÓ (360 C4) (National Archaeological Museum) ★, Patission 44 , has an excellent collection of classical statuary, pottery, stone carv-

ings, jewelry and other works of art from excavated sites throughout Greece. Highlights include a gold death mask from the royal tombs at Mykínes, and the 3,500-year-old Minoan frescoes from the island of Thíra.

MOUSÍO LAÏKIS ELLINIKIS TÉCHNIS (360 C2) (Museum of Greek Folk Art), Kidathineon 17, displays traditional Greek costumes and examples of embroidery, weaving, ceramics, woodwork and jewelry.

ODION IRÓDOU ATTIKO (360 B1) (Odeion of Herodes Atticus) is a 5,000-seat theater erected by the Romans in about AD 161. Best seen from the Akropolis above, it is open only for performances during the Athens Festival.

OLYMPION DHIOS (360 C1) (Temple of Olympian Zeus) was the largest temple in ancient Greece. Begun in the 6th century BC, it was finally completed by the Roman emperor Hadrian in AD 132.

PÍLI ADHRIANOÚ (360 C1) (Arch of Hadrian) was built in honor of the Roman emperor in about AD 132 to mark the separation of Roman Athens from the Hellenic city of Theseus.

PIRÉAS (Piraeus), 14 kilometers (8½ miles) west, is linked to the city by subway, and also by a series of residential and industrial suburbs. In antiquity the port was connected to Athens by the famed walls of Themistocles, replaced in the 4th century BC by the existing classical walls.

Attractions include one of the Mediterranean's busiest harbors, and the seafood restaurants of the smaller harbor of Mikrolímano (or Tourkolimano). An archaeological museum displays items from classical and Roman times, and there is also a maritime museum.

STADION (361 D1) is an ancient stone stadium dating to the 4th century BC. It was restored for the first modern

Olympic games in 1896, and has seating for up to 70,000 spectators.

THÉATRO DHIONISSOU (360 B1) (Theater of Dionysius) was built in the 6th century BC and renovated later in antiquity. Athenians filled the theater's 17,000 seats to see works by Aeschylus, Sophocles, Euripides and Aristophanes.

VIZANDINÓ MOUSÍO (361 D2) (Byzantine Museum), Vasilissis Sofias 22, presents a rich collection of Early Christian and Byzantine artifacts.

POLEMIKO MOUSÍO (361 D2), Vasilissis Sofias, has exhibits pertaining to Greek military achievements from ancient to modern times.

AEGEAN ISLANDS

There are more than 1,000 islands in the Aigaio Pélagos (Aegean Sea), many of which are ideal for sunning, swimming, fishing and boating.

The Kiklades (Cyclades), the southwestern group of Aegean islands, received their name in antiquity because they formed a circle around the sacred island of Dílos (see p.355 B2–C1). Places of interest include the classical ruins on Dílos, Kéa and Kímolos; the Byzantine churches on Kýthnos, Páros and Sífnos; and the caves on Antíparos. The islands can be very busy in July and August.

There are more islands in the Dodekanisos (Dodecanese) group than their name – which means 12 – implies (p.355 C1). Their position in the southeast made them vulnerable to invasions by Venetians and Turks, while adding to their rich history. There are large resorts on Ródos and Kós.

In the northern Aegean the large, forested islands of Chíos, Lésvos, and Sámos face the Turkish coast and are less frequented (p.355 C2). The Sporádes group lie nearer the Greek mainland and are green and mountainous (p.355 B2). Further north, Thásos and Samothráki are accessible from the mainland ports of Kavála and Alexandroúpoli (p.355 B3).

Islands in the Aegean Sea listed under their own names are Chíos (Khíos), Dílos (Délos), Kálymnos,

---

ÁGIO ÓROS

From the 9th century, religious zealots came to Ágio Óros (Holy Mountain) to live as hermits. The highest point on this mountainous peninsula is Mount Áthos at 2,033 meters (6,670 feet).

Visitors to the area must obtain a permit from the Ministry of Foreign Affairs in Athens or the Office of the Governor-General in Thessaloníki. Female visitors are not permitted and males under 21 years must be accompanied by their fathers, unless part of a student group and accompanied by an older supervisor. Most people satisfy their curiosity from a nearby beach, or a boat trip around the peninsula.

Kárpathos, Kós (Cos), Lésvos (Lesbos), Mílos (Melos), Mýkonos (Mikonos), Náxos, Pátmos, Ródos (Rhodes), Sámos, Samothráki, Thásos and Thíra (Thera).

AETOLIA AND EPIROS (355 A2–3)

The two main western regions of Greece lie between the Píndos mountain range and the Ionian Sea. Although visited less frequently than the rest of the country, they have much to offer travelers. In the far south Náfpaktos is graced by a Venetian castle and there are classical ruins at Strátos. The English poet Lord Byron died of fever at Mesolóngi in 1824; he had recently arrived in Greece to promote the fight for independence.

The more remote area of Epiros in the north has fine remains of the Hellenistic period at Dodóni and Mesopótamo, and the Roman city of Nikópoli lies near Préveza. Igoumenítsa is the main port for the Ionian Islands, while the mountain road from **Ioánnina** to **Kalampáka** offers dramatic scenery.

GREECE

AÍGINA (355 B2)
CENTRAL GREECE *pop. 10,000*
Zeus abducted the nymph Aegina to this scenic island, and it is from this legend that Aígina derives its name. In antiquity the island was an important maritime center that vied briefly with Athína for supremacy on the seas. Today it is a popular tourist destination and a prime producer of pistachio nuts. Aígina can be reached by ferry from Piréas.

The island's capital and principal port is also named Aígina. Nearby to the north is the well-preserved Temple of Aphaía, erected about 500 BC.

ÁRGOS (355 B2)
PELOPONISSOS *pop. 21,000*
As one of the principal cities of classical Greece, Árgos ruled a state covering the northeastern Peloponissos (Peloponnese). Over the centuries this city vied with Spárti for rule of this peninsula.

Today Árgos is a major tourist destination and has a number of ancient ruins. At the foot of Mount Larissa are Roman baths with marble fixtures, mosaics and statuary; a 20,000-seat theater dating from the 3rd or 4th century BC; and the Roman odeion, which has several mosaics. On the summit is a 13th-century Frankish castle. The town has a fine archaeological museum, with outstanding bronze armor, pottery, and a terracotta figurine dating from the 5th millennium BC.

Excursions can be made to the ancient sites of Mykínes, 17 kilometers (10½ miles) north, and to Neméa, 30 kilometers (18½ miles) north. The latter, where Herakles (Hercules) slew the Nemean Lion, possesses several outstanding temple ruins. Some 8 kilometers (5 miles) east of Árgos is Tiryns. This is the legendary birthplace of Herakles in Greek mythology, and there are impressive remains of cyclopean walls and a palace dating from the 13th century BC.

Also of interest is ancient Lerna, 10 kilometers (6 miles) south at Míloi, where Herakles slew the legendary

Hydra. Remains of a Bronze Age palace survive overlying a neolithic house.

ÁRTA (355 A2)
EPIROS *pop. 33,000*
The ancient capital of Pyrrhus, the king of Epiros, later became the seat of the Byzantine Despotate of Epiros during the 13th century and 14th centuries. The medieval castle beside the River Árachthos and the church of Panagia Parigoritissa survive from this period. The town's old bridge is 17th-century.

CENTRAL GREECE (355 B2)
Ancient Athína (Athens), followed by Thíva (Thebes), established a hegemony over much of Greece in the 5th and 4th centuries BC. Remains of this time are pervasive and make Attikí (Attica), or central Greece, the most important tourist region. Here are the classical monuments of **Athens**, the battlefield of Marathónas, and the shrines of **Delfoí** and **Elefsína**.

The Apollo Coast, the country's major seaside resort area, stretches south from Piréas (Piraeus) to the Temple of Poseidon at **Soúnio**. Among the more notable resorts are Glyfáda, with its golf course; pine-edged Várkiza; picturesque Lagonsi; and Vouliagméni, with remains of the Temple of Apollo nearby. Other places of interest are the classical ruins at Vravróna (Brauron).

Except for Delfoí, the rest of central Greece is visited less frequently by tourists. Sights of interest include the medieval *kastra* (castles) at Ámfissa, Lamía and Leivádia; the spas at Loutrá Ypátis and Kámena Voúrla; and the ancient battlefield at the pass of Thermopýles (Thermopylae). The former glory of Thíva is displayed in the town's small museum.

CHANIÁ (355 B1)
KRÍTI *pop. 63,000*
Chaniá is the island's second city and former capital. It lies on the site of the Minoan town of Kydonía which is being revealed by excavations. Finds from this

and later periods are displayed in the city's archaeological museum.

In the 13th century Chianiá became a Venetian city, and it fell to the Turks in 1645. The attractive harbor with its defences, lighthouse and dockyard survive from the Venetian occupation. Nearby is the delightful old Turkish quarter, with its narrow lanes and striking façades. Also of interest is the Firkás Naval Museum. The port of Soúda to the east is one of the greatest natural harbors in the Mediterranean.

CHÍOS (355 C2)
AEGEAN ISLANDS *pop. 54,000*
Homer taught on Chíos in the 9th century BC, and by the following century it had become a prosperous maritime center. Chíos (Khíos) remains a wealthy island today, largely due to shipping and mastik, a resin used in chewing gum. The lively port of Chíos is based around one of several medieval *kastra*, or castles, on the island, and has excellent museums devoted to archaeology, folklore and the Byzantine period.

Other places of interest include remains of a classical temple at Káto Fána, the 11th-century Byzantine church of Néa Moní, and the medieval walls of Pyrgi.

CORFU – *see Kérkyra on p.368.*

CORINTH – *see Kórinthos on p.369.*

CRETE – *see Kríti on p.369.*

DELFOÍ (355 B2) ★
CENTRAL GREECE *pop. 2,400*
These classical ruins are perhaps the most beautiful and impressive in Greece. The high and low were drawn from all over the ancient world to receive the wisdom of the oracle at the Sanctuary of Pythian Apollo, and visitors continue to be attracted to the site. Here, too, is the stadium where the Pythian Games were once held.

The Sacred Precinct forms a large square in the heart of Delfoí (Delphi),

entered by the Sacred Way. Here mortals came into contact with the gods.

Dominating the site are the ruins of the Temple of Apollo, dating from the 4th century BC. Here the Pythia, seated on a tripod, offered prophecies under the influence of intoxiating fumes.

MOUSEION DELFON (Museum of Delfoí) has an excellent collection of finds recovered from the site. Highlights of the artworks include the bronze *Charioteer* and the *Sphinx of Naxians*. Also notable are statues which were formerly attached to the pediment of the Temple of Apollo.

PIGI KASTALIAS (Castalian Spring) flows from between two towering crags to the east of the Sacred Precinct. Suppliants purified themselves in its waters before approaching the sanctuary.

DÍLOS (355 B2)
AEGEAN ISLANDS
Ancient Dílos (Délos) was largely a shrine dedicated to Apollo, traditionally the birthplace of the god and his sister Artemis, the huntress. Its oracle was second only to that of Delfoí, and the ancient Greeks endowed the island with a complex of monuments, temples and settlements.

Today the entire island, the smallest of the Kiklades (Cyclades), is protected as an archaeological site and can be visited only by a daytrip, usually from Mýkonos. There are no accommodations for tourists. It is difficult to cover the vast ruins in the time allowed: be sure to see the Terrace of the Lions, where the majestic marble beasts once guarded the Sacred Lake. Other highlights include several houses with mosaic floors, the sanctuary area, the Egyptian temples, and the Archaeological Museum. The panoramic view from Mount Kynthos is worth the climb.

ELEFSÍNA (355 B2)
CENTRAL GREECE *pop. 23,000*
Elefsína (Eleusis) is an industrial town,

EPÍDAVROS

23 kilometers (14½ miles) northwest of Athína. This was formerly the location of an ancient temple to Demeter, goddess of agriculture; festivals of planting and harvest took place here, culminating in an annual torchlight procession from Athína. It was also the center of the Mysteries of Eleusis, a religious cult whose initiates were sworn to secrecy.

The main attraction today is the Telesterion, the hall of initiation and the mysteries, built on the site of the Temple of Demeter in the 5th century BC. There is a museum nearby.

ELEUSIS – *see Elefsína on p.365.*

EPÍDAVROS (355 B2) ★
PELOPONISSOS
The small settlements and harbors of Néa Epídavros and Palaía Epídavros lie on the east coast of the Argolis peninsula, overlooking the Saronikós Kólpos (Saronic Gulf). The former has remains of a medieval castle built by the Franks, while the latter lies near the remains of the ancient city of Epidauros.

The ruins of the Sancturay of Epidauros are 19 kilometers (12 miles) inland, set within a broad valley amid pine trees. This was a major religious and health center with a temple devoted to Asklepios. The theater, built in the 4th century BC, is one of the best preserved in Greece with seating for 14,000; it is famous for its perfect acoustics, and is the venue for a festival of ancient drama in summer. There is a small archaeological museum.

HERAKLION – *see Irakleío below.*

HYDRA/ÍDHRA – *see Ýdra on p.377.*

▲ IOÁNNINA (355 A3)
EPIROS *pop. 90,000*
The origins of this regional center, on the shores of Lake Pamvotis, lie in the Middle Ages. During the 13th century it developed as a Byzantine capital, but from the 15th century onward Ioánnina was under Ottoman rule. The picturesque old town has mosques, a bazaar, and the Tomb of Ali Pasha, a ruthless adventurer who made Ioánnina his headquarters between 1788 and 1822. The Archaeological Museum contains artifacts from prehistory to the Byzantine period.

DODÓNI, 21 kilometers (13 miles) southwest, is the site of Greece's oldest oracle. From about 2000 BC to the 4th century AD, the ancients came here to consult Zeus, king of the gods. There are several ancient and historic ruins, including the *Akropolis*, a stadium, and a Byzantine basilica. The large theater, dating from the 3rd century BC, hosts a festival of ancient drama in August.

IONIAN ISLANDS (355 A2-3)
The mythical nymph Io, having incurred the jealousy of Hera, Zeus' queen, plunged into the sea in fearful flight. From this legend the sea and islands off the west coast of Greece have become known as Ionian.

The strongest influence on these islands has been Venetian. They were largely ruled by this Italian republic from the 14th to the 18th century, only Lefkáda falling under Turkish rule. Napoléon appropriated the islands in the early 19th century, but after his defeat they became a British protectorate until they were united with Greece in 1864.

Kérkyra (Corfu) is one of the most beautiful islands in Greece, and therefore very popular. Kefalloniá, the largest island, has dense pine forests on its mountain slopes. Paxoí, the smallest, is an idyllic getaway with two charming villages, isolated coves and sea caves. Homer made Itháki (Ithaca) famous in his *Odyssey*. The attraction of Zákynthos (Kakinthos) is its beautiful gardens and wild flowers. Kýthira lies apart from the main group, south of the Peloponissos.

IRAKLEÍO (355 B1) ★
KRÍTI *pop. 125,000*
Irakleío (Heraklion), medieval Candia, is the largest city and principal port of Kríti

(Crete). With its fine archaeological museum and the nearby Palace of Knosós, it is also the modern gateway to the ancient Minoan civilization. For this reason the sprawling, noisy, commercial center must be visited. Its other attractions include the Venetian fortress in the harbor, emblazoned with the Lion of St. Mark; the ornate Morosini Fountain; and the 16th-century church of Agía Ekateríni, now a museum with a collection of icons by Damaskinós.

ARCHEOLOGIKON MOUSEIO (Archaeology Museum) holds the finest collection of Minoan art and artifacts in the world. The crowning glory of the museum is the magnificent Hall of Frescoes, reassembled from the ruins of Knosós.

KNOSÓS, 5 kilometers (3 miles) south, was the capital of a powerful Minoan civilization during the 2nd millenium BC. From Greek mythology Knosós is associated with King Minos, and within its labyrinth Theseus is believed to have slain the Minotaur.

Its palace, the third on the site, was the largest and most splendid of all the Minoan palaces. The collapse of this Bronze Age civilization in the 15th century BC led to the destruction of this and many other contemporary sites on Crete. The history of Knosós has been recovered by a series of excavations, begun in 1900 by Sir Arthur Evans.

ITHÁKI (355 A2)
IONIAN ISLANDS *pop. 5,000*
The unspoiled island of Itháki (Ithaca) is the legendary home of Odysseus, the ancient hero of Homer's *Odyssey*, who set out for Troy and returned after many trials to rescue his faithful wife, Penelope, from evil suitors.

Vathy, the island's capital, is an attractive town and a good base for exploring the coutryside and places made famous in Homer's epic poem. These include the Grotto of the Nymphs, a stalactite cave west of Vathy, in which the hero hid his treasure; and the Arethusa Fountain, a spring at the southern end of the island where the swineherd Eumaeus welcomed home Odysseus. North of Vathy, Moni Katheron offers magnificent views, and Kióni and Frikes are charming fishing villages.

KAKINTHOS – *see Zákynthos on p.377.*

see Zákynthos on p.377.

▲ KALAMÁTA (355 A2)
PELOPONISSOS *pop. 42,000*
The port of Kalamáta (Kalámai), capital of Messenia, bears the scars of a major earthquake in 1986. Its 13th-century castle, however, survived and offers fine views, while the old town between it and the River Nedhon remains the most interesting part of the city.

ARHEA MESSÍNI, ancient Messenia, is 35 kilometers (22 miles) northwest at the foot of Mount Ithomi. Founded in 369 BC, this classical city is partially occupied by the village of Mavrommati. Points of interest include the city walls, the theater, stadium and the Temple of Asklepios.

KALAMPÁKA (355 A3) ★
THESSALIA *pop. 12,000*
Situated on the broad plain of Thessaly, Kalampáka (Kalambáka) has a fine Byzantine cathedral with a marble pulpit and 12th-century frescoes.

METÉORA is a huge rock mass 9 kilometers (6 miles) north of Kalambáka. Natural erosion has caused the formation of massive pillars of stone that range from 26 to 90 meters (85 to 295 feet) high, on top of which are perched remarkable medieval monasteries. St. Anthanasíos founded the Great Meteoron, one of the first monasteries here, in the 14th century. By the 16th century there were 24 monasteries, of which 12 remain and four are still inhabited.

It is a long climb to the top, and each monastery is closed one day a week. Agios Stefanos is easiest to reach via a footbridge; it contains fine icons. The Great Meteoron is the highest monastery

GREECE

and a fine example of late Byzantine architecture, noted for its 12-sided dome and frescoes. Also worth visiting is Varlaam with a 15th-century chapel.

KÁLYMNOS (355 C2)
AEGEAN ISLANDS *pop. 17,000*

The sponge divers of Kálymnos still maintain their traditional profession, despite the depletion of the sponge beds in recent times. Kálymnos (Pothiá) is the island's main town, with colourful buildings. The scenic coastline is punctuated with coves and sea caves, while good beaches attract a growing tourist industry. Inland the island is largely barren and mountainous, except for the fertile Valley of Vathi where there are orchards and vineyards.

KARPÁTHOS (355 C1)
AEGEAN ISLANDS *pop. 6,000*

This pleasant little island sees fewer tourists than its larger neighbors of Kríti and Ródos. Traditional customs are preserved here in the native costumes and festive weddings. The northern part of the island has a spectacular coastline as well as some charming villages.

▲ KAVÁLA (355 B3)
MAKEDONIA *pop. 57,000*

The regional town of Kavála stands on the site of the Roman port of Neaopolis, and is now the center of Greece's tabocco industry. Sights include the 16th-century Kamares aqueduct, the Archaeological Museum, the Islamic Imaret, and the house of Muhammed Ali, pasha of Egypt from 1805–49.

FÍLIPPI, or Philíppi, is 16 kilometers (10 miles) northwest. This ancient city was founded in 361 BC on the site of an earlier settlement. It was soon taken over by Philip of Macedon in 356 BC who renamed the city after himself. Filippi became a Roman colony in 42 BC, when Julius Caeser's assassins, Brutus and Cassius, were defeated here. The apostle St. Paul first preached on European soil at Fílippi in AD 49.

The extensive ruins of the city include the Roman forum and a public latrine with marble seats intact. There are also remains from the Byzantine period. Classical drama is performed in the ancient theater in summer.

KÉRKYRA (355 A3) ★
IONIAN ISLANDS *pop. 115,000*

Kérkyra (Corfu) is one of the most beautiful islands in Greece. Its hilly interior is covered with trees, flowering shrubs and olive groves, earning it the title of "Emerald Isle." There are also magnificent beaches, from pebbly coves to vast

---

OLIVES

Olives and their oil are one of the basic staples of Greek life, and have been so for centuries. Evident in Minoan art, and described by Homer in both the *Iliad* and the *Odyssey*, cultivation of the olive began around 5,000 years ago. Before coming into general culinary use olive oil was revered: it was awarded to the greatest athletes and used by the aristocracy as an oil to smooth on after bathing.

Produced in a variety of different shapes, sizes and colors, the choice can be daunting to the tourist. Kalamata are the most famous Greek olives – black, elegant, glossy, meaty and firm.

---

stretches of sand. The northern coast has pretty fishing villages at Kalámi and Agios Stéphanos, while Sidári on the north coast has striking rock formations. The summit of Mount Pantókrator is the island's highest peak, and the coves of Palaiokastrítsa on the west are pretty but overcrowded. The southern half of the island has booming beach resorts.

KÉRKYRA is the island's capital, its elegant architecture and striking fortifications dating from the Venetian occupation.

The headland fort is separated from the medieval old town by the Spianada, a huge esplanade bordered on the west by the Liston, an early 19th-century arcade.

ACHILLEION PALACE, 9 kilometers (6 miles) south at Gastoúri, was built in 1890–91 as a retreat for the Empress Elisabeth of Austria.

ARCHEOLOGIKON MOUSEION, Vraila 5, houses archaeological finds, including the restored Gorgon pediment from the 6th-century BC Temple of Artemis.

AGIOS SPYRÍDON, west of the Spianada, was built in 1589–96 to house the remains of St. Spyrídon, the 4th-century bishop and patron saint of Kérkyra.

THE PALACE OF ST. MICHAEL AND ST. GEORGE, north of the Spianada, now houses the Museum of Asiatic Art. It was originally built for the British in 1819.

KHÍOS – see Chíos on p.365.

KÓRINTHOS (355 B2) ★
PELOPONISSOS pop. 22,600
From the 8th century BC, Kórinthos (Corinth) developed as an important commerical and sea power, with satellite ports on the Corinth and Saronic gulfs. The Romans destroyed Corinth in 146 BC and 102 years later built a new city that rose to become the capital of the province of Achaia. The apostle St. Paul established a Christian congregation at Corinth in the early 50s AD. The city declined following the effects of earthquakes in 522 and 551, and the modern center was developed after the earthquake of 1858.

CORINTH is 7 kilometers (4½ miles) southwest of the modern city. Here are remains of the Temple of Apollo, the *agora* (marketplace) and a theater; there are also several Roman ruins, including the odeion and the Fountain of Peirene. A museum displays artifacts from the site. The *Acrocorinth*, the mountain overlooking the ancient city, was once the site of the Temple of Aphrodite. The Byzantines built a fortress here, later modified by the Franks, Venetians and Turks.

CORINTH CANAL measures over 6 kilometers (4 miles) long and 25 meters (82 feet) wide, with walls towering 90 meters (295 feet) high. Only one ship at a time can cross the narrow passage that separates the mainland from the Peloponissos. A canal was planned in the 1st century AD but the present channel was only completed in 1893.

KÓS (355 C1)
AEGEAN ISLANDS pop. 20,000
Hippocrates, the most famous of all physicians, was born on Kós (Cos) about 460 BC. Throughout antiquity the island developed as a center of healing. Today, visitors come to Cos to view the ancient ruins and medieval buildings, and to relax at the seaside resorts.

ASCLEPEION, 4 kilometers (2½ miles) west of Kós, was a sanctuary to Asclepius, god of healing, and his descendants. Treatment here was based on principles ascribed to Hippocrates. The remains of temples and baths date from the 4th century BC to Roman times.

KÓS, the island's capital and main port, is a popular resort. The ancient city has been largely destroyed by earthquakes, but remnants of the Roman city survive. The harbor is guarded by the 15th-century Castle of the Knights, and nearby is the local museum. Other places of interest include the Early Christian church of Agios Ioánnis Pródhromos, and an 18th-century mosque.

▲ KRÍTI (355 B1) ★
Kríti (Crete) is the largest and most historically important Greek island. Prior to the development of classical civilization on the mainland, this beautiful island was the center of the Minoan civilization that flourished from about 3000 to

1400 BC. This had distinctive forms of art, architecture and writing, and ruins of Minoan palaces survive at Knosós, Mália, Faistós and Zákros.

From 67 BC until 824 Crete came under Roman then Byzantine control. A large number of churches were founded before the Arab occupation between 824 and 961. A second Byzantine period was followed by Venetian rule from 1204 until the Turkish conquest in 1669.

Sights include the Byzantine churches at Gortys and Kristá, and the Venetian fortifications at **Chaniá** and Réthymno.

Crete has a number of excellent beaches, and the interior is renowned for its lovely scenery. **Irakleío** (Heraklion) is the island's capital and largest city.

FARÁNGI SAMARIÁS (Samariás Gorge) is Europe's longest gorge, extending 18

TURTLES AND TOURISTS: AT LOGGERHEADS

On the beaches of Zákynthos, Kríti and the Peloponissos, the females of the endangered loggerhead turtle *Caretta caretta* emerge from the sea at night to lay their eggs in underground nests. The disturbance of modern tourism, pollution and motorboats all take their toll. Like tourists, the turtles make use of the beaches from June to August - but unlike tourists only one out of a thousand will reach their reproductive age of 30 years.

---

kilometers (11 miles) from the White Mountains to the sea. The hike down is spectacular but grueling – along steep paths and across the boulder-strewn riverbed. Good walking shoes are a must. The narrowest point, called the Iron Gates, measures only 3 meters (10 feet) across while sheer rock walls on either side soar 300 meters (1,000 feet) high. Due to the level of the river, the

gorge is only open between May and October, and a day should be allowed for a walk along its length.

RÉTHYMNO is dominated by an impressive 16th-century fortress which looks down over the old town with its Venetian and Turkish buildings.

LÉSVOS (355 C2) ★
AEGEAN ISLANDS *pop. 97,000*

In the early 7th century BC, Lésvos (Lesbos) was the center of literary activity that produced the lyric poetry of Sappho and her contemporaries.

Lesbos is a rugged island with outstandingly scenery. There are many good beaches, including those at Plomári, Sígri, Vaterá and around the Gulf of Yera. In the Middle Ages the island was occupied by Byzantines, Genoese and Venetians who erected impressive fortresses at Ántissa, Ayasso, Eresós, Kalloní, Messagros, Míthymna, Mytilíni and Vigla.

Other places of interest include the Early Christian basilicas of Agía Khalinádhos and Ipsilométopo; the ancient ruins at Eresós; and the spa of Loutrópoli Termís.

MAKEDONIA AND THRÁKI (355 B3)

Greece's two northern regions form an area of contrast between the Balkans and the shores of the Aegean, with forested mountains, fertile lowlands and good beaches.

Alexander the Great set out from Makedonia (Macedonia) in the 4th century BC to conquer Persia. He crossed Thráki (Thrace), the traditional bridge between Europe and Asia, and advanced as far as India. Macedonia and Thrace were later occupied by the Romans, Byzantines and the Turks.

Thessaloníki, the second-largest city in Greece and Macedonia's capital, is a good center for exploring the region's attractions, which range from the ancient sites of Fílippi, Pélla and Vergína to the medieval and Byzantine monasteries on the peninsula of Ágio Óros (*see p.363*).

The lakeside resort of Kastoría and the mountain village of Flórina provide opportunities for sport and relaxation. Oros Ólympos, legendary abode of the gods, is southwest of Kateríni.

Byzantine churches are found throughout Thrace, and the towns of Xánthi and Komotiní, with their lovely mosques, minarets and open-air cafés, are characteristically oriental.

MEGALÓPOLI (355 A2)
PELOPONISSOS *pop. 4,700*
Megalópoli, which means "great city," was founded in 371 BC as a bulwark against the advancing Spartans.

ARTHEA MEGALÓPOLI, the ancient city, is 1 kilometer (½ mile) north of the modern center. The 21,000-seat theater was one of the largest in ancient Greece, and the Thersileion, an impressive assembly hall, could accommodate 16,000. Other sights include the slight remains of the the Temple of Zeus Soter.

MYKÍNES (355 B2) ★
PELOPONISSOS
The town "rich in gold" of Homeric legend, Mykínes (ancient Mycenae) is one of the most well-known classical sites in Greece. Legend claims it was founded by Perseus, who built the massive walls with the aid of the Cyclops. The city soon became the capital of a great empire. Agamemnon set out from Mycenae to conquer Troy, only to return to die at the hands of Aegisthus, the seducer of his wife, Clytemnestra.

Heinrich Schliemann, believing that Homer's epics had some basis in fact, excavated Mycenae in 1874–76. His finds included a rich treasure of gold artifacts which can now be seen in the National Archaeological Museum in Athína. But Mycenae's legendary past has only entered the realm of history with a series of later excavations that still continue.

The city reached its zenith during the late Bronze Age, between about 1400 and 1200 BC. After the demise of the Minoan civilization on Kríti, the Myceneans became the dominant force in the region until their own decline around 1100 BC.

ARCHAEOLOGICAL SITE includes all of Mycenae. The *acropolis*, protected in part by the Cyclopean walls, is entered through the Lion Gate that was added about 1250 BC; above the entrance is a carved relief of two lions. Within are the foundations of a great palace, and a circular royal cemetery whose grave finds are now among the treasures at Athína.

Outside the *acropolis* the remains of nine *tholos*, or beehive tombs, have been discovered. The most impressive is the so-called Treasury of Atreus, dating from about 1350 BC; the domed chamber is over 13 meters (43 feet) high.

MÍLOS (355 B1)
AEGEAN ISLANDS *pop. 4,500*
Mílos (Melos) is one of the most colorful islands of the Kiklades (Cyclades). Mílos, its capital, also known as Pláka, has a Frankish castle and the 13th-century church of Thalassítra. The famous Venus de Milo, a classical sculpture of Aphrodite now on display in the Louvre in Paris, was discovered on the island.

MONEMVASÍA (355 B1) ★
PELOPONISSOS
Monemvasía is a 13th-century Byzantine town, 59 kilometers (36½ miles) southeast of Spárti. It is positioned behind an enormous rock, and is reached by a causeway from the new town (Gefyra) on the mainland. The only entrance is through a narrow tunnel; its name, Moni Emvasis, means "single entrance."

At its peak, Monemvasía was an important port with 60,000 inhabitants, including many noble families. Today its narrow alleyways, medieval buildings and Byzantine churches are largely populated by tourists.

Of note are the great vaulted cathedral, built in 1293, and the church of Agios Pávlos, built in 956, converted into a mosque, and now a small museum.

GREECE

MOUNT ÁTHOS – *see Ágio Óros on p.363.*

MYCENAE – *see Mykínes on p.371.*

MÝKONOS (355 B2) ★
AEGEAN ISLANDS *pop. 5,500*

Bright, white houses, windmills and churches are the hallmarks of Mýkonos (Mikonos). The island is a fashionable resort, its many beaches offering excellent swimming.

MÝKONOS, the island's chief port and town, has a cosmopolitan character. Places of interest include the busy harbor and the Archaeological Museum, which displays artifacts from the island of Dílos. The beautiful church of Paraportianí is an outstanding example of Cycladic architecture.

The nearest beaches are at Ornos, 3 kilometers (2 miles) south, and Agios Stefanos, 3 kilometers (2 miles) north. The island is one of the few places in Greece that offers scuba diving.

NÁFPLIO (355 B2)
PELOPONISSOS *pop. 10,600*

The port for Árgos in antiquity, Náfplio is today the chief city of the Argolis, a farming region. With its narrow streets and Venetian buildings, the city provides a charming setting on the Argolikós Kólpos. The Palamídi, an 18th-century fortress, offers an excellent viewpoint. The 12th-century monastic church of Zoodochos Pigi lies 2 kilometers (1 mile) southeast.

Náfplio makes a good base for exploring the sights of the Argolis, including Árgos, Tiryns, Mykínes and Epídavros.

NÁXOS (355 C2)
KIKLADES *pop. 15,000*

Scenic Náxos is the largest island of the Kiklades (Cyclades), with a mountainous interior and fine sandy beaches. It was famed in antiquity for its fine, white marble, and at Flerio the quarries have two unfinished *kouri* (sculptures) from the 6th century BC. Of the same period is the Temple of Apollo on Palatia, an islet in Náxos harbor. Several Byzantine churches and monasteries survive, the more notable at the villages of Apíranthos and Khalkí.

NÁXOS, the island's capital, was the seat of a Venetian duchy from 1207 until 1566 when the island was seized by the Turks. The town has a warren of lanes which leads up to the Venetian castle. The cathedral dates from the 13th century and there is a good local museum.

OLYMPÍA (355 A2) ★
PELOPONISSOS

According to Greek mythology, the hero Herakles (Hercules) chose this beautiful site for the Olympic Games, within a sacred grove of olive and plane trees at the confluence of two rivers.

From 776 BC to AD 393, the Olympic Games, dedicated to Zeus, were the most important events in the Hellenic world. Today the sacred flame is still kindled at Olympía, and is borne by runners to the modern games which were revived at Athína in 1896.

HOLY ALTIS (grove) contains most of the ruins of ancient Olympía, including the gymnasium, stadium, hippodrome, temples of Zeus and Hera, and the fountain of Herod Atticus.

MOUSEION OLYMPÍAS has one of the country's best sculpture collections. It includes the *Hermes* by Praxiteles and carved friezes from the Temple of Zeus.

OROS ÓLYMPOS (355 A3)
MAKEDONIA

Situated 89 kilometers (55½ miles) southwest of Thessaloníki, and north of Lárisa, Oros Ólympos (Mount Ólympos) is the legendary home of the Greek gods and was not scaled by man until 1913. The name is given to the whole limestone mountain range of which Ólympos is the highest peak in Greece at 2,911 meters (9,551 feet).

PÁTMOS (355 C2)
AEGEAN SEA *pop. 2,800*

St. John is believed to have composed *The Book of Revelation* during his exile on Pátmos in AD 95. The Cave of St. Anne, between Skála and Pátmos, is reputedly the place where the saint lived, and subsequently the island became a site of Christian pilgrimage. The cave now lies within the grounds of the Convent of the Apocalypse.

PÁTMOS (Chora) is the island's principal settlement, an attractive village with whitewashed houses dating from the 16th and 17th centuries. The fortified Monastery of St. John Theologos towers over the village. This was founded in 1088 by St. Christodoulos, and is one of the wealthiest monasteries in the world. It has outstanding frescoes and icons, a rich treasury of silver, gold and jeweled artifacts, and a priceless collection of illuminated manuscripts in the library.

▲ PÁTRA (355 A2)
PELOPONISSOS *pop. 142,000*

Pátra (Patras), capital of the Peloponissos and one of Greece's largest cities, is a busy port. Among its places of interest are Agios Andreas, a modern church that contains a relic of St. Andrew; the odeion, a restored Roman theater; and the medieval castle.

Excursions can be made to Girokomion, a 9th-century monastery 3 kilometers (2 miles) south; to the Achaia Clauss Winery, 8 kilometers (5 miles) outside of town; and to the late 15th-century Castle of the Morea at Río, 11 kilometers (7 miles) east. The beach of Chrisi Akú, is 3 kilometers (2 miles) from Pátra.

A good time to visit the city is during the three-week pre-Lenten carnival.

PIRÉAS – *see Athína on on p.362.*

PELOPONISSOS (355 A2–B2)
The mountainous southern peninsula of Greece derives its name from the "island of Pelops," a figure in Greek mythology.

It is joined to the mainland by the isthmus at Kórinthos, which is now cut by a modern canal.

In the 2nd millenium BC, the Peloponissos (Peloponnese) witnessed the developement of the Bronze Age civilization centered on **Mykínes** (Mycenae). Following its collapse, there arose the city-states of **Spárti** (Sparta) and **Kórinthos** (Corinth) during the 1st millenium BC. Impressive remains survive at each of these sites, and further classical ruins can be seen at **Árgos**, **Olympía** and **Epídavros**. The peninsula later came under Roman, Byzantine, Venetian and Turkish rule, from which a wealth of historic monuments survive. Of note are the Byzantine churches at Mystrás, near Spárti, and **Monemvasía**. Spring and fall are best times to explore the ancient sites, which lie mostly inland and become extremely hot in summer.

The Peloponnese has some of Greece's finest beaches, and the Saronic and Ionian islands are easily reached from its ports. Magnificent scenery is found everywhere: the various landscapes range from the forested hills and lush fruit groves of the north to the rugged mountains of the remote Máni region in the south.

PÝLOS (355 A1)
PELOPONISSOS *pop. 2,800*

Pýlos (Pílos) is a major seaport on the southwestern coast of the Peloponissos. It sits on the Bay of Navarino, a large natural harbor sheltered on the west by the island of Sfaktiría. It was here in 1827 that a combined fleet of British, French and Russian ships defeated the Turko-Egyptian fleet and ensured the progress toward Greek independence. On Sfaktiría are several monuments to the allied forces.

The modern town is dominated by the restored Neokastro, a Turko-Venetian fortress that succeeded the 13th-century Paleokastro on the promontory across the bay. The latter occupies the site of Old Pýlos, the classical town once known as Koryfási.

ANÁKTORA NESTOROS (Palace of Nestor), 14 kilometers (8½ miles) north near the village of Chóra, was the seat of Nestor, Homer's wise king in Greek mythology. Excavated since 1952, it has proved to be the best-preserved of the Mycenean palaces, dating from about 1400 BC; it was destroyed by fire two centuries later. Artifacts and frescoes from the site can be seen in the museum at Chóra.

RÓDOS (355 C1)
AEGEAN ISLANDS *pop. 88,000*

Situated 20 kilometers (12½ miles) from the southwest coast of Turkey, Ródos (Rhodes) is one of the most popular of the Aegean islands. Its fertile and scenic landscape encompasses picturesque mountain villages, fine beaches and crowded resorts. Highlights include the Valley of the Butterflies, and many ancient ruins and medieval monuments.

The island rose to prominence as a commercial center at the end of the 2nd millenium BC, during the late Bronze Age. In 408 BC its three city-states, Líndos, Ialissos and Kámeiros, united to found the city of Rhodes. The citizens built the Colossus of Rhodes about 290 BC, a giant bronze statue of the sun-god Helios reputed to have stood 60 cubits (about 90 feet) high; one of the Seven Wonders of the World, it was destroyed by an earthquake in 225 BC.

Following the establishment of Byzantine rule from the 5th century, Rhodes was conquered by the Knights Hospitallers in 1309. Their castles at Líndos and Rhodes can still be seen. In 1522 the island fell to the Turks, and the Knights left for Kríti and then Malta. In 1912 Rhodes was taken by Italy and only became a Greek island in 1947.

Ródos (city of Rhodes) is one of Europe's largest inhabited medieval towns. Its impressive architecture is a legacy from the occupation by the Knights Hospitallers between 1309 and 1522. The Knights were a military and religious order founded in the late 11th century to care for and protect pilgrims en route to the Holy Land. During the Middle Ages they became a powerful and wealthy institution. From 1912 the Italians restored many of the city's historic buildings and built the modern town to the north.

ACROPOLIS, southwest of the medieval city, is the site of several classical ruins including a stadium, theater and two temples.

MEDIEVAL CITY is enclosed by impressive walls rebuilt in the 15th and 16th centuries. They were designed to use and resist artillery, and extend over 4 kilometers (2½ miles). There is a guided tour of the ramparts twice a week.

The city is divided into two areas. The Collachium, or Knights' quarter, lies to the north. This contains the 13th-century Byzantine church of Panagia ton Kastrou, which became the cathedral of the Knights. Later it was converted into a mosque and is now a museum of Byzantine artifacts. Other sights include the Hospital of the Knights, the Palace of the Grand Masters, and remains of the Temple of Aphrodite dating from the 3rd century BC.

Tó the south is the Chóra, the city's Turkish quarter. This contains the Mosque of Sulieman, rebuilt in 1808, the Turksih Library, and the 16th-century Palace of the Castellan. There was also a vibrant Jewish quarter nearby until World War II.

ODOS IPPOTON, the Street of the Knights, has been faithfully restored and is lined with the seven inns that served the various nationalities of Knights.

PALATI IPPOTON RODOU, the Palace of the Grand Masters, was the stronghold of the Knights, built in the 14th century. Reconstructed in 1939–43, it now contains a museum.

RHODES MUSEUM occupies the 15th-century Hospital of the Knights. This building once cared for members of the order and ailing pilgrims. The archaeological collection consists of artifacts ranging from the Bronze Age to the Middle Ages, including the famed *Aphrodite of Ródos*.

SALONICA – *see Thessaloníki on p.376.*

SÁMOS (355 C2)
AEGEAN ISLANDS *pop. 32,600*
In Greek mythology Sámos was the birthplace of Hera, wife of Zeus. The Heraion on the south coast was one of the most important sanctuaries to the goddess, the temple ruins dating from the 6th century BC to the Roman period. The island was more certainly the birthplace of Pythagoras in about 560 BC. The resort of Pythagóreio, on the site of the ancient city of Samos, is named after the philosopher and mathematician.

Also of interest is the Tunnel of Eupalinos, completed in 524 BC, and the modern town and capital Sámos, which has an archaeological museum.

SAMOTHRÁKI (355 C3)
AEGEAN ISLANDS *pop. 2,900*
This small island off the coast of Thráki (Thrace) is rich in natural beauty. Homer claimed that Poseidon watched the Trojan War from the summit of Mount Fengári; at 1,600 meters (5,249 feet), visitors can today share the extensive view. In antiquity the island was a center for the mythological cult of the goddess Cybele.

PALAIÓPOLI was an ancient city-state situated on the north coast of the island. Little now remains of the city but there are ruins of the Sanctuary of the Great Gods. The existing remains date from the 4th and 3rd centuries BC with Roman additions. There is a museum on the site.

SANTORINI – *see Thíra on p.377.*

SOÚNIO (355 B2)
CENTRAL GREECE
Cape Soúnio was in antiquity a strategic location guarding the entrance to the Saronikós Kólpos (Saronic Gulf). Now it is a major tourist location along the Apollo Coast.

TEMPLE OF POSEIDON overlooks the sea from its rocky promontory. This ruined, marble structure was erected in the 5th century BC; 15 Doric columns still stand and nearby are remains of two smaller temples. The headland was visited by the English poet Lord Byron.

SPÁRTI (355 A2)
PELOPONISSOS *pop. 12,000*
Spárti (Sparta) began its rise to power in the 8th century BC, when it conquered the ancient country of Messinia to gain control of the southern Peloponissos. By the 5th century BC this city-state, where daily life was regulated in a militaristic fashion, was able to challenge and defeat Athína, thereby assuming the leadership of Greece.

In the Middle Ages the ruined city was refounded by the Byzantines as Lakedaimonia, only to be superceded by the nearby medieval town of Mystrás. This became the Byzantine capital of the Despotate of Morea, a magnificent center of art and learning until it passed to the Turks in 1460. Sparta was rebuilt in the 19th century, which subsequently lead to the decline and abandonment of Mystrás, now an archaeological site. The modern city of Sparta retains few monuments of its ancient glory; the most notable ruins are the Temple of Artemis Orthia, a theater, and remains of the Byzantine settlement on the *acropolis*.

MYSTRÁS, 6 kilometers (3½ miles) west of Sparta, lies below a Frankish castle built in 1249. It once housed 45,000 people but today Mystrás is an atmospheric ghost town of churches, mansions and monasteries. There are several late Byzantine churches with superb frescoes. The Mitrópolis, the 14th-century cathedral dedicated to St. Dimitríos, was the coronation site of the last Byzantine emperor in 1448. The finest church is the Pantánassa, built in 1365 and now a

GREECE

nunnery. Also of interest is the Agii Theodori, with a central octagon, and the 14th-century Palace of the Despots.

THÁSOS (355 B3)
AEGEAN ISLANDS *pop. 16,000*
The fine beaches, wooded mountain slopes and picturesque villages on the island of Thásos attract visitors seeking a relaxed atmosphere.

LIMÉNAS, or Thásos, the capital of the island, has grown up amid the ruins of the ancient city of Thásos. The classical remains include the *agora* (marketplace), theater, the city walls and several temples; the Sanctuary of Pan has a relief of the god. The site museum has a collection of sculptures and artifacts.

THERA – *see Thíra on p.377.*

THESSALÍA (355 B3)
This northeast region of Greece was home to the centaur in Greek mythology, a creature half man and half horse. The coastline along the Thermaïkos Kólpos (Gulf of Thermai) has many fine beaches, while the verdant peninsula south of Mount Pílio has several quiet resorts. One of the most scenic routes in Greece is the Vale of Tempi, which lies between the upland areas of mounts Ólympos and Óssa.

▲ THESSALONÍKI (355 B3) ★
MAKEDONIA *pop. 871,500*
Thessaloníki, formerly Salonika, was founded in 315 BC by Kassander and named after his wife, a half-sister of Alexander the Great. It became the capital of the Roman province of Makedonia in 146 BC, and later was second in importance to Constantinople within the Byzantine empire. The city fell under Turkish rule from 1430 until 1912, becoming part of modern Greece in the following year.

A fire in 1917 and bombing during World War II destroyed many of the historic buildings, and the city was rebuilt on a grid plan. Despite the damage, Thessaloníki has some of the best examples of Byzantine art and architecture; numerous churches contain mosaics, frescoes and icons.

AGIA SOPHIA, junction of Agia Sofias and Ermou, is a restored 8th-century Byzantine church. Notable among the mosaics is the 10th-century Ascension scene in the dome.

AGIOS DIMITRÍOS, Agiou Dimitriou, is the largest church in Greece. It is dedicated to the city's patron saint, Dimitrius, who is believed to have been martyred on the site. The restored 5th-century basilica has marble columns and contains superb mosaics representing the saint, while the crypt contains the saint's tomb.

ARCHAEOLOGICAL MUSEUM, on Platía Xanthi, contains finds from the Royal Tomb of Vergina. These superb treasures of the classical kings of Makedonia include a gold wreath, armor and a ceremonial shield.

LEVKÓS PÍRGOS (White Tower), beside the harbor, was built about 1430 at the southern angle of the city's defenses.

PANAGIA ACHEIROPOEITOS, Agia Sofias, is a Byzantine basilica dating from the 5th century. The name means "made without hands," a reference to a miraculous icon. The church contains fine frescoes and mosaics.

PILI GALERIOU (Arch of Galerius), spanning Egnatias, is a Roman triumphal arch erected to celebrate the victory of the Emperor Galerius over the Persians in AD 297.

PÉLLA is 38 kilometers (23½ miles) northwest of Thessaloníki. This is the site of the ancient capital of Makedonia, founded in the late 5th century BC. It was the birthplace of Alexander the Great in 356 BC. Excavations since 1957 have uncovered remains of the *agora* (marketplace) and a palace nearby.

THÍRA (355 C1) ★
AEGEAN ISLANDS *pop. 8,000*

The volcanic island of Thíra (Thera), known also as Santorini, is the most southerly of the Kiklades (Cyclades) and a popular tourist destination. There are dramatic sea cliffs, and black volcanic beaches that are excellent for swimming. The shape of the island with its islets was the result of a massive volcanic eruption about 1500 BC.

The south of the island has two important archaeological sites. The Bronze Age settlement at Akrotíri dates from the early 2nd millenium BC; its well-preserved buildings are due to burial under volcanic ash. The ruins of ancient Thera date mainly from the 3rd century BC to the Byzantine period.

Thíra, or Fira, the island's capital, has been restored following an earthquake in 1956. The town is perched on cliffs overlooking the natural harbor to the west, formerly the crater of the volcano.

TRÍPOLI (355 A2)
PELOPONISSOS *pop. 21,300*

The modern town of Trípoli lies at the crossroads of the main routes across the Peloponissos. It is the capital of Arkadia, a pastoral region of quiet beauty. Although the town has no major attractions, there is a good archaeological museum.

TEGEA, 8 kilometers (5 miles) south at Aléa, is the site of a classical city and the later Byzantine city of Nikli. Remains include the Temple of Athena Alea dating from the 4th century BC, and an Early Christian basilica with mosaics.

TEMPLE OF APOLLO EPIKOURIOS, near Andrítsaina 70 kilometers (43½ miles) west, is reached by a scenic drive along narrow winding roads. Built about 425 BC, this well-preserved temple is worth seeing despite the remote location.

ÝDRA (355 B2)
CENTRAL GREECE *pop. 3,000*

The narrow, rocky island of Ýdra (Hydra) lies off the east coast of the Peloponissos. Despite the lack of beaches, in recent years it has become a fashionable, cosmopolitan resort, as well as a tour stop for cruise boats from Athína. To avoid the crowds, a visit outside the busy summer months is recommended. No cars are allowed on the island.

In the 18th and 19th centuries Ýdra was the base for prosperous merchant families who built the beautiful Italianate mansions of the island. The sea captains renounced their maritime trade in 1821 to play an important role in the Greek War of Independence.

ZÁKYNTHOS (355 A2)
IONIAN ISLANDS *pop. 30,000*

A volcanic island of exceptional natural beauty, Zákynthos (Zante or Kakinthos) was called the "flower of the East" by its onetime Venetian rulers. Fertile in the east, the western half of the island is barren and mountainous. Zákynthos is also one of the most important breeding areas in the Mediterranean for the endangered loggerhead turtles, now further threatened by tourism (*see p. 370*).

Beyond the town of Zákynthos, places of interest include the medieval monastery at Anafonítra, with surviving wall paintings; the pretty, 12th-century church of Ayia Paraskeví at Volímes; the spectacular Blue Grotto Cave at the northern tip of the island; and the white limestone cliffs at Kerí in the south.

ZÁKYNTHOS, the island's capital, was attractively rebuilt in its former Venetian character following a disastrous earthquake in 1953. The churches of Agios Nikólaos and Agios Dionysíos have been beautifully restored.

A museum of Byzantine and post-Byzantine art contains masterpieces of the Ionian school and a collection of superb *templos* (carved icon screens). The ruined Venetian *kastro* (castle) on the hill above the town affords fine views across the harbor to the west coast of the Greek mainland.

REPUBLIC OF IRELAND

CONVERSATION MATTERS IN IRELAND, TIME LESS SO. A JOURNEY FROM HOME TO STORE CAN TAKE HALF A MORNING ... AND WHY NOT? A STRANGER WILL NOT BE UNKNOWN FOR LONG, ESPECIALLY IN A PUB, WHERE DRINK FLOWS AND MUSIC PLAYS.

THE LAND IS GREEN, WELL-WATERED BY THE ATLANTIC RAIN, THOUGH EVEN ON THE WETTEST DAY THE IRISH WILL MERELY REMARK THAT IT IS "A BIT SOFT." FOUR SEASONS IN ONE DAY, THEY CLAIM, ESPECIALLY IN THE WEST ALONG THE TOWERING CLIFFS OF MOHER, THE RING OF KERRY AND THE OFFSHORE ARAN ISLANDS.

DUBLIN, THE CAPITAL, HAS THE FEEL OF A VILLAGE AND THE BEST OF ITS ATTRACTIONS CAN BE ENJOYED ON FOOT. STROLL ALONG THE BANKS OF THE LIFFEY RIVER, AND WALK ACROSS TO THE OTHER SIDE OVER THE ELEGANT HALFPENNY BRIDGE.

Left MAGNIFICENT VIEWS OVER DARRYNANE, IN COUNTY KERRY
Above left A TRALEE (TRADITIONAL MUSIC) IS OFTEN PLAYED IN PUBS
Above right THE SOUTH CROSS AT KELLS

Things to Know

- **Area:** 70,285 square kilometers (27,137 square miles)
- **Population:** 3,548,000
- **Capital:** Dublin
- **Languages:** English and Gaelic
- **Religion:** Ireland has both Church of Ireland (Protestant) and Roman Catholic churches; Dublin has a mosque and a synagogue.
- **Economy:** Agriculture, industry and livestock. Barley, wheat, and other grains; root and green crops; food processing; metals and engineering; textiles, clothing and footwear; electronics; brewing and distilling.
- **Electricity:** 220 volts; adaptor required for non-Continental appliances.
- **Passport Requirements:** Required for U.S. citizens.
- **Visa Requirements:** Not required for stays up to three months.
- **Duty-Free Items:** Up to 200 cigarettes or 100 cigarillos or 50 cigars or 250 grams of tobacco; 2 liters of wine and 1 liter of spirits; 50 grams of perfume; ¼ liter of toilet water; and gifts valued up to £73 in Irish currency. Travelers under 17 are not entitled to tobacco or drinks allowances. Also see *The European Union* on p.9.
- **Currency:** The Irish *pound* is divided into 100 *pence*. Due to currency fluctuations, the exchange rate is subject to frequent change. There are no restrictions on the amount of foreign or Irish currency that may be imported, but large amounts to be re-exported should be declared on entry. Visitors and residents may only export up to £100 in Irish currency and up to £500 in foreign currency in addition to the imported amount declared on entry.
- **Bank Opening Hours:** 10am–12:30pm and 1:30–3pm Monday–Friday. Also 10am–12:30pm and 1:30–5pm Thursday in Dublin; open one evening a week in most other towns.
- **Store Opening Hours:** 9am–5:30pm Monday–Saturday. Stores outside the cities frequently close one day a week

History

Ireland, born of conflict, struggles to survive and prosper in the wake of generations of invasion and the fight for self-determination. Two important characteristics distinguish the struggle for Irish independence; firstly, Ireland has remained staunchly Catholic and is, to an extent, still in a state of political and cultural limbo; secondly, Ireland is neither completely free of British influence nor completely absorbed by English custom.

The Gaels of Western Europe, people of Celtic speech who invaded Ireland in prehistory, formulated the blueprint for Irish society and culture. Druids maintained the social order, and semi-independent kingdoms developed under a high king, whose position was largely ceremonial. This arrangement continued until the 5th century AD, when St. Patrick began to convert the people to Christianity and replaced druid priests with monastic leaders. Between the 5th and 12th centuries, Ireland enjoyed a period of profound cultural, literary and artistic successes. An example is the elaborately decorated gospels called the *Book of Kells*, from the 8th century, on display at Trinity College in Dublin.

The 12th century saw a change in the political situation, which inaugurated nearly 800 years of struggle between the English and Irish, and which continues to have a profound effect today. Henry II, with the support of popes Adrian IV (the only English pope) and Alexander III, invaded and declared himself Lord of Ireland in 1171. This marked the first time that the Church was linked to a foreign administration (thereby terminating Gaelic Ireland's independence).

The following years saw attempts by the English to replace papal loyalty with loyalty to the Crown. Oliver Cromwell's victory over Irish resistance in 1650 brought a ban on the practice of the Catholic faith; it also gave Cromwell the opportunity to seize Catholic lands, which were handed out to British subjects as rewards for loyalty.

The Test Act of 1704 continued the anti-Catholic discrimination, tying the right to hold office to a willingness to receive communion in the (Protestant) Church of Ireland. Irish resentment escalated until 1796, when Theobald Wolfe Tone and the United Irishmen rebelled. Two years later Wolfe Tone and his followers were defeated and British Prime Minister William Pitt began campaigning for a merger of the English and Irish parliaments. In order to secure this, promises were made regarding Catholics' rights to representation. The resultant United Kingdom, created under the 1800 Act of Union, established London as the seat of authority, but denied Catholics access to parliament, a decision based on the laws invoked under the Test Act.

Daniel O'Connell, a young Catholic lawyer, was elected in 1828 to the British

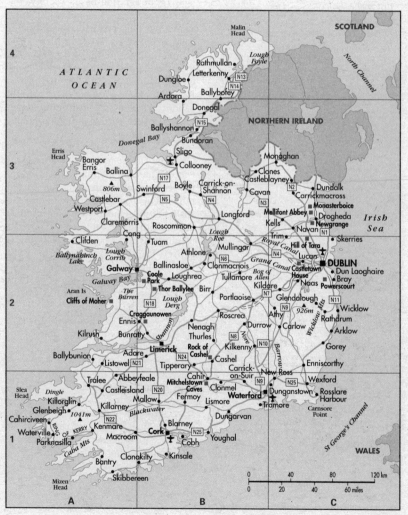

(usually Wednesday or Saturday).
- **BEST BUYS:** Tweeds, linen, woolens, knits, lace, rugs, blankets, woodcarvings, smoking pipes, pottery, jewelry, Connemara marble and Waterford crystal.
- **PUBLIC HOLIDAYS:** January 1; March 17 (St. Patrick's Day); Good Friday; Easter Monday; 1st Monday in June; 1st Monday in August (August Monday); last Monday in October; December 25; December 26 (St. Stephen's Day).
- **USEFUL TELEPHONE NUMBERS:**
Police 999
Fire 999
Ambulance 999
- **NATIONAL TOURIST OFFICES:**
Irish National Tourist Office
345 Park Avenue
New York
NY 10154
Tel: 212/418-0800
Fax: 212/371-9052
Irish Tourist Board
150–151 New Bond Street
London W1Y 0AQ, England
Tel: 0171 493 3201
Fax: 0171 493 9065
Irish Tourist Board
14 O'Connell Street
Dublin, Rebublic of Ireland
Tel: (01) 284 4768
Fax: (01) 284 1751
- **AMERICAN EMBASSY**
42 Elgin Road
Ballsbridge
Dublin 4, Republic of Ireland
Tel: (01) 668 8777
Fax: (01) 668 8274

AUTOMOBILE CLUB
The Automobile Association
(AA) has offices at 23 Rockhill, Blackrock, County Dublin. The symbol ▲ indicates the availability of a AAA-affiliated automobile club branch. Not all auto clubs offer full travel services to AAA members.

Parliament; as a Catholic, however, he was barred from taking his seat under the Act of Union. Fearing the backlash that might occur from the increasing agitation for Catholic emancipation, Parliament yielded to the pressure and revoked the required oath of allegiance to the Church of Ireland. A growing nationalism was emerging within the Catholic community, and talk of home rule escalated. However, the potato famine of the mid-1840s forced the Irish to focus much of their energy on survival – not nationalism. In an agrarian-based society, the potatoes were an economic and dietary staple, but blight and overworked fields led to massive crop failure. The population was reduced by half with more than a million deaths and as many emigrants, mainly to the United States. Resentment over what the Catholic majority viewed as British indifference to their plight further inflamed home-rule sentiment.

Once the famine had subsided, nationalism regained momentum. After several unsuccessful attempts a bill was passed in Parliament granting home rule to the Irish, but it excluded six Ulster counties in the north where Protestants enjoyed a majority. World War I, however, interrupted implementation of the 1914 Home Rule Act. Precipitated by frustration over the postponement, the 1916 Easter Rising was one of the first violent

---

IRISH WHISKEY
Uisce beatha, or "water of life," was supposedly invented by Irish missionary monks, who had gained the knowledge from a Middle Eastern method of making perfume from an *alembic*, or still. It is said that Queen Elizabeth I was partial to a drop of whiskey, a taste probably acquired from Sir Walter Raleigh, who had been presented with a 145-liter (32-gallon) cask of it by the Earl of Cork.

displays by the Irish Republican Army – an organized army of Sinn Féin ("Ourselves Alone") party members who were determined to fight British rule through guerrilla warfare. Although not militarily successful, it proved to be the catalyst for uniting the Irish in their demand for nationhood.

In 1921, the Irish Free State was declared, a self-governing area with its own parliament, though still within the British Commonwealth of Nations. A separate parliament was set up in the six Ulster counties now known as Northern Ireland; the Protestant majority was adamantly opposed to home rule, fearing the Catholic majority to the south. Tensions in the south erupted into civil war over this alliance with the British Commonwealth and the attendant oath to the Crown, planting the seeds of antagonism that brought about the drafting of a new constitution (still under the auspices of the British Commonwealth) in 1937 and, finally, the declaration in 1949 of the Republic of Ireland as an independent nation free of British control. Although the political situation in Northern Ireland remains unresolved, citizens of the Republic have moved forward in their quest for economic stability and international participation.

FOOD AND DRINK

Irish food is wholesome and plentiful. Such favorites as steak, roast beef, mutton and lamb are excellent and always available. The island is also particularly well-known for its seafood – Dublin Bay prawns, lobsters, smoked salmon and oysters are delicacies of exceptional flavor. And, to accompany your feast, how about a pint of Guinness stout followed by a glass of Irish whiskey? Ireland's pubs are renowned, many offering live entertainment that includes traditional music.

SPORTS AND RECREATION

The Irish enthusiasm for sports makes their country ideal for golfers, fishermen and hunters. Fine golf courses are numerous, and both freshwater and saltwater fishing are excellent. Horse racing, soccer and rugby are also extremely popular, although hurling (which is similar to hockey) and Gaelic football are the national games.

GETTING AROUND

Dublin and Shannon airports have international connections, including flights to the U.S. There are car ferry services and catamaran links to Ireland from Britain and France. Some of the most convenient crossings are from Holyhead (Wales) to Dublin and Dun Laoghaire, from Roscoff and Brest (France) to Cork, and from Le Havre, Cherbourg and Brest (France) to Rosslare.

Roads are divided into three categories: national primary, national secondary and regional. Driving is on the left-hand side and roads are narrow. Cyclists, pedestrians and livestock constitute the main driving hazards. Road signs are in Gaelic and English. Seat belts must be worn, and children under 12 must travel in the back seat. Speed limits are 50 k.p.h. (31 m.p.h.) in developed areas, 90 k.p.h. (55 m.p.h.) outside these areas, and 112 k.p.h. (69 m.p.h.) on highways. There are very strict rules against drinking and driving.

ACCOMMODATIONS

Many types of accommodations are available, from first-class luxury hotels to more modest but comfortable second- and third-class establishments. Guest houses are also popular. More information can be obtained from the Irish office of the Automobile Association (see p.382) or the Irish National Tourist Office. Cottages and apartments can also be rented, and there are many campgrounds.

TIPPING

Restaurants and hotels generally include a 15 percent service charge; if not, leave 10 to 15 percent. Tip taxi-drivers 10 percent of the fare, doormen and porters about 50 pence to £1 per bag.

PRINCIPAL TOURING AREAS

Note: For descriptions of attractions in **bold type**, see individual listings.

DONEGAL AND SLIGO

Northwest Ireland is noted for its spectacular indented coast. The cliffs, deep glens and fishing villages of Donegal and the sandy beaches of **Sligo** are shadowed by mountains, and the region is also famous for its castles and lakes.

DUBLIN AND THE EAST COAST

The long, gentle coastline of the Irish Sea attracts thousands of visitors to the beaches and resorts of the east coast, where many remains from prehistory still exist. **Kildare**, with its lush green pastures and ancient bogland, is known as a sporting, racing and hunting region. Louth, Ireland's smallest county, figures in many folktales. Meath is the site of the wooded Blackwater River region – and, of course, there is **Dublin**, the city of James Joyce.

THE MIDLANDS

Central Ireland, unlike the rest of the country, is relatively flat. Of special interest is **Clonmacnois**, Ireland's best-known monastic site. **Athlone** is an excellent departure point for exploring the islands of Lough Ree, several of which bear the ruins of ancient churches.

THE SOUTHWEST

Bordered by rugged coastline and island-strewn bays, Ireland's southwest boasts magnificent mountain scenery best seen from the circular Ring of Kerry drive on the Iveragh Peninsula. County Tipperary has some interesting historic buildings, the most notable being the Rock of Cashel, and the region also includes the popular castle at **Blarney**. The towns of **Adare**, **Killarney**, **Limerick** and **Waterford** feature some fine old buildings, while recreational facilities are available at Glenbeigh, **Kenmare** and **Lismore**.

THE WEST COAST

Historic **Galway** makes an ideal base for touring this lake-studded region on the shores of the Atlantic. The 200-meter (656-foot) **Cliffs of Moher**, the limestone-dominated Burren and mountainous Connemara all make for rewarding excursions. Some 50 kilometers (31 miles) from Galway, are the **Aran Islands**, the setting for some historic ruins and an area where a largely traditional way of life is maintained.

USEFUL EXPRESSIONS IN IRISH

Bord Fáilte (Irish Tourist Board) – pronounced *bord fawlcha*
Céad míle fáilte ("a hundred thousand welcomes") – *kay-d mille fawlcha*
céilídh (Irish dance night) – *kaylee*
Gaeltacht (Irish-speaking region) – pronounced *gale-tackt*
Garda Síochána (police) – *gawrda shee-kawnah*
poteen (alcohol distilled from potatoes, illegal and often dangerous) – *potcheen*
sláinte (cheers, good health) – *slawn-cha*
slán (good-bye) – *slawn*
Taoiseach (Prime Minister) – *teeshock*
uisce beatha (whiskey, literally "water of life") – *ishka baha*
Mná means women and **Fir** means men on public restroom doors.

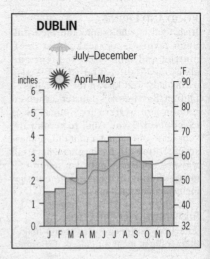

DUBLIN

July–December

April–May

PLACES OF INTEREST

▲ DUBLIN ★

COUNTY DUBLIN *pop. 1,025,300*

Dublin, the capital of the Republic of Ireland, has one of the loveliest settings in Europe. On Dublin Bay, the "Town of the Hurdle Ford" – *Baile Atha Cliath* in Gaelic – is sheltered to the north by the rocky mass of Howth Head. The Liffey River cuts through the city and is crossed by many picturesque bridges. The name Dublin is derived from *dubhlinn*, the Gaelic word for "black pool."

First mentioned by the great map-maker Ptolemy in AD 140, Dublin claims a long and turbulent history. Following centuries of invasions by Vikings, Normans and English, the city became a center of agitation for Irish independence, culminating in the Easter Rising of 1916, when the Irish Volunteers seized the General Post Office. Although this rebellion was crushed, Dublin became the focus for the often violent struggles that followed. Today, an elected city council and the city manager make up Dublin Corporation, which administers the city.

Dublin has produced some of the world's greatest literary figures. Most notably, it was the birthplace and home of James Joyce, whose writings are predominantly based in Dublin. George Bernard Shaw was born at No. 33 Synge Street in 1856. Other natives of the city include Oscar Wilde, who attended Trinity College, and Jonathan Swift, who served as Dean of St. Patrick's Cathedral.

Compact Dublin combines age-old charm with modern facilities. With the exception of two cathedrals and a few historic churches, most of the architecture dates from the 18th century, when the city enjoyed special prominence. Also of interest are the Georgian houses that line Merrion Square. American visitors will be especially interested in Leinster House and Dublin Castle: the Irish-born architect of the White House, James Hoban, borrowed many of its features from these buildings.

Perhaps the most outstanding feature of Dublin is the traditional pub, where visitors can relax over a pint of hearty Irish brew. Many pubs attract artists, writers, actors and students; there is often singing and the atmosphere is loud and friendly.

Dublin offers many recreational facilities. There are fine parks, including attractive St. Stephen's Green and Phoenix Park; the National Botanic Gardens are also of interest. Hunting, fishing, golfing, horse racing and greyhound racing are popular, and there are several bowling greens. Fine beaches nearby include Malahide, 14 kilometers (8½ miles) northeast, and Killiney, 16 kilometers (10 miles) south, both popular with Dubliners. Powerscourt Estate in Enniskerry (see p.399), about 19 kilometers (12 miles) from Dublin, is also a popular excursion.

Annual events include the St. Patrick's Day Parade and related festivities on March 17, the world-renowned Dublin Horse Show in August, and the Theatre Festival in October.

ABBEY THEATRE (The National Theatre), Lower Abbey Street, presents plays by the giants of Irish literature. William

Butler Yeats and Augusta Lady Gregory were instrumental in its founding in 1904, three years after the birth of Irish literary theater. The Peacock Theatre annex gives lunchtime and evening performances.

BANK OF IRELAND (Old Parliament House), College Green, was designed to house the Irish Parliament but made redundant by the 1800 Act of Union.

CHESTER BEATTY LIBRARY AND GALLERY OF ORIENTAL ART, 20 Shrewsbury Road, Ballsbridge, contains a rare collection of

Islamic manuscripts and miniatures, oriental paintings, Western prints, rare books and historic documents donated to the city by Irish-American mining engineer Sir Alfred Chester Beatty.

CHRIST CHURCH CATHEDRAL, Lord Edward Street, near Winetavern Street, was founded in 1038 by Sitric Silkenbeard, the first Christian Viking King of Dublin. Largely rebuilt since then, it retains its medieval crypt.

CUSTOM HOUSE, near the junction of Gardiner Street Lower and Amiens, was

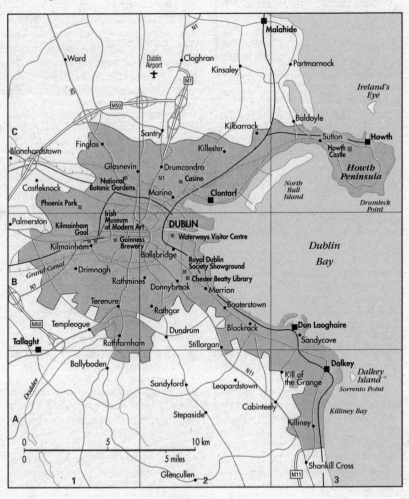

built in 1791 and is one of Dublin's finest buildings. Gutted by fire in 1921, it was restored and is still in use.

DUBLIN CASTLE, with two towers and a partial wall, is the city's most outstanding legacy of the Middle Ages. Of interest are the Record Tower, state apartments, Church of the Most Holy Trinity, and remains of Norman and Viking defenses. The inauguration of the President of Ireland and related ceremonies are held in St. Patrick's Hall.

DUBLIN CIVIC MUSEUM, 58 South William Street, has old maps, pictures, models and archaeological finds that trace the city's history from Viking times.

DUBLIN NATURAL HISTORY MUSEUM, Upper Merrion Street, displays a comprehensive collection of native Irish species and exotic animals.

DUBLIN WRITERS' MUSEUM, 18–19 Parnell Square North, displayed in two restored 18th-century buildings, records Dublin's literary heritage from the 8th-century *Book of Kells* to the present.

FOUR COURTS, Inns Quay, beside the river, houses the Irish Law Courts. Built in 1785 and damaged in 1922 during the Civil War, it has been restored.

GENERAL POST OFFICE, O'Connell Street, was the headquarters of the Irish Volunteers during the Easter Rising of 1916. The 1818 structure was partially destroyed by fire but later rebuilt. A plaque and statue commemorate the Easter Rising.

GUINNESS BREWERY, St. James Gate, was founded in 1759. Its original 9,000-year lease will not require renewal for quite some time! One of the largest breweries in the world, it produces beer from original yeast strains.

GUINNESS HOP STORE, Crane Street, was established in 1876 as a hop store and

---

BILLY-IN-THE-BOWL

The mid-18th century was a worrying time for residents of Stoneybatter in northwest Dublin. Billy-in-the-Bowl was born with no legs, but by sitting in an iron bowl and propelling himself with his arms, he was fully able to get around. Unfortunately, he used his well-developed upper-body strength to seize sympathetic passers-by and strangle them for their purses. Once the long arm of the law finally caught up with him, he was sentenced to "as much hard labor as his condition would allow" for the rest of his days.

---

now houses The World of Guinness exhibition. The history of the well-known brew is depicted through an exhibition, while the Cooperage displays barrel-maker's tools and oak casks; visitors can also see the Transport Gallery or taste Guinness beer at the Sample Bar.

HOWTH CASTLE, 14 kilometers (8½ miles) northeast, is known for its attractive gardens and a rhododendron walk, at its best in May and June.

HUGH LANE MUNICIPAL GALLERY, Parnell Square, occupies Charlemont House, a Georgian mansion. Inside are collections of Irish works, and art from the modern French and British schools.

LEINSTER HOUSE, Kildare Street, a Georgian mansion built for the Duke of Leinster in 1745, is now the home of the Irish Parliament. Visits are by guided tour only.

MALAHIDE CASTLE, 13 kilometers (8 miles) northeast, is 12th-century and one of Ireland's oldest castles. Tours take in Irish period furniture and portrait collections. Additional paintings from the National Gallery of Ireland depict Irish life during the last few centuries.

MANSION HOUSE, Dawson Street, residence of the lord mayors of Dublin since 1715, saw the signing of the 1919 Irish Declaration of Independence and the 1921 Anglo-Irish truce.

NATIONAL BOTANIC GARDENS, located 4 kilometers (2½ miles) north at Glasnevin, encompass 20 hectares (49½ acres) of grounds planted with over 20,000 common and rare species of flowers, shrubs and trees.

NATIONAL GALLERY OF IRELAND ★, Merrion Square, contains the work of masters of most European schools, including Rembrandt, El Greco, Goya, Sir Joshua Reynolds and Degas. Portraits of Irish national figures line the staircase.

GUINNESS

Dublin in 1759 saw one Arthur Guinness establish a brewery, where he began to experiment with a beverage from London. This brew was made with roasted barley and named "porter" after its popularity with Covent Garden porters. Forty years later, all production efforts were concentrated on this distinctive drink, and in the early 1800s an even stronger, extra stout beer was produced. It was this rich, black liquid with a creamy head that soon gained world renown.

NATIONAL MUSEUM ★, Kildare Street, houses the Treasury with its masterpieces of Celtic and medieval metalwork; these include the Tara Brooch and the Ardagh Chalice (both 8th-century), and the 12th-century Cross of Cong. Other displays illustrate Viking and Norman times, the 1916 Easter Rising and the Irish Civil War.

PHOENIX PARK ★ covers 690 hectares (1,704 acres) in the west of Dublin. Within it are the People's Gardens, the Zoological Gardens, the Magazine Fort, and the residences of the President of Ireland and the U.S. ambassador. The Zoological Gardens, founded in 1830, contains an extensive collection of plants and birds.

ROYAL HOSPITAL/IRISH MUSEUM OF MODERN ART, Military Road, Kilmainham, is one of the finest 17th-century buildings in Ireland. The museum includes international and Irish art of the 20th century.

ST. AUDOEN'S CHURCH, High Street, is the oldest parish church in Dublin, which is 12th-century; three of its oldest bells were cast in 1423. Nearby is the 1215 St. Audoen's Arch, the only surviving gate in the city's walls.

ST. MARY'S PRO-CATHEDRAL, Marlborough Street, designed by exiled patriot John Sweetman, was completed in 1825. The famous Palestrina Choir sings Mass in Latin on Sundays at 11am.

ST. PATRICK'S CATHEDRAL, Patrick Street, was founded in 1190 and restored in the 19th century. Its interior is impressive. Jonathan Swift, dean from 1713 to 1745 and author of *Gulliver's Travels*, is buried in this Protestant cathedral.

TRINITY COLLEGE ★, on College Green, has educated many prominent persons. Although Queen Elizabeth I granted a charter to a group of Dubliners in 1591, no structures from that period remain. Most of the present buildings were erected in the 18th century, and the Palladian façade was added in 1759; the oldest building is the red-brick Rubrics.

College Library, completed in 1732, has an impressive collection of books and manuscripts. The brilliantly illuminated 8th-century *Book of Kells*, once kept at the monastery of Kells in County Meath, is on display.

ADARE (381 B2)
COUNTY LIMERICK pop. 800

Adare is an enchanting little village with half-timbered houses, thatched cottages, good hunting and fishing, and interesting ecclesiastical ruins.

BLACK ABBEY, northeast of Adare, is a 14th-century Augustinian friary noted for its west window, Tudor Rose Tower and 15th-century cloister.

WHITE MONASTERY of Trinitarian monks of the Order for the Redemption of Christian Captives is the only known house of this order in Ireland. The monastery was founded in 1230 and enlarged 42 years later.

ARAN ISLANDS (381 A2) ★
COUNTY GALWAY pop. 1,500
The three main islands that make up Aran lie 48 kilometers (30 miles) west of Galway, connected by ferry services and regular flights. These islanders are resourceful subsistence farmers, working "made" ground of sand and seaweed in a rugged and treeless landscape.

Some residents, especially those on the island of Inishmaan, continue to spin and weave their own clothing. Islanders also still use the *currach*, a small boat of ancient design made of tarred canvas stretched over a wicker frame.

The three islands have ruins of ancient forts, monasteries and churches. Foremost among several prehistoric sites is Dun Aengus on Inishmore, a semicircular fort built at the edge of a 90-meter (295-foot) cliff. Another of Inishmore's prehistoric forts is well-preserved Dun Eochaill near the village of Oghil. Ninth-century Teampall Bheanain is said to be the world's smallest church: it measures less than 3.5 meters (11 feet) in length. On Inishmaan are Dun Conor, a well-preserved stone fort, and the cottage in which the writer J. M. Synge lived during his stay on the islands. Inisheer, the smallest of the islands, has a ruined castle inside a prehistoric fort.

ARKLOW (381 C2)
COUNTY WICKLOW pop. 8,000
Arklow stands at the mouth of the Avoca River. In days past, the community was a busy shipping and fishing center; today it is one of the foremost seaside resorts on the eastern coast, with sandy beaches and facilities for golf, tennis, boating, fishing and shooting. In town there is a memorial to Father Michael Murphy, who led a local rebellion that was crushed by the British in 1798.

ATHLONE (381 B2)
COUNTY WESTMEATH pop. 9,500
Athlone, on the Shannon River near Lough Ree, is a point of departure for river excursions. The great tenor John McCormack was born here in 1884, and the museum in the town's 13th-century Norman castle documents his life.

BALLINA (381 A3)
COUNTY MAYO pop. 6,900
Ballina lies on the Moy River near loughs Conn and Cullin. The town is a golfing and fishing center; it also offers boating, swimming, shooting, mountain climbing and trekking. The Ballina (Moy) Salmon Festival is held in July.

To the east rise the long ridges of the Ox Mountains, site of the country's peat bogs and one of the area's major fuel sources. Rosserk Abbey, 8 kilometers (5 miles) north of Ballina, is a well-preserved 15th-century Franciscan friary.

BALLINASLOE (381 B2)
COUNTY GALWAY pop. 6,500
Dating from before the 12th century, Ballinasloe is a thriving market town known for its livestock fairs. Ireland's "travelers" elect their "king" at the renowned Ballinasloe Horse Fair in October. Sights include ruined churches and castles, as well as the battlefield of Aughrim, where Irish forces fought for the Stuarts against William of Orange in 1691. A museum has articles from the battle and archaeological artifacts.

BALLYNAHINCH LAKE (381 A2)
COUNTY GALWAY
Ballynahinch Lake, a well-known fishing center in Connemara, is surrounded by pleasant mountain scenery.

CLONFERT ABBEY, founded in the 6th century by St. Brendan "the Navigator," lies 10 kilometres (6 miles) south. The ruins and rebuilt edifices include an intact Irish Romanesque doorway.

BANTRY (381 A1)
COUNTY CORK *pop. 2,900*

Bantry is a quaint town on Bantry Bay, which was the site of French naval invasions in the 17th and 18th centuries. Bay fishing offers rewarding catches.

BANTRY HOUSE, southwest, is a Georgian mansion set in terraced Italianate gardens overlooking the bay. The house is richly furnished with art and antiques, including a tapestry made for Marie Antoinette. The French Armada Exhibition Centre, housed in a renovated courtyard, relates the history of the failed French invasion led by Irish rebel Wolfe Tone in 1796.

BLARNEY (381 B1)
COUNTY CORK *pop. 2,000*

BLARNEY CASTLE AND GARDENS is home to the Blarney Stone, famed for the eloquence it is said to impart to those who kiss it. The stone is in the upper tower of the castle, and the visitor, held by the feet, must lean backwards down a shaft to receive the "gift of the gab."

BUNDORAN (381 B3)
COUNTY DONEGAL *pop. 1,600*

One of Ireland's principal coastal resorts, Bundoran stands on the southern shore of Donegal Bay, framed by the Sligo Leitrim Mountains. It is believed that the first recorded history of Ireland was compiled in Bundrowes (just west of town) by the Abbot of Donegal and three other scholar-friars, who labored from 1630 to 1636 to chronicle the 4,500 previous years. Their effort is called the *Annals of the Four Masters*.

THE FOUR MASTERS MEMORIAL, situated to the north in Donegal, is a 7.5-meter (25-foot) obelisk bearing the names of the four scholastic monks who compiled the *Annals*: Michael O'Clery, Peregrine O'Clery, Peregrine Duignan and Fearfeasa O'Mulconry.

BUNRATTY (381 B2)
COUNTY CLARE

The village of Bunratty is known both for its castle and for Bunratty Folk Park. The latter contains farmhouses and craft shops, re-erected and furnished to reflect 19th-century rural Irish life.

BUNRATTY CASTLE, dating from the mid-15th century, is Ireland's most complete medieval castle. It houses the Lord Gort Collection of furniture, art objects, and paintings and tapestries dating from before 1650. The castle hosts "medieval banquets," complete with serving wenches.

CAHIR (381 B1)
COUNTY TIPPERARY *pop. 2,100*

A hunting and fishing center, Cahir gets its name from the *caher*, or stone fort, that once stood there. The town is a good starting point for touring in the Galtee Mountains.

CAHIR CASTLE, located on an island in the Suir River, is one of Ireland's best-preserved castles. It dates mainly from the 15th century, although its oldest parts were built in 1164. The fully restored structure has two courts, a massive square, a keep and a great hall.

CASHEL (381 B2) ★
COUNTY TIPPERARY *pop. 2,500*

ROCK OF CASHEL, a 60-meter (197-foot) hill, was the seat of the Munster kings from AD 370 to 1101. Legend states that the Devil took a bite from the Slieve Bloom Mountains (leaving a gap known as the Devil's Bit) and spat forth this limestone outcrop when surprised by St. Patrick. The Rock is crowned by a number of impressive medieval buildings, the oldest being the 27-meter (89-foot) Round Tower that dates from the 10th century. Cormac's Chapel, begun in 1127, is a fine example of Irish Romanesque architecture. The roofless 13th-century cathedral is the largest building on the summit. A replica of a 12th-century high cross stands at the spot where St. Patrick baptized King Aengus, Ireland's first Christian king, in the 5th century. The original cross is in the museum in the 15th-century Hall of the Vicars.

CASTLETOWN HOUSE (381 C2) ★
COUNTY KILDARE

Situated at Celbridge, 7 kilometers (4½ miles) west of Lucan, this is considered by many to be Ireland's finest Georgian country house. Designed in the Palladian style by Italian architect Alessandro Galilei in 1722, the restored house contains excellent plasterwork by the Francini brothers, Irish furniture and paintings of the period, the Pompeian Long Gallery with its Venetian chandeliers, and an 18th-century print room.

CAVAN (381 B3)
COUNTY CAVAN pop. 3,300

Cavan is the capital of its county. In ancient times it was the territory of the O'Reillys, rulers of East Breany, with whom many historic sites are connected. A belfry tower from the 14th-century Franciscan friary still stands. Other places of interest include a crystal factory and a local folk museum.

CEANANNUS MÓR (KELLS) (381 C3)
COUNTY MEATH pop. 3,700

Originating as a 6th-century monastic settlement founded by St. Columcille (Columba), Ceanannus Mór (Gaelic for Kells) is today a market town. *The Book of Kells*, an 8th-century manuscript, is an heirloom of the town's monastery; it is now in the Trinity College Library in Dublin (see p.388), but a facsimile is in St. Columba's Church.

The round tower in the Church of Ireland churchyard is a fine example of this type of structure, with its five windows pointing to the five ancient roads leading into town. South Cross, near the round tower, is the most interesting of Ceanannus Mór's five high crosses:

erected around the 9th century, it is ornately sculptured. Market Cross, used as a gallows in 1798, stands in the town center.

CLIFDEN (381 A2)
COUNTY GALWAY pop. 800

Clifden, the main town of the Connemara region, overlooks Ardbear Bay and is an excellent base for excursions. Good bathing, riding, tennis and fishing can be enjoyed. The Connemara Pony Show is in mid-August.

CLIFFS OF MOHER (381 A2) ★
COUNTY CLARE

These awe-inspiring sheer cliffs, which stretch for 8 kilometers (5 miles) along the coast of Clare, are home to a variety of sea birds. At the northeast end, the cliffs' highest point, you will find O'Brien's Tower, a folly built by 19th-century member of parliament Sir Cornelius O'Brien. The nearby visitor center offers displays on local history, legends, bird life and geology. Not far away is Spanish Point, where the Spanish Armada foundered in 1588.

CLONMACNOIS (381 B2) ★
COUNTY OFFALY

Founded by St. Ciaran in AD 545, the monastic city of Clonmacnois flourished as a religious and scholastic center until its destruction in the 16th century.

Many of the country's kings, saints and scholars are buried here, including St. Ciaran and the last High King of Ireland.

Standing by a bend of the Shannon River, the ruins of Clonmacnois include two round towers, eight churches and a cathedral; there are also many carved gravestones and several of Ireland's famed high crosses, decorated with biblical scenes interlaced with imaginary beasts. O'Rourke's Tower, dating from AD 964, is 18 meters (59 feet) high.

CLONMEL (381 B1)
COUNTY TIPPERARY pop. 12,400

Walled Clonmel is on the Suir River, shadowed by the Comeragh Mountains.

REPUBLIC OF IRELAND

The birthplace of 18th-century novelist Laurence Sterne, author of *Tristram Shandy*, it has preserved several interesting Georgian buildings, including the classical courthouse. The town is also the site of the National Breeders' Stakes, which attract greyhound enthusiasts from March to April.

COBH (381 B1)

COUNTY CORK *pop. 8,400*

Cobh, a seaport on Great Island, was the point of departure for many Irish emigrants bound for the New World, leaving the port in the dreaded "coffin ships." Many of the great transatlantic liners also berthed here, including the ill-fated *Titanic* and *Lusitania*. Cobh's past is vividly re-created in the Queenstown Project heritage center.

THE SINKING OF THE
LUSITANIA

Sailing from New York to Liverpool during World War I, a civilian ship called the *Lusitania* went down off Cobh. Naturally, the Germans were blamed, but a recent allegation suggests the Allies contrived and carried out the attack to persuade the United States to enter the war. Both suspicion and casualties increased due to the unusual absence of patrolling British warships, and by the fact that the German government had placed advertisements in New York papers warning passengers not to take the sailing. Some passengers survived, but nearly 1,200 died.

CATHEDRAL OF ST. COLMAN, a fine Victorian high-Gothic structure, stands on the hilltop dominating the town. Designed by Augustus Pugin in 1868, it is ornately decorated with blue granite. The cemetery contains the graves of writers John Tobin and the Rev. Charles Wolfe as well as many victims of the 1915 *Lusitania* tragedy.

CONG (381 A2)

COUNTY MAYO *pop. 200*

Cong lies on a neck of land between Lough Mask and Lough Corrib. Cong Abbey, dating from the 12th century, was an important monastic center for over 700 years. Nearby are numerous stone caves formed by a subterranean river connecting the two lakes.

COOLE PARK (381 B2)

COUNTY GALWAY

Dramatist Augusta Lady Gregory entertained William Butler Yeats and Edward Martyn at Coole House in Gort, where plans for Dublin's 1904 Abbey Theatre were formulated. Although the house was demolished during the 1930s, the grounds of the estate have survived, as has the "autograph tree," a copper beech carved with the initials of such famous visitors as Yeats, George Bernard Shaw and George Russell.

▲ CORK (381 B1)

COUNTY CORK *pop. 410,400*

Cork, Ireland's third-largest city, lies on the Lee River at the landward end of a fine harbor. The city has main avenues lined with boutiques and department stores, as well as winding cobblestone streets, little stores and stalls. Cork also provides a center from which to tour the southwest coast of Ireland.

CORK PUBLIC MUSEUM, Fitzgerald Park, illustrates the city's history in a Georgian mansion north of the university.

CRAWFORD MUNICIPAL ART GALLERY, Emmet Place, is housed in the former Georgian Custom House; its collections include 18th- and 19th-century paintings, sculpture, silver and stained glass.

ST. ANNE'S OF SHANDON, Church Street, was built between 1722 to 1726 and is famed for its bells, immortalized in the lines of the ballad: "...the bells of Shandon that sound so grand on the pleasant waters of the River Lee." Visitors can ring the carillon daily.

REPUBLIC OF IRELAND

ST. FIN BARRE'S CATHEDRAL, Bishop Street, stands on a 1,300-year-old ecclesiastical site. Built in Gothic revival style in 1870, the cathedral features a 75-meter (246-foot) tower, figures from the parable of the Wise and Foolish Virgins, mosaic work and a wrought-iron baptismal font.

UNIVERSITY COLLEGE is one of the constituent colleges of the National University of Ireland, headquartered in Dublin. The college's predominantly Tudor Gothic buildings were erected in the 19th century. The library has a collection of early printed books, stones inscribed with ogham (an early writing form), and geological and natural history exhibits. Honan Chapel is 12th-century Hiberno-Romanesque in style.

THE PAPER

The first edition of the *Cork Examiner* appeared in August, 1841, just before the Potato Famine. As most of the population of Cork were too poor to buy papers, and many were illiterate anyway, it seemed a crazy venture. However, through those harrowing times and others, "the paper" – as it is known locally – has never lost a single day's printing. As a distinguished and dignified piece of journalism, Cork's daily newspaper seems to epitomize the independent spirit of the city.

CRAGGAUNOWEN (381 B2) ★
COUNTY CLARE
The Craggaunowen Project, 10 kilometers (6 miles) southeast of Ennis, contains a full-scale reconstruction of a *crannóg*, a Bronze Age lake dwelling. The brainchild of art historian and archaeologist John Hunt, the project includes a reconstructed ring-fort and replicas of furniture, tools and utensils. Also displayed is the *Brendan*, a replica of the leather boat used, according to tradition,

by St. Brendan "the Navigator" in about the 6th century.

DROGHEDA (381 C3)
COUNTY LOUTH *pop. 23,600*
Drogheda, a picturesque port on the Irish Sea, has borne the impact of several invasions. It is a good point from which to explore the Boyne Valley, where Protestant William of Orange defeated Catholic James Stuart in 1690. The well-marked battlefield can be toured.

Important prehistoric and monastic sites near Drogheda include the famous Newgrange burial cairn and Mellifont Abbey.

ST. LAURENCE'S GATE is the only remaining portal in Drogheda's town walls. This 13th-century gate is considered to be one of the best-preserved in the country.

DUNDALK (381 C3)
COUNTY LOUTH *pop. 29,100*
Dundalk, the capital of County Louth, has weathered the passing of Celtic, Norman, Jacobite and Williamite armies. Its early 19th-century courthouse and town hall are striking, and an immense old windmill is an impressive landmark. South of the town is the Proleek Dolmen megalithic tomb. Recreational pursuits include golf, tennis, fishing, hunting and horse racing.

DUNGANSTOWN (381 C1)
COUNTY WEXFORD
The village of Dunganstown is the ancestral home of the Kennedy family; John F. Kennedy's great-grandfather was born in a cottage here. Nearby, at Slieve Coillte, is the John Fitzgerald Kennedy Memorial Park, financed by the Irish government and Irish-American societies. The 252-hectare (622-acre) park is a vast arboretum with around 5,000 varieties of trees and shrubs.

DUN LAOGHAIRE (381 C2)
COUNTY DUBLIN *pop. 54,500*
Dun Laoghaire (pronounced "dunleary"), a landing point for ferries from

Britain, is a popular coastal resort 13 kilometers (8 miles) southeast of the capital. The 100-hectare (247-acre) harbor, with its massive piers, took 50 years to build. James Joyce once lived southwest of the city, at Sandycove.

JAMES JOYCE TOWER, built by the British in 1804 as a defence against a possible invasion by Napoléon, has walls 2.5 meters (8 feet) thick and an original entrance 3 meters (10 feet) above the ground, formerly reached by rope ladder.

In 1904, the tower was the temporary home of James Joyce, who depicted this setting in the opening scene of *Ulysses*. The building now houses a museum devoted to the author.

PINK TROUT

You may see the odd roadside sign depicting a fish, with the legend "Save the Sea Trout." These refer to local concerns about fish-farming and its effects on the wild species. One theory is that sea lice from the farmed fish are spreading into wild shoals and wiping them out. One thing you can be sure of, however, is that the fish on your plate is more likely to have been fed pink-tinted food pellets than to have swum free.

ENNIS (381 B2)
COUNTY CLARE *pop. 6,200*
Ennis, the chief town of County Clare, is an excellent center for excursions to nearby castles and abbeys. Ennis Abbey, founded in 1241, has some 14th-century sculptures. Quin Abbey, dating from 1402, lies 10 kilometers (6 miles) east.

GALWAY (381 A2)
COUNTY GALWAY *pop. 37,800*
The capital of County Galway, this town was conquered by the Normans in the 13th century. It is an excellent starting point for exploring the west coast (including the Connemara region, Lough Corrib and the Aran Islands) and

there are fine resorts and beaches at nearby Salthill.

The Galway Races in July and August and the Galway Oyster Festival in September attract many visitors. The Blessing of the Sea ceremony in August signals the start of the herring season.

COLLEGIATE CHURCH OF ST. NICHOLAS was built by Norman settlers in 1320. Local legend has it that Christopher Columbus heard Mass here before he set off on his voyage to the New World.

JOHN FITZGERALD KENNEDY MEMORIAL PARK, in the center of Eyre Square, commemorates the U.S. president and his visit to the city in 1963.

LYNCH'S CASTLE is a well-preserved example of a 16th-century merchant's house and has a mullioned façade.

SALMON WEIR BRIDGE is the place to watch shoals of salmon, as they make their way upstream to spawn from mid-April to early July.

SPANISH ARCH CIVIC MUSEUM, in the southwest quarter, dates from the days when Spain and Ireland had trading ties. Galway City Museum, at the arch, is devoted to the city's history.

UNIVERSITY COLLEGE is one of the constituent colleges of the National University of Ireland. The library contains old city records and rare books.

GLENDALOUGH (381 C2)
COUNTY WICKLOW
In the 6th century, St. Kevin came to the wild, beautiful Vale of Glendalough to live the life of a hermit. After he built a monastery in Glendalough the region became a prominent center of learning. Besides the sites connected with the saint, there are many places of interest dating from the 11th and 12th centuries.

SAINT KEVIN'S KITCHEN, dating from the 6th century, is the the well-preserved ruin of an Early Christian barrel-vaulted oratory. Many of the slabs bear interesting decorations and inscriptions.

HILL OF TARA (381 C2)
COUNTY MEATH

The Hill of Tara, 8 kilometers (5 miles) northeast of Trim, is the site of what was once the religious and cultural capital of pre-Christian Ireland. Dating from 2000 BC, the hill was the seat of the High Kings until AD 1022. It supposedly witnessed St. Patrick's lighting of the Paschal fire on Easter, AD 433. Among the remains are the Mound of Hostages, a passage grave in which the skeleton of a boy wearing a necklace of bronze, amber and jet was found, and a stone pillar thought to be the Coronation Stone of Kings.

KENMARE (381 A1)
COUNTY KERRY pop. 1,100

Kenmare, on the Ring of Kerry, lies at the head of Kenmare Bay. Excellent opportunities for ocean and freshwater fishing, swimming and boating are available, as are hiking, mountain climbing, horseback riding, golf and tennis. Specialties for shoppers are the woolens produced by local weavers.

KILDARE (381 C2)
COUNTY KILDARE pop. 4,200

A center of the Irish horse breeding and training industry, Kildare dates from AD 470, when St. Brigid founded a double monastery here.

IRISH NATIONAL STUD (Tully Estate), situated 2 kilometers (1 mile) east, was set up in 1902 by Colonel William Hall and has since produced many prominent racehorses. Visitors can see the horses being exercised and groomed.

The Irish Horse Museum traces the history of the horse in Ireland. Among the displays is the skeleton of steeplechaser Arkle.

Japanese Gardens, in the grounds, were created by the Japanese gardener Eida and his son Minoru between 1906

and 1910. Their design symbolically portrays man's progress from birth to eternity.

ST. BRIGID'S CATHEDRAL, a 19th-century restoration of the original 1223 structure, contains interesting antiquities.

KILKENNY (381 B2) ★
COUNTY KILKENNY pop. 9,500

A pre-Norman town on the Nore River, Kilkenny combines a distinctive old world atmosphere with modern features. Dominating the city from its highest point is St. Mary's Cathedral, an early Gothic revival edifice dating from 1843.

DUNMORE CAVE is 11 kilometers (7 miles) north, and one of the finest limestone caves in Ireland; its "Market Cross" stalagmite is more than 6 meters (20 feet) high. The bones of over 40 people were found here; they are thought to have died after seeking refuge from a Viking attack.

JERPOINT ABBEY, to the southeast near Thomas-town, is a ruined Gothic Cistercian abbey with a 12th-century Romanesque nave. The cloisters are decorated with human figures, and the church contains some medieval tomb effigies.

KILKENNY CASTLE was the ancestral stronghold of the Butler family until this century. It was originally a 12th-century Norman fortress, but most of the present building dates from the early 19th century. The hammer-beamed picture gallery, lined with portraits, is impressive, and the castle stables house the Kilkenny Design Workshops, where local artists produce a range of high-quality craft items.

KILKENNY COLLEGE is the 200-year-old successor to St. John's College, where William Congreve, George Farquhar, Jonathan Swift, John Banim and George Berkeley studied.

KYTELER'S INN is the restored medieval home of Dame Alice Kyteler, who was condemned as a witch and charged with killing four husbands in 1324. She escaped to Scotland, leaving her maid to take her place at the stake.

ROTHE HOUSE, constructed in 1594, is an excellent example of Tudor architecture. It contains a costume gallery, a museum and a library.

ST. CANICE'S CATHEDRAL occupies the site of an earlier church, the round tower of which still stands. Inside the cathedral are 16th-century sepulchral monuments. St. Canice's Library contains 3,000 volumes from the 16th and 17th centuries.

SHEE ALMS HOUSE, Rose Inn Street, was built in the late 16th century and now houses City Scope, a *son et lumière* show featuring a three-dimensional scale model of 17th-century Kilkenny, plus the tourist information office.

KILLARNEY (381 A1)
COUNTY KERRY *pop. 7,700*

The bustling market town of Killarney is one of Ireland's most popular tourist spots. The surrounding countryside, including the three lakes of Killarney south of the town, is renowned for its scenery; the lakes' many islands, especially Innisfallen with its 7th-century abbey ruins, are favorite destinations by boat. Killarney is a good starting point for a drive along the Ring of Kerry, one of Europe's finest coastal drives.

The trip to the Gap of Dunloe, traditionally reached by horseback, is equally rewarding. Here is some of the area's most beautiful scenery: Macgillycuddy's Reeks, Ireland's highest mountains; the the Tomies and Purple mountains; Cummeenduff, also called Black Valley; and Upper Lake, with the wooded crags of Eagle's Nest. The descent from the gap, 242 meters (794 feet) above sea-level, can also be accomplished by boat, leaving Upper Lake via the 'Coleman's Eye' channel and 'Long Range' strait,

shooting the rapids at Old Weir Bridge, and finishing at Ross Castle. Boatmen demonstrate a bugle's echo against the great crag of Eagle's Nest.

CATHEDRAL OF ST. MARY, New Street, was built in 1846 under the direction of noted English architect Augustus Pugin. A cruciform limestone church, it has a massive stone tower.

KILLARNEY NATIONAL PARK, the former Muckross Estate, is 4 kilometers (2½ miles) south. Donated to the Irish government by its American owners, the 4,450-hectare (10,988-acre) park incorporates most of the county's lake district.

Muckross Abbey, on the eastern shore of Lough Leane, suffered the depredations of Cromwell's troops, who left it roofless in 1652. The 15th-century Franciscan abbey remains well-preserved.

Muckross House, the 19th-century neo-Tudor mansion of this former private estate, has a separate entrance for motorists 5 kilometers (3 miles) south of Killarney off the N71. It now contains a museum of Kerry folklore, and in the basement craft center a weaver, blacksmith and potter demonstrate their trades. The grounds include rhododendrons, azaleas and a rock garden.

ROSS CASTLE is 3 kilometers (2 miles) southwest, overlooking Lough Leane. This 14th-century Irish fort figured prominently in the Cromwellian Wars. It is closed to the public, but boat rentals are available for lake trips.

KILLORGLIN (381 A1)
COUNTY KERRY *pop. 1,300*

The small fishing town of Killorglin is known for its annual three-day Puck Fair in August. The festivities include a goat named Puck being crowned "king" of the town in a colorful traditional ceremony.

KINSALE (381 B1) ★
COUNTY CORK *pop. 1,800*

Overlooking the winding estuary of the Bandon River, Kinsale has an old-world appearance with its narrow streets, ruins and Georgian houses. The local museum, housed in the town's Dutch-style 17th-century courthouse, contains exhibits related to the sinking of the *Lusitania*. Also of interest are the 12th-century Norman St. Multose Church; remains of the 1314 Carmelite friary; Desmond Castle, which held French prisoners during the Napoleonic War; and star-shaped Charles Fort (1677).

The town, famed for its restaurants, hosts an international Gourmet Festival in the first week of October, attracting discerning diners from around the world.

Excursions can be made to the Old Head of Kinsale, site of the 1915 sinking of the *Lusitania* (see *Cobh* on p.392), and to Ballinspittle, where excavations have indicated that the Ballycatten ring-fort dates from about AD 600.

LIMERICK (381 B2)
COUNTY LIMERICK *pop. 60,700*

Limerick is the gateway to the Shannon Valley and the excellent fishing area of Lough Derg. The city dates from the 9th century, when the Danes made it a base. As a seat of the kings of Munster, it suffered many attacks during the Middle Ages.

The nickname "City of the Violated Treaty" stems from forgotten promises of religious tolerance following the Williamite victory over the Jacobites in Limerick in 1691. The Treaty Stone, on which the treaty is said to have been signed, is on a pedestal on the west side of Thomond Bridge. Portions of original city walls and old gateways recall those turbulent days.

Georgian buildings embellish the modern side of Limerick. St. John's Square, constructed in about 1751, is noteworthy for its unusual layout and architecture. The ruins of Mungret, a 7th-century monastery, are 5 kilometers (3 miles) from Limerick on the coast road.

GOOD SHEPHERD CONVENT, Good Shepherd Lane, is where Limerick lace is made. Visitors can view the process.

HUNT MUSEUM is on the grounds of the University of Limerick, 5 kilometers (3 miles) from Limerick. Among the treasures in its collection of Celtic and medieval antiquities are the Antrim Cross and a Bronze Age shield.

KING JOHN'S CASTLE, on the east side of Thomond Bridge, is a 13th-century Norman castle with an imposing twin-towered gatehouse and battle-scarred walls. The castle's history is explored in the visitor center, where archaeological finds are also displayed.

ST. JOHN'S CATHEDRAL is a 19th-century Gothic structure, with a spire that rises 85 meters (279 feet). Of interest are a Madonna by Benzoni and the statue of Patrick Sarsfield, who was a hero of the siege of 1690 to 1691.

ST. MARY'S CATHEDRAL was originally built as a palace in the 12th century. Among its most interesting features are the high tower, Romanesque doorway, 15th-century choir stalls and ornately carved 15th-century misericords. In summer the cathedral is the setting for a *son et lumière* show highlighting episodes from the city's history.

ST. SAVIOUR'S, a 19th-century Dominican church, houses many treasures; these include a 17th-century statue of Our Lady thought to have been brought from Flanders by Patrick Sarsfield, the cross of a 17th-century bishop, the 1639 Kilmallock Dominican Chalice, the 1647 Sarsfield Chalice, and a 1951 fresco by Father Aengus Buckley.

LISMORE (381 B1)
COUNTY WATERFORD *pop. 1,100*

Lismore, noted for its excellent fishing, dates from the 7th century, when St. Carthage founded a monastery here that became one of the renowned universities of Europe. Chemist Robert Boyle and dramatist and poet William Congreve were born in Lismore. An audiovisual presentation in the award-winning heritage center relates the history of the town. Also of interest are two cathedrals: St. Cathage's (Church of Ireland) and the Roman Catholic cathedral.

LISMORE CASTLE, the Irish seat of the Dukes of Devonshire, was once the home of Sir Walter Raleigh. Built by Prince John in 1185, the castle was extensively remodeled in the 19th century. The gardens are open during the summer.

MELLIFONT ABBEY (381 C3)
COUNTY LOUTH

Located 8 kilometres (5 miles) west of Drogheda, this is the 12th-century ruin of the first Cistercian house established in Ireland. Among the remains are a Romanesque cloister, a two-story

---

ST. OLIVER PLUNKETT

St. Oliver Plunkett, Archbishop of Armagh and Primate of All Ireland, lived from 1629 to 1681 and was canonized in 1976. He lived in the troubled years when Catholicism was being suppressed by the English. In 1678, Plunkett was arrested after anti-Catholic conspirator Titus Oates falsely alleged that he was plotting to bring French soldiers into Ireland. Although he had won the friendship of Ulster's Protestant clergy, Plunkett was executed on July 1, 1681, in London for treason, his offense being simply that he was an unrepentant Catholic. After the execution, Plunkett's severed head was rescued and taken back to Ireland, where it now resides in the Catholic Church of St. Peter, Drogheda.

---

octagonal lavabo (or washing place) and a 13th-century chapter house.

MONASTERBOICE (381 C3)
COUNTY LOUTH

This celebrated monastic site, located 8 kilometers (5 miles) northwest of

Drogheda, includes three high crosses, a 30-meter (98-foot) round tower, two churches, a tombstone and a sundial. The elaborately sculptured crosses vary in height from 5 to 6.5 meters (16 to 21 feet). Muirdeach's Cross, one of the finest high crosses in Ireland, is thought to have been made in the 10th century.

MULLINGAR (381 B2)
COUNTY WESTMEATH *pop. 7,900*

The fishing center of Mullingar also has facilities for golf, tennis, racket ball, horseback riding, hunting, swimming and sailing.

CATHEDRAL OF CHRIST THE KING was built in 1936, its twin towers dominating the landscape. The mosaics of saints Patrick and Anne, near the high altar, were designed by the Russian Boris Anrep. An ecclesiastical museum houses the vestments of St. Oliver Plunkett, unjustly executed for treason in London in 1681.

NEWGRANGE (381 C3) ★
COUNTY MEATH

Newgrange lies in the valley of the Boyne and is the site of a 5,000-year-old megalithic tomb. Around 11 meters (36 feet) high and covering 0.4 hectare (1 acre) of ground, it is surrounded by an incomplete circle of stones; the front walls of the mound are faced with brilliant white quartz stones. A burial chamber with a funnel-shaped roof is connected to the tomb by a long passageway, and on the morning of the winter solstice, the rays of the sun penetrate a narrow slit in the stone and illuminate it for about 15 minutes – a phenomenon reproduced artificially for visitors at the end of guided tours. There is an information center on the grounds.

Less well-known than Newgrange are the burial cairns of Dowth and Knowth, both situated only a few miles away.

PARKNASILLA (381 A1)
COUNTY KERRY

On the Ring of Kerry, Parknasilla overlooks the island-studded Kenmare River, an ocean estuary. Because of the effects of the Gulf Stream and Parknasilla's sheltered location, this exotic place has subtropical plants. Nearby Sneem is a charming village with several interesting churches. St. Michael's is the most notable; dated 1865, it contains the grave of Father Michael Walsh, the Father O'Flynn of the celebrated song.

POWERSCOURT (381 C2) ★
COUNTY WICKLOW

Near the village of Enniskerry stands Powerscourt Estate, the site of Ireland's best-known gardens. An impressive drive leads to the shell of a Palladian mansion, which was sadly gutted by fire in 1974. Laid out in the Victorian era, the gardens feature ornate sculptures, fountains and terraces. About 6 kilometers (3½ miles) south is the spectacular

---

A LUCKY LUNCHEON

In 1821, King George IV announced that he would visit magnificent Powerscourt House, built on land granted by James I. In anticipation of the visit, a path from the house to the waterfall on the grounds was laid out, and as the waterfall was not deemed dramatic enough for a king, an artificial lake with sluice gates was created at the top of the fall for greater effect. However, George IV delighted so much in the banquet at the mansion that insufficient time was left to admire the waterfall. Perhaps this was just as well, for when the sluice gates were opened the platform intended for the king was destroyed by the great flood of water.

Powerscourt Waterfall; at 120 meters (394 feet), it is the highest in Ireland.

RATHMULLAN (381 B4)
COUNTY DONEGAL pop. 600

The popular resort of Rathmullan, is a picturesque village with a sandy beach backed by high hills. It has also been the stage for important events in Irish history. In 1587, Ulster chieftain "Red" Hugh O'Donnell, Earl of Tyrconnell, was captured in Rathmullan harbor after being lured on board a disguised English ship. Twenty years later, Rathmullan witnessed the Flight of the Earls, the exile of Ulster's nobility. A heritage center recounts these events.

ROSSLARE (381 C1)
COUNTY WEXFORD pop. 800

Rosslare is a popular vacation resort, with 10 kilometers (6 miles) of fine beaches. It is also noted for its 18-hole championship golf course and other sporting facilities. Rosslare Harbour, the terminus of car ferries from Fishguard in Wales and Le Havre and Cherbourg in France, is about 8 kilometers (5 miles) south.

Our Lady's Island, joined to the mainland by a causeway, has been a place of pilgrimage for centuries; it has a 12th-century Norman castle and ruined Augustinian priory. The Saltee Islands, off Kilmore Quay, together form a bird sanctuary.

SKERRIES (381 C2)
COUNTY DUBLIN pop. 5,800

Skerries is a highly popular resort, with a fine sandy beach and a dry climate. Golf, tennis, fishing and water sports abound. Three small islands – St. Patrick's, Colt and Shenick's – are worth exploring.

SLIGO (381 B3)
COUNTY SLIGO pop. 17,200

Surrounded by the Ox Mountains, Sligo is where William Butler Yeats spent many years. The poet is buried in a churchyard at Drumcliff near the ruins of a monastery founded by St. Columba in AD 574; his epitaph, a quotation from one of his best-known poems, reads: "Cast a cold Eye On Life, on Death. Horseman, pass by."

The Yeats Memorial Building, Hyde Bridge, hosts the annual Yeats International Summer School in August. The County Museum in Stephen Street includes Yeats memorabilia, while the County Art Gallery has paintings by the poet's father and brother.

The area around Sligo Bay is also known for interesting archaeological remains, which include the ruins of 13th-century Sligo Abbey. Other places of interest are Doorly Park's walking paths and racecourse, the town hall, the courthouse, ancient St. John's Church and Summerhill College.

Boat excursions can be made to Aghamore on Lough Gill, to the Lake Isle of Innisfree, and past the Dooney Rock to Dromahair, site of a feudal castle.

CARROWMORE, about 5 kilometers (3 miles) from Sligo, has one of the largest groups of megalithic remains in Western Europe, with dolmens, stone circles and about 60 tombs. The oldest dolmen is thought to date back to 4000 BC.

CREEVYKEEL COURT CAIRN, on the Sligo–Burdoran Road, is a neolithic court-tomb dating from about 3000 BC. It was excavated by a Harvard archaeological expedition in 1935, and many of the finds are in the National Museum in Dublin.

LISSADELL HOUSE is a Georgian mansion overlooking Sligo Bay. William Butler Yeats was a frequent guest of the Gore-Booth family, who resided in this house.

THOR BALLYLEE (381 B2)
GALWAY

This 14th-century Norman tower house was the residence of poet William Butler Yeats between 1917 and 1928.

The tower, which has been restored to appear as it was when Yeats lived there, houses an interpretive center with audiovisual presentations and displays of the poet's work. Visitors can climb up to the tower by "the narrow winding stair," an image common in Yeats' poetry.

TIPPERARY (381 B2)
COUNTY TIPPERARY pop. 5,000

Although Tipperary dates from the 12th century it has few historic remains. The town lies in the Golden Vale of Tipperary, the subject of Jack Judge's song from World War I, with the Galtee mountain range to the south. Hiking, climbing, fishing and hunting are popular pastimes in this region.

TRALEE (381 A1)
COUNTY KERRY pop. 16,500

Tralee is the starting point for trips to the remote Dingle Peninsula, a beautiful expanse of mountains with spectacular sea views. In late August, the Festival of Kerry features a week of celebrations culminating in a beauty contest to select the "Rose of Tralee." The town is also home to Siamsa Tíre, the National Folk Theatre of Ireland.

TRIM (381 C2)
COUNTY MEATH pop. 3,500

An agricultural town in the Boyne Valley, one of the oldest ecclesiastical centers in Ireland. Of the original walls enclosing the town, only two gates remain. The towering 38-meter (125-foot) 13th-century Yellow Steeple is the last remnant of an Augustinian abbey.

TRIM CASTLE, founded in the 12th century, is the largest Norman fortress in Ireland, its 20-meter (66-foot) walls and adjoining towers covering about 1 hectare (2½ acres).

WATERFORD (381 B1)
COUNTY WATERFORD pop. 38,500

World-renowned as the home of a lead-crystal glass industry, Waterford is also a large seaport with a fine harbor. Founded by Norsemen in the 10th century, it retains its anglicized Norse name.

Places of interest include the 18th-century Cathedral of the Holy Trinity, Christ Church Cathedral, and the ruins of Blackfriars Abbey, a Dominican friary founded in 1226. The council chamber in the city hall has a striking Waterford glass chandelier made in 1802, a copy of which can be found in Independence Hall in Philadelphia. The famous Waterford Glass Factory is sited about 2 kilometers

(1 mile) south of the town.

Tramore, 11 kilometers (7 miles) from town, is a modern resort, and Dunmore East a popular picnic spot with opportunities for water sports and deep-sea fishing. Waterford itself hosts the two-week International Light Opera Festival from mid-September to early October.

FRENCH CHURCH, dating from 1240, aquired its name when it was used by Huguenot refugees in the 18th century. Remains of this national monument include the 15th-century tower, chancel, belfry and east window.

REGINALD'S TOWER, built in 1003 by Vikings, is a circular 24-meter (79-foot) tower with walls 3 meters (10 feet) thick. Restored in 1819, it now serves as a municipal museum.

WATERVILLE (381 A1)
COUNTY KERRY *pop. 500*
Waterville is renowned for its championship golf course and for the excellent game fishing at nearby Lough Currane. Staigue Fort, to the southeast, is a well-preserved *cashel* (stone ring-fort) dating from around 1000 BC.

DERRYNANE HOUSE, located 16 kilometers (10 miles) south near Caherdaniel, is a former home of Daniel O'Connell, "The Liberator," first of the great 19th-century Irish leaders. The surrounding 130-hectare (32-acre) park provides superb scenery.

WESTPORT (381 A3)
COUNTY MAYO *pop. 3,400*
A major salt-water fishing center on Clew Bay, Westport is an attractive wooded town. Excursions can be made to Achill Island, Ireland's largest; to the mountain of Croagh Patrick, site of a pilgrimage on the last Sunday in July; and to Clare Island with its precipitous cliffs.

WESTPORT HOUSE is a handsome Georgian mansion on Westport Quay, just over 2 kilometers (1 mile) from the

town. Designed for the Marquess of Sligo by 18th-century architects Richard Cassels and James Wyatt, the house boasts exquisite Georgian and Victorian furniture, antique silver, Waterford glass and superb family portraits.

WEXFORD (381 C1)
COUNTY WEXFORD *pop. 11,400*
Wexford is an ancient seaport with narrow, winding streets and a medieval atmosphere. It was fortified under the Normans; the Westgate Tower, the remains of the town wall and the bullring date from that period.

In Crescent Quay, overlooking the harbor, a bronze statue commemorates Commodore John Barry, the local-born founder of the U.S. Navy. The world-renowned Wexford Opera Festival held in late October and early November features international opera singers.

IRISH NATIONAL HERITAGE PARK, at nearby Ferrycarrig, re-creates Ireland's history up to Anglo-Norman times. The open-air site includes replicas of Stone Age settlements, ring-forts and a Norman castle.

JOHNSTOWN CASTLE, 5 kilometers (3 miles) southwest, is a 19th-century mansion incorporating the remains of a 15th-century castle. It now houses a research center of the Agriculture Institute and the Irish Agricultural Museum, and its attractive grounds are open to the public.

SELSKAR ABBEY, near Westgate Tower, is now a ruin. In 1172 King Henry II did 40 days' penance at the abbey for the murder of Thomas à Becket.

WESTGATE, a 13th-century town gate, is the setting for the Wexford Medieval Experience – an audiovisual display that recounts the town's early history.

WEXFORD WILDFOWL RESERVE lies on the north shore of Wexford harbor. Among the birds that winter on the mudflats are Greenland white-fronted geese.

ITALY

IT IS IMPOSSIBLE TO DISLIKE THE
ITALIANS. THEY MAY BE THE MOST
INCONSIDERATE DRIVERS IN THE
WORLD, AND PUNCTUALITY IS FOR
THE MOST PART LACKING. BUT THEY ARE ALSO
PASSIONATE, FRIENDLY AND SYMPATHETIC, WITH A
LOVE OF PEOPLE, GOOD FOOD AND DRINK, AND LIFE
ITSELF. ITALIANS LOVE THEIR COUNTRY AS WELL,
AND WHO CAN BLAME THEM? ITALY MAY NOT LIE AT
THE GEOGRAPHICAL HEART OF EUROPE, BUT IT LIES
AT THE HEART OF EUROPEAN CULTURE AND ONCE
RULED ONE OF THE LARGEST EMPIRES EVER KNOWN.
FROM THE TOP OF ITS BOOT TO THE TIP OF ITS TOE,
ITALY OFFERS AN EMBARRASSMENT OF RICHES. TO
THE NORTH LIE THE ALPS AND THE ITALIAN LAKES;
TO THE WEST GENOA; TO THE EAST THE CANALS OF
VENICE. TO THE SOUTH LIE TUSCANY AND UMBRIA,
WITH THE GLORIOUS ART TREA-
SURES OF FLORENCE. ROME,
NAPLES AND CAPRI LEAD ON TO
RUGGED, UNSPOILED CALABRIA.

Left THE MAGNIFICENT DUOMO IN FLORENCE DOMINATES PIAZZA DEL DUOMO
Above left GONDOLIERS IN VENICE ARE A COLORFUL SIGHT
Above right GUARDS AT VATICAN CITY PROTECT A POPULATION OF 200

THINGS TO KNOW

- **AREA:** 301,225 square kilometers (116,303 square miles)
- **POPULATION:** 57,772,000
- **CAPITAL:** Roma (Rome)
- **LANGUAGE:** Italian
- **RELIGION:** Roman Catholic.
- **ECONOMY:** Tourism, industry, agriculture, machinery, food, tobacco, textiles, mercury, wheat, rice, citrus fruits, grapes, olives, wine.
- **PASSPORT REQUIREMENTS:** Required for U.S. citizens.
- **VISA REQUIREMENTS:** Not required for stays up to three months, after which a three-month extension can be obtained.
- **DUTY-FREE ITEMS:** 200 cigarettes or 50 cigars or 250 grams of tobacco; 2 liters of wine and 1 liter of spirits; fine perfume, up to ½ liter; two still cameras with up to 10 rolls of film for each, one movie camera with 10 rolls of movie film, one video camera; other goods up to $230 in value (from outside the E.U.). Also see *The European Union* on p.9.
- **CURRENCY:** The currency unit is the Italian *lira*. Due to currency fluctuations, the exchange rate is subject to frequent change. There is no limit on the amount of foreign currency that can be brought into the country, but all such monies must be declared.
- **BANK OPENING HOURS:** 8:30am–1:30pm and 3–4pm Monday–Friday.
- **STORE OPENING HOURS:** 8:30 or 9am–7:30 or 8pm Monday–Saturday, with a siesta between 1 and 4pm. Many stores in Rome are closed Monday mornings.
- **MUSEUM OPENING HOURS:** State museums open 9am–2pm Tuesday–Saturday, 9am–1pm Sunday, closed Monday. Times vary, so check locally.
- **SPECIAL REGULATIONS:** Numbered fiscal receipts (*ricevuta fiscale*) are issued for certain goods and services. They indicate the price charged and the total cost after adding Value Added Tax (V.A.T.), a tax on non-essential items. Tourists should be sure to obtain such receipts, as they are required by law.

HISTORY

Because of its vast shoreline and strategic location, Italy has long been the target of invasion. Phoenicians, Carthaginians and Greeks all established colonies, and the Etruscans, a mysterious race of unknown origin, came to dominate central Italy. By the end of the 5th century BC, however, the Romans had ousted the Etruscan kings and started on the path of world conquest.

Victory over Carthage in the bitter Punic Wars (260–146 BC) gave Rome control of the Mediterranean. As the boundaries of the Roman Empire expanded, so did the ambitions and wealth of the ruling patrician class. When tensions with the lower classes escalated into revolt, a hero emerged to restore order – Julius Caesar. His successor, Octavius, took the title of Emperor in 27 BC, and the empire flourished until the death of Aurelius in AD 180, when decline set in.

In subsequent centuries a weakening Rome was ruled by foreign kings and invaded by barbarians. Emperor Constantine's conversion to Christianity in AD 315 enabled the growth of papal power. Independent states and sovereign kingdoms developed, controlled by influential families such as the Medici. Art, literature and architecture flourished under their patronage, giving birth to the Renaissance. From the end of the 15th century French, Austrian and Spanish armies fought for control of the peninsula. After years of conflict, citizens began to appeal for one unified government in a nationalist movement called the *Risorgimento*, or resurrection. The foreign powers were expelled and the kingdom of Italy was finally united under Victor Emmanuel II in 1861.

In the climate of economic chaos and social unrest that followed World War I, Italians embraced the Facist leader Benito Mussolini, who promised to restore order and stability. "Il Duce" led Italy into World War II, but after several defeats he fell from power and the new democratic government sided with the Allies in 1943

Postwar Italy became a democratic republic and has been administered by more than 50 governments since. American aid and membership in the European Community led to economic recovery until inflation, unemployment and terrorism in the late 1970s brought another troubled period. In April 1993, the Italian people voted overwhelmingly for sweeping electoral reforms designed to root out corruption and weaken the influence of powerful party leaders. In March 1994, the conservative "Freedom Alliance" won the general elections, and in May media magnate Silvio Berlusconi was named prime minister. His coalition government was short-lived, however, with Berlusconi himself resigning after accusations of bribery.

FOOD AND DRINK

Pasta, the national staple, comes in a variety of sizes and shapes, and risotto, or rice dishes, are also popular. The classic Neapolitan pizza is made with tomato sauce, mozzarella cheese and anchovies. *Prosciutto*, a dark, spicy ham usually served on melon, is a favorite appetizer, while *antipasto*, the Italian *hors-d'oeuvre*, is often a meal in itself. Tempting desserts range from fresh fruit to *gelati* (ice-cream). Regional wines can be excellent and good value, and the meal's end is properly celebrated by drinking one or more cups of aromatic *espresso* coffee.

SPORTS AND RECREATION

A number of outstanding mountain resorts make Italy a major destination for skiers, and the Alpine regions of the north are also excellent for climbing. The Italian Riviera in the northwest, the Versilia, the Tyrrhenian coast, Sicily, Sardinia, and the Adriatic coast (including famous resorts like Rimini, Riccione, Grado, Lignano and Jesolo Lido) have fine bathing facilities. Soccer

is by far the favorite national sport; bicycle racing also arouses national enthusiasm, particularly during May, when the Tour of Italy takes to the roads.

GETTING AROUND

The *autostrade* is a comprehensive network of highways that reaches most of the country. Most are toll roads. Main and secondary roads are generally good, even in the mountains. Nevertheless, the roads can be very congested, especially in the cities.

The wearing of seat belts is mandatory. Children under three must use a seat fitted with a suitable restraint system. Speed limits are 50 k.p.h. (31 m.p.h.) in town, 90 k.p.h. (55 m.p.h.) out of town and 130 k.p.h. (81 m.p.h.) on the highways. Visiting motorists must pay fines for driving violations on the spot in Italian *lire*.

ACCOMMODATIONS

Hotels in Italy are classified into five categories. Regional and provincial tourist offices publish a list of hotels and guest houses and their ratings annually.

AUTOMOBILE CLUB
Automobile Club d'Italia
(A.C.I.), Via Marsala 8, 00185
Rome, tel: (06) 49981, has
branch offices in various cities
throughout Italy.
The symbol ▲ beside a city name
indicates the presence of an AAA-
affiliated automobile club branch.
Not all auto clubs offer full travel
services to AAA members.

Campeggiare in Italia lists campgrounds and youth hostels throughout Italy. For more information contact Federcampeggio, Casella Postale n. 23, 50041 Calenzano, Florence; tel: (055) 882391. For a list of youth hostels contact A.I.G. (Associazione Italiana Allerghi per la Gioventù), Via Cavour 44, 00184 Roma; tel: (06) 487 1152.

- **BEST BUYS:** Leather goods, gloves, Venetian glass, jewelry, prints, silk, silver, straw products, porcelain.
- **PUBLIC HOLIDAYS:** January 1; January 6; Easter Monday; April 25 (WW II Liberation Day); May 1 (Labor Day); August 15 (Assumption Day); November 1 (All Saints' Day); December 8 (Immaculate Conception); December 25–26.
- **USEFUL TELEPHONE NUMBERS:**
  Police (*Carabinieri*) 112
  Emergency numbers:
  Police 113
  Fire 113
  Ambulance 113
  Car breakdown 116
- **NATIONAL TOURIST OFFICES:**
  Italian Government Travel Office
  630 Fifth Avenue, Suite 1565
  Rockefeller Center
  New York
  NY 10111
  Tel: 212/245-4822
  Fax: 212/586-9249
  Italian Government Travel Office
  2400 Wilshire Boulevard
  Suite 550
  Los Angeles
  CA 90025
  Tel: 310/820-0098
  Fax: 310/820-6357
  Italian State Tourist Office
  1 Princes Street
  London W1 8AY
  England
  Tel: 0171-408 1254
  Fax: 0171-493 6695
  Italian State Tourist Board
  (E.N.I.T.)
  Via Marghera 2
  00185 Rome,
  Italy
  Tel: (39 6) 49 711
  Fax: (39 6) 446 3379
- **AMERICAN EMBASSY:**
  Via Vittorio Veneto 119a
  Palazzo Margherita
  00187 Rome, Italy
  Tel: (39 6) 46 741
  Fax: (39 6) 488 2672

TIPPING

A service charge of 10–15 percent is usually added to a restaurant bill, and it is customary to leave a small extra tip. Tip taxi drivers about 10 percent of the fare. Gas-station attendants, theater ushers, hairdressers, bellhops and hotel staff get 1,000–2,000 *lira*.

PRINCIPAL TOURING AREAS

Note: For descriptions of attractions in **bold type**, see individual listings.

CAMPANIA AND THE SOUTH

The mountains of southern Campania sweep toward the coast in a series of fertile fields. The broad Bay of Naples is the historic and economic heart of the region, sheltering the islands of **Capri** and **Ischia**. The volcano of Mount Vesuvius towers over **Napoli**, or Naples, which is the capital of the region.

On the other side of the Sorrentine Peninsula lies the famous **Amalfi** coast. Farther south are the quieter regions of Basilicata and Calabria and, along the eastern side, Puglia.

EMILIA-ROMAGNA

This exuberant region takes its name from the Via Emilia, the main north–south link road built by the Romans in 187 BC. The vigorous medieval communes of this region became splendid capitals of the Renaissance: **Ferrara**, **Módena**, **Piacenza** and **Parma**. **Bologna**, with its old red-brick buildings, has been a famous seat of learning since the Middle Ages.

Ravenna, last capital of the western Roman Empire, is a treasure trove of Byzantine mosaic art, while **Rímini** is the best known of the region's lively Adriatic resorts.

LAZIO, ABRUZZO AND MOLISE

Lazio (Latio) is characterized by a central, rolling plain ringed by blue, misty mountains. The great historic capital of **Roma**, or Rome, lies at its heart. Abruzzo, a region of rugged scenery, remote villages and a splendid national park, borders the Adriatic, with its smaller neighbor Molise to the south.

LIGURIA

Liguria stretches along the western coast from the French frontier to the Gulf of Genoa. **Génova**, or Genoa, dominated the trade of the eastern Mediterranean for centuries and is still Italy's largest trading port. To the north and south lie the resorts of the Italian Riviera, while inland are a number of excellent centers offering winter sports.

LOMBARDIA

This attractive region originates at the foot of the Alps and unfolds into a broad plain studded with natural and man-made lakes. These clear blue lakes, plied by steamers, reflect graceful towns. It is also home to such fine old cities as **Milano** (Milan), **Mantova** (Mantua), **Pavia** and **Bergamo**, and to smaller towns such as **Como**, **Cremona** and **Bréscia**.

PIEDMONT AND VALLE D'AOSTA

Surrounded on three sides by the Alps, the northern Piedmont region forms a giant amphitheater that attracts those who come to ski, hike or relax at the resorts. Further south is an area rich in history, agriculture and industry, the latter centered on **Torino**, or Turin. Just north of Piedmont is Valle d'Aosta, Italy's prime winter sports region.

SICILIA AND SARDEGNA

Sicilia, or Sicily, the largest and one of the most beautiful islands in the Mediterranean, is an archaeological treasure house, and rich in tradition. **Sardegna**, or Sardinia, is famed for its Emerald Coast, with miles of unspoiled beaches. The

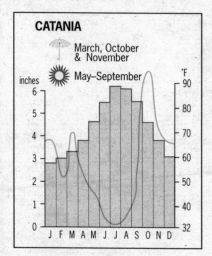

CATANIA

March, October & November

May–September

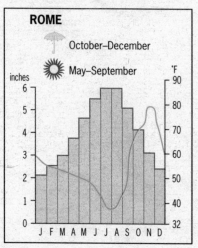

ROME

October–December

May–September

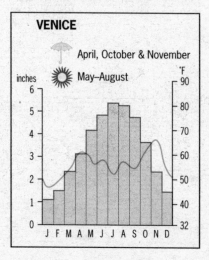

VENICE

April, October & November

May–August

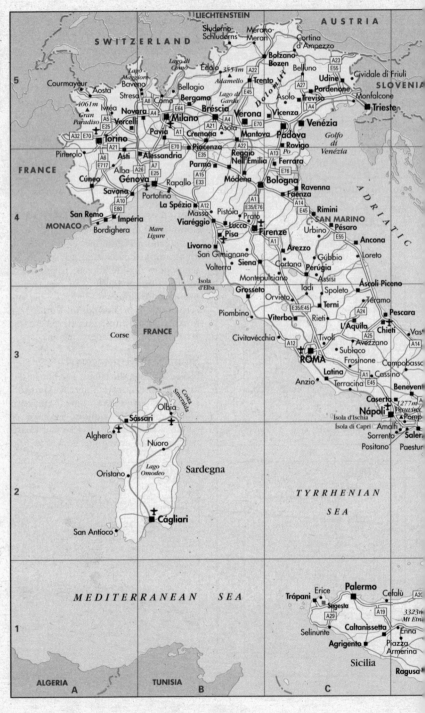

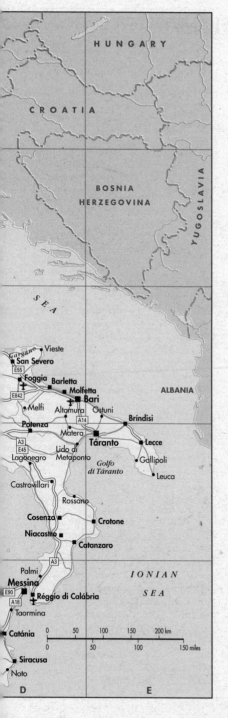

island is littered with thousands of mysterious stone dwellings called *nuraghi*.

TOSCANA, MARCHE AND UMBRIA

Nature at its friendliest marks Toscana (Tuscany), where gentle mountains and rich forests are bathed in misty vapor and soft light. Set within this magnificent garden is the flower of the Renaissance, **Firenze**, or Florence, the city which produced that period's greatest figures. Tuscany offers more ancient treasures in the medieval cities of **Siena** and **Lucca**, and newer resorts such as Viaréggio and busy Livorno.

The Marche and Umbria regions border on Tuscany and in a way complete it, forming a natural continuation of this attractive area. The hilly Marche side of the Apennines slopes to the sea, terminating in a long row of vacation towns. Gentle, rolling Umbria was the cradle of the Franciscan movement, and **Assissi** the home of its founder, St. Francis.

VENETO AND TRENTINO-ALTO ADIGE

Veneto embraces the upper basin of the Adriatic, forming a great semicircle; most of the region is a flourishing, fertile plain dotted with such important cities as **Verona**, **Vicenza** and **Padova**, or Padua. The Veneto is famed for wines, and the countryside is full of vineyards.

Mulberry orchards are also typical of this region, providing food for the worms that produce luxurious Italian silks. In the watery center of the Adriatic crescent is **Venézia**, or Venice, a graceful city of canals, doges, *palazzi* and *piazze*.

Trentino-Alto Adige lies between Veneto and the Venoste, Breonie and Aurine Alps. The high, rugged country includes the Dolomites, sheer vertical projections rising to jagged peaks. Situated in this area are the three contrasting resort towns of Bolzano, turn-of-the-century **Merano**, and the historic city of **Trento**.

USEFUL EXPRESSIONS IN ITALIAN

hello	ciao (on the telephone, **pronto**)
good morning	**buongiorno**
good evening	**buona sera**
good night	**buona notte**
good bye	**arrivederci, ciao, arrivederla** (formal)
please	**per favore, per piacere**
thank you	**grazie**
yes/no	**sì/no**
excuse me	**mi scusi**
excuse me (in a crowd)	**permesso**
I'm sorry	**mi dispiace**
you're welcome	**prego**
How are you?	**Come stai/sta?**
I'm fine	**Sto bene**
Do you speak English?	**Parla inglese?**
I don't understand.	**Non capisco.**
What is the time?	**Che ore sono?**
How much is that?	**Quant'è?**
Where are the restrooms?	**Dove sono i gabinetti?**
I'd like ...	**Vorrei ...**
The check, please.	**Il conto, per favore.**
Is service included?	**É compreso il servizio?**
Can you help me, please?	**Per favore, mi aiuta?**
I want to go to...	**Vorrei andare a...**
Where are we?	**Dove siamo?**
Are we far from...?	**Siamo lontani da...?**
Do you take credit cards?	**Accetta carta di credito?**
Where is the nearest bank?	**Dov'è la banca più vicina?**
where	**dove**
when	**quando**
how	**come**
hot/cold	**caldo/freddo**
open/closed	**aperto/chiuso**
yesterday	**ieri**
today	**oggi**
tomorrow	**domani**
to the left	**a sinistra**
to the right	**a destra**

straight ahead	**sempre diritto**
vacant/occupied	**libero/occupato**
airport	**aeroporto**
train	**il treno**
platform	**il binario**
bus stop	**la fermata**
ticket	**il biglietto**
gas station	**la stazione di rifornimento**
police station	**il posto di polizia**
post office	**l'ufficio postale**
hotel	**l'albergo**
restaurant	**il ristorante**
doctor	**il medico**
pharmacy	**la farmacia**
church	**la chiesa**
museum	**il museo**

DAYS OF THE WEEK

Sunday	**domenica**
Monday	**lunedì**
Tuesday	**martedì**
Wednesday	**mercoledì**
Thursday	**giovedì**
Friday	**venerdì**
Saturday	**sabato**

NUMBERS

1	**uno/una**
2	**due**
3	**tre**
4	**quattro**
5	**cinque**
6	**sei**
7	**sette**
8	**otto**
9	**nove**
10	**dieci**
20	**venti**
30	**trenta**
40	**quaranta**
50	**cinquanta**
60	**sessanta**
70	**settanta**
80	**ottanta**
90	**novanta**
100	**cento**
1,000	**mille**

ROMA *(408 C3) pop. 2,775,250*

The Colosseo, or Colosseum, proved an impressive blueprint for future stadiums.

HISTORY

Legend tells us that Roma (Rome) was founded by Romulus and Remus, twin sons of the god Mars who were nursed by a wolf. More reliable sources date the inception of the city from the 8th century BC, when a village was founded on the banks of the Tiber River by the Etruscans as a meeting-place and market. The settlement prospered and grew into a fortified kingdom, the last ruler of which was the infamous Tarquinius "the Proud." In 509 BC the Etruscans were overthrown, and the Roman Republic was created.

Internal political struggles failed to halt the city's expansion, and the republic became an empire. The Republic foundered during the 1st century BC, and 13 years of civil war succeeded Julius Caesar's assassination in 44 BC. Caesar's adopted son Octavius (Augustus Caesar) led one faction to victory around 30 BC, and took the title of Emperor. The Roman legions swept outward, conquered all of Italy and spread across the Mediterranean lands until, by the end of the 2nd century AD, their empire encompassed most of the known world. Meanwhile, art flourished, monumental buildings were erected and great public works undertaken. The Pantheon, the best preserved of the ancient Roman structures, dates from this time, as do the ruined Colosseo, parts of the Foro Romano, and Trajan's victory column.

By the the time of the death of Emperor Marcus Aurelius in AD 180, the strains of maintaining such a huge

---

ROMULUS AND REMUS

According to legend, the twins were the children of Rhea, a vestal virgin, and the god Mars. Abandoned on the Palatine hill, they were suckled by a wolf before being adopted by a shepherd. In adulthood, the brothers were told by Mars to found a settlement on the Palatine. Unable to agree on a name or on who should rule, they invoked the gods to settle the matter, but the signs were inconclusive; in the ensuing fight Romulus killed Remus.

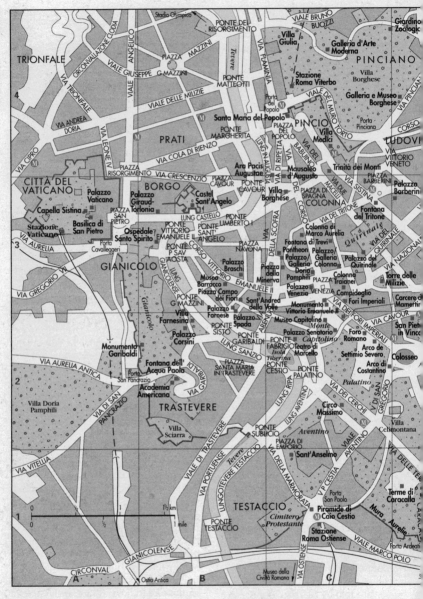

empire were apparent and decline set in. The attrition accelerated in the 4th century with the death of Constantine, when the Empire was split into eastern and western halves, and power moved out of Rome to Constantinople. Goths, then Vandals, plundered the city; by AD 476 the Western Empire ceased to exist.

With the emergence of Rome as the capital of Western Christianity, the city once again began an ascent to glory. This culminated in its role as one of the main centers of the Renaissance in the 15th century, a "rebirth" of painting,

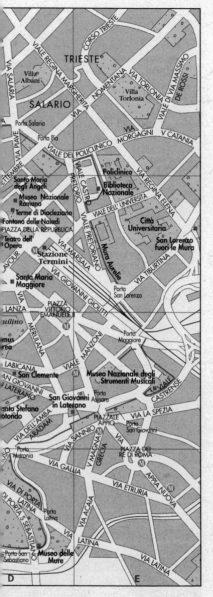

with Rome still in the hands of French troops, who supported the Pope. In 1870 the city of Rome was finally liberated, and took over from Florence the role of state capital.

During the 19th and early 20th centuries, both church and state vied for ownership of Rome. In 1929 "the Roman Question" was resolved with the signing of the Lateran Treaty by Benito Mussolini and Cardinal Gaspari. Under the agreement, a Vatican city-state under papal rule was created within Rome. Toward the end of World War II, Rome was declared an open city and as a result was saved from wholesale destruction.

Since the establishment of the Republic of Italy in 1946, the city has grown both in population and unplanned building, its tentacles spreading into the hinterland. The center, however, with its churches, ancient palaces and monuments, spacious parks, tree-lined boulevards, fountains, outdoor cafés and elegant shops, makes Rome one of the world's most attractive cities. Cultural diversity also contributes to Rome's popularity with visitors. During the social season, from November to May, there is a wide range of offerings in opera, concerts and theater. Special events in Rome include the Good Friday Procession, the Flower Festival in mid-June, and the Festa de Noiantri in Trastevere in July.

THE FOUNTAINS OF ROME

Rome has more fountains than any other city in the world. Many of them are masterpieces of design and sculpture, such as Bernini's Fontana dei Quattro Fiumi in Piazza Navona, and the ever-popular Fontana di Trevi.
Two other fountains to look for are Bernini's Fontana delle Api in Piazza Barberini, which includes three bees (*api*), Barberini family emblems; and the Fontana della Barcaccia, which takes the form of a half-sunken boat.

sculpture and architecture that would profoundly affect succeeding generations of artists.

By the 19th century, Rome had become a provincial backwater, but was soon to regain prominence. The unified Kingdom of Italy was created in 1861,

ITALY

GETTING THERE
BY CAR

Ancient history deemed that all roads led to Rome. A glance at any map assures today's traveler that things have not changed – roads radiate from Rome like spokes from a hub.

From the northwest, the *autostrada* from Civitavecchia (A12) angles down the coast, connecting with Via Aurelia (SS1) and entering the city from the west. Continuing clockwise, the Via Cassia (SS2), Flaminia (SS3), Autostrada del Sole (A1) and Via Salaria (SS4) lead into the northern outskirts.

Via Tiburtina (SS5), Autostrada L'Aquila (A24) and Via Casilina (SS6) are the eastern approaches to Rome, while the Autostrada del Sole (A1) and Via Appia Nuova (SS7) make their way into the southeastern section of the city.

From the south and southwest, respectively, the Coast Road to Naples (SS148) and Via del Mare (SS8) complete the main approach routes to Rome. All these routes join the Gran Raccordo Anulare (Circular Road) some 12 kilometers (7½ miles) from the city center, allowing motorists to bypass the center and enter from the most convenient direction.

Note: Most *autostrade* are toll roads.

BY PLANE, TRAIN AND BUS

The Leonardo da Vinci Airport, at Fiumicino, serves Rome. Train service to and from the airport is available at Roma-Ostiense railroad station, at Piazzale dei Partigiani. The trip includes shuttle bus service from the Roma–Ostiense railroad station to main Termini railroad station (Piazza dei Cinquecento) and vice versa.

The Stazione Termini is the most important train station in Rome. Ticket offices are to the right of the entrance; the *albergo diurno* (offering such travel amenities as baths, barber service, hairdressing, pressing and cleaning) and the subway station are in the basement. Trolleys are available for carrying luggage.

C.I.T. Bus Terminal, Piazza della Republica 64, serves Intercity buses from Naples, Florence, Venice and Milan.

GETTING AROUND
STREET SYSTEM

For the uninitiated, driving on Rome's narrow, winding streets can be a nightmare. Numerous areas in the center of the city have been restricted to bus and taxi traffic or have been pedestrianized. There are many one-way streets. If you must drive, be alert at all times and let the passengers do the sightseeing. The best tip is to stick to the main avenues. Avoid the rush hours – 7:30–9am, 12:30–2:30pm and 4:30–8:30pm. A detailed street map, available at tourist centers, is essential. Also check driving restrictions for foreign motorists.

PARKING

On-street parking, except during the Italian holiday month of August, is scant. A wise policy is not to depend on it, and take public transportation instead.

CAR RENTAL

Vehicles can be rented in the Rome area with or without drivers; car-rental agencies are listed in the telephone directory under the heading *Autonoleggio*.

TAXIS

A good way to enjoy sightseeing is to take a taxi. Cab stands are at most busy intersections and at piazzas; taxis do not cruise. For assistance, telephone Radio-taxi (check telephone numbers in the Rome telephone directory). It is best to use only metered taxis. Additional charges are made for luggage, for service during late-night and early-morning hours, and for trips to or from the airport.

PUBLIC TRANSPORTATION

Public transportation in Rome is fast and inexpensive. Bus and train tickets are bought in advance from automatic machines or newsstands with an A.T.A.C. sticker. Board at the back and cancel the ticket in the stamping machine. Among the most important lines are the 64, running through the center of the city from the Stazione Termini to the Basilica di San Pietro, and the 87, through Piazza di Spagna from Piazza Cavour to St. John Lateran.

There are two underground, or subway, lines: the "A" line, from Ottaviano to Anagnina, with stops at Anagnina, Cinecitta, Subaugusta, Giulio Agricola, Lucio Sestio, Numidio Quadrato, Porta Furba, Arco de Travertino, Colli Albani, Furio Camillo, Ponte Lungo, Re di Roma, S. Giovanni, Manzoni, Vittorio E., Termini, Repubblica, Barberini, Spagna and Flaminio; and the "B" line, from Rebibbia to Eur, with stops at Rebibbia, P. Mammolo, S. M. Soccorso, Pietralata, M. Tiburtini, Quintiliani, Tiburtina FS (railroad station) Bologna, Policlinico, C. Pretorio, Termini FS (railroad station), Cavour, Colosseo, Circo Massimo, Piramide, Garbatella, Basilica St. Paolo, Marconi, Magliana, E.U.R. Palasport, E.U.R. Fermi and Laurentina.

WHAT TO DO
SIGHTSEEING
The best way to see Rome properly is on foot, as many of the smaller streets and monuments are inaccessible to vehicular traffic. Always remember to cross the road on the striped sections.

CARRIAGE TOURS
Every visitor should take a horse-drawn carriage at least to the Villa Borghese, the Gianicolo and the Via Appia. Fares can be expensive; extra charges are made for night rides and luggage.

SPORTS AND RECREATION
Like most Italians, Romans are passionate about soccer, or *calcis*. Home teams A.S. Roma and Lazio play on alternate Sunday afternoons at the Stadio Olimpico from September to May. Basketball, also played at the professional level, can be enjoyed at the Palazzo dello Sport, E.U.R.

Horse racing is another Roman preoccupation. Flat racing and steeplechasing are held at the Ippodromo della Capanelle, trotting at the Ippodromo di Tordi Valle. An annual May event is the Rome International Horse Show.

Rome has many swimming pools. The Piscine delle Rosa in E.U.R. is an outdoor pool open in summer. Romans also enjoy the beaches at Ostia, Fregene (both very dirty and crowded), Santa Marinella and San Severo (the latter two further north and more salubrious).

WHERE TO SHOP
The elegant shops of Rome will afford unlimited pleasure, but, as always, it pays to comparison shop. The main shopping area is formed by the Via Frattina, Piazza di Spagna, Via Condotti and the Via Sistina. The Via Condotti, opposite the Piazza di Spagna, is comparable to Fifth Avenue in New York City. There are also elegant specialty shops along the Via Veneto. For something different, you might enjoy the busy flea market held on Sunday mornings at Porta Portese. Some of the best buys in Rome are sportswear, silks, leather goods (particularly shoes, handbags and gloves), silverware, table linens and jewelry. Most shops are open from 8:30 or 9am to 1pm and from 3:30 or 4pm to 7:30 or 8pm. Many are closed on Monday mornings.

WHERE TO STAY – WHERE TO EAT
With hotels of all classes available in Rome, there are accommodations to suit every pocket. Careful consideration should be given to the location of your hotel and to individual preferences.

Many fashionable hotels are in the area bounded by Via Veneto, Piazza Barberini and Trinità dei Monti (near the Spanish Steps). The area around the central railroad station offers a variety of less expensive hotels. For those wishing to avoid the traffic in the city center, hotels near the Via Aurelia (south of the Vatican) or to the north, in the vicinity of the Villa Borghese near the Via Flaminia or Salaria, are recommended.

Shoppers will probably opt to stay between Piazza di Spagna and Via del Corso or on more moderately priced Via Cola di Rienzo, across the Tevere (Tiber River). Hotels between Via del Corso and the Tiber or near Via Fori Imperiali are convenient for those wishing to explore the narrow streets, open-air markets and famous landmarks of the historic center.

Excellent food is as inherent to Rome as its ancient monuments. *Ristoranti* and *trattorie* are numerous, and vary from the most elegant to the most informal and from the native to the international.

Traditionally, an Italian meal consists of pasta, followed by a meat or fish course and dessert (fresh fruit), accompanied by red or white wine. Reservations are advised at all restaurants. Bars are a good place to start the day with a cappuccino and *cornetto* (pastry), or an afternoon sandwich. To get served, first pay for your order at the cash register, then give your slip to the barman. It is cheaper to eat and drink standing up, as there is a service charge if you sit down.

ENTERTAINMENT

NIGHTLIFE

As in any great city, nightlife in Rome can be as varied as the visitor. Movie theaters are numerous and offer films of all kinds in both Italian and English.

Nightclubs are expensive but offer entertainment ranging from sipping a drink in an elegant atmosphere to dancing or quaffing beer with gregarious students. Most clubs close during stretches of summer, particularly August.

Note: The mention of any area or establishment in the preceding sections is for information only and does not imply endorsement by AAA.

THEATER AND CONCERTS

The concert season in Rome runs from October to June. Noted soloists can be heard at the Accademia di Santa Cecilia at Via della Conciliazione 4 or Via dei Greci 18. The Accademia Filarmonica perform at the Teatro Olimpico.

Opera is a festive occasion in Rome. The Teatro dell'Opera features productions from late November until June, and the Terme di Caracalla stages open-air opera from July through August.

Theatergoing in Rome focuses upon revivals of classics, especially Italian versions of Shakespeare. Smaller establishments present music-hall productions, political satires and parodies. The Commedia Napolitana features musical revues; the Greek Theater at Ostia Antica presents classic outdoor theater.

ESPECIALLY FOR CHILDREN

Rome is a fine vacation spot for children of all ages. The list below is a sample of suitable attractions.

Having learned the origin of Rome, youngsters can appreciate the she-wolf caged on the Capitoline Hill steps; the animal maintains a 3,000-year-old tradition. The Foro Romano, the Colosseo, with its memories of bloodthirsty games, and the frescoed catacombs will all stimulate young imaginations. Visit the Luna Amusement Park at E.U.R., take a boat ride to Ostia Antica, enjoy a puppet show on the Pincio, or combine a picnic at the Villa Borghese with a visit to the zoo or the children's cinema, Dei Piccoli.

For play opportunities, try the myriad fountains of Rome. Horse-drawn carriage rides are appealing to all ages.

PLACES OF INTEREST

ACCADEMIA AMERICANA (412 B2), above the Paolina Fountain on the Gianicolo, is a 20th-century palace built to resemble a Roman *palazzo*. It is the home and studio of many American musicians, painters, scholars, sculptors and writers, and contains a library and museum.

ARA PACIS AUGUSTAE (412 B4), near Via di Ripetta, was constructed by order of the Senate from 13 to 9 BC as a tribute to the peace that reigned throughout the Empire at that time. There are superb bas-reliefs.

ARCO DI COSTANTINO (412 C2), at the end of Piazzale del Colosseo between the Caelian and Palatine hills, commemorates Constantine's victory over Maxentius in AD 312. It is a triple arch, and

★ Rome's Highlights ★

Basilica di San Pietro   (see p.445)
Cappella Sistina   (see p.445)
Castel Sant'Angelo   (see p.417)
Colosseo   (see p.418)
Fontana di Trevi   (see p.418)
Foro Romano   (see p.418)
Pantheon   (see p.419)
Santa Maria Maggiore   (see p.420)
Villa Borghese   (see p.421)
Villa Giulia   (see p.421)

ITALY

many of its reliefs were made from fragments of other monuments.

ARCO DI SETTIMIO SEVERO (412 C2), Foro Romano, was erected as a tribute to Emperor Septimius Severus and his sons, Caracalla and Publius Septimius Geta, for their outstanding battle achievements. Later, Caracalla murdered his brother and wrote a new inscription deleting Geta's name, but traces of the old inscription are still visible.

CAMPIDOGLIO (412 C3), the sacred hill of ancient Rome, holds the imposing Piazza del Campidoglio, designed by Michelangelo. The piazza is enclosed by the Palazzo Senatorio, Palazzo dei Conservatori and Palazzo Nuovo, which together form the Museo Capitolino, which has a fine collection of classical sculpture.

CARCERE DI MAMERTINO (San Pietro in Carcere) (412 C2) is beneath the church of San Giuseppe dei Falegnami. It served as a dungeon for captives awaiting execution; St. Peter was imprisoned here.

CASTEL SANT' ANGELO (412 B3) ★, Lungotevere Castello, is a huge edifice with thick walls and a tower. Erected by Emperor Hadrian as a mausoleum and later used as a prison, barracks and papal fortress, it is now a museum with military relics and works of art.

CATACOMBS, the subterranean cemeteries surrounding Rome, were used by early Christians for meetings and worship. In AD 313, Constantine ended Christian persecution, and major tombs were transferred to nearby churches.

Priscilla Catacombs, Via Salaria (413 D4), has 2nd-century frescoes; the *Virgin and Child with Isiah* is the oldest-known painting of the Virgin Mary.

San Callisto, Rome's largest system of catacombs, was the papal burial place in the 3rd century. The tomb of St. Cecilia, with frescoes from the 7th and 8th centuries, is particularly imposing. Like the San Sebastiano catacombs, these lie beside Via Appia Antica (413 D1).

San Sebastiano has frescoes and stuccoed tombs, some pre-Christian. The Basilica di San Sebastiano is above. The bodies of apostles Peter and Paul were temporarily kept here in the 3rd century.

CIMITERO PROTESTANTE (412 C1), Via Caio Cestio, is a peaceful, shady spot set within a grove of cypress trees. It shelters the grave of John Keats and the ashes of Percy Bysshe Shelley, along with the remains of other expatriates.

CIRCO MASSIMO (Circus Maximus) (412 C2), Via del Circo Massimo, was the largest Roman circus, holding 300,000. Begun around 326 BC, it was much modified during its existence. Used first for chariot races, later as the site of Christian slaughter and games, it was destroyed by fire; a grassy hollow is all that remains.

COLONNA DI MARCO AURELIO (412 C3), Piazza Colonna, consists of 27 drums of sculptured marble. Grand bas-reliefs portray Marcus Aurelius' 2nd-century victories over the Germans; a statue of St. Paul surmounts the column and replaces an earlier one of Aurelius.

COLONNA TRAIANEI (Trajan's Column) (412 C3), in the Forum of Trajan, one of the Fori Imperiali, is among the city's most striking monuments. It was erected in AD 113 and dedicated to the Emperor for his victory over the Dacians (a tribe of present-day Romania).

ITALY

COLOSSEO (Colosseum) (412 D2) ★, begun about AD 72, is the best-known structure remaining from ancient Rome. It was capable of holding over 50,000 to view gladiatorial contests, hunts, mock naval battles and perhaps Christian martyrdoms. Many of the materials of this magnificent edifice were later used in the construction of various churches and palaces.

DOMUS AUREA (Golden House) (413 D2), near the Colosseum, was Nero's palace built after the burning of Rome in AD 64. Little remains today, and Trajan's baths (unexcavated) cover much of the site.

FONTANA DI TREVI (412 C3) ★ is one of the most impressive of Rome's many fountains. The waters play about a sculpture of Neptune, the sea god, riding in a winged chariot drawn by horses led by marble tritons. Traditionally, visitors throw a coin in the fountain if they wish to return to Rome.

FORO ROMANO (412 C2) ★, center of public life in Rome until the 2nd century AD, is crowded with the jumbled ruins of basilicas, temples and other buildings, including the Arch of Septimius Severus (see p.417); the temples of Saturn (a Roman god), Castor and Pollux (Helen of Troy's twin brothers), Julius Caesar (erected on the spot where Caesar was cremated), Vesta (the vestal virgins) and Emperor Antoninus and Empress Faustina; the Arch of Titus; and the well-preserved Curia, where the Senate met.

GALLERIA E MUSEO BORGHESE (412 D4) ★, in the Casino of the Villa Borghese (see p.421), houses the paintings and sculptures collected by the Borghese family and now owned by the state. This outstanding collection includes sculptures by Bernini and Canova, and paintings by Titian, Raphael and Botticelli.

GALLERIA COLONNA (412 C3), Via della Pilotta 17 in the Palazzo Colonna, comprises a great private collection of largely late-Renaissance and baroque paintings, with works by Tintoretto and Van Dyck displayed in a spectacular setting.

GALLERIA D'ARTE MODERNA (412 C4), Viale delle Belle Arti 131, contains a collection of Italian and foreign art from the 19th century to the present. The 20th-century Italian wing has works by Marino Marini, Giacomo Manzù, and the Futurists Boccioni and de Chirico.

GIANICOLO (Janiculum) (412 B3), Rome's highest hill (though not one of the original seven), offers a spectacular view of the city. It also includes a small park containing the lovely Paolina Fountain. On the summit is an imposing equestrian statue of Antonio Garibaldi by Gallori.

ISOLA TIBERINA (412 C2), near the Teatro di Marcello, is a boat-shaped island. To enhance this illusion, the Romans created a stone bow at one end and erected an obelisk to serve as a mast. The island can be reached via the Ponte Fabricio, the oldest bridge in Rome (62 BC).

MAUSOLEO D'AUGUSTO (413 C3), Piazza Augusto Imperatore, a circular structure like the Castel Sant'Angelo, for which it was a model, contains the crypts of emperors Augustus, Claudius, Nerva and Tiberius, as well as other members of this royal family. It has been used as a fortress, bullring and concert hall.

MONUMENTO VITTORIO EMANUELE II (412 C3), Piazza Venezia, is a huge Bréscian marble work by Giuseppe Sacconi (1911). Dedicated to Italian unity, it contains the tomb of the Unknown Soldier.

MURA AURELIE (412 E3), a wall begun by Emperor Aurelian in AD 271, encircled the seven hills of Rome: Aventine, Caelian, Capitoline, Esquiline, Palatine, Quirinal and Viminal. Extensive sections remain intact.

MUSEO BARRACCO (412 B3), near Campo dei Fiori, houses ancient sculpture, including Assyrian, Babylonian, Egyptian, Etruscan, Greek and Roman art.

MUSEO CAPITOLINO (412 C2), Piazza del Campidoglio, is a most Roman museum, with many masterpieces of classical sculpture in both sections (see *Campidoglio*, p.417). Look for the *Dying Gaul*, *Capitoline Venus* (in Palazzo Nuovo), the *Spinario* and *Capitoline Wolf* (Palazzo dei Conservatori).

MUSEO DELLA CIVILTÀ ROMANA, Piazzale Giovanni Agnelli, E.U.R., documents daily life in Rome from its beginnings through the Empire.There is an excellent model of the city in the 4th century, with its great monuments intact.

MUSEO NAZIONALE ROMANO (413 D3), in the newly restored Palazzo Massimo near Piazza della Repubblica, displays some of the world's finest antique sculptures and mosaics.

OSTIA ANTICA, the ancient Roman port, is a whole excavated city and the best-preserved Roman town after Pompeii. Ostia is 30 minutes from Rome by train or car. The setting among pines is delightful, and there is much to see: baths, an amphitheater and a Roman bar.

PALATINO (412 C2) was the first of Rome's seven hills to be inhabited. It is a peaceful spot, dotted with fragmentary ruins including the imperial palaces Domus Augustana, Domus Tiberiana (within the Farnese Gardens) and Domus Severiana, and the "Stadium" built by Domitian.

PALAZZO BARBERINI (412 D3), Via delle Quattro Fontane, is an impressive 17th-century structure including the splendid baroque Gran Salon. It houses the Galleria Nazionale d'Arte Antica, a magnificent collection of paintings by the great masters. There are works by Raphael, Holbein and El Greco.

PALAZZO FARNESE (412 B3), Piazza Farnese, is one of the prettiest palaces in

Rome. It was begun by Antonio da Sangallo the Younger in 1514 and completed by Michelangelo in 1546. The palace now houses the French Embassy and is not regularly open to the public.

PALAZZO DEL QUIRINALE (412 C3), on Via del Quirinale, was a former palace of kings and popes; it is now the residence of Italy's president. The palace is closed to the public, but a changing of the guard ceremony, complete with a brass band, takes place outside daily at 6pm.

PALAZZO VENEZIA (412 C3), abutting the Piazza Venezia, is a 15th-century palace that was once a papal residence and later the home of Benito Mussolini. A small museum houses an exceptionally fine collection of Renaissance sculptures.

PALAZZO-GALLERIA DORIA PAMPHILI (412 C3) is a huge palace, part of which is open to the public; it contains four galleries crammed with fine paintings. The collection's prize exhibit is the portrait by Velásquez of Pope Innocent X.

PANTHEON (412 C3) ★, Piazza della Rotonda, is the best-preserved monument of ancient Rome. First built by Marcus Agrippa (son-in-law of Augustus) as a temple dedicated to the seven planetary gods, it was replaced in its present form by Hadrian around AD 125. In AD 609 it was consecrated and became the Church of Santa Maria dei Martiri.

The exterior is brick; the interior, green and white marble. Sunlight streams in through a 9-meter (30-foot) opening at the top of the impressive concrete dome, an extraordinary achievement of the Roman engineers. The church floor slopes toward the center, where drains catch the rainwater. Bronze tiles that once covered the interior are gone; some were melted down to make the columns of Bernini's baldacchino in the Basilica di San Pietro.

PIAZZA CAMPO DEI FIORI (412 B3) is one of Rome's most enjoyable squares, the

ITALY

scene of a picturesque daily food and flower market and a place to relax while observing everyday Roman life.

PIAZZA NAVONA (412 B3), off Corso del Rinascimento, occupies the site of the great hippodrome built by Emperor Domitian. A typical 17th-century Roman square, it is a favorite city meeting-place. In the center, Bernini's famous Fontana dei Quattro Fiumi (Fountain of the Four Rivers) fronts Borromini's Church of St. Agnes in Agony.

PIAZZA DELLA MINERVA (412 C3), near the Pantheon, has perhaps Bernini's most charming public work: a marble elephant toting an obelisk taken from a temple of Isis. The Church of Santa Maria Sopra Minerva is Rome's only Gothic church, built in 1280 over an earlier church, itself on the ruins of a temple to Minerva.

PIAZZA MATTEI, Via dei Falegnami, contains the delightful Fontanna delle Tartaraghe (Fountain of the Tortoises), sculpted by Taddeo Landini in the 16th century, with tortoises added by Bernini.

PIAZZA DELLA REPUBBLICA (413 D3), off the Via Nazionale, has seen better days, but is distinguished by the Fontana delle Naiadi (Fountain of the Naiads) (1901). The Terme di Diocleziano can be found within the Church of Santa Maria degli Angeli.

PIAZZA DI SANTA MARIA IN TRASTEVERE (412 B2) is the heart of one of the oldest sections of the city. It fronts the first church in Rome, a basilica based on a chapel founded in the 3rd century BC.

PIAZZA DI SPAGNA (412 C3) is one of Rome's most popular spots, best known for the elegant "Spanish Steps." At the top is the church of Trinità dei Monti.

PIRAMIDE DI CAIO CESTIO (412 C1), in the Protestant Cemetery, was erected in 12 BC and is 27 meters (89 feet) tall. It is the tomb of Caius Cestius.

SANT' ANDREA DELLA VALLE (412 B3), Corso Vittorio Emanuele II, is a beautiful 17th-century church with the second-largest dome in Rome. The first act of Puccini's *Tosca* is set in the church.

SAN CLEMENTE (413 D2), Via di San Giovanni in Laterano, has the finest medieval interior in Rome. Beneath it lie the remains of a 1st-century Roman palace and a 3rd-century Mithraic temple.

SAN GIOVANNI IN LATERANO (413 D2), Piazza di Porta San Giovanni, is the Cathedral of Rome. The impressive façade is adorned with 16 huge statues of Christ, the Apostles and the saints; the interior contains many relics and artworks. The Lateran Palace adjoins the cathedral, and the Baptistery is the earliest in the world. Opposite the palace stands the Scala Santa, the staircase believed to have come from Pontius Pilate's house in Jerusalem.

SAN LORENZO FUORI LE MURA (413 E3), located off Via Tiburtina, was formed by two churches built end to end: San Lorenzo, erected by Constantine, and Madonna Della Vergine, built by Pope Sixtus III. It has 6th-century mosaics and a 13th-century marble choir.

SANTA MARIA DEGLI ANGELI (412 D3), on Piazza della Repubblica, was the central hall of the Terme di Diocleziano, transformed into a church by Michelangelo.

SANTA MARIA MAGGIORE (413 D3) ★, Piazza di Santa Maria Maggiore, dates from the 5th century but has been twice restored. Inside, 40 columns line the nave, and there are 5th-century mosaics. The ceiling was gilded by Giuliano da Sangallo with the first gold brought from the New World by Christopher Columbus. Mass has been celebrated here daily since the 5th century.

SANTA MARIA DEL POPOLO (412 C4) was supposedly built on the site of Nero's tomb in 1099 as a kind of exorcism. The present church is noteworthy for two dramatic masterpieces of saints Peter and Paul by Caravaggio, Pinturrichio's frescoes on the choir ceiling, and Raphael's *Cappella Chigi*.

SAN PAOLO FUORI LE MURA, near Porta San Paolo (414 C1), was originally constructed over the tomb of St. Paul. It is an authentic reconstruction of the original, destroyed by fire in 1823. This church is one of the four patriarchal basilicas, along with San Giovanni in Laterano, Santa Maria Maggiore and the Basilica di San Pietro.

SAN PIETRO IN VINCOLI (412 D2), Piazza di San Pietro in Vincoli, was created in AD 432 to house the chains that bound St. Peter after his arrest in Rome. The relics themselves are visible under the main altar, but the church's chief attraction is the statue of Moses by Michelangelo. It was originally intended for a tomb for Pope Julius II, never completed.

SANTO STEFANO ROTONDO (413 D2), in Via di Santo Stefano Rotondo, dates from the 5th century and was once one of Christendom's most important churches. The granite and marble interior is decorated with medieval frescoes showing horrific scenes of torture and butchery.

TEATRO DI MARCELLO (412 C2), near Via del Teatro di Marcello, was begun by order of Julius Caesar and completed by Caesar Augustus. It went out of use in the 3rd century, when bloodthirsty entertainment at the Colosseum was more popular than the dramas performed here.

TERME DI CARACALLA (412 D1), along Via delle Terme di Caracalla, were luxurious baths with a stadium, extensive galleries, libraries, and facilities for 2,000 bathers. Percy Bysshe Shelley composed part of *Prometheus Unbound* here.

TERME DI DIOCLEZIANO (413 D3), on the Piazza della Repubblica, were once the largest baths in Rome, with a capacity of 3,000. The ruins are incorporated in the church of Santa Maria degli Angeli and the Museo Nazionale Romano.

TORRE DELLE MILIZIE (412 C3), Via 4 Novembre, next to Trajan's Market, believed to be the tower where Nero fiddled while Rome burned, was in fact the lookout tower for a 13th-century fortress.

VATICAN CITY – *see p.445*.

VIA APPIA ANTICA (412 D1), the ancient Roman highway to Brindisi, is flanked by cypress trees, monuments, tombs, marbles and statues reflecting past glories. The road, still partially paved with Roman cobbles, starts from Porta San Sebastiano.

VILLA ADRIANA – *see Tivoli on p.443*.

VILLA BORGHESE (412 C4) ★, one of the loveliest parks in the city, faces Porta Pinciana at the top of Via Veneto. No cars are allowed, but Rome's largest underground carpark is near the entrance. The park itself contains temples, statues, fountains, a zoo and the Galleria Borghese (see p.418). The nearby Pincio, an exquisite botanical garden, was created by the early 19th-century architect Giuseppe Valadier.

VILLA DORIA PAMPHILI (412 A2) is on the Gianicolo hill, off the Via Aurelia Antica. Rome's largest park, it covers hundreds of hectares with lawns, woods, fountains and lakes, and is a good place to escape the crowds.

VILLA D'ESTE – *see Tivoli on p.443*.

VILLA GIULIA (412 C4) ★, Viale delle Belle Arti, near the Galleria Borghese, houses the Museo Nazionale Etrusco, an extensive collection of Etruscan art and artifacts. Its best-known exhibit is the *Sarcophagus of the Married Couple*, a touching sculptural portrait of connubial happiness. The villa itself is a delightful Renaissance country house.

ITALY

PLACES OF INTEREST

AMALFI (408 D2)
CAMPANIA pop. 5,800

At one time this delightful town was the center of commerce and shipping on the Mediterranean. It became the first independent Italian maritime republic and reached its zenith in the 11th century.

During the 1230s, however, Genoa and Pisa tumbled Amalfi from its position of power. The sea eroded its harbor away, and the city evolved into the pleasant holiday center of today.

THE AMALFI COAST DRIVE

The southern part of the Sorrentine Peninsula is one of the most beautiful coastlines in Europe, and to drive the precipitous Corniche Road that winds along it is an unforgettable experience. The road runs from Sorrento via Positano and Amalfi to Salerno, giving glimpses of small resorts and tiny fishing hamlets en route.

DUOMO DI SANT' ANDREA (Cathedral of St. Andrew), Piazza del Duomo, dates from the 10th century. The body of St. Andrew reposes in the crypt. The cloisters date from the 13th century.

GROTTA DELLO SMERALDO (Emerald Grotto) is 12 kilometers (7½ miles) west. Reflected light turns the grotto's clear water and stalactites a rich green.

▲ ANCONA (408 C4)
MARCHE pop. 103,200

The Adriatic seaport of Ancona was founded in the 4th century BC by Greeks from Syracuse and colonized by Rome a century later. Like many Italian cities, it was an independent republic during the Middle Ages, but from 1532 to 1860 it formed part of the papal states.

Ancona suffered severe damage during World War II and in a later earthquake, although some of its ancient monuments survived or were restored. Today this busy commercial and industrial city is noted as a resort and for the manufacture of accordions and guitars.

ARCO DI TRAIANO (Arch of Trajan) was erected in AD 115 to honor the emperor who developed the port.

DUOMO DI SAN CIRIACO (Cathedral of St. Cyriacus) dominates the city and harbor. The sturdy Romanesque structure incorporates the Byzantine Greek-cross floor plan; two lions of Verona marble guard its Gothic entrance.

MUSEO NAZIONALE DELLE MARCHE, in the 16th-century Palazzo Ferretti, provides a comprehensive survey of the archaeology of the Marche region.

▲ AOSTA (408 A5)
VALLE D'AOSTA pop. 36,100

A leading holiday resort as well as the capital of the region, Aosta was founded around 25 BC by the Romans, and Roman walls still partially enclose the old city. The remnants of a theater, amphitheater, forum and impressive double gateway are among the remains to be seen. The 1st-century Arco di Augusto (Arch of Augustus) lies on Via Sant'Anselmo, near the old Roman bridge.

Dwarfed by the surrounding Alps, Aosta is the Italian terminus of three highways to France and Switzerland. A cable car runs from Aosta to the winter-sports area at Pila. To the south is the scenic Gran Paradiso National Park.

COLLEGIATA DI SANT'ORSO (Collegiate Church of St. Orso) shows the work of different centuries from the 8th (the crypt), to the 12th (the nave) and the 15th (the fantastically carved choir stalls). The carved capitals of the Romanesque cloister depict biblical events and an old folk fable.

▲ L'AQUILA (408 C3)
ABRUZZO pop. 68,300
Against the bulky backdrop of the Gran Sasso, L'Aquila, capital of the Abruzzo, rises behind its ramparts. Today it is a major resort, popular in both winter and summer. Of note is the Fontana delle 99 Cannelle (Fountain of the 99 Spouts). This recalls a local legend, which tells the tale that the town was created when Frederick II combined the populations of 99 villages. To perpetuate the tale, the clock tower of the Palazzo di Giustizia chimes 99 times every evening.

BASILICA DI SAN BERNARDINO DA SIENA crowns a small piazza stairway on Via San Bernardino. The Renaissance façade dates from 1527, the rest of the structure from the mid-1400s.

BASILICA DI SANTA MARIA DI COLLE-MAGGIO, at the end of the Piazza Collemaggio, is the town's finest church. The Romanesque structure was begun in the late 13th century; the façade, noted for its rose windows, was added later.

CASTELLO, a 16th-century Spanish fort-ress, dominates the town. It houses the National Museum of the Abruzzo.

▲ AREZZO (408 C4)
TOSCANA pop. 91,900
The familiar "do-re-mi-fa-so" originated in Arezzo as part of the first system of musical notation, invented by Guido d'Arezzo in the 11th century. The poet

Petrarch was born in this village, as was Giorgio Vasari, a painter, sculptor and architect who chronicled the lives of various Renaissance artists.

At the end of August, Giostra del Saraceno, a tournament in which mount-ed lancers charge a dummy, is held in Arezzo's Piazza Grande. This spectacle involves thousands of citizens all clad in medieval garb.

CHIESA DI SAN FRANCESCO, a 14th-centu-ry Gothic structure, contains one of Tuscany's great art treasures in the choir chapel: the fresco cycle Legend of the Holy Cross by Piero della Francesca, painted between 1453 and 1464.

DUOMO, begun in 1277, stands above the main square, Piazza Grande. It contains another fresco by Piero della Francesca, Mary Magdalen, and the massive tomb of Bishop Guido Tarlati.

MUSEO ARCHEOLOGICO (Archaeological Museum), Via Magaritone 10, is next to the Roman amphitheater. It displays frag-ments of locally produced 1st-century vases and Etruscan figures.

SANTA MARIA DELLA PIEVE, a parish church on the Piazza Grande, was built in the 12th–14th centuries. The delicate arcades of its Romanesque façade reveal the Pisan influence.

▲ ÁSCOLI PICENO (408 C3)
MARCHE pop. 52,800
The Picini tribe founded the town, which was destroyed by the Romans in the 1st century BC and rebuilt in a checkerboard pattern. Medieval Ascoli Piceno is best viewed from the Roman Ponte Solesta, which arches 24 meters (79 feet) above the Tronto River.

PIAZZA DEL POPOLO (People's Square) forms the attractive center of the old town. The flagstone piazza is bordered by the 13th-century Palazzo del Popolo, destroyed by fire and remodelled in the 16th century; the venerable Chiesa di

San Francesco (Church of St. Francis), and the 16th-century Loggia dei Mercanti (Merchants' Loggia). On the first Sunday in August the locals dress in medieval costume for the Tournament of the Quintana festival held here.

ÁSOLA (408 B6)

VENETO *pop. 3,500*

At the foot of the Dolomites, surrounded by wooded countryside, this is one of the prettiest medieval towns in the region. The Museo Civico houses memorabilia of poet Robert Browning and actress Eleonore Duse. The Castello was also home to Caterina Cornaro, 15th-century queen, who was given Ásola in return for surrendering Cyprus to the Venetians.

ASSISI (408 C4) ★

UMBRIA *pop. 25,000*

A gentle landscape outside its walls and a history of gentle saints within characterize serene Assisi, birthplace of St. Francis and St. Clare.

Assisi has changed little since the days of St. Francis, but tourism has brought inevitable crowds and commercialism. Nevertheless, it is a charming town. The Rocca Maggiore, a 14th-century castle, offers a sweeping view, and on the town's main square is the 1st-century Temple of Minerva and the medieval town hall.

BASILICA DI SAN FRANCESCO, consecrated in 1253, consists of two churches sur-

---

ST. FRANCIS OF ASSISI

St. Francis was born in 1182. Like many 12th-century males he spent his youth womanizing and wining, until a nearly fatal illness converted him to a life of poverty, penitence and prayer. In 1210 he founded the mendicant Franciscan Order. St. Clare, a devoted follower of Francis, established the Order of Poor Clares in 1212 and retired to the nearby Convento di San Damiano.

---

mounting a crypt. In the upper basilica are Giotto's magnificent frescoes, showing 28 scenes from the life of St. Francis in imaginative detail. The lower church contains frescoes by Simone Martini, Cimabue and Pietro Lorenzetti. The tomb of St. Francis is in the crypt.

CHIESA DI SANTA CHIARA (Church of St. Clare), completed in 1265, is dedicated to the founder of the Clarissines or Poor Clares. The saint's open tomb is in the crypt.

DUOMO DI SAN RUFINO (Cathedral of St. Rufinus) is a Romanesque building noted for its belltower and façade. The interior houses the font where both St. Francis and St. Clare were baptized.

▲ ASTI (408 A4)

PIEMONTE *pop. 73,800*

Asti, in the Tárano wine-producing region, lends its name to the popular sparkling wine Asti Spumante. An old Roman town, it rivalled Milan for power and wealth as one of the most important city-republics in the Middle Ages.

Traces of Asti's past can be seen in the city's many towers, including those of the 14th-century Gothic cathedral. The Collegiate Church of San Secundo, near the Town Hall, was built in the 13th and 14th centuries; it has a Romanesque tower and Gothic decorations. On the third Sunday in September, Asti holds its *palio*, a bareback horse race said to be the oldest in Italy, originating in 1275.

▲ BARI (409 D3)

PUGLIA *pop. 335,400*

A major seaport, modern industrial Bari, Puglia's capital, spreads gridlike around its medieval core. The Castello (castle), first built by the Normans in 1131, is among the many interesting buildings in the old quarter. A number of *trulli*, the strange conical dwellings for which the region is known, can be seen at Alberobello and Fasano, about 55 kilometers (34 miles) southeast of Bari.

BASILICA DI SAN NICOLA (Basilica of St. Nicholas), built 1087–1197 on the site of a Byzantine governor's residence, incorporates two towers from the earlier structure. Look for the magnificent bishop's throne of marble, and the relics of St. Nicholas, the original Santa Claus.

CATTEDRALE DI SAN SABINO, built in 1170, also incorporates elements of earlier Byzantine edifices.

BARLETTA (409 D3)
PUGLIA *pop. 89,000*
Barletta, a large agricultural and commercial center on the Adriatic, has a 12th to 14th-century cathedral and two good beaches.

CASTEL DEL MONTE, about 26 kilometers (16 miles) south, is a commanding octagonal castle with a tower at each angle; it was built by Emperor Frederick II.

CASTELLO, in Barletta, is another of Frederick II's castles, built on the foundations of a Norman fortress and with 16th-century Spanish bastions.

COLOSSO, in front of the church of San Sapolcro, stands over 5 meters (16 feet) high. Believed to represent the Byzantine emperor Valentinian, it is the biggest bronze statue from ancient times in existence.

BAVENO (408 B5)
PIEMONTE *pop. 4,400*
Baveno is a quiet resort on Lake Maggiore. Excursions can be made to unspoiled Isola Superiore; Isola Bella, known for its Palazzo Borromeo; and Isola Madre.

▲ BERGAMO (408 B5)
LOMBARDIA *pop. 117,000*
Beautifully situated at the foot of the Alps, Bergamo has two parts: the old hill town, the Città Alta, surrounded by Venetian city walls; and the Città Bassa, or lower town, the modern industrial district on the plain.

In the 12th century Bergamo became the seat of a Lombard duchy, later passing into Venetian hands. The Commedia dell'Arte form of theater developed here in the 16th century, and the town was also known for its school of painting.

CITTÀ ALTA has at its heart the superb medieval Piazza Vecchia, complete with a fountain. Palazzo della Ragione, built in 1199 and reconstructed in the 16th century, is one of the oldest palaces in Italy.

Battistero (Baptistery), an octagonal structure dating from the 14th century, was once part of Santa Maria Maggiore.

Cappella Colleoni (Colleoni Chapel), the mausoleum of the *condottiere* (mercenary soldier) Bartolomeo Colleoni, was completed in 1476. Richly sculptured marble marks the façade. Inside are delicately carved bas-reliefs; the ceiling frescoes were added by Giovanni Battista Tiepolo in the 18th century.

Santa Maria Maggiore was begun in 1137. While the outside is unimposing, the interior was lavishly decorated in the 16th and 17th centuries, including fine choir-stalls, stucco-work and tapestries.

CITTÀ BASSA
Accademia Carrara (Carrara Academy) includes paintings from the Bergamasque and Venetian schools, among other works by great Italian masters.

▲ BOLOGNA (408 B4) ★
EMILIA-ROMAGNA *pop. 412,000*
One of Italy's oldest cities, Bologna was first recorded as the Etruscan village of Felsina. The Romans occupied it in 189 BC, their legacy is a regular grid of streets in the city centre. The university, founded in the 13th century, is the oldest in Europe.

Today, Bologna is a major commercial and cultural center. Its medieval streets make for pleasant wandering among red-brick houses with tiled roofs and balconies, elegant arcades and strange leaning towers. The Via Zamboni is noted for its lovely private *palazzi*.

BASILICA DI SAN PETRONIO (Basilica of St. Petronius), honoring the city's patron saint, was begun in 1390 on a grandiose scale but was never completed. The red and white marble façade displays the town's heraldic colors. The style is primarily Gothic, and the transeptless nave is huge: its interior measures 58 by 131 meters (190 by 430 feet). Look for the unusual zodiacal sundial that uses sunlight shining through a hole in the roof to measure time.

CHIESA DI SANTO STEFANO consists of several distinct sanctuaries. Of particular interest are the Church of St. Vitalis and Agricola, built from the 8th to the 11th centuries, and the Church of the Holy Sepulcher, dating from the 12th century. The basin in which Pontius Pilate reputedly washed his hands of the Crucifixion (actually 8th-century) is in a courtyard behind the latter.

CIVICO MUSEO BIBLIOGRAFICO MUSICALE (Musical Bibliographical Museum), Piazza Rossini, contains collections of rare books, antique musical scores and autographs of well-known composers.

FONTANA DEL NETTUNO (Neptune's Fountain; 1566), by Giambologna and one of the finest fountains of the 16th century, occupies the piazza of the same name.

MUSEO CIVICO ARCHEOLOGICO (Municipal Archaeological Museum), Via dell'Archiginnasio 2, faces the east side of San Petronio and displays a particularly fine collection of Egyptian, Etruscan and Roman antiquities.

PALAZZO DEL PODESTÀ (Governor's Palace) is across the Piazza Maggiore from San Petronio. The Renaissance façade has some fine stonework. It is the creation of Aristotle Fioravantí, who later designed the Kremlin in Moscow. Across the plazza, the huge brick Palazzo Comunale has a clock tower by Fioravantí Fioravantí, Aristotle's father.

PINACOTECA NAZIONALE (National Picture Gallery), Via delle Belle Arti 56, houses one of Europe's finest collections, with special emphasis on the work of the Bolognese School from the 14th to 17th centuries, including Raphael's *St. Cecilia*. There are also works by Francesco del Cossa and Tintoretto.

TORRE ASINELLI AND TORRE GARISENDA, both leaning towers, are in the Piazza di Porta Ravegnana. The former, 96 meters (315 feet) high, rewards a 498-step climb with a good view over the city; the latter is 50 meters (164 feet) high.

UNIVERSITÀ, at Via Zamboni and Via Trombetti, dates from the 5th century and became Europe's first university.

▲ BRÉSCIA (408 B5)
LOMBARDIA *pop. 191,000*

The demand for fine armor and swords made Bréscia one of the wealthiest cities in Italy during the Middle Ages. Still a busy industrial and agricultural hub, Lombardia's second city has a pleasant location, but unattractive rebuilding since World War II detracts from the historic center.

The Museum of the Roman Age and the Museum of Christian Art are part of a cluster of museums around the Via dei Musei that house antiquities and a variety of ecclesiastical displays.

LOGGIA, the 16th-century town hall, is an unusual building with an open portico and marble decorations. On the same square are two late 15th-century palaces.

PINACOTECA TOSIO-MARTINENGO, Piazza Maretto, displays masterpieces by Brescian artists.

ROTONDA, Piazza del Duomo, is the old cathedral. Outwardly dwarfed by the marble *duomo nuovo*, or new cathedral, the Romanesque structure houses a fine bishop's sarcophagus of rose-coloured marble Additional sarcophagi are to be found in the 11th-century crypt.

▲ BRINDISI (408 E3)
PUGLIA *pop. 95,400*
In medieval times Brindisi was an embarkation point for the Holy Land; nowadays, it is a main ferry port for Greece. A 20-meter (66-foot) high, 1st-century BC marble column close to the harbor marks the end of the Appian Way.

CAPRI (ÍSOLA DI) (408 C2)
CAMPANIA *pop. 12,700*
The isle of Capri has drawn visitors from Roman emperors to modern tourists. It has an excellent year-round climate and a wide variety of landscapes.

The island can be reached from Naples by boat or hydrofoil. Accommodations on the island are limited; day trips are a popular way to visit.

ANACAPRI is the name given to the town and to the whole western part of the island. Both are dominated by 596-meter (1,955-foot) Monte Solaro, the highest point on Capri; the summit commands a panorama extending all the way from the Bay of Naples to the mountains of Calabria.

CAPRI TOWN is reached by funicular from the Marina Grande dock. It has a 17th-century monastery and the Giardino di Augusto (garden), provides wonderful views.

GROTTA AZZURRA (Blue Grotto), 4 kilometers (2½ miles) from Anacapri on the northern coast, is the best of the island's grottoes. It measures nearly 30 meters (98 feet) high, 55 meters (180 feet) long and 15 meters (49 feet) wide. Refracted sunlight turns the water in the cavern an intense, cobalt blue, best seen in the morning.

VILLA IOVIS (Jove's Villa), Via Tiberio, the remains of Emperor Tiberius' lavish villa, tops Monte Tiberio. From the promenade there are panoramic views of the surrounding countryside. The steep climb to the villa takes about an hour.

▲ CASERTA (408 D3)
CAMPANIA *pop. 71,300*
Caserta was the 18th-century showplace of the Kingdom of Naples. During World War II the town became the headquarters of Allied Forces in the Mediterranean.

LA REGGIA (Royal Palace) was intended to be the Versailles of the Bourbon kings of Naples and Sicily. Built 1752–74, the 1,200-room palace has four courts and 34 staircases. The palace borders a 100-hectare (247-acre) landscaped park.

CASSINO (408 C3)
LAZIO *pop. 34,500*
Cassino's monastery of Montecassino, founded by St. Benedict in AD 529 as headquarters of the Benedictine movement, featured prominently in the battle for liberation of the area by the Allies in World War II.

▲ CATANZARO (409 D2)
CALABRIA *pop. 97,000*
Busy Catanzaro, Calabria's capital, stands on a high cliff within sight of the Ionian Sea. Behind it rises the Sila Massif, a plateau that reaches 2,533 meters (8,310 feet). Excursions can be made southward along the Ionian coast and around the "toe" of Italy to Reggio Calabria.

CINQUETERRE
LIGURIA
The Cinqueterre ("Five Lands") is the collective name for the five tiny, timeless villages nestled in the rugged cliffs above the Ligurian coast. For centuries they were accessible only by sea, and the best way to admire them is on a boat trip from La Spézia (408 B4) or Portovenere.

CITTÀ DEL VATICANO – *see Vatican City on p.445*

CIVIDALE DEL FRIULI (408 C5)
FRIULI-VENEZIA GIULIA *pop. 9,000*
Founded by Julius Caesar, Cividale del Friuli is one of the few places in Italy to

ITALY

still show the legacy of the Lombards, a Teutonic tribe that swept into Italy after the fall of the Roman Empire. The carved stucco arch on the Tempietto Lombardo is a fine example of Lombard art. The 15th-century cathedral contains other examples.

▲ COMO (408 B5)
LOMBARDIA *pop. 85,700*
Como is at the extreme southern end of Lake Como, its green banks providing an appealing contrast to the distant snow-capped mountain range.

DUOMO is a splendid Gothic-Renaissance marble cathedral. The façade was decorated by the Rodari brothers; fine tapestries hang inside.

CORTONA (408 C4)
TUSCANY *pop. 3,200*
Cortona sits on Monte Egidio, and the views from its ramparts are among the best in Tuscany. In addition to its crumbling Duomo, churches include 13th-century Sant'Agostino; 14th-century San Nicolò, with an altarpiece by Luca Signorelli, who was born here; and the Renaissance Santa Mariadel Calcinaio. Renaissance art is on display in the Museo Diocesano, and Etruscan artifacts at the Palazzo Casali.

▲ CREMONA (408 B5)
LOMBARDIA *pop. 72,900*
This quiet, agricultural town, noted for its medieval appearance, was where Antonio Stradivari and other noted violin-makers perfected their art during the 16th to 18th centuries. Claudio Monteverdi, whose *Orfeo* is considered to have laid the groundwork for modern opera, was born in Cremona, and there is a musical college named after him.

MUSEO CIVICO (Civic Museum), Via Ugolani, is in the late-Renaissance Palazzo Affaitati. The museum houses Roman remains, as well as violins, and paintings by the 16th-century Cremona School of artists.

MUSEO STRADIVARIANO (Stradivarius Museum), Via Palestro 17, exhibits more than 700 examples of violin, plans, models, molds and tools belonging to violin-maker Antonio Stradivari.

PIAZZA DEL COMUNE (Town Square) is Cremona's magnificent medieval square, bordered on one side by the fine sculptured façade of the Duomo. The 13th-century Torrazzo, at 115 meters (377 feet) high, is one of the tallest towers in Italy. The octagonal Battistero (Baptistery), the Loggia dei Militi (Soldier's Loggia) and the Palazzo Comunale (Town Hall), containing violins by Stradivari and the Amati family, are also on the square.

ELBA (ÍSOLA D') (408 B3)
TOSCANA
Largest island of the Tuscan archipelago in the Tyrrhenian Sea, mountainous Elba can be reached by ferry from Piombino and Livorno. The island's highest point is 1,019-meter (3,343-foot) Monte Capanne, and its largest beach is Marina di Campo on the southern coast. Elba is best known as the island where Napoléon Bonaparte spent 10 months of exile in 1814–15.

PORTOFERRAIO is the main town of Elba. The Misericordia Church has a bronze reproduction of Napoléon Bonaparte's death mask. Napoléon's rooms at Palazzina dei Mulini, and his summer house, San Martino Villa, with fine views, can both be visited.

FAENZA (408 C4)
EMILIA-ROMAGNA *pop. 54,000*
Faenza, on the banks of the Lamone River, is famous for its faience, or majolica pottery. Faience masterpieces are on display at the Museo Internazionale delle Ceramiche, which details the history of ceramic pottery. The display includes pieces by Picasso and Chagall.

The Piazza della Libertà is dominated by the early Renaissance cathedral, with its unfinished façade.

▲ **FERRARA** (408 C4)
EMILIA-ROMAGNA *pop. 138,200*

An agricultural and industrial center on a broad plain, Ferrara still preserves a Renaissance atmosphere, recalling its heyday as the seat of the powerful Este family (1264–1598).

Great patrons of the arts, the Este imported Roger van der Weyden, Paolo Veronese and Pisanello to Ferrara, forming the basis for the Ferrara School of painting.

CASTELLO ESTENSE is the moated 14th-century castle of the Este family. The grim dungeons once held Parisina, wife of Duke Nicolò III, and her lover before they were executed.

DUOMO, the 12th-century cathedral, has a marble façade with a carved portal depicting the Last Judgement. Unusual 12th-century bas-reliefs, statues by Jacopo della Quercia and works by Cosimo Tura are in the museum.

PALAZZO DEI DIAMANTI is covered with blocks of marble faceted like diamonds. Ferraran paintings are displayed in the Pinacoteca Nazionale.

PALAZZO DI LUDOVICO IL MORO (Palace of Ludovico the Moor) houses an archaeological museum with Etruscan and Greek items.

PALAZZO SCHIFANOIA, Via Scandiana 23, built in the 15th century, was the summer palace of the Este. The frescoes in the Sala dei Mesi (Hall of Months) depict arcadian scenes.

▲ **FIRENZE** (408 B4) ★
TOSCANA *pop. 403,300*

Firenze, or Florence, was founded by Julius Caesar in 59 BC. In the 6th century it was conquered by the Lombards, who ruled the city for 200 years before it came under the control of the Holy Roman Empire. In 1115, Florence became an independent city-state.

The first period of Florentine art, with Romanesque church architecture, began between the 11th and 12th centuries. During the following century the townspeople were divided between the papal party (Guelphs) and the imperial party (Ghibellines) in a split that would last hundreds of years.

In 1252, the gold florin was first minted in Florence. This was the first coin to be used extensively for trading and banking, and formed the standard medium of exchange until the 16th century.

The early 15th century brought the beginning of the Renaissance. The powerful Medici family, bankers who became rulers, were enthusiastic patrons of the arts. Brunelleschi in architecture, Donatello in sculpture and Masaccio in painting all broke new ground in early 15th-century Florence. In the High Renaissance of the early 16th century, four of the greatest names in Italian art – Botticelli, Leonardo da Vinci, Raphael and Michelangelo – all worked here.

Few visitors leave Florence untouched by its beauty. One can stroll for hours just enjoying the scenery, window-shopping, pausing among the sellers of second-hand books and scrutinizing the open-air stalls that decorate the streets.

Events in Florence include Scoppio del Carro (Explosion of the Cart – fireworks) on Easter Sunday, a music festival in May and June, and the football games in 16th-century costume in late June to celebrate the feast day of St. John the Baptist.

Some 8 kilometers (5 miles) north is Fiesole, with spectacular views back over Florence. The 11th-century cathedral here has carvings by Mino da Fiesole, and the Teatro Romano, where classical plays are still performed, dates from 80 BC.

BATTISTERO (Baptistery) (430 C2), decorated in Romanesque style, was originally built in the 5th century. The 14th-century bronze doors are world-renowned, especially the East Doors, Lorenzo Ghiberti's "Gates of Paradise." These doors are replicas: the originals have been moved to the Museo dell'Opera del Duomo.

CHIESA DI SANTA CROCE (430 E1), on the southeast side of the old town, was built in the 14th century but with a 19th-century façade, contains fine monuments

and the tombs of Michelangelo, Niccolo Machiavelli, Galileo and many others; it also has frescoes by Giotto, and father and son Taddeo and Agnolo Gaddi.

CHIESA DI SAN LORENZO (430 C4) is one of the best expressions of Renaissance

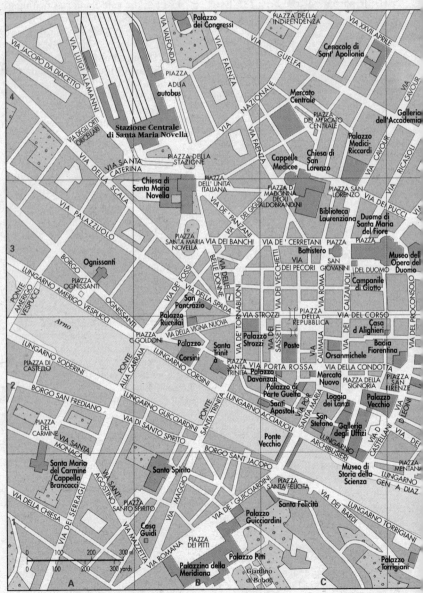

religious architecture. The interior by Filippo Brunelleschi is fine, but the main attraction is the Medici Chapel behind the church and the tombs there, sculpted by Michelangelo. He also designed the extraordinary Biblioteca Laurenziana containing several thousand manuscripts.

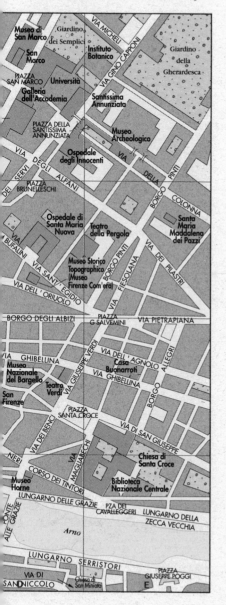

CHIESA DI SANTA MARIA DEL CARMINE (430 A1) is a must for the frescoes in its Brancacci Chapel. This cycle of paintings by Masaccio, depicting biblical scenes, was completed by Filippino Lippi after Masaccio's early death.

CHIESA DI SANTA MARIA NOVELLA (430 B3), which was begun in 1278, has some of Florence's greatest Renaissance paintings: Masaccio's innovative *Trinity*; Orcagna's altarpiece; and Ghirlandaio's charming frescoes of the lives of the Virgin and John the Baptist. Also worth seeing are the Cappella Strozzi, with frescoes by Filippino Lippi, and the cloisters with Uccello's *Noah's Flood*.

CHIESA DI SAN MINIATO is Florence's most impressive Romanesque church. The marble façade and superb interior are 11th century.

DUOMO DI SANTA MARIA DEL FIORE (430 C3), in the Gothic style, features Brunelleschi's vast dome, a miracle of early engineering. The 14th-century Campanile (bell-tower), to a design by Giotto, stands 80 meters (262 feet) high.

GALLERIA DELL'ACCADEMIA (430 D4), Via Ricasoli 60, has a fine collection of Michelangelo sculptures, including the original *David*. There is also a *Pietà*, and an incomplete *St. Matthew*.

GALLERIA DEGLI UFFIZI (430 C2), Piazzale degli Uffizi, houses one of the richest collections of masterpieces in the world. The gallery is in the Uffizi Palace, built in the 1560s. The collection was founded by the Medici family, and bequeathed to the city in 1737. As well as paintings by artists including Bellini, Titian and Canaletto, the gallery also houses sculpture, jewelry and early scientific instruments. Highlights include the *Annunciation* of Simone Martini, the *Birth of Venus* and *Primavera* in the Botticelli rooms, Leonardo da Vinci's *Annunciation*, Michelangelo's *Doni Tondo* and Titian's *Venus of Urbino*.

MUSEO NAZIONALE DEL BARGELLO (430 D2), Via del Proconsolo 4, holds a rich collection of Renaissance sculpture, with works by Brunelleschi, Cellini, Donatello, Giotto, Giambologna, Michelangelo, and Luca Della Robbia.

MICHELANGELO'S DAVID

The original of the world's most reproduced piece of sculpture, on display in the Galleria dell' Accademia (see p.431), is not seen as its creator intended – as a piece of public sculpture. For this, you should view the replica outside the Palazzo Vecchio. In the gallery, David's head, hands and arms clearly are out of proportion; the deliberate distortions give a monumental effect.

MUSEO DI SAN MARCO (430 D4), Piazza San Marco 2, housed in the Monastery of St. Mark, is a repository of works by Fra Angelico, who was a monk here (1436–7). Besides his frescoes *in situ* – including the wonderful *Annunciation* – there are works from other Florentine churches.

PALAZZO MEDICI-RICCARDI (430 C4), Via Cavour 1, was built for Cosimo the Elder by Michelozzo in 1444.

The chapel is the only surviving feature of the original design, with Gozzoli's *Journey of the Magi* fresco.

PALAZZO PITTI (430 B1), in 15th-century Renaissance style, houses six museums, of which the Galleria Palatine is the most important. Its noted collection of 11 Raphaels includes the *Madonna of the Chair* and the *Grand Duke's Madonna*, as well as works by Filippo Lippi, Titian, Fra Bartolommeo, Andrea del Sarto, Rubens, Tintoretto and Van Dyck.

PIAZZA DELLA SIGNORIA (430 C2) is dominated by the Palazzo Vecchio, built in the 14th century to house the *signoria*, Florence's ruling council. The nearby

Loggia della Signoria (or dei Lanzi) houses two famous sculptures: Cellini's *Perseus* and Giambologna's *Rape of the Sabines*.

PONTE VECCHIO (Old Bridge) (430 C2) dates from the 10th century. It is lined with jewelers' and silversmiths' shops.

FLORENCE – *see Firenze on p.429.*

GARGANO (409 D3)
PUGLIA
The wild, rocky peninsula of Gargano is the spur in Italy's boot. Religious sites include: Monte Sant' Angelo and San Marco. There are salt lakes at Lesina and Varano, and evidence of prehistoric man at Péschici. Vieste and Mattinata are popular beach resorts, and inland is the great Umbra Forest.

MONTE SANT' ANGELO, a site of Christian pilgrimage is perched on top of a limestone cliff. The unusual Sanctuary of St. Michael occupies the spot where the saint is said to have miraculously appeared to shepherds in a cave.

▲ GÉNOVA (408 B4)
LIGURIA *pop. 679,000*
Italy's leading seaport and chief commercial center, Génova (Genoa), is laid out along the seashore like an amphitheater. Medieval churches, 16th-century palaces and modern commercial streets justify the city's nickname of "La Superba" (The Proud).

GALLERIA DI PALAZZO BIANCO, Via Garibaldi 11, is Genoa's most important art gallery, with impressive works by Flemish, Dutch and local masters.

GALLERIA DI PALAZZO ROSSO, Via Garibaldi 18, displays tapestries, furniture and major works of art, including portraits by Anthony Van Dyck.

MUSEO DEL TESORO DI SAN LORENZO, in the cathedral of San Lorenzo, is a treasury of relics, including the *Sacro Catino*, believed to be the Holy Grail.

PALAZZO DUCALE (Ducal Palace), Piazza Matteotti, dating from the 13th century, was the palace of the Genoese Doges.

SAN AGOSTINO, Piazzo Sarzano, was built 1260–82. Badly damaged during World War II, it is now restored. Next to the church is the original triangular cloister, containing a sculpture museum.

GUBBIO (408 C4)
UMBRIA
Medieval Gubbio is renowned for its ancient festivals. Taking place on 15 May is The Feast of the Candles, in which three teams race uphill to the Abbey of St. Ubaldo carrying huge candle-shaped pillars; the Palio della Balestra, a crossbow tournament, is held on the last Sunday in May.

PALAZZO DEI CONSOLI, a massive Gothic building, dominates the town. In the museum here the Tavole Eugubine (Gubbio Tablets) are held – ancient bronze plaques bearing inscriptions in Etruscan, Umbrian and Latin.

HERCULANEUM – see Nápoli on p.435.

ISCHIA (ÍSOLA D') (408 C3)
CAMPANIA pop. 44,000
A volcanic island in the Bay of Naples, Ischia is rich in therapeutic mineral waters. It can be reached by boat or hydrofoil from Naples.

▲ LECCE (409 E2)
PUGLIA pop. 100,700
Lecce is remarkable for its many beautiful baroque buildings, notably the cathedral and the Basilica di Santa Croce. There are also the remains of a Roman theater and an amphitheater.

LORETO (408 C4)
MARCHE pop. 10,600
With 3 million visitors annually, Loreto is one of Italy's major pilgrimage sites.

SANTUARIO DELLA SANTA CASA is said to have been the Nazareth home of the Virgin Mary carried here in the 13th century by angels. The 15th-century façade of the church built around the house is particularly fine.

▲ LUCCA (408 B4)
TOSCANA pop. 85,900
Lucca is one of Tuscany's finest cities, boasting a cathedral, many historic buildings, and massive Renaissance walls with three gates intact. A Roman street grid survives within the ramparts.

CHIESA DI SAN MICHELE, dates from the 12th century and has a glorious façade with columned galleries. Inside are paintings by Filippo Lippi and Luca della Robbia.

DUOMO, the cathedral was founded in the 6th century and also has a tiered façade. It contains what is supposed to be a true effigy of Christ.

▲ MANTOVA (408 B5)
LOMBARDIA pop. 50,800
Mantova (Mantua), was the seat of Italy's Gonzaga family and their court from the 14th to 18th centuries. They built the immense Palazzo Ducale, which still contains some of their art collection.

CASTELLO DI SAN GIORGIO, facing the Ducal Palace, is a 14th-century Gonzaga fortress known for the Camera degli Sposi, a matrimonial room containing superb frescoes by Andrea Mantegna.

PALAZZO DELL TE is another Gonzaga palace, built around 1527. It contains many frescoed rooms, including the Sala dei Cavalli, adorned with paintings of royal horses and the extraordinary Sala dei Giganti (Room of the Giants).

▲ MATERA (409 D2)
BASILICATA pop. 55,800
Much of Matera's old quarter is built into the rock that forms the base of the hill supporting the 13th-century town cathedral. There are good views of the

caves and stone stairways of the old quarter and the desolate gorge below from the Strada Panoramica dei Sassi. Most of the houses here, known as *sassi*, are hewn from the rock.

MELFI (409 D3)
BASILICATA *pop. 13,900*

The Normans captured Melfi in 1041 and made it their first southern Italian capital. In 1059 Robert Guiscard was recognized by Pope Nicholas II as Duke of Apulia and Calabria in the eight-towered castle at the top of the town; today there is a museum of antiquities here. The cathedral was rebuilt after an earthquake, but its 12th-century campanile survived.

MERANO (408 B5)
TRENTINO-ALTO ADIGE *pop. 33,800*

Merano is a major health and vacation resort at the foot of the Val Venosta. It has a mild climate and its medicinal waters have been lauded since the 4th century BC.

▲ MILANO (408 B5)
LOMBARDIA *pop. 1,370,000*

Capital of high fashion and finance, Milano (Milan) is Italy's leading commercial and industrial center. Thoroughly modern in appearance, the city is also a storehouse of artistic treasures, its greatest being Leonardo da Vinci's *Last Supper*.

Milan came to prominence in the 4th century, and was destroyed by Frederick Barbarossa in the 12th century. Rebuilt, the city came under the influence of the wealthy Viscontis in the 14th century, and later the powerful Sforzas. Claimed by Spain in 1535, it was assigned to Austria in 1713, and finally became part of the Kingdom of Italy in 1859.

CASTELLO SFORZESCO, Piazza Castello, a 15th-century palace, houses the unfinished *Pietà Rondanini* by Michelangelo, and medieval and Renaissance collections in the Museo d'Arte Antica.

The art gallery includes works by Bellini, Correggio and Tintoretto; there are also collections of decorative arts and musical instruments.

DUOMO is the largest Gothic cathedral in Italy, its spire topped by the golden *Madonnina*, 108 meters (354 feet) above the ground. The exterior is adorned with 2,000 marble statues and 135 spires. A museum in the nearby Palazzo Reale houses statues, sketches and relics.

MUSEO POLDI PEZZOLI, Via Manzoni 12, is a small palace with displays of paintings, jewelry, arms and clocks.

PINACOTECA AMBROSIANA, Piazza Pio XI 2, has an outstanding collection of paintings dating from the 14th century. Of particular interest are a still-life by Caravaggio and works by Raphael and Leonardo da Vinci.

PINACOTECA DI BRERA, Via Brera 28, one of Italy's most important art gal-

---

SHOPPING IN MILAN

Milan is Italy's capital of design and high fashion, and is *the* place to shop for quality clothes, accessories and luxury goods.
The "Quadrilatero d'Oro" (Golden Quadrilateral), the area defined by Via Monte Napoleone, Via della Spiga, Via Borgo Spesso and Via Sant'Andrea, contains the top designer shops. For shopping – or simply strolling – in elegant surroundings, visit the 19th-century Galleria Vittorio Emanuele.

---

leries, contains such masterpieces as Andrea Mantegna's *Dead Christ* and a magnificent *Pietà* by Giovanni Bellini.

SANTA MARIA DELLE GRAZIE, a 15th-century Renaissance church, houses one of the world's most famous works of religious art, the *Last Supper* by Leonardo da Vinci, on the refectory wall.

TEATRO ALLA SCALA is one of the best-known opera houses in the world. Built in 1776, its acoustics are considered by many to be perfect. Statues of Bellini, Donizetti, Rossini and Verdi grace the foyer. The Museo Teatrale next door tells the history of the theater.

▲ MÓDENA (408 B4)
EMILIA-ROMAGNA *pop. 174,700*
Formerly the capital of the great Duchy of Este, Módena has an attractive core of old arcaded streets and large squares.

DUOMO is a Romanesque masterpiece dedicated to St. Geminian, Módena's patron saint. The sculptured decoration, including the bas-relief doorways and rood screen, dates from the 13th century.

MONTEPULCIANO (408 C4)
TOSCANA *pop. 14,400*
This small medieval town has an impressive array of *palazzi*, three of which border its main square, Piazza Grande. The unfinished façade of the Duomo commands the square's fourth side, with interior statues by Michelozzo di Bartolomeo. Palazzo Comunale, the town hall, is a large 14th-century building with fine views from the tower. The Church of San Biagio, to the west of the town, is one of Italy's finest Renaissance churches.

▲ NÁPOLI (408 C3) ★
CAMPANIA *pop. 1,067,000*
Nápoli, or Naples lies on the enchanting Bay of Naples, overshadowed by the cone of Mount Vesuvius. The city is the commercial, cultural and artistic center of southern Italy, and an important port on the Mediterranean.

CERTOSA DI SAN MARTINO, a former Carthusian monastery in the Neapolitan baroque style, is now a museum.

DUOMO SAN GENNARO, Via del Duomo, contains the treasure of the patron saint of Naples and fragments of a what was a 4th-century basilica.

ERCOLANO (Herculaneum), lying 7 kilometers (4½ miles) southeast of Naples, was buried by mud when Vesuvius erupted in AD 79. Though smaller than Pompeii, it is better preserved, some buildings standing two stories high. Of note are the houses of Deer, Telephus and Samnite, and the temples of Diana, Mercury and Venus.

MOUNT VESUVIUS is 1,277 meters (4,190 feet) high and still an active volcano. Eruptions have occurred since AD 79 (when Pompeii and Herculaneum were destroyed), most recently in 1944. Visitors can climb to the rim of the crater.

MUSEU ARCHEOLOGICO NAZIONALE contains the best finds from Pompeii and Herculaneum. There are wall paintings and mosaics from these and other Campanian sites on the upper floor. The *Battle of Issus, Alexander the Great's famous battle*, mosaic is particularly fine.
PALAZZO REALE DI CAPODIMONTE, to the north of the city, is a former royal palace.

THE GENUINE PIZZA
Pizza originated in Naples in the 18th century, and only one cooked in a wood-fired brick oven can claim to be genuine. Traditional toppings include tomatoes, mozzarella and fresh basil, in the colors of the Italian flag and created in honor of Queen Margherita.

It houses the National Gallery, an outstanding collection with over 500 works.

POMPEII (408 D3) is at the foot of Mount Vesuvius, whose eruption buried it in volcanic ash in AD 79. Excavations have revealed life in this city as it was nearly 2,000 years ago.

Look for the Antiquarium, Forum, Stabian Baths, Casa dei Vettii and Villa of the Mysteries. Ornamental mural designs representing four different periods retain brilliant colors.

TEATRO SAN CARLO, Via Vittorio Emanuele III, was built in 1737 and is a grand opera house.

ORVIETO (408 C3)
UMBRIA *pop. 21,500*
This hill town has preserved its medieval appearance; the renowned Orvieto wine is produced here.

DUOMO, started in the 13th century, is one of Italy's finest Gothic cathedrals. Its façade is adorned with mosaics, carved stonework and statuary; inside is Luca Signorelli's *Last Judgement*.

POZZO DI SAN PATRIZIO (St. Patrick's Well) was dug in 1537 by order of Pope Clement VII de Medici, to supply the town with water in case of siege.

▲ PADOVA (408 C5)
VENETO *pop. 212,900*
According to legend, Padova (Padua), was founded by Antenore, a Trojan prince; under the Romans, it became one of the Empire's richest cities. Destroyed by the Lombards in AD 602, it flourished again as a Venetian territory during the Middle Ages. Today it is a busy, sprawling city, much rebuilt after World War II bomb damage.

BASILICA DI SANT' ANTONIO is a fine 13th-century Roman-Gothic building with Byzantine cupolas. Relics of St. Anthony, who is buried here, are displayed in the treasury chapel; bronze reliefs by Donatello embellish the high altar.

CAPPELLA DEGLI SCROVEGNI, Corso Garibaldi, houses one of Italy's great fresco cycles, Giotto's 38 scenes from the lives of Christ and the Virgin Mary, painted in 1303–9.

GATTAMELATA, Piazza del Santo, is a fine bronze equestrian statue (1453) by Donatello of Erasmo da Narni, the great Venetian *condottiere* whose nickname was "Gattamelata" (spotted cat).

MUSEO CIVICO (Civic Museum), Piazza Eremitani, is housed in the restored Monastery of Eremitani. A varied collection of archaeological items, sculptures, coins and paintings is displayed.

PALAZZO DELLA RAGIONE, near the Piazza delle Frutta, is the vast 13th-century law court. In the attic salon are 15th-century frescoes and the Stone of Dishonor.

PAESTUM (408 D2)
CAMPANIA *pop. 900*
Paestum was once the ancient Greek city of Poseidonia. All that remains is a handful of well-preserved temples: the Temple of Neptune, the Basilica and the Temple of Ceres. The museum contains architectural fragments, sculpture and tomb paintings.

▲ PARMA (408 B4)
EMILIA-ROMAGNA *pop. 169,400*
Parma, a busy commercial and agricultural center, is said to enjoy the highest standard of living in Italy. It is notable for the numerous monuments and art collections that recall its past as capital of the Duchy of Farnese.

Correggio was born just east of Parma, and left notable frescoes in the cathedral, the Church of San Giovanni Evangelista, and the Camera di San Paolo. The composer Verdi was born here, and the conductor Arturo Toscanini.

BATTISTERO is a 12th-century octagonal baptistery built of Veronese pink marble. Benedetto Antelami's Romanesque sculptures are particularly expressive.

DUOMO is a superb Romanesque cathedral containing Correggio's great fresco *The Assumption*. The sculptured episcopal throne and *Deposition* bas-relief are by Benedetto Antelami.

PALAZZO DELLA PILOTTA houses the National Gallery, displaying paintings by Correggio and his pupil Parmigianini. Other artists represented are El Greco,

Leonardo da Vinci, Holbein, Giovanni Battista Tiepolo and Van Dyck. Also within the palace are the Teatro Farnese (an important 17th-century Italian theater), the Palatine Library and the Bodoni Museum.

▲ PAVIA (408 B5)
LOMBARDIA pop. 75,600

Pavia, a former Lombard capital, had a stirring history before it came under the aegis of the Visconti and Sforza families of Milan. It is now a fascinating old town of medieval streets and buildings.

CERTOSA DI PAVIA, a 1376 Carthusian monastery 10 kilometers (6 miles) north of Pavia, is a masterpiece of Renaissance art. The façade of the monastery is decorated with marble slabs and delicate sculptures. Painted portraits of monks peer down from the first chapel.

SAN MICHELE is a 12th-century coronation church with a majestic façade of rich ornaments and figural reliefs in a series of bands, surmounted by a gabled gallery. Medieval emperors were crowned here.

SAN PIETRO IN CIEL D'ORO, built in 1132, holds relics of St. Augustine and the tomb of the philosopher Boethius.

▲ PERÚGIA (408 C4)
UMBRIA pop. 149,000

Capital of its region, Perúgia held strategic importance for the Etruscans and Romans. It has early fortifications, including the remains of two Etruscan gates. Events include the Umbria Jazz Festival (July) and the Umbria Sacred Music Festival (September).

COLLEGIO DEL CAMBIO, Corso Vannucci 25, is the old 15th-century stock exchange building. Frescoes by Perugino, teacher of Raphael, and his pupils adorn the council chamber.

DUOMO, Piazza Dante, was built in the Gothic style 1345–1490, but the interior is baroque. The wrought-iron grilles are of interest, and a chapel is reputed to contain the Virgin Mary's wedding ring.

FONTANA MAGGIORE, Piazza IV Novembre, is an ornate fountain dating from 1278. Sculptures are by Nicola Pisano and his son, Giovanni.

GALLERIA NAZIONALE DELL' UMBRIA, Palazzo dei Priori, exhibits Umbrian and Tuscan masterpieces.

ORATORIO DI SAN BERNARDINO, Via dei Priori, is a fine Renaissance-style church in marble built in 1461. Scenes from the life of the saint and figures of angel musicians decorate the façade.

PALAZZO DEI PRIORI (Sala dei Notari), Piazza IV Novembre, is a grandiose palace dating from the 13th century. The great staircase leads to a marble pulpit from which the priors addressed the township.

SAN PIETRO, Corso Cavour, has been rebuilt several times since its original construction in the 10th century.
It is a graceful church with an unusual bell tower; the 16th-century stalls display carvings of the saints and Renaissance ornamentation.

▲ PÉSARO (408 C4)
MARCHE pop. 87,700

The beach resort of Pésaro is best known for its summertime Rossini music festival and for ceramics. Pésaro was the home of composer Gioacchino Rossini, and his house is open to visitors. The town's principal building is the 16th-century Palazzo Ducale; the main art treasure is Bellini's *Coronation of the Virgin* in the Museo Civico.

▲ PIACENZA (408 B5)
EMILIA-ROMAGNA pop. 101,000

Founded by the Romans in 219 BC to defend the banks of the Po River, Piacenza was ruled in turn by northern Italy's leading families. Peace came

ITALY

during the Renaissance under the Farnese. Visitors can still see the Farnese Palace, an impressive 16th-century structure that now houses the Museo Civico.

Among the town's other attractions are the 12th-century Lombard-Romanesque cathedral with baroque frescoes by Barbieri Guercino, the 13th-century town hall in Lombard style, and the two splendid equestrian statues in Piazza dei Cavalli.

▲ PISA (408 B4) ★
TOSCANA *pop. 95,400*
Pisa is one of the finest towns in Italy, a veritable storehouse of famous buildings. Major sights form the Campo dei Miracoli (Field of Miracles); the Piazza dei Cavalieri is also interesting for its 16th- and 17th-century architecture. The Gioco del Ponte, a medieval parade, is held on the last Sunday in June.

BATTISTERO (1278), a massive circular baptistery with an intriguing pulpit by Nicola Pisano, is known for its unusual echo-making qualities.

CAMPANILE, or Torre Pendente, the "Leaning Tower of Pisa," was begun in 1173 as a bell-tower for the cathedral. The white marble tower is 55 meters (180 feet) tall, and has leaned ever since it was built. The tower became too dangerous and was closed to visitors in 1990; efforts are being made to stabilize it.

DUOMO, opposite the "Leaning Tower," is an enormous marble cathedral in Romanesque-Pisan style. The bronze door panels by Bonnano Pisano (about 1180) depict the life of Christ. The pulpit is the work of Giovanni Pisano.

MUSEO NAZIONALE, in the 15th-century Monastery of St. Matthew, contains medieval sculptures and painting.

MUSEO DELL' OPERA DEL DUOMO contains sculpture, paintings and church vestments from the cathedral and baptistery.

SANTA MARIA DELLA SPINA (St. Mary of the Thorn) is in Roman-Gothic style. The outer ornamentation illustrates the Pisan School of art.

▲ PISTOIA (408 B4)
TOSCANA *pop. 90,000*
This provincial capital has a superb medieval center, its many buildings including the Church of Sant'Andrea, with a fine sculptured pulpit; the Palazzo Pretorio; the Hospital del Ceppo, known for its terracotta frieze by Giovanni della Robbia; and the church of San Bartolomeo in Pantano.

The cathedral of San Zeno is one of the most impressive buildings of all, combining Romanesque and baroque architecture. The Gothic Palazzo del Comune is also impressive; inside is the Museo Civico, displaying local paintings, sculptures and artifacts.

POMPEII – *see Nápoli on p.435.*

PORTOFINO (408 B4)
LIGURIA *pop. 600*
Sheltered below Monte Portofino, this pretty, colorful seaside town has become a popular (and expensive) gathering place for the rich and famous.

POSITANO (408 D2)
CAMPANIA *pop. 2,600*
Delightful Positano, with its pink and white villas, has become one of the most exclusive resorts on the Amaffi coast.

RAPALLO (408 B4)
LIGURIA *pop. 29,700*
One of the best-known and most attractive resorts on the Italian Riviera, Rapallo is popular all year round.

Several medieval monuments are preserved, including the castle (used for exhibitions), and a convent, which is now a theater.

RAVELLO (408 D2)
CAMPANIA *pop. 2,400*
Picturesque Ravello, some 350 meters (1,148 feet) above Amalfi, affords a mag-

nificent view of the Amalfi coast.

The romantic Villa Cimbrone, with its lush gardens, as well as the ancient cathedral, are both of interest.

VILLA RUFOLO, built in the 11th century, inspired Richard Wagner to compose his opera *Parsifal*. Its lovely gardens are the setting for a Wagner festival, which takes place each summer.

RAVENNA (408 C4) ★
EMILIA-ROMAGNA *pop. 137,000*
Briefly the capital of the Western Roman Empire, then capital of the Byzantine exarchate of Ravenna from the 6th to the 8th centuries, the city is famous for its glorious mosaics of the Byzantine era.

Among its many other attractions are the Archepiscopal Chapel in the Museum of the Archbishop's Palace and the Basilica of St. Apollinare at Classe, 4 kilometers (2½ miles) away.

BATTISTERO DEGLI ORTODOSSI, known as the Neonian Baptistery, has some of Ravenna's oldest mosaics and was a Roman bathhouse before becoming a church in the 5th century.

MAUSOLEO DI GALLA PLACIDIA, Via Fiandrini, built in the 5th century, is noted for its wonderfully rich blue-and-gold mosaics.

SANT'APOLLINARE NUOVO, a 6th-century church, is known for its procession of mosaic saints and martyrs along the wall of the nave on the men's side of the building. On the wall of the women's side is a procession of 22 virgins led by the Magi.

SAN VITALE, an octagonal church built in 546, is spectacularly decorated with brightly colored mosaics of blue, green and gold, including depictions of the Byzantine emperor Justinian, his wife Theodora and their court.

Adjoining the monastery is the Museo Nazionale, housing an interesting array of antiquities.

▲ RÉGGIO DI CALÁBRIA (409 D1)
CALÁBRIA *pop. 179,000*
MUSEO NAZIONALE, Piazza de Nava, is Réggio's only noteworthy attraction. It contains terracotta sculptures, votive tablets and paintings by Antonello da Messina; its highlight is the Bronzi di Riaca, two 5th-century BC bronze figures recovered from the sea off Réggio.

▲ RÍMINI (408 C4)
EMILIA-ROMAGNA *pop. 130,000*
Rímini is a large, brash seaside resort well known for its excellent beach. The city also contains Roman ruins and Renaissance works of art. It was here that Julius Caesar defied the Roman senate by marching across the Rubicon and on to Rome.

ARCO D'AUGUSTO (Arch of Augustus), was built in 27 BC to commemorate the building of the Via Flaminia.

PONTE DI TIBERIO (Bridge of Tiberius), also known as the Bridge of Augustus, spans the Marecchia River at the end of Corso d'Augusto. Made of Istrian travertine, the 63-meter (207-foot) bridge has five arches. Completed in AD 20, the bridge remains in use today.

TEMPIO MALATESTIANO, was erected by Sigismondo Malatesta, who ruled Rímini in the 15th century. The temple features frescoes by Piero della Francesca and a painted cross thought to be the work of Giotto.

ROMA (ROME) – *see p.411*.

▲ SALERNO (408 D2)
CAMPANIA *pop. 145,000*
Salerno, a busy port with an interesting medieval core, was the scene of the 1943 Allied landing during World War II.

SAN GIMIGNIANO (408 B4)
TOSCANA *pop. 7,000*
High on a hilltop, San Giminiano is one of the best-preserved medieval towns in Italy. The walled city once had 72 tow-

ITALY

ers, 14 of which are still standing. You can climb the Torre Grossa in Piazza del Popolo.

COLLEGIATA, the cathedral, contains frescoes by early Renaissance artists. Best of all are those by Domenico Ghirlandaio in the Santa Fina chapel.

VIA SAN MATTEO is a charming, narrow medieval street lined with ancient houses. It leads to the fine Romanesque church of Sant'Agostino, which is decorated with frescoes by Benozzo Gozzoli.

SARDEGNA (408 B2)

Sardegna (Sardinia), is enjoying increased popularity among travelers, who have discovered the island's distinct and colorful culture. Largely mountainous, Sardinia also offers attractive beaches, coves and grottoes, and sophisticated resorts on the Costa Smeralda.

The prehistoric inhabitants of Sardinia left relics of a unique and mysterious culture: tiny rock-cut tombs; "giants' tombs," characterized by huge, stone slabs; and *nuraghi*, curious stone fortresses and towers. Later came the Phoenicians, Carthaginians, Romans, Vandals, Byzantines and Arabs. The Spanish ruled Sardinia from 1479 to 1720, when the Piedmont dukes of Savoy gained control.

ALGHERO (408 A2), is a busy seaside resort and fishing village. Its Catalan heritage is reflected in many buildings, churches, fortifications and cultural events. There are prehistoric sites, grottoes and caves nearby, notably Neptune's Grotto at Capo Caccia.

▲ CÁGLIARI (408 B2) is the large capital and chief seaport of Sardinia. The city dates back to Phoenician times and there are the remains of a Roman amphitheater. The Duomo, on the Piazza Palazzo, was built in the 12th century, but was given a baroque interior in the 17th century and a mock-Romanesque façade in 1933.

The Museo Archeologico Nazionale houses both an archaeological museum and a picture gallery. Particularly interesting are the bronze statuettes from the Nuraghic civilization.

COSTA SMERALDA (408 B3) (Emerald Coast), the picturesque coast of northeastern Sardinia, was developed by the Aga Khan in the 1960s. A mecca for the jet set, it is ideal for watersports.

▲ NUORO (408 B2), stands near the foot of Mount Ortobene. Atop the 955 meter (3,133 feet) peak is a statue of Christ the Redeemer, the goal of a procession on the Feast of the Redeemer on August 29. Sardinia's foremost folk museum, the Museo Etnografico, is located here.

OLBIA (408 B3), is an ancient city, founded by the Carthaginians and once under Roman rule. Although this port is a major gateway to Sardinia, there is little to see beyond the Romanesque cathedral of San Simplicio, center for Olbia's main festival in mid-May.

▲ SASSARI (408 A3), though a modern town, has a medieval center and some fine relics of the past. Among them is the Duomo, with its baroque façade. Look also for the ornate Fonte del Rosello, a late-Renaissance fountain, and the 18th-century Ducal Palace, now the town hall. The Museo Sanna, in the modern town, is an archaeological museum.

SICILIA (408 C1-D1) ★

Sicilia, or Sicily, one of the most beautiful islands in the Mediterranean, is also the largest. It was part of Magna Graecia, the ancient Greek Empire, from about 800 to 300 BC. After suffering the rule of Romans, Arabs, Normans, the French and the Spanish, Sicily gained a degree of autonomy in 1947, having its own Assembly in Palermo.

Sicily has vast stretches of beautiful scenery, from volcanic Mount Etna to sandy beaches (though parts of the coast have been spoiled by industrial development). Some of the islands off Sicily still offer peaceful, unspoiled retreats.

Sicily has a rich archaeological store: Greek temples and theaters, Roman mosaics, paleolithic cave art and rock-cut tombs of the Bronze Age period. The later architectural heritage is also rich, with Norman churches, Swabian castles and some superb baroque buildings.

▲ AGRIGENTO (408 C1), founded by the Greeks as Akragas in 581 BC, has, in its Valley of Temples, one of Europe's great archaeological sites: the Greek Tempio della Concordia (Temple of Concord). The base and 34 columns are visible from a considerable distance. There are four other temples on the site. About a kilometer (½ mile) away is the Museo Archeologico Regionale (Archaeological Museum), containing a fine collection of artifacts recovered in this area.

▲ CATÁNIA (408 D1), Sicily's second city, stands at the southern foot of Mount Etna, which has destroyed it several

Mount Etna is Europe's tallest and most active volcano; it experienced its tenth major eruption of the century in December 1991. It is possible to visit the summit during less active periods. The area is a designated National Park.

▲ ENNA (408 D1), perched on a crag at 915 meters (3,001 feet), has a genial climate, even in summer. The Citadel, or Castello de Lombardia, is a medieval fortress with mighty ramparts and six towers, the tallest of which provides an excellent viewpoint. The 14th-century Duomo has its own museum, the Museo Alessi.

▲ MESSINA (409 D1), is the gateway to Sicily, and there are regular passenger- and car-ferry services from the Italian mainland. The city is completely modern, having been destroyed by an earthquake in 1908. The reconstructed cathedral has a large astronomical clock in the campanile – it chimes at noon, with a delightful array of moving figures. The Museo Regionale has two paintings by Caravaggio, and other notable works from the 13th to 16th centuries.

NOTO (409 D1), is one of the gems of Sicily, a town completely rebuilt in baroque style after the earthquake of 1693.

▲ PALERMO (408 C1), is the capital, largest city and principal port of Sicily. Although poverty and neglect make parts of Palermo uninviting, the city's location and varied architecture do much to compensate for this. Several splendid buildings date from the time of Roger, King of Sicily, who first united the Greek, Arabic and Norman influences of southern Italy in the 12th century.

Capella Palatina (Palatine Chapel), Palermo's jewel, is part of the Palace of the Normans, now the Sicilian Parliament building. Built by Roger II in 1132, it has lavish Arab-Norman decoration.

The Cattedrale was consecrated in 1185. Its 18th-century interior is dull,

---

THE SICILIAN MAFIA

Sicily's history of foreign domination and the consequent distrust of and isolation from the rest of the country provided a fertile soil for a form of local – and lawless – authority. Before World War II Mussolini tried ruthlessly to eradicate the Mafia. It was the Allies who revived the organization, enlisting Mafia help in the invasion of Sicily and afterwards giving control of towns to men with Mafia connections.

---

times. Catánia's streets and attractive buildings date from the reconstruction following the major earthquake of 1693. Castello Ursino (1287) now houses the Civic Museum.

The Duomo, originally Norman, was remodeled in baroque style. The church of San Nicolò is Sicily's largest.

but contains Norman royal tombs and a rich treasury.

Chiesa della Martorana, Piazza Bellini, was built in 1143. The original church, now bearing a 17th-century façade, contains some fine Byzantine mosaics.

Chiesa di San Giovanni degli Eremiti (Church of St. John of the Hermits), entirely Arabic in appearance, was built in 1132. A peaceful garden with 13th-century cloisters adjoins the church.

Duomo in Monreale (Cathedral in Monreale) 8 kilometers (5 miles) south, is an outstanding Norman cathedral. Magnificent 12th-century mosaics depict Christ enthroned, and biblical events. The decoration of the adjoining cloisters reinforces the Moorish style.

Museo Archeologico Nazionale, in a 16th-century monastery at Piazza Olivella, contains an important collection of Sicilian artifacts including prehistoric cave paintings.

PIAZZA ARMERINA (408 D1), near Enna, contains monuments of the Norman and Aragonese periods, as well as baroque churches and palaces. A baroque 17th century cathedral can be seen at the highest point in the city.

However, most visitors come to see the Imperial Roman Villa at Casale, 6 kilometers (3½ miles) southwest of the city. The ruins, which date from the 4th century, include columned courtyards, baths and personal apartments. Most spectacular, however, are the mosaics.

SEGESTA, an ancient town in western Sicily, is the site of a 5th-century BC temple and a Hellenistic theater.

SELINUNTE (408 C1), south of Segesta, was a flourishing Greek city in the 5th century BC. Destroyed by Carthaginians in the 4th century BC, the city was later inhabited by Arabs and Byzantines.

Earthquakes worked the final destruction. The ruins of eight Doric temples were found in the sacred precinct; two have been reconstructed, with others in progress.

▲ SIRACUSA (409 D1) (Syracuse), was the bulwark of Greek civiliszation in the 4th century BC and the rival of Athens, Carthage and Rome.

Città Vechia (Old City), its narrow streets lined with medieval and baroque buildings, spreads over the island of Ortygia, first settled in 734 BC. The Duomo dates from the 7th-century but incorporates in its structure columns from the 5th-century BC Temple of Athena that first occupied the site. The Fonte Aretusa is a freshwater spring on a waterfront terrace. The Museo Regionale d'Arte Medioevale e Moderna (Regional Museum of Medieval and Modern Art), situated in the Palazzo Bellomo, contains a fine collection of paintings.

Parco Archeologico della Neapoli, along the northern edge of the city, contains both Greek and Roman ruins. The Roman amphitheater dates from the 2nd century; the Catacombe di San Giovanni includes the crypt of San Marziano, which was part of the island's first cathedral; and the Latomia del Paradiso, the "Paradise Quarry," is noted for an echo in the grotto called the "Ear of Dionysius".

The 15,000-seat Teatro Greco (Greek Theater), cut out of the rock, is remarkable and classical drama is still presented here. A particularly fine collection of archaeological artifacts is displayed at the purpose-built Museo Nuevo Archeologico, east of the Parco.

TAORMINA (409 D1), is Sicily's most popular resort. Above the town is a Greek theater, remodeled by the Romans.

▲ SIENA (408 B4) ★
TOSCANA *pop. 55,000*

Siena is fascinating both for its medieval atmosphere, and for the number and richness of its artistic possessions. The city flourished in the 12th and 13th centuries, when it became a major centre of trade in Europe. Twice a year Siena holds its Palio, a historic pageant and horse race (see box opposite).

DUOMO is a masterpiece of Italian Romanesque-Gothic architecture striped in black and white marble. The campanile dates from the late 13th century. Off the left aisle the Liberia Piccolomini, built during the late 15th century, contains frescoes and portraits by Pinturicchio. Behind the cathedral stands the baptistery, with a 16th-century Gothic façade.

MUSEO DELL'OPERA METROPOLITANA houses paintings and sculptures, including the *Maestà* by Duccio di Buonisegna.

PALAZZO PUBBLICO (Town Hall), on the Piazza del Campo, is an elegant Gothic structure. It houses the Museo Civico with frescoes by Martini, Lorenzetti and

---

THE PALIO

The most famous horse race in Italy is held twice a year, on July 2 and August 16. Siena's Palio has existed since the Middle Ages and is an expression of the rivalry between the city's 17 *contrade,* or districts, which command total allegiance from their inhabitants. Ten *contrade* are selected by lot to take part, and thereafter the competitiveness increases up to the day of the race, with parades and pageantry during the preceding days. The bareback race around the Campo lasts barely 90 seconds.

---

other pre-Renaissance artists. The Torre del Mangia (tower), is next to the palace.

PINACOTECA NAZIONALE, Via San Pietro 29, has the city's largest collection of Sienese art.

SORRENTO (408 D2)
CAMPANIA *pop. 17,500*
Sorrento stands amid lemon groves on a natural terrace above the Bay of Naples. The beauty of this popular holiday resort has drawn visitors for centuries. The

Museo Correale, in a former palace, contains local crafts and archaeological finds.

SPOLETO (408 C3)
UMBRIA *pop. 38,000*
Spoleto's history goes back more than 2,500 years, and much of its past has left visible traces. Most important are the ruins of the Roman theater and amphitheater; the Museo Archeologico, and the Ponte delle Torri, a 14th-century aqueduct.

From mid-June to mid-July the town hosts the Festival dei Due Mondi (Festival of Two Worlds), an annual celebration of music, dance and theater.

DUOMO, at one end of the long Piazza del Duomo, was rebuilt in 1175. A fine mosaic dominates the 13th-century façade. Inside are frescoes by Filippo Lippi, who is buried in the cathedral.

SUBIACO (408 C3)
LAZIO *pop. 6,800*
In the 5th century, St. Benedict retired to a cave here to write his *Rule*, the foundation on which much of western monasticism is based. Of the 12 monasteries founded nearby, two survive, including the Convento di San Benedetto which incorporates the cave.

▲ TÁRANTO (409 E2)
PUGLIA *pop. 213,300*
A Spartan colony in the 8th century BC, Táranto is now a large industrial port and naval base. The Città Vecchia (Old Town), with its castle, cathedral and lively fish market, is on a central island.

MUSEO NAZIONALE, Corso Umberto 1, is found in the New Town and contains a wealth of material on the art and civilization of Magna Graecia.

TIVOLI (408 C3)
LAZIO *pop. 52,000*
Set on a high hilltop, Tivoli was important in Roman times for its travertine marble, from which much of imperial Rome was built. The town was also a popular retreat from the city.

VILLA ADRIANA (Hadrian's Villa), 7 kilometers (4½ miles) south, was the largest and richest of the Roman villas. In the beautiful gardens, the colonnaded Teatro Marittimo stands in a lagoon.

VILLA D'ESTE, on the site of a Benedictine monastery, was redesigned as a retreat for Cardinal Ippolito d'Este in 1549. The formal gardens are the principal attraction today.

TODI (408 C3)
UMBRIA *pop. 6,200*
Todi's three concentric sets of town walls are respectively Etruscan, Roman and medieval. The central Piazza del Popolo is a medieval showpiece ringed with elegant palaces and a Romanesque cathedral. Near the public gardens is Santa Maria della Consolazione which is considered to be one of Italy's finest Renaissance churches.

▲ TORINO (408 A5)
PIEMONTE *pop. 962,500*
Torino (Turin), rose to importance after the Savoy dukes made it their capital in 1574. The Savoy rulers – who took the title of Kings of Piedmont in the 18th century – were to become the royal family of Italy after unification. Today it is an attractive, modern city, and also home to some of Italy's largest manufacturers, including the Fiat and Lancia factories.

DUOMO SAN GIOVANNI, a Renaissance cathedral, houses the controversial *Turin Shroud*, a cloth believed to be imprinted with the image of the crucified Christ. A replica is displayed.

MUSEO DELL' AUTOMOBILE CARLO BISCARETTI DI RUFFIA, south of town at *Corso Unità d'Italia 40*, displays an outstanding collection of over 400 automobiles, including early Fiats.

PALAZZO DELL' ACCADEMIA DELLE SCIENZE is just off the Piazza San Carlo. The huge 17th-century palace contains two excellent museums. Galleria Sabauda is particularly well endowed with paintings by Flemish and Dutch masters. The Collezione Gualino is an outstanding collection of 15th- to 16th-century Florentine furniture, paintings and sculptures. Museo Egizio contains an important collection of ancient Egyptian art. A complete funerary chamber, effigies of Rameses II and a host of everyday objects is displayed.

PALAZZO MADAMA, Piazza Castello, houses the Museo Civico dell' Arte, with its varied collection of decorative art. In addition, there are furnished 18th-century rooms, a Venetian state barge used by the kings of Sicily, fabrics, ivories, porcelain and stained glass.

PALAZZO REALE, Piazza Castello, was the residence of the Savoy princes until 1865. It has lavishly decorated state apartments and displays of arms and armor. The peaceful Giardino Reale (Royal Garden) lies behind the palace.

▲ TRENTO (408 B5)
TRENTINO-ALTO ADIGE *pop. 103,100*
Formerly part of the Austrian Tyrol, Trento presents a fascinating blend of the Germanic and Mediterranean worlds in its culture, languages and cuisine. It was the seat from 1545 to 1563 of the Council of Trent, which sought to modernize the Catholic Church as part of the Counter-Reformation. The 13th-century cathedral, where the Council sometimes met, is of particular interest.

CASTELLO DEL BUON CONSIGLIO, Via Bernardo Clesio, was once the home of the city's bishop princes. Frescoed salons house the varied collections of the Museo Provinciale d'Arte, including bronzes, ceramics and a fresco cycle.

▲ TREVISO (408 C5)
VENETO *pop. 81,200*
The ancient walled city of Treviso is now a busy provincial capital. In the old quarter are the Palazzo dei Trecento and the Loggia dei Cavalieri, both

in Romanesque style, and the cathedral, with paintings by Titian. Restoration followed World War II bomb damage.

CHIESA DI SAN NICOLÒ, a 14th-century church, has frescoes by Tommaso da Modena, and unusual decorated tombs.

▲ TRIESTE (408 C5)
FRIULI-VENEZIA GIULIA *pop. 225,500*
Situated on a beautiful stretch of coastline, Trieste was once the main port of the Austro-Hungarian Empire, and only became part of Italy in 1918.

CATTEDRALE DI SAN GIUSTO was built in the 14th century. The church is a mixture of styles and contains Byzantine mosaics and medieval frescoes.

TURIN – *see Torino on p.444.*

▲ UDINE (408 C5)
FRIULI-VENEZIA GIULIA *pop. 94,300*
Erected upon a mound said to have been built by the army of Attila the Hun, Udine contains elegant buildings, including the Palazzo del Comune.

CASTELLO (Castle), overlooking the town, was built in the early 16th century. The Museo Civico houses paintings by various Italian masters.

MUSEUM FRIULIANO DELLE ARTE E TRADIZIONI POPULARI, Via Viola 3, has a collection of regional costumes, crafts and art.

PIAZZA DELLA LIBERTÀ, in the center of town, has fine colonnades, statues and a grand fountain.

URBINO (408 C4)
MARCHE *pop. 15,400*
Imposing walls and gates still enclose Urbino, an old city balanced on a steep hill. Narrow, winding streets contain Renaissance buildings, a small university, old churches and a palace. In the 15th century Urbino possessed one of the most cultured courts in Italy under the Montefeltro dukes. The painter Raphael was born here; his home on Via Rafaello is open to view.

PALAZZO DUCALE, built for Federico da Montefeltro in 1465, is a magnificent Renaissance palace. It houses the Galleria Nazionale delle Marche, with two masterpieces by Piero della Francesca.

VATICAN CITY (412 A3) ★
Vatican City (Città del Vaticano), the worldwide centre of the Roman Catholic Church, is an independent sovereign state governed by the Pope and the College of Cardinals. The 43-hectare (106-acre) state was created in 1929 by the Lateran Treaty, and about 200 people live within its walls.

The Via della Conciliazione is the main approach to the Vatican. It leads to the famous Piazza San Pietro, created by Giovanni Lorenzo Bernini. Twin Doric colonnades topped with statues of saints and martyrs flank either side; a 26-meter (85-foot) high obelisk rises from the center. At the head of the square is the Basilica di San Pietro; to the right is the Palazzo Vaticano.

BASILICA DI SAN PIETRO (St. Peter's Basilica) ★ was built over the tomb of St. Peter between 1506 and 1626, replacing an earlier, 4th-century construction.

The enormous interior, which has standing room for 100,000, is richly adorned with art. Of special note are *La Pietà*, the great sculpture by Michelangelo; the 13th-century statue of St. Peter, with its foot worn smooth by pilgrims' kisses; and the 26-meter (85-foot) bronze baldachin, or canopy, by Bernini, over the high altar and presumed tomb of St. Peter. The dome, designed by Michelangelo and finished 24 years after his death by Giacomo della Porta, can be reached by an elevator.

CAPPELLA SISTINA (Sistine Chapel) ★ is renowned for its ceiling, painted over the course of four years with scenes from the

Old Testament by Michelangelo. The artist's *Last Judgement*, completed more than 20 years later, is behind the altar. The chapel walls are lavishly decorated with fine frescoes by some of the great artists of the Renaissance, including Botticelli. Christ's life is depicted on the right wall; on the left is the life of Moses.

PALAZZO VATICANO (Vatican Palace), a complex of many buildings, covers 5.5 hectares (13½ acres) and contains about 1,400 rooms. To see all the museums you will need at least a day. There are color-coded routes to follow.

Biblioteca Apostolica Vaticana is one of the world's richest libraries, which contains ancient papyri, and manuscripts in the handwriting of Michelangelo, Petrarch, and Luther among others, many of them beautifully illuminated. Capella di Nicolo V is worth a look for Fra Angelico's lovely frescoes.

Museo Gregoriano Etrusco contains a particularly fine collection of artifacts from the Etruscan civilization.

Museo Pio-Clementino contains the best of the Vatican's classical sculpture collection, including the *Laocoön*, the *Apollo Belvedere* and the athlete figure known as the *Apoxyomenos*.

Pinacoteca displays Italian paintings dating from the 13th to the 17th century. It is notably strong in the schools of Siena, Umbria and the Marches.

PAPAL AUDIENCES

General audiences with His Holiness are usually held on Wednesday at 11am, either in St. Peter's Square or the Audiences Room, and in summer at Castel Gandolfo. To participate in a general audience, you must apply to the office of the Prefetto della Casa Pontificia at the Vatican. Americans should apply to the North American College, Via dell' Umilta 30. Catholics are asked to take a letter of introduction from their parish priest.

The Stanze di Raffaello were decorated by Raphael (and his pupils) for Pope Julius II. The magnificent frescoes include the famous *School of Athens*.

▲ VENÉZIA (408 C5) ★
VENETO *pop. 309,400*
See map on p.448.

Venézia (Venice), is singular among the world's cities. It is built over a sprawling archipelago 4 kilometers (2½ miles) from the mainland, encompassing 118 islands separated by more than 150 canals.

Refugees fleeing the Barbarian hordes founded the first Venetian settlement in the 5th century. By the 13th century, the Republic of St. Mark dominated trade in the eastern Mediterranean and ruled an empire that extended from the Dalmatian coast to Crete, Cyprus and several Aegean islands. However, the advance of the Turks in the East, and the discovery of America and other trade routes in the West crippled the Venetian economy, and decline set in.

Despite these troubles, Venice entered its artistic golden age from the 16th to the 18th centuries: many magnificent structures were erected, and painters Giovanni Bellini, Titian, Tintoretto and others gained world renown. Napoléon Bonaparte finally overthrew the old republic in 1797, and the new nation-state of Italy annexed the city and its dominions in 1866.

Visitors can drive into Venice via the Ponte della Libertà to the Piazzale Roma. There are parking lots and garages in the area and visitors should use these, as any illegally parked cars will be towed away. Private boat, gondola and *vaporetto* (water bus) connections to Venice proper are available.

Trips can be made to the Lido, a fashionable seaside resort; to the islands of Murano, known for its exquisite blown glass; to Burano, known for intricate lace; and to Torcello, with its fine medieval monuments.

BASILICA DI SAN MARCO (449 D2), a Byzantine masterpiece, was begun as a tomb for St. Mark, whose body was reputedly stolen from Alexandria by two Venetians in AD 828. Above the main doors are gilded copper replicas of the well-known *Four Horses*.

CANAL GRANDE (448 C2), the main thoroughfare through the city, and always busy with water-borne traffic, is an impressive sight, and lined with more than 200 palaces.

COLLEZIONE GUGGENHEIM (448 C1), Calle Cristoforo, is a superb collection of modern art amassed by millionaire Peggy Guggenheim.

VENETIAN GLASS

Venice's glass industry has been based on the island of Murano since 1291, when it was moved out of Venice itself because of the fire risk. The glass-blowing furnaces still glow today, and many workshops can be visited.

GALLERIA DELL'ACCADEMIA (448 C1), Campo della Carita, is the city's finest art gallery. It presents Venetian painting, with works by artists such as Giovanni Bellini and Andrea Mantegna.

PALAZZO DUCALE (Doge's Palace) (449 D2) is an imposing construction built in the 14th century in Venetian-Gothic style. It was the seat of government of the Republic and the home of the doges. Tintoretto's *Paradise* adorns a wall of the grand council chamber.

PIAZZA SAN MARCO (St. Mark's Square) (449 D2), the heart of Venice, is an immense square bordered on three sides by palatial arcades lined with outdoor cafés and shops. Gondolas (which have been painted black since the passage of a 1562 law to curtail ostentation) can be hired at the water's edge.

PONTE DI RIALTO (448 D2) is one of the three bridges that cross the Canal Grande

(until 1854 it was the only crossing point). It is lined with luxury shops.

PONTE DEI SOSPIRI (Bridge of Sighs) (449 D2) joins the Palazzo Ducale with the prisons. Completed around 1600, the bridge's name recalls the despairing sighs of criminals led from the prisons to their execution.

SAN GIÓRGIO MAGGIORE (449 E1) is situated on a small island across the lagoon. It contains two of Tintoretto's masterpieces: *Last Supper* and *Shower of Manna*.

SANTA MARIA GLORIOSA DEI FRARI (448 B2) houses Titian's *Assumption* and Bellini's *Madonna and Child with Saints*.

SANTA MARIA DELLA SALUTE (448 C1), dedicated to the Virgin Mary after the plague of 1630, contains paintings by Titian.

SCUOLA GRANDE DI SAN ROCCO (448 B2), completed in 1560, is one of the great Venetian *scuole*, establishments set up to help the city's needy. It contains over 50 paintings by Tintoretto.

VENICE – *see Venézia on p.446*.

▲ VERONA (408 B5)
VENETO *pop. 255,800*

Verona is known for its Roman, medieval and Renaissance buildings, and famously forms the backdrop in Shakespeare's *Two Gentlemen of Verona* and *Romeo and Juliet*. Casa di Giulietta (Juliet's House) on Via Cappello has the romantic, if not authentic, balcony. During July and August, operas are presented at the impressive Roman amphitheater.

ARCHE SCALIGERE, by Santa Maria Antica, are the tombs of the della Scala family, who ruled Verona in the 13th and 14th centuries.

ARENA, Piazza Bra, is a massive Roman ampitheater seating 22,000.

ITALY

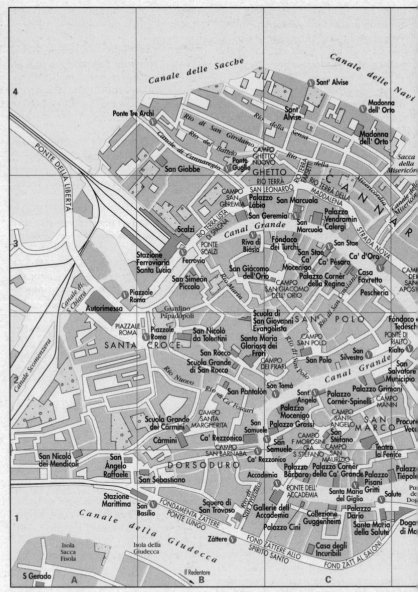

Canale delle Sacche

Canale delle Navi

Sant' Alvise

Madonna dell' Orto

4

Ponte Tre Archi

Sant' Alvise

Madonna dell' Orto

PONTE DELLA LIBERTA

Rio di San Girolamo

Rio della Sensa

Canale di Cannaregio

Rio dei Battelo

CAMPO GHETTO NUOVO

Ponte Guglie

RIO TERRA FARSETTI

Rio della Misericordia

Sacca della Misericordia

San Giobbe

GHETTO

RIO TERRA

CANNAREGIO

RIO TERRA DELLA MADDALENA

Canale della Misericordia

San Geremia

CAMPO SAN GEREMIA

Palazzo Lábia

San Leonardo

San Marcuola

3

Scalzi

RIO TERRA LISTA DI SPAGNA

PONTE SCALZI

Canal Grande

San Marcuola

Palazzo Vendramin Calergi

STRADA NOVA

Riva di Biásio

Fóndaco dei Turchi

San Stae

San Stae

Ca' d'Oro

CAMPO DEI SANT'APOST

Stazione Ferroviaria Santa Lucia

Ferrovia

San Simeòn Piccolo

San Giàcomo dell'Orio

Mocenigo

Ca' Pésaro

Casa Favretto

Pescheria

Piazzale Roma

Rio Marin

CAMPO SAN GIACOMO DELL' ORIO

Palazzo Cornèr della Regina

Canale di S. Chiara

Autorimessa

Giardino Papadópoli

Scuola di San Giovanni Evangelista

SAN POLO

Fóndaco Tedeschi

PIAZZALE ROMA

Piazzale Roma

San Nicolò da Tolentini

Santa Maria Gloriosa dei Frari

CAMPO SAN POLO

PONTE DI RIALTO

Rialto

SANTA CROCE

San Rocco

Rio di San Polo

San Polo

San Silvestro

San Salvatore Municipio

Canale Scomenzera

Scuola Grande di San Rocco

CAMPO DEI FRARI

Rio Nuovo

Rio di Ca' Fóscari

San Pantalòn

San Tomà

Canal Grande

Sant' Angelo

Palazzo Cornèr-Spinelli

Palazzo Grimani

CAMPO MANIN

Scuola Grande dei Carmini

CAMPO SANTA MARGHERITA

Palazzo Mocenigo

Palazzo Grassi

San Samuele

Palazzo Corner

SAN MARCO

Procura Vecc

Cármini

Ca' Rezzonico

San Samuele

San Stéfano

CAMPO F MOROSINI GIA S STEFANO

SANT' ANGELO

CAMPO SAN MAURIZIO

Teatro la Fenice

San Nicolò dei Mendícoli

San Àngelo Raffaele

DORSODURO

CAMPO SAN BARNABA

Ca' Rezzonico

Palazzo Cornèr della Ca' Grande

Palazzo Tiépolo

San Sebastiano

Accademia

Palazzo Bárbaro

Palazzo Pisani

Santa Maria Gritti

Palazzo

Stazione Marittima

San Basilio

PONTE DELL' ACCADEMIA

Santa Maria del Giglio

Salute

Pu de Do

Squero di San Trovaso

Gallerie dell' Accademia

Palazzo Dario

Santa Maria della Salute

Doga di M

1

FONDAMENTA ZATTERE

PONTE LUNGO

Collezione Guggenheim

Casa degli Incurabili

Canale della Giudecca

Zàttere

Palazzo Cini

FOND ZATTERE ALLO SPIRITO SANTO

Isola Sacca Fisola

Isola della Giudecca

Il Redentore

FOND ZATT AI SALONI

S Gerado

A

B

C

BASILICA DI SAN ZENO MAGGIORE is a magnificent Romanesque church. Its features include a huge rose window, 12th-century bronze door panels with biblical scenes, Mantegna's *Madonna and Saints*, and on the north side of the basilica, beautiful cloisters.

CASTELVECCHIO, Corso Cavour, a 14th-century palace, houses the Museo Civico d'Arte.

CHIESA DI SANT'ANASTASIA, a Gothic church built 1290–1481 with a double portal and richly decorated interior.

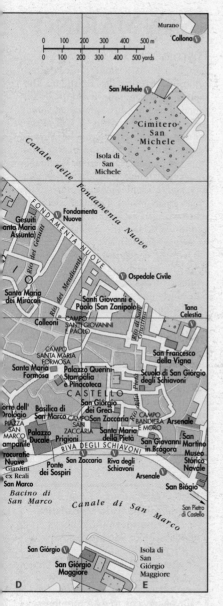

PIAZZA DELLE ERBE is the city's most delightful square, bordered by medieval townhouses and palaces, and with a central fountain. A market has operated here for over 2,000 years.

PIAZZA DEI SIGNORI is surrounded by 12th-century civic buildings. In the center is a monument to Dante. The Torre dei Lamberti (tower), part of the Palazzo dell Regione (Town Hall), offers excellent views of the city.

TEATRO ROMANO (Roman Theater), was built during the reign of Augustus. Nearby is an archaeological museum.

▲ VICENZA (408 C5)
VENETO *pop. 108,000*
Vicenza is renowned for its beautiful 16th century buildings by Andrea Palladio.

BASILICA PALLADIANA, Piazza dei Signori, was Palladio's first public building. It is a massive structure with two stories of grand colonnades.

PALAZZO CHIERICATI, Piazza Matteotti, is crowned with many statues; it houses the Museo Civico, displaying archaeological exhibits, and a picture gallery.

TEATRO OLIMPICO, Piazza Matteotti, is a charming 16th-century, classical Renaissance theater.

▲ VITERBO (410 C3)
LAZIO *pop. 60,200*
Viterbo, the main city of northern Lazio, was important as a papal residence from 1257 to 1281, when it rivaled Rome. The charm of Viterbo's medieval quarter is still evident. The city is also famous for its nearby thermal springs.

CATTEDRALE DI SAN LORENZO is a simple Romanesque building with a Gothic campanile.

PALAZZO DEI PAPI (Papal Palace) dates from 1266. Slender columns and delicate arches create a lacy effect.

DUOMO was originally a Roman basilica. The present cathedral was begun in the 12th century and the Gothic nave dates from the 15th century. Titian's *Assumption of the Virgin* is in the first chapel on the left, and outside the cathedral is an Early Christian mosaic.

THINGS TO KNOW

- **AREA:** 62 square kilometers (24 square miles)
- **POPULATION:** 23,000
- **CAPITAL:** San Marino
- **LANGUAGE:** Italian
- **ECONOMY:** Agriculture, tourism, printing of postage stamps, grain, coins, wine and textiles.
- **ELECTRICITY:** 220 volts, Continental two round-pin plugs. Adaptor/transformer required for non-Continental appliances.
- **PASSPORT REQUIREMENTS:** Required for U.S. citizens.
- **VISA REQUIREMENTS:** Not required for stays up to three months, after which a three-month extension can be obtained.
- **DUTY-FREE ITEMS:** *See Italy.*
- **CURRENCY:** Currency units are the Italian *lira* and the San Marino *lira*. Due to currency fluctuations, exchange rates are subject to frequent change.
- **BANK OPENING HOURS:** 8:30am–1:30pm and 3–4pm Monday–Friday.
  STORE OPENING HOURS: 8:30 or 9am–7:30 or 8pm Monday–Saturday, with a siesta between 1 and 4pm.
- **PUBLIC HOLIDAYS:** January 1; January 6; Easter Monday; April 25 (World War II Liberation Day); May 1 (Labor Day); August 15 (Assumption Day); November 1 (All Saints' Day); December 8 (Immaculate Conception); 25–26 December.
- **USEFUL TELEPHONE NUMBERS:**
  Police 113
  Fire 113
  Ambulance 113
- **NATIONAL TOURIST OFFICE:**
  Consulate General of the Republic of San Marino
  186 Lehrer Avenue
  New York, NY 11003
  Tel: 516/242-2212; fax: 516/7751-5897
- **AMERICAN EMBASSY:**
  Via Vittorio Veneto 119a
  Palazzo Margherita
  00187 Rome
  Tel: (396) 46 741
  Fax: (396) 488 2672

SAN MARINO

HISTORY

San Marino is a small independent republic, covering just 62 square kilometers (24 square miles), and totally surrounded by Italy. It was founded around AD 300 when Marinus, a Dalmatian stonemason, fled to the heights of Monte Titano to escape persecution from the emperor Diocletian. With other refugees he founded a Christian community, and the land was bequeathed to the group by its owner, Donna Felicissima, who was also a convert. Marinus was cannonized, and the enclave became known as San Marino.

Over the centuries, this little-known republic maintained its freedom in isolation from the rest of the world. San Marino was finally recognized as a sovereign state by the Congress of Vienna in 1815.

San Marino is governed by the Grand and General Council, whose 60 members are elected every five years. Executive powers are held by the Congress of State, and these officials are selected by and from the Grand Council every six months. Communist-led coalitions ruled from 1947 to 1957 and 1978 to 1986. A small army is kept for ceremonial purposes.

AUTOMOBILE CLUB
Federazione Auto Motoristica Sammarinese (Automobile Federation of San Marino), which has an office at Via Gingno Serravalle 99, San Marino, is the club in San Marino affiliated with AAA. Not all auto clubs offer full travel services to AAA members.

GETTING AROUND

San Marino is easily reached by car. The main approach is highway 72 from Rimini, but there are two alternate secondary roads. Road 258 links Rimini and

Sansepolcro, and a narrow, unclassified road connects Sansepolcro and Urbino. Automobiles are not allowed within the town walls. Instead, park in the lower town of Borgomaggiore and take the cable car up to the capital. Insurance requirements and traffic regulations are the same as those for Italy.

ACCOMMODATIONS

Most people visit San Marino on a day trip from Rimini. For those who want to stay longer, a range of accommodations is available. The tourist office next to the cable car station on Contrade Omagnano can provide information.

TIPPING

Restaurants and hotels in San Marino often add service charges to their bills, but check to make sure. If no charge has been added, tip 10 to 15 percent. For small services, the equivalent of 75¢ to $1.50 is appropriate.

LANGUAGE

For a list of useful words and phrases in Italian, see p.410.

Guaita Rock and Tower, a magnificent sight.

PLACES OF INTEREST

▲ SAN MARINO (408 C2)

pop. 3,000

Red-roofed stone houses and old ramparts add to the medieval character of San Marino, the nation's capital on the western slope of Monte Titano. A major road connects San Marino to Rimini, Italy, 24 kilometers (15 miles) northeast.

Although automobiles are prohibited within the town walls, a tour on foot can include the 19th-century Basilica di San Marino, where St. Marinus, the nation's patron saint, is buried, and the Palazzo dei Valloni, which houses the national library. A variety of small stores, many of which stay open late into the night, line San Marino's narrow streets, and there are panoramic views of the area around.

PALAZZO DEL GOVERNO is the 19th-century Gothic-style government headquarters facing the Piazza della Libertà. The building contains two portraits of St. Marinus, one of which is by Guercino.

ROCCHE'S three tower fortresses were strategically built on the three peaks of Monte Titano to guard against invasion. These carefully preserved citadels are connected by a path and offer a panorama of the countryside, the Italian city of Rimini and magnificent views across the Adriatic Sea; sometimes the Dalmatian Coast can be seen. The first tower, Guaita, and the second tower, Cesta, can be visited. Inside Cesta is the Ancient Weapons Museum.

SAN FRANCESCO, the Church of St. Francis, was erected in the 14th century on the site of an older church.

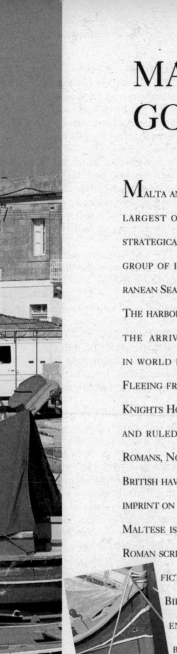

MALTA AND GOZO

MALTA AND GOZO ARE THE LARGEST OF A SMALL, YET STRATEGICALLY IMPORTANT, GROUP OF ISLANDS SITUATED IN THE MEDITERRANEAN SEA BETWEEN SICILY AND AFRICA. THE HARBORS AROUND MALTA'S COASTS HAVE SEEN THE ARRIVAL OF MANY ILLUSTRIOUS NAMES IN WORLD HISTORY, STARTING WITH ST. PAUL. FLEEING FROM SULEIMAN THE MAGNIFICENT, THE KNIGHTS HOSPITALLERS LEFT RHODES FOR MALTA AND RULED IT FOR ALMOST 300 YEARS. GREEKS, ROMANS, NORMANS, ARABS, ITALIANS, FRENCH AND BRITISH HAVE SINCE INVADED, RULED, AND LEFT AN IMPRINT ON THE ISLANDS' HISTORY.

MALTESE IS SPOKEN LIKE ARABIC, YET WRITTEN IN ROMAN SCRIPT. PLACE-NAMES SEEM DRAWN FROM A FICTIONAL WORLD: XAGĦRA, MARSAXLOKK, BIRŻEBBUĠA. BUT THE LANDSCAPE IS REAL ENOUGH, WITH ROCKY COVES, BEACHES, BLUE SEAS, AND LEMON TREES BLOWN BY THE HOT SIROCCO WIND FROM AFRICA.

Left MARSAXLOKK BAY HAS KEPT ITS CHARM DESPITE THE ARRIVAL OF TOURISTS
Above left COLORFUL FISHING BOATS ARE SEEN ALL OVER THE ISLAND
Above right THIS CHURCH IN MDINA SHOWS A TYPICAL RELIGIOUS DETAIL

THINGS TO KNOW

- **AREA:** 316 square kilometers (122 square miles)
- **POPULATION:** 369,500
- **CAPITAL:** Valletta
- **LANGUAGES:** Maltese and English.
- **PASSPORT REQUIREMENTS:** Required for U.S. citizens.
- **VISA REQUIREMENTS:** Not required for stays up to three months.
- **DUTY-FREE ITEMS:** 200 cigarettes or equivalent cigars and tobacco; one bottle spirits and one bottle wine; reasonable quantity perfume; personal goods.
- **CURRENCY:** The Maltese *lira*, divided into 100 *cents*, and each cent into 10 *mils*. Exchange rate is subject to change.
- **BANK OPENING HOURS:**
  8:30am–12:30pm Monday–Friday, 8:30am–12 noon Saturday.
  Opening and closing times are ½ hour earlier mid-June to September.
- **STORE OPENING HOURS:** 9am–1pm and 3:30–7pm Monday–Saturday.
- **PUBLIC HOLIDAYS:** January 1; February 10 (St Paul's Shipwreck); March 19 (St Joseph's Day); Good Friday; March 31 (Freedom Day); May 1 (Labor Day); June 7; June 29 (Feast of Saints Peter and Paul); August 15; September 8 (Our Lady of Victories); September 21 (Independence Day); December 8 (Immaculate Conception); December 13 (Republic Day); December 25.
- **NATIONAL TOURIST OFFICES:**
  Malta National Tourist Office
  Empire State Building, 350 5th Avenue, Suite 4412, New York, NY 10118
  Tel: 212/695-9520; fax: 212/695-8229
  Malta National Tourist Office
  36–8 Picadilly, London W1V 0PP, England
  Tel: 0171 292 4900; fax 0171 734 1880
  National Tourist Organization
  280 Republic Street, Valletta;
  Tel: 356 224444; fax: 356 220401
- **AMERICAN EMBASSY:**
  Development House, Third Floor, St. Anne Street,
  Floriana, Malta
  Tel: 356 235961; fax: 356 243229

HISTORY

The first settlers on this small group of islands arrived from Sicily about 7,000 years ago. Malta's many prehistoric sites are remarkably well-preserved: the island's great megalithic monuments, which contain some of the oldest free-standing statues in the world, were built between 4000 and 2000 BC. These temples and tombs housed a wealth of stone idols, carvings, pottery and implements, much of which is preserved the Museum of Archaeology in Valletta.

The first historical people to colonize the islands were the Phoenicians in the early 7th century BC. The Carthaginians ruled from 515 to 218 BC, but their domination was brought to a sudden end by Roman annexation. The islanders acquired a degree of self-government under Roman rule, minting their own coinage and controlling domestic affairs. Maltese ruins from this period indicate a high degree of wealth and sophistication.

With the fall of the Roman Empire, Malta came under control of the Byzantine Empire and then, in 870, fell to the Arabs. Various European rulers held sway until 1530 when the Knights Hospitallers were granted the islands by the Holy Roman Emperor. Having repulsed the Turks in the Great Siege, the Knights occupied and protected the islands until the Napoleonic Wars. This period ended in 1814 when Malta gained its last overseer – the British. The country achieved independence in 1964, becoming a member of the British Commonwealth. Ten years later Malta became a republic, and in 1979 British forces finally left.

FOOD AND DRINK

Although hotels and restaurants generally serve European or English food, the local specialties are well worth trying. Fish is abundant and includes tuna, grouper, swordfish and seabass. Lampuki, which shoal around Malta in the fall, are often prepared in a pie. Typical Maltese meat dishes are *bragioli*, similar to beef olives; rabbit stew; and *timpana*, a meat and macaroni pie. Interesting dishes are made from pumpkin dried on rooftops. The local grapes are pressed into fine wines, and Maltese beer is popular too.

SPORTS AND RECREATION

Ideally located in the unpolluted blue waters of the Mediterranean, Malta enjoys a hot, dry summer of clear skies and sea breezes. The winter season, from November to March, is mild. Opportunities for outdoor activities abound, including riding, shooting, fishing and water sports. Sailing regattas are held from May to October. Many hotels have swimming pools and a few also have tennis courts. The Marsa Sports Club, within a 10-minute drive of Valletta, has facilities for tennis, golf, cricket, polo, racket ball and badminton; it offers weekly membership to tourists. Soccer is Malta's most popular spectator sport, while horse racing and water polo offer great competition during their respective seasons.

More leisurely pursuits include touring Valletta's harbor in a cruiser or a traditional rowing boat; attending an open-air performance at the St. Anton Gardens; or participating in the colorful February Carnival, held just before Lent.

GETTING AROUND

Luqa International Airport, 6 kilometers (4 miles) south of Valetta, has flights to and from major European cities. The Grand Harbor at Valetta is Malta's main seaport. Car and passenger ferry services connect Malta to Réggio di Calabria, Naples, Genoa and Liverno in Italy, and to Catania and Palermo on Sicily.

Malta and Gozo are linked by frequent ferry crossings, as well as a faster, passenger-only hovercraft service. There is also a helicopter service. Buses connect Malta's towns and villages with Valletta. Taxis are metered, and can also be hired for a day's touring. *Karozzini* (horse-drawn cabs) are popular for sightseeing, but it is best to agree on the fare before you get in.

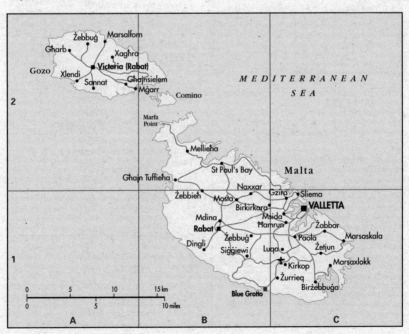

Road conditions are good between major towns, but minor roads are often poorly surfaced, winding and narrow. Good roads lead to the beaches, mainly on the northwest coast. Parking is difficult in Valletta and Mdina, and illegally parked vehicles will be fined. There are many car-rental firms with economical rates. Gas, however, is expensive. Service stations close at 6 or 7pm, and many also close on Sunday.

Driving is on the left. The wearing of seat belts is mandatory, as are crash helmets for motorcyclists. Speed limits are 40 k.p.h. (25 m.p.h.) in urban areas and 65 k.p.h. (40 m.p.h.) on highways. There are no on-the-spot fines.

AUTOMOBILE CLUB
M.T.C. Touring Services, 47 Ta' Xbiex Seafront, Msida. The **Touring Club (Malta)** is at Philcyn House, Ursuline Sisters Street, G'Mangia. The symbol ▲ beside a city name indicates the presence of a AAA-affiliated automobile club branch. Not all auto clubs offer full travel services to AAA members.

ACCOMMODATIONS
Malta classifies its hotels from one to five stars. There are also complexes, guest houses, apartments and villas. Most accommodations are near the coast; all room rates include breakfast. There are no official campgrounds in Malta.

SPECIAL EVENTS
Malta's carnival celebrations are held in early February. Dating back to 1535, they offer brass bands and folk-dancing competitions in Valletta's Freedom Square. More solemn is the Good Friday procession held in many of the Maltese towns and villages, when life-size statues and costumed participants enact scenes from the life and Passion of Christ. Joyful processions follow on Easter Sunday. Village feast days and public holidays are lively affairs, with parades, fireworks and bands.

TIPPING
A 15 percent tax is added to restaurant bills. If a service charge is also included leave a small tip, otherwise a 10 to 15 percent tip is standard.

USEFUL EXPRESSIONS IN MALTESE

good morning	bonju
good evening	bonswa
yes/no	iva/le
please	jekk joghgbok
thank you	grazzi
excuse me	skuzzi
how much...?	kemm...?

NUMBERS

1	wiehed
2	tnejn
3	tlieta
4	erbgħa
5	hamsa
6	sitta
7	sebgħa
8	tmienja
9	disgħa
10	għaxra

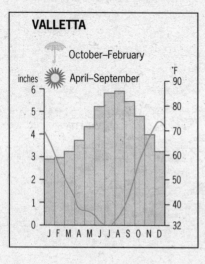

VALLETTA

October–February

April–September

inches / °F

PLACES OF INTEREST

▲ VALLETTA (455 C1) ★
MALTA *pop. 15,500*

Valletta, the capital of Malta, is most reminiscent of the Knights Hospitallers. The city was built by the French Grand Master of the Knights, Jean de la Valette, after the epic Turkish siege of 1565. Rising sheer from its rocky promontory, Valletta's historic city commands an excellent view over the Grand and Marsamxett harbors.

Across the harbor from Valletta are Vittoriosa, Cospicua, and Senglea, known collectively as the Three Cities. The Knights settled in Vittoriosa before Valletta was built, and constructed churches, chapels, forts and inns. The cities bore the brunt of the Turkish siege, and more recently came under attack during World War II. Further information on the history of Valletta and the surrounding area can be obtained at the Malta National Tourist Office in Freedom Square.

AUBERGE DE CASTILE ET LÉON, Castile Place, is a baroque-style palace built in 1741. The finest and best-preserved of the original eight palaces of the Knights Hospitallers, it now houses several government departments, including the offices of Malta's prime minister.

GĦAR DALAM ★, 11 kilometers (7 miles) south on the road to Birżebbuġa, is a natural cave that contained the fossilized remains of many extinct species, such as dwarf elephants and hippopotamuses, which roamed the island some 250,000 years ago. Neolithic pottery has also been discovered here. A small museum displays a fascinating collection of the animal bones found in the cave.

HYPOGEUM OF HAL SAFLIENI ★, 6 kilometers (4 miles) south in Paola, is a complex of underground chambers and corridors once used for multiple burials and rituals. These catacombs were built in three levels down to a depth of nearly 12 meters (39 feet) below the surface. The remains of some 7,000 human bodies, along with their personal ornaments, were discovered on the lower level. The highest level is the oldest, dating to around 3000 BC. Statuettes, pottery and ornaments from the chambers can be seen in Valletta's Museum of Archaeology (see below).

MANOEL THEATRE, Old Theatre Street, was built in 1731, and is one of the oldest, surviving theaters in Europe. It is now the main venue for music, opera, dance and drama; the season lasts from October to May.

NATIONAL MUSEUM OF ARCHAEOLOGY, Republic Street, is housed in the Auberge de Provence. It contains impressive finds from Malta's archaeological sites.

Prehistoric artifacts from the Tarxien Temples, Haġar Qim, and Hypogeum of Hal Saflieni are displayed on the ground floor, along with fascinating small-scale reconstructions of the various temple complexes. The top floor contains Phoenician and Punic antiquities.

MALTA AND GOZO

NATIONAL MUSEUM OF FINE ARTS, South Street, is housed in a 16th-century palace and contains paintings from medieval Italian to modern Maltese. The basement holds memorabilia of the Knights Hospitallers, including portraits, sculpture, ceramics and silverware.

NATIONAL WAR MUSEUM, Fort St. Elmo, contains a replica of the *Faith*, one of the three Gloster Gladiator aircraft that defended the island in World War II. Another highlight is the George Cross awarded to Malta by King George VI on April 15, 1942 for the bravery of her people during the war. Also on display is a large collection of uniforms, weapons and military vehicles.

PALACE OF THE GRAND MASTERS ★, Republic Street, was designed by Gerolamo Cassar and completed in 1574. Its features include luxuriously furnished state apartments with portraits of the Grand Masters and European monarchs, as well as the Tapestry Chamber which is lined with Gobelin tapestries. The palace is now the presidential office and Malta's Parliament House.

The armoury at the palace contains arms and armor of various periods with descriptions, including the suits of celebrated warriors and Turkish shields taken during the 1565 siege.

ST. JOHN'S CO-CATHEDRAL ★, St. John's Square, was built for the Knights in 1573–7 by Gerolamo Cassar. No expense was spared in the decoration of the walls and chapels. The crypt houses the tombs of the first 12 Grand Masters of St. John. In the oratory is Michelangelo Caravaggio's masterpiece, *The Beheading of St. John*.

A museum displays illuminated missals, sacred vestments and Flemish tapestries based upon cartoons by Peter Paul Rubens and Nicolas Poussin.

TARXIEN TEMPLES ★, lying 6 kilometers (3½ miles) south in Paola, are probably the best-preserved examples of megalithic temples on Malta. Dating between 3500 and 2500 BC, this monumental complex has three interconnecting main temples and the remains of an older temple; the chambers are decorated with carvings and contain elaborate altars for animal sacrifice. Finds from the site can be seen in the National Museum of Archaeology (see p.457).

UPPER BARRACCA GARDENS, near Castile Place, provide an excellent panorama of the Grand Harbour.

MDINA (455 B1) ★
MALTA *pop. 400*

The medieval town of Mdina, rising above the plains of central Malta, is also known as the "Silent City." This former capital of Malta is tightly packed with palaces and mansions, many of which still belong to Maltese nobility. The city walls command a superb view over the island. While some of the buildings and walls were built in the Middle Ages, the town's history goes back even further. The Cathedral of St. Paul is thought to occupy the site of the house of Publius, the Roman governor who was converted to Christianity by St. Paul.

Other buildings of interest are the old Seminary, which houses the Cathedral Museum, the dungeons and the medieval Palazzo Falzon. Visitors can watch Mdina glass-blowers practicing their craft at the Ta'Qali Crafts Village about 2 kilometers (1 mile) from the city.

ST. PAUL'S CATHEDRAL ★, destroyed by an earthquake in 1693, was rebuilt by Lorenzo Gafà in 1697–1702. The impressive dome, visible from afar, is arguably the finest in Malta. The Cathedral Museum contains various art treasures, including paintings, prints, silverware, and a fine collection of woodcuts by Albrecht Dürer.

NATIONAL MUSEUM OF NATURAL HISTORY ★, at Vilhena Palace, has seven sections displaying local and foreign collections of skeletons, fish, insects, birds, shells, fossils and geological specimens. The palace, built by Grand Master Vilhena in the 18th century, was used as a military hospital from 1860 until the 1960s.

RABAT (455 B1) ★
MALTA *pop. 13,400*

Rabat's early history is confirmed by the remains of a Roman villa. In this time Rabat and Mdina were one city. The ditch protecting Mdina and making Rabat its suburb was dug by the Arabs. Today a bustling town, Rabat is visited for its churches, Roman remains and the extensive catacombs beneath its streets. The 4th-century Christian catacombs contain canopied graves and saddle-backed tombs cut in imitation of Greek sarcophagi. An unusual feature of the Maltese catacombs is the presence of rock *agape* tables, where mourners partook of farewell meals.

Rabat and adjacent Mdina are most lively on June 29, during the Feast of St. Peter and St. Paul.

MUSEUM OF ROMAN ANTIQUITIES, Museum Road, displays evidence of the Roman rule of Malta between 218 BC and the 5th century AD. Highlights include a number of mosaic floors.

ST. AGATHA AND ST. PAUL'S CATACOMBS, on the southwest edge of Rabat, are typical of the underground Christian cemeteries that were common in the 4th and 5th centuries.

ST. PAUL'S GROTTO ★, a cave below the Chapel of St. Publius (adjoining the Church of St. Paul), is where St. Paul is said to have lived during his three-month stay on the island after a shipwreck in AD 60. A marble statue of St. Paul lies below dimly-lit catacombs.

VERDALA CASTLE ★, 2 kilometers (1 mile) southeast, is a late 16th-century summer palace of the Grand Master Verdalle. Today it is used for visiting foreign dignitaries and by the president as a summer residence.

The palace stands within the Buskett Gardens, which include vineyards and orange and lemon groves; they are open to the public on Tuesday and Friday.

SLIEMA (455 C1)
MALTA *pop. 13,500*

This coastal resort, together with the neighboring St. Julian-St. George area, is Malta's largest town. Sliema encompasses some of the island's most frequented spots, including a 3-kilometer (2-mile) seafront promenade and an attractive hotel district sprinkled with stores and cafés. There are no sandy beaches, but smooth rocks on the north side afford good swimming. In St. Julian's Bay is the Dragonara Palace Casino, a 19th-century mansion whose elegant rooms form the setting for baccarat, boule, blackjack and roulette. Sliema has the largest concentration of hotels in Malta and the best choice of facilities. The Yacht Marina offers modern facilities for boating.

VICTORIA (RABAT) (455 A2) ★
GOZO *pop. 6,400*

Named after Queen Victoria on the occasion of her Diamond Jubilee in 1897, the capital of Gozo is often referred to by its older name of Rabat. It is the geographical, political and cultural center of the island.

On a hill dominating the town are the ruins of an ancient citadel known as Gran Castello. Inside the walls are a late 17th-century cathedral, the old Bishop's Palace, the Law Courts and several small museums. The Feast of St. George on July 18 and the Feast of the Assumption on August 15 are celebrated with an array of festivities.

GGANTIJA PREHISTORIC TEMPLE ★, about 3 kilometers (2 miles) east on the Xaghra plateau, is the finest Copper Age monument on Gozo. The two adjoining megalithic temples are well-preserved, with some of the walls still standing over 5 meters (16 feet) high. The setting, affording a glorious panorama over the island, is worth a visit in itself.

THE NETHERLANDS

Nowhere in Europe do image and reality clash as they do in the Netherlands. For a land with a traditional image of windmills, cheeses, tulips and clogs, it is one of the most liberal countries in Europe. While drugs are not legal, they are tolerated.

Amsterdam, the city of bicycles and canals, boasts many art museums, with famous works by Rembrandt and van Gogh. Sights range from its picturesque gabled houses and flower market to the infamous red-light district. If Holland surprises, so will its people, especially for their friendliness, their easygoing nature, and a command of the English language to put most native speakers to shame.

Left Tulips and windmills – emblems of the Dutch countryside
Above left Cycling is the ideal way to get around Amsterdam
Above right Why not try a pair of clogs for size?

Things to Know

- **Area:** 40,844 square kilometers (15,770 square miles)
- **Population:** 15,423,000
- **Capital:** Amsterdam
- **Language:** Dutch
- **Religion:** Roman Catholic, Protestant
- **Economy:** Industry, commerce, agriculture. Light machinery, chemicals, textiles, food processing, shipbuilding, petroleum products, natural gas; trade and finance, tourism; farms (often small, producing mostly cattle), flower bulbs and blossoms, fruits and vegetables.
- **Electricity:** 220 volts, Continental two-pin plug. Adaptor and/or transformer required for U.S. appliances.
- **Passport Requirements:** Required for U.S. citizens.
- **Visa Requirements:** Not required for stays up to three months.
- **Duty-Free Items:** 200 cigarettes or 50 cigars or 100 cigarillos or 250 grams of tobacco; 1 liter of spirits over 22 proof or 2 liters of fortified or sparkling wine; 2 liters of still table wine; ¼ liter of toilet water; 60 milliliters of perfume; two still cameras with 24 rolls of film; two movie cameras with 10 rolls of film; one video camera; personal goods worth up to about $225 (if arriving from outside the European Union). See also *The European Union* on p.9.
- **Currency:** The currency unit is the *guilder*, or *florin*, divided into 100 *cents*. Remember that the exchange rate is subject to frequent change. There is no limit on the import or export of Dutch or foreign currency, but the export of Dutch silver coins is limited.
- **Bank Opening Hours:** 9am–4 or 5pm Monday–Friday, sometimes to 8pm on late-night shopping evenings.
- **Store Opening Hours:** Stores are normally open from 8:30 or 9am–5:30 or 6pm Monday–Friday, 8:30 or 9am–4 or 5pm Saturday. Many are closed for a half day each week, but the day varies with location. Many places have late shopping on Thursday or Friday. In Amsterdam stores may remain open until 10pm.

History

The Netherlands began to assume a national identity in the 15th century, when the dukes of Burgundy consolidated their control over the region of the Low Countries. The marriage of a Burgundian daughter, Mary, to the Austrian Maximilian I brought about Habsburg rule in 1477. Maximilian's son married a Spanish princess, and his grandson, Philip II, succeeded as king of Spain and prince of the Netherlands in 1555. Philip's introduction of Counter-Reformation policies was resisted by the Protestant majority in the north of the country who finally revolted.

Prince William of Orange, the Silent, became the leader in the struggle for independence. Despite the declaration of the United Provinces of the Netherlands in 1579, under the Treaty of Utrecht, war with Spain lasted until 1648 when the Spanish crown finally acknowledged Dutch independence. The Netherlands under the House of Orange then entered a golden age, becoming a leading maritime power.

Dutch explorers began to establish colonies and chart new routes to the Far East. New York was founded as New Amsterdam in 1629, while the Dutch East India Company became the largest trading company in the world.

Competition for command of the seas brought the Netherlands into conflict with other European powers. Hostilities with England and France were brought to a successful conclusion for the Dutch by William III who, through his marriage to Mary Stuart, daughter of James II, went on to become king of England in 1689.

The influence of the French Revolution spread to the Netherlands in 1795 when it became the Batavian Republic, a French protectorate. After Napoléon's defeat the House of Orange was restored as a monarchy, the new kingdom including Begium and Luxembourg. This union was shortlived, and following Belgian independence in 1839 the Netherlands was reformed toward a parliamentary state. In 1848 a constitutional monarchy under the parliament of the States General was established. This system of government continues to the present day.

Occupied by Germany during World War II, the Netherlands dropped its neutral status after the war and joined the North Atlantic Treaty Organization (N.A.T.O.). In 1957 the nation was a founder member of the European Economic Community, which has since become the European Union. In 1986 Flevoland, created from land reclaimed from the sea, was declared the country's newest province.

FOOD AND DRINK

Traditional Dutch food includes *erwtensoep,* a thick pea soup with ham or bacon, and *stamppotten,* a combination of

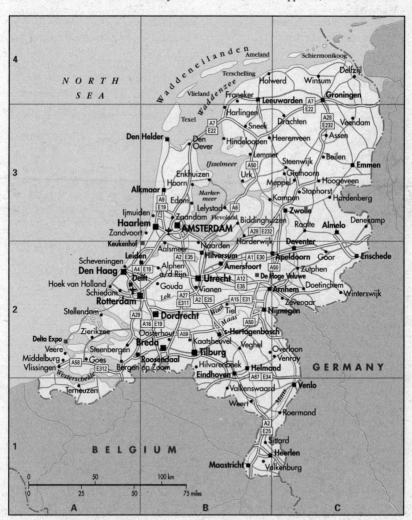

- **BEST BUYS:** Delft pottery, crystal, silver, pewter, wooden shoes, costumed dolls, fashions, antiques, flower bulbs, diamonds from the diamond-cutting center of Amsterdam.
- **PUBLIC HOLIDAYS:** January 1; Good Friday; Easter Monday; April 30 (Queen's Birthday Celebration); May 5 (Liberation Day); Ascension Day; Whitmonday; December 25–26.
- **USEFUL TELEPHONE NUMBERS:**
  Police 0611
  Fire 0611
  Ambulance 0611
- **NATIONAL TOURIST OFFICES:**
  Netherlands Board of Tourism
  21st Floor
  355 Lexington Avenue
  New York
  NY 10017
  Tel: 212/370-7367
  Fax: 212/370-9507
  Netherlands Board of Tourism
  9841 Airport Boulevard
  10th Floor
  Los Angeles
  CA 90045
  Tel: 310/348-9333
  Fax: 310/348-9344
  Netherlands Board of Tourism
  18 Buckingham Gate
  London
  SW1E 6LB
  England
  Tel: 0891-717 777
  Fax: 0171-828 7941
  V.V.V. Tourist Office
  P.O. Box 3901
  1001 AS Amsterdam
  The Netherlands
  Tel: 900 3403 4066
  Fax: 20 625 2869
- **AMERICAN EMBASSY:**
  Lange Voorhout 102
  2514 EJ Den Haag
  The Netherlands
  Tel: (070) 310 9209
  Fax: (070) 361 4688

vegetables with sausage. *Rijsttafel* is served in the many Indonesian restaurants, an exotic meal consisting of a choice of 15 to 40 spicy side dishes served with rice. Excellent Dutch cheese is available in many varieties. Pancakes with sweet or savory fillings, waffles, pastries, and *poffertjes* (doughnuts) are found everywhere.

Two types of tourist menus are recommended. Restaurants with a set-price tourist menu have a blue sign with a white fork, while the *Netherlands Dis* restaurants, serving traditional Dutch or regional fare, display a red, white and blue soup tureen. Tourist offices supply brochures listing the establishments participating in these schemes. An authentic *bruine café* (brown café) is the place to sample fine Dutch beers or *jenever* (juniper), Dutch gin.

SPORTS AND RECREATION

The Netherlands is ideal for many vacation activities. Its lakes and coastline offer fishing, canoeing, sailing, and a variety of water sports. The V.V.V. tourist offices have maps and details on numerous cycling and walking routes and tours. There are over 90 golf clubs; contact the Dutch Golf Federation, Rijnzathe 8, De Meern, tel: 030 662 1888. Soccer is the country's most popular spectator sport.

GETTING AROUND

The country's main airport is Schiphol, 14 kilometers (8½ miles) southwest of Amsterdam; there are train links to the capital, or south to Den Haag and Rotterdam. Car rentals can be found at the airport and in all main cities.

The major ferry ports of Vlissingen, Rotterdam and Hoek van Holland offer good connections to the British ports of Sheerness, Harwich and Hull; trips takes from 7 to 14 hours. Ferries also serve many parts of the country, including Zeeland, Flanders, some islands of Zuid Holland, and the islands of

---

AUTOMOBILE CLUB
Koninklijke Nederlandse Toeristenbond
(A.N.W.B.), Wassenaarseweg 220, 2596 EC's-Gravenhage; tel: (31-70) 314 71 47, has branch offices in various cities throughout the Netherlands. The symbol ▲ beside a place-name indicates the presence of a AAA-affiliated automobile club branch. Not all auto clubs offer full travel services to AAA members.

Waddeneilanden to the north of the mainland. There are direct rail connections to the Netherlands from all over Europe, and major highway routes from France, Begium and Germany.

Roads in the Netherlands are well signposted and well maintained. The green E symbol indicates an international highway, the red A indicates a national highway. Other main roads are marked by a yellow signpost with the letter N. Some of the most scenic routes are the minor roads along the canals.

Car seat belts must be worn, including passengers in the back seat. Children aged 4 to 12 must sit in the back, and those under 4 must use an approved child safety seat. All vehicles must carry an emergency triangle.

Unless signs indicate otherwise, speed limits are 50 k.p.h. (31 m.p.h.) in urban areas, 80 k.p.h. (49 m.p.h.) out of town, and 120 k.p.h. (74 m.p.h.) on highways. Do not park on roads signposted "*Stop-Verbod*," on access roads to the main highways, along a yellow line, or on a black-and-white line beside a bus stop; use designated parking areas and put enough money in the meter. Traffic regulations are strictly enforced with fines, wheel clamps and towing. There are free park-and-ride areas on the outskirts of Amsterdam with frequent connections to the city.

A *strippenkaart* (strip card) is available for travel on buses, trams and metros nationwide. Each card is valid for one zone of travel on the national zone system, and they can be purchased at rail stations, V.V.V. tourist offices, newsstands and post offices.

ACCOMMODATIONS
Dutch hotels are classified from one to five stars. Reservations should be made well in advance in summer, particularly in Amsterdam. The Netherlands Reservation Center (N.R.C.), provides a free hotel booking service; N.R.C., P.O. Box 404, 2260 AK Leidschendam; tel: 070 317 5454, fax: 070 320 2611.

Visitors can make hotel reservations in person through the local V.V.V. tourist offices for a small fee. They also have bed-and-breakfast listings, but these cannot usually be booked in advance. There are 38 youth hostels in the Netherlands, which are open to travelers of all ages, including families, who possess an International Youth Hostel card.

There are hundreds of campgrounds throughout the country. Reservations and information are available from V.V.V. tourist offices and the Stichting Vrije Recreatie, Broekseweg 75-77, 4231 VD Meerkerk; tel: 0183 352741.

TIPPING
A service charge is added to hotel and restaurant bills, and taxi fares; taxi drivers expect an extra tip of 10 percent, or round up the fare to the next *guilder*.

PRINCIPAL TOURING AREAS
Note: For descriptions of attractions in **bold type,** see individual listings.

ZEELAND
This southwestern province is a large delta region of islands and peninsulas popular for bird-watching, fishing and water sports. **Middelburg**, the provincial

ON YOUR BIKE

The bicycle is part of the Dutch way of life. By using the extensive network of *fietspaden* (cycle paths), totaling some 10,000 kilometers (6,215 miles), it is one of the best means of getting around.

If you are so inclined, you could tour the entire country on these well-signposted routes – they even have their own crossings and traffic lights.

A particularly breathtaking route is the road along the top of the Aasluitdijk, the dam across the IJsselmeer. However, in high winds this 30-kilometer (19-mile) ride can be a little hair-raising, to say the least.

capital, and the historic trading ports of **Zierikzee** and **Veere** are of interest.

HOLLAND AND UTRECHT

The provinces of Noord-Holland, Zuid-Holland and Utrecht contain the country's main tourist destinations. This region is also known as the Randstad (ring town) from the crescent formed by **Amsterdam, Aalsmeer, Delft, Den Haag, Rotterdam** and **Utrecht**. Beyond these centers lies the quintessential Dutch landscape of bulb fields, dikes, sand dunes and windmills.

The scenic area of heath, lakes and woodlands southeast of Amsterdam, known as Gooiland, makes a pleasant excursion from the cities and is popular for water sports. Along the coast, white sandy beaches stretch from Hoek van Holland (Hook of Holland) to the island of **Texel**.

FLEVOLAND

The country's newest province is based on a series of *polders*, land reclaimed from the IJsselmeer (formerly the Zuiderzee). The marshes and reedbeds make this a prime wildlife area, with lakes and channels for boating and water sports.

IJSSEL VALLEY

Noted for its castles, the IJssel Valley is a peaceful region of forests, orchards and meadows. In the picturesque village of Giethoorn, north of **Zwolle**, canal boats are the only means of transport. Staphorst, one of the country's most unusual villages, is renowned for its strict religious customs.

THE NORTH

The provinces of Friesland, Groningen and Drenthe form a major dairy area with many canals, lakes, marshes and attractive market towns. **Groningen** is a lively university city.

THE SOUTH

The southern provinces are less visited by tourists yet have much to offer. Noord-Brabant is a mainly industrial region opposite the Belgian border. The historic cities of 's-Hertogenbosch and **Breda** are of most interest, as well as the Biesbosch National Park. Industrial **Maastricht** is a convenient base from which to explore Limburg, a province with a rich and fascinating architectural tradition.

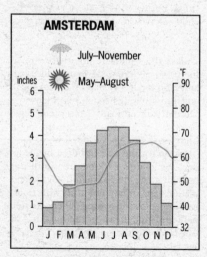

AMSTERDAM

July–November

May–August

USEFUL EXPRESSIONS IN DUTCH

Note: You'll find that virtually everyone in the Netherlands speaks English fluently, particularly in Amsterdam. Indeed, English is rapidly becoming the first language of Amsterdam. Signs are written in Dutch and English, and menus are printed in several languages, so confusion is rare.

hello	dag
good morning	goedemorgen
good afternoon	goedemiddag
good evening	goedenavond
good night	goedenacht
good-bye	tot ziens
please/thank you	alstublieft/dank u
yes	ja
no	nee
excuse me	pardon
you're welcome	tot uw dienst
Do you speak English?	Spreekt u Engels?
I don't understand.	Ik begrijp het niet.
What is the time?	Hoe laat is het?
How much is that?	Was kost dit?
Do you take credit cards?	Accepteert u kredietkaarten?
Where are the restrooms?	Waar zijn de toiletten?
I'd like ...	Ik wil graag ...
Can you help me, please?	Kunt u mij helpen, alstublieft?
where	waar
when	wanneer
how	hoe
old/new	oud/nieuw
open/closed	open/dicht
yesterday	gisteren
today	vandaag
tomorrow	morgen
no entry	verboden toegang
post office	het postkantoor
pharmacy	de apotheek
mailbox	de brievenbus
postcard	de briefkaart
telephone booth	de telefooncel
hotel	het hotel
gas station	het benzinestation
traffic lights	de verkeerslichten
trailer	de aanhangwagen
baker	de bakker
bookshop	de boekwinkel

department store	het warenhuis
liquor store	de slijterij
accident	het ongeluk
ambulance	de ziekenwagen
blister	de blaar
burn	de brandwond
cold	de verkoudheid
contact lenses	de contactlenzen
dentist	de tandarts
earache	de oorpijn
fever	de koorts
first aid	eerste hulp
hay fever	de hooikoorts
headache	de hoofdpijn
hospital	het ziekenhuis
migraine	de migraine
painkiller	de pijnstiller
sore throat	de zere keel
temperature	de temperatuur
toothache	de kiespijn
doctor	de dokter

DAYS OF THE WEEK

Sunday	zondag
Monday	maandag
Tuesday	dinsdag
Wednesday	woensdag
Thursday	donderdag
Friday	vrijdag
Saturday	zaterdag

NUMBERS

1	een	21	eenentwintig
2	twee	22	tweeëntwintig
3	drie	30	dertig
4	vier	40	veertig
5	vijf	50	vijftig
6	zes	60	zestig
7	zeven	70	zeventig
8	acht	80	tachtig
9	negen	90	negentig
10	tien	100	honderd
20	twintig	1,000	duizend

PLACES OF INTEREST

▲ AMSTERDAM (463 B3) ★
NOORD-HOLLAND *pop. 722,350*
The cosmopolitan city of Amsterdam consists of 70 islands separated by 80 kilometers (49½ miles) of canals, and connected by more than 1,000 bridges. Perhaps the best introduction to its charm, therefore, is a canal cruise on one of the glass-topped boats that depart from the convenient downtown docks.

The historic inner city contains many places of interest, including the 14th-century St. Nicolaaskerk, or Oude Kerk, the medieval weigh-house, and Centraal Station built in 1889.

Two of Amsterdam's outstanding parks are Vondelpark and Amsterdamse Bos southeast of the city center. Also of interest are the University of Amsterdam, founded 1632, and the Free Reformed University, founded 1880.

Since the time of Rembrandt, Amsterdam has been a center for the arts, and the city is celebrated for its museums – there are more than 40.

The Muziektheater is home to the Netherlands Opera Company and the National Ballet, while the highly acclaimed symphony orchestra performs at the Concertgebouw. Most dramatic productions are given in Dutch, with the exception of opera, which is sung in the original language. For the majority of ballet, music, opera and theater performances, seats can be reserved in advance from the Amsterdam Uit Buro at Leidseplein 26.

There are several movie theaters where foreign movies are frequently shown, and there is also plenty of lively (and often loud) nightlife.

Amsterdam is a shopper's city too. Antique shops are along the Spiegelgracht and the Rokin offer everything from porcelain to pewter, while the World Trade Center at Strawinskylaan 1 is a modern shopping and business complex with boutiques and eateries. The many small stores alongside the canals are popular and well worth exploring.

Trips can be taken to the flower centers of Aalsmeer, 12 kilometers (7½ miles) southwest, and Haarlem 12 kilometers (7½ miles) west. The drive south from Haarlem to Leiden or north to Den Helder takes in much of the country's bulb-growing area; the best time for this excursion is from spring to fall. There are cheese markets near Amsterdam at Alkmaar, Edam and Gouda.

Nearby Marken and Volendam are picturesque fishing villages, noted for the traditional costumes worn by their inhabitants.

AMSTERDAM HISTORISCH MUSEUM (470 C3), Kalverstraat 92, contains numerous historic drawings, maps and prints of the city. The museum is housed in the former Municipal Orphanage, which was founded in 1580.

ANNE FRANKHUIS (470 B3) ★, Prinsengracht 263, is the merchant's house where Anne Frank wrote her poignant diary. She and her family hid here from the Germans between 1942–44, prior to their imprisonment in Nazi concentra-

THE NETHERLANDS

tion camps. The rooms where the family hid have been left as they were in 1944, and the first floor is now used for exhibits by the Anne Frank Foundation.

BEGIJNHOF (470 C2–3), on a tiny side street between Kalverstraat 130 and 132, was founded in 1346 as a convent for the Beguines, or lay nuns. Their houses surround a tree-shaded courtyard: No. 34, Het Houten Huis (The Wooden House), dates from 1470, and is the oldest domestic building in the city.

DIAMOND-CUTTING WORKSHOPS are scattered throughout the city, and most of them are open to the public. The largest is Van Moppes Diamant at Albert Cuypstraat 2–6; visitors are shown every phase of diamond cutting, shaping and polishing.

HEINEKEN BRAUWERIJ (Heineken Brewery Museum) (470 C1), Stadhouderskade 78, is a restored brewery. Guided tours on weekdays explore the historic brewhouse and stables.

KONINKLIJK PALEIS (470 C3) (Royal Palace), Dam, is the city residence of Queen Beatrix. Built 1648–62 by Jacob Van Campen as the town hall, the building became a royal palace in 1808 when Louis Bonaparte made it his residence. The royal apartments contain a wealth of 17th-century marble sculpture and Empire-style furniture.

MUNTTOREN (470 C2), Muntplein, means "Mint Tower." The name derives from the mint established here in the early 17th century. The tower dates from 1490 and was part of the city's fortifications.

MUSEUM AMSTELKRING (470 C3), Oudezijds Voorburgwal 40, is also known as Ons Lieve Heer Op Solder (Our Lord in the Attic). It is a well-preserved example of a 17th-century merchant's house, with a baroque church hidden in its attic. Houses of this kind were common during the 16th and 17th

centuries when Catholic worship was forbidden, and only practiced in secret.

MUSEUM HET REMBRANDTHUIS (470 C2–3), Jodenbreestraat 4–6, was Rembrandt's home from 1639 to 1658. It contains a large collection of his etchings, period furniture and memorabilia.

MUSEUM WILLET-HOLTHUYSEN (470 C2), Herengracht 605, is a splendid 17th-century canal house with carved wood and painted ceilings. It is furnished with contemporary silver, porcelain, glass and furniture, and has a formal garden.

NEDERLANDS SCHEEPVAARTMUSEUM (471 E3) ★ (Maritime Museum), Kattenburgerplein 1, is housed in the former naval arsenal and presents the maritime history of the country through model ships, paintings, maps and artifacts. A replica of the *The Amsterdam*, a three-masted trading ship, is moored on the quay.

NIEUWE KERK (470 C3), Dam. Begun in 1468, the "New Church" was rebuilt in the Renaissance style following a fire in 1645. It has been the site of coronations since the 19th century, and is also used for concerts.

OUDE KERK (470 C3), Oudekerksplein 23, is the city's oldest surviving church, consecrated in 1306. Particularly noteworthy are the original bell tower, and the 16th- and 17th-century stained glass.

RIJKSMUSEUM (470 B1) ★ (National Museum), Stadhouderskade 42, is one of Europe's major museums. The famous collections include colonial and national artifacts, along with Dutch and Flemish paintings from the 15th to the 19th centuries. Among the masterpieces in this vast collection are Rembrandt's *The Night Watch* and *The Jewish Bride*, and several works by Jan Vermeer.

RIJKSMUSEUM VINCENT VAN GOGH (470 B1) ★, Paulus Potterstraat 7, presents an important collection of some 200 paint-

ings and 500 drawings by Vincent van Gogh. The museum illustrates the artist's prolific but tormented career up to his suicide in 1890 at the age of 37. Van Gogh's use of color had a profound influence on 20th-century art. Works by Gauguin and Monet are also on view.

WESTERKERK (470 B3) (West Church), on the corner of Westermarkt and Prinsengracht, was built 1620–31. Its elegant tower, popularly known as "Langer Jan" (Long John), is the tallest in the city; it rises to 86 meters (282 feet) and is topped by a crown.

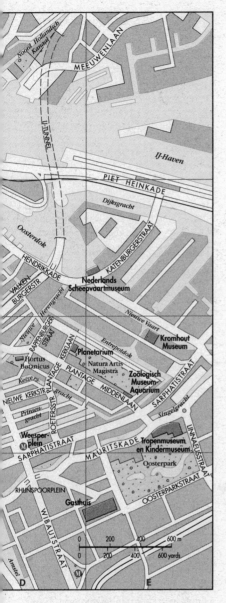

RED-LIGHT DISTRICT

Like other port cities, Amsterdam has had commercial sex available for many centuries. In the 17th century prostitutes had to pay rent to the city bailiff. He therefore had a vested interest in ensuring that they did not stray from the area; if they did, he sent a drum-and-flute-playing guard to expose both client and prostitute, thus driving them back to their designated area. The red-light district is still here, but it is now a viable tourist attraction as well. You will be as safe as in any other large city, provided that you take precaution against theft and do not take photographs.

AALSMEER (463 B2)

NOORD-HOLLAND *pop. 22,200*

Aalsmeer is a small town devoted to flower-growing. Blooms of every imaginable variety are cut early each morning and taken to Aalsmeer's flower market, the largest in the world.

AALSMEER FLOWER MARKET, covering 45 hectares (111 acres), sells millions of blossoms each day by auction. They are sorted into lots for the buyers who place bids electronically; by 9:30am all have been sold, and they are then flown to European cities for resale the same day. Visitors can view the proceedings from a gallery, but it is advisable to arrive before 8am to avoid the crowds.

▲ ALKMAAR (463 B3)

NOORD-HOLLAND *pop. 93,000*

Alkmaar is an attractive old town of historic buildings and canals. It is famous for its cheese maket, a colorful event held every Friday morning on the Waagplein; here colourful rounds of Gouda and red-skinned Edam are piled high for buyers to inspect and sample before they bargain.

ZOÖLOGISCH MUSEUM-AQUARIUM (471 E2), Plantage Kerklaan 40, is the city zoo, housing over 6,000 animals. It has the country's largest aquarium, and there are geological and zoological museums on the site. Notable features include the tropical house and a planetarium.

To complete the sale, porters dressed in the traditional clothes of their cheese guild haul the cheeses on sledges to the Waag (weighing house), and on to the stalls or warehouses of the buyers.

KAASMUSEUM (Cheese Museum), on the upper floor of the Waag, explains the cheese-making process and has displays of antique cheese- and butter-making implements.

▲ AMERSFOORT (463 B2)
UTRECHT pop. 114,900

Athough Amersfoot is now an industrial center, it still retains much of its medieval core. The restored Kopplepoort, a water-gate dating from the early 15th century, spans the Eem River at the northern end of town, while the Onze Lieve Vrouwe Toren (Tower of Our Lady), an impos-ing Gothic tower rising 102 meters (335 feet), survives from a former 15th-cen-tury church. Also of note are the Gothic church of St. Joriskerk, and the hospice of St. Pietersen-Bloklands Gast-huis from the 14th-century.

MUSEUM FLEHITE, Westsingel 50, has dis-plays of prehistoric and medieval artifacts from the region. The museum also has collections of Delftware and Chinese porcelain.

▲ APELDOORN (463 C2)
GELDERLAND pop. 150,000

Located in the Veluwe region, this large and modern town was a small village until development in the 1960s. It is now called the "Garden City" because of the many parks and gardens incorpo-rated into its growth. Nonetheless, Apeldoorn still retains some historic churches and buildings, and possesses several museums.

BERG EN BOS is a scenic park with 397 hectares (980 acres) of woods, meadows and floral displays, The Apenheul is popular, an enclosure where monkeys can roam free and gorillas enjoy a natural habitat on a wooded island.

HET LOO PALACE, Koninklijk Park, is the city's main attraction. This 17th-century palace was built for Prince William III, and the Dutch royal family lived here until 1975. It is now a museum honoring the House of Orange, and houses art-works and memorabilia from the royal collection. The splendid formal gardens are patterned after those at Versailles.

▲ ARNHEM (463 B2)
GELDERLAND pop. 134,200

Arnhem, on the Neder Rijn (Lower Rhine), lies in an attractive region of gar-dens and orchards. Heavily bombed during World War II, it has been rebuilt with wide avenues and numerous parks.

AIRBORNE MUSEUM, Utrechtseweg 232, commemmorates the disastrous Battle of Arnhem in World War II. In September 1944 the Allies attempted to gain control of the Rhine bridges in Operation Market Garden.

BURGERS' ZOO, Schelmseweg 85, has created remarkable natural habitats where indigenous animals can roam freely. These include a tropical rainfor-est, a covered desert, a wolf wood, and a safari park.

NEDERLANDS OPENLUCHT MUSEUM, Schelmseweg 89, off highway N 93, is a delightful open-air museum where tradi-tional Dutch buildings have been reconstructed from their original loca-tions. They include farms, a paper mill, factories, stores and old Dutch houses.

▲ BREDA (463 B2)
NOORD-BRABANT pop. 130,000

The attractive town of Breda was the scene of an important event in the Dutch struggle for independence. It was here in 1566 that the Compromise of Breda was issued in protest against Spanish rule. Many subsequent battles were fought here.

The town of Zundert, 13 kilometers (8 miles) south, is notable as the birth-place of Vincent van Gogh.

STEDELIJK EN BISSCHOPPELIJK MUSEUM (Municipal and Episcopal Museum), Grote Markt 19, has exhibits on Breda's history, as well as displays of religious art, including embroidered vestments.

DELFT (463 A2)
ZUID-HOLLAND *pop. 93,200*
The cobbled streets and the canals lined with medieval and Renaissance houses make this one of the Netherlands' most charming towns. Delft is famous for its blue-and-white pottery, inspired by the Chinese porcelain brought back by Dutch trading ships in the 17th century. The painter Jan Vermeer was born here in 1632, and later established the Delft school of painting.

HET PRINSENHOF, St. Agathaplein 1, was formerly a convent built around 1400. It became the headquarters of William the Silent during the Dutch uprising against Spanish rule; William was assassinated here in 1584. The Prinsenhof is now a museum housing ceramics, paintings, tapestries, silver and historical exhibits.

NIEUWE KERK, Markt, dates from the late 14th century, and contains the baroque tomb of William the Silent; his descendants are buried in the crypt. There are scenic views from the top of the tower, which is over 107 meters (351 feet) high; its splendid carillon, created in 1663, rings out through the town every hour.

OUDE KERK, beside the Oude Delft canal, is a large church dating from the 13th century; Vermeer is buried inside.

DE PORCELEYNE FLES (The Porcelain Jar), Rotterdamseweg 196, has been producing Delftware since 1653 and still uses traditional methods of production. Visitors can watch potters and artists at work, and buy examples of their craft in the factory showroom.

▲ DORDRECHT (463 B2)
ZUID-HOLLAND *pop. 16,000*
Located on the Oude Maas, a major waterway, Dordrecht is a busy port and yachting centre. The area around the harbor, Nieuwe Haven, has fine 17th- and 18th-century buildings.

DORDRECHT MUSEUM, Museumstraat 40, has a good collection of paintings by artists born in the town, including lively 17th-century waterfront scenes.

GROTE KERK, Grotekerksplein, built in the Brabant Gothic style, dates from the late 15th century. This "Great Church" is one of the country's largest, with a 72-meter (236-foot) tower housing 49 bells. The impressive choir stalls date from 1538 to 1541.

EDAM (463 B3)
NOORD-HOLLAND *pop. 26,250*
The historic seaport of Edam, with its canals, bridges and pleasant façades, is world famous for its cheese. The story of its production is told at the old Waag (weighing house). A cheese market is held in Edam on Wednesday mornings during the summer.

EDAMS MUSEUM, Damplein 8, occupies a 16th-century house with an unusual floating cellar, built by a retired ship's captain who longed for the feel of the sea. The town's museum contains portraits of three local characters known for their unusual physique.

GROTE KERK, Grote Kerkstraat, is a late Gothic church built in the 15th century, which has since been restored. It contains a number of windows with beautiful 17th-century stained glass, as well as furnishings of the same period.

ENKHUIZEN (463 B3) ★
NOORD-HOLLAND *pop. 16,100*
Until the Zuiderzee was enclosed to form the IJsselmeer in 1932, Enkhuizen was a prosperous seaport. It is a pretty town of canals, with well-preserved buildings dating from the 15th to the 17th centuries. The painter Paulus Potter was born in the town in 1625.

ZUIDERZEEMUSEUM, Wierdijk, has two parts. The Buitenmuseum is an open-air museum reached by boat, and comprises 135 traditional buildings reconstructed here. The indoor Binnenmuseum presents the maritime history of the Zuiderzee area, including model ships, old fishing boats and folk artifacts.

▲ ENSCHEDE (463 C2)
OVERIJSSEL *pop. 147,700*

Enschede, on the Twente Canal, is the main town of a largely industrial region opposite the German border. The Rijksmuseum Twente has a good art collection, and there is a textile museum devoted to the town's main industry.

FRANEKER (463 B4)
FRIESLAND *pop. 20,700*

This attractive, historic town was the cultural center of the north of the Netherlands from the 16th to the early 19th centuries. Pieter Stuyvesant, the colonial governor of New York, studied at its renowned university.

PLANETARIUM EISE EISINGA, Eise Eisingastraat 3, was the home of a local wool-comber and astronomer, Eise Eisinga, who built a planetarium in his living-room in 1774-81.

▲ GOUDA (463 B2)
ZUID-HOLLAND *pop. 70,900*

Situated on the Hollandse IJssel River, Gouda is famed for its cheese, waffles, candles, pottery and clay tobacco pipes. A colorful cheese and handicrafts market is held on the main square on Thursday mornings in summer.

The town is a good base for exploring the surrounding countryside. The Reeuwijk Lakes to the north offer excellent water sports, and at Oudewater to the east the weighing house of 1595 was once used for weighing alleged witches.

HET CATHARINA GASTHUIS (Hospice of St. Catherine), Oosthaven 9, was founded in 1310 as an almshouse for pilgrims. The present building dates from 1665, when

it became a hospital until 1910. It now houses the town museum containing period rooms, a picture gallery, historical artifacts, and the old infirmary with its surgical instruments.

ST. JANSKERK, Markt, is also known as Grote Kerk. The present structure was built in the 15th and 16th centuries. Its nave is illuminated by 70 magnificent stained-glass windows that date from the 16th century.

▲ GRONINGEN (463 C4)
GRONINGEN *pop. 169,600*

Groningen is a provincial capital with a prestigious university that was founded in 1614. It is also an important commercial and industrial center.

GRONINGEN MUSEUM is housed in a new complex of buildings at Musemeiland. Notable among the collections is the remarkable display of Chinese porcelain recovered in 1985 from the Dutch ship *Geldermalsen*, which sank in the South China Seas in 1572.

NOORDELIJK SCHEEPVAARTMUSEUM (Northern Maritime Museum), Brugstraat 24, occupies two 16th-century merchants' houses. It illustrates the region's maritime history from the Middle Ages to the present, with models of ships, paintings, navigational instruments, and various nautical artifacts.

▲ DEN HAAG (463 A2) ★
ZUID-HOLLAND *pop. 445,300*

Den Haag (The Hague) is an elegant city of large squares, broad streets, and stately 18th- and 19th- century buildings. It is the seat of the country's government, the official residence of Queen Beatrix, and the home of the International Court of Justice. Officially known as 's-Gravenhage, it is the Netherlands' most cosmopolitan city.

The city's royal palaces can be visited on a guided tour, and information on canal cruises and other excursions is available from V.V.V. tourist offices.

In July The Hague is the host for the North Sea Jazz Festival at the Nederlands Congresgebouw; this event attracts top artists from around the world. The seaside resort of Scheveningen is about 3 kilometers (2 miles) north of the city.

BINNENHOF is a group of historic courtyard buildings on the site of the castle built about 1250 by Count William II of Holland. They now house the two chambers of the Netherlands' Houses of Parliament. The medieval Ridderzaal, or Hall of the Knights, is the site of the state opening of Parliament.

GEMEENTEMUSEUM, Stadhouderslaan 4, was built in 1935 and exhibits 19th- and 20th-century art, including a collection of modern works by the Dutch artist Piet Mondrian. There are also displays of musical instruments, costumes, decorative art and Delftware.

MAURITSHUIS ROYAL, Korte Vijverberg 8, is a classical-style mansion built in 1633-34. It houses a magnificent art gallery with a fine collection of 17th-century Dutch masters; highlights include Rembrandt's *The Anatomy Lesson of Dr. Tulp*, and Jan Vermeer's *View of Delft*.

PANORAMA MESDAG, Zeestraat 65, is an impressive late 19th-century cyclorama with a circumference of 124 metres (407 feet). It was painted by the Dutch artist H.W. Mesdag with a small team, and depicts the popular seaside resort of Scheveningen in about 1881.

VREDESPALEIS, Carnegieplein 2, is the home of the International Court of Justice. It was built in 1908–13 with funds donated by the Scottish philanthropist Andrew Carnegie.

▲ HAARLEM (463 B3) ★
NOORD-HOLLAND *pop. 150,000*
Haarlem is a historic town with attractive streets and courtyards, several museums, and many fine buildings surviving from the 15th century. Several notable build-

QUEEN BEATRIX
Amid great controversy, Queen Beatrix was crowned on April 30, 1980. The festivities did not go according to plan: protesters, objecting to the cost of the investiture and seeking to highlight the housing crisis, fought with police, which resulted in a full-scale riot.

The second richest woman in Europe after Queen Elizabeth II of the United Kingdom, the queen has since won the respect and affection of the people. She promotes Dutch interests at home and abroad, and says of her job: "The kingdom is something to be marketed, just like oranges." This modern royal family live in Den Haag amid extensive parkland; guided tours take in the lovely 17th-century Huis ten Bosch (House in the Woods).

ings can be found around the Grote Markt: 17th-century almshouses, the Vleeshal (meat market), the Grote Kerk, built between the 14th and 16th centuries, and the medieval Stadhuis (town hall). Haarlem is a large bulb-growing center. At Lisse, 15 kilometers (9½ miles) south, are the Keukenhof Gardens, with 28 hectares (69 acres) of colorful flower beds, canals and lakes.

DE HALLEN, Grote Markt, were formerly the city's fish and meat markets (Vishal and Vleeshal). The ornate Vleeshal, built in 1603 by Lieven de Key, is a superb example of Dutch Renaissance architecture. They are now used for temporary art exhibitions.

FRANS HALS MUSEUM, Groot Heiligland 62, includes a fine collection of works by the Dutch painter Frans Hals. The artist lived in Haarlem most of his life, and spent his last years in poverty in this almshouse, built by Lieven de Key in 1608. The museum's collections range from Renaissance to Modern art.

TEYLER'S MUSEUM, Spaarne 16, is the oldest museum in the Netherlands, founded in 1778. It includes drawings and paintings by Dutch and European artists from the Renaissance onwards, notably a collection of 25 drawings by Michelangelo.

THE HAGUE – see Den Haag on p.474.

▲ DEN HELDER (463 B3)
NOORD-HOLLAND pop. 61,000

Located at the northern tip of Noord-Holland, Den Helder is a scenic tourist destination within the country's main bulb-growing area. The car ferry to the island of Texel leaves from here.

Den Helder is also the Netherlands' main naval base, and for three days in midsummer the Royal Dutch Navy invites the public to view the fleet.

In Schagen, 12 kilometers (7½ miles) south, the Old Dutch Market is a colorful spectacle of crafts, costumes and folk-dancing.

HELDERS MARINEMUSEUM HET TORENTJE, Hoofdgracht 14, illustrates the history of the Royal Dutch Navy with displays on its ships, uniforms and weaponry.

▲ 's-HERTOGENBOSCH (463 B2)
NOORD-BRABANT pop. 125,000

This provincial capital, known also as Den Bosch, is now an industrial and commercial center. Historic places of interest include the Gothic St. Janskathedraal, the baroque town hall, and the 16th- and 17th-century town fortifications. The artist Hieronymus Bosch was born here in about 1450.

DE EFTELING RECREATION PARK, 24 kilometers (15 miles) west, is a family theme park drawing more than a million visitors a year. The complex includes thrill and fantasy rides based on traditional fairy tales and legends.

NOORDBRABANTS MUSEUM, Verwerstraat 41, occupies an 18th-century mansion, the former residence of the governors of Noord-Brabant. It contains archaeological finds, paintings, local coins and historic documents.

ST. JANSKATHEDRAAL ★, Parade, is the finest, and largest, medieval church in the Netherlands. The oldest part is the Romanesque west tower, but the rest is a rich Gothic rebuilding from the 14th to the early 16th century; the ornately carved choir stalls date from 1480.

DE HOGE VELUWE (463 B2) ★
GELDERLAND

De Hoge Veluwe is the Netherlands' largest enclosed national park, situated 10 kilometers (6 miles) northwest of Arnhem. It contains 5,500 hectares (13,580 acres) of dunes, heath and mixed woodland, providing a varied habitat for boar, deer, wild sheep, and numerous species of birds. Also in the park is St. Hubertus hunting lodge, designed by the famous Dutch architect H.P. Berlage; built 1914–20, it symbolises the patron saint of hunting.

RIJKSMUSEUM KRÖLLER-MÜLLER, within the park, contains paintings and sculptures that were bequeathed to the nation, along with the park, by Anton and Hélène Kröller-Müller. The collection includes a large number of works by Vincent van Gogh. A sculpture park surrounding the main gallery contains pieces by August Rodin, Henry Moore and Barbara Hepworth.

HOORN (463 B3)
NOORD-HOLLAND pop. 61,750

Hoorn, once a major seaport, is now a popular resort with two yacht harbors on the IJsselmeer. The well-preserved town center has many fine Renaissance buildings, including the Waag (weighing house) and the Proostenhuis; the latter, built in 1632, houses the Westfries Museum and has displays on local history. The Hoofdtoren (watch tower) and

Oosterpoort (west gate) survive from the town's medieval fortifications.

▲ LEEUWARDEN (463 B4)
FRIESLAND *pop. 88,000*

Leeuwarden, capital of the dairy province of Friesland, lies within a region of lakes and canals. The inner town, enclosed by canals, contains the Renaissance Waag (weighing house) built 1595-98, the medieval Grote Kerk, and the leaning Oldehove Toren, a 16th-century brick tower whose adjoining church was never completed.

Leeuwarden has the largest cattle market in the Netherlands.

FRIES MUSEUM, Turfmarkt 24, has displays of artifacts illustrating the history and culture of Friesland.

▲ LEIDEN (463 B2)
ZUID-HOLLAND *pop. 116,220*

The historic town of Leiden has long been a center of culture. The university founded in 1575 is the oldest in the country, and there are several notable museums. Rembrandt was born here in 1606, and many other Dutch painters, including Jan Steen, lived and worked in Leiden.

This attractive city on the Oude Rijn (Old Rhine) also has a special place in American history. The Pilgrims migrated here from England in their search for religious freedom. They lived in Leiden for ten years before joining the voyage of the *Mayflower*, which sailed from Plymouth, England in 1620.

MOLENMUSEUM DE VALK (Windmill Museum), 2e Binnenvestgracht 1, presents the history and workings of Dutch windmills in a seven-story stone flour mill built in 1743.

RIJKSMUSEUM VAN OUDHEDEN (National Museum of Antiquities), Rapenburg 28, has a world-famous collection of prehistoric, Egyptian, Greek and Roman artifacts. The memorable displays of Egyptian antiquities include mummies,

sarcophagi, and the reconstructed Nubian temple of Taffah.

RIJKSMUSEUM VOOR VOLKENKUNDE (National Museum of Ethnology), Steenstraat 1, explores the various cultures of the world. The former Dutch colony of Indonesia is highlighted with wonderful puppets, masks, costumes and temple bells.

LELYSTAD (463 B3)
FLEVOLAND *pop. 60,800*

The capital of Flevoland is a modern city founded in 1967. It is named after Dr. Cornelius Lely, the engineer who masterminded the reclamation of the Netherland's newest province.

FLEVOHOF is a 150-hectare (370-acre) complex re-creating a Dutch agricultural and horticultural community. It features two working farms where visitors can experience "learning by doing" through sorting eggs, making butter and cheese, and practicing other rural activities.

RIJKSMUSEUM VOOR SCHEEPSARCHELOGIE (Museum of Ship Archaeology), Vossemeerdijk 21, traces the maritime history of the former Zuiderzee through the excavations of some 400 shipwrecks found during land reclamation.

LISSE – *see Haarlem on p.475*.

▲ MAASTRICHT (463 B1) ★
LIMBURG *pop. 118,320*

Founded by the Romans at a crossing of the Maas, the provincial capital of Limburg is one of the oldest and most vibrant cities in the Netherlands. The narrow province is bordered by both Belgium and Germany, and its history and culture have also been influenced by Spain and France. Most the city's population is multilingual.

In December 1991 the city was the scene for the Maastricht Treaty, the Treaty on European Union agreed by member states of the European Community; it came into effect in 1993.

THE NETHERLANDS

BONNEFANTENMUSEUM, Avenue Cérmamique 250, contains archaeological finds from the region, including artifacts dating from Roman and medieval times. There is a remarkable scale model of Maastricht in 1748. The museum's art collection includes works by the Flemish painters Brueghel the Elder and Younger, Rubens, and van Orley.

HELPOORT (Hell Gate), junction of St. Bernardusstraat and Het Bat, is the oldest surviving city gate in the country, dating from about 1229.

KAZEMETEN (Casemates), Waldeck Park, form part of the fortifications that extend for 10 kilometers (6 miles) around the city. The Casemates, built between 1575 and 1825, consist of a series of underground passages and powder stores. Near the entrance is a bronze statue of d'Artagnan, the real-life musketeer who was killed during a siege of the town in 1673.

ONZE LIEVE VROUWEBASILIEK (Basilica of Our Lady), Vrouweplein, was founded upon Roman foundations in about 1000. The fortress-like west work survives from the original church.

ST. SERVAASBASILEK was built over the grave of St. Servatius, the first bishop of Maastricht. The present structure dates mainly from the 11th to the 13th centuries, and is a fine example of Romanesque architecture. The Treasury contains a rich collection of religious artifacts, including a medieval reliquary containing the remains of St. Servatius.

▲ MIDDELBURG (463 A2)
ZEELAND *pop. 40,000*

The provincial capital of Zeeland has been well-restored after heavy damage during World War II. Many of the historic buildings around the Markt have since been totally rebuilt.

ABDIJKERKEN (Abbey Churches), Onderdentoren, is a complex of restored medieval churches and religious buildings. In 1574, during the revolt against Spain, the monastery was converted into a seat of provincial government. The tower of Lange Jan (Long John) provides visitors with excellent views.

STADHUIS (Town Hall), Markt, is a fine example of 15th-century Flemish architecture, now restored. The original 16th-century façade contains 25 statues of the counts and countesses of Zeeland.

NAARDEN (463 B2)
NOORD-HOLLAND *pop. 16,500*

This historic grid-plan town beside the IJsselmeer has become an island within the concentric moats of its impressive fortifications. These follow a star-shaped plan constructed 1675–85 in accordance with the principles of the French military engineer Sébastien le Prestre de Vauban. The Vestingmuseum, Westwalstraat 6, presents the history of the fortress town, which has been given the status of a national monument.

MUIDERSLOT, 7 kilometers (4½ miles) northwest in Muiden, is a moated castle built in 1370 on the site of a ruined 13th-century fortress.

The restored interior reflects its heyday during the 17th century, when the poet Pieter Hooft hosted literary gatherings here. The herb and plum gardens are also of interest.

▲ NIJMEGEN (463 B2)
GELDERLAND *pop. 144,700*

Nijmegan, on the south bank of the Waal, is one of the Netherlands' oldest cities, founded by the Romans about 2,000 years ago. Charlemagne established the Valkhof Palace here in the 8th century, while the surviving palace chapels date from the 12th century.

The town was extensively damaged during World War II, but several notable buildings survive. These include the Renaissance Waag (weighing house), the 16th-century town hall, and St. Stevenskerk, a late Gothic building.

BEVRIJDINGSMUSEUM 1944 (Liberation Museum), Keizer Traianusplein 35, tells the story of Operation Market Garden and the later events which led to the liberation of the Netherlands during World War II.

OVERLOON (463 B2)
NOORD-BRABANT *pop. 8,000*

The small town of Overloon has been rebuilt since World War II. In October 1944 it was site of one of the fiercest battles of the war, and was devastated by Allied and German shellfire. Set in a woodland park nearby to the east, the National Oorlogs-en Verzetsmuseum (War and Resistence Museum) commemorates the battle with displays of tanks, vehicles and weapons; a chapel honors those who gave their lives.

▲ ROTTERDAM (463 A2) ★
ZUID-HOLLAND *pop. 597,650*

Rotterdam, the country's second largest city, is one of the biggest commercial ports in the world. Its center has been rebuilt following the destruction caused by German bombs in 1940, and is now known for its experimental modern architecture; architect Piet Blom's Kijk-Kubus, a group of bizarre cube-shaped houses, is an example of the many striking buildings that can be found in the Oudehaven area.

Delfshaven, once a separate port town, became part of Rotterdam in 1886. Its 17th-century buildings and narrow docks survive to recall the time when the Pilgrim Fathers departed from here aboard the *Speedwell*; they abandoned the ailing ship at Plymouth, England, and joined the *Mayflower*.

Boat trips can be taken to Europoort, west of the city. This can also be reached by car along the Rotterdamse Havenroute, an 80-kilometer (49½-mile) round tour that shows the enormous size of the port.

BOYMANS-VAN BEUNINGEN MUSEUM, Museumpark 18–20, contains an outstanding and diverse collection of art from the Middle Ages to the present day. These include works by Hubert and Jan van Eyck, Rembrandt, van Gogh, Picasso and Salvador Dali.

DIERENPARK BLIJDORP (Blijdorp Zoo), Van Aerssenlaan 49, is among the top modern zoos in Europe, specializing in the breeding of endangered species.

Man-made rain forests harbor tropical birds, and rare animals include European bison and pygmy hippopotami.

THE LOCALS

While there are exceptions to every rule, the Dutch are generally renowned for their tolerance and liberal attitudes. The expression laissez-faire sums up the feelings of many citizens: their strong belief in the rights of individuals, and opposition to officialdom and interference.

When this personal freedom is exploited and threatened, however, the Dutch unite. In the 1980s parts of Amsterdam and Rotterdam were becoming unsafe for visitors. The local people therefore formed community action groups and, with the assistance of the authorities, worked to rejuvenate the run-down areas that had become the haunt of drug pushers and addicts.

EUROMAST, Parkhaven 20, is a 185-meter (607-foot) tower, with a revolving glass Space Cabin that affords a spectacular panorama of the city of Rotterdam.

MARITIEM MUSEUM PRINS HENDRIK, Leuvehaven 1. The museum explores the city's maritime history with displays of model ships, maps and navigational instruments. Visitors can also tour the small fleet of historic ships moored outside in the Leuvehaven, including *De Buffel*, an ironclad vessel built in the late 19th century for the Dutch navy.

MILLS OF KINDERDIJK, 20 kilometers (12 miles) east, are a group of 19 windmills built between 1722 and 1761 to drain water from the polders. They now form the largest concentration of windmills in the country, and are protected as national monuments.

OUDE KERK, Aelbrechtstolk 22 in Delfshaven, is the church where the Pilgrim Fathers held a service before setting sail for the New World.

TOY-TOY MUSEUM, Groene Wetering 41, has a collection of rare 19th- and 20th-century dolls from France, Germany and England, and mechanical toys dating back to 1700.

SCHEVENINGEN – *see Den Haag on p.474.*

▲ SCHIEDAM (463 A2)
ZUID HOLLAND *pop. 73,640*
The historic port of Schiedam, founded in the 13th century, now lies in the shadow of Rotterdam. The city still has several medieval buildings, including the early 15th-century church of St. Janskerk. Schiedam is known today for its *jenever* distilleries, producing traditional Dutch gin flavored with juniper.

TEXEL (463 B3)
NOORD-HOLLAND *pop. 13,200*
Texel, the largest island of the Waddeneilanden, is reached by ferry from Den Helder, and is now a popular resort for visitors who enjoy swimming, windsurfing, cycling and walking. De Koog, with its long sandy beach, is the main resort; the nearby Ecomare natural history museum has a seal sanctuary. Den Burg is the main market town.
The island is one of Europe's most important bird-breeding areas.

▲ UTRECHT (463 B2) ★
UTRECHT *pop. 235,630*
Utrecht is the provincial capital and one of the oldest towns in the Netherlands. Remains of a Roman settlement have

been discovered near the cathedral, which was founded in about 695 by St. Willibrord. The university was established in 1636. The city is now a busy commercial center and has one of the largest shopping malls in Europe.

THE FRISIAN ISLANDS

As you travel northeast, the five Frisian islands become smaller, wilder and more remote.
Texel is the most southerly island and the only one where you will find automobiles in any number. It can be busy on summer weekends, as sunbathers and windsurfers pour out of the cities. Vlieland, which attracts naturists and birdwatchers, has the largest nudist beach in Europe.
Many vessels have been wrecked on the sandbanks of Terschelling, one of the most famous being the *Lutine*; the ship's bell was the only part to be recovered and is still rung at Lloyd's, the London insurance market, whenever a ship is lost at sea.

The historic town center lies within an extensive moat and is crossed by the Oude Gracht (Old Canal). This is lined with attractive high-gabled houses, medieval cellars and lively cafés.

CENTRAAL MUSEUM, Agnietenstraat 1, is housed in the buildings of a medieval convent and has exhibits illustrating the history of Utrecht. Other displays include paintings by the Utrecht school of artists, and a 12th-century ship.

DOMKERK (Cathedral), Domplein, was built between 1254 and 1517 on the site of an earlier church. A storm destroyed the nave in 1674, leaving only the Gothic choir and transepts, and the peaceful 14th-century cloisters which link the cathedral with the university. Detached from the church since 1674, the 14th-century Domtoren (Cathedral Tower) is the tallest church tower in the Netherlands at 112 meters (367 feet). Visitors can climb to a platform near the top for splendid views of the city.

NATIONAAL MUSEUM VAN SPEELKLOK TOT PIEREMENT (From the Musical Clock to the Barrel Organ), Buurkerkhof 10, is a delightful museum illustrating the history of mechanical musical instruments. Exhibits date back to the 18th century and include music boxes, and dance, fairground and street organs.

NEDERLANDS SPOORWEGMUSEUM (Dutch Railway Museum), Maliebaanstation, presents the history of Dutch railroads and trams within in a former railroad station built in 1874. The collection contains original locomotives, carriages and wagons.

RIETVELD-SCHRÖDERHUIS, Prins Hendriklaan 50a, is a striking, modern house built in 1924 for Mrs. Truus Schröder-Schräder by Gerrit Rietveld, one of the leading architects in De Stijl, a famous Dutch art movement.

Although viewing is by appointment only, the imaginative interior design is well worth seeing. The house is now designated as a World Heritage Site.

RIJKSMUSEUM HET CATHARIJNECONVENT, Nieuwegracht 63, housed in a 16th-century Carmelite convent, traces the history of Christianity in the Netherlands through an extensive collection of religious artifacts.

VALKENBURG (463 B1)
LIMBURG pop. 18,070
Situated within the the beautiful Guel Valley, Valkenburg is a popular resort and spa dominated by the ruins of a medieval castle founded in the 12th century. The town is best known for the man-made cave system on Cauberg, with murals and sculptures dating from the 15th century to the 1960s. Other attractions include the mineral springs at

Thermae 2,000, and a fairy-tale entertainment park for children.

VEERE (463 A2)
ZEELAND pop. 5,090
Veere flourished as a port between the 14th and 18th centuries, when it traded in fish, linen, salt and Scottish wool. The elegant 16th-century Schotse Huizen (Scottish Houses) beside the harbor were once the homes of Scottish merchants; the buildings now contain the town museum. Today, the harbor only serves pleasure craft.

Also of interest is the late medieval Grote Kerk, and the 15th-century Stadhuis (Town Hall).

ZIERIKZEE (463 A2)
ZEELAND pop. 10,150
An important trading port in the Middle Ages, Zierikzee is now a popular yachting resort.

Sites of interest include the medieval Nobelport (Nobel Gate), one of the three surviving town gates; the elegant 17th-century merchants' houses lining the old canals; and the 16th-century 's Gravensteen, a prison until 1923 and now a maritime museum.

DELTA EXPO, 15 kilometers (9½ miles) west, is reached from the mainland by highway. This permanent exhibition explains the development of the Delta Plan, a response to the disastrous flood of 1953. It is housed on the storm barrier, part of the remarkable engineering project which involved the construction of a series of dams and dykes to protect the region from inundation by the sea.

▲ ZWOLLE (463 C3)
OVERIJSSEL pop. 100,760
This provincial capital is surrounded by ramparts and a moat. Sights within the historic center include the 15th-century Onze Lieve Vrouwekerk (Church of Our Lady), the contemporary Stadhuis (town hall), noted for its Gothic marriage hall, and the Provinciaal Overijssels Museum located in a 16th-century house.

PORTUGAL

The shadow of Spain has kept Portugal partly hidden, and those who find it delight in its culture, countryside, mountainous interior and ancient villages.

Portugal seems almost all shoreline, from the remote rural areas of the north to the sun-drenched sandy beaches of the Algarve. This long coastline has made Portugal a nation of fishermen and seafarers; many of the greatest maritime explorers were Portuguese, including Vasco da Gama. Successful navigators returned, bringing their influences with them, and nowhere are these more evident than in the vibrant capital city of Lisbon, with its parks, churches, and cobbled streets, mosaics and monuments, *FADO* music in back-street bars, and mix of crumbling grandeur and startling new buildings.

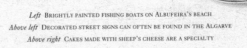

Left Brightly painted fishing boats on Albufeira's beach
Above left Decorated street signs can often be found in the Algarve
Above right Cakes made with sheep's cheese are a specialty

THINGS TO KNOW

- **AREA:** 94,250 square kilometers (36,390 square miles).
- **POPULATION:** 10,600,000
- **CAPITAL:** Lisboa (Lisbon)
- **LANGUAGES:** Portuguese
- **ECONOMY:** tourism, agriculture, production of wine, textiles, fish, cork, leather goods and olive oil.
- **PASSPORT REQUIREMENTS:** Required for U.S. citizens.
- **VISA REQUIREMENTS:** Not required for stays up to 60 days.
- **DUTY-FREE ITEMS:** 200 cigarettes or 100 cigarillos or 50 cigars or 250 grams tobacco (for non-European visitors: 400 cigarettes or 200 cigarillos or 100 cigars or 500 grams tobacco); however, if on the way to Portugal a stopover of more than 24 hours is made in any European country, the duty-free allowance is reduced. 2 liters of wine; 1 liter of spirits; ¼ liter of eau de cologne; 50 grams perfume; 100 grams of tea or 40 grams of tea extract; personal goods to be used during the stay; and gifts and souvenirs to a value of 7,500$00 (to 3,750$00 for those under 15). See also *The European Union* on p.9.
- **CURRENCY:** The currency unit is the *escudo*, divided into 100 *centavos*. In writing, the *escudo* is shown with a centrally placed dollar sign between the *escudo* and *centavo* amounts; for example, 3$20. Due to currency fluctuations, the exchange rate is subject to frequent change. There are no restrictions on the importation of local or foreign currency, but amounts exceeding the equivalent of 1,000,000 *escudos* must be declared upon arrival. Any amount of foreign currency may be exported provided it was declared on entry, but no more than 1,000,000 *escudos* may be exported. *Note:* foreign visitors entering Portugal must have a minimum of 10,000 *escudos* and a further 3,000 *escudos* for each day of their intended stay in the country. These amounts can be in any currency.

HISTORY

Although Portugal traces its origins to prehistoric times, the country's role in the history of Western civilization began with Roman occupation in the 2nd century BC. In turn, the Roman settlements were invaded by the Visigoths, who were later Christianized. Moslem rule came with the Moors, an Islamic people who ruled Portugal up until the 12th century. Portugal's first king, Afonso Henriques, drove the Moors from the city of Santarém in 1147 and, banding with passing Crusaders, took the capital, Lisboa, or Lisbon. About a century later, the last of the Moors were ousted.

In the early 15th century, Prince Henry the Navigator inspired a period of great exploration. During the late 16th century, Portugal fell under Spanish domination, but recovered its independence in 1640 and regained prosperity during the 18th century.

In the 19th century, the country was ravaged first by the Napoleonic Wars and later by civil strife. In 1908, King Carlos I was assassinated in Lisbon, and Portugal became a republic. For much of the 20th century Portugal was subject to a military dictatorship. There was a brief socialist revolution in 1974, but free elections were held in 1976. In 1989, Portugal's parliament officially abolished the socialist economy and called for the denationalization of industry.

FOOD AND DRINK

Cooking in Portugal is considered a fine art, which ranks the cuisine with the best in Europe. The Portuguese excel in preparing lobster, shrimp, prawn, crab, clam, mussel and oyster dishes. Also delicious are tuna, sardines, and *bacalhau*, salted dried cod. Other specialties are *caldo verde*, a soup made of potatoes and cabbage, and *gaspacho*, the tomato and cucumber soup of the Algarve.

Portuguese desserts are varied and typically very rich; *arroz doce* is probably the most common after-dinner choice. The national drink is wine, produced all over the country. Port and Madeira are served before and after meals. Portuguese beer is also popular.

SPORTS AND RECREATION

Golf is inexpensive in the large cities and the better resorts; costs are reasonable even at the Estoril Country Club. Estoril also offers swimming, as do a lot of resorts all along the coast. In the Serra da Estréla Mountains, in central Portugal, the ski season is from December through March.

The most popular spectator sport is soccer, and games are played in stadiums throughout the country every Sunday from September through June.

GETTING AROUND

Public transportation is generally inexpensive. Prices are comparatively low on the streetcar and subway systems; the lowest fares can be obtained by purchasing a series of 10 or 20 tickets at one time.

Airports at Faro and Porto have made the Algarve coast and the northern districts more easily accessible. Europabus is also a convenient method of travel.

Motorists will find that a well-maintained network of national highways, designated by the letters EN followed by a number, reaches virtually all corners of Portugal. A large section of the auto-estrada (highway) is open, with

---

BULLFIGHTING

In Portugal a bullfight is called a *tourada*. It is considered an art rather than a sport and differs from the Spanish *corrida*. As a result of a mishap that took place in the 18th century, the bull is never killed. The star of the show is the *cavaleiro* (horseman), who shows off his skills on horseback. When the bull is deemed exhausted, a group of eight men known as *forcados* perform a series of maneuvers to master the bull, including an attempt to seize its horns.

Touradas are held in Lisbon on Thursdays and Sundays from Easter Sunday to October.

---

more under construction; tolls are charged on most sections. The driver and all passengers must wear seat belts, if available. Children under 12 must occupy rear seats unless wearing an appropriate restraint. Speed limits are 50 k.p.h. (31 m.p.h.) in town, 90 k.p.h. (55 m.p.h.) on out-of-town roads and 120 k.p.h. (75 m.p.h.) on highways. A visitor who has held a driver's license for under one year must not exceed 90 k.p.h. (55 m.p.h.). All motorists are required to pay on-the-spot fines for violations in Portuguese *escudos*.

ACCOMMODATIONS

Hotels in Portugal are ranked from two to five stars. The government has encouraged the construction of well-equipped hotels, particularly in the Algarve region. *Pousadas*, modern, state-owned hotels, are converted historic buildings that are often set in scenic areas. *Estalagems* are small, well-appointed inns that are privately owned but supervised by the Ministry of Tourism. Lists of *pousadas* and *estalagems* can be obtained from tourist offices; these inns are usually very busy, especially in summer, so reserving well in advance is advised.

AUTOMOBILE CLUB
Automovel Club de Portugal
(A.C.P., Automobile Club of Portugal) has its headquarters at rua Rosa Araújo 24, 1250 Lisboa; tel: (01) 356 3931. The symbol ▲ indicates the presence of a AAA-affiliated automobile club branch. Not all auto clubs offer full travel services to AAA members.

- **BANK OPENING HOURS:** 8:30am–3pm Monday–Friday. Closed national holidays. One bank at Sacavém International Airport and one in downtown Lisbon are open daily 24 hours.
- **STORE OPENING HOURS:** 9am–1pm and 3–7pm Monday–Friday, 9am–1pm Saturday. Some large shopping complexes open daily 9am–midnight (most are in Lisbon).
- **BEST BUYS:** Cork products, Madeira lace, hand-knit woolen sweaters, hand-sewn Arraiolos rugs, sterling silver, gold and filgree jewelry, antiques, embroidered material, leather goods, port and Madeira wine, pottery, folk crafts, ceramic tiles.
- **PUBLIC HOLIDAYS:** January 1; Shrove Tuesday; Good Friday; April 25 (Liberty Day); May 1 (Labor Day); Corpus Christi; June 10 (National Day); August 15 (Assumption); October 5 (Proclamation of the Republic); November 1(All Saints' Day); December 1 (Independence Day); December 8 (Immaculate Conception); December 25.
- **USEFUL TELEPHONE NUMBERS:** Police **115**; Fire **115**; Ambulance **115**.
- **NATIONAL TOURIST OFFICES:** Portuguese National Tourist Office 590 Fifth Avenue, Fourth Floor New York, NY 10036 Tel: 212/354-4403 Fax: 212/764-6137 Portuguese National Tourist Office 22–25a Sackville Street London W1X 1DE, England Tel: 0171 494 1441 Fax: 0171 494 1868
- **LOCAL TOURIST OFFICES:** Lisbon: Praça dos Restauradores (Palácio Foz). Tel: (01) 346 3643 Estoril: Arcadas do Parque. Tel: (01) 468 0113 Cascais: Avenida Dom Carlos 1. Tel: (01) 486 8204
- **AMERICAN EMBASSY:** Av. das Forças Armadas 1600 Lisboa Portugal Tel: (01) 726 6600

Guesthouses, or *pensões*, are readily available. *Solares de Portugal* is a scheme of government-checked accommodations, divided into *casas antiguas* (historic buildings), *casas rusticas* (small country houses), and *quintas e herdades* (farms and country estates). Mostly located in the Minho province, some date as far back as the 15th century. Information on these can be obtained from the Portuguese National Tourist Office (see *Things to Know*).

Youth hostels' minimum age is usually seven years. Some hostels allow only male or only female guests. There are good campgrounds near the major cities. Automovel Club de Portugal can book tent sites, recreational vehicle hookups, etc., for travelers. An International Camping Carnet is recommended.

TIPPING
Portuguese hotels and most restaurants include a 10 percent service fee in bills, but service personnel expect another 5 to 10 percent; use your discretion. Taxi drivers are tipped 10 percent.

PRINCIPAL TOURING AREAS

Note: For descriptions of attractions in **bold type**, see individual listings.

THE ALGARVE
Separated from the rest of the country by the Caldeirão and Monchique mountains, the Algarve is Portugal's southernmost province. A number of resort complexes have sprung up, but little has spoiled the white sandy beaches for which the Algarve is known. Towns such as **Olhão** preserve memories of the past in their churches, palaces, and white "sugar cube" houses.

The Algarve's prettiest area begins with the seaport of **Faro**. Popular neighboring cities are Silves and scenic **Portimão**. **Sagres**, which preserves mementos of Prince Henry the Navigator, faces Africa on Portugal's southwestern tip.

MADEIRA AND THE AZORES

Ilha da Madeira, or Madeira Island, is a paradise island bathed in sunshine off the northwest coast of Africa. The **Ilhas dos Açores**, or the Azores Islands, with their hot-water springs and green pastures, consist of nine islands 1,280 kilometers (800 miles) west of Portugal. Mists, mountains, and whitewashed houses lend them an unusual beauty.

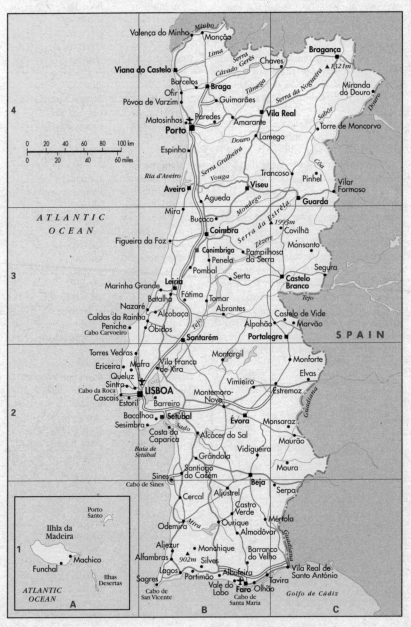

ATLANTIC OCEAN

SPAIN

Valença do Minho
Minho
Monção
Lima
Serra Gerês
Chaves
Bragança
▲ 1321m
Viana do Castelo
Cávado
Serra da Nogueira
Miranda do Douro
Barcelos
Braga
Tâmega
Ofir
Guimarães
Póvoa de Varzim
Vila Real
Sabor
Douro
Matosinhos
Paredes
Amarante
Torre de Moncorvo
Porto
Douro
Lamego
Espinho
Côa
Ria d'Aveiro
Serra Gralheira
Vouga
Trancoso
Pinhel
Vilar Formoso
Aveiro
Viseu
Agueda
Mondego
Guarda
Mira
Buçaco
Serra da Estrela
▲ 1993m
Figueira da Foz
Coimbra
Covilhã
Conimbriga
Zêzere
Monsanto
Penela
Pampilhosa da Serra
Pombal
Serta
Segura
Marinha Grande
Leiria
Castelo Branco
Batalha
Fátima
Tomar
Tejo
Nazaré
Alcobaça
Abrantes
Caldas da Rainha
Castelo de Vide
Peniche
Óbidos
Alpalhão
Marvão
Cabo Carvoeiro
Santarém
Portalegre
Torres Vedras
Montargil
Monforte
Ericeira
Mafra
Vila Franca de Xira
Elvas
Queluz
Vimieiro
Sintra
Cabo da Roca
LISBOA
Montemor-o-Novo
Estremoz
Cascais
Estoril
Barreiro
Guadiana
Bacalhoa
Setúbal
Évora
Monsaraz
Sesimbra
Costa da Caparica
Sado
Alcácer do Sal
Mourão
Baía de Setúbal
Vidigueira
Grândola
Moura
Sines
Santiago do Cacém
Cabo de Sines
Beja
Serpa
Cercal
Aljustrel
Castro Verde
Odemira
Mira
Ourique
Mértola
Guadiana
Almodôvar
Aljezur
Monchique
Barranco do Velho
Alfambras
▲ 902m
Silves
Vila Real de Santo António
Lagos
Portimão
Albufeira
Tavira
Sagres
Vale do Lobo
Faro
Olhão
Cabo de San Vicente
Cabo de Santa Maria
Golfo de Cádiz

0 20 40 60 80 100 km
0 20 40 60 miles

Ilhla da Madeira
Porto Santo
Funchal
Machico
Ilhas Desertas
ATLANTIC OCEAN

4
3
2
1

A B C

PORTUGAL

LISBON AND CENTRAL PORTUGAL

The colorful houses high on the steep, narrow streets of **Lisboa**, or Lisbon, give the capital a special charm. **Estoril**, with its fine beach, is only a short drive away, and beyond lies **Sintra**, or Cintra, known for its pretty setting and stately palaces.

Southeast of Lisbon is ancient **Setúbal**, which is an important port and fishing center. Nearby are the ruins of the Roman city of Troia. On the coast north of Lisbon is the fishing village of **Nazaré**.

Near the center of the country, the Beira provinces comprise cool mountains, sun-scorched plains, and villages perched on the granite slopes of the Serra da Estréla Mountains.

NORTHERN PORTUGAL

Douro province, whose capital is **Porto**, or Oporto, is known for its port wine. Visitors can wander through bottle-lined, dark caves where the wine is made. This part of the country has streams and rivers, woods, lush greenness and a general impression of great prosperity.

In the north is the mountainous province of Mingo, where grapes and grain are important. **Braga**, the provincial capital, has a fine cathedral.

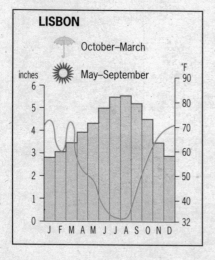

USEFUL EXPRESSIONS IN PORTUGUESE

hello	olá
good-bye	adeus
good morning	bom dia
good afternoon	boa tarde
good night	boa noite
please	por favor
thank you	obrigada (f)
	obrigado (m)
yes/no	sim/não
why/when	porquê/quando
how/what	como/o que
Do you speak English?	Fala inglês?
I do not understand	Nâo compreendo
You're welcome	De nada
Excuse me	Com licença
How much is ...?	Quanto é ...?
What time is it?	Que horas sâo?
today	hoje
tomorrow	amanhã
yesterday	ontem
where is ...?	Onde é ...?
I would like ...	Queria ...
restroom	casa de banho
old/new	velho/novo
cheap/expensive	barato/caro
open/closed	aberto/fechado

DAYS OF THE WEEK

Sunday	domingo
Monday	segunda-feira
Tuesday	terça-feira
Wednesday	quarta-feira
Thursday	quinta-feira
Friday	sexta-feira
Saturday	sábado

NUMBERS

1	uma (f), um (m)
2	daus (f), dois (m)
3	três
4	quatro
5	cinco
6	seis
7	sete
8	oito
9	nove
10	dez

PLACES OF INTEREST

The Bairro Alto area lies north of Baixa. The ancient part of this district contains the Church of São Roque and the Chapel of São João Baptista. Alfama, the oldest part of the city, dates from the Moorish occupation of the 8th to 12th century.

Museums in the Belém and Ajuda districts include the Museu Nacional dos Coches, the Padrao dos Descobrimentos, the Mosteiro dos Jerónimos, and the Torre de Belém.

Visitors to Lisbon can purchase the Tourist Ticket, which offers unlimited use of all city buses, streetcars, subways, and cable cars.

▲ LISBOA (487 B2) ★

ESTREMADURA *pop. 1,100,100*

Portugal's capital city, Lisboa, or Lisbon, reaches out to the sea from its sheltered position by the Tejo River. Lisbon's seven hills provide a varied setting, and charm is everywhere in the tiled roofs and softly colored houses. Lisbon International Airport, (also called Portula de Sacauém), is 8 kilometers (5 miles) north of the city.

The legendary founder of Lisbon was Ulysses, but the theory of Phoenician origin is probably more realistic. Occupiers in later years included the Romans, Visigoths, and beginning in the 8th century, the Moors.

On the morning of All Saints' Day in 1755, an earthquake struck Lisbon, killing about 40,000 people. The royal minister, the Marques de Pombal, began the rebuilding, and his layout of a carefully planned street system is still in use.

Lisbon can be roughly divided into six districts. Baixa is the central business district. Its two main streets, Rua Garrett – also called the Chiado – and Rua Augusta, are lined with fashionable stores; among the attractions are Rossio Square and the National Theatre of Dona Maria II. East of Baixa is Eastern Lisbon, which has the ancient Castelo São Jorge, and the Sé (Cathedral).

CASTELO DE SÃO JORGE (491 E2) ★, Largo do Chão da Feira and Largo do Menino de Deus, is in the Alfama district near the Tejo River. Constructed by the Visigoths in the 5th century, rebuilt by the Moors in the 9th century and modified during the reign of Afonso I, it has dominated Lisbon life for 1,500 years from the city's highest hill.

MOSTEIRO DOS JERÓNIMOS (490 A1), Praça do Império, Belém, is an early 16th-century Hieronymite monastery built by order of Manuel I, using the riches of the trade with India. It survived the 1755 earthquake.

IGREJA DE SANTA MARIA DE BELÉM (490 A1) houses a Cross of the Holy Order, a statue of Prince Henry the Navigator, and the tomb of Vasco de Gama.

ATTRACTION SCHEDULES IN PORTUGAL

Museums in Portugal are generally open 10am–6pm Tuesday–Sunday, with some closing for lunch between 12:30 and 2pm. Palaces are usually open 10am–5pm Wednesday–Monday. Museums and palaces are closed on public holidays. Other attractions often follow this schedule.

PORTUGAL

PORTUGAL

MUSEU CALOUSTE GULBENKIAN (491 D3) ★ is in a modern building on Avenida de Berna near Praça de Espanha. The museum's displays date from Egyptian antiquity to the present and include sculptures, furniture, ceramics, tapestries, jewelry, and paintings including works by Rembrandt, Gainsborough, Manet and Renoir.

TRADITIONAL MUSIC

Fados form a distinctive part of Portugal's folklore. Showing influences of the early songs of the troubadours and the sailors, the *fado* has a deeply melancholic air, relating to love, passions, destiny, with the singer, or *fadista*, accompanied by one or two guitarists. The old quarter of Lisbon is a good place in which to hear the traditional *fados*. They are also popular, in a slightly different style, in Coimbra, where they are often performed by the students.

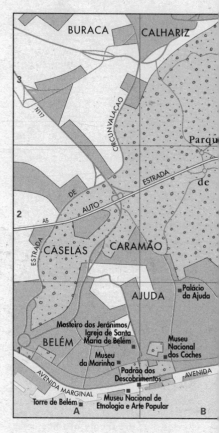

MUSEU-ESCOLA DE ARTES DECORATIVAS (Museum-Academy of Decorative Arts) (491 E2), in an Alfama palace on Largo das Portas do Sol, is a study in 18th- and 19th-century Portuguese design. Precious furniture, silver and rugs combine in lavish displays.

MUSEU MILITAR (Military Museum) (491 E2), Largo dos Caminhos de Ferro, Santa Apolónia, contains a display of arms and armor from the 15th century onwards.

MUSEU NACIONAL DE ARTE ANTIGA (National Museum of Ancient Art) (491 C1), facing the port at Rua Janelas Verdes 9, is Portugal's most outstanding art gallery. Renowned for its collection of Portuguese pictures, the museum also has pottery, porcelain, silverware, and superb western European paintings.

MUSEU NACIONAL DOS COCHES (National Coach Museum) (490 B1), in the 18th-century former riding school of Belém Palace, on Praça Alfonso de Albuquerque, contains an outstanding collection of state coaches and carriages of the 17th to 19th centuries.

PADRÃO DOS DESCOBRIMENTOS (490 A1), in Belém, is a monument to the discoveries of Prince Henry the Navigator. His statue stands at the prow of a stone ship overlooking the Tejo River; behind him crowd Portuguese explorers, religious figures and representatives of all walks of life who took part in the discoveries. At the monument's base are a compass and a mosaic map of the world as it was known to Prince Henry.

PRAÇA DO COMÉRCIO (491 E2), also called the Terreiro do Paço, is one of the country's loveliest squares.

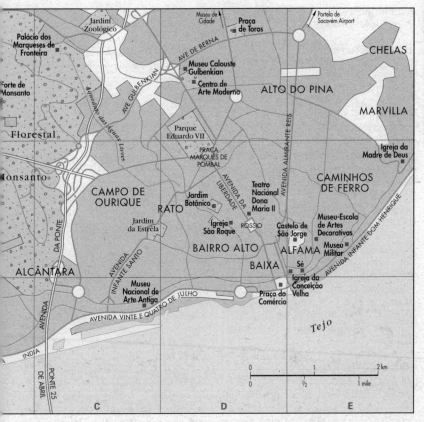

SÉ (490 E2), the Cathedral of Lisbon, towers over the Tejo River in the Alfama district. Tours are available, except during Mass.

ALBUFEIRA (487 B1)
ALGARVE *pop. 15,000*
From a small, picturesque fishing village, Albufeira has developed into a busy resort. It has still retained its charm, however, with cobbled streets leading uphill to the old village. There are good views, a fine swimming beach, and an attractive boating cove where the fishermen work.

ALCOBAÇA (487 B3)
ESTREMADURA *pop. 11,400*
The Cistercian community that settled in Alcobaça in the 12th century exer-

cised a powerful influence throughout medieval Portugal. Mosteiro de Santa Maria (Santa Maria Monastery), founded by King Afonso I in 1178 and restored several times, retains its noble character.

▲ AVEIRO (487 B4)
BEIRA LITORAL *pop. 40,000*
Aveiro's canals and lagoons are suggestive of Holland or Venice. In fact, Aveiro is often referred to as the "Venice of Portugal."

AZORES ISLANDS – *see Ilhas dos Açores on p.494.*

BARCELOS (487 B4)
MINHO *pop. 9,700*
Barcelos is known for its brightly colored *Galo de Barcelos*, or pottery roosters,

which have become a ubiquitous Portuguese symbol.

BATALHA (487 B3) ★
BEIRA LITORAL *pop. 7,700*

In 1385, João I of Portugal defeated Juan I of Castile in a battle waged at Aljubarrota, 15 kilometers (9 miles) south of Batalha at Aljubarrota. As a result, the young king secured 200 years of independence from Spain. In gratitude, João vowed tò build a great church to the Virgin Mary, which has grown into the present monastery.

MOSTEIRO DA BATALHA, the monastery João I dedicated to Santa Maria da Vitória, was begun in Gothic design. Later rulers expanded and embellished the Gothic themes.

The chapter house was built without supporting shafts, an architectural feat that gave rise to legends. It contains Portugal's Tomb of the Unknown Soldier and the tomb of Prince Henry the Navigator.

▲ BRAGA (487 B4)
MINHO *pop. 87,000*

Braga is the capital of the province of Minho. It has been a religious center since the 5th century and pilgrimages are made to Braga each year. Among the town's architectural highlights is the 11th-century Manueline cathedral, with its beautiful chapels, tombs, statues and religious treasures.

PARQUE NACIONAL DA PENEDA-GERÊS (National Park of Peneda-Gerês) is an extensive park northeast of Braga, between the provinces of Minho and Tras-os-Montes.

BRAGANÇA (487 C4)
TRAS-OS-MONTES *pop. 15,600*

The ancient town of Bragança has a magnificent medieval fortress encircled by formidable walls. Evidence of the town's Moorish background can be seen in the architecture of its five-sided, 12th-century town hall.

CASCAIS (487 A2)
ESTREMADURA *pop. 29,900*

Cascais is a fashionable Atlantic resort that retains the simple charm of a fishing village while having one of the country's finest beaches, Praia do Guincho.

CINTRA – *see Sintra on p.497.*

CINTRA – *see Sintra on p.497.*

▲ COIMBRA (487 B3) ★
BEIRA LITORAL *pop. 89,700*

Once the capital of Portugal, Coiumbra was a powerful city under the Romans and in the 16th century became the artistic and intellectual center of the country. Much of the city's life still revolves around the university, founded in 1290.

CONIMBRIGA, 14 kilometers (9 miles) south, is the site of a recently excavated Roman city, famous for its well-preserved mosaics.

IGRERA DE SANTA CRUZ (Church of the Holy Cross), built in the 16th century, contains the tombs of the first two kings of Portugal.

MUSEU DE MACHADO DE CASTRO is a fine art museum in a former palace (restored in 1592), containing paintings, sculptures and ceramics from the 13th and 14th centuries.

PORTUGAL DOS PEQUENINOS (Portugal for Little Children) is a children's attraction with tiny castles, cathedrals and cottages.

SÉ VELHA (Old Cathedral) is a 12th-century Romanesque church.

ELVAS (487 C2)
ALTO ALENTEJO *pop. 14,000*

Elvas is enclosed by impressive 17th-century ramparts. The remarkable four-tiered Amoreira Aqueduct, constructed in 1498–1622, carries water to Elvas.

ESTORIL (487 A2)
ESTREMADURA *pop. 25,200*

Estoril, connected to Lisbon by an excellent electric train system, is

PORTUGAL

Portugal's largest and most fashionable seaside resort. It is known for its casinos.

▲ ÉVORA (487 B2) ★
ALTO ALENTEJO *pop. 37,900*

From 1165 to 1580, when Portugal was at the height of its power and prestige, Evora was the preferred seat of the country's kings.

Decline began, however, when Spain conquered Portugal in 1580; Évora never recovered its former eminence.Today it is a major tourist attraction and cultural center, given World Heritage status by U.N.E.S.C.O.

Surrounded by walls that date mostly from the 14th and 17th centuries, Évora's older sections are primarily Moorish, characterized by hanging gardens, patios, and alleys with arches.

ERMIDA DE SÃO BRÁS is a Gothic-Mudejar hermitage south of the city walls near the station. Multiple turrets surmounted by spires decorate this fortress-like building, which was founded around 1485.

IGREJA DE SÃO FRANCISCO, Rua da República, is near the town center. The church is typical of the local Gothic-Manueline style of 1480–1510, with a baroque altar and a nave topped with arches of various designs. In the macabre Chapel of Bones, the skulls and bones of 5,000 monks cover the walls and pillars.

MUSEU REGIONAL (Regional Museum), Largo Marqués de Marialva, is in the old archbishop's palace next to the cathedral.

SÉ, in the town center on Largo Marqués de Marialva, is Évora's cathedral. Begun in 1186, the Gothic church has a neo-classical main chapel and Renaissance choir stalls. The treasury in the chapter house has a fine collection of gold and silver work, paintings, sculptures, and vestments.

TEMPLO ROMANO (Roman Temple), Largo Bonde de Vila-Flor, faces a garden near the cathedral. Probably dedicated to Diana in the 2nd century AD, this Corinthian temple of Estremoz marble was used as a fortress in medieval times. It was excavated during the 19th century.

▲ FARO (487 B1)
ALGARVE *pop. 33,700*

Capital of the Algarve province, the port of Faro occupies an enviable setting midway along the southern coast.

The town has a number of temples and monuments. The most important are the ancient cathedral; the Church of Our Lady of Carmo, with its Chapel of Bones; the Chapel and Museum of St Antonio; and the Convent of Our Lady of Assunçao, with its noteworthy cloister. Faro also has a local museum.

FÁTIMA (487 B3)
RIBATEJO *pop. 7,300*

The Sanctuary here (see p.494) is one of Europe's most revered shrines, second only to Lourdes in France.

FUNCHAL – *see Ilha da Madeira on p.494.*

GUARDA (487 C4)
BEIRA ALTA *pop. 18,000*

Fortified in the late 12th century by Sancho I, Guarda, known as the "City of Health," is on the northeastern slope of the Estrela Mountains. It is one of the oldest and highest towns in Portugal.

GUIMARÃES (487 B4)
MINGO *pop. 25,000*

Founded by the Celts in 500 BC, Guimarães was the birthplace of the first king of Portugal and was the country's first capital. The town is surrounded by Moorish fortifications and ancient architecture.

LAGOS (487 B1)
ALGARVE *pop. 11,700*

Popular as a vacation resort today, Lagos was the starting point for Henry the Navigator's 15th-century expeditions to Africa. Places of interest include the old slave market in the Praça da República (Republic Square).

PORTUGAL

PONTA DE PIADED, a rugged promontory with some of the most striking multicolored rock formations in the Algarve, is just 3 kilometers (2 miles) south.

ILHAS DOS AÇORES
pop. 250,000

Still serene and unspoiled, the Ilhas dos Açores, or Azores Islands, offer numerous opportunities for relaxation. When discovered in the 15th century they were uninhabited; today a small population ensures their continuing tranquility.

Covered with vegetation and groves of fruit trees, the nine islands extend for almost 600 kilometers (345 miles) across the Atlantic Ocean, 1,280 kilometers (800 miles) west of Portugal. São Miguel, Tirceira, and Faial are served by nonstop flights from Lisbon. A regional airline connects all the islands, which are also linked by ferryboats.

The island group has only a handful of beaches, but fishing and scuba diving are popular alternatives to swimming. Any activity, however, is enjoyed in a lush and striking landscape and a climate that is warm and sunny from May to September.

On São Miguel, the largest island, Ponta Delgada houses over half of the Azores' inhabitants. This cosmopolitan capital city, with its black-and-white mosaic sidewalks, is a convenient excursion center.

Angra do Heroismo, capital of Terceira, is a pretty, flower-bedecked town with cobbled streets. Vila do Porto, capital of Santa Maria island, is noted for its old houses and its 16th-century church.

ILHA DA MADEIRA (487 A1) ★
pop. 100,000

Off the coast of Morocco is Portugal's "other world," Ilha da Madeira, or Madeira Island. The largest island in the Madeira archipelago, with an area of 740 square kilometers (286 square miles), it lies some 900 kilometers (563 miles) southwest of Lisbon. Entirely volcanic in origin, Madeira's peaks stretch out of the sea from their "valleys" in the ocean depths. The volcanic soil combines with a mild climate to produce abundant colorful vegetation.

Although reportedly known to other nations in earlier times, the Madeira archipelago was rediscovered in the early part of the 15th century by Portugal, and colonization began. Today, the islands are an integral part of Portugal.

Madeira Island is an elongated stretch of land reaching east and west. Along the center runs a mountain chain, a spectacular contrast to the fertile coastal lands where sugarcane, bananas and grapes flourish. Terraces of farmland extend into the hills, adding tiers of green beauty to the landscape. Although there are no real beaches, hotels usually have large swimming pools. Its ideal climate brings Madeira fame as a year-round resort.

Madeira exports a superb embroidery that carries the island's name, as does the wine, which many feel ranks among the world's best. Wicker baskets and furniture also show fine craftsmanship.

Ilha do Pôrto Santo is the only other inhabited island in the archipelago.

▲ FUNCHAL has a population of about 120,000. Ilha da Madeira's capital, it has a wide selection of resort hotels. Watersports, golf and tennis are available.

A Madeiran way to tour the city is by bullock-pulled sled; the descent by wicker toboggan at the nearby town of Monte is another popular ride.

Igreja de Santa Maria Maior, near the waterfront, is a striking 18th-century white stucco church with a contrasting black lava scroll design in baroque style.

Mercado dos Lavradores (Laborer's Market), on the eastern edge of town, has vendors in colorful costumes selling local produce and craftwork.

Sé (Cathedral), done in white stucco with contrasting black basalt and red tufa rock, was begun in the 15th century by the Knights of the Order of Christ, who led many of Portugal's expeditions of discovery.

LAMEGO (487 B4)
BEIRA ALTA pop. 10,000
A land of orchards and vineyards, the Lamego region produces sparkling wines. The town's famous shrine of Nossa Senhora dos Remédios attracts pilgrims from all parts of the country; the main annual pilgrimage is on September 8.

MADEIRA ISLAND – see Ilha da Madeira on p.494.

MARVÃO (487 C3)
ALTO ALENTEJO pop. 300
Marvão, on a precipitous hill near the Spanish border, has steep streets, fine wrought-iron balconies, and the ruins of a 13th-century castle. A high stone wall surrounds the village, indicating its great military importance during the Middle Ages. The views are astonishing. Cars should be parked in the parking lot at the entrance to town.

NAZARÉ (487 B3)
ESTREMADURA pop. 13,200
The picturesque seaside village of Nazaré is known for its clothes, customs and traditions. The fishermen dress in brilliant checked shirts and pants, the women in long dresses. In addition to the fishermen's quarter, the Sítio – a village set on a very high cliff and reached by a funicular – is worth visiting, especially for its breathtaking views.

OLHÃO (487 B1)
ALGARVE pop. 34,600
Olhão resembles a North African town more than a European one. The narrow streets are bordered by blank, high walls and white, cubical houses, making it one of the most unusual towns in Europe. Olhão's distinctive appearance has attracted many artists.

OPORTO – see Porto below.

PORTIMÃO (487 B1)
ALGARVE pop. 27,000
Portimão has a bustling harbor lined with fishing boats.

PRAIA DA ROCHA, a seaside resort 3 kilometers (2 miles) north, has a mild climate, picturesque beaches of white and yellow sand, and unusual rock formations sometimes suggestive of statues. Boat excursions can be made to Lagos (see p.493).

THE BLOSSOMS OF THE ALGARVE
In January and February, the Algarve is transformed into a fairyland of white and pale pink almond blossoms. According to legend, the almond trees were planted long ago by a Moorish chieftain to please his wife, who yearned for the snows of her native Scandinavia. One fine day the princess awoke and was delighted to find the area covered in blossoms, resembling snow.

▲ PORTO (487 B4) ★
DOURO LITORAL pop. 335,900
Porto, or Oporto, is Portugal's second-largest city, occupying an imposing position on the right bank of the Douro River. Three magnificent bridges span

PORTUGAL

the river, and from the riverbank rise steep streets with tiers of pastel-colored houses and white churches lined with bright blue tiles.

In Roman times, Oporto was two distinct cities, Oporto and Cale, whose combined names gave the nation of Portugal its name. Also deriving its name from this ancient source is the port wine for which Oporto is known. From vineyards far up the Douro Valley, grapes are brought to the suburb of Vila Nova de Gaia for blending and ageing. Visitors are welcome at the big, dark warehouses where vats and barrels wait out the years as the wines mature.

A little more than 20 kilometers (12½ miles) northwest of Oporto are the beach resorts of Póvoa de Varzim and Vila do Conde. Both are old fishing villages, and many unusual local customs remain.

IGREJA DOS CLÉRIGOS, the 18th-century Church of the Clergy, is an example of restrained baroque design. Its tower, Torre dos Clérigos, has massive yet seemingly delicate stone carvings. There is an excellent view from its summit.

IGREJA SÃO FRANCISCO (Saint Francis Church), facing Largo de São Francisco, is a 14th-century Gothic church. It retains its original rose window, and also a wealth of 17- and 18th-century gilded woodcarvings.

MUSEU SOARES DOS REIS, Rua de Dom Manuel II 56, is a national museum. Once the 18th-century Carrancas Palace, the museum's exhibits include wrought gold and silver, ceramics, religious articles, paintings and sculptures.

SÉ, the cathedral, was formerly a fortress-church. Good examples of the original Romanesque design of the cathedral are its twin towers and wonderful 13th-century rose window. The Gothic cloister was a 14th-century addition, and in the 17th and 18th centuries, architects made numerous alterations. The Chapel of the Holy Sacrament has a superb altar.

PORT

One of Portugal's best-known drinks is undoubtedly the sweet, fortified wine known as port, derived from vines cultivated in the Upper Douro. These days, the cut grapes are mostly crushed mechanically, followed by the fermenting process. Later, a fortifying brandy is added. The wine is then placed in casks and stored in cellars, where it continues to mature. The resulting wine is then shipped all over the world from Oporto, hence the name.

The Ponte de Dom Luis bridge over the Douro River connects Oporto with Vila de Gaia, where the wine can be sampled.

QUELUZ (487 A2)
ESTREMADURA pop. 47,900
QUELUZ PALACE, built in the 18th century, was the sumptuous residence of Queen Maria I. Features include the rose stucco façade, the guard's room, and the throne room, famed for its mirrored doors and Venetian chandeliers. The gardens have lavish flower displays, sculpted hedges, lakes, fountains and statues.

SAGRES (487 B1) ★
ALGARVE pop. 2,600
In the windy coastal town of Sagres, Henry the Navigator lived and mapped out the routes taken by the first Portuguese explorers.

FORTALEZA, beyond the village and port, is believed to be Prince Henry's former residence and where he founded his Navigation School. A 30-minute movie chronicles the major events of the Age of Discoveries.

▲ SETÚBAL (487 B2)
ESTREMADURA pop. 97,800
The Setúbal area dates from Roman times. At low tide the foundations of Roman villas are still visible through the

sand, and from time to time Roman coins or pottery are found.

IGREJA DE JESUS, a late 15th-century church, is the earliest building in the town.

SINTRA (487 A2) ★
ESTREMADURA *pop. 21,000*
Abundant vegetation gives a lush beauty to the hillside setting of ancient Sintra, or Cintra. In sharp contrast, man-made fortresses crown the stern, bare stone peak of Serra de Sintra, high above the town.

CASTELO DOS MOUROS (Castle of the Moors), begun in the 8th century, looks down from nearby mountain heights. It was captured from the Moors in 1147, marking the return of Christianity. It is now partially ruined.

QUINTA DE MONSERRATE, near Sintra, is a castle with an outstanding botanical garden.

PALÁCIO DA PENA (Pena Palace), like the Castelo dos Mouros, towers over the town from a spectacular height. It is a fascinating 19th-century creation, built by Fernando II on the site of an old monastery. A large and lovely park surrounds the castle.

PALÁCIO NACIONAL DE SINTRA (Sintra National Palace), in the center of town, is a royal palace with a special dignity. Its two huge, cone-shaped chimneys are the most prominent landmarks in Sintra. The palace interiors are lavishly decorated and include a fine example of *azulejos*, or brightly colored tiles.

TOMAR (487 B3) ★
RIBATEJO *pop. 15,000*
Tomar is one of the prettiest towns in Portugal, with narrow, winding streets opening unexpectedly onto wide squares. Built long before the era of the automobile, local thoroughfares are seldom wider than a single lane.

Among Tomar's attractions are many beautiful churches, including the Convent of Christ, which contains a magnificent series of cloisters. The 12th-century convent was built by the Knights Templar, a powerful religious-military order. In the Jewish quarter, a synagogue houses the Portuguese-Hebrew Museum.

The Festa dos Tabuleiros, or Trays Festival, is held irregularly. It features a religious procession in which hundreds of girls parade through the old part of town, balancing elaborately decorated towers on their heads.

VALE DO LOBO (487 B1)
FARO (ALGARVE)
Located some 14 kilometers (9 miles) west of Faro, this well-planned development consists of villas and apartments, swimming pools, bars and restaurants, attractively set among pine trees. The resort offers high quality facilities for golf, tennis and other sports.

VIANA DO CASTELO (487 B4)
MINHO *pop. 16,000*
On the left bank of the Lima River, Viana do Castelo has been celebrated for its beauty since Roman times. Radiating from the square are narrow, paved streets lined with old granite houses, lively Renaissance mansions and wrought-iron balconies.

Cod fishing first brought prosperity in the 16th century, and later on wine and fruit exports helped contribute to the fine public buildings. Viana do Castelo is now as well known for its crafts and folk costumes as it is for its beaches.

▲ VILA REAL (487 B4)
TRÁS-OS-MONTES *pop. 13,900*
Vila Real, overlooking the Corgo and Cabril gorges, is an ancient town in a fertile wine region. The cathedral and other churches are interesting.

VILA REAL, the residence of the Counts of Vila Real, is one of Europe's great country houses, with beautiful furnishings and many works of art. Next to the palace is a baroque chapel, built in 1750.

DENMARK

Mainland Denmark (Jutland/Jylland) reaches right up into the North Sea. It is low-lying and fertile, with extensive pasture for livestock and a long coastline that provides excellent fishing.

A bridge links Jutland with Funen (Fyn), Denmark's second region.

The third is Zealand (Sjælland), on which stands Copenhagen (København).

The easygoing people have established an excellent system of education, health and social welfare, which causes them to turn their backs a little on the European Union.

Copenhagen has been the capital of the country since the 15th century, when it was also the capital of Norway and Sweden. The largest and liveliest of the Zealand region's cities, its Tivoli Gardens have been a magnet for locals and visitors alike for the last century and a half.

Left København, Denmark's capital, has a very attractive and colorful old harbor, known as Nyhavn
Above The Little Mermaid on København's waterfront is a sailor's dream

499

THINGS TO KNOW

- **AREA:** 42,930 square kilometers (16,633 square miles)
- **POPULATION:** 5,134,000
- **CAPITAL:** København (Copenhagen)
- **LANGUAGE:** Danish
- **ECONOMY:** Industry, agriculture, meat and dairy products. Fishing and tourism are also important.
- **PASSPORT REQUIREMENTS:** Required for U.S. citizens.
- **VISA REQUIREMENTS:** Not required for stays up to three months total in the Scandinavian countries (Denmark, Finland, Iceland, Norway, Sweden).
- **DUTY-FREE ITEMS:** See *The European Union* on p.9.
- **CURRENCY:** The currency unit is the Danish *krone*, divided into 100 *øre*. Due to currency fluctuations, the exchange rate is subject to frequent change. There is no limit on the import or export of foreign or Danish currency.
- **BANK OPENING HOURS:** 9:30am–4pm Monday–Wednesday and Friday, 9:30am–6pm Thursday (in Copenhagen).
- **PUBLIC HOLIDAYS:** January 1; Maundy Thursday; Good Friday; Easter Sunday and Monday; fourth Friday after Easter (Great Prayer Day); Ascension Day; Whitsunday and Whitmonday; June 5 – half day (Constitution Day); December 25–26.
- **NATIONAL TOURIST OFFICES:**
Danish Tourist Board
655 Third Avenue, 18th floor
New York, NY 10017
Tel: 212/949-2333
Fax: 212/855-9726
Turistrådet
Bernstorffsgade 1
1577 Copenhagen V, Denmark
Tel: 33 11 13 25
Fax: 33 93 49 69
- **AMERICAN EMBASSY:**
Dag Hammarskjöldsalle 24
DK-2100 Copenhagen Ø
Denmark
Tel: 31 42 31 44
Fax: 35 43 02 23

HISTORY

Danish ships led the way when the Viking conquest of Western Europe and the British Isles began between the 8th and 10th centuries. During this period the sailing and shipbuilding fame of the Norsemen spread throughout the continent. The Kalmar Union of Denmark, Sweden and Norway was created in 1397 under Queen Margrethe I and lasted until Sweden broke away in 1523.

Seventeenth-century Denmark witnessed the establishment of a monarchy under Christian V, and several defeats by Sweden. In the 19th century, Norway was lost to Sweden, and the provinces of Schleswig and Holstein were surrendered in battles with Prussia. The country has been a constitutional monarchy since a new constitution in 1849 ended the absolute power of the crown.

FOOD AND DRINK

One meal a day, normally *frokost* (lunch), consists of *smørrebrød* – open sandwiches of fish, herring, meat, paté, cheese and/or salads on different kinds on rye bread with butter. The hot meal of the day, *aftensmad* or *middag* (dinner) could be a fish or a meat course followed by dessert. A typical main dish would be *flaekesteg med rødkål* (roast pork with red cabbage and sucker browned potatoes), or *stegt rødspaette med persillesovs* (fried plaice with parsley or a white sauce flavored with parsley). The Danes are proud of their hams, cheeses and pastries. *Snaps (Aalborg akvavit)* is the

---

AUTOMOBILE CLUB
Forenede Danske Motorejere
(F.D.M., Federation of Danish Motorists); Firskovvej 32, P.O. Box 500, 2800 Lyngby, has branches in cities throughout Denmark. The symbol ▲ indicates the presence of a AAA-affiliated automobile club branch. All auto clubs offer full travel services to AAA members.

national drink, and Danish beer has an international reputation for its high quality.

SPORTS AND RECREATION

Denmark has fine facilities for most land and water sports. Tennis and riding clubs are plentiful, and many cities have golf courses. Soccer is the favorite spectator sport. In this seafaring nation, all water sports are extremely popular on the bays, lakes and streams.

GETTING AROUND

Ferries are essential links between highway and railroad stops on the major islands. Reservations may be necessary, especially in summer. On land, you can buy a number of bus and rail combination packages from Danish State Railways (D.S.B.) and other companies. Major cities sell special travel cards for use on buses and trains, which may include discounts on museum entrance fees. Bicycles, popular throughout the country,

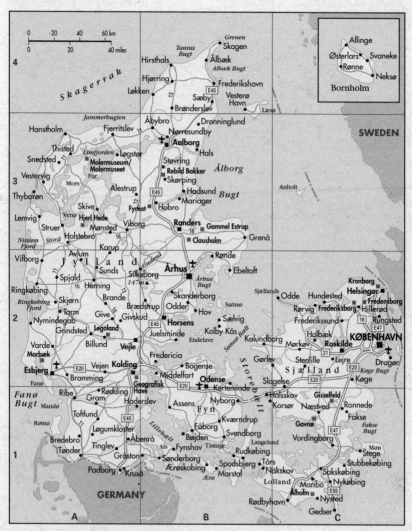

can be rented from D.S.B. Local tourist offices also have information about bicycle rental. Car rental services operate from the major cities. A motorboat or horse-cab tour is a good way to see Copenhagen.

You can drive to Denmark by traveling north from Germany and entering at either Kruså or Padborg, or by taking the car ferry from Puttgarden to Rødbyhavn. Ferries also operate directly from Harwich or Newcastle-upon-Tyne, England, to Esbjerg on the west coast of Jylland.

Roads in Denmark are generally very good and well-marked. Main highways are marked with green and white signs bearing numbers with the prefix E. Primary roads are designated by one- or two-digit numbers on yellow signs, and secondary roads are labeled with three-digit numbers on white signs.

Front- and rear-seat occupants must wear seat belts if fitted. A child under seven years must use a suitable restraint system; it is recommended that a child under three years sits in a baby seat and does not travel in front. All motorists must drive with low-beam headlights on during the day. Visiting motorists are required to pay on-the-spot fines for motoring violations. Speed limits are 50 k.p.h. (31 m.p.h.) in town, 80 k.p.h. (50 m.p.h.) on out-of-town roads and 100 k.p.h. (62 m.p.h.) on highways, unless otherwise posted.

ACCOMMODATIONS

Hotels are not classified in Denmark. Many establishments offer breakfast and include Value Added Tax (V.A.T.) and service charges in their room rates. Several international hotel chains operate in Denmark and issue vouchers with discounts at certain periods. *Kroer* are small country inns, many of which are very old; they offer comfortable lodgings and good food for reasonable rates. The Danish National Tourist Board publishes a list of hotels, and local tourist offices have details of country houses, farms and homes with guest rooms; breakfast may not be included in the room rate.

Over 100 *vandrerhjem* (hostels) also serve travelers in Denmark with accommodations of a high standard. The country has more than 500 campgrounds; some campgrounds have cottages that can be rented. The F.D.M. (see *Automobile Club* on p.500) operates about 25 camping areas that welcome members of other automobile clubs. An International Camping Carnet or Danish Camping Carnet, which can be purchased at all Danish campgrounds, is required.

TIPPING

Restaurant checks often include a gratuity charge. Tips are included in taxi fares, but railroad porters, washroom and coat-check attendants expect small tips.

PRINCIPAL TOURING AREAS

Note: For descriptions of attractions in **bold type**, see individual listings.

The government of Denmark has formulated a number of tours called the Green Roads. These tours avoid expressways and include all major points of interest, as well as many others.

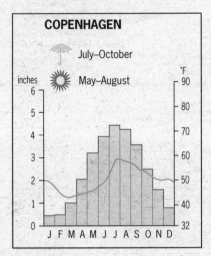

COPENHAGEN

July–October

May–August

inches / °F

KØBENHAVN – ODENSE – RIBE – ESBJERG

Green Road North leads from **København** (Copenhagen) on the eastern coast of the east island of Sjælland (Zealand), and proceeds southwest through medieval **Roskilde** and Slagelse, the site of a Viking garrison, to the port of Korsør. From Korsør, a ferry runs to Fyn Island and crosses a waterway known as Store Bælt (the Big Belt). At **Nyborg**, the site of the oldest castle in Denmark, the road winds northward along the coast to Kerteminde, and then curves to **Odense**, capital of Fyn and home of the storyteller Hans Christian Andersen. The route then passes through Hindevad, on to Middelfart and the Lille Bælt Bridge to the Jylland (Jutland) Peninsula, the Danish mainland.

South of the fjord-head city of **Kolding**, the road passes by quaint Christiansfeld then veers across the moors through Rødding to **Ribe**. A short distance up the west coast is the major port of **Esbjerg**.

Grand Southern Green Road leaves the Green Road North at **Nyborg**, and goes directly to Odense. Turning south, the route passes close to the beautiful Egeskov manor house at Kvaerndrup. The tour continues south through the château country of Fyn to **Svendborg**, then heads west through Ollerup to the 18th-century town of **Fåborg**. Next is Bøjden and a ferry to Fynshav, on the island of Als.

The route then cuts across the base of the peninsula via **Sønderborg**, Gråsten and Kollund, to **Tønder**, where the medieval past is remembered in its museum and in the charm of its main street. It rejoins the Green Road West route in nearby Møgeltønder and continues to **Esbjerg**.

KRUSÅ – FREDERIKSHAVN

This tour runs the length of Jylland (Jutland) from the German border at Flensburg. From **Frederikshavn**, centre of a beach resort area, ships sail to Göteborg, Sweden, and Oslo, Norway.

Green Road East follows a path along the east coast of the peninsula. From Kruså it reaches the important fjord port of Åbenrå via a loop through Gråsten, the dowager Queen's summer residence, and **Sønderborg**. The road proceeds due north past Christiansfeld, **Kolding** and Vejle, to the industrial port of Horsens.

From **Århus**, Denmark's second-largest city, the route continues to **Randers** and Mariager, on Mariager Fjord. Here it turns inland along the fjord to Hobro, then runs north to Rebild. **Aalborg** is the next large city before the route bears northeast to Sæby and **Frederikshavn**.

Green Road West leaves Kruså and travels through **Tønder** and **Ribe** – a side trip can be made to **Esbjerg** – to Varde. Here it turns northwest to the beach resort of Nymindegab, then travels along the narrow strand between the Ringkøbing Fjord and the sea, to Søndervig and **Ringkøbing**.

Leaving the dunelands, the route goes east to **Holstebro** and north to **Skive**, where it turns northwest. It follows the northwest shore of the great Limfjorden, where the largest island, Mors, has

DENMARK

interesting geological deposits and good oysters! The road veers east to Åbybro where it turns north.

A final arch through Løkken and the commercial center of Hjørring takes the tour to end at **Skagen**, on the peninsula's tip.

RØDBYHAVN – KØBENHAVN – HELSINGØR

Rødbyhavn, on Lolland Island near Rødby, is the main ferry port from Puttgarden, on Fehmarn Island in Germany. From **Helsingør**, or Elsinore, a ferry crosses to Helsingborg, Sweden. The two tours described below begin at Rødbyhavn.

Green Road East starts on Lolland and leads from Rødbyhavn east to **Nysted**, noted for its antique automobile collection at Ålholm Castle. The tour route then turns north and proceeds by bridge to **Nykøbing**, on the island of Falster, and Stubbekøbing, where there is a ferry to Bogø Island and a bridge leading to the steep chalk cliffs on the island of Møn. The road crosses the eastern bulge of Sjælland (Zealand) through Praestø to **Køge**, where there are several fine manors. It curves along Køge Bay to **København** (Copenhagen). North of the capital city it follows the coast to Elsinore, passing resorts and historic sites. An extension proceeds west along the northern coast of Zealand, through Holbæk and other resorts, ending on the peninsula of Sjællands Odde.

Green Road West heads north across the island of Lolland from Rødbyhavn to Maribo and Knuthenborg Safari Park, then east through Sakskøbing. It crosses the Storstrøms bridge to Vordingborg, Sjælland, and continues north to the medieval town of **Næstved**.

From Næstved the route meanders through Gisselfeld Manor to **Køge**. Beyond Copenhagen it reaches Elsinore by way of **Hillerød** and Fredensborg.

USEFUL EXPRESSIONS IN DANISH

hello/good morning	godmorgen
good-bye	farvel
good afternoon	goddag
good evening	godaften
please/thank you	vær så venlig/tak
yes/no	ja/nej
excuse me	undskyld
you're welcome	åh, jeg be'r
Does anyone here speak English?	Er der nogen her der taler engelsk?
I don't understand	Jeg forstår ikke
Where are the restrooms?	Hvor er toilettet?
Do you take credit cards?	Tager de kreditkort?
How much is that?	Hvor meget koster dat?
What time is it?	Hvad er klokken?
where/when	hvor/hvornår
how	hvordan
yesterday	i går
today/tomorrow	i dag/i morgen
What does this mean?	Hvad betyder dette?
cheap/expensive	billig/dyr
open/closed	åben/lukket
vacant/occupied	ledig/optaget
good/bad	god/dårlig

DAYS OF THE WEEK

Sunday	søndag
Monday	mandag
Tuesday	tirsdag
Wednesday	onsdag
Thursday	torsdag
Friday	fredag
Saturday	lørdag

NUMBERS

1	en
2	to
3	tre
4	fire
5	fem
6	seks
7	syv
8	otte
9	ni
10	ti

PLACES OF INTEREST

DENMARK

★ HIGHLIGHTS ★	
Århus	(see p.507)
Fåborg	(see p.508)
Helsingør (Elsinore)	(see p.509)
Hillerød	(see p.509)
Humlebæk	(see p.510)
København	(see p.505)
(Copenghagen)	
Odense	(see p.511)
Rungsted	(see p.512)
Karen Blixen	(see p.512)
Museum	
Skagen	(see p.512)
Svendborg	(see p.513)
Egeskov Slot	(see p.513)

COPENHAGEN – *see København below.*

▲ KØBENHAVN ★
SJÆLLAND *pop. 1,450,000*

Although Vikings and fishermen had known this site for years as Havn (Harbor), the founding of København, or Copenhagen, dates from 1167. As commerce flourished, the name was changed to Køpmannæhafn (Merchants' Harbor); in 1443, the city became capital of the Kingdom of Denmark.

Home to a quarter of Denmark's population, the capital city is a focus for commerce, culture and industry and has a cosmopolitan atmosphere.

Copenhagen has impressive theaters, museums and churches, but its best-loved attractions include the Tivoli Gardens, the Langelinie harbor with its Lille Havfrue ("Little Mermaid") statue, and the busy shopping promenade of Strøget.

A canal tour is a relaxing way to get your bearings. Guided tours of Tuborg and Carlsberg breweries, as well as the Royal Copenhagen china factory, are popular tourist trips. The Copenhagen Card offers travel on buses and trains in Copenhagen and nearby, as well as admission to over 60 museums, and other discounts. Kastrup, Copenhagen's international airport, is 10 kilometers (6 miles) south.

AMALIENBORG (507 D3), Amaliegade, has been the royal palace since 1794. When the Queen is at home, guard changes are at noon. Closed to the public.

MUSEET FOR DANMARKS FRIHEDSKAMP (Danish Resistance Museum) (507 D4), Churchillparken, has collections of objects relating to World War II.

KØBENHAVNS BYMUSEET (Copenhagen City Museum) (506 A1), Vesterbrogade 59, describes the history of the city.

LILLE HAVFRUE (Little Mermaid) (507 E4), the well-known statue on the harbor promenade, is the symbol of the city.

NATIONALMUSEET (506 C2), Ny Vestergade 10, has special collections presenting Denmark from the Ice Age through the Viking period to the present.

ORLOGSMUSEET (The Royal Naval Museum) (507 D2), Overgaden Oven Vandet 58A, details the history of the navy, in a renovated naval hospital.

ROSENBORG SLOT (506 C3) Øster Voldgade 4A, a Renaissance building erected by Christian IV, contains the Danish crown jewels and other treasures.

RUNDETÅRN (Round Tower) (506 C3), Købmagergade 52A, was built in 1643 by Christian IV. Erected to adjoin the Church of the Trinity, it was used as an observatory.

STATENS MUSEUM FOR KUNST (Royal Museum of Fine Arts) (506 C4), Solvgade, houses the national collection of 16th-century works by Danish artists as well as works by French and Dutch old masters.

TIVOLI (506 B2) is considered to be the heart of Copenhagen. This 8-hectare (20-acre) pleasure garden has been a celebrated amusement park since 1843. In addition to rides, there are free con-

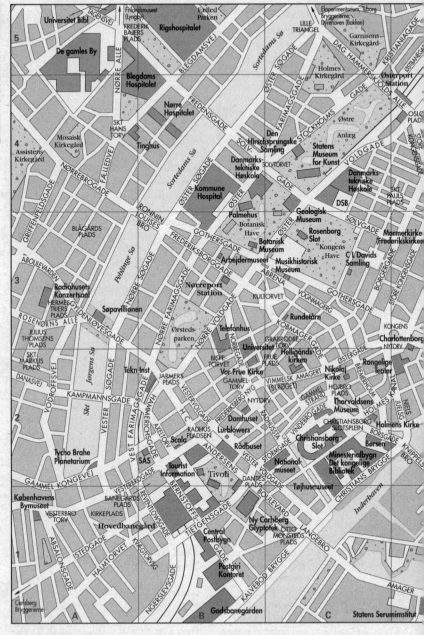

certs, puppet shows, ballet performances, illuminated gardens, fireworks, parades, and supervised playgrounds. Restaurants and cafés add to its charm.

TYCHO BRAHE PLANETARIUM (506 A2) Kongevej 10, was named after the renowned 16th-century Danish astronomer. Interesting star shows are given.

▲ AALBORG (501 B3)
JYLLAND *pop. 155,000*

Aalborg is a highly industrialized transportation center and is known for manufacturing *akvavit*, Denmark's national drink. Aalborg's modern architecture contrasts with such structures as the 15th-century Holy Ghost Monastery and the 16th-century Aalborghus Castle. The many entertainment spots and colorful cafés give hard-working Aalborg a light-hearted atmosphere.

NORDJYLLANDS KUNSTMUSEUM (North Jutland Art Museum), Kong Christians Alle 50, was designed mainly by Finnish architect Alvar Ålto. Collections feature Danish art of the 20th century, as well as works by Picasso and Le Corbusier.

▲ ÅRHUS (501 B2) ★
JYLLAND *pop. 250,000*

Denmark's second-largest city, Århus is a popular resort. The city has been an episcopal center since the 10th century. Many very old structures can still be seen, including the early medieval Vor Frue Kirke (Church of Our Lady), in contrast to the modern city hall.

GAMLE BY (Old Town), Viborgvej, is an open-air museum with a fascinating collection of more than 70 17th- and 18th-century houses, brought here from all over Denmark.

DOMKIRKE (Cathedral), Store Torv/ Bispetorv, begun in 1201, has an intricately carved pulpit and some fine frescoes. The altar tryptich dates from before the Reformation – an unusual survival.

ÆRØSKOBING (501 B1)
ÆRO *pop. 1,200*

Ærøskobing, on Ærø Island, has a museum displaying more than 400 model ships in bottles. Hammerichs Hus is a merchant's house displaying various items from South Jylland (Jutland) and nearby islands. The town itself has many 17th- and 18th-century houses, which line the cobbled streets.

VOR FRELSERS KIRKE (Our Savior's Church) (506 D1) Prinsessegade, is a baroque church with an external staircase around the spire.

DENMARK

BILLUND (501 A2)
JYLLAND *pop. 4,600*

LEGOLAND, near Billund airport and the factory where Lego toys are made, is a children's park erected from more than 35 million Lego bricks. Features include miniature re-creations of a Danish town and prominent buildings and sights from around the world.

There is a large collection of antique dolls and dolls' houses. Concerts, plays and movies are presented in the 200-seat children's theater.

BORNHOLM ISLAND (501 C4)
pop. 47,200

The easternmost Danish island in the Baltic Sea is seven hours journey from Copenhagen by ferry. The island has been Danish since 1660. Four 12th-century round churches that remain today were constructed as fortifications against attacks by pagan islanders; the church at Østerlars is particularly notable.

At the northern tip of the island, on a steep seaside cliff, are the ruins of 13th-century Hammershus Castle. White sand beaches, smokehouses for herring, pastel-painted homes, and a countryside ideal for walking and cycling add to Bornholm's charm.

ELSINORE – *see Helsingør on p.509.*

▲ ESBJERG (501 A2)
JYLLAND *pop. 80,000*

Esbjerg, one of Denmark's most important fishing ports, is a vital import-export and industrial center. After the port was built in the late 19th century, the city grew quickly from a tiny village. Today, the lively fish auction halls, said to be the largest in Northern Europe, can be visited on weekdays during the summer, and there is an interesting fisheries museum. Esbjerg is a point of departure for passenger ships bound for Great Britain and for Denmark's Faerøerne (Faroe) Islands, more than 1,000 kilometers (625 miles) northwest in the seas of the Atlantic.

FANØ, a few miles southeast of Esbjerg and easily reached by ferry, was a center for shipbuilding in the era of sail. The island's sandy beach runs for 16 kilometers (10 miles) and is popular. Relatively peaceful, Fanø is a good place to camp.

FÅBORG (501 B1) ★
FYN *pop. 18,000*

Fåborg, an 18th-century market town, is well-preserved, with streets and some houses dating from the late 18th century. Of interest are the clock tower, the Art Museum of Funen Painters, the western town gate and the 12th-century Horne Kirke, a round church.

MARKETS, FAIRS AND FESTIVALS

Market days are a regular weekly feature all over Denmark, with the market square or pedestrianized street filled with decorated stalls piled high with local produce. Many towns hold junk fairs and flea markets – there's a junk market in Esbjerg on the first Saturday of each month. Agricultural fairs are very popular at Roskilde and Åbenrå (both in June), when cattle, horses and sheep are for sale. In addition, there are Norse fairs, Viking markets, and tilting festivals. Many coastal towns have Harbor or Herring festivals, and everywhere there is music to suit all tastes, often performed in fine settings such as castles and parks. Midsummer Day is celebrated with bonfires. For more information contact the relevant local tourist office.

FAERØERNE
pop. 41,600

More than 1,000 kilometers (620 miles) from Denmark's west coast lie the Faerøerne, or Faroe Islands, a triangle of 18 windswept islands, 17 of which are inhabited. The best time to visit is mid-May through September. Tórshavn, the capital, is on Streymoy.

Sea birds flock in their thousands to the craggy seaside cliffs, especially near Vestmanna on Streymoy. Ancient structures can still be seen in villages clustered around old churches. Modern towns reflect the Faroes' dependence on the fishing industry.

A network of buses, ships and ferries links towns and villages. Rental cars are available from Tórshavn and the main airport on the island of Vágar. Car ferries sail weekly from the Danish mainland, and there are daily flights from Copenhagen.

FAROE ISLANDS – *see Faerøerne above.*

FREDERICIA (501 B2)
JYLLAND *pop. 29,000*
A fortified town, built by King Frederik III in 1649 to defend the Jylland (Jutland) Peninsula. The ramparts are among the best-preserved in Europe.

▲ FREDERIKSHAVN (501 B4)
JYLLAND *pop. 28,000*
Frederikshavn's fine natural harbor has made it a busy fishing port and the main gateway to Denmark from Norway and Sweden. The town was fortified in the 17th century to assure safe commerce with Norway. The nearby coast has popular beaches.

FREDERIKSSUND (501 C2)
SJÆLLAND *pop. 14,050*
Frederikssund is noted for its annual 16-day Viking Festival, held late June through early July.

JÆGERPRIS SLOT was a royal summer residence until the death of King Frederik VII, when it was passed to Countess Danner, his wife. The rooms are richly furnished.

HELSINGØR (501 C2) ★
SJÆLLAND *pop. 57,000*
Immortalized by Shakespeare, who chose its castle for the setting of *Hamlet*,

Helsingør, or Elsinore, has a story apart from that of the "melancholy Dane." It is a seaport, a resort, and a ship-building and commercial center, with ferry routes to nearby Sweden.

Today, Elsinore's old half-timbered houses are reminders of the past, but the city is located in a popular beach area where such modern resorts as Hornbæk share the white-sand coast with villages, fishing harbors and woods.

SANKT MARIL KIRKE (St. Mary's Church) is an abbey church, featuring an organ used by the baroque composer Dietrich Buxtehude.

KRONBORG SLOT still seems to be haunted by the tragic story of Hamlet. The castle's Renaissance grace and its great size, especially its ramparts, are as impressive today as they were in Shakespeare's time.

MARIENLYST SLOT is an interesting local history museum featuring 16th- to 20th-century paintings.

▲ HILLERØD (501 C2) ★
SJÆLLAND *pop. 34,400*
FREDERIKSBORG, a large castle that uses a lake as its moat, was completed in the early 17th century by Christian IV. Kings were crowned in the sumptuous chapel. The castle is now a National-Historical Museum, with a wealth of antiques and paintings that illustrate the history of Denmark.

▲ HOLBÆK (501 C2)
SJÆLLAND *pop. 21,500*
Founded in 1270, Holbæk is a port, a trade center, and a good base for trips to Odsherred, the area that surrounds the town and stretches some 70 kilometers (44 miles) to the west.

▲ HOLSTEBRO (501 A3)
JYLLAND *pop. 30,100*
Holstebro, on the Storå River, dates from the 13th century. The Museum of Art contains modern Danish art and

DENMARK

works by Matisse and Picasso. An unusual church in the town is built around an inner courtyard.

HUMLEBÆK (501 C2) ★
LOUISIANAMUSEET, Humlebæk, has a fine collection of contemporary art that includes works by Henry Moore, Max Ernst, and Alberto Giacometti, both indoors and in a landscaped garden.

KØGE (501 C2)
SJÆLLAND *pop. 35,000*
Picturesque Køge is noted for its half-timbered houses, especially the one at

---

DIGGING UP THE PAST

In a land where the Iron Age, Bronze Age and Stone Age are gradually yielding their treasures, it is not surprising that the Danes are so enthusiastic about re-creating the past. Apart from excellent museum collections, such as finds from the Stone Age at Aalborg Historical Museum, from the Iron Age at Silkeborg, and from the Bronze Age at the National Museum in Copenhagen, other centers have re-created realistic dwellings.
The Historical-Archeological Center at Lejre has reconstructed an Iron Age village, and at Hollufgård near Odense, reproductions of early prehistoric houses have been built.

Kirkstræde 20, built in 1527 and Denmark's oldest date-marked house. There are some fine castles in the area.

▲ KOLDING (501 A2)
JYLLAND *pop. 58,000*
Amid some of the most spectacular scenery in Denmark, Kolding is on a fjord that cuts into the eastern shore of Jylland. Southeast of the town, Geografiske Have (Geographical Garden) contains plants and flowers from around the world.

MARSTAL (501 B1)
ÆRØ *pop. 4,000*
The largest town on the picturesque island of Aerø, Marstal is linked by ferry to Rudkøbing, on the neighboring island of Langeland. The Søfartsmuseum (Maritime Museum) has ship models and mementos of the sailing era.

▲ NÆSTVED (501 C1)
SJÆLLAND *pop. 38,200*
A thriving industrial center, Næstved has kept its medieval charm with its many half-timbered houses. Every Wednesday morning, the brightly costumed royal cavalry ride through town blowing trumpets.

NAKSKOV (501 B1)
LOLLAND *pop. 16,400*
Nakskov is the main town and harbor on Lolland and still has many picturesque half-timbered houses. Many visitors come to the island for its excellent beaches.

NYBORG (501 B1)
FYN *pop. 18,000*
An old fortress town, Denmark's capital in the Middle Ages, Nyborg is the terminus of the ferries that cross the 32-kilometer (20-mile) wide Store Bælt to Sjælland (Zealand).

NYBORG SLOT (Nyborg Castle), dating from 1170, is one of the oldest royal castles in Scandinavia. It was the seat of the Danish parliament until 1413.

▲ NYKØBING (501 C1)
FALSTER *pop. 26,000*
Nykøbing, the main town on the island of Falster, is on Guldborg Sound. Tsar's House commemorates a visit by Peter the Great of Russia.

NYSTED (501 C1)
LOLLAND *pop. 1,970*
ÅLHOLM SLOT, a large 12th-century castle, is noted for its museum of antique automobiles, where 200 vehicles from the period 1886 to 1936 are displayed.

HANS CHRISTIAN ANDERSEN

Born in Odense in 1805 – his childhood home can be visited – Hans Andersen was orphaned at the age of 10. His ambition was to go on the stage, and at 14 he went to Copenhagen and tried, unsuccessfully, to become an actor. So he started to write plays instead (most of which are lost) and then to travel widely. After he visited Italy he wrote a book about childhood in Rome as if it were his own. This was a great success, and he then began to write the fairy tales for which he became so famous.

▲ ODENSE (501 B2) ★
FYN *pop. 170,000*

Odense, the third-largest city in Denmark, is the capital of the island of Fyn (Funen). One of Scandinavia's oldest settlements, it dates from the 9th century. Odense has two faces: the fairytale appearance of its streets and houses, and the modern visage of manufacture, commerce and shipping. Hans Christian Andersen was born here in 1805.

BRANDTS KLÆDEFABRIK CULTURAL CENTER, Brandt's Pasage 37, is an old textile mill that is now a museum and entertainment complex, with the museums of Photographic Art, Graphic Art and the Press, an art gallery, and a movie theater.

CARL NIELSEN MUSEET, Claus Bergs Gade 11, is a museum devoted to Denmark's most famous composer and his wife, the sculptress Anne Marie.

HANS CHRISTIAN ANDERSENS HUS, Hans Jensens Stræde 37–45, was the storyteller's birthplace. There is a musum of his life, with manuscripts, a multimedia show, and recordings of some of his tales.

SANKT HANS KIRKE (St. Hans Church), Nørregade 42, is from the 14th century and has Denmark's only open-air pulpit.

SANKT KNUDS KIRKE (St. Canute's Church), Flalchauen, is 13th- to 14th-century Gothic and has the tomb of the 11th-century martyr King Canute the Holy.

▲ RANDERS (501 B3)
JYLLAND *pop. 60,000*

An old town ringed by parks, on the Nørre and Gudenå rivers, both good for canoeing and fishing. Interesting buildings line the narrow streets; of special note is 15th-century St. Morten's Church.

GAMMEL ESTRUP, a castle east of Randers near Auning, is one of Denmark's most magnificent 15th-century manor houses. It contains the Jyllands Herragårds museum (Jutland's Manor House Museum). Collections are of national interest and focus on folklore, painting, furniture, tapestries and china.

Dansk Landbrugesmuseum (Danish Agricultural Museum) is housed in the farm buildings of the castle.

REBILD BAKKER, about 40 kilometers (25 miles) north, has the Danish-American Emigration Museum, featuring a replica Abraham Lincoln log cabin.

RIBE (501 A1)
JYLLAND *pop. 8,000*

A cathedral town founded by Vikings in about AD 860, Ribe is Denmark's oldest community. The entire medieval center, with over 500 buildings, is beautifully preserved by the Danish National Trust.

DOMKIRKE (Cathedral) was built during the 12th century. It combines late Romanesque and early Gothic styles.

VIKING AND MEDIEVAL MUSEUM, Odinsplads, re-creates a Viking settlement, complete with workshops, a replica ship, sounds and smells.

SANKT CATHARINÆ KIRKE OG KLOSTER (St. Catherine's Church and Abbey) were founded by the Dominicans (Black Friars) in 1228. It is one of Denmark's best-preserved abbeys.

DENMARK

RINGKØBING (501 A2)
JYLLAND *pop. 8,400*
Founded in 1250, Ringkøbing is a fjord-side town surrounded by dunes. The well-preserved town center boasts a town hall and a museum containing some remarkable prehistoric finds. A beach is 9 kilometers (5½ miles) away.

SOMMERLAND WEST, 7 kilometers (4½ miles) north of town at Hee, is a wildlife and bird sanctuary, a children's amusement park and a Viking village with demonstrations of weaving, baking and archery.

RØMØ (501 A1)
JYLLAND *pop. 816*
Linked to the mainland by a causeway, Rømø is a popular seaside resort. The island's west coast supports a rich variety of bird species and has fine beaches.

NATIONALMUSEETS KOMMANDØRGAARD, at nearby Toftum, portrays the lifestyle of Rømø's prosperous 18th-century commanders (whalers).

▲ ROSKILDE (501 C2)
SJÆLLAND *pop. 50,000*
Roskilde, on Roskilde Fjord, was the capital city of Denmark from the 10th century until 1443, and was the king's residence until the 15th century.

PALÆSAMLINGERNE (Palace Collections), Staendertorvet 3E, features exhibits of furniture and paintings in the east wing of the former Bishop's Palace.

DOMKIRKE (Cathedral) is an 800-year-old cathedral containing the centuries-old tombs of 38 Danish kings and queens.

ROSKILDE MUSEUM, 18 Skt. Ols Gade, is a museum of cultural history containing local costumes, embroidery and toys.

VIKINGESKIBSHALLEN (Viking Ship Hall), Strandengen, is a glass-sided museum housing five ancient ships that were raised from Roskilde Fjord in 1962.

RUDKØBING (501 B1)
LANGELAND *pop. 7,000*
Rudkøbing is the largest town on Langeland Island, with many timber-framed and 18th-century houses. The of grounds of Tranekær Castle, north of town, are open.

RUNGSTED (501 C2) ★
SJÆLLAND *pop. 6,100*
KAREN BLIXEN MUSEUM is the birthplace of the Danish author whose pen name was Isak Dinesen. Her best-known work is *Out of Africa*. The house has elegant rooms that have been left untouched since Blixen's death in 1962.

▲ SILKEBORG (501 A2)
JYLLAND *pop. 34,180*
On the banks of Denmark's longest river and surrounded by beautiful countryside, Silkeborg is one of the country's leading holiday centers. About 25 kilometers (16 miles) southeast is Skanderborg, which has a small museum and the remains of a medieval castle. On the way to Skanderborg are forests and a chain of scenic lakes.

JUTLAND AUTOMOBILE MUSEUM, about 25 kilometers (16 miles) northeast at Gjern, has a collection of some 135 restored vintage cars, dating from 1900 to 1942.

SILKEBORG MUSEUM, Hovedgården, exhibits stone implements, ancient jewelry and glass. The museum's most important exhibit is the well-preserved head of the 2,200-year-old Tollund Man, who was found in a peat bog.

SKAGEN (501 B4) ★
JYLLAND *pop. 12,000*
The fishing center of Skagen has flourished at the gateway between the Kattegat and the North Sea since the Middle Ages. During the 19th century the town became a cultural center; interest in the arts continues as artists are drawn to the extended daylight of Denmark's northernmost town. The area is also a popular seaside resort.

THE VIKINGS

Ships found at Roskilde forts and burial grounds have provided many clues about these warlike people who lived in Denmark around 1,000 years ago. Among the most exciting finds are the four ring forts at Trelleborg, Aggersborg, Nonnebakken and Fyrkat. The ring at Fyrkat was used for about 20 years, and consisted of a circular rampart, covered with wooden palisades, which was protected from the outside by a moat. Streets led to the houses, each inhabited by about 50 people, which were grouped around squares. Smaller buildings are likely to have been workshops and storerooms. Viking graves here have yielded pots, spindles, rings and keys, proving that the Vikings were not always at war and had achieved a high degree of technical skill.

Viking finds are to be seen at the Hobro Museum and at the large burial site at Lindholm Hoje, near Aalborg.

SKAGEN FORTIDSMINDER is an open-air museum with several buildings furnished to show the hard lives of fisherfolk and lifeboat men of the last two centuries.

SKAGEN MUSEUM, Brøndumvej, displays Danish paintings, and sculpture created by local artists between 1830 and 1930.

▲ SKIVE (501 A3)
JYLLAND *pop. 20,100*
An industrial town on the Skivefjord whose medieval church boasts 16th-century frescoes. The local museum displays antiquities and a modern art collection.

HJERL HEDES FRILANDSMUSEUM, southwest, is an open-air museum showing the development of the Danish village from 1500 to 1900. Buildings have been moved here from all over Denmark.

▲ SØNDERBORG (501 B1)
JYLLAND *pop. 25,900*
Sønderborg is a busy commercial, industrial and educational center on the island of Als. Its castle, Sønderberg Slot, has an interesting chapel and museum.

STEGE (501 C1)
MØN *pop. 2,220*
Stege is a pleasant country town with some old buildings. On the eastern side of Møn Island are chalk cliffs carved by erosion into peculiar conical shapes.

▲ SVENDBORG (501 B1)
FYN *pop. 37,500*
The harbor town and yachting resort of Svendborg dates from the 12th century. A bridge connects Svendborg to the islands of Tåsinge and Langeland, and there is a frequent ferry service to the small nearby islands, which are good for swimming.

EGESKOV SLOT ★, 15 kilometres (9½ miles) north at Kværndrup, is one of Denmark's most romantic castles. Built in a lake on a foundation of oak piles, the 16th-century mansion has round corner towers and conical roofs. Inside is a series of period furnished rooms and old workshops. There is also a floral park and a museum of antique cars and airplanes.

TØNDER (501 A1)
JYLLAND *pop. 8,000*
Tønder has been known for its lace industry since the 17th century. Displays of lace and locally made silver can be seen in the Tønder Museum.

▲ VIBORG (501 A3)
JYLLAND *pop. 29,400*
Historic Viborg's setting is the lake area around the Dollerup Hills. Hans Tausen's religious movement, which began the Danish Reformation in the 16th century, originated in this town.

DOMKIRKE (Cathedral), built in 1120–80 and said to be one of the largest granite churches in Europe, retains only its original Romanesque crypt.

FINLAND

Finland's neighbors are Sweden to the west and Russia to the east. Their past influence can still be felt, not least in Swedish remaining alongside Finnish as an official language. Despite this, Finnish culture is unique.

Much of Finland's surface is water, with most of it in the lakelands in the south. Lake Inari, however, covering 1,000 square kilometers (386 square miles), is in the extreme north. This is Lappland, land of the midnight sun and the northern lights.

The capital, Helsinki, which has a seafaring background, is built on a series of peninsulas linked by bridges over the inlets. Ferries journey to the nearby islands, and to Suomenlinna (Finland's Castle); built in 1748, it is now so large that it spreads across several islands and provides today's Finns with parks, walks and museums.

Left Finland's northern lakeland region is breathtakingly beautiful
Above A far superior way to get around – take a ride with a reindeer

Things to Know

- **Area:** 337,113 square kilometers (130,160 square miles)
- **Population:** 5,100,000
- **Capital:** Helsinki (Helsingfors)
- **Language:** Finnish and Swedish.
- **Economy:** Machinery and forest products. Tourism, shipbuilding, and textile industries are also important.
- **Passport Requirements:** Required for U.S. citizens.
- **Visa Requirements:** Not required for stays up to three months total in the Scandinavian countries.
- **Duty-Free Items:** 200 cigarettes or 250 grams of other tobacco products; 2 liters of beer and 2 liters of wine, or 1 liter of wine and 1 liter of spirits; cameras and a reasonable amount of film; televisions; bicycles and other sports goods.
- **Currency:** The currency unit is the Finnish *markka*, divided into 100 *penni*. Due to currency fluctuations, the exchange rate is subject to frequent change. Unlimited amounts of foreign and Finnish currency may be imported.
- **Bank Opening Hours:** 9:15am–4:15pm Monday–Friday.
- **Public Holidays:** January 1; January 6; Good Friday; Easter Monday; May 1 (Labor Day); first Saturday after Ascension Day; Saturday nearest June 24 (Midsummer's Day); first Saturday in November (All Saints' Day); December 6 (Independence Day); December 25–26.
- **National Tourist Offices:**
  Finnish National Tourist Board
  655 Third Avenue
  New York, NY 10017
  Tel: 212/949-2333
  Fax: 212/983-5260
  Finnish Tourist Board Head Office
  P.O. Box 625
  00101 Helsinki, Finland
  Tel: (09) 4030 1300
  Fax: (09) 4030 1301
- **American Embassy:**
  Itäinen Puistotie 14
  00140 Helsinki, Finland
  Tel: (09) 171 931
  Fax: (09) 174 681

History

Two thousand years ago, the area that is now Finland was inhabited by nomadic Sami (Lapps). Beginning about 100 BC, people of Finno-Ugric stock settled in the area, and most of the Sami retreated to the north. Three major groups – the Finns, Tavastians and Karelians – established themselves, but it was not until the arrival of Swedish crusaders that Finland became unified. However, although Sweden was largely responsible for the introduction of Christianity to the country, in the form of Catholicism, Russians also preached Orthodoxy in the east.

For 600 years after the 12th-century Peace of Nöteborg, most of Finland was ruled by Sweden. However, the country was allowed to develop its own social order and language.

The eastern frontier was frequently harassed by Russia. In 1809, Tsar Alexander I invaded and Finland was granted virtual autonomy as a grand duchy of Russia. Finland established its independence during the turmoil that followed World War I and the Russian Revolution. However, by the end of World War II, Finland had been forced to cede territories in the north and the southeast (Karelia) to the U.S.S.R. Rapid reconstruction and economic progress took place during the postwar years.

Modern Finland is a parliamentary democracy, with highest powers vested in a president and in a single-chamber parliament. The country was the first European nation to grant women political rights equal to those enjoyed by men.

Food and Drink

Fish is at the heart of Finnish cuisine, and an array of dishes is built around salmon, whitefish and Baltic herring. Crawfish, in season from late July to September, are enthusiastically consumed. Finnish cookery also includes a variety of meats and soups. Regional dishes include *kalakukko*, a pie of fish and pork, and *karjalan piirakka*, a rye pastry stuffed with rice or potato and eaten with egg butter. Reindeer meat is prepared in many different ways.

Finnish restaurants have been greatly influenced by Swedish, Russian and French cooking, and visitors find the results pleasing. Many still serve *voileipäpöytä*, the Finnish version of the Swedish *smörgåsbord*, for lunch. Distinctive Finnish beverages are vodka, and liqueurs flavoured with *mesimarja* (arctic bramble), *lakka* (cloudberry) and *polar* (cranberry).

SPORTS AND RECREATION

Not surprisingly, water-related sports are those most enjoyed by Finns. Boating and fishing continue all year, and the sea and lakes are warm enough for swimming during the summer. The water also attracts boating and canoeing enthusiasts. Less energetic visitors can take excursions on lake steamers. Northern Finland offers salmon, perch and other catches for summertime fishermen. Larger towns provide tennis, riding and horse racing. International track events are held in Helsinki's Olympic Stadium.

In winter, Finland is a magnet for cross-country skiers, and the Finlandia Ski Race draws some 10,000 participants each winter. Other activities are ice fishing, ice skating and snowmobiling. Tours by reindeer-drawn sleighs are available in Lappland.

Finland has approximately one sauna for every five Finns, so visitors are never far from one of these warm, wood-lined rooms. When water is tossed onto stones topping a special stove, the resulting steam causes the room's occupants to perspire. This is traditionally followed by a cooling dip in a lake or the sea.

GETTING AROUND

A steamer network provides ferry and excursion services. Major train routes are concentrated in the south; Finnrail passes are available for three, five, or ten days of unlimited travel at a discount. Finnair, the international and internal airline, connects all major cities. In Helsinki and elsewhere, buses and streetcars are inexpensive with the purchase of multiple-journey tickets. Taxis and rental cars are plentiful, but not cheap.

Magnificent scenery rewards driving in Finland. Roads are uncrowded and well-maintained, though most routes in the far north are graded gravel, not paved. The overland trip is accomplished by driving through Sweden or Norway to Lappland, though many prefer to take their cars directly to Helsinki by ship. Departures are from Stockholm, Sweden; from Travemünde, Germany; and from Tallin, Estonia.

FINLAND

The use of seat belts in vehicles so equipped is mandatory for drivers and passengers. Motorists must drive with headlights on low beam at all times during the day when outside towns. Speed limits are 50 k.p.h. (31 m.p.h.) in town, between 60 k.p.h. (37 m.p.h.) and 100 k.p.h. (62 m.p.h.) on country roads, depending on road quality, and 120 k.p.h. (74 m.p.h.) on highways. Parking violation fines are paid with Finnish *markkas* or traveler's checks at post offices.

ACCOMMODATIONS
Although Finland does not classify its hotels, several chains offer high-quality lodging. Among these are Arctia Hotels, Best Western, Cumulus, Rantasipi and Sokos. Hotel prices are high by international standards, but there is a wide choice of alternative lodgings. Finnish Tourist Board offices give out a "Budget Accommodation" brochure listing many of these. From June 1 to August 31, buildings usually used as student accomodations open as hotels. About 500 farms have guest rooms, and many private houses offer bed and breakfast.

There are about 150 youth and family hostels, some open only in summer. Some provide meals, or guests can normally use the kitchen.

Campers have a choice of about 200 campgrounds approved by the Finnish Travel Association. Most have chalets that can be rented. Although camping away from officially designated grounds is allowed, you must first obtain permission from the landowner. An International Camping Carnet is recommended.

TIPPING
A service charge is included in restaurant checks and taxi fares; tips are not necessary. Railroad porters, bell staff and coat checkers, however, do expect tips.

PRINCIPAL TOURING AREAS

Note: For descriptions of attractions in **bold type**, see individual listings.

THE LAKELAND AND FORESTS
Most of Finland's thousands of lakes are in an area stretching from the eastern border to within 96 kilometers (60 miles) of the western coast. Many lakes are linked by waterways that are popular for excursions. The eastern section of this region is dominated by Lake Saimaa, a vast series of interconnected lakes dotted with about 33,000 islands. This wild expanse, amounting to 25 percent of the country's area, is broken by Kuopio and **Jyväskylä**, lake-based cities popular for water sports. **Tampere** is the lakeland's largest city.

The area north of the lakeland along the eastern border is remote and largely unspoiled, and is a popular destination for canoeists and hikers.

> AUTOMOBILE CLUB
> **Autoliitto** (Automobile and Touring Club of Finland) has offices at Hämeentie 105 A, 00550 Helsinki. The symbol ▲ indicates the presence of a AAA-affiliated automobile club branch. Not all auto clubs offer full travel services to AAA members.

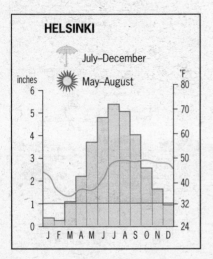

HELSINKI

July–December

May–August

inches / °F

THE NORTH

The northern third of Finland is much more than snow and northern lights. Plants live a complete cycle during the three summer months, then are replaced by the blazing colors of the Lappland autumn; midwinter brings dramatic displays of the northern lights. In the northeasternmost section dwell about 4,000 Sami, many of whom still herd reindeer that graze freely for most of the year.

The provincial capital is **Rovaniemi**, only 10 kilometers (6 miles) from the Arctic Circle. Although the province is sparsely settled, its four cities are easily accessible by daily air and rail services.

THE SOUTHERN COAST

Finland's southern coast stretches from Pori, on the Baltic Sea, to the eastern border. Low, red or gray granite rocks characterize the coast, but there are a few sandy beaches; because there are almost no tides, the seashore resembles a lakeshore. Off the southwest coast are the **Åland** (Ahvenanmaa in Finnish) Islands, over 30,000 granite islands, islets and reefs.

The **Helsinki** (Helsingfors in Swedish) metropolitan area to the southeast is the most densely populated region, with about 750,000 inhabitants. The coast along the Gulf of Finland has several ports and former garrison towns.

THE WESTERN COAST

Along the Gulf of Bothnia, from **Kemi** to **Pori**, the western coast is lined with farms and good, sandy beaches. The region has the country's sunniest and driest climate. Picturesque old wooden houses grace many of the towns, where local traditions are kept alive through annual festivals. Between **Vaasa** and Kokkola are islands with old fishing villages. **Turku** (Åbo in Swedish), the old capital, is Finland's second city, and the heart of the Swedish-speaking area. Oula is the main center for scientific research, commerce and education.

USEFUL EXPRESSIONS IN FINNISH

Finnish has no relationship to the other Scandinavian languages, although some Finns speak Swedish. Pronunciation corresponds to the spelling, with the first syllable always stressed.

good morning	hyvää huomenta
good evening	hyvää iltaa
good night	hyvää yötä
good-bye	hyvästi
yes/no	kyllä/ei
please	olkaa hyvä
thank you	kiitos
excuse me	anteeksi
you're welcome	ei kestä
Does anyone here speak English?	Puhuuko kukaan täällä englantia?
I don't understand	En ymmärrä
Where are the restrooms?	Missä on w.c.?
Do you take credit cards?	Voinko maksaa luottokorttejä?
How much is that?	Mitä se maksaa?
What time is it?	Mitä kello on?
when	milloin
where	missä
how	kuinka
how long	kuinka kauan
how far	kuinka kaukana
yesterday	eilen
today	tänään
tomorrow	huomenna
good/bad	hyvä/huono
cheap/expensive	halpa/kallis
open/closed	avoin/suljettu
old/new	vanha/uusi
hot/cold	kuuma/kylmä
big/small	suuri/pieni
left/right	vasen/oikea
early/late	aikainen/myöhäinen

DAYS OF THE WEEK

Sunday	sunnuntai
Monday	maanantai
Tuesday	tiistai
Wednesday	keskiviiko
Thursday	torstai
Friday	perjantai
Saturday	lauantai

PLACES OF INTEREST

FINLAND

▲ **HELSINKI/HELSINGFORS (517 A1) ★**
UUSIMAA *pop.500,000*

The capital and leading seaport of Finland is bounded on the north by fields and forests and on the south by the Gulf of Finland. The commercial, industrial and political heart of the nation, it is also a historical city.

Helsinki (known by Swedish-speaking Finns as Helsingfors) was founded by King Gustav Vasa of Sweden in 1550 as a trading center, but the city did not begin to flourish until the Suomenlimma fortress was built in the 18th century. With this protection from invasion, Helsinki gained importance in international shipping and trading. Few early buildings remain, mainly because most were built of wood and were destroyed by fires and invaders.

The great, wide thoroughfare of Mannerheimintie was named after General Mannerheim, Finland's leader during World War II. Near its south end is Esplanadi, an old-fashioned tree-lined promenade, leading to South Harbor. Mannerheimintie itself is a great shopping street, with many fine buildings and statues.

Major Finnish academic institutions, as well as the country's finest museums, theaters and orchestras have their headquarters in Helsinki. The Helsinki Festival, held in late summer, provides a showcase for some of Finland's finest music, dance and arts programs.

A remarkable feature of Helsinki is its wealth of greenery and uncluttered space. The central city abounds in parks, and plans for future development ensure that at least 30 percent of the total metropolitan area will remain free of construction.

The Helsinki Card offers unlimited travel in the metropolitan area on buses, trams, trains and the metro area. The card also gives discounts for car and bicycle rentals, guided walking tours, and several restaurants, as well as free admission to various museums and sights. It is valid for one to three days and can be purchased from the City Tourist Office, Pohjoisesplanadi 19; all major hotels; the Hotel Booking Center in the Railroad Station; and Stockmann's department store.

FINLANDIATALO ★, Mannerheimintie, is the magnificent national concert hall, designed by Alvar Aalto. Both Helsinki's symphony orchestras perform here, as well as many visiting orchestras and performers. It has a fine view over Töölönlahti, a beautiful lake. A little further on is the new National Opera House (opened 1994), a lovely white and glass building with superb acoustics, which also overlooks the lake.

KANSALLIS MUSEO, Mannerheimintie 34, is Finland's national museum and covers every era of Finland's history. Stone Age, Bronze Age and Iron Age artifacts evoke the life of the earliest inhabitants. Other sections deal with the Finnish folk cultures, medieval and modern history.

KAUPPATORI (Market Square) ★ is the site of Helsinki's principal year-round market, close to South Harbor. Fresh produce and flowers are sold in the outdoor stalls, and dairy products and meat in the covered hall; freshly caught fish are sold from boats moored along the quayside.

THE RAILROAD STATION ★ is a striking pinkish, granite building, with a green clocktower, all designed by Elie Saarinen. Today it also houses a metro stop and an underground shopping mall. On the north of the station square is the National Theater; a statue of Finland's national writer, Aleksis Kivi, stands in front of it.

SENAATINTORI (Senate Square) ★ is the site of several important buildings. On the north side is the great white stone cathedral Tuomiokirkko; on the west, Helsinki's university; and on the east, Government Palace. Most of the imposing structures were designed by architect Carl Ludwig Engel. The university has botanical gardens and museums of zoology, mineralogy, medicine, agriculture and paleontology.

SUOMENLINNA, nicknamed the Gibraltar of the North, is the great island-fortress at the entrance to Helsinki's harbor. Suomenlinna now has parks, seaside walks, pavilions, restaurants and an open-air theater. Two military museums are housed in sections of the former fortress.

USPENSKIN KATEDRAALI (Uspenskin Cathedral) ★ is a large Orthodox cathedral that towers above Katajanokka Hill and the island it occupies.

VALTION TAIDEMUSEO (Finnish National Gallery), Kaiuokatu 2–4, is the principal art gallery. The neo-Renaissance building comprises four individual sections: the Ateneum (Museum of Finnish Art), the Museum of Foreign Art, the Museum of Contemporary Art and the Central Art Archive.

ÅLAND ISLANDS/AHVENANMAA
(517 A1)

pop. 25,000

The 6,500 granite islands, islets and reefs of the Åland Islands (Ahvenanmaa in Finnish), lie in the southern Gulf of Bothnia, between Finland and Sweden. The archipelago, totaling some 30,000 isles, covers about 6,084 square kilometers (2,349 square miles), but less than a fifth of this is above water. Seafarers from Sweden settled in these islands early in the Middle Ages; runic inscriptions and other archaeological finds have provided clues about the lives of these first nhabitants.

Today, the islands, with their strong Swedish heritage, are an autonomous province of Finland. The citizenry fly their own flag, elect their own parliament, have their own postage stamps, and formulate most of their own political and economic policies. Populated by fishermen and farmers, the area attracts many summer vacationers who come to fish, swim and hike.

Mariehamn (Maarianhamina in Finnish) is the provincial capital and principal port, with frequent ferry services to Finland and Sweden. Most hotels and many of the man-made attractions are in this town. Interesting cave formations are near Geta, while the fortress ruins of Kastelholm and the Borgboda Viking fort are in the Sund district.

ÅLAND MUSEO, Öhbergsvägen 1, Mariehamn, is the province's museum of local history. Collections feature Stone Age artifacts and later items.

BOMARSUND, Sund, is the site of a fortress begun by the Russians in 1830. A Franco-British naval force captured and razed the stronghold in 1854. Scattered but impressive ramparts remain here.

KASTELHOLMS SLOTT (Kastelholm Ruins), Sund, was built by the Swedes in the 14th century to strengthen their position in the Baltic.

FINLAND

POMMERN, a four-masted barque in Mariehamn's harbor, is now a museum. It was the last of the graceful vessels that carried cargoes of grain from Australia to England until the 1930s.

ESPOO/ESBO (517 A1) ★
UUSIMAA *pop. 179,000*

Coastal Espoo in southern Finland was first settled more than 5,000 years ago. Emerging as an independent country parish in the 13th century, it was later absorbed as a suburb of Helsinki. However, in 1972, Espoo obtained its town charter and is now the second-largest city in the country.

Interesting for its natural features and recreational opportunities, Espoo also has man-made attractions. Among the oldest structures is the stone parish church, dating from the 15th century. Espoo Manor, now privately owned, was founded by the Swedish King Gustav Vasa in the 16th century. The University of Technology at Otaniemi has ultra-modern buildings, designed by the well-known architect Alvar Aalto.

The city's best-known attraction is the garden city of Tapiola. This innovative community has become a prototype for planned towns around the world; houses, businesses, recreational and other facilities for more than 16,000 residents exist in a beautiful, carefully planned setting.

GALLEN-KALLELA MUSEO, Leppävaara, Tarvaspää, was the studio and home of Finnish artist Akseli Gallen-Kallela until his death in 1931. Built by the artist between 1911 and 1913, the turreted, gray stone and concrete structure contains more than 100 of his drawings, oils and graphics.

HVITTRÄSK ★, Kirkonummi, built in 1902 as studios and homes by the architects Eliel Saarinen, Armas Lindgren and Herman Gesellius, is a superb group of stone and timber buildings that blend into the countryside. There are art exhibits, and Saarinen's house contains the original furnishings.

HÄMEENLINNA (517 A1) ★
HÄME *pop. 43,000*

Hämeenlinna is surrounded by forested cliffs and long, narrow ridges of coarse gravel in the Lake Vanajavesi basin. Originally a garrison town, Finland's oldest inland settlement is now an educational center. On the lake is Aulangon Puisto, a recreational playground and the southern terminus of the Silver Line watercoach.

AULANGON PUISTO (Aulanko Forest Park) ★ is north of town on the former Karlberg Estate. Once barren and stony, this national park now supports both

A LAND OF FESTIVALS

Finland must have more festivals per capita than any country: not invented celebrations aimed at tourists, but genuine festivals. These are often rooted in the strong Labor movement that bred the Valkeakoski Festival of Workers' Music, with many marching bands, and the old fire brigades, who got together for music and dance. The biggest, Kaustinen Folk Music Festival, attracts an audience of 92,000 that comes not just to listen, but to learn and play. There is also a rock festival at Ruissalo and a jazz one at Pori. The first classical festival, Savonlinna Opera Festival, began in 1912 – its castle setting the most dramatic anywhere. Close to the border with Russia is the Kuhmo Chamber Music Festival, played against the silence of forest and hill. The Korsholm Festival, based at Vaasa, is now linked to Umeå Festival on the Swedish side of the Gulf of Bothnia.

vegetation and animal life. Aulanko has a big, modern hotel, a golf course, tennis courts, saunas, beaches, ski trails, campsites, youth hostels, a sightseeing tower and a fairy-tale castle.

HÄMEEN LINNA (Häme Castle) ★ is in the center of town. It was built more than 700 years ago by Birger Jarl, the ruler of Sweden from 1248 to 1266, on what was then the shore of Lake Vanajavesi.

IITTALA GLASS WORKS, 5 kilometers (3 miles) northeast, demonstrates the art of glass-blowing and sells some of Finland's best glassware.

SIBELIUS' BIRTHPLACE ★, Hallituskatu 11, contains the piano, harmonium, violin and numerous manuscripts of Finland's great composer Jean Sibelius, born here in 1865. There are also pictures of the young composer with his two siblings playing trios, and other memorabilia.

HANKO (517 A1) ★
UUSIMAA *pop. 10,700*
Hanko, which has the only free port in Finland, is at the southernmost tip of the country. The city is described in old documents as the most pleasant and secure harbor in which a ship could dock. In the late 1800s, Hanko became a major embarkation point for Finnish emmigrants to the United States and Canada. Now it is a resort, popular for the Baltic Sea air, good beaches and high cliffs.

GÄDDTARMEN, Tullholmarna Island, bears evidence of the region's history. In this natural harbor are rock inscriptions dating from as early as 1400; about 400 of them have been restored.

IMATRA (517 B1)
KYMI *pop. 33,000*
Imatra has been a tourist center since the 19th century, when the rapids of the Vuoksi River drew such visitors as Catherine the Great, Alexandre Dumas and Richard Wagner. Although the rapids are now controlled by Finland's largest hydroelectric plant, the waters are allowed to follow their old course through the center of town on summer evenings. During the week-long International Big Band Music Festival in July, various performances and concerts take place.

A major landmark in Imatra is the Church of the Three Crosses, designed by Alvar Aalto, which features a high belfry representing an arrow fired into the ground. It has three huge crosses and 103 windows, only three of which have the same shape.

PIETARSAARI/JAKOBSTAD (517 A2)
VAASA *pop. 20,000*
Pietarsaari (Jakobstad in Swedish) is known for its tobacco industry, which has been the town's mainstay since 1762. The Rettig (Strengberg) cigarette factory, is the world's second-oldest such factory in operation.

NANOQ (Arctic Museum), at Fäboda, 6 kilometers (4½ miles) west, displays artifacts from Arctic cultures, hunting equipment dating from the 17th century, and items from Arctic expeditions.

JÄRVENPÄÄ (517 B1) ★
UUSIMAA *pop. 33,500*
Finnish composer Jean Sibelius spent most of his life in Järvenpää. Sibelius channeled his love of nature, mythology and northern Finland's landscapes into compositions that greatly contributed to both the symphonic repertoire and the growth of Finnish nationalism.

AINOLA was the home of Sibelius and his wife Aino for 53 years; they are buried under a huge, plain gravestone in the quiet garden. Inside, the composer's piano stands in the drawing room, along with other exhibits.

▲ JYVÄSKYLÄ (517 B2)
KESKI-SUOMI *pop. 71,000*
Jyväskylä was founded in 1837 and led a peaceful academic existence until 1934, when manufacturing took precedence. Industry is balanced by several museums and the Jyväskylä Arts Festival, in early June, which includes musical events and art exhibitions.

ALVAR AALTO MUSEO, Alvar Aalto Katu 7, displays the sketches, drawing, designs and furniture of Alvar Aalto, the great Finnish artist, architect and designer.

▲ KEMI (517 A3)
LAPPI *pop. 26,000*

The southernmost community in Lappland, Kemi is an excellent point from which to view the *aurora borealis* (northern lights) in early and mid-winter.

KOTKA (517 B1)
KYMI *pop. 57,000*

The fortress ruins of Kukouri attest to Kotka's role in history. The late 18th-century bastion and Russian garrison town preceding the present town were virtually eliminated by a British fleet in 1855. Modern Kotka did not appear until later that century, when the deep, natural harbors rendered the spot ideal for an expanding timber industry.

Kotka has spacious parks and interesting architecture. Notable buildings include the Työvaentalo, or Workers' House, designed by Eliel Saarinen, and a cellulose factory by Alvar Aalto.

The city's oldest structure is the Russian Orthodox Church of St. Nicholas, built in 1795 for use by personnel of the Russian naval base. A small museum on the islet of Varissaari commemorates a 1790 naval battle in which Finnish-Swedish forces defeated the Russians. Surviving from the early 19th century is the Imperial Tsar's Fishing Lodge at Langinkoski.

A maritime festival is held during August each year. In summer, local residents as well as outsiders head for Kaunissaari, 20 kilometers (12½ miles) southwest of Kotka in the Gulf of Finland. The island has pine forests and sandy beaches; a fishing village offers indoor lodgings for those who do not wish to camp.

▲ LAHTI (517 B1)
HÄME *pop. 95,000*

Lahti was founded in 1905 on the site of a former trading post on Lake Vesijärvi, on the extensive Salpausselkä ridge system, the setting for major world skiing championships. Lahti Sports Center has some of Finland's best winter sports facilities, with a superb view from the top of the highest ski-jump, and first-class cross-country and downhill skiing in several centers, plus annual winter games in March. One of Finland's most modern cities, Lahti is well-planned, with innovative architecture that creates an impression of light and space in an urban area; visitors might never suspect it is home to several large manufacturing concerns.

In addition to its sports facilities, Lahti offers refreshing lake scenery and water activities. The city has a number of museums devoted to history, skiing and art. The last church designed by Alvar Aalto, the Ristinkirkko, is in the middle of the city. Nearby in Hollola is a medieval church and the Pyhäniemi Art Manor.

Local events include the annual Midnight Sun Song Festival, Organ Week, and Writers' Festival held in June.

LAPPEENRANTA (517 B1)
KYMI *pop. 55,000*

Founded in the mid-17th century, Lappeenranta first functioned as a Swedish garrison on the Russian border. After mineral springs were discovered in 1824, the town gained repute as a summer vacation spot. Today, Lappeenranta is South Karelia's main town and is better-known for its position on the Saimaa Canal, at the end of an extensive network of lakes. The town's old fortress contains a local history museum, an art museum, and the oldest Orthodox church in Finland.

MARIEHAMN/MAARIANHAMINA –
see Åland Islands/Ahvenanmaa on p.521.

MIKKELI (517 B1)
MIKKELI *pop. 32,000*

At the intersection of several major roads is Mikkeli, capital of Mikkeli province and center of trade in the South Savo. On the shore of Lake Saimaa, the town becomes a lively resort in summer; in winter it is popular for skiing.

Mikkeli, founded in 1838, was the site of Field Marshal von Mannerheim's headquarters during the fighting with the U.S.S.R. in World War II, and now has a museum that chronicles the period in Finnish history.

▲ OULU (517 B3)
OULU pop. 105,000
An old trading and shipping post at the mouth of the Oulujoki River, Oulu has been important since medieval times, and because of its early commercial activities, the town was once fortified.

Today, Oulu is the sixth-largest town in Finland. It has one of the world's most modern paper factories and is also a leader in advanced information technology. Visitors to the Tictomaa Science center can experience the latest in virtual reality and the electronic future. A university and several other schools contribute to Oulu's reputation. The city offers many opportunities for boating, swimming and other water sports.

Turkansaari, set on an island in the Oulujoki River, is an open-air museum, with typical folk buildings.

▲ PORI (517 A1)
TURKU-PORI pop. 77,000
On the lower course of the Kokemäenjoki River, Pori was established in 1558. Founded at the point where the river flows into the sea, the center of town is now 20 kilometers (12½ miles) from the coast. Most of the city occupies the left bank of the river and is connected to its smaller part by a majestic old bridge. After a major fire in 1852, the town was modernized, but unusual architectural sights remain, including the Venetian-style town hall.

The old town has one attraction of very contemporary interest – the Pori International Jazz Festival, held each year during the second weekend of July, takes place in Kirjurinluoto Park and the Eteläranta shoreline.

▲ PORVOO/BORGÅ (517 B1) ★
UUSIMAA pop. 20,000
Picturesque Porvoo (Borgå in Swedish) is a fashionable center for artists and media people, who commute to Helsinki from here. Quaint 18th-century buildings with colorful roofs and an early 15th-century Gothic cathedral are reminders of the town's past. Other interesting sites are the 1764 Old Town Hall, a historical museum and the Edelfelt-Vallgren Art Museum.

J.L. RUNEBERG'S HOME, Aleksanterinkatu 3, was the home of the Finnish national poet, Johan Ludvig Runeberg, from 1852 to 1877. The house has been restored to its original appearance.

▲ RAUMA (517 A1) ★
TURKU-PORI pop. 38,500
The brightly painted wooden buildings in Rauma's old town date from the 18th century, but the town was founded 500

THE SAUNA

The world's best saunas are in Finland, where they have been used for 2,000 years. The country has well over half a million saunas, not counting those in private houses, lakeside summer cabins, or communal saunas, in which each family has its own time. The family sauna is an important pivot of family life and a social ritual with guests.

Finnish saunas are hot, up to 100°C (212°F) – invariably too much for foreigners – and are generally followed by a dip in a plunge pool, along with a beer or soft drink to replace the liquid. Except for families, saunas are usually single sex. Best of all is a lakeside summer house with a wood-fired sauna built over the lake, the after-sauna plunge a simple dive into the water below.

FINLAND

years earlier at a trade route junction. Two distinctive local characteristics originated in the 17th century: the fine lace made in the town, and the unique Rauma language, a mixture of Latin, old Dutch, Estonian, Swedish and English. It now thrives as a center of word-processing and metal industries.

In addition to the old town, attractions include the Rauma Museum; the Church of the Holy Cross, a 15th-century Franciscan monastery church; and Marela House, a 19th-century shipowner's home. The annual Lace Week is held at the end of July.

ROVANIEMI (517 B3) ★
LAPPI *pop. 34,000*
The capital of Finnish Lappland, this Arctic town at the confluence of two rivers has become the north's principal city. Fur trading and reindeer herding, once common activities, were largely supplanted by lumber operations towards the end of the 19th century.

The Arktikum houses the Arctic Center and the Lappland Provincial Museum. The Lappland Forestry Museum and the Ethnographic Museum are on the outskirts of town. Pöykkölä Museum preserves 19th-century farm buildings near the river, 3 kilometers (2 miles) south. Rovaniemi's biggest winter attractions are snowmobiling and sledding behind teams of reindeer or huskies. Riverboat trips and white-water rafting are popular in summer.

SAVONLINNA (517 B2)
MIKKELI *pop. 28,500*
The frontier town of Savonlinna, sacked and destroyed many times during its turbulent history, is now a popular resort. The medieval fortress has become a monument, and festivals have replaced sieges. The best time to visit is in July, during Savonlinna Music Summer, which features concerts and an outdoor opera.

OLAVINLINNA is one of the best medieval frontier fortress in Finland. The castle was built by Erik Axelsson Tort in the 15th century to protect Savonlinna from Russia. Completely restored, the fortress is now a national monument.

▲ TAMPERE (517 A1) ★
HÄME *pop. 175,000*
The northernmost point of a triangle that it forms with Turku and Helsinki, Tampere is the largest Finnish inland city, situated on an isthmus between two large lakes. The city is a major center for lake traffic and cruises. Although highly industrialized, beautiful Tampere has benefited from astute city planning. Old factory areas, such as Finlaysons (founded by a Scot, James Finlayson), became almost towns within a town; Finlayson's hospital, factory, school and church still stand and should not be missed and neither should nearby Finlayson Palatsi.

The bustle of business and manufacture is balanced by the serenity of leafy parks and rows of old wooden houses. Numerous museums cover local history, art, natural science, dolls and sports. Architect Lars Sonck designed Tampere Cathedral in 1907, in National Romantic style. Kalevala Church is an amazing modern building, rising like a sail, with a soaring interior and a vast organ.

Annual events include the Tampere Film Festival, held in February and March; the Tampere International Theater Festival in August; and the Tampere Jazz Happening in November. Pispala Schottis, an international folk dance festival, takes place in early June every other even year.

TAMPERE HALL ★ is a spectacular blue-white building, with a lobby fountain. The main hall holds 2,000.

▲ TURKU/ÅBO (517 A1) ★
TURKU-PORI *pop. 158,000*
Turku, Åbo in Swedish, was the capital of Finland during Swedish rule. It was the commercial center of what was then called Osterland (Eastern Land), long before the name Finland came into use. It is still a trade center, as well as the site of Finland's greatest historical treasures.

Despite devastating fires over the centuries, the last in 1827, much of old Turku remains, including the medieval castle and cathedral.

LUOSTARINMÄKI HANDWERKMUSEUM (Handicrafts Museum) features more than 30 workshops that display different trades and their histories from the 18th and 19th centuries.

THE ORTHODOX CATHEDRAL, which served a Russian community during Grand Duchy days, is now Greek Orthodox, with a congregation of 2,000. It has all the rich beauty of an Orthodox cathedral and many fine paintings.

RUISSALO ISLAND, reached swiftly by boat or bridge, has the best beaches, and is home to an odd mix of rock music and art. The 19th-century Villa Roma holds a summer exhibition of top-class painting, glass and textiles, and, also in summer, the island hosts Ruisrock, the world's oldest rock music festival.

SIBELIUS MUSEO, Piispankatu 17, displays musical instruments and the manuscripts of Jean Sibelius.

TUOMIOKIRKKO (Cathedral), by the Aura River, was consecrated in 1290 and guided the religious life of Finland for centuries. It is one of northern Europe's most outstanding historical monuments.

TURUN LINNA (Turku Castle), west of town near Kanavaniemi Harbor, dates from the late 13th century, with parts built in the 14th and 16th centuries. It was restored between 1946 and 1961.

WÄINO AALTONEN MUSEUM, Östra Strandgatan, holds works by the famous artist, including the huge statues of *Peace* and *Faith*.

▲ VAASA/VASA (517 A2) ★
VAASA *pop. 54,000*
Busy Vaasa, Vasa in Swedish, on the Gulf of Bothnia, is characterized by seashore parks, broad boulevards and long green esplanades. Founded in 1606, the city was almost destroyed by fire in 1852, but was reconstructed and modernized. Now it is an important seaport and a manufacturing and arts center. The Korsholm Music Festival takes place in late June and early July.

BRAGEGÅRDEN MUSEO, Hietalahti, is an open-air museum with exhibits relating to Finnish domestic traditions. Displays highlight the seal-hunting tradition.

OSTROBOTHNIA MUSEO, Museokatu 3, displays feature centuries of Vaasa and regional culture. The 19th- and 20th-century Finnish art collection is supplemented by 16th- and 17th-century Italian, Dutch, Flemish and German works of art.

THE KALEVALA

This marvelous collection of poetry and prose, often described as Finland's national poem, or Finland's epic poem, played a significant role in raising the Finns' sense of their own nationality. In the Grand Duchy days, the writer Elias Lönnrot embarked on a great journey to record Finland's traditional stories and poems before they were lost, traveling into Karelia and other parts where the oral tradition was still strong. Then, welding together this collection, he produced the *Kalevala,* a mixture of heroic deed, violence, grief and passion, with something of the style of a Norse saga. Its impact, which was startling, became even stronger when the painter Askeli Gallen-Kallela produced a series of some 100 great paintings portraying vivid *Kalevala* scenes, which decorated the Finnish Pavilion at the Paris Exhibition in 1900. It was as if Finland was declaring its desire for independence to the world.

ICELAND

Iceland was born out of volcanic action, leaving a landscape that was an apt setting for Jules Verne's *Journey to the Centre of the Earth*. It is a land of peaks, geysers, glaciers, lakes, and astonishing scenery that would take your breath away if the cold had not already done so.

In fact, it is not as cold as might be expected, although the winter gloom is relieved only in the day for a few hours and at night by the eerie glow of the northern lights. In summer the sun scarcely sets, making this strange land even stranger at the sunlit midnight hour.

Less than one percent of the land is cultivated, the people turning instead to the sea to provide a livelihood. In Reykjavík, the capital, it is Icelandic culture you find, with museums devoted to names little-known elsewhere: Jónsson and Sveinsson.

Left Thingvellir church and farmhouse, where the declaration of the Icelandic republic was made in 1944

Above left There are signs of volcanic activity everywhere in Iceland

Above right Lief Eriksson, the Icelandic navigator, in Viking costume

THINGS TO KNOW

- **AREA**: 103,000 square kilometers (39,768 square miles)
- **POPULATION**: 266,786
- **CAPITAL**: Reykjavík
- **LANGUAGE**: Icelandic
- **ECONOMY**: Agricultural, with cattle and sheep ranching. Fish-processing industries account for the majority of exports.
- **PASSPORT REQUIREMENTS**: Required for U.S. citizens.
- **VISA REQUIREMENTS**: Not required for stays of up to three months total in the Scandinavian countries.
- **DUTY-FREE ITEMS**: 200 cigarettes or 250 grams of tobacco; 1 liter of spirits up to 47 percent alcohol; 1 liter of wine up to 21 percent alcohol; reasonable amounts of clothing and camping equipment.
- **CURRENCY**: The currency unit is the Icelandic *krona*, divided into 100 *eyrir*. Due to currency fluctuations, the exchange rate is subject to change. There is no limit on the import of foreign or Icelandic currency.
- **BANK OPENING HOURS**: 9:15am–4pm Monday–Wednesday and Friday; 9:15am–4pm and 5–6pm Thursday.
- **BEST BUYS**: Wool, whalebone carvings, sealskin articles, ceramics, silverwork, sheepskin and ponyskin rugs.
- **PUBLIC HOLIDAYS**: January 1; Maundy Thursday; Good Friday; Easter Monday; First Day of Summer; May 1 (Labor Day); Ascension Day; Whitmonday; June 17 (National Day); Bank Holiday, first Monday in August; December 24–26; December 31.
- **NATIONAL TOURIST OFFICES**: Icelandic National Tourist Board 655 Third Ave New York, NY 10017 Tel: 212/949-2333; fax: 212/983-5260 Icelandic Tourist Information: Gimli Laekjargata 3 101 Reykjavik, Iceland Tel: 552 7488; fax: 562 4749
- **AMERICAN EMBASSY**: Laufásvegur 21 101 Reykjavík, Iceland Tel: 562 9100; fax: 562 9110

HISTORY

Living evidence of geological movement, 20-million-year-old Iceland widens almost an inch a year. Although the island was inhabited briefly during the 8th century AD by Irish hermits, permanent settlement did not begin until 874 when a Norwegian, Ingólfur Arnarson, arrived. In 930, the homesteaders formed a legislature, the Althing.

The Icelanders embarked upon further exploration; Eiríkur Thorvaldsson, dubbed "the Red," colonized Greenland from about 986. Eiríkur's son, Leif Eiríksson, reached North America about AD 1000, and established a colony called Vinland. It was also at this time that Christianity was adopted.

From the 10th to the 14th centuries, a literary form, the Icelandic Saga, was developed in the native language. It was used to spin stories of the gods, record historical events, such as blood feuds and battles between rival chieftains, and glorify heroes. In 1262, Iceland's leaders asked the King of Norway to impose peace, and in 1380, Denmark took over as the soverign power. In 1800, the last - vestige of the democratic commonwealth, the Althing, was formally abolished.

A 19th-century independence movement led, in 1874, to the restoration of the Althing as an elected legislative power. Iceland was declared a republic on June 17, 1944. Today it is governed by the 60-member Althing, with a premier and a president who is head of state. In 1980, Vigdís Finnbogadóttir became the first woman to be elected as president of a European country.

FOOD

Although international cuisine is readily available, visitors should sample the local fare. Seafood and lamb are staples and are utilized in such dishes as *hangikjöt* (smoked mutton), *saltfbkur* (salt cod), *humar* (a small lobster delicacy), and *hardfiskur* (dried fish). A tasty treat, at least according to Icelanders, is *svid* (sheep's head). Other Icelandic favorites are *blódmör* (blood sausage); *lifrarpylsa* (liver sausage); and *skyr* (sheep's milk cheese). Snacks that go well with *schnapps* are herring, pickled whale blubber and *hákarl* (dried shark). The traditional Christmas feast is *rjúpa*.

SPORTS AND RECREATION

Winter skiing is pursued at Akureyri, Isafjördur and Siglufjördur and there is summer skiing in the Kerlingarfjöll region and near Langjökull glacier. Golf is also popular. Icelanders are enthusiastic campers, and it seems as if every family has an all-terrain vehicle. The weather can be unpredictable and antimosquito measures are essential.

Rich in wildlife, Iceland has well-stocked lakes and rivers that attract fishing enthusiasts; permits are required and can usually be obtained on the spot. Birdwatching, hiking and horseback riding are all good ways to enjoy the invigorating air and see the countryside.

GETTING AROUND

Iceland has no railroads. Roads within and near the main towns are paved, as is most of the route around the island. Others are graded gravel or lava. Routes across the interior are only open in summer. Rental cars are available; four-wheel-drive vehicles are recommended. Regular bus routes crisscross all the inhabited regions, and the Omnibus Passport, which can only be purchased in Iceland, allows one to four weeks of unlimited travel on scheduled routes. The Full-Circle Passport allows one trip around the main island perimeter road.

Because of road conditions and natural obstructions such as glaciers and lava fields, air travel is often considerably more convenient. Icelandair, its subsidiaries, and smaller airlines operate a network of internal flights to all popula-

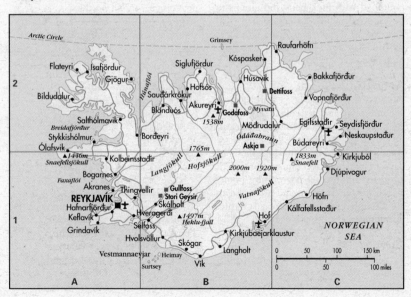

REYKJAVÍK

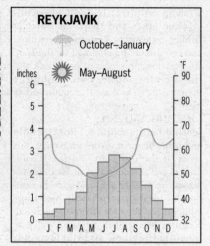

October–January

May–August

inches

°F

| J F M A M J J A S O N D |

tion centres. Discounts are available for multi-flights within Iceland. State Shipping Department steamers ply the waters between all ports, and various ferry companies have services across the fjords. Taxis are also available.

The Touring Club of Iceland operates huts equipped with beds and cooking facilities in uninhabited areas, where travelers may stay. Refuge huts are equipped with fuel, beds and rations to be used *only* during an emergency. The best way to travel through the interior is by four-wheel-drive vehicle, accompanied by an experienced guide.

ACCOMMODATIONS

Only Reykjavík has large hotels; most accommodations in Iceland are small, simple and plentiful. Camping gear can be rented in Reykjavík. Edda Hotels are good value, often converted for the holidays from school accommodations, with good food and often swimming pools. Youth hostels operate and are open to all, though reservations are advisable. Farmhouses are also popular.

TIPPING

Service fees are included in most bills; tipping is not expected and may even be resented.

USEFUL EXPRESSIONS IN ICELANDIC

hello	góðan daginn
good-bye	bless
please	gjörðu svo vel
thank you	takk fyrir
yes/no	já/nei
Does anyone here speak English?	Er einhver hér sem talar ensku?
I don't understand.	Ég skil ekki.
Where are the restrooms?	Hvar er snyrtingin?
Do you take credit cards?	Takið pér kredit kort?
How much is that?	Hvað kostar petta?
I'd like...	Mig myndi langa...
What time is it?	Hvað er klukkan?
left	vinstri
right	hœgri
passport	vegabréf
telephone	sími
church	kirkja
bridge	brú
doctor	læknir
hospital	spítali
information office	upplýsingaskrifstofa
museum	safn
pharmacy	apótek
police station	lögreglustöð
post office	pósthús
store	búð
supermarket	stórmarkaður
bus	straetisvagn
gas	bensín
early/late	snemma/seint
easy	auðvelt
difficult	erfitt
free (vacant)	laus
occupied	upptekin
open/closed	opið/loka
good/bad	gott/slæmt
cheap/expensive	ódýrt/dýrt

DAYS OF THE WEEK

Sunday	sunnudagur
Monday	mánudagur
Tuesday	thriðjudagur
Wednesday	miðvikudagur
Thursday	fimmtudagur
Friday	föstudagur
Saturday	laugardagur

PLACES OF INTEREST

▲ REYKJAVÍK (531 A1) ★

pop. 97,000

Reykjavík (Bay of Smoke) was so named in AD 874, when Iceland's first Norse colonist, Ingólfur Arnarson, sighted the numerous hot springs on the Seltjarnarnes Peninsula. Today, this remarkably pollution-free city on Faxa Bay is a major seaport, the capital of Iceland and the home of 40 percent of the country's population.

Reykjavík's predominantly 20th-century architecture presents a clean and attractive appearance. There are only a few chimneys and heat is almost exclusively supplied by steam piped from nearby hot springs. It gives Reykjavík several magnificently hot, outdoor swimming pools. The sunsets in this smokeless city can be spectacular.

Reykjavík has a wide choice of eating-places, serving international and local cuisine. Nightlife centers on the hotels and restaurants. Food and drink tends to be expensive. For its small population, Iceland is remarkably rich in arts and culture, with several art and sculpture galleries in Reykjavík, in addition to the National Gallery. There are two main theaters: the National, which is open only in winter, and the City Theatre.

Places of interest include the National Library, Archives and National Art Gallery, and the Museum of Natural History. The Danish baroque Parliament Building and the small Lutheran cathedral face the Austurvöllur, the main square. The botanical gardens in Laugardalur are open in the summer. Shoppers seek out Austurstræti.

ÁRBAEJARSAFN, is a folk museum on Reykjavík's eastern outskirts. Its center is the Árbaer farmhouse, surrounded by other late 19th-century structures, including a sod-and-stone church.

ÁSMUNDUR SVEINSSON GALLERY, Sigtún, is a gallery exhibiting a collection of original sculpture by Sveinsson, the famous Icelandic sculptor.

BLUE LAGOON ★, 48 kilometers (30 miles) southwest of Reykjavík, near the fishing village of Grindavik, is a pool of mineral-rich geothermal salty water. The lagoon's amazing blue color and its warmth attract more than 100,000 visitors each year, to splash and soak. The water is beneficial to sufferers of certain skin diseases, and there is a special skin clinic here.

GULLFOSS (Golden Falls) ★ is 123 kilometers (76 miles) east. The waters of the Hvítá River cascade 27.5 meters (90 feet) through a rocky gorge.

HEKLU-FJALL (Mount Hekla), 120 kilometers (77 miles) east, is a famous active volcano. In times past it was believed to be the entrance to hell but is now a major tourist attraction. The spectacular view from the summit is accessible by a long but fairly easy climb.

HVERAGERDI ★, 40 kilometers (25 miles) south, is the centre of the horticulture industry, where the greenhouses are heated by steam from local hot springs. The complex also has an excellent hotel – an unusual and pleasant place to stay.

KJARVALSSTAðIR, in Miklatún Park, has works by the painter Johannes Kjarval.

SKÁLHOLT ★, 85 kilometers (53 miles) east, has had a Christian church since the 11th century. The present simple, modern church on this site today displays the work of famous artists.

LISTASAFN EINARS JÓNSSONAR (Art Museum of Einar Jónsson) Njaroargata, displays works by Iceland's most prominent sculptor.

STORI GEYSIR ★, 118 kilometers (74 miles) east, has given its name to similar hot springs all over the world. Although its performance today is erratic, it gained international fame centuries ago by regularly projecting a column of boiling water nearly 70 meters (230 feet) into the air. The geyser is set in a scenic area where numerous smaller hissing springs and rumbling craters constantly expel hot steam, water and mud.

THINGVELLIR ★, 50 kilometers (31 miles) east, is regarded as a sacred place by Icelanders because in AD 930, the world's oldest extant legislative body, the Althing, first convened at this site.

Of special note are the speaker's rock and a few remains of the sod-and-brick shelters that the deputies raised and used as dwelling places during their two-week assemblies.

Possessing some of the most outstanding scenery, this national park ranks among Iceland's most popular tourist destinations.

THJÖDMINJASAFNID (National Museum of Iceland), Suourgata, displays a collection of medieval art objects. Noteworthy exhibits include silverwork, national costumes and Viking artifacts.

SNÆFELLSNES PENINSULA ★ is situated 240 kilometers (150 miles) north of Reykjavík. The peninsula has the cone-shaped Snæfellsjökulla, a 1,446-meter (4,744-foot) ice-covered extinct volcano, which was Jules Verne's starting point for *Journey to the Centre of the Earth*.

To the north, Stykkisholmur (a peninsula) offers spectacular boat tours through the offshore islands.

A car-ferry also runs across the bay to Brjánslækur on the northern side, saving a 240-kilometer (150-mile) drive.

ÓLAFSVIK, along the Snaefellsnes Peninsula's northern coast, held Iceland's first trading license from 1687. Today, its main industry is fishing, and among its attractions it offers a lively harbor, the Gamla Pakkhúsid (Old Packing House), a trading house dating from 1844, and a beautiful, modern church.

THE ICELAND HORSE

These sturdy, surefooted little beasts are pure descendants of the animals brought from Norway as long ago as the 9th century. No horses have been imported into Iceland for over 800 years – it is now illegal to do so – and this means that these small horses, little bigger than ponies but strong enough to carry a large man, have changed little over the years, though they have adapted well to a harsh terrain. These sturdy horses served until World War II as the main means of transport, and are still used in the September *réttir*, the sheep round-up. Horseback riding is popular with Icelanders, as are the many riding tours for visitors.

ÁKUREYRI (531 B2)
pop. 14,100

Akureyri, the chief city of northern Iceland, is at the mouth of the scenic Eyjafjördur, 60 kilometers (38 miles) from the open sea.

Until recent times a small trading post, Akureyri has evolved into an attractive, modern town and a thriving commercial center. Of special interest are the botanical gardens, established in 1912, and the modern Lutheran church.

Akureyri is also a major winter sports resort. The slopes of Mount Hlídarfjall provide skiing well into May; ice skating, hiking and fishing are also popular.

Roads connecting Akureyi with Reykjavík are mostly asphalted or paved. The 430-kilometer (269-mile) trip takes about eight hours and there are daily flights from the capital.

ASKJA, 230 kilometers (144 miles) southeast, is a large caldera, or depression. It attracted world attention in 1875 when it was the site of a tremendous volcanic explosion. Several minor eruptions have occurred since, the last in 1961.

The summit offers a spectacular view of Vatnajökull, which is Europe's largest glacier. Covering more than 8,340 square kilometers (3,220 square miles), Vatnajökull is also a center of volcanic activity.

DETTIFOSS ★, 134 kilometers (84 miles) east, is Iceland's highest waterfall. Here the swift waters of the Jökulsá á Fjöllum River cascade nearly 44 meters (144 feet) through rocky surroundings.

GODAFOSS ★ is situated 49 kilometers (30 miles) east, on the Skjálfandi River. The "Falls of the Gods" received its name in AD 1000 when Thorgeir, president of the Althing, threw images of the pagan gods into the river, and turned to Christianity.

MÝVATN is a spectacular lake situated 104 kilometers (65 miles) east. The lake is bordered by extensive lava fields, which is evidence that the area was once a center of volcanic activity. No major eruption has occurred since 1729; a brief one in 1975 created a lava flow into uninhabited wilderness. The shallow lake, which is only 4 meters (13 feet) deep, is studded with immense lava blocks in strange shapes. Among the more notable are Dimmuborgir (Black Castles), a series of rocks, caves and canyons on the eastern shore.

HEIMAY – *see Vestmannaeyjar below.*

SURTSEY – *see Vestmannaeyjar below.*

▲ VESTMANNAEYJAR (531 B1)
pop. 4,800

Off Iceland's southern coast, the Vestmannaeyjar, or Westmann Islands, are of volcanic origin. According to legend, their name was derived from some Irish slaves – called the West Men because of their homeland west of Scandinavia – who fled to this Atlantic landfall to escape their Viking masters in the 9th century.

Although sparsely covered with vegetation, most of the islands are surrounded by cliffs that teem with a variety of bird life. Opportunities for birdwatching are excellent. The local tradition of hanging from ropes over the cliffs to gather eggs is mainly practiced as a sport nowadays. However, strict regulations govern the hunting and filming of nesting birds.

HEIMAY, the largest and only inhabited island, was Iceland's chief fishing center until January 1973, when a volcanic eruption split the earth near the port of Vestmannaeyjar. The island's 5,000 inhabitants were evacuated by the local fishing fleet and 300 of the 1,400 houses were buried under ash. Since that time, there have been no further eruptions, and most inhabitants have returned, but island topography and the town have both changed.

During the first weekend in August, a festival of song and dance takes place to mark the restoration of Icelandic sovereignty in 1874.

SURTSEY, the newest of the Westmann Islands, was created in November 1963 when a volcanic eruption shook the North Atlantic. The island is still an active volcano beneath a cooling crust.

Boat trips can be made around Surtsey, but special permission must be obtained to land. Sightseeing flights over the island can be arranged.

NORWAY

Norway has more coast-line (over 20,000 kilometers – 13,000 miles) for its size than any other country in the world. A third of Norway lies inside the Arctic Circle, the land of the Lapps and reindeer, but the rest has forests and fjords that slice into the high, craggy mountains. The Jotunheimen range, the Home of the Giants, is aptly named, for here is the highest point in Scandinavia, the prominent Glittertinden.

Norway has one of the lowest population densities in the world. Almost 500,000 people live in the capital, Oslo, a modern, clean city that preserves many old buildings. From its position at the head of a fjord, ferries leave Oslo for the offshore islands. In summer the sun does not set until almost midnight.

Left Cruise ships venture inland as far as Geirangerfjord
Above left Wooden houses line the waterfront at Bergen
Above Fishing is one of main industries in Norway

THINGS TO KNOW

- **AREA:** 324,219 square kilometers (125,181 square miles)
- **POPULATION:** 4,300,000
- **CAPITAL:** Oslo
- **LANGUAGE:** Norwegian
- **ECONOMY:** Oil processing, paper and food manufacturing. Fishing, shipbuilding and hydroelectric power production are also important. Small farming.
- **PASSPORT REQUIREMENTS:** Required for U.S. citizens.
- **VISA REQUIREMENTS:** Not required for stays up to three months total in the Scandinavian countries (Denmark, Finland, Iceland, Norway and Sweden).
- **DUTY-FREE ITEMS:** 400 cigarettes or 50 cigars or 500 grams of tobacco; 1 liter of spirits; 1 liter of wine; cameras and a reasonable amount of film; personal goods that have been used. Visitors must be at least 20 years old to import or export spirits; 18 for wine or beer.
  Note: Instead of being reimbursed by mail for Value Added Tax (V.A.T.) paid in Norway, tourists are repaid in cash as they leave the country. When buying items with a total value exceeding 300 *krone* at Norwegian stores that display the "Tax Free for Tourists" sign, visitors are issued a check for the amount they are due. Provided the items have not been used, the money is returned to them at refund offices at all international airports, border stations and ships on presentation of a passport.
- **CURRENCY:** The currency unit, the Norwegian *krone*, is divided into 100 *øre*. Due to currency fluctuations, the exchange rate is subject to frequent change. There are no restrictions on the import of foreign or Norwegian currency, but it is recommended that any large amount be declared on arrival in case it needs to be exported later. No more than 5,000 *krone* may be exported.
- **BANK OPENING HOURS:** 8:15am–3pm Monday–Friday (3:30pm in winter); some banks are open until 5pm on Thursday.

HISTORY

Norwegian history recalls a people who reacted to the difficulties of the land with genius and daring. With only a small percentage of the land tillable, the Vikings sought their fortune at sea, raiding throughout Europe from AD 800 to 1100. As fearless as their warlike gods, tall, blond, blue-eyed Vikings in leather and metal helmets brandished battle-axes as they crossed the seas in their longships to conquer other lands.

In their path the Vikings left awakened trade and evidence of their culture. The Viking story form, the saga, recorded their adventures and was incorporated into the literature of many parts of the world. Returning to Norway with new wealth and cultural impulses, the Viking people moved toward unification under one powerful leader who could subdue their many chiefs.

The martyrdom of King Olav II (St. Olav) in 1030 marked the establishment of Christianity throughout Norway. For more than 400 years the country was united with Denmark and later with Sweden. A constitution was established in 1814, but Norway was forced into a new union with Sweden. After a peaceful separation from Sweden in 1905, the Norwegian parliament, the *Storting*, elected Prince Charles of Denmark to be its king.

King Harald V is the present king of Norway. The country's royal family is a treasured part of Norwegian life. On Constitution Day in Oslo thousands of school children parade up the grand avenue Karl Jogansgate to the Palace Gardens. Embracing the active Norwegian lifestyle, the royal family sails, skis and personally congratulates such champions as the skiers at mammoth Holmenkollen Ski Jump in Oslo.

FOOD AND DRINK

Norwegians prepare salmon and trout for the table using recipes evolved over

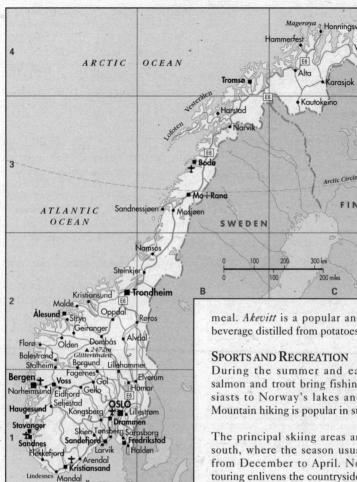

meal. *Akevitt* is a popular and potent beverage distilled from potatoes.

SPORTS AND RECREATION

During the summer and early fall, salmon and trout bring fishing enthusiasts to Norway's lakes and rivers. Mountain hiking is popular in summer.

The principal skiing areas are in the south, where the season usually lasts from December to April. Nordic ski touring enlivens the countryside, and ski jumping attracts competitors and spectators. Even summer skiing is possible, at Stryn, Galdhøpiggen and also places further north.

GETTING AROUND

For pleasure as well as practicality, steamers and cruise ships are popular ways to see the lakes, fjords and islands. Many itineraries are offered; the longest is a tour of 34 ports that lasts 11 days.

Internal ferry services are less important now than in the past because of the system of improved and modern roads, but the ferries are useful for short trips.

the centuries. Perhaps the crowning achievement is smoked salmon, which is often a highlight of the Norwegian *koldtbord*, an abundant buffet found at many hotels. A smaller version of the *koldtbord* is the *smørbrød*, the Norwegian open-faced sandwich. Tempting appetites are such distinctive foods as reindeer steaks, *fårikål* (lamb and cabbage stew), *kjøttkaker* (meat cakes) and goats-milk cheeses. Fresh from the dew of their mountain home, *multer* (cloudberries) bring their unique flavor to top off a

- **STORE OPENING HOURS:** 9am–4 or 5pm Monday–Wednesday and Friday, 9am–6, 7 or 8pm Thursday, 9am–1, 2 or 3pm Saturday; store hours may be shortened in midsummer.
- **BEST BUYS:** Silver and enamelware, ceramics, woodcarvings and furniture; sweaters, glass, ski clothes and equipment.
- **PUBLIC HOLIDAYS:** January 1; Maundy Thursday; Good Friday; Easter Monday; May 1 (May Day); Ascension Day; May 17 (National Day); Whitmonday; December 25; December 26 (Boxing Day).
- **NATIONAL TOURIST OFFICES:**
  Scandinavian National Tourist Board
  655 Third Avenue.
  New York
  NY 10017
  Tel: 212/949-2333
  Fax: 212/983-5260
  Norway Information Center
  Drammensveien 40
  P.O. Box 2893 Solli
  N-0230 Oslo
  Tel: (22) 92 52 00
  Fax: (22) 56 05 05
- **AMERICAN EMBASSY:**
  Drammensveien 18
  N-0255 Oslo 2
  Norway
  Tel: (22) 44 85 50; fax: (22) 44 33 63

AUTOMOBILE CLUBS
Kongelig Norsk Automobilklub
(K.N.A.), Drammensveien 20-C,
0255 Oslo
Norges Automobil-Forbund
(N.A.F.), Storgaten 2,
0155 Oslo
These clubs have branch offices in various cities throughout Norway. The symbol ▲ beside a name indicates the presence of a AAA-affiliated automobile club branch. Not all auto clubs offer full travel services to AAA members.

Norway's internal air network connects 50 airports, some small. Railroads generally parallel the main roads; the Oslo–Bergen railroad offers tourist trains with special commentaries in English. Larger cities sell tourist cards, which give unlimited travel on buses and streetcars for a specified number of days.

The national highways, or *motorveig*, are hard surfaced and concentrated in the south and along the coast; secondary roads are gravel surfaced. Low speeds are recommended for the narrow roads of western Norway. During the winter months some roads are not suitable for driving. Drivers entering Oslo, Bergen and Trondheim must pay a toll. There are also tolls for bridges, ferries and some general roads. Road information is available from the Oslo Tourist Office, telephone (22) 83 00 50, or the Norges Automobil-Forbund Information Center in Oslo, telephone (22) 34 14 00.

Speed limits are 50 k.p.h. (31 m.p.h.) in town and 80–90 k.p.h. (49–55 m.p.h.) on out-of-town roads, including highways. Motorists must drive with low-beam headlights on during the day, and all vehicles must be equipped with replacement bulbs. Seat belt use is mandatory for drivers and passengers; children under seven years must use a suitable seat restraint. Visiting motorists will be required to pay fines for motoring violations on the spot with Norwegian *krone*.

ACCOMMODATIONS
Although Norway does not grade its hotels, standards are high – as are the prices. Establishments that cater mainly to international tourists are the *turisthotell* or *høyfjellshotell* (mountain hotels); *pensjonater* (pensions) or *fjellstuer* (mountain lodges); and *turiststasjoner* (tourist stations). *Gards* (farms that accept guests) are normally very well run and offer excellent opportunities to become acquainted with Norwegians.

Most hotel chains offer the use of discount cards. The major discount programs are the Fjord Pass, Best Western Hotel Check and Scandinavian BonusPass. The Scandinavian National Tourist Boards can provide more information.

Norway's 1,400 campgrounds are graded from one to five stars. While an International Camping Carnet is not required, some sites might still ask for it. Many sites have cabins available for rent. On the Lofoten Versterålen (Lofoten Islands), fishing cottages are frequently available for rent during the summer. Youth hostels welcome visitors of all ages and often have family rooms.

TIPPING

Restaurants include a service fee in the bill, but you can add 5 to 10 percent if service is excellent. Tip porters 5 *krone* per bag and chambermaids and other service personnel about 5 *krone* each.

PRINCIPAL TOURING AREAS

Note: For descriptions of attractions in **bold type**, see individual listings.

MOUNTAINS AND VALLEYS OF THE SOUTH

Bustling **Oslo**, encircled by hills and overlooking a region of lakes and forests, is a scenic starting point for a tour of the southern mountains and valleys. Many roads lead from Oslo to such resorts as **Arendal** and the village of Fevik; also worth visiting are **Larvik** and Sandefjord.

Northeast of Oslo is Norway's largest lake, 99-kilometer (62-mile) Mjøsa, leading toward the northwest into the fabled valley of Gudbrandsdal. Smaller lakes are scattered over the valley, and the climate is relatively mild. On old family farms, customs and speech remain almost unchanged by modern life.

Gudbrandsdal is part of the legend of the tall-story teller Peer Gynt, immortalized

by Ibsen and Grieg, as are the Jotunheim Mountains to the west. Their name means "Home of the Giants," and a view of these awe-inspiring peaks proves the aptness of the name. The Oslo–Bergen railroad offers panoramic views, as do the mountain roads. Hikers can find challenging terrain in the Jotunheim.

THE SOUTHERN FJORD COUNTRY

Fjords, the essence of Norway, cut inland for 200 kilometers (125 miles). They are at their loveliest when the orchards blossom in May and June, the peak tourist season, but Gulf Stream waters and winds make fjord vacations practical all year. In the southwest corner of fjord country, green farmland hugs the edge of steep cliffs. **Stavanger**'s wooden buildings and narrow, winding streets reflect its medieval origin. Today this major seaport is a focal point of the oil industry, adding modern ways of living to its traditions.

A short distance north around the coast, beautiful Hardangerfjord justifies its reputation as the inspiration of many artists. Sharing the view of Hardangerfjord are picturesque villages like Øystese, Ulvik, Lofthus, Kinsarvik and Eidfjord. Near Eidfjord is Voringsfossen, Norway's most famous waterfall.

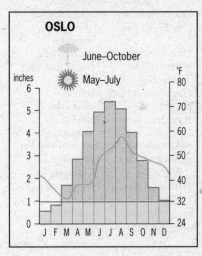

OSLO

June–October

May–July

NORWAY

North of Hardangerfjord is **Bergen**, Norway's second-largest city, a busy port and cultural center. A first glimpse of Bergen is not easily forgotten. It is set among seven mountains, and within the town, brightly painted houses seem to be stacked up against the steep slopes.

The longest fjord is Sognefjord. Deep in its many branches are fascinating towns like Gudvangen, Stalheim and Laerdal. Farther north is Nordfjord, which takes its water from an inland glacier.

The Trondheimsfjord area is filled with natural beauty and historical sites that are reminders of medieval days of religious and political leadership in the area. The royal town of **Trondheim**, Norway's third-largest city, stands just at the entrance of the long, narrow area that leads to Norway's northland.

THE NORTH

Whether traveling by car or steamer, a trip to the roof of Europe is an unforgettable experience. This land beyond the Arctic Circle, where the sun shines 24 hours a day from May to August, is one of weird rock formations and endless moors.

It is also the land of the Sami (Lapps), who follow the reindeer herds to the coast each spring. In the fall, they return to the inland plateau, to which Alta, a small cluster of hamlets, is the gateway.

Hammerfest, in Norway's far northern extremities, is inhabited by hardy of people accustomed to living on the fringes of the earth. From Hammerfest you can continue into the Arctic on the island of Magerøya.

USEFUL EXPRESSIONS IN NORWEGIAN

hello/good morning	god morgen	old/new	gammel/ny
good-bye	adjø	church	kirke
good afternoon	god dag	museum	museum, museet
good evening	god kveld	town hall	rådhuset
please/thank you	vennligst/takk	post office	postkontor
yes/no	ja/nei	station	jernbanestasjon
excuse me	unnksyld	bank	bank
you're welcome	ingen årsak	credit card	kredittkort
Does anyone here speak English?	Er det noen her som snakker engelsk?	doctor	lege
		right/left	til høyre/til venstre
		straight ahead	rett fram
I don't understand.	Jeg forsår ikke.	breakdown	motorstopp
Where are the restrooms?	Hvor er toalettet?	gas station	bensinstasjon
		street	gate
How much is that?	Hvor mye koster det?	square	plass
		tower	tårn
What time is it?	Hvor mange er klokken?		
where/when/how	hvor/når/hvordan		
yesterday/today/ tomorrow	i går/i dag/ i morgen		
What does this mean?	Hva betyr dette?		
cheap/expensive	billig/dyr		
open/closed	åpen/lukket		

DAYS OF THE WEEK

Sunday	søndag
Monday	mandag
Tuesday	tirsdag
Wednesday	onsdag
Thursday	torsdag
Friday	fredag
Saturday	lørdag

PLACES OF INTEREST

snowcapped peaks. It is the country's leading industrial and cultural center and its chief port.

Visitors to Oslo will find a full range of attractions among the many art galleries, museums, nightclubs, restaurants, movies (with films shown in English) and theaters. The National Theater stages productions of Norwegian classics, while more experimental theater productions take place at the Central Theater and the Open Theater.

The purchase of an Oslo Kort (Oslo Card) entitles visitors to travel on streetcars, buses, and railroads (N.S.B.) as well as many other discounts. Cards, which are valid for one to three days, are sold at many outlets.

▲ OSLO (539 A1) ★
OSLO *pop. 500,000*
Oslo, Norway's capital, is at the head of Oslofjord, encircled by wooded hills and

AKERSHUS SLOTT (543 B1) ★, entered from Festningsplassen, is a large fortress overlooking the harbor, and one of Norway's principal medieval monu-

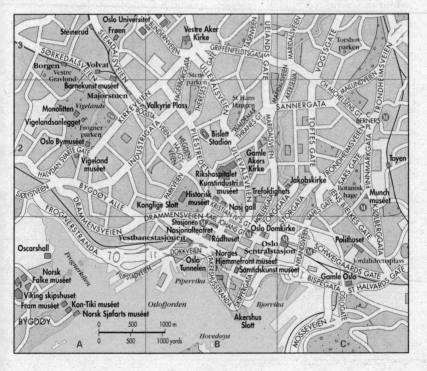

ments. Constructed in the 14th century, it was rebuilt in the 17th century to withstand ships' cannon.

BARNEKUNST MUSÉET (International Museum for Children's Art) (543 A3), Lille Froensvei 4, displays children's art from more than 180 countries. There are various activities available for children.

DOMKIRKE (Cathedral) (543 B1), Stortorvet 1, was completed in 1699 and restored in the 19th century; the altarpiece and pulpit date from 1690.

FRAM MUSÉET (543 A1), Bygdøynes, contains the beautifully kept ship *Fram*. She was built for Fridtjof Nansen's expeditions of 1893–96 and 1898–1902 to the Arctic, and carried Roald Amundsen on his voyage to Antarctica, where he reached the South Pole in 1911.

FROGNERPARKEN (Vigelandsparken) (543 A2) is the site of the renowned Vigeland sculptures. The Norwegian sculptor Gustav Vigeland created a world of human beings and animals in stone, plaster and bronze.

HISTORISK MUSÉET (543 B2), University of Oslo, Frederiksgt 2, comprises three museums, including the Ethnographic Museum and the Myntkabinettet, a collection of coins and medals.

The Oldsalssamling, the university's antique collection, displays weapons, ornaments and household items from the Stone Age to the present.

HOLMENKOLLEN ★ is just behind the city, the site of international skiing events and a famous ski jump. A simulator gives visitors an idea of what it is like to make a jump.

Ski muséet (Ski Museum), Kongevei 5, presents the 2,500-year history of this Norwegian sport.

KONGELIGE SLOTT (Royal Palace) (543 B2) can be found at Drammensvei 1 in Oslo's central park. Although the interior

of the palace is closed to the public, the colorful changing of the guard can be seen daily at 1:30pm.

KON-TIKI MUSÉET (543 A1), Bygdøynesvei 36, exhibits the raft that Thor Heyerdahl used to substantiate his claim that prehistoric South Americans settled the Polynesian islands.

The museum also houses *Ra II*, Heyerdahl's second craft, a reed boat that he built in Egypt to test the theory that this sort of boat could have reached the Americas before Columbus.

KUNSTINDUSTRI MUSÉET (Museum of Applied Arts) (543 B2), St. Olavsgt 1, has exhibits from Norway and other countries dating from the 7th century to the present. The 12th-century Baldishol Tapestry is one of only five remaining Romanesque tapestries in the world.

MUNCH MUSÉET (543 C2) ★, Tøyengata 53, houses the city's art collection left by the painter Edvard Munch. It contains thousands of his paintings, graphic plates, drawings, prints and sculptures, as well as his books, letters and private papers.

NASJONALGALLERIET (National Gallery) (543 B2), at Universitetsgt 13, emphasizes Norwegian painting, sculpture, drawing and engraving, but also includes works by Van Gogh, Matisse and Cezanne. Two rooms are devoted to Munch.

NORGES HJEMMEFRONT MUSÉET (Norwegian Resistance Museum) (543 B1), Akershus, depicts the German occupation of Norway during World War II.

NORSK FOLKE MUSÉET (Norwegian Folk Museum) (543 A1) at Museumsvei 10, Bygdøy, preserves over 150 antique buildings from all over Norway, including the Gal stave church from around 1200. Urban areas from 1700 and 1800 are re-created, and there are art exhibits.

NORSK SJØFARTS MUSÉET (Norwegian Maritime Museum) (543 A1), Bygdøynesvei 37, exhibits Norwegian maritime traditions through the ages. *Gjøa*, the vessel Amundsen used to navigate the Northwest Passage, is on display.

RÅDHUSET (Oslo City Hall) (543 B1) ★, Rådhusplassen, is an impressive contemporary building with two square towers. Norway's leading artists contributed to its decoration in the 1930s and 1940s.

VIKING SKIPSHUSET (Viking Ship Museum) (543 A1), Huk Aveny 38, Bygdøy, houses three Viking ships, found along the Oslofjord.

▲ ÅLESUND (539 A2) ★
MØRE OG ROMSDAL *pop. 40,500*
Ålesund's major attraction is the scenic wonder of its fjords and peaks, including Mount Aksla in the center of the town, with some 418 steps to the top. The surrounding area has fine fishing, caves, cliffs, white beaches and attractive little harbors. The best island is Runde, where 200 bird species have been recorded on its cliffs.

In 1904, most of Ålesund's center was destroyed by fire. The rebuilding drive was led by Kaiser Willhelm II of Germany, a regular visitor to the town. Art nouveau was the prevailing fashion of the day, and the architects seized upon their chance to create a whole new town in the style.

▲ ARENDAL (539 A1)
AUST-AGDER *pop. 12,000*
On the southern coast of the Nidelven, Arendal is an inviting excursion center with a mixture of ancient and modern streets and buildings. Trinity Church's soaring spire and the 19th-century town hall, housing a portrait gallery, are highlights of Arendal's diverse architecture.

▲ BERGEN (539 A1) ★
BERGEN *pop. 210,000*
Bergen was founded in 1070 by King Olav Kyrre and became the capital of Norway in the 13th century. The city has long been an important shipping and commercial center.

Although periodically ravaged by fire, many fine examples of medieval and Renaissance architecture remain. The broad avenues and open spaces are testimonials to the city planners, who designed the thoroughfares in such a way as to prevent the rapid spread of flames.

The chief event during the tourist season, and the cultural event of the year, is the Bergen International Festival, which takes place in late May and early June. This festival of music, drama, folklore, opera and ballet takes place in the Grieghallenn, named after Bergen's famous son, the composer Edward Grieg.

In addition to those listed below, points of interest in and around Bergen include the Bergen Art Gallery; Bergen Fisheries, Theatrical and Natural

---

NATIONAL DAY
Unless you are on foot, it is difficult to get around a Norwegian community on May 17. No matter how small the village, it is certain to have its own parade, and in Oslo the streets are packed with people walking toward the Royal Palace. They are a brilliant sight, many in the unique and beautiful national dress or *bunad*, which varies from region to region, is not just worn as a costume or by dancers, but as formal dress wear. For every parade, the colors are the Norwegian flag's red, blue, and white, carried by children, with parents carrying children too small to walk, all singing patriotic songs.

In Oslo, so many file past the Royal Family, that it takes hours but, whether it be Oslo in the May sun, northern Norway in the snow, or anywhere else in the world, on May 17, Norwegians will celebrate Norway.

NORWAY

History museums; Rosenkrantz Tower, built in 1563; and Bergen Cathedral.

BERGENHUS is a 12th-century fortress that guards Bergen's harbor. It contains several interesting medieval monuments, including the 16th-century Rosenkrantz Tower.

Haakonshallen (Haakon's Hall) is Norway's most venerated secular building. Erected by King Haakon IV Haakonsson as a wedding and coronation palace, this restored 13th-century structure is used on formal occasions.

BRYGGEN ★, the Hanseatic Wharf, now on the U.N.E.S.C.O. list of World Heritage Sites, is a wide quay facing the harbor. In the gabled wooden houses, Bergen's German merchants conducted business during the Hanseatic period. This all-male enclave maintained strict laws and never mingled with the community. Most of the buildings were destroyed by the fire of 1702, but have since been reconstructed. Some of the workshops are open.

Bryggens muséet has the earliest archaeological remains from Bergen's medieval past. There are also re-creations of medieval rooms, from the days when Bergen was a small seafaring town.

Hanseatisk muséet (Hanseatic Museum) is one of the oldest timber buildings on the Bryggen. Furnished in 16th-century style, it depicts the cold daily life of the merchants and young apprentices. Dining and work rooms and the youngsters' tiny box beds remain.

Schötsuene, Øvregt 50, were the merchants' assembly rooms, well-warmed for social life. The long central table has both Bible and cane, for this was also the apprentices' school.

FISKETORGET (Fish Market) has an array of busy, crowded stalls selling fish (salmon is the specialty), flowers, fruits and vegetables.

FLØYEN is one of the seven hills surrounding Bergen. The 319-meter (1,050-foot) peak, reached by funicular, affords a superb view as well as miles of lakes, trees and trails.

GAMLE BERGEN (Old Bergen), Elsero, is a lovely open-air museum facing Sandviken harbor. It has more than 35 old wooden houses with interiors based on establish dwellings and stores from the 18th to the 20th centuries.

MARIA KIRKE (St. Mary's Church), built before 1150, is Bergen's oldest building and one of the finest churches in Norway.

RASMUS MEYER'S COLLECTION, Rasmus Meyers Allé 7, includes works by Edvard Munch. It was bequeathed to the city by a business magnate.

TROLDHAUGEN (Hill of Trolls) is at Hopsvegen, 8 kilometers (5 miles) south overlooking Lake Nordå. In beautiful grounds, this was the summer home of the composer Edvard Grieg for the last 22 years of his life. He and his wife are buried here. The house is furnished as it was in Grieg's time, with his grand piano in the drawing room. Grieg's *hytte* (small cabin), where he worked, overlooks the lake. There is also a concert hall.

UNIVERSITET (University of Bergen) opened in 1948. On the grounds are the city's botanical gardens and several fine museums, including the Museum of Natural History. Sjøfarts muséet (Maritime Museum), Sydneshaugen, has displays pertaining to shipping history from the Viking period through modern times, and the Historisk Museum (Historical Museum), Sydneshaugen, has collections from prehistory to the present, with rare medieval religious art.

▲ BODØ (539 B3)
NORDLAND *pop. 37,000*
Bodø is just north of the Arctic Circle in the land of the midnight sun, where there is constant daylight from late April to mid-August. The town is set against an impressive backdrop of high moun-

LEAVING FOR A BETTER LIFE

In 1825, the Norwegian sloop, *Restauration*, took 52 passengers and crew from Stavanger to North America. By the end of the century, 750,000 Norwegians had left the country. The first group had religious motives and aimed to establish a classless society. Later, poverty and lack of opportunity drove people out. The American Homestead Law of 1862, which granted land to immigrants, turned the early trickle into a flood, and many who had been farm laborers in Norway became farm owners. Many settled in Illinois, where the icy winters were something they could deal with, as well as heading for Iowa, Minnesota and Wisconsin. Where they settled, Norwegian schools, language, and other customs remained for many generations and today you have only to read Garrison Keillor's *Lake Wobegon Days* to realize that, in some places, the traditions live on.

BORGUND STAVKIRKE, built in 1150, is one of the oldest Christian buildings in Scandinavia. Distinguished by its superimposed roofs and conical turret, it also incorporates several pagan elements.

SUNNMØRE MUSÉET is an open-air museum with 30 old timber dwellings, a medieval church and an excavated Viking town. It also has a collection of boats, some of them over 600 years old.

URNES STAVKIRKE, built in 1130–50, is thought to be the oldest stave church in Norway; parts of an even older church were used in its construction.

▲ FAGERNES (539 A1)
OPPLAND *pop. 1,800*
Fagernes is one of Norway's foremost mountain resorts, partially encircling an extension of the lovely Strandefjord.

VALDRES FOLKE MUSÉET, just outside the town, is a collection of about 70 wooden buildings dating from 1200 to 1850. Folk dancing programs, accompanied by Hardanger fiddles and other instruments unique to Norway, are given to celebrate the region's rich musical tradition.

▲ FREDRIKSTAD (539 A1)
ØSTFOLD *pop. 27,200*
On the eastern shore of Oslofjord, Fredrikstad's elaborate Old Town fortifications date from the 17th century and the continual wars between the Swedes and the Danes.

GEILO (539 A1)
BUSKERUD *pop. 2,000*
One of the largest winter sports resorts in Scandinavia, Geilo maintains many ski slopes for beginners and experts.

GEIRANGER (539 A2)
MØRE OG ROMSDAL *pop. 4,800*
At the head of the Geirangerfjord is the charming village of Geiranger. North, on the way to Valldal, are the beautiful waterfalls De Syv Søstre (The Seven Sisters), and Brudesløret (Bridal Veil).

tains that provide splendid views of the surrounding countryside.

In addition to the nearby mountains, Bodø's attractions include the town's modern cathedral, distinguished by the beauty of its architecture and stained glass; the Nordland Museum, with displays of local arts and crafts; and the 13th-century Bodin Church, 3 kilometers (2 miles) outside town, which contains a magnificently carved altarpiece from 1670.

BORGUND (539 A2)
SOGN OG FJORDANE *pop. 1,200*
Borgund is known for its fine stave church and its fish ladder. At the ladder, about 2.5 kilometers (1½ miles) east on E68, the persistent salmon fight their way up the steps to their spawning grounds located upstream.

▲ Halden (539 A1)

ØSTFOLD *pop. 26,100*

Halden is a border town that withstood numerous Swedish attacks during the 17th and 18th centuries. The Fredriksten Fort still dominates the settlement and is a major tourist attraction. Inside are restaurants and museums; the ramparts afford views of the Swedish borderlands.

Hammerfest (539 C4)

FINNMARK *pop. 9,500*

Hammerfest claims to be the world's northernmost town. Having long made its living from fishing, it is now Norway's main trawler port. It was the first European town to have electric street lighting, installed in 1891. The unusual new church, built in 1961, has a shape inspired by the traditional wooden fish-drying racks.

▲ Haugesund (539 A1)

ROGALAND *pop. 28,000*

Once a major fishing center, Haugesund now derives its income from the oil industry. The town gained historical fame when Harald Håfagre united Norway during a series of battles between AD 872 and 930. Haugesund hosts the Norwegian Film Festival.

Honningsvåg (539 C4)

FINNMARK *pop. 3,400*

Honningsvåg is the northwesternmost village in Norway. Reached by ferry from Repvag or by steamer from Tromsø, it sits on a green mountainside behind a fine harbor. Bus excursions to the North Cape provide spectacular sights of the midnight sun over the Arctic Ocean.

▲ Kongsberg (539 A1)

BUDKERUD *pop. 20,000*

Formerly a silver-mining center on the Lågen River, Kongsberg maintains a miniature train that carries tourists through the mining tunnels. Other sites include Lågendal Museum, the Arsenal, the Royal Mint and the Norwegian Mining Museum. The baroque church is Norway's largest.

▲ Kristiansand (539 A1) ★

VEST-AGDER *pop. 66,300*

On a peninsula at the estuary of the Otra River, Kristiansand is Norway's second-largest port and the capital of the south coast area. Built by King Christian IV of Denmark in 1641, it is now an important center of nickel refining. Kristiansand Folk Museum and Ravnedal Municipal Park are of interest.

KRISTIANSAND DOMKIRKE ★, Kirkegata, is a 17th-century Gothic cathedral, rebuilt in 1895. It contains an attractive altarpiece by Eilif Petersen, as well as statues of the Four Evangelists.

THE COASTAL EXPRESS

Every evening, a Coastal Express *(Hurtigruten)* steamer sails out of Bergen's fjord harbor, the start of a 2,300-kilometer (1,250-nautical-mile) trip north, across the Arctic Circle, around North Cape, to Kirkenes on the Russian border, with some 40 stops on the way there and back. At one time, this was the only way to travel in northern Norway, when winter closed the mountain roads; the *Hurtigruten* reached its centenary in 1994. Today, there are popular 11-day tours for visitors, though Norwegians still hop on and off, using the boats as buses between the ports. Passengers can disembark to explore places such as Trondheim, Hammerfest, and Trollfjord. Then there is the North Cape, the highlight of the voyage. There is a lot of fun on board, the most festive occasion coming at the crossing of the Arctic Circle, with Santa Claus on deck and certificates for everyone.

KRISTIANSAND DYREPARK ★, is the largest zoo in Norway, a 45-hectare (111-acre) park that also includes a fairytale village based on stories by a popular children's author, a tropical rain forest, fairgrounds and an alpine pasture farm.

KRISTIANSAND KANON MUSÉET displays one of the largest guns in the world. Its range extends over some 56 kilometers (35 miles).

ODDERRØY, an island in the harbor connected to the mainland by a bridge, bears the remains of several ancient fortresses, including Christiansholm, built by Frederik III in 1674, which is now a venue for art exhibits.

VEST-AGDER FYLKES MUSÉET, Kongsgård, is an open-air museum with some 30 dwellings. Dating from 1600, they display collections of folk furniture, textiles and antique church relics.

▲ KRISTIANSUND (539 B2)
MØRE OG ROMSDAL *pop. 17,900*
Kristiansund is built on three islands connected by bridges and ferry boats. A busy fishing port, it is the home of a trawling fleet. The marketplace, broad streets and brightly painted houses give Kristiansund a charming appearance. Excursion boats tour Kristiansund's three islands.

GAMLE BYEN (Old Town), has an old customs house, the town's first hospital and school, and old warehouses.

LARVIK (539 A1)
VESTFOLD *pop. 9,000*
A delightful seaside resort on the North Sea at the mouth of the Lågen River, Larvik is a center for bathing, boating and salmon fishing. Nearby Lade Farris is known for its natural mineral springs. Over 100 Viking burial mounds can be found in the area.

LARVIK KIRKE, on Kirkestredet, is a 17th-century church with an attractive interior noted for its numerous paintings, including one by Lucas Cranach.

LILLEHAMMER (539 A1) ★
OPPLAND *pop. 22,800*
Norway's best-known resort, Lillehammer is at the northern edge of Mjøsa, the country's largest lake.

A favorite spot for people who love the outdoors, Lillehammer offers a full spectrum of sporting opportunities. Popular summer activities are fishing, horseback riding, swimming, boating and waterskiing. The *Skibladner*, Norway's only remaining paddle steamer, offers cruises on Mjøsa in summer. In winter, lifts transport skiers to nearby slopes. Lillehammer hosted the 1994 Winter Olympic Games.

AULESTAD, 19 kilometers (12 miles) north, was the home of the great Norwegian poet, dramatist and novelist Bjørnstjerne Bjørnson, who wrote the Norwegian national anthem. It is now a museum.

HELLERISTRINGER (Rock Sculptures) are at Drotten, 10 kilometers (6 miles) north. These 4,000-year-old monuments are embellished with animal motifs.

MAIHAUGEN constitutes one of the largest open-air museums in Europe. Over 130 fascinating traditional buildings from the Gudbrandsdal contain thousands of utensils and articles of furniture.

LOFOTEN VESTERÅLEN (539 B3)
NORDLAND *pop. 27,000*
A wall of mountains interrupted by narrow fjords and navigable sounds makes up the Lofoten Vesterålen (Lofoten Islands). Fishermen congregate from January to March for the cod migration, swimmers enjoy waters warmed by the Gulf Stream in the summer, and mountaineers find a variety of challenging climbs all year. The Røst cluster of about 365 islands makes up one of the largest bird sanctuaries in Europe.

NORWAY

▲ MOLDE (539 A2)
MØRE OG ROMSDAL *pop. 21,500*

Beautiful Molde, "City of Roses," is set amid the mountains and fjords of central Norway. The town has attractive parks and flower gardens and is a good base for boating, fishing and mountain climbing.

Boat tours travel to the island resort of Hjertøya, to the picturesque fishing villages of Bud and Bjørnsund on the Atlantic coast and to the holy island of Veøy, with its medieval stone church.

Other attractions include the orchard town of Andalsnes, a noted fishing resort to the southwest. Rødven is known for its 14th-century stave church, and for Mardalsfoss, a 300-meter (984-foot) waterfall at Eikesdalen that is one of Europe's highest. A scenic tour can be made to Geiranger (see p.547) by way of the *Trollstigveien*, or Path of Trolls, which zigzags up steep mountain slopes.

NARVIK (539 B3)
NORDLAND *pop. 18,000*

Narvik is a busy port primarily concerned with exporting iron ore. The town suffered considerable damage during World War II, but has since been rebuilt. It is now a popular tourist destination because of its mountain setting and views of the midnight sun.

RØROS (539 B2) ★
SØR-TRØNDELAG *pop. 3,300*

Røros, with its many unpainted timber houses, looks much as it did when the first copper mines opened in 1644. Slag heaps, a smelter and poor mining houses make the 1,000 or so buildings authentic enough to gain Røros a place on the U.N.E.S.C.O. list of World Heritage Sites. The stone church with its white steeple is very fine. Røros Museum, in the Smelting Works, has mining displays, and underground tours descend to 50 meters (160 feet) below Olav's Gruva (Olav's Mine), some 14 kilometers (9 miles) west, with all its machinery. Røros is also a winter sports center. Other points of interest include Korthaugen Fortress, erected in 1711.

▲ SKIEN (539 A1)
TELEMARK *pop. 46,700*

Industrialized Skien, on the north bank of the Skienselv, was the birthplace of dramatist Henrik Ibsen in 1828. The farm where he grew up is just north of town and is preserved as a monument.

▲ STAVANGER (539 A1) ★
ROGALAND *pop. 100,000*

When Harald Håfagre won the Battle of Hafrsfjord near Stavanger in AD 872, he united Norway for the first time. The old city, the country's fourth largest, has become a major port and oil production center. Modern Stavanger is a charming blend of fishing village and modern city, sprinkled with parks, gardens and lakes.

Points of interest include the Stavanger Museum, with historical and zoological exhibits, and the Kongsgård, a former royal manor that is now a school. Market Square is lined with fish, fruit and vegetable stalls.

GAMLE STAVANGER (Old Stavanger) is preserved from the late 17th and 18th centuries, with more than 150 wooden houses, cobbled streets and old-fashioned street lamps. This is no museum; people live here and take pride in keeping their homes in character.

HERMETIKK MUSÉET (Canning Museum). Until World War II, Stavanger prospered on sardine processing, and had 70 canning factories. Once a working factory, the museum has curing ovens and guides who demonstrate a life of threading, smoking and packing sardines.

SJOFARTS MUSÉET (Maritime Museum), close to the harbor, deals with the town's maritime history, from sailing ships to oil platforms. Its old store has goods that would have been sold in the 1930s, and the owner's office and comfortable apartment remain as they were then.

STAVANGER DOMKIRKE, a 12th-century cathedral at Haakon VII's Gate, is one of Norway's most attractive churches.

Rebuilt in about 1300 with a Gothic chancel by English craftsmen, this structure has a pulpit with some interesting woodcarvings dating from 1658.

VISTEHOLA is a cave at Randaberg, 10 kilometers (6 miles) from Stavanger. It is believed to be the oldest homestead in Scandinavia. Excavations have uncovered ancient animal skeletons and tools made of horn and bone.

▲ TØNSBERG (539 A1)
VESTFOLD *pop. 33,000*
Tønsberg is the oldest town in Scandinavia, founded before AD 871. This ancient fortress city on the coast south of Oslo is now an important shipping center.

▲ TROMSØ (539 B4) ★
TRØMS *pop. 53,000*
Tromsø is the largest town in northern Norway. It has the world's most northerly university and a lively student life. The study of the *aurora borealis* (northern lights), observed especially in December and January, is made by the Auroral Observatory (Rockefeller-sponsored). Expeditions to the Arctic island of Spitzbergen are possible.

ISHAVSKATEDRALEN (Arctic Cathedral) is coated in aluminum and said to symbolize Norwegian nature, culture and faith. It is a perfect example of modern architecture and contains one of the largest stained-glass windows throughout Europe. In the center of the town is the original Domkirke (Cathedral), one of Norway's biggest wooden churches.

NORDLYSPLANETARIET (Northern Lights Planetarium) presents *Arctic Lights*, a representation of the *aurora borealis*, or northern lights.

POLARMUSEET (Polar Museum) celebrates the Arctic in vivid pictures, along with memorabilia of explorers and other interesting aspects of Arctic life, including a Sami exhibit.

▲ TRONDHEIM (539 A2) ★
SØR-TRØNDELAG *pop. 140,000*
Founded in AD 997, Trondheim is the principal city in north-central Norway. This is known as the Royal Town because Norwegian kings are crowned in the cathedral. Excellent sailing, fishing and skiing are available nearby.

ERKEBISPEGÅRDEN, bordering Bispegt, was formerly the Archbishop's Palace, built in the 12th century.

KRISTIANSTEN FESTNING, off Brubakken, is the town fortress built by General Caspar de Cicignon in 1676–82.

NIDAROS DOMKIRKE (Nidaros Cathedral), next to Erkebispegården, is one of Europe's finest Gothic buildings. It was built in the early 11th century and is noted for its interesting sculptures. In ancient times, the cathedral was used for royal coronations, and since 1988 it has housed the crown jewels of Norway, a beautiful regalia, on display to visitors in summer.

RINGVE MUSIKHISTORISK MUSÉET (Ringve Museum of Musical History), Ringve Mansion at Lade, contains instruments of the type played by Beethoven and Mozart, demonstrated by guides who play them. Oriental countries are represented by exotic instruments of fine mosaic and ivory.

▲ VOSS (539 A1)
HORDALAND *pop. 14,100*
Voss is a center of traditional Norwegian culture, a place to see old dances performed in authentic dress. Voss has also produced a remarkable number of Hardanger fiddle-players as well as other musicians and artists. As a resort, it has fine facilities for skiing and summer water sports.

VANGSKYRKJA is a church built by King Magnus the Lawmaker in 1277. The octagonal steeple is unique, and inside the church are rich decorations.

NORWAY

SWEDEN

THE LARGEST OF THE SCANDINAVIAN COUNTRIES, SWEDEN'S DOMINANCE, PAST AND PRESENT, IS SOMETIMES RESENTED BY ITS NEIGHBORS. OFTEN AT WAR IN THE PAST, SWEDEN REMAINED NEUTRAL THROUGHOUT THE TWO WORLD WARS AND HAS RETAINED A COOL AND PROSPEROUS PRESENCE. SWEDEN IS SCENICALLY RICH TOO. COVERING 1,600 KILOMETERS (1,000 MILES) BY 500 KILOMETERS (310 MILES), IN THE NORTH IT SHARES MOUNTAINS WITH NORWAY, WHILE FARTHER SOUTH ARE THE LAKES, INCLUDING HUGE LAKE VÄNERN. THERE ARE ABOUT 100,000 LAKES SCATTERED THROUGHOUT SWEDEN, AND WITH FOREST COVERING 60 PERCENT OF THE COUNTRY THERE WOULD SEEM TO BE LITTLE ROOM FOR ANYTHING ELSE BUT WOOD AND WATER. STOCKHOLM IS SWEDEN'S CAPITAL, SPRAWLED OVER ISLANDS AND AROUND INLETS, WITH AN OLD TOWN OF 16TH- AND 17TH-CENTURY BUILDINGS.

Left GAMLA STAN, STOCKHOLM'S OLD TOWN, IS FULL OF WATERFRONTS AND
NARROW LANES, THE MOST BEAUTIFUL OF SCANDINAVIA'S CAPITALS
Above ORUST HAS MANY PRETTY FISHING VILLAGES LIKE HÄLLVIKSSTRAND

THINGS TO KNOW

- **AREA:** 449,963 square kilometers (173,731 square miles).
- **POPULATION:** 8,692,000
- **CAPITAL:** Stockholm
- **LANGUAGE:** Swedish
- **ECONOMY:** Industry, trade, forestry, machinery, iron, steel, wood and paper products, iron ore (especially Lappland); farmland produces cattle, grains, potatoes, sugar beets.
- **PASSPORT REQUIREMENTS:** Required for U.S. citizens.
- **VISA REQUIREMENTS:** Not required for stays up to three months total in the Scandinavian countries (Denmark, Finland, Iceland, Norway and Sweden)
- **DUTY-FREE ITEMS:** 200 cigarettes or 100 cigarillos or 250 grams of tobacco, 1 liter of wine and 1 liter of spirits (or 2 liters of wine), 2 liters of beers, perfume for personal use, cameras and a reasonable amount of film, one video camera.
- **CURRENCY:** The currency unit, the Swedish *krona*, is divided into 100 *öre*. Due to currency fluctuations, the exchange rate is subject to frequent change. No limit on import or export of foreign currency.
- **BANK OPENING HOURS:** 9:30am–3pm Monday–Friday; many banks remain open until 5:30 or 6pm on Monday or Thursday. In small towns and rural areas bank hours are 10am–2pm Monday–Friday.
- **STORE OPENING HOURS:** 9am–6pm Monday–Friday; on Saturday stores open at 9am and close between 1 and 4pm. In some larger towns, department stores remain open until 8pm; some also open Sunday.
- **BEST BUYS:** Glassware, ceramics and pottery; furniture and carved wood; stainless steel, silver and other metal items; textiles, rugs and wall hangings; and reindeer souvenirs from Lappland.
- Note: Sweden has a system for cash refunds of Value Added Tax (V.A.T.). Visitors who show a passport when making a purchase in a shop displaying the "Tax Free for Tourists" sign will

HISTORY

The first settlers moved in to Sweden in about 12,000 BC when hunter-gatherers crossed a land bridge from continental Europe. By 1500 BC the population was trading with the Danube Basin and the Mediterranean. From the 9th to the 11th centuries Swedish Vikings controlled trade across the Baltic and ranged as far south as Constantinople.

By the end of the 11th century Christianity had replaced paganism and the country was unified under a single ruler. The first Swedish parliament, the bicameral *Riksdag*, was established in the year 1435.

In the early 1600s Sweden became a great northern European power seeking control over the Baltic Sea and the western trade routes of the Russian empire. Impoverished by wars in the 18th and early 19th centuries, Sweden adopted policies of non-alignment and neutrality that continue unbroken.

Nineteenth-century Sweden was a poor country whose population more than doubled despite heavy emigration. There were many democratic changes including compulsory free education, equal rights of inheritance for men and women, religious freedom and parliamentary reforms. In the last half of the century Sweden's industrialization began, based upon iron ores and forests.

In the 20th century Sweden has experienced almost continuous economic growth and increased prosperity. In 1932 the Social Democratic Party gained control of the government, a control that it has maintained with only two short breaks since.

Somewhat delayed by World War II, in which Sweden remained neutral, social welfare laws were enacted establishing pensions, health insurance, a tax reorganisation that redistributed wealth, and educational reforms and expansions.

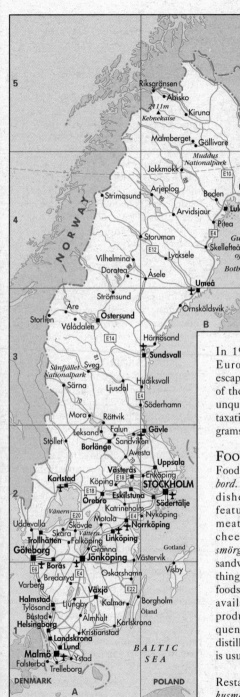

In 1994, Sweden voted to join the European Union. Sweden has not escaped the general economic problems of the 1990s, however, and the previous unquestioned support for relatively high taxation and generous social welfare programs may be changing.

FOOD AND DRINK

Food in Sweden often means a *smörgåsbord*. This wide selection of hot and cold dishes served buffet style usually features pickled or smoked herring, meats, sausages, fish delicacies and cheese. Another Swedish treat is *smörgås*. The *smörgås* is an open faced sandwich and may be covered with anything from lobster to cold turkey. Other foods popular with Swedes are crayfish, available in early fall, seafood, dairy products and pastries. Common thirst quenchers are *aquavit*, a potent drink distilled from potatoes, and beer, which is usually very mild.

Restaurants all over the country serve *husmanskost*, literally "home cooking," receive a check for the V.A.T. amount. Checks can be cashed at airports, on certain ferries and at ferry ports on departure.

- **PUBLIC HOLIDAYS:** January 1; January 6 (Epiphany); Good Friday; Easter Monday; May 1 (Labor Day); Ascension Day; Whitmonday; Midsummer's Day; All Saints' Day; December 25; December 26 (Boxing Day).
- **NATIONAL TOURIST OFFICES:** Scandinavian National Tourist Boards 655 Third Ave. New York, NY 10017 Tel: 212/949-2333 Fax: 212/885-9764 Swedish Travel and Tourism Council 11 Montagu Place London W1H 2AL Tel: 0171 724 5869 Fax: 0171 724 5872 Sweden House Corner Hamngatan/Kungsträdgården Box 7542 S-10393 Stockholm Tel: (08) 789-24-00 Fax: (08) 789-24-50
- **AMERICAN EMBASSY:** Strandvägen 101 11589 Stockholm Sweden Tel: (08) 783-53-00 Fax: (08) 661-19-64

AUTOMOBILE CLUBS
Motormännens Riksförbund (Swedish Automobile Association), Sveavägen 159, Stockholm, and the **Svenska Turistföreningen** (S.T.F., Swedish Touring Club), Stureplan 4C, Stockholm, also have offices in Malmö and Göteborg. The symbol ▲ indicates the presence of a AAA affiliated automobile club branch. Not all auto clubs offer full travel services to AAA members.

---

based on traditional Swedish recipes. Each province has its specialty, which is often served as the dish of the day.

SPORTS AND RECREATION
Avid sports enthusiasts, Swedes have excellent recreational facilities. Lakes and mountains throughout Sweden attract visitors all year for camping, hiking, fishing, boating and swimming. Skiing attracts Swedes and visitors alike in this land ideally suited for miles of cross-country ski trails. The north harbors numerous resorts – Abisko, Åre, Storlien, Riksgränsen and Vålådalen – that offer skiing, skating, ice hockey, tobogganing and curling. Some of Sweden's favorite seaside resorts are Båstad, Falsterbo, Saltsjöbaden, Tylösand and Visby. Sweden has many golf courses and good facilities for tennis. With more than 96,000 fish-filled lakes, Sweden is a fisherman's paradise. Facilities are available at most resorts. Karlstad is especially popular for fishing.

GETTING AROUND
Sweden can be reached by ferry to Göteborg (Gothenburg) from Kiel in Germany, Harwich and Newcastle in England, and Fredrikshavn in Denmark. There also are ferries from Elsinore and Grenå, Denmark, to Helsingborg; and Travemünde, Germany, to Trelleborg. There are also connections from Finland, Estonia, Poland and Norway.

All Sweden's roads are toll free, including the *motortrafikled*, or highway, and *motorväg*, or freeway. Road surfaces in the south are generally good, but those in central and northern areas are often just loose gravel. If the vehicle has seat belts, wearing them is compulsory; a child of seven years or under may not occupy a front seat unless using a suitable restraint system. Low beam lights should be used at all times during the day. Speed limits are 50 k.p.h. (31 m.p.h.) in town, 70–90 k.p.h. (43–55 m.p.h.) on out-of-town roads and 90–110 k.p.h. (55–65 m.p.h.) on *motorväg*. There are no on-the-spot fines.

ACCOMMODATIONS

A wide variety of accommodations is found in Sweden. Though there is no official rating system, Swedish hotels have a particularly good reputation. The Swedish Tourist Board publishes an annual hotel guide, as well as a guide covering less expensive alternatives. Many hotels offer discounted rates in summer and at weekends; summer chalets are slightly less expensive. A number of farms also offer bed and breakfast. Budget-priced accommodations are available in simple rooms that do not include breakfast; a *rum*, or room, sign identifies this type of lodging. Most *turistbyrå*, local tourist offices, will book a *rum* or lodging at a farm. The best deals are found at Sweden's 750 officially approved campgrounds, open in April or May through August; some are even open in winter. An International Camping Carnet is required.

TIPPING

A service charge of 12 to 15 percent is usually included in hotel bills, so there is no need to tip further unless for special attention. The same is true in restaurants, where an 18 percent Value Added Tax (V.A.T.) and service charge are included in the price. Taxi drivers and hairdressers are tipped 10 percent.

PRINCIPAL TOURING AREAS

Note: For descriptions of attractions in **bold type**, see individual listings.

THE WEST COAST AND LAKELANDS

Sweden's lake district is popular all year. The huge lakes Vänern and Vättern, and thousands of smaller waterways, make Götaland excellent for water sports. A boat trip yields spectacular scenery. **Göteborg** (Gothenburg) is a good center for exploring.

THE SOUTH

Skåne is château country; there are more than 200 castles in Sweden's southern-most province. Skåne also offers white sand beaches, fertile farmland and medieval churches.

Filled with reminders from bygone eras are the nature havens of Öland and Götland, large islands off Sweden's southeast coast. From the bridge that links Öland with the mainland at **Kalmar**, it is a short drive to Öland's capital, **Borgholm**. **Visby**, on Götland, is served by air and ferry connections.

THE NORTH

Northern Sweden is like a giant park. Vast lakes and swift streams lure anglers, high mountains beckon skiers, and lovely scenery attracts campers and hikers. **Åre**, Storlien, Vålådalen are popular all year, but especially in the ski season.

In the far north, Lappland's inhabitants still live much as they did centuries ago. Some Sami (Lapp) people depend upon reindeer for survival, and a few still dwell in tents. Popular skiing resorts are **Abisko** and Riksgränsen.

STOCKHOLM AND AROUND

Stockholm is a good starting point for exploring. The nation's capital is a cultural center offering opera, concerts, museums and art galleries, and is within

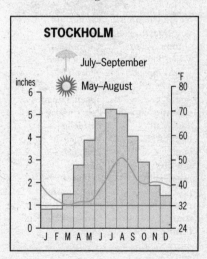

STOCKHOLM

July–September

May–August

driving distance of most of Svealand's attractions. The most outstanding university in Sweden is at **Uppsala**.

DALARNA – FOLKLORE COUNTRY

Dalarna, in Svealand, is renowned for its culture and folklore. The inhabitants still adhere to ancient customs and wear regional costumes on festive occasions. Festivals are numerous, and most villages have midsummer celebrations. The resorts of **Rättvik**, Leksand, **Mora** and Tällberg are surrounded by lakes, birch meadows and green hills.

USEFUL EXPRESSIONS IN SWEDISH

hello/good morning	god morgon	doctor	läkare, doktor
good-bye	adjö	rest rooms	toaletten
good afternoon	god dag	right	till höger
good evening	god kväll	left	till vänster
good night	god natt	straight ahead	rakt fram
please	var så god	breakdown	motorstopp
thank you	tack	gas station	bensinstation
yes/no	ja/nej	street	gatan
excuse me	ursäkta mig	square	platsen
you're welcome	ingen orsak	tower	torn
Does anyone here speak English?	Finns det någon här som talar engelska?	castle	slott
		bridge	bro

I don't understand.	Jag förstår inte.	**DAYS OF THE WEEK**	
Where are the restrooms?	Var är toaletten?	Sunday	söndag
		Monday	måndag
Do you take credit cards?	Kan jag beta la med kredikort?	Tuesday	tisdag
		Wednesday	onsdag
How much is that?	Hur mycket kostar det?	Thursday	torsdag
		Friday	fredag
I'd like...	jag skulle vilja ha	Saturday	lördag
What time is it?	Hur mycket är klockan?		

		NUMBERS	
where/when/how	var/när/hur	1	en, ett
yesterday/today/ tomorrow	igår/idag/ i morgen	2	två
		3	tre
What does this mean?	Vad betyder det här?	4	fyra
		5	fem
cheap/expensive	billig/dyr	6	sex
open/closed	öppen/stängd	7	sju
vacant/occupied	ledig/upptagen	8	åtta
good/bad	bra/dålig	9	nio, nie
old/new	gammal/ny	10	tio, tie
church	kyrkan	20	tjugo
museum	museet	21	tjugo en
town hall	rådhuset	22	tjugo två
post office	postkontoret	30	trettio
newspaper	tidning	40	fyrtio
station	järnvägsstationen	50	femtio
bank	bank	60	sextio

70	sjuttio
80	åttio
90	nittio
100	hundra
1,000	tusen

PLACES OF INTEREST

▲ STOCKHOLM (555 B2) ★

STOCKHOLMS LÄN *pop. 684,500*

Spread over several peninsulas and 14 islands in Lake Mälaren and the Baltic Sea, Stockholm is Sweden's capital and largest city. Canals and bridges lace the "city on the water" founded in the 13th century. Once occupied by the Danes, it has been Swedish territory since 1523.

The city underwent a renaissance in the 18th century, when cultural enrichment followed architectural and governmental expansion. Stockholm's great literary and scientific academies were founded in this period.

A tour of Stockholm should begin with Gamla Stan, the Old Town of Stadsholmen, an island in the center of the city. Conservation has ensured that this area retains its medieval charm and has many government buildings. As most streets are narrow – Mårten Trotzigs Gränd is little more than 1 meter (3 feet) wide – the best way to see Gamla Stan is on foot. Stockholm's nightlife is based in the nightclubs and bars here; by day boutiques and antique shops flourish. Stora Nygt is the principal thoroughfare in this area of the city.

From Stortorget, a large square by the Royal Palace, most attractions of Gamla Stan are within easy reach. Skeppsbron is a quay on the eastern shore that is lined with 17th- and 18th-century trading houses. Other points of interest are Storkyrkan, a 13th-century cathedral, and Tyska Kyrkan, the German Church of St. Gertrude.

Together with Stadsholmen, the islands of Riddarholmen, Helgeandsholmen and Stromsborg make up the "town between the bridges." Helgeandsholmen, or "Island of the Holy Ghost," is the seat of parliament. Riddarholmen, the Island of Knights, is the location of Riddarholms-kyrkan, the royal memorial church since the 17th century.

Across the North Bridge from Stadsholmen is Norrmalm, Stockholm's commercial center. The 18th-century Foreign Office and the Royal Opera are next to Gustav Adolf Torg.

Stockholm's principal shopping area is the Sergelstorget area, a completely

---

THE ART GALLERY UNDERGROUND

Stockholm's *Tunnelbanan* (subway) must be the most beautiful in the world. Its stations are full of art of all sorts. The idea originated in the 1940s, but it was not until 1957 that T-Centralen, the hub of the network, could display the first three by Egon Möller-Nielsen, decorations on track walls made of white clinker and ceramic figures, with glass prisms in patterns and colors. Gradually ticket halls, platforms, ceilings, and even the track walls were covered with wonderful murals gathered in from some 70 artists. People argue about which is the best, but the Akalla train (route 11) is hard to beat – its entrance is like going down into a strange, deep cavern.

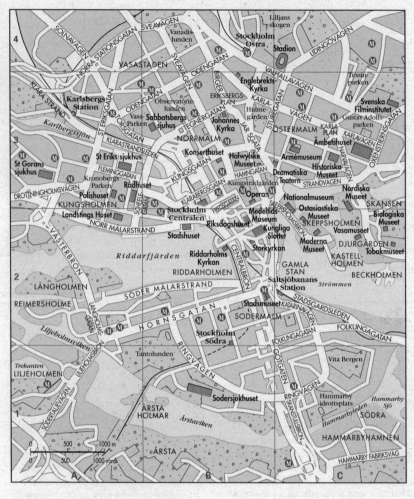

rebuilt section in Central Norrmalm. Several large department stores and Sergelgatan shopping mall are here.

Humlegården, or Hop Garden, the site of the Royal Library, lies to the west of Norrmalm, as does Nybroplan, home to the Royal Dramatic Theater. East of Nybroplan are the Army Museum, the National Museum of History, the Royal Numismatic Collection and, farther east, the Maritime Museum and Technical Museum. The Ethnographic Museum has displays from the Orient and is near Kaknastornet, a 116-meter (380-foot) tower with a panoramic view of the city.

South of Östermalm is Djurgården, or Deer Park, once a royal hunting park. Oak trees, some of them 1,000 years old, grow on the island, which is Stockholm's largest park area. Lundsgröna, also on the island, is a popular amusement park.

Skeppsholmen and Kastellholmen are islands east of Stadsholmen. The two islands once comprised a naval base. Several old military buildings now house the Museum of Modern Art and Asiatic Antiquities.

Tourists in Stockholm can purchase the special ticket *Stockholmskortet*, the "key to Stockholm," which entitles the traveler to transportation on buses, subways and suburban railways, as well as sightseeing trips and admission to 50 of Stockholm's main attractions, including the Royal Palace, the *Vasa* Museum and Gripsholm Castle, all at no extra cost. Valid for 12 to 36 hours, the card is available at the tourist center in Kungsträdgården, and at Hotellcentraler in the Central Railroad Station.

DROTTNINGHOLM ★, is on Lovon, an island west of Stockholm. Surrounded by formal gardens, the 17th-century French-style palace contains portraits of European monarchs. Gustavus III established the Drottningholm Court Theater in the 18th century. After his assassination it lay closed and forgotten until the 1920s, when it was discovered with its 18th-century stage equipment, seating and character intact.

GAMLA STAN (560 B2), the Old Town, is a maze of narrow streets and old buildings, ideal for browsing and shopping.

GRIPSHOLM SLOTT ★, lies 60 kilometers (37 miles) west on an island in Mälaren and is considered to be the "Swedish Pantheon." Dating from 1383, and rebuilt in 1537, the castle served as a refuge for the country's kings. Highlights include a silk and velvet-lined throne, Swedish and Foreign Portrait Galleries and an 18th-century theater. Extensive gardens and a deer park surround the castle.

HAGA PARK MUSEUM AND GUSTAV IIIs PAVILJONG, Haga was Gustav III's retreat, a graceful pavilion, with beautiful interiors.

HISTORISKA MUSEUM (560 C3) ★, Narvaväg 13–17, houses many Viking and medieval treasures.
The Gold Room, in a vault some 7 meters (23 feet) below ground, contains rare gold from as early as the 5th century and is a new addition to an already fine collection recalling Sweden's past.

KAKNÄSTÅRNET ★, north of Djurgården. The television/radio tower at some 150 meters (492 feet) is Stockholm's tallest building. The restaurant near the top commands the best view of the city.

KUNGLIGA SLOTTET (560 B2) ★, the Royal Palace in Gamla Stan, was built in 1697–1754. Art collections, tapestries and marble statuary occupy the 608 rooms. The king's silver throne is in the Hall of State, and the Swedish crown jewels are in the Treasury. A summer highlight is the daily changing of the guard.

NORDISKA MUSEET (Nordic Museum) (560 C3), on Djurgården, depicts folk art and daily life in Scandinavia since 1500. It also houses the Royal Armory.

ROSENDALS SLOTT, on Djurgården, was built in the 1820s as a royal summer residence. The original interiors are well preserved.

SKANSEN ★, on Djurgården, is one of the world's oldest open-air museums. About 150 buildings date from several periods; the grounds comprise a zoo, parks and gardens.

STRINDBERGMUSEET, Drottninggatan 85, was the home of the dramatist August Strindberg from 1908 until his death in 1912. Exhibits chronicle his life.

ULRIKSDAL CASTLE ★, Solna, was used by King Gustav VI Adolf and Queen Louise (the parents of the King Carl XVI Gustav) from 1923–73, whose apartments, together with earlier rooms, are displayed with beautiful antiques. The park has a splendid 17th-century conservatory.

VASAMUSEET (560 C2) ★, Djurgården, houses the restored 17th-century warship *Vasa*. At the time the world's largest warship, the 70-meter (230-foot) *Vasa* sank in Stockholm harbor on her maiden voyage in 1628. She was recovered in 1961 and has now been carefully restored to her original condition.

SWEDEN

ABISKO (555 B5) ★
LAPPLAND

Abisko is a well-known resort on Lake Torneträsk, a narrow body of water that extends almost to the Norwegian border. Abisko's location at the entrance to Abisko National Park and at the start of the 394-kilometer (245-mile) Royal Trail (Kungsleden), makes it a popular destination for hikers, campers, skiers and for summer boat trips and water sports.

BJÖRKLIDEN, some 7 kilometers (4½ miles) north of Abisko, has the highest mountain station in Sweden, at some 1,200 meters (3,937 feet). Here, they ski all year, and sunbathe in summer, when the lower snow-free slopes are covered with rare and beautiful plants.

ÅRE (555 A3)
JÄMTLAND *pop. 9,900*

The Jämtland village of Åre, one of Sweden's top ski resorts, lies at the foot of 1,350-meter (4,429-foot) Mount Åre in a lush valley of the same name.

BORGHOLM (555 A1) ★
ÖLAND *pop. 11,600*

The principal town on the island of Öland is, like the whole island, a summer resort. Its climate and bathing facilities attract visitors. Places of interest include Solliden, a summer residence of the Swedish royal family. Built in 1906, it has Italian gardens and is open daily.

Characterisitcs of Öland Island include a variety of plant life, many species of visiting birds and over 400 windmills. There are 16 primitive forts, including the ruins of one at Gråborg that has walls 8 meters (26 feet) high and dates from AD 500. There are several Viking burial grounds on the island, with Stone Age tombs at Resmo and Bronze Age burial mounds at Mysinge Hog. The Trollskogen, or Enchanted Forest, is a thick pine grove threaded by pleasant hiking trails.

BORGHOLM SLOTTET, overlooking Borgholm, originated as a medieval stronghold and was rebuilt as a Renaissance palace in the 16th century. Though ravaged by fire in 1806, Borgholm remains the biggest and most imposing ruined fortress in Sweden.

EKETORP was a fortified settlement in the late Iron Age and Viking era dating from around AD 300–1200. Huts and buildings re-creating the village illustrate the life of the people whose graves have been excavated nearby.

▲ ESKILSTUNA (555 A2)
SÖDERMANLAND *pop. 89,500*

Industrial Eskilstuna is noted for its modern architecture and scenic location. Places of interest include Stora Sunby Slottet, the only Norman fortress in Sweden, and People's Park, which has the country's second largest zoo.

The Rademacher Smithy has well-preserved forges; the quality of Eskilstuna knives, scissors, and measuring tools is widely respected.

FALKÖPING (555 A2)
VÄSTERGÖTLAND *pop. 31,900*

Falköping is a good base for exploring Västergötland. Contrasting with the region's modern farms are remarkable runic stones, old churches and graves dating from the Stone Age.

▲ FALUN (555 A2) ★
DALARNA *pop. 54,600*

Falun, capital of Dalarna, is noted for its copper mine, which has been operated by the same company since 1288. The mine helped Sweden to attain military superiority in northern Europe in the 16th and 17th centuries by providing copper for cannonballs. Visitors can descend the 50-meter (164-foot) elevator shaft and take a guided tour.

CARL LARSSON'S HOME at Sundborn, some 10 kilometers (6 miles) from Falun, commemorates a famous Dalarna painter, who specialized in domestic scenes. His family left the house as it was, with the 19th century interiors that inspired him. There are also tours of Sundborn Kyrka and the parsonage, which have Larsson collections.

▲ GÖTEBORG (555 A2) ★
GÖTEBORGS OCH BOHUSLÄN
pop. 483,400

Göteborg, or Gothenburg, is Sweden's second largest city. Situated on the Göta River, its busy, attractive harbor, can be explored by boat.

Tree-lined streets and parks add to the city's charm. Slottsskogen, a forested area, has a deer park, open-air museum, biological museum and playgrounds. The green Allé extends more than 2 kilometers (1 mile) beyond the moat.

Gothenburg was founded in 1621 by the warrior king, Gustav II Adolf. His statue stands in the square that bears his name, Gustav Adolf Torg. The Old Town surrounding the square is a delightful section with Dutch-built canals and old buildings. Points of interest include the garrison overlooking the harbor, the town hall, cathedral, Kristine Kyrka (German church) and warehouses of the Swedish East India Company.

Good theaters and concert halls, museums, restaurants and shops dot the city. The Götaplatsen, a square, is the cultural heart of the city, with the municipal theater, concert hall and art gallery. Gothenburg's main thoroughfare for shopping is Kungsportsavenyen, known simply as Avenyn.

Facilities in Gothenburg include fishing, sailing, golf and tennis. Excursions depart to the numerous off-shore islands, including the resort of Marstrand, noted for its medieval fortress and annual regatta. Comfortable steamers ply wide lakes past areas noted for their scenic beauty.

Gothenburg offers tourists *Göteborgskortet*, a special discount card that gives free travel on buses and trams, free parking and sightseeing tours, a free boat tour to Denmark and admission to museums, nightspots and other attractions. It includes discounts at car rental agencies, hotels and restaurants. Valid from 12 to 36 hours, *Göteborgskortet* can be purchased at the tourist information office at Kungsportsplatsen 2.

KONSTMUSEET, on Götaplatsen, has collections of works by old masters, French Impressionists and modern artists, with particular emphasis on Scandinavian artists, including Larsson and Zora, who, in the late 19th century gathered at Skagen in northern Denmark.

KRONHUSET, Kronhusgt 1, dates from 1650 and is the city's oldest building. Once an arsenal, it is now a historical museum and has exhibits on the development of the area since ancient times. Beside Kronhuset, two large buildings were once artillery workshops, and are now Kronhusbodarna, shops and workshops which demonstrate and sell craftware and delicious old-fashioned cakes and spice buns.

LISEBERG is one of Sweden's biggest and best outdoor amusement parks, dating back to 1923 and the Gothenburg Exhibition.

THE GÖTA CANAL

Many Swedes travel the Göta Canal each year, spending four to five days on one of the elegant old 19th-century canal boats that glide slowly along a waterway linking Gothenburg and Stockholm.

The original purpose of this engineering miracle through several lakes including Lake Mälaren and the Great Lakes, Vänern and Vättern, was to carry timber, iron and other products to the growing industries along its banks.

Today the boats take Swedish and foreign passengers on a peaceful, relaxing trip with time to stop at an interesting church or enjoy a meal at one of the many *Herrgård* (manor houses) dotted throughout these long-inhabited areas.

SWEDEN

TRÄDGÅRDSFÖRENINGEN has beautiful formal gardens, with fine statues by Scandinavian sculptors, an elegant palm house dating from 1878, as well as water, camellia, and Mediterranean houses.

GRÄNNA (555 A2)
SMÅLAND *pop. 3,800*
Gränna is a popular vacation center in the orchard district on the eastern shores of Lake Vättern. In late May or early June, a rally for ballooning enthusiasts takes place.

▲ HALMSTAD (555 A1)
HALLAND *pop. 81,000*
Capital of fertile Halland, Halmstad was a meeting place for Danish and Swedish leaders when the two countries were united. Older sections of the city still maintain a distinctly Danish air. The 16th-century Halmstad Slottet now serves as the governor's residence. Norreport, or North Gate, is a fortification dating from 1605. Hallandsgården, an open-air museum, and 14th-century Halmstad Kyrka are both worth visiting.

▲ HELSINGBORG (555 A1)
SKÅNE *pop. 110,800*
Helsingborg, on the Oresund, is a picturesque seaport founded in 1085. The Kärnan, an 11th-century tower-fortress, provides views of the channel and the Danish coast. Kulla-Gunnarstorp is an old château, and Krapperup is the castle home of the Gyllenstierna family, the Guildensterns of Shakespeare's *Hamlet*.

▲ JÖNKÖPING (555 A2)
SMÅLAND *pop. 112,800*
Jönköping is on the southern edge of Lake Vättern. A match museum is on the site of a 19th-century factory where the first safety match was made and struck.

The Kristine Kyrka dates from 1673; the town hall, built in the 17th century, contains the Museum of the Småland Archaeological Society, which displays religious art treasures. Habo Kyrka, a gabled wooden church built in 1680, has an attractive painted interior.

STADSPARKEN is an extensive nature reserve where the attractions rival those of Skansen Park in Stockholm.

KALMAR (555 A1)
SMÅLAND *pop. 56,800*
The site of the Union of Kalmar, an agreement uniting Sweden, Denmark and Norway in 1397, Kalmar is the ancient key to Sweden. In medieval times, whoever controlled this fortress ruled Sweden. Today it is one of the country's most popular tourist resorts.

The older sections of the city occupy an island and contain remnants of the ancient city walls, several parks and a 17th-century cathedral. The cathedral is in Kvarnholmen, the oldest part of town. Excursions can be made to nearby Öland Island (see *Borgholm* on p.562) and to the internationally known glassworks at Strömsbergshyttan, Orrefors and Kosta.

KALMAR SLOTT, one of Sweden's outstanding Renaissance castles, was begun in the 12th century. Kalmar has lavish courts, a rococo chapel, a dungeon, medieval battlements, round towers and a surrounding moat. The museum's most important exhibit is the remains of the *Kronan*, a warship sunk here in 1676 by a Danish-Dutch fleet. Discovered in 1980, divers still bring up new treasures showing life on a 17th-century vessel.

KARLSKRONA (555 A1)
BLEKINGE *pop. 59,300*
Karlskrona, Sweden's principal naval base, occupies a series of islands. Impressive buildings line its wide streets, and include the Varvsmuseet, or Shipyard Museum, formerly a sailor's barracks, and Holy Trinity Church. There is also an evocative emigrants' monument, *Karl-Oskar och Kristina*, in memory of those who left Sweden.

KIRUNA (555 B5)
LAPPLAND *pop. 26,200*
In terms of land area, Kiruna is one of the largest cities in the world. Its city limits encompass 5,000 square kilo-

meters (1,931 square miles) of the richest iron ore region in the world; two huge mines, Kirunavaara and Luossavaara; and countless reindeer herds. About 160 kilometers (100 miles) north of the Arctic Circle, Kiruna is in the "land of the midnight sun," where constant daylight reigns from the end of May to mid-July. The city itself is a small mining and market center.

Despite its northern location, Kiruna has a mild climate suitable for boating, hiking, fishing, skiing and climbing in season. Of special interest is Kiruna Kyrka, built like a Lapp hut. Excursions can be made into the countryside, where the nomadic Lapps still live much as they did centuries ago.

▲ LINKÖPING (555 A2)
ÖSTERGÖTLAND pop. 126,300
Inhabited since the Bronze Age, Linköping is the capital of Östergötland province. It is one of Sweden's foremost literary and religious centers, as well as home to SAAB and Svenska industries.

The Romanesque and Gothic cathedral, built in the 13th century, dominates the city. Places of interest are the City and Provincial Museum, which displays modern architectural techniques; the Church of St. Lars, with paintings by the Swedish peasant artist Pehr Hoerberg; and the 1734 Lutheran bishop's palace.

LUND (555 A1) ★
SKÅNE pop. 92,000
Historic Lund was founded in 1035 by King Knut (Canute) of Denmark and England. In 1103, it became the seat of the archbishop of all Scandinavia. Soon after, the city flourished as a major religious center and, briefly, as the capital of Denmark. Sweden permanently incorporated the city in 1658.

Today Lund is a growing industrial city and the cultural and intellectual center of southern Sweden. On April 30, Walpurgis Eve, students stage a colorful procession and engage in boisterous merrymaking. City attractions include the Museum of Cultural History. The castle of Trollenäs,

near Eslövis, is easily reached from Lund and the village of Dalby.

DOMKYRKAN, a 12th-century Romanesque structure, is considered one of the most beautiful cathedrals in Sweden. Its huge astronomical clock, dating from 1380, records the position of the stars and features a procession of wooden figures that parade every day at noon and 3pm.

▲ MALMÖ (555 A1) ★
SKÅNE pop. 236,600
The major port and industrial center of Malmö has preserved many of its old buildings. The town hall dates from the 16th century; the governor's residence dates from the 18th century. Gothic St. Peter's Church has superb ceiling paintings and an intricate, working clock. The Malmö Museum is on Malmöhus Slottet.

Tourists can buy *Malmökortet*, a card that entitles the bearer to free bus

---

ALLEMANSRÄTT

Allemansrätt (Everyone's Right) is an ancient right in Sweden and other Nordic countries. It means that you can walk, ski or ride anywhere and not be turned back by a landowner, and can pick any wild berries, mushrooms and flowers that are not protected species. You can swim, sail, moor a boat and go ashore anywhere except close to a house or on land in a prohibited (usually military) area.
The other side of all this liberty is that everyone must be sensible. It is not permitted to walk over a garden, nor to disturb or destroy anything, fires must be controlled and camping close to a house is not welcomed. A single, discreet tent for one night is fine, but people using groups of tents, or staying for a long time should ask first. Driving off-road is not acceptable, but this is a small price to pay for this generous *Allemansrätt*.

rides and parking in the city, as well as discounts on rail travel and sightseeing tours. The card also provides free admission to museums, nightspots and other attractions. Valid from 12 to 36 hours, it can be bought at the Malmö Tourist Office at Skeppsbron 2 and hotels in Malmö.

Skåne is Sweden's château country and can easily be explored from Malmö. Many of the 250 *Herrgård* (manor houses) and castles are open to the public, for use as hotels, for concert venues, or as museums.

MORA (555 A3)
DALARNA *pop. 20,900*

Mora, on Lake Siljan, has memorials to early 20th-century artist Anders Zorn and King Gustav Vasa. The house where

Zorn was born still stands; the Zorn Museum contains some of his works.

The *Vasaloppet* is a skiing event held annually to honor King Gustav Vasa. In 1521, the town's inhabitants rejected the future king's leadership but, after changing their minds, sent two skiers to halt his flight to Norway. Now skiers from all over the world come to Mora, usually on the first Sunday in March, to race across the 85-kilometer (53-mile) route traversed by those messengers nearly 500 years ago.

▲ NORRKÖPING (555 A2)
ÖSTERGÖTLAND *pop. 120,700*

Sweden's foremost textile-manufacturing city, Norrköping has several attractive parks by the Motala River. Gamla Torget, or old square, has some quaint old houses, but the city is noted principally as an excursion center.

ÖSTERSUND (555 A3)
JAMTLAND *pop. 59,000*

A commercial and industrial center, Östersund is on a hill overlooking the island of Frösön in Lake Storsjön. The Jämtli is an open air museum that has displays of cultural and historical interest.

RÄTTVIK (555 A3) ★
DALARNA *pop. 11,400*

An attractive resort on Lake Siljan, Rättvik appeals to hikers, cyclists, sailors and fishermen in summer and skiers in early spring. It is the focus of folk song and dance, with a midsummer festival centered on the 14th-century church beside the lake. Gammelgård is an open-air museum with reconstructed buildings, period furniture and traditional costumes on display.

THE SWEDISH SKÅL

The Swedes, other Scandinavians tell you, are very formal, and their attitude to the drinking toast, the *skål*, sums it up. At a dinner party it is not acceptable to pick up your glass as it is filled to take a gulp. Swedes expect to wait until the host (usually) or hostess raises a glass and says: *Välkommen och skål* (Welcome and skål). Then comes the difficult part, because the idea is to catch everyone's eye in turn, and to *skål* before the first sip. Later, various guests will propose toasts and everyone goes through the communal *skål* again. One person may also later raise a glass to another, and make a more private *skål*.

One thing not to forget is that no one should *skål* the hostess for the first hour. This is because she is supposed to be organizing the next course! Remember that this is informal – a formal occasion is even stricter about where and when to *skål*!

SKARA (555 A2)
VÄSTERGÖTLAND *pop. 13,700*

Important as a religious center in the Middle Ages, Skara has preserved its 14th-century cathedral, an impressive Gothic building. The Västergötland Museum and the open-air museum present a picture of regional history.

▲ **UMEÅ** (555 B3)
VÄSTERBOTTEN *pop. 94,900*
A thriving industrial and commercial port on the Umeälv River, the university town of Umea is known for its wooden goods. Northeast are the restored buildings of the Gammlia Open Air Museum. There is a skiing museum in Lars Fägrares Gård, and also a county museum depicting Sami (Lapp) life.

▲ **UPPSALA** (555 B2) ★
UPPLAND *pop. 174,500*
The name Uppsala has long been synonymous with learning: one of Europe's outstanding educational centers, the University of Uppsala, was founded in 1477.

GAMLA UPPSALA (Old Uppsala) is 5 kilometers (3 miles) to the north and is the former Swedish Viking capital. The Tingshögen served as the court mound where medieval laws were made and administered. Viking kings were also chosen at this site, and three are buried nearby in mounds known as the "Pyramids of Scandinavia."

LINNETRÄDGÅRDEN contains the townhouse, the grounds and the botanical gardens of Carolus Linnaeus, the father of modern botany. Many of his possessions are exhibited. Hammerby, just southeast of Uppsala center, was the great botanist's summer home, a charming 18th-century building, half manor/half farm. The small botanic garden delights gardeners.

UPPSALA UNIVERSITET has educated many prominent persons, including Carolus Linnaeus. A good time to visit the university is April 30, Walpurgis Eve, when Uppsalais host to Sweden's traditional student festival. The library, Carolina Rediviva, has an outstanding collection. Its greatest treasure is the *Codex Argentus*, the "Silver Bible." Dating from AD 500, this is the earliest surviving work in ancient Gothic, an eastern Germanic language.

▲ **VÄSTERÅS** (555 A2)
VÄSTMANLAND *pop. 120,800*
An old town on Lake Mälaven, Västerås became industrialized early in the 20th century and now mainly manufactures electrical goods. Elements of the past persist, however, in the 13th-century cathedral, which contains Belgian and German 15th- and 16th-century decorations, and the 13th-century castle, which contains a museum of local history.

▲ **VÄXJÖ** (555 A1) ★
SMÅLAND *pop. 70,700*
Växjö is an ancient religious settlement that has evolved into an important industrial and educational center. The restored cathedral dates from the 12th century, and the Utvandrarnas Hus, or Emigrant's House, documents the 19th-century exodus of thousands of citizens to the United States. The Småland Museum includes an exhibit on the local glass-blowing trade. Växjö lies at the eastern limit of Småland's "kingdom of glass," the area between here and Kalmar, which has 16 of Sweden's most famous glassworks. The works have museums and shops and demonstrations of glass-blowing.

VISBY (555 B1)
GOTLAND *pop. 21,300*
The island of Gotland lies about 80 kilometers (50 miles) off the southeast coast of Sweden. Visby, the capital, is one of Sweden's outstanding tourist attractions. By the 13th century, the city was a powerful commercial center and a key member of the Hanseatic League, minted its own coins, and had a code of law.

The principal attractions in Visby are its medieval fortifications. The city is surrounded on three sides by a 13th-century stone wall 3 kilometers (2 miles) long. This has 38 towers, including the 12th-century Kruttornet which overlooks the harbor. Various ruined medieval churches also remain, and the Church of St. Maria, which served the German merchant community in the city's heyday, is still in use for worship.

SPAIN

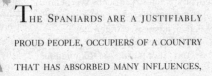

THE SPANIARDS ARE A JUSTIFIABLY PROUD PEOPLE, OCCUPIERS OF A COUNTRY THAT HAS ABSORBED MANY INFLUENCES, YET HAS ALWAYS RETAINED A STRONG SENSE OF ITS OWN IDENTITY. FRINGED BY GOLDEN BEACHES, IT HAS AN INTERIOR WITH MOUNTAIN RANGES AS GRAND AS THEIR NAMES ARE DRAMATIC.

A VISIT SHOULD NOT BE CONFINED TO THE COAST OR THE CAPITAL, MADRID. SEVILLE HAS THE ALCÁZAR PALACE, BUILT BY THE MOORS IN 1181, WHILE THE MOSQUE IN CÓRDOBA DATES BACK TO THE 8TH CENTURY. GRANADA HAS THE INCOMPARABLE ALHAMBRA PALACE, AND NEARBY ARE THE MOUNTAINS OF THE SIERRA NEVADA. BARCELONA AND MADRID ALSO VIE FOR ATTENTION. BARCELONA, FOUNDED IN THE 3RD CENTURY BC, IS THE CENTER OF CATALAN CULTURE AND HOSTED THE 1992 OLYMPIC GAMES. MADRID IS A CITY OF BOULEVARDS AND PLAZAS, AND IS HOME TO THE PRADO MUSEUM.

Left GAUDÍ'S CASA BATLLÓ, IN BARCELONA, HAS AN AMAZING ROOFLINE
Above left A TYPICAL ICON, AT THE IGLESIA SAN SEBASTIAN IN ESTELPA
Above right THIS BULL IS ADVERTISING SHERRY, SPAIN'S FAMOUS EXPORT

THINGS TO KNOW

- **AREA:** 504,781 square kilometers (194,896 square miles)
- **POPULATION:** 40,358,400
- **CAPITAL:** Madrid
- **LANGUAGES:** Spanish, Basque, Catalan and Galician.
- **ECONOMY:** Industry, mining, tourism, agriculture, forestry, machinery, chemicals, steel, textiles, shoes, shipbuilding, coal, iron, potatoes, cattle, wine. Tourism is important.
- **PASSPORT REQUIREMENTS:** Required for U.S. citizens.
- **VISA REQUIREMENTS:** Not required for stays up to 90 days.
- **DUTY FREE ITEMS:** 200 cigarettes, 50 cigars or 250 grams of tobacco; 2 liters of wine and 1 liter of alcohol over 22 proof or 2 liters up to 22 proof; 50 grams of perfume; ¼ liter of toilet water; one still camera with 10 rolls of film; one video camera; personal jewelry; portable tape recorder; sports equipment. See also *The European Union* on p.9.
- **CURRENCY:** The unit of currency is the Spanish *peseta*. Due to currency fluctuations, the exchange rate is subject to frequent change. There is no limit on the import of foreign currency, but the amount exported cannot exceed the amount imported. There is no limit on the import of *pesetas*, but amounts exceeding 1 million *pesetas* must be declared on entry. No more than 1 million *pesetas* may be exported.
- **BANK OPENING HOURS:** 9am–2pm Monday–Friday, also 9am–1pm Saturday, October–May.
- **STORE OPENING HOURS:** 9:30am–1:30pm and 3:30 or 4:30pm–8:30pm Monday–Friday, 9am–1pm Saturday.
- **BEST BUYS:** Jewelry, woodcarvings, Toledo ware, Talavera porcelains, *mantillas*, linen, gloves, lace, leather goods, perfume, all types of pottery and glassware.
- **PUBLIC HOLIDAYS:** January 1; January 6 (Epiphany); March 19 (St. Joseph's Day); Maundy Thursday; Good Friday;

HISTORY

The Moorish reign, which began in the 8th century, left a pronounced mark on Spain. The Moors built cities, libraries and universities that were the intellectual showpieces of Europe.

By the late 13th century, the Moslem government had been overthrown by Christian forces. The 1469 marriage of Ferdinand II of Aragon and Isabella of Castile united the Christian kingdoms. Granada, the last Moslem kingdom, was captured in 1492 – the same year the "Catholic Kings" sponsored Christopher Columbus' departure for the New World.

The riches that the New World brought made Spain the greatest European power of the next century. However, decline followed and Spain suffered from costly wars and poor government.

In 1808, France's Napoléon Bonaparte gained control of Spain and appointed his brother Joseph king but, with British and Portuguese help, France was expelled in the subsequent War of Independence of 1808–13. An internal struggle for the throne followed, and the ensuing Carlist Wars ended with the return of the Bourbons in 1876.

By the 1930s, Spanish life and politics were deeply polarized. The February 1936 election of a coalition led by the left touched off a military coup organized by conservatives and the army. From this developed the Spanish Civil War of 1936–39. The Nationalists (the rebels) were commanded by General Franco and had help from Fascist Italy and Nazi Germany. The Republicans accepted aid from the Soviet Union as well as volunteers from other countries. The Nationalists won the bitter struggle.

Franco was now the leader of a nation impoverished and embittered by a long, costly war. Franco remained neutral during World War II, but did send some military assistance to Hitler. After Franco's death in 1975, Spain became a monarchy again and King Juan Carlos I was sworn in.

Democratic governments since then have maintained Spain's membership of N.A.T.O. and brought Spain into the European Union.

FOOD AND DRINK

Spanish cuisine might be a surprise. The menus are as varied as those in France and Italy, meals are usually substantial and as inexpensive as anywhere in western Europe. There are several regional specialties: the north is noted for sauces, the Castilian plateau for roasts, and the southeast for rice dishes. A national fondness for seafood means shrimp, clam, crawfish and crab are available everywhere.

Gazpacho, a cold soup of tomato, seasoned with garlic, has become internationally celebrated. *Paella,* especially good in Valencia, is a casserole of rice, saffron, peas and pimento, with seafood and chicken added. *Tortilla española*, an omelette as only the Spanish make it, is a combination of eggs, potatoes and onions. Fruit-flavored *Sangriá* and other wines are commonly served; beer is also popular. *Jerez* (sherry) is available in a wide range of flavors and degrees of sweetness.

Lunch is served from 1:30pm onwards, but 3pm is the most popular time. Dinner in a restaurant hardly ever begins before 9:30pm, except in the state-owned *paradores* (hotels), where it is served from 8:30 to 11pm. *Hosterías,* state-operated restaurants, serve regional specialties. *Tapas,* substantial snacks, are available at most cafés.

SPORTS AND RECREATION

A *corrida,* or bullfight, is neither a fight nor a sport. It is rather an artistic pageant and drama. Bullfighting was first known on the island of Crete 4,000 years ago.

Since the 18th century, bullfighting in Spain has been a profession, but only recently has the pay compensated for the risks. The season is from Easter through October. Bullfights are held in Madrid on Sundays, holidays and many Saturdays. The summer festivals of smaller towns offer other chances to see this spectacle.

Bullfights are an integral part of Spain's heritage. Some people find these spectacles inhumane, so the option to attend should be a strictly personal decision. If you don't wish to watch a bullfight, but would like to enjoy some of the color and excitement of the event, the *apartado,* where the animals are selected by emissaries of the matadors, is an alternative. This ritual enables spectators to view the proceedings from the lower tiers of the ring without having to witness the outcome of the fight.

Spaniards are enthusiastic about *fútbol* (soccer), and on Sundays from October to May stadiums all over the country overflow with shouting fans. Madrid's racetrack, the Zarzuela, has horse racing in the spring and fall; Seville's Pineda course, from April through September.

The Valderrama golf course in Cádiz hosted the 1997 Ryder Cup, and is one of the many excellent courses in Spain. Tennis and swimming are available in all the large cities and resorts, and Spain has many opportunities for sailing and other water sports. Hunting and fishing opportunities are among the best in Europe. Some 607,000 hectares (1½ million acres) have been set aside as national and game preserves. Mountainous regions, such as the Pyrénées and the Cantábrica ranges in the north, and the Sierra Nevada in the south, are fine hiking and climbing areas and also have the main ski resorts.

GETTING AROUND

Travelers in Spain have a choice of transportation. The government rail network R.E.N.F.E., which covers the entire country, is efficient and inexpensive. Several

Easter Monday; May 1; Ascension Day; Corpus Christi; July 25 (St. James' Day); August 15 (Assumption Day); October 12 *(Día de la Hispanidad)*; November 1 (All Saints' Day); December 6 (Constitution Day); , December 8 (Immaculate Conception); December 25. Many attractions and places of interest are closed on major religious holidays.

- USEFUL TELEPHONE NUMBERS:
  Madrid, Barcelona and other main cities:
  Police 091 (in other towns call the operator)
  Ambulance 092
  Fire 080
- NATIONAL TOURIST OFFICES:
  National Tourist Office of Spain
  665 Fifth Avenue
  New York, NY 10103
  Tel: 212/265-8822
  Fax: 212/265-8864
  Spanish Tourist Office
  8383 Wilshire Boulevard, Suite 960
  Beverley Hills
  Los Angeles CA 90211
  Tel: 213/658-7192
  Fax: 213/658-1061
  Tourist Office of Spain
  1221 Brickell Avenue
  Miami,
  Florida 33131
  Tel: 305/358-1992
  Fax: 305/358-8223
  Spanish Tourist Office
  57–58 St. James's Street
  London SW1A 1LD
  England
  Tel: 0171 499 1169/0901
  Fax: 0171 629 4257
- AMERICAN EMBASSY:
  Serrano 75
  Madrid
  Spain
  Tel: (1) 577 4000
  Fax: (1) 577 5735

AUTOMOBILE CLUB
Real Automóvil Club de España
(R.A.C.E.,Royal Automobile Club of Spain), José Abascal 10, 28003 Madrid, has branch offices in various cities throughout Spain. The symbol ▲ indicates the presence of an AAA-affiliated automobile club branch. Not all auto clubs offer full travel services to AAA members.

Several bus lines have moderately priced package tours and the airlines Iberia and Aviaco link the major cities.

The best roads in Spain are the *autopistas*, limited-access dual highways, which are designated by the letter A followed by a number. Aside from a few toll-free stretches around Barcelona and Madrid, tolls are charged. The other dependable thoroughfares are the *nacional* roads that are designated with an N. Generally in good condition, these are wide two-lane highways. Roads other than these are designated C for *comarcal*, or regional, are usually narrow and not quite as well-maintained.

Speed limits are 50 k.p.h. (31 m.p.h.) in town, 90–100 k.p.h. (56–62 m.p.h.) on out-of-town roads and 120 k.p.h. (75 m.p.h.) on the *autopistas*.

The use of seat belts is compulsory. Children under 12 may not occupy a front seat unless using a suitable restraint system. Expect to pay for gas with cash, as credit cards are not widely accepted at service stations. It is compulsory to carry a spare set of bulbs, fuses and a spare tire; and it is advisable to carry a warning triangle in the event of a breakdown or accident. Visiting motorists are required to pay on the spot fines with Spanish *pesetas*. An International Driving Permit is required. Insurance cover should include a Bail Bond.

ACCOMMODATIONS

Hotels in Spain are graded from one- to five-star, with five stars being the highest rating. Classifications are posted on signs outside each establishment. Just as pilgrims to Santiago de Compostela in the Middle Ages found the road lined with priories and hospices, so too can today's visitors to Spain find accommodations and refreshments through the nationwide network of *paradores*. Some of these state-operated hotels are housed in beautifully restored castles, palaces and convents. Privately-owned country inns and hotels are usually simple, but serve three meals a day. Spas and health resorts normally have accommodations for travelers. Youth hostels give priority to those under 26.

Of Spain's 700 campgrounds, over 100 are on the Costa Brava. They are ranked in four categories. For more information contact Federación Española de Empresarios de Campings y C.V., San Bernardo 97–99, Edificio Colomina 3U, 28015 Madrid; or the National Tourist Office of Spain. An International Camping Carnet is advised but not compulsory; however, some campgrounds may give a reduced rate if you have one.

TIPPING

Hotels and restaurants in Spain add a 15 percent service charge to their bills, but service personnel expect an additional 5 to 10 percent. Tip taxi drivers 5 percent of the fare, porters 50 pesetas.

PRINCIPAL TOURING AREAS

Note: For descriptions of attractions in **bold type**, see individual listings.

ANDALUCIA

The region stretching from the Portuguese border almost to **Cartagena** and inland past **Córdoba** was the seat of Moorish power, and later the launching site for voyages in the age of discovery. From Portugal to the Strait of Gibraltar is a land of sandy beaches, sunny skies, pine forests and olive groves: the Costa de la Luz. From the strait to **Almería** lies the Costa del Sol, site of the long, narrow, flower-bedecked streets of ancient **Cádiz**. The beaches in the provinces of Cádiz and Málaga are low and sandy; those south of **Granada** are more rugged. The country's major resorts are west of **Málaga** and include **Torremolinos**, **Marbella**, and Fuengirola. A cliff-hugging highway runs east from Málaga through the banana groves surrounding Almuñécar to the rugged mountains at **Almería**. Mostly ignored by the tourist crowds, this coast abounds with lush gardens and terraced fields, solitary coves and clean beaches.

From the coast, the land rises to the southern edge of Spain's vast and arid central plateau. Here is **Granada**, once the heart of Moorish Spain and retaining the sumptuous architecture epitomized by the famed Alhambra. **Sevilla**, or Seville, has a centuries-old blend of architectural styles. **Córdoba**, the cathedral city of Jaén and the old bridge of **Ronda** are all historic sites with much to offer the visitor.

MURCIA AND VALENCIA

Extending along the eastern coast roughly from **Cartagena** to Castellón de la Plana is the historic Levante, where the Phoenicians landed long ago to trade for minerals dug by Iberians and Celts.

From Cartagena to just south of **Valencia**, the Costa Blanca offers an interesting mixture of beaches, mountains and farmland. The land surrounding Cartagena is fairly flat, rising to the rugged mountains near **Alicante**.

Inland is Murcia. Arabic words strongly color the local dialect, and the architecture hints of the town's 8th-century Moorish origin. Alicante harks back to the Carthaginian colony of the 3rd century BC through the oriental flavor of the palm trees that line its waterfront.

The Costa del Azahar, stretching from Valencia to Castellón de la Plana, takes its name from the orange blossoms that scent the air. A continuous mountain chain stands guard close to the waters of this area. The great seaport of Valencia contains many fine old buildings and claims possession of the Holy Grail.

CATALONIA

Catalonia, most commercial of Spain's regions, borders France; its cuisine compares favorably with that of its neighbor. The celebrated Monastery of **Montserrat** is a highlight, with its spectacular mountian setting and **Girona** (Gerona) is noted for its baroque cathedral; however,

sophisticated **Barcelona**, second-largest city in Spain, is the east's greatest pride.

The Costa Brava, or "wild coast," has long been a big tourist attraction with its beautiful inlets and hidden caves. Some of the best opportunities for fun in the sun occur in the resort towns of Bagur,

Blanes, Lloret de Mar, Palamós, Rosas and San Feliú de Guixols.

ARAGON AND NAVARRE
Inland from Catalonia is Aragon and to its west, Navarre. Once an independent kingdom, Aragon united with Spain in the 15th century. Dominated by its capital **Zaragoza**, this hot, mountainous and largely infertile region stretches from the Pirineos (Pyrénées) nearly to Valencia.

Navarre was a Christian stronghold during the Moorish occupation of Spain. The major city is **Pamplona**, the site of the colorful Fiesta de San Fermin, during which bulls run through the city's streets. South of Navarre is the province of La Rioja, which produces excellent wines.

THE BASQUE PROVINCES
The Basque region, stretching along the coast from Navarre to just past **Bilbao**, or Bilbo in Basque, is the seat of an ancient culture. The inhabitants of this area are thought to be descendants of the original settlers of the Iberian Peninsula.

The administrative headquarters of the region during the Spanish Civil War, Bilbao is an industrial center and an excellent departure point for excursions into the adjoining countryside. South east is **Vitoria**, or Gasteiz in Basque, thought by some to resemble an English country village. Small mountain communities that have changed little since the time of Christopher Columbus dot the countryside. **San Sebastián**, or Donostia in Basque, is on the coast 19 kilometers (12 miles) from France. The Cornisa Cantabrica, as Spain's northern coast is known, is characterized in this area by steep forested cliffs and sandy beaches.

CASTILE
Reaching west from the Basque provinces past Santander and extending south to Andalusia are the Castilian regions, historically divided between **Segovia** and **Madrid** into Old Castile and New Castile. Isolated from outside influences,

SPAIN

much of the region has changed little since the time of Cervantes. Though sun-baked in summer, the area can be bitterly cold in winter. The most popular time to visit is during the spring *fiesta* season.

In Old Castile are **Burgos**, with its most Spanish of Spanish Gothic cathedrals, and **Valladolid**, home of Cervantes. **Segovia** has a Roman aqueduct that still carries water, and Logroño is the center of a fertile wine-producing region. The cathedrals of Palencia and walls of **Avila** are other highlights of the region.

New Castile is the site of modern Madrid, whose principal attraction is the Prado Museum. El Greco's **Toledo**, whose ancient buildings reflect Moorish and Roman influences, is worth an extended visit.

EXTREMADURA AND LEÓN

Between New Castile and the Portuguese border lies Extremadura, a region of lush lowlands and plains dotted with castles. Andalusia is to the south.

Built in the lowlands by the Moors, **Badajoz** reflects the occupation by both Moors and Christians. Although its founding pre-dates the birth of Christ, the palaces, towers and narrow winding

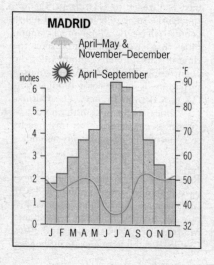

MADRID

April–May & November–December

April–September

inches

6
5
4
3
2
1
0

°F
90
80
70
60
50
40
32

J F M A M J J A S O N D

streets of **Cáceres** suggest the city's medieval heritage. South is Merída, once the capital of the Roman province of Lusitania, now the site of one of Spain's finest archeological museums and many Roman ruins.

The León region lies inland, north of Extremadura and west of Old Castile. This area contains the many medieval buildings of León and the Romanesque architecture of Zamora. The ancient university, twin cathedrals and unusual Casa de las Conchas of **Salamanca** are also interesting.

GALICIA AND ASTURIAS

Rugged and little-known Galicia and Asturias in northwestern Spain have a wealth of beautiful scenery. Summers on the beaches are cool and pleasant, and there is excellent river fishing.

Galicia, known as the "Ireland of Iberia," is a green and charming region in the country's far northwestern corner. It preserves its Celtic background in culture and such old cities as Ferrol, now the country's main shipbuilding center, as well as **La Coruña**, noted for its Tower of Hercules.

The region's chief attraction is beautiful **Santiago de Compostela**, which, with Jerusalem and Rome, was one of the "sainted cities" of the Middle Ages. The town is at its most colorful during the Feast of St. James in July, but the best time to tour the rest of the area is in May, June, September and October.

Asturias, between Galicia and the tip of Old Castile, still has evidence of the Celtic settlements that pre-dated the Roman occupation. Asturians, who boast of playing the bagpipe centuries before the Scots, relive their ancient origins in colorful costumes and dances on *fiesta* days. The battlefield of Covadonga, where the struggle of the Christian reconquest began, is a landmark for Spanish nationalism.

BALEARIC AND CANARY ISLANDS

The beaches, resorts and scenery of the **Islas Baleares**, or Balearic Islands, in the Mediterranean and the **Islas Canarias**, or Canary Islands, in the Atlantic have long made Spain popular with vacationers.

Off the east coast of Spain, the popular Balearic Islands of **Mallorca, Menorca, Ibiza**, Formentera and Cabrera, have unspoiled beaches, picturesque towns and a mild climate.

Mountainous Mallorca, lively Ibiza, and the more tranquil Menorca are the leading resort areas.

Equally interesting are the volcanic Canary Islands rising steeply from the Atlantic off the northwest African coast. There are seven islands with scenery ranging from lush jungles to stark desert. The cities of **Las Palmas**, on Gran Canaria, and **Santa Cruz**, on Tenerife, are the most popular vacation spots.

USEFUL EXPRESSIONS IN SPANISH

PRONUNCIATION TIPS

a – as in t<u>a</u>r
e – as in l<u>e</u>t
i – as in mar<u>i</u>ne
o – as in T<u>o</u>m
u – as in r<u>u</u>le
b and **v** – similar, like a soft 'b'
c – like 'th' in <u>th</u>in before 'e' or 'i'; otherwise as in <u>c</u>at
g – like 'ch' in lo<u>ch</u> before 'e' or 'i'; otherwise as in <u>g</u>et
j – like 'ch' in lo<u>ch</u>
ll – like 'lli' in mi<u>lli</u>on
ñ – like 'ni' in o<u>ni</u>on
r – strong and rolled, **rr** more so
z – like 'th' in <u>th</u>in

hello	**hola**
good morning	**buenos días**
good evening	**buenas tardes**
good night	**buenas noches**
good-bye	**adiós**
please/thank you	**por favor/gracias**
yes/no	**sí/no**
excuse me	**perdón**
you're welcome	**de nada**
I am sorry, I don't speak Spanish	**lo siento, pero no hablo español**
Does anyone here speak English?	**¿Hay alguien aqui que hable inglés?**
I do not understand.	**No comprendo.**
What is the time?	**¿Qué hora es?**
How much is that?	**¿Cuánto cuesta esto?**

Where are the restrooms?	**¿Dónde están los servicios?**
I'd like ...	**Quisiera ...**
Can you help me, please?	**¿Puede usted ayùdeme, por favor?**
where/when/how	**dónde/cuándo/cómo**
open/closed	**abierto/cerrado**
big/small	**grande/pequeño**
Do you take credit cards?	**¿Acepta usted tarjetas de crédito?**
yesterday/today/ tomorrow	**ayer/hoy/ mañana**
to the left	**a la izquierda**
to the right	**a la derecha**
vacant/occupied	**libre/ocupado**

DAYS OF THE WEEK

Sunday	**domingo**
Monday	**lunes**
Tuesday	**martes**
Wednesday	**miercoles**
Thursday	**jueves**
Friday	**viernes**
Saturday	**sábado**

NUMBERS

1	uno	9	nueve
2	dos	10	diez
3	tres	20	veinte
4	cuatro	30	treinta
5	cinco	40	cuarenta
6	seis	50	cincuenta
7	siete	100	cien
8	ocho	1,000	mil

PLACES OF INTEREST

SPAIN

▲ MADRID ★

MADRID *pop. 3,010,500*
(See map on p.580)

(See map on p.580)

Although the rest of Spain is rich in ancient history, modern Madrid manages to hide its past. The colorful capital was once a Moorish fortress, but had become a relatively unknown village before Philip II formally established it as the seat of government in 1561.

The older section has narrow streets and picturesque 17th-century buildings. The royal Casa de la Panadería, built in 1672, is one of the oldest edifices on the historic Plaza Mayor.

Many visitors begin their sightseeing at the Puerta del Sol, a starting point for the major thoroughfare of the Calle de Alcalá. This street, which contains the Museo d'Academia Real de Bellas Artes des San Fernando, an art and music academy housing works by Murillo and Goya, intersects the Paseo del Prado, which is known for the Museo del Prado. Dominating the Calle de Bailén at the west end of town is the Palacio Real (Royal Palace).

A cultural as well as geographic center, Madrid is noted for the arts. The National Orchestra presents regular concerts at the Royal Theater. Devotees can easily spend at least a day in the nearby Prado, and there are more than 20 other museums in the city. Operettas, top dance groups and musical revues can be seen at the Teatro de la Zarzuela; the Teatro Español produces the best of Spanish classical theater. Nightclubs feature flamenco music and dance.

The bullfighting season in Madrid lasts from Easter to October. Golf is played at 10 courses. Soccer is a favorite diversion; horse racing can be seen at Hippodrome de la Zarzuela (racecourse).

Madrid is an ideal place for shopping. The best stores are on La Gran Vía, Calle de Alcalá, Carrera San Jerónimo, Calle de Serrano and Calle de Sevilla. Jewelry, pottery, linens, leather goods, and lace *mantillas* are popular items. El Rastro, on Ribera de Curtidores, is a famous flea market offering thousands of secondhand bargains. The market is best visited on Sunday morning. Try Calle del Prado for antiques.

BIBLIOTECA NACIONAL (National Library) (581 D3), entered from Paseo de Recoletos, the library contains more than one million volumes, in addition to many early manuscripts.

TAPAS

The popularity of *tapas* bars has spread both within and outside Spain. *Tapar* means to cover, in a general sense, and so *tapas* relates to the time when drinks were covered by a small plate with a snack on top. These days *tapas* are served separately and include a great variety of small dishes, ranging from olives, Spanish ham or omelette slices, to tasty meat or seafood snacks.

Madrid is renowned for its lively bars, a number of which are located around the old Plaza Mayor. A round of the *tapas* bars, each with its own character, is a most enjoyable way of spending an evening, either before or instead of dinner.

CATEDRAL DE SAN ISIDRO (580 C1), on Calle de Toledo near Plaza Mayor, was built 1622–64 by the Jesuits.

MUSEO CERRALBO (580 B3), Ventura Rodríguez 17, was bequeathed to the state by the Marquis Cerralbo. There are paintings by El Greco, José Ribera, Titian and Van Dyck. A collection of arms, china and tapestries is also shown.

MUSEO D'ACADEMIA REAL DE BELLES ARTES DE SAN FERNANDO (580 C2), Alcalá 13, in the restored Palace of Juan de Goyeneche, houses 16th- to 19th-century paintings and sculpture with works by El Greco, Murillo, Goya and Velázquez.

MUSEO DEL PRADO (580 D2) ★, Paseo del Prado, in an 18th-century building, houses one of the most complete and valuable collections of paintings in the world. Its masterpieces include works by Velázquez, Ribera, Murillo, Goya, El Greco, Rubens, Titian, Fra Angelico, Raphael, Correggio, Tintoretto, Van Dyck and other masters. The museum contains classical sculptures as well as coin, enamel, gold and silver collections.

MUSEO THYSSEN-BORNEMISZA (580 B2), Paseo del Prado 8, houses the splendid private collection of Baron Thyssen-Bornemisza. Paintings range from works by Fra Angélico, Van Eyck and Rembrandt to Impressionist works by Renoir, Manet and Van Gogh.

PALACIO REAL (ROYAL PALACE) (580 B2), in the Plaza de Oriente, is beautifully decorated and richly furnished. The palace was erected in the 18th century on the site of a 9th-century fortress. There is a grand marble staircase, a scarlet and gold throne room, with an intricate ceiling and 800 valuable tapestries.

EL PARDO is 14 kilometers (9 miles) northwest off highway N4. This extensive, thickly wooded natural park surrounding the village of El Pardo harbors an abundance of large and small game.

Nearby Pardo Palace was built by Carlos V around a royal shooting lodge.

PARQUE DEL RETIRO (581 D2), a 130-hectare (320-acre) park, includes a lake, fountains, and a series of shady walks, carriage drives and bridle paths.

PLAZA DE COLON (581 D3), has a monument to Columbus. There is a theater and arts center underground.

PLAZA MONUMENTAL, Patio de Caballos, is the larger of the city's two bullrings. Bullfights are staged on Sunday and some Thursdays from Easter through October. The Bullfighting Museum on the Plaza de Toros de Ventas contains paintings, engravings and models.

ALCALÁ DE HENARES (574 C3)
MADRID *pop. 166,000*
Alcalá de Henares enjoys a distinguished reputation as the birthplace of Miguel de Cervantes, creator of *Don Quixote*; of Catherine of Aragon, first wife of King Henry VIII of England; and of Ferdinand I, King of Aragon in 1412–16. The University of Madrid, although later transferred to the capital, originated in the Colegio Mayor de San Ildefonso, founded in the late 15th century. The old university buildings have been restored and are still in scholastic use. Of particular interest are the exquisite façade of the Colegio, the Magistral Church and the Archbishop's Palace.

Miguel de Cervantes Saavedra was born in Alcalá de Henares in 1547. He reached fame with his masterpiece *Don Quixote* published in two parts, in 1605 and 1615. Memories of Cervantes survive in the house of his birth and in the baptistry of the Church of Santa María la Mayor, which has his birth certificate.

▲ ALICANTE (575 D2)
ALICANTE *pop. 265,500*
Founded by the Carthaginians in 325 BC, Alicante was captured by the Romans in 210 BC, and subsequently occupied by the Moors in AD 718–1246. Considered

SPAIN

the tourist capital of the Costa Blanca, Alicante is noted for its historical monuments and its mild climate; it is also the commercial port for Madrid. In June the parades from a colorful festival dedicated to San Juan fill the city's streets.

Old and new Alicante meet near the city center. In the newest districts, hotels, restaurants and shops line such streets as the Rambla and attractive multi-colored Explanada de España. A number of interesting buildings fill the town's old quarter, including the baroque town hall, the Renaissance cathedral and the 15th- and 16th-century church, Santa María.

beneath towering mountains. It is dominated by the Alcazába and the ruined Castillo de San Cristobal, which stands on an adjoining hill. Paseo de Almería is the city's main shopping thoroughfare.

ALCAZÁBA overlooks the city. Built in the 8th century, this Moorish fortress is Almería's most important monument. Of the battlements that surrounded it, only the 15th-century Torre de Homenaje, or Tower of Homage, remains.

CATEDRAL, Plaza de la Catedral, was built between 1524 and 1543. Although it has a Renaissance façade, the cathedral is principally Gothic in style. It contains paintings by Cano and Murillo.

▲ AVILA (574 B3)

AVILA *pop. 46,300*

Surrounded on three sides by mountains, historic Avila maintains its medieval appearance. For centuries this former Roman outpost was the object of a Moorish-Christian struggle, until the construction of its walls in 1090 brought it permanently under Christian control. The completely walled city honors St. Teresa with a church and convent. Other sights are the cathedral and the Church of San Pedro. Nearby are scenic Sierra de Gredos and El Arenal.

CATEDRAL, Plaza de la Catedral, is a church and fortress which forms part of the town's ancient ramparts. Dating

---

Alicante lends itself to sports and leisure activities, with tennis courts, a bullring, yachting club and good beaches.

▲ ALMERÍA (574 C1)

ALMERÍA *pop. 155,100*

Roman harbor, Moorish stronghold and Spanish port, Almería overlooks the sea

---

SAINT TERESA OF AVILA

Avila is the birthplace of Saint Teresa, who was known for her visions and mystical writings. She became a Carmelite nun when she was 18 and spent some 30 years in the Convent of the Incarnation in Avila, becoming prioress in her later years. In the chapel on the site of her birthplace are writings and relics. Saint Teresa was canonized in 1622.

from the 12th century, the Romanesque and Gothic structure has an unusual red and yellow stone interior.

REAL MONASTERIO DE SANTO TOMAS, Plaza de Granada, houses the alabaster tomb of Prince John, the only son of Ferdinand and Isabella.

THE WALLS, begun in 1090, are the best preserved in Spain. They average 10 meters (33 feet) in height and have a perimeter of 2,535 meters (8,287 feet). Forming a hexagon around the town, they are strengthened by 88 bastions and towers and crowned by embrasures. There is access to the walkway on top through the *parador* (hotel).

▲ BADAJOZ (574 B2)
BADAJOZ *pop. 114,400*

Badajoz was founded in the 11th century by the Moors. On the Guadiana River near the border of Portugal, it has continued to be a frontier outpost; even the churches and houses present a fortified appearance. The old quarter is surrounded by medieval walls and can be entered through the 16th-century Puerta de las Palmas, which faces the Puente de las Palmas, an impressive bridge. Inside are narrow streets, broad plazas and parks.

ALCAZÁBA overlooks the city. Badajoz's Moorish rulers established themselves on the summit of Orinaca in the 11th century. Attractions include gardens, the ruins of a medieval castle and the Museo Arqueológico's Roman statues.

BALEARIC ISLANDS – *see p.598.*

▲ BARCELONA (575 E3) ★
BARCELONA *pop. 1,712,350*

Barcelona is the capital of historic Catalonia. It was founded in the 3rd century BC by Hamilcar Barca of Carthage and later ruled by Romans, Visigoths, Moors and Franks. After Catalonia united with Aragon in the Middle Ages, Barcelona became a commercial center. Now a leading Mediterranean seaport,

Barcelona is the country's second-largest city and its greatest industrial center. Tree-lined boulevards, gardens, fountains, well-designed public buildings and stores lend an air of elegance.

From the Barri Gòtic (Gothic quarter) to the Modernista (art nouveau) creations of architects such as Antonio Gaudí in the 19th and 20th centuries, the city is a delight. It is filled with museums displaying special collections from musical instruments to ceramics.

The pedestrianized Ramblas, lined with trees and flower stalls, runs from the Plaça de Catalunya to the harbor. Near the Columbus Monument, the palm-lined Passeig de Colom leads from the waterfront to the hill of Montjuïc, where some of the best museums and the Olympic Stadium are located. North of Plaça de Catalunya is the modern district of Eixample, with wide streets and many Gaudí buildings.

CATEDRAL (583 C2), Plaça de la Seu, exemplifies Mediterranean Gothic architecture. It was built 1248–98, but the façade was not finished until the 19th century. It is dedicated to the martyr Santa Eulàlia, whose tomb lies in the crypt. The highlight is the cloister, filled with palm trees and lush vegetation.

IGLESIA DE SANT PAU DEL CAMP (583 B2), Carrer de Sant Pau, is dedicated to St. Paul. This is one of Barcelona's oldest churches, an early Romanesque structure dating from the 10th century.

MONTJUÏC (583 B1), crowned by an 18th-century castle, has many attractions on its steep, green hillsides, including five museums, an amusement park, and buildings from the 1929 International Exhibition. The fountains at the Palau Nacional are illuminated at night.

MUSEO D'HISTÒRIA DE LA CIUTAT (583 C2), Plaça del Rei, is Barcelona's local history museum. Housed in a 15th-century building, excavations reveal the ancient Roman city.

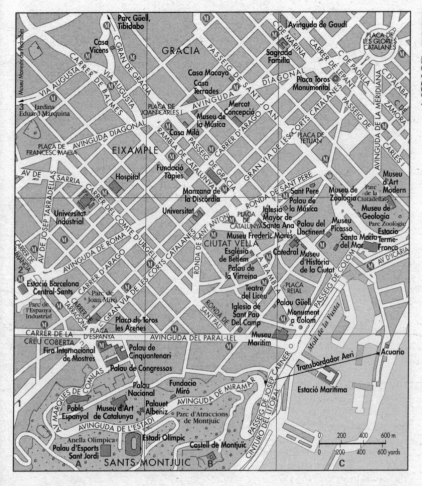

MUSEO PICASSO (583 C2), 15 Calle de Montcada, contains many drawings, paintings and engravings by Spain's most famous modern artist. The Picasso Museum is housed in the Gothic palaces of Berenguer d'Aguilar and Castellet.

PALAU DE LA VIRREINA (583 B2), 99 Rambla, is an outstanding baroque palace dating from 1776, which is now used as an exhibition hall.

PARC GÜELL, at the north end of the Gràcia quarter, was conceived as a utopian suburb at the turn of the century. Here Gaudí's imaginative genius was indulged with surreal park benches, columns, and fairy-tale buildings, one of which contains a small Gaudí museum.

PARC DE LA CIUTADELLA (583 C2), a park laid out in the early 18th century, containins multiple attractions. Museums, monuments and statues, a lovely waterfall, Spain's largest zoo and an attractive baroque church are within its walls.

PLAÇA DE CATALUNYA (583 B2) is the largest and busiest square. Embellished with attractive gardens and impressive groups of sculptures, it is a good starting point for a walking tour of the city.

POBLE ESPANYOL (Spanish Village) was built for the 1929 World's Fair, held at Montjuïc. Working craftsmen, whose wares can be purchased, populate the streets, squares and houses.

TEMPLO EXPIATORIO DE LA SAGRADA FAMILIA (583 C3), is Gaudí's great unfinished cathedral. Its startling spires are the city's star attraction. He began work in 1883 and finished the eastern end, which represents the Nativity, before his untimely death in 1926 (he was run over by a tram). Work to complete the cathedral continues amid great controversy, for Gaudí left no plans.

TIBIDABO, just outside the city, is a high mountain affording a view of Barcelona, surrounding villages and the sea. It is the site of an amusement park and a funicular railroad.

TORRE DE COLLSEROL is a modern communications tower built for the 1992 Summer Olympics. A viewing gallery on the 10th level is accessible by a glass elevator departing from within Tibidabo.

BETANZOS (574 A4)
LA CORUÑA pop. 12,000
Medieval Betanzos lies in a picturesque region at the confluence of the Mendo and Mandeo Rivers. The narrow old streets are lined with churches; among the most interesting are the Santa María del Azogue and the 14th-century Church of San Francisco.

BILBAO (574 C4)
VIZCAYA pop. 384,000
A major industrial center, Bilbao, or Bilbo in Basque, is also a strategic port in the Basque country. Most of the city's attractions are concentrated in the old town along the Nervion River. It is here, in the narrow, paved streets of Siete Calles, or Seven Streets, where many of Bilbao's busy bars and restaruants are to be found. Also in this picturesque part of Bilbao are attractive old buildings and the collonnaded square of Plaza Nueva.

MUSEO DE BELLAS ARTES, in a park at the end of Grand Via, specializes in Spanish and Basque art. Of special note are the works by El Greco, Goya and José Ribera. Renaissance Dutch and Italian artists are also represented.

▲ BURGOS (574 C4)
BURGOS pop. 161,500
Burgos is synonymous with the name El Cid. Born in the nearby village of Vivar, this Spanish national hero spent much of his life in Burgos, from where he embarked on his 11th-century campaign which resulted in remarkable victories over the Moors.

Founded in AD 884, Burgos was the capital of Castile until the 16th century, when its political prestige was lost to the newly declared capital, Madrid.

A wealth of medieval architecture characterizes Burgos, and the city is principally visited by travelers interested in its Romanesque fortifications, Gothic churches and Renaissance mansions. The oldest quarter is on the slopes of Cerro de San Miguel, site of castle ruins.

CARTUJA DE MIRAFLORES, Paseo de la Quinta, is 4 kilometers (2½ miles) east. Founded by Juan II of Castile in the 15th century, this Carthusian monastery resembles a medieval fortress. The monks are known for the rosaries they make from thousands of rose petals.

CATEDRAL, Plaza de Santa María, dominates the Burgos skyline. One of Spain's most outstanding Gothic structures, this magnificent church, begun in 1221 was completed in the mid-13th century.

The cathedral art includes a painting of Mary Magdalene by Leonardo da Vinci and numerous gold, ivory and silver items. Also present is the tomb of the 11th-century Spanish hero, El Cid.

CONVENTO DE LAS HUELGAS, Paseo de la Isla, is 1 kilometer (½ mile) west of town. Alfonso VIII, who converted this former summer palace to a Cistercian convent in 1180, is buried here.

MONASTERIO DE SAN PEDRO DE CARDEÑA, 11 kilometers (7 miles) southeast of Burgos is this 17th-century monastery. El Cid came in exile to this stern abbey and his remains rested in the monastery from 1099 until 1919.

MUSEO ÁRQUEOLÓGICO, Calle Miranda, is housed in the Casa de Miranda, a superb example of a 16th-century nobleman's mansion, with a lovely Renaissance courtyard. Its archaeological displays range from Roman times to the 18th century.

▲ CÁCERES (574 B2)
CÁCERES *pop. 72,700*
Roman settlement, Moorish metropolis and Spanish fortress, Cáceres is one of the best-preserved feudal towns in Europe. The old quarter is surrounded by medieval fortifications with towers and gates. Inside, along narrow streets and broad plazas, are buildings from the 15th to 18th centuries.

The best religious architecture includes the Gothic churches of Santa María and San Mateo, on squares of the same names. Next to the latter is the lovely Casa de las Cigüenas (House of the Storks), with its original tower, now used by the military services.

Casa de las Veletas (House of the Weather Vanes), the former Moorish Alcázar, houses the town museum. Superb palaces include the Golfines de Arriba, the Episcopal Palace, and the Golfines de Abajo.

▲ CÁDIZ (574 B1)
CÁDIZ *pop. 156,900*
Phoenicians from Tyre founded Cádiz in about 1100 BC. Carthaginians captured the colony 600 years later and were followed by Romans, Visigoths and Moors. In 1262 the city became a part of Christian Spain. After the discovery of America, it was the headquarters of the Spanish treasure fleet and became the wealthiest port in western Europe.

On a peninsula extending into the Atlantic, Cádiz exudes a maritime atmosphere. The old city, where numerous flat-roofed white houses have Moorish watchtowers, is the site of most attractions. The Church of San Felipe Neri has a painting by Murillo; the Santa Cueva chapel has wall paintings by Goya. Among other points of interest are the Catedral Vieja, or Old Cathedral, dating from the 13th century, and the old fortress and lighthouse at San Sebastián west of the city.

Cádiz is the cultural and recreational center of the Costa de la Luz. The city has one theater, a 14,000-seat bullring and some long sandy beaches, including La Victoria, Cortadura and La Caleta. It is an ideal headquarters for exploring the Costa de la Luz, a major resort area, and the "white towns" inland.

CATEDRAL NUEVA, built between 1772 and 1838, is of Andalusian baroque architectural style. It contains a magnificent collection of sculptures and art objects.

HOSPITAL DE MUJERES, the former women's hospital, is a fine baroque building. The chapel houses El Greco's *Ecstasy of St. Francis*.

MUSEO DE BELLAS ARTES has one of Spain's richest art exhibits, including works by Francisco de Zurbarán.

CANARY ISLANDS – see p.600.

CARTAGENA (575 D1)
MURCIA *pop. 179,700*
Cartagena was founded by the Carthaginians in the 3rd century BC, but the Romans transformed it into a major port and prosperous mining center. Today it is Spain's chief naval base.

CONSUEGRA (574 C2)
TOLEDO *pop. 9,900*
Deep in the heart of La Mancha, Consuegra has windmills, and an old ruined castle standing on the hilltop. The village has an attractive square surrounded by buildings of note and is the burial place of Diego, son of El Cid.

SPAIN

▲ CÓRDOBA (574 B2) ★
CÓRDOBA *pop. 302,200*

In the 10th century, Córdoba was one of the great cities of the world. Its caliphs exercised political and religious authority over an empire that included much of Spain and North Africa; its schools and libraries attracted scholars and artists. This former Moorish metropolis

---

THE WINDMILL ROUTE OF LA MANCHA

To capture the flavor of Don Quixote-land, with its vast, flat plains and windmills, head for Consuegra, south east of Toledo, and join the N420 east. You will pass a host of typical Manchegan villages, such as Puerto Lápice, Alcázar de San Juan, Campo de Criptana, El Toboso (legendary House of the Lady Dulcinea) and Mota del Cuervo, complete with windmills galore!

---

and its art treasures are among Spain's principal tourist attractions. The climate is usually temperate, although July and August can be torrid.

Probably of Carthaginian origin, Córdoba became a Roman colony in 152 BC. After periods of Vandal and Visigothic control, the Moors occupied the city in AD 711. Forty-five years later, the city was made the capital of Moorish Spain by Abd-al-Rahman I.

The 10th century was Córdoba's golden age. Renowned for its great library, university and mosque, the city was the home of outstanding scientists, mathematicians, astronomers, geographers, theologians and philosophers. The arts flourished, while architects and craftsmen increased the city's splendor (it is still famous for its silverwork today). But decline set in following a period of political turmoil in the 11th century, and Córdoba never recovered its prestige.

Most places of interest are in the old city surrounding the Mezquita. The best way to see this area of narrow streets and

whitewashed houses is on foot. Stroll down the quaint alleys called *callejas:* Flores, Rincones de Oro, Los Arquillos, Los Siete Infantes de Lara, La Luna and Junio Galión are the most interesting. Judería is the former Jewish quarter.

The city is also noted for its plazas; Corredera, the best known, is surrounded by 17th-century arcades. Potro has a 16th-century fountain and an inn that dates from the time of Cervantes. Many others face churches. Neo-classical Santa Victoria and 16th-century San Salvador flank Plaza del Salvador. A Capuchin convent fronts Los Dolores. The Convento de la Merced looks upon Colón, and 18th-century La Magdalena faces the plaza of the same name.

Other attractions include old fortifications and churches. The ruined Alcázar citadel dates from Moorish times. The Sevilla, Portilla and Almodovar gates are the only remains of Córdoba's medieval walls. Several churches reflect a range of architectural styles and periods. The 14th-century synagogue, the only remaining Jewish house of worship in Andalucia, contains fine stucco work.

MEZQUITA, in the Arab city facing the Roman bridge, is a former mosque that is now a cathedral. Built in the 8th century on the site of a Roman temple and Visigothic church, the Zeca, or House of Purification, grew in splendor until the 10th century when it was one of Islam's most outstanding religious structures. In the 13th century it was consecrated to the Assumption of Mary. Despite subsequent additions, it still looks much as it did in its heyday in the Moorish times.

The building's most outstanding attraction is the Mihrab, an octagonal prayer niche topped with a dome carved from a single block of white marble. It is especially noted for its mosaics. The 16th-century Capilla Mayor and most of the other Christian chapels contain interesting art objects.

MUSEO MUNICIPAL TAURINO Y DE ARTE CÓRDOBES, Plaza Bulas, is in the Casa de las Bulas in the Barrio de la Judería. Its displays include traditional Córdoban arts, leatherwork and silverwork. The bullfighting section has memorabilia of the four native Córdoban matadors known as the "Caliphs," as well as posters, trophies and uniforms.

MUSEO PROVINCIAL DE BELLAS ARTES, Plaza del Potro in the city center, has paintings by such noted Spanish and foreign masters as Murillo, Zurbarán, Goya, Raphael, Titian and Rubens.

PUENTE ROMANO spans the Guadalquivir River in front of the Mezquita. Built during the time of Julius Caesar, the bridge has been restored several times and is still in use. Note the Arab waterwheels downstream.

RUINAS DE MEDINA AZAHARA are 10 kilometers (6 miles) west off highway C431. In the sumptuous retreat built by Córdoban caliphs in the 10th century, Abd-al-Rahman III and his successors held court. Attractions include the Royal or Viziers' Hall, mosque and a museum with outstanding art.

▲ La Coruña (574 A4)
CORUÑA *pop. 252,400*
An important cultural center and largest town and port in Galicia, La Coruña (A Coruña) has a rich historical background. Wide streets and modern buildings distinguish the city, although the old town districts still preserve traces of the past. The 12th-century, Romanesque Church of Santiago is the oldest church. It stands in the old town north of the harbor, where the 13th- to 15th-century Church of Santa Maria del Campo is also of interest.

TORRE DE HERCULES (Tower of Hercules) is a 57-meter (187-foot) Roman lighthouse. Although the lighthouse is said to have been built by a Celtic chieftain in the 2nd century AD, some historians believe it existed many centuries before Christ.

▲ Cuenca (574 C3)
CUENCA *pop. 42,800*
The town of Cuenca lies on a spectacular rocky spur of land between the Júcar River and its tributary, the Huécar. Over the centuries, these rivers have carved deep ravines, creating a stark, wild landscape. In the Barrio del Castillo, the castle district and old quarter, houses known as *casas colgadas*, or "hanging houses," cling to the sides and edges of these steep slopes.

The government has restored three of Cuenca's hanging houses and declared them National Monuments.

CATEDRAL, Plaza Mayor, is a National Monument dating from the 12th century. The church was begun in Norman Gothic style and finished with Anglo-Norman elements; its wrought-iron grilles and tapestries are noteworthy.

THE CUENCA MUSEUM, in La Casa del Curato opposite the hanging house, displays archaeological finds. The Roman period rooms are especially outstanding.

THE DIOCESAN MUSEUM OF SACRED ART, on the ground floor of the Episcopal Palace, houses an impressive collection of religious and modern art and valuable objects from the cathedral and other churches within the Diocese of Cuenca. Among the treasures are paintings by El Greco, a 14th-century Byzantine diptych, and a display of early carpets and tapestries, once a flourishing local industry in Cuenca.

MUSEO DE ARTE ABSTRACTO ESPAÑOL, in a hanging house on Calle Canonigos, has a curious Gothic interior and a lovely Mudéjar ceiling. Its unusual art collection includes works by some of Spain's most important abstract artists.

El Escorial (574 C3) ★
MADRID *pop. 6,900*
SAN LORENZO DEL ESCORIAL is the magnificent monastery and summer palace inspired and built by King Philip II in

SPAIN

the foothills of the Guadarrama Mountains. Constructed with uncemented granite blocks and completed in 1584, the complex includes a monumental, austere domed church surrounded by chapels, each decorated by such masters as Benvenuto Cellini.

The Royal Pantheon of black marble and bronze, contains the tombs of Spanish kings and queens; in the chapter halls is an art collection that includes works by El Greco, Hieronymus Bosch, Titian, Tintoretto and others. The library houses a rare collection of 2,700 manuscripts and 40,000 books. The rooms of Maderas Finas, or Fine Woods, are royal apartments from the 17th century, decorated with inlaid woods.

VALLE DE LOS CAIDOS (Valley of the Fallen) commemorates the Spanish Civil War with a 148-meter (485-foot) cross towering above a green valley. Below the cross, a crypt and chapel are carved into the granite mountainside.

GIRONA (575 E4)
GIRONA pop. 74,800
Colorful Girona (Gerona) is crossed by the Onyar River and an international railroad line. Originally an Iberian stronghold in the 4th century, Girona has since passed through several hands.

During medieval times the Jewish community settled in El Cail, an area with steep, narrow streets. The Museu d'Art has fine paintings and ceramics.

BANYS ARABS (Arabian Baths) are in a Romanesque building and are based on the Roman public baths.

CATEDRAL, dating from 1312, is a mixture of architectural styles. The cloister and part of the tower remain from the earlier Romanesque building. Housed in the cathedral, the Capitular Museo contains the 11th-century *Tapestry of the Creation*.

L'ESGLESIA DE SANT FELIU, built in the 14th to 17th centuries, is known for its octagonal bell tower decorated in the Gothic style. Notable treasures include eight pagan and Christian sarcophagi.

MONESTIR DE SANT PERE DE GALLIGANTS, a monastery that dates from the 11th and 12th centuries, houses a noteworthy archaeological museum. The cloister is an excellent example of Catalonian Romanesque architecture.

GRANADA (574 C1) ★
GRANADA pop. 265,300
It is still possible to fall under the spell of Granada. Indeed, this magnificent city, so rich in relics of its past, is one of Spain's outstanding tourist attractions. Splendid Moorish palaces and fortifications contrast sharply with churches of more recent origin. The Alhambra, the Moorish citadel overlooking the city, is among the world's most highly regarded architectural creations.

Granada rose to fame in 1238 when the Moors moved the seat of their diminishing dominions to this Andalucian city. It then became a cultural capital, boasting world-renowned artists, architects and scholars.

Much of Granada's Moslem past can be seen in the Albaicín, the old quarter facing the Alhambra across the Darro. This section of the city contains private dwellings, narrow streets and plazas, remains of Moorish fortifications and the Arab baths. Santa Isabel la Real, a former mosque, is now a church with a Gothic portal. The 13th-century tower of Gothic San Juan de los Reyes is a former minaret, and the church courtyard of 16th-century El Salvador was once part of a mosque.

Although not as old as the Albaicín, Granada's other districts contain their own distinctive reminders of the past, many reflecting Christian interests. Attractions in the Antequeruela, the area south west of the Alhambra, include interesting churches, most notably Nuestra Señora de las Angustias, in addition to the 16th-century Morisco-style Casa de los Tiros.

Among Granada's annual celebrations are colorful religious processions during Corpus Christi, Holy Week and other feasts. But the chief attraction is the International Festival of Music and Dance. Held in late June and early July, it features concerts and ballets.

ALHAMBRA is Spain's outstanding symbol of Moorish heritage and, as a result, one of the country's most visited tourist attractions. The 13th-century ruler al-Ahmer began construction of the first palace on this plateau overlooking Granada in 1238. During the next 100 years its extravagance increased with successive rulers, and this magnificent complex became a world-renowned center of Moslem art, culture and politics. Although the name properly belongs only to the palace, it is usually applied to the entire fortified complex.

ALAMEDA DE LA ALHAMBRA is an attractive park that encompasses the southern portions of the Alhambra. At this site the Moors planted orange and myrtle trees; the Duke of Wellington added a grove of English elms in 1812.

ALCAZÁBA is the oldest part of the Alhambra. The Moorish caliphs built this citadel in the 11th century on the Alhambra's precipitous western end. Only the massive outer walls, towers and ramparts remain.

GENERALIFE is the former summer retreat of Moorish kings. Although physically distinct from the rest of the Alhambra, this 14th-century palace is usually visited along with the rest of the Moorish complex. It is noted for its maze of terraces, grottoes, flowing fountains and pools.

PALACIO ARABE, also called the Casa Real, or the Royal Palace, is the most magnificent structure of the Alhambra. The interior of this splendid 14th-century palace is a seemingly endless procession of intricately carved ceilings, arches, columns and fountains, beautiful sculptures and brightly tiled floors and walls.

Visitors enter the Palacio Arabe through the Patio de los Arrayanes, or Courtyard of Myrtles, which contains an impressive marble colonnade and pool. The chief attraction is the Patio de los Leones, or Courtyard of the Lions. Surrounded by many white marble columns and paved with colored tiles, it contains the Fountain of the Lions.

Other points of interest in the palace include the Sala de Abencerrajes, with its lofty, brightly colored, domed ceiling; the Mirador de Lindaraja, or Daraxa, decorated with paneled ceiling and arabesques; and the Sala de las Dos Hermanas or Hall of the Two Sisters, a domed room with a fountain. The beautiful Sala de los Embajadores, the largest room, was the sultans' reception room.

PALACIO DE CARLOS V is next to the Palacio Arabe. Begun in 1526, this Renaissance palace was never finished. It houses a museum depicting the artistic history of Granada and the National Museum of Hispanic-Moorish Art.

CAPILLA REAL (Royal Chapel) is attached to the south side of the cathedral. Erected in 1506–17 as a mausoleum for Ferdinand V and Isabella I, this Gothic church has housed their remains since 1521. Of special note are the crown and scepter of Isabella, and her art collection of Flemish paintings.

LA CARTUJA, 1.5 kilometers (1 mile) on the Calle Real de la Cartuja. Begun in 1516, the Carthusian monastery was called the Christian Alhambra because of its beautiful stucco work. Only the cloisters, church and sacristy remain. All three contain interesting paintings.

CATEDRAL, in the city center in the Moslem town, is dedicated to Santa María de la Encarnación. Diego de Siloé began this memorial to the Reconquest in 1528; it was finished in 1703. The Renaissance exterior is embellished with jasper and colored marble and is topped with an impressive dome.

▲ HUELVA (574 A1)
HUELVA pop. 139,100

After the King of Portugal rejected Christopher Columbus' scheme for a western voyage in 1484, Columbus came for help to this city at the confluence of the Odiel and Tinto rivers. The discoverer is commemorated by an annual festival early in August.

In spite of origins linked to the Phoenicians, Huelva exhibits a modern appearance. The city center, La Placeta, bustles with stores and cafés. Notable among the old churches are the 1605 La Merced; San Pedro, with traces of a former mosque; and Concepción, with two paintings by Zurbarán.

Visitors can sample the region's distinctive cuisine. Such fish dishes as *choco con habas*, squid with broad beans, are among the specialties.

The Convento de la Virgen de la Cinta, 2 kilometers (1½ miles) south east, contains a series of faïence tiles depicting the discovery of America. From Palos de la Frontera, 10 kilometers (6 miles) southeast of Huelva, Columbus set sail after recruiting a crew in front of the 15th-century Iglesia de San Jorge.

DONANA NATIONAL PARK, 32 kilometers (20 miles) east, is one of the most important and extensive national parks in the whole of Europe. Visits are by guided tour only; reservations are essential.

JEREZ DE LA FRONTERA (574 B1)
CÁDIZ pop. 183,300

Sherry takes it name from Jerez de la Frontera, known for wines of all kinds. Jerez is surrounded by vineyards and has wine cellars open to thirsty visitors.

Dating from before Roman times, Jerez also offers an old quarter of white-washed houses.

Attractions include remains of the old Arab walls, the 11th-century Alcázar as well as two churches, Gothic San Marcos and baroque Colegiata.

▲ MÁLAGA (574 B1)
MÁLAGA pop. 555,500

Capital of the Costa del Sol, the resort area of Spain's southern coast, Málaga is popular with tourists all year. The Phoenicians founded a port here in the 12th century BC. Romans, Visigoths and Moors followed, and in 1487 the city became a part of Christian Spain.

The birthplace of Pablo Picasso is in the Plaza de la Merced. Several old churches include Gothic Sagrario, with interesting 16th-century altar decora-

---

SHERRY

Jerez de la Frontera is famous for *jerez* (sherry) which has been produced here since the 18th century. The four main types are the extra dry *fino*, more full-bodied *amontillado*, golden *oloroso* and sweet *dulce*. Wine-tasting rounds of the *bodegas* are always enjoyable. A wine harvest festival, held here in early September, includes *flamenco* among its joyous celebrations.

---

tions; 15th-century Santiago, with a Mudéjar tower; and medieval Victoria, which contains a tomb with some macabre decorations.

ALCAZÁBA, on Calle de la Alcazábiella, was the palace of Málaga's Moorish kings. Reconstructed, it houses the Museo Arqueológico and its gardens.

MUSEO DE BELLAS ARTES, San Agustino 6, is a fine art museum in an ancient palace. It contains Roman mosaics and early works by Picasso.

MARBELLA (574 B1)
MÁLAGA pop. 80,600

Marbella is the fashionable centre for the wealthy who visit the Costa del Sol. The fortifications above the old town offer a pleasant stroll, and pretty restaurants can be found around Plaza de los Naranjos (Square of Orange Trees).

MONTSERRAT (575 E3) ★
BARCELONA *pop. 200*

The monastery of Montserrat commands a spectacular setting amid the jagged peaks and monolithic rocks of a massif rising 1,200 meters (3,940 feet) above the Llobregat River. The mountain is associated with many legends, including the Holy Grail.

Montserrat was founded in AD 880 by the Benedictines after the discovery of an icon, the Black Virgin, supposedly hidden by St. Peter in a nearby cave. It became Spain's second pilgrimage center after Santiago de Compostela; there are major pilgrimages twice a year.

The most thrilling approach to the monastery is by the aerial cable car from the rail station, or take the funicular higher up the mountain, where there are stunning views. Paths lead to the caves and hermitages near the summit.

▲ ORENSE (574 A4)
ORENSE *pop. 107,000*

Little remains of ancient Orense (Ourense); it was destroyed by the Moors during the 8th century, but the hot springs that gave Orense its name first attracted the Romans.

One of the oldest surviving buildings in the city is the 12th-century cathedral, whose Portico of Paradise and rich decorations are typical of that period. Yet another notable structure is the seven-arch bridge across the Miño River. One of Spain's most impressive spans, it was built by Bishop Lorenzo in 1230.

▲ OVIEDO (574 B4)
OVIEDO *pop. 192,300*

Ancient Oviedo was once capital of the kingdom of Asturias, later to become Oviedo Province. Founded in the 8th century around a monastery, the town retains many splendid buildings dating from the 8th to the 12th centuries. Two museums display archaeological finds that pre-date the Roman occupation.

CATEDRAL, a 14th-century Gothic building, has an 80-meter (265-foot) tower decorated with filigree. The building also has fine carved portals and beautiful stained-glass windows.

PAMPLONA (574 D4)
NAVARRA *pop. 182,400*

The author Ernest Hemingway made Pamplona the setting for his novel *The Sun Also Rises*, and the Fiesta de San Fermín he described is the city's outstanding tourist attraction. Each day during a week in July, the bulls run through the streets preceded by young men running for their lives. Other activities include bullfights and general merrymaking.

LA ESCOLONÍA

The monastery of Montserrat is renowned for both its library and music. The music school, with its boys' choir *La Escolonía,* dates back to the 13th century and is the oldest in Europe. The boys sing like angels and to hear a performance (given daily) can be a very moving experience.

CATEDRAL is Pamplona's most outstanding monument. Although founded in 1120, this French Gothic church dates mainly from the 14th and 15th centuries.

SAN SATURNINO, is the town's oldest, and finest, Romanesque building.

RONDA (574 B1)
MÁLAGA *pop. 33,900*

Ronda is a picturesque town flanking the deep gorge of the Guadalevín River from atop a rocky plateau. Its spectacular setting and famous bridge, the Puente Nuevo, linking the old town with the new, makes this a great attraction. The old town is on the south side of the ravine; its attractions include Roman ruins, the old Arab Quarter and Santa María la Mayor, a cathedral that combines Gothic and Renaissance influences. North of the river is the "new" town, the site of 15th-century residences and the 18th-century bullring.

SPAIN

▲ **SALAMANCA** (574 B3)
SALAMANCA *pop. 160,500*

Salamanca has had a long and colorful history marked by Roman settlement and struggles between Christians and Moors. The great days of this city on the Tormes River, however, began in the 13th century with the founding of the university, which became a leading European learning center. The majestic old cathedral towering above the city is the principal landmark; the Palacio Monterrey, on the Plaza Agustinas, is a 16th-century seignorial mansion.

A good time to visit Salamanca is during *fiesta* time in mid-September, when it comes alive with fairs, bullfights, parades, folklore, livestock exhibitions and an international horse show.

CATEDRAL NUEVA (New Cathedral), Plaza de Anaya, was begun in 1513 and finished two centuries later, resulting in an unusual combination of architectural styles. Its principal feature is the ornamental detail of the façade with its bas-reliefs of the Nativity and Adoration.

CATEDRAL VIEJA (Old Cathedral), surrounded on three sides by the new cathedral, is a 12th-century church with magnificent chapels and tombs. The Patio Chico, or small patio, offers a view of the remarkable Romanesque apses and the Torre del Gallo, or Cock Tower. The most outstanding feature is the dome, with scenes from the Apocalypse.

PLAZA MAYOR, the heart of the city in both location and spirit, is one of the most beautiful portico squares in Spain. Surrounded by 18th-century baroque buildings, it was originally constructed for use as a bullring.

UNIVERSIDAD, near the Plaza Mayor, is the oldest is Spain. Its outstanding Plateresque façade is intricately carved floral decorations, with shields and medallions, most notably one that portrays Ferdinand and Isabella, the "Catholic Kings."

▲ **SAN SEBASTIÁN** (574 C4)
GUIPÚZCOA *pop. 181,800*

The white buildings of San Sebastián, or Donostia in Basque, provide a pleasant contrast to the green fields and mountains surrounding this leading summer resort. The city's harbor bustles with fishing boats and La Concha, a large sandy beach, offers sporting activities.

The city is divided into two areas. The old quarter has interesting buildings, including two churches, 16th-century San Vicente and 18th-century Santa María. The newer district faces La Concha and its promenade. The Avenida de la Libertad, with nightclubs and stores, is the main thoroughfare.

San Sebastián is host to several festivals during the summer: the two week *Festivales de España* features musical events; Basque Week celebrates local traditions, arts and crafts.

MUSEO MUNICIPAL DE SAN TELMO, a former monastery in the old town dating from the 16th century, with murals by José María Sert, a noted Catalan artist.

SANTIAGO DE COMPOSTELA
(574 A4) ★
LA CORUÑA *pop. 93,700*

For centuries, Santiago de Compostela has been one of the world's great pilgrimage sites. According to tradition, the Apostle St. James (Santiago) was beheaded in Palestine and his body brought to Spain for burial. In 1813, a hermit discovered the tomb, which radiated light and song in the forest. A shrine was built, and later, the great cathedral.

Santiago was at its height of popularity in the 11th to the 13th centuries. The town was declared a Holy City in the same vein as Jerusalem and Rome. The Año Santo (Holy Year) celebrations are held when the Feast of St. James, July 25, falls on a Sunday; the next festival will be held in 1999.

CATEDRAL, is one of the most magnificent in Spain. Rebuilt in the 11th and 12th centuries in Romanesque style with an overlay of baroque carving, the edifice also combines delicate Gothic with elegant plateresque.

The bones of the Apostle St. James the Elder are kept in a crypt under the high altar, which is decorated with baroque gold and silver.

MUSEO, in the cloister by the cathedral, contains archaeological remains, valuable liturgical ornaments and fine tapestries.

CONVENTO DE SAN FRANCISCO is believed to have been founded by St. Francis of Assisi when he came here on a pilgrimage in 1214.

MONASTERIO DE SAN MARTIN PINARIO was founded by monks who served in the cathedral. It was one of the most important in Galicia, with a resplendent baroque high altar.

SANTA MARIA LA REAL DEL SAR, on the city outskirts, is of Romanesque architecture with an enchanting cloister surrounded by pillars with richly carved capitals. The walls and columns of this beautiful church lean at a peculiar angle,

---

THE INCENSE OF SANTIAGO DE COMPOSTELA

The spectacle of the *Botafumeiro* ritual, which happens on feast days and special occasions in the cathedral of Santiago de Compostela, should not be missed. This huge incense burner is brought out and hung from the transept dome. It then swings to the eaves with eight men clinging madly on to it by a rope.

The tradition goes back to the times when the presence of vast numbers of pilgrims who came to worship at the shrine necessitated strong fumigation!

---

but no one has been able to decide whether this is the result of faulty foundations or the intent of the builders.

SANTILLANA DEL MAR (574 C4)
SANTANDER *pop. 3,800*

Santillana del Mar grew up around the 6th-century Monastery of Santa Juliana and was recently declared a national monument. Besides the adjacent Caves of Altamira, the town is noted for a 12th-century Romanesque Collegiate Church and numerous residences bearing coats of arms and emblems.

A short distance away are the Cuevas de Altamira (Altamira Caves) which contain prehistoric wall paintings of bison, horses, deer and other animals, which are between 13,000 and 25,000 years old. A limited number of visitors are allowed in each day.

▲ SEGOVIA (574 C3) ★
SEGOVIA *pop. 54,800,*

On the Eresma and Clamores rivers in the central Guadarrama mountains, Segovia has been inhabited since before the Roman Conquest. Isabella I was proclaimed queen in Segovia in 1474, and much of the town appears to have changed little in succeeding centuries. A walk on the ramparts dividing the upper and lower towns affords a good view of twisting streets leading to picturesque plazas and interesting churches.

The 16th-century Carmelite convent houses the tomb of St. John of the Cross. The Chapter House has Gobelin tapestries and a fine coffered ceiling. Northwest near the village of Santa María la Real de Nieva is 15th-century Coca Castle, one of Spain's finest and best-preserved castles.

La Granja de San Ildefonso, 12 kilometers (7 miles) southeast, is an elaborate palace and estate with gardens similar to those at Versailles in France.

ACUEDUCTO ROMANO, town center, was built in the 1st century AD and is one of the world's best-preserved Roman remains. The perfectly fitting granite blocks form 118 arches reaching a height of 29 meters (95 feet) in the Plaza del Azoguejo. The aqueduct still carries water to part of the city.

SPAIN

ALCÁZAR, Plaza del Alcázar, is a remarkable 13th-century palace serving as Segovia's principal landmark. Enhanced by magnificent chambers added in a 15th-century renovation, it was gutted by fire in 1862 and later rebuilt. The Throne, Gallery, and Pineapple Rooms feature period furniture and motifs.

CATEDRAL, Plaza Catedral, has earned the nickname "Lady of Cathedrals" for its graceful elegance. The 16th-century church is an excellent example of Spanish Gothic; its museum contains masterpieces by Van Dyck, Morales and Benvenuto Cellini.

▲ SEVILLA (574 B1) ★
SEVILLA pop. 714,000
Sevilla (Seville), capital of Andalucia, is an outstanding Spanish city full of culture and history. Situated on the banks of the Guadalquiver, the only navigable river in Spain, it has been an important port since ancient times.

Founded by the Iberians 3,000 years ago, Seville became a major Roman settlement and the birthplace of the emperors Trajan and Hadrian. But it was during five centuries of Moorish rule that Seville flourished. After the reconquest in 1248, Seville became a royal court for various Christian kings, including Ferdinand and Isabella, who sponsored Columbus' voyage to the New World. Columbus returned here triumphant in 1493, and thereafter Seville monopolized trade with the Americas.

In the 17th century, Cervantes conceived his hero, Don Quixote, while imprisoned in Seville. This romantic city gave birth to many great cultural characters, from Próspero Merimé's Carmen to Rossini's Barber of Seville. The city is also renowned as the capital of *flamenco*, and for its arcaded bullring and outstanding *toreadors*.

Squares and streets are lined with orange trees, whose fruit is used to make bitter marmalade. The old city comprises charming neighborhoods perfect for strolling, the best known is the Barrio de Santa Cruz. the pretty houses along its narrow streets have flower-filled balconies, and cool inner patios and courtyards can sometimes be glimpsed behind the walls.

Another fine place to wander is the shady Parque de María Luisa. Nearby, on Calle de San Fernando, is the massive Fábrica de Tabacos, a former tobacco factory built in the 18th century, which now houses the university. The 18th-century baroque Palacio de San Telmo, designed as a nautical school and now the seat of the regional government, is near the San Telmo bridge. In Plaza Nueva, the 16th-century plateresque *ayuntamiento* (town hall), can be visited two days a week.

Seville's many beautiful churches include Gothic San Pedro, where Velázquez was baptized; Mudéjar-style Santa Ana in the Triana district; San Marco, with a fine minaret tower; Churrigueresque San Salvador on Calle de Las Sierpes and, further along, San Lorenzo, with a splendid high altar.

Among the convents and monasteries are 15th-century Santa Paula, with a striking ceramic façade and Santa Clara, with its 13th-century tower from the former palace of Don Fadrique. Near the cathedral is the the 17th-century Hospital de la Caridad, with several paintings by Murillo in the chapel alongside two hideous scenes of death by Valdés Leal.

Holy Week is the most remarkable of the city's annual festivities, with elaborate street processions that have taken place since the 16th century. Following Easter, Seville celebrates its *feria* (fair), with parades, bullfights, music, dancing and revelry. Other feast days such as Corpus Christi and Epiphany also attract large crowds – reserve accommodations.

In the summer Seville is one of the hottest places in Europe, so a visit in spring or fall may be preferable. There is also a high incidence of petty crime, and visitors should take particulare care with valuables or, better still, leave them in the hotel safe.

ALCÁZAR is near the cathedral in the Plaza del Triunfo. Seville's Moorish sovereigns began construction of a fortress palace in 1181. From that period, however, only the impressive Patio del Yeso remains. Under the stewardship of 14th-century Pedro the Cruel and later monarchs, Moorish architects built lavish courts, apartments and gardens.

ARCHIVO DE INDIAS, Plaza del Triunfo, is in the Renaissance Casa Lonja, the former merchants' exchange. Noted for its red marble staircase, the building houses the Archives of the Indies, and a collection of books, maps, manuscripts and documents depicting the history of Spain's vanished New World empire.

FLAMENCO

While good *flamenco* may be seen in Madrid, Málaga, or countless places, it has close associations with Seville, and a good *tablao*, or performance, can be unforgettable. The gypsy and Moorish origins of *flamenco* are from Andalucía, with the *cante jondo*, literally "deep song," considered the heart and soul of flamenco, relating to passions, deep emotions, unhappiness in love and other such human feelings! A good performance has terrific atmosphere and plenty of high drama.

CASA DE PILATOS (Pilate's House), Calle de Aguilas, is a 16th-century Mudéjar palace, built as a reproduction of Pontius Pilate's Praetorium in Jerusalem.

CATEDRAL, Avénida de la Constitución, is the largest cathedral in Spain and third largest in Christendom. Begun in 1402, the Gothic church is dedicated to Santa María de la Sede. Priceless paintings, 15th-century choir stalls and chapels enclosed by exquisite iron screens decorate the interior. In the south transept is the tomb of Christopher Columbus.

During the festivals of Corpus Christi and the Immaculate Conception, altar boys stage a ceremony that includes a dance with castanets. A magnificent Almohad bronze door leads from the street into the ablutions courtyard of the former mosque.

Torre de la Giralda, in the north-west corner of the cathedral, dominates Seville's skyline. Built in 1184 as a minaret, the 92-meter (300-foot) tower now houses the church's 25 bells.

HOSPITAL DE LOS VENERABLES SACERDOTES, in the Barrio de Santa Cruz, opened in 1675 as the Paupers' House of the Venerable Priests. It now contains a museum and a baroque church.

ITALICA is an ancient Roman city 8 kilometers (5 miles) north on highway N630 at Santiponce. The remains of an amphitheater, villas, theater and streets can still be seen in this settlement, which was also the birthplace of the emperors Trajan and Hadrian.

MUSEO DE BELLAS ARTES, Plaza del Museo 9, is one of the oldest museums in Spain. Housed in a former convent the collection includes works by El Greco, Goya and Velázquez.

TARRAGONA (575 E3)
TARRAGONA *pop. 110,900*
With its air of ancient history, Tarragona is the most pleasant of the larger towns on the Costa Dorada. The medieval upper town is encircled by Roman walls, while the lower town is scattered with fine Roman remains including a forum.

ARCO DE BARA, 20 kilometers (12 miles) north on highway N340, was built in the 2nd century by the Romans. The two stone pillars of the arch are carved to form false Corinthian columns.

CATEDRAL, in the city center, is a skilful blend of Romanesque and Gothic architecture. The façade of the 12th-century building features a rose window and magnificent sculptures; the decorations on the main altar are superb.

PUENTE DEL DIABLO (Devil's Bridge) is a Roman aqueduct 4 kilometers (2½ miles) from Tarragona on highway N240. The well-preserved, double-arched structure is one of the most impressive Roman remains in Spain.

▲ TOLEDO (574 C3) ★
TOLEDO *pop. 60,200*

As El Greco painted it, Toledo was a divine city illuminating medieval Spain; as the Romans and Moors saw it, the town was an excellent site for a walled fortress. But today's visitor remembers the city for its rich heritage, so well-preserved that the urban area has been named a National Monument. Capital of the province of the same name, Toledo lies on the central Spanish plain. The Tagus River hugs the town on three sides, much like a castle moat.

An excursion into the almost inexhaustible architectural treasury that is Toledo might begin from either of two bridges spanning the Tagus, each at the foot of the medieval town. The outer walls, of Moorish, Visigothic and Christian origins, contain well-preserved gateways. From the picturesque Zocodover Square in the center of town, the main street, Comercio, leads to the celebrated cathedral. Other sights in the environs are mosques, Mudéjar synagogues, Christian churches and several museums, parks and *paseos*. The 15th-century Castillo de Guadamur, 14 kilometers (9 miles) southwest, is one of Spain's finest and best-preserved castles.

The craftsmen of Toledo are nearly as well-known as its sights. Artisans still produce damascened work in the style inherited from the Moors, as well as traditional bullfighters' swords and modern military swords.

EL ALCÁZAR, Cuesta del Alcázar, overlooks the city. Built in its present form by Charles V, the fortress stands on the site of a 3rd-century Roman palace. This plateresque citadel was nearly destroyed during the Civil War. It has since been restored and is a National Monument.

CASA Y MUSEO DEL GRECO is in the Judería. El Greco lived in this vicinity, and this well-preserved mansion houses many of his personal effects. The museum has a collection of his paintings.

CATEDRAL, begun in 1226, was completed in the late 1400s. The Spanish Gothic church is celebrated for its Mudéjar decorations and more than 750 stained-glass windows. Also renowned are the Treasury and Sacristy, which contain works by Van Dyck, El Greco, Velázquez and Goya.

HOSPITAL DE TAVERA, north on the road to Madrid, is a restored 16th-century hospital with a pharmacy, church and exquisite patio. Adjoining the main building is the Palace of the Dukes of Lerma; the art collection contains the last picture painted by El Greco.

MEZQUITA DEL CRISTO DE LA LUZ is opposite the Puerta del Sol. Built as a mosque in the 10th century and converted to Christian use after the reconquest, this Moorish structure contains some 12th-century Christian frescoes.

SANTO TOMÉ, Calle Santo Tomé, is a 14th-century Mudéjar church with a notable spire. El Greco's most renowned work, *The Burial of Count Orgaz*, can be seen in one of the chapels.

SINAGOGA DE SANTA MARIA LA BLANCA, Judería near the Calle de los Reyes Católicos, is Spain's oldest synagogue.

TORREMOLINOS (574 B1)
MÁLAGA *pop. 27,500*

The first of the booming vacation resorts on the Costa del Sol, Torremolinos has long been a favorite with visitors seeking sun and sand. After sunbathing, sightseeing and shopping, there is the lively nightlife of the bars and discos.

SPAIN

▲ VALENCIA (575 D2)

VALENCIA *pop. 749,600*

A sunny garden city surrounded by orange groves, Valencia lies on the Turia River. Excellent communications link the third largest city in Spain to Barcelona and Madrid. Like its two sisters, Valencia's turbulent history has included past occupation by the Romans, Moors and French.

Valencia's many churches include the cathedral; the convent of Santo Domingo, with its outstanding Gothic cloister; and the Renaissance Colegio del Patriarca, with a collection of fine tapestries and paintings. Civic buildings include the Lonja de Mercado, the 18th-century Palacio de Justicia and the Casa de las Rocas, which houses *rocas* or chariots. The picturesque flower market and botanical gardens are worth a visit, as are the museums, including the National Ceramics Museum.

Valencia is most memorable during its colorful holidays. The noisiest and happiest is Las Fallas, which celebrates the coming of spring. The Festival of St. James in July is also important.

CATEDRAL, on Plaza de la Virgen, is a 13th-century Gothic building with a baroque façade and octagonal bell tower, the Torre del Miguette. Its great treasure is the Santo Cáliz ("holy chalice"), which is beleived to be the Holy Grail.

▲ VALLADOLID (574 B3)

VALLADOLID *pop. 333,200*

Valladolid, Spain's former capital, was the residence of the kings of Castile in the 15th century before Philip II made Madrid his capital. A university city of modern appearance, it is in the heart of Old Castile. Ferdinand and Isabella were married here, Philip II was born here, and Columbus died here. Among its highlights is the grand house where Cervantes lived (1603–06).

MUSEO NACIONAL DE ESCULTURA (National Museum of Sculpture), on Cadenas de San Gregorio, contains the best and most representative pieces of Spanish polychrome woodwork.

VITORIA (574 C4)

ALAVA *pop. 206,700*

Historic Vitoria, or Gasteiz in Basque, was founded by the Visigoths in AD 581. The city was fortified by Sancho the Wise of Navarre in 1181.

Vitoria is divided into two districts. There are Gothic mansions, complete with heraldic escutcheons over the doors, which line narrow streets in the old district; while in the newer area is picturesque La Florida park.

CATEDRAL DE SANTA MARIA was founded in 1180 and reconstructed in the 14th century. It has a 17th-century tower and paintings by Van Dyck and Rubens.

SAN MIGUEL is a 14th-century Gothic church. Of particular interest are the beautiful altar and the jasper Virgen Blanca de Vitoria, the White Virgin of Vitoria.

▲ ZARAGOZA (575 D3)

ZARAGOZA *pop. 600,500*

Although it pre-dates the Roman occupation, Zaragoza is best-known for its association with the artist, Francisco José de Goya, born in this province at Fuentedotos. Many of his paintings, as well as works by other renowned artists, are displayed in the city.

BASILICA DE NUESTRA SEÑORA DEL PILAR is a baroque structure with cupolas and blue tiles. There are splendid frescoes by Francisco José de Goya and Francisco Bayeu in the choir; a treasury contains gold plate and jewels.

CASTILLO DE ALJAFERÍA is an 11th-century Moorish castle whose original walls and oratory, or chapel, still stand.

MUSEO PROVINCIAL DE BELLAS ARTES exhibits a collection of paintings by Goya and El Greco's *St. Francis*.

SPAIN

ISLAS BALEARES

(575 E2)

Carthaginians, Romans, Vandals and Arabs have over the centuries invaded the Islas Baleares, or Balearic Islands. In modern times the 16 islands are besieged by invaders of a different sort – tourists. As a result, cosmopolitan resorts offer visitors sandy beaches, lively nightlife and sports.

The beaches of the Balearic Islands are the principal attractions, and the four major islands – Formentera, Ibiza, Mallorca and Menorca – have countless sand-rimmed coves. If you are looking for uncrowded beaches, head for the smaller isles, such as Formentera, or the more remote parts of Ibiza and Menorca.

The interiors of the islands also are worth visiting. In quaint hill villages and valleys, old customs prevail, including traditional folk dancing. Local craftsmen produce handmade shoes, gloves and other leather goods, embroideries, wood carvings, glassware, ceramics, wrought-iron items and raffia. There is a steamer service from Barcelona and Valencia to Mallorca, Menorca and Ibiza, which are also accessible by air. Various watercraft serve the other islands from Palma de Mallorca.

IBIZA (575 E2)
ISLAS BALEARES *pop. 50,000*

The gleaming white sand beaches of Ibiza make this island second only to Mallorca in popularity with tourists. Among Ibiza's most popular resorts are San Antonio on the west coast, Santa Eulalia, northeast of Ibiza town, and Portinatx, which lies on the north coast.

IBIZA, on the island of the same name, was founded by the Carthaginians more than 2,600 years ago, but most of its antiquities are of more recent origin. The attractive old town, Dalt Villa, is situated on a hill; the town walls date from the 16th century.

MALLORCA (575 E1)
ISLAS BALEARES *pop. 613,800*

Largest of the Balearic Islands, Mallorca is the most frequently visited. Its shores are rimmed with fine sandy beaches, the interior has exceptional mountain scenery, and its capital Palma, is a resort of world renown. The island's southwest is favored by tourists. The beaches around Palma have heavy resort development and there are hundreds of clubs, hotels and restaurants.

Although less visited than the southwest, the rest of Mallorca is just as interesting. In the interior are quaint hill villages. Along the south and east coasts are such fine beaches as Cala d'Or, a lovely cove where pine trees grow to the water's edge. On the north coast are the popular seaside resorts of Alcúdia and Puerto Pollensa, and Formentor, a stunning area of pine woods.

The west coast provides some of Mallorca's most spectacular scenery. From the rugged cliffs and caves of Cala San Vicente in the north to the great stone mass of the Dragonera islet in the south, the mountains climb to heights of more than 900 meters (2,950 feet).

ALCÚDIA, an ancient town with a Roman theater and a medieval city gate, Alcúdia was the last stronghold of the Moors when Jaime the Conqueror landed in the western part of the island. It lies at the northern end of the Bay of Alcúdia.

ARTÁ, a pleasant hillside town, has a small archaeological museum and is next to several prehistoric settlements where some megalithic remains can be seen. The excellent beach of Cala Ratjada is 10 kilometers (6 miles) west.

Cuevas De Arta are 9 kilometers (6 miles) east. These impressive caves descend more than 390 meters (1,280 feet) and contain some of Mallorca's largest subterranean rock formations.

DEYÁ, set on a hill, has long been the haunt of writers and artists. One of its most famous guests was the poet Robert

Graves, who made it his permanent home and was buried here in 1985. It continues to attract art lovers as well as the rich and famous.

MANACOR is noted for the production of Mallorca pearls. The factory where the artificial pearls are made and the town's archaeological museum can be visited.

Cueva De Los Hams (Cave of the Fishhooks) is 11 kilometers (7 miles) east. The cave follows the course of a former underground river and owes its name to the strange limestone formations.

Cuevas Del Drach (Limestone Caverns) are 13 kilometers (8 miles) east near Porto Cristo. They extend more than 1.5 kilometers (1 mile) and contain one of Europe's largest underground lakes.

▲ PALMA (575 E1) *(pop. 297,000)*, once a great maritime power, is now a cosmopolitan resort and the chief city of the Balearic Islands. It enjoys a magnificent seaside setting on the Bahía de Palma and attracts vacationers to its beaches, shopping stalls and nightclubs. Because it is within driving distance of all of Mallorca's points of interest, it is a convenient center for exploring the island.

A tour of Palma should include the old city, an area of narrow streets, many open to pedestrian traffic only. Attractions include the Arco de la Almudaina, a Moorish arch; Baños Arabes, the 11th-century Arab baths; such churches as Gothic San Francisco and baroque Montesión; and several other old buildings. This area is also Palma's principal shopping district.

The newest districts encompass elegant stores, luxurious hotels, lively nightclubs with colorful cabarets, fine restaurants and multilingual movie houses. During the summer season there are bullfights in the 18,000-seat coliseum, Coliseo Balear, as well as horse racing and *jai alai* (pelota) events.

And, of course, there are beaches. To the east, the sands of the Ribera de Levante extend 13 kilometers (8 miles) from Ciudad Jardín to El Arenal. To the

west is the Ribera de Poniente and beyond are Santa Ponsa and Cala Fornells; the latter, one of Mallorca's less crowded beaches, is 20 kilometers (12 miles) from Palma.

La Almudaina, the former residence of Moorish governors and later of Mallorcan kings, is the official reception hall of the king of Spain. Little remains of the Arab influence; the building was reconstructed in the 16th century. The two courtyards are of special interest.

Ayuntamiento, Plaza de Cort, is Palma's 16th-century town hall. Its style a blend of Italian Renaissance and baroque, the building contains a library and a picture gallery.

Castillo De Bellver is on a pine-clad hill west of town. Construction of this fortress began in the 13th century. Since then it has served primarily as a military stronghold and prison.

Catedral, known as La Seu, facing the bay, dominates Palma's skyline. Begun in 1230, this large Gothic church has numerous carvings, frescoes, paintings and other art objects. It also contains the tombs of Mallorcan kings and a museum with displays of religious relics and jewelry.

MENORCA (575 E2)
ISLAS BALEARES *pop. 64,000*

Pretty Menorca, northeast of Mallorca and second-largest of the Islas Baleares, is noted for its beaches. These fine sandy expanses range from crowded, popular Cala Santa Galdana to almost deserted Cala Mezquida. Indeed, the entire north and south coast of the island is lined with rugged coves and quiet bathing spots.

Menorca's places of interest include 350-meter (1,148-foot) Monte Toro; the archaeological site of Naveta de Tudons, which has some megalithic monuments; and the Old World port of Ciudadela, with its interesting cathedral.

The capital, Mahon, has an archaeological museum with a variety of exhibits. Menorca is also known for its *caldereta de lagosta*, a lobster specialty and a favorite of King Juan Carlos I, and *mahonesa*, a local creation better known as mayonnaise.

SPAIN

ISLAS CANARIAS

(575 E1)

Off the Atlantic coast of Africa, the Islas Canarias, or Canary Islands, have been a favorite vacation spot throughout the 20th century. The scenery varies from lush tropical jungles to stark, arid deserts. There are beaches of white sand, black sand and shingle. More than 900 varieties of flowering plant grow, and the 220 species of bird include the native canary.

During the ancient and medieval periods, the Guanches inhabited the Canary Islands, but during the Spanish conquest of 1401–96, the aboriginal population decreased. Nevertheless, evidence of their ultimate absorption into the population is suggested by many of the islanders' family names.

Of the seven major islands, Gran Canaria, La Palma, Tenerife, Lanzarote and Fuerteventura are the most tourist-oriented, offering modern facilities and beaches. Those seeking solitude should head for El Hierro, Fuerteventura, volcanic Lanzarote, or La Gomera. Of special interest to shoppers is the islands' status as free ports.

LA GOMERA (575 D1)
ISLAS CANARIAS *pop. 17,500*
La Gomera is a round island of steep-sided mountains with a large central massif, the Alto de Garajonay, rising to 1,487 meters (4,878 feet) at its center. Its dense forests of silver laurel are protected by the Garajonay national park, while banana plantations dot the lush valleys.

Ancient customs are preserved here, such as the unique whistling language, *el silbo*, that islanders use to communicate from mountain to mountain.

Tourism is relatively recent on La Gomera – it is less crowded and can only be reached by boat from Tenerife and other islands. The capital, San Sebastián, is where Columbus stopped in 1492 on his way to discover the New World. The house where he stayed, the church where he prayed, and the Torre del Conde fortress tower commemorate his presence. Other places of interest include the villages of Hermigua and Chipude, known for its handmade pottery; the Los Organos rock formations; and the fine beaches at Valle Gran Rey and Playa Santiago.

GRAN CANARIA (575 E1)
ISLAS CANARIAS *pop. 700,000*
Gran Canaria, the Canary Islands' most populous and third largest island, is a mixture of several continents. From 1,979-meter (6,496-foot) Roque Nublo in the interior to the coasts, plants of Europe, Africa and the Americas thrive, including palm, pine, grape, coffee, sugar cane, banana, almond and tomato. The best beaches on the island are in the south, an area of considerable development.

Of interest are the southern resorts of San Agustín, Playa de Inglés and Maspalomas, all with fine beaches; the interior towns of Tejeda and San Bartolomé de Tirajana, which are surrounded by rugged rocky peaks; and the southwestern village of Mogán and its nearby seaside cliffs.

▲ LAS PALMAS (575 E1) (*pop. 342,000)* is a cosmopolitan resort, port and metropolis on Gran Canaria, which enjoys a setting between mountains and the sea. The city boasts numerous shops offering a variety of items at bargain prices. Nearby are fine beaches, including Las Canteras, a wide, sandy expanse protected from currents by a natural volcanic reef offshore. Puerto de la Luz is 5 kilometers (3 miles) north, and the airport is 26 kilometers (16 miles) south.

Casa de Colón is the former governor's palace. Christopher Columbus stayed here before embarking on his first voyage to the New World. The building now houses artifacts from the time of Columbus. The Canary Museum has an important anthropology section with mummies of the ancient Guanches.

LANZAROTE (575 E1)
ISLAS CANARIAS *pop. 80,000*

As recently as the 19th century, Lanzarote's numerous volcanoes spewed rivers of molten lava. Even today, fissures in the desert-like slopes of Montaña del Fuego, the Mountain of Fire, are hot enough to fry eggs. With more than 300 volcanic cones, Lanzarote is one of the most beautiful islands in the Canaries. Red, black and white sand beaches, many remarkably uncrowded, line its shores. Despite a dry climate, the island abounds with vineyards and fruit plantations. Arrecife, the chief town, has two fortresses: San Gabriel and San José.

LA PALMA (575 D1)
ISLAS CANARIAS *pop. 80,000*

Emerald-tinted forests and aquamarine waters combine to make La Palma a gem of the Canaries. La Caldera de Taburiente, a giant volcanic crater, dominates the island's interior. A national park surrounding the crater is filled with immense pine groves. The 2,398-meter (7,871-foot) Roque de los Muchachos and the more accessible La Cumbrecita lookout point afford excellent views.

SANTA CRUZ (575 D1) (*pop. 18,000*), on the island of La Palma, surveys the sea from the slopes of a volcanic crater, a location that curves impressively like an amphitheater. Modern buildings line the attractive avenues alongside old colonial houses with wooden balconies.

TENERIFE (575 E1)
ISLAS CANARIAS *pop. 428,000*

Largest of the Canary Islands, Tenerife is also one of the most beautiful. Its scenery varies from the fertile valleys of Orotava and Güimar to the lava fields of Las Cañadas.

The northeast has attracted most tourists up to now, but development in the south is increasing.

Places of interest include the popular year-round swimming resorts of Puerto de la Cruz, Playa de las Americas and Los Cristianos. Among the most notable beaches are Playa de Medano, 90 kilometers (56 miles) from Santa Cruz, and Los Realejos.

LAS CAÑADAS DEL TEIDE, an ancient volcanic cone 2,000 meters (6,562 feet) above sea level, is a national park in the center of the island. Its 80-kilometer (50-mile) circumference is covered with colored lava fields and jutting rock formations. Dominating this strange landscape is the 3,718-meter (12,198-foot) Pico de Teide, the highest point in Spain. A funicular railroad runs to the summit, from where, on a clear day, you can see all the islands.

LA OROTAVA (*pop. 31,400*), best visited during June, is situated in the beautiful Orotava Valley on Tenerife. It is an old town of steep steps, red-tiled roofs and grand houses.

Set among lush banana plantations and pine groves overshadowed by snow-capped Teide, the town is the scene of the most colorful festival in the Canaries. During Corpus Christi, the inhabitants carpet streets and plazas with flowers for the religious procession. Four days later, during the Romeria de San Isidro, they dress in colorful costumes for a parade.

PUERTO DE LA CRUZ (*pop. 39,200*) is the destination for most tourists visiting Tenerife. Hotels, restaurants and nightclubs abound in the city's modern surroundings. Along the Avenida de Colón are natural pools of water and a spectacular lido built into the sea. The black volcanic sand beaches of the north coast are nearby.

▲ SANTA CRUZ (574 E1) (*pop. 220,000*). During the Napoleonic Wars, the British Admiral Lord Nelson lost a battle while attempting to take this city; his captured flags are still treasured relics in the military museum in the Paso Alto castle.

This bustling metropolis is better known for its harbor, colorful parks and plazas and crowded shopping stalls.

THINGS TO KNOW

- **AREA:** 467 square kilometers (180 square miles)
- **POPULATION:** 64,300
- **CAPITAL:** Andorra la Vella
- **LANGUAGES:** Catalan is the official language; French and Spanish also spoken.
- **PASSPORT REQUIREMENTS:** Advised for U.S. visitors. Spanish and French borders require a valid passport.
- **VISA REQUIREMENTS:** Not required for stays of up to three months.
- **DUTY-FREE ITEMS:** No restrictions on goods brought into or taken out of Andorra; however, visitors entering or leaving Spain or France must comply with these countries' regulations.
- **CURRENCY:** The currency units are the Spanish *peseta* and the French *franc*. Due to currency fluctuations, the exchange rate is subject to frequent change. No limit on currency brought into or taken out of Andorra.
- **BANK OPENING HOURS:** 9am–1pm, 3–5pm Monday–Friday, 9am–noon Saturday.
- **BEST BUYS:** Cameras, electronic equipment, watches, porcelain, crystal, perfume, costumed dolls, woodcarvings, flags, leather jackets, jewelry, sports items. As a duty-free zone, Andorra offers low prices on all goods.
- **PUBLIC HOLIDAYS:** January 1; January 6 (King's Day); March 19; Good Friday; May 1; Whitmonday; August 15 (Assumption Day); September 8 (Andorran National Feast Day); December 25–26. Villages celebrate local holidays and saints' days.
- **NATIONAL TOURIST OFFICES:** There are no tourist offices for Andorra in the United States. The best place to obtain information is the Spanish Tourist Office. *(See p.572.)*
  Andorra Delegation in Britain
  63 Westover Road
  London SW18 2RF, England
  Tel: 0181 874 4806
- **AMERICAN EMBASSY** The are no embassies or consulates in Andorra. *(See p.572.)*

ANDORRA
(575 E4)

HISTORY

Located in the heart of the Pirineos (Pyrénées) Andorra has historic ties with both Spain and France. Until 1993, when it became an independent state, it was co-principality of both countries, owing tribute under a 13th-century feudal agreement. This is reflected in its culture, cuisine and the use of both languages, although Catalan is the official language.

Its economy is based on tourism and commerce. Andorra's status as a tax-free zone attracts day-trippers from across its borders as well a vacationers who come to enjoy the sporting facilities and the scenery.

SPORTS AND RECREATION

Andorra's high altitude and sunny climate is ideal for year-round recreation. It has five ski resorts, as well as 30 kilometers (19 miles) of ski tracks. There are many sports centers, from the Ice Palace skating rink in Canillo to the Olympic swimming pool in Serradells. Mountain biking, golfing, climbing and hiking or horseback riding are among the popular summer activities.

GETTING AROUND

Highway C1313 from Spain via Seo de Urgel leads to Andorra, and becomes CG1. The N22 from France (CG2 in Andorra) is occasionally closed due to snow in winter.

Children under 10 may not travel in the front seat. Speed limits are 40 k.p.h. (25 m.p.h.) in town and 90 k.p.h. (55 m.p.h.) out of town, depending on conditions. Visiting motorists must pay fines for violations on the spot with Spanish *pesetas* or French *francs*.

ACCOMMODATIONS

Andorra has over 50 *pensions* and 200 hotels, many have resort facilities such as swimming pools, tennis courts and golf courses. Andorra's campgrounds are open all year.

PLACES OF INTEREST

▲ ANDORRA LA VELLA
pop. 21,800, elev. 1,029m. (3,376 ft.)

The capital of Andorra enjoys a beautiful setting at the confluence of two mountain streams, surrounded by towering peaks. Its 12th-century church has fine wood carvings and is one of numerous Romanesque churches, bridges and shrines scattered through the country.

The town is the main shopping center for duty-free goods. Shopping is one of the main attractions of Andorra. Department stores are open full time, even on public holidays, and smaller stores are open on Sunday morning. The best buys are spirits, cigarettes and perfume; cameras and electrical goods are not always bargains. It is also a good place to fill up with gas.

CASA DE LA VALL (House of the Valley), a 16th-century stucco building, is the seat of government.

CANILLO
pop. 2,400, elev. 1,559m. (5,118ft.)

This medieval village near the waterfall of Les Moles, has slate-roofed houses, old mills and an unusual seven-armed Gothic cross. Beyond the village, the Romanesque church of San Joan des Caselles has a striking bell tower.

ENCAMP
pop. 10,100, elev. 1,265m. (4,153ft.)

A cable lift runs from Encamp to Lake Engolasters, offering spectacular panoramas of the surrounding mountains and the Valira River. About 6 kilometers (4 miles) beyond the town is the attractive chapel of Sant Roma de les Bons.

AUTOMOBILE CLUB
The Automobil Club d'Andorra (Automobile Club of Andorra) is at rue Babot Camp 4, Andorra la Vella. Not all auto clubs offer full travel services to AAA members.

NOTRE DAME DE MERITXELL, north of town, is the site of an annual pilgrimage in September. According to legend, a wooden image of the Virgin Mary was discovered under a blooming rose bush.

LA MASSANA
pop. 5,500, elev. 1,240m. (4,068ft.)

This pretty mountain town, known for its Romanesque art, is a fine place to wander around. Some 3 kilometers (2 miles) outside of town is the Pont di Sant Antoni, an ancient stone bridge spanning the gorge.

LES ESCALDES
pop. 15,200, elev. 1,054m. (3,458ft.)

Les Escaldes is known for its thermal springs, which are pumped into hotels. The Caldea spa complex has various pools, baths and fountains. The waters are available to the public from a fountain in the village square.

ORDINO
pop. 1,700, elev. 1,304m. (4,281ft.)

Ordino has a beautiful 16th-century village church and well-preserved Spanish-style homes. Casa Rosell has a dovecote and private chapel. Classical music festivals take place in the town.

Nearby, Casamanya climbs to over 2,000 meters (6,560 feet), providing magnificent views.

CASA PLANDOLIT dates to the early 1600s. The house contains wine and meat cellars, a chapel, a music room, a bakery and wrought-iron balconies, and has pleasant gardens. Paintings and period furnishings are on show.

SANT JULIÁ DE LÓRIA
pop. 7,550, elev. 939m. (3,081ft.)

Exceptionally beautiful woodlands laced with roads and footpaths surround Sant Juliá de Lória. It was a commercial center as early as the Middle Ages, due to its geographical position near Spain's northern plains.

THINGS TO KNOW

- **AREA:** 6 square kilometers (2½ square miles)
- **POPULATION:** 32,000
- **CAPITAL:** Gibraltar
- **LANGUAGES:** English and Spanish
- **ECONOMY:** Port commerce, tourism, financial services.
- **PASSPORT REQUIREMENTS:** Required for U.S. citizens
- **VISA REQUIREMENTS:** Not required.
- **CURRENCY:** The currency unit, the Gibraltar pound, is divided into 100 pence (p). The exchange rate is subject to frequent change. No restrictions on import of currency, but only currency declared on arrival may be exported. United Kingdom and Gibraltar government notes and coins are legal tender.
- **BANK OPENING HOURS:** 9am–3:30pm Monday–Thursday; 9am–3:30pm and 4:30–6pm Friday.
- **STORE OPENING HOURS:** 9am–7pm Monday–Friday; 9am–1pm Saturday.
- **BEST BUYS:** Perfume, cameras, crystal, cigars, cigarettes, electrical goods, jewelry, watches, ceramics and luxury items from other European countries.
- **PUBLIC HOLIDAYS:** January 1; Commonwealth Day; Good Friday; Easter Monday; first Monday in May (May Day); last Monday in May (Spring Bank Holiday); June 8 (the Queen's Birthday); last Monday in August (Late Summer Bank Holiday); December 25–26.
- **NATIONAL TOURIST OFFICES:**
  Gibraltar Information Bureau
  710 The Madison Offices
  1155 15th Street NW
  Washington, DC 20005
  Tel: 202/452-1108; Fax: 202/872-8543
  Gibraltar Information Bureau
  Arundel Great Court
  179 The Strand
  London WC2R 1EH, England
  Tel: 0171 836 0777
- **AMERICAN EMBASSY:**
  24 Grosvenor Square
  London W1A 1AE, England
  Tel: 0171 499 9000

GIBRALTAR

(574 B1)

HISTORY

The Straits of Gibraltar link the Atlantic to the Mediterranean. To ancient seafarers, the 426-meter (1,400-foot) high rock of Jurassic limestone was one of the Pillars of Hercules, which marked the edge of the known world. In AD 711, the Moorish forces of Tarik ibn Ziyad landed here before embarking on their conquest of Spain. It became known as Jebel Tarik (Mountain of Tarik), later corrupted to Gibraltar.

The Moors maintained their stronghold until taken by the Spanish in 1462, It was ceded to the British in 1713 after the War of the Spanish Succession. Since then, this crown colony has withstood 14 seiges and served as a strategic naval base. In recent years Gibraltar's status has been disputed diplomatically by Britain and Spain. It is largely self-governed, and at present the population remains under British rule.

SPORTS AND RECREATION

Both the Mediterranean and the Atlantic shores offer good swimming. Other water sports include game fishing, yacht and boat charter, sailing, scuba diving and water-skiing. Land-based activities includes tennis and horseback riding.

GETTING AROUND

The frontier crossing from Spain is open 24 hours a day. There are daily scheduled flights from the U.K., and a daily ferry service to and from Tangier in Morocco.

Driving is on the right. Seat belts are not compulsory; a child should not sit in a front seat. Speed limits are 30 k.p.h. (18 m.p.h.) in town and 50 k.p.h. (31 m.p.h.) outside of town. Roads on the Upper Rock are narrow and winding. Alternatively, there are bus and taxi tours. Much of Gibraltar Town is pedestrianized, so it is advisable to park outside the city walls. Visiting motorists are required to pay fines for parking violations on the spot in Gibraltar pounds.

PLACES OF INTEREST

GIBRALTAR TOWN, set beneath the northwestern corner of the Rock, melds the blue-helmeted policemen and red mailboxes of Britain with Oriental bazaars and international restaurants. The town has been fortified over the centuries, and much of the old garrison still stands. Points of interest include the Casino; the Gibraltar Museum, with its anthropological, coin and stamp collections; and the busy harbor.

Gibraltar is one of the busiest cruise ports in the western Mediterranean and has three marinas. Main Street is a tax-free shopping area, and along with the usual duty-free goods, there are British and European chain stores. Nightlife ranges from international retaurants and nightclubs to the glamorous Casino. Accommodations range from bed-and-breakfast to international hotels. There are no campgrounds on the Rock.

ALAMEDA BOTANICAL GARDENS, at the south end of town off Europa Road, is a park with subtropical vegetation, scenic walks and fine view of the sea. Opened in 1816, the gardens contain a wide array of flowers, trees and shrubs, as well as an open-air theater.

APES' DEN, Queens Gate, halfway up the Rock, is the best spot for viewing the Barbary apes, the only wild monkeys found on the continent of Europe. Residents of the Rock for centuries, they are free to roam as they choose but tend to frequent the upper cliffs. The Den is one of their favorite spots. Legend has it that British rule will end when the apes are gone from the Rock.

EUROPA POINT, south of Europa Road, is the southernmost tip of Gibraltar. On a clear day the coast of Africa can be seen. The lighthouse here was opened in 1841 and stands 49 meters (160 feet) above the high watermark. Now fully automated, its light is visible from a distance of 27 kilometers (17 miles).

THE GALLERIES are northeast at the end of Queens Road. During the French and Spanish Great Siege of 1779–83, military miners dug these tunnels 115 meters (370 feet) into the Rock, where they mounted four cannons in small windows called notches. During World War II, the system of tunnels was expanded to form a 48-kilometer (30-mile) labyrinth. Many of the tunnels can be explored. Life-size models depict scenes during the Great Siege.

MOORISH BATH, under the Gibraltar Museum, is an outstanding example of Moroccan architecture. The 14th-century structure with its 16-sided vaulted roof incorporates hot and cold baths and a steam room.

ROCK OF GIBRALTAR is the crown colony's chief attraction. Views of Europe, Africa and the Mediterranean are the reward of a six-minute cable car ride to the summit. A large sundial can be seen below the north face. The fare includes the cable car round trip, a stop at the Apes' Den, and entry to the nature reserve and St. Michael's Cave. The ride begins at the boarding station in the Grand Parade at the southern end of Main Street.

ST. MICHAEL'S CAVE, is southeast of town on a side road off Queens Road. Not fully explored until 1936–38, this immense cavern is 250 meters (820 feet) above sea level. According to a local legend Gibraltar was once linked to Africa by a subterranean passage at this site. Concerts are frequently held in the upper hall, where colored lights illuminate spectacular stalagmites and stalactites. The cave's origins go back to the warm glacial period, some 250,000 years ago.

Birdwatchers should note that in spring and fall, Gibraltar becomes a busy staging post for hundreds of thousands of birds who are migrating between Europe and Africa.

SWITZERLAND

SWITZERLAND IS UNITED BY ITS DIVISIONS: ONE OF THE MOST PROSPEROUS ECONOMIES IN EUROPE HAS BEEN PRODUCED BY THIS NATION, DIVIDED FIRST OF ALL INTO FOUR DIFFERENT LANGUAGE GROUPS – GERMAN, FRENCH, ITALIAN AND ROMANSCH – AND SECONDLY INTO TWO RELIGIOUS GROUPS – PROTESTANT AND CATHOLIC. THERE IS LESS DIVERSITY IN THE SCENERY, HOWEVER, MOST OF THE COUNTRY BEING GIVEN TO THE VARIOUS ALPINE MOUNTAIN RANGES THAT DOMINATE THE SOUTHERN AND CENTRAL REGIONS. BETWEEN THE ALPS AND THE JURA LIES THE SWISS PLATEAU, WHERE MOST OF THE PEOPLE LIVE; IT RUNS BETWEEN TWO HUGE LAKES, LAKE CONSTANCE IN THE NORTHEAST, AND LAKE GENEVA IN THE SOUTHWEST.

Left THERE ARE FANTASTIC VIEWS TO BE HAD FROM THE PRETTY MOUNTAIN-TOP CHALETS IN THE BERNESE OBERLAND
Above THE ALPHORN IS A SURVIVING TRADITION IN APPENZELL

THINGS TO KNOW

- **AREA:** 41,287 square kilometers (15,941 square miles)
- **POPULATION:** 6,900,000
- **CAPITAL:** Bern
- **LANGUAGES:** French, German, Italian and Romansch
- **RELIGION:** Switzerland is essentially divided between Roman Catholics and Protestants. Other denominations are represented in the larger cities, however.
- **ECONOMY:** Processing industry; chief exports are machinery, chemicals and watches. Forests, waterpower, some farming (mainly dairy). Tourism (particularly skiing).
- **ELECTRICITY:** Standard current is 220-volts AC; 50-cycles – supplied from sockets designed for three-pin round plugs.
- **PASSPORT REQUIREMENTS:** A valid passport is required for U.S. citizens.
- **VISA REQUIREMENTS:** Not required provided visitors do not become employed at any time.
- **DUTY-FREE ITEMS:** 400 cigarettes or 100 cigars or 500 grams tobacco; 2 liters of wine and 1 liter of liquor; two still cameras, or one movie camera and one still camera; a reasonable amount of film for personal use only; one video camera and normal accessories. Half of these quantities are allowed for visitors entering from another European country, except for wines and spirits.
- **CURRENCY:** The unit of currency is the Swiss *franc*, divided into 100 *centimes*. Due to currency fluctuations, the exchange rate is subject to change. There are no import or export restrictions for Swiss or foreign currency.
- **BANK OPENING HOURS:** 8:15am or 8:30am–4:30pm Monday–Friday; exchange of currency daily until 10pm at large railroad stations and airports.
- **STORE OPENING HOURS:** 8am–noon and 2–6:30pm Monday–Friday (open during lunch in large cities); 8am–4 or 5pm Saturday; some close Monday mornings.

HISTORY

Today a land of peaceful prosperity, Switzerland has a history of invasion. In pre-Christian times, the Helvetians and other Celtic tribes crossed the Rhine River and established settlements along the lakes of this mountainous land. Inevitably, the Romans conquered, their era lasting 400 years. During the decline of the Roman Empire the Burgundians and Franks invaded; it was during the Frankish period that Christianity was introduced.

The Habsburgs entered the picture in 1273, when Rudolf of Habsburg became German Emperor. He soon reigned over the whole of central Europe and the

Alpine lands, but the Habsburg rule was an unpopular one, and the cities and cantons that make up present-day Switzerland began to yearn for freedom. When Rudolf died, the forest cantons of Uri, Unterwalden and Schwyz (which gave Switzerland its name) united and freed themselves from Habsburg domination, forming the nucleus of the Swiss Confederation; its independence was recognized in 1684, while other towns and villages were still struggling to free themselves. These years of bitter war and invasion by greedy neighbors left the Swiss with a strong sense of independence and a conviction that neutrality – which still prevails – was essential for their country's survival.

Switzerland remains ready to defend itself, however, with a citizen army comprising every able-bodied male – each of whom keeps his gun at home.

Switzerland is made up of a confederation of 26 cantons. National authority rests in a bicameral parliament and a federal council with seven members and a presidency which rotates between them for one-year terms. Each canton is, in fact, a sovereign state with its own government and control over its own internal affairs.

FOOD AND DRINK

As Switzerland is multicultural, each region has its own specialty. However,

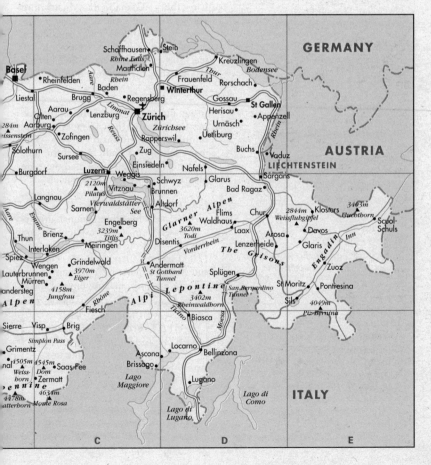

- **BEST BUYS:** Watches, clocks, chocolate, cheese, toys, music boxes, handkerchiefs, handicrafts, embroideries.
  Note: It is against U.S. customs regulations to bring liqueur-filled confections into the United States.
- **PUBLIC HOLIDAYS:** New Year's Day; January 2; Epiphany; Good Friday; Easter Monday; Ascension Day; Whitmonday; December 25–26. Some cantons may celebrate additional holidays such as May 1, Corpus Christi, All Saints' Day and August 1 (National Day), among others.
- **USEFUL TELEPHONE NUMBERS:**
  Police: 117
  Fire: 118
  Ambulance: 144
- **NATIONAL TOURIST OFFICES:**
  Swiss National Tourist Office
  608 Fifth Ave
  New York
  NY 10020
  Tel: 212/757-5944
  Swiss National Tourist Office
  222 North Fepulveda Building
  Suite 1570
  El Segundo
  Los Angeles
  CA 90245
  Tel: 310/335-5980
  Swiss National Tourist Office
  Swiss Centre
  Swiss Court
  London W1V
  Tel: 0171 734 1921
  Schweizerische Verkehrszentrale
  (Swiss National Tourist Office)
  Bellariastrasse 38
  CH-8017 Zürich
  Switzerland
  Tel: (01) 2881111
- **AMERICAN EMBASSY:**
  Jubiläumsstrasse 93
  CH-3005 Bern
  Switzerland
  Tel: (03) 3577234

râclette and *fondue* originated in Switzerland and must not be missed. For dessert, try *leckerli* (honey biscuits) or the famous Swiss chocolate.

Among the most popular wines are *Dôle*, *Nostrano* and *Maienfelder* (red); *Dézalay*, *Yvorne* and *Fendant* (white). The fruit brandies, *Schnapps*, are also very popular.

SPORTS AND RECREATION
Mountaineering and skiing head the list of sporting activities in Switzerland. Guides for mountain climbing trips can be engaged by the day, week or month; the mountaineering school at Rosenlaui, near Meiringen, will provide full information. Major ski resorts include Davos, Engelberg, Gstaad, St. Moritz and Verbier. Generally, the ski season continues from December through late-March, but at resorts above 1,524 meters (5,000 feet) this extends to mid-May. Skiing is also possible all year round at the high glacier resorts.

In summer, a network of efficiently waymarked footpaths attracts casual ramblers and mountain hikers. The many lakes offer endless opportunities for watersports of all kinds, and there are plenty of lidos and swimming pools.

GETTING AROUND
Switzerland's four international airports – at Basel, Bern, Genève (Geneva) and Zürich – link the country with around 110 foreign cities. Both Geneva and Zürich airports have stations on the railroad network, making onward travel

---

AUTOMOBILE CLUB
The Touring Club Suisse
(T.C.S.), rue Pierre Fatio 9, 1211 Genève, has offices in cities throughout Switzerland.
The symbol ▲ indicates the presence of a AAA-affiliated automobile club branch. Not all clubs offer full travel services to AAA members.

easy. A fly-rail system enables baggage to be checked in at overseas airports to a range of rail destinations within Switzerland (and vice-versa).

All Swiss trains are electric, reasonably fast, reliable, and connected to most parts of the country. Tunnels, rack and pinion railroads, and cable cars have overcome the obstacles to travel posed by some of Europe's highest mountains. Numerous concessions – particularly the Swiss Pass – minimize the cost of rail travel for the visitor.

The Swiss Pass is also valid on steamer services and alpine postbuses. Steamer services operate on the larger lakes, while the bright yellow postbuses carry both mail and passengers to areas inaccessible by rail. Public transportation in cities is well-developed, with trams as well as buses in the larger of them.

The road system in Switzerland is excellent, though mountain roads involve hairpin bends and postbuses demanding their right of way. The challenge of the Alpine passes has largely been removed, however, by the building of tunnels.

Motoring laws are much the same as for the rest of Europe. All occupants of cars must use seat belts, and children under 12 may not travel in the front seat. Speed limits are 50 k.p.h. (31 m.p.h.) in built-up areas, 80 k.p.h. (49 m.p.h.) out of town, and 120 k.p.h.(74 m.p.h.) on highways. To use the latter you must buy a *vignette* from a customs point or main post office. Motoring offenses are liable to on-the-spot fines.

ACCOMMODATIONS
Standards of lodging in Switzerland are among the highest in the world. The Swiss Hotel Association rates hotels from one to five stars, (five being the highest), and the Swiss National Tourist Office can provide a list of accommodations. In many areas there is also a choice of chalets, apartments and youth hostels.

Campers can take their pick of about 450 campgrounds, many in scenic areas near resorts or along major roads.

TIPPING
Restaurants, hotels and taxi fares all include a 15 percent gratuity in their bills, so extra tipping is discretionary.

LANGUAGE
Useful terms in all three main languages – German, French and Italian – can be found in the relevent country section.

PRINCIPAL TOURING AREAS

Note: For descriptions of attractions in **bold type**, see individual listings.

THE BERNESE OBERLAND AND CENTRAL SWITZERLAND
The Bernese Oberland, "aristocrat of Alpine scenery," contains nine valleys and several lakes. Here, you can bathe in a lake surrounded by fig trees and vineyards, then, within three hours, take to the ski slopes. The lakes at **Brienz** and **Thun** are popular both for rowing and swimming, and **Interlaken** is a good base for exploring the mountains.

Southeast of Interlaken is **Grindelwald**; at no other place in the Alps do the glaciers so closely approach the lush vegetation of the countryside. To the south rises the great wall of rock formed by the world-renowned trio of *Jungfrau, Eiger* and *Mönch* (Maiden, Ogre and Monk).

Northwest lies the ancient city of **Bern**, capital of the Swiss Federation. Bordering a lovely lake is bustling **Luzern** (Lucerne), a main excursion center for resorts such as **Engelberg** and Andermatt; boat trips also leave regularly for a number of nearby historic villages.

EASTERN SWITZERLAND
Bordering on Liechtenstein, Germany and Austria, this part of Switzerland consists of two distinct regions.

In the southeast is mountainous Graubünden (or Grisons), containing some of the highest valleys in the country and such world-famous resorts as **St. Moritz, Davos** and **Pontresina**. Also of interest are **Arosa**, with its lakes, and the capital city of **Chur**, surrounded by wooded mountains. Well-maintained roads wind through the breathtaking scenery of this part of Switzerland.

Northeastern Switzerland includes the canton of **Appenzell** – an area of rolling countryside famous both for its fruit and for the cows that wear large bells around their necks. From the 2,005-meter (6,578-foot) summit of the Säntis mountain you can enjoy one of the finest views in the country. The abbey town of **St. Gallen** is known for the delicate hand embroidery it produces. To the west is the ancient town of **Winterthur**, guarded by the castles that overlook it from surrounding hills.

SOUTHERN SWITZERLAND

With Ticino's almost Mediterranean climate and Italian-speaking people you could almost believe that you were in Italy, but this southernmost canton has been linked politically to Switzerland since the Middle Ages.

The Sottoceneri region is one of contrasts, varying from Lugano – a bustling city with a lake and beaches – and the charming villages of surrounding valleys. **Bellinzona**, capital of the canton, and the northern valley form a second area, while a third is composed of lakeside **Lorano** and its neighboring valleys. There is an excellent beach 4 kilometers (2½ miles) from Locarno, in Ascona.

SOUTHWEST SWITZERLAND

This region is divided into two distinct areas – the area around Lac Léman (Lake Geneva) to the west and the Valais and Upper Rhône River Valley to the east.

The beauty of Lake Geneva has often been celebrated in the arts. Paddle steamers shuttle across it, serving French and Swiss ports. Neighboring **Vevey** and **Montreux** have long been popular resorts, and villages surrounded by vineyards rise 305 meters (1,000 feet) from the lakeside. To the south is the Mont Blanc mountain range, extending into the heart of Europe.

The Valais region begins at the east end of Lake Geneva. The numerous valleys branching off the long, deep valley of the Rhine lead to some picturesque and spectacular scenery.

ZÜRICH AND THE NORTH

German-speaking **Zürich**, with its fine stores, luxury hotels and restaurants, is an industrial and cultural center, and the largest city in Switzerland. Gardens and villas extend from the center of the city to the summit of the encircling hill.

The verdant countryside of northern Switzerland has its own fascination, with many charming villages and small historic towns. The Rhine runs westward from Bodensee (Lake Constance) forming the border with Germany for much of its course and crashing over famous falls near the old town of **Schaffhausen**. **Basel**, the country's second-largest city, has a historic core as well as modern industries and commerce.

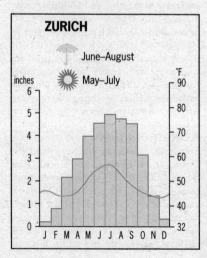

ZURICH

🌂 June–August

☀ May–July

PLACES OF INTEREST

★ HIGHLIGHTS ★	
Basel	(see p.614)
Bern	(see p.613)
Davos	(see p.615)
Genève	(see p.616)
Lausanne	(see p.619)
Luzern	(see p.620)
Montreux	(see p.621)
St. Moritz	(see p.623)
Zermatt	(see p.624)
Zürich	(see p.625)

▲ BERN (608 B2) ★
BERN *pop. 127,500*

Bern has been capital of the Swiss confederation since 1848. According to legend, this city on the banks of the Aare River received its name when Berthold V, Duke of Zähringen, told his followers that the city would be named after the first animal he killed. Thus the "Bear of Bern" became its trademark.

Turreted buildings, beautiful fountains and miles of arcaded sidewalks decorate the old town like illustrations in a fairy tale, while the figures in the Clock Tower re-enact the world's oldest horological play. Other highlights of Bern are the 15th-century town hall and the Gothic cathedral. Some of the finest viewpoints over the city and its surroundings are from such immaculately maintained parks as the Rosengarten (Rose Garden).

The opera and theater seasons are late September through June. Operas and ballets are presented at the Stadttheatre, and concerts at a number of other halls.

Bern is the principal departure point for trips to the Bernese Oberland; daily tours of varying duration are offered. The region's lakeside roads afford incomparable views, and other well-maintained roads lead upward to the funicular railroad stations.

BÄRENGRABEN, off Nydeggbrücke on the east bank of the Aare, is the city's bear pit. The inhabitants – who amuse visitors for the price of a carrot – have been an attraction since the late 15th century.

BERNISCHES HISTORISCHES MUSEUM (Bernese Historical Museum), housed in a mock-Gothic building, highlights the history of the city and canton of Bern.

BUNDESHAUS (Federal Palace) offers extensive views of the Bernese Alps from the terrace of its domed Florentine Renaissance-style building.

KUNSTMUSEUM (Fine Arts Museum) has one of the best collections of both Swiss and international painting. Paul Klee was a native of Bern, and there is an extensive collection of his works.

MÜNSTER (Cathedral of St. Vincent) is considered the most beautiful ecclesiastical building in Switzerland. Built between 1421 and 1571, it has notable stained-glass windows and a superbly carved main portal depicting the Last Judgement.

SCHWEIZERISCHES ALPINES MUSEUM (Swiss Alpine Museum) contains fascinating exhibits on the natural history of the Alps and the story of mountaineering.

ZEITGLOCKENTURM (Clock Tower) dates from the 12th century; it was rebuilt in stone after a fire in 1405, and its astrological clock and mechanical figure-play were added in 1530.

APPENZELL (609 D3)
APPENZELL INNER-RHODEN
pop. 5,000, elev. 780m. (2,559ft.)

Set in rich meadow countryside, the picturesque little capital of Appenzell retains many of its old customs. On the last Sunday of April, residents attend the Landsgemeinde – an open-air meeting at which citizens vote directly on the laws by which they are governed. Colorful processions to and from the mountains take place as farmers move

SWITZERLAND

their cattle onto Alpine pastures for eight to twelve weeks in the summer. The area's mountains are accessible by cable car and hiking trail.

Arosa (609 D2)
GRAUBÜNDEN *pop. 2,600, elev. 1,875m. (6,152ft.)*
Arosa is known world-wide as a winter sports resort, attracting thousands of enthusiasts to its ski school (one of the largest in the country), four practice slopes, ice hockey and skating rinks, toboggan runs and curling facilities.

Ascona (609 D1)
TICINO *pop. 5,000*
Ascona lies on a protected bay at the northern end of mainly Italian Lake Maggiore. The town began as a fishing village, but its mild climate slowly transformed it into a popular vacation spot. Narrow streets and alleys are lined with antique and arts-and-crafts shops.

▲ Baden (609 C3)
AARGAU *pop. 15,700*
Baden is Switzerland's oldest spa and health resort. Old Town is medieval, though much of it was rebuilt in the 18th century following an attack by an army from Bern. Dominated by the ruins of Stein Castle, the town is picturesquely sited on the Limmat River.

LANDVOGTEISCHLOSS (Bailiffs' Castle) dates from the 15th century. The museum in the keep displays arms, period furniture and local costumes; the upper floor gives fine views of the Old Town.

SCHWEIZER KINDERMUSEUM (Swiss Children's Museum), Oelrainstrasse 29, promotes and conducts research into children's culture. Exhibits portray the world of childhood over the past 200 years.

▲ Basel (609 B3) ★
BASEL-STADT *pop. 200,000*
As Switzerland's second-largest city, Basel has both economic and historic importance. Sprawling on both banks of a wide curve of the Rhine, it is the meeting place of three countries – Switzerland, France and Germany. The Vosges and Jura mountains in France and the Black Forest in Germany are nearby.

Basel was the home of the German painter Hans Holbein the Younger and the Dutch humanist Erasmus (who paved the way for the Reformation). Its university, built in 1460, is the oldest in Switzerland. Proud of its history, Basel is also a progressive city: it is a large inland port; a center of international banking; and the site of many highly developed pharmaceutical and chemical industries.

The lively three-day Fasnacht Carnival in February or March, and the Swiss Industries Fair in the spring, are of special interest. So too is the fall fair, celebrating the city's accomplishments.

HISTORISCHES MUSEUM (History Museum), Barfüsserplatz, is housed in a 14th-century Franciscan church. Its collection of religious and art pieces tell the story of Basel and its surroundings from the Middle Ages onwards.

KUNSTMUSEUM (Fine Arts Museum), St. Albangraben 16, is the city's pride and joy. One of Europe's great art galleries, it has modern art by Picasso, Braque, Léger and Arp as well as 15th- and 16th-century pieces by Konrad Witz, Nikolaus Manuel and the Holbeins.

MÜNSTER (Cathedral), Münsterplatz, was erected in the 11th century, destroyed in the 14th and 15th centuries, and completely restored in the 19th century; with twin towers and patterned roof tiles, it is one of the city's great landmarks.

RATHAUS (Town Hall), a red sandstone 16th-century town hall dominating the market square, is enhanced by frescoes and carvings on its walls and ceilings.

ZOOLOGISCHER GARTEN (Zoo), is perhaps the finest in the country, set in a spacious park near the city center. The children's zoo is delightful.

▲ BELLINZONA (609 D1)

TICINO *pop. 17,300*

Bellinzona, capital of the Ticino canton, is the gateway to Italian Switzerland, and consequently it has a distinct Italian atmosphere. Its strategic importance is emphasized by the three castles that guard it. The Castello Grande, Montebello and di Sasso Corbaro are splendid examples of fortification design; the last two contain museums.

▲ BIEL-BIENNE (608 B3)

BERN *pop. 51,000*

Known for its watchmaking, Biel-Bienne is an important industrial and commercial center. The Old Quarter still bears the stamp of its historic past with many fine old buildings and medieval fountains.

BRIENZ (609 C2)

BERN *pop. 3,000*

On the northern shore of Lake Brienz, this quaint village with wooden houses and narrow alleyways is well-known for its wood carving. It lies at the foot of the Brienzer Rothorn, which rises to 2,350 meters (7,710 feet), and has a promenade running alongside the lake.

BALLENBERG (Swiss Open Air Museum) is a 63-hectare (155-acre) living-history museum with 70 original farmhouses dating from the 16th century. All the buildings were dismantled and moved from various parts of the country for re-erection here. Furnished in period, they form the background to arts and crafts demonstrations by costumed workers.

BRIENZER ROTHORN BAHN is a rack railroad, which climbs almost to the top of the Brienzer Rothorn and is still worked by steam engines built as long ago as the 1890s. It is one of the most spectacular rides in the Swiss Alps.

▲ LA CHAUX-DE-FONDS (608 B3)

NEUCHÂTEL *pop. 37,375, elev. 992m. (3,255ft.)*

La Chaux-de-Fonds is the center of the country's watchmaking industry; its underground Horological Museum boasts more than 3,000 exhibits from all over the world. Famous car designer Louis Chevrolet (1870 to 1941) was born here.

▲ CHUR (609 D2)

GRAUBÜNDEN *pop. 30,000*

As the guardian of Alpine routes since 15 BC, Chur is probably the country's oldest settlement. Although mountains surround this ancient city, there are direct connections to most of the ski resorts in the region.

A train excursion running southeast from Chur, to the Engadine Valley of the Rhaetian Alps, passes the picturesque village of Filisur – near to which are Greifenstein Castle and "La Chanzla," a huge rock with a 10-meter (33-foot) painting of the Devil.

KUNSTMUSEUM (Fine Arts Museum) Postplatz, contains pictures by artists from the canton of Graubünden – of whom there are many.

RHÄTISCHES MUSEUM is devoted to the art and folklore of Graubünden, with paintings and sculptures from the 18th century to the present, as well as a noteworthy collection of prehistoric artifacts.

CRANS MONTANA (608 B1)

VALAIS *pop. 2,400, elev. 1,470m. (4,823ft.)*

Situated above the Rhône valley, with majestic views of the Alps from Mont Blanc to the Matterhorn, Crans Montana offers year-round skiing on the Plaine Morte glacier. The town boasts one of the finest golf courses in Europe and plays host to many tournaments.

DAVOS (609 E2) ★

GRAUBÜNDEN *pop. 11,200, elev. 1,560m. (5,118ft.)*

The countryside surrounding Davos, one of the highest towns in Europe, is ideal for both downhill and cross-country skiing. Once famous as spas specialising in the treatment of tuberculosis, Davos-Dorf and Davos-Platz are now internationally renowned as winter sports resorts, boasting Europe's largest ice-skating rink and two ski schools; the Parsennbahn funicular railroad takes skiers up to Weissfluhjoch, the departure point for several runs. The town is also a focal point of scientific research and a center of the arts.

KIRCHNER MUSEUM contains the world's largest collection of the works of German expressionist painter Ernst Ludwig Kirchner.

▲ DELÉMONT (608 B3)
JURA *pop. 12,000*
Delémont, the capital of the Jura canton, is a renowned watchmaking center. Despite its modern appearance, the town retains some of its 16th-century character, especially around the town hall and the Church of St. Marcellus.

EINSIEDELN (609 D3)
SCHWYZ *pop. 11,700, elev. 910m. (2,986ft.)*
Einsiedeln is the site of Switzerland's most famous monastery, one of Europe's most important places of pilgrimage. Inside the Holy Chapel, built over the site of the hut where a saintly hermit called Meinrad lived in the 9th century, is a Black Madonna; this tiny wooden statuette holding the Infant Christ is an object of great veneration.

ENGELBERG (609 C2)
OBWALDEN *pop. 3,300, elev. 1,050m. (3,445ft.)*
This vacation resort at the foot of Mount Titlis is especially popular for winter sports; skiing can be enjoyed December through June, thanks to the Titlis glacier. In summer there are regularly scheduled events of music, theater and colorful folk entertainment. The 12th-century Benedictine Abbey has one of the largest pipe organs in Switzerland.

FLIMS WALDHAUS (609 D2)
GRAUBÜNDEN *pop. 2,300, elev. 1,140m. (3,740ft.)*
This sheltered, terraced resort of Flims

offers year-round attractions for tourists. Winter sports like skiing, ice-skating, curling and tobogganing are replaced in the summer by mountaineering, hiking through pine woods, horseback riding, tennis, and swimming in Lake Cauma, which is heated by underground hot water springs.

▲ FRIBOURG (608 B2)
FRIBOURG *pop. 33,000*
The capital of its French and English speaking canton, this historic city on the Saane River is the home of Switzerland's only bilingual Catholic university. The old town has a graceful medieval atmosphere, while the modern part bustles with fine homes and schools. Chocolate is made here.

CATHÉDRALE ST.-NICOLAS, begun in 1283, took five centuries to complete. Of note are the tower, the frescoed tympanum, a monumental pipe organ and fine sculptures.

MUSÉE D'ART ET D'HISTOIRE (Museum of Art History), rue de Morat 12, displays examples of Fribourg's art and artistic crafts from the Middle Ages to the latter part of the 18th century. Late Gothic sculptures and paintings, as well as works by contemporary artist Jean Tingueley, are also on show.

▲ GENÈVE (608 A1) ★
GENÈVE *pop. 173,000*
Genève (Geneva) has all the advantages of a big city as well as a magnificent lakeside and mountain setting. Whether seen from the carillon tower in the cathedral or from the deck of a steamer as it crosses Lac Léman (Lake Geneva), it is equally beautiful.

Geneva has earned its place in world history through the efforts of great reformers and thinkers. They include Calvin (1509–64), who made the city the "Protestant Rome," Jean-Jacques Rousseau (1712–78), who prepared the way for the French Revolution, and Henri Dunant (1828–1910), who persuaded governments to sign the Geneva Convention, thereby limiting the effects of war and leading to the foundation of the International Red Cross, whose headquarters are still in Geneva.

The modern city faces the lake, while the old town, the Vieille Ville, huddles around the cathedral, embracing a maze of antique shops and bistros. In summer, Geneva assumes an international atmosphere as visitors stroll along the quays and spend time in the cafés. Much of the activity centers on the Quai du Mont-Blanc, the departure point for the paddle steamers that go across the lake.

In August, the city holds its four-day Fête de Genève, complete with fireworks, singing, street dancing and parades. The Escalade, in mid-December, involves horse riders in period costumes, country markets, folk music and parades.

Year-round concert schedules include the Orchestre de la Suisse Romande at the Victoria Hall during winter, and opera at the Grand-Théâtre, near the Conservatoire, from October to May.

Geneva is the European headquarters of the United Nations and the international headquarters of the World Health Organization.

CATHÉDRALE DE ST.-PIERRE (617 B2), rue St.-Pierre, dates from the 12th century and was partly rebuilt in the 15th century. John Calvin's Chair commemorates the celebrated theologian, who lived in Geneva during the mid-16th century.

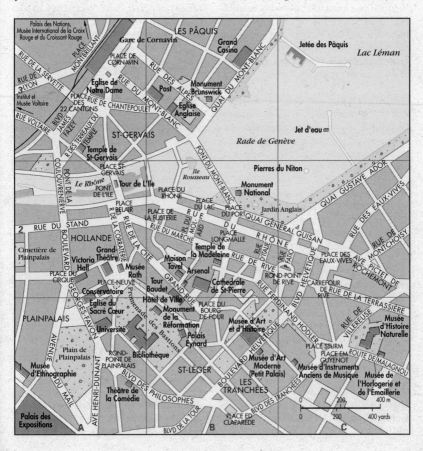

Of particular note are the flamboyant Chapel of the Maccabees, with its fine stained glass, and the North Tower, which offers a view of the Alps and Lake Geneva.

HÔTEL DE VILLE (Town Hall) (617 B1), Grande-Rue. In 1864, the Geneva Convention, founding the International Red Cross, was signed in what is now the Alabama Room (named after the 1871 arbitration between America and Britain).

JET D'EAU (617 C3), During the summer months, this towering spray of water – 145 meters (476 feet) high – provides a landmark that can be seen for miles.

MAISON TAVEL (617 B2), rue du Puits St. Pierre 6, is a museum housed in a building dating from the 12th century and illustrating the history of the city from the 14th to 19th century. In the attic, visitors can see a relief map that represents Geneva during the 1850s.

MUSÉE D'ART ET D'HISTOIRE (Museum of Art and History) (617 B1), rue Charles-Galland 2, is one of Switzerland's great museums, an immense building housing coins, paintings, sculpture, clocks and watches, and archaeological exhibits.

MUSÉE DE L'HORLOGERIE ET DE L'ÉMAIL-LERIE (Watch and Clock Museum) (617 C1), route de Malagnou 15, exhibits clocks, watches, and music boxes dating from the 16th century onwards.

MUSÉE D'HISTOIRE NATURELLE (Natural History Museum) (617 C1), route de Malagnou 1, is one of the most important in Europe. Representations of dinosaurs in their natural habitats are particularly fascinating, and the science library has over 150,000 reference documents.

MUSÉE D'INSTRUMENTS ANCIENS DE MUSIQUE (Museum of Ancient Musical Instruments) (617 C1), rue Francois Lefort 23, displays a wide range of 16th- to 19th-century European instruments.

GRINDELWALD (609 C2)
BERN *pop. 4,000, elev. 1,057m. (3,468ft.)*
Grindelwald, spread out over a sunny plateau, is one of the most popular year-round resorts in Switzerland. To the south are some of the great peaks of the Bernese Oberland, the Jungfrau and the Eiger, and the Grindelwald Glacier reaches almost to the village. All the popular winter sports facilities are available from December to March and the town also has an excellent climbing and mountaineering school.

GRUYÈRES (608 B2)
FRIBOURG *pop. 1,400, elev. 830m. (2,723ft.)*
Despite its seemingly precarious location, Gruyères lies safe behind its medieval ramparts. A 12th-century castle dominates this town, which owes its international reputation to the cheese that bears its name.

SWISS CHEESE
Swiss cheese is famous, its flavor enhanced by the flower-rich pastures grazed by the country's cows. More than one hundred varieties are produced, though about three-quarters of the nation's appetite for cheese is satisfied by four big names – Gruyère, Emmenthal, Tilsit and Appenzeller.

GSTAAD (608 B2)
BERN *pop. 2,000, elev. 1,056m. (3,465ft.)*
Forests, mountains and glaciers surround fashionable Gstaad, which boasts 16th-century houses in the old part of town. As one of the leading winter and summer resorts in Switzerland, it has many community sports facilities; for those interested in viewing Alpine scenery, gondola rides are available in summer.

INTERLAKEN (609 C2)
BERN *pop. 5,100*
A Swiss health and pleasure resort, Interlaken combines the attraction of an international vacation spot with the

charm of a rustic village. The town lies between the lakes of Thun and Brienz, with a famous view of the Jungfrau rising at the end of the valley.

Interlaken was founded in 1133 by Augustinian monks and evolved into a popular resort during the 17th century. Essentially an excursion centre and the gateway to the Bernese Oberland, it also provides an important rail connection to the Jungfraujohn – Europe's highest railroad station at 3,453 meters (11,329 feet).

THE SWISS ARMY

Though every able-bodied Swiss male is still a citizen soldier, and the army, once mobilized, is one of the largest in Europe, the forces no longer enjoy the prestige they earned while manning the frontiers during the long years of World War II, effectively deterring any attack the Axis powers might have been tempted to make.
The result of a recent referendum showed that the majority of young adults were in favor of abolishing the army altogether.

KANDERSTEG (609 B2)
BERN *pop. 1,100, elev. 1,200m. (3,937ft.)*
Surrounded by the spectacular scenery of the Bernese Oberland, the old village of Kandersteg stands among the meadows of the valley floor. One of the finest walks in Switzerland leads along an ancient pack-horse route to the Gemmi Pass. A chairlift takes visitors most of the way up to the Oeschinensee, a beautiful small lake set amongst the rock wall of the Oberland.

▲ LAUSANNE (608 A2) ★
VAUD *pop. 116,000*
Lausanne, the capital of the French-speaking canton of Vaud, has many distinctions. Built on several hills, the town rises nearly 244 meters (800 feet) and is the second-largest city on Lake

Geneva. The home of the Swiss High Courts of Justice, the site of a great university and thriving cultural center, its exuberance has attracted foreigners since the 18th century.

Lausanne's concert and theater season runs from September to April. Plays in French are presented at Le Théâtre Municipal, where the International Festival of Lausanne takes place in May and June. Opera, ballet, concerts, and performances by guest artists are held at the Théâtre du Beaulieu.

As well as hosting many scientific congresses and the National Autumn Agricultural, Industrial and Trade Fair, the city is also the headquarters of the International Olympic Committee.

CATHÉDRALE (Cathedral of Notre Dame) is one of the finest Gothic churches in Switzerland. Its many noteworthy features include an elaborately carved south door, 13th-century stalls and a rose window. It is one of the few places in the world that still keeps a night watch, a custodian calling out the hours throughout the night.

MUSÉE DE L'ÉLYSÉE (Élysée Museum), avenue de l'Élysée 18, an 18th-century mansion, has four floors of exhibits dedicated to the history of photography.

MUSÉE OLYMPIQUE (Olympic Museum) chronicles the history of the modern Olympic Games using photographs, medals, flags and other memorabilia. The International Olympic Committee was founded in Lausanne in 1915.

PALAIS DE RUMINE, close to the cathedral, houses Lausanne University as well as several museums that deal with the fine arts, natural history and botany.

LAUTERBRUNNEN (609 C2)
BERN *pop. 3,400, elev. 797m. (2,615ft.)*
A favorite center for mountain climbing, Lauterbrunnen is also a busy tourist center known for its spectacular waterfalls and mountain torrents. It is the starting

point of the railroad to the Jungfrau, where the highest station in Europe commands one of the most magnificent views in the world. Nearby, the Trümmelbach Falls descend in five cascades through a narrow gorge below the Jungfrau, and Staubbach Falls drop nearly 305 meters (1,000 feet).

LENZBURG (609 C3)
AARGAU pop. 13,800

The small industrial town of Lenzburg lies on the Aare River in a region that is peppered with castles. Nearby are the strongholds of Hallwil and Lenzburg, both dating from the 11th century.

▲ LOCARNO (609 D1)
TICINO pop. 14,100

Locarno, on the north shore of Lake Maggiore, has a mild climate and rich vegetation. Immortalized in Ernest Hemingway's novel, *A Farewell to Arms*, it is especially festive during the International Film Festival in August. Lake trips can be made to Ascona, Brissago, and (across the Italian border) Stresa and the Borromean isles.

CASTELLO VISCONTI, Piazza Castello, is a medieval castle that features Roman relics as well as temporary exhibits. The archaeological museum is of interest.

SAN VITTORE, Via della Collegiata, one of several fascinating churches in Locarno, is a fine example of 12th-century Romanesque architecture.

▲ LUGANO (609 D1)
TICINO pop. 29,000

Lugano, the largest town in the canton of Ticino, is on the shore of Lake Lugano; the hotels and villas beyond give it an international air, but the old town is thoroughly Italian in character. A March to October bill of concerts includes free jazz festivals in July and late August, and there is a huge fireworks display on the lake towards the end of July. The Festival of the Grape Harvest, with folk music performances, is held from late September to early October.

Excursions can be made to the 925 meter-high (3,035 feet) Monte Bré and Monte San Salvatore, 911 meters (2,990 feet). A regular steamer service connects many places on Lake Lugano.

CHIESA DE SANTA MARIA DEGLI ANGIOLI, a former convent constructed in 1499, has frescoes by Bernardino Luini (including the *Crucifixion*).

LA VILLA FAVORITA is a stately 17th-century mansion housing the Thyssen Collection, one of the finest private collections in Europe.

▲ LUZERN (609 C3) ★
LUZERN pop. 60,000

Luzern (Lucerne), the capital of its canton, is considered one of the most beautiful cities in the country. Located on the shores of Lake Luzern, its medieval heritage is evident in the 14th-century city walls and watchtowers, the fine old churches and houses, and above all, in the unusual covered bridges that span the Reuss.

In 1992, Lucerne suffered a great loss, when the 14th-century Kapellbrücke, or Chapel Bridge, was destroyed by fire. Built in 1333, it was Europe's oldest covered bridge and connected the two parts of the Old Town. It has subsequently been fully restored.

An International Music Festival takes place here from August to September (during which time it is essential to have booked rooms in advance). Opera is presented from September to April in the Stadttheater, which also offers plays and comedies in German. An open-air market lines both river banks on Tuesdays and Saturdays.

The classic excursion from Lucerne is to Mount Pilatus, a 2,120-meter (7,000-foot) pyramidal crag to which legend says Pontius Pilate was wafted by the Devil after the Crucifixion. It is reached by the world's steepest cogwheel mountain railroad from Alpnachstad, but you will be rewarded by a fine view.

SWITZERLAND

HISTORISCHES MUSEUM (History Museum), Pfistergasse 24, is housed in a 16th-century arsenal. Exhibits include antique armor, uniforms, costumes, coins and the medieval Gothic fountain that originally stood in the wine market.

MUSEGGMAUER, the largest complex of medieval fortifications remaining in Switzerland, consists of nine towers and a substantial section of the city wall. Part of the wall and the Schirmer, Mannli and Zyt towers are open to the public from May through October.

VERKEHRSHAUS (Transport Museum) is one of the largest, most modern and most fascinating transportation museums in Europe. Exhibits include automobiles, airplanes, ships, locomotives, space vehicles and a planetarium.

MEIRINGEN (609 C2)
BERN *pop. 2,800*
The principal town of the Hasli Valley and a popular Alpine resort, Meiningen is ideally situated for touring the eastern parts of the Bernese Oberland.

AARE GORGE is the deep, narrow gorge through which the Aare River passes; a specially constructed footpath traces this astonishing phenomenon.

MONTREUX (608 B2) ★
VAUD *pop. 20,400*
Set at the east end of Lake Geneva, the cosmopolitan town of Montreux is a year-round health and pleasure resort (though at its liveliest during the summer). Famous for its superb location, it also enjoys a mild climate – protected as it is from the north by wooded and vine-clad slopes. The high points of its extensive program of concerts, plays and variety shows are the Montreux Jazz Festival (July) and the Music Festival (September).

The 2,042-meter (6,699-foot) Rochers-de-Naye offers a great view of the Alps and Lake Geneva.

CHÂTEAU DE CHILLON is an imposing 13th-century fortress and former prison. Built on a jagged rock rising out of the lake, the castle was immortalized by Lord Byron in *The Prisoner of Chillon*. It is one of the best-preserved and most popular medieval castles in Europe.

MORGES (608 A2)
VAUD *pop. 13,000*
Morges, an elegant little harbor town on Lake Geneva, was once one of the lake's most important commercial ports. Located at the center of the wine-growing district of La Côte it holds a tulip festival from April to May.

MUSÉE MILITAIRE (Military Museum) is housed in the huge, four-towered castle. It contains collections of uniforms, weapons, flags and lead soldiers.

MÜRREN (609 C2)
BERN *pop. 350, elev. 1,096m. (3,596ft.)*
The highest village of the Bernese Oberland, Mürren is perched on a high rocky shelf overlooking the Lauterbrunnen Valley; it can only be reached by mountain railroad from Lauterbrunnen and by cable car from Stechelberg. Another cable car takes visitors to the revolving restaurant at the summit of the Schilthorn, some 3,048 meters (10,000 feet) high.

MURTEN (608 B2)
FRIBOURG *pop. 4,700*
Murten, on the eastern shore of the Murtensee, has retained its medieval ramparts; these boast 12 fortified towers, two main gates, and one of Switzerland's oldest clocks. From the tops of the walls you can look out over the town's rooftops to the lake below.

▲ NEUCHÂTEL (608 B2)
NEUCHÂTEL *pop. 32,000*
Capital city of the canton of the same name, Neuchâtel spreads for 5 kilometers (3 miles) along the shore of its lake at the foot of Chaumont. Set among vineyards, this picturesque town is also

SWITZERLAND

noted for banking, watchmaking, and the Institute for Horological Research.

MUSÉE CANTONAL D'ARCHÉOLOGIE (Canton Museum of Archaeology) has many exhibits found in local caves; these date back some 50,000 years.

MUSÉE D'ART ET D'HISTOIRE (Art and History Museum) contains a large collection of works by French Impressionist painters and a good selection of Swiss art. There are also displays of pottery, clocks, coins and automated figures.

NYON (608 A2)
VAUD *pop. 15,400*
The ancient port of Nyon dominates a hillside overlooking Lake Geneva. The old town has remnants of medieval buildings, gardens and walks.

PONTRESINA (609 E2)
GRAUBÜNDEN *pop. 2,000, elev. 1,775m. (5,823ft.)*
One of the great mountain centers of the Alps and a much-frequented year-round resort, Pontresina is a starting point for glacier climbs and walking excursions to the Bernina group and the upper Engadine. As well as intense sunshine and a healthy climate the village offers innumerable opportunities for skiing tours in the surrounding mountains.

▲ RAPPERSWIL (609 D3)
ST. GALLEN *pop. 7,000*
Rapperswil is built on a little peninsula jutting into Zürichsee (Lake Zürich). It has charming streets and a massive 13th-century castle with a museum devoted to Polish exiles in Switzerland – a reminder of the years when the town was virtually the capital of a Poland that had been absorbed by Russia, Prussia and Austria.

▲ ST. GALLEN (609 D3)
ST. GALLEN *pop. 72,000*
St. Gallen originated as a Benedictine monastery, founded in 612 by the Irish hermit monk Gallus. A natural gateway

HIGH-ALTITUDE HEALTH
Temples throbbing, gasping for breath and nauseated, you barely notice the sparkling snow or the spectacular view below.
You might be suffering from Acute Mountain Sickness (A.M.S.). Usually striking at around 2,500 meters (8,002 feet), A.M.S. is your body's way of coping with the reduced oxygen of high altitudes.
Among the symptoms are headaches, shortness of breath, loss of appetite, insomnia and lethargy. Some people complain of temporary weight gain or swelling of the face, hands and feet.
If your A.M.S. is severe, stop ascending; you will recover in a few days. A quick descent will end the suffering immediately.
You can reduce the impact of high altitude by being in top condition. If you smoke or suffer from heart or lung ailments, consult your physician. Alcohol and certain drugs will intensify the symptoms. A gradual ascent with a few days' acclimatization is best, if you have time. On the way up, eat light, nutritious meals and drink lots of water. A spicy, high-carbohydrate diet may ease the effects of low oxygen and encourage you to drink more. But beware of those crystal-clear mountain streams where parasites might lurk. Boil such water for at least 10 minutes.
Other high-altitude problems are sunburn and hypothermia; dress in layers to protect yourself from the intense sun and fluctuations in temperature.
Finally, after you unwind in the sauna or whirlpool bath at your hotel, remember to stand up carefully, for the heat relaxes your blood vessels and lowers your blood pressure.

to Switzerland from Germany or Austria, the town is now a main industrial center known for its 600-year textile industry.

INDUSTRIE UND GEWERBEMUSEUM (Textile Museum), Vadianstrasse 2, is renowned for its needlework collection, one of the most complete in Europe; the lacework and embroidery exhibit spans a total of five centuries.

STIFTSBIBLIOTHEK (Abbey Library) contains more than 100,000 books and manuscripts dating from the Middle Ages. The superb rococo rooms have delicate woodwork and painted ceilings.

ST.-MAURICE (608 B1)
VALAIS *pop. 3,500*

The ancient town of St.-Maurice stands among mountains on the west bank of the Rhône, its restored 6th-century abbey church is one of the oldest in Switzerland. The treasury is one of Europe's richest, with many precious objects dating from the earliest days of Christianity.

ST. MORITZ (609 E2) ★
GRAUBÜNDEN *pop. 5,100, elev. 1,856m. (6,089ft.)*

One of the most acclaimed resorts in Europe, the mineral spa of St. Moritz stands ringed by high mountains in the upper Engadine Valley, on the shores of Lake St. Moritz. Winter sports include bobsledding on the Cresta Run, ski jumping, curling and skating, and a comprehensive range of summer recreation facilities is also available. The town has an excellent museum devoted to the life of the region – among the country's most fascinating, with villages unrivaled for their wonderful traditional architecture.

▲ SCHAFFHAUSEN (609 C3)
SCHAFFHAUSEN *pop. 34,000*

Capital of the northernmost canton of Switzerland, the idyllic medieval town of Schaffhausen stands on the Rhine River. Frescoed houses line the winding streets of some of its older sections; Ritter House, with frescoes by Tobias Stimmer, and Munot, a massive 16th-century fortress are particularly noteworthy.

At nearby Neuhausen, the mighty 152-meter (500-foot) wide Rhine River plunges over its 23-meter (75-foot) high falls, the most powerful in Europe.

THE ROMANSCH LANGUAGE

About 40,000 Swiss, nearly all of them in the canton of Graubünden, speak Romansch as their first language. Romansch is a direct descendant of the Latin brought to these Alpine valleys by Roman legions 2,000 years ago, and although superficially similar to Italian, it is a quite distinct language in its own right. Its survival is all the more remarkable because of its division into many, very different, dialects.

▲ SCHWYZ (609 C2)
SCHWYZ *pop. 13,600*

As a founding member, Schwyz had the honour of giving both its name and flag to the Swiss Confederation. Today, this quiet little town is home to the Bundesbriefmuseum (Federal Charters Museum), which holds the Oath of Eternal Alliance (the Swiss declaration of independence) along with paintings and other records of the period.

▲ SION (608 B1)
VALAIS *pop. 26,000*

Flanked by two vast rocks – the Tourbillon and Valère – Sion presents a striking appearance. The Tourbillon is crowned by castle ruins, while the fortified church on the Valère, which houses the world's oldest working pipe organ, is one of Switzerland's finest sights.

The capital of the Valais canton has many fine medieval buildings; the orange-colored town hall, dating from the 17th century, is particularly striking. Archaeological excavations have shown that Neolithic people lived in this area 5,000 years ago.

SWITZERLAND

▲ SOLOTHURN (609 B3)
SOLOTHURN *pop. 15,300*
Located at the foot of the Jura Mountains, on the banks of the Aare River, Solothurn is the site of one of the oldest Roman settlements north of the Alps.

Old Town has some of the finest baroque buildings in Switzerland, including the Jesuitenkirche (Jesuit Church) and St. Urtsenkathedrale (St. Ursus Cathedral). Parts of the town's fortifications are still intact, including the Krummturm (Twisted Tower). Among Solothurn's several museums is the Naturmuseum (Natural History Museum), great for children, the Kunstmuseum (Fine Art Museum), with good Swiss paintings of various periods, and the Zeughaus (Arsenal), with a huge collection of weapons.

SPIEZ (609 B2)
BERN *pop. 11,300*
Attractively located on the shores of Lake Thun, this resort has preserved much of its medieval charm.

Reached by a chair lift, nearby Weissenstein, at 1,275 meters (4,183 feet), offers a panoramic view of Switzerland, extending from the Säntis in the east to Mont Blanc in the west.

THUN (609 B2)
BERN *pop. 39,000*
One of the most enchanting old towns in Switzerland, Thun overlooks Lake Thun and has a fine view of 3,610-meter (11,845-foot) Blümlisalp and other summits of the Bernese Oberland.

THUN CASTLE is reached by way of an unusual covered staircase. Tapestries are on display in a museum in one of the castle's four round towers.

VERBIER (608 B1)
VALAIS *pop. 2,100, elev. 1,524m. (5,000ft.)*
First used by skiers in 1925, Verbier is a fashionable resort on the high Verbier Plateau. Positioned in the heart of one of the world's largest skiing areas (known as the Four Valleys), it boasts excellent ski runs and facilities. Summer activities include swimming, paragliding, hanggliding, mountain-bicycling and golf.

VEVEY (608 B2)
VAUD *pop. 15,600*
Vevey is a "Swiss Riviera" resort with more than 8 kilometers (5 miles) of promenades along the shore of Lake Geneva. It is at the center of the splendid terraced vineyards of the lake's north shore, and every 25 years the town is the scene of what is perhaps the most spectacular of European folk festivals – the *Fête des Vignerons* (Winegrowers' Festival).

Vevey's other mainstay is chocolate, and the Nestlé corporation has its headquarters here.

WENGEN (609 C2)
BERN *pop. 1,000, elev. 1,274m. (4,180ft.)*
On a sheltered terrace at the foot of the Jungfrau, Wengen is superbly positioned as one of the most elegant resorts on the Bernese Oberland. Private cars are not permitted, but Wengen is nevertheless one of the most accessible places in the Alps, linked by mountain railroad to Lauterbrunnen (via the Kleine Scheidegg) as well as to Jungfraujoch. It is also at the center of a magnificent network of waymarked footpaths.

▲ WINTERTHUR (609 D3)
ZÜRICH *pop. 87,600*
Winterthur was founded in the 11th century by the counts of Kyburg, who granted it a charter with special privileges. The Reinhart Gallery has a superb collection of Swiss and European art.

SCHLOSS KYBURG Kyburg Castle, 6 kilometers (4 miles) south, passed from the counts of Kyburg to the Habsburgs. Displays in the 10th-century castle highlight antique furniture and arms.

ZERMATT (609 C1) ★
VALAIS *pop. 5,500, elev. 1,620m. (5,315ft.)*
Zermatt, known as a mountaineering center, gained recognition during the

period of heroic attempts to conquer the 4,477-meter (14,690-foot) Matterhorn. This pyramidal mountain mass on the Swiss-Italian border forms an incomparable backdrop to the village.

ALPINE MUSEUM contains equipment and documents relating to the first successful ascent of the Matterhorn in 1865. A scale model of the massive mountain and reconstructions of old Zermatt add to an understanding of the town.

GORNERGRAT RACK-RAILWAY, the highest open-air railroad in Europe, provides a magnificent view of the Matterhorn and its glistening glaciers.

▲ ZUG (609 C3)
ZUG *pop. 22,700*

A picturesque old town superbly set on the lake of the same name, this little cantonal capital with a distinctly medieval flavor retains its early defense towers.

▲ ZÜRICH (609 C3) ★
ZÜRICH *pop. 344,000*

Switzerland's largest city is a world industrial leader whose air of prosperity blends with natural beauty and historical interest. Gardens slope down to the Zürichsee (Lake Zürich), mingling green with blue and setting off the white-capped mountains.

The University of Zürich, where Albert Einstein studied, has a zoological museum; Carl Jung taught at the Polytechnic Institute.

During the International June Festival Weeks, the city echoes with orchestral music, opera, ballet, and drama. For full year-round schedules of opera, concerts, theater and ballet, see the *Zürich Weekly Bulletin*.

Most stores radiate from the busy, centrally located Bahnhofstrasse, one of Europe's foremost avenues for luxury shopping. Fine jewelry, Swiss watches, high-fashion clothing and other luxury items abound in the exclusive stores.

Excursions can be made to the Zürichberg (686 meters /2,250 feet), or to the Uetliberg (873 meters /2,865 feet), with their magnificent views and picnic grounds. Of the steamer excursions on Lake Zurich, the four-hour trip to Rapperswil is one of the best.

GROSSMÜNSTER, has twin Romanesque towers that dominate the Zürich landscape; the south tower is surmounted by an enormous statue of the Emperor Charlemagne.

KUNSTHAUS (Fine Arts Museum), Heimplatz 1, has a fine collection of Swiss, French and German paintings from the 13th century to the present, as well as the largest collection of Edward Munch paintings outside Scandinavia.

LINDENHOF, above the Limmat River, is a favorite walking destination and provides a view of Zürich's old quarter. The hill once supported a Roman settlement.

ST. PETERSKIRCHE, the parish church of Zürich, has a massive late Gothic steeple surmounted by Europe's largest clockface, measuring 9 meters (30 feet).

SCHWEIZERISCHES LANDESMUSEUM (Swiss National Museum), facing the railroad station, houses an extraordinarily rich collection of artifacts illustrating all aspects of the country's history since prehistoric times.

HOLD THE FRONT PAGE

Zürich is the home of one of the world's great newspapers, the *Neue Zürcher Zeitung* (*New Zürich News* or *N.Z.Z.*). Tabloid in format but sober in appearance and style, the *N.Z.Z.* monitors the doings of Zürich and its canton with the same thoroughness that it devotes to world finance, politics and culture. Learned articles on trends in academic philosophy may be interestingly juxtaposed with headlines like "Village barn burns; forty pigs die."

THINGS TO KNOW

- **AREA:** 160 square kilometers (62 square miles)
- **POPULATION:** 30,600
- **CAPITAL:** Vaduz
- **LANGUAGE:** German
- **ECONOMY:** Banking, agriculture, tourism, and the publication and sale of postage stamps.
- **PASSPORT REQUIREMENTS:** Required for U.S. citizens.
- **VISA REQUIREMENTS:** Not required provided visitors do not become employed.
- **DUTY-FREE ITEMS:** 400 cigarettes or 100 cigars or 500 grams tobacco; 2 liters of alcohol under 15% proof; 1 liter of alcohol over 15% proof; two still cameras; two movie cameras; one video camera with accessories; and personal goods to the value of 100 Swiss *francs*.
- **CURRENCY:** The unit of currency is the Swiss *franc*, divided into 100 *centimes*. Due to currency fluctuations, the exchange rate is subject to frequent change. There are no restrictions on the import or export of currency.
- **BANK OPENING HOURS:** 8am–noon and 1:30–4:30pm Monday–Friday.
- **PUBLIC HOLIDAYS:** January 1 and January 2; January 6 (Epiphany); Shrove Tuesday; March 19 (Feast of St Joseph); Good Friday; Easter Monday; May 1 (Labor Day); Ascension Day; Whitmonday; Corpus Christi; August 15 (Feast of the Assumption); Nativity of our Lady; September 8, (Immaculate Conception); November 1 (All Saints Day); December 25; December 26 or closest weekday (Boxing Day).
- **NATIONAL TOURIST OFFICES:**
  Swiss National Tourist Office
  608 Fifth Ave
  New York, NY 10020
  Tel: 212/757-5944; Fax: 212/262-6116
  Liechtensteinische Fremdenverkehrs-zentrale (Liechtenstein Tourist Board)
  Städtle 37
  9490 Vaduz, Liechtenstein
  Tel: (75) 232-1443; Fax: (75) 232-0806
- **AMERICAN EMBASSY:**
  See *Switzerland* p.610.

LIECHTENSTEIN

HISTORY

The principality of Liechtenstein was founded in 1719, independence was achieved in 1866, and the House of Liechtenstein has ruled ever since. United economically with Switzerland since 1923, the country is the world's only German-speaking monarchy. The 1986 elections were the first in which women could vote.

GETTING AROUND

Liechtenstein, with its breathtaking scenery and imposing castles, attracts many tourists. The capital is Vaduz.

There are no border formalities for visitors entering Liechtenstein from Switzerland. Visitors entering from Austria are subject to normal procedures.

The nearest airport to Vaduz is at Zürich, a 130-kilometer (80-mile) drive away. Good bus connections operate to Liechtenstein from railroad stations at Sargans and Buchs in Switzerland and Feldkirch in Austria; there is also a good internal bus service (though only one rail station, at Nendeln).

Liechtenstein's roads are well-maintained. The valley towns are linked by a route that parallels the Rhine, and modern roads climb to the Alpine resorts. Insurance requirements and traffic regulations are as those for Switzerland.

ACCOMMODATIONS

Liechtenstein hotels that belong to the Swiss Hotel Association are classified using a system of one to four stars; breakfast is usually included in the price. You can also find accommodations in chalets and inns and camping is available at Triesen, and Bendern.

TIPPING

Most hotels, restaurants and taxis charge a service fee of 15 percent, so tipping is usually not necessary.

PLACES OF INTEREST

▲ VADUZ (609 D3)

VADUZ *pop. 5,000*

Medieval Vaduz is one of the smallest capitals in the world. Its single main thoroughfare runs along the edge of the Rhine River, and a few residential streets climb the precipitous hills to the prince's castle, originally built in the 12th century (not open to visitors). Scattered over the area are vineyards whose fruit, under skilled hands, becomes fine wine.

Home to one-sixth of Liechtenstein's population, Vaduz is a major administrative center where small-scale factories often border open meadows.

ENGLANDERBAU (English Building), Städtle 37, houses the Liechtenstein State Art Collection. It also stages temporary exhibitions of world-renowned works from the Prince of Liechtenstein's private collection, one of the oldest and most comprehensive in Europe.

LIECHTENSTEINISCHES LANDESMUSEUM (National Museum), Städtle 43, has archaeological finds, carvings, coins, weapons, and other objects that bring to life the history of this tiny state.

BRIEFMARKENMUSEUM (Postage Stamp Museum), Städtle 37, traces philatelic history. Founded in 1930, it has a large collection of Liechtenstein stamps dating back to 1912, and temporary and permanent exhibits showcase stamps from around the world. There are also original sketches, designs, and other material related to the production of stamps.

WILDSCHLOSS (Ruine Schalun), is a 13th-century castle said to be the former seat of robber barons. It is a half-hour's scenic walk from Vaduz.

TRIESENBERG

TRIESENBERG *pop 2,400*

WALSER HEIMATMUSEUM (Local Walser Museum) exhibits historical items from the 13th-century Walser community that first settled in this area. Among its highlights are a display of wood engravings by prominent local artist Rudolf Schadler, and a slide show on the Alpine areas of Liechtenstein.

Das Rote Haus in Vaduz, a typical example of the beautiful villages in Liechtenstein

Within Great Britain and Ireland
Miles 147 Average time (excluding stops): 2.47

On the Continent
Kilometers 583 Average time (excluding stops): 5.44

At the Restaurant

DUTCH		FRENCH		GERMAN	
water	water	water	eau	water	Wasser
coffee	koffie	coffee	café	coffee	Kaffee
tea	thee	tea	thé	tea	Tee
milk	melk	milk	lait	milk	Milch
beer	bier	beer	bière	beer	Bier
wine	wijn	wine	vin	wine	Wein
cider	appelwijn	bread	pain	bread	Brot
bread	brood	eggs	œuf	eggs	Eier
eggs	eieren	fish	poisson	fish	Fisch
soup	soep	meat	viande	beef	Rindfleisch
fish	vis	beef	bœuf	beefsteak	Beefsteak
lobster	kreeft	pork	porc	pork	Schweinefleisch
beef	rundvlees	lamb	agneau	ham	Schinken
pork	varkensvlees	ham	jambon	chicken	Huhn
ham	ham	chicken	poulet	rice	Reis
chicken	kip	rice	riz	potatoes	Kartoffeln
rice	rijst	potatoes	pommes de	vegetables	Gemüse
potatoes	aardappelen		terre	green peas	Grune Erbsen
cabbage	kool	vegetables	légumes	salad	Salat
green peas	doperwten	salad	salade	tomatoes	Tomaten
vegetables	groenten	tomatoes	tomates	mushrooms	Pilz
salad	salade	lettuce	laitue	cheese	Käse
tomatoes	tomaten	mushrooms	champignons	fruit	Frucht
mushrooms	champignons	cheese	fromage	pastries	Gebäck
cheese	kaas	fruit	fruit	ice-cream	Eis
fruit	fruit	pastries	patisseries	cookies	Kekse
pastries	gebak	ice-cream	glace	orange	Orange
ice-cream	ijs	orange	orange	apple	Apfel
cookies	beschult	apple	pomme	banana	Banane
orange	sinaasappel	banana	banane	pear	Birne
apple	appel	sugar	sucre	cherries	Kirschen
banana	banaan	cream	crème	strawberries	Erdbeeren
sugar	suiker	salt	sel	sugar	Zucker
cream	room	pepper	poivre	cream	Sahne
salt	zout	garlic	ail	salt	Salz
pepper	peper	butter	beurre	pepper	Pfeffer
garlic	knoflook	knife	couteau	garlic	Knoblauch
butter	boter	fork	forchette	butter	Butter
knife	mes	spoon	cuillère	knife	Messer
fork	vork	glass	verre	fork	Gabel
spoon	lepel	cup	tasse	spoon	Löffel
glass	glas	plate	assiette	glass	Glas
cup	kopje	napkin	serviette	cup	Tasse
plate	bord	roasted	rôti	plate	Teller
napkin	servet	fried	frit	napkin	Serviette
rare	half rauw	rare	saignant	rare	blutig
medium	gaar	medium	à point	medium	Halbengleich
well-done	gebakken	well-done	bien cuit	well-done	Durch

Can I see the menu?
Geeft u mij de kaart?
How much is the meal?
Hoeveel kost de maaltijd?
Is service included?
Is de bediening inbegrepen?
The bill, please.
De rekening, alstublieft.

Can I see the menu?
Est-ce que je peux voir le menu?
How much is the meal?
Quel est le prix du repas?
Is service included?
Le service est-il compris?
The bill, please.
L'addition, s'il-vous plaît.

Can I see the menu?
Zeigen Sie mir die Speisekarte?
How much is the meal?
Was kostet die Mahlzeit?
Is service included?
Ist die Bedienung inbegriffen?
The bill, please.
Die Rechnung, bitte.

AT THE RESTAURANT

ITALIAN		SPANISH		SWEDISH	
water	acqua	water	agua	water	vatten
coffee	caffè	coffee	café	coffee	kaffe
tea	tè	tea	té	tea	te
milk	latte	milk	leche	milk	mjölk
beer	birra	beer	cerveza	beer	öl
wine	vino	wine	vino	wine	vin
bread	pane	bread	pan	bread	bröd
soup	zuppa	soup	sopa	soup	soppa
eggs	uova	eggs	huevos	egg	ägg
omelette	frittata	omelette	tortilla	fish	fisk
fish	pesce	fish	pescado	lobster	hummer
beef	manzo	lobster	langosta	beef	oxkott
beefsteak	bistecca	beef	vaca	beefsteak	biffstek
pork	maiale	beefsteak	bistec	pork	flask
ham	prosciutto	pork	cerdo	ham	skinka
lamb	agnello	ham	jamón	mutton	farkött
chicken	pollo	lamb	cordero	chicken	kyckling
rice	riso	chicken	pollo	rice	ris
potatoes	patate	rice	arroz	potatoes	potatis
vegetables	verdura	potatoes	patatas	vegetables	grönsaker
salad	insalata	vegetables	legumbres	cabbage	kål
tomatoes	pomodori	salad	ensalada	salad	sallad
lettuce	lattuga	tomatoes	tomates	tomatoes	tomater
mushrooms	funghi	lettuce	lechuga	green peas	gröna ärtor
cheese	formaggio	mushrooms	hongos	mushroom	svamp
fruit	frutta	cheese	queso	cheese	ost
pastries	pasticceria	fruit	frutas	fruit	frukt
ice-cream	gelato	pastries	pasteleria	pastries	kakor
orange	arancia	ice-cream	helado	ice-cream	glass
apple	mela	orange	naranja	orange	apelsinsaft
banana	banana	apple	manzana	apple	äpple
sugar	zucchero	banana	plàtano	banana	banan
cream	panna	sugar	azúcar	sugar	socker
salt	sale	salt	sal	salt	salt
pepper	pepe	pepper	pimienta	pepper	peppar
garlic	aglio	garlic	ajo	garlic	vitlök
butter	burro	butter	mantequilla	butter	smör
knife	coltello	knife	cuchillo	knife	kniv
fork	forchetta	fork	tenedor	fork	gaffel
spoon	cucchiaio	spoon	cuchara	spoon	sked
glass	bicchiere	glass	vaso	glass	glas
cup	tazza	cup	taza	cup	kopp
plate	piatto	plate	plato	plate	tallrik
napkin	tovagliolo	napkin	servilleta	napkin	servett
rare	al sangue	rare	poco pasado	rare	latt stek kott
medium	cotto a puntino	medium	a punto	medium	lagom
well-done	ben cotto	well-done	bien pasado	well-done	val kokat

ITALIAN

Can I see the menu?
Mi faccia vedere la lista delle vivande, per favore?
How much is the meal?
Qual è il prezzo del pasto?
Is service included?
Il servizio è compreso?
The bill, please.
Il conto, per favore.

SPANISH

Can I see the menu?
¿Muestreme la carta, por favor?
How much is the meal?
¿Cuánto cuesta el cubierto?
Is service included?
¿Está incluido el servicio?
The bill, please.
La cuenta, por favor.

SWEDISH

Can I see the menu?
Var god och visa mig matsedeln?
How much is the meal?
Hur mycket kostar måltiden?
Is service included?
Är det inklusive betjaning?
The bill, please.
Notan, var vanlig.

USEFUL PHRASES AT THE RESTAURANT

PORTUGUESE

water	água
coffee	café
tea	chá
milk	leite
beer	cerveja
wine	vinho
bread	pão
egg	ovo
fish	peixe
beef	vaca
beefsteak	bife
pork	porco
ham	presunto
lamb	carneiro
chicken	frango
rice	arroz
potatoes	batatas
vegetables	legumes
salad	salada
tomatoes	tomates
lettuce	alface
mushrooms	cogumelos
cheeses	queijos
fruits	frutas
pastries	pastelaria
ice-cream	gelados
cookies	biscoitos
orange	laranja
apple	maçã
banana	banana
sugar	açúcar
cream	natas
salt	sal
pepper	pimenta
butter	manteiga
knife	faca
fork	garfo
spoon	colher
glass	copo
cup	chávena
plate	prato
napkin	guardanapo
rare	em sangue
medium	passado
well-done	bem passado

Can I see the menu?
Mostre-me a ementa?
How much is the meal?
Qual é o preço da refeição?
Is service included?
O serviço está incluída?
The bill, please.
A conta, por favor.

HELPFUL PHRASES ON THE ROAD

DUTCH

I want to go to ...
Ik wil naar ...
May I park here?
Mag ik hier stoppen?
Go straight ahead.
Rijdt u rechtdoor.
To the right.
Rechts
To the left.
Links
How far is ...
Hoever hier vandaan is ...

a garage?	een garage?
a gas station?	een benzine station?
a doctor?	een dokter?
a police station?	een politie-bureau?
a phone box?	een telefooncel?
a post office?	een postkantoor?

FRENCH

I want to go to ...
Je voudrais aller à ...
May I park here?
Puis-je stationner ici?
Go straight ahead.
Roulez tout droit.
to the right.
à droite
to the left.
à gauche
How far is ...
A quelle distance se trouve ...

a garage?	un garage?
a gas station?	un poste à essence?
a doctor/hospital?	un médecin/hôpital
a police station?	un poste de police?
a phone box?	une cabine?
a post office?	la poste?

GERMAN

I want to go to ...
Ich möchte nach ... gehen.
May I park here?
Kann ich hier anhalten?
Go straight ahead.
Fahren Sie gerade aus.
To the right.
Nach rechts
To the left.
Nach links
How far is ...
Wie weit ist es ...

a garage?	zu einer Garage?
a gas station?	zu einer Tankstelle?
a doctor?	zu einem Arzt?
a police station?	zur Polizei?
a phone box?	zu einer Telefon?
a post office?	zur Post?

ITALIAN

I want to go to ...
Vorrei andare a ...
May I park here?
Posso fermarmi qui?
Go straight ahead.
Vada sempre diritto.
To the right.
A destra
To the left.
A sinistra
How far is ...
A che distanza se trova ...

a garage?	un garage?
a gas station?	un distributore di benzina?
a doctor?	un medico?
a police station?	un posto di polizia?
a phone box?	una cabina?
a post office?	l'ufficio postale?

SPANISH

I want to go to ...
Quiero ir a ...
May I park here?
¿Puedo detenerme aqui?
Go straight ahead.
Siga el camino recto.
to the right.
a la derecha
to the left.
a la izquierda
How far is ...
¿A que distancia esta ...

a garage?	un garage?
a gas station?	una estacion de gasolina?
a doctor?	un médico?
a police station?	una comisaría de policía?
a phone box?	una cabina?
a post office?	la oficina de correos?

INDEX

INDEX

When You Really Need to Speak Their Language...